# Principles of
# Risk Management and Insurance

# The Pearson Series in Finance

**Bekaert/Hodrick**
*International Financial Management*

**Berk/DeMarzo**
*Corporate Finance**

**Berk/DeMarzo**
*Corporate Finance: The Core**

**Berk/DeMarzo/Harford**
*Fundamentals of Corporate Finance**

**Brooks**
*Financial Management: Core Concepts**

**Copeland/Weston/Shastri**
*Financial Theory and Corporate Policy*

**Dorfman/Cather**
*Introduction to Risk Management and Insurance*

**Eiteman/Stonehill/Moffett**
*Multinational Business Finance*

**Fabozzi**
*Bond Markets: Analysis and Strategies*

**Fabozzi/Modigliani**
*Capital Markets: Institutions and Instruments*

**Fabozzi/Modigliani/Jones**
*Foundations of Financial Markets and Institutions*

**Finkler**
*Financial Management for Public, Health, and Not-for-Profit Organizations*

**Frasca**
*Personal Finance*

**Gitman/Zutter**
*Principles of Managerial Finance**

**Gitman/Zutter**
*Principles of Managerial Finance— Brief Edition**

**Goldsmith**
*Consumer Economics: Issues and Behaviors*

**Haugen**
*The Inefficient Stock Market: What Pays Off and Why*

**Haugen**
*The New Finance: Overreaction, Complexity, and Uniqueness*

**Holden**
*Excel Modeling in Corporate Finance*

**Holden**
*Excel Modeling in Investments*

**Hughes/MacDonald**
*International Banking: Text and Cases*

**Hull**
*Fundamentals of Futures and Options Markets*

**Hull**
*Options, Futures, and Other Derivatives*

**Hull**
*Risk Management and Financial Institutions*

**Keown**
*Personal Finance: Turning Money into Wealth**

**Keown/Martin/Petty**
*Foundations of Finance: The Logic and Practice of Financial Management**

**Kim/Nofsinger**
*Corporate Governance*

**Madura**
*Personal Finance**

**Marthinsen**
*Risk Takers: Uses and Abuses of Financial Derivatives*

**McDonald**
*Derivatives Markets*

**McDonald**
*Fundamentals of Derivatives Markets*

**Mishkin/Eakins**
*Financial Markets and Institutions*

**Moffett/Stonehill/Eiteman**
*Fundamentals of Multinational Finance*

**Nofsinger**
*Psychology of Investing*

**Ormiston/Fraser**
*Understanding Financial Statements*

**Pennacchi**
*Theory of Asset Pricing*

**Rejda/McNamara**
*Principles of Risk Management and Insurance*

**Seiler**
*Performing Financial Studies: A Methodological Cookbook*

**Smart/Gitman/Joehnk**
*Fundamentals of Investing**

**Solnik/McLeavey**
*Global Investments*

**Stretcher/Michael**
*Cases in Financial Management*

**Titman/Keown/Martin**
*Financial Management: Principles and Applications**

**Titman/Martin**
*Valuation: The Art and Science of Corporate Investment Decisions*

**Weston/Mitchel/Mulherin**
*Takeovers, Restructuring, and Corporate Governance*

# Principles of
# RISK MANAGEMENT
# AND INSURANCE

### GEORGE E. REJDA

### MICHAEL J. MCNAMARA

## TWELFTH EDITION

**PEARSON**

Boston  Columbus  Indianapolis  New York  San Francisco  Upper Saddle River
Amsterdam  Cape Town  Dubai  London  Madrid  Milan  Munich  Paris  Montréal  Toronto
Delhi  Mexico City  São Paulo  Sydney  Hong Kong  Seoul  Singapore  Taipei  Tokyo

Editor in Chief: Donna Battista
Acquisitions Editor: Katie Rowland
Editorial Project Manager: Emily Biberger
Editorial Assistant: Elissa Senra-Sargent
Director of Marketing: Maggie Moylan Leen
Director of Production: Erin Gregg
Managing Editor: Jeff Holcomb
Associate Managing Editor: Karen Carter
Senior Operations Supervisor: Evelyn Beaton
Senior Operations Specialist: Carol Melville
Art Director, Text and Cover Design: Jonathan Boylan
Permissions Specialist: Samantha Graham
Cover Photo: Shutterstock/Chudakov
Media Director: Susan Schoenberg
Full-Service Project Management: GEX Publishing Services
Printer/Binder: RR Donnelley
Cover Printer: RR Donnelley

Credits and acknowledgments borrowed from other sources and reproduced, with permission, in this textbook appear on the appropriate page within text.

**Library of Congress Cataloging-in-Publication Data**
Rejda, George E.
  Principles of risk management and insurance / George E. Rejda, Michael J. McNamara. -- Twelfth edition.
    pages cm
  Includes index.
  ISBN 978-0-13-299291-6 (casebound)
1. Insurance. 2. Risk (Insurance) 3. Risk management. I. McNamara, Mike. II. Title.
  HG8051.R44 2014
  368--dc23
                            2012049473
10 9 8 7 6 5

ISBN 10: 0-13-299291-4
ISBN 13: 978-0-13-299291-6

# CONTENTS

Preface   xv

| PART ONE | BASIC CONCEPTS IN RISK MANAGEMENT AND INSURANCE |

## CHAPTER 1   RISK AND ITS TREATMENT   1

Definitions of Risk   2
Chance of Loss   3
Peril and Hazard   4
Classification of Risk   5
Major Personal Risks and Commercial Risks   7
Burden of Risk on Society   12
Techniques for Managing Risk   12

Summary   15 ▪ Key Concepts and Terms   16 ▪ Review Questions   16 ▪ Application
Questions   17 ▪ Internet Resources   18 ▪ Selected References   18 ▪ Notes 18

Case Application   15

INSIGHT 1.1: FINANCIAL IMPACT ON DISABLED INDIVIDUALS CAN BE STAGGERING,
        SAYS NEW STUDY   9

## CHAPTER 2   INSURANCE AND RISK   19

Definition of Insurance   20
Basic Characteristics of Insurance   20
Characteristics of an Ideally Insurable Risk   22
Two Applications: The Risks of Fire and Unemployment   24
Adverse Selection and Insurance   26
Insurance and Gambling Compared   26
Insurance and Hedging Compared   26
Types of Insurance   27
Benefits of Insurance to Society   31
Costs of Insurance to Society   32

Summary   35 ▪ Key Concepts and Terms   36 ▪ Review Questions   36 ▪ Application
Questions   36 ▪ Internet Resources   37 ▪ Selected References   37 ▪ Notes 37

Case Application   35

INSIGHT 2.1: INSURANCE FRAUD HALL OF SHAME—SHOCKING EXAMPLES OF INSURANCE
        FRAUD   33

INSIGHT 2.2: DON'T THINK INSURANCE FRAUD IS COMMITTED ONLY BY HARDENED CROOKS   34

Appendix  Basic Statistics and the Law of Large Numbers   39

## CHAPTER 3   INTRODUCTION TO RISK MANAGEMENT   43

Meaning of Risk Management   44
Objectives of Risk Management   44
Steps in the Risk Management Process   45

Implement and Monitor the Risk Management Program   54
Benefits of Risk Management   55
Personal Risk Management   55

Summary   58 ▪ Key Concepts and Terms   59 ▪ Review Questions   59 ▪ Application
Questions   59 ▪ Internet Resources   60 ▪ Selected References   61 ▪ Notes 61

Case Application   57

INSIGHT 3.1: ADVANTAGES OF SELF INSURANCE   50

CHAPTER 4   ADVANCED TOPICS IN RISK MANAGEMENT   62
The Changing Scope of Risk Management   63
Insurance Market Dynamics   68
Loss Forecasting   71
Financial Analysis in Risk Management Decision Making   76
Other Risk Management Tools   78

Summary   81 ▪ Key Concepts and Terms   82 ▪ Review Questions   82 ▪ Application
Questions   82 ▪ Internet Resources   82 ▪ Selected References   83 ▪ Notes   84

Case Application   80

INSIGHT 4.1: THE WEATHER DERIVATIVES MARKETS AT CME GROUP: A BRIEF HISTORY   73

PART TWO   THE PRIVATE INSURANCE INDUSTRY

CHAPTER 5   TYPES OF INSURERS AND MARKETING SYSTEMS   86
Overview of Private Insurance in the Financial Services Industry   87
Types of Private Insurers   88
Agents and Brokers   93
Types of Marketing Systems   95
Group Insurance Marketing   98

Summary   99 ▪ Key Concepts and Terms   99 ▪ Review Questions   99 ▪ Application
Questions   100 ▪ Internet Resources   100 ▪ Selected References   101 ▪ Notes   102

Case Application   98

INSIGHT 5.1: SHOW ME THE MONEY—HOW MUCH DO INSURANCE SALES AGENTS
EARN?   94

CHAPTER 6   INSURANCE COMPANY OPERATIONS   103
Insurance Company Operations   104
Rating and Ratemaking   104
Underwriting   105
Production   108
Claims Settlement   108
Reinsurance   110
Alternatives to Traditional Reinsurance   115
Investments   116
Other Insurance Company Functions   117

Summary   119 ▪ Key Concepts and Terms   119 ▪ Review Questions   119 ▪ Application
Questions   120 ▪ Internet Resources   121 ▪ Selected References   121 ▪ Notes   122

Case Application   118

INSIGHT 6.1: BE A SAVVY CONSUMER—CHECK THE INSURER'S CLAIMS RECORD BEFORE
              YOU BUY   111

CHAPTER 7    **FINANCIAL OPERATIONS OF INSURERS    123**

Property and Casualty Insurers   124
Life Insurance Companies   130
Rate Making in Property and Casualty Insurance   131
Rate Making in Life Insurance   135

Summary   136 ▪ Key Concepts and Terms   137 ▪ Review Questions   137 ▪ Application
Questions   138 ▪ Internet Resources   138 ▪ Selected References   139 ▪ Notes   139

Case Application   136

INSIGHT 7.1: HOW PROFITABLE IS THE PROPERTY AND CASUALTY INSURANCE
              INDUSTRY?   129

CHAPTER 8    **GOVERNMENT REGULATION OF INSURANCE    141**

Reasons for Insurance Regulation   142
Historical Development of Insurance Regulation   144
Methods for Regulating Insurers   145
What Areas Are Regulated?   146
State Versus Federal Regulation   151
Modernizing Insurance Regulation   156
Insolvency of Insurers   157
Credit-Based Insurance Scores   158

Summary   160 ▪ Key Concepts and Terms   160 ▪ Review Questions   161 ▪ Application
Questions   161 ▪ Internet Resources   162 ▪ Selected References   163 ▪ Notes   163

Case Application   159

INSIGHT 8.1: QUALITY OF INFORMATION PROVIDED TO CONSUMERS ON AUTO
              AND HOMEOWNERS INSURANCE VARIES WIDELY AMONG STATE INSURANCE
              DEPARTMENTS   143

INSIGHT 8.2: WIDE RATE DISPARITY REVEALS WEAK COMPETITION IN INSURANCE   153

PART THREE    **LEGAL PRINCIPLES IN RISK AND INSURANCE**

CHAPTER 9    **FUNDAMENTAL LEGAL PRINCIPLES    165**

Principle of Indemnity   166
Principle of Insurable Interest   169
Principle of Subrogation   170
Principle of Utmost Good Faith   172
Requirements of an Insurance Contract   174
Distinct Legal Characteristics of Insurance Contracts   175
Law and the Insurance Agent   177

Summary 179 ▪ Key Concepts and Terms 180 ▪ Review Questions 180 ▪ Application Questions 181 ▪ Internet Resources 182 ▪ Selected References 182 ▪ Notes 182

Case Application 179

INSIGHT 9.1: CORPORATION LACKING INSURABLE INTEREST AT TIME OF DEATH CAN RECEIVE LIFE INSURANCE PROCEEDS 171

INSIGHT 9.2: AUTO INSURER DENIES COVERAGE BECAUSE OF MATERIAL MISREPRESENTATION 172

INSIGHT 9.3: INSURER VOIDS COVERAGE BECAUSE OF MISREPRESENTATIONS IN PROOF OF LOSS 173

CHAPTER 10   ANALYSIS OF INSURANCE CONTRACTS 184

Basic Parts of an Insurance Contract 185
Definition of "Insured" 187
Endorsements and Riders 189
Deductibles 189
Coinsurance 190
Coinsurance in Health Insurance 192
Other-Insurance Provisions 192

Summary 195 ▪ Key Concepts and Terms 195 ▪ Review Questions 196 ▪ Application Questions 196 ▪ Internet Resources 197 ▪ Selected References 197 ▪ Notes 197

Case Application 194

INSIGHT 10.1: WHEN YOU DRIVE YOUR ROOMMATE'S CAR, ARE YOU COVERED UNDER YOUR POLICY? 188

PART FOUR   LIFE AND HEALTH RISKS

CHAPTER 11   LIFE INSURANCE   198

Premature Death 199
Financial Impact of Premature Death on Different Types of Families 200
Amount of Life Insurance to Own 201
Types of Life Insurance 208
Variations of Whole Life Insurance 213
Other Types of Life Insurance 221

Summary 225 ▪ Key Concepts and Terms 226 ▪ Review Questions 226 ▪ Application Questions 227 ▪ Internet Resources 228 ▪ Selected References 229 ▪ Notes 230

Case Application 224

INSIGHT 11.1: WHY DOES THE UNITED STATES LAG BEHIND MANY FOREIGN COUNTRIES IN LIFE EXPECTANCY? 200

INSIGHT 11.2: CASH-VALUE LIFE INSURANCE AS AN INVESTMENT—DON'T IGNORE TWO POINTS 212

INSIGHT 11.3: BE A SAVVY CONSUMER—FOUR LIFE INSURANCE POLICIES TO AVOID 222

CHAPTER 12   LIFE INSURANCE CONTRACTUAL PROVISIONS   231

Life Insurance Contractual Provisions 232
Dividend Options 238
Nonforfeiture Options 239
Settlement Options 241
Additional Life Insurance Benefits 246

Summary  251  ▪ Key Concepts and Terms  251  ▪ Review Questions  252  ▪ Application Questions  252  ▪ Internet Resources  253  ▪ Selected References  254  ▪ Notes  254

Case Application  250

INSIGHT 12.1: IS THIS DEATH A SUICIDE?  234

INSIGHT 12.2: SELECTION OF THE BEST DIVIDEND OPTION IN A PARTICIPATING WHOLE LIFE POLICY  240

INSIGHT 12.3: ACCELERATED DEATH BENEFITS—REAL LIFE EXAMPLE  249

INSIGHT 12.4: WHAT IS A LIFE SETTLEMENT? EXAMPLES OF ACTUAL CASES  249

CHAPTER 13  BUYING LIFE INSURANCE  255
Determining the Cost of Life Insurance  256
Rate of Return on Saving Component  260
Taxation of Life Insurance  262
Shopping for Life Insurance  263

Summary  266  ▪ Key Concepts and Terms  266  ▪ Review Questions  267  ▪ Application Questions  267  ▪ Internet Resources  268  ▪ Selected References  268  ▪ Notes  268

Case Application  266

INSIGHT 13.1: BE CAREFUL IN REPLACING AN EXISTING LIFE INSURANCE POLICY  259

Appendix  Calculation of Life Insurance Premiums  269

CHAPTER 14  ANNUITIES AND INDIVIDUAL RETIREMENT ACCOUNTS  275
Individual Annuities  276
Types of Annuities  277
Longevity Insurance  282
Taxation of Individual Annuities  283
Individual Retirement Accounts  284
Adequacy of IRA Funds  288

Summary  291  ▪ Key Concepts and Terms  292  ▪ Review Questions  292  ▪ Application Questions  292  ▪ Internet Resources  293  ▪ Selected References  293  ▪ Notes  293

Case application 1  290

Case application 2  290

INSIGHT 14.1: ADVANTAGES OF AN IMMEDIATE ANNUITY TO RETIRED WORKERS  278

INSIGHT 14.2: BELLS AND WHISTLES OF VARIABLE ANNUITIES  281

INSIGHT 14.3: TEN QUESTIONS TO ANSWER BEFORE YOU BUY A VARIABLE ANNUITY  284

INSIGHT 14.4: WILL YOU HAVE ENOUGH MONEY AT RETIREMENT? MONTE CARLO SIMULATIONS CAN BE HELPFUL  289

CHAPTER 15  HEALTH-CARE REFORM; INDIVIDUAL HEALTH INSURANCE COVERAGES  295
Health-Care Problems in the United States  296
Health-Care Reform  303
Basic Provisions of the Affordable Care Act  303
Individual Medical Expense Insurance  309
Individual Medical Expense Insurance and Managed Care Plans  311
Health Savings Accounts  312
Long-Term Care Insurance  313
Disability-Income Insurance  316

Individual Health Insurance Contractual Provisions    319

Summary   321 ▪ Key Concepts and Terms   322 ▪ Review Questions   322 ▪ Application
Questions   323 ▪ Internet Resources   323 ▪ Selected References   324 ▪ Notes   325

Case Application   321

INSIGHT 15.1: HOW DOES U.S. HEALTH SPENDING COMPARE WITH OTHER COUNTRIES?   298

INSIGHT 15.2: MORE THAN SEVENTY PERCENT OF THE UNINSURED HAVE GONE WITHOUT HEALTH
         COVERAGE FOR MORE THAN A YEAR   300

CHAPTER 16    EMPLOYEE BENEFITS: GROUP LIFE AND HEALTH
              INSURANCE   327
Meaning of Employee Benefits   328
Fundamentals of Group Insurance   328
Group Life Insurance Plans   330
Group Medical Expense Insurance   332
Traditional Indemnity Plans   333
Managed Care Plans   334
Key Features of Group Medical Expense Insurance   336
Affordable Care Act Requirements and Group Medical Expense Insurance   337
Consumer-Directed Health Plans   340
Recent Developments in Employer-Sponsored Health Plans   340
Group Medical Expense Contractual Provisions   343
Group Dental Insurance   344
Group Disability-Income Insurance   345
Cafeteria Plans   346

Summary   348 ▪ Key Concepts and Terms   349 ▪ Review Questions   350 ▪ Application
Questions   350 ▪ Internet Resources   351 ▪ Selected References   352 ▪ Notes   352

Case Application   348

INSIGHT 16.1: WHAT ARE THE FINANCIAL IMPLICATIONS OF LACK OF COVERAGE?   339

CHAPTER 17    EMPLOYEE BENEFITS: RETIREMENT PLANS   353
Fundamentals of Private Retirement Plans   354
Types of Qualified Retirement Plans   357
Defined-Benefit Plans   358
Defined-Contribution Plans   360
Section 401(k) Plans   360
Profit-Sharing Plans   363
Keogh Plans for the Self Employed   364
Simplified Employee Pension   365
SIMPLE Retirement Plans   365
Funding Agency and Funding Instruments   365
Problems and Issues in Tax-Deferred Retirement Plans   366

Summary   368 ▪ Key Concepts and Terms   369 ▪ Review Questions   369 ▪ Application
Questions   370 ▪ Internet Resources   370 ▪ Selected References   371 ▪ Notes   371

Case Application   368

INSIGHT 17.1: SIX COMMON 401(K) MISTAKES   361

**CHAPTER 18    SOCIAL INSURANCE    372**

Social Insurance    373

Old-Age, Survivors, and Disability Insurance    375

Types of Benefits    376

Medicare    384

Impact of the Affordable Care Act on Medicare    389

Problems and Issues    390

Unemployment Insurance    392

Workers Compensation    395

Summary    399 ▪ Key Concepts and Terms    400 ▪ Review Questions    400 ▪ Application Questions    401 ▪ Internet Resources    402 ▪ Selected References    403 ▪ Notes    403

Case Application    399

INSIGHT 18.1: TAKING SOCIAL SECURITY: SOONER MIGHT NOT BE BETTER    381

INSIGHT 18.2: WHAT ARE YOUR SOLUTIONS FOR REFORMING SOCIAL SECURITY?    392


**PART FIVE    PERSONAL PROPERTY AND LIABILITY RISKS**

**CHAPTER 19    THE LIABILITY RISK    405**

Basis of Legal Liability    406

Law of Negligence    407

Imputed Negligence    409

*Res Ipsa Loquitur*    410

Specific Applications of the Law of Negligence    410

Current Tort Liability Problems    412

Summary    421 ▪ Key Concepts and Terms    421 ▪ Review Questions    422 ▪ Application Questions    422 ▪ Internet Resources    423 ▪ Selected References    424 ▪ Notes    424

Case Application    420

INSIGHT 19.1: JUDICIAL HELLHOLES 2011–2012    415


**CHAPTER 20    HOMEOWNERS INSURANCE, SECTION I    426**

Homeowners Insurance    427

Analysis of Homeowners 3 Policy (Special Form)    431

Section I Coverages    432

Section I Perils Insured Against    437

Section I Exclusions    440

Section I Conditions    442

Section I and II Conditions    447

Summary    448 ▪ Key Concepts and Terms    449 ▪ Review Questions    449 ▪ Application Questions    450 ▪ Internet Resources    451 ▪ Selected References    451 ▪ Notes    452

Case Application    448

INSIGHT 20.1: LESSON TO BE LEARNED FROM APARTMENT FIRE    430

INSIGHT 20.2: HOW DO I TAKE A HOME INVENTORY AND WHY?    443

INSIGHT 20.3: THE BIG GAP BETWEEN REPLACEMENT COST AND ACTUAL CASH VALUE CAN EMPTY YOUR WALLET    444

**CHAPTER 21**  **HOMEOWNERS INSURANCE, SECTION II**  **453**

Personal Liability Insurance  454
Section II Exclusions  457
Section II Additional Coverages  460
Section II Conditions  462
Endorsements to a Homeowners Policy  462
Cost of Homeowners Insurance  465

Summary  473 ▪ Key Concepts and Terms  473 ▪ Review Questions  473 ▪ Application
Questions  474 ▪ Internet Resources  475 ▪ Selected References  475 ▪ Notes  476

Case Application  472

INSIGHT 21.1: DOG BITES HURT, SO DO LAWSUITS  455

INSIGHT 21.2: TRYING TO SAVE MONEY? AVOID THE FIVE BIGGEST INSURANCE MISTAKES!  471


**CHAPTER 22**  **AUTO INSURANCE**  **477**

Overview of Personal Auto Policy  478
Part A: Liability Coverage  479
Part B: Medical Payments Coverage  483
Part C: Uninsured Motorists Coverage  485
Part D: Coverage for Damage to Your Auto  489
Part E: Duties After an Accident or Loss  497
Part F: General Provisions  498
Insuring Motorcycles and Other Vehicles  499

Summary  500 ▪ Key Concepts and Terms  500 ▪ Review Questions  500 ▪ Application
Questions  501 ▪ Internet Resources  503 ▪ Selected References  503 ▪ Notes  504

Case Application  499

INSIGHT 22.1: RECESSION MARKED BY BUMP IN UNINSURED MOTORISTS  485

INSIGHT 22.2: TOP 10 REASONS TO PURCHASE THE RENTAL CAR DAMAGE WAIVER  491

INSIGHT 22.3: NO CALL, NO TEXT, NO UPDATE BEHIND THE WHEEL: NTSB CALLS FOR NATIONWIDE
BAN ON PEDS WHILE DRIVING  494


**CHAPTER 23**  **AUTO INSURANCE AND SOCIETY**  **505**

Approaches for Compensating Auto Accident Victims  506
Auto Insurance for High-Risk Drivers  516
Cost of Auto Insurance  517
Shopping for Auto Insurance  522

Summary  527 ▪ Key Concepts and Terms  528 ▪ Review Questions  528 ▪ Application
Questions  529 ▪ Internet Resources  529 ▪ Selected References  530 ▪ Notes  530

Case Application  527

INSIGHT 23.1: FILING AN AUTO CLAIM WITH THE OTHER PARTY'S INSURANCE COMPANY  510

INSIGHT 23.2: PROTECT YOURSELF: INSURING YOUR TEEN DRIVER  520

INSIGHT 23.3: INCREASING THE COLLISION DEDUCTIBLE TO SAVE MONEY—SOME IMPORTANT
CONSIDERATIONS  523


**CHAPTER 24**  **OTHER PROPERTY AND LIABILITY INSURANCE COVERAGES**  **532**

ISO Dwelling Program  533
Mobile Home Insurance  535
Inland Marine Floaters  535
Watercraft Insurance  536

Government Property Insurance Programs   538
Title Insurance   543
Personal Umbrella Policy   545

Summary   548 ▪ Key Concepts and Terms   549 ▪ Review Questions   549 ▪ Application Questions   550 ▪ Internet Resources   551 ▪ Selected References   551 ▪ Notes   552

Case Application   548

INSIGHT 24.1: DISPELLING MYTHS ABOUT FLOOD INSURANCE   541

INSIGHT 24.2: TITLE INSURANCE: PROTECTING YOUR HOME INVESTMENT AGAINST UNKNOWN TITLE DEFECTS   544


PART SIX          COMMERCIAL PROPERTY AND LIABILITY RISKS

CHAPTER 25   COMMERCIAL PROPERTY INSURANCE   554
Commercial Package Policy   555
Building and Personal Property Coverage Form   557
Causes-of-Loss Forms   559
Reporting Forms   560
Business Income Insurance   561
Other Commercial Property Coverages   564
Transportation Insurance   567
Businessowners Policy (BOP)   571

Summary   574 ▪ Key Concepts and Terms   575 ▪ Review Questions   575 ▪ Application Questions   576 ▪ Internet Resources   577 ▪ Selected References   578 ▪ Notes   578

Case Application   573

INSIGHT 25.1: EXAMPLES OF EQUIPMENT BREAKDOWN CLAIMS   566

CHAPTER 26   COMMERCIAL LIABILITY INSURANCE   580
General Liability Loss Exposures   581
Commercial General Liability Policy   582
Employment-Related Practices Liability Insurance   588
Workers Compensation Insurance   589
Commercial Auto Insurance   592
Aircraft Insurance   594
Commercial Umbrella Policy   595
Businessowners Policy   597
Professional Liability Insurance   597
Directors and Officers Liability Insurance   599

Summary   600 ▪ Key Concepts and Terms   602 ▪ Review Questions   602 ▪ Application Questions   603 ▪ Internet Resources   604 ▪ Selected References   604 ▪ Notes   604

Case Application   600

INSIGHT 26.1: BASIC FACTS ABOUT WORKERS COMPENSATION   590

CHAPTER 27   CRIME INSURANCE AND SURETY BONDS   606
ISO Commercial Crime Insurance Program   607
Commercial Crime Coverage Form (Loss-Sustained Form)   608
Financial Institution Bonds   613
Surety Bonds   614

Summary  617 ▪ Key Concepts and Terms  618 ▪ Review Questions  618 ▪ Application Questions  619 ▪ Internet Resources  619 ▪ Selected References  620 ▪ Notes  620

Case Application  616
INSIGHT 27.1: SMALL BUSINESS CRIME PREVENTION GUIDE  610

**Appendix A   Homeowners 3 (Special Form)   621**

**Appendix B   Personal Auto Policy   646**

**Glossary   660**

**Index   678**

# PREFACE

This text deals with risk and its treatment. Since the last edition of *Principles of Risk Management and Insurance* appeared, several unprecedented events have occurred that clearly demonstrate the destructive presence of risk in our society. In 2010, one of the most devastating earthquakes in recent history struck poverty-stricken Haiti, causing enormous human suffering, an estimated 316,000 deaths, one million homeless people, and widespread property destruction. In 2011, a deadly earthquake hit Japan that caused a devastating tsunami and a nuclear accident crisis. More than 18,000 people died, thousands more are missing, and estimated property damage may exceed $300 billion. During the same period, the Obama Administration introduced legislation to reform a broken health-care delivery system. Despite formidable opposition by the Republicans, and heated and bitter debate, Congress enacted the Affordable Care Act in March 2010. The new law extends health insurance coverage to millions of uninsured people, provides subsidies to purchase insurance, and prohibits certain abusive practices by insurers.

Finally, in 2012, a deranged gunman randomly killed 12 people and wounded at least 58 others in a theater in Aurora, Colorado. This tragic act again highlights the fact that spree killings are not isolated events, and that the risk of death or injury is markedly present.

Flash forward to the present. The economy and housing markets are slowly recovering from the second most severe economic downswing in the nation's history; although declining, unemployment remains at historically high levels; and a dysfunctional Congress remains hopelessly deadlocked because of deeply held ideological beliefs by its members. The Affordable Care Act remains controversial, and Republicans in Congress are determined to repeal it. The House has already enacted legislation to repeal the Affordable Care Act. To say that we live in a risky and dangerous world is an enormous understatement.

The twelfth edition of *Principles of Risk Management and Insurance* discusses these issues and other insurance issues as well. As in previous editions, the text is designed for a beginning undergraduate course in risk management and insurance with no prerequisites. The twelfth edition provides an in-depth treatment of major risk management and insurance topics. Coverage includes a discussion of basic concepts of risk and insurance, introductory and advanced topics in risk management, functional and financial operations of insurers, legal principles, life and health insurance, property and liability insurance, employee benefits, and social insurance. In addition, the new Affordable Care Act is discussed in depth. Once again, the twelfth edition places primary emphasis on insurance consumers and blends basic risk management and insurance principles with consumer considerations. With this user-friendly text, students can apply basic concepts immediately to their own personal risk management and insurance programs.

## KEY CONTENT CHANGES IN THE TWELFTH EDITION

Thoroughly revised and updated, the twelfth edition provides an in-depth analysis of current insurance industry issues and practices, which readers have come to expect from *Principles of Risk Management and Insurance*. Key content changes in the twelfth edition include the following:

- *Health-care reform.* Chapter 15 has an in-depth discussion of the broken health-care delivery system in the United States, which led to enactment of the Affordable Care Act.
- *Enactment of the Affordable Care Act.* Chapters 15 and 16 discuss the major provisions of the new Affordable Care Act and its impact on individual and group health insurance coverages. Primary attention is devoted to provisions that have a major financial impact on individuals, families, and employers.

- *New homeowners insurance policies.* The Insurance Services Office (ISO) has introduced a new 2011 edition of the homeowners insurance policies that are widely used throughout the United States. Chapters 20 and 21 discuss important changes in homeowners insurance, especially the Homeowners 3 policy.
- *Updated discussion of life insurance marketing.* The section on life insurance marketing and distribution systems has been completely updated and substantially rewritten. Chapter 5 discusses the current distribution systems and marketing practices of life insurers.
- *New developments in employer-sponsored health insurance plans.* Employers continue to grapple with the rapid increase in group health insurance premiums and continually seek new solutions for holding down costs. Chapter 16 discusses new developments in group health insurance to contain higher health-care costs and premiums.
- *Impact of the Affordable Care Act on Medicare.* Chapter 18 discusses important provisions of the Affordable Care Act that have a direct impact on the Medicare program. These provisions are designed to control cost and make Medicare a more efficient program in protecting seniors against the risk of poor health.
- *New Insight boxes.* The twelfth edition contains a number of new and timely Insight boxes. Insights are valuable learning tools that provide real-world applications of a concept or principle discussed in the text.
- *Technical accuracy.* As in previous editions, numerous experts have reviewed the text for technical accuracy, especially in areas where changes occur rapidly. The twelfth edition presents technically accurate and up-to-date material.

## SUPPLEMENTS

The twelfth edition provides a number of supplements to help busy instructors save time and teach more effectively. The following supplements are available to qualified adopters through the Instructor's Resource Center at pearsonhighered.com/irc.

**Companion Web Site.** The twelfth edition has an Internet site at pearsonhighered.com/rejda that allows students to work through a variety of exercises and to take a self-assessment quiz after studying the chapter material. Students can use the Internet to view real world examples of risk and insurance concepts discussed in the text.

**Printed Instructor's Manual and Test Item File.** Designed to reduce start-up costs and class preparation time, a comprehensive instructor's manual contains teaching notes; outlines; and answers to all end-of-chapter review, application, and case questions. The test bank, prepared by Professor Michael J. McNamara of Washington State University, enables instructors to construct objective exams quickly and easily.

**Computerized Test Bank.** In addition to the printed test bank, these same questions are also available in Word, PDF, and TestGen formats. The easy-to-use TestGen software is a valuable test preparation tool that allows busy professors to view, edit, and add questions.

**PowerPoint Presentation.** Prepared by Professor Patricia Born of Florida State University, this tool contains lecture notes that reflect the new edition. It also includes the complete set of figures from the textbook. Depending on interest, instructors can choose among hundreds of slides to assist in class preparation.

**Study Guide.** Also prepared by Michael J. McNamara, this study tool helps students analyze and internalize the topics learned in class. Every chapter includes an overview, learning objectives, outline, and extensive self-test with answers. The self-test section contains short answer, multiple choice, true/false, and case application questions that challenge students to apply the principles and concepts covered in the twelfth edition.

## ACKNOWLEDGMENTS

A market-leading textbook is never written alone. I owe an enormous intellectual debt to many professionals for their kind and gracious assistance. In particular, Professor Michael McNamara, Washington State University, is a new coauthor of the text. Professor McNamara is an outstanding scholar and researcher who has made significant contributions to the twelfth edition. As a result, the new edition is a substantially improved educational product.

In addition, numerous educators, risk management experts, and industry personnel have taken time out of their busy schedules to review part or all of the twelfth edition, to provide supplementary materials, to make valuable comments, to answer questions, or to provide other assistance. They include the following:

Burton T. Beam, Jr., The American College (retired)

Patricia Born, Florida State University

Nick Brown, Chief Underwriting Officer, Global Aerospace, United Kingdom

Ann Costello, University of Hartford

Joseph Fox, Asheville-Buncombe Technical Community College

Edward Graves, The American College

Eric Johnsen, Virginia Tech

J. Tyler Leverty, University of Iowa

Rebecca A. McQuade, Director of Risk Management, PACCAR, Inc.

William H. Rabel, University of Alabama

Johnny Vestal, Texas Tech

Eric Wiening, Insurance and Risk Management/ Author-Educator, Consultant

Millicent W. Workman, Research Analyst, International Risk Management Institute, Inc. (IRMI), and Editor, *Practical Risk Management*

I would also like to thank Kelly Morrison at GEX Publishing Services and Donna Battista, Katie Rowland, Emily Biberger, Karen Carter, Elissa Senra-Sargent at Pearson for their substantive editorial comments, marketing insights, and technical suggestions.

The views expressed in the text are those solely of the authors and do not necessarily reflect the viewpoints or positions of the reviewers whose assistance I am gratefully acknowledging.

Finally, the fundamental objective underlying the twelfth edition remains the same as in the first edition—I have attempted to write an intellectually stimulating and visually attractive textbook from which students can learn and professors can teach.

*George E. Rejda, Ph.D., CLU*
*Professor Emeritus*
*Finance Department*
*College of Business Administration*
*University of Nebraska—Lincoln*

# CHAPTER 1

# RISK AND ITS TREATMENT

*"When we take a risk, we are betting on an outcome that
will result from a decision we have made, though we do not
know for certain what the outcome will be."*

Peter L. Bernstein
Against the Gods: The Remarkable Story of Risk

## LEARNING OBJECTIVES

**After studying this chapter, you should be able to**

◆ Explain the historical definition of risk.

◆ Explain the meaning of loss exposure.

◆ Understand the following types of risk:

    Pure risk
    Speculative risk
    Diversifiable risk
    Enterprise risk

◆ Identify the major pure risks that are associated with financial insecurity.

◆ Show how risk is a burden to society.

◆ Explain the major techniques for managing risk.

*Shannon, age 28, is employed as a bank teller for a commercial bank in Omaha, Nebraska. She is a single parent with two preschool children. Shortly after the bank opened on a Saturday morning, two men armed with handguns entered the bank and went to Shannon's window and demanded money. When a bank guard entered the premises, one gunman became startled and shot Shannon in the chest. She died while being transported to a local hospital.*

*Shannon's tragic and untimely death shows that we live in a risky and dangerous world. The news media report daily on similar tragic events that clearly illustrate the widespread presence of risk in our society. Examples abound—a tornado destroys a small town; a gunman enters a classroom at a local college and kills seven students; a drunk driver kills four people in a van on a crowded expressway; a river overflows, and thousands of acres of farm crops are lost. In addition, people experience personal tragedies and financial setbacks that cause great economic insecurity—the unexpected death of a family head; catastrophic medical bills that bankrupt the family; or the loss of a good paying job during a business recession.*

*In this chapter, we discuss the nature and treatment of risk in our society. Topics discussed include the meaning of risk, the major types of risk that threaten our financial security, the burden of risk on the economy, and the basic methods for managing risk.*

## DEFINITIONS OF RISK

There is no single definition of risk. Economists, behavioral scientists, risk theorists, statisticians, and actuaries each have their own concept of risk. However, risk historically has been defined in terms of uncertainty. Based on this concept, risk *is defined as uncertainty concerning the occurrence of a loss.* For example, the risk of being killed in an auto accident is present because uncertainty is present. The risk of lung cancer for smokers is present because uncertainty is present. The risk of flunking a college course is present because uncertainty is present.

Employees in the insurance industry often use the term *risk* in a different manner to identify the property or life that is being considered for insurance. For example, in the insurance industry, it is common to hear statements such as "that driver is a poor risk," or "that building is an unacceptable risk."

Finally, in the economics and finance literature, authors often make a distinction between risk and uncertainty. The term "risk" is often used in situations where the probability of possible outcomes can be estimated with some accuracy, while "uncertainty" is used in situations where such probabilities cannot be estimated.[1] As such, many authors have developed their own concept of risk, and numerous definitions of risk exist in the professional literature.[2]

Because the term *risk* is ambiguous and has different meanings, many authors and corporate risk managers use the term "loss exposure" to identify potential losses. A loss exposure *is any situation or circumstance in which a loss is possible, regardless of whether a loss occurs.* Examples of loss exposures include manufacturing plants that may be damaged by an earthquake or flood, defective products that may result in lawsuits against the manufacturer, possible theft of company property because of inadequate security, and potential injury to employees because of unsafe working conditions.

Finally, when the definition of risk includes the concept of uncertainty, some authors make a careful distinction between objective risk and subjective risk.

### Objective Risk

**Objective risk** (also called degree of risk) *is defined as the relative variation of actual loss from expected loss.* For example, assume that a property insurer has 10,000 houses insured over a long period and, on average, 1 percent, or 100 houses, burn each year. However, it would be rare for exactly 100 houses to burn each year. In some years, as few as 90 houses may burn; in other years, as many as 110 houses may burn. Thus, there is a variation of 10 houses from the expected number of 100, or a variation of 10 percent. This relative variation of actual loss from expected loss is known as objective risk.

Objective risk declines as the number of exposures increases. More specifically, *objective risk varies inversely with the square root of the number of cases under observation.* In our previous example, 10,000 houses were insured, and objective risk was 10/100, or 10 percent. Now assume that 1 million houses are insured. The expected number of houses that will burn is now 10,000, but the variation of actual loss from expected loss is only 100. Objective risk is now 100/10,000, or 1 percent. Thus, as the square root of the number of houses increased from 100 in the first example to 1000 in the second example (10 times), objective risk declined to one-tenth of its former level.

Objective risk can be statistically calculated by some measure of dispersion, such as the standard deviation or the coefficient of variation. Because objective risk can be measured, it is an extremely useful concept for an insurer or a corporate risk manager. As the number of exposures increases, an insurer can predict its future loss experience more accurately because it can rely on the law of large numbers. The **law of large numbers** *states that as the number of exposure units increases, the more closely the actual loss experience will approach the expected loss experience.* For example, as the number of homes under observation increases, the greater is the degree of accuracy in predicting the proportion of homes that will burn. The law of large numbers is discussed in greater detail in Chapter 2.

### Subjective Risk

**Subjective risk** *is defined as uncertainty based on a person's mental condition or state of mind.* For example, assume that a driver with several convictions for drunk driving is drinking heavily in a neighborhood bar and foolishly attempts to drive home. The driver may be uncertain whether he will arrive home safely without being arrested by the police for drunk driving. This mental uncertainty is called subjective risk.

The impact of subjective risk varies depending on the individual. Two persons in the same situation can have a different perception of risk, and their behavior may be altered accordingly. If an individual experiences great mental uncertainty concerning the occurrence of a loss, that person's behavior may be affected. High subjective risk often results in conservative and prudent behavior, while low subjective risk may result in less conservative behavior. For example, assume that a motorist previously arrested for drunk driving is aware that he has consumed too much alcohol. The driver may then compensate for the mental uncertainty by getting someone else to drive the car home or by taking a cab. Another driver in the same situation may perceive the risk of being arrested as slight. This second driver may drive in a more careless and reckless manner; a low subjective risk results in less conservative driving behavior.

## CHANCE OF LOSS

Chance of loss is closely related to the concept of risk. **Chance of loss** *is defined as the probability that an event will occur.* Like risk, "probability" has both objective and subjective aspects.

### Objective Probability

**Objective probability** *refers to the long-run relative frequency of an event based on the assumptions of an infinite number of observations and of no change in the underlying conditions.* Objective probabilities can be determined in two ways. First, they can be determined by deductive reasoning. These probabilities are called *a priori probabilities*. For example, the probability of getting a head from the toss of a perfectly balanced coin is 1/2 because there are two sides, and only one is a head. Likewise, the probability of rolling a 6 with a single die is 1/6, since there are six sides and only one side has six dots.

Second, objective probabilities can be determined by inductive reasoning rather than by deduction. For example, the probability that a person age 21 will die before age 26 cannot be logically deduced. However, by a careful analysis of past mortality experience, life insurers can estimate the probability of death and sell a five-year term life insurance policy issued at age 21.

### Subjective Probability

**Subjective probability** *is the individual's personal estimate of the chance of loss.* Subjective probability need not coincide with objective probability. For example, people who buy a lottery ticket on their birthday may believe it is their lucky day and overestimate the small chance of winning. A wide variety of factors can influence subjective probability, including a person's age, gender, intelligence, education, and the use of alcohol or drugs.

In addition, a person's estimate of a loss may differ from objective probability because there may be ambiguity in the way in which the probability is perceived. For example, assume that a slot machine in a casino requires a display of three lemons to win. The person playing the machine may perceive the probability of winning to be quite high. But if there are 10 symbols on each reel and only one is a lemon, the objective probability of hitting the jackpot with three lemons is quite small. Assuming that each reel spins independently of the others, the probability that all three will simultaneously show a lemon is the product of their individual probabilities (1/10 × 1/10 × 1/10 = 1/1000). This knowledge is advantageous to casino owners, who know that most gamblers are not trained statisticians and are therefore likely to overestimate the objective probabilities of winning.

### Chance of Loss Versus Objective Risk

Chance of loss can be distinguished from objective risk. Chance of loss is the probability that an event that causes a loss will occur. Objective risk is the relative variation of actual loss from expected loss. *The chance*

*of loss may be identical for two different groups, but objective risk may be quite different.* For example, assume that a property insurer has 10,000 homes insured in Los Angeles and 10,000 homes insured in Philadelphia and that the chance of a fire in each city is 1 percent. Thus, on average, 100 homes should burn annually in each city. However, if the annual variation in losses ranges from 75 to 125 in Philadelphia, but only from 90 to 110 in Los Angeles, objective risk is greater in Philadelphia even though the chance of loss in both cities is the same.

## PERIL AND HAZARD

The terms *peril* and *hazard* should not be confused with the concept of risk discussed earlier.

### Peril

**Peril** *is defined as the cause of loss.* If your house burns because of a fire, the peril, or cause of loss, is the fire. If your car is damaged in a collision with another car, collision is the peril, or cause of loss. Common perils that cause loss to property include fire, lightning, windstorm, hail, tornado, earthquake, flood, burglary, and theft.

### Hazard

A **hazard** *is a condition that creates or increases the frequency or severity of loss.* There are four major types of hazards:

- Physical hazard
- Moral hazard
- Attitudinal hazard (morale hazard)
- Legal hazard

**Physical Hazard**   A **physical hazard** *is a physical condition that increases the frequency or severity of loss.* Examples of physical hazards include icy roads that increase the chance of an auto accident, defective wiring in a building that increases the chance of fire, and a defective lock on a door that increases the chance of theft.

**Moral Hazard**   **Moral hazard** *is dishonesty or character defects in an individual that increase the frequency or severity of loss.* Examples of moral hazard in insurance include faking an accident to collect from an insurer, submitting a fraudulent claim, inflating the amount of a claim, and intentionally burning unsold merchandise that is insured. Murdering the insured to collect the life insurance proceeds is another important example of moral hazard.

Moral hazard is present in all forms of insurance, and it is difficult to control. Dishonest individuals often rationalize their actions on the grounds that "the insurer has plenty of money." This view is incorrect because the insurer can pay claims only by collecting premiums from other insureds. Because of moral hazard, insurance premiums are higher for everyone.

Insurers attempt to control moral hazard by the careful underwriting of applicants for insurance and by various policy provisions, such as deductibles, waiting periods, exclusions, and riders. These provisions are examined in Chapter 10.

**Attitudinal Hazard (Morale Hazard)** Attitudinal hazard *is carelessness or indifference to a loss, which increases the frequency or severity of a loss.* Examples of attitudinal hazard include leaving car keys in an unlocked car, which increases the chance of theft; leaving a door unlocked, which allows a burglar to enter; and changing lanes suddenly on a congested expressway without signaling, which increases the chance of an accident. Careless acts like these increase the frequency and severity of loss.

The term *morale hazard* has the same meaning as attitudinal hazard. *Morale hazard* is a term that appeared in earlier editions of this text to describe someone who is careless or indifferent to a loss. However, the term *attitudinal hazard* is more widely used today and is less confusing to students and more descriptive of the concept being discussed.

**Legal hazard** Legal hazard *refers to characteristics of the legal system or regulatory environment that increase the frequency or severity of losses.* Examples include adverse jury verdicts or large damage awards in liability lawsuits; statutes that require insurers to include coverage for certain benefits in health insurance plans, such as coverage for alcoholism; and regulatory action by state insurance departments that prevents insurers from withdrawing from a state because of poor underwriting results.

## CLASSIFICATION OF RISK

Risk can be classified into several distinct classes. They include the following:

- Pure and speculative risk
- Diversifiable risk and nondiversifiable risk
- Enterprise risk

### Pure Risk and Speculative Risk

**Pure risk** *is defined as a situation in which there are only the possibilities of loss or no loss.* The only possible outcomes are adverse (loss) and neutral (no loss). Examples of pure risks include premature death, job-related accidents, catastrophic medical expenses, and damage to property from fire, lightning, flood, or earthquake.

**Speculative risk** *is defined as a situation in which either profit or loss is possible.* For example, if you purchase 100 shares of common stock, you would profit if the price of the stock increases but would lose if the price declines. Other examples of speculative risks include betting on a horse race, investing in real estate, and going into business for yourself. In these situations, both profit and loss are possible.

It is important to distinguish between pure and speculative risks for three reasons. First, private insurers generally concentrate on insuring certain pure risks. With certain exceptions, private insurers generally do not insure speculative risks. However, there are exceptions. Some insurers will insure institutional portfolio investments and municipal bonds against loss. Also, enterprise risk management (discussed later) is another exception where certain speculative risks can be insured.

Second, the law of large numbers can be applied more easily to pure risks than to speculative risks. The law of large numbers is important because it enables insurers to predict future loss experience. In contrast, it is generally more difficult to apply the law of large numbers to speculative risks to predict future loss experience. An exception is the speculative risk of gambling, where casino operators can apply the law of large numbers in a most efficient manner.

Finally, society may benefit from a speculative risk even though a loss occurs, but it is harmed if a pure risk is present and a loss occurs. For example, a firm may develop new technology for producing inexpensive computers. As a result, some competitors may be forced into bankruptcy. Despite the bankruptcy, society benefits because the computers are produced at a lower cost. However, society normally does not benefit when a loss from a pure risk occurs, such as a flood or earthquake that devastates an area.

## Diversifiable Risk and Nondiversifiable Risk

**Diversifiable risk** *is a risk that affects only individuals or small groups and not the entire economy.* It is a risk that can be reduced or eliminated by diversification. For example, a diversified portfolio of stocks, bonds, and certificates of deposit (CDs) is less risky than a portfolio that is 100 percent invested in stocks. Losses on one type of investment, say stocks, may be offset by gains from bonds and CDs. Likewise, there is less risk to a property and liability insurer if different lines of insurance are underwritten rather than only one line. Losses on one line can be offset by profits on other lines. Because diversifiable risk affects only specific individuals or small groups, it is also called *nonsystematic risk* or *particular risk.* Examples include car thefts, robberies, and dwelling fires. Only individuals and business firms that experience such losses are affected, not the entire economy.

In contrast, **nondiversifiable risk** *is a risk that affects the entire economy or large numbers of persons or groups within the economy.* It is a risk that cannot be eliminated or reduced by diversification. Examples include rapid inflation, cyclical unemployment, war, hurricanes, floods, and earthquakes because large numbers of individuals or groups are affected. Because nondiversifiable risk affects the entire economy or large numbers of persons in the economy, it is also called *systematic risk* or *fundamental risk.*

The distinction between a diversifiable and nondiversifiable (fundamental) risk is important because government assistance may be necessary to insure nondiversifiable risks. Social insurance and government insurance programs, as well as government guarantees or subsidies, may be necessary to insure certain nondiversifiable risks in the United States. For example, the risks of widespread unemployment and flood are difficult to insure privately because the characteristics of an ideal insurable risk (discussed in Chapter 2) are not easily met. As a result, state unemployment compensation programs are necessary to provide weekly income to workers who become involuntarily unemployed. Likewise,

the federal flood insurance program makes property insurance available to individuals and business firms in flood zones.

## Enterprise Risk

**Enterprise risk** *is a term that encompasses all major risks faced by a business firm. Such risks include pure risk, speculative risk, strategic risk, operational risk, and financial risk.* We have already explained the meaning of pure and speculative risk. *Strategic risk* refers to uncertainty regarding the firm's financial goals and objectives; for example, if a firm enters a new line of business, the line may be unprofitable. *Operational risk* results from the firm's business operations. For example, a bank that offers online banking services may incur losses if "hackers" break into the bank's computer.

Enterprise risk also includes financial risk, which is becoming more important in a commercial risk management program. **Financial risk** *refers to the uncertainty of loss because of adverse changes in commodity prices, interest rates, foreign exchange rates, and the value of money.* For example, a food company that agrees to deliver cereal at a fixed price to a supermarket chain in six months may lose money if grain prices rise. A bank with a large portfolio of Treasury bonds may incur losses if interest rates rise. Likewise, an American corporation doing business in Japan may lose money when Japanese yen are exchanged for American dollars.

Enterprise risk is becoming more important in commercial risk management, which is a process that organizations use to identify and treat major and minor risks. In the evolution of commercial risk management, some risk managers are now considering all types of risk in one program. **Enterprise risk management** *combines into a single unified treatment program all major risks faced by the firm.* As explained earlier, these risks include pure risk, speculative risk, strategic risk, operational risk, and financial risk. By packaging major risks into a single program, the firm can offset one risk against another. As a result, overall risk can be reduced. As long as all risks are not perfectly correlated, the combination of risks can reduce the firm's overall risk. In particular, if some risks are negatively correlated, overall risk can be significantly reduced. Chapter 4 discusses enterprise risk management in greater detail.

Treatment of financial risks typically requires the use of complex hedging techniques, financial derivatives, futures contracts, options, and other financial instruments. Some firms appoint a chief risk officer (CRO), such as the treasurer, to manage the firm's financial risks. Chapter 4 discusses financial risk management in greater detail.

## MAJOR PERSONAL RISKS AND COMMERCIAL RISKS

The preceding discussion shows several ways of classifying risk. However, in this text, we emphasize primarily the identification and treatment of pure risk. Certain pure risks are associated with great economic insecurity for both individuals and families, as well as for commercial business firms. This section discusses (1) important personal risks that affect individuals and families and (2) major commercial risks that affect business firms.

### Personal Risks

**Personal risks** *are risks that directly affect an individual or family.* They involve the possibility of the loss or reduction of earned income, extra expenses, and the depletion of financial assets. Major personal risks that can cause great economic insecurity include the following:[3]

- Premature death
- Insufficient income during retirement
- Poor health
- Unemployment

**Premature Death**    Premature death *is defined as the death of a family head with unfulfilled financial obligations.* These obligations include dependents to support, a mortgage to be paid off, children to educate, and credit cards or installment loans to be repaid. If the surviving family members have insufficient replacement income or past savings to replace the lost income, they will be exposed to considerable economic insecurity.

Premature death can cause economic insecurity only if the deceased has dependents to support or dies with unsatisfied financial obligations. Thus, the death of a child age seven is not "premature" in the economic sense since small children generally are not working and contributing to the financial support of the family.

There are at least four costs that result from the premature death of a family head. First, the human life value of the family head is lost forever. *The* **human life value** *is defined as the present value of the family's share of the deceased breadwinner's future earnings.* This loss can be substantial; the actual or potential human life value of most college graduates can easily exceed $500,000. Second, additional expenses may be incurred because of funeral expenses, uninsured medical bills, probate and estate settlement costs, and estate and inheritance taxes for larger estates. Third, because of insufficient income, some families may have trouble making ends meet or covering expenses. Finally, certain noneconomic costs are also incurred, including emotional grief, loss of a role model, and counseling and guidance for the children.

**Insufficient Income During Retirement**    The major risk associated with retirement is insufficient income. The majority of workers in the United States retire before age 65. When they retire, they lose their earned income. Unless they have sufficient financial assets on which to draw, or have access to other sources of retirement income, such as Social Security or a private pension, a 401(k) plan, or an individual retirement account (IRA), they will be exposed to considerable economic insecurity.

The majority of workers experience a substantial reduction in their money incomes when they retire, which can result in a reduced standard of living. *For example, according to the 2012 Current Population Survey, estimated median money income for all households in the United States was $50,054 in 2011. In contrast, the estimated median income for households with a householder aged 65 and older was only $33,118 in 2010, or 34 percent less.*[4] This amount generally is insufficient for retired workers who have substantial additional expenses, such as high uninsured medical bills, catastrophic long-term costs in a skilled nursing facility, or high property taxes.

In addition, most retired workers have not saved enough for a comfortable retirement. During the next 15 years, millions of American workers will retire. However, an alarming number of them will be financially unprepared for a comfortable retirement. According to a 2012 survey by the Employee Benefit Research Institute, the amounts saved for retirement are relatively small. *The survey found that 55 percent of the retirees who responded to the survey reported total savings and investment of less than $25,000,* *which did not include their primary residence or any defined benefit plan. Only 15 percent reported saving $250,000 or more for retirement (see Exhibit 1.1).* In general, these amounts are relatively small and will not provide a comfortable retirement.

Finally, many retired people are living in poverty and are economically insecure. New poverty data show that poverty among the aged is more severe than the official rate indicates. For 2011, the official poverty rate by the Census Bureau showed that only 8.7 percent of those aged 65 and over were counted poor. However, the official figure does not include the value of food stamps, payroll taxes, the earned income tax credit, work-related expenses, medical costs, child care expenses, and geographical differences. The Census Bureau has developed a supplemental poverty measure that includes these factors and shows that the poverty rate for the aged is significantly higher than is commonly believed. *The new measure showed that the poverty rate for the aged 65 and older was 15.1 percent or about 74 percent higher than the official rate.*[5]

**Poor Health**   Poor health is another major personal risk that can cause great economic insecurity. The risk of poor health includes both the payment of catastrophic medical bills and the loss of earned income. The costs of major surgery have increased substantially in recent years. An open heart operation can cost more than $300,000, a kidney or heart transplant can cost more than $500,000, and the costs of a crippling accident requiring several major operations, plastic surgery, and rehabilitation can exceed $600,000. In addition, long-term care in a nursing home can cost $100,000 or more each year. Unless you have adequate health insurance, private savings and financial assets, or other sources of income to meet these expenditures, you will be exposed to great economic insecurity. At the present time, millions of Americans are uninsured and cannot afford to pay for medical care, or delay seeking needed medical care, or are ruined financially because of catastrophic medical bills and declare bankruptcy. Economic insecurity from poor health and the problems of the uninsured are discussed in greater detail in Chapter 15.

The loss of earned income is another major cause of financial insecurity if the disability is severe. In cases of long-term disability, there is substantial loss of earned income; medical bills are incurred; employee benefits may be lost or reduced; and savings are often depleted. There is also the additional cost of providing care to a disabled person who is confined to the home.

Most workers seldom think about the financial consequences of long-term disability. The probability of becoming disabled before age 65 is much higher than is commonly believed, especially by the young. According to the Social Security Administration, studies show that a 20-year-old worker has a 3 in 10 chance of becoming disabled before reaching the full retirement age.[6] Although disability for a specific individual cannot be predicted, the financial impact of total disability on savings, assets, and the ability to earn an income can be severe. In particular, the loss of earned income during a lengthy disability can be financially devastating (see Insight 1.1).

**EXHIBIT 1.1**

**Total Savings and Investment Reported by Retirees, Among Those Providing a Response (not including value of primary residence or defined benefit plans)**

| | 2002 | 2007 | 2008 | 2009 | 2010 | 2011 | 2012 |
|---|---|---|---|---|---|---|---|
| Less than $1,000 | | | | 23% | 27% | 28% | 28% |
| | | 32% | 51% | | | | |
| $1,000–$9,999 | 45% | | | 17 | 15 | 14 | 19 |
| $10,000–$24,999 | | 13 | 9 | 16 | 14 | 12 | 8 |
| $25,000–$49,999 | 7 | 10 | 9 | 13 | 11 | 6 | 9 |
| $50,000–$99,999 | 14 | 11 | 6 | 9 | 6 | 11 | 8 |
| $100,000–$249,999 | 19 | 20 | 13 | 10 | 15 | 12 | 12 |
| $250,000 or more | 15 | 14 | 12 | 12 | 12 | 17 | 15 |

SOURCE: Employee Benefit Research Institute and Mathew Greenwald & Associates, Inc. 2002–2012. Retirement Confidence Surveys.

## INSIGHT 1.1

### Financial Impact on Disabled Individuals Can Be Staggering, Says New Study

The financial impact on individuals who become disabled can be staggering if they lack disability insurance—as high as 20 times a person's annual salary, finds a new study released today by the nonprofit LIFE Foundation and America's Health Insurance Plans (AHIP). Conducted by the global consulting firm Milliman, Inc., the study, titled "The Impact of Disability", is a rare look at the consequences facing individuals who become disabled and can't work, and the level to which various types of disability income protection can help to reduce the financial impact. The findings reveal that in the absence of insurance, a majority of Americans would likely have to make difficult financial decisions, or even drastic lifestyle changes, in order to cover the costs associated with disability, regardless of whether the disability is short- or long-term.

#### The Cost of Disability Hits Single, Low Income, and Long-Term Disabled the Hardest

Examining four representative scenarios of newly disabled individuals, *the study found, for example, that the financial impact of a disability—equal to lost income plus expenses—to be as high as nearly $1 million for a 40-year-old, single male earning $50,000 per year who suffers a long-term disability lasting untill age 65—nearly 20 times his pre-disability earnings.* The study also shows that the costs associated with short-term disabilities can be quite significant—equaling one to nearly two times income in some cases for a disability lasting just two years.

The study by Milliman found that those hit hardest by the costs resulting from a disability are single individuals, who do not have a second income to rely on; lower-income individuals, because added expenses are greater relative to the lost income; and those who suffer longer-term disabilities, since both income and expenses tend to increase with inflation, raising the cost of disability over time.

Further illustrating the stark financial reality outlined by these findings is the fact that as a result of the recession, many Americans have less savings and investments to fall back on should they become disabled and can't work. According to a recent national survey conducted by LIFE, more than a quarter (27%) of Americans admit they would begin having difficulty supporting themselves financially "immediately" following a disability, while nearly half (49%) would reach that point within a month.

"Our experience tells us that if you become disabled and don't have disability insurance, you're going to have a very rough go of it. This study quantifies the impact of a disability so working Americans can get a better understanding of financial difficulties they'll likely face without proper insurance coverage," said Marvin H. Feldman, CLU, ChFC, RFC, president and CEO of the LIFE Foundation. "Disability Insurance provides a financial safety net that can be counted on to replace lost income if you were suddenly out of work due to illness or injury."

#### The Value and Availability of Sources of Disability Income Protection

The study also shows that various sources of disability insurance provide valuable income replacement to help cover the high costs of disability and keep life on track for people who can't work due to a disabling illness or injury.

In fact, private disability insurance plans, such as employer-sponsored (primarily group) or individual coverage, can reduce the cost of a disability by 70–80%. Individual disability coverage, in combination with employer- or government-sponsored insurance programs, can reduce the financial cost of disability by 80–95%.

The study also makes clear that while government-sponsored disability insurance—either through Workers' compensation or Social Security—is available to many working Americans, it can be difficult to qualify for. Workers' Compensation insurance is limited to disabilities that occur on the job, but a vast majority (90%) occur outside the workplace and are therefore not covered by Workers' Compensation programs. In recent years, only about 45% of initial applications for Social Security benefits have been approved, and the average monthly benefit, $1,062, is barely above the poverty level.

"The Social Security Disability Insurance (SSDI) program can be one source of disability income for many Americans, but this is no guarantee that disabled individuals will be eligible for SSDI," said Karen Ignagni, President and CEO of HIP. "Working Americans and their families can benefit from the value that private disability income insurance provides."

#### The Non-Financial Impact of Disability

The study also examines the non-financial impacts associated with disability. While difficult to articulate and quantify, they are often tied to an individual's overall happiness and sense of self-worth, and can be exacerbated by the financial strain that occurs when a disabled person is overwhelmed with expenses in the absence of sufficient income. The availability of benefits from government programs and private insurance during a period of disability can also mitigate the severity of the non-financial costs.

"Not only does a disability take a financial toll, but it also has an impact emotionally and psychologically on the individual and affects the family as well," said Ignagni. "Private disability coverage helps not only to address the financial toll, but it also allows a person to focus on recovery and rehabilitation."

SOURCE: Life and Health Foundation for Education (LIFE), Press Release, "Financial Impact on Disabled Individuals Can Be Staggering, Says New Study," May 15, 2009.

**Unemployment**   The risk of unemployment is another major threat to economic security. Unemployment can result from business cycle downswings, technological and structural changes in the economy, seasonal factors, imperfections in the labor market, and other causes as well.

At the time of this writing, the United States is slowly recovering from one of the most severe recessions in its history, exceeded only by the Great Depression of the 1930s. In June 2012, the unemployment rate was 8.2 percent and 12.7 million workers were unemployed. As a result, millions of unemployed workers are currently experiencing serious problems of economic insecurity. Extended unemployment can cause economic insecurity in at least three ways. First, workers lose their earned income and employer-sponsored health insurance benefits. Unless there is adequate replacement income or past savings on which to draw, an unemployed worker will be exposed to economic insecurity. Second, because of economic conditions, hours of work may be cut, and the worker is employed part time. The reduced income may be insufficient in terms of the worker's needs. Finally, if the duration of unemployment is extended over a long period, past savings and unemployment benefits may be exhausted.

## Property Risks

Persons owning property are exposed to **property risks**—the risk of having property damaged or lost from numerous causes. Homes and other real estate and personal property can be damaged or destroyed because of fire, lightning, tornado, windstorm, and numerous other causes. There are two major types of loss associated with the destruction or theft of property: direct loss and indirect or consequential loss.

**Direct Loss**   A **direct loss** *is defined as a financial loss that results from the physical damage, destruction, or theft of the property.* For example, if you own a home that is damaged by a fire, the physical damage to the home is a direct loss.

**Indirect or Consequential Loss**   An **indirect loss** *is a financial loss that results indirectly from the occurrence of a direct physical damage or theft loss.* For example, as a result of the fire to your home,

you may incur additional living expenses to maintain your normal standard of living. You may have to rent a motel or apartment while the home is being repaired. You may have to eat some or all of your meals at local restaurants. You may also lose rental income if a room is rented and the house is not habitable. These additional expenses that resulted from the fire would be a **consequential loss**.

## Liability Risks

**Liability risks** are another important type of pure risk that most persons face. Under our legal system, you can be held legally liable if you do something that results in bodily injury or property damage to someone else. A court of law may order you to pay substantial damages to the person you have injured.

The United States is a litigious society, and lawsuits are common. Motorists can be held legally liable for the negligent operation of their vehicles; homeowners may be legally liable for unsafe conditions on the premises where someone is injured; dog owners can be held liable if their dog bites someone; operators of boats can be held legally liable because of bodily injury to boat occupants, swimmers, and water skiers. Likewise, if you are a physician, attorney, accountant, or other professional, you can be sued by patients and clients because of alleged acts of malpractice.

Liability risks are of great importance for several reasons. *First, there is no maximum upper limit with respect to the amount of the loss.* You can be sued for any amount. In contrast, if you own property, there is a maximum limit on the loss. For example, if your car has an actual cash value of $20,000, the maximum physical damage loss is $20,000. But if you are negligent and cause an accident that results in serious bodily injury to the other driver, you can be sued for any amount—$50,000, $500,000, $1 million or more—by the person you have injured.

*Second, a lien can be placed on your income and financial assets to satisfy a legal judgment.* For example, assume that you injure someone, and a court of law orders you to pay damages to the injured party. If you cannot pay the judgment, a lien may be placed on your income and financial assets to satisfy the judgment. If you declare bankruptcy to avoid payment of the judgment, your credit rating will be impaired.

*Finally, legal defense costs can be enormous.* If you have no liability insurance, the cost of hiring an attorney to defend you can be staggering. If the suit goes to trial, attorney fees and other legal expenses can be substantial.

## Commercial Risks

Business firms also face a wide variety of pure risks that can financially cripple or bankrupt the firm if a loss occurs. These risks include (1) property risks, (2) liability risks, (3) loss of business income, and (4) other risks.

**Property Risks**   Business firms own valuable business property that can be damaged or destroyed by numerous perils, including fires, windstorms, tornadoes, hurricanes, earthquakes, and other perils. Business property includes plants and other buildings; furniture, office equipment, and supplies; computers and computer software and data; inventories of raw materials and finished products; company cars, boats, and planes; and machinery and mobile equipment. The firm also has accounts receivable records and may have other valuable business records that could be damaged or destroyed and expensive to replace.

**Liability Risks**   Business firms today often operate in highly competitive markets where lawsuits for bodily injury and property damage are common. The lawsuits range from small nuisance claims to multimillion-dollar demands. Firms are sued for numerous reasons, including defective products that harm or injure others, pollution of the environment, damage to the property of others, injuries to customers, discrimination against employees and sexual harassment, violation of copyrights and intellectual property, and numerous other reasons. In addition, directors and officers may be sued by stockholders and other parties because of financial losses and mismanagement of the company.

**Loss of Business Income**   Another important risk is the potential loss of business income when a covered physical damage loss occurs. The firm may be shut down for several months because of a physical damage loss to business property because of a fire, tornado, hurricane, earthquake, or other perils.

During the shutdown period, the firm would lose business income, which includes the loss of profits, the loss of rents if business property is rented to others, and the loss of local markets.

In addition, during the shutdown period, certain expenses may still continue, such as rent, utilities, leases, interest, taxes, some salaries, insurance premiums, and other overhead costs. Fixed costs and continuing expenses that are not offset by revenues can be sizeable if the shutdown period is lengthy.

Finally, the firm may incur extra expenses during the period of restoration that would not have been incurred if the loss had not taken place. Examples include the cost of relocating temporarily to another location, increased rent at another location, and the rental of substitute equipment.

**Other Risks**   Business firms must cope with a wide variety of additional risks, summarized as follows:

- *Crime exposures.* These include robbery and burglary; shoplifting; employee theft and dishonesty; fraud and embezzlement; computer crimes and Internet-related crimes; and the piracy and theft of intellectual property.
- *Human resources exposures.* These include job-related injuries and disease of workers; death or disability of key employees; group life and health and retirement plan exposures; and violation of federal and state laws and regulations.
- *Foreign loss exposures.* These include acts of terrorism, political risks, kidnapping of key personnel, damage to foreign plants and property, and foreign currency risks.
- *Intangible property exposures.* These include damage to the market reputation and public image of the company, the loss of goodwill, and loss of intellectual property. For many companies, the value of intangible property is greater than the value of tangible property.
- *Government exposures.* Federal and state governments may pass laws and regulations that have a significant financial impact on the company. Examples include laws that increase safety standards, laws that require reduction in plant emissions and contamination, and new laws to protect the environment that increase the cost of doing business.

## BURDEN OF RISK ON SOCIETY

The presence of risk results in certain undesirable social and economic effects. Risk entails three major burdens on society:

- The size of an emergency fund must be increased.
- Society is deprived of certain goods and services.
- Worry and fear are present.

### Larger Emergency Fund

It is prudent to set aside funds for an emergency. However, in the absence of insurance, individuals and business firms would have to increase the size of their emergency fund to pay for unexpected losses. For example, assume you have purchased a $300,000 home and want to accumulate a fund for repairs if the home is damaged by fire, hail, windstorm, or some other peril. Without insurance, you would have to save at least $50,000 annually to build up an adequate fund within a relatively short period of time. Even then, an early loss could occur, and your emergency fund may be insufficient to pay for the loss. If you are a middle- or low-income earner, you would find such saving difficult. In any event, the higher the amount that must be saved, the more current consumption spending must be reduced, which results in a lower standard of living.

### Loss of Certain Goods and Services

A second burden of risk is that society is deprived of certain goods and services. For example, because of the risk of a liability lawsuit, many corporations have discontinued manufacturing certain products. Numerous examples can be given. Some 250 companies in the world once manufactured childhood vaccines; today, only a small number of firms manufacture vaccines, due in part to the threat of liability suits. Other firms have discontinued the manufacture of certain products, including asbestos products, football helmets, silicone-gel breast implants, and certain birth-control devices, because of fear of legal liability.

In addition, as a result of the September 11, 2001, terrorist attacks, Congress feared that companies manufacturing anti-terrorism technologies (such as airport security devices) would not manufacture their products for fear of being sued if the technology failed.

To deal with this risk, Congress included a provision in the Homeland Security Act of 2002, which limits the legal liability of companies that produce anti-terrorism technology. Without this provision, many anti-terrorism technologies would not be produced because the liability risk is too great.

### Worry and Fear

The final burden of risk is that of worry and fear. Numerous examples illustrate the mental unrest and fear caused by risk. Parents may be fearful if a teenage son or daughter departs on a ski trip during a blinding snowstorm because the risk of being killed on an icy road is present. Some passengers in a commercial jet may become extremely nervous and fearful if the jet encounters severe turbulence during the flight. A college student who needs a grade of C in a course to graduate may enter the final examination room with a feeling of apprehension and fear.

## TECHNIQUES FOR MANAGING RISK

Techniques for managing risk can be classified broadly as either risk control or risk financing. **Risk control** *refers to techniques that reduce the frequency or severity of losses*. **Risk financing** *refers to techniques that provide for the funding of losses*. Risk managers typically use a combination of techniques for treating each loss exposure.

### Risk Control

As noted above, risk control is a generic term to describe techniques for reducing the frequency or severity of losses. Major risk-control techniques include the following:

- Avoidance
- Loss prevention
- Loss reduction

**Avoidance** Avoidance is one technique for managing risk. For example, you can avoid the risk of being mugged in a high crime area by staying out of the vicinity; you can avoid the risk of divorce by not marrying; and a business firm can avoid the risk of being sued for a defective product by not producing the product.

Not all risks should be avoided, however. For example, you can avoid the risk of death or disability in a plane crash by refusing to fly. But is this choice practical or desirable? The alternatives—driving or taking a bus or train—often are not appealing. Although the risk of a plane crash is present, the safety record of commercial airlines is excellent, and flying is a reasonable risk to assume.

**Loss Prevention**   Loss prevention aims at reducing the probability of loss so that the frequency of losses is reduced. Several examples of personal loss prevention can be given. Auto accidents can be reduced if motorists take a safe-driving course and drive defensively. The number of heart attacks can be reduced if individuals control their weight, stop smoking, and eat healthy diets.

Loss prevention is also important for business firms. For example, strict security measures at airports and aboard commercial flights can reduce acts of terrorism. Boiler explosions can be prevented by periodic inspections by safety engineers; occupational accidents can be reduced by the elimination of unsafe working conditions and by strong enforcement of safety rules; and fires can be prevented by forbidding workers to smoke in a building where highly flammable materials are used. In short, the goal of loss prevention is to reduce the probability that losses with occur.

**Loss Reduction**   Strict loss prevention efforts can reduce the frequency of losses; however, some losses will inevitably occur. Thus, the second objective of loss control is to reduce the severity of a loss after it occurs. For example, a department store can install a sprinkler system so that a fire will be promptly extinguished, thereby reducing the severity of loss; a plant can be constructed with fire-resistant materials to minimize fire damage; fire doors and fire walls can be used to prevent a fire from spreading; and a community warning system can reduce the number of injuries and deaths from an approaching tornado.

From the viewpoint of society, loss control is highly desirable for two reasons. *First, the indirect costs of losses may be large, and in some instances can easily exceed the direct costs*. For example, a worker may be injured on the job. In addition to being responsible for the worker's medical expenses and a

certain percentage of earnings (direct costs), the firm may incur sizable indirect costs: a machine may be damaged and must be repaired; the assembly line may have to be shut down; costs are incurred in training a new worker to replace the injured worker; and a contract may be canceled because goods are not shipped on time. By preventing the loss from occurring, both indirect costs and direct costs are reduced.

*Second, the social costs of losses are reduced*. For example, assume that the worker in the preceding example dies from the accident. Society is deprived forever of the goods and services the deceased worker could have produced. The worker's family loses its share of the worker's earnings and may experience considerable grief and economic insecurity. And the worker may personally experience great pain and suffering before dying. In short, these social costs can be reduced through an effective loss-control program.

### Risk Financing

As stated earlier, risk financing refers to techniques that provide for the payment of losses after they occur. Major risk-financing techniques include the following:

- Retention
- Noninsurance transfers
- Insurance

**Retention**   Retention is an important technique for managing risk. Retention means that an individual or a business firm retains part of all of the losses that can result from a given risk. Risk retention can be active or passive.

- **Active Retention**   Active risk retention means that an individual is consciously aware of the risk and deliberately plans to retain all or part of it. For example, a motorist may wish to retain the risk of a small collision loss by purchasing an auto insurance policy with a $500 or higher deductible. A homeowner may retain a small part of the risk of damage to the home by purchasing a homeowners policy with a substantial deductible. A business firm may deliberately retain the risk of petty thefts by employees, shoplifting, or the spoilage of perishable goods by purchasing a property insurance policy with a sizeable deductible. In these cases, a conscious decision is made to retain part or all of a given risk.

Active risk retention is used for two major reasons. First, it can save money. Insurance may not be purchased, or it may be purchased with a deductible; either way, there is often substantial savings in the cost of insurance. Second, the risk may be deliberately retained because commercial insurance is either unavailable or unaffordable.

- **Passive Retention** Risk can also be retained passively. Certain risks may be unknowingly retained because of ignorance, indifference, laziness, or failure to identify an important risk. Passive retention is very dangerous if the risk retained has the potential for financial ruin. For example, many workers with earned incomes are not insured against the risk of total and permanent disability. However, the adverse financial consequences of total and permanent disability generally are more severe than the financial consequences of premature death. Therefore, people who are not insured against this risk are using the technique of risk retention in a most dangerous and inappropriate manner.

**Self-Insurance** Our discussion of retention would not be complete without a brief discussion of self-insurance. Self-insurance *is a special form of planned retention by which part or all of a given loss exposure is retained by the firm.* Another name for self-insurance is self-funding, which expresses more clearly the idea that losses are funded and paid for by the firm. For example, a large corporation may self-insure or fund part or all of the group health insurance benefits paid to employees.

Self-insurance is widely used in corporate risk management programs primarily to reduce both loss costs and expenses. There are other advantages as well. Self-insurance is discussed in greater detail in Chapter 3.

In summary, risk retention is an important technique for managing risk, especially in modern corporate risk management programs, which are discussed in Chapters 3 and 4. Risk retention, however, is appropriate primarily for high-frequency, low-severity risks where potential losses are relatively small. Except under unusual circumstances, risk retention should not be used to retain low-frequency, high-severity risks, such as the risk of catastrophic medical expenses, long-term disability, or legal liability.

**Noninsurance Transfers** Noninsurance transfers are another technique for managing risk. The risk is transferred to a party other than an insurance company. A risk can be transferred by several methods, including:

- Transfer of risk by contracts
- Hedging price risks
- Incorporation of a business firm

*Transfer of Risk by Contracts* Undesirable risks can be transferred by contracts. For example, the risk of a defective television or stereo set can be transferred to the retailer by purchasing a service contract, which makes the retailer responsible for all repairs after the warranty expires. The risk of a rent increase can be transferred to the landlord by a long-term lease. The risk of a price increase in construction costs can be transferred to the builder by having a guaranteed price in the contract.

Finally, a risk can be transferred by a **hold-harmless clause.** For example, if a manufacturer of scaffolds inserts a hold-harmless clause in a contract with a retailer, the retailer agrees to hold the manufacturer harmless in case a scaffold collapses and someone is injured.

*Hedging Price Risks* Hedging price risks is another example of risk transfer. Hedging is a technique for transferring the risk of unfavorable price fluctuations to a speculator by purchasing and selling futures contracts on an organized exchange, such as the Chicago Board of Trade or New York Stock Exchange.

For example, the portfolio manager of a pension fund may hold a substantial position in long-term United States Treasury bonds. If interest rates rise, the value of the Treasury bonds will decline. To hedge that risk, the portfolio manager can sell Treasury bond futures. Assume that interest rates rise as expected, and bond prices decline. The value of the futures contract will also decline, which will enable the portfolio manager to make an offsetting purchase at a lower price. The profit obtained from closing out the futures position will partly or completely offset the decline in the market value of the Treasury bonds owned. Of course, interest rates do not always move as expected, so the hedge may not be perfect. Transaction costs also are incurred.

However, by hedging, the portfolio manager has reduced the potential loss in bond prices if interest rates rise.

***Incorporation of a Business Firm***   Incorporation is another example of risk transfer. If a firm is a sole proprietorship, the owner's personal assets can be attached by creditors for satisfaction of debts. If a firm incorporates, personal assets cannot be attached by creditors for payment of the firm's debts. In essence, by incorporation, the liability of the stockholders is limited, and the risk of the firm having insufficient assets to pay business debts is shifted to the creditors.

**Insurance**   For most people, insurance is the most practical method for handling major risks. Although private insurance has several characteristics, three major characteristics should be emphasized. First, *risk transfer* is used because a pure risk is transferred to the insurer. Second, the *pooling technique* is used to spread the losses of the few over the entire group so that average loss is substituted for actual loss. Finally, the risk may be reduced by application of the *law of large numbers* by which an insurer can predict future loss experience with greater accuracy. These characteristics are discussed in greater detail in Chapter 2.

---

## CASE APPLICATION

Michael is a college senior who is majoring in marketing. He owns a high-mileage 2003 Ford that has a current market value of $2500. The current replacement value of his clothes, television, stereo, cell phone, and other personal property in a rented apartment totals $10,000. He uses disposable contact lenses, which cost $200 for a six-month supply. He also has a waterbed in his rented apartment that has leaked in the past. An avid runner, Michael runs five miles daily in a nearby public park that has the reputation of being extremely dangerous because of drug dealers, numerous assaults and muggings, and drive-by shootings. Michael's parents both work to help him pay his tuition.

For each of the following risks or loss exposures, identify an appropriate risk management technique that could have been used to deal with the exposure. Explain your answer.

a. Physical damage to the 2003 Ford because of a collision with another motorist
b. Liability lawsuit against Michael arising out of the negligent operation of his car
c. Total loss of clothes, television, stereo, and personal property because of a grease fire in the kitchen of his rented apartment
d. Disappearance of one contact lens
e. Waterbed leak that causes property damage to the apartment
f. Physical assault on Michael by gang members who are dealing drugs in the park where he runs
g. Loss of tuition assistance from Michael's father who is killed by a drunk driver in an auto accident

---

## SUMMARY

- There is no single definition of risk. Risk historically has been defined as uncertainty concerning the occurrence of a loss.

- A loss exposure is any situation or circumstance in which a loss is possible, regardless of whether a loss occurs.

- Objective risk is the relative variation of actual loss from expected loss. Subjective risk is uncertainty based on an individual's mental condition or state of mind.

- Chance of loss is defined as the probability that an event will occur; it is not the same thing as risk.

- Peril is defined as the cause of loss. Hazard is any condition that creates or increases the chance of loss.

- There are four major types of hazards. Physical hazard is a physical condition that increases the frequency or severity of loss. Moral hazard is dishonesty or character defects in an individual that increase the chance of loss. Attitudinal hazard (morale hazard) is carelessness or indifference to a loss that increase the frequency or severity of loss. Legal hazard refers to characteristics of the legal system or regulatory environment that increase the frequency or severity of losses.

■ A pure risk is a risk where there are only the possibilities of loss or no loss. A speculative risk is a risk where either profit or loss is possible.

■ Diversifiable risk is a risk that affects only individuals or small groups and not the entire economy. It is a risk that can be reduced or eliminated by diversification. In contrast, nondiversifiable risk is a risk that affects the entire economy or large numbers of persons or groups within the economy, such as inflation, war, or a business recession. It is a risk that cannot be eliminated or reduced by diversification.

■ Enterprise risk is a term that encompasses all major risks faced by a business firm. Enterprise risk management combines into a single unified treatment program all major risks faced by the firm. Such risks include pure risk, speculative risk, strategic risk, operational risk, and financial risk.

■ Financial risk refers to the uncertainty of loss because of adverse changes in commodity prices, interest rates, foreign exchange rates, and the value of money.

■ The following types of pure risk can threaten an individual's financial security:

Personal risks

Property risks

Liability risks

■ Personal risks are those risks that directly affect an individual. Major personal risks include the following:

Premature death

Insufficient income during retirement

Poor health

Unemployment

■ A direct loss to property is a financial loss that results from the physical damage, destruction, or theft of the property.

■ An indirect, or consequential, loss is a financial loss that results indirectly from the occurrence of direct physical damage or theft loss. Examples of indirect losses are the loss of use of the property, loss of profits, loss of rents, and extra expenses.

■ Liability risks are extremely important because there is no maximum upper limit on the amount of the loss; a lien can be placed on income and assets to satisfy a legal judgment; and substantial court costs and attorney fees may also be incurred.

■ Business firms face a wide variety of major risks that can financially cripple or bankrupt the firm if a loss occurs. These risks include property risks, liability risks, loss of business income, and other risks.

■ Risk entails three major burdens on society:

The size of an emergency fund must be increased.

Society is deprived of needed goods and services.

Worry and fear are present.

■ Risk control refers to techniques that reduce the frequency or severity of losses. Major risk-control techniques include avoidance, loss prevention, and loss reduction.

■ Risk financing refers to techniques that provide for the funding of losses after they occur. Major risk-financing techniques include retention, noninsurance transfers, and insurance.

## KEY CONCEPTS AND TERMS

Attitudinal (morale) hazard (5)
Avoidance (12)
Chance of loss (3)
Direct loss (10)
Diversifiable risk (6)
Enterprise risk (6)
Enterprise risk management (6)
Financial risk (6)
Hazard (4)
Hedging (14)
Hold-harmless clause (14)
Human life value (7)
Incorporation (15)
Indirect, or consequential, loss (10)
Law of large numbers (3)
Legal hazard (5)
Liability risks (10)
Loss exposure (2)

Loss prevention (13)
Moral hazard (4)
Nondiversifiable risk (6)
Noninsurance transfers (14)
Objective probability (3)
Objective risk (3)
Peril (4)
Personal risks (7)
Physical hazard (4)
Premature death (7)
Property risks (10)
Pure risk (5)
Retention (13)
Risk (2)
Risk control (12)
Risk financing (12)
Self-insurance (14)
Speculative risk (5)
Subjective probability (5)
Subjective risk (3)

## REVIEW QUESTIONS

1. a. Explain the historical definition of risk.
   b. What is a loss exposure?
   c. How does objective risk differ from subjective risk?

2. a. Define chance of loss.
   b. What is the difference between objective probability and subjective probability?

3. a. What is the difference between peril and hazard?
   b. Define physical hazard, moral hazard, attitudinal hazard, and legal hazard.

4. a. Explain the difference between pure risk and speculative risk.
   b. How does diversifiable risk differ from nondiversifiable risk?

5. a. Explain the meaning of enterprise risk.
   b. What is financial risk?

6. a. What is enterprise risk management?
   b. How does enterprise risk management differ from traditional risk management?

7. List the major types of pure risk that are associated with economic insecurity.

8. Describe the major social and economic burdens of risk on society.

9. Explain the difference between a direct loss and an indirect or consequential loss.

10. Identify the major risks faced by business firms.

11. a. Briefly explain each of the following risk-control techniques for managing risk:
      1. Avoidance
      2. Loss prevention
      3. Loss reduction
    b. Briefly explain each of the following risk-financing techniques for managing risk:
      1. Retention
      2. Noninsurance transfers
      3. Insurance

## APPLICATION QUESTIONS

1. Assume that the chance of loss is 3 percent for two different fleets of trucks. Explain how it is possible that objective risk for both fleets can be different even though the chance of loss is identical.

2. Several types of risk are present in the American economy. For each of the following, identify the type of risk that is present. Explain your answer.

   a. The Department of Homeland Security alerts the nation of a possible attack by terrorists.
   b. A house may be severely damaged in a fire.
   c. A family head may be totally disabled in a plant explosion.
   d. An investor purchases 100 shares of Microsoft stock.
   e. A river that periodically overflows may cause substantial property damage to thousands of homes in the floodplain.
   f. Home buyers may be faced with higher mortgage payments if the Federal Reserve raises interest rates at its next meeting.
   g. A worker on vacation plays the slot machines in a casino.

3. There are several techniques available for managing risk. For each of the following risks, identify an appropriate technique, or combination of techniques, that would be appropriate for dealing with the risk.
   a. A family head may die prematurely because of a heart attack.
   b. An individual's home may be totally destroyed in a hurricane.
   c. A new car may be severely damaged in an auto accident.
   d. A negligent motorist may be ordered to pay a substantial liability judgment to someone who is injured in an auto accident.
   e. A surgeon may be sued for medical malpractice.

4. Andrew owns a gun shop in a high crime area. The store does not have a camera surveillance system. The high cost of burglary and theft insurance has substantially reduced his profits. A risk management consultant points out that several methods other than insurance can be used to handle the burglary and theft exposure. Identify and explain two noninsurance methods that could be used to deal with the burglary and theft exposure.

5. Risk managers use a number of methods for managing risk. For each of the following, what method for handling risk is used? Explain your answer.
   a. The decision not to carry earthquake insurance on a firm's main manufacturing plant
   b. The installation of an automatic sprinkler system in a hotel
   c. The decision not to produce a product that might result in a product liability lawsuit
   d. Requiring retailers who sell the firm's product to sign an agreement releasing the firm from liability if the product injures someone

## INTERNET RESOURCES

- The **American Risk and Insurance Association (ARIA)** is the premier professional association of risk management and insurance educators and professionals. ARIA is the publisher of *The Journal of Risk and Insurance* and *Risk Management and Insurance Review*. Links are provided to research, teaching, and other risk and insurance sites. Visit the site at

  aria.org

- The **Risk Theory Society** is an organization within the American Risk and Insurance Association that promotes research in risk theory and risk management. Papers are distributed in advance to the members and are discussed critically at its annual meeting. Visit the site at

  aria.org/rts

- The **Huebner Foundation and Geneva Association** act as an international clearinghouse for researchers and educators in insurance economics and risk management. The Huebner foundation, formerly at the University of Pennsylvania, provides graduate fellowships to promising scholars in the areas of risk management and insurance education. The Geneva Association is an international organization that promotes research dealing with worldwide insurance activities. At the time of writing, the Huebner Foundation announced that it is moving to Georgia State University. Visit the site at

  huebnergeneva.org

- The **Insurance Information Institute** is a trade association that provides consumers with information relating to property and casualty insurance coverages and current issues. Visit the site at

  iii.org

- The **Society for Risk Analysis (SRA)** provides an open forum for all persons interested in risk analysis, including risk assessment, risk management, and policies related to risk. SRA considers threats from physical, chemical, and biological agents and from a variety of human activities and natural events. SRA is multidisciplinary and international. Visit the site at

  sra.org

## SELECTED REFERENCES

Bernstein, Peter L. *Against the Gods: The Remarkable Story of Risk*. New York: Wiley, 1996.

Employee Benefit Research Institute. "EBRI's 2012 Retirement Confidence Survey: Job Insecurity, Debt, Weigh on Retirement Confidence, Savings," *EBRI Issue Brief, No. 369,* March 13, 2012.

*The Insurance Fact Book 2012,* New York: Insurance Information Institute.

Rejda, George E. "Causes of Economic Insecurity." In *Social Insurance and Economic Security,* 7th ed. M.E. Sharpe, Inc., Armonk New York, 2012, pp. 5–14.

Wiening, Eric A. *Foundations of Risk Management and Insurance.* Boston, MA: Pearson Custom Publishing, 2005.

## NOTES

1. American Academy of Actuaries, Risk Classification Work Group. *On Risk Classification,* A Public Policy Monograph (Washington, DC: American Academy of Actuaries, 2011), note 2, p.1.
2. Risk has also been defined as (1) variability in future outcomes, (2) chance of loss, (3) possibility of an adverse deviation from a desired outcome that is expected or hoped for, (4) variation in possible outcomes that exist in a given situation, and (5) possibility that a sentient entity can incur a loss.
3. George E. Rejda, *Social Insurance and Economic Security,* 7th ed. (M.E. Sharpe, Inc.,: Armonk, New York, 2012), 5–14.
4. U.S. Census Bureau, *Income, Poverty, and Health Insurance Coverage in the United States: 2011* (Washington, DC: US Government Printing Office, September 2012), Table 1.
5. U.S. Census Bureau, *Income, Poverty, and Health Insurance Coverage in the United States" 2011* (Washington, DC, September 2012). The supplemental poverty measure is discussed in U.S. Census Bureau, "The Research Supplemental Poverty Measure: 2011," Current Population Reports, P60-244, November 2012. See Table 1.
6. *Disability Benefits,* SSA Publication No. 05-10029, July 2011.

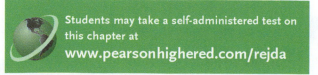

# CHAPTER 2

# INSURANCE AND RISK

*"Insurance: An ingenious modern game of chance in which the player is permitted to enjoy the comfortable conviction that he is beating the man who keeps the table."*

Ambrose Bierce

## LEARNING OBJECTIVES

**After studying this chapter, you should be able to**

◆ Explain the basic characteristics of insurance.

◆ Explain the law of large numbers.

◆ Describe the characteristics of an ideally insurable risk from the viewpoint of a private insurer.

◆ Identify the major insurable and uninsurable risks in our society.

◆ Describe the major types of insurance.

◆ Explain the social benefits and social costs of insurance.

*Michael and Ashley graduated from a southern university, married, and moved to Miami, Florida. Like many married couples, they wanted to save money for a down payment on a house. Shortly after they rented an apartment, a burglar broke into the premises and stole a wide screen television, laptop computer, camera, jewelry, and cash stashed in a dresser drawer. The loss exceeded $15,000. The couple had no insurance. As a result, their goal of accumulating a down payment received a serious setback. The couple made the common mistake of paying inadequate attention to risk and insurance in their financial plans.*

*In Chapter 1, we identified major risks that can cause financial insecurity. For most people, private insurance is the most important technique for managing risk. Consequently, you should understand how insurance works. In this chapter, we examine the basic characteristics of insurance, characteristics of an ideally insurable risk, major types of insurance, and the social benefits and costs of insurance.*

## DEFINITION OF INSURANCE

There is no single definition of insurance. Insurance can be defined from the viewpoint of several disciplines, including law, economics, history, actuarial science, risk theory, and sociology. But each possible definition will not be examined at this point. Instead, we will examine the common elements that are typically present in any insurance plan. However, before proceeding, a working definition of insurance—one that captures the essential characteristics of a true insurance plan—must be established.

After careful study, the Commission on Insurance Terminology of the American Risk and Insurance Association has defined insurance as follows.[1] **Insurance** *is the pooling of fortuitous losses by transfer of such risks to insurers, who agree to indemnify insureds for such losses, to provide other pecuniary benefits on their occurrence, or to render services connected with the risk.* Although this lengthy definition may not be acceptable to all insurance scholars, it is useful for analyzing the common elements of a true insurance plan.

## BASIC CHARACTERISTICS OF INSURANCE

Based on the preceding definition, an insurance plan or arrangement typically includes the following characteristics:

- Pooling of losses
- Payment of fortuitous losses
- Risk transfer
- Indemnification

### Pooling of Losses

Pooling or the sharing of losses is the heart of insurance. **Pooling** *is the spreading of losses incurred by the few over the entire group, so that in the process, average loss is substituted for actual loss.* In addition, pooling involves the grouping of a large number of exposure units so that the law of large numbers can operate to provide a substantially accurate prediction of future losses. Ideally, there should be a large number of similar, but not necessarily identical, exposure units that are subject to the same perils. Thus, pooling implies (1) the sharing of losses by the entire group and (2) prediction of future losses with some accuracy based on the law of large numbers.

The primary purpose of pooling, or the sharing of losses, is to reduce the variation in possible outcomes as measured by the standard deviation or some other measure of dispersion, which reduces risk. For example, assume that two business owners each own an identical storage building valued at $50,000. Assume there is a 10 percent chance in any year that each building will be destroyed by a peril, and that a loss to either building is an independent event. The expected annual loss for each owner is $5000 as shown below:

$$\text{Expected loss} = .90 \times \$0 + .10 \times \$50,000$$
$$= \$5000$$

A common measure of risk is the standard deviation, which is the square root of the variance. The standard deviation (SD) for the expected value of the loss is $15,000, as shown below:

$$SD = \sqrt{.90(0 - \$5000)^2 + .10(\$50,000 - \$5000)^2}$$
$$= \$15000$$

Suppose instead of bearing the risk of loss individually, the two owners decide to pool (combine) their loss exposures, and each agrees to pay an equal share of any loss that might occur. Under this scenario, there are four possible outcomes:

| Possible Outcomes | Probability |
| --- | --- |
| Neither building is destroyed | $.90 \times .90 = .81$ |
| First building destroyed, second building no loss | $.10 \times .90 = .09$ |
| First building no loss, second building destroyed | $.90 \times .10 = .09$ |
| Both buildings are destroyed | $.10 \times .10 = .01$ |

If neither building is destroyed, the loss for each owner is $0. If one building is destroyed, each owner pays $25,000. If both buildings are destroyed, each owner must pay $50,000. The expected loss for each owner remains $5000 as shown below:

$$\text{Expected loss} = .81 \times \$0 + .09 \times \$25,000$$
$$+ .90 \times \$25,000 + .01 \times \$50,000$$
$$= \$5,000$$

Note that while the expected loss remains the same, the probability of the extreme values, $0 and $50,000, have declined. The reduced probability of the extreme values is reflected in a lower standard deviation (SD) as shown below:

$$SD = \sqrt{\begin{array}{l} .81(0 - \$5000)^2 + .09(\$25,000 - \$5000)^2 \\ + .09(\$25,000 - \$5000)^2 \\ + .01(\$50,000 - \$5000)^2 \end{array}}$$

$$SD = \$10,607$$

Thus, as additional individuals are added to the pooling arrangement, the standard deviation continues to decline while the expected value of the loss remains unchanged. For example, with a pool of 100 insureds, the standard deviation is $1500; with a pool of 1000 insureds, the standard deviation is $474; and with a pool of 10,000, the standard deviation is $150.

In addition, by pooling or combining the loss experience of a large number of exposure units, an insurer may be able to predict future losses with greater accuracy. From the viewpoint of the insurer, if future losses can be predicted, objective risk is reduced. Thus, another characteristic often found in many lines of insurance is risk reduction based on the law of large numbers.

The law of large numbers states that the greater the number of exposures, the more closely will the actual results approach the probable results that are expected from an infinite number of exposures.[2] For example, if you flip a balanced coin into the air, the a priori probability of getting a head is 0.5. If you flip the coin only 10 times, you may get a head eight times. Although the observed probability of getting a head is 0.8, the true probability is still 0.5. If the coin were flipped 1 million times, however, the actual number of heads would be approximately 500,000. Thus, as the number of random tosses increases, the actual results approach the expected results.

A practical illustration of the law of large numbers is the National Safety Council's prediction of the number of motor vehicle deaths during a typical holiday weekend. Because millions of vehicles are on the road, the National Safety Council has been able to predict with some accuracy the number of motorists who will die during a typical Fourth of July weekend. For example, assume that 500 to 700 motorists are expected to die during a typical July 4th weekend. Although individual motorists cannot be identified, the actual number of deaths for the group of motorists as a whole can be predicted with some accuracy.

However, for most insurance lines, actuaries generally do not know the true probability and severity of loss. Therefore, estimates of both the average frequency and the average severity of loss must be based on previous loss experience. If there are a large number of exposure units, the actual loss experience of the past may be a good approximation of future losses. As we noted earlier, as the number of exposure units increases, the relative variation of actual loss from expected loss will decline. Thus, actuaries can predict future losses with a greater degree of accuracy. This concept is important because an insurer must charge a premium that will be adequate for paying all losses and expenses during the policy period. The lower the degree of objective risk, the more confidence an insurer has that the actual premium charged will be sufficient to pay all claims and expenses and provide a margin for profit.

A more rigorous statement of pooling and the law of large numbers can be found in the appendix at the end of this chapter.

### Payment of Fortuitous Losses

A second characteristic of private insurance is the payment of fortuitous losses. A **fortuitous loss** *is one that is unforeseen and unexpected by the insured and occurs as a result of chance*. In other words, the loss must be accidental. The law of large numbers is based on the assumption that losses are accidental and occur randomly. For example, a person may slip on an icy sidewalk and break a leg. The loss would be fortuitous.

### Risk Transfer

Risk transfer is another essential element of insurance. With the exception of self-insurance, a true insurance plan always involves risk transfer. **Risk transfer** *means that a pure risk is transferred from the insured to the*

*insurer, who typically is in a stronger financial position to pay the loss than the insured*. From the viewpoint of the individual, pure risks that are typically transferred to insurers include the risk of premature death, excessive longevity, poor health, disability, destruction and theft of property, and personal liability lawsuits.

### Indemnification

A final characteristic of insurance is indemnification for losses. **Indemnification** *means that the insured is restored to his or her approximate financial position prior to the occurrence of the loss*. Thus, if your home burns in a fire, a homeowners policy will indemnify you or restore you to your previous position. If you are sued because of the negligent operation of an automobile, your auto liability insurance policy will pay those sums that you are legally obligated to pay. Similarly, if you become seriously disabled, a disability-income insurance policy will restore at least part of the lost wages.

## CHARACTERISTICS OF AN IDEALLY INSURABLE RISK

Private insurers generally insure only pure risks. However, some pure risks are not privately insurable. From the viewpoint of a private insurer, an insurable risk ideally should have certain characteristics. There are ideally six characteristics of an **insurable risk**:

- There must be a large number of exposure units.
- The loss must be accidental and unintentional.
- The loss must be determinable and measurable.
- The loss should not be catastrophic.
- The chance of loss must be calculable.
- The premium must be economically feasible.

### Large Number of Exposure Units

*The first requirement of an insurable risk is a large number of exposure units*. Ideally, there should be a large group of roughly similar, but not necessarily identical, exposure units that are subject to the same peril or group of perils. For example, a large number of frame dwellings in a city can be grouped together for purposes of providing property insurance on the dwellings.

The purpose of this first requirement is to enable the insurer to predict loss based on the law of large numbers. Loss data can be compiled over time, and losses for the group as a whole can be predicted with some accuracy. The loss costs can then be spread over all insureds in the underwriting class.

## Accidental and Unintentional Loss

*A second requirement is that the loss should be accidental and unintentional;* ideally, the loss should be unforeseen and unexpected by the insured and outside of the insured's control. Thus, if an individual deliberately causes a loss, he or she should not be indemnified for the loss.

The loss should be accidental because the law of large numbers is based on the random occurrence of events. A deliberately caused loss is not a random event because the insured knows when the loss will occur. Thus, prediction of future experience may be highly inaccurate if a large number of intentional or nonrandom losses occur.

## Determinable and Measurable Loss

*A third requirement is that the loss should be both determinable and measurable.* This means the loss should be definite as to cause, time, place, and amount. Life insurance in most cases meets this requirement easily. The cause and time of death can be readily determined in most cases, and if the person is insured, the face amount of the life insurance policy is the amount paid.

Some losses, however, are difficult to determine and measure. For example, under a disability-income policy, the insurer promises to pay a monthly benefit to the disabled person if the definition of disability stated in the policy is satisfied. Some dishonest claimants may deliberately fake sickness or injury to collect from the insurer. Even if the claim is legitimate, the insurer must still determine whether the insured satisfies the definition of disability stated in the policy. Sickness and disability are highly subjective, and the same event can affect two persons quite differently. For example, two accountants who are insured under separate disability-income contracts may be injured in an auto accident, and both may be classified as totally disabled. One accountant, however, may be stronger willed and more determined to return to work. If that accountant undergoes rehabilitation and returns to work, the disability-income benefits will terminate.

Meanwhile, the other accountant would still continue to receive disability-income benefits according to the terms of the policy. In short, it is difficult to determine when a person is actually disabled. However, all losses ideally should be both determinable and measurable.

The basic purpose of this requirement is to enable an insurer to determine if the loss is covered under the policy, and if it is covered, how much should be paid. For example, assume that Shannon has an expensive fur coat that is insured under a homeowners policy. It makes a great deal of difference to the insurer if a thief breaks into her home and steals the coat, or the coat is missing because her husband stored it in a dry-cleaning establishment but forgot to tell her. The loss is covered in the first example but not in the second.

## No Catastrophic Loss

*The fourth requirement is that ideally the loss should not be catastrophic.* This means that a large proportion of exposure units should not incur losses at the same time. As we stated earlier, pooling is the essence of insurance. If most or all of the exposure units in a certain class simultaneously incur a loss, then the pooling technique breaks down and becomes unworkable. Premiums must be increased to prohibitive levels, and the insurance technique is no longer a viable arrangement by which losses of the few are spread over the entire group.

Insurers ideally wish to avoid all catastrophic losses. In reality, however, that is impossible, because catastrophic losses periodically result from floods, hurricanes, tornadoes, earthquakes, forest fires, and other natural disasters. Catastrophic losses can also result from acts of terrorism.

Several approaches are available for meeting the problem of a catastrophic loss. First, reinsurance can be used by which insurance companies are indemnified by reinsurers for catastrophic losses. **Reinsurance** *is an arrangement by which the primary insurer that initially writes the insurance transfers to another insurer (called the reinsurer) part or all of the potential losses associated with such insurance.* The reinsurer is then responsible for the payment of its share of the loss. Reinsurance is discussed in greater detail in Chapter 6.

Second, insurers can avoid the concentration of risk by dispersing their coverage over a large geographical area. The concentration of loss exposures in a geographical area exposed to frequent floods, earthquakes, hurricanes, or other natural disasters can result in periodic catastrophic losses. If the loss exposures are geographically dispersed, the possibility of a catastrophic loss is reduced.

Finally, financial instruments are now available for dealing with catastrophic losses. These instruments include catastrophe bonds, which are designed to help fund catastrophic losses. Catastrophe bonds are discussed in Chapters 4 and 6.

### Calculable Chance of Loss

A *fifth requirement is that the chance of loss should be calculable.* The insurer must be able to calculate both the average frequency and the average severity of future losses with some accuracy. This requirement is necessary so that a proper premium can be charged that is sufficient to pay all claims and expenses and yields a profit during the policy period.

Certain losses, however, are difficult to insure because the chance of loss cannot be accurately estimated, and the potential for a catastrophic loss is present. For example, floods, wars, and cyclical unemployment occur on an irregular basis, and prediction of the average frequency and severity of losses is difficult. Thus, without government assistance, these losses are difficult for private carriers to insure.

### Economically Feasible Premium

A *final requirement is that the premium should be economically feasible.* The insured must be able to afford the premium. In addition, for the insurance to be an attractive purchase, the premiums paid must be substantially less than the face value, or amount, of the policy.

To have an economically feasible premium, the chance of loss must be relatively low. One view is that if the chance of loss exceeds 40 percent, the cost of the policy will exceed the amount that the insurer must pay under the contract.[3] For example, an insurer could issue a $1000 life insurance policy on a man age 99, but the pure premium would be close to that amount, and an additional amount for expenses would also have to be added. The total premium would exceed the face amount of insurance.

Based on the preceding requirements, most personal risks, property risks, and liability risks can be privately insured because the ideal characteristics of an insurable risk generally can be met. In contrast, most market risks, financial risks, production risks, and political risks are difficult to insure by private insurers.[4] These risks are speculative, and the ideal characteristics of an insurable risk discussed earlier are more difficult to meet. In addition, the potential of each risk to produce a catastrophe loss is great; this is especially true for political risks, such as the risk of war. Finally, calculation of a proper premium may be difficult because the chance of loss cannot be accurately estimated. For example, insurance that protects a retailer against loss because of a change in consumer tastes, such as a style change, generally is not available. Accurate loss data are not available. Thus, it would be difficult to calculate an accurate premium. The premium charged may or may not be adequate to pay all losses and expenses. Since private insurers are in business to make a profit, certain risks are difficult to insure because of the possibility of substantial losses.

## TWO APPLICATIONS: THE RISKS OF FIRE AND UNEMPLOYMENT

You will understand more clearly the requirements of an insurable risk if you can apply these requirements to a specific risk. For example, consider the risk of fire to a private dwelling. This risk can be privately insured because the requirements of an insurable risk are generally fulfilled (see Exhibit 2.1).

Consider next the risk of unemployment. How well does the risk of unemployment meet the ideal requirements of an insurable risk? As is evident in Exhibit 2.2, the risk of unemployment does not completely meet the requirements.

First, predicting unemployment is difficult because of the different types of unemployment and labor. There are professional, highly skilled, semiskilled, unskilled, blue-collar, and white-collar workers. Moreover, unemployment rates vary significantly by occupation, age, gender, education, marital status, city, state, and a host of other factors, including government programs and economic policies that frequently change. In addition, the outsourcing of jobs to foreign countries by major corporations is another major problem in the United States, which makes the risk of unemployment more difficult to measure and insure privately. Also, the duration of unemployment varies widely among the different groups. Because a large number of workers can become unemployed

**EXHIBIT 2.1**
**Risk of Fire as an Insurable Risk**

| Requirements | Does the risk of fire satisfy the requirements? |
| --- | --- |
| 1. Large number of exposure units | Yes. Numerous exposure units are present. |
| 2. Accidental and unintentional loss | Yes. With the exception of arson, most fire losses are accidental and unintentional. |
| 3. Determinable and measurable loss | Yes. If there is disagreement over the amount paid, a property insurance policy has provisions for resolving disputes. |
| 4. No catastrophic loss | Yes. Although catastrophic fires have occurred, all exposure units normally do not burn at the same time. |
| 5. Calculable chance of loss | Yes. Chance of fire can be calculated, and the average severity of a fire loss can be estimated in advance. |
| 6. Economically feasible premium | Yes. Premium rate per $100 of fire insurance is relatively low. |

**EXHIBIT 2.2**
**Risk of Unemployment as an Insurable Risk**

| Requirements | Does the risk of unemployment satisfy the requirements? |
| --- | --- |
| 1. Large number of exposure units | Not completely. Although there are a large number of employees, predicting unemployment is often difficult because of the different types of unemployment and different types of labor. |
| 2. Accidental and unintentional loss | Not always. Some unemployment is due to individuals who voluntarily quit their jobs. |
| 3. Determinable and measurable loss | Not completely. The level of unemployment can be determined, but the measurement of loss may be difficult. Most unemployment is involuntary because of layoffs or because workers have completed temporary jobs. However, some unemployment is voluntary; workers voluntarily change jobs because of higher wages, a change in careers, family obligations, relocation to another state, or other reasons. |
| 4. No catastrophic loss | No. A severe national recession or depressed local business conditions in a town or city could result in a catastrophic loss. |
| 5. Calculable chance of loss | Not completely. The different types of unemployment in specific occupations can make it difficult for actuaries to estimate the chance of loss accurately. |
| 6. Economically feasible premium | Not completely. Adverse selection, moral hazard, policy design, and the potential for a catastrophic loss could make the insurance too expensive to purchase. Some plans, however, will pay unemployment benefits in certain cases where the unemployment is involuntary, and the loss payments are relatively small, such as waiver of life insurance premiums for six months, or payment of credit card minimum payments for a limited period. |

at the same time, a potential catastrophic loss is also present. And because certain types of unemployment occur irregularly, it may be difficult to calculate the chance of loss accurately. For these reasons, the risk of widespread unemployment is difficult to insure by private insurers. However, unemployment can be insured by social insurance programs. Social insurance programs are discussed later in the chapter.

## ADVERSE SELECTION AND INSURANCE

When insurance is sold, insurers must deal with the problem of adverse selection. **Adverse selection** *is the tendency of persons with a higher-than-average chance of loss to seek insurance at standard (average) rates, which if not controlled by underwriting, results in higher-than-expected loss levels.* For example, adverse selection can result from high-risk drivers who seek auto insurance at standard rates, from persons with serious health problems who seek life or health insurance at standard rates, and from business firms that have been repeatedly robbed or burglarized and seek crime insurance at standard rates. If the applicants for insurance with a higher-than-average chance of loss succeed in obtaining the coverage at standard rates, we say that the insurer is "adversely selected against." If not controlled by underwriting, adverse selection can result in higher-than-expected loss levels.

Adverse selection can be controlled by careful underwriting. **Underwriting** *refers to the process of selecting and classifying applicants for insurance.* Applicants who meet the underwriting standards are insured at standard or preferred rates. If the underwriting standards are not met, the insurance is denied, or an extra premium must be paid, or the coverage offered may be more limited. Insurers frequently sell insurance to applicants who have a higher-than-average chance of loss, but such applicants must pay higher premiums. The problem of adverse selection arises when applicants with a higher-than-average chance of loss succeed in obtaining the coverage at standard or average rates.

Policy provisions are also used to control adverse selection. Examples are the suicide clause in life insurance and the preexisting conditions clause in individual medical expense policies prior to enactment of the Affordable Care Act, also known as "Obamacare." These policy provisions are discussed in greater detail later in the text when specific insurance contracts are analyzed.

## INSURANCE AND GAMBLING COMPARED

Insurance is often erroneously confused with gambling. There are two important differences between them. *First, gambling creates a new speculative risk, while insurance is a technique for handling an already existing pure risk.* Thus, if you bet $500 on a horse race, a new speculative risk is created, but if you pay $500 to an insurer for a homeowners policy that includes coverage for a fire, the risk of fire is already present. No new risk is created by the transaction.

*The second difference is that gambling can be socially unproductive, because the winner's gain comes at the expense of the loser.* In contrast, insurance is always socially productive, because neither the insurer nor the insured is placed in a position where the gain of the winner comes at the expense of the loser. Both the insurer and the insured have a common interest in the prevention of a loss. Both parties win if the loss does not occur. Moreover, frequent gambling transactions generally never restore the losers to their former financial position. In contrast, insurance contracts restore the insureds financially in whole or in part if a loss occurs.

## INSURANCE AND HEDGING COMPARED

In Chapter 1, we discussed the concept of hedging, by which risk can be transferred to a speculator through the purchase of a futures contract. An insurance contract, however, is not the same thing as hedging. Although both techniques are similar in that risk is transferred by a contract, and no new risk is created, there are some important differences between them. *First, an insurance transaction typically involves the transfer of pure risks because the characteristics of an insurable risk generally can be met.* However, hedging is a technique for handling speculative risks that may be uninsurable, such as protection against a decline in the price of agricultural products and raw materials.

*A second difference between insurance and hedging is that insurance can reduce the objective risk of an insurer by application of the law of large numbers.* As the number of exposure units increases, the insurer's prediction of future losses improves because the relative variation of actual loss from expected loss will decline. Thus, many insurance transactions reduce objective risk. In contrast, hedging typically involves only risk transfer, not risk reduction. The risk of adverse price fluctuations is transferred to speculators who believe they can make a profit because of superior knowledge of market conditions. The risk is transferred, not reduced, and prediction of loss generally is not based on the law of large numbers.

# TYPES OF INSURANCE

Insurance can be classified as either private or government insurance. Private insurance includes life and health insurance and property and liability insurance. Government insurance includes social insurance programs and other government insurance plans.

## Private Insurance

**Life Insurance**   At the end of 2010, 917 life insurers were doing business in the United States, down from a peak of 2343 in 1988. The decline is due to mergers and consolidations to reduce operating costs and general overhead and to increase efficiency.[5]

**Life insurance** pays death benefits to designated beneficiaries when the insured dies. The benefits pay for funeral expenses, uninsured medical bills, estate taxes, and other expenses. The death proceeds can also provide periodic income payments to the deceased's beneficiary. Life insurers also sell annuities, individual retirement account (IRA) plans, 401(k) plans, and individual and group retirement plans. Some life insurers also sell (1) individual and group health insurance plans that cover medical expenses because of sickness or injury; (2) disability income plans that replace income lost during a period of disability; and (3) long-term care policies that cover care in nursing facilities.

**Health Insurance**   Although many life insurers described above also sell some type of individual or group health insurance plan, the health insurance industry overall is highly specialized and controlled by a relatively small number of insurers. About 35 health insurers write most individual and group health insurance plans sold today. These companies include Blue Cross Blue Shield Association, AETNA, UnitedHealth Group, and WellPoint. Medical expense plans pay for hospital and surgical expenses, physician fees, prescription drugs, and a wide variety of additional medical costs. Health insurance plans are covered in greater detail in Chapters 15–16.

**Property and Liability Insurance**   In 2010, there were 2689 property and liability insurers in the United States.[6] **Property insurance** indemnifies property owners against the loss or damage of real or personal property caused by various perils, such as fire, lightning, windstorm, or tornado. **Liability insurance** covers the insured's legal liability arising out of property damage or bodily injury to others; legal defense costs are also paid.

Property and liability insurance is also called property and casualty insurance. In practice, nonlife insurers typically use the term *property and casualty insurance* (rather than property and liability insurance) to describe the various coverages and operating results. **Casualty insurance** *is a broad field of insurance that covers whatever is not covered by fire, marine, and life insurance; casualty lines include auto, liability, burglary and theft, workers compensation, and health insurance.*

Exhibit 2.3 identifies the major property and casualty coverages sold today. Although there is some overlap, the various coverages can be grouped into two major categories—personal lines and commercial lines.

1. *Personal Lines.* **Personal lines** *refer to coverages that insure the real estate and personal property of individuals and families or provide them with protection against legal liability.* Major personal lines include the following:
   - *Private passenger auto insurance* protects the insured against legal liability arising out of auto accidents that cause property damage or bodily injury to others. Auto insurance also includes physical damage insurance on a covered auto for damage or loss resulting from a collision, theft, or other perils. Medical expense coverage and uninsured motorist coverage are also available.
   - *Homeowners insurance* is a package policy that provides property insurance and personal liability insurance in one policy. There are a number of homeowners policies available that cover the dwelling, other structures, and personal property against loss or damage from numerous perils, including fire, lightning, windstorm, or tornado. The policies also include theft coverage and personal liability insurance. A homeowners policy is an example

**EXHIBIT 2.3**
**Property and Casualty Insurance Coverages**

1. Personal lines
   - Private passenger auto insurance
   - Homeowners insurance
   - Personal umbrella liability insurance
   - Earthquake insurance
   - Flood insurance
2. Commercial lines
   - Fire and allied lines insurance
   - Commercial multiple-peril insurance
   - General liability insurance
   - Products liability insurance
   - Workers compensation insurance
   - Commercial auto insurance
   - Accident and health insurance
   - Inland marine and ocean marine insurance
   - Professional liability insurance
   - Directors and officers liability insurance
   - Boiler and machinery insurance (also known as mechanical breakdown, equipment breakdown, or systems breakdown coverage)
   - Fidelity bonds and surety bonds
   - Crime insurance
   - Other coverages

of a *multiple-line policy*, which refers to state legislation that allows insurers to write property and casualty lines in one policy.

- *Personal umbrella liability insurance* provides protection against a catastrophic lawsuit or judgment. Coverage applies on an excess basis after any underlying insurance coverages are exhausted. Policy limits typically range from $1 million to $10 million.
- *Earthquake insurance* covers damage that can result from the shaking and cracking of buildings and damage to personal property in an earthquake. Homeowners policies and business insurance policies do not cover damage from earthquake. However, coverage can be obtained by an endorsement to the policy or by a separate policy.
  - *Federal flood insurance* is a federal program that provides coverage for flood losses to homeowners and business firms in

flood zones. Flood losses are excluded under standard homeowners and renters policies. Flood insurance is typically sold by participating property and casualty insurers.

2. *Commercial Lines.* **Commercial lines** *refer to property and casualty coverages for business firms, nonprofit organizations, and government agencies.* Major commercial lines include the following:

- *Fire insurance* covers losses caused by fire and lightning; it is usually sold as part of a package policy, such as a commercial multiple-peril policy. *Allied lines* refer to coverages that are usually purchased with fire insurance, such as coverage for windstorm, hail, and vandalism. Indirect losses can also be covered, including the loss of business income, rents, and extra expenses.
- *Commercial multiple-peril insurance* is a package policy, which can be written to include property insurance, general liability insurance, business income insurance, equipment breakdown insurance, and crime insurance.
- *General liability insurance* covers the legal liability of business firms and other organizations that arise out of property damage or bodily injury to others. Legal liability can arise out of the ownership of business property, sale or distribution of products, and manufacturing or contracting operations. However, general liability insurance does not include products liability insurance, which is a separate line.
- *Products liability insurance* covers the legal liability of manufacturers, wholesalers, and retailers to persons who are injured or incur property damage from defective products.
- *Workers compensation insurance* covers workers for a job-related accident or disease. The insurance pays for medical bills, disability income benefits, rehabilitation benefits, and death benefits to the dependents of an employee whose death is job-related.
- *Commercial auto insurance* covers the legal liability of business firms arising out of the ownership or operation of business vehicles. It also includes physical damage insurance on covered business vehicles for damage or loss resulting from a collision, theft, or other perils.

- *Accident and health insurance* is also sold by some property and casualty insurers. This line is similar to the health insurance coverages sold by life and health insurers.
- *Inland marine insurance* covers goods being shipped on land, which include imports, exports, domestic shipments, and instrumentalities of transportation (for example, bridges, tunnels, and pipelines). Inland marine insurance also covers personal property such as fine art, jewelry, and furs.
- *Ocean marine insurance* covers ocean-going vessels and their cargo from loss or damage because of perils of the sea; contracts are also written to cover the legal liability of shippers and owners.
- *Professional liability insurance* provides protection against malpractice lawsuits or lawsuits that result from a substantial error or omission. Professional liability insurance covers the professional acts or omissions of physicians, surgeons, attorneys, accountants, and other professionals. For example, *medical malpractice insurance* covers physicians and other health-care providers for liability claims arising out of harm or injury to patients.
- *Directors and officers (D&O)* liability insurance provides financial protection for the directors and officers and the corporation if the directors and officers are sued for mismanagement of the company's affairs.
- *Boiler and machinery insurance (also known as mechanical breakdown, equipment breakdown, or systems breakdown coverage)* is a highly specialized line that covers losses due to the accidental breakdown of covered equipment. Such equipment includes steam boilers, air conditioning and refrigeration equipment, and electrical generating equipment.
- *Fidelity bonds* cover loss caused by the dishonest or fraudulent acts of employees, such as embezzlement and the theft of money. *Surety bonds* provide for monetary compensation in the case of failure by bonded persons to perform certain acts, such as failure of a contractor to construct a building on time.
- *Crime insurance* covers the loss of money, securities, and other property because of burglary, robbery, theft, and other crime perils.

- *Other coverages* include *aircraft insurance*, which provides physical damage insurance on covered aircraft and liability coverage for legal liability arising out of the ownership or operation of aircraft. *Credit insurance* covers manufacturers and wholesalers against loss because an account receivable is uncollectible. *Financial guaranty insurance* guarantees the payment of principal and interest on debt instruments issued by the insured. *Private mortgage insurance* (PMI) guarantees the mortgage lender for a loss up to certain limits for a property foreclosure if the borrower defaults on the mortgage.

## Government Insurance

Numerous government insurance programs are in operation at the present time. Government insurance can be divided into social insurance programs and other government insurance programs.

**Social Insurance**   Social insurance programs are government insurance programs with certain characteristics that distinguish them from other government insurance plans. These programs are financed entirely or in large part by mandatory contributions from employers, employees, or both, and not primarily by the general revenues of government. The contributions are usually earmarked for special trust funds; the benefits, in turn, are paid from these funds. In addition, the right to receive benefits is ordinarily derived from or linked to the recipient's past contributions or coverage under the program; the benefits and contributions generally vary among the beneficiaries according to their prior earnings, but the benefits are heavily weighted in favor of low-income groups. Moreover, most social insurance programs are compulsory. Covered workers and employers are required by law to pay contributions and participate in the programs. Finally, eligibility requirements and benefit rights are usually prescribed exactly by statute, leaving little room for administrative discretion in the award of benefits.[7]

Major social insurance programs in the United States include the following:

- Old-Age, Survivors, and Disability Insurance (Social Security)
- Medicare
- Unemployment insurance

- Workers compensation
- Compulsory temporary disability insurance
- Railroad Retirement Act
- Railroad Unemployment Insurance Act

*Old-Age, Survivors, and Disability Insurance,* commonly known as Social Security, is a massive public income-maintenance program that provides retirement, survivor, and disability benefits to eligible individuals and families.

*Medicare* is part of the total Social Security program and covers the medical expenses of most people age 65 and older and certain disabled people younger than age 65.

*Unemployment insurance* programs provide weekly cash benefits to eligible workers who experience short-term involuntary unemployment. Regular state unemployment benefits are typically paid up to 26 weeks after certain eligibility requirements are met. In recent years, temporary emergency unemployment programs have also been enacted to provide additional weeks of benefits to beneficiaries who have exhausted their regular benefits during severe business recessions. In addition, extended benefits also may be available to unemployed workers in states with high unemployment who exhaust their regular benefits. Unemployment insurance is discussed in Chapter 18.

As stated earlier, *workers compensation insurance* covers workers against a job-related accident or disease. Although workers compensation is a casualty line sold by private insurers, it is also an important form of social insurance. The social insurance aspects of workers compensation are discussed in Chapter 18.

In addition, *compulsory temporary disability insurance,* which exists in five states, Puerto Rico, and the railroad industry, provides for the partial replacement of wages that may be lost because of a temporary nonoccupational disability.[8]

The *Railroad Retirement Act* provides retirement benefits, survivor benefits, and disability income benefits to railroad workers who meet certain eligibility requirements.

Finally, the *Railroad Unemployment Insurance Act* provides unemployment and sickness benefits to railroad employees.

**Other Government Insurance Programs**   Other government insurance programs exist at both the federal and state level. However, these programs do not have the distinguishing characteristics of social insurance programs. Important federal insurance programs include the following:

- The *Federal Employees Retirement System (FERS)* provides retirement, survivor, and disability benefits to federal employees hired after 1983.
- The *Civil Service Retirement System* provides retirement, survivor, and disability benefits to federal employees hired before 1984.
- The *Federal Deposit Insurance Corporation (FDIC)* provides insurance on checking and savings accounts in commercial banks, credit unions, and savings and loan association.
- The *Pension Benefit Guaranty Corporation (PBGC)* is a federal corporation that guarantees (up to certain limits) the pension benefits of workers if a private defined-benefit pension plan is terminated.
- The *National Flood Insurance Program (NFIP)* makes property insurance available (up to certain limits) to homeowners and business firms who reside in flood zones.
- *Other federal programs* include various life insurance programs to veterans, federal crop insurance, war risk insurance, and numerous additional programs.

A wide variety of insurance programs also exist at the state level. They include the following:

- As stated earlier, *state workers compensation programs* provide medical, disability, rehabilitation, and survivor benefits if workers are injured or die as a result of a job-related accident or disease.
- *State children's health insurance programs (SCHIP)* are joint state-federal programs that provide low-cost health insurance to low-income children and families.
- The majority of states have *high-risk pools* that make health insurance available to persons who are uninsurable or substandard in health.
- *Residual market plans (also called shared or involuntary market plans)* exist in a number of states, which provide insurance to high-risk policyholders in certain states who may have difficulty in obtaining basic insurance in the standard market. These plans include (1) FAIR

(Fair Access to Insurance) Plans, which provide basic property insurance to high-risk policyholders; (2) Beach and Windstorm Plans that provide windstorm and hurricane coverage to property owners along the Atlantic and Gulf Coast seaboard; (3) Citizens Property Insurance Company (CPIC) that makes available coverage to property owners in Florida for windstorm, hurricanes, and certain other perils; and (4) Citizens Property Insurance Corporation that provides insurance to policyholders in Louisiana.

- *Other state programs* include the California Earthquake Authority, Florida Hurricane Catastrophe Fund, Maryland Automobile Insurance Fund, and the State Life Insurance Fund in Wisconsin.

# BENEFITS OF INSURANCE TO SOCIETY

The major social and economic benefits of insurance include the following:

- Indemnification for loss
- Reduction of worry and fear
- Source of investment funds
- Loss prevention
- Enhancement of credit

## Indemnification for Loss

Indemnification permits individuals and families to be restored to their former financial position after a loss occurs. As a result, they can maintain their financial security. Because insureds are restored either in part or in whole after a loss occurs, they are less likely to apply for public assistance or welfare benefits, or to seek financial assistance from relatives and friends.

Indemnification to business firms also permits firms to remain in business and employees to keep their jobs. Suppliers continue to receive orders, and customers receive the goods and services they desire. The community also benefits because its tax base is not eroded. In short, the indemnification function contributes greatly to family and business stability and therefore is one of the most important social and economic benefits of insurance.

## Reduction of Worry and Fear

A second benefit of insurance is that worry and fear are reduced. This is true both before and after a loss. For example, if family heads have adequate amounts of life insurance, they are less likely to worry about the financial security of their dependents in the event of premature death; persons insured for long-term disability do not have to worry about the loss of earnings if a serious illness or accident occurs; and property owners who are insured enjoy greater peace of mind because they know they are covered if a loss occurs. Worry and fear are also reduced after a loss occurs, because the insureds know that they have insurance that will pay for the loss.

## Source of Investment Funds

The insurance industry is an important source of funds for capital investment and accumulation. Premiums are collected in advance of the loss, and funds not needed to pay immediate losses and expenses can be loaned to business firms. These funds typically are invested in shopping centers, hospitals, factories, housing developments, and new machinery and equipment. The investments increase society's stock of capital goods, and promote economic growth and full employment. Insurers also invest in social investments, such as housing, nursing homes, and economic development projects. In addition, because the total supply of loanable funds is increased by the advance payment of insurance premiums, the cost of capital to business firms that borrow is lower than it would be in the absence of insurance.

## Loss Prevention

Insurance companies are actively involved in numerous loss-prevention programs and also employ a wide variety of loss-prevention personnel, including safety engineers and specialists in fire prevention, occupational safety and health, and products liability. Some important loss-prevention activities that property and casualty insurers strongly support include the following:

- Highway safety and reduction of auto accidents and deaths
- Fire prevention
- Reduction of work-related injuries and disease

- Prevention of auto thefts
- Prevention and detection of arson losses
- Prevention of defective products that could injure the user
- Prevention of boiler explosions
- Educational programs on loss prevention

The loss-prevention activities reduce both direct and indirect, or consequential, losses. Society benefits, because both types of losses are reduced.

### Enhancement of Credit

A final benefit is that insurance enhances a person's credit. Insurance makes a borrower a better credit risk because it guarantees the value of the borrower's collateral or gives greater assurance that the loan will be repaid. For example, when a house is purchased, the lending institution normally requires property insurance on the house before the mortgage loan is granted. The property insurance protects the lender's financial interest if the property is damaged or destroyed. Similarly, a business firm seeking a temporary loan for Christmas or seasonal business may be required to insure its inventories before the loan is made. If a new car is purchased and financed by a bank or other lending institution, physical damage insurance on the car may be required before the loan is made. Thus, insurance can enhance a person's credit.

## COSTS OF INSURANCE TO SOCIETY

Although the insurance industry provides enormous social and economic benefits to society, the social costs of insurance must also be recognized. The major social costs of insurance include the following:

- Cost of doing business
- Fraudulent claims
- Inflated claims

### Cost of Doing Business

One important cost is the cost of doing business. Insurers consume scarce economic resources—land, labor, capital, and business enterprise—in providing insurance to society. In financial terms, an expense loading must be added to the pure premium to cover the expenses incurred by insurance companies in their daily operations. *An expense loading is the amount needed to pay all expenses, including commissions, general administrative expenses, state premium taxes, acquisition expenses, and an allowance for contingencies and profit.* In 2010, property and casualty insurers incurred underwriting costs of about 28 percent for each underwriting dollar for sales and administration, taxes, licenses and fees. In 2010, life insurers incurred costs of 17 percent of expenditures for operating expenses, taxes, and investment expenses.[9] As a result, total costs to society are increased. For example, assume that a small country with no property insurance has an average of $100 million of fire losses each year. Also assume that property insurance later becomes available, and the expense loading is 30 percent of losses. Thus, total costs to this country are increased to $130 million.

However, these additional costs can be justified for several reasons. First, from the insured's viewpoint, uncertainty concerning the payment of a covered loss is reduced because of insurance. Second, the costs of doing business are not necessarily wasteful, because insurers engage in a wide variety of loss-prevention activities. Finally, the insurance industry provides jobs to millions of workers in the United States. However, because economic resources are used up in providing insurance to society, a real economic cost is incurred.

### Fraudulent Claims

A second cost of insurance comes from the submission of fraudulent claims. Examples of fraudulent claims include the following:

- Auto accidents are faked or staged to collect benefits.
- Dishonest claimants fake slip-and-fall accidents.
- Phony burglaries, thefts, or acts of vandalism are reported to insurers.
- False health insurance claims are submitted to collect benefits.
- Dishonest policyholders take out life insurance policies on unsuspecting insureds and later arrange to have them killed.

The payment of such fraudulent claims results in higher premiums to all insureds. The existence of insurance also prompts some insureds to deliberately cause a loss to profit from insurance. These social costs fall directly on society.

Some types of insurance fraud are especially outrageous. The Coalition Against Insurance Fraud has established a "hall of shame" for insurance scams that are strikingly shocking, brazen, and outrageous (see Insight 2.1).

## Inflated Claims

Another cost of insurance relates to the submission of inflated or "padded" claims. Although the loss is not intentionally caused by the insured, the dollar amount of the claim may exceed the actual financial loss. Examples of inflated claims include the following:

- Attorneys for plaintiffs sue for high-liability judgments that exceed the true economic loss of the victim.

- Insureds inflate the amount of damage in auto collision claims so that the insurance payments will cover the collision deductible.
- Disabled persons often malinger to collect disability-income benefits for a longer duration.
- Insureds exaggerate the amount and value of property stolen from a home or business.

Inflated claims must be recognized as an important social cost of insurance. Premiums must be increased to pay the additional losses. As a result, disposable income and the consumption of other goods and services are reduced.

## Cost to Society of Fraudulent and Inflated Claims

According to the Insurance Information Institute, industry estimates of fraud are about 10 percent of the property and casualty incurred losses and loss adjustment expenses each year. Based on this

---

## INSIGHT 2.1

### Insurance Fraud Hall of Shame—Shocking Examples of Insurance Fraud

The Coalition Against Insurance Fraud compiles annually a list of insurance fraud cases that are especially shocking, brazen, and outrageous. The following is a summary of several shocking cases:

- **Sinister seniors.** Two elderly women befriended two homeless men in Los Angeles and took out $3 million of life insurance on the men, naming themselves as beneficiaries. Helen Golay and Olga Rutterschmidt then had cars run down and kill the two men. Both women received life without parole.

- **Killing street people for life insurance.** Richard James is a Guyanese-American life insurance agent who conspired to take out fraudulent life insurance policies on Guyanese street people in the New York City area. He had them killed for the payouts. Four street people were killed in a scheme that netted more than $1 million. James and a crony are headed to prison for life.

- **Crooked cop shoots himself.** A passerby found Los Angeles District police officer Jeff Stenroos lying on the ground near his open door. He claimed he was shot by a car-burglary suspect with a ponytail and black leather jacket. But the shooting was a hoax. Stenroos shot himself in his bulletproof vest and then filed a fraudulent workers compensation claim.

- **Torching his home and children die.** Timothy Nicholls torched his home to get insurance money to pay his mounting debt to a motorcycle gang that supplied him with methamphetamines. Three children died of smoke inhalation. Nichols received life in prison.

- **Playing with fire backfires.** Victor and Olga Barriere wanted to burn their rickety home for the insurance. The couple was stuck with a $315,000 mortgage and a decaying home that nobody wanted to buy. They hired handyman Thomas Trucious to torch the place for an insurance payoff. The plan backfired. The handyman was a rank amateur who blew up the house in a searing fireball, fatally engulfing himself in flames and endangering homes in the neighborhood.

- **Nursing home hellholes.** Robert Wachter ran three nursing homes in Missouri. Residents were denied water, food, and sanitation. He billed Medicare and Medicaid for many of the same services. Some residents died of neglect. Wachter received 18 months in federal prison and fines of $750,000.

SOURCE: Adaptation of selected cases from *Hall of Shame's No-Class of 2011 Dishonored; Amazing Disgrace: 2008 Shamers Dishonored;*, and *Newsroom, Top Swindlers of 2007*, Coalition Against Insurance Fraud, at insurancefraud.org.

estimate, property and casualty insurance fraud exceeded $30 billion each year over the five-year period from 2006 to 2010. In addition, according to the Federal Bureau of Investigation (FBI), health-care fraud is an estimated 3 to 10 percent of total health-care spending. This includes both private and public fraud. According to the Centers for Medicare and Medicaid Services estimated health-care fraud amounted to between $77 billion and $259 billion in 2010.[10]

Some people commit insurance fraud because they are greedy, need large amounts of cash for various purposes, and view insurers as easy targets. Others want to reduce their out-of-pocket costs when a loss occurs, such as covering their deductible, or want to "get back" at insurers who may be perceived as unfair. The end result is higher insurance premiums for all policyholders.

Most Americans think insurance fraud is committed only by career criminals and large crime rings, such as auto-theft rings, chop shops, and dishonest doctors and lawyers. This restricted view of insurance fraud is incorrect. Many Americans who otherwise think they are basically honest often engage in a variety of actions that clearly fall within the category of insurance fraud (see Insight 2.2).

Although fraudulent and inflated claims must be recognized as a social cost of insurance, the economic benefits of insurance generally outweigh these costs. Insurance reduces worry and fear; the indemnification function contributes greatly to social and economic stability; financial security of individuals and firms is preserved; and from the perspective of insurers, objective risk in the economy is reduced. The social costs of insurance can be viewed as the sacrifice that society must make to obtain these benefits.

## INSIGHT 2.2

### Don't Think Insurance Fraud Is Committed Only by Hardened Crooks

So, you think insurance fraud is committed only by hardened crooks and large crime rings?

Actually, many normally honest people also commit fraud. Maybe even your church-going uncle ... that helpful neighbor across the street ... a friendly store owner downtown.

People sometimes "just fudge a bit" or tell "little white lies" when they apply for insurance or make a claim.

They may not even think this is real insurance fraud. "Heck, it's only a few dollars," or "Nobody's really being hurt," or "I've paid my premiums for years, and now it's my turn."

Well guess again. Try this quiz. If you check "yes" for any question, you may have committed insurance fraud.

| Yes or No | Have you ever knowingly: |
|:---:|:---|
| ☐ ☐ | said you drive fewer miles to work than you really do, when applying for auto coverage? |
| ☐ ☐ | said you never use your car for work though you actually do, when applying for auto coverage? |
| ☐ ☐ | said you park your car in a garage when you actually park it on the street, when applying for auto coverage? |
| ☐ ☐ | said you live in a different location than you really do, when applying for auto coverage? |
| ☐ ☐ | let a body shop pad your car repair bill to recoup your deductible when making an auto claim? |
| ☐ ☐ | inflated the value of possessions stolen from your home or car when making a claim? |
| ☐ ☐ | inflated the value of jewelry or other goods you lost when making a claim? |
| ☐ ☐ | asked a repairman to pad a bill for damage to your home so you could recoup your deductible? |
| ☐ ☐ | said your business has fewer employees than it really does, when you applied for workers compensation coverage? |
| ☐ ☐ | said your employees have safer jobs than they really do, when you applied for workers compensation coverage? |
| ☐ ☐ | fudged your medical history so you seem healthier on your life insurance application? |
| ☐ ☐ | said you don't smoke even though you really do, when applying for life insurance coverage? |
| ☐ ☐ | said an injury you received at home or while playing sports was work-related so you could collect workers compensation coverage? |
| ☐ ☐ | stayed home even though you're healed, so you could keep collecting workers compensation? |

SOURCE: Reprinted with permission of the Coalition Against Insurance Fraud, insurancefraud.org.

## CASE APPLICATION

There are numerous definitions of insurance. Based on the definition of insurance stated in the text, indicate whether each of the following guarantees is considered insurance.

    a. A new television is guaranteed by the manufacturer against defects for 90 days.

    b. A new set of radial tires is guaranteed by the manufacturer against road defects for 50,000 miles.

    c. A builder of new homes gives a 10-year guarantee against structural defects in the home.

    d. A cosigner of a note agrees to pay the loan balance if the original debtor defaults on the payments.

    e. A large group of homeowners agrees to pay for losses to homes that are damaged or destroyed by fire during the year.

## SUMMARY

- There is no single definition of insurance. However, a typical insurance plan contains four elements:

  > Pooling of losses
  >
  > Payment of fortuitous losses
  >
  > Risk transfer
  >
  > Indemnification

  Pooling means that the losses of the few are spread over the group, and average loss is substituted for actual loss. Fortuitous losses are unforeseen and unexpected and occur as a result of chance. Risk transfer involves the transfer of a pure risk to an insurer. Indemnification means that the victim of a loss is restored in whole or in part by payment, repair, or replacement by the insurer.

- The law of large numbers states that the greater the number of exposures, the more likely the actual results will approach the expected results. The law of large numbers permits an insurer to estimate future losses with some accuracy.

- From the viewpoint of a private insurer, an insurable risk ideally should have certain characteristics.

  > There must be a large number of exposure units.
  >
  > The loss must be accidental and unintentional.
  >
  > The loss must be determinable and measurable.
  >
  > The loss should not be catastrophic.
  >
  > The chance of loss must be calculable.
  >
  > The premium must be economically feasible.

- Most personal risks, property risks, and liability risks can be privately insured, because the requirements of an insurable risk generally can be met. However, most market risks, financial risks, production risks, and political risks generally are difficult to insure privately.

- Adverse selection is the tendency of persons with a higher-than-average chance of loss to seek insurance at average rates, which, if not controlled by underwriting, results in higher-than-expected loss levels.

- Insurance is not the same as gambling. Gambling creates a new speculative risk, whereas insurance deals with an existing pure risk. Also, gambling may be socially unproductive, because the winner's gain comes at the expense of the loser. Insurance is socially productive because both the insured and insurer benefit if the loss does not occur.

- Insurance is not the same as hedging. Insurance involves the transfer of a pure risk, whereas hedging involves the transfer of a speculative risk. Also, insurance may reduce objective risk because of the law of large numbers. Hedging typically involves only risk transfer and not risk reduction.

- Insurance can be classified into private and government insurance. Private insurance consists of life and health insurance and property and liability insurance. Government insurance consists of social insurance and other government insurance programs.

- The major benefits of insurance to society are as follows:

  > Indemnification for loss
  >
  > Reduction of worry and fear
  >
  > Source of investment funds
  >
  > Loss prevention
  >
  > Enhancement of credit

- Insurance imposes certain costs on society, which include the following:

  > Cost of doing business
  >
  > Fraudulent claims
  >
  > Inflated claims

## KEY CONCEPTS AND TERMS

Adverse selection (26)
Casualty insurance (27)
Commercial lines (28)
Expense loading (32)
Fidelity bonds (29)
Fortuitous loss (22)
Indemnification (22)
Inland marine insurance (29)
Insurance (20)
Law of large numbers (21)
Liability insurance (27)
Life insurance (27)

Ocean marine insurance (29)
Personal lines (27)
Pooling (20)
Property insurance (27)
Reinsurance (23)
Requirements of an
 insurable risk (24)
Risk transfer (22)
Social insurance (29)
Surety bonds (29)
Underwriting (26)

## REVIEW QUESTIONS

1. Explain each of the following characteristics of a typical insurance plan.
   a. Pooling of losses
   b. Payment of fortuitous losses
   c. Risk transfer
   d. Indemnification

2. Explain the law of large numbers.

3. Pure risks ideally should have certain characteristics to be insurable by private insurers. List the six characteristics of an ideally insurable risk.

4. Identify the approaches that insurers can use to deal with the problem of catastrophic loss exposures.

5. Why are most market risks, financial risks, production risks, and political risks considered difficult to insure by private insurers?

6. a. What is the meaning of adverse selection?
   b. Identify some methods that insurers use to control for adverse selection.

7. What are the two major differences between insurance and gambling?

8. What are the two major differences between insurance and hedging?

9. a. Identify the major fields of private insurance.
   b. Identify several property and casualty insurance coverages.

10. a. Explain the basic characteristics of social insurance programs.
    b. Identify the major social insurance programs in the United States.

## APPLICATION QUESTIONS

1. Compare the risks of (i) fire with (ii) war in terms of how well they meet the requirements of an ideally insurable risk.

2. a. Private insurers provide social and economic benefits to society. Explain the following benefits of insurance to society.
   (1) Indemnification for loss
   (2) Enhancement of credit
   (3) Source of funds for capital investment and accumulation
   b. Explain the major costs of insurance to society.

3. Buildings in flood zones are difficult to insure by private insurers because the ideal requirements of an insurable risk are difficult to meet.
   a. Identify the ideal requirements of an insurable risk.
   b. Which of the requirements of an insurable risk are not met by the flood peril?

4. Private insurance provides numerous coverages that can be used to meet specific loss situations. For each of the following situations, identify a private insurance coverage that would provide the desired protection.
   a. Emily, age 28, is a single parent with two dependent children. She wants to make certain that funds are available for her children's education if she dies before her youngest child finishes college.
   b. Danielle, age 16, recently obtained her driver's license. Her parents want to make certain they are protected if Danielle negligently injures another motorist while driving a family car.
   c. Jacob, age 30, is married with two dependents. He wants his income to continue if he becomes totally disabled and unable to work.
   d. Tyler, age 35, recently purchased a house for $200,000 that is located in an area where tornadoes frequently occur. He wants to make certain that funds are available if the house is damaged or destroyed by a tornado.
   e. Nathan, age 40, owns an upscale furniture store. Nathan wants to be protected if a customer is injured while shopping in the store and sues him for the bodily injury.

## INTERNET RESOURCES

- The **American Insurance Association (AIA)** is an important trade and service organization that represents approximately 300 insurers. The site lists available publications, position papers on important issues in property and casualty insurance, press releases, insurance-related links, and names of state insurance commissioners. Visit the site at

  aiadc.org/aiapub/

- The **Coalition Against Insurance Fraud** is an alliance of consumer, law enforcement, and insurance industry groups that attempt to reduce insurance fraud through public education and action. Numerous examples of fraudulent claims are listed. Visit this interesting site at

  insurancefraud.org/

- The **Insurance Information Institute (III)** has an excellent site for obtaining information on property and casualty insurance. III provides timely consumer information on auto, homeowners, and business insurance, submission of claims and rebuilding after catastrophes, and ways to save money. The site contains background material and information for the news media, including television, newspapers, and radio. Visit this important site at

  iii.org

- **Insure.com** provides timely information on auto insurance, homeowners insurance, life and health insurance, disability insurance, and other types of insurance. Rate quotes can be obtained online for major lines of insurance. The site provides valuable information to consumers on most types of insurance. Visit the site at

  insure.com

- The **Insurance Journal** is a definitive online source of timely information on the property/casualty industry. A free online newsletter is available that provides breaking news on important developments in property and casualty insurance. Visit the site at

  insurancejournal.com

- The **Insurance Research Council (IRC)** is a division of the Institutes. IRC is an independent, nonprofit research organization supported by leading property and casualty insurance companies and associations. IRC provides timely and reliable information based on extensive data collection and analyses and examines important public policy issues that affect insurers, customers, and the general public. IRC is devoted solely to research and communication of its research findings. Visit the site at

  insurance-research.org/

- **InsWeb** operates an online insurance marketplace that enables consumers to get quotes for numerous insurance products, including auto, homeowners, and renters insurance, term insurance, and individual health insurance. Overall, it is an excellent source of information for consumers. Visit the site at

  insweb.com

- The **International Risk Management Institute (IRMI)** seeks to be the premier authority in providing expert advice and practical strategies on risk management and insurance. IRMI has a large online library with information on numerous risk management and insurance topics. Visit the site at

  irmi.com

- The **National Association of Mutual Insurance Companies** is a trade association that represents mutual insurance companies involved in property and casualty insurance. Visit the site at

  namic.org

## SELECTED REFERENCES

*The Financial Services Fact Book 2012,* New York: Insurance Information Institute, 2012.

*The Insurance Fact Book 2012,* New York: Insurance Information Institute, 2012.

*Life Insurers Fact Book 2011,* Washington, DC: American Council of Life Insurers, 2011.

*Risk Management and Insurance*, 2nd ed., Compiled from publications by Charles M. Nyce and George E. Rejda, Boston, MA: Pearson Custom Publishing, 2008.

## NOTES

1. *Bulletin of the Commission on Insurance Terminology of the American Risk and Insurance Association,* (October 1965).

2. Robert I. Mehr and Sandra G. Gustavson, *Life Insurance: Theory and Practice,* 4th ed. (Plano, TX: Business Publications, 1987), p. 31.

3. Robert I. Mehr, *Fundamentals of Insurance,* 2nd ed. (Homewood, IL: Richard D. Irwin, 1986), p. 43.

4. Market risks include the risks of adverse price changes in raw materials, general price level changes (inflation), changes in consumer tastes, new technology, and increased competition from competitors. Financial risks include the risks of adverse price changes in the price of securities, adverse changes in interest rates, and the inability to borrow on favorable terms. Production risks include shortages of raw materials, depletion of natural resources, and technical problems in production. Political risks include the risks of war, acts of terrorism, government uprisings, adverse government regulations, and the nationalization of foreign plants by a hostile government.

5. American Council of Life Insurers, *Life Insurers Fact Book 2011,* Washington, D.C., 2011, Table 1.7. Available at acli.com

6. *The Insurance Fact Book 2012,* New York: Insurance Information Institute, p. v.

7. George E. Rejda, *Social Insurance and Economic Security,* 7th ed. (Armonk, New York M.E. Sharpe, Inc., 2012), pp. 15-17.

8. The five states are California, Hawaii, New Jersey, New York, and Rhode Island.

9. *The Insurance Fact Book 2012,* New York: Insurance Information Institute, p. 38; *Life Insurers Fact Book 2011,* Table 5.1.

10. Insurance Information Institute, "Insurance Fraud," March 2012. This article is periodically updated.

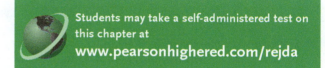

Students may take a self-administered test on this chapter at
**www.pearsonhighered.com/rejda**

# APPENDIX

# BASIC STATISTICS AND THE LAW OF LARGE NUMBERS

The application of probability and statistics is crucial in the insurance industry. Insurance actuaries constantly face a tradeoff when determining the premium to charge for coverage: the premium must be high enough to cover expected losses and expenses, but low enough to remain competitive with premiums charged by other insurers. Actuaries apply statistical analysis to determine expected loss levels and expected deviations from these loss levels. Through the application of the law of large numbers, insurers reduce their risk of adverse outcomes.

In this appendix, we review some statistical concepts that are important to insurers, including probability, central tendency, and dispersion. Next, we examine the law of large numbers and how insurance companies apply it to reduce risk.

## PROBABILITY AND STATISTICS

To determine expected losses, insurance actuaries apply probability and statistical analysis to given loss situations. The probability of an event is simply the long-run relative frequency of the event, given an infinite number of trials with no changes in the underlying conditions. The probability of some events can be determined without experimentation. For example, if a "fair" coin is flipped in the air, the probability the coin will come up "heads" is 50 percent, and the probability it will come up "tails" is also 50 percent. Other probabilities, such as the probability of dying during a specified year or the probability of being involved in an auto accident, can be estimated from past loss data.

A convenient way of summarizing events and probabilities is through a probability distribution. A probability distribution lists events that could occur and the corresponding probability of each event's occurrence. Probability distributions may be discrete, meaning that only distinct outcomes are possible, or continuous, meaning that any outcome over a range of outcomes could occur.[1]

Probability distributions are characterized by two important measures: central tendency and dispersion. Although there are several measures of central tendency, the measure most often employed is the mean ($\mu$) or expected value ($EV$) of the distribution.[2] *The mean or expected value is found by multiplying each outcome by the probability of occurrence, and then summing the resulting products:*

$$\mu \text{ or } EV = \sum X_i P_i$$

For example, assume that an actuary estimates the following probabilities of various losses for a certain risk:

| Amount of Loss ($X_i$) | | Probability of Loss ($P_i$) | | $X_iP_i$ |
|---|---|---|---|---|
| $ 0 | × | .30 | = | $ 0 |
| $360 | × | .50 | = | $180 |
| $600 | × | .20 | = | $120 |
| | | $\Sigma X_iP_i$ | = | $300 |

Thus, we could say that the mean or expected loss given the probability distribution is $300.

Although the mean value indicates central tendency, it does not tell us anything about the riskiness or dispersion of the distribution. Consider a second probability-of-loss distribution:

| Amount of Loss ($X_i$) | | Probability of Loss ($P_i$) | | $X_iP_i$ |
|---|---|---|---|---|
| $225 | × | .40 | = | $ 90 |
| $350 | × | .60 | = | $210 |
| | | $\Sigma XiPi$ | = | $300 |

This distribution also has a mean loss value of $300. However, the first distribution is riskier because the range of possible outcomes is from $0 to $600. With the second distribution, the range of possible outcomes is only $125 ($350 – $225), so we are more certain about the outcome with the second distribution.

Two standard measures of dispersion are employed to characterize the variability or dispersion about the mean value. These measures are the variance ($\sigma^2$) and the standard deviation ($\sigma$). The variance of a probability distribution is the sum of the squared differences between the possible outcomes and the expected value, weighted by the probability of the outcomes:

$$\sigma^2 = \sum P_i(X_i - EV)^2$$

So the variance is the average squared deviation between the possible outcomes and the mean. Because the variance is in "squared units," it is necessary to take the square root of the variance so that the central tendency and dispersion measures are in the same units. The square root of the variance is the standard deviation. The variance and standard deviation of the first distribution are as follows:

$$\sigma^2 = .30(0 - 300)^2 + .50(360 - 300)^2$$
$$+ .20(600 - 300)^2$$
$$= 27,000 + 1,800 + 18,000$$
$$= 46,800$$
$$\sigma = \sqrt{46,800} = 216.33$$

For the second distribution, the variance and standard deviation are:

$$\sigma^2 = .40(225 - 300)^2 + .60(350 - 300)^2$$
$$= 2,250 + 1,500$$
$$= 3,750$$
$$\sigma = \sqrt{3,750} = 61.24$$

Thus, while the means of the two distributions are the same, the standard deviations are significantly different. *Higher standard deviations, relative to the mean, are associated with greater uncertainty of loss; therefore, risk is higher. Lower standard deviations, relative to the mean, are associated with less uncertainty of loss; therefore, risk is lower.*

The two probability distributions used in the discussion of central tendency and dispersion are "odd" in that only three and two possible outcomes, respectively, could occur. In addition, specific probabilities corresponding to the loss levels are assigned. In practice, estimating the frequency and severity of loss is difficult. Insurers can employ both actual loss data and theoretical loss distributions in estimating losses.[3]

## LAW OF LARGE NUMBERS

Even if the characteristics of the population were known with certainty, insurers do not insure populations. Rather, they select a sample from the population and insure the sample. Obviously, the relationship between population parameters and the characteristics of the sample (mean and standard deviation) is important for insurers, since actual experience may vary significantly from the population parameters. The characteristics of the sampling distribution help to illustrate the law of large numbers, the mathematical foundation of insurance.

It can be shown that the average losses for a random sample of $n$ exposure units will follow a normal distribution because of the Central Limit Theorem, which states:

> If you draw random samples of $n$ observations from any population with mean $\mu_x$ and standard deviation $\sigma_x$, and $n$ is sufficiently large, the distribution of sample means will be approximately normal, with the mean of the distribution equal to the mean of the population $\mu_{\bar{x}} = \mu_x$, and the standard error of the sample mean $\sigma_{\bar{x}}$ equal to the standard deviation of the population $(\sigma_x)$ divided by the square root of $n$ $(\sigma_{\bar{x}} = \sigma_x/\sqrt{n})$. This approximation becomes increasingly accurate as the sample size, $n$, increases.

The Central Limit Theorem has two important implications for insurers. First, it is clear that the sample distribution of means does not depend on the population distribution, provided $n$ is sufficiently large. *In other words, regardless of the population distribution (bimodal, unimodal, symmetric, skewed right, skewed left, and so on), the distribution of sample means will approach the normal distribution as the sample size increases.* This result is shown in Exhibit A2.1.

The normal distribution is a symmetric, bell-shaped curve. It is defined by the mean and standard deviation of the distribution. About 68 percent of the distribution lies within one standard deviation of the mean, and about 95 percent of the distribution lies within two standard deviations of the mean. The normal curve has many statistical applications (hypothesis testing, confidence intervals, and so on) and is easy to use.

The second important implication of the Central Limit Theorem for insurers is that the standard error of the sample mean distribution declines as the sample size increases. Recall that the standard error is defined as

$$\sigma_{\bar{x}} = \sigma_x/\sqrt{n}$$

In other words, the standard error of the sample mean loss distribution is equal to the standard deviation of the population divided by the square root of the sample size. Because the population standard deviation is independent of the sample size, *the standard error of the sampling distribution, $\sigma_{\bar{x}}$ can be reduced by simply increasing the sample size.*

This result has important implications for insurers. For example, assume that an insurer would like to select a sample to insure from a population where the mean loss is $500 and the standard deviation is $350. As the insurer increases the number of units insured $(n)$, the standard error of the sampling distribution $\sigma_{\bar{x}}$ will decline. The standard error for various sample sizes is summarized below:

| $n$ | $\sigma_{\bar{x}}$ |
|---|---|
| 10 | 110.68 |
| 100 | 35.00 |
| 1,000 | 11.07 |
| 10,000 | 3.50 |
| 100,000 | 1.11 |

Thus, as the sample size increases, the difference between actual results and expected results decreases. Indeed, $\sigma_{\bar{x}}$ approaches zero as $n$ gets very large. This result is shown graphically in Exhibit A2.2.

**EXHIBIT A2.1**
**Sampling Distribution Versus Sample Size**

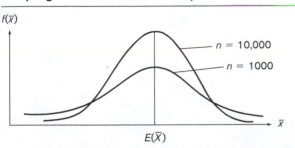

**EXHIBIT A2.2**
**Standard Error of the Sampling Distribution Versus Sample Size**

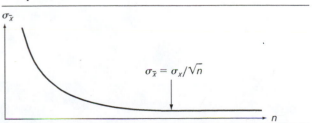

Obviously, when an insurer increases the size of the sample insured, underwriting risk (maximum insured losses) increases because more insured units could suffer a loss. The underwriting risk for an insurer is equal to the number of units insured multiplied by the standard error of the average loss distribution, $\sigma_{\bar{x}}$. Recalling that $\sigma_{\bar{x}}$ is equal to $\sigma_x/\sqrt{n}$, we can rewrite the expression for underwriting risk as:

$$n \times \sigma_{\bar{x}} = n \times \sigma_x/\sqrt{n} = \sqrt{n} \times \sigma_x$$

Thus, while underwriting risk increases with an increase in the sample size, it does not increase proportionately.

Insurance companies are in the loss business—they expect some losses will occur. It is the deviation between actual losses and expected losses that is the major concern. By insuring large samples, insurers reduce their objective risk. There truly is "safety in numbers" for insurers.

## NOTES

1. The number of runs scored in a baseball game is a discrete measure as partial runs cannot be scored. Speed and temperature are continuous measures as all values over the range of values can occur.

2. Other measures of central tendency are the median, which is the middle observation in a probability distribution, and the mode, which is the observation that occurs most often.

3. Introductory statistics texts discuss several popular theoretical distributions, such as the binomial and Poisson distributions, that can be used to estimate losses. Another popular distribution, the normal distribution, is discussed next under the "Law of Large Numbers."

# CHAPTER 3

# INTRODUCTION TO RISK MANAGEMENT

*"The essence of risk management lies in maximizing the areas where we have some control over the outcome while minimizing the areas where we have absolutely no control over the outcome …"*

Peter L. Bernstein
*Against the Gods: The Remarkable Story of Risk*

## LEARNING OBJECTIVES

**After studying this chapter, you should be able to**

◆ Define risk management and explain the objectives of risk management.

◆ Describe the steps in the risk management process.

◆ Explain the major risk-control techniques, including
   Avoidance
   Loss prevention
   Loss reduction

◆ Explain the major risk-financing techniques, including
   Retention
   Noninsurance transfers
   Insurance

◆ Apply the principles of risk management to a personal risk management program.

*Delbert Williams is the owner and operator of Del's Diner, a popular restaurant in downtown Chicago. Last month, Del's meat supplier recalled some hamburger for fear of E. coli contamination. One of Del's cooks was recently injured in a kitchen fire and a waitress is complaining about pain in her elbow from carrying serving trays. Del noticed two weeks ago that there was $60 missing from the cash register, and this week another $80 is missing. Del's has an excellent take-out business, and the diner is considering providing delivery to a limited area using a vehicle owned by the diner. Del's bookkeeper suggested that Delbert should establish a risk management program to address the many loss exposures faced by the business. Risk management is a process that identifies and analyzes loss exposures, and uses a variety of techniques, including insurance, to treat these loss exposures. Delbert hopes that by implementing a risk management program, losses will decline and the business will be better prepared when losses occur.*

*The above example shows how a business firm could benefit from a risk management program. Today, risk management is widely used by corporations, small employers, nonprofit organizations, and state and local governments. Families and students can also benefit from a personal risk management program.*

*In this chapter—the first of two dealing with risk management—we discuss the fundamentals of traditional risk management. The following chapter discusses the newer forms of risk management that are rapidly emerging, including enterprise risk management and financial risk management. In this chapter, we discuss the meaning of risk management, objectives of risk management, steps in the risk management process, and the various techniques for treating loss exposures. The chapter concludes with a discussion of personal risk management.*

## MEANING OF RISK MANAGEMENT

**Risk management** *is a process that identifies loss exposures faced by an organization and selects the most appropriate techniques for treating such exposures.* Because the term *risk* is ambiguous and has different meanings, risk managers typically use the term *loss exposure* to identify potential losses. As stated in Chapter 1, a **loss exposure** *is any situation or circumstance in which a loss is possible, regardless of whether a loss actually occurs.* In the past, risk managers generally considered only pure loss exposures faced by the firm. However, new forms of risk management are emerging that consider both pure and speculative loss exposures. This chapter discusses only the traditional treatment of pure loss exposures. The newer forms of risk management—such as enterprise risk management—are discussed in Chapter 4.

## OBJECTIVES OF RISK MANAGEMENT

Risk management has important objectives. These objectives can be classified as follows:[1]

- Pre-loss objectives
- Post-loss objectives

### Pre-Loss Objectives

Important objectives before a loss occurs include economy, reduction of anxiety, and meeting legal obligations.

*The first objective means that the firm should prepare for potential losses in the most economical way.* This preparation involves an analysis of the cost of safety programs, insurance premiums paid, and the costs associated with the different techniques for handling losses.

*The second objective is the reduction of anxiety.* Certain loss exposures can cause greater worry and fear for the risk manager and key executives. For example, the threat of a catastrophic lawsuit because of a defective product can cause greater anxiety than a small loss from a minor fire.

*The final objective is to meet any legal obligations.* For example, government regulations may require a firm to install safety devices to protect workers from harm, to dispose of hazardous waste materials properly, and to label consumer products appropriately. Workers compensation benefits must also be paid to injured workers. The firm must see that these legal obligations are met.

### Post-Loss Objectives

Risk management also has certain objectives after a loss occurs. These objectives include survival of the firm, continued operations, stability of earnings, continued growth, and social responsibility.

*The most important post-loss objective is survival of the firm.* Survival means that after a loss occurs, the firm can resume at least partial operations within some reasonable time period.

*The second post-loss objective is to continue operating.* For some firms, the ability to operate after a loss is extremely important. For example, a public utility firm must continue to provide service. Banks, bakeries, and other competitive firms must continue to operate after a loss. Otherwise, business will be lost to competitors.

*The third post-loss objective is stability of earnings.* Earnings per share can be maintained if the firm continues to operate. However, a firm may incur substantial additional expenses to achieve this goal (such as operating at another location), and perfect stability of earnings may be difficult to attain.

*The fourth post-loss objective is continued growth of the firm.* A company can grow by developing new products and markets or by acquiring or merging with other companies. The risk manager must therefore consider the effect that a loss will have on the firm's ability to grow.

*Finally, the objective of social responsibility is to minimize the effects that a loss will have on other persons and on society.* A severe loss can adversely affect employees, suppliers, customers, creditors, and the community in general. For example, a severe loss that shuts down a plant in a small town for an extended period can cause considerable economic distress in the town.

## STEPS IN THE RISK MANAGEMENT PROCESS

There are four steps in the risk management process (see Exhibit 3.1):

- Identify loss exposures
- Measure and analyze the loss exposures
- Select the appropriate combination of techniques for treating the loss exposures
- Implement and monitor the risk management program

Each of these steps is discussed in some detail in the sections that follow.

**EXHIBIT 3.1**
**Steps in the Risk Management Process**

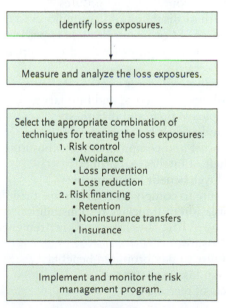

Identify loss exposures.

Measure and analyze the loss exposures.

Select the appropriate combination of techniques for treating the loss exposures:
1. Risk control
   - Avoidance
   - Loss prevention
   - Loss reduction
2. Risk financing
   - Retention
   - Noninsurance transfers
   - Insurance

Implement and monitor the risk management program.

## Identify Loss Exposures

The first step in the risk management process is to identify all major and minor loss exposures. This step involves a painstaking review of all potential losses. Important loss exposures include the following:

1. Property loss exposures
   - Building, plants, other structures
   - Furniture, equipment, supplies
   - Computers, computer software, and data
   - Inventory
   - Accounts receivable, valuable papers, and records
   - Company vehicles, planes, boats, and mobile equipment
2. Liability loss exposures
   - Defective products
   - Environmental pollution (land, water, air, noise)
   - Sexual harassment of employees, employment discrimination, wrongful termination, and failure to promote
   - Premises and general liability loss exposures
   - Liability arising from company vehicles
   - Misuse of the Internet and e-mail transmissions
   - Directors' and officers' liability suits
3. Business income loss exposures
   - Loss of income from a covered loss
   - Continuing expenses after a loss
   - Extra expenses
   - Contingent business income losses
4. Human resources loss exposures
   - Death or disability of key employees
   - Retirement or unemployment exposures
   - Job-related injuries or disease experienced by workers
5. Crime loss exposures
   - Holdups, robberies, and burglaries
   - Employee theft and dishonesty
   - Fraud and embezzlement
   - Internet and computer crime exposures
   - Theft of intellectual property
6. Employee benefit loss exposures
   - Failure to comply with government regulations
   - Violation of fiduciary responsibilities
   - Group life, health, and retirement plan exposures
   - Failure to pay promised benefits
7. Foreign loss exposures
   - Acts of terrorism
   - Plants, business property, inventory
   - Foreign currency and exchange rate risks
   - Kidnapping of key personnel
   - Political risks
8. Intangible property loss exposures
   - Damage to the company's public image
   - Loss of goodwill and market reputation
   - Loss or damage to intellectual property
9. Failure to comply with government laws and regulations

A risk manager can use several sources of information to identify the preceding loss exposures. They include the following:

- *Risk analysis questionnaires and checklists.* Questionnaires and checklists require the risk manager to answer numerous questions that identify major and minor loss exposures.
- *Physical inspection.* A physical inspection of company plants and operations can identify major loss exposures.
- *Flowcharts.* Flowcharts that show the flow of production and delivery can reveal production and other bottlenecks as well as other areas where a loss can have severe financial consequences for the firm.
- *Financial statements.* Analysis of financial statements can identify the major assets that must be protected, loss of income exposures, and key customers and suppliers.
- *Historical loss data.* Historical loss data can be invaluable in identifying major loss exposures.

In addition, risk managers must keep abreast of industry trends and market changes that can create new loss exposures and cause concern. Major risk management issues include rising workers compensation costs, effects of mergers and consolidations by insurers and brokers, increasing litigation costs, financing risk through the capital markets, cyber and privacy risks, supply-chain security, repetitive motion injury claims, and climate change. Protection of company assets and personnel against acts of terrorism is another important issue.

## Measure and Analyze the Loss Exposures

The second step is to measure and analyze the loss exposures. It is important to measure and quantify the loss exposures in order to manage them properly.

This step requires an estimation of the frequency and severity of loss. **Loss frequency** *refers to the probable number of losses that may occur during some given time period.* **Loss severity** *refers to the probable size of the losses that may occur.*

Once the risk manager estimates the frequency and severity of loss for each type of loss exposure, the various loss exposures can be ranked according to their relative importance. For example, a loss exposure with the potential for bankrupting the firm is much more important in a risk management program than an exposure with a small loss potential.

In addition, the relative frequency and severity of each loss exposure must be estimated so that the risk manager can select the most appropriate technique, or combination of techniques, for handling each exposure. For example, if certain losses occur regularly and are fairly predictable, they can be budgeted out of a firm's income and treated as a normal operating expense. If the annual loss experience of a certain type of exposure fluctuates widely, however, an entirely different approach is required.

Although the risk manager must consider both loss frequency and loss severity, severity is more important because a single catastrophic loss could destroy the firm. Therefore, the risk manager must also consider all losses that can result from a single event. Both the maximum possible loss and probable maximum loss must be estimated. The **maximum possible loss** *is the worst loss that could happen to the firm during its lifetime.* The **probable maximum loss** *is the worst loss that is likely to happen.* For example, if a plant is totally destroyed by a flood, the risk manager estimates that replacement cost, debris removal, demolition costs, and other costs will total $25 million. Thus, the maximum possible loss is $25 million. The risk manager also estimates that a flood causing more than $20 million of damage to the plant is so unlikely that such a flood would not occur more than once in 100 years. The risk manager may choose to ignore events that occur so infrequently. Thus, for this risk manager, the probable maximum loss is $20 million.

Catastrophic losses are difficult to predict because they occur infrequently. However, their potential impact on the firm must be given high priority. In contrast, certain losses, such as physical damage losses to vehicles, occur with greater frequency, are usually relatively small, and can be predicted with greater accuracy.

## 3 Select the Appropriate Combination of Techniques for Treating the Loss Exposures

The third step in the risk management process is to select the appropriate combination of techniques for treating the loss exposures. These techniques can be classified broadly as either risk control or risk financing.[2] **Risk control** *refers to techniques that reduce the frequency or severity of losses.* **Risk financing** *refers to techniques that provide for the funding of losses.* Risk managers typically use a combination of techniques for treating each loss exposure.

**Risk Control**   As noted above, risk control is a generic term to describe techniques for reducing the frequency or severity of losses. Major risk-control techniques include the following:

- Avoidance
- Loss prevention
- Loss reduction

*Avoidance*   **Avoidance** *means a certain loss exposure is never acquired or undertaken, or an existing loss exposure is abandoned.* For example, flood losses can be avoided by building a new plant on high ground, well above a floodplain. A pharmaceutical firm that markets a drug with dangerous side effects can withdraw the drug from the market to avoid possible legal liability.

The major advantage of avoidance is that the chance of loss is reduced to zero if the loss exposure is never acquired. In addition, if an existing loss exposure is abandoned, the chance of loss is reduced or eliminated because the activity or product that could produce a loss has been abandoned. Abandonment, however, may leave the firm with a residual liability exposure from the sale of previous products.

Avoidance has two major disadvantages. First, the firm may not be able to avoid all losses. For example, a company may not be able to avoid the premature death of a key executive. Second, it may not be feasible or practical to avoid the exposure. For example, a paint factory can avoid losses arising from the production of paint. Without paint production, however, the firm will not be in business.

*Loss Prevention*   **Loss prevention** *refers to measures that reduce the frequency of a particular loss.* For example, measures that reduce truck accidents include driver training, zero tolerance for alcohol or drug abuse, and strict enforcement of safety rules. Measures that reduce lawsuits from defective products include installation of safety features on hazardous products, placement of warning labels on dangerous products, and use of quality-control checks.

**Loss Reduction**    Loss reduction *refers to measures that reduce the severity of a loss after it occurs*. Examples include installation of an automatic sprinkler system that promptly extinguishes a fire; segregation of exposure units so that a single loss cannot simultaneously damage all exposure units, such as having warehouses with inventories at different locations; rehabilitation of workers with job-related injuries; and limiting the amount of cash on the premises.

**Risk Financing**    As stated earlier, risk financing refers to techniques that provide for the payment of losses after they occur. Major risk-financing techniques include the following:

- Retention
- Noninsurance transfers
- Commercial insurance

**Retention**    Retention *means that the firm retains part or all of the losses that can result from a given loss*. Retention can be either active or passive. Active risk retention means that the firm is aware of the loss exposure and consciously decides to retain part or all of it, such as collision losses to a fleet of company cars. Passive retention, however, is the failure to identify a loss exposure, failure to act, or forgetting to act. For example, a risk manager may fail to identify all company assets that could be damaged in an earthquake.

Retention can be effectively used in a risk management program under the following conditions:[3]

- *No other method of treatment is available.* Insurers may be unwilling to write a certain type of coverage, or the coverage may be too expensive. Also, noninsurance transfers may not be available. In addition, although loss prevention can reduce the frequency of loss, all losses cannot be eliminated. In these cases, retention is a residual method. If the exposure cannot be insured or transferred, then it must be retained.

- *The worst possible loss is not serious.* For example, physical damage losses to vehicles in a large firm's fleet will not bankrupt the firm if the vehicles are separated by wide distances and are not likely to be simultaneously damaged.
- *Losses are fairly predictable.* Retention can be effectively used for workers compensation claims, physical damage losses to cars, and shoplifting losses. Based on past experience, the risk manager can estimate a probable range of frequency and severity of actual losses. If most losses fall within that range, they can be paid out of the firm's income.

**Determining Retention Levels**    If retention is used, the risk manager must determine the firm's **retention level**, *which is the dollar amount of losses that the firm will retain*. A financially strong firm can have a higher retention level than one whose financial position is weak.

Although a number of methods can be used to determine the retention level, only two methods are summarized here. First, a corporation can determine the maximum uninsured loss it can absorb without adversely affecting the company's earnings. One rough rule is that the maximum retention can be set at 5 percent of the company's annual earnings before taxes from current operations.

Second, a company can determine the maximum retention as a percentage of the firm's net working capital—for example, between 1 and 5 percent. Net working capital is the difference between a company's current assets and current liabilities. Although this method does not reflect the firm's overall financial position for absorbing a loss, it does measure the firm's ability to fund a loss.

**Paying Losses**    If retention is used, the risk manager must have some method for paying losses. The following methods are typically used:[4]

- *Current net income.* The firm can pay losses out of its current net income and treat losses as expenses for that year. A large number of losses could exceed current income, however, and other assets may have to be liquidated to pay losses.
- *Unfunded reserve.* An unfunded reserve is a bookkeeping account that is charged with actual or expected losses from a given exposure.

- *Funded reserve.* A funded reserve is the setting aside of liquid funds to pay losses. A self-insurance program (discussed later) that is funded is an example of a funded reserve. However, if not required to do so, many businesses do not establish funded reserves because the funds may yield a higher return by being used elsewhere in the business. In addition, contributions to a funded reserve are not income-tax deductible. Losses, however, are tax deductible when paid.

- *Credit line.* A credit line can be established with a bank, and borrowed funds may be used to pay losses as they occur. Interest must be paid on the loan, however, and loan repayments can aggravate any cash-flow problems a firm may have.

**Captive Insurer**    Losses can also be paid by a captive insurer. A **captive insurer** *is an insurer owned by a parent firm for the purpose of insuring the parent firm's loss exposures.* There are different types of captive insurers. A **single parent captive** (also called a **pure captive**) is an insurer owned by only one parent, such as a corporation. An **association or group captive** is an insurer owned by several parents. For example, corporations that belong to a trade association may jointly own a captive insurer.

Globally, there were an estimated 6000 captive insurance companies in 2010. Many captive insurers are located in the Caribbean because of the favorable regulatory climate, relatively low capital requirements, and low taxes. In the U.S., over 25 states have enacted captive insurance company statutes. Vermont remains the leader in U.S.-based captives with nearly 600 active companies in 2012. This total includes 42 of the Fortune 100 companies and 18 of the 30 companies that comprise the Dow Jones Industrial Average. Other popular domestic domiciles include Utah, Kentucky, Montana, and Delaware; each of which had double-digit growth in business between 2010 and 2011.[5]

Captive insurers are formed for several reasons, including the following:

- *Difficulty in obtaining insurance.* The parent firm may have difficulty obtaining certain types of insurance from commercial insurers, so it forms a captive insurer to obtain the coverage. This pattern is especially true for global firms that often cannot purchase certain coverages at reasonable rates from commercial insurers.

- *Favorable regulatory environment.* Some captives are formed offshore to take advantage of a favorable regulatory environment and to avoid undesirable financial solvency regulations. However, captives are regulated under the insurance laws of the domicile, and in many domiciles, the regulation of captive insurers is rigorous. In particular, in Bermuda and Vermont, the regulation of captives is viewed as not being lax and permissive.[6]

- *Lower costs.* Forming a captive may reduce insurance costs because of lower operating expenses, avoidance of an agent's or broker's commission, and retention of interest earned on invested premiums and reserves that commercial insurers would otherwise receive. Also, the problem of wide fluctuations in commercial insurance premiums is avoided.

- *Easier access to a reinsurer.* A captive insurer has easier access to reinsurance because reinsurers generally deal only with insurance companies, not with insureds. A parent company can place its coverage with the captive, and the captive can pass the risk to a reinsurer.

- *Formation of a profit center.* A captive insurer can become a source of profit if it insures other parties as well as the parent firm and its subsidiaries. It should be noted that there are costs involved in forming a captive insurance company and that this option is not feasible for many organizations. A firm is putting its capital at risk when it insures through its captive.

**Income Tax Treatment of Captives**    The Internal Revenue Service (IRS) earlier took the position that premiums paid to a *single parent captive (pure captive)* are not income-tax deductible. The IRS argued that there is no substantial transfer of risk from an economic family to an insurer, and that the premiums paid are similar to contributions to a self-insurance reserve, which are not deductible.

However, as a result of a number of complex court decisions and IRS rulings, premiums paid to captive insurers may be tax deductible under certain conditions. It is beyond the scope of this text to discuss in detail each of these rulings. However, according to actuarial consulting firm, Towers Watson (formerly Towers Perrin, Tillinghast), premiums paid to captives are not income-tax deductible unless some or all of the following factors are present:[7]

- The transaction is a *bona fide* insurance transaction, and the captive insurer takes some risk under a defensible business plan.
- The captive insurer's owner is organized such that subsidiaries, and not the parent, pay premiums to the captive insurer under a "brother–sister" relationship. (The term "brother–sister" refers to separate subsidiaries owned by the same parent, such as a captive insurer and an operating subsidiary.)
- The captive insurer writes a substantial amount of unrelated business. (If a captive insurer receives 30 percent or more of the premiums from unrelated third parties, many tax experts view this requirement as being met.) In addition, premiums for certain employee benefits are considered to be "unrelated business" if they are structured properly.
- Ownership of the captive insurer is structured so that the insureds are not the same as the shareholders.

Finally, premiums paid to a *group captive* are usually income-tax deductible because the large number of insureds creates an essential element of insurance, which is the pooling of loss exposures over a large group.

*Self-Insurance*  Self-insurance is widely used in risk management programs. As stated in Chapter 1, **self-insurance** *is a special form of planned retention by which part or all of a given loss exposure is retained by the firm.* Another name for self-insurance is self-funding.

Self-insurance is widely used in workers compensation insurance. Self-insurance is also used by employers to provide group health, dental, vision, and prescription drug benefits to employees. Firms often self-insure their group health insurance benefits because they can save money and control health-care costs. There are other benefits of self-insurance as well (see Insight 3.1).

Finally, self-insured plans are typically protected by some type of *stop-loss* limit that caps the employer's out-of-pocket costs once losses exceed certain limits. For example, an employer may self-insure workers compensation claims up to $1 million and purchase excess insurance for the amount exceeding $1 million.

*Risk Retention Groups (RRGs)*  Federal legislation allows employers, trade groups, governmental units, and other parties to form risk retention groups. A **risk retention group** *is a group captive that can write any type of liability coverage except employers' liability, workers compensation, and personal lines.* For example, a group of physicians may find medical

---

## INSIGHT 3.1

### Advantages of Self Insurance

A self-funded employee benefit plan has a number of advantages over a more traditional insured plan. They include:

- The self-funded plan may be **tailored to fit** the needs of the group.
- The self-funded plan has **lower fixed costs** than a fully insured plan. Most expenses are variable based on the actual claims.
- The self-funded employer may use the independent, managed-care measures, such as preferred provider organizations, pre-certification, and utilization review, that **save the most money,** rather than simply those the carrier offers.
- Any leftover funds in the claim account may be reconciled against future contributions.

- **Interest earned** on the claim account is considered income to a non-qualified plan. A qualified plan may use this interest for future benefit payment.
- Benefit plan administration through a professional third-party administrator is **reasonably and competitively priced.** Only slightly more involvement by the employer is required, such as verifying eligibility, printing employee communication materials, and distributing claim checks.
- Self-funding with stop-loss coverage **simplifies budgeting** because the employer always knows its maximum expenditure for group health coverage.
- Administrative services such as claims handling are often **simpler, faster,** and performed on a more personal and professional basis. Bureaucratic red tape is eliminated.

SOURCE: TPA of Georgia.

malpractice liability insurance difficult to obtain or too expensive to purchase. The physicians can form a risk retention group to insure their medical malpractice loss exposures.

Risk retention groups are exempt from many state insurance laws that apply to other insurers. Nevertheless, every risk retention group must be licensed as a liability insurer in at least one state.

**Advantages and Disadvantages of Retention** The risk retention technique has both advantages and disadvantages in a risk management program.[8] The major advantages are as follows:

- *Save on loss costs.* The firm can save money in the long run if its actual losses are less than the loss component in a private insurer's premium.
- *Save on expenses.* The services provided by the insurer may be provided by the firm at a lower cost. Some expenses may be reduced, including loss-adjustment expenses, general administrative expenses, commissions and brokerage fees, risk-control expenses, taxes and fees, and the insurer's profit.
- *Encourage loss prevention.* Because the exposure is retained, there may be a greater incentive for loss prevention.
- *Increase cash flow.* Cash flow may be increased because the firm can use some of the funds that normally would be paid to the insurer at the beginning of the policy period.

The retention technique, however, has several disadvantages:

- *Possible higher losses.* The losses retained by the firm may be greater than the loss allowance in the insurance premium that is saved by not purchasing insurance. Also, in the short run, there may be great volatility in the firm's loss experience.
- *Possible higher expenses.* Expenses may actually be higher. Outside experts such as safety engineers may have to be hired. Insurers may be able to provide risk control and claim services at a lower cost.
- *Possible higher taxes.* Income taxes may also be higher. The premiums paid to an insurer are immediately income-tax deductible. However, if retention is used, only the amounts paid out for losses are deductible, and the deduction cannot be taken until the losses are actually paid. Contributions to a funded reserve are not income-tax deductible.

**Noninsurance Transfers** Noninsurance transfers are another risk-financing technique. **Noninsurance transfers** *are methods other than insurance by which a pure risk and its potential financial consequences are transferred to another party.* Examples of noninsurance transfers include contracts, leases, and hold-harmless agreements. For example, a company's contract with a construction firm to build a new plant can specify that the construction firm is responsible for any damage to the plant while it is being built. A firm's computer lease can specify that maintenance, repairs, and any physical damage loss to the computer are the responsibility of the computer firm. A firm may insert a hold-harmless clause in a contract, by which one party assumes legal liability on behalf of another party. For example, a publishing firm may insert a hold-harmless clause in a contract, by which the author, not the publisher, is held legally liable if the publisher is sued for plagiarism.

In a risk management program, noninsurance transfers have several advantages:[9]

- The risk manager can transfer some potential losses that are not commercially insurable.
- Noninsurance transfers often cost less than insurance.
- The potential loss may be shifted to someone who is in a better position to exercise loss control.

However, noninsurance transfers have several disadvantages:

- The transfer of potential loss may fail because the contract language is ambiguous. Also, there may be no court precedents for the interpretation of a contract tailor-made to fit the situation.
- If the party to whom the potential loss is transferred is unable to pay the loss, the firm is still responsible for the claim.
- An insurer may not give credit for the transfers, and insurance costs may not be reduced.

**Insurance** Commercial insurance is also used in a risk management program. Insurance is appropriate for loss exposures that have a low probability of loss but the severity of loss is high.

If the risk manager uses insurance to treat certain loss exposures, five key areas must be emphasized:[10]

- Selection of insurance coverages
- Selection of an insurer

■ Negotiation of terms
■ Dissemination of information concerning insurance coverages
■ Periodic review of the insurance program

*First, the risk manager must select the insurance coverages needed.* The coverages selected must be appropriate for insuring the major loss exposures identified in step one. To determine the coverages needed, the risk manager must have specialized knowledge of commercial property and liability insurance contracts. Commercial insurance is discussed in Chapters 25 through 27.

The risk manager must also determine if a deductible is needed and the size of the deductible. A **deductible** *is a provision by which a specified amount is subtracted from the loss payment otherwise payable to the insured.* A deductible is used to eliminate small claims and the administrative expense of adjusting these claims. As a result, substantial premium savings are possible. In essence, a deductible is a form of risk retention.

Most risk management programs combine the retention technique discussed earlier with commercial insurance. In determining the size of the deductible, the firm may decide to retain only a relatively small part of the maximum possible loss. The insurer normally adjusts any claims, and only losses in excess of the deductible are paid.

Another approach is to purchase **excess insurance**—*a plan in which the insurer does not participate in the loss until the actual loss exceeds the amount a firm has decided to retain.* A firm may be financially strong and may wish to retain a relatively larger proportion of the maximum possible loss. The retention limit may be set at the probable maximum loss (not maximum possible loss). For example, a retention limit of $1 million may be established for a single fire loss to a plant valued at $25 million. The $1 million would be viewed as the probable maximum loss. In the unlikely event of a total loss, the firm would absorb the first $1 million of loss, and the commercial insurer would pay the remaining $24 million.

*Second, the risk manager must select an insurer or several insurers.* A number of important factors come into play here, including the financial strength of the insurer, risk management services provided by the insurer, and the cost and terms of protection. The insurer's financial strength is determined by the size of the policyholders' surplus, underwriting and investment results, adequacy of reserves for outstanding liabilities, types of insurance written, and the quality of management. Several trade publications are available to the risk manager for determining the financial strength of a particular insurer. One of the most important rating agencies is the A.M. Best Company, which rates insurers based on their relative financial strength.

The risk manager must also consider the availability of risk management services in selecting a particular insurer. An insurance agent or broker can provide the desired information concerning the risk management services available from different insurers. These services include risk-control services, assistance in identifying loss exposures, and claim adjustment services.

The cost and terms of insurance protection must be considered as well. All other factors being equal, the risk manager would prefer to purchase insurance at the lowest possible price. Many risk managers will solicit competitive premium bids from several insurers to get the broadest possible coverage and terms at the most cost-effective price.

*Third, after the insurer or insurers are selected, the terms of the insurance contract must be negotiated.* If printed policies, endorsements, and forms are used, the risk manager and insurer must agree on the documents that will form the basis of the contract. If a specially tailored **manuscript policy**[11] is written for the firm, the language and meaning of the contractual provisions must be clear to both parties. In any case, the various risk management services the insurer will provide must also be determined. Finally, the premiums may be negotiable between the firm and insurer. In many cases, an agent or broker will be involved in the negotiations.

*In addition, information concerning insurance coverages must be disseminated to others in the firm.* The firm's employees and managers must be informed about the insurance coverages, the various records that must be kept, and the risk management services that the insurer will provide. Those persons responsible for reporting a loss must also be informed of the process for reporting claims and the appropriate contact information. The firm must comply with policy provisions concerning how notice of a claim is to be given and how the necessary proof of loss will be presented.

*Finally, the insurance program must be periodically reviewed.* This review is especially important when the firm has a change in business operations or is involved in a merger or acquisition of another firm. The review includes an analysis of agent and broker relationships, coverages needed, quality of risk control services provided, whether claims are paid promptly, and numerous other factors. Even the basic decision—whether to purchase insurance or retain the risk—must be reviewed periodically.

*Advantages of Insurance*    The use of commercial insurance in a risk management program has certain advantages.[12]

- The firm will be indemnified after a loss occurs. The firm can continue to operate and fluctuations in earnings are minimized.
- Uncertainty is reduced, which permits the firm to lengthen its planning horizon. Worry and fear are reduced for managers and employees, which should improve performance and productivity.
- Insurers can provide valuable risk management services, such as risk-control services, loss exposure analysis, and claims adjusting.
- Insurance premiums are income-tax deductible as a business expense.

*Disadvantages of Insurance*    The use of insurance also entails certain disadvantages and costs.

- The payment of premiums is a major cost because the premium consists of a component to pay losses, an amount to cover the insurer's expenses, and an allowance for profit and contingencies. There is also an opportunity cost. Under the retention technique discussed earlier, the premium could be invested or used in the business until needed to pay claims. If insurance is used, premiums must be paid in advance, and the opportunity to use the funds is forgone.
- Considerable time and effort must be spent in negotiating the insurance coverages. An insurer or insurers must be selected, policy terms and premiums must be negotiated, and the firm must cooperate with the risk-control activities of the insurer.
- The risk manager may have less incentive to implement loss-control measures because the insurer will pay the claim if a loss occurs. Such

a lax attitude toward risk control could increase the number of noninsured losses as well.

**Which Technique Should Be Used?**    In determining the appropriate technique or techniques for handling loss exposures, a matrix can be used that classifies the various loss exposures according to frequency and severity. This matrix can be useful in determining which risk management method should be used (see Exhibit 3.2).

The first loss exposure is characterized by both low frequency and low severity of loss. One example of this type of exposure would be the potential theft of office supplies. This type of exposure can be handled by retention because the loss occurs infrequently and, when it does occur, it seldom causes financial harm.

The second type of exposure is more serious. Losses occur frequently, but severity is relatively low. Examples of this type of exposure include physical damage losses to automobiles, workers compensation claims, shoplifting, and food spoilage. Loss prevention should be used here to reduce the frequency of losses. In addition, because losses occur regularly and are predictable, the retention technique can also be used. However, because small losses in the aggregate can reach sizable levels over a one-year period, excess insurance could also be purchased.

The third type of exposure can be met by transfer, including insurance. As stated earlier, insurance is best suited for low-frequency, high-severity losses. High severity means that a catastrophic potential is present, while a low probability of loss indicates that the purchase of insurance is economically feasible. Examples of this type of exposure include fires, explosions, natural disasters, and liability lawsuits.

**Exhibit 3.2**
**Risk Management Matrix**

| Type of Loss | Loss Frequency | Loss Severity | Appropriate Risk Management Technique |
|---|---|---|---|
| 1. | Low | Low | Retention |
| 2. | High | Low | Loss prevention and retention |
| 3. | Low | High | Transfer |
| 4. | High | High | Avoidance |

The risk manager could also use a combination of retention and commercial insurance to deal with these exposures.

The fourth and most serious type of exposure is one characterized by both high frequency and high severity. This type of exposure is best handled by avoidance. For example, a pharmaceutical company might be concerned about the harmful side effects of a new drug that it is developing. The exposure to liability arising from this drug can be avoided if the drug is not produced and sold.

### Market Conditions and Selection of Risk Management Techniques

The risk management techniques shown in Exhibit 3.2 are general guidelines that risk managers modify depending on market conditions in the insurance markets. In property and casualty insurance, an *underwriting cycle* exists, which is the term used to describe the cyclical pattern in underwriting standards, amount of premiums charged, and profitability in the industry. In particular, "hard" or "soft" market conditions can influence the selection of the risk management techniques used to treat loss exposures. During a period of hard market conditions, profitability is declining, or the industry is experiencing underwriting losses. As a result, underwriting standards tighten, premiums increase, and insurance becomes expensive and more difficult to obtain. Because of unfavorable market conditions, a risk manager may decide to retain more of a given loss exposure and cut back on the amount of insurance purchased.

In contrast, in a soft market, profitability is improving, underwriting standards loosen, premiums decline, and insurance is easier to obtain. Insurance may be viewed as relatively inexpensive. Because of favorable market conditions, a risk manager may decide to retain less of a given loss exposure and increase the amount of insurance purchased. The underwriting cycle is discussed in greater detail in Chapter 4.

## IMPLEMENT AND MONITOR THE RISK MANAGEMENT PROGRAM

At this point, we have discussed three of the four steps in the risk management process. The fourth step is to implement and monitor the risk management program. This step begins with a policy statement.

A **risk management policy statement** is necessary to have an effective risk management program. This statement outlines the risk management objectives of the firm, as well as company policy with respect to treatment of loss exposures. It also educates top-level executives in regard to the risk management process; establishes the importance, role, and authority of the risk manager; and provides standards for judging the risk manager's performance.

In addition, a **risk management manual** may be developed and used in the program. The manual describes in some detail the risk management program of the firm and can be a very useful tool for training managers, supervisors, and new employees who will be participating in the program. Writing the manual also forces the risk manager to state precisely his or her responsibilities, objectives, available techniques, and the responsibilities of other parties. A risk management manual often includes a list of insurance policies, agent and broker contact information, who to contact when a loss occurs, emergency contact numbers, and other relevant information.

### Cooperation with Other Departments

The risk manager does not work alone. Other functional departments within the firm are extremely important in identifying loss exposures, methods for treating these exposures, and ways to administer the risk management program. These departments can cooperate in the risk management process in the following ways:

- *Accounting.* Internal accounting controls can reduce employee fraud and theft of cash. Accounting can also provide information on the tax treatment of risk finance alternatives.
- *Finance.* Information can be provided showing the effect that losses will have on the firm's balance sheet and profit and loss statement.
- *Marketing.* Accurate packaging and product-use information can prevent lawsuits. Safe distribution procedures can prevent accidents.
- *Production.* Quality control can prevent the production of defective goods and lawsuits. Effective safety programs in the plant can reduce injuries and accidents.
- *Human resources.* This department is responsible for employee benefit programs, retirement programs, safety programs, and the company's hiring, promotion, and dismissal policies.

This list indicates how the risk management process involves the entire firm. Indeed, without the active cooperation of the other departments, the risk management program will fail. It is essential for there to be open communication between the risk management department and other functional areas of the firm.

### Periodic Review and Evaluation

To be effective, the risk management program must be periodically reviewed and evaluated to determine whether the objectives are being attained or if corrective actions are needed. In particular, risk management costs, safety programs, and loss-prevention programs must be carefully monitored. Loss records must also be examined to detect any changes in frequency and severity. Retention and transfer decisions must also be reviewed to determine if these techniques are being properly used. Finally, the risk manager must determine whether the firm's overall risk management policies are being carried out, and whether the risk manager is receiving cooperation from other departments.

## BENEFITS OF RISK MANAGEMENT

The previous discussion shows that the risk management process involves a complex and detailed analysis. Despite the complexities, an effective risk management program yields substantial benefits to the firm or organization. Major benefits include the following:

- A formal risk management program enables a firm to attain its pre-loss and post-loss objectives more easily.
- The cost of risk is reduced, which may increase the company's profits. The **cost of risk** is a risk management tool that measures certain costs. These costs include premiums paid, retained losses, loss control expenditures, outside risk management services, financial guarantees, internal administrative costs, and taxes, fees, and other relevant expenses.
- Because the adverse financial impact of pure loss exposures is reduced, a firm may be able to implement an enterprise risk management program that treats both pure and speculative loss exposures.
- Society also benefits since both direct and indirect (consequential) losses are reduced. As a result, pain and suffering are reduced.

In conclusion, it is clear that risk managers are extremely important to the financial success of business firms in today's economy. In view of their importance, risk managers are paid relatively high salaries. A recent survey found average total risk manager compensation (salary plus bonus) was $138,100 in 2011. The survey found variation in compensation levels across industries and a positive relationship between risk manager compensation and the size of the firm.[13] The financial crisis and large loss events (e.g. the 9/11 terrorist attacks and Hurricane Katrina) helped to focus attention on the critical role of risk management.

## PERSONAL RISK MANAGEMENT

The principles of corporate risk management are also applicable to a personal risk management program. **Personal risk management** *refers to the identification and analysis of pure risks faced by an individual or family, and to the selection and implementation of the most appropriate technique(s) for treating such risks.* Personal risk management considers other methods for handling risk in addition to insurance.

### Steps in Personal Risk Management

A personal risk management program involves four steps: (1) identify loss exposures, (2) measure and analyze the loss exposures, (3) select appropriate techniques for treating the loss exposures, and (4) implement and review the risk management program periodically.

**Identify Loss Exposures**   The first step is to identify all loss exposures that can cause serious financial problems. Serious financial losses can result from the following:

1. Personal loss exposures
   - Loss of earned income to the family because of the premature death of the family head
   - Insufficient income and financial assets during retirement

- Catastrophic medical bills and the loss of earnings during an extended period of disability
- Loss of earned income from unemployment
- Identity theft

2. Property loss exposures
   - Direct physical damage to a home and personal property because of fire, lightning, windstorm, flood, earthquake, or other causes
   - Indirect losses resulting from a direct physical damage loss, including extra expenses, moving to another apartment or home during the period of reconstruction, loss of rents, and loss of use of the building or property
   - Theft of valuable personal property, including money and securities, jewelry and furs, paintings and fine art, cameras, computer equipment, coin and stamp collections, and antiques
   - Direct physical damage losses to cars, motorcycles, and other vehicles from a collision and other-than-collision losses
   - Theft of cars, motorcycles, or other vehicles

3. Liability loss exposures
   - Legal liability arising out of personal acts that cause bodily injury or property damage to others
   - Legal liability arising out of libel, slander, defamation of character, and similar exposures
   - Legal liability arising out of the negligent operation of a car, motorcycle, boat, or recreational vehicle
   - Legal liability arising out of business or professional activities
   - Payment of attorney fees and other legal defense costs

**Analyze the Loss Exposures**   The second step is to measure and analyze the loss exposures. The frequency and severity of potential losses should be estimated so that the appropriate techniques can be used to deal with the exposure. For example, the chance that your home will be destroyed by a fire,

tornado, or hurricane is relatively small, but the severity of the loss can be catastrophic. Such losses should be insured because of their catastrophic potential. On the other hand, if loss frequency is high, but loss severity is low, such losses should not be insured (such as minor scratches and dents to your car). Other techniques such as retention are more appropriate for handling these types of small losses. For example, minor physical damage losses to your car can be retained by purchasing collision insurance with a deductible.

**Select Appropriate Techniques for Treating the Loss Exposures**   The third step is to select the most appropriate techniques for treating each loss exposure. The major methods are avoidance, risk control, retention, noninsurance transfers, and insurance.

1. *Avoidance.* Avoidance is one method for treating a loss exposure. For example, you can avoid being mugged in a high-crime area by staying out of the area. You can avoid the loss from the sale of a home in a depressed real estate market by renting instead of buying.
2. *Risk control.* Risk control refers to activities that reduce the frequency or severity of loss. For example, you can reduce the chance of an auto accident by driving within the speed limit, taking a safe driving course, and driving defensively. Car theft can be prevented by locking the car, removing the keys from the ignition, and installing anti-theft devices.

   Risk control can also reduce the severity of a loss. For example, wearing a helmet reduces the severity of a head injury in a motorcycle accident. Wearing a seat belt reduces the severity of an injury in an auto accident. Having a fire extinguisher on the premises can reduce the severity of a fire.
3. *Retention.* Retention means that you retain part or all of a loss. As noted earlier, risk retention can be active or passive. Active risk retention means you are aware of the risk and plan to retain part or all of it. For example, you can retain small collision losses to your car by buy-

ing a collision insurance policy with a deductible. Likewise, you can retain part of a loss to your home or to personal property by buying a homeowners policy with a deductible.

Risk can also be retained passively because of ignorance, indifference, or laziness. This practice can be dangerous if the retained risk could result in a catastrophic loss. For example, many workers are not insured against the risk of long-term disability, even though the adverse financial consequences from a long-term permanent disability generally are more severe than the financial consequences of premature death. Thus, workers who are not insured against this risk are using risk retention in a potentially dangerous manner.

4. *Noninsurance transfers.* Noninsurance transfers are methods other than insurance by which a pure risk is transferred to a party other than an insurer. For example, the risk of damage to rental property can be transferred to the tenant by requiring a damage deposit and by inserting a provision in the lease holding the tenant responsible for damages. Likewise, the risk of a defective television can be transferred

to the retailer by purchasing an extended-warranty contract that makes the retailer responsible for labor and repairs after the warranty expires.

5. *Insurance.* In a personal risk management program, most people rely heavily on insurance as the major method for dealing with risk. Common purchases include life insurance, health insurance, homeowners insurance, auto insurance, and a personal umbrella liability policy. The use of insurance in a personal risk management program is discussed in greater detail later in the text when specific insurance contracts are analyzed.

### Implement and Monitor the Program Periodically

The final step is to implement the personal risk management program and review the program periodically. At least every two or three years, you should determine whether all major loss exposures are adequately covered. You should also review your program at major events in your life, such as a divorce, birth of a child, purchase of a home, change of jobs, or death of a spouse or family member.

---

## CASE APPLICATION

City Bus Corporation provides school bus transportation to public schools in Lancaster County. City Bus owns 50 buses that are garaged in three different cities within the county. The firm faces competition from two larger bus companies that operate in the same area. Public school boards generally award contracts to the lowest bidder, but the level of service and overall performance are also considered.

a. Briefly describe the steps in the risk management process that should be followed by the risk manager of City Bus.

b. Identify the major loss exposures faced by City Bus.

c. For each of the loss exposures identified in (b), identify a risk management technique or combination of techniques that could be used to handle the exposure.

d. Describe several sources of funds for paying losses if retention is used in the risk management program.

e. Identify other departments in City Bus that would also be involved in the risk management program.

## SUMMARY

- Risk management is a process to identify loss exposures faced by an organization or individual and to select the most appropriate techniques for treating such exposures.

- Risk management has several important objectives. Pre-loss objectives include the goals of economy, reduction of anxiety, and meeting legal obligations. Post-loss objectives include survival of the firm, continued operation, stability of earnings, continued growth, and social responsibility.

- There are four steps in the risk management process:

    Identify loss exposures.

    Measure and analyze the loss exposures.

    Select the appropriate combination of techniques for treating the loss exposures.

    Implement and monitor the risk management program.

- Risk control refers to techniques that reduce the frequency or severity of losses. Major risk-control techniques include avoidance, loss prevention, and loss reduction.

- Risk financing refers to techniques that provide for the funding of losses after they occur. Major risk-financing techniques include retention, noninsurance transfers, and commercial insurance.

- Avoidance means that a loss exposure is never acquired or an existing loss exposure is abandoned. Loss prevention refers to measures that reduce the frequency of a particular loss. Loss reduction refers to measures that reduce the severity of a loss after it occurs.

- Retention means that the firm retains part or all of the losses that result from a given loss exposure. This technique can be used if no other method of treatment is available, the worst possible loss is not serious, and losses are fairly predictable. Losses can be paid out of the firm's current net income; an unfunded or funded reserve can be established to pay losses; a credit line with a bank can provide funds to pay losses; or the firm can form a captive insurer.

- The advantages of retention are the saving of money on insurance premiums, lower expenses, greater incentive for loss prevention, and increased cash flow. Major disadvantages are possible higher losses that exceed the loss component in insurance premiums, possible higher expenses if loss-control and claims personnel must be hired, and possible higher taxes.

- A captive insurer is an insurer that is owned and established by a parent firm for the purpose of insuring the parent firm's loss exposures. Captive insurers are often formed because of difficulty in obtaining insurance, or to take advantage of a favorable regulatory environment. They can also provide for lower costs; easier access to a reinsurer; and the formation of a profit center.

- Self-insurance or self-funding is a special form of planned retention by which part or all of a given loss exposure is retained by the firm.

- Noninsurance transfers are methods other than insurance by which a pure risk and its financial consequences are transferred to another party.

- Noninsurance transfers have several advantages. The risk manager may be able to transfer some uninsurable exposures; noninsurance transfers may cost less than insurance; and the potential loss may be shifted to another party who is in a better position to exercise loss control.

- Noninsurance transfers also have several disadvantages. The transfer of a potential loss may fail because the contract language is ambiguous; the firm is still responsible for the loss if the party to whom the potential loss is transferred is unable to pay the loss; and an insurer may not give sufficient premium credit for the transfers.

- Commercial insurance can also be used in a risk management program. Use of insurance involves the selection of insurance coverages, selection of an insurer, negotiation of contract terms with the insurer, dissemination of information concerning the insurance coverages, and periodic review of the insurance program.

- The major advantages of insurance include indemnification after a loss occurs, reduction of uncertainty, availability of valuable risk management services, and the income-tax deductibility of the premiums. The major disadvantages of insurance include the cost of insurance, time and effort that must be spent in negotiating for insurance, and a possible lax attitude toward loss control because of the existence of insurance.

- A risk management program must be properly implemented and administered. This effort involves preparation of a risk management policy statement, close cooperation with other individuals and departments, and periodic review of the entire risk management program.

- The principles of corporate risk management can also be applied to a personal risk management program.

## KEY CONCEPTS AND TERMS

Association or group
  captive (49)
Avoidance (47)
Captive insurer (49)
Cost of risk (55)
Deductible (52)
Excess insurance (52)
Loss exposure (44)
Loss frequency (47)
Loss prevention (47)
Loss reduction (48)
Loss severity (47)
Manuscript policy (52)
Maximum possible
  loss (47)
Noninsurance transfers (51)

Personal risk management
  (55)
Probable maximum loss (47)
Retention (48)
Retention level (48)
Risk control (47)
Risk financing (47)
Risk management (44)
Risk management
  manual (54)
Risk management policy
  statement (54)
Risk retention group (50)
Self-insurance (50)
Single parent captive
  (pure captive) (49)

## REVIEW QUESTIONS

1. What is the meaning of risk management?

2. Explain the objectives of risk management both before and after a loss occurs.

3. Describe the steps in the risk management process.

4. a. Identify the sources of information that a risk manager can use to identify loss exposures.
   b. What is the difference between the maximum possible loss and probable maximum loss?

5. a. Explain the meaning of risk control.
   b. Explain the following risk-control techniques.
      1. Avoidance
      2. Loss prevention
      3. Loss reduction

6. a. Explain the meaning of risk financing.
   b. Explain the following risk-financing techniques.
      1. Retention
      2. Noninsurance transfers
      3. Insurance

7. What conditions should be fulfilled before retention is used in a risk management program?

8. a. What is a captive insurer?
   b. Explain the advantages of a captive insurer in a risk management program.

9. a. What is self-insurance?
   b. What is a risk retention group?

10. a. Explain the advantages of using insurance in a risk management program.
    b. Explain the disadvantages of using insurance in a risk management program.

## APPLICATION QUESTIONS

1. Scaffold Equipment manufactures and sells scaffolds and ladders that are used by construction firms. The products are sold directly to independent retailers in the United States. The company's risk manager knows that the company could be sued if a scaffold or ladder is defective, and someone is injured. Because the cost of products liability insurance has increased, the risk manager is considering other techniques to treat the company's loss exposures.
   a. Describe the steps in the risk management process.
   b. For each of the following risk management techniques, describe a specific action using that technique that may be helpful in dealing with the company's products liability exposure.
      1. Avoidance
      2. Loss prevention
      3. Loss reduction
      4. Noninsurance transfers

2. The Swift Corporation has 5000 sales representatives and employees in the United States who drive company cars. The company's risk manager has recommended to the firm's management that the company should implement a partial retention program for physical damage losses to company cars.
   a. Explain the advantages and disadvantages of a partial retention program to the Swift Corporation.
   b. Identify the factors that the Swift Corporation should consider before it adopts a partial retention program for physical damage losses to company cars.
   c. If a partial retention program is adopted, what are the various methods the Swift Corporation can use to pay for physical damage losses to company cars?
   d. Identify two risk-control measures that could be used in the company's partial retention program for physical damage losses.

3. Avoidance is a risk-control technique that can be used effectively in a risk management program.
   a. What is the major advantage of using the technique of avoidance in a risk management program?
   b. Is it possible or practical for a firm to avoid all potential losses? Explain your answer.

4. A risk management program must be implemented and periodically monitored to be effective. This step requires the preparation of a risk management policy statement. The cooperation of other departments is also necessary.
   a. What benefits can the firm expect to receive from a well-prepared risk management policy statement?
   b. Identify several departments within a firm that are especially important in a risk management program.

5. Chris and Karen are married and own a three-bedroom home in a large Midwestern city. Their son, Christian, attends college away from home and lives in a fraternity house. Their daughter, Kelly, is a senior in high school. Chris is an accountant who works for a local accounting firm. Karen is a marketing analyst and is often away from home several days at a time. Kelly earns extra cash by babysitting on a regular basis.

   The family's home contains household furniture, personal property, a computer that Chris uses to prepare business tax returns on weekends, and a laptop computer that Karen uses while traveling. The Swifts also own three cars. Christian drives a 2004 Ford; Chris drives a 2009 Pontiac for both business and personal use; and Karen drives a 2011 Toyota and a rental car when she is traveling. Although the Swifts have owned their home for several years, they are considering moving because of the recent increase in violent crime in their neighborhood.
   a. Describe briefly the steps in the personal risk management process.
   b. Identify the major pure risks or pure loss exposures to which Chris and Karen are exposed with respect to each of the following:
      1. Personal loss exposures
      2. Property loss exposures
      3. Liability loss exposures
   c. With respect to each of the loss exposures mentioned above, identify an appropriate personal risk management technique that could be used to treat the exposure.

## INTERNET RESOURCES

- **Captive.com** provides considerable information about captive insurers. The site provides answers to frequently asked questions about captives. The site also has experts who will answer questions pertaining to captives or alternative retention techniques. Visit the site at

  captive.com

- **The Institutes** are a leading provider of educational material and property and liability insurance designation programs. In addition to the American Institute for Chartered Property Casualty Underwriters (CPCU) designation, the Institutes provide several associate programs, including the Associate in Risk Management (ARM) program. Visit the site at

  aicpcu.org

- The **International Financial Risk Institute (IFRI)** provides financial risk management opportunities for senior risk practitioners, especially the chief risk officers of the world's major financial institutions, to discuss and exchange ideas on the principles and practical application of financial risk management. Visit the site at

  riskinstitute.ch

- The **International Risk Management Institute (IRMI)** seeks to be the premier authority in providing expert advice and practical strategies for risk management, insurance, and legal professionals. IRMI has a large online library with information about property and liability insurance and risk management. Visit the site at

  irmi.com

- The **Nonprofit Risk Management Center** conducts research and provides education on risk management and insurance issues that are of special concern to nonprofit organizations. The organization provides technical assistance, a newsletter, online software programs, and conferences related to risk management and insurance. Visit the site at

  nonprofitrisk.org

- The **Public Risk Management Association** represents risk managers of state and local governmental units. The organization provides practical training and education for risk managers in the public sector. Visit the site at

  primacentral.org

- The **Risk Management Society (RIMS)** is the premier professional association in the United States for risk managers and corporate buyers of insurance. RIMS discusses common risk management issues, supports loss-prevention activities, and makes known to insurers the insurance needs of its members. RIMS has local chapters in major cities and publishes *Risk Management* magazine. Visit the site at
  rims.org

- The **Self-Insurance Institute of America** is a national association that promotes self-insurance as an alternative method for financing losses. The organization publishes technical articles on self-insurance, holds educational conferences, and promotes the legislative and regulatory interests of the self-insurance industry at both the federal and state levels. Visit the site at
  siia.org

## SELECTED REFERENCES

Baranoff, Etti G., Scott E. Harrington, and Gregory R. Niehaus. *Risk Assessment,* 1st ed. Malvern, PA: American Institute for Chartered Property Casualty Underwriters/Insurance Institute of America, 2005.

Elliott, Michael W. *Fundamentals of Risk Financing,* 1st ed. Malvern, PA: American Institute for Chartered Property Casualty Underwriters/Insurance Institute of America, 2002.

Elliott, Michael W. (editor), *Risk Management Principles and Practices*, Malvern, PA: American Institute for Chartered Property Casualty Underwriters, 2012.

Harrington, Scott. E., and Gregory R. Niehaus. *Risk Management and Insurance,* 2nd ed. Boston, MA: Irwin/McGraw-Hill, 2004.

Risk and Insurance Management Society. *The 2008 Financial Crisis, A Wakeup Call for Enterprise Risk Management,* 2008.

Wade, Jared, "The Risks of 2012," *Risk Management,* January/February 2012, pp. 36-42.

Wiening, Eric A. *Foundations of Risk Management and Insurance.* Malvern, PA: American Institute for Chartered Property Casualty Underwriters/Insurance Institute of America, 2002.

Wiening, Eric A., and George E. Rejda. *Risk Management and Insurance.* Boston, MA: Pearson Custom Publishing, 2005.

## NOTES

1. Robert I. Mehr and Bob A. Hedges, *Risk Management: Concepts and Applications* (Homewood, IL: Richard D. Irwin, 1974), chs. 1–2; see also Eric A. Wiening, *Foundations of Risk Management and Insurance* (Malvern, PA: American Society for Chartered Casualty Property Underwriters/Insurance Institute of America, 2002), ch. 3, and George L. Head and Stephen Horn II, *Essentials of Risk Management,* 3rd ed., vol. 1 (Malvern, PA: Insurance Institute of America, 1997), pp. 70–79.

2. This section is based on Head and Horn, pp. 36–44, and C. Arthur Williams, Jr., et al., *Principles of Risk Management and Insurance,* 2nd ed., vol. 1 (Malvern, PA: American Institute for Property and Liability Underwriters, 1981), chs. 2–3.

3. Williams et al., pp. 125–126.

4. Head and Horn, pp. 40–42.

5. Statistics presented in this paragraph were obtained from vermontcaptive.com, captiveexperts.com, captive.com, and propertycasualty360.com

6. Towers Perrin, Tillinghast, Captives 101: Managing Cost and Risk, October 2003.

7. Ibid.

8. Williams et al., pp. 126–133.

9. Ibid., pp. 103–104.

10. Ibid., pp. 107–123, 146–151.

11. A manuscript policy is one specifically designed for a firm to meet its specific needs and requirements.

12. Williams et al., pp. 108–116.

13. "Risk Manager Compensation Survey," *National Underwriter Property and Casualty*, May 2, 2011.

Students may take a self-administered test on this chapter at
**www.pearsonhighered.com/rejda**

# CHAPTER 4

# ADVANCED TOPICS IN RISK MANAGEMENT

*"The field of risk management is constantly changing. Risk managers must understand the implications of the changes, analyze how such changes affect their risk management program, look for ways to incorporate new techniques and tools into their analysis and design, and continue to broaden their knowledge of emerging trends and the financial aspects of risk management."*

Millicent Workman, CPCU
Director of Training and Education,
International Risk Management Institute (IRMI),
and Editor, *Practical Risk Management*

## LEARNING OBJECTIVES

**After studying this chapter, you should be able to**

◆ Explain the meaning of financial risk management and enterprise risk management.

◆ Describe how the risks of terrorism and climate change impact risk management.

◆ Describe the impact of the underwriting cycle and consolidation in the insurance industry on the practice of risk management.

◆ Explain capital market risk financing alternatives, including risk securitization through catastrophe bonds and weather options.

◆ Explain the methods that a risk manager employs to forecast losses.

◆ Show how financial analysis can be applied to risk management decision making.

◆ Describe other risk management tools that may be of assistance to risk managers.

*"So what's new at DE?" Valerie Williams asked Joan Brinson. Williams retired from her position as risk manager with Diversified Enterprises (DE) four years ago. Brinson, who was second-in-command in the risk management department, was named her successor. DE is a U.S.-based global company, comprised of a regional airline, a banking and mortgage lending division, a defense products division, an agricultural products division, and a hotel/resort division.*

*"Just about everything is new," replied Brinson. "A year after you left, my title was changed to Chief Risk Officer, and my responsibilities were drastically altered. The new CEO thought enterprise risk management would be a perfect fit for the company, and he was right. I'm being asked to consider risks we never considered before—fuel prices, terrorism, company reputation, the supply chain, interest rates, currency exchange rates, and climate change-- just to name a few. In addition to the insurance program and loss control, I oversee a hedging program for the fuel used by the planes in the airline division and we're using weather options to manage risk in the hotel and ag products divisions.*

*"Wow!" replied Williams. "What's the insurance market like these days?"*

*"We got spoiled during the soft market. The market is hardening and prices are rising. Remember the insurance broker we used when you were here? I really liked the service they provided and Mark Edwards, the lead broker on the account, was my go-to guy. Well, that brokerage was acquired last year, and Mark got laid off. My position is challenging, but at least there's never a dull moment!"*

*This chapter builds on the discussion of risk management in Chapter 3 and discusses some advanced topics in risk management. Topics discussed include the changing scope of risk management, insurance market dynamics, loss forecasting, financial analysis in risk management decision making, and application of several risk management tools. A problem set based on some of the quantitative material presented in this chapter is available at the companion website: pearsonhighered.com/rejda.*

## THE CHANGING SCOPE OF RISK MANAGEMENT

Traditionally, risk management was limited in scope to pure loss exposures, including property risks, liability risks, and personnel risks. An interesting trend emerged in the 1990s, however, as many businesses began to expand the scope of risk management to include speculative financial risks. Some businesses have gone a step further, expanding their risk management programs to consider all risks faced by the organization and the strategic implications of the risks.

### Financial Risk Management

Business firms face a number of speculative financial risks. **Financial risk management** *refers to the identification, analysis, and treatment of speculative financial risks.* These risks include the following:

- Commodity price risk
- Interest rate risk
- Currency exchange rate risk

**Commodity Price Risk** Commodity price risk *is the risk of losing money if the price of a commodity changes.* Producers and users of commodities face commodity price risks. For example, consider an agricultural operation that will have thousands of bushels of grain at harvest time. At harvest, the price of the commodity may have increased or decreased, depending on the supply and demand for grain. Because little storage is available for the crop, the grain must be sold at the current market price, even if that price is low. In a similar fashion, users and distributors of commodities face commodity price risks. Consider a cereal company that has promised to deliver 500,000 boxes of cereal at an agreed-upon price in six months. In the meantime, the price of grain—a commodity needed to produce the cereal—may increase or decrease, altering the profitability of the transaction. The first part of Exhibit 4.1 shows how futures contracts can be used to hedge a commodity price risk.

## EXHIBIT 4.1

### Managing Financial Risk—Two Examples

---

#### 1. Hedging a Commodity Price Risk Using Futures Contracts

A corn grower estimates in May that his production will total 20,000 bushels of corn, with the harvest completed by December. Checking the price of futures contracts, he notices that the price of December corn is $4.90 per bushel. He would like to hedge the risk that the price of corn will be lower at harvest time and can do so by the appropriate use of futures contracts. Because corn futures contracts are traded in 5000 bushel units, he would sell four contracts in May totaling 20,000 bushels in the futures market. In December, he would buy four contracts to offset his futures position. As demonstrated below, it doesn't matter whether the price of corn has increased or decreased by December. By using futures contracts and ignoring transaction costs, he has locked-in total revenue of $98,000.

| **If the market price of corn drops to $4.50 per bushel in December:** | | |
|---|---|---|
| Revenue from sale of corn | $20,000 \times \$4.50$ = | $90,000 |
| Sale of four contracts at $4.90 in May | 98,000 | |
| Purchase of four contracts at $4.50 in December | 90,000 | |
| Gain on futures transaction | | 8000 |
| Total revenue | | $98,000 |
| **If the market price of corn increases to $5.00 per bushel in December:** | | |
| Revenue from sale of corn | $20,000 \times \$5.00$ = | $100,000 |
| Sale of four contracts at $4.90 in May | 98,000 | |
| Purchase of four contracts at $5.00 in December | 100,000 | |
| Loss on futures transaction | | (2000) |
| Total revenue | | $98,000 |

#### 2. Using Options to Protect Against Adverse Stock Price Movements

Options on stocks can be used to protect against adverse stock price movements. A call option gives the owner the right to buy 100 shares of stock at a given price during a specified period. A put option gives the owner the right to sell 100 shares of stock at a given price during a specified period. While there are many options strategies used to reduce risk, one simple alternative is discussed here: buying put options to protect against a decline in the price of stock that is already owned.

Consider someone who owns 100 shares of a stock priced at $43 per share. The owner may be concerned that the price of the stock will fall. At the same time, however, the owner may not wish to sell the stock as the sale would trigger taxation of a capital gain. In addition, the owner may believe that the price of the stock could increase. The stockholder could purchase a put option to reduce the risk of a price decline.

Assume there is a put option available with a strike (exercise) price of $40. The owner of the stock could purchase the option. If the price of the stock increases, the stock owner has lost the purchase price of the option (called the premium), but the stock price has increased. But what if the price of the stock declines, say to $33 per share? In the absence of the put option, the stock owner has lost $10 ($43–$33) per share on paper. As owner of the put option, however, the stock holder has the right to sell 100 shares at $40 per share. Thus, the option is "in the money" by $7 per share ($40–$33), ignoring the option premium. The put option could be sold to offset the paper loss. Using put options in this way protects against losing money if the price of the stock declines.

**Interest Rate Risk**    Financial institutions are especially susceptible to interest rate risk. **Interest rate risk** *is the risk of loss caused by adverse interest rate movements.* For example, consider a bank that has loaned money at fixed interest rates to home purchasers through 15- and 30-year mortgages. If interest rates increase, the bank must pay higher interest rates on deposits while the mortgages are locked-in at lower interest rates. Similarly, a corporation might issue bonds at a time when interest rates are high. For the bonds to sell at their face value when issued, the coupon interest rate must equal the investor-required rate of return. If interest rates later decline, the company must still pay the higher coupon interest rate on the bonds.

**Currency Exchange Rate Risk**    The currency exchange rate is the value for which one nation's currency may be converted to another nation's currency. For example, one Canadian dollar might be worth the equivalent of two-thirds of one U.S. dollar. At this currency exchange rate, one U.S. dollar may be converted to one and one-half Canadian dollars.

U.S. companies that have international operations are susceptible to currency exchange rate risk. **Currency exchange rate risk** *is the risk of loss of value caused by changes in the rate at which one nation's currency may be converted to another nation's currency.* For example, a U.S. company faces currency exchange rate risk when it agrees to accept a specified amount of foreign currency in the future as payment for goods sold or work performed. Likewise, U.S. companies with significant foreign operations face an earnings risk because of fluctuating exchange rates. When a U.S. company generates profits abroad, those gains must be translated back into U.S. dollars. When the U.S. dollar is strong (that is, when it has a high value relative to a foreign currency), the foreign currency purchases fewer U.S. dollars and the company's earnings therefore are lower. A weak U.S. dollar (that is, when it has a low value relative to a foreign currency) means that foreign profits can be exchanged for a larger number of U.S. dollars, and consequently the firm's earnings are higher.

**Managing Financial Risks**    The traditional separation of pure and speculative risks meant that different business departments addressed these risks. Pure risks were handled by the risk manager through risk retention, risk transfer, and risk control. Speculative risks were handled by the finance division through contractual provisions and capital market instruments. Examples of contractual provisions that address financial risks include call features on bonds that permit bonds with high coupon rates to be retired early and adjustable interest rate provisions on mortgages through which the interest rate varies with interest rates in the general economy. A variety of capital market approaches are also employed, including options contracts, forward contracts, futures contracts, and interest rate swaps.[1] The second part of Exhibit 4.1 shows how options can help to manage the risk of a decrease in the price of common stock that an investor owns.

During the 1990s, some businesses began taking a more holistic view of the pure and speculative risks faced by the organization, hoping to achieve cost savings and better risk treatment solutions by combining coverage for both types of risk. In 1997, Honeywell became the first company to enter into an "integrated risk program" with American International Group (AIG).[2] *An* **integrated risk program** *is a risk treatment technique that combines coverage for pure and speculative risks in the same contract.* At the time, Honeywell was generating more than one-third of its profits abroad. Its integrated risk program provided traditional property and casualty insurance, as well as coverage for currency exchange rate risk.

In recognition of the fact that they are treating these risks jointly, some organizations have created a new position. *The* **chief risk officer (CRO)** *is responsible for the treatment of pure and speculative risks faced by the organization.*[3] Combining responsibilities in one area permits treatment of the risks in a unified, and often more economical way. For example, the risk manager may be concerned about a large self-insured property claim. The financial manager may be concerned about losses caused by adverse changes in the exchange rate. Either loss, by itself, may not harm the organization if the company has a strong balance sheet. The occurrence of both losses, however, may damage the business more severely. An integrated risk management program can be designed to consider both contingencies by including a double-trigger option. *A* **double-trigger option** *is a provision that provides for payment only if two specified losses occur.* Thus payments would be made only if a large property claim and a large exchange rate loss occurred. The cost of such coverage is less than the cost of treating each risk separately.

## Enterprise Risk Management

**Background and Use** Encouraged by the success of financial risk management, some larger organizations took the next logical step. **Enterprise risk management** *is a comprehensive risk management program that addresses an organization's pure risks, speculative risks, strategic risks, and operational risks.* Pure and speculative risks were defined previously. *Strategic risk* refers to uncertainty regarding an organization's goals and objectives, and the organization's strengths, weaknesses, opportunities, and threats. *Operational risks* develop out of business operations, including the manufacture and distribution of products and providing services to customers. By packaging all of these risks in a single risk management program, the organization offsets one risk against another, and in the process reduces its overall risk. As long as the risks combined are not perfectly and positively correlated, the combination of loss exposures reduces risk. Indeed, if some of the risks are negatively correlated, risk can be reduced significantly.

Many examples of such combinations of risk could be cited. Consider a simple illustration, a petroleum company that owns and operates a refinery and service stations. Assume the business also sells heating oil to business and residential customers. During summer months, the company may agree to deliver heating oil to customers in the fall at a specified price. Between summer and the delivery date, the price of heating oil may increase. Considering this risk in isolation and assuming the company lacks sufficient storage, the company may use heating oil futures contracts to hedge the company's price risk. However, recall that the company also has service stations which provide a natural hedge position. If the price of fuel increases in the summer months, the company will make money on its service station operations but lose money covering the promised heating oil delivery. Likewise, if the price of heating oil and gasoline decreases between the summer and fall, the company will make money delivering the fuel oil at a price higher than the market price at a time when service stations operations may not be profitable.

To what extent have large businesses adopted enterprise risk management programs? Each year,

the Risk Management Society (RIMS) and the world's largest insurance broker, Marsh, publish the "Excellence in Risk Management" report. The report provides results of a survey of risk management professionals concerning current issues and practices. The survey found that in 2010, 80 percent of the respondents had developed or were in the process of developing an enterprise risk management program. Seventeen percent of the respondents said their ERM program was fully integrated and addressed risks all across the organization.[4] Organizations adopt ERM for several reasons. Among the reasons often cited are: holistic treatment of risks facing the organization, competitive advantage, positive impact on revenues, a reduction in earnings volatility, and compliance with corporate governance guidelines.

Reasons cited in an earlier RIMS/Marsh survey for not adopting an ERM program include: not a priority, risk is managed at the operational or functional level, senior management does not see the need, lack of personnel resources, and lack of demonstrated value.[5] The value proposition for ERM is interesting. For smaller organizations, and organizations with limited financial exposure, an ERM program may not make sense. A recent study examining ERM adoption by insurance companies found that ERM adoption enhanced the firm's value, with a premium of about 20 percent.[6] The most recent "Excellence in Risk Management" report compared the views of C-suite respondents (chief executive officers, chief financial officers, etc.) with the views of risk managers.[7] The results of the study were interesting, and a gap in expectations was detected. When asked about the primary focus area for developing risk management capabilities, C-suite respondents stressed the importance of strategic thinking rather than strengthening enterprise risk management capabilities. Given the ERM adoption rate reported earlier for these larger firms, it appears that C-suite respondents take ERM expertise as somewhat of a given. In contrast, risk management respondents had a narrower focus, emphasizing integrating risk management with operations and focusing more on short-term activities rather than the broader, strategic view.

The presence of an ERM program does not guarantee that an organization will be successful. A survey of executives of 316 financial services executives prior to the financial crisis revealed that 18 percent of the respondents had well–formulated and fully implemented ERM programs and 71 percent had an

ERM strategy that was in the implementation stage.[8] Even with an enterprise risk management program in place and a Chief Risk Officer, insurer American International Group (AIG) needed a federal government bailout to prevent the company from becoming insolvent. AIG's near-demise was caused by loan guarantees called credit default swaps issued by its financial products division.

**Emerging Risks**   As noted, ERM programs are designed to address all of the risks faced by an organization. Two emerging risks that merit additional discussion are terrorism-related losses and losses attributable to climate change.

*Terrorism Risk*   While the terrorist attacks on 9/11 served as a wake-up call to many, the risk of terrorism is not new. The World Trade Center was attacked previously (1993) and the Murrah Federal Building in Oklahoma City was attacked in 1995. Foreign and domestic terrorists can attack property directly through bombs and other explosives, or they can stage a cyber-attack on an organization's sensitive data (e.g., bank records, credit card numbers, and social security numbers) or introduce a virus into the computer system. Another risk from terrorists is a "CRBN" attack—use of chemicals, radioactive material, biological material, and nuclear material. An example of a chemical attack would be the release of a lethal gas, such as sarin. Radioactive material would be released in a radiological attack. Terrorists could release a contagious disease or anthrax spores in a biological attack. Nuclear material could also be used by terrorists. These materials could be used with conventional explosives in an attack. For example, a dirty bomb combines explosives with radiological material. The results of such an attack could be devastating.[9]

The risk of terrorism can be addressed through risk control and insurance. Numerous risk control measures can be deployed. For example, physical barriers may be erected to prevent suicide bombers from using a vehicle to reach a building. Screening devices can check for metal (weapons) and also test air samples to see if explosives are present. Computer networks can be protected by impenetrable fire walls to prevent a cyber-attack. Key company personnel can be instructed on how to reduce the probability of being kidnapped by terrorists.

Prior to the 9/11 attack, terrorism exclusions were not common in commercial insurance policies. After the 9/11 attacks, insurers began to exclude losses attributable to terrorism. Congress passed the Terrorism Risk Insurance Act (TRIA) in 2002 to create a federal backstop for terrorism claims. This Act was extended in 2005, and again in 2007 through the Terrorism Risk Insurance Program Reauthorization Act (TRIPRA). Terrorism insurance coverage is available through standard insurance policies or through separate, stand-alone coverage. Organizations with the greatest exposure (e.g., large metropolitan office buildings, defense contractors, ports, etc.) often purchase coverage for terrorism losses. Insurance underwriting has evolved to consider the terrorism risk. For example, workers compensation underwriters consider whether employees are concentrated at one location or geographically dispersed.

*Climate Change Risk*   Losses attributable to natural catastrophes have increased significantly in recent years.[10] Such losses include earthquakes, hurricanes, tsunamis, typhoons, droughts, floods, and tornadoes. Many of these losses are attributable to the changing climate, which in turn may be attributable to carbon emissions. Greater volatility in weather patterns has occurred in recent years—wider temperature ranges, droughts, floods, and an increase in the frequency and severity of storms. The increased losses when storms occur are also related to demographic factors. For example, much of the population growth in the U.S. is in areas that are exposed to greater risk from hurricanes (e.g., coastal Florida, Texas, and South Carolina).

Governments, insurers, and businesses have all responded to this increased risk. Governments have sought to reduce carbon emissions by restricting the amount of carbon dioxide released by businesses. Several carbon trading markets developed through which companies that are below their emissions limit can sell credits to companies above the standard. Other governmental approaches to dealing with climate change are tougher zoning and building code requirements for structures in areas where the hazard is greater. Insurers have also responded by providing discounts for energy efficient ("green") buildings and premium credits for structures with superior loss control. Businesses must be careful about where they locate structures, risk control measures deployed, and in procuring the appropriate insurance coverage given the increased risk. Businesses may also employ weather derivatives, discussed later in this chapter, to address climate change risk.

# INSURANCE MARKET DYNAMICS

Chapter 3 discussed the various methods of dealing with risk. When property and liability loss exposures are not eliminated through risk avoidance, losses that occur must be financed in some way. The risk manager must choose between two methods of funding losses: *risk retention* and *risk transfer*. Retained losses can be paid out of current earnings, from loss reserves, by borrowing, or through a captive insurance company. Risk transfer shifts the burden of paying for losses to another party, most often a property and liability insurance company. Decisions about whether to retain risks or to transfer them are influenced by conditions in the insurance marketplace. Three important factors influencing the insurance market are:

- The underwriting cycle
- Consolidation in the insurance industry
- Capital market risk financing alternatives

## The Underwriting Cycle

For many years, a cyclical pattern has been observed in a number of underwriting results and profitability measures in the property and liability insurance industry. *This cyclical pattern in underwriting stringency, premium levels, and profitability is referred to as the* **underwriting cycle**. *Property and liability insurance markets fluctuate between periods of tight underwriting standards and high premiums, called a* **"hard"** *insurance market, and periods of loose underwriting standards and low premiums, called a* **"soft"** *insurance market.*

A number of measures can be used to ascertain the status of the underwriting cycle at any point in time. Exhibit 4.2 shows the combined ratio for the property and liability insurance industry over time. *The* **combined ratio** *is the ratio of paid losses and loss adjustment expenses plus underwriting expenses to premiums.* If the combined ratio is greater than 1 (or 100 percent), underwriting operations are

**EXHIBIT 4.2**

**Combined Ratio for All Lines of Property and Liability Insurance, 1956–2011***

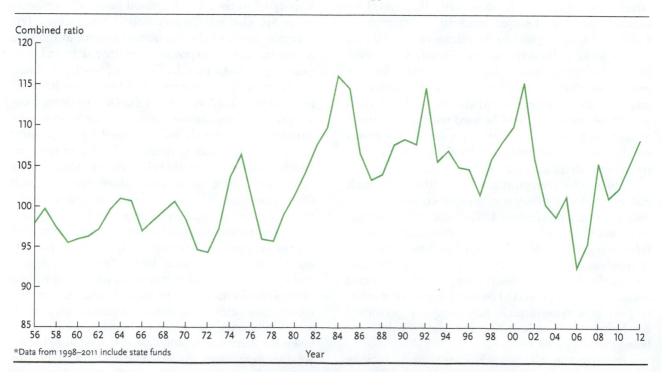

*Data from 1998–2011 include state funds

unprofitable. For example, the combined ratio of 107 for 2002 indicates that for every $1.00 that insurers collected in premiums, they paid out $1.07 in claims and expenses. If the combined ratio is less than 1 (or 100 percent), insurance companies are making money on underwriting operations. The combined ratio of 92.5 in 2006 indicates a 7.5 cent underwriting profit per dollar of premium collected.

Risk managers must consider current premium rates and underwriting standards when making their retention and transfer decisions. When the market is "soft," insurance can be purchased at favorable terms (for example, lower premiums, broader coverage, removal of exclusions). In a "hard" market, more retention is used because some insurance coverages are limited in availability or may not be affordable. The continued soft market of the late 1990s, for example, led some risk managers to purchase multiple-year insurance contracts in an effort to lock in favorable terms.

What causes these price fluctuations in property and liability insurance markets? Although a number of explanations have been offered,[11] two obvious factors affect property and liability insurance pricing and underwriting decisions:

- Insurance industry capacity
- Investment returns

**Insurance Industry Capacity**   In the insurance industry, **capacity** *refers to the relative level of surplus.* **Surplus** *is the difference between an insurer's assets and its liabilities.* When the property and casualty insurance industry is in a strong surplus position, insurers can reduce premiums and loosen underwriting standards because they have a cushion to draw on if underwriting results prove unfavorable. Given the flexibility of financial capital and the competitive nature of the insurance industry, other insurers often follow suit if one insurer takes this step. As competition intensifies, premiums are reduced further, and underwriting standards are applied less stringently. Underwriting losses begin to mount for insurers because inadequate premiums have been charged. Underwriting losses reduce insurers' surplus, and at some point, premiums must be raised and underwriting standards tightened to restore the depleted surplus. These actions will lead to a return to profitable underwriting, which helps to replenish the surplus.

When adequate surplus is restored, insurers once again are able to reduce premiums and loosen underwriting standards, causing the cycle to repeat.

External factors (such as earthquakes, hurricanes, and large liability awards) may increase the level of claims, reducing surplus. The insurance market was hardening when the 9/11 terrorist attacks occurred in 2001. Insured losses from the destruction of the World Trade Center and other buildings by terrorists totaled about $32.5 billion ($40 billion in 2010 dollars).[12]

The 9/11 attacks produced what in the insurance industry is called a "clash loss." *A* **clash loss** *occurs when several lines of insurance simultaneously experience large losses.* The terrorist attacks created large losses for life insurers, health insurers, and property and liability insurers. A second major recent shock to insurance industry capacity resulted from claims related to Hurricane Katrina in 2005. Insured losses from Hurricane Katrina totaled $45 billion in 2010 dollars.[13]

The U.S. property and casualty insurance industry sustained a loss of over $13 billion in 2001 and industry surplus declined by 8.5 percent that year. Combined ratios of 115.7 in 2001 and 107.2 in 2002 forced insurers to tighten underwriting standards and raise premiums, causing surplus to grow. Even with claims from Hurricane Katrina and other hurricanes, the industry posted a profit and an 8.8 percent growth in surplus in 2005. Insurance prices, in general, started to decline in 2006. Insurers posted record underwriting profits in 2006 and 2007. The combined ratio of 92.4 in 2006 produced an underwriting profit of $31.1 billion. The combined ratio of 95.5 in 2007 produced an underwriting profit of $19 billion. These favorable underwriting results combined with strong investment income created a record industry surplus. Surplus grew by 15 percent in 2006 and 6.8 percent in 2007, reaching a total of over $537 billion at year-end 2007. Underwriting results from 2007–2011 were unfavorable. The continued soft market and high losses pushed the combined ratio to 105.2 in 2008 and 108.2 in 2011. While investment income offset the underwriting losses, net income and surplus declined in 2011 as the market began to harden.[14]

**Investment Returns**   Would you sell insurance if, for every dollar you collected in premiums, you expected to pay 78 cents in losses and 30 cents in expenses?

That payout rate would lead to a loss of 8 cents per dollar of premiums collected. Property and casualty insurance companies can, and often do, sell coverages at an expected loss, hoping to offset underwriting losses with investment income. In reality, insurance companies are in two businesses: underwriting risks and investing premiums. If insurers expect favorable investment results, they can sell their insurance coverages at lower premium rates, hoping to offset underwriting losses with investment income. This practice is known as cash flow underwriting.

During the period from 1980 to date, the annual combined ratio has rarely been below 100. Insurers frequently lost money on their underwriting activities and relied on investment income to offset underwriting losses. After the total rate of return on invested assets fell to 2.2 percent in 2002, the rate of return increased to 8.3 percent in 2003, followed by four years of returns in the 5.2 percent to 6.7 percent range. Given the increase in funds available for investment generated by increased underwriting profits, net investment income was $50.1 billion in 2005, $53.1 billion in 2006, and $58.1 billion in 2007. Net investment income was lower in the next four years, reaching a low of $49.9 billion in 2010 and $51.4 billion in 2011.[15] The recent low-interest rate environment made it difficult for insurers to find favorable yields on fixed-income securities.

### Consolidation in the Insurance Industry

While changes occur in insurance product markets, changes also happen among the organizations operating in this sector of the economy. In the financial services industry, the consolidation trend is continuing. **Consolidation** *means the combining of business organizations through mergers and acquisitions*. A number of consolidation trends have changed the insurance marketplace for risk managers:

- Insurance company mergers and acquisitions
- Insurance brokerage mergers and acquisitions
- Cross-industry consolidations

**Insurance Company Mergers and Acquisitions**
Given the market structure of the property and liability insurance industry (numerous companies, relatively low barriers to entry given the flexibility of financial capital, and relatively homogenous

products), insurance company consolidations do not have severe consequences for risk managers. Risk managers may notice, however, that the marketplace is populated by fewer but larger, independent insurance organizations as a result of consolidation. Two excellent examples are the mergers of Travelers Property Casualty Insurance Company with The St. Paul Companies in 2004, and Liberty Mutual Group's acquisition of Safeco Corporation in 2008. In 2010, there were 60 property and casualty insurer mergers valued at $6.42 billion.[16]

**Insurance Brokerage Mergers and Acquisitions**
Unlike the consolidation of insurance companies, consolidation of insurance brokerages does have consequences for risk managers. **Insurance brokers** *are intermediaries who represent insurance purchasers. Insurance brokers offer an array of services to their clients, including attempting to place their clients' business with insurers*. Clearly, a risk manager wants to obtain insurance coverages and related services under the most favorable financial terms available. Periodically, risk managers contact several insurance agents and insurance brokers in an effort to obtain competitive insurance coverage bids. The number of large, national insurance brokerages has declined significantly in recent years because of consolidation. For example, before consolidation, a risk manager could obtain coverage bids from the Sedgwick Group, Johnson & Higgins, and Marsh & McLennan. Today, these formerly independent organizations are all part of Marsh & McLennan Companies, Inc. In 2008, the third-largest broker, Willis Group Holdings, Limited, acquired the eighth-largest broker, Hilb Rogal & Hobbs Company. In 2010, Aon, the second-largest insurance broker acquired Hewitt Associates, Inc.

**Cross-Industry Consolidation** Consolidation in the financial services arena is not limited to mergers between insurance companies or between insurance brokerages. Boundaries separating institutions with depository functions, institutions that underwrite risk, and securities businesses were enacted in Depression-era legislation. The divisions between banks, insurance companies, and securities firms began to blur in the 1990s. The U.S. Congress formally struck down the barriers with passage of the Financial Services Modernization Act of 1999 (also known by the names of the bill's sponsors, Gramm-Leach-Bliley). Several illustrations include Northwestern Mutual Life Insurance Company's acquisition of mutual fund manager Frank Russell Company, State Farm Insurance and Mutual of Omaha initiating banking operations, and Wells Fargo's foray into the insurance brokerage business through the acquisition of ACO Brokerage, parent company of Acordia, Inc.

## Capital Market Risk Financing Alternatives

Insurers and risk managers are looking increasingly to the capital markets to assist in financing risk. Two capital market risk financing arrangements include risk securitization and insurance options.[17]

**Securitization of Risk**   An important development in insurance and risk management is the use of risk securitization. **Securitization of risk** *means that insurable risk is transferred to the capital markets through creation of a financial instrument, such as a catastrophe bond, futures contract, options contract, or other financial instrument.* The impact of risk securitization upon the insurance marketplace is an immediate increase in capacity for insurers and reinsurers. Rather than relying upon the capacity of insurers only, securitization provides access to the capital of many investors.

Insurers were among the first organizations to experiment with securitization. USAA Insurance Company, through a subsidiary, issued a catastrophe bond in 1997 to protect the company against catastrophic hurricane losses. **Catastrophe bonds** *are corporate bonds that permit the issuer to skip or defer scheduled payments if a catastrophic loss occurs.* Under the terms of the USAA bond, investors were paid principal and interest provided that hurricane losses during a time period did not exceed a specified level. Principal and interest would be lost, however, if hurricane claims exceeded a trigger point.

Exhibit 4.3 shows the number of catastrophe bond issues and the size of the risk capital made available from these bonds from 1997–2011.

**Insurance Options**   Exhibit 4.1, discussed earlier, showed how traditional options on common stock, put options and call options, could be used in a financial risk management application. Another class of options, insurance options, can be used in risk management. *An* **insurance option** *is an option that derives value from specific insurable losses or from an index of values.* The profitability of many businesses is determined in large part by weather conditions. Utility companies, farmers, ski resorts, and other businesses face weather-related risk and uncertainty. A growing number of businesses are turning to weather derivatives for assistance in managing this risk. *A* **weather option** *provides payment if a specified weather contingency (e.g., temperature above a certain level or rainfall below a specified level) occurs.* To learn more about the weather derivatives market, which is based at the Chicago Mercantile Exchange (CME), see Insight 4.1.[18]

# LOSS FORECASTING

The risk manager must also identify the risks the organization faces, and then analyze the potential frequency and severity of these loss exposures. Although loss history provides valuable information, there is no guarantee that future losses will follow past loss trends. Risk managers can employ a number of techniques to assist in predicting loss levels, including the following:

- Probability analysis
- Regression analysis
- Forecasting based on loss distributions

## Probability Analysis

Chance of loss is the possibility that an adverse event will occur. The probability $(P)$ of such an event is equal to the number of events likely to occur $(X)$ divided by the number of exposure units $(N)$. Thus, if a vehicle fleet has 500 vehicles and on average 100 vehicles suffer physical damage each year, the probability that a fleet vehicle will be damaged in any given year is:

$$P(\text{physical damage}) = 100/500 = .20 \text{ or } 20\%$$

Some probabilities of events can be easily deduced (for example, the probability that a fair coin will come up "heads" or "tails"). Other probabilities (for example, the probability that a male age 50 will die before reaching age 60) may be estimated from prior loss data.

The risk manager must also be concerned with the characteristics of the event being analyzed. Some events are **independent events**—*the occurrence does not affect the occurrence of another event.* For example, assume that a business has production

**EXHIBIT 4.3**

**Catastrophe Bonds: Annual Number of Transactions and Issue Size**

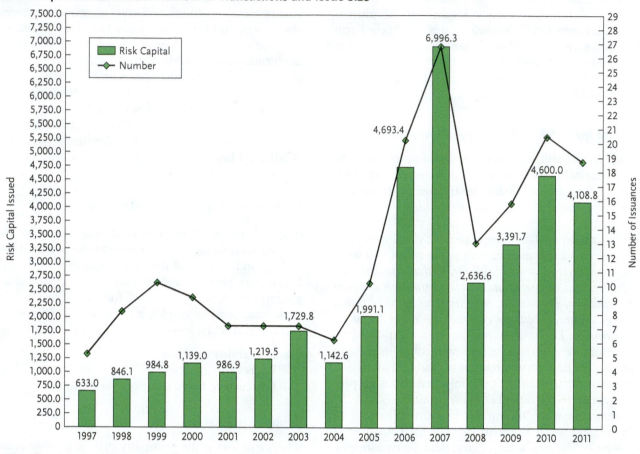

\* All dollar amounts in USD millions.

SOURCE: Adapted and updated from "Catastrophe Bond Update: First Quarter 2012," Guy Carpenter, May 2012. GC Securities Proprietary Data Base, March 31, 2012. Used with permission from Guy Carpenter & Company, LLC.

facilities in Louisiana and Virginia, and that the probability of a fire at the Louisiana plant is 5 percent and that the probability of a fire at the Virginia plant is 4 percent. Obviously, the occurrence of one of these events does not influence the occurrence of the other event. If events are independent, the probability that they will occur together is the product of the individual probabilities. Thus, the probability that both production facilities will be damaged by fire is:

$P$(fire at Louisiana plant)
$\times P$(fire at Virginia plant) $= P$(fire at both plants)

$$= .04 \times .05 = .002 \text{ or } .2\%$$

Other events can be classified as **dependent events**—*the occurrence of one event affects the occurrence of the other.* If two buildings are located

close together, and one building catches on fire, the probability that the other building will burn is increased. For example, suppose that the individual probability of a fire loss at each building is 3 percent. The probability that the second building will have a fire given that the first building has a fire, however, may be 40 percent. What is the probability of two fires? This probability is a conditional probability that is equal to the probability of the first event multiplied by the probability of the second event given that the first event has occurred:

$$P(\text{fire at one bldg}) \times P\left(\begin{array}{c}\text{fire at second bldg given}\\ \text{fire at first bldg}\end{array}\right)$$

$$= P(\text{both burn})$$
$$.03 \times .40 = .012 \text{ or } 1.20\%$$

## INSIGHT 4.1

## The Weather Derivatives Markets at CME Group: A Brief History

On August 24, 1897, in an editorial in the Hartford *Courant*, Mark Twain wrote, "Everybody talks about the weather but nobody does anything about it!" If Mr. Twain had lived long enough, he would have had to revise his quote.

One-hundred and two years after that famous quote was printed, the public was given the rare opportunity to do something, more about the weather than just talk about it. This Fundamental Business Driver provides the historical timeline of Weather product innovations by the Chicago Mercantile Exchange (CME)Group.

What is the difference between weather and climate?

**Weather** is the day-to-day state of the atmosphere, and is short-term (minutes to weeks) in variation. Universally, weather is thought of as the combination of temperature, humidity, precipitation, cloudiness, visibility and wind.

It is important to understand the difference between weather and climate when trading weather because it depends on the type of trade a user wants to establish. A weekly trader of weather is only concerned with the short-term outlook for weather. Monthly and seasonal traders will want to view long term climate patterns. Traders will look back at climate data from 10, 15, 30 or more years before initiating a position.

*Climate* is defined as statistical weather information that describes the variation of weather at a given place for a specified period. In popular usage, it represents the synthesis of weather; officially it is the weather of an area averaged over some time period plus statistics of weather extremes.

The weather futures markets available at CME began trading in 1999. At the initial launch, two standard temperature contracts—Heating Degree Days (HDDs) and Cooling Degree Days (CDDs)—were listed for trading for ten U.S. cities. (See Table 1 for current listings of all weather cities, which now includes nearly 50 locations worldwide.) These contracts were monthly futures and options, and reflected the accumulated differences between the average daily temperature and a "base" temperature of 65 degrees Fahrenheit for each day in a calendar month.

Any new and unique product has a steep learning curve, and weather fits the term "unique" perfectly. But as the marketplace began to realize the advantages of hedging weather exposure on a centralized market, trading began to increase and so too did the demand for additional locations and products. The collapse of Enron also encouraged the adoption of standardized exchange-traded futures and options by participants in the over-the-counter (OTC) market for weather.

By 2003, the CME Group weather market had gained modest traction among the 10 original locations and the market demanded an additional five U.S. locations. Additionally, seasonal strip contracts were introduced to allow market participants to hedge seasonal weather and have the flexibility to string together any combination of months, as long as there were a minimum of two consecutive and a maximum of seven months. In addition, market participants discovered that a "strip" of options for individual calendar months did not provide the same hedging performance as an option on the entire strip. As a point of reference, the heating season runs from November through March and the cooling season is May through September. There are also "shoulder months" that can either be a heating or cooling month, and those transition months are October and April.

It was also in 2003 that CME Group weather products went global, with the launch of monthly and seasonal (HDD) and cumulative average temperature (CAT) contracts for six European locations. In addition, contracts for two Pacific Rim locations were added to the product line-up.

More milestones for CME Group's weather suite occurred in 2005 with the introduction of a Frost contract for Amsterdam. This contract was developed in response to contractual provisions of construction workers in the Netherlands that halt work based on frost events, and therefore Dutch construction firms face a specialized form of weather risk. CME Group's suite of exchange-traded contracts were patterned after a large OTC deal that was done the previous year.

Market participation was gaining traction and the need for different types of weather contracts continued to grow. CME also launched the first precipitation contract based on snowfall for the U.S in 2005. In addition, more locations were added to the temperature-based product suite, bringing the U.S. total to 18 locations and the European total to nine. The following year, CME Group expanded its presence into Canada with six Canadian locations based on HDD, CDD and CAT (cumulative average temperature) contracts. CDD contracts were added to the European listings, and seasonal strip contracts were added for U.S. Snowfall.

The innovation continued in 2007 with the addition of Weekly Average Temperature contracts on 18 U.S. locations. These contracts were designed to capture shorter-term temperature variations during the work week, Monday through Friday.

Australian temperature-based contracts joined the CME Group product family in 2008, along with several more U.S. and European locations. Further enhancements and additions occurred in 2009, 2010 and 2011, including binary contracts for U.S. Snowfall that pay a fixed amount when a given amount of snowfall occurs, and U.S. Rainfall contracts that provide precipitation risk management during the spring, summer and fall months. New and innovative weather products are continually being researched and discussed with

*(Continued)*

## INSIGHT 4.1 (Continued)

market participants, as shown in Table 2 below. Some of the ideas that are being actively discussed include solar radiation, wind and extreme temperature. CME Group is also investigating new locations in other parts of the world not already covered by current offerings.

The weather market is still quite young, but since the initial launch of the basic HDD and CDD contracts a little more than a decade ago, innovation has been a driving force in providing financial protection against weather conditions that people could only talk about 100 years ago.

### Table 1
### Current Cities Available for Trading

| 24 U.S. Cities | 6 Canadian Cities | 3 Australian Cities |
|---|---|---|
| Atlanta | Calgary | Bankstown, Sydney |
| Chicago | Edmonton | Brisbane Aero |
| Cincinnati | Montreal | Melbourne Regional |
| New York | Toronto | |
| Dallas | Vancouver | |
| Philadelphia | Winnipeg | |
| Portland | | |
| Tucson | | |
| Des Moines | | |
| Las Vegas | | |
| Detroit | | |
| Minneapolis | 11 European Cities | 3 Japanese Cities |
| Houston | London | Tokyo |
| Sacramento | Paris | Osaka |
| Salt Lake City | Amsterdam | Hiroshima |
| Baltimore | Berlin | |
| Boston | Essen | |
| Colorado Springs | Stockholm | |
| Jacksonville | Barcelona | |
| Little Rock | Rome | |
| Los Angeles | Madrid | |
| Raleigh | Oslo-Blindern | |
| Durham | Prague | |
| Washington D.C | | |

### Table 2
### Examples of Potential Weather Risks

| Economic Sector | Hedgeable Weather Risks |
|---|---|
| Energy | Reduced and/or excessive demand |
| Hedge Funds | Making profits on volatile markets |
| Agriculture | Crop yield, handling, storage, pests |
| Offshore | Storm frequency/severity |
| Insurance | Increased claims, premium diversification |
| Entertainment | Postponements, reduced attendance |
| Retailing | Reduced demand of weather-sensitive products |
| Construction | Delays, incentive/ disincentive clauses |
| Transportation | Budget overruns, delays |
| Manufacturing | Reduced demand, increased raw material costs |
| Governments | Budget overruns |

Source: Courtesy of CME Group; http://www.cmegroup.com/

Events may also be mutually exclusive. *Events are* **mutually exclusive** *if the occurrence of one event precludes the occurrence of the second event.* For example, if a building is destroyed by fire, it cannot also be destroyed by flood. Mutually exclusive probabilities are additive. If the probability that a building will be destroyed by fire is 2 percent and the probability that the building will be destroyed by flood is 1 percent, then the probability the building will be destroyed by either fire or flood is:

$P$(fire destroys bldg) + $P$(flood destroys bldg)

$\qquad\qquad$ = $P$(fire or flood destroys bldg)

$\qquad$ .02 + .01 = .03 or 3%

If the independent events are not mutually exclusive, then more than one event could occur. Care must be taken not to "double-count" when determining the probability that at least one event will occur. For example, if the probability of minor fire damage is 4 percent and the probability of minor flood damage is 3 percent, then the probability of at least one of these events occurring is:

$\qquad$ $P$(minor fire) + $P$(minor flood)

$\qquad$ − $P$(minor fire and flood) = $P$(at least one event)

$\qquad$ .04 + .03 − (.04 × .03) = .0688 or 6.88%

Assigning probabilities to individual and joint events and analyzing the probabilities can assist the risk manager in formulating a risk treatment plan.

### Regression Analysis

Regression analysis is another method for forecasting losses. **Regression analysis** *characterizes the relationship between two or more variables and then uses this characterization to predict values of a variable.* One variable—the dependent variable—is hypothesized to be a function of one or more independent variables. It is not difficult to envision relationships that would be of interest to risk managers in which one variable is dependent upon another variable. For example, consider workers compensation claims. It is logical to hypothesize that the number of workers compensation claims should be positively related to some variable representing employment (for example, the number of employees, payroll, or hours worked). Likewise, we would expect the number of physical damage claims for a fleet of vehicles to increase as the size of the fleet increases or as the number of miles driven each year by fleet vehicles increases.

The first panel in Exhibit 4.4 provides data for a company's annual payroll in thousands of dollars and the corresponding number of workers compensation claims during the year. In the second panel of Exhibit 4.4, the number of claims is plotted against payroll. Regression analysis provides the coordinates of the line that best fits the points in the chart.[19] This line will minimize the sum of the squared deviations of the points from the line. Our hypothesized relationship is as follows:

$$\begin{array}{c}\text{Number of}\\\text{workers}\\\text{compensation}\\\text{claims}\end{array} = B_0 + (B_1 \times \text{Payroll [in thousands]})$$

where $B_0$ is a constant and $B_1$ is the coefficient of the independent variable.

The regression results provided at the bottom of Exhibit 4.4 were obtained using spreadsheet software. The coefficient of determination, R-square, ranges from 0 to 1 and measures the model fit. An R-square value close to 1 indicates that the model does a good job of predicting Y values. By substituting the estimated payroll for next year (in thousands), the risk manager estimates that 509 workers compensation claims will occur in the next year.

### Forecasting Based on Loss Distributions

Another useful tool for the risk manager is loss forecasting based on loss distributions. *A* **loss distribution** *is a probability distribution of losses that could occur.* Forecasting by using loss distributions works well if losses tend to follow a specified distribution and the sample size is large. Knowing the parameters that specify the loss distribution (for example, mean, standard deviation, and frequency of occurrence) enables the risk manager to estimate the number of events, severity, and confidence intervals. Many loss distributions can be employed, depending on the pattern of losses. As noted at the start of the chapter, a problem set for this chapter is provided at the companion website. The first section of the problem set discusses loss forecasting based on the normal

EXHIBIT 4.4

**Relationship Between Payroll and Number of Workers Compensation Claims**

| Year | Payroll in thousands | Workers compensation claims |
|------|------|------|
| 2001 | $ 400 | 18 |
| 2002 | 520 | 26 |
| 2003 | 710 | 48 |
| 2004 | 840 | 96 |
| 2005 | 1200 | 110 |
| 2006 | 1500 | 150 |
| 2007 | 1630 | 228 |
| 2008 | 1980 | 250 |
| 2009 | 2300 | 260 |
| 2010 | 2900 | 300 |
| 2011 | 3400 | 325 |
| 2012 | 4000 | 412 |

Regression results: $Y = -6.1413 + .1074 X$, $R^2 = .9519$

Predicted number of claims next year, if the payroll is $4.8 million:

$Y = -6.1413 + (.1074 * 4800)$

$Y = 509.38$

distribution, a widely used distribution. To access the problem set, visit the site at: pearsonhighered.com/rejda.

## FINANCIAL ANALYSIS IN RISK MANAGEMENT DECISION MAKING

Risk managers must make a number of important decisions, including whether to retain or transfer loss exposures, which insurance coverage bid is best, and whether to invest in risk control projects. The risk manager's decisions are based on economics—weighing the costs and benefits of a course of action to see whether it is in the economic interests of the company and its stockholders. Financial analysis can be applied to assist in risk management decision making. To make decisions involving cash flows in different time periods, the risk manager must employ time value of money analysis.

### The Time Value of Money

Because risk management decisions will likely involve cash flows in different time periods, the time value of money must be considered. *The* **time value of money** *means that when valuing cash flows in different time periods, the interest-earning capacity of money must be taken into consideration.* A dollar received today is worth more than a dollar received one year from today because the dollar received today can be invested immediately to earn interest. Therefore, when evaluating cash flows in different time periods, it is important to adjust dollar values to reflect the earning of interest.

A lengthy discourse on the time value of money is beyond the scope of this text.[20] Instead, we will limit our treatment to the valuation of single cash flows.

Suppose you open a bank account today and deposit $100. The value of the account today—the present value—is $100. Further assume that the bank is willing to pay 4 percent interest, compounded annually, on your account. What is the account balance one year from today? At that time, you would have your original $100, plus an additional 4 percent of $100, or $4 in interest:

$$\$100 + (\$100 \times .04) = \$104$$

Factoring, you would have:

$$\$100 \times (1 + .04) = \$104$$

Thus, if you multiply the starting amount (the present value, or $PV$) by 1 plus the interest rate ($i$), it will give you the amount one year from today (the future value, or $FV$):

$$PV \times (1 + i) = FV$$

If you wish to know the account balance after two years, simply multiply the balance at the end of the first year by 1 plus the interest rate. In this way, we arrive at the simple formula for the future value of a present amount:

$$PV (1 + i)^n = FV, \text{ where "}n\text{" is the number of time periods}$$

In the second year, not only will you earn interest on the original deposit, but you will also earn interest on the $4 in interest you earned in the first period. *Because you are earning interest on interest (compound interest), the operation through which a present value is converted to a future value is called* **compounding**.

Compounding also works in reverse. Assume that you know the value of a future cash flow, but you want to know what the cash flow is worth today, adjusting for the time value of money. Dividing both sides of our compounding equation by $(1 + i)^n$ yields the following expression:

$$PV = \frac{FV}{(1 + i)^n}$$

Thus, if you want to know the present value of any future amount, divide the future amount by 1 plus the interest rate, raised to the number of periods. *This operation—bringing a future value back to present value—is called* **discounting**.

### Financial Analysis Applications

In many instances, the time value of money can be applied in risk management decision making. We will consider two applications:

- Analyzing insurance coverage bids
- Risk-control investment decisions

**Analyzing Insurance Coverage Bids**    Assume that a risk manager would like to purchase property insurance on a building. She is analyzing two insurance coverage bids. The bids are from comparable insurance companies, and the coverage amounts are the same. The premiums and deductibles, however, differ. Insurer A's coverage requires an annual premium of $90,000 with a $5000 per-claim deductible. Insurer B's coverage requires an annual premium of $35,000 with a $10,000 per-claim deductible. The risk manager wonders whether the additional $55,000 in premiums is warranted to obtain the lower deductible. Using some of the loss forecasting methods just described, the risk manager predicts the following losses will occur:

| Expected Number of Losses | Expected Size of Losses |
|---|---|
| 12 | $5000 |
| 6 | $10,000 |
| 2 | over $10,000 |
| $n = 20$ | |

Which coverage bid should she select, based on the number of expected claims and the magnitude of these claims? For simplicity, assume that premiums are paid at the start of the year, losses and deductibles are paid at the end of the year, and 5 percent is the appropriate interest (discount) rate.

With Insurer A's bid, the expected cash outflows in one year would be the first $5000 of 20 losses that are each $5000 or more, for a total of $100,000 in deductibles. The present value of these payments is

$$PV = \frac{100,000}{(1 + .05)^1} = 95,238$$

The present value of the total expected payments ($90,000 insurance premium at the start of the year plus the present value of the deductibles) would be $185,238.

With Insurer B's bid, the expected cash outflows for deductibles at the end of the year would be

$$(\$5000 \times 12) + (\$10,000 \times 6) + (\$10,000 \times 2) = \$140,000$$

The present value of these deductible payments is

$$PV = \frac{140,000}{(1 + .05)^1} = \$133,333$$

The present value of the total expected payments ($35,000 insurance premium at the start of the year plus the present value of the deductibles) would be $168,333. Because the present values calculated represent the present values of cash outflows, the risk manager should select the bid from Insurer B because it minimizes the present value of the cash outflows.

**Risk-Control Investment Decisions**  Risk-control investments are undertaken in an effort to reduce the frequency and severity of losses. Such investments can be analyzed from a capital budgeting perspective by employing time value of money analysis. **Capital budgeting** *is a method of determining which capital investment projects a company should undertake.* Only those projects that benefit the organization financially should be accepted. If not enough capital is available to undertake all of the acceptable projects, then capital budgeting can assist the risk manager in determining the optimal set of projects to consider.

A number of capital budgeting techniques are available.[21] Methods that take into account time value of money, such as net present value and internal rate of return, should be employed. *The* **net present value (NPV)** *of a project is the sum of the present values of the future net cash flows minus the cost of the project.*[22] *The* **internal rate of return (IRR)** *on a project is the average annual rate of return provided by investing in the project.* Cash flows are generated by increased revenues and reduced expenses. To calculate the NPV, the cash flows are discounted at an interest rate that considers the rate of return required by the organization's capital suppliers and the riskiness of the project. A positive net present value represents an increase in value for the firm; a negative net present value would decrease the value of the firm if the investment were made.

For example, the risk manager of an oil company that owns service stations may notice a disturbing trend in premises-related liability claims. Patrons may claim to have been injured on the premises (e.g., slip-and-fall injuries near gas pumps or inside the service station) and sue the oil company for their injuries. The risk manager decides to install camera surveillance systems at several of the "problem" service stations at a cost of $85,000 per system. The risk manager expects each surveillance system to generate an after-tax net cash flow of $40,000 per year for three years. The present value of $40,000 per year for three years discounted at the appropriate interest rate (we assume 8 percent) is $103,084. Therefore, the *NPV* of this project is

$$NPV = PV \text{ of future cash flows} - \text{Cost of project}$$
$$= \$103,084 - \$85,000 = \$18,084$$

As the project has a positive net present value, the investment is acceptable.

Alternatively, the project's internal rate of return could be determined and compared to the company's required rate of return on investment. The IRR is the interest rate that makes the net present value equal zero. In other words, when the IRR is used to discount the future cash flows back to time zero, the sum of the discounted cash flows equals the cost of the project. For this project, the IRR is 19.44 percent. As 19.44 percent is greater than the required rate of return, 8 percent, the project is acceptable.

Although the cost of a project is usually known with some certainty, the future cash flows are merely estimates of the benefits that will be obtained by investing in the project. These benefits may come in the form of increased revenues, decreased expenses, or a combination of the two. Although some revenues and expenses associated with the project are easy to quantify, other values—such as employee morale, reduced pain and suffering, public perceptions of the company, and lost productivity when a new worker is hired to replace an injured experienced worker—are difficult to measure.

## OTHER RISK MANAGEMENT TOOLS

Our discussion of advanced risk management topics would not be complete without a brief discussion of some other risk management tools. We will divide our discussion into five parts:

- Risk management information systems (RMIS)
- Risk management intranets
- Risk maps
- Value at risk (VAR) analysis
- Catastrophe modeling

## Risk Management Information Systems (RMIS)

A key concern for risk managers is accurate and accessible risk management data. *A* **risk management information system (RMIS)** *is a computerized database that permits the risk manager to store, update, and analyze risk management data and to use such data to predict and attempt to control future loss levels.* Risk management information systems may be of great assistance to risk managers in decision making. Such systems are marketed by a number of vendors, or they may be developed in-house.[23]

Risk management information systems have multiple uses. With regard to property exposures, the database may include a listing of a corporation's properties and the characteristics of those properties (construction, occupancy, protection, and exposure), property insurance policies, coverage terms, loss records, a log of fleet vehicles (including purchase dates, claims history, and maintenance records), and other data. On the liability side, the database may contain a listing of claims, the status of individual claims (pending, filed, in litigation, being appealed, or closed), historic claims, exposure bases (payroll, number of fleet vehicles, number of employees, and so on), and liability insurance coverages and coverage terms.

Organizations with many employees often find risk management information systems of great assistance in tracking employees, especially in the area of workers compensation claims. For example, a business with production facilities across the country may self-insure its workers compensation program but hire a third party to administer the program. In addition to settling claims, the third party administrator (TPA) may provide detailed claims records to the company that become part of the company's database. Armed with these data, the risk manager can perform a number of analyses, such as examining the number of injuries incurred by geographic region, by type of injury or body part (for example, laceration or lower back injury), by job classification, and by employee identification number. Such an analysis may reveal, for example, that the injury rate is greater in the Southwest region or that a small number of employees account for a disproportionately high number of claims. In turn, the risk manager may use the results in measuring the effectiveness of risk-control investments and in targeting additional risk-control efforts. Accurate workers compensation records are also important if the business decides to purchase private insurance because past performance must be documented to obtain lower premiums from insurers.

## Risk Management Intranets

Some risk management departments have established their own Web sites, which include answers to "frequently asked questions" (FAQs) and a wealth of other information. In addition, some organizations have expanded the traditional risk management Web site into a risk management intranet. *An* **intranet** *is a private network with search capabilities designed for a limited, internal audience.* For example, a software company that sponsors trade shows at numerous venues each year might use a risk management intranet to make information available to interested parties within the company. Through the intranet, employees can obtain a list of procedures to follow (formulated by the risk management department) along with a set of forms that must be signed and filed before the event can be held (such as hold-harmless agreements).

## Risk Maps

Some organizations have developed or are developing sophisticated "risk maps." **Risk maps** *are grids detailing the potential frequency and severity of risks faced by the organization.* Construction of these maps requires risk managers to analyze each risk that the organization faces before plotting it on the map. Use of risk maps varies from simply graphing the exposures to employing simulation analysis to estimate likely loss scenarios. In addition to property, liability, and personnel exposures, financial risks and other risks that fall under the broad umbrella of "enterprise risk" may be included on the risk map.[24]

## Value at Risk (VAR) Analysis

A popular risk assessment technique in financial risk management is value at risk (VAR) analysis. **Value at risk (VAR)** *is the worst probable loss likely to occur in a given time period*

## CASE APPLICATION

Great West States (GWS) is a railroad company operating in the Western United States. Juanita Salazar is risk manager of GWS. At the direction of the company's chief executive officer, she is searching for ways to handle the company's risks in a more economical way. The CEO stressed that Juanita should consider not only pure risks but also financial risks. Juanita discovered that a significant financial risk facing the organization is a commodity price risk—the risk of a significant increase in the price of fuel for the company's locomotives. A review of the company's income and expense statement showed that last year about 28 percent of its expenses were related to fuel oil.

Juanita was also asked to determine whether the installation of a new sprinkler system at the corporate headquarters building would be justified. The cost of the project would be $40,000. She estimates the project would provide an after-tax net cash flow of $25,000 per year for three years, with the first of these cash flows coming one year after investment in the project.

GWS is considering expanding its routes to include Colorado, New Mexico, Texas, and Oklahoma. The company is concerned about the number of derailments that

might occur. Juanita ran a regression with "thousands of miles GWS locomotives traveled" as the independent variable and "number of derailments" as the dependent variable. Results of the regression are as follows:

$$Y = 2.31 + .022X$$

With the expansion, GWS trains will travel an estimated 640,000 miles next year.

a. With regard to the fuel price risk:
   1. Discuss how Juanita could use futures contracts to hedge the price risk.
   2. Discuss how a double-trigger, integrated risk management plan could be employed.
b. What is the net present value (NPV) of the sprinkler system project, assuming the rate of return required by GWS investors is 10 percent?
c. How many derailments should Juanita expect next year, assuming the regression results are reliable and GWS goes ahead with the expansion plan?

(*Hint:* Be careful of scale factors when considering the independent variable.)

---

*under regular market conditions at some level of confidence.* Value-at-risk analysis is often applied to a portfolio of assets, such as a mutual fund or a pension fund. It is similar to the concept of "maximum probable loss" in traditional property and liability risk management discussed in the previous chapter.[25] For example, a mutual fund may have the following VAR characteristics: there is a 5 percent probability that the value of the portfolio may decline by $50,000 on any single trading day. In this case, the worst probable loss is $50,000, the time period is one trading day, and the level of confidence is 95 percent. Based on a VAR estimate, the risk level could be increased or decreased, depending on risk tolerance. Value at risk can also be employed to examine the risk of insolvency for insurers. VAR can be determined in a number of ways, including using historical data and running a computer simulation. While VAR is used in financial risk management, a growing number of organizations are considering

financial risk under the broadened scope of risk management.

### Catastrophe Modeling

Record-setting catastrophic losses occurred in the United States in 2005. Insured catastrophic losses were $62.3 billion ($68.9 billion in 2010 dollars).[26] Most of these claims were a result of Hurricane Katrina and other hurricanes that year. Catastrophic losses can also result from earthquakes, terrorist attacks, hurricanes, and other storms. Insured losses from the tornado that hit Joplin, Missouri in 2011 were expected to be $2.8 billion, making it the costliest tornado since 1950.[27] The possibility of catastrophic losses and the impact of such losses upon insurers and other businesses have focused attention on catastrophe modeling.

**Catastrophe modeling** *is a computer-assisted method of estimating losses that could occur as a result of a catastrophic event.* Input variables include such factors as seismic data, meteorological data, historical losses, and values exposed to loss (e.g., structures, population, business income, etc.). The output from the computer analysis is an estimate of likely results from the occurrence of a catastrophic event, such as a category 5 hurricane or an earthquake of magnitude 7.8 on the Richter scale.

Catastrophe models are employed by insurers, brokers, ratings agencies, and large companies with exposure to catastrophic loss. An insurance company with hurricane exposure on the Eastern Seaboard or Gulf Coast, or earthquake exposure in California, may use catastrophe modeling to estimate possible aggregate losses from a disaster. Insurance brokerages, as a service to their customers, may offer catastrophe modeling services. Organizations that assess the financial viability of insurers, such as A. M. Best, use catastrophe models to determine risk potential and reserve adequacy. Some private companies also use catastrophe models in their risk management programs.

A number of organizations provide catastrophe modeling services, including RMS (Risk Management Solutions), AIR (Applied Insurance Resources, a subsidiary of the Insurance Services Office), EQECAT (a subsidiary of ABSG Consulting, Inc.), and Impact Forecasting (a center of excellence within Aon Benefield). In addition to catastrophic losses caused by hurricanes and earthquakes, RMS also provides modeling for terrorism losses and infectious diseases.

## SUMMARY

- Financial risk management is the identification, analysis, and treatment of speculative financial risks. Such risks include commodity price risk, interest rate risk, and currency exchange rate risk.

- An integrated risk program is a risk treatment technique that combines coverage for pure and speculative risks within the same contract.

- Enterprise risk management is a comprehensive risk management program that addresses an organization's pure, speculative, strategic, and operational risks.

- Two important emerging risks considered in an enterprise risk management program are the risks of terrorism and climate change.

- A cyclical pattern—called the underwriting cycle—has been observed in underwriting stringency, premium levels, and profitability in the property and casualty insurance industry. In a "hard" insurance market, premiums are high and underwriting standards are tight. In a "soft" insurance market, premiums are low and underwriting standards are loose.

- Two important factors that affect property and casualty insurance company pricing and underwriting decisions are the level of capacity in the insurance industry and investment returns.

- The insurance industry has been experiencing consolidation through insurance company mergers and acquisitions, insurance brokerage mergers and acquisitions, and cross-industry consolidation.

- Insurers, reinsurers, and others are using capital market risk financing alternatives. These arrangements include securitizing risk by issuing catastrophe bonds and insurance options.

- Risk managers can use a number of techniques to predict losses. These techniques include probability analysis, regression analysis, and forecasting by using loss distributions.

- When analyzing events, the characteristics of the events must be considered. Events may be independent, dependent, or mutually exclusive.

- Regression analysis is a method of characterizing the relationship that exists between two or more variables and then using the characterization as a predictor.

- In analyzing cash flows in different periods, the time value of money must be considered.

- Changing a present value into a future value is called compounding; determining the present value of a future amount is called discounting.

- Risk managers can apply time value of money analysis in many situations, including insurance coverage bid analysis and loss-control investment analysis.

- A risk management information system (RMIS) is a computerized database that permits risk managers to store and analyze risk management data and to use such data to predict future losses.

- Risk managers may use intranets, risk maps, value at risk (VAR) analysis, and catastrophe modeling in their risk management programs.

## KEY CONCEPTS AND TERMS

Capacity (69)
Capital budgeting (78)
Catastrophe bond (71)
Catastrophe modeling (80)
Chief risk officer (CRO) (65)
Clash loss (69)
Combined ratio (68)
Commodity price risk (63)
Compounding (77)
Consolidation (70)
Currency exchange rate risk (65)
Dependent events (72)
Discounting (77)
Double-trigger option (65)
Enterprise risk management (66)
Financial risk management (63)
"Hard" insurance market (68)
Independent events (71)
Insurance brokers (70)
Insurance option (71)
Integrated risk program (65)
Interest rate risk (65)
Internal rate of return (IRR) (78)
Intranet (79)
Loss distribution (75)
Mutually exclusive events (75)
Net present value (NPV) (78)
Regression analysis (75)
Risk management information system (RMIS) (79)
Risk maps (79)
Securitization of risk (71)
"Soft" insurance market (68)
Surplus (69)
Time value of money (76)
Underwriting cycle (68)
Value at risk (VAR) (79)
Weather option (71)

## REVIEW QUESTIONS

1. Name three speculative financial risks that may be considered by a risk manager.

2. How does enterprise risk management differ from traditional risk management?

3. What is the underwriting cycle? Differentiate between a "hard" and a "soft" insurance market.

4. What is meant by "consolidation" in the insurance industry?

5. How does securitization of risk increase capacity in the property and casualty insurance industry?

6. a. Why is loss forecasting necessary when making a decision about whether to retain or transfer loss exposures?
   b. What techniques can a risk manager use to predict future losses?

7. What is the danger of simply using past losses to estimate future losses?

8. Why is time value of money analysis used in risk management decision making?

9. What variables are difficult to quantify when analyzing investments in risk-control projects?

10. a. What is a risk management information system (RMIS)?
    b. What is a risk management intranet?

## APPLICATION QUESTIONS

1. Integrated risk management programs are new to many risk managers and the insurance companies that offer such programs. What additional expertise, aside from knowledge of property and casualty insurance, must an insurance company possess to offer integrated risk management products?

2. A risk manager self-insured a property risk for one year. The following year, even though no losses had occurred, the risk manager purchased property insurance to address the risk. What is the best explanation for the change in how the risk was handled, even though no losses had occurred?

3. Why do insurance brokerage mergers and acquisitions have a greater influence on corporate risk managers than do property and casualty insurance company mergers and acquisitions?

4. a. What would be the effect of ignoring the time value of money when making risk management decisions?
   b. What does the net present value of a loss control investment really represent to the owners of the organization?

5. During a "hard" insurance market, a manufacturing company decided to self-insure its workers compensation loss exposure. The company hired a third party to administer the workers compensation claims. Even though the risk was being self-insured, the risk manager insisted that the third-party administrator maintain meticulous records. When asked why such detailed records were necessary, the risk manager replied, "So we have a good story to tell an insurance company next year." What did the risk manager mean?

## INTERNET RESOURCES

■ The **International Risk Management Institute (IRMI)** seeks to be the premier authority in providing expert advice and practical strategies relating to insurance and risk management. IRMI has a large online library with information on many insurance and risk management topics. Visit the site at

irmi.com

■ The **Nonprofit Risk Management Center** provides assistance and services to nonprofit organizations. The organization publishes a newsletter, easy-to-read publications, and informative briefs on frequently asked questions related to risk management and insurance. The organization also offers consulting services and risk audits. Visit the site at

nonprofitrisk.org

■ The **Public Risk Management Association** represents risk managers of state and local governmental units. The organization provides practical training and education for risk managers in the public sector; publishes a magazine, a newsletter, and detailed issue-specific publications; and provides cutting-edge updates on federal regulations and legislation. Visit the site at

primacentral.org

■ The **Risk Management Society (RIMS)** is the premier professional association in the United States for risk managers and corporate buyers of insurance. RIMS provides a forum for the discussion of common risk management issues, supports loss-prevention activities, and makes known to insurers the insurance needs of its members. RIMS has local chapters in major cities and publishes *Risk Management* magazine. Visit the site at

rims.org

■ The **Self-Insurance Institute of America** is a national association that promotes self-insurance as an alternative method for financing losses. The organization publishes technical articles on self-insurance, holds educational conferences, and promotes the legislative and regulatory interests of self-insurance at both the federal and state levels. Visit the site at

siia.org

■ The **Casualty Actuarial Society (CAS)** promotes the application of actuarial science to property, casualty, and similar loss exposures. To learn more about the CAS, its research, and its publications, access the site at

casact.org

■ The **Insurance Information Institute (III)** is an excellent resource. The III provides a wealth of information about the property and casualty insurance industry, as well as reports on timely topics. The III also provides information on the financial services industry. Visit the site at

iii.org

■ Two industry education organizations provide professional designation programs in risk management. The **American Institute for CPCU** ("The Institutes") offers the "Associate in Risk Management" (ARM) designation. The **National Alliance for Insurance Education and Research** offers the "Certified Risk Manager" (CRM) designation. For information about these professional designations, visit the sites at

aicpcu.org and scic.com

## SELECTED REFERENCES

Berthelsen, Richard G., Michael W. Elliot, and Connor M. Harrison, *Risk Financing*, 4th ed. (American Institute for CPCU—Insurance Institute of America, 2006).

"The Bigger Picture—Enterprise Risk Management in Financial Services Organizations," a report from *The Economist* Intelligence Unit, September 2008.

"Excellence in Risk Management IX—Bridging the Gap: Be Visible, Be Valuable, Be Strategic," Marsh and The Risk Management Society, 2012.

Harrington, Scott E., and Gregory R. Niehaus, *Risk Management and Insurance*, 2nd ed. McGraw Hill/Irwin, 2004.

Kunreuther, Howard C. and Erwann O. Michel-Kerjan, *At War with the Weather—Managing Large-Scale Risks in a New Era of Catastrophes*, MIT Press, 2009.

Ross, Stephen A., Randolph W. Westerfield, and Bradford Jordan, *Fundamentals of Corporate Finance*, 9th ed. McGraw-Hill/Irwin 2010.

"Spotlight on ERM," *Risk Management* magazine, 2007. This issue includes nine articles on enterprise risk management.

"2011 RIMS Benchmark Survey," Risk and Insurance Management Society, 2011.

Woodhouse, Antony, and Amber Mills, "Sea Change vs. Hot Air: What You Need to Know about Climate Change, *Risk Management*, March 2009, pp. 32-36.

## NOTES

1. See an investments text for a detailed explanation of these capital market instruments.

2. As reported in "Who Needs Derivatives?" by Caroyln T. Geer, *Forbes Magazine,* April 21, 1997.

3. To learn more about the positioning, role, and job of a chief risk officer (CRO), see "The Chief Risk Officer: What Does It Look Like and How Do You Get There?" *Risk Management,* September 2005, pp. 34–38; "Implementing Enterprise Risk Management: The Emerging Role of the Chief Risk Officer," International Risk Management Institute (IRMI), Inc., Web site January 2002; also visit the International Financial Risk Institute Web site.

4. Statistics were taken from the 2011 RIMS Benchmark Survey of risk managers as quoted in "The ERM Tipping Point—ERM has Reached Critical Mass—Time to Get on Board," by Carol A. Fox, *Risk Management,* Nov. 2011, pp. 22-24. This same issue of *Risk Management* has stories on how Caterpillar, a federal home loan bank, and a state government department utilize ERM.

5. "Viewing Risk Management Strategically," Excellence in Risk Management V—An Annual Survey of Risk Management Issues and Practices, The Risk and Insurance Management Society (RIMS) and Marsh, Inc., 2008, p. 8.

6. "The Value of Enterprise Risk Management," by Robert E. Hoyt and Andre P. Liebenberg, *Journal of Risk and Insurance*, Vol. 78, No. 4 (2011), pp. 795-822.

7. "Excellence in Risk Management IX—Bridging the Gap: Be Visible, Be Valuable, Be Strategic," Marsh and The Risk Management Society, 2012.

8. Survey results were taken from "The Bigger Picture—Enterprise Risk Management in Financial Services Organizations," a report from *The Economist* Intelligence Unit, September, 2008, p. 4.

9. See "A Risk and Economic Analysis of Dirty Bomb Attacks on the Ports of Los Angeles and Long Beach," by H. Rosoff and D. von Winderfeldt, *Risk Analysis,* Vol. 27, No. 2 (2007), pp. 533-546.

10. See Chapter 1 of *At War with the Weather—Managing Large-Scale Risks in a New Era of Catastrophes* by Howard C. Kunreuther and Erwann O. Michel-Kerjan, (MIT Press, 2009).

11. For a review of the literature on underwriting cycles see Mary A. Weiss, "Underwriting Cycles: A Synthesis and Further Directions," *Journal of Insurance Issues,* 2007, Vol. 30, No. 1, pp. 31–45.

12. Insurance Information Institute, "9/11: The Tenth Anniversary."

13. Ibid.

14. Statistics reported in this paragraph were taken from various tables in Chapter 4 of the Insurance Information Institute's *The Insurance Fact Book 2012, and* various editions of A.M. Best Company's publication *Best's Aggregates & Averages—Property Casualty.* The most recent data are from *2012 Best's Aggregates & Averages—Property/Casualty*, pages 80, 81, and 368.

15. Ibid.

16. U.S. Insurance-Related Mergers and Acquisitions, 2001-2010, Insurance Information Institute's, *The Insurance Fact Book 2012*, p. 21.

17. For a discussion of capital market approaches for dealing with risk, including risk securitization and derivatives, see *Risk Financing*, by Richard G. Berthelsen, Michael W. Elliot, and Connor M. Harrison, 4th ed. (2006), American Institute for CPCU—Insurance Institute of America.

18. Also see: "Taming Mother Nature—How Weather Risk Management has Helped Offset the Elements," *Risk Management,* June 2009, pp. 33-36.

19. The line that best fits the data minimizes the sum of the squared deviations of the points from the line. Business statistics and econometrics textbooks provide a more detailed discussion of regression analysis.

20. Introductory business finance textbooks discuss the time value of money in greater detail. The time value of money calculations displayed here may also be performed using a financial calculator. Such calculators ease financial computations as the time value of money functions are preprogrammed.

21. Net present value and internal rate of return are discussed here. Some other methods are the payback method, discounted payback, and accounting rate of return. Net present value is preferred by many people because it employs the time value of money, uses the appropriate cash flow, and provides a dollars and cents answer that is easy to interpret.

22. The relevant cash flow measure captures increased revenues and decreased expenses. Depreciation is not subtracted directly as it is a noncash expense. Depreciation is considered, however, when determining the tax liability.

23. The International Risk Management Institute's *RMIS Review* provides comparative vendor information and a process for selecting an RMIS.

24. To learn more about risk mapping, see "Where do you go from risk mapping?" Strategy@Risk.com/October 19, 2010.

25. Value at risk is discussed in many contexts by many authors. For a representative discussion, see Chapter 2 of *Making Enterprise Risk Management Pay Off,* Thomas L. Barton, William G. Shenkir, and Paul L. Walker, Prentice Hall, 2002; and "Value at Risk (VAR): The New Benchmark for Managing Market Risk," Giuseppe Tardivo, *Journal of Financial Management and Analysis,* January 2002, pp. 16–26. For an interesting discussion of some problems with reliance on Value-at-Risk, see Chapters 6 and 7 of *Plight of the Fortune Tellers—Why We Need to Manage Financial Risk Differently* by Riccardo Rebonato, 2007.

26. "Insured Losses, U.S. Catastrophes, 2001-2010," *The Insurance Fact Book 2012,* Insurance Information Institute: New York: Insurance Information Institute (iii.org), p. 128.

27. "Records: Joplin Twister was Costliest Since 1950," Advisen FPN, May 19, 2012.

# CHAPTER 5

# TYPES OF INSURERS AND MARKETING SYSTEMS

*"Insurers are increasingly using multiple distribution channels to sell their products."*

Insurance Information Institute

## LEARNING OBJECTIVES

**After studying this chapter, you should be able to**

◆ Describe the major types of private insurers, including the following:

| | |
|---|---|
| Stock insurers | Lloyd's of London |
| Mutual insurers | Blue Cross and Blue Shield plans |
| Reciprocal exchanges | Health maintenance organizations |

◆ Explain why some life insurers have demutualized or formed holding companies.

◆ Describe the major distribution systems for selling life insurance.

◆ Describe the major distribution systems in property and casualty insurance, including the following:

| | |
|---|---|
| Independent agency system | Direct writer |
| Exclusive agency system | Mixed systems |
| Direct response system | |

*Kristin, age 32, is a widow with two sons, ages 3 and 1. Her husband died recently from pancreatic cancer. The amount of life insurance on his life was insufficient for paying the funeral costs and other medical bills not covered by insurance. After assessing her situation, Kristin believes she should purchase additional life insurance. A friend suggests the purchase of life insurance from a mutual insurer because policyholders may receive dividends. Kristin has no idea what a mutual insurer is and how a mutual insurer differs from other insurers. She is not alone in her confusion. Many consumers also do not understand the differences among insurers.*

*Thousands of life and health insurers and property and casualty insurers are doing business in the United States today. As part of the financial services industry, private insurers have a profound impact on the American economy. Private insurers sell financial and insurance products that enable individuals, families, and business firms to attain a high degree of protection and economic security. The insurance industry also provides millions of jobs for workers and is an important source of capital to business firms. Indemnification for losses is one of the most important economic functions of insurers; insureds are restored completely or partially to their previous financial position, thereby maintaining their economic security.*

*In this chapter, we discuss the role of private insurance companies in the financial services industry. Topics discussed include an overview of the financial services industry, the major types of private insurers, the major marketing methods for selling insurance, and the role of agents and brokers in the sales process.*

## OVERVIEW OF PRIVATE INSURANCE IN THE FINANCIAL SERVICES INDUSTRY

The financial services industry consists of thousands of financial institutions that provide financial products and services to the public. Financial institutions include commercial banks, savings and loan institutions, credit unions, life and health insurers, property and casualty insurers, mutual funds, securities brokers and dealers, private and state pension funds, various government-related financial institutions, finance companies, and other financial firms.

There are various ways of measuring the relative importance of private insurance in the financial services industry. One common method is to determine the percentage of industry assets held by each financial sector. Exhibit 5.1 shows the amount of assets held by various financial institutions in 2010. Assets in the financial service industry totalled $60.8 trillion. The banking sector held 27 percent of the total assets; the securities sector accounted for 21 percent of the assets; and the insurance industry held 11 percent of the total assets. However, this figure is somewhat misleading and understates the relative financial importance of the insurance industry because private insurers also control a large amount of private pension assets (shown separately in Exhibit 5.1).

The financial services industry is changing rapidly. Two trends clearly stand out—consolidation

**Exhibit 5.1**
**Assets of Financial Services Sectors, 2010 ($ billions)**

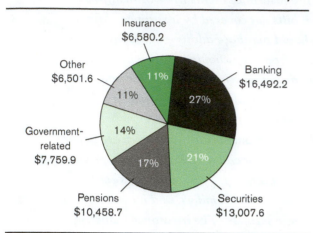

NOTE: Data are from the Board of Governors of the Federal Reserve System.

SOURCE: Insurance Information Institute, *Financial Services Fact Book*, 2012, p.v.

and convergence of financial products and services. *Consolidation* means that the number of firms in the financial services industry has declined over time because of mergers and acquisitions. Because of competitive reasons, the number of commercial banks, securities dealers and brokerage firms, life and health insurers, and property and casualty insurers has declined significantly over time.

*Convergence* means that financial institutions can now sell a wide variety of financial products that earlier were outside their core business area. Because of the Financial Modernization Act of 1999, financial institutions, including insurers, can now compete in other financial markets that are outside their core business area. For example, many life insurers sell substantial amounts of life insurance and annuities through banks. Some insurers have established banks and savings institutions chartered by the Office of Thrift Supervision (OTS). Other insurers have established financial holding companies that allow them to engage in banking activities.

## TYPES OF PRIVATE INSURERS

A large number of private insurers are currently doing business in the United States. In 2010, 1061 life and health insurers were doing business in the United States.[1] These insurers sell a variety of life and health insurance products, annuities, mutual funds, pension plans, and related financial products. Exhibit 5.2 shows the top 17 U.S. life and health insurance groups ranked by revenues in 2010.

In 2010, 2689 property and casualty insurers were also doing business in the United States.[2] These insurers sell property and casualty insurance and related lines, including inland marine coverages and surety and fidelity bonds. Exhibit 5.3 shows the top 19 U.S. property and casualty insurers ranked by revenues in 2010.

There are various ways of classifying insurance companies. In terms of legal ownership and structure, the major types of private insurers can be classified as follows:

- Stock insurers
- Mutual insurers
- Lloyd's of London
- Reciprocal exchanges
- Blue Cross and Blue Shield plans
- Health maintenance organizations (HMOs)
- Other types of private insurers

### Stock Insurers

A **stock insurer** *is a corporation owned by stockholders.* The objective is to earn profits for the stockholders. The stockholders elect a board of directors, who in turn appoint executive officers to manage the corporation. The board of directors has ultimate responsibility for the corporation's financial success. If the business is profitable, dividends can be declared and paid to the stockholders; the value of the stock may also increase. Likewise, the value of the stock may decline if the business is unprofitable.

### Mutual Insurers

A **mutual insurer** *is a corporation owned by the policyholders.* There are no stockholders. The policyholders elect a board of directors, who appoint executives to manage the corporation. Because relatively few policyholders bother to vote, the board of directors has effective management control of the company.

A mutual insurer may pay dividends to the policyholders or give a rate reduction in advance.

**EXHIBIT 5.2**
## Top U.S. Life/Health Insurance Groups by Revenues, 2010[i] ($ millions)

| Rank | Group | Revenues | Assets |
|------|-------|----------|--------|
| 1 | MetLife | $52,717 | $730,906 |
| 2 | Prudential Financial | 38,414 | 539,854 |
| 3 | New York Life Insurance | 34,947 | 199,646 |
| 4 | TIAA-CREF | 32,225 | 417,332 |
| 5 | Massachusetts Mutual Life Insurance | 25,647 | 188,449 |
| 6 | Northwestern Mutual | 23,384 | 180,038 |
| 7 | Aflac | 20,732 | 101,039 |
| 8 | Lincoln National | 10,411 | 193,824 |
| 9 | Unum Group | 10,193 | 57,308 |
| 10 | Genworth Financial | 10,089 | 112,395 |
| 11 | Guardian Life Insurance Co. of America | 10,051 | 46,122 |
| 12 | Principal Financial | 9,159 | 145,631 |
| 13 | Reinsurance Group of America | 8,262 | 29,082 |
| 14 | Thrivent Financial for Lutherans | 7,471 | 62,760 |
| 15 | Mutual of Omaha Insurance | 5,724 | 24,986 |
| 16 | Pacific Life | 5,603 | 115,992 |
| 17 | Western & Southern Financial Group | 4,921 | 36,465 |

[i]Revenues for insurance companies include premium and annuity income, investment income and capital gains or losses but exclude deposits. Based on companies and categories in the Fortune 500. Each company is assigned only one category, even if it is involved in several industries.
SOURCE: Fortune; Insurance Information Institute, *Financial Services Fact Book*, 2012, p. 105.

**EXHIBIT 5.3**
## Top U.S. Property/Casualty Companies by Revenues, 2010 ($ millions)

| Rank | Group | Revenues | Assets |
|------|-------|----------|--------|
| 1 | Berkshire Hathaway | $136,185 | $372,229 |
| 2 | American International Group | 104,417 | 683,443 |
| 3 | State Farm Insurance Cos. | 63,177 | 192,794 |
| 4 | Liberty Mutual Insurance Group | 33,193 | 112,350 |
| 5 | Allstate | 31,400 | 130,874 |
| 6 | Travelers Cos. | 25,112 | 105,181 |
| 7 | Hartford Financial Services | 22,383 | 318,346 |
| 8 | Nationwide | 20,265 | 148,702 |
| 9 | United Services Automobile Association (USAA) | 17,946 | 94,262 |
| 10 | Progressive | 14,963 | 21,150 |
| 11 | Lowes (CNA) | 14,621 | 76,277 |
| 12 | Chubb | 13,319 | 50,249 |
| 13 | Assurant | 8,528 | 26,397 |
| 14 | Amarican Family Insurance Group | 6,492 | 16,788 |
| 15 | Fidelity National Finacial | 5,740 | 7,888 |
| 16 | Auto-Owners Insurance | 5,396 | 15,316 |
| 17 | Erie Insurance Group | 4,890 | 14,344 |
| 18 | W.R.Berkley | 4,724 | 17,529 |
| 19 | American Financial Group | 4,497 | 32,454 |

SOURCE: Fortune; Insurance Information Institute, *Financial Services Fact Book*, 2012, p. 89.

In life insurance, a dividend is largely a refund of a redundant premium that can be paid if the insurer's mortality, investment, and operating experience are favorable. However, because the mortality and investment experience cannot be guaranteed, dividends legally cannot be guaranteed.

There are several types of mutual insurers, including the following:

- Advance premium mutual
- Assessment mutual
- Fraternal insurer

**Advance Premium Mutual**   Most mutual insurers are advance premium mutuals. *An advance premium mutual is owned by the policyholders; there are no stockholders, and the insurer does not issue assessable policies.* Once the insurer's surplus (the difference between assets and liabilities) exceeds a certain amount, the states will not permit a mutual insurer to issue an assessable policy. The premiums charged are expected to be sufficient to pay all claims and expenses. Any additional costs because of poor experience are paid out of the company's surplus.

In life insurance, mutual insurers typically pay annual dividends to the policyholders. In property and casualty insurance, dividends to policyholders generally are not paid on a regular basis. Instead, such insurers may charge lower initial or renewal premiums that are closer to the actual amount needed for claims and expenses.

**Assessment Mutual**   *An* assessment mutual *has the right to assess policyholders an additional amount if the insurer's financial operations are unfavorable.* Relatively few assessment mutual insurers exist today, partly because of the practical problem of collecting the assessment. Those insurers that still market assessable policies are smaller insurers that operate in limited geographical areas, such as a state or county, and the coverages offered are limited.

**Fraternal Insurer**   A fraternal insurer *is a mutual insurer that provides life and health insurance to members of a social or religious organization.* This type of insurer is also called a "fraternal benefit society." To qualify as a fraternal benefit society

under the state's insurance code, the insurer must have some type of social or religious organization in existence. In addition, it must be a nonprofit entity that does not issue common stock; it must operate solely for the benefit of its members or beneficiaries; and it must have a representative form of government with a ritualistic form of work. Examples include the Knights of Columbus, Woodmen of the World Life, and Thrivent Financial.

Fraternal insurers sell only life and health insurance to their members. The assessment principle was used originally to pay death claims. Today, most fraternal insurers operate on the basis of the level premium method and legal reserve system that commercial life insurers use. Fraternal insurers also sell term life insurance and annuities. Because fraternal insurers are nonprofit or charitable organizations, they receive favorable tax treatment.

**Changing Corporate Structure of Mutual Insurers**
The corporate structure of mutual insurers—especially life insurers—has changed significantly over time. Three trends are clearly evident:

1. *Increase in company mergers.* We noted earlier that the number of active life insurers has declined significantly in recent years. Most of the decline is due to company mergers and acquisitions. A merger means that one insurer is absorbed by another insurer or that two or more existing insurers are blended into an entirely new company. Mergers occur because insurers wish to reduce their operating costs and general overhead costs. They also occur because some insurers wish to acquire a line of new insurance, enter a new area of business, or become larger and benefit from economies of scale.

2. *Demutualization.* **Demutualization** *means that a mutual insurer is converted into a stock insurer.* Some mutual insurers have become stock insurers for the following reasons:[3]

   - The ability to raise new capital is increased.
   - Stock insurers have greater flexibility to expand by acquiring new companies or by diversification.
   - Stock options can be offered to attract and retain key executives and employees.
   - Conversion to a stock insurer may provide tax advantages.

3. *Mutual holding company.* Demutualization is cumbersome, expensive, and slow, and it requires the approval of regulatory authorities. As an alternative, many states have enacted legislation that allows a mutual insurer to form a holding company. A **holding company** *is a company that directly or indirectly controls an authorized insurer.* A mutual insurer is reorganized as a holding company that owns or acquires control of stock insurance companies that can issue common stock (see Exhibit 5.4). The mutual holding company owns at least 51 percent of the subsidiary stock insurer if the latter issues common stock.

Mutual holding companies have both advantages and disadvantages. Proponents present the following advantages:

- Insurers have an easier and less expensive way to raise new capital to expand or remain competitive.
- Insurers can enter new areas of insurance more easily, such as a life insurer acquiring a property and casualty insurer.
- Stock options can be given to attract and retain key executives and employees.

Critics of mutual holding companies, however, present the following counterarguments:

- Policyholders could be financially hurt by the change; the mutual holding structure could result in a reduction of dividends and other financial benefits to the policyholders.

- Critics also argue that a conflict of interest may arise between top management and the policyholders. For example, top management may be given company stock or stock options for earning higher operating profits, which could result in lower dividends or higher premiums.

## Lloyd's of London

**Lloyd's of London** is not an insurer, but is the world's leading insurance market that provides services and physical facilities for its members to write specialized lines of insurance. It is a market where members join together to form syndicates to insure and pool risks. Members include some of the world's major insurance groups and companies listed on the London Stock Exchange, as well as individuals (called Names), and limited partnerships.

Lloyd's is also famous for insuring unusual exposure units, such as a prize for a hole-in-one at a golf tournament, or injury to a Kentucky Derby horse-race winner. These unusual exposures, however, account for only a small part of the total business.

Lloyd's of London has several important characteristics.[4] *First, as stated earlier, Lloyd's technically is not an insurance company, but is a society of members (corporations, individuals, and limited partnerships) who underwrite insurance in syndicates.* Lloyd's by itself does not write insurance; the insurance is actually written by syndicates that belong to Lloyd's. In this respect, Lloyd's conceptually is similar to the New York Stock Exchange, which does not buy or sell securities, but provides a marketplace and other services to its members who buy and sell securities.

*Second, as stated earlier, the insurance is written by the various syndicates that belong to Lloyd's.* At the end of 2010, 85 syndicates were registered to conduct business at Lloyd's. Each syndicate is headed by a managing agent who manages the syndicate on behalf of the members who receive profits or bear losses in proportion to their share in the syndicate. The syndicates tend to specialize in marine, aviation, catastrophe, professional indemnity, and auto insurance coverages. Also, Lloyd's is a major player in the international reinsurance markets. As noted earlier, the unusual exposure units that have made Lloyd's famous account for only a small fraction of the total business. Likewise, life insurance accounts only for a small fraction of the total business and is limited to short-term contracts.

**EXHIBIT 5.4**
**Mutual Holding Company Illustration**

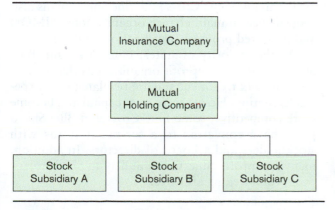

*Third, new individual members or Names who belong to the various syndicates now have limited legal liability.* Individual Names earlier had unlimited legal liability and pledged their personal fortune to pay their agreed-upon share of the insurance written as individuals. However, because of catastrophic asbestosis liability losses in the early 1990s, many Names could not pay their share of losses and declared bankruptcy. As a result, no new Names with unlimited legal liability are admitted today.

*Corporations with limited legal liability and limited liability partnerships are also members of Lloyd's of London.* Corporations and partnerships were permitted to join Lloyd's in order to raise new capital, which has substantially increased the ability of Lloyd's to write new business.

*Members must also meet stringent financial requirements.* Individual members are high net worth individuals. Each member, whether individual or corporate, must supply capital to support its underwriting at Lloyds. All premiums go into a premium trust fund, and withdrawals are allowed only for claims and expenses. Members must also deposit additional funds if premiums do not cover the claims, and the venture is a loss. A central guarantee fund is also available to pay claims if the members backing a policy go bankrupt and cannot meet their obligations.

*Finally, Lloyd's is licensed only in a small number of jurisdictions in the United States.* In the other states, Lloyd's must operate as a nonadmitted insurer. This means that a surplus lines broker or agent can place business with Lloyd's, but only if the insurance cannot be obtained from an admitted insurer in the state. Despite the lack of licensing, Lloyd's does a considerable amount of business in the United States. In particular, Lloyd's of London reinsures a large number of American insurers and is an important professional reinsurer.

## Reciprocal Exchange

A reciprocal exchange is another type of private insurer. *A* **reciprocal exchange** (**also called an interinsurance exchange**) *can be defined as an unincorporated organization in which insurance is exchanged among the members (called subscribers).* In its basic form, insurance is exchanged among the members; each member of the reciprocal insures the other members and, in turn, is insured by them. Thus, there is an exchange of insurance promises—hence the name reciprocal exchange.

In addition, a reciprocal is managed by an attorney-in-fact. The attorney-in-fact is usually a corporation that is authorized by the subscribers to seek new members, pay losses, collect premiums, handle reinsurance arrangements, invest the funds, and perform other administrative duties. However, the attorney-in-fact is not personally liable for the payment of claims and is not the insurer. The reciprocal exchange is the insurer.

Most reciprocals are relatively small and account for only a small percentage of the total property and casualty insurance premiums written. In addition, most reciprocals specialize in a limited number of lines of insurance. However, a few reciprocals are multiple-line insurers that are large.

## Blue Cross and Blue Shield Plans

Blue Cross and Blue Shield plans are another type of insurer organization. In most states, Blue Cross plans generally are organized as nonprofit, community-oriented prepayment plans that provide coverage primarily for hospital services. Blue Shield plans generally are nonprofit, prepayment plans that provide payment for physicians' and surgeons' fees and other medical services. In recent years, most Blue Cross and Blue Shield plans have merged into single entities. However, a few separate Blue Cross plans and Blue Shield plans are still in operation.

Although most members are insured through group plans, individual and family coverages are also available. Blue Cross and Blue Shield plans also sponsor health maintenance organizations (HMOs) and preferred provider organizations (PPOs).

In the majority of states, Blue Cross and Blue Shield plans are nonprofit organizations that receive favorable tax treatment and are regulated under special legislation. However, to raise capital and become more competitive, some Blue Cross and Blue Shield plans have converted to a for-profit status with stockholders and a board of directors. In addition, many nonprofit Blue Cross and Blue Shield plans own profit-seeking affiliates.

## Health Maintenance Organizations

HMOs are organized plans of health care that provide comprehensive health-care services to their members. HMOs provide broad health-care services to a specified group for a fixed prepaid fee; however, many HMOs today also have cost-sharing provisions, such as deductibles and copayments, and cost control is heavily emphasized. In addition, the choice of health-care providers may be restricted, and less costly forms of treatment are often provided. The characteristics of HMOs will be discussed in greater detail in Chapter 16.

## Other Private Insurers

In addition to the preceding, other types of private insurers merit a brief discussion. These include captive insurers and savings bank life insurance.

**Captive Insurers**    As noted in Chapter 3, *a captive* **insurer** *is an insurer owned by a parent firm for the purposes of insuring the parent firm's loss exposures.* There are different types of captive insurers. A *single parent captive* (also called a *pure captive)* is an insurer owned by one parent, such as a corporation. The captive can be an *association captive*, which is owned by several parents. For example, business firms that belong to a trade association may own a captive insurer.

Captive insurers are becoming more important in commercial property and casualty insurance, and thousands of captive insurers exist today. As noted in Chapter 3, captive insurers are formed because (1) a parent firm may have difficulty in obtaining insurance; (2) some captives are formed offshore to take advantage of a favorable regulatory environment; (3) the parent's insurance costs may be lower; (4) a captive insurer makes access to reinsurers easier; (5) the captive insurer may be a source of profit to the parent if other parties are insured as well; and (6) there may be income-tax advantages to the parent under certain conditions. The characteristics of captives have already been discussed in Chapter 3, so additional treatment is not needed here.

**Savings Bank Life Insurance**    Savings Bank Life Insurance (SBLI) refers to life insurance that was sold originally by mutual savings banks in three states: Massachusetts, New York, and Connecticut. Today, SBLI is also sold to consumers over the phone or through Web sites in those states, and to consumers who reside in other states as well, including Maine, New Hampshire, New Jersey, Pennsylvania, and Rhode Island. The objective of SBLI is to provide low-cost life insurance to consumers by holding down operating costs and the payment of high sales commissions to agents. SBLI is discussed in greater detail in Chapter 11.

# AGENTS AND BROKERS

A successful sales force is the key to success in the financial services industry. Most insurance policies sold today are sold by agents and brokers.

## Agents

When you buy insurance, you will probably purchase the insurance from an agent. An **agent** is someone who legally represents the principal and has the authority to act on the principal's behalf. The principal represented is the insurance company.

An agent has the authority to represent the insurer based on express authority, implied authority, and apparent authority. *Express authority* refers to the specific powers that the agent receives from the insurer. *Implied authority* means the agent has the authority to perform all incidental acts necessary to exercise the powers that are expressly given. *Apparent authority* is the authority the public reasonably believes the agent possesses based on the actions of the principal.[5] The principal is legally responsible for the acts of an agent whenever the agent is acting within the scope of express, implied, or apparent authority. This includes wrongful and fraudulent acts, omissions, and misrepresentations so long as the agent is acting within the scope of his or her authority granted or implied by the principal.[6]

There is an important difference between a property and casualty insurance agent and a life insurance agent. A property and casualty agent has the power to bind the insurer immediately with respect to certain types of coverage. This relationship can be created by a *binder, which is temporary insurance until the policy is actually written.* Binders can be oral or written. For example, if you telephone an agent and request

## INSIGHT 5.1

### Show Me the Money—How Much Do Insurance Sales Agents Earn?

The median annual wage of insurance sales agents was $46,770 in May 2010. The median wage is the wage at which half the workers in an occupation earned more than that amount and half earned less. The lowest 10 percent earned less than $25,940, and the top 10 percent earned more than $115,340.

Many independent agents are paid by commission only. Sales workers who are employees of an agency or an insurance carrier may be paid in one of three ways: salary only, salary plus commission, or salary plus bonus.

In general, commissions are the most common form of compensation, especially for experienced agents. The amount of the commission depends on the type and amount of insurance sold and on whether the transaction is a new policy or a renewal. When agents meet their sales goals or when an agency meets its profit goals, agents usually get bonuses. Some agents involved with financial planning receive a fee for their services, rather than a commission.

Insurance sales agents usually determine their own hours of work and often schedule evening and weekend appointments for the convenience of their clients. Some sales agents meet with clients during business hours and then spend evenings doing paperwork and preparing presentations to prospective clients. Most agents work full-time and some work more than 40 hours per week.

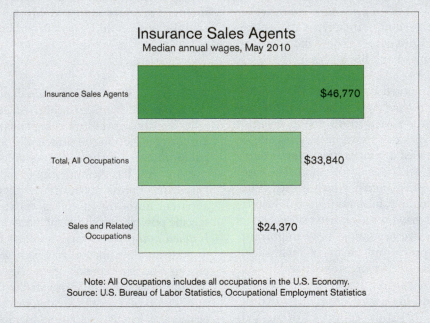

**Insurance Sales Agents**
Median annual wages, May 2010

| | |
|---|---|
| Insurance Sales Agents | $46,770 |
| Total, All Occupations | $33,840 |
| Sales and Related Occupations | $24,370 |

Note: All Occupations includes all occupations in the U.S. Economy.
Source: U.S. Bureau of Labor Statistics, Occupational Employment Statistics

SOURCE: Excerpted from Bureau of Labor Statistics, U.S. Department of Labor, Occupational Outlook Handbook, 2012–13 Edition, Insurance Sales Agents, on the Internet at http://www.bls.gov/ooh/sales/insurance-sales-agents.htm (visited March 30, 2012).

insurance on your motorcycle, the agent can make the insurance effective immediately. In contrast, a life insurance agent normally does not have the authority to bind the insurer. The agent is merely a soliciting agent who induces persons to apply for life insurance. The applicant for life insurance must be approved by the insurer before the insurance becomes effective.

Finally, some college students have an interest in insurance sales as a career. Insight 5.1 discusses the earnings of insurance agents for 2010.

### Brokers

In contrast to an agent who represents the insurer, a **broker** *is someone who legally represents the insured* even though he or she receives a commission from the insurer. A broker legally does not have the authority to bind the insurer. Instead, he or she can solicit or accept applications for insurance and then attempt to place the coverage with an appropriate insurer. But the insurance is not in force until the insurer accepts the business.

As stated earlier, a broker is paid a commission by insurers where the business is placed. Many brokers are also licensed as agents, so that they have the authority to bind their companies when acting as agents.

Brokers are extremely important in commercial property and casualty insurance. Large brokerage firms have knowledge of highly specialized insurance markets, provide risk management and loss-control services, and handle the accounts of large corporate insurance buyers.

Brokers are also important in the surplus lines markets. *Surplus lines refer to any type of insurance for which there is no available market within the state, and the coverage must be placed with a nonadmitted insurer. A* **nonadmitted insurer** *is an insurer not licensed to do business in the state. A* **surplus lines broker** *is a special type of broker who is licensed to place business with a nonadmitted insurer.* An individual may be unable to obtain the coverage from an admitted insurer because the loss exposure is too great, or the required amount of insurance is too large. A surplus lines broker has the authority to place the business with a surplus lines insurer if the coverage cannot be obtained in the state from an admitted company.

Finally, brokers are important in the area of employee benefits, especially for larger employers. Large employers often obtain their group life and medical expense coverages through brokers. As indicated earlier, brokers also play a major role in the marketing of property and casualty insurance to large national accounts.

## TYPES OF MARKETING SYSTEMS

Marketing systems refer to the various methods for selling and marketing insurance products. These methods of selling are also called *distribution systems.* Insurers employ actuaries, claims adjusters, underwriters, and other home office personnel, but unless insurance policies are profitably sold, the insurer's financial survival is unlikely. Thus, an efficient distribution system is essential to an insurance company's survival.

### Life Insurance Marketing

Distribution systems for the sale of life insurance have changed dramatically over time. Traditional methods for selling life insurance have been substantially modified, and new marketing models have emerged. It is beyond the scope of the text to discuss all distribution methods in detail. However, the major life insurance distribution systems used today can be classified as follows:[7]

- Personal selling systems
- Financial institution distribution systems
- Direct response system
- Other distribution systems

**Personal Selling Systems**  The majority of life insurance policies and annuities sold today are through **personal selling distribution systems**, which are systems in which commissioned agents solicit and sell life insurance products to prospective insureds. Life insurance and annuities are complex products, and knowledgeable agents are needed to explain and sell the various products. Personal selling distribution systems include the following:

- *Career agents*. Career agents are full-time agents who usually represent one insurer and are paid on a commission basis. These agents are also called *affiliated agents* because they sell primarily the life insurance products of a single insurer. Under this system, insurers recruit new agents and provide financing, training, supervision, and office facilities. Commissions on the sale of life insurance typically range from 40 to 90 percent of the first-year's premium. Renewal commissions for policies in force are much lower, such as 2 to 5 percent, and are paid for a limited number of years. Despite aptitude tests, the attrition rate for new life insurance agents is high. The five-year retention rate is typically less than 15 percent for many insurers.
- *Multiple Line Exclusive Agency System*. Under this system, agents who sell primarily property and casualty insurance also sell individual life and health insurance products. These agents are also called *captive agents*. Under this system, agents represent only one insurer or group of insurers that are financially interrelated or under common ownership. For example, an agent may sell an auto or homeowners policy to a client. Depending on the client's needs and insurance products available, the agent can also sell life insurance, health insurance, annuities, mutual funds, individual retirement accounts, and other

products as well. State Farm Mutual and Allstate are examples of this system.

- *Independent Property and Casualty Agents.* Independent property and casualty agents are independent contractors who represent several insurers and sell primarily property and casualty insurance. In addition to property and casualty insurance, many independent agents also sell life and health insurance to their clients.
- *Personal-Producing General Agent (PPGA).* Some independent agents place substantial amounts of business with one insurer and enter into a special financial arrangement with that insurer. **A personal-producing general agent (PPGA)** is an independent agent who receives special financial consideration for meeting minimum sales requirements. PPGAs often have the option of recruiting and training sub-agents. In such cases, the PPGA receives an overriding commission based on the amount of insurance sold by the sub-agents.[8]
- *Brokers.* Life insurance and annuities are also sold by brokers. *Brokers* are independent agents who do not have an exclusive contract with any single insurer or an obligation to sell the insurance products of a single insurer. Although brokers may place a substantial amount of business with a particular insurer, they have no obligation to sell a certain amount of insurance for that insurer.[9] Brokers usually enter into separate agency contracts with each insurer in which business is placed.

**Financial Institution Distribution Systems**   Many insurers today use commercial banks and other financial institutions as a distribution system to market life insurance and annuity products. Commerical banks are becoming increasingly more important in the marketing of fixed and variable annuities, and to a lesser degree, life insurance.

In addition, other financial institutions and investment firms, such as Charles Schwab, Fidelity Investments, and The Vanguard Group, also make life insurance products and annuities available to their clients.

**Direct Response System**   The **direct response system** is a marketing system by which life and health insurance products are sold directly to consumers without a face-to-face meeting with an agent. Potential customers are solicited by television, radio, mail, newspapers, and the Internet. Some insurers use telemarketing to sell their products while others advertise extensively on television. Many insurers have Web sites through which life and health insurance can be sold directly to the consumer.

The direct response system has several advantages to insurers. Insurers gain access to large markets; acquisition costs can be held down; and uncomplicated products, such as term insurance, can be sold effectively. One disadvantage, however, is that complex products are often difficult to sell because an agent's services may be required.

**Other Distribution Systems**   Life insurers also use a variety of additional distribution systems to sell their products. They include the following:

- *Worksite Marketing.* Under this system, individual producers go into a business firm, and, with the approval of management, conduct sales interviews on site with employees interested in purchasing life insurance products or annuities. There are few direct costs or fees to employers, and this method is especially appropriate for low-income and middle-income markets.
- *Stock Brokers.* Many stock brokers are also licensed to sell life insurance products and fixed and variable annuities. As a result, stock brokers can better meet both the investment needs and life insurance needs of clients.
- *Financial Planners.* Financial planners provide advice to clients on investments, estate planning, taxation, wealth management, and insurance. Some financial planners are licensed to sell life insurance, and many career life insurance agents are also financial planners who offer financial planning in their analysis of needs.

### Property and Casualty Insurance Marketing

The major distribution systems for marketing property and casualty insurance include the following:

- Independent agency system
- Exclusive agency system
- Direct writer
- Direct response system
- Multiple distribution systems

**Independent Agency System** The **independent agency system**, which is sometimes called the American agency system, has several basic characteristics. *First, the independent agency is a business firm that usually represents several unrelated insurers.* Agents are authorized to write business on behalf of these insurers and in turn are paid a commission based on the amount of business produced.

*Second, the agency owns the expirations or renewal rights to the business.* If a policy comes up for renewal, the agency can place the business with another insurer if it chooses to do so. Likewise, if the contract with an insurer is terminated, the agency can place the business with other insurers that the agency represents.

*Third, the independent agent is compensated by commissions that vary by line of insurance.* The commission rate on renewal business generally is the same as that paid on new business. If a lower renewal rate were paid, the insurer may lose business, because the agent would have a financial incentive to place the insurance with another insurer at the time of renewal.

In addition to selling, independent agents perform other functions. They are frequently authorized to adjust small claims. Larger agencies may also provide loss control services to their insureds, such as accident prevention and loss control engineers. Also, for some lines, the agency may bill the policyholders and collect the premiums. However, most insurers use *direct billing*, by which the policyholder is billed directly by the insurer. This is particularly true of personal lines of insurance, such as auto and homeowners.

**Exclusive Agency System** *Under the* **exclusive agency system**, *the agent represents only one insurer or a group of insurers under common ownership.* The agent may be prohibited by contract from representing other insurers. In the property and casualty industry, insurers that use this system are also called "direct writers." However, as discussed later, there is a technical distinction between the exclusive agency system and direct writers.

Agents under the exclusive agency system do not usually own the expirations or renewal rights to the policies. There is some variation, however, in this regard. Some insurers do not give their agents any ownership rights in the expirations. Other insurers may grant limited ownership of expirations while the

agency contract is in force. In addition, the contract usually permits the insurer to buy the expiration list from the exclusive agent to establish its value if the agency contract is terminated.[10] In contrast, under the independent agency system, the agency has complete ownership of the expirations.

Another difference is the payment of commissions. Exclusive agency insurers generally pay a lower commission rate on renewal business than on new business. This approach results in a strong financial incentive for the agent to write new business and is one factor that helps explain the historical growth of exclusive agency insurers. In contrast, as noted earlier, insurers using the independent agency system typically pay the same commission rate on new and renewal business.

Also, exclusive agency insurers provide strong support services to new agents. A new agent usually starts as an employee during a training period to learn the business. After the training period, the agent becomes an independent contractor who is then paid on a commission basis.

**Direct Writer** As stated earlier, insurers that use the exclusive agency system are also called direct writers by the trade press and property and casualty insurers. However, there is a technical distinction between them. *Technically, a* **direct writer** *is an insurer in which the salesperson is an employee of the insurer, not an independent contractor.* The insurer pays all the selling expenses, including the employee's salary. Similar to exclusive agents, an employee of a direct writer usually represents only one insurer.

Employees of direct writers are usually compensated on a "salary plus" arrangement. Some companies pay a basic salary plus a commission directly related to the amount of insurance sold. Others pay a salary and a bonus that represent both selling and service activities of the employee. In contrast, the agents that sell for exclusive agency insurers, such as State Farm and Allstate, generally, are not salaried employees but are independent contractors who are paid commissions based on the amount of business produced.

**Direct Response System** Property and casualty insurers also use the direct response system to sell insurance. A direct response insurer sells directly to the public by television, telephone, mail, newspapers, and other media. Property and casualty insurers also operate Web sites that provide considerable consumer information and premium quotes.

The direct response system is used primarily to sell personal lines of insurance, such as auto and homeowners insurance. It is not as useful in the marketing of commercial property and casualty coverages because of complexity of contracts and rating considerations.

**Multiple Distribution Systems**   The distinctions between the traditional marketing systems are breaking down as insurers search for new ways to sell insurance. To increase their profits, many property and casualty insurers use more than one distribution system to sell insurance. These systems are referred to as **multiple distribution systems**. For example, some insurers that have traditionally used the independent agency system now sell insurance directly to consumers over the Internet or by television and mail advertising. Other insurers that have used only exclusive agents (also called captive agents) in the past to sell insurance are now using independent agents as well. Other insurers are marketing property and casualty insurance through banks and to consumer groups through employers and through professional and business associations. The lines between the traditional distribution systems will continue to blur in the future as insurers develop new systems to sell insurance.

# GROUP INSURANCE MARKETING

In addition to the preceding, many insurers use group marketing methods to sell individual insurance policies to members of a group. These groups include employers, labor unions, trade associations, and other groups. In particular, substantial amounts of new individual life insurance, annuities, long-term-care insurance, and other financial products are sold to employees in employer–employee groups. Employees pay for the insurance by payroll deduction. Workers no longer employed can keep their insurance in force by paying premiums directly to the insurer.

Life insurers typically sell and service group life insurance products through *group representatives* who are employees who receive a salary and incentive payments based on group sales, persistency, and profitability of the business.

Some property and casualty insurers use mass merchandising plans to market their insurance. **Mass merchandising** is a plan for selling individually underwritten property and casualty coverages to group members; auto and homeowners insurance are popular lines that are frequently used in such plans. As noted earlier, individual underwriting is used, and applicants must meet the insurer's underwriting standards. Rate discounts may be given because of a lower commission scale for agents and savings in administrative expenses. In addition, employees typically pay for the insurance by payroll deduction. Finally, employers do not usually contribute to the plans; any employer contributions result in taxable income to the employees.

## CASE APPLICATION

Commercial Insurance is a large stock property and liability insurer that specializes in the writing of commercial lines of insurance. The board of directors has appointed a committee to determine the feasibility of forming a new subsidiary insurer that would sell only personal lines of insurance, primarily homeowners and auto insurance. The new insurance company would have to meet certain management objectives. One member of the board of directors believes the new insurer should be legally organized as a mutual insurer rather than as a stock insurer. Assume you are an insurance consultant who is asked to serve on the committee. To what extent, if any,

would each of the following objectives of the board of directors be met by formation of a mutual property and casualty insurer? Treat each objective separately.

a. Commercial Insurance must legally own the new insurer.
b. The new insurer should be able to sell common stock periodically in order to raise capital and expand into new markets.
c. The policies sold should pay dividends to the policyholders.
d. The new insurer should be licensed to do business in all states.

## SUMMARY

- There are several basic types of insurers:

    Stock insurers

    Mutual insurers

    Lloyd's of London

    Reciprocal exchange

    Blue Cross and Blue Shield Plans

    Health maintenance organizations (HMOs)

    Captive insurers

    Savings bank life insurance

- An *agent* is someone who legally represents the insurer and has the authority to act on the insurer's behalf. In contrast, a *broker* is someone who legally represents the insured.

- *Surplus lines* refer to any type of insurance for which there is no available market within the state, and the coverage must be placed with a nonadmitted insurer. A *nonadmitted insurer* is a company not licensed to do business in the state. A *surplus lines broker* is a special type of broker who is licensed to place business with a nonadmitted insurer.

- Several distribution systems are used to market life insurance. They include:

    Personal selling systems

    Financial institution distribution systems

    Direct response system

    Other distribution systems

- Several distribution systems are used to market property and casualty insurance. They include:

    Independent agency system

    Exclusive agency system

    Direct writer

    Direct response system

    Multiple distribution systems

- Many insurers use group insurance marketing methods to sell individual insurance policies to members of a group. Employees typically pay for the insurance by payroll deduction. Workers no longer employed can keep their insurance in force by paying premiums directly to the insurer.

## KEY CONCEPTS AND TERMS

Advance premium mutual (90)

Agent (93)

Assessment mutual (90)

Broker (94)

Captive agent (95)

Captive insurer (93)

Demutualization (90)

Direct response system (96)

Direct writer (97)

Exclusive agency system (97)

Fraternal insurer (90)

Holding company (91)

Independent agency system (97)

Lloyd's of London (91)

Mass merchandising (98)

Multiple distribution systems (98)

Multiple line exclusive agency system (95)

Mutual insurer (88)

Nonadmitted insurer (95)

Personal-producing general agent (96)

Personal selling systems (95)

Reciprocal exchange (92)

Savings bank life insurance (SBLI) (93)

Stock insurer (88)

Surplus lines broker (95)

## REVIEW QUESTIONS

1. Describe the basic characteristics of stock insurers.

2. a. Describe the basic features of mutual insurers.
   b. Identify the major types of mutual insurers.

3. The corporate structure of mutual insurers has changed over time. Briefly describe several trends that have had an impact on the corporate structure of mutual insurers.

4. Explain the basic characteristics of Lloyd's of London.

5. Describe the basic characteristics of a reciprocal exchange.

6. Explain the legal distinction between an agent and a broker.

7. Describe briefly the following distribution systems in the marketing of life insurance.
   a. Personal selling systems
   b. Financial institution distribution systems
   c. Direct response system
   d. Other distribution systems

8. Describe briefly the following distribution systems in the marketing of property and casualty insurance.
   a. Independent agency system
   b. Exclusive agency system
   c. Direct writer
   d. Direct response system
   e. Multiple distribution systems

9. Who owns the policy expirations or the renewal rights to the business under the independent agency system?

10. What is a mass-merchandising plan in property and liability insurance?

## APPLICATION QUESTIONS

1. A group of investors are discussing the formation of a new property and liability insurer. The proposed company would market a new homeowners policy that combines traditional homeowner coverages with unemployment benefits if the policyholder becomes involuntarily unemployed. Each investor would contribute at least $100,000 and would receive a proportionate interest in the company. In addition, the company would raise additional capital by selling ownership rights to other investors. Management wants to avoid the expense of hiring and training agents to sell the new policy and wants to sell the insurance directly to the public by selective advertising in personal finance magazines.
   a. Identify the type of insurance company that best fits the above description.
   b. Identify the marketing system that management is considering adopting.

2. Compare a stock insurer to a mutual insurer with respect to each of the following:
   a. Parties who legally own the company
   b. Right to assess policyholders additional premiums
   c. Right of policyholders to elect the board of directors

3. A luncheon speaker stated that "the number of life insurers has declined sharply during the past decade because of the increase in company mergers and acquisitions, demutualization of insurers, and formation of mutual holding companies."
   a. Why have mergers and acquisitions among insurers increased over time?
   b. What is the meaning of *demutualization?*
   c. Briefly explain the advantages of demutualization of a mutual life insurer.
   d. What is a mutual holding company?
   e. What are the advantages of a mutual holding company to an insurer?

4. A newspaper reporter wrote that "Lloyds of London is an association that provides physical facilities and services to the members for selling insurance. The insurance is underwritten by various syndicates who belong to Lloyd's." Describe Lloyd's of London with respect to each of the following:
   a. Liability of individual members and corporations
   b. Types of insurance written
   c. Financial safeguards to protect insureds

5. Property and casualty insurance can be marketed under different marketing systems. Compare the independent agency system with the exclusive agency system with respect to each of the following:
   a. Number of insurers represented by the agent
   b. Ownership of policy expirations
   c. Differences in the payment of commissions

## INTERNET RESOURCES

- The **American College** is an accredited, nonprofit educational institution that provides graduate and undergraduate education, primarily on a distance learning basis, to people in the financial services field. The organization awards the professional Chartered Life Underwriter (CLU) designation, the Chartered Financial Consultant (ChFC) designation, and other professional designations. Visit the site at

  theamericancollege.edu

- The **American Council of Life Insurers (ACLI)** represents the life insurance industry on issues dealing with legislation and regulation. ACLI also publishes statistics on the life insurance industry in an annual fact book. Visit the site at

  acli.com

- The **American Fraternal Alliance** is the recognized leader in the fraternal benefit system. The Fraternal Alliance is the voice of fraternal benefit societies on legislative and regulatory issues. Visit the site at

  fraternalalliance.org

- The **American Insurance Association (AIA)** is an important trade association that represents property and casualty insurers. The site lists available publications, position papers on important issues in property and casualty insurance, press releases, insurance-related links, and names of state insurance commissioners. Visit the site at

  aiadc.org

- The **Insurance Information Institute (III)** has an excellent site for obtaining information on the property and casualty insurance industry. It provides timely consumer information on auto, homeowners, and commercial insurance, and other types of property and casualty insurance. Visit the site at

iii.org

■ The **Insurance Information Institute (III)** also publishes an online fact book on the financial services industry. The publication provides detailed financial information on the role of insurers in the financial services industry. Visit the site at

iii.org/financial

■ The **Institutes** (also known as **the American Institute for CPCU)** is an independent, nonprofit organization that offers educational programs and professional certification to people in all segments of the property and casualty insurance business. The organization awards the professional CPCU designation and other designations. Visit the site at

aicpcu.org

■ The **Insurance Journal** is a definitive online source of timely information on the property/casualty industry. A free online newsletter is available that provides breaking news on important developments in property and casualty insurance. Visit the site at

insurancejournal.com

■ **Insure.com** provides a considerable amount of timely information on the insurance industry. The stories reported are directed toward insurance consumers. Consumers can get premium quotes on life, health, auto, and homeowners insurance. Visit the site at

insure.com

■ **InsWeb** offers insurance quotes from the nation's strongest insurers. You can obtain quotes for auto and homeowners insurance, term life insurance, individual health insurance, and other products as well. Visit the site at

insweb.com

■ **LIMRA** is the principal source of industry sales and marketing statistics in life insurance. Its site provides news and information about LIMRA and the financial

services field, conducts research, and produces a wide range of publications. Visit the site at

limra.com

■ **Lloyd's of London** provides a considerable amount of information about its history and chronology, global insurance operations, financial results, and key events on its Web site. The site also provides information to the news media. Visit the site at

lloyds.com

■ The **National Association of Mutual Insurance Companies** is a trade association that represents mutual property and casualty insurance companies. Visit the site at

namic.org

■ **Towers Watson** is one of the world's largest actuarial and management consulting firms. Towers Watson provides a substantial amount of information on the insurance industry and advises other organizations on risk financing and self-insurance. Visit the site at

towerswatson.com

## SELECTED REFERENCES

Black, Kenneth, Jr., and Harold D. Skipper, Jr. *Life Insurance,* 13th ed. Upper Saddle River, NJ: Prentice-Hall, 2000, chs. 23–24.

*The Financial Services Fact Book 2012,* New York: Insurance Information Institute, 2012.

Graves, Edward E., ed. *McGill's Life Insurance,* 8th ed. Bryn Mawr, PA: The American College, 2011; chs. 22–23.

*The Insurance Fact Book 2012,* New York: Insurance Information Institute, 2012.

*Life Insurers Fact Book, 2011,* Washington, DC: American Council of Life Insurers, 2011.

LOMA (Life Office Management Association), *Insurance Company Operations,*3rd ed., Atlanta, GA: LL Global, Inc. 2012, Ch. 11.

Viswanathan, Krupa S., and J. David Cummins, "Ownership Structure Changes in the Insurance Industry: An Analysis of Demutualization," *Journal of Risk and Insurance,* Vol. 70, No. 3 (September 2003), pp. 401–437.

## NOTES

1. Insurance Information Institute, *The Insurance Fact Book 2012,* (New York: Insurance Information Institute, 2012), p.v.
2. Ibid.
3. Edward E. Graves, ed., *McGill's Life Insurance,* 8th ed. (Bryn Mawr, PA: The American College, 2011), pp. 22.9–22.11.
4. This section is based on *Lloyd's Quick Guide 2011,* Lloyd's of London at lloyds.com and *Lloyd's of London,* Wikipedia, the free encyclopedia.
5. Edward E. Graves, and Burke A. Christensen, *McGill's Legal Aspects of Life Insurance,* 7th ed. (Bryn Mawr, PA: The American College, 2010), pp. 6.3–6.5.
6. Ibid., p. 6.7.
7. This section is based on LOMA (Life Office Management Association). *Insurance Company Operations,* 3rd ed. (Atlanta, GA: LL Global, Inc. 2012), Ch. 11; and Graves, McGill's Life Insurance, Ch. 23.
8. LOMA, *Insurance Company Operations,* 3rd ed., p. 11.8.
9. Ibid., p. 11.8.
10. Constance M. Luthardt and Eric A. Wiening, *Property and Liability Insurance Principles,* 4th ed., 5th printing (Malvern, PA: American Institute for Chartered Property Casualty Underwriters/Insurance Institute of America), 2005, p. 4.11.

# CHAPTER 6

# INSURANCE COMPANY OPERATIONS

*"People who work for insurance companies do a lot more than sell insurance."*

Insurance Information Institute

## LEARNING OBJECTIVES

**After studying this chapter, you should be able to**

◆ Explain the ratemaking function of insurers.

◆ Explain the steps in the underwriting process.

◆ Describe the sales and marketing activities of insurers.

◆ Describe the steps in the process of settling a claim.

◆ Explain the reasons for reinsurance and the various types of reinsurance treaties.

◆ Explain the importance of insurance company investments and identify the various types of investments of insurers.

*Michael, age 26, is a political science major at a large university in Illinois. The placement director has an annual job fair where recruiters from different business firms interview students for possible employment. Michael signed up for an interview with a property insurer to learn about job opportunities. The recruiter explained that job openings exist in several areas, and that the company hires new employees with a wide variety of educational backgrounds. Michael is surprised to learn of the wide range of jobs in the property and casualty insurance industry. Jobs are available in ratemaking, underwriting, sales, claims, finance, information technology, accounting, legal, and other areas as well.*

*To make insurance available to the public, insurers must perform a wide variety of specialized functions or operations. In this chapter, we discuss the major functional operations of insurers, including ratemaking, underwriting, production, claim settlement, reinsurance, and investments. The financial operations of insurers are discussed in Chapter 7.*

## INSURANCE COMPANY OPERATIONS

The most important insurance company operations consist of the following:

- Ratemaking
- Underwriting
- Production
- Claim settlement
- Reinsurance
- Investments

Insurers also engage in other operations, such as accounting, legal services, loss control, and information systems.

The sections that follow discuss each of these functional areas in some detail.

## RATING AND RATEMAKING

**Ratemaking** *refers to the pricing of insurance and the calculation of insurance premiums.* The premium paid by the insured is the result of multiplying a rate determined by actuaries by the number of exposure units, and then adjusting by various rating plans (a process called rating). A *rate* is the price per unit of insurance. An *exposure unit* is the unit of measurement used in insurance pricing, which varies by line of insurance. For example, when you buy gas for your car, the rate per gallon multiplied by the number of gallons purchased equals the amount paid. Likewise, in property and casualty insurance, the rate times the number of exposure units determines the premium paid. We discuss this concept and ratemaking in greater detail in Chapter 7.

Insurance pricing differs considerably from the pricing of other products. When other products are sold, the company generally knows in advance the costs of producing those products, so that prices can be established to cover all costs and yield a profit. However, the insurance company does not know in advance what its actual costs are going to be. The total premiums charged for a given line of insurance may be inadequate for paying all claims and expenses during the policy period. It is only after the period of protection has expired that an insurer can determine its actual losses and expenses. Of course, the insurer hopes that the premium it charges plus investment income will be sufficient to pay all claims and expenses and yield a profit.

The person who determines rates and premiums is known as an **actuary**. An actuary is a highly skilled mathematician who is involved in all phases of insurance company operations, including planning, pricing, and research. In life insurance, the actuary studies important statistical data on births, deaths, marriages, disease, employment, retirement, and accidents. Based on this information, the actuary determines the premiums for life and health insurance policies and annuities. The objectives are to calculate premiums that will make the business profitable, enable the company to compete effectively with other insurers, and allow the company to pay claims and expenses as they occur. A life insurance actuary must also determine the legal reserves a company needs for future obligations.[1]

Professional certification as a life insurance actuary is attained by passing a series of examinations administered by the Society of Actuaries, which qualifies the actuary as a Fellow of the Society of Actuaries.

In property and casualty insurance, actuaries also determine the rates for different lines of insurance. Rates are based on the company's past loss experience and industry statistics. Statistics on hurricanes, tornadoes, fires, crime rates, traffic accidents, and the cost of living are also carefully analyzed. Many companies use their own loss data in establishing the rates. Other companies obtain loss data from advisory organizations, such as the Insurance Services Office (ISO). These organizations calculate historical or prospective loss costs that individual companies can use in calculating their own rates.

Actuaries in property and casualty insurance also determine the adequacy of loss reserves,[2] allocate expenses, and compile statistics for company management and for state regulatory officials.

To become a certified actuary in property and casualty insurance, an actuarial science student must pass a series of examinations administered by the Casualty Actuarial Society. Successful completion of the examinations enables the actuary to become a Fellow of the Casualty Actuarial Society.

# UNDERWRITING

**Underwriting** *refers to the process of selecting, classifying, and pricing applicants for insurance.* The underwriter is the person who decides to accept or reject an application.

## Statement of Underwriting Policy

Underwriting starts with a clear statement of underwriting policy. An insurer must establish an underwriting policy that is consistent with company objectives. The objective may be a large volume of business with a low profit margin or a smaller volume with a larger margin of profit. Classes of business that are acceptable, borderline, or prohibited must be clearly stated. The amounts of insurance that can be written on acceptable and borderline business must also be determined.

The insurer's underwriting policy is determined by top-level management in charge of underwriting. The underwriting policy is stated in detail in an *underwriting guide* that specifies the lines of insurance to be written; territories to be developed; forms and rating plans to be used; acceptable, borderline, and prohibited business; amounts of insurance to be written; business that requires approval by a senior underwriter; and other underwriting details.

## Basic Underwriting Principles

Underwriting is based on a number of principles. Three important principles are as follows:

- Attain an underwriting profit.
- Select prospective insureds according to the company's underwriting standards.
- Provide equity among the policyholders.

*The primary objective of underwriting is to attain an underwriting profit.* The objective is to produce a profitable book of business. The underwriter constantly strives to select certain types of applicants and to reject others so as to obtain a profitable portfolio of business.

*The second principle is to select prospective insureds according to the company's underwriting standards.* This means that the underwriters should select only those insureds whose actual loss experience is not likely to exceed the loss experience assumed in the rating structure. For example, a property insurer may wish to insure only high-grade factories, and expects that its actual loss experience will be well below average. Underwriting standards are established with respect to eligible factories, and a rate is established based on a relatively low loss ratio.[3] Assume that the expected loss ratio is established at 70 percent, the ratio of losses plus loss adjustment expenses to earned premiums, and the rate is set accordingly. The underwriters ideally should insure only those factories that can meet stringent underwriting requirements, so that the actual loss ratio for the group will not exceed 70 percent.

The purpose of the underwriting standards is to reduce adverse selection against the insurer. There is an old saying in underwriting, "select or be selected against." *Adverse selection is the tendency of people with a higher-than-average chance of loss to seek insurance at standard (average) rates, which if not controlled by underwriting, will result in higher-than-expected loss levels.*

*A final underwriting principle is equity among the policyholders.* This means that equitable rates should be charged, and that each group of policyholders should pay its own way in terms of losses and expenses. Stated differently, one group of policyholders should not unduly subsidize another group. For example, a group of 20-year-old persons and a group of 80-year-old persons should not pay the same premium rate for individual life insurance. If identical rates were charged to both groups, younger persons would be subsidizing older persons, which would be inequitable. Once the younger persons became aware that they were being overcharged, they would seek other insurers whose classification systems are more equitable. The first insurer would then end up with a disproportionate number of older persons, and the underwriting results would be unprofitable. Thus, because of competition, there must be rate equity among the policyholders.

## Steps in Underwriting

After the insurer's underwriting policy is established, it must be communicated to the sales force. Initial underwriting starts with the agent in the field.

**Agent as First Underwriter** This step is often called field underwriting. The agent is told what types of applicants are acceptable, borderline, or prohibited. For example, in auto insurance, an agent may be told not to solicit applicants who have been convicted for drunk driving, who are single drivers under age 21, or who are young drivers who own high-powered sports cars. In property insurance, certain exposures, such as bowling alleys and restaurants, may have to be submitted to a company underwriter for approval.

In property and casualty insurance, the agent often has authority to bind the company immediately, subject to subsequent disapproval of the application and cancellation by a company underwriter. Thus, it is important that the agent follow company policy when soliciting applicants for insurance.

In life insurance, the agent must also solicit applicants in accordance with the company's underwriting policy. The agent may be told not to solicit applicants who are active drug addicts or alcoholics, or who work in hazardous occupations.

## Sources of Underwriting Information

The underwriter requires certain information in deciding whether to accept or reject an applicant for insurance. Important sources of information include the following:

- *Application.* The type of information required depends on the type of insurance requested. In property insurance, the application provides information on the physical features of the building, including type of construction, occupancy of the building, quality of fire protection, exposures from surrounding buildings, whether the building has a sprinkler system, and other loss control features.

  In life insurance, the application indicates the age; gender; weight; occupation; personal and family health history; any hazardous hobbies, such as skydiving; and the amount of insurance requested.

- *Agent's report.* Many insurers require the agent or broker to give an evaluation of the prospective insured. In property insurance, the agent or broker may submit an application that does not completely meet the underwriting standards of the company. In such cases, the agent's evaluation of the applicant is especially important.

  In life insurance, the agent may be asked how long he or she has known the applicant, the applicant's annual income and net worth, whether the applicant plans to surrender or exchange an existing life insurance policy for the new policy, and whether the application is the result of the agent's solicitation.

- *Inspection report.* In property insurance, the company may require an inspection report by some outside agency, especially if the underwriter suspects moral hazard. An outside firm investigates the applicant for insurance and makes a detailed report to the company.

In life insurance, the report may provide information on the applicant's financial condition, marital status, outstanding debts or delinquent bills, felony convictions, any drinking or drug problems, whether the applicant has ever declared bankruptcy and additional information as well.

- *Physical inspection.* In property insurance and casualty insurance, the underwriter may require a physical inspection before the application is approved. For example, in workers compensation insurance, the inspection may reveal unsafe working conditions, such as dangerous machinery; violation of safety rules, such as not wearing goggles when a grinding machine is used; and an excessively dusty or toxic plant.
- *Physical examination.* In life insurance, a physical exam may be required to determine if the applicant is overweight; has high blood pressure; or has any abnormalities in the heart, respiratory system, urinary system, or other parts of the body. An *attending physician's report* may also be required, which is a report from a physician who has treated the applicant in the past.

As part of the physical exam, a life insurer may request a report from MIB Group, Inc. (**Medical Information Bureau report**). Companies that belong to this trade association report any health impairments, which are recorded and made available to member companies. For example, if an applicant has high blood pressure, this information would be recorded in the MIB files. The files, however, do not reveal the underwriting decision made by the submitting company.

**Making an Underwriting Decision** After the underwriter evaluates the information, an underwriting decision must be made. There are three basic underwriting decisions with respect to an initial application for insurance:

- Accept the application
- Accept the application subject to certain restrictions or modifications
- Reject the application

First, the underwriter can accept the application and recommend that the policy be issued. A second option is to accept the application subject to certain restrictions or modifications. Several examples

illustrate this second type of decision. Before a crime insurance policy is issued, the applicant may be required to place iron bars on windows or install an approved burglar alarm system; the applicant may be refused a homeowners policy and offered a more limited dwelling policy; a large deductible may be inserted in a property insurance policy; or a higher rate for life insurance may be charged if the applicant is substandard in health. If the applicant agrees to the modifications or restrictions, the policy is then issued.

The third decision is to reject the application. However, excessive and unjustified rejection of applications reduces the insurer's revenues and alienates the agents who solicited the business. If an application is rejected, the rejection should be based on a clear failure to meet the insurer's underwriting standards.

Many insurers now use computerized underwriting for certain personal lines of insurance that can be standardized, such as auto and homeowners insurance. As a result, underwriting decisions can be expedited.

### Other Underwriting Considerations

Other factors are considered in underwriting. They include the following:

- *Rate adequacy and underwriting.* Property and casualty insurers are more willing to underwrite new business for a specific line if rates are considered adequate. However, if rates are inadequate, prudent underwriting requires a more conservative approach to the acceptance of new business. If moral hazard is excessive, the business generally cannot be insured at any rate.

In addition, in commercial property and casualty insurance, the underwriters have a considerable impact on the price of the product. A great deal of negotiation over price takes place between line underwriters and agents concerning the proper pricing of a commercial risk.

Finally, the critical relationship between adequate rates and underwriting profits or losses results in periodic underwriting cycles in certain lines of insurance, such as commercial general liability and commercial multiperil insurance. If rates are adequate, underwriting profits are higher, and underwriting is more liberal. Conversely, when rates are inadequate, underwriting losses occur, and underwriting becomes more restrictive.

- *Reinsurance and underwriting*. Availability of reinsurance may result in more liberal underwriting. However, if reinsurance cannot be obtained on favorable terms, underwriting may be more restrictive. Reinsurance is discussed in greater detail later in the chapter.
- *Renewal underwriting*. In life insurance, policies are not cancellable. In property and casualty insurance, most policies can be canceled or not renewed. If the loss experience is unfavorable, the insurer may either cancel or not renew the policy. Most states have placed restrictions on the insurer's right to cancel.

## PRODUCTION

The term **production** refers to the sales and marketing activities of insurers. Agents who sell insurance are frequently referred to as **producers**. This word is used because an insurance company can be legally chartered, personnel can be hired, and policy forms printed, but no business is produced until a policy is sold. The key to the insurer's financial success is an effective sales force.

### Agency Department

Life insurers have an agency or sales department. This department is responsible for recruiting and training new agents and for the supervision of general agents, branch office managers, and local agents.

Property and casualty insurers have marketing departments. To assist agents in the field, special agents may also be appointed. A *special agent* is a highly specialized technician who provides local agents in the field with technical help and assistance with their marketing problems. For example, a special agent may explain a new policy form or a special rating plan to agents in the field.

In addition to development of an effective sales force, an insurance company engages in a wide variety of marketing activities. These activities include development of a marketing philosophy and the company's perception of its role in the marketplace; identification of short-run and long-run production goals; marketing research; development of new products to meet the changing needs of consumers and business firms; development of new marketing strategies; and advertising of the insurer's products.

### Professionalism in Selling

The marketing of insurance has been characterized by a distinct trend toward professionalism in recent years. This means that the modern agent should be a competent professional who has a high degree of technical knowledge in a particular area of insurance and who also places the needs of his or her clients first. The professional agent identifies potential insureds, analyzes their insurance needs, and recommends a product to meet their needs. After the sale, the agent has the responsibility of providing follow-up service to clients to keep their insurance programs up to date. Finally, a professional agent abides by a code of ethics.

Several organizations have developed professional designation programs for agents and other personnel in the insurance industry. In life and health insurance, The American College has established the **Chartered Life Underwriter (CLU)** program. An individual must pass certain professional examinations to receive the CLU designation.

The American College also awards the **Chartered Financial Consultant (ChFC)** designation for professionals who are working in the financial services industry. To earn the ChFC designation, students must also pass professional examinations.

A similar professional program exists in property and casualty insurance. The American Institute for CPCU has established the **Chartered Property Casualty Underwriter (CPCU)** program. The CPCU program also requires an individual to pass professional examinations.

Other professionals are also important in the insurance industry. Many financial planners are also licensed as insurance agents. The **Certified Financial Planner (CFP)** designation is granted by the Certified Financial Planner Board of Standards, Inc. Many agents in property and liability insurance have been awarded the **Certified Insurance Counselor (CIC)** designation sponsored by the National Alliance for Insurance Education & Research.

## CLAIMS SETTLEMENT

Every insurance company has a claims division or department for adjusting claims. This section of the chapter examines the basic objectives in adjusting claims, the different types of claim adjustors, and the various steps in the claim-settlement process.

## Basic Objectives in Claims Settlement

From the insurer's viewpoint, there are several basic objectives in settling claims.[4]

- Verification of a covered loss
- Fair and prompt payment of claims
- Personal assistance to the insured

*The first objective in settling claims is to verify that a covered loss has occurred.* This step involves determining whether a specific person or property is covered under the policy, and the extent of the coverage. This objective is discussed in greater detail later in the chapter..

*The second objective is the fair and prompt payment of claims.* If a valid claim is denied, the fundamental social and contractual purpose of protecting the insured is defeated. Also, the insurer's reputation may be harmed, and the sales of new policies may be adversely affected. Fair payment means that the insurer should avoid excessive claim settlements and should resist the payment of fraudulent claims, because they will ultimately result in higher premiums.

The states have passed laws that prohibit unfair claims practices. These laws are patterned after the National Association of Insurance Commissioners' Model Act. Some unfair claim practices prohibited by these laws include the following:[5]

- Refusing to pay claims without conducting a reasonable investigation.
- Not attempting in good faith to provide prompt, fair, and equitable settlements of claims in which liability has become reasonably clear.
- Compelling insureds or beneficiaries to institute lawsuits to recover amounts due under its policies by offering substantially less than the amounts ultimately recovered in suits brought by them.

*A third objective is to provide personal assistance to the insured after a covered loss occurs.* Aside from any contractual obligations, the insurer should also provide personal assistance after a loss occurs. For example, the claims adjustor could assist the agent in helping a family find temporary housing after a fire occurs.

## Types of Claims Adjustors

The person who adjusts a claim is known as a **claims adjustor**. The major types of adjustors include the following:

- Agent
- Company adjustor
- Independent adjustor
- Public adjustor

An **insurance agent** often has authority to settle small first-party claims up to some maximum limit. A first-party claim is a claim submitted by the insured to the insurer, such as a small theft loss by the insured. The insured submits the claim directly to the agent, who has the authority to pay up to some specified amount. This approach to claims settlement has several advantages: it is speedy, it reduces adjustment expenses, and it preserves the policyholder's goodwill.

A **company adjustor** can settle a claim. The adjustor is usually a salaried employee who represents only one company. After notice of the loss is received, the company adjustor will investigate the claim, determine the amount of loss, and arrange for payment.

An **independent adjustor** can also be used to adjust claims. *An independent adjustor is an organization or individual that adjusts claims for a fee.* Claims personnel are highly trained individuals who adjust claims on a full-time basis. Property and casualty insurers often use independent adjustors when a catastrophic loss occurs in a given geographical area, such as a hurricane, and a large number of claims are submitted at the same time.

In addition, independent adjustors include individuals who reside in certain geographical areas where the volume of claims is too low to justify the expense of a branch office with full-time adjustors.

A **public adjustor** can be involved in settling a claim. *A public adjustor represents the insured rather than the insurance company and is paid a fee based on the amount of the claim settlement.* A public adjustor may be employed by the insured if a complex loss situation occurs and technical assistance is needed, and also in those cases where the insured and insurer cannot resolve a dispute over a claim.

## Steps in Settlement of a Claim

There are several important steps in settling a claim:

- Notice of loss must be given.
- The claim is investigated.
- A proof of loss may be required.
- A decision is made concerning payment.

**Notice of Loss**　The first step is to notify the insurer of a loss. A provision concerning notice of loss is usually stated in the policy. A typical provision requires the insured to give notice immediately or as soon as possible after the loss has occurred. For example, the homeowners policy requires the insured to give immediate notice; a medical expense policy may require the insured to give notice within 30 days after the occurrence of a loss, or as soon afterward as is reasonably possible; and the personal auto policy requires that the insurer must be notified promptly of how, when, and where the accident or loss happened. The notice must also include the names and addresses of any injured persons and of witnesses.

**Investigation of the Claim**　After notice is received, the next step is to investigate the claim. An adjustor must determine that a covered loss has occurred and must also determine the amount of the loss. A series of questions must be answered before the claim is approved. The most important questions include the following:[6]

- Did the loss occur while the policy was in force?
- Does the policy cover the peril that caused the loss?
- Does the policy cover the property destroyed or damaged in the loss?
- Is the claimant entitled to recover?
- Did the loss occur at an insured location?
- Is the type of loss covered?
- Is the claim fraudulent?

The last question dealing with fraudulent claims is especially important. Insurance fraud is widespread, especially in auto and health insurance. Dishonest people frequently submit claims for bodily injuries that have never occurred.

**Filing a Proof of Loss**　An adjustor may require a proof of loss before the claim is paid. A proof of loss is a sworn statement by the insured that substantiates the loss. For example, under the homeowners policy, the insured may be required to file a proof of loss that indicates the time and cause of the loss, interest of the insured and others in the damaged property, other insurance that may cover the loss, and any change in title or occupancy of the property during the term of the policy.

**Decision Concerning Payment**　After the claim is investigated, the adjustor must make a decision concerning payment. There are three possible decisions. *The claim can be paid*. In most cases, the claim is paid promptly according to the terms of the policy. *The claim can be denied*. The adjustor may believe that the policy does not cover the loss or that the claim is fraudulent. Finally, *the claim may be valid, but there may be a dispute* between the insured and insurer over the amount to be paid. In the case of a dispute, a policy provision may specify how the dispute is to be resolved. For example, if a dispute concerning the value of lost or damaged property arises under the homeowners policy, both the insured and insurer select a competent appraiser. The two appraisers select an umpire. If the appraisers cannot agree on an umpire, a court will appoint one. An agreement by any two of the three is then binding on all parties.

When there is disagreement over the claim settlement, consumers may file a complaint with the state insurance department. The National Association of Insurance Commissioners (NAIC) now has a Web site that permits consumers to check the complaint record of individual insurers (see Insight 6.1).

# REINSURANCE

Reinsurance is another important insurance operation. This section discusses the meaning of reinsurance, the reasons for reinsurance, and the different types of reinsurance contracts.

## Definitions

**Reinsurance** *is an arrangement by which the primary insurer that initially writes the insurance transfers to another insurer (called the reinsurer) part or all of the potential losses associated with such insurance.* The primary insurer that initially writes the insurance is called the **ceding company**. The insurer that accepts

### Be a Savvy Consumer—Check the Insurer's Claims Record Before You Buy

Consumers often experience considerable frustration in their efforts to obtain accurate and timely information on complaints against specific insurers. Some state insurance departments provide detailed information on complaints and rank the insurers operating in the state based on a complaint index. However, not all states provide easily accessible complaint data to the public.

The National Association of Insurance Commissioners (NAIC) has a Web site that provides a wealth of information to consumers with respect to complaints against specific insurers. *Go to the NAIC Consumer Information Source (CIS) at https://eapps.naic.org/cis/. Type in the company name, state, and business type. After locating the company, click on Closed Complaints.* Note that this Web site and address may change if the NAIC makes changes to its current site.

The information provided is based on closed consumer complaint reports. Four types of complaint data are available:

- *Complaint counts by state.* This source shows the total number of complaints in each state for a specific insurer. For example, one national auto insurer that advertises extensively on television received 1172 complaints for private passenger auto insurance from all persons in 2011.
- *Complaint counts by code.* This source shows the total number of complaints by type of coverage, reason the complaint was filed, and final decisions regarding the complaints.
- *Complaint ratio report.* This source is valuable because it compares a specific insurer with all insurers nationally using a single index number. This source compares the ratio of the insurer's market share of complaints to the insurer's market share of premiums for a specific policy type. For example, in 2011, the national median complaint ratio for private passenger auto insurance was 1.00. The above insurer received a score of 0.35, which was below the national median.
- *Closed complaint trend report.* This source shows whether complaints against the insurer are increasing or decreasing. The information presented shows the total number of complaints in the database for consecutive years with the percentage change in complaint counts between years. For example, the total number of complaints from all persons for the above insurer increased from 1114 in 2010 to 1172 in 2011, or a 5 percent increase.

Information on complaints is especially valuable if you are shopping around for auto, homeowners, or health insurance and want to avoid insurers that have bad reputations for paying claims or for providing other services to policyholders.

part or all of the insurance from the ceding company is called the **reinsurer**. The amount of insurance retained by the ceding company for its own account is called the **retention limit** or **net retention**. The amount of insurance ceded to the reinsurer is known as the **cession**. Finally, the reinsurer in turn may reinsure part or all of the risk with another insurer. This is known as a **retrocession**. In this case, the second reinsurer is called a **retrocessionaire**.

### Reasons for Reinsurance

Reinsurance is used for several reasons. The most important reasons include the following:

- Increase underwriting capacity
- Stabilize profits
- Reduce the unearned premium reserve
- Provide protection against a catastrophic loss

Reinsurance also enables an insurer to retire from a territory or class of business and to obtain underwriting advice from the reinsurer.

**Increase Underwriting Capacity** Reinsurance can be used to increase the insurance company's underwriting capacity to write new business. The company may be asked to assume liability for losses in excess of its retention limit. Without reinsurance, the agent would have to place large amounts of insurance with several companies or not accept the risk. This is awkward and may create ill will on behalf of the policyholder. Reinsurance permits the primary company to issue a single policy in excess of its retention limit for the full amount of insurance.

**Stabilize Profits** Reinsurance is used to stabilize profits. An insurer may wish to avoid large fluctuations in annual financial results. Loss experience can fluctuate widely because of social and economic conditions, natural disasters, and chance. Reinsurance can be used to stabilize the effects of poor loss experience. For example, reinsurance may be used to cover a large exposure. If a large, unexpected loss occurs, the reinsurer would pay that portion of the loss in excess of some specified limit. Another arrangement would be to have the reinsurer reimburse the ceding insurer for losses that exceed a specified loss ratio during a given year. For example, an insurer may wish to stabilize its loss ratio at 70 percent. The reinsurer then agrees to reimburse the ceding insurer for part or all the losses in excess of 70 percent up to some maximum limit.

### Reduce the Unearned Premium Reserve

Reinsurance can be used to reduce the unearned premium reserve. For some insurers, especially newer and smaller companies, the ability to write large amounts of new insurance may be restricted by the unearned premium reserve requirement. *The* **unearned premium reserve** *is a liability item on the insurer's balance sheet that represents the unearned portion of gross premiums on all outstanding policies at the time of valuation.* In effect, the unearned premium reserve reflects the fact that premiums are paid in advance, but the period of protection has not yet expired. As time goes on, part of the premium is considered earned, while the remainder is unearned. It is only after the period of protection has expired that the premium is fully earned.

As noted earlier, an insurer's ability to grow may be restricted by the unearned premium reserve requirement. This is because the entire gross premium must be placed in the unearned premium reserve when the policy is first written. The insurer also incurs relatively heavy first-year acquisition expenses in the form of commissions, state premium taxes, underwriting expenses, expenses in issuing the policy, and other expenses. In determining the size of the unearned premium reserve, there is no allowance for these first-year acquisition expenses, and the insurer must pay them out of its surplus. Policyholders' surplus is the difference between assets and liabilities.[7]

For example, a one-year property insurance policy with an annual premium of $1200 may be written on January 1. The entire $1200 must be placed in the unearned premium reserve. At the end of each month, one-twelfth of the premium, or $100, is earned and the remainder is unearned. On December 31, the entire premium is fully earned. However, assume that first-year acquisition expenses are 30 percent of the gross premium, or $360. This amount will come out of the insurer's surplus up front. Thus, the more business it writes, the greater is the short-term drain on its surplus. A rapidly growing insurer's ability to write new business could eventually be impaired. Acquisition expenses must be paid up front, but offsetting income is realized with the passage of time.

Reinsurance reduces the level of the unearned premium reserve required by law and temporarily increases the insurer's surplus position. As a result, the ratio of policyholders' surplus to net written premiums is improved, which permits the insurer to continue to grow.

### Provide Protection Against a Catastrophic Loss

Reinsurance also provides financial protection against a catastrophic loss. Insurers often experience catastrophic losses because of hurricanes and other natural disasters, industrial explosions, commercial airline disasters, and similar events. Reinsurance can provide considerable protection to the ceding company that experiences a catastrophic loss. The reinsurer pays part or all of the losses that exceed the ceding company's retention up to some specified maximum limit.

The tragic terrorist attacks on September 11, 2001, show clearly the importance of reinsurance. Losses from the destruction of the World Trade Center and other buildings by terrorists totaled about $31.6 billion ($39.5 billion in 2008 dollars) when the attacks occurred.[8] Reinsurers paid a large part of the total losses. Congress provided additional backup by enacting the Terrorism Risk Insurance Act (TRIA) of 2002, which provides federal reinsurance to property and casualty insurers if future terrorist losses exceed certain levels. TRIA was extended for an additional seven years in December 2007 and is scheduled to expire at the end of 2014. The legislation is now called the Terrorism Risk Insurance Program Reauthorization Act (TRIPRA) of 2007.

Hurricane Katrina in 2005 is another example of the importance of reinsurance. Insured property losses totaled $41.1 billion ($41.5 billion in 2010 dollars).[9] Reinsurers paid a large part of the loss, which significantly reduced the losses retained by primary insurers.

**Other Reasons for Reinsurance** An insurer can also use reinsurance to retire from the business or from a given line of insurance or territory. Reinsurance permits the insurer's liabilities for existing insurance to be transferred to another carrier; thus, policyholders' coverage remains undisturbed.

Finally, reinsurance allows an insurer to obtain the underwriting advice and assistance of the reinsurer. An insurer may wish to write a new line of insurance, but it may have little experience with respect to underwriting the line. The reinsurer can often provide valuable assistance with respect to rating, retention limits, policy coverages, and other underwriting details.

## Types of Reinsurance

There are two principal types of reinsurance: (1) facultative reinsurance and (2) treaty reinsurance.

**Facultative Reinsurance** Facultative reinsurance *is an optional, case-by-case method that is used when the ceding company receives an application for insurance that exceeds its retention limit.* Reinsurance is not automatic. The primary insurer negotiates a separate contract with a reinsurer for each loss exposure for which reinsurance is desired. However, the primary insurer is under no obligation to cede insurance, and the reinsurer is under no obligation to accept the insurance. But if a willing reinsurer is found, the primary insurer and reinsurer can then enter into a valid contract.

Facultative reinsurance is often used when the primary insurer has an application for a large amount of insurance. Before the application is approved, the primary insurer determines whether reinsurance is available. If reinsurance is available and other underwriting standards are met, the policy can then be written.

Facultative reinsurance has the advantage of flexibility because it can be tailored to fit any type of case, it can increase the capacity of the primary insurer to write large amounts of insurance, and it can help stabilize the financial operations of the primary insurer by shifting part of a large loss to the reinsurer.

Facultative reinsurance, however, has several disadvantages. There is some uncertainty because the primary insurer does not know in advance whether a reinsurer will accept any part of the insurance. There can also be a problem of delay because the policy will not be issued until reinsurance is obtained. Finally, during periods of poor loss experience, reinsurance markets tend to tighten, and facultative reinsurance may be more costly and more difficult to obtain.

**Treaty Reinsurance** Treaty reinsurance *means the primary insurer has agreed to cede insurance to the reinsurer, and the reinsurer has agreed to accept the business.* All business that falls within the scope of the agreement is automatically reinsured according to the terms of the treaty.

Treaty reinsurance has several advantages to the primary insurer. It is automatic, and no uncertainty or delay is involved. It is also economical, because it is not necessary to shop around and negotiate reinsurance terms before the policy is written.

Treaty reinsurance could be unprofitable to the reinsurer. The reinsurer generally has no knowledge about the individual applicant and must rely on the underwriting judgment of the primary insurer. The primary insurer may write bad business and then reinsure it. Also, the premium received by the reinsurer may be inadequate. Thus, if the primary insurer has a poor selection of risks or charges inadequate rates, the reinsurer could incur a loss. However, if the primary insurer consistently cedes unprofitable business to its reinsurers, the ceding insurer will find it difficult to operate because reinsurers will not want to do business with it.

## Methods for Sharing Losses

There are two basic methods for sharing losses: (1) pro rata and (2) excess-of-loss. Under the pro rata method, the ceding company and reinsurer agree to share losses and premiums based on some proportion. Under the excess-of-loss method, the reinsurer pays only when covered losses exceed a certain level.

The following reinsurance methods for the sharing of losses are examples of both methods:

- Quota-share treaty
- Surplus-share treaty
- Excess-of-loss reinsurance
- Reinsurance pool

**Quota-Share Treaty** Under a **quota-share treaty**, the ceding company and reinsurer agree to share premiums and losses based on some proportion.

*The ceding company's retention is stated as a percentage rather than as a dollar amount.* For example, assume that Apex Fire Insurance and Geneva Re enter into a quota-share arrangement by which losses and premiums are shared 50 percent and 50 percent. Thus, if a $100,000 loss occurs, Apex Fire pays $100,000 to the insured but is reimbursed by Geneva Re for $50,000.

Premiums are also shared based on the same agreed-on percentage. However, the reinsurer pays a **ceding commission** to the primary insurer to help compensate for the expenses incurred in writing the business. Thus, in the previous example, Geneva Re would receive 50 percent of the premium less a ceding commission that is paid to Apex Fire.

The major advantage of quota-share reinsurance is that the primary insurer's unearned premium reserve is reduced. For smaller insurers and other insurers that wish to reduce the drain on surplus, a quota-share treaty can be especially effective. The principal disadvantage is that a large share of potentially profitable business is ceded to the reinsurer.

**Surplus-Share Treaty**   Under a **surplus-share treaty,** the reinsurer agrees to accept insurance in excess of the ceding insurer's retention limit, up to some maximum amount. *The retention limit is referred to as a line and is stated as a dollar amount.* If the amount of insurance on a given policy exceeds the retention limit, the excess insurance is ceded to the reinsurer up to some maximum limit. The primary insurer and reinsurer then share premiums and losses based on the fraction of total insurance retained by each party. Each party pays its respective share of any loss regardless of its size.

For example, assume that Apex Fire Insurance has a retention limit of $200,000 (called a line) for a single policy, and that four lines, or $800,000, are ceded to Geneva Re. Apex Fire now has a total underwriting capacity of $1 million on any single exposure. Assume that a $500,000 property insurance policy is issued. Apex Fire takes the first $200,000 of insurance, or two-fifths, and Geneva Re takes the remaining $300,000, or three-fifths. These fractions then determine the amount of loss paid by each party. If a $5000 loss occurs, Apex Fire pays $2000 (two-fifths), and Geneva Re pays the remaining $3000 (three-fifths). This arrangement can be summarized as follows:

| | |
|---|---|
| Apex Fire | $200,000 (1 line) |
| Geneva Re | 800,000 (4 lines) |
| Total underwriting capacity | $1,000,000 |
| *$500,000 policy issued* | |
| Apex Fire | $200,000 (2/5) |
| Geneva Re | $300,000 (3/5) |
| *$5000 loss occurs* | |
| Apex Fire | $2000 (2/5) |
| Geneva Re | $3000 (3/5) |

Under a surplus-share treaty, premiums are also shared based on the fraction of total insurance retained by each party. However, the reinsurer pays a ceding commission to the primary insurer to help compensate for the acquisition expenses.

The principal advantage of a surplus-share treaty is that the primary insurer's underwriting capacity on any single exposure is increased. The major disadvantage is the increase in administrative expenses. The surplus-share treaty is more complex and requires greater record keeping.

**Excess-of-Loss Reinsurance**   Excess-of-loss reinsurance *is designed largely for protection against a catastrophic loss.* The reinsurer pays part or all of the loss that exceeds the ceding company's retention limit up to some maximum level. Excess-of-loss reinsurance can be written to cover (1) a single exposure, (2) a single occurrence, such as a catastrophic loss from a tornado, or (3) excess losses when the primary insurer's cumulative losses exceed a certain amount during some stated time period, such as a year. For example, assume that Apex Fire Insurance wants protection for all windstorm losses in excess of $1 million. Assume that Apex Fire enters into an excess-of-loss arrangement with Franklin Re to cover single occurrences during a specified time period. Franklin Re agrees to pay all losses exceeding $1 million but only to a maximum of $10 million. If a $5 million hurricane loss occurs, Franklin Re would pay $4 million.

**Reinsurance Pool** Reinsurance can also be provided by a reinsurance pool. A **reinsurance pool** *is an organization of insurers that underwrites insurance on a joint basis.* Reinsurance pools have been formed because a single insurer alone may not have the financial capacity to write large amounts of insurance, but the insurers as a group can combine their financial resources to obtain the necessary capacity. For example, the combined hull and liability loss exposures on a large commercial jet can exceed $500 million if the jet should crash. Such high limits are usually beyond the financial capability of a single insurer. However, a reinsurance pool for aviation insurance can provide the necessary capacity. Reinsurance pools also exist for nuclear energy exposures, oil refineries, marine insurance, insurance in foreign countries, and numerous other types of exposures.

The method for sharing losses and premiums varies depending on the type of reinsurance pool. Pools work in two ways.[10] First, each pool member agrees to pay a certain percentage of every loss. For example, if one insurer has a policyholder that incurs a $500,000 loss, and there are 50 members in the pool, each insurer would pay 2 percent, or $10,000 of the loss, depending on the agreement.

Another arrangement is similar to the excess-of-loss arrangement. Each pool member pays for its share of losses below a certain amount. Losses exceeding that amount are then shared by all members in the pool.

# ALTERNATIVES TO TRADITIONAL REINSURANCE

Many insurers and reinsurers are now using the capital markets as an alternative to traditional reinsurance. The financial capacity of the property and casualty industry to pay catastrophic losses from hurricanes, earthquakes, and other natural disasters is limited. Rather than rely solely on the limited financial capacity of the insurance industry to pay catastrophic claims, some insurers and reinsurers are using the capital markets to gain access to the capital of institutional investors. Having access to the capital markets substantially increases the funds available to pay catastrophe losses.

## Securitization of Risk

There is an increasing use of the securitization of risk to obtain funds to pay for a catastrophe loss. **Securitization of risk** means *that an insurable risk is transferred to the capital markets through the creation of a financial instrument, such as a catastrophe bond, futures contract, options contract, or other financial instrument.* These instruments are also called risk-linked securities that transfer insurance-related risks to the capital markets. Insurers were among the first financial institutions to experiment with the securitization of risk.

## Catastrophe Bonds

Catastrophe bonds are an excellent example of the securitization of risk. **Catastrophe bonds** *are corporate bonds that permit the issuer of the bond to skip or reduce scheduled interest payments if a catastrophic loss occurs.* The bonds are complex financial instruments issued by insurers and reinsurers and are designed to provide funds for catastrophic natural disaster losses. The bonds pay relatively high interest rates and help institutional investors to diversify their portfolios because natural disasters occur randomly and are not correlated with the stock market or other economic factors.

Catastrophe bonds are made available to institutional investors in the capital markets through an entity called a *special purpose reinsurance vehicle (SPRV),* which is specifically established for that purpose. The insurer purchases reinsurance from the SPRV and pays reinsurance premiums to the SPRV. The SPRV issues the catastrophe bonds, holds the premiums collected from insurers and the proceeds from the bond sales in a trust, and invests the funds in U.S. Treasuries or other high-quality assets. The bonds pay relatively high interest rates. *However, if a catastrophic loss occurs, the investors could forfeit the interest and even the principal, depending on how the bonds are structured.*

Catastrophe bonds are typically purchased by institutional investors seeking higher-yielding, fixed-income securities. The bonds generally are not available for direct purchase by individual retail investors. Insurers to date have transferred only a small portion of their catastrophe loss exposures to the capital markets. However, catastrophe bonds are growing in importance and are now considered by many to be a standard supplement to traditional reinsurance.

## INVESTMENTS

The investment function is extremely important in the overall operations of insurance companies. Because premiums are paid in advance, they can be invested until needed to pay claims and expenses.

### Life Insurance Investments

Assets held by life insurers have increased substantially over time. In 2010, U.S. life insurers held $5.3 trillion in assets (see Exhibit 6.1). The funds available for investment are derived primarily from premium income, investment earnings, and maturing investments that must be reinvested.

A life insurer divides its assets into two accounts. The assets in the *general account* support the contractual obligations for guaranteed fixed dollar benefits, such as life insurance death benefits. The assets in the *separate account* support the liabilities for investment-risk products, such as variable annuities, variable life insurance, and private pension benefits.

State laws place restrictions on the types of assets in the general account. Because of the long-term nature of life insurance products, most investments are in bonds, mortgages, and real estate; only a small percentage of the assets is invested in stocks. In contrast, state laws generally have fewer restrictions on the investment of assets in the separate account. As such, 80 percent of the assets in the separate account were invested in stocks in 2010 (see Exhibit 6.2).

Life insurance investments have an important economic and social impact on the nation for several reasons. First, life insurance contracts are long-term, and the liabilities of life insurers extend over long periods of time, such as 50 or 60 years. Thus, safety of principal is a primary consideration. Consequently, as stated earlier, the majority of investments in the general account are in bonds.

Second, investment income is extremely important in reducing the cost of insurance to policyholders because the premiums can be invested and earn interest. The interest earned on investments is reflected in the payment of dividends to policyholders, which reduces the cost of life insurance.

Finally, life insurance premiums also are an important source of capital funds to the economy. These funds are invested in shopping centers, housing developments, office buildings, hospitals, new plants, and other economic and social ventures.

**Exhibit 6.1**
**Growth of Life Insurers' Assets**

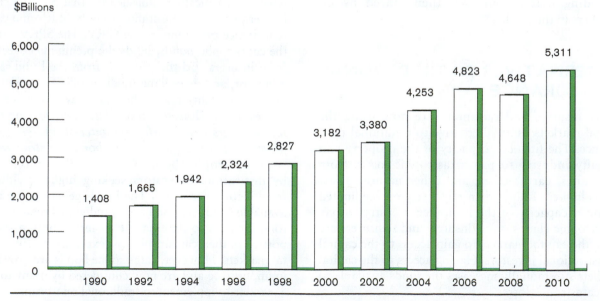

Source: American Council of Life Insurers, *Life Insurers Fact Book 2011*, Figure 2.1

**Asset Distribution of Life Insurers, 2010**

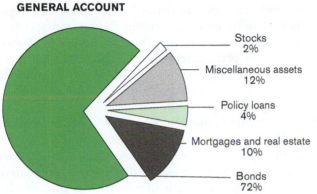

GENERAL ACCOUNT

Stocks
2%

Miscellaneous assets
12%

Policy loans
4%

Mortgages and real estate
10%

Bonds
72%

SEPARATE ACCOUNT

Stocks
80%

Bonds
13%

Miscellaneous assets
6%

Mortgages and real estate
1%

SOURCE: American Council of Life Insurers, *Life Insurers Fact Book 2011*, Figure 2.2.

## Property and Casualty Insurance Investments

In 2010, property and casualty insurance company investments totaled $1.32 trillion.[11] Most assets are invested in securities that can be quickly sold to pay claims if a major catastrophe occurs—primarily in high-quality bonds, stocks, and cash rather than real estate (see Exhibit 6.3).

Two important points must be stressed when the investments of property and casualty insurers are analyzed. *First, in contrast to life insurance, property insurance contracts generally are short-term in nature.* The policy period in most contracts is one year or less, and property claims are usually settled quickly. Also, in contrast to life insurance claims, which are generally fixed in amount, property insurance claim payments can vary widely depending on catastrophic losses, inflation, medical costs, construction costs, auto repair costs, economic conditions, and changing value judgments by society. For these reasons, the investment objective of liquidity is extremely important.

*Second, investment income is extremely important in offsetting unfavorable property and casualty underwriting experience.* The investment of capital and surplus funds, along with the funds set aside for loss reserves and the unearned premium reserve, generate investment earnings that usually permit an insurer to continue its insurance operations despite an underwriting deficit.

**Investments, Property/Casualty Insurers, 2010**

INVESTMENTS BY TYPE[1]

Real estate 0.74%
Preferred stock 1.34%
Other 9.17%
Cash and short-term investments
6.51%

Bonds
66.40%

Common stock
15.85%

SOURCE: National Association of Insurance Commissioners (NAIC) Annual Statement Database, via Highline Data, LLC. Copyrighted Information. No portion of this work may be copied or reproduced without the express written permission of Highline Data, LLC. Excerpted from Insurance Information Institute, *The Insurance Fact Book 2012*, p. 45.

## OTHER INSURANCE COMPANY FUNCTIONS

Insurers also perform other functions. They include information systems, accounting, legal, and loss-control services.

### Information Systems

**Information systems** are extremely important in the daily operations of insurers. These **systems** depend heavily on computers and new technology.

Computers have revolutionized the insurance industry by speeding up the processing and storage of information and by eliminating many routine tasks. Computers are widely used in accounting, policy processing, premium notices, information retrieval, telecommunications, simulation studies, market analysis, training and education, sales, and policyholder services. Information can quickly be obtained on premium volume, claims, loss ratios, investments, and underwriting results.

## Accounting

The accounting department is responsible for the financial accounting operations of an insurer. Accountants prepare financial statements, develop budgets, analyze the company's financial operations, and keep track of the millions of dollars that flow into and out of a typical company each year. Periodic reports are prepared dealing with premium income, operating expenses, claims, investment income, and dividends to policyholders. Accountants prepare statutory annual statements that must be filed with state insurance departments. If the company is publicly traded, accountants must also prepare accounting statements based on Generally Accepted Accounting Principles (GAAP) for investors.

## Legal Function

Another important function of insurance companies is the legal function. In life insurance, attorneys are widely used in advanced underwriting and estate planning. Attorneys also draft the legal language and policy provisions in insurance policies and review all new policies before they are marketed to the public. Other activities include providing legal assistance to actuarial personnel who testify at rate hearings; reviewing advertising and other published materials; providing general legal advice concerning taxation, marketing, investments, and insurance laws; and lobbying for legislation favorable to the insurance industry.

Attorneys must also keep abreast of the frequent changes in state and federal laws that affect the company and its policyholders. These include laws affecting consumers, cost disclosure, affirmative action programs, truth in advertising, and similar legislation. Finally, attorneys must keep up with current court cases and legal precedents.

## Loss-Control Services

**Loss control** is an important part of risk management, and a typical property and casualty insurer provides numerous loss-control services. These services include advice on alarm systems, automatic sprinkler systems, fire prevention, occupational safety and health, prevention of boiler explosions, and other loss-prevention activities. In addition, loss-control specialists can provide valuable advice on the construction of a new building or plant to make it safer and more resistive to damage, which can result in a substantial rate reduction. Loss-control specialists can also assist underwriters.

## CASE APPLICATION

Reinsurance can be used by an insurer to solve several problems. Assume you are an insurance consultant who is asked to give recommendations concerning the type of reinsurance plan or arrangement to use. For each of the following situations, indicate the type of reinsurance plan or arrangement that the ceding insurer should use, and explain the reasons for your answer.

a. Company A is an established insurer and is primarily interested in having protection against a catastrophic loss arising out of a single occurrence.

b. Company B is a rapidly growing new company and desires a plan of reinsurance that will reduce the drain on its surplus because of the expense of writing a large volume of new business.

c. Company C has received an application to write a $50 million life insurance policy on the life of the chief executive officer of a major corporation. Before the policy is issued, the underwriter wants to make certain that adequate reinsurance is available.

d. Company D would like to increase its underwriting capacity to underwrite new business.

## SUMMARY

- Ratemaking refers to the pricing of insurance. Insurance rates are determined by actuaries.

- Underwriting refers to the process of selecting, classifying, and pricing applicants for insurance. There are several important underwriting principles:

  Attain an underwriting profit.

  Select prospective insureds according to the company's underwriting standards.

  Provide equity among the policyholders.

- In determining whether to accept or reject an applicant for insurance, underwriters have several sources of information. Important sources include the application, agent's report, inspection report, physical inspection, and a physical examination in life insurance.

- Production refers to the sales and marketing activities of insurers. Agents who sell insurance are called producers.

- From the insurer's viewpoint, there are several basic objectives in settling claims:

  Verification of a covered loss

  Fair and prompt payment of claims

  Personal assistance to the insured

- The person who adjusts a claim is known as a claims adjustor. The major types of adjustors are as follows:

  Agent

  Company adjustor

  Independent adjustor

  Public adjustor

- Several steps are involved in settling a claim:

  Notice of loss must be given to the company.

  The claim is investigated by the company.

  A proof of loss may be required.

  A decision is made concerning payment.

- Reinsurance is used for several reasons:

  To increase the company's underwriting capacity

  To stabilize profits

  To reduce the unearned premium reserve

  To provide protection against a catastrophic loss

- Facultative reinsurance is an optional case-by-case method by which the primary company negotiates a separate agreement with the reinsurer for each loss exposure that the primary company wants to reinsure. Reinsurance is not automatic. The primary company is under no obligation to cede insurance, and the reinsurer is under no obligation to accept. In contrast, under treaty reinsurance, if the business falls within the scope of the agreement, the primary company must cede insurance to the reinsurer, and the reinsurer must accept the ceded coverage.

- Reinsurance arrangements for the sharing of losses include the following:

  Quota-share treaty

  Surplus-share treaty

  Excess-of-loss treaty

  Reinsurance pool

- Other important insurance company operations include investments, information systems, legal services, and loss-control services.

## KEY CONCEPTS AND TERMS

Actuary (104)
Catastrophe bonds (115)
Ceding commission (114)
Ceding company (110)
Certified Financial Planner (CFP) (108)
Certified Insurance Counselor (CIC) (108)
Cession (111)
Chartered Financial Consultant (ChFC) (108)
Chartered Life Underwriter (CLU) (108)
Chartered Property Casualty Underwriter (CPCU) (108)
Claims adjustor (109)
Company adjustor (109)
Excess-of-loss reinsurance (114)
Facultative reinsurance (113)
Independent adjustor (109)
Information systems (117)

Insurance agent (109)
Loss control (118)
Medical Information Bureau report (107)
Producers (108)
Production (108)
Public adjustor (109)
Quota-share treaty (113)
Ratemaking (104)
Reinsurance (110)
Reinsurance pool (115)
Reinsurer (111)
Retention limit (net retention) (111)
Retrocession (111)
Retrocessionaire (111)
Securitization of risk (115)
Surplus-share treaty (114)
Treaty reinsurance (113)
Underwriting (105)
Unearned premium reserve (112)

## REVIEW QUESTIONS

1. How does ratemaking, or the pricing of insurance, differ from the pricing of other products?

2. a. Define the meaning of underwriting.
   b. Briefly explain the basic principles of underwriting.
   c. Identify the major sources of information available to underwriters.

3. Briefly describe the sales and marketing activities of insurers.

4. Explain the basic objectives in the settlement of claims.

5. Describe the steps involved in the settlement of a claim.

6. Briefly describe the following types of claims adjustors:
   a. Agent
   b. Company adjustor
   c. Independent adjustor
   d. Public adjustor

7. a. What is the meaning of reinsurance?
   b. Briefly explain the reasons for reinsurance.
   c. Explain the meaning of "securitization of risk."

8. Distinguish between facultative reinsurance and treaty reinsurance.

9. Briefly explain the following types of reinsurance methods for sharing losses:
   a. Quota-share treaty
   b. Surplus-share treaty
   c. Excess-of-loss reinsurance
   d. Reinsurance pool

10. Briefly describe the following insurance company operations:
    a. Information systems
    b. Accounting
    c. Legal services
    d. Loss control

# APPLICATION QUESTIONS

1. Delta Insurance is a property insurer that entered into a surplus-share reinsurance treaty with Eversafe Re. Delta has a retention limit of $200,000 on any single building, and up to nine lines of insurance may be ceded to Eversafe Re. A building valued at $1,600,000 is insured with Delta. Shortly after the policy was issued, a severe windstorm caused a $800,000 loss to the building.
   a. How much of the loss will Delta pay?
   b. How much of the loss will Eversafe Re pay?

   c. What is the maximum amount of insurance that Delta can write on a single building under the reinsurance agreement? Explain your answer.

2. Liability Insurance Company writes a substantial amount of commercial liability insurance. A large construction company requests $100 million of liability insurance to cover its business operations. Liability Insurance has a reinsurance contract with Bermuda Re that enables the coverage to be written immediately. Under the terms of the contract, Liability Insurance pays 25 percent of the losses and retains 25 percent of the premium. Bermuda Re pays 75 percent of the losses and receives 75 percent of the premium, less a ceding commission that is paid to Liability Insurance. Based on the preceding, answer the following questions:
   a. What type of reinsurance contract best describes the reinsurance arrangement that Liability Insurance has with Bermuda Re?
   b. If a $50 million covered loss occurs, how much will Bermuda Re have to pay? Explain your answer.
   c. Why does Bermuda Re pay a ceding commission to Liability Insurance?

3. Property Insurance Company is a new property insurer. The company is growing rapidly because of a new homeowners policy that combines traditional homeowner coverages with insurance that pays off the mortgage if the insured dies or becomes totally disabled. Premiums written have increased substantially; new agents have been hired; and the company is considering expanding into additional states. However, its growth has been hampered by statutory accounting rules that require an insurer to write off immediately its first-year acquisition expenses but do not allow full recognition of premium income until the policy period has expired. In this case, explain how reinsurance will enable Property Insurance to continue to grow in an orderly fashion.

4. Felix is a property claims adjustor for a large property insurer. Janet is a policyholder who recently notified the company that the roof of her home incurred substantial damage because of a recent hail storm. Janet owns her home and is insured under a standard homeowners policy with no special endorsements. What questions should Felix ask before the claim is approved for payment by his company?

# INTERNET RESOURCES

- The **American Council of Life Insurers (ACLI)** represents the life insurance industry on issues dealing with legislation and regulation. ACLI also publishes statistics on the life insurance industry in an annual fact book. Visit the site at

  acli.com

- **The American College** is an accredited, nonprofit educational institution that provides graduate and undergraduate education, primarily on a distance learning basis, to people in the financial services industry. The organization awards the professional Chartered Life Underwriter (CLU) designation, the Chartered Financial Consultant (ChFC) designation, and other professional designations. Visit the site at

  theamericancollege.edu

- The **American Insurance Association (AIA)** is an important trade association that represents property and casualty insurers. The site lists available publications, position papers on important issues in property and casualty insurance, press releases, insurance-related links, and names of state insurance commissioners. Visit the site at

  aiadc.org

- The **Institutes** (also known as the **American Institute for CPCU**) is an independent, nonprofit organization that offers educational programs and professional certification to people in all segments of the property and casualty insurance business. The organization awards the professional CPCU designation and other designations. Visit the site at

  aicpcu.org

- The **Insurance Information Institute (III)** is an excellent site for obtaining information on the property and liability insurance industry. It provides timely consumer information on auto, homeowners, and business insurance, and other types of property and liability insurance. Visit the site at

  iii.org

- The **Life Office Management Association (LOMA)** provides extensive information dealing with the management and operations of life insurers and financial services companies. Visit the site at

  loma.org

- **LIMRA** is the principal source of industry sales and marketing statistics in life insurance. Its site provides news and information about LIMRA and the financial services field, conducts research, and publishes a wide range of publications. Visit the site at

  limra.com

- The **National Association of Insurance Commissioners (NAIC)** provides considerable information on complaints against specific insurers. Go to NAIC Consumer Information Source, type in the company name, state, and business type. After locating the company, click on Closed Complaints. Visit the site at

  https://eapps.naic.org/cis/

- The **National Association of Mutual Insurance Companies** is a trade association that represents mutual insurance companies in property and casualty insurance. Visit the site at

  namic.org

- **Towers Watson** is one of the world's largest actuarial and management consulting firms. Towers Watson provides a substantial amount of information on the insurance industry and advises other organizations on risk financing and self-insurance. Visit the site at

  towerswatson.com

# SELECTED REFERENCES

Black, Kenneth, Jr., and Harold D. Skipper, Jr. *Life Insurance,* 13th ed. Upper Saddle River, NJ: Prentice-Hall, 2000, chs. 25–26.

Bouriaux, Sylvie and Richard MacMinn. "Securitization of Catastrophe Risk: New Developments in Insurance-Linked Securities and Derivatives." *The Journal of Insurance Issues*, Vol. 32, No. 1 (Spring 2009), pp. 1–34.

"Catastrophes: Insurance Issues," *Issues Updates,* Insurance Information Institute, April 2012. This source is periodically updated.

Cummins, J. David. "Reinsurance for Natural and Man-Made Catastrophes in the United States: Current State of the Market and Regulatory Reforms." *Risk Management & Insurance Review,* Vol. 10, No. 2 (Fall 2007), pp. 179–220.

Graves, Edward E., ed. *McGill's Life Insurance,* 8th ed. Bryn Mawr, PA: The American College 2011, chs. 17–18, 22–23.

*The Financial Services Fact Book 2012,* New York: Insurance Information Institute.

*The Insurance Fact Book 2012,* New York: Insurance Information Institute.

*Life Insurers Fact Book 2011,* Washington, DC: American Council of Life Insurers, 2011.

Myhr, Ann E. and James J. Markham. *Insurance Operations, Regulation, and Statutory Accounting,* 2nd ed., Malvern, PA: American Institute for Chartered Property Casualty Underwriters/Insurance Institute of America, 2004.

Orsina, Miriam A. and Gene Stone. *Insurance Company Operations,* 3rd ed., Atlanta, GA: LOMA Education and Training, 2012.

"Reinsurance," *Issues Updates.* Insurance Information Institute, April 2012. This source is periodically updated.

Webb, Bernard L., et al. *Insurance Operations and Regulation,* 1st ed., Malvern, PA: American Institute for Chartered Property Casualty Underwriters/Insurance Institute of America, 2002.

## NOTES

1. A legal reserve is a liability item on a company's balance sheet that measures the insurer's obligations to its policyholders. State laws require a company to maintain policy reserves at a level sufficient to pay all policy obligations as they fall due.

2. In property and casualty insurance, a loss reserve is an estimated liability item that represents an amount for claims reported but not yet paid, claims in the process of settlement, and claims that have already occurred but have not been reported.

3. A loss ratio is the ratio of incurred losses and loss adjustment expenses to earned premiums. For example, if incurred losses and loss adjustment expenses are $70 and earned premiums are $100, the loss ratio is 0.70, or 70 percent.

4. For additional information on claims settlement, see Bernard L. Webb, et al., *Insurance Operations and Regulation,* 1st ed. (American Institute for Chartered Property Casualty Underwriters/Insurance Institute of America, 2002), chs. 13–15.

5. Webb, et al., pp. 13.48–13.49.

6. Robert I. Mehr, Emerson Cammack, and Terry Rose, *Principles of Insurance,* 8th ed. (Homewood, IL: Richard D. Irwin, 1985), pp. 616–617.

7. Technically, for a stock insurer, policyholders' surplus is the sum of capital stock (value of the contributions of original stockholders), plus surplus (the amount paid in by the organizers in excess of the par value of the stock), plus any retained earnings. In the case of a mutual insurer, there is no capital account. Policyholders' surplus is the excess of assets over liabilities.

8. Insurance Information Institute, "Terrorism Risk and Insurance," *Issues Updates,* August 2011. This source is periodically updated.

9. Insurance Information Institute, *The Insurance Fact Book 2012,* p. 133.

10. *Sharing the Risk,* 3rd ed. (New York: Insurance Information Institute, 1989), pp. 119–120.

11. *The Insurance Fact Book 2012,* (New York: Insurance Information Institute), p. 44.

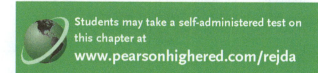

Students may take a self-administered test on this chapter at
**www.pearsonhighered.com/rejda**

# CHAPTER 7

# FINANCIAL OPERATIONS OF INSURERS

*"To manage an insurance enterprise successfully, you must understand the volatility inherent in each portfolio of risks and investments. Further, you must understand the impact that unexpected volatility has on the balance sheet, income statement, and cash flows."*

Mike Keyes,
Chairman of the Board and former CEO,
Oregon Mutual Insurance Company

## LEARNING OBJECTIVES

**After studying this chapter, you should be able to**

◆ Understand the three major sections of the balance sheet for a property and casualty insurance company: assets, liabilities, and policyholders' surplus.

◆ Identify the sources of revenues and types of expenses incurred by a property and casualty insurance company.

◆ Explain how profitability is measured in the property and casualty insurance industry.

◆ Understand the balance sheet and income and expense statement of a life insurance company, and explain how profitability is measured in the life insurance industry.

◆ Explain the objectives of rate making in the property and casualty insurance industry and discuss the basic rate-making methods, including judgment rating, class rating, and merit rating.

*"* So how did XYZ Insurance Company get into trouble?" board member Lexi Armstrong asked.

"They wrote too much property insurance in a tight geographic area and they did not purchase reinsurance. Those wind and hail storms last summer really did a number on their policyholders and on their financial statements," responded ABC Insurance Company president, Brian Fallon.

This exchange occurred at the quarterly board meeting of ABC Insurance Company. President Fallon asked the board of directors to consider acquiring XYZ Insurance Company. A major rating service just lowered XYZ Insurance Company's rating because of large losses from storms the previous summer. XYZ Insurance Company limited its underwriting to homeowners insurance and small business coverage in one state. ABC Insurance Company writes most of its coverage in areas where earthquake risk is important. Where XYZ writes coverage there is little earthquake risk.

"Take a good look at XYZ's financial statements," Fallon said to the board. They have high-quality assets in their investment portfolio. Our surplus can easily absorb their losses from last summer. Once we acquire the company, our agents will be able to cross-sell to existing XYZ policyholders, offering auto insurance, umbrella policies, and other coverages XYZ does not market. We'll be able to write more business while reducing our earthquake exposure. This acquisition is a no-brainer!"

This chapter discusses the financial operations of insurers. Specific topics discussed are insurance company balance sheets, income statements, profitability measures, and rate-making methods.

In Chapter 2, the two sides of the private insurance industry, property and casualty insurance and life and health insurance, were discussed. The discussion of the financial operations of insurers is organized in the same way. First, we consider the financial statements for property and casualty insurance companies and for life insurance companies. Then, we discuss rate making in property and casualty insurance and in life insurance.

## PROPERTY AND CASUALTY INSURERS

To understand the financial operations of an insurance company, it is necessary to examine the insurer's financial statements. Two important financial statements are the balance sheet and the income and expense statement.[1]

### Balance Sheet

A **balance sheet** *is a summary of what a company owns (assets), what it owes (liabilities), and the difference between total assets and total liabilities (owners' equity).* A balance sheet shows these values on a specific date. This financial statement is called a balance sheet because the two sides of the financial statement must be equal:

Total assets = Total liabilities + Owners' equity

Exhibit 7.1 shows the balance sheet for the ABC Insurance Company at the end of 2012. Note how the company's total assets equal the company's total liabilities plus owners' equity (policyholders' surplus).

**Assets** The primary assets for an insurance company are financial assets. An insurance company invests premium dollars and retained earnings in

**Exhibit 7.1**
**ABC Insurance Company**

ABC Insurance Company
Balance Sheet
December 31, 2012

| Assets: | | Liabilities: | |
|---|---|---|---|
| Bonds | $250,000,000 | Loss Reserves | $120,000,000 |
| Common Stock | 80,000,000 | Unearned Premiums | 101,000,000 |
| Real Estate | 20,000,000 | Loss Adjustment Expenses | 14,000,000 |
| Cash & Short-term Investments | 12,000,000 | Commissions Payable | 9,000,000 |
| Mortgage-backed Securities | 30,000,000 | Other Liabilities | 11,000,000 |
| Total Invested Assets | $392,000,000 | Total Liabilities | 255,000,000 |
| | | | |
| Premiums Receivable | 29,600,000 | Surplus and Capital | |
| Data Processing Equipment | 400,000 | Paid-in Surplus | 16,000,000 |
| Other Assets | 18,000,000 | Unassigned Surplus | 169,000,000 |
| | | | |
| Total Admitted Assets | $440,000,000 | Total Liabilities and Surplus | $440,000,000 |

financial assets. These investments also provide an important source of income for an insurer. As with most insurance companies, ABC's primary investment holding is bonds. Other investments are in common and preferred stock, real estate, mortgage-backed securities, marketable securities, and cash/cash equivalents. The company's assets total $440 million.

**Liabilities** While the assets of an insurance company are relatively straightforward, the liabilities are more complex. An insurer is required by law to maintain certain reserves on its balance sheet. Because premiums are paid in advance, but the period of protection extends into the future, an insurer must establish reserves to assure that premiums collected in advance will be available to pay future losses. A property and casualty insurer is required to maintain two principal types of financial reserves:

1. *Loss Reserves.* The loss reserve is a large liability item on a property and casualty insurance company's balance sheet. A **loss reserve** *is the estimated cost of settling claims for losses that have already occurred but that have not been paid as of the valuation date.* More specifically, the *loss reserve is an estimated amount for (1) claims reported and adjusted but not yet paid, (2) claims reported and filed, but not yet adjusted, and (3) claims for losses incurred but not yet reported to the company.* The loss reserve is especially important to a casualty insurer because bodily injury and property

damage liability claims may take a long time to settle, especially if litigation is involved. In contrast, property insurance claims, such as auto collision and other physical damage claims and homeowners dwelling and personal property insurance claims, are settled more quickly; hence loss reserves are relatively small for property insurance. ABC's loss reserves are $120 million.

Loss reserves in property and casualty insurance can be classified as case reserves, reserves based on the loss ratio method, and reserves for incurred-but-not-reported claims.

**Case reserves** *are loss reserves that are established for each individual claim when it is reported.* Major methods of determining case reserves include the following: the judgment method, the average value method, and the tabular method.[2]

- Under the *judgment method,* a claim reserve is established for each individual claim. The amount of the loss reserve can be based on the judgment of someone in the claims department or estimated using a computer program. Many insurers use computer programs that apply guidelines to calculate the size of the loss reserve. The details of an individual claim are entered, and a computer algorithm estimates the size of the required loss reserve.
- When the *average value method* is used, an average value is assigned to each claim. This method is used when the number of claims is

large, and the average claim amount is relatively small. Loss reserves for auto physical damage claims are often based on this method.

- Under the *tabular value method,* loss reserves are determined for claims for which the amounts paid depend on life expectancy, duration of disability, and similar factors. This method is often used to establish loss reserves involving permanent disability, partial permanent disability, survivor benefits, and similar claims. The loss reserve is called a tabular reserve because the duration of the benefit period is based on data derived from mortality and morbidity tables.

The case reserves just discussed establish loss reserves for individual claims. In contrast, *the* **loss ratio method** **(loss reserves)** *establishes aggregate loss reserves for a specific coverage line. Under the loss ratio method, a formula based on the expected loss ratio is used to estimate the loss reserve.* The expected loss ratio is multiplied by premiums earned during a specified time period. Loss and loss-adjustment expenses paid to date are then subtracted from the ultimate loss figure to determine the current loss reserve. The loss ratio method is required for certain lines of insurance, such as workers compensation, where the expected loss ratio ranges from 65 percent to 75 percent of earned premiums.

Some losses occur near the end of the accounting period but are not reported until the next period. *The* **incurred-but-not-reported (IBNR) reserve** *is a reserve that must be established for claims that have already occurred but have not yet been reported to the insurer.* For example, some accidents may occur on the final day of the accounting period. A loss reserve is needed for these losses that will not be reported until the next accounting period.

2. *Unearned Premium Reserve. The* **unearned premium reserve** *is a liability item that represents the unearned portion of gross premiums on all outstanding policies at the time of valuation.* An insurer is required by law to place the entire gross premium in the unearned premium reserve when the policy is first written, and to place renewal premiums in the same reserve. ABC Insurance Company's unearned premium reserve is $101 million.

*The fundamental purpose of the unearned premium reserve is to pay for losses that occur during the policy period.* Premiums are paid in advance, but the period of protection extends into the future. To assure policyholders that future losses will be paid, the unearned premium reserve is required.

*The unearned premium reserve is also needed so that premium refunds can be paid to policyholders in the event of coverage cancellation.* If the insurer cancels the policy, a full pro rata premium refund based on the unexpired portion of the policy term must be paid to the policyholder. Thus, the unearned premium reserve must be adequate so premium refunds can be made in the event of cancellation.

*Finally, if the business is reinsured, the unearned premium reserve serves as the basis for determining the amount that must be paid to the reinsurer for carrying the reinsured policies until the end of their terms.* In practice, however, the amount paid to the reinsurer may be considerably less than the unearned premium reserve, as the reinsurer does not incur heavy first-year acquisition expenses in acquiring the reinsured policies.

Several methods can be used to calculate the unearned premium reserve. Only one method is described here. Under the **annual pro rata method,** it is assumed that the policies are written uniformly throughout the year. For purposes of determining the unearned premium reserve, it is assumed that all policies are written on July 1, which is the average issue date. Therefore, on December 31, the unearned premium reserve for all one-year policies is one-half of the premiums attributable to these policies. For two-year policies, the unearned premium reserve is three-fourths of the premium income, and for three-year policies, it is five-sixths of the premium income.

Several other liabilities merit mention. There are costs associated with settling and paying reserved claims. ABC Insurance Company estimates that the **loss-adjustment expenses** to settle the reserved claims are $14 million. Other important liability items include commissions owed to agents selling ABC products and taxes owed to the government.

**Policyholders' Surplus** Policyholders' surplus *is the difference between an insurance company's assets and liabilities.* It is not calculated directly—it is the "balancing" item on the balance sheet. If the insurer were to pay all of its liabilities using its assets, the amount remaining would be policyholders' surplus. ABC Insurance Company's paid-in capital and surplus total $185 million. This value is 42 percent of the company's total assets.

Surplus can be thought of as a cushion that can be drawn upon if liabilities are higher than expected. Recall that loss reserves are an estimate of future losses, but that actual losses could easily exceed the estimate. Obviously, the stronger an insurance company's surplus position, the greater is the security for its policyholders. Surplus represents the paid-in capital of investors plus retained income from insurance operations and investments over time. The level of surplus is also an important determinant of the amount of new business that an insurance company can write.[3]

## Income and Expense Statement

The **income and expense statement** *summarizes revenues received and expenses paid during a specified period of time.* Exhibit 7.2 shows the income and expense statement for ABC Insurance Company for 2012.

**Revenues**   Revenues are cash inflows that the company can claim as income. *The two principal sources of revenues for an insurance company are premiums and investment income.* As noted in the discussion of the unearned premium reserve, premiums are not considered wholly earned until the period of time for which the premiums were paid has passed. The premiums written that appear on the income and expense statement reflect the premiums for coverage that was placed on the books during the year. **Earned premiums** *represent the portion of the premiums for which insurance protection has been provided.*

**EXHIBIT 7.2**
**ABC Insurance Company**

| ABC Insurance Company Income and Expense Statement January 1, 2012–December 31, 2012 | | |
|---|---|---|
| **Revenues:** | | |
| Premiums Written* | $206,000,000 | |
| Premiums Earned | | $205,000,000 |
| | | |
| Investment Income: | | |
| Interest | 14,000,000 | |
| Dividends | 2,400,000 | |
| Rental Income | 600,000 | |
| Gain on Sale of Securities | 1,000,000 | |
| Total Investment Income | | 18,000,000 |
| Total Revenues | | $223,000,000 |
| **Expenses:** | | |
| Net Losses Incurred | 133,600,000 | |
| Loss Adjustment Expenses | 14,000,000 | |
| Total Losses and Loss Adj. Expenses | | 147,600,000 |
| | | |
| Commissions | 18,000,000 | |
| Premium Taxes | 5,050,000 | |
| General Insurance Expenses | 41,590,000 | |
| Total Underwriting Expenses | | 64,640,000 |
| Total Expenses | | 212,240,000 |
| | | |
| Net Income Before Taxes | | 10,760,000 |
| Federal Income Tax | | 3,260,000 |
| Net Income | | 7,500,000 |

*Premiums written reflect coverage put in force during the accounting period.

Insurance premiums are paid in advance for a specified period of protection. With the passage of time, an insurer "earns" the premium and can claim it as income under insurance accounting rules.

The second major source of income is investment income. Given the size of ABC's bond portfolio, it is not surprising that interest income is the major source of investment income. The company also received dividend income on stocks owned and rental income on real estate the company owned. The company also sold some securities for more than the original purchase price and realized a capital gain. The company's total revenues for 2012 were $223 million.

**Expenses** Partially offsetting the company's revenues were the company's expenses, which are cash outflows from the business. The major expenses for ABC Insurance Company were the cost of adjusting claims and paying the insured losses that occurred. The company paid $133.6 million in losses and $14 million in loss-adjustment expenses during 2012, for a total of $147.6 million.

Underwriting expenses are the other major category of expenses. These expenses consist of commissions that ABC paid agents for selling the company's products, premium taxes, and general expenses. These items total $64.64 million in 2012. ABC Insurance Company's total expenses in 2012 were $212.24 million.

The company's taxable income (total revenues minus total expenses) was $10.76 million. The company paid $3.26 million in federal income taxes. The company's net income after taxes was $7.5 million. This money can be returned to stockholders through dividends or be used to increase the investment portfolio. If added to the investment portfolio, the company's total assets will increase relative to its total liabilities, and policyholders' surplus will increase.

## Measuring Profit or Loss

One way of measuring the performance of an insurance company is to consider how the company did in its core business, underwriting risks.[4] A simple measure that can be used is the insurance company's loss ratio. *The* **loss ratio** *is the ratio of incurred losses and loss adjustment expenses to premiums earned.* The formula and the loss ratio for ABC Insurance Company are:

$$\text{Loss ratio} = \frac{\text{Incurred losses} + \text{Loss adjustment expenses}}{\text{Premiums earned}}$$

$$= \frac{147,600,000}{205,000,000}$$

$$= .720$$

The loss ratio for individual coverage lines can be determined, as well as the overall loss ratio for the company. The loss ratio is often in the 65 percent to 75 percent range, but an insurer does not know at the beginning of the coverage period what the ultimate loss ratio will be.

A second important performance measure is the expense ratio. *The* **expense ratio** *is equal to the company's underwriting expenses divided by written premiums.* The expense ratio for ABC Insurance Company is:

$$\text{Expense ratio} = \frac{\text{Underwriting expenses}}{\text{Premiums written}}$$

$$= \frac{64,640,000}{206,000,000}$$

$$= .314$$

As with the loss ratio, the expense ratio can be determined for individual coverage lines and in the aggregate. Underwriting expenses include acquisition costs (commissions), general expenses, and underwriting costs. Some coverages, such as personal lines, are less costly to underwrite. Underwriting costs for large commercial accounts may be much higher. Obviously, a low expense ratio is preferred by insurers. Expense ratios are usually in the 25 percent to 40 percent range.

For an overall measure of underwriting performance, the combined ratio can be calculated. *The* **combined ratio** *is the sum of the loss ratio and expense ratio.*[5] The combined ratio for ABC Insurance Company is 1.034:

$$\text{Combined ratio} = \text{Loss ratio} + \text{Expense ratio}$$

$$\text{Combined ratio} = .720 + .314 = 1.034$$

The combined ratio is one of the most common measures of underwriting profitability. *If the combined ratio exceeds 1 (or 100 percent), it indicates an underwriting loss. If the combined ratio is less than 1 (or 100 percent), it indicates an underwriting profit.* In the case of ABC Insurance Company, for every $100 in premiums the company collected, the company paid out $103.40 in claims and expenses.

At this point, it is important to recall the asset holdings of insurance companies. The investments an insurer makes in bonds, stocks, real estate, and other investments generate investment income. *A property and casualty insurance company can lose money on its underwriting operations, but still report positive net income if the investment income offsets the underwriting loss.* The **investment income ratio** *compares net investment income to earned premiums.* The formula and the ratio for the ABC Insurance Company are provided below:

$$\text{Investment income ratio} = \frac{\text{Net investment income}}{\text{Earned preminus}}$$

$$= \frac{18,000,000}{205,000,000}$$

$$= .088$$

To determine the company's total performance (underwriting and investments), the overall operating ratio can be calculated. *The* **overall operating ratio** *is equal to the combined ratio minus the investment income ratio.* This ratio and the result for ABC are presented below:

$$\text{Overall operating ratio} = \text{Combined ratio} - \text{Investment income ratio}$$

$$= 1.034 - .088$$

$$= .946 \text{ or } 94.6\%$$

At first glance, it may seem incorrect to subtract the investment income ratio from the combined ratio. However, recall that a combined ratio in excess of 100 percent indicates an underwriting loss and that investment income can reduce or totally offset an underwriting loss. ABC Insurance Company's combined ratio was 103.4. The company's investment income ratio was 8.8 percent, producing an overall operating ratio of 94.6. An overall operating ratio of less than 100 indicates that the company, overall, was profitable. If the overall operating ratio exceeds 100, it means that investment income was not enough to offset the underwriting loss.

### Recent Underwriting Results

As noted in Chapter 4, the combined ratio in the U.S. property and casualty insurance industry has been less than 100 percent in only three years between 1980 and 2011. The combined ratios of 92.4 and 95.6 in 2006 and 2007, respectively, created record underwriting profits. The combined ratio, however, climbed back above 100 in 2008, reaching 105.2 and was 108.2 in 2011. The 2011 combined ratio was the highest measure since 2001. The underwriting loss was attributable to insured losses and increased loss adjustment expenses. Although net investment income increased from 2010 to 2011, policyholders' surplus declined.[6]

The property and casualty insurance industry has not been highly profitable over time. The industry has lagged profitability benchmarks for various industry groups in most years. The two best years in the past decade for overall profitability were 2006 and 2007 when the property and casualty industry provided competitive returns.[7] Insight 7.1 discusses the profitability of property and casualty insurance relative to some peer groups over time.

# LIFE INSURANCE COMPANIES

## Balance Sheet

The balance sheet for a life insurance company is similar to the balance sheet of a property and casualty insurance company. The discussion that follows focuses on the major differences.

**Assets**   Like the property and casualty insurance companies discussed earlier, the assets of a life insurance company are primarily financial assets. However, there are three major differences between the assets of a property and casualty insurance company and the assets of a life insurance company. The first major difference is the average duration of the investments. The matching principle states that an organization should match the maturities of its sources and uses of funds. Most property and casualty insurance contracts are relatively short-term, often for one year or six months. Permanent life insurance contracts, however, may be in force for 40 or 50 years, or even longer. As the matching principle suggests, life insurance company investments, on average, should be of longer duration than property and casualty insurance company investments. Note that life insurance companies invest more heavily in bonds, mortgages, and real estate than do property and casualty insurance companies. Property and casualty insurance companies place greater emphasis on liquidity, holding larger relative positions in cash and marketable securities.

The second major difference is created by the savings element in cash-value life insurance. Permanent life insurance policies develop a savings element over time called the cash value, which may be borrowed by the policyholder. When life insurance premiums are calculated, it is assumed that the life insurer will have the funds available to earn investment income. If a policyholder borrows the cash value, the life insurer must forgo the investment income that could have been earned on this money. Life insurance companies charge interest on life insurance policy loans, and this interest-bearing asset is called "contract loans" or "policy loans" on a life insurer's balance sheet. It can be thought of as an interest-earning account receivable from the policyholder.

The third major difference in assets between a property and casualty insurer and a life insurance company is that a life insurance company may have separate account assets. To protect policyholders, state laws place limitations on a life insurance company's general investments. Separate account investments are not subject to these restrictions. Life insurers use separate accounts for assets backing interest-sensitive products, such as variable annuities, variable life insurance, and universal-variable life insurance.

**Liabilities**   Policy reserves are the major liability item of life insurers. Under the level-premium method of funding cash-value life insurance, premiums paid during early years are higher than necessary to pay death claims, while those paid in later years are insufficient to pay death claims. The excess premiums collected in early years of the contract must be accounted for and held for future payment as a death claim to the beneficiary. The excess premiums paid during the early years result in the creation of a policy reserve. *Policy reserves are a liability item on the balance sheet that must be offset by assets equal to that amount.* Policy reserves are considered a liability item because they represent an obligation of the insurer to pay future policy benefits. The policy reserves held by an insurer plus future premiums and future interest earnings will enable the insurer to pay all future policy benefits if the company's experience conforms to the actuarial assumptions used in calculating the reserve. Policy reserves are often called *legal reserves* because state insurance laws specify the minimum basis for calculating them. Reserves in life insurance are discussed in greater detail in the Appendix to Chapter 13.

Two other life insurance company reserves merit discussion—the reserve for amounts held on deposit and the asset valuation reserve (AVR).[8] *The* **reserve for amounts held on deposit** *is a liability that represents funds owed to policyholders and to beneficiaries.* Given the nature of the life insurance business, it is common for life insurers to hold funds on deposit for later payment to policyholders and beneficiaries. For example, a beneficiary may select a fixed-period or fixed-amount settlement option under a life insurance policy, or a policyholder may select the accumulate-at-interest dividend option.

As noted earlier, statutory accounting rules emphasize the solvency of insurers. As such, the surplus position of a life insurer is crucial. The surplus, however, is determined in large part by the value of the assets the insurer holds. Given that the assets are largely financial assets, their values are subject to considerable fluctuation. *The* **asset valuation reserve** *is a statutory account designed to absorb asset value fluctuations not caused by changing interest rates.* The net effect of this reserve is to smooth the company's reported surplus over time.

**Policyholders' Surplus**  As with property and casualty insurance companies, policyholders' surplus is the difference between a life insurer's total assets and total liabilities. Given the long-term nature of the life insurance industry, conservative long-term investments, and the lower risk of catastrophic losses in the life insurance industry, policyholders' surplus is less volatile in the life insurance industry than in the property and casualty insurance industry.

### Income and Expense Statement

The income and expense statement for a life insurance company is similar to the statement reviewed earlier for a property and casualty insurance company. The major sources of revenues are premiums received for the various products sold (e.g., ordinary life insurance, group life insurance, annuities, and health insurance) and income from investments. As with property and casualty insurers, investment income can take the form of periodic cash flows (interest, dividends, and rental payments) and realized capital gains or losses.

Like a property and casualty insurance company, claims payments are a major expense for a life insurance company. Payments consist of death benefits paid to beneficiaries, annuity benefits paid to annuitants, matured endowments paid to policyholders, and benefits paid under health insurance policies (medical benefits and disability income payments). Those policyholders who choose to terminate their cash-value life insurance coverage are paid surrender benefits, another expense for life insurers. Increased reserves, general insurance expenses, agents' commissions and licenses, premium taxes, and fees round out the list of important expenses.

A life insurer's net gain from operations before dividends and taxes is the insurer's total revenues less the insurer's total expenses. *A life insurer's* **net gain from operations** *(also called net income) equals total revenues less total expenses, policyholder dividends, and federal income taxes.*

### Measuring Financial Performance

A number of measures can be used to gauge the financial performance of the life insurance industry. For example, pre-tax or after-tax net income could be compared to total assets. An alternative measure is the rate of return on policyholders' surplus, similar to a return on equity (ROE) ratio. Using this measure, the life insurance industry has provided higher rates of return in seven of 10 years over the past decade with less volatility, as compared to the property and casualty insurance industry.[9]

## RATE MAKING IN PROPERTY AND CASUALTY INSURANCE

Given the competitive nature of the insurance industry, premiums charged by insurance companies are important. Before examining specific rate-making methods in property and casualty insurance, the objectives of rate making are discussed.

### Objectives in Rate Making

Rate making, or insurance pricing, has several basic objectives. Because insurance rates, primarily property and casualty insurance rates, are regulated by the states, certain statutory and regulatory requirements must be met. Also, due to the overall goal of profitability, certain business objectives must be stressed. Thus, rate-making goals can be classified into two categories: regulatory objectives and business objectives.

**Regulatory Objectives**  The goal of insurance regulation is to protect the public. States enact rating laws that require insurance rates to meet certain standards. In general, rates charged by insurers must be adequate, not excessive, and not unfairly discriminatory.

The first regulatory requirement is that rates must be adequate. *This means the rates charged by insurers should be high enough to pay all losses and expenses.* If rates are inadequate, an insurer may become insolvent and unable to pay claims. As a result, policyholders, beneficiaries, and third-party claimants may be harmed. However, rate adequacy is complicated by the fact that an insurer does not know its actual costs when a policy is sold. The premium is paid up front, but it may not be sufficient to pay all claims and expenses during the policy period. It is only after the period of protection has expired that an insurer can determine its actual costs.

The second regulatory requirement is that rates must not be excessive. *This means that the rates should not be so high that policyholders are paying more than the actual value of their protection.* Exorbitant insurance prices are not in the public interest.

The third regulatory objective is that the rates must not be unfairly discriminatory. *This means that exposures that are similar with respect to losses and expenses should not be charged significantly different rates.*[10] For example, consider two men, both age 30, who live in the same neighborhood. Each owns a late-model sedan and has a clean driving record. If they purchase the same insurance coverage from the same insurer, they should not be charged different rates. However, if the loss exposures are substantially different, it is fair to charge different rates. Consider two other auto insurance buyers. The first is 45, he has a clean driving record, and he drives a four-year-old sedan. The second is 20, and he drives a new sports car. He has been arrested for speeding twice and for causing an accident by running a stop sign. It is fair, in this case, to charge the second man a higher rate for his coverage because of the higher probability of loss.

**Business Objectives** Insurers are also guided by business objectives in designing a rating system. The rating system should meet all of these objectives: simplicity, responsiveness, stability, and encouragement of loss control.[11]

The rating system should be easy to understand so that producers can quote premiums with a minimum amount of time and expense. This is especially important in the personal lines market, where relatively small premiums do not justify a large amount of time and expense in the preparation of premium quotations. In addition, commercial insurance purchasers should understand how their premiums are determined so that they can take active steps to reduce their insurance costs.

Rates should be stable over short periods of time so that consumer satisfaction can be maintained. If rates change rapidly, insurance consumers may become irritated and dissatisfied. They may then look to government to control the rates or to enact a government insurance program.

Rates should also be responsive over time to changing loss exposures and changing economic conditions. To meet the objective of rate adequacy, the rates should increase when loss exposures increase. For example, as a city grows, auto insurance rates should increase to reflect greater traffic and increased frequency of auto accidents. Likewise, rates should reflect changing economic conditions. Thus, if inflation causes liability awards to increase, liability insurance rates should rise to reflect this trend.

Finally, the rating system should encourage loss-control activities. Loss-control efforts are designed to reduce the frequency and severity of losses. This point is important because loss control tends to keep insurance affordable. Profits are also stabilized. As you will see later, certain rating systems provide a strong financial incentive for the insured to engage in loss control.

## Basic Rate-Making Definitions

You should be familiar with some basic terms that are widely used in rate making. A **rate** *is the price per unit of insurance.* An **exposure unit** *is the unit of measurement used in insurance pricing.* The exposure unit varies by line of insurance. For example, in fire insurance, the exposure unit is $100 of coverage; in product liability, it is $1000 of sales; and in auto collision insurance, it is one car-year, which is one car insured for a year.

The **pure premium** *refers to that portion of the rate needed to pay losses and loss-adjustment expenses.* The **loading** *refers to the amount that must be added to the pure premium for other expenses, profit, and a margin for contingencies.* The **gross rate** *consists of the pure premium and a loading element.* Finally, the **gross premium** *paid by the insured consists of the gross rate multiplied by the number of exposure units.* Thus, if the gross rate is 10 cents per $100 of property insurance, the gross premium for a $500,000 building would be $500.

## Rate-Making Methods

There are three basic rate-making methods in property and casualty insurance: judgment, class, and merit rating. Merit rating, in turn, can be broken down into schedule rating, experience rating, and retrospective rating. Thus, the basic rating methods can be conveniently classified as follows:[12]

> Judgment rating
> Class rating
> Merit rating
> > Schedule rating
> > Experience rating
> > Retrospective rating

**Judgment Rating**   Judgment rating *means that each exposure is individually evaluated, and the rate is determined largely by the judgment of the underwriter.* This method is used when the loss exposures are so diverse that a class rate cannot be calculated, or when credible loss statistics are not available.

Judgment rating is widely used in ocean marine insurance and in some lines of inland marine insurance. Because ocean-going vessels, ports, cargoes, and waters traveled are diverse, some ocean marine rates are determined largely by the judgment of the underwriter.

**Class Rating**   The second type of property and casualty rating is class rating. Most rates used today are class rates. **Class rating** *means that exposures with similar characteristics are placed in the same underwriting class, and each is charged the same rate.* The rate charged reflects the *average loss experience* for the class as a whole. Class rating is based on the assumption that future losses to insureds will be determined largely by the same set of factors. For example, major classification factors in homeowners insurance include construction material, age of the home, and protective devices (e.g., smoke detectors and fire extinguishers). Accordingly, newly constructed masonry homes with protective devices are not placed in the same underwriting class with older wood-frame homes that may not have protective devices.

The major advantage of class rating is that it is simple to apply. Also, premium quotations can be quickly obtained. As such, it is ideal for the personal lines market.

Class rating is also called *manual rating*. Class rating is widely used in homeowners insurance, private passenger auto insurance, workers compensation, and life and health insurance.

There are two basic methods for determining class rates: the **pure premium method** and the **loss ratio method.**

1. *Pure Premium Method.* As stated earlier, the pure premium is that portion of the gross rate needed to pay losses and loss-adjustment expenses. *The pure premium can be determined by dividing the dollar amount of incurred losses and loss-adjustment expenses by the number of exposure units.* Incurred losses include all losses paid during the accounting period, plus amounts held as reserves for the future payment of losses that have already occurred during the same period. Thus, incurred losses include all losses that occur during the accounting period whether or not they have been paid by the end of the period. Loss-adjustment expenses are the expenses incurred by the company in adjusting losses during the same accounting period.

To illustrate how a pure premium can be derived, assume that in auto collision insurance, 500,000 autos in a given underwriting class generate incurred losses and loss-adjustment expenses of $33 million over a one-year period. The pure premium is $66. This can be illustrated by the following:

$$\text{Pure premium} = \frac{\text{Incurred losses and loss adjustment expenses}}{\text{Number of exposure units}}$$

$$= \frac{\$33,000,000}{500,000}$$

$$= \$66$$

The final step is to add a loading for expenses, underwriting profit, and a margin for contingencies. The expense loading is usually expressed as a percentage of the gross rate and is called the expense ratio. The final gross rate can be determined by dividing the pure premium by one minus the expense ratio. For example, if expenses are 40 percent of the gross rate, the final gross rate is $110. This can be illustrated by the following:[13]

$$\text{Gross rate} = \frac{\text{Pure premium}}{1 - \text{Expense ratio}}$$

$$= \frac{\$66}{1 - .40} = \$110$$

2. *Loss Ratio Method. Under the loss ratio method, the actual loss ratio is compared with the expected loss ratio, and the rate is adjusted accordingly.* The actual loss ratio is the ratio of incurred losses and loss-adjustment expenses to earned premiums.[14] The expected loss ratio is the percentage of the premium that can be expected to be used to pay losses. For example, assume that a line of insurance has incurred losses and loss-adjustment expenses of $800,000 and earned premiums of $1 million. The actual loss ratio is 0.80 or 80 percent. If the expected loss ratio is 0.70 or 70 percent, the rate must be increased 14.3 percent. This can be illustrated by the following:

$$\text{Rate change} = \frac{A - E}{E}$$

where A = Actual loss ratio
E = Expected loss ratio

$$= \frac{0.80 - 0.70}{0.70}$$

$$= 0.143, \text{ or } 14.3\%$$

**Merit Rating**  The third principal type of rating in property-casualty insurance is merit rating. **Merit rating** *is a rating plan by which class rates (manual rates) are adjusted upward or downward based on individual loss experience.* Merit rating is based on the assumption that the loss experience of a particular insured will differ substantially from the loss experience of other insureds. Thus, class rates are modified upward or downward depending on individual loss experience. There are three types of merit rating plans: schedule rating, experience rating, and retrospective rating.

1. *Schedule Rating. Under a* **schedule rating** *plan, each exposure is individually rated. A basis rate is determined for each exposure, which is then modified by debits or credits for undesirable or desirable physical features.* Schedule rating is based on the assumption that certain physical characteristics of the insured's operations will influence the insured's loss experience. Thus, the physical characteristics of the exposure to be insured are extremely important in schedule rating.

Schedule rating is used in commercial property insurance for large, complex structures, such as an industrial plant. Each building is individually rated based on several factors, including construction, occupancy, protection, exposure, and maintenance.

- *Construction* refers to the physical characteristics of the building. A building may be constructed with wood frame, brick, fire-resistive, or fireproof materials. A frame building is charged a higher rate than a brick building or fire-resistive building. Also, tall buildings and buildings with large open areas may receive debits because of the greater difficulty of extinguishing or containing a fire.
- *Occupancy* refers to the use of the building. The probability of a fire is greatly influenced by the use of the structure. For example, open flames and sparks from torches and welding equipment can quickly cause a fire. Also, if highly combustible materials or chemicals are stored in the building, a fire will be more difficult to contain.
- *Protection* refers to the quality of the city's water supply and fire department. It also includes protective devices installed in the insured building. Rate credits are given for a fire alarm system, security guard, fire doors, automatic sprinkler system, fire extinguishers, and similar protective devices.
- *Exposure* refers to the possibility that the insured building will be damaged or destroyed by a peril, such as fire that starts at an adjacent building and spreads to the insured building. The greater the exposure from surrounding buildings, the greater are the charges applied.
- *Maintenance* refers to the housekeeping and overall upkeep of the building. Debits are applied for poor housekeeping and maintenance. Thus, debits may be given for oily rags near a heat source or debris strewn on the grounds of the plant.

2. *Experience Rating. Under* **experience rating,** *the class or manual rate is adjusted upward or downward based on past loss experience.* The most distinctive characteristic of experience rating is that *the insured's past loss experience is used to determine the premium for the next policy period.* The loss experience over the last three years is typically used to determine the premium for the next policy year. If the insured's loss experience is better than the average for the class as a whole, the class rate is reduced. If the loss experience is worse than the class average, the rate is increased. In determining the magnitude of the rate change, the actual loss experience is modified by a *credibility factor* based on the volume of experience.[15]

For example, assume that a retail firm has a general liability insurance policy that is experience rated. Annual premiums are $30,000, and the expected loss ratio is 30 percent. If the actual loss ratio over the years is 20 percent, and the credibility factor (C) is .29, the firm will receive a premium reduction of 9.7 percent. This reduction is illustrated below:

$$\text{Premium change} = \frac{A - E}{E} \times C$$

$$= \frac{.20 - .30}{.30} \times .29$$

$$= -9.7\%$$

Thus, the premium for the next policy period is $27,090. Obviously, experience rating provides a financial incentive to reduce losses, because premiums can be reduced by favorable loss experience.

Experience rating is generally limited to larger firms that generate a sufficiently high volume of premiums and more credible loss experience. Smaller firms are normally ineligible for experience rating. The rating system is frequently used in general liability insurance, workers compensation, commercial auto liability insurance, and group health insurance.

3. *Retrospective Rating. Under a* **retrospective rating** *plan, the insured's loss experience during the current policy period determines the actual premium paid for that period.* Under this rating plan, a provisional premium is paid at the start of the policy period. At the end of the period, a final premium is calculated based on actual losses that occur during the policy period. There is a minimum and a maximum premium that must be paid. In practice, the actual premium paid generally will fall somewhere between the minimum and maximum premium, depending on the insured's loss experience during the current policy period.

Retrospective rating is widely used by large firms in workers compensation insurance, general liability insurance, auto liability and physical damage insurance, and burglary and glass insurance.

## RATE MAKING IN LIFE INSURANCE

The discussion of rate making thus far has been limited to property and casualty insurance. Rate making is also important for life insurance companies, especially given the long-term nature of many life insurance contracts.

Life insurance actuaries use a mortality table or individual company experience to determine the probability of death at each attained age. The probability of death is multiplied by the amount the life insurer will have to pay if death occurs to determine the expected value of the death claims for each policy year. These annual expected values are then discounted back to the beginning of the policy period to determine the net single premium (NSP). The NSP is the present value of the future death benefit. Since most insureds pay life insurance premiums in installments, the NSP must be converted into a series of periodic level premiums to determine the net level premium. This is done through a mathematical adjustment that is discussed in the Appendix to Chapter 13. After the net level premium is calculated, a loading for expenses is added to determine the gross premium. The Appendix to Chapter 13 discusses each of these steps in greater detail.

## CASE APPLICATION

Carolyn is senior vice president of finance and chief actuary for Rock Solid Insurance Company (RSIC). Lonnie is double-majoring in finance and mathematics at State University. Lonnie applied for an internship with Rock Solid, and he is working for the company during the summer before the start of his senior year of college. Curious to learn what Lonnie knew about insurance company financial statements and ratemaking, Carolyn prepared a quiz for Lonnie to take on his first day on the job. See if you can help Lonnie answer these questions.

1. At year-end last year, Rock Solid had total liabilities of $640 million and total assets of $900 million. What was the company's policyholders' surplus?

2. Explain how it is possible for Rock Solid to have $500 million in written premiums last year and $505 million in earned premiums last year.

3. Rock Solid's net underwriting result last year was a $540,000 loss. Explain how it is possible that Rock Solid was required to pay income taxes.

4. Rock Solid provides collision coverage for one year on 50,000 autos located in a specific territory within the state. During the one-year period, the company expects to pay $10 million in incurred losses and loss-adjustment expenses for these 50,000 autos. Based on this information, what is the pure premium?

5. The pure premium per unit of personal liability insurance for one group of prospective purchasers is $300. If Rock Solid wants to allow for a 40 percent expense ratio for this line of coverage, what gross rate per unit of coverage should be charged?

## SUMMARY

- A balance sheet summarizes what a company owns (assets), what it owes (liabilities), and the difference between these two values (owners' equity).

- For an insurance company, the major assets are financial assets, which are investments in bonds, stocks, real estate, mortgage-backed securities, and marketable securities, as well as cash.

- An insurer's liabilities are called reserves. The loss reserve is the estimated cost of settling claims. Loss reserves in property and casualty insurance can be classified as case reserves, reserves established using the loss ratio method, and reserves for incurred-but-not-reported (IBNR) claims.

- Another important reserve for property and casualty insurers is the unearned premium reserve. This reserve equals the unearned portion of gross premiums for outstanding policies at the time of valuation.

- The difference between an insurer's total assets and total liabilities is called policyholders' surplus. Policyholders' surplus consists of paid-in capital at stock companies, plus retained profits from insurance operations and investments over time. Surplus represents a margin of safety for policyholders.

- The major sources of revenue for an insurance company are premiums and investment income. The major expenses are loss payments, loss-adjustment expenses, and other expenses including commissions, premium taxes, and general insurance company expenses.

- To determine an insurer's net income, total expenses are subtracted from total revenues. Policyholder dividends, if any, are deducted to determine taxable income, and federal income taxes are levied on taxable income.

- The loss ratio is the ratio of a property and casualty insurer's incurred losses and loss-adjustment expenses to earned premiums. The expense ratio is the ratio of the insurer's underwriting expenses to written premiums.

- The combined ratio is the sum of the loss ratio and the expense ratio. A combined ratio greater than 1 (or 100 percent) indicates an underwriting loss, and a combined ratio less than 1 (or 100 percent) indicates an underwriting profit.

- An insurance company can lose money on its underwriting operations and still be profitable if the investment income offsets the underwriting loss.

- The assets of life insurance companies tend to be of longer duration than the assets of property and casualty insurers. As a policyholder may borrow the cash value, life insurance policy loans are an asset for life insurers. Life insurers maintain separate accounts for the assets backing interest-sensitive products, such as variable annuities.

- The major liability item for a life insurance company is the policy reserve. Two other important reserves are the reserve for amounts held on deposit and the asset valuation reserve.

- A life insurer's net gain from operations equals total revenues, less total expenses, policyholder dividends, and federal income taxes.

- Insurance rates are regulated to make sure they are adequate, not excessive, and not unfairly discriminatory. Business objectives of rating systems include simplicity, responsiveness, stability, and encouragement of loss control.

- The rate is the price per unit of insurance and the exposure unit is the measurement base used. The pure premium is the portion of the premium needed to pay claims and loss adjustment expenses. The loading covers expenses, profit, and other contingencies. The gross rate is the sum of the pure premium and the loading element.

- Three major rating methods are used in property and casualty insurance: judgment, class, and merit rating.

- Judgment rating means that each exposure is individually evaluated, and the rate is determined largely by the underwriter's judgment.

- Class rating means that exposures with similar characteristics are placed in the same underwriting class, and each is charged the same rate. The rate charged reflects the average loss experience for the class as a whole. Most personal lines of insurance are class rated.

- Merit rating is a rating plan by which class rates are adjusted upward or downward based on individual loss experience. It is based on the assumption that the loss experience of an individual insured will differ substantially from the loss experience of other insureds.

- There are three principal types of merit rating plans:

    Schedule rating

    Experience rating

    Retrospective rating

- Under schedule rating, each exposure is individually rated, and debits and credits are applied based on the physical characteristics of the exposure to be insured. Experience rating means that the insured's past loss experience is used to determine the premium for the next policy period. Retrospective rating means the insured's loss experience during the current policy period determines the actual premium paid for that period.

- Life insurance actuaries determine the probability of death in any given year, and based on this probability determine the expected value of the loss payment. These expected future payments are discounted back to the start of the coverage period and summed to determine the net single premium. The net single premium may be leveled to convert to installment premiums. A loading for expenses is added to determine the gross premium.

## KEY CONCEPTS AND TERMS

Annual pro rata
  method (126)
Asset valuation
  reserve (131)
Balance sheet (124)
Case reserves (125)
Class rating (133)
Combined ratio (128)
Earned premiums (127)
Expense ratio (128)
Experience rating (135)
Exposure unit (132)
Gross premium (132)
Gross rate (132)
Income and expense
  statement (127)
Incurred-but-not-reported
  (IBNR) reserve (126)
Investment income ratio (129)
Judgment rating (133)
Loading (132)
Loss-adjustment
  expenses (126)

Loss ratio (128)
Loss ratio method
  (of determining loss
  reserves) (126)
Loss ratio method
  (of rating) (133)
Loss reserve (125)
Merit rating (134)
Net gain from
  operations (131)
Overall operating
  ratio (129)
Policyholders'
  surplus (126)
Pure premium (132)
Pure premium method (133)
Rate (132)
Reserve for amounts held
  on deposit (130)
Retrospective rating (135)
Schedule rating (134)
Unearned premium
  reserve (126)

## REVIEW QUESTIONS

1. a. What are the three major sections of a balance sheet?
   b. What is the balance sheet equation?

2. a. What types of assets appear on the balance sheet of an insurance company?
   b. Why are the liabilities of a property and casualty insurance company difficult to measure?

3. a. What are the two major sources of revenue for a property and casualty insurance company?
   b. What are the major expenses of a property and casualty insurance company?

4. a. How is the combined ratio of a property and casualty insurance company calculated, and what does the combined ratio measure?

   b. How is it possible for a property and casualty insurance company to be profitable if its combined ratio exceeds one (or 100 percent)?

5. Name three ways in which the assets of a life insurance company differ from the assets of a property and casualty insurance company.

6. What do the reserves on a life insurance company's balance sheet represent?

7. What are the major categories of expenses for a life insurance company?

8. a. What are the major regulatory objectives that must be satisfied in insurance rate making?

   b. What are the major business objectives?

9. In the context of rate making, explain the meaning of:
   a. rate
   b. exposure unit
   c. pure premium
   d. gross premium

10. Briefly describe the following methods for determining a class rate:
    a. pure premium method
    b. loss ratio method

11. Explain the following methods of merit rating:
    a. schedule rating
    b. experience rating
    c. retrospective rating

## APPLICATION QUESTIONS

1. Based on the following information, determine the policyholders' surplus for XYZ Insurance Company:

   | | |
   |---|---|
   | Total invested assets | $50,000,000 |
   | Loss reserves | 40,000,000 |
   | Total liabilities | 70,000,000 |
   | Bonds | 35,000,000 |
   | Unearned premium reserve | 25,000,000 |
   | Total assets | 90,000,000 |

2. Based on the following information, determine Mutual Life Insurance Company's gain from operations before income taxes and dividends to policyholders:

   | | |
   |---|---|
   | Total premium income | $20,000,000 |
   | Licenses, taxes, and fees | 580,000 |

   | | |
   |---|---|
   | Death benefits paid | 6,000,000 |
   | Net investment income | 3,000,000 |
   | Commissions paid | 5,900,000 |
   | General insurance expense | 2,500,000 |
   | Surrender benefits paid | 800,000 |
   | Annuity benefits paid | 1,600,000 |

3. A large casualty insurer writes a substantial amount of private passenger auto insurance. An actuary analyzed claims data for a specific class of drivers for a recent one-year policy period. The claims data showed that the insurer paid out $30 million for incurred losses and loss-adjustment expenses for each 100,000 cars insured for one year. Based on the pure premium method, calculate the pure premium.

4. For the past calendar year, a property insurer reported the following financial information for a specific line of insurance:

   | | |
   |---|---|
   | Premiums written | $25,000,000 |
   | Expenses incurred | 5,000,000 |
   | Incurred losses and loss-adjustment expenses | 14,000,000 |
   | Earned premiums | 20,000,000 |

   a. What was the insurer's loss ratio for this line of coverage?

   b. Calculate the expense ratio for this line of coverage.

   c. What was the combined ratio for this line of coverage?

5. a. Why are property and casualty insurance companies required to maintain loss reserves?

   b. Briefly explain the following methods for determining loss reserves:
      1. judgment method
      2. average value method
      3. tabular method

   c. What is the incurred-but-not-reported (IBNR) loss reserve?

## INTERNET RESOURCES

- The **American Academy of Actuaries** is a public policy and communications organization for all actuaries in the United States. Their site provides timely studies on important insurance problems and issues. Visit the site at actuary.org

- The **American Council of Life Insurers** is a Washington DC–based trade association representing the interests of member companies. The council prepares *The Life*

*Insurers Fact Book* annually, and this excellent resource is available online. Visit the site at

acli.com

- The **American Society of Pension Professionals & Actuaries** is an organization formed to educate pension actuaries, consultants, and other professionals in the employee benefits field. Visit the site at

  asppa.org

- The **Casualty Actuarial Society** is a professional organization that promotes education in actuarial science and provides statistics on property and casualty insurance. Visit the site at

  casact.org

- The **Conference of Consulting Actuaries** is an organization that consists of consulting actuaries in all disciplines. Visit the site at

  ccactuaries.org

- The **Insurance Information Institute** is an excellent primary source for information, statistics, and analysis on topics in property and casualty insurance. Visit the site at

  iii.org

- **Insurance Journal,** *The National Property Casualty Magazine,* is a free online journal that provides local and national news on the property and casualty insurance industry. Breaking news and current developments are sent daily to subscribers. Visit the site at

  insurancejournal.com

- The **Insurance Services Office (ISO)** provides statistical information, actuarial analysis and consulting, policy language, and related information to organizations in the property and casualty insurance markets. Visit the site at

  iso.com

- The **Society of Actuaries** is a professional organization that educates and qualifies individuals to become actuaries, provides continuing education programs, and enforces a professional code of conduct. Membership is obtained by successful completion of a rigorous set of exams leading to the designation of Associate or Fellow in the Society. Visit the site at

  soa.org

- **Towers Watson** is one of the world's largest actuarial and management consulting firms. The company provides a substantial amount of information on the insurance industry and advises other organizations on risk financing and self-insurance. Visit the site at

  towerswatson.com

## SELECTED REFERENCES

Black, Kenneth, Jr., and Harold D. Skipper, Jr. *Life Insurance,* 13th ed., Upper Saddle River, NJ: Prentice Hall, 2000, chs. 27–30.

Graves, Edward E., ed. *McGill's Life Insurance,* 8th ed., Bryn Mawr, PA: The American College, 2011.

*The Insurance Fact Book 2012,* New York: Insurance Information Institute, 2012.

*The Life Insurers Fact Book 2011,* Washington, DC: American Council of Life Insurers, 2011.

Myhr, Ann E. and James J. Markham. *Insurance Operations, Regulation, and Statutory Accounting,* 1st ed., Malvern, PA: American Institute for Chartered Property Casualty Underwriters / Insurance Institute of America, 2003.

Webb, Bernard L., et al., *Insurance Operations and Regulations,* 1st ed., Malvern, PA: American Institute for Chartered Property Casualty Underwriters/ Insurance Institute of America, 2002.

Wiening, Eric A. *Foundations of Risk Management and Insurance,* 1st ed., Malvern, PA: American Institute for Chartered Property Casualty Underwriters/ Insurance Institute of America, 2002.

## NOTES

1. Simplified versions of the financial statements are presented in this chapter. In practice, the financial statements are more complex. Insurers are required to use statutory accounting rules for the financial statements prepared for regulators. Financial statements may also be prepared using Generally Accepted Accounting Principles (GAAP). Statutory accounting is conservative and emphasizes insurer solvency.

2. For a detailed discussion of loss reserves, see Bernard L. Webb, et al., *Insurance Operations and Regulation,* 1st ed. (Malvern, PA: American Institute for Chartered Property Casualty Underwriters/Insurance Institute of America, 2002), ch. 12.

3. Under statutory accounting, expenses are recognized immediately while premium income is earned over

a period of time. An insurance company, therefore, is immediately placed in a negative position when it writes a policy as acquisition expenses must be charged immediately. Surplus can also be considered from a leverage perspective. Obviously, the more coverage written per dollar of surplus, the greater the policyholder leverage.

4. This section is based on Eric A. Wiening, *Foundations of Risk Management and Insurance,* 1st ed., Malvern, PA: American Institute for Chartered Property Casualty Underwriters/Insurance Institute of America, 2002. The author drew heavily on the material presented in ch. 5, especially pp. 5.21 through 5.26, in preparing this section.

5. The observant reader may note that the denominators in the loss ratio and the expense ratio are different—premiums earned for the loss ratio and premiums written for the expense ratio. This version of the combined ratio is called the "trade basis" combined ratio. A second version, the "statutory" combined ratio, uses earned premiums in both denominators. Although the statutory combined ratio is mathematically correct, the trade basis better matches income and expenses.

6. Combined ratios were provided by *2012 Best's Aggregates and Averages—Property and Casualty,* p. 368. The investment income increase and surplus decline are from pages 80 and 81 of the same publication.

7. As shown in the table on page 39 of *The Insurance Fact Book 2012* (New York: Insurance Information Institute).

8. See Kenneth R. Black, Jr. and Harold D. Skipper, Jr., *Life Insurance,* 13th ed. (Upper Saddle River, NJ: Prentice Hall, 2000), pp. 914–915 for a discussion of these and other life insurer policy reserves.

9. As shown in the table on page 39 of *The Insurance Fact Book 2012,* New York: Insurance Information Institute.

10. Robert J. Gibbons, George E. Rejda, and Michael W. Elliott, *Insurance Perspectives* (Malvern, PA: American Institute for Chartered Property Casualty Underwriters, 1992), p. 119.

11. Bernard L. Webb, Connor M. Harrison, and James J. Markham, *Insurance Operations,* 2nd ed., Vol. 2 (Malvern, PA: American Institute for Chartered Property Casualty Underwriters, 1997), pp. 89–90.

12. The basic rate-making methods are discussed in some detail in Webb et al., Chs. 10 and 11. Also see Bernard L. Webb, J. J. Launie, Willis Park Rokes, and Norman A. Baglini, *Insurance Company Operations,* 3rd ed., Vol. 2 (Malvern, PA: American Institute for Property and Liability Underwriters, 1984), chs. 9 and 10.

13. An equivalent method for determining the final rate is to divide the pure premium by the permissible loss ratio. The permissible loss ratio is the same as the expected loss ratio. If the expense ratio is .40, the permissible loss ratio is $1 - .40$, or .60. Thus if the pure premium of $66 is divided by the permissible loss ratio of .60, the resulting gross rate is also $110.

$$\text{Gross rate} = \frac{\text{Pure premium}}{\text{Permissible loss ratio}} = \frac{\$66}{.60} = \$110$$

14. Earned premiums, as discussed earlier in the chapter, are premiums actually earned by a company during the accounting period, rather than the premiums written during the same period.

15. The credibility factor, C, refers to the statistical reliability of the data. It ranges from 0 to 1 and increases as the number of claims increases. If an actuary believes that the data are highly reliable and can accurately predict future losses, a credibility factor of 1 can be used. However, if the data are not completely reliable as a predictor of future losses, a credibility factor of less than 1 is used.

# CHAPTER 8

# GOVERNMENT REGULATION OF INSURANCE

*"There are serious shortcomings in state laws and regulatory activities with respect to protecting the interests of insurance consumers."*

U.S. Government Accountability Office

## LEARNING OBJECTIVES

**After studying this chapter, you should be able to**

◆ Explain the major reasons why insurers are regulated.

◆ Identify key legal cases and legislative acts that have had an important impact on insurance regulation.

◆ Identify the major areas of insurance that are regulated.

◆ Explain the objectives of rate regulation and the different types of rating laws.

◆ Explain the major arguments for and against state regulation of insurance.

◆ Describe some approaches for modernizing the regulation of insurance.

*Brent, age 23, was in an auto accident where he was at fault. His car was damaged beyond repair. Although Brent had collision insurance on the vehicle, his insurer denied payment of the collision claim on the grounds that a policy provision had been violated. A friend suggested that Brent contact the state insurance department for assistance. After investigating the incident, the state insurance department representative concluded that the claim should be paid. The claim was later settled to Brent's satisfaction.*

*One important function of state insurance departments is to protect consumers. In the above case, the state insurance department helped Brent resolve his claim dispute with the insurance company. To protect consumers, the states regulate the market activities of insurers. Certain federal laws also apply to insurers.*

*In this chapter, we discuss the fundamentals of insurance regulation. Topics covered include the reasons why insurers are regulated, the various methods for regulating insurers, the areas that are regulated, and the continuous controversy over state versus federal regulation of insurance. The chapter concludes with a discussion of current issues in insurance regulation and recommendations for modernizing insurance regulation.*

## REASONS FOR INSURANCE REGULATION

Insurers are regulated by the states for several reasons, including the following:

- Maintain insurer solvency
- Compensate for inadequate consumer knowledge
- Ensure reasonable rates
- Make insurance available

### Maintain Insurer Solvency

Insurance regulation is necessary to maintain the solvency of insurers. Solvency is important for several reasons. First, premiums are paid in advance, but the period of protection extends into the future. If an insurer goes bankrupt and a future claim is not paid, the insurance protection paid for in advance is worthless. Therefore, to ensure that claims will be paid, the financial strength of insurers must be carefully monitored.

A second reason for stressing solvency is that individuals can be exposed to great economic insecurity if insurers fail and claims are not paid. For example, if the insured's home is totally destroyed by a hurricane and the loss is not paid, he or she may be financially ruined. Thus, because of possible financial hardship to insureds, beneficiaries, and third-party claimants, regulation must stress the solvency of insurers.

Finally, when insurers become insolvent, certain social and economic costs are incurred. Examples include the loss of jobs by insurance company employees, a reduction in premium taxes paid to the states, and a "freeze" on the withdrawal of cash values by life insurance policyholders. These costs can be minimized if insolvencies are prevented.

Insurer solvency is an important issue that is discussed in greater detail later in the chapter.

## Compensate for Inadequate Consumer Knowledge

Regulation is also necessary because of inadequate consumer knowledge. Insurance contracts are technical, legal documents that contain complex clauses and provisions. Without regulation, an unscrupulous insurer could draft a contract so restrictive and legalistic that it would be worthless.

Also, most consumers do not have sufficient information for comparing and determining the monetary value of different insurance contracts. It is difficult to compare dissimilar policies with different premiums because the necessary price and policy information is not readily available. For example, individual health insurance policies vary widely by cost, coverages, and benefits. The average consumer would find it difficult to evaluate a particular policy based on the premium alone.

Without good information, consumers cannot select the best insurance product. This failure can reduce the impact that consumers have on insurance markets as well as the competitive incentive of insurers to improve product quality and lower price. Thus, regulation is needed to produce the same market effect that results from knowledgeable consumers who are purchasing products in highly competitive markets.

Finally, some agents are unethical, and state licensing requirements are minimal. Thus, regulation is needed to protect consumers against unscrupulous agents.

All states maintain Web sites that provide consumers with information on a variety of insurance-related topics. The quality of the information, however, varies widely among the states. A Consumer Federation of America study shows wide differences among the states, especially in the information provided on auto and homeowners insurance (see Insight 8.1).

## Ensure Reasonable Rates

Regulation is also necessary to ensure reasonable rates. Rates should not be so high that consumers are being charged excessive prices. Nor should they be so low that the solvency of insurers is threatened. In most insurance markets, competition among insurers results in rates that are not excessive. Unfortunately, this result is not always the case. In some insurance markets with relatively small numbers of insurers,

---

## INSIGHT 8.1

### Quality of Information Provided to Consumers on Auto and Homeowners Insurance Varies Widely Among State Insurance Departments

A Consumer Federation of America (CFA) study shows that there are wide differences in the quality of information provided to consumers, especially information on auto and homeowners insurance.[a] CFA graded the 50 states from excellent to inadequate. Only six states received the highest grade of "excellent." The results of the study are summarized as follows:

- **Excellent (6 states)**: California, Georgia, Kansas, Oklahoma, Texas, and Utah.
- **Good (12 states)**: Alaska, Arizona, Arkansas, Colorado, Delaware, Florida, Maine, Missouri, New Jersey, Ohio, Oregon, and Wisconsin.
- **Fair (14 states and D.C.)**: District of Columbia, Illinois, Kentucky, Louisiana, Maryland, Michigan, Montana, New Hampshire, New York, North Carolina, North Dakota, Pennsylvania, South Carolina, Virginia, and Washington.
- **Inadequate (18 states)**: Alabama, Connecticut, Hawaii, Idaho, Indiana, Iowa, Massachusetts, Minnesota, Mississippi, Nebraska, Nevada, New Mexico, Rhode Island, South Dakota, Tennessee, Vermont, West Virginia, and Wyoming.

CFA concludes that consumers who purchase auto or homeowners insurance can potentially save hundreds of dollars annually and avoid serious problems in settling claims if they obtain the information from the best Web sites.

[a]Consumer Federation of America, News Release, *Study Finds Significant Differences in Auto and Home Insurance Information Provided by States to Consumers*, November 10, 2008.

such as credit and title insurance, rate regulation is needed to protect consumers against excessive rates. Regulation also protects consumers against some insurers who may attempt to increase rates to exorbitant levels after a natural disaster occurs so as to recoup their underwriting losses.

## Make Insurance Available

Another regulatory goal is to make insurance available to all persons who need it. Insurers are often unwilling to insure all applicants for a given type of insurance because of underwriting losses, inadequate rates, adverse selection, and a host of additional factors. However, the public interest may require regulators to take actions that expand private insurance markets so as to make insurance more readily available. If private insurers are unable or unwilling to supply the needed coverages, then government insurance programs may be necessary.

# HISTORICAL DEVELOPMENT OF INSURANCE REGULATION

In this section, the development of insurance regulation by the states is briefly reviewed. You should pay careful attention to certain landmark legal decisions and legislative acts that have had a profound impact on insurance regulation.

## Early Regulatory Efforts

Insurance regulation first began when state legislatures granted charters to new insurers, which authorized their formation and operation. The new insurers were initially subject to few regulatory controls. The charters required only that the companies issue periodic reports and provide public information concerning their financial conditions.

The creation of state insurance commissions was the next step in insurance regulation. In 1851, New Hampshire became the first state to create a separate insurance commission to regulate insurers. Other states followed suit. In 1859, New York created a separate administrative agency headed by a single superintendent who was given broad licensing and investigative powers. Thus, initial insurance regulation developed under the jurisdiction and supervision of the states.

## Paul v. Virginia

The case of **Paul v. Virginia** in 1868 was a landmark legal decision that affirmed the right of the states to regulate insurance.[1] Samuel Paul was an agent in Virginia who represented several New York insurers. Paul was fined for selling fire insurance in Virginia without a license. He appealed the case on the grounds that Virginia's law was unconstitutional. He argued that because insurance was interstate commerce, only the federal government had the right to regulate insurance under the commerce clause of the U.S. Constitution. The Supreme Court disagreed. The Court ruled that issuance of an insurance policy was not interstate commerce. Therefore, the insurance industry was not subject to the commerce clause of the Constitution. *Thus, the legal significance of* Paul v. Virginia *was that insurance was not interstate commerce, and that the states rather than the federal government had the right to regulate the insurance industry.*

## South-Eastern Underwriters Association Case

The precedent set in *Paul v. Virginia,* which held that insurance is not interstate commerce, was overturned by the Supreme Court in 1944. The **South-Eastern Underwriters Association (SEUA)** was a cooperative rating bureau that was found guilty of price fixing and other violations of the Sherman Antitrust Act. *In the landmark case of* U.S. v. South-Eastern Underwriters Association, *the Supreme Court ruled that insurance was interstate commerce when conducted across state lines and was subject to federal regulation.*[2] The Court's decision that insurance was interstate commerce and subject to federal antitrust laws caused considerable turmoil for the industry and state regulators. The decision raised serious doubts concerning the legality of private rating bureaus and the power of the states to regulate and tax the insurance industry.

## McCarran-Ferguson Act

To resolve the confusion and doubt that existed after the SEUA decision, Congress passed the **McCarran-Ferguson Act** (Public Law 15) in 1945. *The McCarran-Ferguson Act states that continued regulation and taxation of the insurance industry by the states are in the public interest. It also states that* *federal antitrust laws apply to insurance only to the extent that the insurance industry is not regulated by state law.* Therefore, as long as state regulation is in effect, federal antitrust laws will not apply to insurance. However, the exemption from antitrust laws is not absolute. For example, the Sherman Act forbids any acts or agreements to boycott, coerce, or intimidate. In these areas, insurers are still subject to federal law.

At present, the states still have the primary responsibility for regulating insurance. However, Congress can repeal the McCarran-Ferguson Act, which would then give the federal government primary authority over the insurance industry. There have been strong pressures from some politicians and consumer groups to repeal the McCarran-Ferguson Act, but Congress to date has not done so. This important issue is discussed later in the chapter.

### Financial Modernization Act of 1999

More recently, the **Financial Modernization Act of 1999** (also called the Gramm-Leach-Bliley Act) has had a significant impact on insurance regulation. The legislation changed federal law that earlier prevented banks, insurers, and investment firms from competing fully in other financial markets outside their core area. As a result, insurers can now buy banks; banks can underwrite insurance and sell securities; brokerage firms can sell insurance; and a company that wants to provide insurance, banking, and investment services through a single entity can form a new holding company for that purpose.

The legislation had several areas of regulation, which caused additional complexity, some overlap, and regulatory gaps in the regulatory process. As a result, state insurance departments continue to regulate the insurance industry, state and federal bank agencies regulate banks and thrifts, the Securities and Exchange Commission regulates the sale of securities, and the Federal Reserve has umbrella authority over bank affiliates that engage in risky activities such as underwriting insurance and developing real estate. As a result, regulation of the insurance industry has become more complex because of different levels of regulation at the state and federal level and the overlap of regulatory functions.

## METHODS FOR REGULATING INSURERS

Three principal methods are used to regulate insurers: legislation, courts, and state insurance departments.

### Legislation

All states have insurance laws that regulate the operations of insurers. These laws regulate (1) formation of insurance companies, (2) licensing of agents and brokers, (3) financial requirements for maintaining solvency, (4) insurance rates, (5) sales and claim practices, (6) taxation, and (7) rehabilitation or liquidation of insurers. Also, laws have been passed to protect the rights of consumers, such as laws restricting the right of insurers to terminate insurance contracts and laws making insurance more widely available.

Insurers are also subject to regulation by certain federal agencies and laws. Only a few are mentioned here. The Federal Trade Commission has authority to regulate mail-order insurers in those states where they are not licensed to do business. The Securities and Exchange Commission has issued regulations concerning the sale of variable annuities and variable life insurance and has jurisdiction over the sale of insurance company securities to the public. The Employee Retirement Income Security Act of 1974 (ERISA) applies to the private pension plans of insurers.

### Courts

State and federal courts periodically hand down decisions concerning the constitutionality of state insurance laws, the interpretation of policy clauses and provisions, and the legality of administrative actions by state insurance departments. As such, the court decisions can affect the market conduct and operations of insurers in an important way.

### State Insurance Departments

All states, the District of Columbia, and U.S. territories have a separate insurance department or bureau. An insurance commissioner, who is elected or appointed by the governor, has the responsibility to administer state insurance laws. Through administrative rulings, the state insurance commissioner wields considerable power over insurers doing business in the state. The insurance commissioner has the power to hold hearings, issue cease-and-desist orders, and revoke or suspend an insurer's license to do business.

The state insurance commissioners belong to an important organization known as the **National Association of Insurance Commissioners (NAIC)**. The NAIC, founded in 1871, meets periodically to discuss industry problems that might require legislation or regulation. The NAIC has drafted model laws in various areas and has recommended adoption of these proposals by state legislatures. Although the NAIC has no legal authority to force the states to adopt the recommendations, most states have adopted all or part of them.

# WHAT AREAS ARE REGULATED?

Insurers are subject to numerous laws and regulations. The principal areas regulated include the following:

- Formation and licensing of insurers
- Solvency regulation
- Rate regulation
- Policy forms
- Sales practices and consumer protection
- Taxation of insurers

## Formation and Licensing of Insurers

All states have requirements for the formation and licensing of insurers. A new insurer is typically formed by incorporation. The insurer receives a charter or certificate of incorporation from the state, which authorizes its formation and legal existence.

After being formed, insurers must be licensed to do business. The licensing requirements for insurers are more stringent than those imposed on other new firms. If the insurer is a capital stock insurer, it must meet certain minimum capital and surplus requirements, which vary by state and by line of insurance. A new mutual insurer must meet a minimum surplus requirement (rather than capital and surplus, as there are no stockholders) and must meet other requirements as well.

A license can be issued to a domestic, foreign, or alien insurer. A **domestic insurer** is an insurer domiciled in the state; it must be licensed in the state as well as in other states where it does business. A **foreign insurer** is an out-of-state insurer that is chartered by another state; it must be licensed to do business in

the state. An **alien insurer** is an insurer chartered by a foreign country. It must also meet certain licensing requirements to operate in the state. For example, Mutual of Omaha is a domestic insurer in Nebraska. In Iowa, Mutual of Omaha is considered a foreign insurer. Lloyd's of London would be considered an alien insurer when operating in Nebraska.

## Solvency Regulation

In addition to minimum capital and surplus requirements, insurers are subject to other financial regulations designed to maintain solvency.

**Admitted Assets**   Insurers are required by law to file certain financial statements in an annual report to regulators. The Annual Statement is based on statutory accounting principles (SAP), which differ from generally accepted accounting principles (GAAP).

An insurer must have sufficient assets to offset its liabilities. Based on statutory accounting principles, only admitted assets can be shown on the insurer's balance sheet. **Admitted assets** *are assets that an insurer can show on its statutory balance sheet in determining its financial condition.* All other assets are nonadmitted assets.

Most assets are classified as admitted assets. These assets include cash, bonds, common and preferred stocks, mortgages, real estate, and other legal investments. Nonadmitted assets include premiums overdue by 90 or more days, office furniture and equipment, and certain investments or amounts that exceed statutory limits for certain types of securities. Nonadmitted assets are excluded because their liquidity is uncertain.

**Reserves**   **Reserves** *are liability items on an insurer's balance sheet and reflect obligations that must be met in the future.* The states have regulations for the calculation of reserves. The various methods for calculating reserves were discussed in Chapter 7.

**Surplus**   The surplus position is also carefully monitored. **Policyholders' surplus** *is the difference between an insurer's assets and its liabilities.* It is an item on the balance sheet that represents an insurer's net worth under statutory accounting principles.

In property and casualty insurance, policyholders' surplus is important for several reasons. First, the amount of new business an insurer can write is limited by the amount of policyholders' surplus. One conservative rule is that a property insurer can safely write $1 of new net premiums for each $1 of policyholders' surplus. Second, policyholders' surplus is necessary to offset any substantial underwriting or investment losses. Finally, policyholders' surplus is required to offset any deficiency in loss reserves that may occur over time.

In life insurance, policyholders' surplus is less important because of the substantial safety margins in the calculation of premiums and dividends, conservative interest assumptions used in calculating legal reserves, conservative valuation of investments, greater stability in operations over time, and less likelihood of a catastrophic loss.

**Risk-Based Capital**  To reduce the risk of insolvency, life and health insurers must meet certain risk-based capital standards based on a model law developed by the NAIC. The NAIC has drafted a similar model law for property and casualty insurers. Only the standards for life insurers are discussed here.

*Risk-based capital (RBC) means that insurers must have a certain amount of capital, depending on the riskiness of their investments and insurance operations. Insurers are monitored by regulators based on how much capital they have relative to their risk-based capital requirements.* For example, insurers that invest in less-than-investment-grade corporate bonds ("junk bonds") must set aside more capital than if Treasury bonds were purchased.

The risk-based capital requirements in life insurance are based on a formula that considers four types of risk:

- *Asset risk.* Asset risk is the risk of default of assets for affiliated investments; the parent company must hold an equivalent amount of risk-based capital that provides protection against the financial downturn of affiliates. The asset risk also represents the risk of default for bonds and other debt assets and a loss in market value for equity (common stock) assets.
- *Insurance risk.* Insurance risk is the equivalent of underwriting risk and reflects the amount of surplus needed to pay excess claims because of random fluctuations and inaccurate pricing for

future claim levels (risk of fluctuations in mortality experience).

- *Interest rate risk.* Interest rate risk reflects possible losses due to changing interest rates. The impact of interest rate changes is greatest on those products where the contractual guarantees favor the policyholders and where policyholders are likely to respond to changes in interest rates by withdrawing funds from the insurer. Examples include a decline in the market value of assets supporting contractual obligations because of a rise in interest rates, and liquidity problems caused by policyholders withdrawing funds because of changing interest rates.
- *Business risk.* Business risk represents the wide range of general business risks that life insurers face, such as guaranty fund assessments and insolvency because of bad management.

The NAIC requires a comparison of a company's total adjusted capital with the amount of required risk-based capital. *Total adjusted capital* is essentially the company's net worth (assets minus liabilities) with certain adjustments.

Certain regulatory and company actions must be taken if an insurer's total adjusted capital falls below its required RBC levels. The corrective action levels for life insurers are summarized as follows:

| RBC Ratio (%) | Zone | Action |
|---|---|---|
| 125% and above | Adequate | None |
| 100% to 124% | Red flag | Insurer must conduct trend test |
| 75% to 99% | Company action | Insurer must file plan with regulator outlining corrective steps |
| 50% to 74% | Regulatory action | Regulator must examine insurer and order corrective steps |
| 35% to 49% | Authorized control | Regulator may seize insurer if necessary |
| Below 35% | Mandatory control | Regulator must seize insurer |

SOURCE: "Insurance Companies' Risk-Based Capital Ratios," *The Insurance Forum*, Vol. 39, No. 8 (August 2012), p. 73. © 2012.

The effect of the RBC requirements is to raise the minimum amount of capital for many insurers and decrease the chance that a failing insurer will exhaust its capital before it can be seized by regulators. Thus, the overall result is to limit an insurer's financial risk and reduce the cost of insolvency. As a practical matter, the vast majority of insurers have total adjusted capital that exceeds their risk-based capital requirements.

**Investments** Insurance company investments are regulated with respect to types of investments, quality, and percentage of total assets or surplus that can be invested in different investments. The basic purpose of these regulations is to prevent insurers from making unsound investments that could threaten the company's solvency and harm the policyholders.

Life insurers typically invest in common and preferred stocks, bonds, mortgages, real estate, and policy loans. The laws generally place maximum limits on each type of investment based on a percentage of assets or surplus.

Property and casualty insurers typically invest in common and preferred stock, tax-free municipal and special revenue bonds, government and corporate bonds, cash, and other short-term investments. The percentage of assets invested in real estate is relatively small (less than 1 percent in 2010). Most assets are invested in highly liquid securities—for example, high-quality stocks and bonds rather than real estate—that can be sold quickly to pay claims if a catastrophe loss occurs.

**Dividend Policy** In life insurance, the annual gain from operations can be distributed in the form of dividends to policyholders, or it can be added to the insurer's surplus for present and future needs. Many states limit the amount of surplus a participating life insurer can accumulate. The purpose of this limitation is to prevent life insurers from accumulating a substantial surplus at the expense of dividends to policyholders.

**Reports and Examinations** Annual reports and examinations are used to maintain insurer solvency. Each insurer must file an annual report with the state insurance department in states where it does business. The report provides detailed financial information to regulatory officials with respect to assets, liabilities, reserves, investments, claim payments, risk-based capital, and other information.

Insurance companies are also periodically examined by the states. Depending on the state, domestic insurers generally are examined one or more times every three to five years by the state insurance department. However, state regulations have the authority to conduct an examination at any time when considered necessary. Licensed out-of-state insurers are also periodically examined.

**Liquidation of Insurers** If an insurer is financially impaired, the state insurance department assumes control of the company. With proper management, the insurer may be successfully rehabilitated. If the insurer cannot be rehabilitated, it is liquidated according to the state's insurance code.

Most states have adopted the Insurers Supervision, Rehabilitation, and Liquidation Model Act drafted by the NAIC in 1977 or similar types of legislation. The act is designed to achieve uniformity among the states in the liquidation of assets and payment of claims of a defunct insurer and provides for a comprehensive system for rehabilitation and liquidation.

If an insurer becomes insolvent, some claims may still be unpaid. All states have **guaranty funds** that provide for the payment of unpaid claims of insolvent property and casualty insurers. In life insurance, all states have enacted guaranty laws and guaranty associations to pay the claims of policyholders of insolvent life and health insurers.

The **assessment method** is the major method used to raise the necessary funds to pay unpaid claims. Insurers are generally assessed after an insolvency occurs. New York is an exception because it maintains a permanent preassessment solvency fund, which assesses property and casualty insurers prior to any insolvency. A few states have preassessment funds for workers compensation. Insurers can recoup part or all of the assessments paid by special state premium tax credits, refunds from the state guaranty funds, and higher insurance premiums. The result is that taxpayers and the general public indirectly pay the claims of insolvent insurers.

The guaranty funds limit the amount that policyholders can collect if an insurer goes broke. For example, in life insurance, a typical state guaranty fund has a $100,000 limit on cash values, a $100,000 limit on an annuity contract, and a $300,000 limit on the combined benefits from all policies. Some state funds also do not protect out-of-state residents when an insurer domiciled in the state goes broke.

## Rate Regulation

Rate regulation is an important regulatory area. As noted in Chapter 7, property and casualty insurance rates must be adequate, not excessive, and not unfairly discriminatory. Rate regulation, however, is far from uniform. Some states have more than one rating law, depending on the type of insurance. The principal types of rating laws are the following:[3]

- Prior-approval laws
- Modified prior-approval law
- File-and-use law
- Use-and-file law
- Flex-rating law
- State-made rates
- No filing required

**Prior-Approval Law**   Under a **prior-approval law**, rates must be filed and approved by the state insurance department before they can be used. In most states, if the rates are not disapproved within a certain period, such as 30 or 60 days, they are deemed to be approved.[4]

Insurers have criticized prior-approval laws on several grounds. There is often considerable delay in obtaining a needed rate increase, because state insurance departments are often understaffed. The rate increase granted may be inadequate, and rate increases may be denied for political reasons. In addition, the statistical data required by the state insurance department to support a rate increase may not be readily available.

**Modified Prior-Approval Law**   Under a **modified prior-approval law**, if the rate change is based solely on loss experience, the insurer must file the rates with the state insurance department, and the rates may be used immediately (i.e., file-and-use). However, if the rate change is based on a change in rate classifications or expense relationships, then prior approval of the rates may be necessary (i.e., prior-approval). The insurance department can disapprove the rate filing at anytime if the filing does not comply with the law.

**File-and-Use Law**   Under a **file-and-use law**, insurers are required only to file the rates with the state insurance department, and the rates can be used

immediately. Regulatory authorities have the authority to disapprove the rate filing if it violates state law. This type of law overcomes the problem of delay that exists under a prior-approval law.

**Use-and-File Law**   A variation of file-and-use is a **use-and-file law**. Under this law, insurers can put into effect immediately any rate changes, but the rates must be filed with the regulatory authorities within a certain period after first being used, such as 15 to 60 days.

**Flex-Rating Law**   Under a **flex-rating law**, prior approval of rates is required only if the rate increase or decrease exceeds a specified range. Rate changes of 5 to 10 percent are typically permitted without prior approval. The purpose of a flex-rating law is to allow insurers to make rate changes more rapidly in response to changing market conditions.

**State-Made Rates**   A small number of states earlier prescribed state-made rates that applied to specific lines of insurance.

Massachusetts earlier prescribed state-made rates for private passenger automobile insurance. However, in 2008, the Massachusetts law was changed to "managed competition." Insurers are free to determine their own rates. The rates, however, can be disapproved if they are viewed as excessive. An independent actuarial firm reviews the rates filed by insurers to determine if the rates are in compliance with the law.

In addition, a few states, including Florida and Texas, specify the rates that title insurers in the state can charge for title insurance.

**No Filing Required**   Under the **no filing required** system, insurers are not required to file their rates with the state insurance department. However, insurers may be required to furnish rate schedules and supporting data to state officials. A fundamental assumption is that market forces will determine the price and availability of insurance rather than the discretionary acts of regulatory officials.

**Commercial Lines Deregulation**   Many states have passed legislation that exempts insurers from filing rates and policy forms for large commercial accounts with the state insurance department for approval.

In most states, the legislation applies to commercial auto, general liability, and commercial property lines. Proponents of deregulation of commercial lines believe that insurers can design new products more quickly to meet the specific insurance needs of corporations; insurers can save money because rates and policy forms do not have to be filed for a commercial account with offices in several states; and risk managers can get specific coverages more quickly.

**Life Insurance Rate Regulation**   Life insurance rates are not directly regulated by the states. Rate adequacy in life insurance is indirectly achieved by laws that require legal reserves to be at least a minimum amount. Minimum legal reserve requirements indirectly affect the rates that must be charged to pay death claims and expenses.

## Policy Forms

The regulation of policy forms is another important area of insurance regulation. Because insurance contracts are technical and complex, the state insurance commissioner has the authority to approve or disapprove new policy forms before the contracts are sold to the public. The purpose is to protect the public from misleading, deceptive, and unfair provisions.

## Sales Practices and Consumer Protection

The sales practices of insurers are regulated by laws concerning the licensing of agents and brokers, and by laws prohibiting twisting, rebating, and unfair trade practices.

**Licensing of Agents and Brokers**   All states require agents and brokers to be licensed. Depending on the type of insurance sold, applicants must pass one or more written examinations. The purpose is to ensure that agents have knowledge of the state insurance laws and the contracts they intend to sell. If the agent is incompetent or dishonest, the state insurance commissioner has the authority to suspend or revoke the agent's license.

All states have legislation requiring the continuing education of agents. The continuing education requirements are designed to upgrade an agent's knowledge and skills and keep the agent up to date.

**Unfair Trade Practices**   Insurance laws prohibit a wide variety of unfair trade practices, including misrepresentation, twisting, rebating, deceptive or false advertising, inequitable claim settlement, and unfair discrimination. The state insurance commissioner has the legal authority to stop insurers from engaging in unfair trade practices and deceptive advertising. Insurers can be fined, an injunction can be obtained, or, in serious cases, the insurer's license can be suspended or revoked.

**Twisting**   All states forbid twisting. **Twisting** *is the inducement of a policyholder to drop an existing policy and replace it with a new one that provides little or no economic benefit to the client.* Twisting laws apply largely to life insurance policies; the objective here is to prevent policyholders from being financially harmed by replacing one life insurance policy with another.

All states have replacement regulations so that policyholders can make an informed decision concerning the replacement of an existing life insurance policy. These laws are based on the premise that replacement of an existing life insurance policy generally is not in the policyholder's best interest. For example, acquisition expenses for the new policy must be paid; a new incontestable clause and suicide clause must be satisfied; and higher premiums based on the policyholder's higher attained age may have to be paid. *In some cases, however, switching policies can be financially justified.* However, deceptive sales practices by some agents of certain insurers have resulted in the replacement of life insurance policies that were financially harmful to the policyholders.

**Rebating**   The vast majority of states forbid rebating. **Rebating** *is giving an individual a premium reduction or some other financial advantage not stated in the policy as an inducement to purchase the policy.* One obvious example is a partial refund of the agent's commission to the policyholder. The basic purpose of anti-rebate laws is to ensure fair and equitable treatment of all policyholders by preventing one insured from obtaining an unfair price advantage over another.

Consumer groups, however, believe that anti-rebating laws are harmful to consumers. Critics argue that (1) rebating will increase price competition and lower insurance rates; (2) present anti-rebating laws protect the incomes of agents rather than consumers; and (3) insurance purchasers are denied the right to negotiate price with insurance agents.

**Complaint Division**    State insurance departments typically have a complaint division or department for handling consumer complaints. The department will investigate the complaint and try to obtain a response from the alleged offending insurer or agency. Most consumer complaints involve claims. An insurer may refuse to pay a claim, or it may dispute the amount payable. Although state insurance departments respond to individual complaints, the departments generally lack direct authority to order insurers to pay disputed claims where factual questions are an issue. *However, you should phone or write your state insurance department if you feel you are being treated unfairly by your insurer or agent.* This is especially true for auto insurance disputes where certain insurers have significantly higher complaint ratios than others.

**Publications and Brochures**    State insurance departments typically provide a wide variety of publications and brochures for consumers. The publications are also available on the insurance department's Web site. The publications provide considerable information on life, health, auto, homeowners, and long-term care insurance, and other insurance products as well. Many states also publish rate information on auto and homeowners insurance on the Internet so that consumers can make meaningful cost comparisons.

### Taxation of Insurers

Insurers pay numerous local, state, and federal taxes. Two important taxes are the federal income tax and the state premium tax. Insurers pay federal income taxes based on complex formulas and rules established by federal legislation and the Internal Revenue Service. The states also require insurers to pay a premium tax on gross premiums received from policyholders, such as 2 percent of the premium paid.

The primary purpose of the premium tax is to raise revenues for the states, not to provide funds for insurance regulation. Many state insurance departments are underfunded and receive only a small fraction of the premium taxes collected. Critics of state regulation argue that if state regulation is to become more effective, more money must be devoted to insurance regulation.

Most states also have **retaliatory tax laws** that affect premium taxes and other taxes. For example, assume that the premium tax is 2 percent in Nebraska and 3 percent in Iowa. If insurers domiciled in Nebraska are required to pay a 3 percent premium tax on business written in Iowa, then domestic insurers in Iowa doing business in Nebraska must also pay a 3 percent tax on business written in Nebraska even though Nebraska's rate is 2 percent. The purpose of a retaliatory tax law is to protect domestic insurers in the state from excessive taxation by other states where they do business.

## STATE VERSUS FEDERAL REGULATION

The issue of state versus federal regulation has been widely discussed in the professional literature and by insurance regulators and public policy experts for more than 50 years. The states, however, continue to remain the primary supervisory body. However, because of the recent collapse of the financial services industry, especially commercial banks, during the historically severe 2007-2009 economic downswing, critics claim federal regulation would be superior to the present system.

### Advantages of Federal Regulation

Critics maintain that the present system of regulation is broken, unduly complex, and costly, with considerable overlap and duplication in regulation. Major arguments for an increased federal role in insurance regulation include the following:

- *Uniform state laws and regulations.* Federal regulation would provide uniformity in state laws and regulations, which would be less costly and would allow new products to be introduced more rapidly. Under the present system, insurers doing business nationally must follow the laws and regulations of 51 separate jurisdictions, which is costly and time consuming.
- *More effective negotiations of international insurance agreements.* Another argument is that federal regulation is more effective in the

negotiation of international agreements that pertain to insurance regulation. In 2010, Congress enacted the Dodd-Frank Wall Street Reform and Consumer Protection Act to correct abuses in the financial services industry. Part of the Act created the Federal Insurance Office (FIO). The FIO has authority to represent the United States in discussions and negotiations with foreign countries involving insurance regulation. Federal regulators could design standard rules for foreign insurers to follow in the United States and also speak with one voice for American regulators in international insurance agreements.

- *More effective treatment of systemic risk.* Proponents believe federal regulation is more effective than state regulation in the identification and treatment of systemic risk. **Systemic risk** *is the risk of collapse of an entire system or entire market in which the failure of a single entity or group of entities can result in the breakdown of the entire financial system.* The 2007-2009 business recession in the United States was the second worst economic downswing in U.S. history, next to the Great Depression of the 1930s. The downswing was caused largely by systemic risk. During this period, the economy experienced a massive financial meltdown and a brutal stock market crash that wiped out or substantially reduced the life savings of many Americans; the national unemployment rate increased to historically high levels; the economy and monetary system came terrifying close to a catastrophic collapse; the housing market collapsed, and foreclosures increased; more than 100 commercial banks and financial institutions failed or merged with other entities, which produced a credit crunch and a freezing of credit markets; commercial banks and some insurers sold billions of complex derivatives that were largely unregulated and resulted in massive losses to investors worldwide; and state and federal regulation of the financial services industry, including insurance companies, proved inadequate and broken. Proponents maintain that federal regulators could identify and treat systemic risk more effectively in the financial services sector, including any emerging systemic risk in the insurance industry.
- *Greater efficiency of insurers.* Another argument is that federal regulation would enable insurers

to become more efficient. Insurers doing business nationally would have to deal with only one federal agency rather than with numerous state insurance departments. Also, the federal agency would be less likely to yield to industry pressures, especially on issues that reflect the views of local insurers.

## Advantages of State Regulation

Proponents of state regulation offer a number of convincing counterarguments for continued regulation of insurance by the states. They include the following:

- *Quicker response to local insurance problems.* Proponents of state regulation argue that insurance problems vary widely by location, and that state regulators can resolve these problems more quickly than federal officials. Local problems include quick action by state insurance departments in resolving complaints by policyholders and corrective action by regulators in dealing with insurers that violate state law. In contrast, critics argue that federal regulators are not as well prepared to resolve these problems quickly at the local level.
- *Increased costs from dual regulation.* Critics maintain that federal regulation could lead to a dual system of insurance regulation, which would substantially increase the costs of regulation. There would be two separate regulatory systems in each state—the present state system and a new federal system. As a result, both insurers and the federal government would incur high transition costs in moving to a new system. Policyholders and taxpayers would have to pay more because of an additional layer of federal regulation.
- *Poor quality of federal regulation.* Critics argue that the past record of federal regulation is poor, and that state regulation is superior despite its faults. Critics maintain federal regulators have done a poor job in regulating the banking industry, which resulted in the failure or merger of more than 100 banks and other financial institutions during the severe 2007-2009 business recession. Also, critics argue that federal regulation of railroads, airlines, and trucking has been destructive to competition. Critics also maintain that federal regulation has obstructed entry into

specific industries, entrenched the market power of large companies, and created a cozy relationship between regulators and the regulated.

- *Promotion of uniform laws by NAIC.* Proponents of state regulation argue that reasonable uniformity of laws can be achieved by the model laws and proposals of the NAIC. By adopting the model legislation, the various state laws can be made reasonably uniform. However, many policy experts believe that, despite NAIC model laws, there are still wide differences in state laws and regulations, which continue to make compliance and administration more costly and inefficient.

- *Greater opportunity for innovation.* Proponents believe that state regulation provides greater opportunities for innovation in insurance regulation. An individual state can experiment, and if the innovation fails, only that state is affected. In contrast, poor federal legislation would affect all states.

- *Unknown consequences of federal regulation.* Proponents of state regulation argue that state regulation is already in existence, and its strengths and weaknesses are well known. In contrast, the financial and economic consequences of federal regulation on consumers and the insurance industry are not completely known. Also, changing or repealing a flawed federal law or regulation would be costly and time consuming because congressional action may be required. Lobbyists and special interest groups may oppose any proposed regulatory change, which could result in months or even years of delay before the proposed change is enacted if at all.

## Shortcomings of State Regulation

Various congressional committees, the Government Accountability Office (GAO), and consumer experts, however, have assessed the effectiveness of state regulation of insurance and have found serious shortcomings, which include the following:

- *Inadequate protection of consumers.* Critics argue that state insurance departments do not have adequate procedures for determining whether consumers are being treated properly with respect to claim payments, rate setting, and protection from unfair discrimination. In addition, according to J. Robert Hunter, Director of Insurance for Consumer Federation of America, the complexity of insurance products and pricing structures makes it difficult for consumers to comparison shop (see Insight 8.2).

- *Improvements needed in handling complaints.* Although the states prepare complaint ratios (ratio of complaints to premiums) for each insurer, the information may not be readily accessible. Many consumers are not aware of the NAIC Web site that provides information on complaints against insurers.

---

## INSIGHT 8.2

### Wide Rate Disparity Reveals Weak Competition in Insurance

Consider the wide disparities in automobile insurance rate quotes that a thirty-five year old married man in Philadelphia with a clean driving record would receive.[a] Allstate would quote as much as $12,493 for this coverage; Erie Insurance Exchange (an insurer with a better service record than Allstate) would charge $2,500.[b]

Some would say this wide range in price proves a competitive market. It does not. A disparity like this, where prices for the exact same person can vary by a multiple of five, reveals very weak competition in the market. In a truly competitive market, prices fall in a much narrower range around a market-clearing price at the equilibrium point of the supply/demand curve.

There are a number of important reasons why competition is weak in insurance. Several have to do with the consumer's ability to understand insurance:

1. **Complex Legal Documents.** Most products are able to be viewed, tested, "tires kicked" and so on. Insurance policies, however, are difficult for consumers to read and understand—even more difficult than documents for most other financial products. For example, consumers often think they are buying insurance, only to find they've bought a list of exclusions.

2. **Comparison Shopping is Difficult.** Consumers must first understand what is in the policy to compare prices.

*(Continued)*

## INSIGHT 8.2 (Continued)

3. **Policy Lag Time.** Consumers pay a significant amount for a piece of paper that contains specific promises regarding actions that might be taken far into the future. The test of an insurance policy's usefulness may not arise for decades, when a claim arises.

4. **Determining Service Quality is Very Difficult.** Consumers must determine service quality at the time of purchase, but the level of service offered by insurers is usually unknown at the time a policy is bought. Some states have complaint ratio data that help consumers make purchase decisions, and the NAIC has made a national database available that should help, but service is not an easy factor to assess.

5. **Financial Soundness is Hard to Assess.** Consumers must determine the financial solidity of the insurance company. They can get information from A.M. Best and other rating agencies, but this is also complex information to obtain and decipher.

6. **Pricing is Dismayingly Complex.** Some insurers have many tiers of prices for similar consumers—as many as 25 tiers in some cases. Consumers also face an array of classifications that can number in the thousands of slots. Online assistance may help consumers understand some of these distinctions, but the final price is determined only when the consumer actually applies and full underwriting is conducted. At that point, the consumer might be quoted a rate quite different from what he or she expected. Frequently, consumers receive a higher rate, even after accepting a quote from an agent.

7. **Underwriting Denial.** After all that, underwriting may result in the consumer being turned away.

8. **Mandated Purchase.** Government or lending institutions often require insurance. Consumers who must buy insurance do not constitute a "free-market," but a captive market ripe for arbitrary insurance pricing. The demand is inelastic.

9. **Producer Compensations Unknown.** Since many people are overwhelmed with insurance purchase decisions, they often go to an insurer or an agent and rely on them for the decision making process. Hidden commission arrangements may tempt agents to place insureds in the higher priced insurance companies. Contingency commissions may also bias an agent or broker's decision making process.

10. **Incentives for Rampant Adverse Selection.** Insurer profit can be maximized by refusing to insure classes of business (e.g., redlining) or by charging regressive prices. Profit can also be improved by offering kickbacks in some lines such as title and credit insurance.

11. **Antitrust Exemption.** Insurance is largely exempt from antitrust law under the provisions of the McCarran-Ferguson Act.

Compare shopping for insurance with shopping for a can of peas. When you shop for peas, you see the product and the unit price. All the choices are before you on the same shelf. At the checkout counter, no one asks where you live and then denies you the right to make a purchase. You can taste the quality as soon as you get home and it doesn't matter if the pea company goes broke or provides poor service. If you don't like peas at all, you need not buy any. By contrast, the complexity of insurance products and pricing structures makes it difficult for consumers to comparison shop. Unlike peas, which are a discretionary product, consumers absolutely require insurance products, whether as a condition of a mortgage, as a result of mandatory insurance laws, or simply to protect their home, family or health.

[a]For a complete discussion of the anticompetitive activities uncovered by Attorney General Spitzer, see Statement of J. Robert Hunter before the Senate Committee on Governmental Affairs on November 16, 2004 in the hearing entitled, "Oversight Hearing on Insurance Brokerage Practices. Including Potential Conflicts of Interest and the Adequacy of the Current Regulatory Framework."
[b]Buyers Guide for Auto Insurance. Downloaded from the Pennsylvania Insurance Department website on May 12. 2006.

SOURCE: Excerpted from "Testimony of J. Robert Hunter, Director of Insurance, Consumer Federation of America before the Committee on the Judiciary of the United States Senate regarding the McCarran-Ferguson Act: Implications of Repealing the Insurer's Antitrust Exemption," Consumer Federation of America, June 20, 2006.

■ *Inadequate market conduct examinations.* Market conduct examinations refer to insurance department examinations of consumer matters such as claims handling, underwriting, complaints, advertising, and other trade practices. Serious deficiencies have been found in many market conduct examination reports.

■ *Insurance availability.* Many states have not conducted current studies to determine whether property and casualty insurance availability is a serious problem in their states.

■ *Regulators overly responsive to the insurance industry.* Another alleged shortcoming of state regulation is that many state regulators are overly responsive to the insurance industry in their policy decisions, rules, and regulations. Prior to their service as state insurance commissioners, many regulatory officials are employed in the insurance industry. In a large number of states, state insurance commissioners serve in that capacity for a few years and then are hired or rehired by insurance companies at high level management positions after leaving office. Critics claim that state insurance commissioners have close ties to the insurance industry while in office and often make policy decisions that favor insurers at the expense of consumers. It is argued that state insurance commissioners should be fair and objective in their rules and regulations that affect both insurance consumers and the insurance industry, and that close industry ties often result in decisions that favor the insurance industry over consumer concerns.

Consumer groups have made numerous recommendations that would result in greater objectivity and fairness by state insurance commissioners. They include the following:[5]

- In states where regulatory officials are appointed, governors should avoid appointing insurance industry personnel to be state insurance commissioners.
- In states that have elective offices, the states should prohibit insurance companies from contributing to the campaigns of insurance commissioner candidates.
- The NAIC should prohibit former insurance commissioners who currently work in the insurance industry from lobbying former colleagues.
- The NAIC should prohibit former state insurance commissioners from accepting employment in the insurance industry for at least one year after leaving office.

The recommendations that pertain to the NAIC are especially important today because of the prominent role that the NAIC is playing in the implementation of provisions in the new Affordable Care Act ("Obamacare") to reform health care and correct for a broken health-care delivery system in the United States.

## Repeal of the McCarran-Ferguson Act

As noted earlier, the McCarran-Ferguson Act gives the states primary responsibility for regulation of the insurance industry and also provides limited exemption from federal antitrust laws. Because of the shortcomings of state regulation, there is considerable public and political support for repeal of the McCarran-Ferguson Act.

Critics of state regulation present several arguments for repeal of the McCarran-Ferguson Act. They include the following:

- *The insurance industry no longer needs broad antitrust exemption.* Critics argue that the "state action doctrine" has been fully developed and clarified by the Supreme Court. The state action doctrine defines certain activities required by state law that are exempt from federal antitrust activities. Because permissible actions of insurers have been clarified, exemption from the antitrust laws is no longer needed. In addition, it is argued that other industries are not exempt from antitrust laws, and the same should also be true for insurers.
- *Federal regulation is needed because of the defects in state regulation.* Critics argue that federal minimum standards are needed to ensure nondiscrimination in insurance pricing, full availability of essential property and casualty coverages, and elimination of unfair and excessive rate differentials among insureds.

However, many insurers and industry groups believe that repeal of the McCarran-Ferguson Act would be harmful to both the insurance industry and the public. They present the following counterarguments in support of their position:

- *The insurance industry is already competitive.* More than 2600 property and casualty insurers and more than 900 life insurers compete for business at the present time.
- *Small insurers may be harmed.* Small insurers may be unable to compete because they could not develop accurate rates based on their limited loss and expense experience. Thus, they could go out of business or be taken over by larger insurers. Ultimately, a small number of large insurers will control the business, a result exactly opposite of that intended by repeal of the McCarran-Ferguson Act.
- *Insurers may be prevented from developing common coverage forms.* This problem could lead to costly gaps in coverage for insurance buyers and increased litigation between insurers and policyholders. Also, it would be difficult for insureds to know what is covered and excluded if nonstandard forms are used.

# MODERNIZING INSURANCE REGULATION

The insurance industry is part of the overall financial services industry and should not be viewed in isolation when regulation is discussed. Critics believe that the insurance industry is in need of modernization and must be brought up to date.

## Need for Modernization

Critics argue that regulation of the financial services industry is broken, state and federal regulators see only part of a horribly complex system of regulation, regulators are often lax in their oversight of the industries they are supposed to regulate, and critical regulatory gaps and weaknesses in the supervision of insurers exist in the present system. Critics believe that a complete overhaul and restructuring of the financial services regulatory system are necessary, which also includes the insurance industry.

As stated earlier, in 2007–2009, the United States experienced the worst business recession in its history second only to the Great Depression of the 1930s. The recession was caused by numerous factors. The housing market collapsed, and foreclosures increased sharply; the sub-prime real estate market collapsed because many homebuyers with marginal credit records purchased homes they could not afford, or obtained adjustable-rate mortgages they did not understand; and financial institutions generally had lax lending standards and often made predatory and undocumented mortgage loans. Many homeowners relied heavily on home equity loans, used credit cards excessively, and defaulted on their mortgage payments. Banks and some insurance companies sold complex credit default swaps and other derivatives in unregulated markets that resulted in billions of dollars of losses. Commercial banks generally were overleveraged and undercapitalized, many banks failed or were forced to merge with other banks, and credit became difficult to obtain. Although the insurance industry generally weathered the financial meltdown, some insurers were severely impacted. Also, critics believe that lax regulatory oversight at both the state and federal levels contributed to the financial meltdown.

In addition, the American International Group (AIG), a large worldwide insurance holding company, sold billions of complex *credit default swaps* through a subsidiary, which produced massive losses to AIG and to institutional investors around the world.[6] As a result, AIG lost billions of dollars and was close to declaring bankruptcy. The federal government bailed out AIG by injecting billions of taxpayer dollars into the company in the form of federal loans and a large equity stake in the company. The bailout was controversial. Federal officials argued that the AIG bailout was justified because of the worldwide repercussions that would have resulted from the bankruptcy of AIG, and that the global recession would have been severely impacted.

## Dodd-Frank Act and Insurance Regulation

To correct the abuses in the financial services industry, Congress enacted the Dodd-Frank Wall Street Reform and Consumer Protection Act in 2010. The Act contained numerous provisions to reform the financial services industry; to deal with the destabilizing practices of commercial banks, investment firms, mortgage companies, and credit rating agencies; and to provide protection for consumers. The Act also created the Financial Stability Oversight Council (FSOC) to treat systemic risk and to identify nonbank financial companies, including insurers that could increase systemic risk in the economy.

## Federal Insurance Office

The Dodd-Frank Act also created the Federal Insurance Office (FIO), which will have a significant impact on insurance regulation. The FIO has authority to (1) monitor all aspects of the insurance industry, (2) identify gaps in insurance regulation and identify issues that contribute to systemic risk, (3) assist the FSOC in identifying insurers that could create systemic risk, (4) represent the federal government in international discussions dealing with insurance regulation, and (5) negotiate international agreements with foreign countries that pertain to insurance regulation. However, the FIO is not an insurance regulator, and the states remain the dominant supervisory body. The FIO has authority, however, to preempt state law in those areas where state law conflicts with a negotiated international agreement, or treats a foreign insurer less favorably than a U.S. insurer.

The Dodd-Frank Act required the FIO to study and report on the regulation of insurance within

18 months of enactment of the Act (January 23, 2012). At the time of writing, the report is overdue and has not yet been released.

## Optional Federal Charter

Another approach to insurance regulation is an optional federal charter. The American Council of Life Insurers (ACLI) and the American Insurance Association (AIA) have proposed an optional federal charter for insurers as an alternative to the present system of state regulation.[7] Under the ACLI proposal, life insurers would have the option of obtaining either a federal or state charter. Small local insurers may opt for a state charter, while national insurers may prefer a federal charter. *The major argument for a federal charter is that national insurers are at a competitive disadvantage under the present system.* Many new life insurance products are investment products. National insurers are at a competitive disadvantage when they compete nationally with banks and stock brokerage firms. Because of differences and inconsistencies in state laws, it may take as long as two years to get new products approved. A federal charter would enable large life insurers to speed up the development and approval products and make insurers more competitive at the national level.

However, most industry trade associations, producer groups, and consumer advocates are strongly opposed to a federal charter and offer the following counter arguments:

- *As stated earlier, there will be a dual system of insurance regulation, which will substantially increase the cost of insurance regulation.* There may be duplication and overlap under both systems.
- *A new federal regulator would have the power to preempt state laws.* A federal regulator may issue regulations that conflict with existing state laws. This could result in uncertainty and confusion among insurers and policyholders as to which state law should apply.
- *Some consumer groups believe that greater regulation of cash-value products at the state level is needed to protect consumers.* It is argued that a federal charter may result in a "race to the bottom" to lower consumer protection standards if an insurer is licensed at the federal level.

## INSOLVENCY OF INSURERS

Insolvency of insurers is another important regulatory problem. According to the National Conference of Insurance Guaranty Funds, more than 550 property and casualty insurers have become insolvent since the guaranty fund system was established in 1968.[8] Fewer life and health insurers have failed in recent years because of conservative financial management. More recently, only two life and health insurers became impaired in 2011, which was the lowest impairment count for that sector in 50 years.[9]

### Reasons for Insolvencies

Insurers fail for a variety of reasons. Major causes of failure include inadequate reserves for claims, inadequate rates, rapid growth and inadequate surplus, mismanagement and fraud, bad investments, problems with affiliates, overstatement of assets, catastrophe losses, and failure of reinsurers to pay claims.

When an insurer becomes insolvent or financially impaired, state regulators must take appropriate action. With proper management, the insurer may be rehabilitated. If rehabilitation is not feasible, the insurer may be involuntarily liquidated or acquired by a healthy insurer. Other possible regulatory actions include license revocation, cease-and-desist orders, and other actions that restrict an insurer's freedom to do business.

What happens to your policy or unpaid claim if your insurer becomes insolvent? Your policy may be sold to another insurer, and an unpaid claim may be paid by the state's guaranty fund. However, failure of a large insurer may result in delay of several years before all claims are paid, and claims may not be paid in full.

### Methods of Ensuring Solvency

The principal methods of ensuring insurer solvency are the following:

- *Financial requirements.* Insurers must meet certain financial requirements that vary among the states, such as minimum capital and surplus requirements, restrictions on investments, and valuation of loss reserves.
- *Risk-based capital standards.* As noted earlier, insurers must meet the risk-based capital

standards based on a model law developed by the NAIC. The increased capital requirements help to prevent insolvency.

- *Annual financial statements.* Certain annual financial statements must be submitted to state insurance departments in a prescribed manner to provide information on premiums written, expenses, losses, investments, and other information. The financial statements are then reviewed by regulatory officials.
- *Field examinations.* State laws require that insurers must be examined periodically, such as every three to five years. The NAIC coordinates the examination of insurers that do business in several states.
- *Early warning system.* The NAIC administers an early warning system called the Insurance Regulatory Information System (IRIS). Financial ratios and other reports are developed based on information in the annual statement. Based on a review of this information, insurers may be designated for immediate review or targeted for regulatory attention. The system, however, is not perfect. The financial ratios may not identify all troubled insurers. The system also has identified an increasing number of insurers, some of which do not require immediate regulatory attention.
- *FAST system.* The NAIC employs a solvency screening system called FAST (Financial Analysis Solvency Tracking) that prioritizes insurers for additional analysis. Different point values are assigned for the various ranges of financial ratio results. The points are then summed to determine a FAST score for each insurer. Based on their FAST scores, certain insurers are considered a priority for regulatory action.

## CREDIT-BASED INSURANCE SCORES

**Credit-based insurance scores** continue to be an important and controversial regulatory issue. *The majority of insurers use the applicant's credit record for purposes of underwriting and rating in auto and homeowners insurance.* The insurance score is derived from the applicant's credit history and is combined with other underwriting factors.

Depending on the insurance score, the applicant may be placed in a lower or higher rating class or denied insurance.

The use of insurance scores in underwriting and rating is controversial. Proponents offer the following arguments:

- *There is a high correlation between an applicant's credit record and future claims experience.* Studies show that applicants with poor credit records are more likely to submit more auto or homeowners claims than applicants with good or superior credit records. Insurance scores enhance the ability of insurers to predict future claims experience with greater accuracy.
- *Insurance scores benefit consumers.* Insurers maintain that underwriting and rating can be more accurate and objective. A Federal Trade Commission study concluded that insurance scores permit insurers to evaluate risk with greater accuracy, which might make them more willing to insure higher-risk consumers for whom otherwise an appropriate premium could not be determined. As a result, higher-risk insureds pay higher premiums, and lower-risk insureds pay lower premiums.[10]
- *Most consumers have good credit scores and benefit from credit scoring.* Consumers with good credit records may qualify for lower rates or obtain coverage that otherwise might be difficult to obtain. Insurers maintain that more than 50 percent of the policyholders pay lower premiums because of good credit.[11]

Critics of insurance scores, however, present the following counterarguments:

- *The use of credit data in underwriting or rating discriminates against minorities and other groups.* Critics claim that African Americans and Hispanics are overrepresented among consumers with the lowest credit scores and pay more for their insurance as a result. Critics also argue that credit-based insurance scores hurt certain groups. These groups include low-income people who may be unable to obtain credit; the unemployed who may fall behind in paying their bills; the sick and disabled who may be late with their monthly credit card payments; female-headed families with children who do not receive child-support payments, or the payments are late; and applicants for insurance who do not use credit but pay cash for their purchases.

However, insurers deny that insurance scores discriminate against minorities and certain groups because income, race, or ethnic background are not used in the underwriting process. A Texas Department of Insurance study found a strong relationship between credit scores and claims experience; the study also concluded that there is no evidence of any dissimilar or unequal impact on any minority or socioeconomic group because the underwriting process does not consider income, race, or ethnic background. As such, regardless of differences in income, race, or ethnic background, all identically situated individuals would be charged the same amount for auto or homeowners insurance under a rating plan that permits the use of credit data in personal lines underwriting.[12]

In addition, an FTC report concluded that credit scores cannot easily be used as a proxy for race and ethnic origin.[13] Likewise, a Federal Reserve study on credit concluded that credit scores were not proxies or substitutes for race, ethnicity, or gender.[14] Additional research on the problem of discrimination should clarify the issue.

- *Credit-based insurance scores may penalize consumers unfairly during business recessions.*

At the time of writing, the United States is slowly recovering from a severe recession in 2007–2009. During this recession, millions of workers lost their jobs; many homeowners defaulted on their mortgage payments; millions of homeowners lost their homes; bankruptcies skyrocketed; and many unemployed workers incurred high credit card debts, or obtained money from nontraditional lenders at high rates of interest. All of these factors had a negative impact on insurance scores. Critics argue that consumers are already impacted severely by a business recession, and that it is cruel and unfair to penalize them a second time by higher premiums because of insurance scoring.[15]

To protect consumers, most states have enacted legislation that regulates the use of credit-based insurance scores. Typical laws require insurers to file an underwriting model that includes insurance scores with the state insurance department, the number of factors that can be used to calculate an insurance score may be limited, insurers are prohibited from penalizing consumers who do not use credit or have no credit history, insurers are usually prohibited from using insurance scores as the sole determinant in underwriting and rating, and insurers must inform consumers if credit information is used in underwriting or rating.[16]

## CASE APPLICATION

Ashley is an actuary who is employed by the Nebraska Department of Insurance. Her duties include monitoring the financial position of insurance companies doing business in Nebraska. Based on an analysis of annual financial statements that insurers are required to submit, she discovered that Mutual Life Insurance has a risk-based capital ratio of 75 percent. Based on this information, answer the following questions:

a. What is the purpose of requiring insurers to meet risk-based capital requirements?

b. What regulatory action, if any, should the Nebraska Department of Insurance take with respect to Mutual Life Insurance?

c. Would your answer to part (b) change if the risk-based capital ratio for Mutual Life Insurance fell to 30 percent? Explain your answer.

d. Mutual Life Insurance has 25 percent of its assets invested in common stocks. Assume the stocks are sold, and the proceeds are invested in U.S. government bonds. What effect, if any, will this investment change have on the risk-based capital ratio of Mutual Life Insurance? Explain your answer.

## SUMMARY

- The insurance industry is regulated for several reasons:

    To maintain insurer solvency

    To compensate for inadequate consumer knowledge

    To ensure reasonable rates

    To make insurance available

- The insurance industry is regulated primarily by the states. The McCarran-Ferguson Act states that continued regulation and taxation of the insurance industry by the states are in the public interest.

- Three principal methods are used to regulate the insurance industry:

    Legislation

    Courts

    State insurance departments

- The principal areas that are regulated include the following:

    Formation and licensing of insurers

    Solvency regulation

    Rate regulation

    Policy forms

    Sales practices and consumer protection

    Taxation of insurers

- Property and casualty insurance rates must be adequate, reasonable (not excessive), and not unfairly discriminatory. The principal types of rating laws are as follows:

    Prior-approval law

    Modified prior-approval law

    File-and-use law

    Use-and-file law

    Flex-rating law

    State-made rates

    No filing required

- Insurers must pay a state premium tax on gross premiums. The primary purpose is to raise revenues for the state, not to provide funds for insurance regulation.

- State versus federal regulation is an issue that has evoked considerable debate. The alleged advantages of federal regulation include the following:

    Uniform state laws and regulations

    More effective negotiation of international insurance agreements

    More effective treatment of systemic risk

    Greater efficiency of insurers

- The advantages of state regulation include the following:

    Quicker response to local insurance problems

    Increased costs from dual regulation

    Poor quality of federal regulation

    Promotion of uniform laws by the NAIC

    Greater opportunity for innovation

    Unknown consequences of federal regulation

- Critics argue that state regulation of insurance has serious shortcomings, including the following:

    Inadequate protection of consumers

    Improvements needed in handling complaints

    Inadequate market conduct examinations

    Insurance availability studies conducted only in a minority of states

    Regulators overly responsive to the insurance industry

- Arguments for repeal of the McCarran-Ferguson Act include the following:

    The insurance industry no longer needs broad antitrust exemption.

    Federal regulation is needed because of the defects in state regulation.

- Arguments in support of the McCarran-Ferguson Act include the following:

    The insurance industry is already competitive.

    Small insurers may be harmed.

    Insurers may be prevented from developing common coverage forms

- Several current issues in insurance regulation include the following:

    Modernizing insurance regulation

    Insolvency of insurers

    Credit-based insurance scores

## KEY CONCEPTS AND TERMS

Admitted assets (146)

Alien insurer (146)

Assessment method (148)

Credit-based insurance score (158)

Domestic insurer (146)

File-and-use law (149)
Flex-rating law (149)
Financial Modernization
  Act of 1999 (145)
Foreign insurer (146)
Guaranty funds (157)
McCarran-Ferguson
  Act (144)
Modified prior-
  approval law (149)
National Association of
  Insurance Commissioners
  (NAIC) (146)
No filing required (149)

*Paul v. Virginia* (144)
Policyholders' surplus (146)
Prior-approval law (149)
Rebating (150)
Reserves (146)
Retaliatory tax laws (151)
Risk-based capital
  (RBC) (147)
South-Eastern Underwriters
  Association (SEUA) (144)
Systemic risk (152)
Twisting (150)
Use-and-file law (149)

## REVIEW QUESTIONS

1. Explain why the insurance industry is regulated.

2. Briefly explain the significance of the following legal cases and legislative acts with respect to insurance regulation:
   a. *Paul v. Virginia*
   b. South-Eastern Underwriters Association Case
   c. McCarran-Ferguson Act
   d. Financial Modernization Act of 1999

3. Explain the principal methods for regulating insurance companies.

4. Identify the principal areas of insurance company operations that are regulated by the states.

5. Briefly describe the major types of rating laws.

6. Explain the following actions by agents that are prohibited by state law:
   a. Twisting
   b. Rebating

7. a. Explain the major arguments for federal regulation of the insurance industry.
   b. Explain the major arguments in support of state regulation of the insurance industry.
   c. Describe the shortcomings of state regulation.

8. a. Explain the major arguments for repeal of the McCarran-Ferguson Act.
   b. Explain the major arguments against repeal of the McCarran-Ferguson Act.

9. Identify the major techniques that regulators use to monitor insurance company solvency.

10. Describe the risk-based capital standards that insurers must meet.

## APPLICATION QUESTIONS

1. The Financial Services Company is a large life insurer that sells annuity products to retired people. Company actuaries have designed a new annuity contract that combines lifetime annuity benefits with long-term care in a skilled nursing home. Financial Services wants to market the new annuity nationally in all 50 states. The company faces competition from a national commercial bank that is trying to sell a similar product to Social Security beneficiaries. The CEO of Financial Services believes that the new annuity product could be marketed more efficiently if the company had a federal charter. Several members of the board of directors, however, believe that a federal charter would be undesirable.
   a. What major regulatory obstacle does Financial Services face in trying to market the new annuity product in each state under the present system of state regulation?
   b. Assume that Financial Services has the option of obtaining a federal charter. Explain the advantages, if any, of a federal charter to Financial Services in their efforts to market the new annuity product.
   c. Explain the major arguments against federal charters.

2. Opal, age 75, has a $100,000 ordinary life insurance policy that has a cash value of $35,000. Opal is concerned about the cost of long-term care in a nursing home. A new agent of a national life insurer persuaded her to transfer the $35,000 into a deferred annuity. The agent told Opal that the annuity pays lifetime income benefits and also allows her to withdraw the $35,000 without penalty if she should enter a nursing home. After the policy was issued, Opal had 10 days to change her mind. During the free-look period, a friend of Opal examined the policy. Analysis of the policy showed that only 10 percent of the cash value could be withdrawn each year without penalty. A 7 percent surrender charge would apply to any excess amounts withdrawn. In addition, the income payments were scheduled to start in 10 years when O

attained age 85. Opal filed a complaint against the agent with the state insurance department. An investigation revealed that the agent had made similar misrepresentations to other clients.

a. Based on the above facts, identify the illegal practice in which the agent engaged.

b. What action can the state insurance department take against the dishonest agent?

c. What action can the state insurance department take against the life insurer?

3. Although domiciled in Nebraska, Auto Insurance is licensed to sell auto insurance in 10 states. A different set of rates applies in each state. In five states, prior approval of rates is required. Two states have a file-and-use law, and the remaining three states have a flex-rating law. Auto Insurance has experienced poor underwriting results and needs to increase its rates.

a. Explain how each of the above rating laws would apply to Auto Insurance.

b. Describe some possible problems that Auto Insurance may experience in trying to get its rates increased in a prior-approval state.

4. Janet, age 35, is divorced and has two preschool children. Janet earns only the federal minimum wage, and money is tight. Her former husband failed to make child-support payments for the past three months because he lost his job in a company merger. As a result, Janet fell behind in the payment of her bills and received several threatening letters from collection agencies. Janet believes that she can save money if she switches auto insurers. One auto insurer quoted her a rate that is substantially higher than the rate she is now paying. A company representative explained that Janet is being rated-up because of her poor credit record. Janet is surprised because she has a good driving record and has not been involved in an accident within the last five years.

a. Explain the rationale for charging Janet a higher premium for auto insurance because of a poor credit record.

b. Explain the arguments against using credit-based insurance scores as a rating or underwriting factor in auto insurance.

## INTERNET RESOURCES

- The **Insurance Regulatory Examiners Society** is a nonprofit professional and educational association for insurance company examiners and other professionals working in insurance regulation. Visit the site at

  go-ires.org

- The **National Association of Insurance Commissioners (NAIC)** is an organization of state insurance commissioners that promotes uniformity in state insurance laws and recommends legislation to state legislatures. The Web site for each state insurance department can be accessed through the NAIC Web site. Visit the site at

  naic.org

- The **National Association of Insurance Commissioners (NAIC)** also provides considerable information on complaints against individual insurers. Go to the NAIC Consumer Information Source, and type in the company name, state, and business type. After locating the company, click on "Closed Complaints." Visit the site at

  https://eapps.naic.org/cis

- The **National Conference of Insurance Legislators** is an organization of state legislators whose main area of public policy concern is insurance regulation and legislation. Visit the site at

  ncoil.org

- The **National Organization of Life & Health Insurance Guaranty Associations** (NOLHGA) is a voluntary association of life and health insurance guaranty associations in all 50 states, the District of Columbia, and Puerto Rico. The organization was founded in 1983 when the state guaranty associations needed a mechanism to help them coordinate their efforts to protect policyholders when a life or health insurance company insolvency affects people in many states. Visit the site at

  http://www.nolhga.com/

## SELECTED REFERENCES

American Council of Life Insurers, News Release, *Modernizing Insurance Regulation,* January 2009.

Birnbaum, Birny. "Regulators Should Impose Credit Scoring Moratorium," *National Underwriter,* Property & Casualty Ed., September 1, 2008, pp. 41–42.

Board of Governors of the Federal Reserve System, *Report to the Congress on Credit Scoring and Its Effects on the Availability and Affordability of Credit,* August 2007.

Derrig, Richard A. and Sharon Tennyson, "The Impact of Rate Regulation on Claims: Evidence from Massachusetts Automobile Insurance." *Risk Management and Insurance Review,* Vol. 14, No. 2, 2011, pp. 173–199.

Federal Trade Commission, *Credit-Based Insurance Scores: Impacts on Consumers of Automobile Insurance, A Report to Congress by the Federal Trade Commission,* July 2007.

*The Financial Crisis Inquiry Report: Final Report of the National Commission on the Causes of the Financial and Economic Crisis in the United States.* Washington, DC: U.S. Government Printing Office, January 2011.

Grace, Martin F. and Robert W. Klein, *Alternative Frameworks for Insurance Regulation in the U.S.,* Center for Risk Management and Insurance, Georgia State University, October 7, 2008.

Harrington, Scott E. "Insurance Regulation and the Dodd-Frank Act," *Networks Financial Institute,* Indiana State University, 2011, PB-01, March 2011.

Hartwig, Robert P. *No Evidence of Disparate Impact in Texas Due to Use of Credit Information by Personal Lines Insurers.* New York: Insurance Information Institute, January 2005.

Insurance Information Institute. "Credit Scoring," *Issues Updates.* New York: Insurance Information Institute, February 2012. This source is periodically updated.

Insurance Information Institute. "Insolvencies/Guaranty Funds," *Issues Updates.* New York: Insurance Information Institute, July 2012. This source is periodically updated.

Insurance Information Institute. "Regulation Modernization," *Issues Updates.* New York: Insurance Information Institute, August 2012. This source is periodically updated.

Leverty, J. Tyler. "The Cost of Duplicative Regulation: Evidence from Risk Retention Groups." *The Journal of Risk and Insurance,* Vol. 79, No. 1, March 2012, pp. 105–127.

Schwartzman, Joy and Gail Ross, "The Dodd-Frank Act and the Insurance Industry: Strategic Considerations of U.S. Financial Reform," *Milliman Insight,* September 27, 2010.

Schwartzman, Joy and Michael Schmitz, "Shifting the Regulatory Burden?", *Milliman Insight,* April 21, 2008.

## NOTES

1. 8 Wall 168,183 (1869).
2. 322 U.S. 533 (1944).
3. "Regulation Modernization," *Issues Updates,* Insurance Information Institute, August 2012. This source is periodically updated.
4. Ibid.
5. Warren S. Hersch, "Consumer Watchdog: Most NAIC Commissioners Have Industry Ties," *The National Underwriter, Life & Health,* March 22, 2011.
6. A credit default swap is a financial instrument for dealing with the risk that a debt instrument might default. The buyer of a credit default swap pays premiums for protection against debt default and receives a lump sum payment if the debt instrument is in default. The seller of a credit default swap receives monthly premiums from the buyer, and if the debt instrument defaults, the seller must pay the agreed amount to the buyer.
7. American Council of Life Insurers, *Modernizing Insurance Regulation,* January 2009.
8. National Conference of Insurance Guaranty Funds. *Insolvency Trends, 2012,* winter issue.
9. "Insolvency/Guaranty Funds," *Issues Updates,* Insurance Information Institute, July 2012. This source is periodically updated.
10. Federal Trade Commission, *Credit-Based Insurance Scores: Impacts on Consumers of Automobile Insurance, A Report to Congress by the Federal Trade Commission,* July 2007.

11. "Credit Scoring," *Issues Updates,* Insurance Information Institute, February 2010. This source is periodically updated.

12. Robert P. Hartwig, *No Evidence of Disparate Impact in Texas Due to Use of Credit Information by Personal Lines Insurers,* Insurance Information Institute, January 2005.

13. Federal Trade Commission, *Credit-Based Insurance Scores: Impacts on Consumers of Automobile Insurance, A Report to Congress by the Federal Trade Commission,* July 2007.

14. Board of Governors of the Federal Reserve System. *Report to the Congress on Credit Scoring and Its Effects on the Availability and Affordability of Credit,* August 2007.

15. Birny Birnbaum, "Regulators Should Impose Credit Scoring Moratorium," *National Underwriter,* Property & Casualty Ed., September 1, 2008, pp. 41–42.

16. "Credit Scoring," *Issues Updates,* Insurance Information Institute, February 2012. This source is periodically updated.

Students may take a self-administered test on this chapter at
www.pearsonhighered.com/rejda

# CHAPTER 9

# FUNDAMENTAL LEGAL PRINCIPLES

*"It is unfair to believe everything we hear about lawyers—some of it may not be true."*

Gerald F. Lieberman

**After studying this chapter, you should be able to**

◆ Explain the fundamental legal principles that are reflected in insurance contracts, including:
  Principle of indemnity
  Principle of insurable interest
  Principle of subrogation
  Principle of utmost good faith

◆ Explain how the legal concepts of representations, concealment, and warranty support the principle of utmost good faith.

◆ Describe the basic requirements for the formation of a valid insurance contract.

◆ Show how the nature of insurance contracts differs from that of other contracts.

◆ Explain the law of agency and how it affects the actions and duties of insurance agents.

*Kyle, age 23, has a serious alcohol and substance abuse problem. He has three drunk driving convictions and has been arrested for reckless driving, leaving the scene of an accident, and driving without a license. He recently served a six-month sentence in the county jail for driving on a suspended license. Kyle moved to another state and had to provide proof of insurance to get his car licensed. On the application, Kyle did not reveal his previous accident record and DUI convictions. He stated that he had received only one citation for parking in a no-parking zone. The insurer issued the policy. After drinking for several hours in a local tavern, Kyle was again involved in another auto accident on his way home. The other driver was seriously injured and almost died. The injured driver sued Kyle for her bodily injuries. Kyle's insurer refused to pay the claim on the grounds that Kyle had concealed his previous DUI convictions and also made several material misrepresentations on the application. Kyle's introduction to insurance law was financially painful and costly.*

*As Kyle discovered, insurance law can have substantial legal consequences for you after a loss occurs. When you buy insurance, you expect to be paid for a covered loss. Insurance law and contractual provisions determine whether you are covered and how much will be paid. Insurance contracts are complex legal documents that reflect both general rules of law and insurance law. Thus, you should have a clear understanding of the basic legal principles that underlie insurance contracts.*

*For this chapter, we examine the fundamental legal principles on which insurance contracts are based, legal requirements for a valid insurance contract, and legal characteristics of insurance contracts that distinguish them from other types of contracts. The chapter concludes with a discussion of the law of agency and its application to insurance agents.*

## PRINCIPLE OF INDEMNITY

The principle of indemnity is one of the most important principles in insurance. *The* **principle of indemnity** *states that the insurer agrees to pay no more than the actual amount of the loss; stated differently, the insured should not profit from a loss.* Most property and casualty insurance contracts are contracts of indemnity. If a covered loss occurs, the insurer should not pay more than the actual amount of the loss. A contract of indemnity does not mean that all covered losses are always paid in full. Because of deductibles, dollar limits on the amount paid, and other contractual provisions, the amount paid is often less than the actual loss.

The principle of indemnity has two fundamental purposes. *The first purpose is to prevent the insured from profiting from a loss.* For example, if Kristin's

home is insured for $200,000, and a partial loss of $50,000 occurs, the principle of indemnity would be violated if $200,000 were paid to her. She would be profiting from insurance.

*The second purpose is to reduce moral hazard.* If dishonest policyholders could profit from a loss, they might deliberately cause losses with the intention of collecting the insurance. If the loss payment does not exceed the actual amount of the loss, the temptation to be dishonest is reduced.

### Actual Cash Value

The concept of *actual cash value* supports the principle of indemnity. In property insurance, the basic method for indemnifying the insured is based on the actual cash value of the damaged property at the time of loss. The courts have used a number of methods to determine actual cash value, including the following:

- Replacement cost less depreciation
- Fair market value
- Broad evidence rule

**Replacement Cost Less Depreciation**   Under this rule, **actual cash value** *is defined as replacement cost less depreciation.* This rule has been used traditionally to determine the actual cash value of property in property insurance. It takes into consideration both inflation and depreciation of property values over time. Replacement cost is the current cost of restoring the damaged property with new materials of like kind and quality. Depreciation is a deduction for physical wear and tear, age, and economic obsolescence.

For example, Sarah has a favorite couch that burns in a fire. Assume she bought the couch five years ago, the couch is 50 percent depreciated, and a similar couch today would cost $1000. Under the actual cash value rule, Sarah will collect $500 for the loss because the replacement cost is $1000, and depreciation is $500, or 50 percent. If she were paid the full replacement value of $1000, the principle of indemnity would be violated. She would be receiving the value of a new couch instead of one that was five years old. In short, the $500 payment represents indemnification for the loss of a five-year-old couch. This calculation can be summarized as follows:

$$\text{Replacement cost} = \$1000$$

$$\text{Depreciation} = \$500 \text{ (couch is 50 percent depreciated)}$$

$$\text{Replacement cost} - \text{Depreciation} = \text{Actual cash value}$$

$$\$1000 - \$500 = \$500$$

**Fair Market Value**   Some courts have ruled that fair market value should be used to determine actual cash value of a loss. **Fair market value** *is the price a willing buyer would pay a willing seller in a free market.*

The fair market value of a building may be below its actual cash value based on replacement cost less depreciation. This difference is due to several factors, including a poor location, deteriorating neighborhood, or economic obsolescence of the building. For example, in major cities, large homes in older residential areas often have a market value well below replacement cost less depreciation. If a loss occurs, the fair market value may reflect more accurately the value of the loss. In one case, a building valued at $170,000 based on the actual cash value rule had a market value of only $65,000 when a loss occurred. The court ruled that the actual cash value of the property should be based on the fair market value of $65,000 rather than on $170,000.[1]

**Broad Evidence Rule**   Many states use the broad evidence rule to determine the actual cash value of a loss. *The* **broad evidence rule** *means that the determination of actual cash value should include all relevant factors an expert would use to determine the value of the property.* Relevant factors include replacement cost less depreciation, fair market value, present value of expected income from the property, comparison sales of similar property, opinions of appraisers, and numerous other factors.

Although the actual cash value rule is used in property insurance, different methods are employed in other types of insurance. In liability insurance, the insurer pays up to the policy limit the amount of damages that the insured is legally obligated to pay because of bodily injury or property damage to another. In business income insurance, the amount paid is usually based on the loss of profits plus continuing expenses when the business is shut down because of a loss from a covered peril. In life insurance, the amount paid when the insured dies is generally the face value of the policy.

### Exceptions to the Principle of Indemnity

There are several important exceptions to the principle of indemnity. They include the following:

- Valued policy
- Valued policy laws
- Replacement cost insurance
- Life insurance

**Valued Policy**   *A* **valued policy** *is a policy that pays the face amount of insurance if a total loss occurs.* Valued policies typically are used to insure antiques, fine arts, rare paintings, and family heirlooms. Because of difficulty in determining the actual value of the property at the time of loss, the insured and insurer both agree on the value of the property when the policy is first issued. For example, you may have a valuable antique clock that was owned by your great-grandmother. You may feel that the clock is worth $10,000 and have it insured for that amount. If the clock is totally destroyed in a fire, you would be paid $10,000 regardless of the actual cash value of the clock at the time of loss.

**Valued Policy Laws**   Valued policy laws are another exception to the principle of indemnity.[2] A **valued policy law** *is a law that exists in some states that requires payment of the face amount of insurance to the insured if a total loss to real property occurs from a peril specified in the law.* The specified perils to which a valued policy law applies vary among the states. Laws in some states cover only fire; other states cover fire, lightning, windstorm, and tornado; and some states include all insured perils. In addition, the laws generally apply only to real property, and the loss must be total. For example, a building insured for $200,000 may have an actual cash value of $175,000. If a total loss from a fire occurs, the face amount of $200,000 would be paid. Because the insured would be paid more than the actual cash value, the principle of indemnity would be violated.

The original purpose of a valued policy law was to protect the insured from a dispute with the insurer if an agent had deliberately overinsured property for a higher commission. After a total loss, the insurer might offer less than the face amount for which the policyholder had paid premiums on the grounds that the building was overinsured. However, the importance of a valued policy law has declined over time because inflation in property values has made overinsurance less of a problem. Underinsurance is now the greater problem, because it results in both inadequate premiums for the insurer and inadequate protection for the insured.

Despite their reduced importance, however, valued policy laws can lead to overinsurance and an increase in moral hazard. Most buildings are not physically inspected before they are insured. If an insurer fails to inspect a building for valuation purposes, overinsurance and possible moral hazard may result. The insured may not be concerned about loss prevention, or may even deliberately cause a loss to collect the insurance proceeds. Although valued policy laws provide a defense for the insurer when

fraud is suspected, the burden of proof is on the insurer to prove fraudulent intent. Proving fraud is often difficult. For example, in an older case, a house advertised for sale at $1800 was insured for $10,000 under a fire insurance policy. About six months later, the house was totally destroyed by a fire. The insurer denied liability on the grounds of misrepresentation and fraud. An appeals court ordered the face amount of insurance to be paid, holding that nothing prevented the company from inspecting the property to determine its value. The insured's statement concerning the value of the house was deemed to be an expression of opinion, not a representation of fact.[3]

**Replacement Cost Insurance**   Replacement cost insurance is a third exception to the principle of indemnity. **Replacement cost insurance** *means there is no deduction for physical depreciation in determining the amount paid for a loss.* For example, assume that the roof on your home is 5 years old and has a useful life of 20 years. The roof is damaged by a tornado, and the current cost of replacement is $10,000. Under the actual cash value rule, you would receive only $7500 ($10,000 − $2500 = $7500). Under a replacement cost policy, you would receive the full $10,000 (less any applicable deductible). Because you receive the value of a brand-new roof instead of one that is 5 years old, the principle of indemnity is technically violated.

Replacement cost insurance is based on the recognition that payment of the actual cash value can still result in a substantial loss to the insured, because few persons budget for depreciation. In our example, you would have had to pay $2500 to restore the damaged roof, since it was one-fourth depreciated. To deal with this problem, replacement cost insurance can be purchased to insure homes, buildings, and business and personal property.

**Life Insurance**   Life insurance is another exception to the principle of indemnity. A life insurance contract is not a contract of indemnity but is a valued policy that pays a stated amount to the beneficiary upon the insured's death. The indemnity principle is difficult to apply to life insurance because the actual cash value rule (replacement cost less depreciation) is meaningless in determining the value of a human life. Moreover, to plan for personal and business purposes, such as the need to provide a specific amount of monthly income to the deceased's dependents, a certain amount of life insurance must be purchased before death occurs. For these reasons, a life insurance policy is another exception to the principle of indemnity.

# PRINCIPLE OF INSURABLE INTEREST

The principle of insurable interest is another important legal principle. *The* **principle of insurable interest** *states that the insured must be in a position to lose financially if a covered loss occurs.* For example, you have an insurable interest in your car because you may lose financially if the car is damaged or stolen. You have an insurable interest in your personal property, such as a computer, books, and clothes, because you may lose financially if the property is damaged or destroyed.

## Purposes of an Insurable Interest

To be legally enforceable, all insurance contracts must be supported by an insurable interest. Insurance contracts must be supported by an insurable interest for the following reasons.[4]

- To prevent gambling
- To reduce moral hazard
- To measure the amount of the insured's loss in property insurance

*First, an insurable interest is necessary to prevent gambling.* If an insurable interest were not required, the contract would be a gambling contract and would be against the public interest. For example, you could insure the property of another and hope for a loss to occur. You could similarly insure the life of another person and hope for an early death. These contracts clearly would be gambling contracts and would be against the public interest.

*Second, an insurable interest reduces moral hazard.* If an insurable interest were not required, a dishonest person could purchase property insurance on someone else's property and then deliberately cause a loss to receive the proceeds. But if the insured stands to lose financially, nothing is gained by causing the loss. Thus, moral hazard is reduced. In life insurance, an insurable interest requirement reduces the incentive to murder the insured for the purpose of collecting the proceeds.

*Finally, in property insurance, an insurable interest measures the amount of the insured's loss.* Most property insurance contracts are contracts of indemnity, and one measure of recovery is the insurable interest of the insured. If the loss payment cannot exceed the amount of one's insurable interest, the principle of indemnity is supported.

## Examples of an Insurable Interest

Several examples of an insurable interest are discussed in this section. However, it is helpful at this point to distinguish between an insurable interest in property and casualty insurance and in life insurance.

**Property and Casualty Insurance** *Ownership of property* can support an insurable interest because owners of property will lose financially if their property is damaged or destroyed.

*Potential legal liability* can also support an insurable interest. For example, a dry-cleaning firm has an insurable interest in the property of the customers. The firm may be legally liable for damage to the customers' goods caused by the firm's negligence.

*Secured creditors* have an insurable interest as well. A commercial bank or mortgage company that lends money to buy a house has an insurable interest in the property. The property serves as collateral for the mortgage, so if the building is damaged, the collateral behind the loan is impaired. A bank that makes an inventory loan to a business firm has an insurable interest in the stock of goods, because the goods are collateral for the loan. However, the courts have ruled that unsecured or general creditors normally do not have an insurable interest in the debtor's property.[5]

Finally, a *contractual right* can support an insurable interest. Thus, a business firm that contracts to purchase goods from abroad on the condition that they arrive safely in the United States has an insurable interest in the goods because of the loss of profits if the merchandise does not arrive.

**Life Insurance** The question of an insurable interest does not arise when you purchase life insurance on your own life. The law considers the insurable interest requirement to be met whenever a person voluntarily purchases life insurance on his or her life. Thus, you can purchase as much life insurance as you can afford, subject of course to the insurer's underwriting rules concerning the maximum amount of insurance that can be written on any single life. Also, when you apply for life insurance on your own life, you can name anyone as beneficiary. The beneficiary is not required to have an insurable interest, either at the inception of the policy or time of death, when you purchase life insurance on your own life.[6]

However, if you wish to purchase a life insurance policy on the life of another person, you must have an insurable interest in that person's life. Close family ties or marriage will satisfy the insurable interest requirement in life insurance. For example, a husband can purchase a life insurance policy on his wife and be named as beneficiary. Likewise, a wife can insure her husband and be named as beneficiary. A grandparent can purchase a life insurance policy on the life of a grandchild. However, remote family relationships will not support an insurable interest. For example, cousins cannot insure each other unless a pecuniary relationship is present.

If there is a **pecuniary (financial) interest,** the insurable interest requirement in life insurance can be met. Even when there is no relationship by blood or marriage, one person may be financially harmed by the death of another. For example, a corporation can insure the life of an outstanding salesperson, because the firm's profit may decline if the salesperson dies. One business partner can insure the life of the other partner and use the life insurance proceeds to purchase the deceased partner's interest if he or she dies.

### When Must an Insurable Interest Exist?

*In property insurance, the insurable interest must exist at the time of the loss.* There are two reasons for this requirement. First, most property insurance contracts are contracts of indemnity. If an insurable interest does not exist at the time of loss, the insured would not incur any financial loss. Hence, the principle of indemnity would be violated if payment were made. For example, if Mark sells his home to Susan, and a fire occurs before the insurance on the home is cancelled, Mark cannot collect because he no longer has an insurable interest in the property. Susan cannot collect either under Mark's policy because she is not named as an insured under his policy.

Second, you may not have an insurable interest in the property when the contract is first written but

may expect to have an insurable interest in the future, at the time of possible loss. For example, in ocean marine insurance, it is common to insure a return cargo by a contract entered into prior to the ship's departure. However, the policy may not cover the goods until they are on board the ship as the insured's property. Although an insurable interest does not exist when the contract is first written, you can still collect to the extent of your interest if you have an insurable interest in the goods at the time of loss.

*In contrast, in life insurance, the insurable interest requirement must be met only at the inception of the policy, not at the time of death.* Life insurance is not a contract of indemnity but is a valued policy that pays a stated sum upon the insured's death. Because the beneficiary has only a legal claim to receive the policy proceeds, the beneficiary does not have to show that a financial loss has been incurred by the insured's death. For example, if Michelle takes out a policy on her husband's life and later gets a divorce, she is entitled to the policy proceeds upon the death of her former husband if she has kept the insurance in force. The insurable interest requirement must be met only at the inception of the contract (see Insight 9.1).

## PRINCIPLE OF SUBROGATION

The principle of subrogation strongly supports the principle of indemnity. **Subrogation** *means substitution of the insurer in place of the insured for the purpose of claiming indemnity from a third party for a loss covered by insurance.* Stated differently, the insurer is entitled to recover from a negligent third party any loss payments made to the insured. For example, assume that a negligent motorist fails to stop at a red light and smashes into Megan's car, causing damage in the amount of $5000. If she has collision insurance on her car, her insurer will pay the physical damage loss to the car (less any deductible) and then attempt to collect from the negligent motorist who caused the accident. Alternatively, Megan could attempt to collect directly from the negligent motorist for the damage to her car. Subrogation does not apply unless the insurer makes a loss payment. However, to the extent that a loss payment is made, the insured gives to the insurer any legal rights to collect damages from the negligent third party.

## INSIGHT 9.1

### Corporation Lacking Insurable Interest at Time of Death Can Receive Life Insurance Proceeds

**Legal Facts**

A corporation purchased a $1 million life insurance policy on an officer who was a 20 percent stockholder in the company. Shortly thereafter, the officer sold his stock and resigned. Two years later he died. The insurer paid the death proceeds to the corporation. The personal representative of the deceased insured's estate claimed the insurable interest was only temporary and must continue until death. Is the corporation entitled to the policy proceeds even though it had no insurable interest at the time of death?

**Court Decision**

The court rejected the argument that the corporation's insurable interest must continue until death.[a] Its decision reflects the principle that termination of an insurable interest before the policy matures does not affect the policyholder's right of recovery under a policy valid at its inception. The insurable interest requirement must be met only at the inception of the policy.

[a]*In re Al Zuni Trading*, 947 F.2d 1402 (1991).

SOURCE: Adapted from Buist M. Anderson, *Anderson on Life Insurance, 1992 Supplement* (Boston, MA: Little, Brown, 1992), p. 29. ©1992, Little, Brown and Company.

## Purposes of Subrogation

Subrogation has three basic purposes. *First, subrogation prevents the insured from collecting twice for the same loss.* In the absence of subrogation, the insured could collect from his or her insurer and from the person who caused the loss. The principle of indemnity would be violated because the insured would be profiting from a loss.

*Second, subrogation is used to hold the negligent person responsible for the loss.* By exercising its subrogation rights, the insurer can collect from the negligent person who caused the loss.

*Finally, subrogation helps to hold down insurance rates.* Subrogation recoveries are reflected in the rate-making process, which tends to hold rates below where they would be in the absence of subrogation. Although insurers pay for covered losses, subrogation recoveries reduce the loss payments.

## Importance of Subrogation

You should keep in mind several important corollaries of the principle of subrogation.

1. *The general rule is that by exercising its subrogation rights, the insurer is entitled only to the amount it has paid under the policy.*[8] Some insureds may not be fully indemnified after a loss because of insufficient insurance, satisfaction of a deductible, or legal expenses in trying to recover from a negligent third party. Many policies, however, now have a provision that states how a subrogation recovery is to be shared between the insured and insurer.

In the absence of any policy provision, the courts have used different rules in determining how a subrogation recovery is to be shared. *One view is that the insured must be reimbursed in full for the loss; the insurer is then entitled to any remaining balance up to the insurer's interest, with any remainder going to the insured.*[9] For example, Andrew has a $200,000 home insured for only $160,000 under a homeowners policy. Assume that the house is totally destroyed in a fire because of faulty wiring by an electrician. The insurer would pay $160,000 to Andrew and then attempt to collect from the negligent electrician. After exercising its subrogation rights against the negligent electrician, assume that the insurer has a net recovery of $100,000 (after deduction of legal expenses). Andrew would receive $40,000, and the insurer can retain the balance of $60,000.

2. *After a loss, the insured cannot impair or interfere with the insurer's subrogation rights.* The insured cannot do anything after a loss that interferes with the insurer's right to proceed against a negligent third party. For example, if the insured waives the right to sue the negligent party, the right to collect from the

insurer for the loss is also waived. This could happen if the insured admits fault in an auto accident or attempts to settle a collision loss with the negligent driver without the insurer's consent. If the insurer's right to subrogate against the negligent motorist is adversely affected, the insured's right to collect from the insurer is forfeited.[10]

3. *Subrogation does not apply to life insurance contracts.* Life insurance is not a contract of indemnity, and subrogation has relevance only for contracts of indemnity.

4. *The insurer cannot subrogate against its own insureds.* If the insurer could recover a loss payment for a covered loss from an insured, the basic purpose of purchasing the insurance would be defeated.

## PRINCIPLE OF UTMOST GOOD FAITH

An insurance contract is based on the **principle of utmost good faith**—*that is, a higher degree of honesty is imposed on both parties to an insurance contract than is imposed on parties to other contracts.* This principle has its historical roots in ocean marine insurance. An ocean marine underwriter had to place great faith in statements made by the applicant for insurance concerning the cargo to be shipped. The property to be insured may not have been visually inspected, and the contract may have been formed in a location far removed from the cargo and ship. Thus, the principle of utmost good faith imposed a high degree of honesty on the applicant for insurance.

The principle of utmost good faith is supported by three important legal doctrines: representations, concealment, and warranty.

### Representations

**Representations** *are statements made by the applicant for insurance.* For example, if you apply for life insurance, you may be asked questions concerning your age, weight, height, occupation, state of health, family history, and other relevant questions. Your answers to these questions are called representations.

The legal significance of a representation is that the insurance contract is voidable at the insurer's option if the representation is (1) material, (2) false, and (3) relied on by the insurer.[11] **Material** *means that if the insurer knew the true facts, the policy would not have been issued, or it would have been issued on different terms. False* means that the statement is not true or is misleading. *Reliance* means that the insurer relies on the misrepresentation in issuing the policy at a specified premium.

For example, Joseph applies for life insurance and states in the application that he has not visited a doctor within the last five years. However, six months earlier, he had surgery for lung cancer. In this case, he has made a statement that is false, material, and relied on by the insurer. Therefore, the policy is voidable at the insurer's option. If Joseph dies shortly after the policy is issued, say three months, the company could contest the death claim on the basis of a material misrepresentation. Insight 9.2 provides an additional application of this legal principle.

---

## INSIGHT 9.2

### Auto Insurer Denies Coverage Because of Material Misrepresentation

**Legal Facts**

The insured misrepresented that she had no traffic violation convictions in the prior three-year period. After an accident, a check of her record revealed that she had two speeding tickets in that period. The insurer denied coverage.

**Court Decision**

State law regarding the voiding of insurance requires that the misrepresentation must be material and made with the intent to deceive. The insured claimed that she had forgotten about the two tickets, and therefore had no intent to deceive. The court ruled that it is unlikely she would forget both events. Decision is for the insurer.[a]

[a]*Benton v. Shelter Mutual Ins. Co.,* 550 So.2d 832 (La.App.2 Cir. 1989).

SOURCE: "Misrepresentations in Auto Coverage Applications," *FC&S Bulletins,* Miscellaneous Property section, Fire and Marine volume, July 2004, p. M 35.6.

If an applicant for insurance states an opinion or belief that later turns out to be wrong, the insurer must prove that the applicant spoke fraudulently and intended to deceive the company before it can deny payment of a claim. For example, assume that you are asked if you have high blood pressure when you apply for health insurance, and you answer "no" to the question. If the insurer later discovers you have high blood pressure, to deny payment of a claim, it must prove that you intended to deceive the company. Thus, a statement of opinion or belief must also be fraudulent before the insurer can refuse to pay a claim.

An **innocent misrepresentation** of a material fact, if relied on by the insurer, also makes the contract voidable. An innocent misrepresentation is one that is unintentional. A majority of court opinions have ruled that an innocent misrepresentation of a material fact makes the contract voidable.

Finally, the doctrine of material misrepresentations also applies to statements made by the insured after a loss occurs. If the insured submits a fraudulent proof of loss or misrepresents the value of the items damaged, the insurer has the right to void the coverage (see Insight 9.3).

### Concealment

The doctrine of concealment also supports the principle of utmost good faith. *A concealment is intentional failure of the applicant for insurance to reveal a material fact to the insurer*. Concealment is the same thing as nondisclosure; that is, the applicant for insurance deliberately withholds material information from the insurer. The legal effect of a material concealment is the same as a misrepresentation—the contract is voidable at the insurer's option.

To deny a claim based on concealment, a nonmarine insurer must prove two things: (1) the concealed fact was known by the insured to be material, and (2) the insured intended to defraud the insurer.[12] For example, Joseph DeBellis applied for a life insurance policy on his life. He had an extensive criminal record. Five months after the policy was issued, he was murdered. The death certificate named the deceased as Joseph DeLuca, his true name. The insurer denied payment on the grounds that Joseph had concealed a material fact by not revealing his true identity and that he had an extensive criminal record. In finding for the insurer, the court held that intentional concealment of his true identity was material and breached the obligation of good faith.[13]

### Warranty

The doctrine of warranty also reflects the principle of utmost good faith. *A* **warranty** *is a statement that becomes part of the insurance contract and is guaranteed by the maker to be true in all respects*.[14] For example, in exchange for a reduced premium, a liquor store owner may warrant that an approved burglar alarm system will be operational at all times. A bank may warrant that a guard will be on the premises twenty-four hours a day. Likewise, a business firm may warrant that an automatic sprinkler system will be in working order throughout the term of the policy. A clause describing the warranty becomes part of the contract.

---

## INSIGHT 9.3

### Insurer Voids Coverage Because of Misrepresentations in Proof of Loss

**Legal Facts**

The insured experienced a burglary loss of $9000 and misrepresented the value of the items stolen. The insured provided receipts that showed a purchase price of $900 for a stereo set and $1500 for video equipment. The insurer proved that the stereo set cost only $400, and that the insured had not purchased the video equipment.

**Court Decision**

The court allowed the insurer to void coverage in its entirety. The court ruled that (1) insureds have an obligation to provide the insurer with true receipts, submit to an examination under oath, and provide a sworn proof of loss, and (2) the misrepresentations were material because they were made to mislead, discourage, or deflect the insurer's investigation of the claim.[a]

[a] *Passero v. Allstate Ins. Co.* 554 N.E.2d 384 (Ill. App. lst Dist. 1990).

Source: "Misrepresentation in Proofs of Loss," *FC&S Bulletins*, Miscellaneous Property section, Fire and Marine volume, July 2004, p. M 35.7.

Based on common law, in its strictest form, warranty is a harsh legal doctrine. Any breach of the warranty, even if minor or not material, allowed the insurer to deny payment of a claim. During the early days of insurance, statements made by the applicant for insurance were considered to be warranties. If the statement were untrue in any respect, even if not material, the insurer could deny payment of a claim based on a breach of warranty.

Because strict application of the warranty doctrine harmed many insureds, state legislatures and the courts have softened and modified the harsh common law doctrine of warranty over time. Some modifications of the warranty doctrine are summarized as follows:

- Statements made by applicants for insurance are considered to be representations and not warranties. Thus, the insurer cannot deny liability for a claim if a misrepresentation is not material.
- Most courts will interpret a breach of warranty liberally in those cases where a minor breach affects the risk only temporarily or insignificantly.
- Statutes have been passed that allow the insured to recover for a loss unless the breach of warranty actually contributed to the loss.

## REQUIREMENTS OF AN INSURANCE CONTRACT

An insurance policy is based on the law of contracts. To be legally enforceable, an insurance contract must meet four basic requirements: offer and acceptance, consideration, competent parties, and legal purpose.

### Offer and Acceptance

The first requirement of a binding insurance contract is that there must be an **offer and acceptance** of its terms. In most cases, the applicant for insurance makes the offer, and the company accepts or rejects the offer. An agent merely solicits or invites the prospective insured to make an offer. The requirement of offer and acceptance can be examined in greater detail by making a careful distinction between property and casualty insurance, and life insurance.

In property and casualty insurance, the offer and acceptance can be oral or written. In the absence of specific legislation to the contrary, oral insurance contracts are valid. As a practical matter, most property and casualty insurance contracts are in written form. The applicant for insurance fills out the application and pays the first premium (or promises to pay the first premium). This step constitutes the offer. The agent then accepts the offer on behalf of the insurance company. In property and casualty insurance, agents typically have the power to bind their companies through use of a binder. A **binder** *is a temporary contract for insurance and can be either written or oral.* The binder obligates the company immediately prior to receipt of the application and issuance of the policy. Thus, the insurance contract can be effective immediately, because the agent accepts the offer on behalf of the company. This procedure is usually followed in personal lines of property and casualty insurance, including homeowners policies and auto insurance. However, in some cases, the agent is not authorized to bind the company, and the application must be sent to the company for approval. The company may then accept the offer and issue the policy or reject the application.

In life insurance, the procedures followed are different. A life insurance agent does not have the power to bind the insurer. Therefore, the application for life insurance is always in writing, and the applicant must be approved by the insurer before the life insurance is in force. The usual procedure is for the applicant to fill out the application and pay the first premium. A **conditional premium receipt** is then given to the applicant. The most common conditional receipt is the "insurability premium receipt." If the applicant is found insurable according to the insurer's normal underwriting standards, the life insurance becomes effective as of the date of the application. Some insurability receipts make the life insurance effective on the date of the application or the date of the medical exam, whichever is later.

For example, assume that Aaron applies for a $100,000 life insurance policy on Monday. He fills out the application, pays the first premium, and receives a conditional premium receipt from the agent. On Tuesday morning, he takes a physical examination, and on Tuesday afternoon, he is killed in a boating accident. The application and premium will still be forwarded to the insurer, as if he were still alive. If he is found insurable according to the insurer's underwriting rules, the life insurance is in force, and $100,000 will be paid to his beneficiary.

However, if the applicant for life insurance does not pay the first premium when the application is filled out, a different set of rules applies. Before the life insurance is in force, the policy must be issued and delivered to the applicant, the first premium must be paid, and the applicant must be in good health when the policy is delivered. Insurers also require that there must be no interim medical treatment between submission of the application and delivery of the policy. These requirements are considered to be "conditions precedent"—in other words, they must be fulfilled before the life insurance is in force.[15]

## Consideration

The second requirement of a valid insurance contract is **consideration**—the value that each party gives to the other. The insured's consideration is payment of the premium (or a promise to pay the premium) plus an agreement to abide by the conditions specified in the policy. The insurer's consideration is the promise to do certain things as specified in the contract. This promise can include paying for a loss from an insured peril, providing certain services, such as loss prevention and safety services, or defending the insured in a liability lawsuit.

## Competent Parties

The third requirement of a valid insurance contract is that each party must be **legally competent**. *This means the parties must have legal capacity to enter into a binding contract.* Most adults are legally competent to enter into insurance contracts, but there are some exceptions. Insane persons, intoxicated persons, and corporations that act outside the scope of their authority cannot enter into enforceable insurance contracts. Minors generally lack full legal capacity to enter into a binding insurance contract. Such contracts usually are voidable by the minor, which means the minor can disaffirm the contract. However, most states have enacted laws that allow minors to enter into a valid life insurance contract at a specified age. Depending on the state, the age limit varies from ages 14 to 18; age 15 is the most common.

The insurer must also be legally competent. Insurers generally must be licensed to sell insurance in the state, and the insurance sold must be within the scope of its charter or certificate of incorporation.

## Legal Purpose

A final requirement is that the contract must be for a **legal purpose**. An insurance contract that encourages or promotes something illegal or immoral is contrary to the public interest and cannot be enforced. For example, a drug dealer who sells heroin and other illegal drugs cannot purchase a property insurance policy that would cover seizure of the drugs by the police. This type of contract obviously is not enforceable because it would promote illegal activities that are contrary to the public interest.

# DISTINCT LEGAL CHARACTERISTICS OF INSURANCE CONTRACTS

Insurance contracts have distinct legal characteristics that make them different from other legal contracts. Several distinctive legal characteristics have already been discussed. As we noted earlier, most property and casualty insurance contracts are contracts of indemnity; all insurance contracts must be supported by an insurable interest; and insurance contracts are based on utmost good faith. Other distinct legal characteristics are as follows:

- Aleatory contract
- Unilateral contract
- Conditional contract
- Personal contract
- Contract of adhesion

## Aleatory Contract

An insurance contract is aleatory rather than commutative. An **aleatory contract** *is a contract where the values exchanged may not be equal but depend on an uncertain event.* Depending on chance, one party may receive a value out of proportion to the value that is given. For example, assume that Jessica pays a premium of $600 for a $200,000 homeowners policy. If the home were totally destroyed by fire shortly thereafter, she would collect an amount that greatly exceeds the premium paid. On the other hand, a homeowner may faithfully pay premiums for many years and never have a loss.

In contrast, other commercial contracts are commutative. *A* **commutative contract** *is one in* *which the values exchanged by both parties are theoretically equal.* For example, the purchaser of real estate normally pays a price that is viewed to be equal to the value of the property.

Although the essence of an aleatory contract is chance, or the occurrence of some fortuitous event, an insurance contract is not a gambling contract. Gambling creates a new speculative risk that did not exist before the transaction. Insurance, however, is a technique for handling an already existing pure risk. Thus, although both gambling and insurance are aleatory in nature, an insurance contract is not a gambling contract because no new risk is created.

## Unilateral Contract

An insurance contract is a unilateral contract. *A* **unilateral contract** *means that only one party makes a legally enforceable promise.* In this case, only the insurer makes a legally enforceable promise to pay a claim or provide other services to the insured. After the first premium is paid, and the insurance is in force, the insured cannot be legally forced to pay the premiums or to comply with the policy provisions. Although the insured must continue to pay the premiums to receive payment for a loss, he or she cannot be legally forced to do so. However, if the premiums are paid, the insurer must accept them and must continue to provide the protection promised under the contract.

In contrast, most commercial contracts are *bilateral* in nature. Each party makes a legally enforceable promise to the other party. If one party fails to perform, the other party can insist on performance or can sue for damages because of the breach of contract.

## Conditional Contract

An insurance contract is a **conditional contract**. That is, the insurer's obligation to pay a claim depends on whether the insured or the beneficiary has complied with all policy conditions. **Conditions** *are provisions inserted in the policy that qualify or place limitations on the insurer's promise to perform.* The conditions section imposes certain duties on the insured if he or she wishes to collect for a loss. Although the insured is not compelled to abide by the policy conditions, he or she must do so to collect for an insured loss.

The insurer is not obligated to pay a claim if the policy conditions are not met. For example, under a homeowners policy, the insured must give immediate notice of a loss. If the insured delays for an unreasonable period in reporting the loss, the insurer can refuse to pay the claim on the grounds that a policy condition has been violated.

## Personal Contract

In property insurance, insurance is a **personal contract**, *which means the contract is between the insured and the insurer.* Strictly speaking, a property insurance contract does not insure property, but insures the owner of property against loss. The owner of the insured property is indemnified if the property is damaged or destroyed. Because the contract is personal, the applicant for insurance must be acceptable to the insurer and must meet certain underwriting standards regarding character, morals, and credit.

A property insurance contract normally cannot be assigned to another party without the insurer's consent. If property is sold to another person, the new owner may not be acceptable to the insurer. *Thus, the insurer's consent is required before a property insurance policy can be validly assigned to another party.* In practice, new property owners get their own insurance, so consent of the previous insurer is not required. In contrast, a life insurance policy can be freely assigned to anyone without the insurer's consent because the assignment does not usually alter the risk or increase the probability of death.

Conversely, a loss payment for a property loss can be assigned to another party without the insurer's consent. Although the insurer's consent is not required, the contract may require that the insurer be notified of the assignment of the proceeds to another party.

## Contract of Adhesion

*A* **contract of adhesion** *means the insured must accept the entire contract, with all of its terms and conditions.* The insurer drafts and prints the policy, and the insured generally must accept the entire document and cannot insist that certain provisions be added or deleted or the contract rewritten to suit the insured. Although the contract can be altered by the addition of endorsements and riders or other forms, the contract is drafted by the insurer. To redress the imbalance that exists in such a situation, *the courts have ruled that any ambiguities or uncertainties in the contract are construed against the insurer.* If the policy is ambiguous, the insured gets the benefit of the doubt.

The general rule that ambiguities in insurance contracts are construed against the insurer is reinforced by the principle of reasonable expectations. *The* **principle of reasonable expectations** *states that an insured is entitled to coverage under a policy that he or she reasonably expects it to provide, and that to be effective, exclusions or qualifications must be conspicuous, plain, and clear.*[16] Some courts have ruled that insureds are entitled to the protection that they reasonably expect to have, and that technical restrictions in the contract should be clear and conspicuous. For example, in one case, a liability insurer refused to defend the insured on the grounds that the policy excluded intentional acts. The court ruled that the insurer was responsible for the defense costs. The insured had a reasonable expectation that defense costs were covered under the policy because the policy covered other types of intentional acts.[17]

# LAW AND THE INSURANCE AGENT

An insurance contract normally is sold by an agent who represents the principal (the insurer). An agent is someone who has the authority to act on behalf of someone else. The principal (insurer) is the party for whom action is to be taken. Thus, if Patrick has the authority to solicit, create, or terminate an insurance contract on behalf of Apex Insurance Company, he would be the agent and the Apex Insurance Company would be the principal.

## Law of Agency

Important rules of law govern the actions of agents and their relationship to insureds. They include the following:[18]

- There is no presumption of an agency relationship.
- An agent must have authority to represent the principal.

- A principal is responsible for the acts of agents acting within the scope of their authority.
- Limitations can be placed on the powers of agents.

**No Presumption of an Agency Relationship**    There is no automatic presumption that one person legally can act as an agent for another. Some visible evidence of an agency relationship must exist. For example, a person who claims to be an agent for an auto insurer may collect premiums and then abscond with the funds. The auto insurer is not legally responsible for the person's actions if it has done nothing to create the impression that an agency relationship exists. However, if the person has a business card, rate data, and application blanks supplied by the insurer, then it can be presumed that a legitimate agent is acting on behalf of that insurer.

**Authority to Represent the Principal**    An agent must be authorized to represent the principal. An agent's authority comes from three sources: (1) express authority, (2) implied authority, and (3) apparent authority.

**Express authority** refers to powers specifically conferred on the agent. These powers are normally stated in the **agency agreement** between the agent and the principal. The agency agreement may also withhold certain powers. For example, a life insurance agent may be given the power to solicit applicants and arrange for physical examinations. Certain powers, however, such as the right to extend the time for payment of premiums or the right to alter contractual provisions in the policy, may be denied.

Agents also have **implied authority**. Implied authority refers to the authority of the agent to perform all incidental acts necessary to fulfill the purposes of the agency agreement. For example, an agent may have the express authority to deliver a life insurance policy to the client. It follows that the agent also has the implied power to collect the first premium.

Finally, an agent may bind the principal by **apparent authority**. If an agent acts with apparent authority to do certain things, and a third party is led to believe that the agent is acting within the scope of reasonable and appropriate authority, the principal can be bound by the agent's actions. Third parties have to show only that they have exercised due diligence in determining the agent's authority based on the agent's actual authority or conduct of the principal. For example, an agent for an auto insurer may frequently grant his or her clients an extension of time to pay overdue premiums. If the insurer has not expressly granted this right to the agent and has not taken any action to deal with the violation of company policy, it could not later deny liability for a loss on the grounds that the agent lacked authority to grant the time extension. The insurer first would have to notify all policyholders of the limitations on the agent's powers.

**Principal Responsible for Acts of Agents**   Another rule of agency law is that the principal is responsible for all acts of agents when they are acting within the scope of their authority. This includes fraudulent acts, omissions, and misrepresentations.

*In addition, knowledge of the agent is presumed to be knowledge of the principal with respect to matters within the scope of the agency relationship.* For example, if a life insurance agent knows that an applicant for life insurance is addicted to alcohol, this knowledge is imputed to the insurer even though the agent deliberately omits this information from the application. Thus, if the insurer issues the policy, it cannot later attack the validity of the policy on the grounds of alcohol addiction and the concealment of a material fact.

**Limitations on the Powers of Agents**   Insurers can place limitations on the powers of agents. The limitations are generally effective when they are properly communicated to the policyholder and do not conflict with the law. This is done by a *nonwaiver clause* in the application or policy, which typically states that only certain representatives of the company, such as executive officers, can extend the time to pay premiums or to change the terms of the policy.

## Waiver and Estoppel

The doctrines of waiver and estoppel have direct relevance to the law of agency and to the powers of insurance agents. The practical significance of these concepts is that an insurer legally may be required to pay a claim that it ordinarily would not have to pay.

**Waiver** *is defined as the voluntary relinquishment of a known legal right.* If the insurer voluntarily waives a legal right under the contract, it cannot later deny payment of a claim by the insured on the grounds that such a legal right was violated. For example, assume that an insurer receives an application for insurance at its home office, and that the application contains an incomplete or missing answer. Assume that the insurer does not contact the applicant for additional information, and the policy is issued. The insurer later could not deny payment of a claim on the basis of an incomplete application. In effect, the insurer has waived its requirement that the application be complete by issuing the policy.

The legal term *estoppel* was derived centuries ago from the English common law. **Estoppel** *occurs when a representation of fact made by one person to another person is reasonably relied on by that person to such an extent that it would be inequitable to allow the first person to deny the truth of the representation.*[19] Stated simply, if one person makes a statement of fact to another person who then reasonably relies on the statement to his or her detriment, the first person cannot later deny the statement was made. The law of estoppel is designed to prevent persons from changing their minds to the detriment of another party. For example, assume that an applicant for health insurance tells the agent of a health problem, and the agent assures the applicant that the health problem does not have to be stated in the application. The insurer could be estopped from denying benefits on the grounds that this information was not included in the application.

## CASE APPLICATION

Jeff is a book dealer who purchased a building from Richard. Jeff obtained a loan from the Gateway Bank to purchase the building, which held a mortgage on the building. Jeff planned to store his inventory of books in the building. He also planned to use part of the building for a fast-food restaurant. When Jeff applied for property insurance on the building, he did not tell the agent about the fast-food restaurant because premiums would be substantially higher. Eight months after the policy was issued, a fire occurred in the restaurant that caused substantial damage to the building.

a. Do any of the following parties have an insurable interest in the building at the time of loss? Explain your answer.

   1. Jeff

   2. Richard

   3. Gateway Bank

b. Richard told Jeff he could save money by taking over Richard's insurance instead of purchasing a new policy. Can Richard validly assign his existing property insurance policy to Jeff without notifying the insurer? Explain your answer.

c. Could Jeff's insurer deny coverage for the fire loss based on a material concealment? Explain your answer.

d. Investigation of the fire revealed that an electrician improperly wired an electrical outlet in the restaurant, which caused the fire. Explain how subrogation might apply in this case.

## SUMMARY

- The principle of indemnity states that the insurer should not pay more than the actual amount of the loss; in other words, the insured should not profit from a covered loss.

- There are several exceptions to the principle of indemnity. These exceptions include a valued policy, valued policy laws, replacement cost insurance, and life insurance.

- The principle of insurable interest means that the insured must stand to lose financially if a loss occurs. All insurance contracts must be supported by an insurable interest to be legally enforceable. There are three purposes of the insurable interest requirement:

  To prevent gambling

  To reduce moral hazard

  To measure the amount of loss in property insurance

- In property and casualty insurance, the ownership of property, potential legal liability, secured creditors, and contractual rights can support the insurable interest requirement.

- In life insurance, the question of an insurable interest does not arise when a person purchases life insurance on his or her own life. If life insurance is purchased on the life of another person, there must be an insurable interest in that person's life. Close family ties, blood, marriage, or a pecuniary (financial) interest will satisfy the insurable interest requirement in life insurance.

- In property insurance, the insurable interest requirement must be met at the time of loss. In life insurance, the insurable interest requirement must be met only at the inception of the policy.

- The principle of subrogation means that the insurer is entitled to recover from a negligent third party any loss payments made to the insured. The purposes of subrogation are to prevent the insured from collecting twice for the same loss, to hold the negligent person responsible for the loss, and to hold down insurance rates.

- If the insurer exercises its subrogation rights, the insured generally must be fully restored before the insurer can retain any sums collected from the negligent third party. Also, the insured cannot do anything that might impair the insurer's subrogation rights. However, the insurer can waive its subrogation rights in the contract either before or after the loss. Finally, subrogation does not apply to life insurance contracts.

- The principle of utmost good faith means that a higher degree of honesty is imposed on both parties to an insurance contract than is imposed on parties to other contracts.

- The legal doctrines of representations, concealment, and warranty support the principle of utmost good faith. Representations are statements made by the applicant for insurance. The insurer can deny payment for a claim if the representation is material and false, and is relied on by the insurer in issuing the policy at a specified premium. In the case of statements of belief or opinion, the misrepresentation must also be fraudulent before the insurer can deny a claim. Concealment of a material fact has the same legal effect as a misrepresentation: the contract is voidable at the insurer's option.

- A warranty is a statement of fact or a promise made by the insured, which is part of the insurance contract and must be true if the insurer is to be liable under the contract. Based on common law, any breach of the warranty, even if slight, allowed the insurer to deny payment of a claim. The harsh common law doctrine of a warranty, however, has been modified and softened by court decisions and statutes.

- To have a valid insurance contract, four requirements must be met:

    There must be an offer and acceptance.

    Consideration must be exchanged.

    The parties to the contract must be legally competent.

    The contract must be for a legal purpose.

- Insurance contracts have distinct legal characteristics. An insurance contract is an *aleatory contract* where the values exchanged may not be equal and depend on the occurrence of an uncertain event. An insurance contract is *unilateral* because only the insurer makes a legally enforceable promise. An insurance contract is *conditional* because the insurer's obligation to pay a claim depends on whether the insured or beneficiary has complied with all policy provisions. A property insurance contract is a *personal contract* between the insured and insurer and cannot be validly assigned to another party without the insurer's consent. A life insurance policy is freely assignable without the insurer's consent. Finally, insurance is a *contract of adhesion*, which means the insured must accept the entire contract, with all of its terms and conditions; and if there is an ambiguity in the contract, it will be construed against the insurer.

- Four general rules of agency govern the actions of agents and their relationship to insureds:

    There is no presumption of an agency relationship.

    An agent must have the authority to represent the principal.

A principal is responsible for the actions of agents acting within the scope of their authority.

Limitations can be placed on the powers of agents.

- An agent can bind the principal based on express authority, implied authority, and apparent authority.

- Based on the legal doctrines of waiver and estoppel, an insurer may be required to pay a claim that it ordinarily would not have to pay.

## KEY CONCEPTS AND TERMS

Actual cash value (167)
Agency agreement (177)
Aleatory contract (175)
Apparent authority (177)
Binder (174)
Broad evidence rule (167)
Commutative contract (175)
Concealment (173)
Conditional contract (176)
Conditions (176)
Conditional premium
 receipt (174)
Consideration (175)
Contract of adhesion (176)
Estoppel (178)
Express authority (177)
Fair market value (167)
Implied authority (177)
Innocent
 misrepresentation (173)
Legal purpose (175)
Legally competent (175)
Material fact (172)
Offer and acceptance (174)
Pecuniary (financial)
 interest (170)
Personal contract (176)
Principle of
 indemnity (166)
Principle of insurable
 interest (169)
Principle of reasonable
 expectations (177)
Principle of utmost
 good faith (172)
Replacement cost
 insurance (168)
Representations (172)
Subrogation (171)
Unilateral contract (176)
Valued policy (167)
Valued policy law (168)
Waiver (178)
Warranty (173)

## REVIEW QUESTIONS

1. a. Explain the principle of indemnity.
   b. How is actual cash value calculated?
   c. How does the concept of actual cash value support the principle of indemnity?

2. a. What is a valued policy? Why is it used?
   b. What is a valued policy law?
   c. What is a replacement cost policy?

3. a. Explain the meaning of an insurable interest.
   b. Why is an insurable interest required in every insurance contract?

4. a. Explain the principle of subrogation.
   b. Why is subrogation used?

5. Explain the following legal doctrines:
   a. Misrepresentation
   b. Concealment
   c. Warranty

6. List the four requirements that must be met to form a valid insurance contract.

7. Insurance contracts have certain legal characteristics that distinguish them from other contracts. Explain the following legal characteristics of insurance contracts.
   a. Aleatory contract
   b. Unilateral contract
   c. Conditional contract
   d. Personal contract
   e. Contract of adhesion

8. Explain the general rules of agency that govern the actions of agents and their relationship to insureds.

9. Identify three sources of authority that enable an agent to bind the principal.

10. Explain the meaning of:
    a. Waiver
    b. Estoppel

## APPLICATION QUESTIONS

1. Jake borrowed $800,000 from the Gateway Bank to purchase a fishing boat. He keeps the boat at a dock owned by the Harbor Company. He uses the boat to earn income by fishing. Jake also has a contract with the White Shark Fishing Company to transport tuna from one port to another.
   a. Do any of the following parties have an insurable interest in Jake or his property? If an insurable interest exists, explain the extent of the interest.
      1. Gateway Bank
      2. Harbor Company
      3. White Shark Fishing Company
   b. If Jake did not own the boat but operated it on behalf of the White Shark Fishing Company, would he have an insurable interest in the boat? Explain.

2. Ashley purchased a dining room set for $5000 and insured the furniture on an actual cash value basis. Three years later, the set was destroyed in a fire. At the time of loss, the property had depreciated in value by 50 percent. The replacement cost of a new dining room set at the time of loss was $6000. Ignoring any deductible, how much will Ashley collect from her insurer? Explain your answer.

3. Nicholas owns a laptop computer that was stolen. The laptop cost $1000 when it was purchased five years ago. A similar laptop computer today can be purchased for $500. Assuming that the laptop was 50 percent depreciated at the time the theft occurred, what is the actual cash value of the loss?

4. Megan owns an antique table that has a current market value of $12,000. The table is specifically insured for $12,000 under a valued policy. The table is totally destroyed when a tornado touches down and damages Megan's home. At the time of loss, the table had an estimated market value of $10,000. How much will Megan collect for the loss? Explain your answer.

5. A drunk driver ran a red light and smashed into Kristen's car. The cost to repair the car is $8000. She has collision insurance on her car with a $500 deductible.
   a. Can Kristen collect from both the negligent driver's insurer and her own insurer? Explain your answer.
   b. Explain how subrogation supports the principle of indemnity.

6. One requirement for the formation of a valid insurance contract is that the contract must be for a legal purpose.
   a. Identify three factors, other than the legal purpose requirement, that are essential to the formation of a binding insurance contract.
   b. Explain how each of the three requirements in part (a) is fulfilled when the applicant applies for an auto insurance policy.

7. Nicole is applying for a health insurance policy. She has a chronic liver ailment and other health problems. She honestly disclosed the true facts concerning her medical history to the insurance agent. However, the agent did not include all the facts in the application. Instead, the agent stated that he was going to cover the material facts in a separate letter to the insurance company's underwriting department. However, the agent did not furnish the material facts to the insurer, and

the contract was issued as standard. A claim occurred shortly thereafter. After investigating the claim, the insurer denied payment. Nicole contends that the company should pay the claim because she answered honestly all questions that the agent asked.

   a. On what basis can the insurance company deny payment of the claim?

   b. What legal doctrines can Nicole use to support her argument that the claim should be paid?

## INTERNET RESOURCES

■ **FreeAdvice.com** has a section on insurance law that provides considerable consumer information on topics dealing with insurance law. These topics include auto insurance, health insurance, disability insurance, life insurance law, and numerous other topics. Visit the site at

freeadvice.com

■ The **Legal Information Institute at Cornell University Law School** publishes free legal materials online, creates materials that help people understand the law, and explores new technology to enable people find the law more easily. Visit the site at

law.cornell.edu

■ **Lawyers.com** is an online source for identifying qualified legal counsel. The site contains consumer information on numerous legal topics, including insurance. Visit the site at

lawyers.com

## SELECTED REFERENCES

Anderson, Buist M. *Anderson on Life Insurance.* Boston: Little, Brown, 1991. See also *Anderson on Life Insurance, 1996 Supplement.*

Crawford, Muriel L. *Life and Health Insurance Law,* 8th ed. Boston, MA: Irwin/McGraw-Hill, 1998.

*Fire, Casualty & Surety Bulletins,* Fire and Marine volume, Erlanger, KY: National Underwriter Company. These bulletins contain interesting cases concerning the meaning of actual cash value, insurable interest, and other legal concepts.

Graves, Edward E., and Burke A. Christensen, eds. *McGill's Legal Aspects of Life Insurance*, 7th ed. Bryn Mawr, PA: The American College , 2010.

Lorimer, James J., et al., *The Legal Environment of Insurance,* 4th ed., vols. 1 and 2. Malvern, PA: American Institute for Chartered Property and Liability Underwriters, 1993.

"Two Landmark Anti-Stoli Decisions by the Delaware Surpreme Court." *The Insurance Forum,* Vol. 38, No. 12, December, 2011.

Wiening, Eric A. *Foundations of Risk Management and Insurance*, 1st ed. Malvern, PA: American Institute for Chartered Property Casualty Underwriters/Insurance Institute of America, 2002, chs. 11–19.

Wiening, Eric A. and Donald S. Malecki. *Insurance Contract Analysis*, Malvern, PA: American Institute for Chartered Property Casualty Underwriters, 1992.

## NOTES

1. *Jefferson Insurance Company of New York v. Superior Court of Alameda County,* 475 P. 2d 880 (1970).

2. Valued policy laws are in force in Arkansas, Florida, Georgia, Kansas, Louisiana, Minnesota, Mississippi, Missouri, Montana, Nebraska, New Hampshire, North Dakota, Ohio, South Carolina, South Dakota, Tennessee, Texas, West Virginia, and Wisconsin.

3. *Gamel v. Continental Ins. Co.,* 463 S.W. 2d 590 (1971).

4. Edwin W. Patterson, *Essentials of Insurance Law,* 2nd ed. (New York: McGraw-Hill, 1957), pp. 109–111, 154–159.

5. Patterson, p. 114.

6. Edward E. Graves, and Burke A. Christensen, eds., *McGill's Legal Aspects of Life Insurance,* 7th ed. (Bryn Mawr, PA: The American College, 2010), p. 4.13.

7. Patterson, pp. 147–148.

8. James J. Lorimer et al., *The Legal Environment of Insurance,* 3rd ed., vol. 1 (Malvern, PA: American Institute for Property and Liability Underwriters, 1987), p. 376.

9. Lorimer et al., p. 377.

10. Patterson, p. 149.

11. James J. Lorimer et al., *The Legal Environment of Insurance,* 4th ed., vol. 1 (Malvern, PA: American Institute for Chartered Property Casualty Underwriters, 1993), pp. 202–205.

12. Ibid., pp. 112–115.

13. Ibid., pp. 115–116.

14. Edward E. Graves and Burke A. Christensen, eds., *McGill's Legal Aspects of Life Insurance,* 7th ed. (Bryn Mawr, PA: The American College, 2010), p. 5.1.

15. Ibid., pp. 6.14–6.16.

16. James J. Lorimer et al., *The Legal Environment of Insurance,* 3rd ed., vol. 1 (Malvern, PA: American Institute for Property and Liability Underwriters, 1987), pp. 402–403.

17. Ibid., p. 403.

18. Graves and Christensen, pp. 6.4–6.9.

19. Patterson, pp. 495–496.

20. Muriel L. Crawford, *Life & Health Insurance Law,* 8th ed. (Boston, MA: McGraw-Hill/Irwin, 1998), p. 107.

# CHAPTER 10

# ANALYSIS OF INSURANCE CONTRACTS

*"Let's kill all the lawyers."*
William Shakespeare

## LEARNING OBJECTIVES

**After studying this chapter, you should be able to**

◆ Identify the basic parts of any insurance contract.

◆ Explain the meaning of "insured" in an insurance contract.

◆ Describe the common types of deductibles that appear in insurance contracts, including

Straight deductible
Calendar-year deductible

◆ Explain how coinsurance works in a property insurance contract.

◆ Show how coinsurance works in a health insurance contract.

◆ Explain how losses are paid when more than one insurance contract covers the same loss.

*Jason, age 28, is a marketing analyst who recently moved to Dallas, Texas. Jason is an avid stamp collector and has a collection currently worth $30,000. He rented an apartment and purchased a homeowners policy for renters. The policy insures his personal property but contains a number of limits on certain types of property. While on vacation, a thief broke into his home and stole a wide-screen television, desktop computer, stereo set, two watches, and the stamp collection. Jason became upset when his agent stated that, although the loss is covered, the homeowners policy would pay only $1500 for the theft of the stamp collection. Jason made the common mistake of not reading his homeowners policy and understanding the limits on certain types of property.*

*Like Jason, most policyholders do not read or understand the contractual provisions that appear in their insurance policies. Most people own several policies, including auto and homeowners insurance, as well as life and health insurance. These policies are complex legal contracts that reflect the legal principles discussed in Chapter 9.*

*Although insurance contracts are not identical, they contain a number of similar contractual provisions. In this chapter, we discuss the basic parts of an insurance policy, the meaning of "insured," endorsements and riders, deductibles, coinsurance, and other-insurance provisions. An understanding of these topics will provide you with a foundation for a better understanding of specific insurance policies, discussed later in the text.*

## BASIC PARTS OF AN INSURANCE CONTRACT

Despite their complexities, insurance contracts generally can be divided into the following parts:

- Declarations
- Definitions
- Insuring agreement
- Exclusions
- Conditions
- Miscellaneous provisions

Although all insurance contracts do not necessarily contain all six parts in the order given here, such a classification provides a simple and convenient framework for analyzing most insurance contracts.

### Declarations

The declarations section is the first part of an insurance contract.

**Declarations** *are statements that provide information about the particular property or activity to be insured.* Information contained in the declarations section is used for underwriting and rating purposes and for identification of the property or activity that is insured. The declarations section usually can be found on the first page of the policy or on a policy insert.

In property insurance, the declarations page typically contains information concerning the identification of the insurer, name of the insured, location of the property, period of protection, amount of insurance, amount of the premium, size of the deductible (if any), and other relevant information. In life insurance, although the first page of the policy technically is not called a declarations page, it contains the insured's name, age, premium amount, issue date, and policy number.

### Definitions

Insurance contracts typically contain a page or section of definitions. Key words or phrases have quotation marks (". . .") around them. For example, the insurer is frequently referred to as "we," "our," or "us." The named insured is referred to as "you" and "your." The purpose of the various definitions is to define clearly the meaning of key words or phrases so that coverage under the policy can be determined more easily.

## Insuring Agreement

The insuring agreement is the heart of an insurance contract. *The* **insuring agreement** *summarizes the major promises of the insurer.* The insurer agrees to do certain things, such as paying losses from covered perils, providing certain services (such as loss-prevention services), or agreeing to defend the insured in a liability lawsuit.

There are two basic forms of an insuring agreement in property insurance: (1) named-perils coverage and (2) open-perils coverage (formerly called "all-risks" coverage). *Under a* **named-perils policy,** *only those perils specifically named in the policy are covered.* If the peril is not named, it is not covered. For example, in a homeowners policy, personal property is covered for fire, lightning, windstorm, and certain other named perils. Only losses caused by these perils are covered. Flood damage is not covered because flood is not a listed peril.

Under an **open-perils policy,** all losses are covered except those losses specifically excluded. An open-perils policy is also called a **special coverage policy.** *If the loss is not excluded, then it is covered.* For example, the physical damage section of the personal auto policy covers losses to a covered auto. Thus, if a smoker burns a hole in the upholstery, or a bear in a national park damages the vinyl top of a covered auto, the losses would be covered because they are not excluded.

An open-perils policy generally is preferable to named-perils coverage, because the protection is broader with fewer gaps in coverage. If the loss is not excluded, then it is covered. In addition, a greater burden of proof is placed on the insurer to deny a claim. *To deny payment, the insurer must prove that the loss is excluded. In contrast, under a named-perils contract, the burden of proof is on the insured to show that the loss was caused by a named peril.*

Because the meaning of risk is ambiguous, rating organizations generally have deleted the words "risk of" and "all risks" in their policy forms. In the latest edition of the homeowners forms, the Insurance Services Office has deleted the words "risk of," which appeared in earlier editions. The deletion of any reference to "risk of" or "all-risks" is intended to avoid creating unreasonable expectations among policyholders that the policy covers all losses, even those losses that are specifically excluded.

Life insurance is another example of an open-perils policy. Most life insurance contracts cover all causes of death by accident or by disease except for certain exclusions. The major exclusions are suicide during the first two years of the contract; certain aviation hazard exclusions, such as military flying, crop dusting, or sports piloting; and in some contracts, death caused by war.

## Exclusions

**Exclusions** are another basic part of any insurance contract. There are three major types of exclusions (1) excluded perils, (2) excluded losses, and (3) excluded property.

**Excluded Perils**   The contract may exclude certain perils, or causes of loss. In a homeowners policy, the perils of flood, earth movement, and nuclear radiation or radioactive contamination are specifically excluded. In the physical damage section of the personal auto policy, loss to a covered auto is specifically excluded if the car is used as a public taxi.

**Excluded Losses**   Certain types of losses may be excluded. For example, in a homeowners policy, failure of an insured to protect the property from further damage after a loss occurs is excluded. In the personal liability section of a homeowners policy, a liability lawsuit arising out of the operation of an automobile is excluded. Professional liability losses are also excluded; a specific professional liability policy is needed to cover this exposure.

**Excluded Property**   The contract may exclude or place limitations on the coverage of certain property. For example, in a homeowners policy, certain types of personal property are excluded, such as cars, planes, animals, birds, and fish.

**Reasons for Exclusions**   Exclusions are necessary for the following reasons:[1]

- Certain perils considered uninsurable
- Presence of extraordinary hazards
- Coverage provided by other contracts
- Moral hazard problems
- Attitudinal hazard problems
- Coverage not needed by typical insureds

*Exclusions are necessary because the peril may be considered uninsurable by commercial insurers.* A given peril may depart substantially from the ideal requirements of an insurable risk, as discussed in

Chapter 2. For example, most property and casualty insurance contracts exclude losses for potential catastrophic events such as war or exposure to nuclear radiation. A health insurance contract may exclude losses within the direct control of the insured, such as an intentional, self-inflicted injury. Finally, predictable declines in the value of property, such as wear and tear and inherent vice, are not insurable. "Inherent vice" refers to the destruction or damage of property without any tangible external force, such as the tendency of fruit to rot and the tendency of diamonds to crack.

*Exclusions are also used because extraordinary hazards are present.* A hazard is a condition that increases the chance of loss or severity of loss. Because of an extraordinary increase in hazard, a loss may be excluded. For example, the premium for liability insurance under the personal auto policy is based on the assumption that the car is used for personal and recreational use and not as a taxi. The chance of an accident, and a resulting liability lawsuit, is much higher if the car is used as a taxi for hire. Therefore, to provide coverage for a taxi at the same rate charged for a family car could result in inadequate premiums for the insurer and unfair rate discrimination against other insureds who do not use their vehicles as a taxi.

*Exclusions are also necessary because coverage can be better provided by other contracts.* Exclusions are used to avoid duplication of coverage and to limit coverage to the policy best designed to provide it. For example, a car is excluded under a homeowners policy because it is covered under the personal auto policy and other auto insurance contracts. If both policies covered the loss, there would be unnecessary duplication.

*In addition, certain property is excluded because of moral hazard or difficulty in determining and measuring the amount of loss.* For example, homeowners insurance policies drafted by the Insurance Services Office limit the coverage of money to $200. If unlimited amounts of money were covered, fraudulent claims would increase. Also, loss-adjustment problems in determining the exact amount of the loss would also increase. Thus, because of moral hazard, exclusions are used.

*Exclusions are also used to deal with attitudinal hazard (morale hazard).* Attitudinal hazard is carelessness or indifference to a loss, which increases the frequency or severity of loss. Exclusions force individuals to bear losses that result from their own carelessness.

*Finally, exclusions are used because the coverage is not needed by the typical insured.* For example, most homeowners do not own private planes. To cover aircraft as personal property under a homeowners policy would be grossly unfair to the most insureds who do not own planes because premiums would be substantially higher.

## Conditions

Conditions are another important part of an insurance contract. **Conditions** *are provisions in the policy that qualify or place limitations on the insurer's promise to perform.* In effect, the conditions section imposes certain duties on the insured. If the policy conditions are not met, the insurer can refuse to pay the claim. Common policy conditions include notifying the insurer if a loss occurs, protecting the property after a loss, preparing an inventory of damaged personal property, and cooperating with the insurer in the event of a liability suit.

## Miscellaneous Provisions

Insurance contracts also contain a number of miscellaneous provisions. In property and casualty insurance, miscellaneous provisions include cancellation, subrogation, requirements if a loss occurs, assignment of the policy, and other-insurance provisions. In life and health insurance, typical miscellaneous provisions include the grace period, reinstatement of a lapsed policy, and misstatement of age. Details of these provisions are discussed later in the text when specific insurance contracts are analyzed.

## DEFINITION OF "INSURED"

An insurance contract must identify the person or parties who are insured under the policy. For ease in understanding, the meaning of "insured" can be grouped into the following categories:

- Named insured
- First named insured
- Other insureds
- Additional insureds

### Named Insured

*The* **named insured** *is the person or party named on the declarations page of the policy*. The named insured can be one or more persons or parties. For example, Ron and Kay Lukens may be specifically listed as named insured on the declaration page of their homeowners policy.

The words "you" and "your" appear in many policies and refer to the named insured shown in the declarations. Thus, throughout the entire policy, "you" or "your" refers to the named insured.

### First Named Insured

When more than one person or party is named on the declarations page, the order of names is important. The **first named insured** *is the first name that appears on the declarations page of the policy as an insured*. For example, Tim Jones and Bob Brown own a bookstore and are listed as named insureds under a commercial property policy. Tim is the first named insured.

The first named insured has certain additional rights and responsibilities that do not apply to other named insureds. Additional rights include the right to a premium refund and the receipt of a cancellation notice. However, the first named insured is responsible for the payment of premiums and for complying with notice-of-loss requirements.

### Other Insureds

**Other insureds** *are persons or parties who are insured under the named insured's policy even though they are not specifically named in the policy*. For example, a homeowners policy covers resident relatives of the named insured or any person under age 21 who is in the care of an insured. A homeowners policy also covers resident relatives under age 24 who are full-time students and away from home. Likewise, in addition to the named insured, the personal auto policy also covers the named insured's resident relatives and any other person using the auto with the permission of the named insured (see Insight 10.1).

---

## INSIGHT 10.1

### When You Drive Your Roommate's Car, Are You Covered Under Your Policy?

College students frequently drive cars that are owned by roommates or friends. Will your auto insurance cover you when you drive another person's car? Likewise, you may give permission to your roommate or friend to drive your car. Is your roommate or friend covered under your policy? To answer these questions, we must first examine the definition of "insured" for liability coverage that appears in the 2005 Personal Auto Policy.

*"Insured" as used in this Part means:*[a]

1. *You or any "family member for the ownership, maintenance or use of any auto or trailer."*
2. *Any person using "your covered auto."*
3. *For "your covered auto," any person or organization but only with respect to legal responsibility for acts or omissions of a person for whom coverage is afforded under this Part.*
4. *For any auto or "trailer," other than "your covered auto," any other person or organization but only with respect to legal responsibility for acts or omissions of you or any "family member" for whom coverage is afforded under this Part. This provision applies only if the person or organization does not own or hire the auto or "trailer."*

For example, Chris and Karen Swift are the named insureds under the Personal Auto Policy that contains the above provision. Their son, Patrick, lives in a college dormitory during the school year while away from home. Although he does not live at home currently, he qualifies as a family member since the college stay is temporary, and he regards his parents' home as his permanent residence address.

Patrick drives a Honda titled in his parents' names. Because he is a family member, he clearly is insured under the policy. What happens if Patrick allows his girlfriend to drive the Honda? Although she is not a family member, she nevertheless qualifies as "any person using your covered auto." Thus, the girlfriend is insured as well.

What if Patrick occasionally drives his roommate's car? The car is not furnished for his regular use. Assuming Patrick is a family member under his parents' policy, he is insured while driving any car, including the roommate's car.

Finally, assume that Patrick is involved in an auto accident while delivering Thanksgiving food baskets for a local charity. The injured party sues both Patrick and the charitable organization. Patrick clearly is insured and is covered. Is the charity also "insured" under Patrick's policy? The answer is yes. The definition of insured extends coverage to any person or organization legally responsible for any acts or omissions by an insured. Thus, the charitable organization is insured. Patrick's insurer must defend the charity in the suit.

[a]Insurance Services Office, 2005 Personal Auto Policy.

### Additional Insureds

*An* **additional insured** *is a person or party who is added to the named insured's policy by an endorsement.* As a result, an additional insured acquires coverage under the named insured's policy. For example, Ken owns farmland that is leased to a tenant. Ken is concerned about possible legal liability if the tenant injures someone. Ken can request to be added to the tenant's farm liability policy as an additional insured.

## ENDORSEMENTS AND RIDERS

Insurance contracts frequently contain **endorsements and riders.** The terms *endorsements* and *riders* are often used interchangeably and mean the same thing. *In property and casualty insurance, an endorsement is a written provision that adds to, deletes from, or modifies the provisions in the original contract. In life and health insurance, a rider is a provision that amends or changes the original policy.*

There are numerous endorsements in property and casualty insurance that modify, extend, or delete provisions found in the original policy. For example, a homeowners policy excludes coverage for earthquakes. However, an earthquake endorsement can be added that covers damage from an earthquake or from earth movement.

In life and health insurance, numerous riders can be added that increase or decrease benefits, waive a condition of coverage present in the original policy, or amend the basic policy. For example, a waiver-of-premium rider can be added to a life insurance policy. If the insured becomes totally disabled, all future premiums are waived after an elimination period of six months, as long as the insured remains disabled according to the terms of the rider.

An endorsement attached to a policy generally takes precedence over any conflicting terms in the policy. Also, many policies have endorsements that amend the policy to conform to a given state's law.

## DEDUCTIBLES

A deductible is a common policy provision that requires the insured to pay part of the loss. *A* **deductible** *is a provision by which a specified amount is subtracted from the total loss payment that otherwise would be payable.* Deductibles typically are found in property, health, and auto insurance contracts. A deductible is not used in life insurance because the insured's death is always a total loss, and a deductible would simply reduce the face amount of insurance. Also, a deductible generally is not used in personal liability insurance because the insurer must provide a legal defense, even for a small claim. The insurer wants to be involved from the first dollar of loss so as to minimize its ultimate liability for a claim. Also, the premium reduction that would result from a small deductible in personal types of third-party liability coverages would be relatively small.[2]

### Purposes of Deductibles

Deductibles have several important purposes. They include the following:

- To eliminate small claims
- To reduce premiums
- To reduce moral hazard and attitudinal hazard

*A deductible eliminates small claims that are expensive to handle and process.* For each large claim processed, there are numerous small claims, which can be expensive to process. For example, an insurer may incur expenses of $100 or more in processing a $100 claim. Because a deductible eliminates small claims, the insurer's loss-adjustment expenses are reduced.

*Deductibles are also used to reduce premiums paid by the insured.* Because deductibles eliminate small claims, premiums can be substantially reduced. Insurance is not an appropriate technique for paying small losses that can be better budgeted out of personal or business income. Insurance should be used to cover large catastrophic events, such as medical expenses of $500,000 or more from an extended terminal illness. Insurance that protects against a catastrophic loss can be purchased more economically if deductibles are used. This concept of using insurance premiums to pay for large losses rather than for small losses is often called the **large-loss principle.** The objective is to cover large losses that can financially ruin an individual and exclude small losses that can be budgeted out of the person's income.

Other factors being equal, a large deductible is preferable to a small one. For example, some motorists with auto insurance have policies that contain a $250 deductible for collision losses instead of a $500 or larger deductible. They may not be aware of how expensive the extra insurance really is. For example, assume you can purchase collision insurance on your car with a $250 deductible with an annual premium of $900, while a policy with a $500 deductible has an annual premium of $800. If you select the $250 deductible over the $500 deductible, you have an additional $250 of collision insurance, but you must pay an additional $100 in annual premiums. Using a simple cost-benefit analysis, you are paying an additional $100 for an additional $250 of insurance, which is a relatively expensive increment of insurance. When analyzed in this manner, larger deductibles are preferable to smaller deductibles.

*Finally, deductibles are used by insurers to reduce both moral hazard and attitudinal (morale) hazard.* Some dishonest policyholders may deliberately cause a loss in order to profit from insurance. Deductibles reduce moral hazard because the insured may not profit if a loss occurs.

Deductibles are also used to reduce attitudinal (morale) hazard. Attitudinal hazard is carelessness or indifference to a loss, which increases the chance of loss. Deductibles encourage people to be more careful with respect to the protection of their property and prevention of a loss because the insured must bear a part of the loss.

### Deductibles in Property Insurance

The following deductibles are commonly found in property insurance contracts:

- Straight deductible
- Aggregate deductible

**Straight Deductible**   With a **straight deductible**, *the insured must pay a certain number of dollars of loss before the insurer is required to make a payment.* Such a deductible typically applies to each loss. An example can be found in auto collision insurance. For instance, assume that Ashley has collision insurance on her new Toyota, with a $500 deductible. If a collision loss is $7000, she would receive only $6500 and would have to pay the remaining $500 herself.

**Aggregate Deductible**   Commercial insurance contracts sometimes contain an aggregate deductible. *An* **aggregate deductible** *means that all losses that occur during a specified time period, usually a policy year, are accumulated to satisfy the deductible amount.* Once the deductible is satisfied, the insurer pays all future losses in full. For example, assume that the

policy contains an aggregate deductible of $10,000. Also assume that losses of $1000 and $2000 occur, respectively, during the policy year. The insurer pays nothing because the deductible is not met. If a third loss of $8000 occurs during the same time period, the insurer would pay $1000. Any other losses occurring during the policy year would be paid in full.

### Deductibles in Health Insurance

In health insurance, the deductible can be stated in terms of dollars or time, such as a calendar-year deductible or an elimination (waiting) period.

**Calendar-Year Deductible**   A calendar-year deductible *is a type of aggregate deductible that is found in individual and group medical expense policies.* Eligible medical expenses are accumulated during the calendar year, and once they exceed the deductible amount, the insurer must then pay the benefits promised under the contract. Once the deductible is satisfied during the calendar year, no additional deductibles are imposed on the insured.

**Elimination (Waiting) Period**   A deductible can also be expressed as an elimination period. *An* **elimination (waiting) period** *is a stated period of time at the beginning of a loss during which no insurance benefits are paid.* An elimination period is appropriate for a single loss that occurs over some time period, such as the loss of work earnings. Elimination periods are commonly used in disability-income contracts. For example, disability-income insurance contracts that replace part of a disabled worker's earnings typically have elimination periods of 30, 60, or 90 days, or longer periods.

## COINSURANCE

Coinsurance is a contractual provision that often appears in property insurance contracts. This is especially true of commercial property insurance contracts.

### Nature of Coinsurance

A **coinsurance clause** *in a property insurance contract encourages the insured to insure the property to a stated percentage of its insurable value. If the coinsurance requirement is not met at the time of loss, the insured* *must share in the loss as a coinsurer*. The insurable value of the property is the actual cash value, replacement cost, or some other value described in the valuation clause of the policy. If the insured wants to collect in full for a partial loss, the coinsurance requirement must be satisfied. Otherwise, the insured will be penalized if a partial loss occurs.

A coinsurance formula is used to determine the amount paid for a covered loss. The coinsurance formula is as follows:

$$\frac{\text{Amount of insurance carried}}{\text{Amount of insurance required}} \times \text{Loss} = \frac{\text{Amount of}}{\text{recovery}}$$

For example, assume that a commercial building has an actual cash value of $1,000,000 and that the owner has insured it for only $600,000. If an 80 percent coinsurance clause is present in the policy, the required amount of insurance based on actual cash value is $800,000 (80% × $1,000,000). If a replacement cost policy is used, the required amount of insurance would be based on replacement cost. Thus, if a $100,000 loss occurs, only $75,000 will be paid by the insurer. This calculation can be illustrated as follows:

$$\frac{\$600,000}{\$800,000} \times \$100,000 = \$75,000$$

Since the insured has only three-fourths of the required amount of insurance in force at the time of loss, only three-fourths of the loss, or $75,000, will be paid. Because the coinsurance requirement is not met, the insured must absorb the remaining amount of the loss.

When applying the coinsurance formula, two additional points should be kept in mind. First, the amount paid can never exceed the amount of the actual loss even though the coinsurance formula produces such a result. This case could happen if the amount of insurance carried is greater than the minimum required amount of insurance. Second, the maximum amount paid for any loss is limited to the face amount of insurance.

## Purpose of Coinsurance

*The fundamental purpose of coinsurance is to achieve* **equity in rating**. Most property insurance losses are partial rather than total losses. But if everyone insures

**EXHIBIT 10.1**
**Insurance to Full Value**

Assume that 2000 buildings are valued at $200,000 each and are insured to full value for a total of $400 million of fire insurance. The following fire losses occur:

| | | |
|---|---|---|
| 2 total losses | = | $   400,000 |
| 30 partial losses at $20,000 each | = | $   600,000 |
| Total fire losses paid by insurer | = | $1,000,000 |
| Pure premium rate | = | $\dfrac{\$1,000,000}{\$400,000,000}$ |
| | = | 25 cents per $100 of insurance |

only for the partial loss rather than for the total loss, the premium rate for each $100 of insurance would be higher. This rate would be inequitable to insureds who wish to insure their property to full value. For example, if everyone insures to full value, assume that the pure premium rate for fire insurance is 25 cents for each $100 of insurance, ignoring expenses and the profit allowance of the insurer (see Exhibit 10.1).

However, if each property owner insures only for a partial loss, the pure premium rate will increase from 25 cents per $100 of fire insurance to 40 cents per $100 (see Exhibit 10.2). This rate would be inequitable to property owners who want to insure their buildings to full value. If full coverage is desired, the insured would have to pay a higher

**EXHIBIT 10.2**
**Insurance to Half Value**

Assume that 2000 buildings are valued at $200,000 each and are insured to half value for a total of $200 million of fire insurance. The following fire losses occur:

| | | |
|---|---|---|
| 2 total losses ($400,000) | | |
| Insurer pays only | = | $200,000 |
| 30 partial losses at $20,000 each | = | $600, 000 |
| Total fire losses paid by insurer | = | $800,000 |
| Pure premium rate | = | $\dfrac{\$800,000}{\$200,000,000}$ |
| | = | 40 cents per $100 of insurance |

rate of 40 cents, which we calculated earlier to be worth only 25 cents. This rate would be inequitable. *So, if the coinsurance requirement is met, the insured receives a rate discount, and the policyholder who is underinsured is penalized through application of the coinsurance formula.*

In property insurance, a coinsurance rate of 80 percent is typically used. However, the premium rate decreases as the coinsurance percentage increases. Thus, the premium rate per $100 of insurance decreases if the coinsurance percentage is increased from 80 percent to 90 percent or to 100 percent.

### Coinsurance Problems

Some practical problems arise when a coinsurance clause is present in a policy. First, inflation can result in a serious coinsurance penalty if the amount of insurance is not periodically increased for inflation. The insured may be in compliance with the coinsurance clause when the policy first goes into effect; however, price inflation could increase the replacement cost of the property. The result is that the insured may not be carrying the required amount of insurance at the time of loss, and he or she will then be penalized if a loss occurs. Thus, if a coinsurance clause is present, the amount of insurance carried should be periodically evaluated to determine whether the coinsurance requirement is being met.

Second, the insured may incur a coinsurance penalty if property values fluctuate widely during the policy period. For example, there may be a substantial increase in inventory values because of an unexpected arrival of a shipment of goods. If a loss occurs, the insured may not be carrying sufficient insurance to avoid a coinsurance penalty. One solution to this problem is *agreed value coverage,* by which the insurer agrees in advance that the amount of insurance carried meets the coinsurance requirement. Another solution is a *reporting form,* by which property values are periodically reported to the insurer.

## COINSURANCE IN HEALTH INSURANCE

Health insurance contracts frequently contain a **coinsurance clause,** which is *a provision that requires the insured to pay a specified percentage of covered medical expenses in excess of the deductible.* In particular, individual and group medical expense policies typically have a coinsurance provision that requires the insured to pay a certain percentage of covered medical expenses in excess of the deductible up to some specified annual limit. A typical plan requires the insured to pay 20, 25, or 30 percent of covered expenses in excess of the deductible up to a maximum annual limit. For example, assume that Megan has covered medical expenses in the amount of $50,500, and that she has a major medical policy with a $500 deductible and an 80 percent - 20 percent coinsurance clause. The insurer pays 80 percent of the bill in excess of the deductible, or $40,000, and Megan pays 20 percent, or $10,000 (plus the $500 deductible).

*The purposes of coinsurance in health insurance are (1) to reduce premiums and (2) to prevent overutilization of policy benefits.* Because the insured pays part of the cost, premiums are reduced. In addition, the patient will not demand the most expensive medical services if he or she pays part of the cost.

## OTHER-INSURANCE PROVISIONS

**Other-insurance provisions** typically are present in property and casualty insurance and health insurance contracts. These provisions apply when more than one contract covers the same loss. *The purpose of these provisions is to prevent profiting from insurance and violation of the principle of indemnity.* If the insured could collect the full amount of the loss from each insurer, there would be profiting from insurance and a substantial increase in moral hazard. Some dishonest insureds would deliberately cause a loss to collect multiple benefits.

Some important other-insurance provisions in property and liability insurance include (1) the pro rata liability clause, (2) contribution by equal shares, and (3) primary and excess insurance.

### Pro Rata Liability

**Pro rata liability** is a generic term for a provision that applies when two or more policies of the same type cover the same insurable interest in the property. *Each insurer's share of the loss is based on the proportion that its insurance bears to the total amount of insurance*

**EXHIBIT 10.3**
**Pro Rata Liability Example**

| | | |
|---|---|---|
| Company A | $\dfrac{\$300,000}{\$500,000}$ | or $.60 \times \$100,000 = \$\,60,000$ |
| Company B | $\dfrac{\$100,000}{\$500,000}$ | or $.20 \times \$100,000 = \$\,20,000$ |
| Company C | $\dfrac{\$100,000}{\$500,000}$ | or $.20 \times \$100,000 = \underline{\$\,20,000}$ |
| | Total loss payment | $= \$100,000$ |

*on the property.* For example, assume that Jacob owns a building and wishes to insure it for $500,000. For underwriting reasons, insurers may limit the amount of insurance they will write on a given property. Assume that an agent places $300,000 of insurance with Company A, $100,000 with Company B, and $100,000 with Company C, for a total of $500,000. If a $100,000 loss occurs, each company will pay only its pro rata share of the loss (see Exhibit 10.3). Thus, Jacob would collect $100,000 for the loss, not $300,000.

*The basic purpose of the pro rata liability clause is to preserve the principle of indemnity and to prevent profiting from insurance.* In the preceding example,

if the pro rata liability clause were not present, the insured would collect $100,000 from each insurer, or a total of $300,000 for a $100,000 loss.

## Contribution by Equal Shares

**Contribution by equal shares** is another type of other-insurance provision that often appears in liability insurance contracts. Each insurer shares equally in the loss until the share paid by each insurer equals the lowest limit of liability under any policy, or until the full amount of the loss is paid. For example, assume that the amount of insurance provided by Companies A, B, and C is $100,000, $200,000, and $300,000, respectively. If the loss is $150,000 each insurer pays an equal share, or $50,000 (see Exhibit 10.4).

However, if the loss were $500,000, how much would each insurer pay? In this case, each insurer would pay equal amounts until its policy limits are exhausted. The remaining insurers then continue to share equally in the remaining amount of the loss until each insurer has paid its policy limit in full, or until the full amount of the loss is paid. Thus, Company A would pay $100,000, Company B would pay $200,000, and Company C would pay $200,000 (see Exhibit 10.5). If the loss were $600,000, Company C would pay the remaining $100,000.

**EXHIBIT 10.4**
**Contribution by Equal Shares (Example 1)**

*Amount of Loss = $150,000*

| | Amount of Insurance | Contribution by Equal Shares | Total Paid |
|---|---|---|---|
| **Company A** | $100,000 | $50,000 | $50,000 |
| **Company B** | $200,000 | $50,000 | $50,000 |
| **Company C** | $300,000 | $50,000 | $50,000 |

**EXHIBIT 10.5**
**Contribution by Equal Shares (Example 2)**

*Amount of Loss = $500,000*

| | Amount of Insurance | Contribution by Equal Shares | Total Paid |
|---|---|---|---|
| **Company A** | $100,000 | $100,000 | $100,000 |
| **Company B** | $200,000 | $100,000 + $100,000 | $200,000 |
| **Company C** | $300,000 | $100,000 + $100,000 | $200,000 |

## Primary and Excess Insurance

**Primary and excess insurance** is another type of other-insurance provision. The primary insurer pays first, and the excess insurer pays only after the policy limits under the primary policy are exhausted.

Auto insurance is an excellent example of primary and excess insurance. For example, assume that Bob occasionally drives Jill's car. Bob's policy has a liability insurance limit of $100,000 per person for bodily injury liability. Jill's policy has a limit of $50,000 per person for bodily injury liability. If Bob negligently injures another motorist while driving Jill's car, both policies will cover the loss. *The normal rule is that liability insurance on the borrowed car is primary and any other insurance is considered excess.* Thus, if a court orders Bob to pay damages of $75,000, Jill's policy is primary and pays the first $50,000. Bob's policy is excess and pays the remaining $25,000.

The **coordination-of-benefits provision** in group health insurance is another example of primary and excess coverage. This provision is designed to prevent overinsurance and the duplication of benefits if one person is covered under more than one group health insurance plan.

The majority of states have adopted part or all of the coordination-of-benefits provisions developed by the National Association of Insurance Commissioners (NAIC). The rules are complex, and only two of them are discussed here. *First, coverage as an employee is usually primary to coverage as a dependent.* For example, assume that Jack and Kelly McVay are both employed, and that each is insured as a dependent under the other's group health insurance plan. If Jack incurs covered medical expenses, his policy pays first as primary coverage. He then submits his unreimbursed expenses (such as the deductible and coinsurance payments) to Kelly's insurer. Kelly's coverage then applies as excess insurance. No more than 100 percent of the eligible medical expenses are paid under both plans.

Second, the birthday rule applies to dependents in families where the parents are married or are not separated. Under this rule, *the plan of the parent whose birthday occurs first during the year is primary.* For example, assume that Kelly's birthday is in January, and Jack's birthday is in July. If their daughter is hospitalized, Kelly's plan is primary. Jack's plan would be excess. The purpose of the birthday rule is to eliminate gender discrimination with respect to coverage of dependents.

---

## CASE APPLICATION

Mike took his friend, Donna, out to dinner on her birthday. While driving Donna home, Mike became ill and asked Donna to drive. While driving Mike's car, Donna negligently injured another motorist when she failed to stop at a red light. Mike has an auto insurance policy with a liability insurance limit of $250,000 per person for bodily injury liability. Donna has a similar auto insurance policy with a liability limit of $100,000 per person.

a. If a court awards a liability judgment of $100,000 against Donna, how much, if any, will each insurer pay?

b. If the liability judgment is $300,000, how much, if any, will each insurer pay?

c. Assume that Mike cannot afford to pay the premium and lets his auto insurance policy lapse. At the time of the accident, he is uninsured. If the liability judgment against Donna is $100,000, how much, if any, will Donna's insurer pay?

## SUMMARY

- Insurance contracts generally can be divided into the following parts:

    Declarations

    Definitions

    Insuring agreement

    Exclusions

    Conditions

    Miscellaneous provisions

- Declarations are statements concerning the property or activity to be insured.

- The definitions page or section defines the key words or phrases so that coverage under the policy can be determined more easily.

- The insuring agreement summarizes the promises of the insurer. There are two basic types of insuring agreements:

    Named-perils coverage

    Open-perils coverage

- All policies contain one or more exclusions. There are three major types of exclusions:

    Excluded perils

    Excluded losses

    Excluded property

- Exclusions are necessary for several reasons. Certain perils are considered uninsurable by private insurers; extraordinary hazards may be present; coverage is provided by other contracts; moral hazard and attitudinal (morale) hazard are present to a high degree; and coverage is not needed by the typical insured.

- Conditions are provisions that qualify or place limitations on the insurer's promise to perform. Conditions impose certain duties on the insured if he or she wishes to collect for a loss.

- Miscellaneous provisions in property and casualty insurance include cancellation, subrogation, requirements if a loss occurs, assignment of the policy, and other insurance provisions.

- The contract also contains a definition of "insured." The contract may cover only one person, or it may cover other persons as well even though they are not specifically named in the policy.

- An endorsement, or rider, is a written provision that adds to, deletes from, or modifies the provisions in the original contract. An endorsement or rider normally takes precedence over any conflicting terms in the contract to which the endorsement is attached.

- A deductible requires the insured to pay part of the loss. A specified amount is subtracted from the total loss payment that otherwise would be payable. Deductibles are used to eliminate small claims, to reduce premiums, and to reduce moral hazard and attitudinal (morale) hazard. Examples of deductibles include a straight deductible, aggregate deductible, calendar-year deductible, and elimination (waiting) period.

- A coinsurance clause in property insurance requires the insured to insure the property for a stated percentage of its insurable value at the time of loss. If the coinsurance requirement is not met at the time of loss, the insured must share in the loss as a coinsurer. The fundamental purpose of coinsurance is to achieve equity in rating.

- A coinsurance clause (percentage participation clause) is typically found in individual and group medical expense policies. A typical provision requires the insured to pay 20, 25, or 30 percent of covered expenses in excess of the deductible up to some specified annual limit.

- Other-insurance provisions are present in many insurance contracts. These provisions apply to payment of a loss when more than one policy covers the same loss. The purpose of these provisions is to prevent profiting from insurance and violation of the principle of indemnity. Some important other-insurance provisions include the pro rata liability clause, contribution by equal shares, and primary and excess insurance.

## KEY CONCEPTS AND TERMS

Additional insured (189)

Aggregate deductible (190)

"All-risks" policy (186)

Calendar-year
   deductible (190)

Coinsurance clause (190)

Conditions (187)

Contribution by equal
   shares (193)

Coordination-of-benefits
   provision (194)

Declarations (185)

Deductible (189)

Elimination (waiting)
   period (190)

Endorsements and
   riders (189)

Equity in rating (191)

Exclusions (186)

First named insured (188)

Insuring agreement (186)

Large-loss principle (189)

Named insured (188)

Named-perils policy (186)

Open-perils policy (186)

Other-insurance
   provisions (192)

Other insureds (188)

Primary and excess
   insurance (194)

Pro rata liability (192)

Special coverage
   policy (186)

Straight deductible (190)

## REVIEW QUESTIONS

1. Identify the basic parts of an insurance contract.

2. a. Describe the major types of exclusions typically found in insurance contracts.
   b. Why are exclusions used by insurers?

3. a. Define the term "conditions."
   b. Does the insurer have to pay an otherwise covered loss if the insured fails to comply with the policy conditions? Explain your answer.

4. a. What is the meaning of "named insured"?
   b. Can other parties be insured under a policy even though they are not specifically named? Explain your answer.

5. a. What is an endorsement or rider?
   b. If an endorsement conflicts with a policy provision, how is this problem resolved?

6. a. Describe the following types of deductibles:
   1. straight deductible
   2. calendar-year deductible
   3. aggregate deductible
   b. Explain the purposes of deductibles in property insurance contracts.

7. a. Explain how a coinsurance clause in property insurance works.
   b. What is the fundamental purpose of a coinsurance clause?

8. Describe a typical coinsurance clause in an individual or group medical expense insurance policy.

9. a. What is the purpose of other-insurance provisions?
   b. Give an example of the pro-rata liability clause.

10. Explain the meaning of primary insurance and excess insurance.

*20,000*
*46,000*
*40,000*

## APPLICATION QUESTIONS

1. Michael owns a small plane that he flies on weekends. His insurance agent informs him that aircraft are excluded as personal property under his homeowners policy. As an insured, he feels that his plane should be covered just like any other personal property he owns.
   a. Explain to Michael the rationale for excluding certain types of property, such as aircraft, under the homeowners policy.
   b. Explain some additional reasons why exclusions are present in insurance contracts.

*125000*
*+75 000*

2. a. A manufacturing firm incurred the following insured losses, in the order given, during the current policy year.

| Loss | Amount of Loss |
|------|----------------|
| A | $ 2500 |
| B | 3500 |
| C | 10,000 |

   How much would the company's insurer pay for each loss if the policy contained the following type of deductible?
   1. $1000 straight deductible *1500  2500  9000  7  13,000*
   2. $15,000 annual aggregate deductible
   b. Explain the coordination-of-benefits provision that is typically found in group medical expense plans.

3. Stephanie owns a small warehouse that is insured for $200,000 under a commercial property insurance policy. The policy contains an 80 percent coinsurance clause. The warehouse sustained a $50,000 loss because of a fire in a storage area. The replacement cost of the warehouse at the time of loss is $500,000.
   a. What is the insurer's liability, if any, for this loss? Show your calculations. *25,000*
   b. Assume that Stephanie carried $500,000 of property insurance on the warehouse at the time of loss. If the amount of loss is $10,000, how much will she collect? *10,000*
   c. Explain the theory or rationale of coinsurance in a property insurance contract. *dilute risk*

4. Andrew owns a commercial office building that is insured under three property insurance contracts. He has $100,000 of insurance from Company A, $200,000 from Company B, and $200,000 from Company C.
   a. Assume that the pro rata liability provision appears in each contract. If a $100,000 loss occurs, how much will Andrew collect from each insurer? Explain your answer.
   b. What is the purpose of the other-insurance provisions that are frequently found in insurance contracts?

5. Assume that a $300,000 liability claim is covered under two liability insurance contracts. Policy A has a $500,000 limit of liability for the claim, while Policy B has a $125,000 limit of liability. Both contracts provide for contribution by equal shares.
   a. How much will each insurer contribute toward this claim? Explain your answer.
   b. If the claim were only $50,000, how much would each insurer pay?

6. Ashley has an individual medical expense insurance policy with a $1000 calendar-year deductible and a 20 percent coinsurance clause. Ashley had outpatient surgery to remove a bunion on her foot and incurred medical bills of $10,000. How much will Ashley's insurer pay? How much will Ashley have to pay?

7. The Lincoln Saltdogs is a professional minor league baseball team in the American Association league. The clubhouse is insured for $600,000 under a commercial property insurance policy with an 80 percent coinsurance clause. The current replacement cost of the clubhouse is $1 million. After a playoff game for the league championship, a whirlpool tub for the players shorted out, and a fire ensued. The clubhouse sustained a $100,000 fire loss. Ignoring any deductible, how much will the team's insurer pay for the loss?

## INTERNET RESOURCES

■ The **New York State Department of Financial Services** publishes a number of consumer publications on basic insurance contracts that can be ordered online. The publications are helpful in understanding the various contractual provisions and coverages that appear in homeowners and auto insurance and other insurance contracts. Rating guides are also available. Visit the site at

dfs.ny.gov/

■ The **Wisconsin Office of the Commissioner of Insurance** also makes available consumer publications on specific insurance contracts. These publications are helpful in understanding the contractual provisions and coverages that appear in life, health, auto, and homeowners insurance. Visit the site at

oci.wi.gov

■ The **Insurance Information Institute** provides consumer materials dealing with property and liability insurance. The publications can help you understand the contractual provisions and coverages that appear in homeowners, auto, personal liability, and flood insurance, and other property and casualty insurance coverages. Visit the site at

iii.org

■ The **Texas Department of Insurance** provides a considerable amount of consumer information on auto, homeowners, life and health, and other types of insurance. Rating guides are also available. Visit the site at

www.tdi.texas.gov

## SELECTED REFERENCES

Graves, Edward E., and Burke A. Christensen, eds. *McGill's Legal Aspects of Life Insurance,* 7th ed. Bryn Mawr, PA: The American College, 2010.

Graves, Edward E. "Policy Provisions," *McGill's Life Insurance,* 8th ed. Bryn Mawr, PA: The American College, 2011, Ch. 27.

Lorimer, James J., et al. *The Legal Environment of Insurance,* 4th ed., vols. 1 and 2. Malvern, PA: American Institute for Property and Liability Underwriters, 1993.

Rejda, George E., and Eric A. Wiening, *Risk Management and Insurance,* Boston, MA: Pearson Custom Publishing, 2005, Chs. 9-10.

Wiening, Eric A. *Foundations of Risk Management and Insurance.* Malvern, PA: American Institute for Chartered Property Casualty Underwriters/Insurance Institute of America, 2002, chs. 11–19.

Wiening, Eric A. and Donald S. Malecki. *Insurance Contract Analysis,* Malvern, PA: American Institute for Chartered Property Casualty Underwriters, 1992.

## NOTES

1. Eric A. Wiening, *Foundations of Risk Management and Insurance* (Malvern, PA: American Institute for Chartered Property Casualty Underwriters/Insurance Institute of America, 2002, pp. 11.15–11.18.

2. C. Arthur Williams, Jr., George L. Head, Ronald C. Horn, and G. William Glendenning, *Principles of Risk Management and Insurance,* 2nd ed., vol. 2 (Malvern, PA: American Institute for Property and Liability Underwriters, 1981), pp. 200–201.

Students may take a self-administered test on this chapter at

**www.pearsonhighered.com/rejda**

# CHAPTER 11

# LIFE INSURANCE

*"Death is one of the few things that can be done as easily lying down."*

Woody Allen

*"There are more dead people than living, and their numbers are increasing."*

Eugene Ionesco

*Ryan, age 35, owns a small restaurant in San Francisco, California. He is married and has three children in grade school. Ryan has little discretionary income, and it took considerable effort by a life insurance agent to persuade him to buy a life insurance policy to protect his family. Ryan even tried to cancel the policy several times because his business was strapped for cash. His agent convinced him to pay the premiums from the accumulated cash values to keep the policy in force until his financial position improved. Two years later, Ryan was diagnosed with terminal lung cancer and he died seven months later. After his death, his wife used the policy proceeds to pay burial expenses, eliminate credit card debts, make home improvements, and pay for counseling one daughter who had severe emotional problems in coping with her father's death.*

*In the above case, the life insurance purchased by Ryan kept his family from experiencing economic insecurity after his death. In this chapter, we discuss the risk of premature death and how life insurance can alleviate economic insecurity from premature death. Topics covered include the meaning of premature death, the need for life insurance based on family type, the correct amount of life insurance to own, and a discussion of the major types of life insurance sold today.*

## PREMATURE DEATH

### Meaning of Premature Death

**Premature death** *can be defined as the death of a family head with outstanding unfulfilled financial obligations*, such as dependents to support, children to educate, and a mortgage to pay off. Premature death can cause serious financial problems for the surviving family members because their share of the deceased family head's future earnings is lost forever. If replacement income from other sources is inadequate, or if the accumulated financial assets available to the family are also inadequate, the surviving family members will be exposed to great economic insecurity.

### Costs of Premature Death

Certain costs are associated with premature death. First, the family's share of the deceased breadwinner's future earnings is lost forever. Second, additional expenses are incurred because of funeral expenses, uninsured medical bills, and estate settlement costs. Third, because of insufficient income, some families will experience a reduction in their standard of living. Finally, certain noneconomic costs are incurred, such as intense grief, loss of a parental role model, and counseling and guidance for the children.

### Declining Problem of Premature Death

The economic problem of premature death has declined substantially over time because of an increase in life expectancy. Life expectancy is the average number of years of life remaining to a person at a particular age. *Preliminary data for 2010 show that life expectancy at birth increased to 78.7 years in 2010.*[1] In contrast, in 1970, life expectancy at birth was only 70.8 years, or 10 percent lower. Life expectancy has increased significantly over the past century because of substantial breakthroughs in medical science, rising real incomes, economic growth, and improvements in public health and sanitation.

Although life expectancy has increased over time, the United States lags behind many foreign countries. Insight 11.1 discusses the reasons for the poor showing.

## INSIGHT 11.1

### Why Does the United States Lag Behind Many Foreign Countries in Life Expectancy?

Although life expectancy in the United States has increased over time, the United States lags behind many foreign countries. *In 2010, of some 70 countries with a population of 13 million or more, the United States tied for 11th place in life expectancy at birth, behind France, Germany, Japan, Spain, and the United Kingdom.*[a] The poor showing is due to several factors:

- Obesity is a major factor; more than one-third of U.S. adults (over 72 million) and 17 percent of U.S. children are obese, which results in increased coronary heart disease, diabetes, cancer, hypertension, and other diseases.[b]
- The lifestyle of Americans generally is not conducive to longevity. Americans tend to overeat, diets are high in saturated fat, and millions of Americans lead sedentary lives and fail to exercise.
- Millions of Americans lack health insurance and may not receive needed medical care.

- African Americans and other minority groups have a shorter life expectancy, which pulls down the average.
- Infant mortality rates are relatively high when compared with many industrialized countries. In 2005, the United States ranked 30th in the world in infant mortality, behind most European countries, Canada, Australia, New Zealand, Hong Kong, Singapore, Japan, and Israel.[c] The major cause of the relatively high infant mortality rate in the U.S. is the high percentage of preterm births (birth before 37 weeks of gestation).[d]

[a]U.S. Census Bureau, *Statistical Abstract of the United States: 2012*, Table 1339.
[b]Centers for Disease Control and Prevention, *Obesity, Halting the Epidemic by Making Health Easier, At a Glance, 2011.*
[c]Marian F. MacDorman and T.J. Mathews, "Behind International Rankings of Infant Mortality: How the United States Compares with Europe," NCHS Data Brief Number 23, November 2009.
[d]Ibid.

## Economic Justification for Life Insurance

The purchase of life insurance is economically justified if the insured has earned income, and others are dependent on those earnings for part or all of their financial support. If a family head dies prematurely with dependents to support and outstanding financial obligations, the surviving family members are exposed to great economic insecurity. Life insurance can be used to restore the family's share of the deceased breadwinner's earnings.

# FINANCIAL IMPACT OF PREMATURE DEATH ON DIFFERENT TYPES OF FAMILIES

## Single People

The number of single people has increased in recent years. Younger adults are postponing marriage, often beyond age 30, and many young and middle-aged adults are single again because of divorce. Premature death of single people with no dependents to support or other financial obligations is not likely to create a financial problem for others. Other than needing a modest amount of life insurance for funeral expenses

and uninsured medical bills, *this group does not need large amounts of life insurance*. One exception is a single divorced parent who has child-support obligations. Premature death can create a serious financial problem for the surviving children.

## Single-Parent Families

The number of single-parent families with children under age 18 has increased in recent years because of the large number of children born outside of marriage, divorce, legal separation, and death. Premature death of the single parent can cause great economic insecurity for the surviving children. *The need for large amounts of life insurance on the family head is great.* However, many single parents, especially female-headed households, have incomes below the poverty line. Many of these families are simply too poor to purchase large amounts of insurance.

## Two-Income Earners with Children

Families in which both spouses work outside the home have largely replaced the traditional family in which only one spouse is in the paid labor force. In two-income families with children, the death of one income earner can cause considerable economic insecurity for the surviving family members, because both incomes are necessary to maintain the family's standard of living. *Both income earners need substantial amounts of life insurance.* The life insurance can replace the lost earnings if one family head dies prematurely.

However, in two-income families without children, premature death of one income earner is not likely to cause economic insecurity for the surviving spouse. The need for large amounts of life insurance by income earners within this group is considerably less.

## Traditional Families

Traditional families are families in which only one parent is in the labor force, and the other parent stays at home to take care of dependent children. *The working parent in the labor force needs substantial amounts of life insurance.* If the working spouse dies with an insufficient amount of life insurance, the family may have to adjust its standard of living downward.

In addition, the nonemployed spouse who is caring for dependent children also needs life insurance. The cost of child-care services can be a heavy financial burden to the working spouse if the nonemployed spouse dies prematurely. One study shows that compensating a stay-at-home spouse for services performed in the home would cost almost $117,000 annually.[2]

## Blended Families

A blended family is one in which a divorced spouse with children remarries, and the new spouse also has children. Also, additional children may be born after the remarriage. *The need for life insurance on both family heads is great.* Both spouses generally are in the labor force at the time of remarriage, and the death of one spouse may result in a reduction in the family's standard of living since the family's share of that income is lost.

## Sandwiched Families

A sandwiched family is one in which a son or daughter with children provides financial support or other services to one or both parents. Thus, the son or daughter is "sandwiched" between the younger and older generations. *A working spouse in a sandwiched*

*family needs a substantial amount of life insurance.* Premature death of a working spouse in a sandwiched family can result in the loss of financial support to both the surviving children and the aged parent(s).

Finally, in the family types discussed previously, minor children are typically present who require financial support. Because parents usually support minor children, buying large amounts of life insurance on children is not recommended. *The major disadvantage in insuring minor children is that the family head may be inadequately insured.* Scarce premium dollars that could be used to increase the amount of life insurance on the family head are instead diverted to cover the children.

# AMOUNT OF LIFE INSURANCE TO OWN

Once you determine that you need life insurance, the next step is to calculate the amount of life insurance to own. Some life insurers and financial planners recommend that insureds carry life insurance equal to some multiple of their earnings, such as six to ten times annual earnings. Such rules, however, are meaningless because they do not take into account that the need for life insurance varies widely depending on family size, income levels, existing financial assets, and financial goals.

Three approaches can be used to estimate the amount of life insurance to own:

- Human life value approach
- Needs approach
- Capital retention approach

## Human Life Value Approach

As noted earlier, the family's share of the deceased breadwinner's earnings is lost forever if the family head dies prematurely. This loss is called the human life value. **Human life value** *can be defined as the present value of the family's share of the deceased breadwinner's future earnings.* In its basic form, the human life value can be calculated by the following steps:

1. Estimate the individual's average annual earnings over his or her productive lifetime.
2. Deduct federal and state income taxes, Social Security taxes, life and health insurance premiums,

and the costs of self-maintenance. The remaining amount is used to support the family.

3. Determine the number of years from the person's present age to the contemplated age of retirement.
4. Using a reasonable discount rate, determine the present value of the family's share of earnings for the period determined in step 3.

For example, assume that Richard, age 27, is married and has two children. He earns $50,000 annually and plans to retire at age 67. (For the sake of simplicity, assume that his earnings remain constant.) Of this amount, $20,000 is used for federal and state taxes, life and health insurance, and Richard's personal needs. The remaining $30,000 is used to support his family. This stream of future income is then discounted back to the present to determine Richard's human life value. Using a reasonable discount rate of 5 percent, the present value of 40 annual payments of $1 at the end of each year is $17.16. Therefore, Richard has a human life value of $514,800 ($30,000 × $17.16 = $514,800). This amount represents the present value of the family's share of Richard's earnings that would be lost if he dies prematurely. As you can see, the human life has an enormous economic value when earning capacity is considered. The major advantage of the human life value concept is that it crudely measures the economic value of a human life.

However, the basic human life value described above has several limitations. First, other sources of income are ignored, such as Social Security survivor benefits, income from individual retirement accounts (IRAs), 401(k) plans and private pension death benefits. Second, in the basic model, occupations are not considered, work earnings and expenses are assumed to be constant, and employee benefits are ignored. Third, the amount of money allocated to the family can quickly change because of divorce, birth of a child, or death of a family member. Also, the long run discount rate is critical; the human life value can be substantially increased by assuming a lower rate. Finally, the effects of inflation on earnings and expenses are ignored.

Because of the above limitations, the basic human life value model substantially understates the economic value of a human life. Life Foundation has developed a more accurate and comprehensive human life value model, which considers age and gender, occupational category, increases in earned income, consumption needs, employee benefits, value of services performed in the home, and wages earned by a working spouse. When these factors are considered, the economic value of a human life is significantly higher than the value produced by the basic model. The human life value calculator can be accessed at: lifehappens.org/human-life-value-calculator/.

## Needs Approach

The second method for estimating the amount of life insurance to own is the **needs approach**. The various family needs that must be met if the family head should die are analyzed, and the amount of money needed to meet these needs is determined. The total amount of existing life insurance and financial assets is then subtracted from the total amount needed. The difference, if any, is the amount of new life insurance that should be purchased. The most important family needs are the following:

- Estate clearance fund
- Income during the readjustment period
- Income during the dependency period
- Life income to the surviving spouse
- Special needs
    Mortgage redemption fund
    Educational fund
    Emergency fund
    Mentally or physically challenged family members
- Retirement needs

**Estate Clearance Fund**   An estate clearance fund or cleanup fund is needed immediately when the family head dies. Immediate cash is needed for burial expenses; uninsured medical bills; installment debts; estate administration expenses; and estate, inheritance, and income taxes.

**Income During the Readjustment Period**   The **readjustment period** is a one- or two-year period following the breadwinner's death. During this period, the family should receive approximately the same amount of income received while the family head was alive. The purpose of the readjustment period is to give the family time to adjust its standard of living.

**Income During the Dependency Period**   The **dependency period** follows the readjustment period; it is the period until the youngest child reaches age 18. The family should receive income during this period so that the surviving spouse can remain at home, if necessary, to care for the children. The income needed during the dependency period is substantially reduced if the surviving spouse is already in the labor force and plans to continue working.

**Life Income to the Surviving Spouse**   Another important need is to provide life income to the surviving spouse, especially if he or she is older and has been out of the labor force for many years. Two income periods must be considered: (1) income during the blackout period and (2) income to supplement Social Security benefits after the blackout period. *The* **blackout period** *refers to the period from the time that Social Security survivor benefits terminate to the time the benefits are resumed.* Social Security benefits to a surviving spouse terminate when the youngest child reaches age 16 and start again when the spouse attains age 60.

   If a surviving spouse has a career and is already in the labor force, the need for life income is greatly reduced or even eliminated. However, this conclusion is not true for an older spouse under age 60 who has been out of the labor force for years, and for whom Social Security survivor benefits have temporarily terminated. The need for income during the blackout period is especially important for this group.

**Special Needs**   Families should also consider certain special needs, which include the following:

- *Mortgage redemption fund.* The amount of monthly income needed by surviving family members is greatly reduced when monthly mortgage payments or rent payments are not required.
- *Educational fund.* The family head may wish to provide an educational fund for the children. If the children plan to attend a private college or university, the cost will be considerably higher than at a public institution.
- *Emergency fund.* A family should also have an emergency fund. An unexpected event may occur that requires large amounts of cash, such as major dental work, home repairs, or a new car.

- *Mentally or physically challenged family members.* Additional funds may be needed for educating, training, and caring for mentally or physically challenged children or adult family members.

**Retirement Needs**   Because the family head may survive until retirement, the need for adequate retirement income should also be considered. Most retired workers are eligible for Social Security retirement benefits and may also be eligible for retirement benefits from their employer. If retirement income from these sources is inadequate, you can obtain additional income from cash-value life insurance, individual investments, a retirement annuity, or an individual retirement account (IRA).

## Illustration of the Needs Approach

Exhibit 11.1 provides a worksheet that you can use to determine the amount of life insurance needed. The first part of the worksheet shows the amount needed to meet your various cash needs, income needs, and special needs. The second part analyzes your present financial assets for meeting these needs. The final part determines the amount of additional life insurance needed, which is calculated by subtracting total assets from total needs. For example, Jennifer and Scott Smith are married and have a son, age 1. Jennifer, age 33, earns $60,000 annually as a marketing analyst for a large oil company. Scott, age 35, earns $40,000 as an elementary school teacher. Jennifer would like her family to be financially secure if she dies prematurely.

**Cash Needs**   Jennifer estimates that her family will need at least $15,000 for funeral expenses. Although Jennifer is insured under a group health insurance plan, certain medical services are excluded, and she must pay an annual deductible and coinsurance charges. Thus, she estimates that the family will need $5000 for uninsured medical expenses. She is also making monthly payments on a car loan and credit card debts. The car loan and credit card debts currently total $12,000. In addition, she estimates that the cost of probating her will and attorney fees will be $3000, and that no federal estate taxes will be payable.

**Exhibit 11.1**
## How Much Life Insurance Do You Need?

| What You Will Need | Jennifer Smith | Your Needs |
|---|---|---|
| Cash needs | | |
| Funeral costs | $ 15,000 | $ _____ |
| Uninsured medical bills | 5,000 | $ _____ |
| Installment debts | 12,000 | $ _____ |
| Probate costs | 3,000 | $ _____ |
| Federal estate taxes | 0 | $ _____ |
| State inheritance taxes | 0 | $ _____ |
| Total estate clearance fund | $ 35,000 | $ _____ |
| **Income needs** | | |
| Readjustment period | 24,000 | _____ |
| Dependency period | 180,000 | _____ |
| Life income to surviving spouse | 0 | _____ |
| Retirement income | 0 | _____ |
| Total income needs | $ 204,000 | $ _____ |
| **Special needs** | | |
| Mortgage redemption fund | 200,000 | _____ |
| Emergency fund | 50,000 | _____ |
| College education fund | 150,000 | _____ |
| Total special needs | $ 400,000 | $ _____ |
| Total needs | $ 639,000 | $ _____ |

| What You Have Today | Jennifer Smith | Your Assets |
|---|---|---|
| Checking account and savings | $ 10,000 | $ _____ |
| Mutual funds and securities | 35,000 | $ _____ |
| IRAs and Keogh plan | 20,000 | |
| Section 401(k) plan and employer savings plan | 40,000 | _____ |
| Private pension death benefit | 0 | _____ |
| Current life insurance | 60,000 | _____ |
| Other financial assets | 0 | _____ |
| Total assets | $ 165,000 | _____ |
| **Additional life insurance needed** | | $ _____ |
| Total needs | $ 639,000 | |
| Less total assets | 165,000 | $ _____ |
| **Additional life insurance needed** | $ 474,000 | _____ |
| | | $ _____ |

**Income Needs**    Jennifer also wants to provide monthly income to her family during the readjustment and dependency periods until her son reaches age 18. Jennifer and Scott's net take-home pay is approximately $6000 each month. Jennifer believes that her family can maintain its present standard of living if it receives 75 percent of that amount, or $4500 monthly. Thus, she wants the family to receive $4500 monthly for 17 years during the readjustment and dependency periods.

The family's need for $4500 per month is reduced if other sources of income are available. Scott's net take-home pay is about $2500 monthly. In addition, Scott and his son are eligible for Social Security survivor benefits. Scott's benefits are payable until his son reaches age 16, whereas his son's benefits are payable until age 18. In this example, we will assume that only the son will receive Social Security survivor benefits. Because Scott's earnings substantially exceed the maximum annual limit allowed under the Social Security earnings test, he will lose all of his Social Security survivor benefits. However, his son will continue to receive benefits until age 18. The son will receive an estimated $1000 each month from Social Security until age 18. Thus, the family would receive a total of $3500 monthly from Scott's take-home pay and the son's Social Security benefit. Because their income goal is $4500 monthly, there is a monthly shortfall of $1000. Jennifer's family needs an additional $24,000 to provide monthly income of $1000 during the two-year readjustment period, and another $180,000 to provide monthly income for an additional 15 years during the dependency period. Thus, the family needs a total of $204,000 to meet the monthly goal of $4500 during the readjustment and dependency periods.

If Jennifer considers the time value of money, it will take less than $204,000 of life insurance to meet her income goal. Likewise, if she takes inflation into account, she must increase the amount of life insurance just to maintain the real purchasing power of the benefits. *However, she can ignore both present value and future inflation if she assumes that one offsets the other. Thus, in our example, we assume that the life insurance proceeds are invested at an interest rate equal to the rate of inflation.* Such an assumption builds into the program an automatic hedge against inflation that preserves the real purchasing power of the death benefit. In most cases, however, the death proceeds can be invested at a return exceeding the

rate of inflation. The calculations are also simplified, and the use of present value tables and assumptions concerning future inflation rates are unnecessary.

In addition, Scott is currently in the labor force and plans to continue working if Jennifer should die. Thus, there is no need to provide additional income during the blackout period.

A final need to consider is retirement income. Scott will receive Social Security retirement benefits and a lifetime pension from the school district's retirement plan. He also has an individual retirement account (IRA) that will provide additional retirement income. Jennifer believes that Scott's total retirement income will be sufficient to meet his needs, so he does not need additional retirement income.

In summary, after considering Scott's take-home pay and Social Security survivor benefits, Jennifer determines that she will need an additional $204,000 to meet the income goal of $4500 monthly during the readjustment and dependency periods. Additional income during the blackout period is not needed.

**Special Needs**    Jennifer would like the mortgage to be paid off if she should die. The present mortgage balance is $200,000. She also wants to establish an emergency fund of $50,000 for the family and an educational fund of $150,000 for her son. Thus, her special needs total $400,000.

**Determining the Amount of New Life Insurance Needed**    The next step is to determine the amount of financial assets that can be used to satisfy her needs. Jennifer has a checking account and personal savings in the amount of $10,000. She owns several mutual funds and individual stocks with a current market value of $35,000. She has an individual retirement account with a current balance of $20,000, and $40,000 in a Section 401(k) plan sponsored by her employer. She is also insured for $60,000 under a group life insurance plan. Total financial assets available upon her death are $165,000.

Total family needs are $639,000, but her current financial assets are only $165,000. Thus, Jennifer needs an additional $474,000 of life insurance to protect her family.

The major advantage of the needs approach is that it is a reasonably accurate method for determining the amount of life insurance to own when specific family needs are recognized. The needs approach also considers other sources of income and financial assets. The major disadvantage, however, is that future projections over the insured's lifetime require numerous assumptions and the use of a computer. Dynamic programming models with changing assumptions are complex and usually are not needed by the typical insured.

## Capital Retention Approach

Unlike the needs approach, which assumes liquidation of the life insurance proceeds, the **capital retention approach** preserves the capital needed to provide income to the family. The income-producing assets are then available for distribution later to the heirs.

The amount of life insurance needed based on the capital retention approach can be determined by the following steps:

- Prepare a personal balance sheet.
- Determine the amount of income-producing capital.
- Determine the amount of additional capital needed (if any).

**Prepare a Personal Balance Sheet** The first step is to prepare a personal balance sheet that lists all assets and liabilities. The balance sheet should include all death benefits from life insurance and from other sources. For example, Kevin, age 35, has a wife and two children, ages 3 and 5. Kevin earns $60,000 annually. If he should die, he wants his family to receive $40,000 annually. He also wants to establish an emergency fund and educational fund, and pay off the mortgage, auto loan, and credit card balances. Kevin's personal balance sheet, including death benefits from life insurance and his pension plan, is as follows:

### Assets

| | |
|---|---|
| House | $225,000 |
| Automobiles | 20,000 |
| Personal and household property | 40,000 |
| Securities and investments | 60,000 |
| Checking account | 5,000 |
| Individual and group life insurance | 200,000 |
| 401(k) plan | 70,000 |
| Total | $620,000 |

### Liabilities

| | |
|---|---|
| Mortgage | $100,000 |
| Auto loan | 10,000 |
| Credit cards | 5,000 |
| Total | $115,000 |

**Determine the Amount of Income-Producing Assets** The second step is to determine the amount of income-producing assets. This step is performed by subtracting the liabilities, cash needs, and non-income-producing assets from total assets. Kevin has $55,000 of capital that can produce income for the family. This amount is determined as follows:

| | |
|---|---|
| Total assets | $620,000 |
| Less: | |
| Mortgage payoff | $100,000 |
| Auto loan and credit card debts | 15,000 |
| Final expenses | 15,000 |
| Emergency fund | 50,000 |
| Educational fund | 100,000 |
| Non-income-producing assets (automobiles, personal and household property, value of home) | 285,000 |
| Total deductions | 565,000 |
| Capital now available for income | $ 55,000 |

In the preceding illustration, the home is not an income-producing asset. Unless the home is sold or rented, it ordinarily does not produce cash income for the family. Thus, the home is considered to be part of *non-income-producing assets,* which is subtracted from total assets to arrive at the amount of liquid assets that can produce income for the family.

**Determine the Amount of Additional Capital Needed** The final step is to determine the amount of additional capital needed. This step involves a comparison of the income objective with other sources of income, such as Social Security survivor benefits. In Kevin's case, his family would have an income shortage of $24,250 annually based on his present financial situation. Assuming the liquid assets and life insurance proceeds can be invested to earn at least 5 percent annually, Kevin needs an additional $485,000 of life insurance to meet his financial goals. This calculation is summarized as follows:

| | |
|---|---|
| Income objective for family | $ 40,000 |
| Less: | |
| Income from capital now available ($55,000 × 5%) | –2,750 |
| Social Security survivor benefits | –13,000 |
| Income shortage | $ 24,250 |
| Total new capital required ($24,250/.05) | $485,000 |

The capital retention approach has the advantages of simplicity, ease of understanding, and preservation of capital. In addition, investment income earned on the emergency and educational funds can be used as a partial hedge against inflation, or it can be accumulated to offset rising educational costs. The major disadvantage, however, is that a larger amount of life insurance is required to produce a given amount of income. The family, however, may be unable to afford the additional amount of life insurance.

## Interactive Calculators on the Internet

Many life insurers and premium quoting services have interactive calculators on their Web sites that calculate the amount of life insurance needed. You make assumptions about inflation, rates of return on the death proceeds, amount of income needed by the family, and certain other assumptions. However, the quality of the interactive calculators varies widely. Some calculators are extremely limited, and questions concerning the amount of accumulated assets and other sources of income are often ignored. Other calculators are more detailed and enable you to estimate more accurately the amount of life insurance needed.

In addition, depending on the type of calculator used, the amount of life insurance needed varies widely. *One study of 11 calculators produced recommendations ranging from $73,329 to $3.8 million for a male family head, age 35, and from $0 to $2.3 million for his spouse the same age.*[3] However, despite their limitations, the interactive calculators are worth checking out as a starting point for estimating the amount of life insurance needed.

## Adequacy of Life Insurance for American Families

Most families own insufficient amounts of life insurance. A recent study by LIMRA revealed a more severe problem of underinsurance in the United States than previously existed. *In 2010, only 44 percent of the households in the United States owned any individual life insurance, which was a 50-year low, and 30 percent of U.S. households (35 million) had no life insurance protection at all.*[4] In addition, the average amount of life insurance on individuals with any life insurance is relatively low. In 2010, insured individuals with any life insurance owned on average only $154,000 of total life insurance coverage.[5] After deducting burial expenses and uninsured medical bills, this amount would replace

only about two to three years of disposable income for typical families.

LIMRA also analyzed the reasons why people are underinsured. People delay buying life insurance for three major reasons:

- *Although term insurance premiums have declined to historically low levels, consumers believe life insurance is too expensive to purchase.*
- *Consumers have difficulty in making correct decisions about the purchase of life insurance.*
- *Many consumers simply procrastinate and never get around to buying life insurance.*

Another study sponsored by New York Life shows that many Americans have only about half of the amount of life insurance needed to attain their own self-described financial goals. A survey of 1003 Americans with dependents and household incomes of $50,000 or more revealed a serious problem of underinsurance. *The median amount that respondents reported they needed from their life insurance proceeds to attain their financial goals was $589,378, but the median amount of actual life insurance protection was only $300,000, or a gap of 49 percent.*[6]

Based on the above findings, it is clear that the life insurance industry must do a better job in educating consumers about the need for life insurance, the affordability of life insurance, and the correct amount of life insurance to own.

## Opportunity Cost of Buying Life Insurance

The previous discussion shows that most family heads generally need substantial amounts of life insurance. However, this conclusion must be qualified by considering the opportunity cost of purchasing life insurance. Opportunity cost refers to what the insured policyholder gives up when life insurance is purchased. Since income is limited, the purchase of life insurance reduces the amount of discretionary income available for other high-priority needs. Many families today are heavily in debt and have little savings. Monthly payments on the mortgage, car loans, credit cards, utility costs, food, and taxes absorb most or all of an average family's income. Real wages for most middle-class families have remained relatively constant over the past 20 years. Thus, after payment of other high priority expenses, many family heads have only a limited amount of discretionary income available to purchase life insurance. *As a result, the optimal amount of life insurance that should be purchased may not be possible.* However, as will be pointed out later, families with limited amounts of income to spend on life insurance can purchase inexpensive term insurance.

After determining the amount of insurance to purchase the final step is to select the proper type of life insurance to purchase. The following section discusses the major types of life insurance that are sold today.

## TYPES OF LIFE INSURANCE

From a generic viewpoint, life insurance policies can be classified as either **term insurance** or **cash-value life insurance**. Term insurance provides temporary protection, while cash-value life insurance has a savings component and builds cash values. Numerous variations and combinations of these two types of life insurance are available today.[7]

### Term Insurance

Term insurance has several basic characteristics. First, the period of protection is temporary, such as 1, 5, 10, 20, or 30 years. Unless the policy is renewed, the protection expires at the end of the period.

Most term insurance policies are **renewable**, which means that the policy can be renewed for additional periods without evidence of insurability. The premium is increased at each renewal date and is based on the insured's attained age. The purpose of the renewal provision is to protect the insurability of the insured. However, the renewal provision results in adverse selection against the insurer. Because premiums increase with age, insureds in good health tend to drop their insurance, while those in poor health will continue to renew, regardless of the premium increase. To minimize adverse selection, many insurers have an age limitation beyond which renewal is not allowed, such as age 70 or 80. Some insurers, however, permit term policies to be renewed to age 95 or 99.

Most term insurance policies are also **convertible**, which means the term policy can be exchanged for a cash-value policy without evidence of insurability. There are two methods for converting a term policy. Under the *attained-age method,* the premium charged is based on the insured's attained age at the time of conversion. Under the *original-age method,* the premium charged is based on the insured's original age when the term insurance was first purchased. Most insurers offering the original-age method require the conversion to take place within a certain time period, such as five years, from the issue date of the term policy.

A financial adjustment is also required. Many insurers require policyholders to pay the larger of (1) the difference in reserves (or cash values) under the policies being exchanged, or (2) the difference between the premiums paid on the term policy and those that would have been paid on the new policy, with interest on the difference at a specified rate.[8] The purpose of the financial adjustment is to place the insurer in the same financial position it would have achieved if the policy had been issued at the original age. Because of the financial adjustment required, few term insurance policies are converted based on the original-age method.

Finally, term insurance policies have no cash-value or savings element. Although some long-term policies develop a small reserve, it is used up by the contract expiration date.

**Types of Term Insurance**   A wide variety of term insurance products are sold today. They include the following:

- Yearly renewable term
- 5-, 10-, 15-, 20-, 25-, or 30-year term
- Term to age 65
- Decreasing term
- Reentry term
- Return of premium term insurance

*Yearly renewable term insurance* is issued for a one-year period, and the policyholder can renew for successive one-year periods to some stated age without evidence of insurability. Premiums increase with age at each renewal date. Most yearly renewable term policies also allow the policyholder to convert to a cash-value policy with no evidence of insurability.

Term insurance can also be issued for *5, 10, 15, 20, 25, or 30 years.* The premiums paid during the term period are level, but they increase when the policy is renewed.

A *term to age 65 policy* provides protection to age 65, at which time the policy expires. The policy can be converted to a permanent plan of insurance, but the decision to convert must be exercised before age 65.

*Decreasing term insurance* is a form of term insurance where the face amount gradually declines each year. However, the premium is level throughout the period. In some policies, the premiums are structured so that the policy is fully paid for a few years before the coverage expires. For example, a 20-year decreasing term policy may require premium payments for 17 years. This method avoids paying a relatively large premium for only a small amount of insurance near the end of the term period.

**Reentry term** is a term insurance policy in which renewal premiums are based on select (lower) mortality rates if the insured can periodically demonstrate acceptable evidence of insurability. Select mortality rates are based on the mortality experience of recently insured lives. However, to remain on the low-rate schedule, the insured must periodically show that he or she is in good health and is still insurable. The rates are substantially increased if the insured cannot provide satisfactory evidence of insurability.

*Return of premium term insurance* is a product that returns the premiums at the end of the term period provided the insurance is still in force. Typical periods are 15, 20, 25, or 30 years. Depending on the insurer, there may be a partial refund if the insurance is not kept in force to the end of the period. The amount returned includes only base premiums and does not include any premiums for riders or substandard premiums.

Although this type of insurance is popular with consumers, it has several defects. The return of premiums suggests the insurance is free if the policy remains in force to the end of the term period; the protection is not free when the time value of money is considered. In addition, the insurance is expensive, which can result in a serious problem of underinsurance. For example, the annual premium charged by one insurer for a 15-year, $500,000 term insurance policy issued to a nonsmoking, preferred-risk male, age 32, is only $240. A return of premium policy would cost $985 annually, or 310 percent more. That same premium would buy more than $2 million of protection from the same company.

**Uses of Term Insurance**  Term insurance is appropriate in three situations. *First, if the amount of income that can be spent on life insurance is limited, term insurance can be effectively used.* Substantial amounts of life insurance can be purchased for a relatively modest annual premium outlay (see Exhibit 11.2).

*Second, term insurance is appropriate if the need for protection is temporary.* For example, decreasing term insurance can be used to pay off the mortgage if the family head dies prematurely, or provide income during the dependency period.

*Finally, term insurance can be used to guarantee future insurability.* People may desire large amounts of permanent insurance, but may be financially unable to purchase the needed protection today. Inexpensive term insurance can be purchased, which can be converted later into a permanent cash-value policy without evidence of insurability.

**EXHIBIT 11.2**
**Examples of Term Life Insurance Premiums**

**$500,000 Term Life Insurance Policy**

| | Female Annual Premiums | | | | | | Male Annual Premiums | | | | |
|---|---|---|---|---|---|---|---|---|---|---|---|
| Age | 10 Year | 15 Year | 20 Year | 25 Year | 30 Year | Age | 10 Year | 15 Year | 20 Year | 25 Year | 30 Year |
| 30 | $ 140 | $ 190 | $ 225 | $ 320 | $ 365 | 30 | $ 140 | $ 195 | $ 230 | $ 320 | $ 415 |
| 35 | $ 145 | $ 195 | $ 230 | $ 375 | $ 415 | 35 | $ 145 | $ 195 | $ 255 | $ 375 | $ 465 |
| 40 | $ 195 | $ 260 | $ 315 | $ 505 | $ 525 | 40 | $ 200 | $ 260 | $ 340 | $ 560 | $ 680 |
| 45 | $ 295 | $ 375 | $ 480 | $ 785 | $ 825 | 45 | $ 295 | $ 455 | $ 585 | $ 855 | $ 1,110 |
| 50 | $ 435 | $ 520 | $ 665 | $ 1,055 | $ 1,095 | 50 | $ 450 | $ 690 | $ 955 | $ 1,390 | $ 1,990 |
| 55 | $ 645 | $ 730 | $1,070 | $ 1,670 | $ 2,700 | 55 | $ 685 | $1,025 | $1,470 | $ 2,765 | $ 4,705 |
| 60 | $ 950 | $1,255 | $1,745 | $ 2,845 | $ 6,170 | 60 | $ 1,110 | $ 1,710 | $2,535 | $ 5,735 | $ 7,645 |
| 65 | $1,550 | $2,030 | $3,130 | $ 7,740 | $ 7,950 | 65 | $1,920 | $ 3,360 | $4,970 | $10,045 | $10,045 |
| 70 | $2,425 | $3,885 | $5,845 | $10,990 | $ 10,990 | 70 | $ 4,440 | $5,555 | $9,540 | $ 13,140 | $ 13,140 |

SOURCE: Insure.com

**Limitations of Term Insurance**   Term insurance has two major limitations. *First, term insurance premiums increase with age at an increasing rate and eventually reach prohibitive levels.* For example, in one insurer, a male, age 30, would pay an annual premium of $140 for a $500,000, 10-year term insurance policy. At age 70, this same policy would cost $4400 annually. Thus, term insurance is not suitable for individuals who need large amounts of life insurance beyond age 65 or 70.

*Second, term insurance is inappropriate if you wish to save money for a specific need.* Term insurance policies do not accumulate cash values. Thus, if you wish to save money for a child's college education or accumulate a fund for retirement, term insurance is inappropriate unless it is supplemented with an investment plan.

Decreasing term insurance also has several disadvantages. If you become uninsurable, you must convert the remaining insurance to a permanent plan to freeze the remaining amount of insurance. If the policy is not converted, the insurance protection continues to decline even though you are uninsurable. Moreover, decreasing term insurance does not provide for changing needs, such as birth of a child. Nor does it provide an effective hedge against inflation. Because of inflation, the amount of life insurance in most families should be periodically increased just to maintain the real purchasing power of the original policy.

## Whole Life Insurance

If the insured wants lifetime protection, term insurance is impractical because the coverage is temporary, and the premiums are prohibitive in cost at older ages. In contrast, **whole life insurance** *is a cash-value policy that provides lifetime protection.* Whole life insurance is also called ordinary life insurance. A stated amount is paid to a designated beneficiary when the insured dies, regardless of when the death occurs. Several types of whole life insurance are sold today. Some policies are traditional policies that have been widely sold in the past, whereas new variations of whole life insurance are constantly emerging.

**Ordinary Life Insurance**   Ordinary life insurance *is a level-premium policy that provides cash values and lifetime protection to age 121.* If the insured were to survive to age 121 (highly unlikely), the face amount of insurance would be paid at that time.

Ordinary life insurance has several basic characteristics. *First, as stated earlier, premiums are level throughout the premium-paying period.* As a result, the insured is actuarially overcharged during the early years and undercharged during the later years. The premiums paid during the early years are higher than is actuarially necessary to pay current death claims, whereas those paid in the later years are inadequate for paying death claims. *The excess premiums paid during the early years are accumulated at compound interest and are then used to supplement the inadequate premiums paid during the later years of the policy.* Because state law regulates the method of investing and accumulating the fund, it is referred to as a **legal reserve**. Technically, the legal reserve is a liability item that must be offset by sufficient financial assets. Otherwise, regulatory officials may declare the insurer to be insolvent. Insurers are required to calculate their minimum legal reserve liabilities according to certain standards.

Exhibit 11.3 shows the concept of the legal reserve under an ordinary life policy. The illustration is based on the newer 2001 CSO mortality table. As the death rate increases with age, the legal reserve or savings component steadily increases, and the pure insurance portion called the net amount of risk steadily declines. *The* **net amount at risk** *is the difference between the legal reserve and face amount of insurance.* As a result of an increasing legal reserve and decreasing net amount of risk, the cost of the insurance can be kept within manageable bounds at all ages, and the insurer can provide lifetime protection.[9]

*A second characteristic is the accumulation of* **cash-surrender values**, *which is the amount paid to a policyholder who surrenders the policy.* As noted earlier, under a system of level premiums, the policyholder overpays for the insurance protection during the early years, which results in a legal reserve and the accumulation of cash values.

Cash values should not be confused with the legal reserve. They are not the same thing and are computed separately. Because of the loading for expenses and high first-year acquisition expenses, cash values are initially below the legal reserve. However, the policyholder has the right to borrow the cash value or exercise one of the cash-surrender options. These options are discussed in Chapter 12.

Exhibit 11.3
**Relationship Between the Net Amount at Risk and Legal Reserve (2001 CSO Mortality Table)**

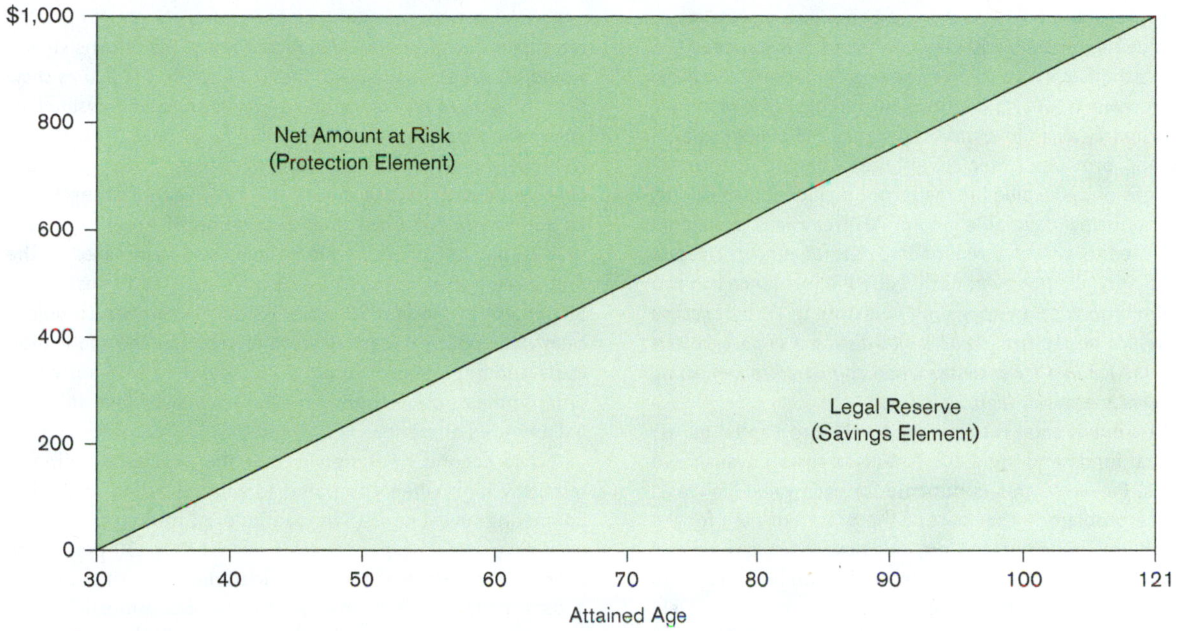

## Uses of Ordinary Life Insurance

*An ordinary life policy is appropriate when lifetime protection is needed.* This means that the need for life insurance will continue beyond age 65 or 70. Some financial planners and consumer experts point out that the average person does not need large amounts of life insurance beyond age 65, because the need for life insurance declines with age. This view is simplistic and misleading. Some persons may need substantial amounts of life insurance beyond age 65. For example, an estate clearance fund is still needed at the older ages; there may be a sizable estate tax problem if the estate is large; a divorce settlement may require the maintenance of a life insurance policy on a divorced spouse, regardless of age; and the policyholder may wish to leave a sizable bequest to a surviving spouse, children, or a charity, regardless of when death occurs. Because an ordinary life policy can provide lifetime protection, these objectives can be realized even though the insured dies at an advanced age.

*Ordinary life insurance can also be used to save money.* Some policyholders wish to meet their protection and savings needs with an ordinary life policy. As stated earlier, ordinary life insurance builds cash values that can be obtained by surrendering the policy or by borrowing the cash value.

Substantial amounts of cash-value life insurance are sold today as an investment and as a method to save money. Insight 11.2 discusses the investment merits of cash value life insurance in greater detail.

## Limitations of Ordinary Life Insurance

*The major limitation of ordinary life insurance is that some people are still underinsured after the policy is purchased.* Because of the savings feature, some people may voluntarily purchase or be persuaded by a life insurance agent to purchase an ordinary life policy when term insurance would be a better choice. For example, assume that Brandon, age 30, is married with two dependents to support. He estimates that he can spend only $500 annually on life insurance. Based on the rates of one insurer, this premium would purchase about $56,000 of ordinary life insurance. The same premium would purchase more than $600,000 of five-year term insurance from many insurers. It is difficult to justify the purchase of ordinary life insurance if it leaves the insured inadequately covered.

## INSIGHT 11.2

### Cash-Value Life Insurance as an Investment—Don't Ignore Two Points

Cash value life insurance is a superb product if you need life-time protection. It is also sold as a saving or investment vehicle. However, you should be cautious in purchasing a whole life policy primarily as an investment because the policy has cash values and provides other advantages. Alleged investment advantages of cash-value life insurance include forced saving, safety of principal, favorable income-tax treatment, protection against creditors, and a reasonable rate of return. Despite these advantages, however, cash-value life insurance has two major limitations as an appealing investment: (1) *the effective rate of return on the cash value is not disclosed to policyholders and (2) the loading for expenses when compared to competing investments is relatively high.*

The annual total return (dividends and capital gains) on mutual funds and individual stocks is readily available to investors. However, this is not true for cash-value life insurance. The problem is that part of the premium pays for the cost of the insurance protection, sales expenses, and administrative expenses, whereas the remainder can be allocated to the cash value. Various techniques, such as the Linton Yield and the yearly-rate-of-return method developed by Professor Joseph Belth, are available to estimate the rate of return on the cash value after deducting the cost of insurance (see Chapter 13). However, most policyholders are not aware of these methods and how they can be used. *Moreover, the life insurance industry has consistently opposed legislation that would require disclosure of the true effective annual rate of return on a cash-value policy.* Some policies, such as universal life insurance, quote a current rate that is credited to the policy, such as 4 or 5 percent, but this is a gross rate and does not reflect the true net rate of return after deducting the cost of insurance and other policy expenses.

Is the annual rate of return on a cash-value reasonable? The Consumer Federation of America has analyzed thousands of cash-value policies for consumers and has issued several reports. One earlier study of 57 cash-value policies showed the following:[a]

| Years Policy Held | Average Annual Rate of Return |
|---|---|
| 5 | −14.5% |
| 10 | 2.3% |
| 15 | 5.1% |
| 20 | 6.1% |

The annual returns are negative during the early years because of relatively high first-year acquisition expenses and other continuing policy expenses. Moreover, because interest rates have declined sharply in recent years, the returns shown would be substantially lower today. *However, the figures show that the annual rate of return can be considered "reasonable" only if you are willing to hold the policy for at least 20 years.* You will lose a considerable amount of money if you surrender or let your policy lapse during the early years. James Hunt, an actuary for the Consumer Federation of America, states that 26 percent of whole life policies are terminated in the first three policy years, 45 percent in the first 10 years, and 58 percent in the first 20 years. As such you need to hold a cash value policy at least 20 years to amortize the acquisition costs and get a decent return.[b] Policyholders who surrender or lapse their policies during the early years will lose substantial amounts of money.

The second limitation is that the expense loading is relatively high when compared to mutual funds and other competing investments. No load indexed mutual funds typically have annual expense ratios of less than .30 percent of assets. In contrast, the expense loading in life insurance is substantially higher, primarily because of commissions and sales expenses. The loading is especially high for the first 10 policy years for variable universal life insurance. For example, the prospectus for one variable universal life policy sold by a leading insurer in 2012 shows that the sales charge is 4 percent of premiums for the first four years and 3 percent for the next six years; however, the policy permits a maximum sales charge of 7.5 percent of premiums. There is an administrative charge of 3.75 percent of premiums for state and local premium taxes and for federal income taxes. In addition, there is a surrender charge of 100 percent of the target premium in the first policy year, which declines to zero in 10 years. There are also transaction charges and other fees as well, such as a cash withdrawal fee of the lesser of $25 or 2 percent of the withdrawal amount. These expenses do not include the investment management fees for investment advisors or managers of the various portfolios in which the premiums are invested. In this policy, investment management fees can range from .38 percent to 1.33 percent of the funds' assets, depending on the funds in which premiums are invested. *As you can see, sales charges, premium taxes, surrender charges, policy fees, administrative fees, and investment management fees can have a severe impact on the annual rate of return on a cash-value policy.*

[a]James H. Hunt, *Analysis of Cash Value Life Insurance Policies*, Consumer Federation of America, July 1997.
[b]James H. Hunt, *Miscellaneous Observations on Life Insurance: Including an Update to 2007 Paper on Variable Universal Life*, Consumer Federation of America, January 2011.

**Limited-Payment Life Insurance**    A limited-payment policy is another type of traditional whole life insurance. The insurance is permanent, and the insured has lifetime protection. The premiums are level, but they are paid only for a certain period. For example, Shannon, age 25, may purchase a 20-year limited payment policy in the amount of $25,000. After 20 years, the policy is completely paid up, and no additional premiums are required even though the coverage remains in force. A paid-up policy should not be confused with one that *matures*. A policy matures when the face amount is paid as a death claim or as an endowment. A policy is *paid-up* when no additional premium payments are required.

The most common limited-payment policies are for 10, 20, 25, or 30 years. A paid-up policy at age 65 or 70 is another form of limited-payment insurance. An extreme form of limited-payment life insurance is **single-premium whole life insurance**, which provides lifetime protection with a single premium. Because the premiums under a limited-payment policy are higher than those paid under an ordinary life policy, the cash values are also higher.

A limited-payment policy should be used with caution. It is extremely difficult for a person with a modest income to insure his or her life adequately with a limited-payment policy. Because of the relatively high premiums, the amount of permanent life insurance that can be purchased is substantially lower than if an ordinary life policy were purchased.

### Endowment Insurance

Endowment insurance is another traditional form of life insurance. **Endowment insurance** pays the face amount of insurance if the insured dies within a specified period; if the insured survives to the end of the endowment period, the face amount is paid to the policyholder at that time. For example, if Stephanie, age 25, purchases a 20-year endowment policy and dies anytime within the 20-year period, the face amount is paid to her beneficiary. If she survives to the end of the period, the face amount is paid to her.

At the present time, endowment insurance is relatively unimportant in terms of total life insurance in force. Endowment insurance accounts for less than 1 percent of the life insurance in force. Most new endowment policies cannot meet the tax definition of life insurance. If this definition is not met,

the investment income credited to the cash-surrender value is subject to current taxation. Thus, adverse tax consequences have discouraged the purchase of new endowment policies, and most life insurers have discontinued the sale of new endowment policies. Even so, many older endowment policies remain in force. Although endowment policies are no longer readily available in the United States, they are popular in many foreign countries.

## VARIATIONS OF WHOLE LIFE INSURANCE

To remain competitive and to overcome the criticisms of traditional cash-value policies, insurers have developed a wide variety of whole life products that combine insurance protection with an investment component. Important variations of whole life insurance include the following:

- Variable life insurance
- Universal life insurance
- Indexed universal life insurance
- Variable universal life insurance
- Current assumption whole life insurance

### Variable Life Insurance

**Variable life insurance** *can be defined as a fixed-premium policy in which the death benefit and cash values vary according to the investment experience of a separate account maintained by the insurer.* The death benefit and cash-surrender values will increase or decrease with the investment experience of the separate account. Although there are different policy designs, variable life policies have certain common features. They are summarized as follows:

- *A variable life policy is a permanent whole life contract with a fixed premium. The premium is level and is guaranteed not to increase.*
- *The entire reserve is held in a separate account and is invested in common stocks or other investments.* The policyholder has the option of investing the cash value in a variety of investments, such as a common stock fund, bond fund, balanced fund, money market fund, or international fund. If the investment experience is favorable, the face amount of insurance is increased.

If the investment experience is poor, the amount of life insurance could be reduced, but it can never fall below the original face amount. A variable life policy must be sold with a prospectus, which is a document that discloses benefit provisions, investment options, expenses, policyholder's rights, and other details about the policy.

■ *Cash-surrender values are not guaranteed, and there are no minimum guaranteed cash values.* The actual cash values depend on the investment experience. Thus, although the insurer bears the risk of excessive mortality and expenses, the policyholder bears the risk of poor investment results.

## Universal Life Insurance

Universal life insurance is another important variation of whole life insurance. **Universal life insurance** (also called flexible premium life insurance) *can be defined as a flexible premium policy that provides protection under a contract that unbundles the protection and saving components.* Except for the first premium, the policyholder determines the amount and frequency of payments. The premiums, less explicit expense charges, are credited to a cash value account (also called an accumulation fund) from which monthly mortality charges are deducted and to which monthly interest is credited. In addition, universal life policies typically have a monthly deduction for administrative expenses.

Universal life insurance has certain characteristics, which include the following:

■ Unbundling of protection and saving component
■ Two forms of universal life insurance
■ Considerable flexibility
■ Cash withdrawals permitted
■ Favorable income-tax treatment

**Unbundling of Component Parts**  A distinct characteristic of universal life insurance is the separation or unbundling of the protection component and the saving component. The policyholder receives an annual statement that shows the premiums paid, death benefit, and value of the cash-value account. The statement also shows the mortality charge and interest credited to the cash-value account.

■ *Premiums.* As noted earlier, except for the first premium, the policyholder determines the frequency and amount of premium payments. Most policies

have a *target premium,* which is a suggested level premium that will keep the policy in force for a specified number of years. However, the policyholder is not obligated to pay the target premium. Most policies also have a *no-lapse guarantee,* which guarantees that the policy will remain in force for a certain number of years, such as 15 or 20 years, if at least the minimum premium is paid. The minimum premium is specified in the policy and, depending on the insurer, may be less than or equal to the target premium.

■ *Mortality charge.* A monthly mortality charge is deducted from the cash value account for the cost of the insurance protection. The cost of insurance is determined by multiplying the applicable monthly mortality rate by the net amount at risk (difference between the current death benefit and cash value). The policy contains a table that shows the maximum rate per $1000 of insurance that the company can charge. Most insurers charge less than the maximum rate. However, the insurer has the right to increase the current mortality charge up to the maximum guaranteed rate stated in the policy.

■ *Expense charges.* Insurers typically deduct 5 to 10 percent of each premium for expenses. There is also a monthly fee for administrative expenses, such as $5 or $6. In addition, there is a relatively high surrender charge that applies if the policy is terminated during the early years. The surrender charge declines annually and disappears after a period of time, such as 10, 15, or 20 years. *As a result, the* policyholder *can lose a substantial amount of money if the policy is surrendered during the early years.* Finally, there is a charge for each partial cash withdrawal, such as $25.

■ *Interest rate.* Interest earnings credited to the cash-value account depend on the interest rate. There are two interest rates. The guaranteed cash value is credited with a contractually *guaranteed minimum interest rate,* such as 3 percent. The cash values, however, may be credited with a higher *current rate,* such as 4 percent. The current rate is not guaranteed but changes periodically depending on market conditions and company experience.

If the policyholder borrows the cash value, the amount borrowed is usually credited with a lower rate of interest. The cash value representing the amount borrowed is credited with either the minimum interest rate or a rate 1 to 2 percent below the policy loan rate.

**Two Forms of Universal Life Insurance** There are two forms of universal life insurance (see Exhibit 11.4). *Option A pays a level death benefit during the early years.* As the cash value increases over time, the net amount at risk declines. However, the death benefit increases during the later years of the policy if the cash value reaches the Internal Revenue limits. If the death benefit did not increase, the policy would not meet the

*corridor test* required by the Internal Revenue Code. As a result, the policy would not receive favorable income-tax treatment. The corridor test is a complex test that disqualifies a policy for favorable income-tax treatment if the cash values are excessive relative to the net amount at risk.

*Option B provides for an increasing death benefit.* The death benefit is equal to a constant net amount at risk plus the accumulated cash value. If the cash value increases over time, the death benefit will increase. Note that an increasing death benefit each year is not guaranteed. The illustration of Option B in Exhibit 11.4 is based on the assumption

**EXHIBIT 11.4**
**Two Forms of Universal Life Insurance Death Benefits**

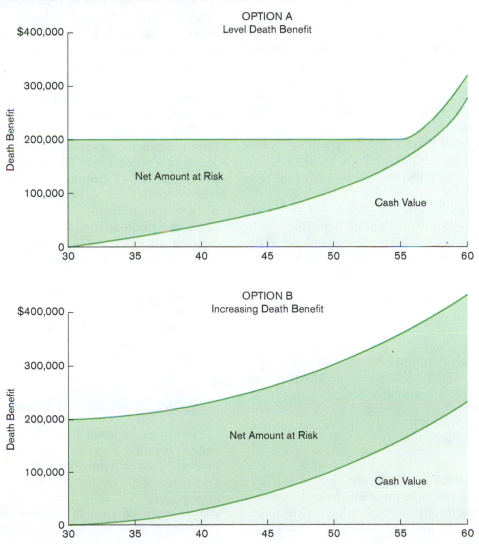

that the policyholder pays at least the target premium and that the interest-rate assumptions are realized. In reality, the premiums paid by the policyholder may vary, and interest rates will change periodically. Thus, actual cash values will fluctuate and could even decline to zero, especially if cash values are used to pay premiums, and interest rates decline. As a result of fluctuations in the cash-value account, the death benefit may fluctuate and may not necessarily increase each year.

**Considerable Flexibility** Compared to traditional whole life products, universal life insurance provides considerable flexibility, which includes the following:

- The policyholder determines the frequency and amount of premium payments. Premiums can be discontinued if there is sufficient cash value to pay mortality costs and expenses.
- The face amount of insurance can be increased with evidence of insurability. However, the face amount of insurance can be reduced with no evidence of insurability.
- The policy can be changed from a level death benefit to a death benefit equal to a specified face amount plus the policy cash value (with evidence of insurability).
- The policyholder can add cash to the policy at any time, subject to maximum guideline limits that govern the relationship between the cash value and the death benefit (tax law limitations).
- Policy loans are permitted at competitive interest rates.
- If the policy permits, additional insureds can be added.

**Cash Withdrawals Permitted** Part or all of the cash value can be withdrawn. Interest is not charged, but the death benefit is reduced by the amount of the withdrawal. Most insurers charge a fee for each cash withdrawal, such as $25. As noted earlier, policy loans are also permitted.

**Favorable Income-Tax Treatment** Universal life insurance enjoys the same favorable federal income-tax treatment as traditional cash-value policies. The death benefit paid to a named beneficiary is normally received income-tax free. Interest credited to the cash-value account is not taxable to the policyholder in the year credited.

**Universal Life Insurance Illustration** To illustrate how universal life insurance works, assume that Jason, age 25, buys a universal life policy with a level death benefit of $100,000. The annual planned premium is $445, which can be changed. For the sake of simplicity, assume that the mortality charge, expense charge, and crediting of interest are made annually. (However, in practice, there is a monthly deduction for mortality and expense charges and monthly crediting of interest.)

Each premium is subject to a 5 percent premium expense charge. The policy has a monthly administrative charge of $6. The policy provides for a maximum mortality charge, but the current mortality charge is only about two-thirds of the maximum rate. The policy has a guaranteed interest rate of 4.5 percent and a current interest rate of 5.5 percent that is not guaranteed.

When Jason pays the first premium of $445, there is a premium expense charge of approximately $22 (5 percent of $445). There is also an administrative charge of $72 ($6 monthly). The first-year mortality charge is $113 ($1.13 per $1000 of the specified $100,000 death benefit). The remaining $238 is credited with $13 of interest (5.5 percent on $238). Thus, the cash-value account at the end of the first year is $251. This calculation is summarized as follows:

| | |
|---|---:|
| Annual premium | $445 |
| Less: | |
| Premium expense charges | −22 |
| Administrative charges | −72 |
| Mortality cost | −113 |
| | $238 |
| Interest at 5.5 percent | +13 |
| Cash value account end of year | $251 |

However, if Jason surrenders the policy at the end of the first year, the surrender value is zero because of the surrender charge. A declining surrender charge applies if the policy is terminated within 16 years after the issue date. Exhibit 11.5 shows in greater detail the cash-value accumulation based on the guaranteed and current interest rates.

## Exhibit 11.5

**$100,000 Universal Life Policy, Level Death Benefit, Male Age 25, Nonsmoker, 5.5 Percent Assumed Interest**

| Age | Year | Premium Outlay | Guaranteed Values (4.5%) | | | Nonguaranteed Projected Values (5.5%) | | |
|-----|------|----------------|-------------------------|-----------|---------------------------|---------------------------------------|-----------|---------------------------|
| | | | Death Benefit | Cash Value | Cash Surrender Value | Death Benefit | Cash Value | Cash Surrender Value |
| 26 | 1 | $445.00 | $100,000 | $222 | $0 | $100,000 | $251 | $0 |
| 27 | 2 | 445.00 | 100,000 | 454 | 0 | 100,000 | 516 | 0 |
| 28 | 3 | 445.00 | 100,000 | 698 | 140 | 100,000 | 796 | 238 |
| 29 | 4 | 445.00 | 100,000 | 953 | 395 | 100,000 | 1,092 | 534 |
| 30 | 5 | 445.00 | 100,000 | 1,219 | 661 | 100,000 | 1,392 | 834 |
| 31 | 6 | 445.00 | 100,000 | 1,498 | 991 | 100,000 | 1,709 | 1,202 |
| 32 | 7 | 445.00 | 100,000 | 1,788 | 1,331 | 100,000 | 2,041 | 1,584 |
| 33 | 8 | 445.00 | 100,000 | 2,079 | 1,673 | 100,000 | 2,393 | 1,987 |
| 34 | 9 | 445.00 | 100,000 | 2,383 | 2,028 | 100,000 | 2,764 | 2,409 |
| 35 | 10 | 445.00 | 100,000 | 2,689 | 2,385 | 100,000 | 3,143 | 2,839 |
| 36 | 11 | 445.00 | 100,000 | 2,994 | 2,740 | 100,000 | 3,542 | 3,288 |
| 37 | 12 | 445.00 | 100,000 | 3,300 | 3,097 | 100,000 | 3,964 | 3,761 |
| 38 | 13 | 445.00 | 100,000 | 3,609 | 3,457 | 100,000 | 4,396 | 4,244 |
| 39 | 14 | 445.00 | 100,000 | 3,919 | 3,818 | 100,000 | 4,853 | 4,752 |
| 40 | 15 | 445.00 | 100,000 | 4,232 | 4,181 | 100,000 | 5,323 | 5,272 |
| 41 | 16 | 445.00 | 100,000 | 4,557 | 4,557 | 100,000 | 5,832 | 5,832 |
| 42 | 17 | 445.00 | 100,000 | 4,872 | 4,872 | 100,000 | 6,369 | 6,369 |
| 43 | 18 | 445.00 | 100,000 | 5,190 | 5,190 | 100,000 | 6,924 | 6,924 |
| 44 | 19 | 445.00 | 100,000 | 5,495 | 5,495 | 100,000 | 7,509 | 7,509 |
| 45 | 20 | 445.00 | 100,000 | 5,790 | 5,790 | 100,000 | 8,114 | 8,114 |
| 46 | 21 | 445.00 | 100,000 | 6,069 | 6,069 | 100,000 | 8,739 | 8,739 |
| 47 | 22 | 445.00 | 100,000 | 6,325 | 6,325 | 100,000 | 9,376 | 9,376 |
| 48 | 23 | 445.00 | 100,000 | 6,568 | 6,568 | 100,000 | 10,025 | 10,025 |
| 49 | 24 | 445.00 | 100,000 | 6,785 | 6,785 | 100,000 | 10,687 | 10,687 |
| 50 | 25 | 445.00 | 100,000 | 6,976 | 6,976 | 100,000 | 11,363 | 11,363 |
| 51 | 26 | 445.00 | 100,000 | 7,133 | 7,133 | 100,000 | 12,052 | 12,052 |
| 52 | 27 | 445.00 | 100,000 | 7,242 | 7,242 | 100,000 | 12,729 | 12,729 |
| 53 | 28 | 445.00 | 100,000 | 7,280 | 7,280 | 100,000 | 13,390 | 13,390 |
| 54 | 29 | 445.00 | 100,000 | 7,241 | 7,241 | 100,000 | 14,033 | 14,033 |
| 55 | 30 | 445.00 | 100,000 | 7,106 | 7,106 | 100,000 | 14,668 | 14,668 |
| 56 | 31 | 445.00 | 100,000 | 6,866 | 6,866 | 100,000 | 15,282 | 15,282 |
| 57 | 32 | 445.00 | 100,000 | 6,498 | 6,498 | 100,000 | 15,873 | 15,873 |
| 58 | 33 | 445.00 | 100,000 | 5,981 | 5,981 | 100,000 | 16,445 | 16,445 |
| 59 | 34 | 445.00 | 100,000 | 5,282 | 5,282 | 100,000 | 16,989 | 16,989 |
| 60 | 35 | 445.00 | 100,000 | 4,370 | 4,370 | 100,000 | 17,483 | 17,483 |

*(Continued)*

EXHIBIT 11.5 (continued)
**$100,000 Universal Life Policy, Level Death Benefit, Male Age 25, Nonsmoker, 5.5 Percent Assumed Interest**

| | | | Guaranteed Values (4.5%) | | | Nonguaranteed Projected Values (5.5%) | | |
| --- | --- | --- | --- | --- | --- | --- | --- | --- |
| Age | Year | Premium Outlay | Death Benefit | Cash Value | Cash Surrender Value | Death Benefit | Cash Value | Cash Surrender Value |
| 61 | 36 | 445.00 | 100,000 | 3,562 | 3,562 | 100,000 | 18,111 | 18,111 |
| 62 | 37 | 445.00 | 100,000 | 2,567 | 2,567 | 100,000 | 18,723 | 18,723 |
| 63 | 38 | 445.00 | 100,000 | 1,362 | 1,362 | 100,000 | 19,298 | 19,298 |
| 64 | 39 | 445.00 | 0* | 0 | 0 | 100,000 | 19,839 | 19,839 |
| 65 | 40 | 445.00 | | | | 100,000 | 20,322 | 20,322 |
| 66 | 41 | 445.00 | | | | 100,000 | 20,819 | 20,819 |
| 67 | 42 | 445.00 | | | | 100,000 | 21,233 | 21,233 |
| 68 | 43 | 445.00 | | | | 100,000 | 21,570 | 21,570 |
| 69 | 44 | 445.00 | | | | 100,000 | 21,824 | 21,824 |
| 70 | 45 | 445.00 | | | | 100,000 | 21,951 | 21,951 |
| 71 | 46 | 445.00 | | | | 100,000 | 21,915 | 21,915 |
| 72 | 47 | 445.00 | | | | 100,000 | 21,721 | 21,721 |
| 73 | 48 | 445.00 | | | | 100,000 | 21,327 | 21,327 |
| 74 | 49 | 445.00 | | | | 100,000 | 20,695 | 20,695 |
| 75 | 50 | 445.00 | | | | 100,000 | 19,772 | 19,772 |
| 76 | 51 | 445.00 | | | | 100,000 | 18,478 | 18,478 |
| 77 | 52 | 445.00 | | | | 100,000 | 16,780 | 16,780 |
| 78 | 53 | 445.00 | | | | 100,000 | 14,574 | 14,574 |
| 79 | 54 | 445.00 | | | | 100,000 | 11,770 | 11,770 |
| 80 | 55 | 445.00 | | | | 100,000 | 8,215 | 8,215 |
| 81 | 56 | 445.00 | | | | 100,000 | 3,685 | 3,685 |
| 82 | 57 | 445.00 | | | | 0* | 0 | 0 |

NOTE: This illustration assumes that the nonguaranteed projected values currently illustrated will continue unchanged for all years shown. This is not likely to occur, and actual results may be more or less favorable. Projected values are based on nonguaranteed elements that are subject to change. Guaranteed values are based on a guaranteed interest rate of 4.5 percent. Projected values are based on a current interest rate of 5.5 percent. Premiums are assumed to be paid at the beginning of the year. Benefits, cash values, and ages are shown at the end of the year.
*Coverage will terminate under current assumptions. Additional premiums would be required to continue coverage.

**Limitations of Universal Life**   Universal life insurance has several limitations. Consumer experts point out the following limitations:[11]

- *Misleading rates of return.* The advertised rates of return on universal life insurance are misleading. For example, insurers may advertise current rates of interest of 3 or 4 percent on universal life policies. *However, the advertised rates are gross rates and not net rates.* The advertised gross

rate overstates the rate of return on the saving component because it does not reflect deductions for sales commissions, expenses, and the cost of the insurance protection. As a result of these deductions, the effective yearly return is substantially lower than the advertised rate and is often negative for several years after the policy is purchased.

- *Decline in interest rates.* Many earlier sales presentations showed sizable future cash values based on relatively high interest rates. However, interest rates have declined significantly over time. *As a result, the earlier cash-value and premium-payment projections based on higher interest rates are misleading and invalid.* Actual cash values will be substantially less than the projected values based on higher interest rates when the policy was first sold.

- *Right to increase the mortality charge.* As stated earlier, insurers can increase the current mortality charge for the cost of insurance up to some maximum limit. Other expenses may be hidden in the mortality charge. If the insurer's expenses increase, the mortality charge could be increased to recoup these expenses. The increase may not be noticed or questioned because the insured may believe the increase is justified because he or she is getting older.
- *Lack of firm commitment to pay premiums.* Another limitation is that some policyholders do not have a firm commitment to pay premiums. As a result, the policy may lapse because of nonpayment of premiums. As stated earlier, premiums can be reduced or skipped in a universal life policy. However, at some point, money must be added to the account, or the policy will lapse.

### Indexed Universal Life Insurance

**Indexed universal life insurance** is a variation of universal life insurance with certain key characteristics.[12] First, there is a minimum interest rate guarantee, which is usually lower than the minimum interest rate guarantee on a regular universal life policy.

Second, additional interest may be credited to the policy based on the investment gains of a specific stock market index, such as the Standard & Poor's 500 index. However, dividends on the S&P 500 index are not included in determining the performance of the stock market.

Third, there is a formula for determining the amount of enhanced (additional) interest credited to the policy; the formula usually places a *cap* on the maximum upper limit of additional interest credited to the policy; the formula may also place a limit on the *participation rate* that applies to the index. That is, the policy may participate in stock market gains at a rate lower than 100 percent of the increase in the stock market index used.

Finally, there is often considerable consumer misunderstanding and unrealistic performance expectations under this type of policy. Some experts believe

that during periods of poor stock market performance, the indexed policy generally will underperform when compared to a regular universal life policy. As stated earlier, dividends on the S&P 500 index are not included in the measurement of stock market gains; this is an important limitation because dividends have accounted for a large part of the increase in the S&P 500 index over time. Also, the minimum interest rate credited to the indexed policy may be 50 to 150 basis points lower than the minimum rate credited to a standard universal life policy. In addition, the formula used to calculate enhanced interest often has maximum limits on the cap and participation rate. These are formidable performance obstacles for the indexed policy to overcome. At best, some experts believe that, in a strong bull market, indexed policies will have crediting rates only slightly above the minimum guaranteed rate.[13]

### Variable Universal Life Insurance

**Variable universal life insurance** is an important variation of whole life insurance. Most variable universal life policies are sold as investments or tax shelters.

Variable universal life insurance is similar to a universal life policy with two major exceptions:

- The policyholder determines how the premiums are invested, which provides considerable investment flexibility.
- The policy does not guarantee a minimum interest rate or minimum cash value. One exception, however, is that the policy may have a fixed-income account, which may guarantee a minimum interest rate on the account value.

**Selection of Investments by Policyholders** *A variable universal life policy allows the* policyholders *to invest the premiums in a wide variety of investments.* The premiums are invested in one or more *separate accounts,* which are similar to mutual funds in their daily operations. Insurers typically have 10 or more separate accounts available. These accounts typically include a common stock fund, bond fund, balanced fund, international fund, real estate fund, money market fund, and other accounts. Some insurers also use the mutual funds of investment companies as subaccounts, such as mutual funds sold by Fidelity Investments and the Vanguard Group. The premiums purchase accumulation units, which reflect the value of the underlying investments.

Policyholders also have the option of switching out of the different funds without incurring an income-tax liability, such as switching out of a bond fund into a money market fund if interest rates are expected to rise.

**No Minimum Interest Rate or Cash Value Guarantees** Unlike a universal life policy, *a variable universal life policy has no guaranteed minimum interest rate and no guaranteed minimum cash value.* When you buy a universal life policy, the cash value account earns a stated rate of interest determined by the insurer from time to time; there is also a minimum interest-rate guarantee. However, when you buy a variable universal life policy, you select one or more separate accounts, and the policy cash values reflect the value of these accounts. There is no minimum interest-rate or cash-value guarantee. However, as stated earlier, a fixed-income account may guarantee a minimum interest rate on the account value, such as 3 percent.

**Relatively High Expense Charges** Variable universal life insurance policies have relatively high expense charges, which reduce the investment returns and erode the favorable tax treatment under the policy. Variable universal life insurance is typically sold as a tax shelter. Investment earnings are not currently taxable as income to the policyholder. If the policy stays in force until death, no federal income taxes are ever payable even if the separate account has sizable capital gains. However, according to the Consumer Federation of America, the various expense charges can more than offset the favorable income-tax treatment that variable universal life insurance now enjoys. A study of variable universal life policies by the Consumer Federation of America (CFA) showed the following charges:[14]

- *Front-end load.* Some policies have front-end loads for sales commissions and expenses, such as 5 percent.
- *Back-end surrender charge.* Policies purchased from agents typically have back-end surrender charges. The surrender charge usually exceeds the first-year premium and declines to zero over a 10- to 20-year period. Many policies have surrender charges that are level for the first five years, and then start to decline.
- *State premium taxes and federal taxes.* State premium taxes that vary by state and federal taxes average about 3 percent of premiums.

- *Investment management fees.* Deductions from the separate accounts are made daily for investment management fees. For the policies studied, investment management fees ranged from .20 percent to 1.62 percent of assets.
- *Mortality and expense charges.* Mortality and expense (M&E) charges are also deducted for certain insurer guarantees. The variable universal life insurer guarantees the death benefit even though the stock market and other markets are declining; the insurer also guarantees future expense charges regardless of inflation. The CFA study showed that M&E charges ranged from .60 percent to .90 percent of the cash value.
- *Administrative costs.* Administrative costs are deducted monthly from the separate accounts, typically $5 to $10.

In addition to the above charges, there is a monthly deduction for the cost of insurance. The applicable mortality rate is multiplied by the net amount at risk (face amount minus the cash value) to determine the insurance charge.

**Substantial Investment Risk** Variable universal life insurance is a risky type of life insurance to own. There is a substantial investment risk that falls entirely on the policyholder. Investment returns vary widely, depending on how the funds are invested. If the investment experience is poor, cash values can decline to zero. This is particularly important for policyholders who are making only minimum premium payments or have discontinued premium payments. If the premiums are invested largely in common stocks and the separate account declines sharply because of a severe stock market decline, such as in 2008–2009, the policyholder may have to pay additional premiums to keep the policy in force.

### Current Assumption Whole Life Insurance

**Current assumption whole life insurance** *(also called interest-sensitive whole life) is a nonparticipating whole life policy in which the cash values are based on the insurer's current mortality, investment, and expense experience.* A nonparticipating policy is a policy that does not pay dividends.

**Common Features** Although current assumption whole life products vary among insurers, they share some common features, summarized as follows:[15]

- *An accumulation account reflects the cash value under the policy.* The accumulation account is credited with the premiums paid less expenses and mortality charges plus interest based on current rates.
- *If the policy is surrendered, a surrender charge is deducted from the accumulation account.* A surrender charge that declines over time is deducted from the accumulation account to determine the net cash-surrender value.
- *A guaranteed interest rate and current interest rate are used to determine cash values.* The minimum cash values are based on the guaranteed interest rate, such as 3 or 4 percent. However, the accumulation account is credited with a higher interest rate based on current market conditions and company experience.
- *A fixed death benefit and maximum premium level at the time of issue are stated in the policy.* (However, under the low-premium version discussed next, both are subject to change.)
- *The premium is periodically redetermined or adjusted based on the actual experience of the block of policies since the last redetermination date. Depending on the policy, the redetermination can be done annually, every two years, or every five years.*

In addition to having the preceding characteristics, current assumption whole life products generally can be classified into two categories: (1) low-premium products and (2) high-premium products.

**Low-Premium Products**    Under the low-premium version, the initial premium is substantially lower than the premium paid for a regular, nonparticipating whole life policy. The low premium is initially guaranteed only for a certain period, such as five years. However, after the initial guaranteed period expires, a *redetermination provision* allows the insurer to recalculate the premium based on the same or different actuarial assumptions with respect to mortality, interest, and expenses (hence, the name "current assumption whole life"). If the new premium is higher than the initial premium, the policyholder generally has the option of paying the higher premium and maintaining the same death benefit. Alternatively, the policyholder can continue to pay the lower premium, but the death benefit is reduced.

**High-Premium Products**    Although premiums are higher under the second category, these policies typically contain a *provision that allows the policyholder to discontinue paying premiums* after a certain time period, such as 10 years. The policy becomes self-sustaining when the accumulation account exceeds the net single premium needed to pay up the contract based on current interest and mortality costs.[16] *However, the policy remains paid up only if current interest and mortality experience remain unchanged or are more favorable than initially assumed.* If the accumulation account falls below the minimum cash-surrender value, additional premiums are required.

Exhibit 11.6 summarizes the basic characteristics of the major forms of life insurance. This chart helps to clarify how the major types of life insurance differ.

## OTHER TYPES OF LIFE INSURANCE

A wide variety of additional life insurance products are sold today. Some policies are designed to meet special needs or have unique features. Others combine term insurance and cash-value life insurance to meet these needs. Still others should be avoided (see Insight 11.3).

### Modified Life Insurance

A **modified life policy** is a whole life policy in which premiums are lower for the first three to five years and higher thereafter. The initial premium is slightly higher than for term insurance, but considerably lower than for a whole life policy issued at the same age.

The major advantage of a modified life policy is that applicants for insurance can purchase permanent insurance immediately even though they cannot afford the higher premiums for a regular whole life policy. Modified life insurance is particularly attractive to persons who expect that their incomes will increase in the future and that higher premiums will not be financially burdensome.

### Preferred Risks

Most life insurers sell policies at lower rates to individuals known as **preferred risks**. These people are individuals whose mortality experience is expected to

## INSIGHT 11.3

### Be a Savvy Consumer—Four Life Insurance Policies to Avoid

For savvy consumers, certain life insurance policies are of doubtful value and should be avoided. They include the following:

- *Flight insurance at airports.* Skip the flight insurance at the airport. This is a limited form of life insurance that covers only the flight. You want to own life insurance that pays off regardless of the cause of death. Moreover, commercial jets seldom crash, so any payoff is doubtful.
- *Credit life insurance.* Credit life insurance pays off a loan if the borrower dies; the bank or lending institution is the beneficiary. According to the Consumer Federation of America, credit life insurance in most states is a "rip-off."[a] Consumers cannot effectively shop for credit life insurance; it is substantially overpriced and is not a low-cost product, it enables lenders to increase the effective yield on a loan, and the loss ratio is relatively low in many states (ratio of benefits paid to premiums). Even though the states regulate credit life insurance, consumer advocates generally believe the insurance is still overpriced. Credit

life insurance from a credit union, however, may be an exception.

- *Accidental death and dismemberment insurance.* This is a limited form of life insurance that pays off only if you die in an accident. You want to own life insurance that pays off regardless of the cause. Death from disease is typically excluded, yet the vast majority of people who die will die as a result of disease, not in an accident.
- *Cash-value policies on children.* Your children usually are not the breadwinners in the family. Although the emotional grief is enormous when a child dies, the family generally does not lose any earned income. Most parents are substantially underinsured, and scarce premium dollars should be used to insure the breadwinners and not the children. If you want insurance on your children for possible burial purposes, call your agent and get an inexpensive term insurance rider added to your present policy.

[a]Consumer Federation of America, *Most Credit Life Insurance Still a Rip-Off*, January 29, 1997.

be lower than average. The policy is carefully underwritten and is sold only to individuals whose health history, weight, occupation, and habits indicate more favorable mortality than the average. The insurer may also require the purchase of a minimum amount of insurance, such as $250,000 or $500,000. If an individual qualifies for a preferred rate, substantial savings are possible.

A discount for nonsmokers is a current example of a preferred risk policy. Most insurers offer substantially lower rates to nonsmokers in recognition of the more favorable mortality that can be expected of this group.

### Second-to-Die Life Insurance

**Second-to-die life insurance** (also called survivorship life) is a form of life insurance that insures two or more lives and pays the death benefit upon the death of the second or last insured. The insurance usually is whole life, but it can be term. Because the death proceeds are paid only upon the death of the second or last insured, the premiums are substantially lower than if two individual policies were issued.

Second-to-die life insurance is widely used at the present time in estate planning. As a result of an unlimited marital deduction, the deceased's entire estate can be left to a surviving spouse free of any federal estate tax. However, when the surviving spouse dies, a sizable state or federal estate tax may be due. A second-to-die policy would provide estate liquidity and the cash to pay estate taxes.

### Savings Bank Life Insurance

**Savings bank life insurance (SBLI)** is a type of life insurance that was sold originally by savings banks in Massachusetts, New York, and Connecticut. SBLI is now sold in most states and in the District of Columbia to consumers over the phone or through Web sites. The objective of SBLI is to provide low-cost life insurance to consumers by holding down operating costs and payment of high sales commissions.

Maximum limits on the amount of life insurance on an individual's life have been substantially raised. In Massachusetts, the amount of term insurance on a single life ranges from $100,000 to $20 million ($500,000 maximum for ages 70-74). In addition, SBLI products in Massachusetts are sold directly to consumers in most

**EXHIBIT 11.6**

**Comparison of Major Life Insurance Contracts**

| | Term Insurance | Ordinary Life Insurance | Variable Life Insurance | Universal Life Insurance | Variable Universal Life Insurance | Current Assumption Whole Life Insurance |
|---|---|---|---|---|---|---|
| **Death benefit paid** | Level or decreasing death benefit | Level death benefit | Guaranteed minimum death benefit plus increased amount from favorable investment returns | Either level or an increasing death benefit | Either level (option A) or variable based on investment returns (option B) | Level death benefit |
| **Cash value** | No cash value | Guaranteed cash values | Cash value depends on investment performance (not guaranteed) | Guaranteed minimum interest rate plus excess interest credited to the account | Cash value depends on investment performance (not guaranteed) | Guaranteed minimum cash value plus excess interest credited |
| **Premiums paid** | Premiums increase at each renewal | Level premiums | Fixed-level premiums | Flexible premiums | Flexible premiums | Premiums paid may vary based on insurer experience; guaranteed maximum premium |
| **Policy loans** | No | Yes | Yes | Yes | Yes | Yes |
| **Partial withdrawal of cash value** | No | No | Permitted in some policies | Yes | Yes | Yes |
| **Surrender charge** | No | No explicit charge stated (reflected in cash values) | Yes | Yes | Yes | Yes |

states, including Maine, New Hampshire, New Jersey, Pennsylvania, and Rhode Island.

In New York, savings bank life insurance was created in 1939. In 1999, a change in the law allowed savings bank life insurance to be sold by one mutual life insurance company. Established in 2000, the company is now called the SBLI USA Mutual Life Insurance Company. However, in 2010, because of difficulty in raising new capital, SBLI USA temporarily discontinued the sale of new life insurance and annuity products. Existing policies, however, are still being serviced.

Savings bank life insurance is also available in Connecticut. However, the Savings Bank Life Insurance Company in Connecticut is now known as Vantis Life. The name was changed to avoid confusion with the Savings Bank Life Insurance Co. of Massachusetts, which is a different insurer. Applicants can purchase up to $5 million of term insurance and up to $5 million in permanent coverage.

### Industrial Life Insurance

Historically, **industrial life insurance** was a class of life insurance that was issued in small amounts; premiums were payable weekly or monthly; and an agent of the company collected the premiums at the insured's home. More than nine out of ten policies were cash-value policies.

Today, industrial life insurance is called **home service life insurance**. In most cases, home collections are no longer made. The policyholder remits the premiums to the agent or to the company. The amount of life insurance per policy generally ranges from $5000 to $25,000. Home service life insurance is relatively unimportant and accounts for less than 1 percent of all life insurance in force.

### Group Life Insurance

**Group life insurance** is a type of insurance that provides life insurance on a group of people in a single master contract. Physical examinations are not required, and certificates of insurance are issued as evidence of insurance.

Group life insurance is important in terms of total life insurance in force. In 2010, group life insurance accounted for 48 percent of all life insurance in force in the United States.[17] Group life insurance is a basic employee benefit that will be discussed in greater detail in Chapter 16.

---

## CASE APPLICATION

Sharon, age 28, is a single parent who earns $30,000 annually as a secretary at a local university. She is the sole support of her son, age 3. Sharon is concerned about the financial well-being of her son if she should die. Although she finds it difficult to save, she would like to start a savings program to send her son to college. She is currently renting an apartment but would like to own a home someday. A friend has told her that life insurance might be useful in her present situation. Sharon knows nothing about life insurance, and the amount of income available for life insurance is limited. Assume you are a financial planner who is asked to make recommendations concerning the type of life insurance that Sharon should buy. The following types of life insurance policies are available:

- Five-year renewable and convertible term
- Life-paid-up-at-age 65
- Ordinary life insurance
- Universal life insurance

a. Which of these policies would best meet the need for protection of Sharon's son if she should die prematurely? Explain your answer.

b. Which of these policies best meets the need to accumulate a college fund for Sharon's son? Explain your answer.

c. Which of these policies best meets the need to accumulate money for a down payment on a home? Explain your answer.

d. What major obstacle does Sharon face if she tries to meet all of her financial needs by purchasing cash-value life insurance?

e. Assume that Sharon decides to purchase the five-year term policy in the amount of $300,000. The policy has no cash value. Identify a basic characteristic of a typical term insurance policy that would help Sharon accumulate a fund for retirement.

# SUMMARY

- Premature death means that a family head dies with outstanding unfulfilled financial obligations, such as dependents to support, children to educate, or a mortgage to pay off.

- At least four costs are associated with premature death:

  There is the loss of the human life value.

  Additional expenses may be incurred, such as funeral expenses, uninsured medical bills, and estate settlement costs.

  Because of insufficient income, some families may experience a reduction in their standard of living.

  Noneconomic costs are incurred, such as the emotional grief of the surviving dependents and the loss of a role model and guidance for the children.

- The purchase of life insurance can be economically justified if a person has an earning capacity, and someone is dependent on those earnings for at least part of his or her financial support.

- The financial impact of premature death varies by family type. Premature death can cause considerable economic insecurity if a family head dies in a single-parent family, in a family with two-income earners with children, or in a traditional, blended, or sandwiched family. In contrast, if a single person without dependents or an income earner in a two-income family without children dies, financial problems for the survivors are less likely to occur.

- The human life value is defined as the present value of the family's share of the deceased breadwinner's future earnings. This approach crudely measures the economic value of a human life.

- The needs approach can be used to determine the amount of life insurance to purchase. After considering other sources of income and financial assets, the various family needs are converted into specific amounts of life insurance. The most important family needs are as follows:

  Estate clearance fund

  Income during the readjustment period

  Income during the dependency period

  Life income to the surviving spouse

  Special needs: mortgage redemption, college education, emergencies, mentally or physically challenged children

  Retirement needs

- The capital retention approach for estimating the amount of life insurance to purchase is based on the assumption that income-producing capital will be preserved and not liquidated.

- *Term insurance* provides temporary protection and is typically renewable and convertible without evidence of insurability. Term insurance is appropriate when income is limited, or when there are temporary needs. Because term insurance has no cash values, it cannot be used for retirement or savings purposes.

- There are several traditional forms of whole life insurance. *Ordinary life insurance* is a form of whole life insurance that provides lifetime protection. The premiums are level and are payable for life. The policy develops an investment or saving element called a cash-surrender value, which results from the overpayment of premiums during the early years. An ordinary life policy is appropriate when lifetime protection is desired or additional savings are desired.

- The legal reserve is a liability item for an insurer that reflects the excess premiums paid during the early years of the policy. The fundamental purpose of the legal reserve is to provide lifetime protection.

- Because a legal reserve is necessary for lifetime protection, cash values become available. Because the insured has paid more than is actuarially necessary during the early years of the policy, he or she should receive something back if the policy is surrendered.

- A *limited-payment policy* is another traditional form of whole life insurance. The insured also has lifetime protection, but the premiums are paid only for a limited period, such as 10, 20, or 30 years, or until age 65.

- *Endowment insurance* pays the face amount of insurance if the insured dies within a specified period. If the insured survives to the end of the endowment period, the face amount of insurance is paid to the policyholder at that time. Endowment insurance is relatively unimportant in the United States because of certain tax disadvantages.

- *Variable life insurance* is a fixed-premium policy in which the death benefit and cash-surrender value vary according to the investment experience of a separate account maintained by the insurer. The entire reserve is held in a separate account and is invested in common stocks or other investments. The cash-surrender values are not guaranteed.

- *Universal life insurance* is another variation of whole life insurance. Conceptually, universal life can be viewed as a flexible-premium policy that provides lifetime protection under a contract that separates the protection and saving components. Universal life insurance has the following features:

  - Unbundling of protection, savings, and expense components
  - Two forms of universal life insurance
  - Considerable flexibility
  - Cash withdrawals permitted
  - Favorable income-tax treatment

- *Variable universal life insurance* is similar to universal life insurance with two major exceptions. First, the cash values can be invested in a wide variety of investments. Second, there is no minimum guaranteed interest rate, and the investment risk falls entirely on the policyholder.

- *Current assumption whole life insurance* is a nonparticipating whole life policy in which the cash values are based on the insurer's current mortality, investment, and expense experience. An accumulation account is credited with a current interest rate that changes over time.

- A *modified life policy* is a whole life policy in which premiums are lower for the first three to five years and are higher thereafter.

- Many insurers sell policies with lower rates to preferred risks. The policies are carefully underwritten and sold only to individuals whose health history, weight, occupation, and habits indicate more favorable mortality than average. Minimum amounts of insurance must be purchased.

- *Second-to-die life insurance* (*survivorship life*) insures two or more lives and pays the death benefit upon the death of the second or last insured.

- *Savings bank life insurance* is sold in Massachusetts, New York, Connecticut, and other states. It is also sold directly to consumers over the phone or Internet.

- *Industrial life insurance* is a type of insurance in which the policies are sold in small amounts, and the premiums earlier were paid to an agent at the policyholder's home.

- *Group life insurance* provides life insurance on people in a group under a single master contract. Physical exami-

nations generally are not required. Group life insurance is a basic employee benefit in employer-sponsored group life insurance plans.

## KEY CONCEPTS AND TERMS

Blackout period (203)
Capital retention approach (206)
Cash-surrender value (210)
Cash-value life insurance (208)
Convertible (208)
Current assumption whole life insurance (220)
Dependency period (203)
Endowment insurance (213)
Estate clearance fund (202)
Group life insurance (224)
Human life value (201)
Indexed universal life insurance (219)
Industrial (home service) life insurance (224)
Legal reserve (210)
Limited-payment policy (213)
Modified life policy (221)
Needs approach (202)
Net amount at risk (210)
Ordinary life insurance (210)
Preferred risks (221)
Premature death (199)
Readjustment period (202)
Reentry term (209)
Renewable (208)
Savings bank life insurance (222)
Second-to-die life insurance (222)
Single-premium whole life insurance (213)
Term insurance (208)
Universal life insurance (214)
Variable life insurance (213)
Variable universal life insurance (219)
Whole life insurance (210)

## REVIEW QUESTIONS

1. a. Explain the meaning of premature death.
   b. Identify the costs associated with premature death.
   c. Explain the economic justification for the purchase of life insurance.

2. Explain the financial impact of premature death on the different types of families in the United States.

3. a. Define the human life value.
   b. Describe the steps in determining the human life value of a family head.

4. a. The needs approach is widely used for determining the amount of life insurance to purchase. Describe the following needs for a typical family head:
   1. Cash needs
   2. Income needs
   3. Special needs

b. Explain the capital retention approach for determining the amount of life insurance to own.

5. a. Briefly explain the basic characteristics of term insurance.
   b. Identify the major types of term insurance sold today.
   c. Explain the situations that justify the purchase of term insurance.
   d. What are the major limitations of term insurance?

6. a. Briefly explain the basic characteristics of ordinary life policies.
   b. Why does an ordinary life insurance policy develop a legal reserve?
   c. Explain the situations that justify the purchase of ordinary life insurance.
   d. What is the major limitation of ordinary life insurance?

7. Describe the basic characteristics of variable life insurance.

8. a. Explain the basic characteristics of universal life policies.
   b. Explain the limitations of universal life insurance.

9. a. What is a variable universal life insurance policy?
   b. How does variable universal life insurance differ from a typical universal life insurance policy?
   c. Identify the various expense charges that policyholders must pay under a variable universal life insurance policy.

10. a. Describe the basic features of current assumption whole life insurance.
    b. What is a preferred risk policy?

## APPLICATION QUESTIONS

1. Richard, age 45, is married with two children in high school. He estimates that his average annual earnings over the next 20 years will be $60,000. He estimates that one-third of his average annual earnings will be used to pay taxes, insurance premiums, and the costs of self-maintenance. The remainder will be used to support his family. Richard wants to calculate his human life value and believes a 6 percent discount rate is appropriate. The present value of $1 payable for 20 years at a discount rate of 6 percent is $11.47. Calculate Richard's human life value.

2. a. The human life value is one method for estimating the amount of life insurance to own. Keeping all other factors unchanged, explain the effect, if any, of each of the following:
   1. The discount rate used to calculate the human life value is increased.
   2. The amount of average annual income going to the family is increased.
   3. The period over which income is paid to the family is reduced.
   b. Explain the limitations of the human life value approach as a method for determining the amount of life insurance to own.

3. Kelly, age 35, is a single parent and has a one-year-old son. She earns $45,000 annually as a marketing analyst. Her employer provides group life insurance in the amount of twice the employee's salary. Kelly also participates in her employer's 401(k) plan. She has the following financial needs and objectives:

| | |
|---|---|
| ■ Funeral costs and uninsured medical bills | $ 10,000 |
| ■ Income support for her son | $2,000 monthly for 17 years |
| ■ Pay off mortgage on home | 150,000 |
| ■ Pay off car loan and credit card debts | 15,000 |
| ■ College education fund for son | 150,000 |

Kelly has the following financial assets:

| | |
|---|---|
| ■ Checking account | $ 2,000 |
| ■ IRA account | 8,000 |
| ■ 401(k) plan | 25,000 |
| ■ Individual life insurance | 25,000 |
| ■ Group life insurance | 90,000 |

a. Ignoring the availability of Social Security survivor benefits, how much additional life insurance, if any, should Kelly purchase to meet her financial goals based on the needs approach? (Assume that the rate of return earned on the policy proceeds is equal to the rate of inflation.)
b. How much additional life insurance, if any, is needed if estimated Social Security survivor benefits in the amount of $800 monthly are payable until her son attains age 18?

4. Janet, age 28, is married and has a son, age 3. She wants to determine how much life insurance she should own based on the capital retention approach. She would like to provide $30,000 each year before

taxes to her family if she should die. She owns a house jointly with her husband that has a current market value of $250,000 and a mortgage balance of $100,000. She also owes $16,000 on a car loan and credit cards. She would like to have the mortgage, car loan, and credit card debts paid off if she should die. She has no investments, and her checking account balance is only $1000. She owns an individual life insurance policy in the amount of $100,000 that her parents purchased for her when she was a baby. Estimated Social Security survivor benefits are $10,000 annually. Janet assumes the life insurance proceeds can be invested at 5 percent interest. Based on the capital retention approach, how much additional life insurance, if any, should Janet purchase to meet her financial goals?

5. Megan, age 32, is married and has a son, age 1. She recently purchased a cash-value life insurance policy that has the following characteristics:

   - The frequency and amount of premium payments are flexible.

   - The insurance and saving components are separate.

   - The interest rate credited to the policy is tied to current market conditions, but the policy guarantees a minimum interest rate.

   - The policy has a back-end surrender charge that declines to zero over some time period.

   Based on the above characteristics, what type of life insurance did Megan purchase? Explain your answer.

6. Todd, age 28, would like to save money for a comfortable retirement. He is considering purchasing a cash-value life insurance policy that has the following characteristics:

   - The premiums are invested in separate investment accounts selected by the policyholder.

   - Interest income and capital gains are not currently taxable to the policyholder .

   - The frequency and amount of premium payments can be changed as financial circumstances change.

   - A mortality and expense (M&E) charge is periodically deducted from the cash value account.

   Based on the above characteristics, what type of life insurance is Todd considering purchasing? Explain your answer.

7. Life insurance policies have different characteristics. For each of the following, identify the life insurance policy that meets the description:
   a. A policy where the face amount of insurance increases if the investment results are favorable
   b. A policy that can be used to insure the human life value of an individual, age 35, at the lowest possible annual premium
   c. A policy that permits the policyholder to determine how the premiums are to be invested
   d. A policy that allows cash withdrawals for a down payment on a home or payment of college tuition
   e. A policy that is sold to applicants whose mortality experience is expected to be lower than average
   f. A policy in which premiums are lower for the first three to five years and higher thereafter, which may appeal to insureds whose incomes are expected to increase
   g. A policy designed to pay estate taxes upon the death of the last surviving spouse

8. Richard, age 35, is married and has two children, ages 2 and 5. He is considering the purchase of additional life insurance. He has the following financial goals and objectives:

   - Pay off the mortgage on his home, which has 25 years remaining

   - Accumulation of a sizeable retirement fund

   - Payment of monthly income to the family if he should die

   - Withdrawal of funds from the policy when the children reach college age

   For each of the following life insurance policies, indicate which of the above financial goals, if any, could be met if the policy is purchased. Treat each policy separately.
   a. Decreasing term insurance
   b. Ordinary life insurance
   c. Universal life insurance
   d. Variable universal life insurance

## INTERNET RESOURCES

- **A. M. Best Co.** is a major rating organization that rates the financial strength of insurance companies. The company also publishes periodicals, reports, and books relating to the insurance industry, including

*Best's Review*. This publication provides considerable information about life insurance products and the insurance industry. Visit the site at

consumerfed.org

ambest.com

- **The American College** offers professional certification and graduate degree programs in the financial services industry. It offers numerous programs and courses leading to the award of professional designations (CLU, ChFC, and others). Visit the site at

theamericancollege.edu

- The **American Council of Life Insurers** represents the life insurance industry on issues dealing with legislation and regulation at the federal and state levels. The site provides consumer information on the uses and types of life insurance. Visit the site at

acli.com

- The **Consumer Federation of America (CFA)** is a nonprofit organization that represents numerous consumer groups. This site is one of the best sources for obtaining meaningful consumer information about life insurance policies and other insurance products. CFA makes available a low-cost life insurance evaluation service by which individual life insurance policies can be evaluated for a small fee. Visit the site at

consumerfed.org

- **InsWeb** provides timely information and premium quotes for life insurance as well as homeowners, auto, and other insurance products. Visit the site at

insweb.com

- Insure.com provides up-to-date information, premium quotes, and other consumer information on life insurance. Visit the site at

insure.com

- The **Life Office Management Association (LOMA)** provides extensive information dealing with the management and operations of life insurers and financial services companies. Visit the site at

loma.org

- **LIMRA** is the principal source of life insurance sales and marketing statistics. The organization provides news and information about the financial services field, conducts research, and publishes a wide range of publications. Visit the site at

limra.com

- The **Life and Health Insurance Foundation for Education (LIFE)** is a nonprofit organization that helps consumers make smart insurance decisions to protect their families. Topics addressed include life, disability, long-term care, and health insurance. The goal is to help consumers better understand these products and the importance of insurance professionals in helping them reach these goals. Visit the site at

lifehappens.org/

- The **National Association of Insurance Commissioners (NAIC)** has a link to all state insurance departments, which provide a considerable amount of consumer information on the types of life insurance discussed in this chapter. Click on "State & Jurisdictions." For starters, check out New York, Wisconsin, and California. Visit the site at

naic.org

- The **National Association of Insurance and Financial Advisors** represents sales professionals in life and health insurance and the financial services industry. The organization promotes ethical standards, supports legislation in the interest of policyholders and agents, and provides agent education seminars. Visit the site at

naifa.org

- The **National Underwriter Company** publishes books and periodicals about life insurance products. The company publishes the *National Underwriter*, Life & Health/ Financial Services edition, a weekly trade publication, which provides timely news about the life insurance industry. Visit the site at

nationalunderwriter.com

- The **Society of Financial Service Professionals** represents individuals who have earned the professional Chartered Life Underwriter (CLU) and Chartered Financial Consultant (ChFC) designations. The site provides timely information on life insurance products. Visit the site at

financialpro.org

## SELECTED REFERENCES

Beam, Burton T., Jr. *Group Benefits: Basic Concepts and Alternatives,*12th ed. Bryn Mawr, PA: The American College, 2010.

Black, Kenneth, Jr., and Harold D. Skipper, Jr. *Life Insurance,* 13th ed. Upper Saddle River, NJ: Prentice-Hall, 2000.

Elger, John F., "Calculating Life Insurance Need: Don't Let the Tools Fool You," *Journal of Financial Service Professionals,* vol. 57, no. 3, May 2003.

Graves, Edward E., ed. *McGill's Life Insurance,* 8th ed. Bryn Mawr, PA: The American College, 2011.

Hunt, James H., *Miscellaneous Observations on Life Insurance: Including an Update to 2007 Paper on Variable Universal Life,* Consumer Federation of America, January 2011.

Hunt, James H., *Variable Universal Life: Worth Buying Now? And Other Types of Life Insurance.* Consumer Federation of America, November 2007.

Retzloff, Cheryl D., *Household Trends in U.S. Life Ownership,* 2010 Report, LIMRA, LL Global, Inc., 2010.

Retzloff, Cheryl D., *Person-Level Trends in U.S. Life Ownership,* 2011 Report, LIMRA, LL Global, Inc., 2011.

Witt, Scott J. "Variable Universal Life—Buyer Beware!" *The Insurance Forum,* vol. 35, no. 11 (November 2008).

## NOTES

1. National Center for Health Statistics, "Deaths: Preliminary Data for 2010," *National Vital Statistics Reports,* vol. 60, no. 4, January 11, 2012, p. 2.

2. "A Mother's Pay? $117,000," The *Wall Street Journal,* May 12, 2008, p. B5.

3. John Elger, "Calculating Life Insurance Need: Don't Let the Tools Fool You," *Journal of Financial Service Professionals,* vol. 57, no. 3 (May 2003), Table 3, p. 40.

4. LIMRA News Center, "Ownership of Individual Life Insurance Falls to 50-Year Low, LIMRA Reports," August 30, 2010.

5. Cheryl D. Retzloff, *Household Trends in U.S. Life Ownership,* 2010 Report, LIMRA, LL Global, Inc., 2010.

6. New York Life press release, *The Life Insurance Gap: a Study in Coverage and Financial Goals, 2009.*

7. This section is based on Edward E. Graves, ed., *McGill's Life Insurance,* 8th ed. (Bryn Mawr, PA: The American College 2011), chs. 1–5; and Kenneth Black, Jr., and Harold D. Skipper, Jr., *Life Insurance,* 13th ed. (Upper Saddle River, NJ: Prentice-Hall, 2000), chs. 4–5.

8. Graves, p. 3.5.

9. The *cost of insurance* is a technical term that is obtained by multiplying the net amount at risk by the death rate at the insured's attained age. Under the level-premium method, the cost of insurance can be kept within reasonable bounds at all ages.

10. This section is based on Graves, ch. 5; Black and Skipper, pp. 114–127; and Joseph M. Belth, ed., "The War Over Universal Life—Part 1," *Insurance Forum,* vol. 8, no. 11 (November 1981).

11. Limitations of universal life are discussed in Joseph M. Belth, ed. "Secondary Guarantees, Marketers, Actuaries, Regulators, and a Potential Financial Disaster for the Life Insurance Business," *Insurance Forum,* vol. 31, nos. 3 & 4 (March/April 2004); "Conseco's Assault on Universal Life Policyholders," *Insurance Forum,* vol. 30, no. 12 (December 2003); "The Likely Failure of a Universal Life Policy," *Insurance Forum,* vol. 28, no. 7 (July 2001); "The War Over Universal Life—Part 1," *Insurance Forum,* vol. 8, no. 11 (November 1981); and "The War Over Universal Life—Part 2," *Insurance Forum,* vol. 8, no. 12 (December 1981).

12. Graves, pp. 5.33–5.34.

13. Ibid., p. 5.34.

14. Consumer Federation of America, *New CFA Report Answers Question—Is Variable Universal Life Insurance Worth It?* February 24, 2003. See also James H. Hunt, *Variable Universal Life: Worth Buying Now? And Other Types of Life Insurance,* Consumer Federation of America, November 2007.

15. This section is based on Graves, pp. 5.34–5.39, and Black and Skipper, pp. 97–101.

16. Black and Skipper, p. 100.

17. *Life Insurers Fact Book 2011* (Washington, DC: American Council of Life Insurers, 2011), p. 65.

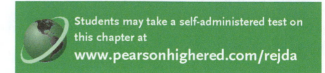

Students may take a self-administered test on this chapter at
**www.pearsonhighered.com/rejda**

# CHAPTER 12

# LIFE INSURANCE CONTRACTUAL PROVISIONS

*"By understanding the contract, the policyowner can make the best use of it and avoid unpleasant surprises."*

Robert I. Mehr, *Fundamentals of Insurance*

## LEARNING OBJECTIVES

**After studying this chapter, you should be able to**

◆ Describe the following contractual provisions that appear in life insurance policies:

  Incontestable clause
  Suicide clause
  Grace period provision

◆ Identify the dividend options that typically appear in participating life insurance policies.

◆ Explain the cash-surrender options (nonforfeiture options) that appear in cash-value policies.

◆ Describe the various settlement options for the payment of life insurance death benefits.

◆ Describe the following riders that can be added to a life insurance policy:
  Waiver of premium rider                Cost-of-living rider
  Guaranteed purchase option             Accelerated benefits rider
  Accidental death benefit rider

*Brandon, age 30, and Ashley, age 28, are married and have a son, age one. One year ago, Brandon purchased a $500,000 term insurance policy that requires an annual premium of $140. Ashley generally pays most bills that are due each month. Two weeks after the second annual premium was due, Brandon died unexpectedly from a massive heart attack. At the time of his death, Ashley had not paid the second annual premium on the policy. She is concerned that the insurer will not pay the death claim because the premium had not been paid. Brandon's life insurance agent, however assured her that the claim would be paid. Brandon died during the grace period for overdue premiums, and the policy was still in force.*

*In the above case, payment of the death benefit was affected by a contractual provision dealing with the grace period. Life insurance policies contain dozens of contractual provisions that affect the policyholder, insured, beneficiary, and payment of the face amount of insurance. Many provisions are mandatory and must be included in every life insurance policy; other provisions are optional.*

*In this chapter, we discuss some common contractual provisions that appear in life insurance policies. The chapter is divided into three major parts. The first part discusses certain contractual provisions that can have a significant financial impact on policyholders and beneficiaries. The second part discusses the various options that appear in life insurance policies, including dividend options, nonforfeiture options, and settlement options. The final part discusses several additional benefits and riders that can be added to a life insurance policy.*

## LIFE INSURANCE CONTRACTUAL PROVISIONS

Life insurance policies contain numerous contractual provisions. This section discusses the major contractual provisions that life insurance consumers should understand.

### Ownership Clause

The owner of a life insurance policy can be the insured, the beneficiary, a trust, or another party. In most cases, the applicant, insured, and owner are the same person. Under the **ownership clause**, *the policyholder possesses all contractual rights in the policy while the insured is living*. These rights include naming and changing the beneficiary, surrendering the policy for its cash value, borrowing the cash value, receiving dividends, and electing settlement options.

These rights generally can be exercised without the beneficiary's consent.

The policy also provides for a change of ownership. The policyholder can designate a new owner by filing an appropriate form with the company.

### Entire-Contract Clause

*The* **entire-contract clause** *states that the life insurance policy and attached application constitute the entire contract between the parties.* All statements in the application are considered to be representations rather than warranties. No statement can be used by the insurer to void the policy unless it is a material misrepresentation and is part of the application. In addition, the insurer cannot change the policy terms unless the policyholder consents to the change.

There are two basic purposes of the entire-contract clause. First, it prevents the insurer from amending the policy without the knowledge or consent of the owner by changing its charter or bylaws. Second, it also protects the beneficiary. A statement made in connection with the application cannot be used by the insurer to deny a claim unless the statement is a material misrepresentation and is part of the application.

## Incontestable Clause

*The* **incontestable clause** *states that the insurer cannot contest the policy after it has been in force two years during the insured's lifetime.* After the policy has been in force for two years during the insured's lifetime, the insurer cannot later contest a death claim on the basis of a material misrepresentation, concealment, or fraud when the policy was first issued. The insurer has two years in which to discover any irregularities in the contract. For example, if Tony, age 25, applies for a life insurance policy, conceals the fact that he has high blood pressure, and dies within the two-year period, the insurer could contest the claim on the basis of a material concealment. But if he dies *after* expiration of the period, the insurer must pay the claim.

The purpose of the incontestable clause is to protect the beneficiary if the insurer tries to deny payment of the claim years after the policy was first issued. Because the insured is dead, he or she cannot refute the insurer's allegations. As a result, the beneficiary could be financially harmed if the claim is denied on the grounds of a material misrepresentation or concealment.

The incontestable clause is normally effective against fraud. If the insured makes a fraudulent misstatement to obtain the insurance, the company has two years to detect the fraud. Otherwise, the death claim must be paid. However, there are certain situations where the fraud is so outrageous that payment of the death claim would be against the public interest. In these cases, the insurer can contest the claim after the contestable period runs out. They include the following:[1]

- The beneficiary takes out a policy with the intent of murdering the insured.
- The applicant for insurance has someone else take a medical examination.
- An insurable interest does not exist at the inception of the policy.

## Suicide Clause

Most life insurance policies contain a suicide clause. *The* **suicide clause** *states that if the insured commits suicide within two years after the policy is issued, the face amount of insurance will not be paid; there is only a refund of the premiums paid.* In some life insurance policies, suicide is excluded for only one year. If the insured commits suicide after the period expires, the policy proceeds are paid just like any other claim.

In legal terms, death is normally considered an unintentional act because of the strong instinct of self-preservation. Thus, there is a presumption against suicide. Consequently, the burden of proving suicide always rests on the insurer. To deny payment of the claim, the insurer must prove conclusively that the insured has committed suicide (see Insight 12.1).

The purpose of the suicide clause is to reduce adverse selection against the insurer. By having a suicide clause, the insurer has some protection against the individual who wishes to purchase life insurance with the intention of committing suicide.

## Grace Period

*A life insurance policy also contains a* **grace period** *during which the policyholder has a period of 31 days to pay an overdue premium.* Universal life and other flexible-premium policies have longer grace periods, such as 61 days. The insurance remains in force during the grace period. If the insured dies within the grace period, the overdue premium is deducted from the policy proceeds.

The purpose of the grace period is to prevent the policy from lapsing by giving the policyholder additional time to pay an overdue premium. The policyholder may be temporarily short of funds or may have forgotten to pay the premium. In such cases, the grace period provides considerable financial flexibility.

## Reinstatement Clause

A policy may lapse if the premium has not been paid by the end of the grace period, or if an automatic premium loan provision is not in effect. *The* **reinstatement provision** *permits the owner to reinstate a lapsed policy.*

## INSIGHT 12.1

### Is This Death a Suicide?

**Facts**

A 20-year-old Marine served in a fighter squadron as a radar technician. He was familiar with .45-caliber semi-automatic pistols and had given instructions on their use. The Marine was a happy-go-lucky, cheerful person who sometimes tried to "shake up" his friends by placing a .45 to his head and pulling the trigger. One day when the Marine was apparently in good spirits, he suddenly put a pistol to his head, said, "Here's to it," to a friend, and pulled the trigger. The gun fired, killing the Marine. The insurance company that insured him claimed the death was a suicide.

**Decision**

The death is not a suicide.

**Reasoning**

The company must prove that the death was intentional. The burden of proof was not met here (Angelus v. Government Personnel Life Ins. Co., 321 P.2d 545 [Wash. 1958]).

SOURCE: *Business Law Text and Cases: The Legal Environment*, 3rd ed., by Frascona, Joseph L., ©1987. Reprinted by permission of Pearson Education, Inc., Upper Saddle River, NJ.

The following requirements must be fulfilled to reinstate a lapsed policy:

- Evidence of insurability is required.
- All overdue premiums plus interest must be paid from their respective due dates.
- Any policy loan must be repaid or reinstated, with interest from the due date of the overdue premium.
- The policy must not have been surrendered for its cash value.
- The policy must be reinstated within a certain period, typically three or five years from the date of lapse.

There are advantages and disadvantages in reinstating a lapsed policy. First, the acquisition expenses incurred in issuing the policy must be paid again if a new policy is purchased. Second, the incontestable period and suicide period under the old policy may have expired; reinstatement of a lapsed policy does not reopen the suicide period, and a new incontestable period generally applies only to statements contained in the application for reinstatement.

A major disadvantage, however, of reinstating a lapsed policy is that a substantial cash outlay is required if the policy lapsed several years earlier. As a practical matter, most lapsed policies are not reinstated because of the required cash outlay.

In addition, most life insurers have reduced premiums over time and have developed new products. As a result, it may be less costly to purchase a new policy even though the insured is older when the new purchase is made.

Finally, the new policy may provide for greater flexibility in the payment of premiums. This is particularly true if the lapsed policy is an older whole life policy where there is limited flexibility in the payment of premiums (other than the grace period and automatic premium loan provisions). However, in a universal life policy, premiums can be reduced or even eliminated if the policy has sufficient cash values. This provides great flexibility in the payment of premiums for policyholders who experience wide fluctuation in disposable income and cash flow throughout the year, such as employment in a seasonal industry; policyholders who lose their jobs in a business recession; or policyholders who need large amounts of cash because of an unexpected emergency.

### Misstatement of Age or Sex Clause

Under the **misstatement of age or sex clause**, *if the insured's age or sex is misstated, the amount payable is the amount that the premiums paid would have purchased at the correct age and sex.* For example, assume that Brent, age 35, applies for a $50,000 whole life policy, but his age is incorrectly stated as 34. If the premium is $16 per $1000 at age 35 and $15 per $1000 at age 34, the insurer will pay only 15/16 of the death proceeds. Thus, only $46,875 would be paid (15/16 × $50,000 = $46,875).

## Beneficiary Designation

The beneficiary is the party named in the policy to receive the policy proceeds. The principal types of beneficiary designations are as follows:

- Primary and contingent beneficiary
- Revocable and irrevocable beneficiary
- Specific and class beneficiary

**Primary and Contingent Beneficiary** A primary **beneficiary** *is the beneficiary who is first entitled to receive the policy proceeds on the insured's death.* More than one party can be named primary beneficiary; however, the amount that each party receives must be specified.

A **contingent beneficiary** *is entitled to the proceeds if the primary beneficiary dies before the insured.* If the primary beneficiary dies before receiving the guaranteed number of payments under an installment settlement option, the remaining payments are paid to the contingent beneficiary.

In many families, the husband will name his wife primary beneficiary (and vice versa), and the children will be named as contingent beneficiaries. However, there is a legal problem when minor children are named as beneficiaries because they lack the legal capacity to receive the policy proceeds directly. Insurers generally will not pay the death proceeds directly to minor children (typically under age 18). Instead, they will require a guardian to receive the proceeds on the minor's behalf. If a court of law appoints a *guardian,* payment of the proceeds may be delayed and legal expenses will be incurred. One solution is to have a guardian named in the will who can legally receive the proceeds on the children's behalf. Another approach is to pay the proceeds to a *trustee* (such as a commercial bank with a trust department), which has the discretion and authority to use the funds for the children's welfare.

The insured's estate can be named as primary or contingent beneficiary. However, many financial planners do not recommend designation of the estate as beneficiary. The death proceeds may be subject to attorney fees and other probate expenses, federal estate taxes, state inheritance taxes, and claims of creditors. Payment of the proceeds may also be delayed until the estate is settled.

**Revocable and Irrevocable Beneficiary** Most beneficiary designations are revocable. A **revocable beneficiary** *means that the* policyholder *reserves the right to change the beneficiary designation without the beneficiary's consent.* The revocable beneficiary has only the expectation of benefits, and the policyholder can change the beneficiary whenever desired. All policy rights under the contract can be exercised without the consent of the revocable beneficiary.

In contrast, *an* **irrevocable beneficiary** *is one that cannot be changed without the beneficiary's consent.* If the policyholder wishes to change the beneficiary designation, the irrevocable beneficiary must consent to the change. However, most policies today provide that the interest of a beneficiary, even an irrevocable beneficiary, terminates if the beneficiary dies before the insured. Thus, if the irrevocable beneficiary dies before the insured, all rights to the policy proceeds revert to the policyholder, who can then name a new beneficiary.

**Specific and Class Beneficiary** A **specific beneficiary** means the beneficiary is specifically named and identified. Under a **class beneficiary**, a specific person is not named but is a member of a group designated as beneficiary, such as "children of the insured." A class designation is appropriate whenever the insured wishes to divide the policy proceeds equally among members of a particular group.

Most insurers restrict the use of a class designation because of the problem of identifying members of the class. Although all insurers permit the designation of children as a class, they will not permit this designation to be used when the class members cannot be identified, or the relationship to the insured is remote. For example, the class designation "my children" means that all children of the insured share in the policy proceeds, whether legitimate, illegitimate, or adopted. But if "children of the insured" is used as the designation, the insured's children by any marriage would be included, but the spouse's children by a former marriage would be excluded. Thus, a class designation must be used with great care.

## Change-of-Plan Provision

Life insurance policies may contain a **change-of-plan provision** that allows policyholders to exchange their present policies for different contracts. The purpose of this provision is to provide flexibility to the policyholders. The original policy may no longer be appropriate if family needs and financial objectives change.

If the change is to a higher-premium policy, such as changing from an ordinary life to a limited-payment policy, the policyholder must pay the difference in the policy reserve under the new policy and the policy reserve under the original policy. Evidence of insurability is not required because the pure insurance protection (net amount at risk) is reduced.

The policyholder may also be allowed to change to a lower-premium policy, such as changing from a limited-payment policy to an ordinary life policy. In such a case, the insurer refunds the difference in cash values under the two policies to the policyholder. Evidence of insurability is required in this type of change because the pure insurance protection is increased (higher net amount at risk).

## Exclusions and Restrictions

A life insurance policy contains remarkably few exclusions and restrictions. Suicide is excluded only for the first two years. During a period of war, some insurers may insert a **war clause** in their policies, which excludes payment if the insured dies as a direct result of war. The purpose of the war clause is to reduce adverse selection against the insurer when large numbers of new insureds may be exposed to death during wartime.

In addition, **aviation exclusions** may be present in some policies. Most newly issued policies do not contain any exclusions with respect to aviation deaths, and aviation death claims are paid like any other claim. However, some insurers exclude aviation deaths other than as a fare-paying passenger on a regularly scheduled airline. Military aviation may also be excluded or be covered only by payment of an extra premium. In addition, a private pilot who does not meet certain flight standards may have an aviation exclusion rider inserted in the policy, or be charged a higher premium.

During the initial underwriting of the policy, the insurer may discover certain undesirable activities or hobbies of the insured. These activities may be excluded or covered only by payment of an extra premium. Some excluded activities are auto racing, skydiving, scuba diving, hang gliding, and travel or residence in a dangerous country.

## Payment of Premiums

Life insurance premiums can be paid annually, semiannually, quarterly, or monthly. If the premium is paid other than annually, the policyholder must pay a carrying charge, which can be relatively expensive when the true rate of interest is calculated. For example, the semiannual premium may be 52 percent of the annual premium and so could be viewed as a carrying charge of only 4 percent. However, the actual charge is 16.7 percent. Assume that your annual premium is $1000. You pay the semiannual premium of $520 and defer payment of $480. Six months later, the $480 and $40 carrying charge are due. This means that you are paying $40 for the use of $480 for six months, which is the equivalent of an annual percentage rate of 16.7 percent.[2]

## Assignment Clause

A life insurance policy is freely assignable to another party. There are two types of assignments. Under an **absolute assignment**, *all ownership rights in the policy are transferred to a new owner*. For example, the policyholder may wish to donate a life insurance policy to a church, charity, or educational institution. This goal can be accomplished by an absolute assignment. The new owner can then exercise the ownership rights in the policy.

Under a **collateral assignment**, *the* policyholder *temporarily assigns a life insurance policy to a creditor as collateral for a loan. Only certain rights are transferred to the creditor to protect its interest, and the* policyholder *retains the remaining rights*. The party to whom the policy is assigned can receive the policy proceeds only to the extent of the loan; the balance of the proceeds is paid to the beneficiary.

The purpose of the assignment clause is to protect the insurer from paying the policy proceeds twice if an unrecorded assignment is presented to the insurer after the death claim is paid to the beneficiary. If the insurer is not notified of the assignment, the proceeds are paid to the named beneficiary when the policy matures as a death claim or endowment. Under general rules of law, the insurer is relieved of any further obligation under the policy, even though a valid assignment is in existence at the insured's death. However, if the insurer is notified of the assignment, a new contract exists between the insurer and assignee (one who receives the assignment, such as a bank), and the insurer then recognizes the assignee's rights as being superior to the beneficiary's rights.

## Policy Loan Provision

Cash-value life insurance contains a **policy loan provision** that allows the policyholder to borrow the cash value. The interest rate is stated in the policy. Older policies typically have a 5 or 6 percent loan rate. Newer policies typically have an 8 percent loan rate. However, all states permit insurers to charge a variable policy loan interest rate based on the National Association of Insurance Commissioner's model bill. If a variable interest rate is used, it can be based on Moody's composite yield on seasoned corporate bonds or some other index that is published regularly in the financial press. Another approach is a policy loan rate equal to the interest rate credited to the cash value plus a specified spread.[3]

Under participating policies, many insurers will reduce the dividend based on the amount of cash value borrowed. This step has the effect of indirectly increasing the effective interest rate on the policy loan. Under interest-sensitive policies, such as universal life and variable universal life, the current interest rate credited to the cash values that are borrowed is typically reduced, which again increases the effective interest rate on the loan.

Interest on a policy loan must either be paid annually or added to the outstanding loan if not paid. If the loan is not repaid by the time the policy matures as a death claim or endowment, the face amount of the policy is reduced by the amount of indebtedness. With the exception of a policy loan to pay a premium, the insurer can defer granting the loan for up to six months, but this is rarely done.

Persons who borrow their cash values often believe that they are paying interest on their own money. *This view is clearly incorrect. The cash value legally belongs to the insurer.* Although you have the contractual right to surrender or borrow the cash value, the cash value legally belongs to the insurer. Interest must be paid on the loan because the insurer assumes a certain interest rate when premiums, legal reserves, dividends, and surrender values are calculated. The insurer's assets must be invested in interest-bearing securities and other investments so that the contractual obligations can be met.

A policyholder *must pay interest on the loan to offset the loss of interest to the insurer.* If the loan had not been granted, the insurer could have earned interest on the funds.

Notice, too, that policy loan provisions may make it necessary for some insurers to keep some assets in lower-yielding, liquid investments to meet the demand for policy loans. Because these funds could have been invested in higher-yielding investments, policyholders who borrow should pay interest because higher yields must be forsaken to maintain liquidity.

**Advantages of Policy Loans**   The major advantage of a policy loan is the relatively low rate of interest that is paid. This is especially true for older contracts. The low policy loan rates of 5, 6, or 8 percent are substantially lower than credit card rates. There is also no credit check on the policyholder's ability to repay the loan; there is no fixed repayment schedule; and the policyholder has complete financial flexibility in determining the amount and frequency of loan repayments.

**Disadvantages of Policy Loans**   The major disadvantage is that the policyholder is not legally required to repay the loan, and the policy could lapse if the total indebtedness exceeds the available cash value. Rather than repay the loan, the policyholder may let the policy lapse or may surrender the policy for any remaining cash value. Finally, if the loan has not been repaid by the time the policy matures, the face amount of insurance is reduced by the amount owed.

## Automatic Premium Loan

The automatic premium loan provision can be added to most cash-value policies. Under the **automatic premium loan provision,** *an overdue premium is automatically borrowed from the cash value after the grace period expires, provided the policy has a loan value sufficient to pay the premium.* The policy continues in force just as before, but a premium loan is now outstanding. Interest is charged on the premium loan at the stated contractual rate. Premium payments can be resumed at any time without evidence of insurability.

The basic purpose of an automatic premium loan is to prevent the policy from lapsing because of nonpayment of premiums. The policyholder may be temporarily short of funds or may forget to pay the premium. Thus, the automatic premium loan provides considerable financial flexibility to the policyholder.

The automatic premium loan provision, however, has two major disadvantages. First, it may be overused. The policyholder may get into the habit of using the automatic premium loan provision too frequently. If the cash values are relatively modest and are habitually borrowed over an extended period, they could eventually be exhausted, and the contract would terminate. Second, the policy proceeds will be reduced if the premium loans are not repaid by the time of death.

## DIVIDEND OPTIONS

Life insurance policies frequently contain dividend options. *If the policy pays dividends, it is known as a* **participating policy**. Both stock and mutual insurers issue participating policies, which give *policyholders* the right to share in the divisible surplus of the insurer. The dividend represents largely a refund of part of the gross premium if the insurer has favorable experience with respect to mortality, interest, and expenses. *In contrast, a policy that does not pay dividends is known as a* **nonparticipating policy**.

Policy dividends are derived from three principal sources: (1) the difference between expected and actual mortality experience; (2) excess interest earnings on the assets required to maintain legal reserves; and (3) the difference between expected and actual operating expenses. Because the dividends paid are determined by the insurer's actual operating experience, they cannot be guaranteed.

There are several ways in which dividends can be taken:

- Cash
- Reduction of premiums
- Dividend accumulations
- Paid-up additions
- Term insurance (fifth dividend option)

### Cash

A dividend is usually payable after the policy has been in force for a stated period, typically one or two years. The policyholder receives a check equal to the dividend, usually on the anniversary date of the policy.

### Reduction of Premiums

The dividend can be used to reduce the next premium coming due. The dividend notice will indicate the amount of the dividend, and the policyholder must then remit the difference between the premium and actual dividend paid. This option is appropriate whenever premium payments become financially burdensome. It can also be used if the policyholder has a substantial reduction in income and expenses must be reduced.

### Dividend Accumulations

The dividend can be retained by the insurer and accumulated at interest. The policy guarantees a minimum interest rate such as 3 percent, but a higher rate may be paid based on current market conditions. The accumulated dividends generally can be withdrawn at any time. If not withdrawn, they are added to the amount paid when the policy matures as a death claim, or the contract is surrendered for its cash value. The dividend generally is not taxable for income-tax purposes. However, the interest income on the accumulated dividends is taxable income and must be reported annually for federal and state income-tax purposes. Thus, the accumulation option may be undesirable for policyholders who wish to minimize income taxes.

### Paid-up Additions

Under the **paid-up additions option**, *the dividend is used to purchase a small amount of paid-up whole life insurance*. For example, assume that Paige, age 22, owns an ordinary life insurance policy. If a dividend of $50 were paid, about $200 of paid-up whole life insurance could be purchased.

The paid-up additions option has some favorable features. First, the paid-up additions are purchased at net rates, not gross rates; there is no loading for expenses. Second, evidence of insurability is not required. Thus, if the insured is substandard in health or has become uninsurable, this option may be appealing because additional amounts of life insurance can be purchased without demonstrating insurability.

## Term Insurance (Fifth Dividend Option)

Some insurers offer a fifth dividend option by which the dividend is used to purchase term insurance. Two forms of this option are typically used. *The dividend can be used to purchase one-year term insurance equal to the cash value of the basic policy, and the remainder of the dividend is then used to buy paid-up additions or is accumulated at interest.* This option may be appropriate if the policyholder regularly borrows the cash value. The face amount of the policy would not be reduced by the amount of any outstanding loans at the time of death.

*A second form of this option is to use the dividend to purchase yearly renewable term insurance.* The actual amount of term insurance purchased depends on the amount of the dividend, the insured's attained age, and the insurer's term insurance rates. However, it is not uncommon for a $40 dividend to purchase $10,000 or more yearly renewable term insurance under this option. Unfortunately, this desirable option is offered by only a small proportion of companies.

## Other Uses of Dividends

The dividends can also be used to convert a policy into a *paid-up contract.* If the paid-up option is used, the policy becomes paid up whenever the reserve value under the basic contract plus the reserve value of the paid-up additions or deposits equal the net single premium for a paid-up policy at the insured's attained age. For example, an ordinary life policy issued at age 25 could be paid up by age 48 by using this option.

The dividend can also be used to *mature a policy as an endowment.* When the reserve value under the basic policy plus the reserve value of the paid-up additions or deposits equal the face amount of insurance, the policy matures as an endowment. For example, a $50,000 ordinary life policy issued at age 25 would mature as an endowment at age 58 by using this option.[4]

Finally, keep in mind that the use of dividend options will vary among policyholders. There is no best dividend option. The best option to use is the one that best meets your financial goals and objectives (see Insight 12.2).

# NONFORFEITURE OPTIONS

If a cash-value policy is purchased, a policyholder pays more than is actuarially necessary for the life insurance protection. Thus, he or she should get something back if the policy is surrendered. The payment to a withdrawing policyholder is known as a nonforfeiture value or cash-surrender value.

All states have standard **nonforfeiture laws** that require insurers to provide at least a minimum nonforfeiture value to policyholders who surrender their policies. There are three **nonforfeiture options** or cash-surrender options:

- Cash value
- Reduced paid-up insurance
- Extended term insurance

## Cash Value

*The policy can be surrendered for its cash value, at which time all benefits under the policy cease.* A policy normally does not build any cash value until the end of the second or third year, although some policies have a small cash value at the end of the first year. The cash values are small during the early years because the relatively high first-year acquisition expenses incurred by the insurer in selling the policy have not yet been recovered. However, over a long period, the cash values accumulate to substantial amounts.

The insurer can delay payment of the cash value for six months if the policy is surrendered. This provision is required by law and is a carryover from the Great Depression of the 1930s, when cash demands on life insurers were excessive. Insurers generally do not delay payment of the cash value.

The cash-surrender option can be used if the insured no longer needs life insurance. Although it is usually not advisable to surrender a policy for cash because other options may be more appropriate, there are circumstances where the cash-surrender option can be used. For example, if an insured is retired and no longer has any dependents to support, the need for substantial amounts of life insurance may be reduced. In such a case, the cash-surrender option could be used if cash is needed.

## INSIGHT 12.2

### Selection of the Best Dividend Option in a Participating Whole Life Policy

In a participating whole life policy, there are typically four dividend options: (1) cash, (2) reduction of premiums, (3) dividend accumulations, and (4) paid-up additions. You may be confused concerning the best dividend option to use. In reality, there is no best dividend option. *The best dividend option is one that best meets your financial goals and objectives.* If money is tight and premiums are financially burdensome, dividends can be paid in cash or used to reduce premiums. If you are substandard in health or uninsurable, the paid-up additions option in a cash-value policy is attractive if you need additional insurance. The paid-up additions are purchased at net rates with no expense loading.

If you have a cash-value policy and wish to accumulate funds for retirement, the paid-up additions option is appropriate. The paid-up additions can also pay up a policy prior to retirement. Another advantage, according to the Consumer Federation of America, is that the interest rate credited to paid-up additions may be higher than the interest rate credited to accumulated dividends retained by the insurer under the interest option.[a]

If income-tax considerations are important, you should not use the **dividend accumulations option**. Although dividends generally are not taxable until they exceed the net premiums paid, interest earnings on the dividends are taxed as ordinary income. In this case, the paid-up additions option is more appropriate because the dividend becomes the legal reserve under the paid-up addition. Interest earnings credited to the legal reserve are not taxed as current income to the policyholder. Moreover, as stated earlier, the interest rate credited to paid-up additions may be higher than the interest rate credited to the accumulated dividends under the dividend accumulations option.

In addition, the paid-up additions option provides a partial hedge against inflation, which can severely erode the purchasing power of the death benefit over a long period of time.

Finally, if you are underinsured and need more life insurance, you can use the paid-up additions option, or the fifth dividend option (term insurance), if it is available. In short, no single dividend option is best for all policyholders. Each policyholder should choose an option best suited to his or her financial situation.

[a]James H. Hunt, *Miscellaneous Observations on Life Insurance: Including an Update to 2007 Paper on Variable Universal Life*, Consumer Federation of America, January 2011.

## Reduced Paid-Up Insurance

Under the **reduced paid-up insurance option**, *the cash-surrender value is applied as a net single premium to purchase a reduced paid-up policy.* The amount of insurance purchased depends on the insured's attained age, the cash-surrender value, and the mortality and interest assumptions stated in the original contract. The reduced paid-up policy is the same as the original policy, but the face amount of insurance is reduced. If the original policy is participating, the reduced paid-up policy also pays dividends.

The reduced paid-up insurance option is appropriate if life insurance is still needed but the policyholder does not wish to pay premiums. For example, assume that Jeremy has a $100,000 ordinary life policy that he purchased at age 37. He is now age 65 and wants to retire, but he does not want to pay premiums after retirement. The cash-surrender value can be used to purchase a reduced paid-up policy of $77,300 (see Exhibit 12.1).

## Extended Term Insurance

Under the **extended term insurance option**, *the net cash-surrender value is used as a net single premium to extend the full face amount of the policy (less any indebtedness) into the future as term insurance for a certain number of years and days.* In effect, the cash value is used to purchase a paid-up term insurance policy equal to the original face amount (less any indebtedness) for a limited period. The length of the term insurance protection is determined by the insured's attained age when the option is exercised, the net cash-surrender value, and the premium rates for extended term insurance. For example, in our earlier illustration,

**EXHIBIT 12.1**
**Table of Guaranteed Values***
**$100,000 Ordinary Life Policy, Male Age 37**

| End of Policy Year | Cash Value | Alternatives to Cash Value | | | | End of Policy Year |
|---|---|---|---|---|---|---|
| | | Paid-Up Insurance | or | Extended Insurance | | |
| | | | | Years | Days | |
| 1 | ***** | *** | | ** | *** | 1 |
| 2 | ***** | *** | | ** | *** | 2 |
| 3 | $400.00 | $2,400 | | 1 | 18 | 3 |
| 4 | 1,400.00 | 7,900 | | 3 | 114 | 4 |
| 5 | 2,400.00 | 12,900 | | 5 | 62 | 5 |
| 6 | 3,500.00 | 17,900 | | 6 | 328 | 6 |
| 7 | 4,500.00 | 22,000 | | 8 | 55 | 7 |
| 8 | 5,600.00 | 26,200 | | 9 | 109 | 8 |
| 9 | 6,800.00 | 30,400 | | 10 | 121 | 9 |
| 10 | 8,000.00 | 34,300 | | 11 | 50 | 10 |
| 11 | 9,300.00 | 38,100 | | 11 | 321 | 11 |
| 12 | 11,000.00 | 43,200 | | 12 | 325 | 12 |
| 13 | 12,900.00 | 48,500 | | 13 | 323 | 13 |
| 14 | 14,800.00 | 53,300 | | 14 | 239 | 14 |
| 15 | 16,700.00 | 57,700 | | 15 | 91 | 15 |
| 16 | 18,700.00 | 61,900 | | 15 | 287 | 16 |
| 17 | 20,700.00 | 65,800 | | 16 | 73 | 17 |
| 18 | 22,700.00 | 69,300 | | 16 | 187 | 18 |
| 19 | 24,800.00 | 72,800 | | 16 | 291 | 19 |
| 20 | 26,900.00 | 75,900 | | 16 | 358 | 20 |
| AGE 60 | 32,300.00 | 69,400 | | 14 | 319 | AGE 60 |
| AGE 65 | 41,700.00 | 77,300 | | 13 | 198 | AGE 65 |

* This table assumes premiums have been paid to the end of the policy year shown. These values do not include any dividend accumulations, paid-up additions, or policy loans.

if Jeremy stopped paying premiums at age 65, the cash value would be sufficient to keep the $100,000 policy in force for another 13 years and 198 days. If he is still alive after that time, the policy is no longer in force.

If the policy lapses for nonpayment of premiums, and the policyholder has not elected another option, the extended term option automatically goes into effect in most policies. This means that many policies are still in force even though some policyholders may mistakenly believe their policies are not in force because of nonpayment of premiums. However, if the automatic premium loan provision has been added to the policy, it has priority over the extended term option.

A whole life or endowment policy contains a table of guaranteed values that indicates the benefits under the three options at various ages.

Exhibit 12.1 illustrates the guaranteed values of one insurer for a $100,000 ordinary life policy issued to a male, age 37.

## SETTLEMENT OPTIONS

**Settlement options** *refer to the various ways that the policy proceeds can be paid.* The policyholder can elect the settlement option prior to the insured's death, or the beneficiary may be granted that right. Most policies permit the cash-surrender value to be paid under the settlement options if the policy is surrendered. The most common settlement options are as follows:

- Cash
- Interest option
- Fixed-period option
- Fixed-amount option
- Life income options

## Cash

When an insured dies, cash is needed immediately for funeral expenses and other expenses. To meet this need, the policy proceeds can be paid in a lump sum to a designated beneficiary or beneficiaries. Interest is paid on the policy proceeds from the date of death to the date of payment. The payment of interest is especially important in those cases where the life insurance proceeds are large, and the proceeds are paid several weeks or months after the insured's death. As a practical matter, most policy proceeds are paid in a lump sum within weeks following the insured's death.

## Interest Option

Under the **interest option**, *the policy proceeds are retained by the insurer, and interest is periodically paid to the beneficiary.* The interest can be paid monthly, quarterly, semiannually, or annually. Most insurers guarantee a minimum interest rate on the policy proceeds retained under the interest option.

The beneficiary can be given withdrawal rights, by which part or all of the proceeds can be withdrawn. The beneficiary may also be given the right to change to another settlement option.

The interest option provides considerable flexibility, and it can be used in a wide variety of circumstances. In particular, it can be effectively used if the funds will not be needed until some later date. For example, educational funds could be retained at interest until the children are ready for college. Meanwhile, the interest income can supplement the family's income.

## Fixed-Period Option

Under the **fixed-period (income for elected period) option**, *the policy proceeds are paid to a beneficiary over some fixed period of time.* Payments can be made monthly, quarterly, semiannually, or annually. Both principal and interest are systematically liquidated under this option. If the primary beneficiary dies before receiving all payments, the remaining payments will be paid to a contingent beneficiary or to the primary beneficiary's estate.

Exhibit 12.2 illustrates the fixed-period option of one insurer for each $1000 of proceeds at a guaranteed interest rate of 3.5 percent. The length of the

**EXHIBIT 12.2**

**Income for Elected Period**
**(minimum monthly payment per $1000 of proceeds)**

| Years | | Years | | Years | | Years | |
|---|---|---|---|---|---|---|---|
| 1 | $84.65 | 5 | $18.12 | 9 | $10.75 | 15 | $7.10 |
| 2 | 43.05 | 6 | 15.35 | 10 | 9.83 | 20 | 5.75 |
| 3 | 29.19 | 7 | 13.38 | 11 | 9.09 | 25 | 4.96 |
| 4 | 22.27 | 8 | 11.90 | 12 | 8.46 | 30 | 4.45 |

period determines the amount of each payment. If the fixed period is five years, a $100,000 policy would provide a monthly income of $1812. However, the monthly benefit would be only $983 if a 10-year period is elected.

The fixed-period option is appropriate in situations where income is needed for a definite time period, such as during the readjustment, dependency, and blackout periods. The fixed-period option, however, should be used with caution. It is extremely inflexible. Partial withdrawals by the beneficiary normally are not allowed because of the administrative expense of recomputing the amount of the payment during the fixed period. However, insurers generally permit the beneficiary to withdraw the commuted value of the remaining payments in a lump sum.

## Fixed-Amount Option

Under the **fixed-amount (income for elected period) option**, *a fixed amount is periodically paid to the beneficiary.* The payments are made until both the principal and interest are exhausted. If excess interest is paid, the period is lengthened, but the amount of each payment is unchanged.

For example, assume that the death benefit is $50,000, the credited interest rate is 4 percent annually, and the desired monthly benefit is $3020. The actual monthly payout schedule would be calculated by the insurer. In this case, the beneficiary would receive $3020 monthly for 17 months. At that time, the principal and interest would be exhausted.

The fixed-amount option provides considerable flexibility. The beneficiary can be given limited or unlimited withdrawal rights, the right to switch the unpaid proceeds to another option, and to increase or decrease the fixed amount. It is also possible to arrange a settlement agreement, by which the periodic payments can be increased at certain times, such as when grown children start college. Unless there is some compelling reason for using the fixed-period option, the fixed-amount option is recommended because of its greater flexibility.

## Life Income Options

Death benefits can also be paid to the beneficiary under a life income option. The cash-surrender value can also be disbursed under a **life income option**. The major life income options are as follows.

**Life Income**  Some insurers include a straight life annuity option on their policies. *Under this option, installment payments are paid only while the beneficiary is alive and cease on the beneficiary's death.* Although this option provides the highest amount of installment income, there may be a substantial forfeiture of the proceeds if the beneficiary dies shortly after the payments start. Because there is no refund feature or guarantee of payments, other life income options are usually more desirable.

**Life Income with Guaranteed Period**  Under this option, the beneficiary receives a life income with a guaranteed period of payments. *If the primary beneficiary dies before receiving the guaranteed number of years of payments, the remaining payments are paid to a contingent beneficiary.* For example, assume that Megan is receiving $2000 monthly under a life income option, and the guaranteed period is 10 years. If Megan dies after receiving only one year of payments, the remaining nine years of payments will be paid to a contingent beneficiary or to her estate.

Exhibit 12.3 shows the life income option of one insurer with guaranteed periods ranging from 5 to 20 years for each $1000 of insurance proceeds. Females receive lower periodic payments because of a longer life expectancy. For example, assume that Megan is the beneficiary of a $100,000 policy. If her adjusted age is 60, she will receive $468 monthly for life with a guaranteed period of 5 years.

**Life Income with Guaranteed Total Amount**  Under this option, the beneficiary receives a lifetime income, and the total amount paid is guaranteed.

*If the beneficiary dies before receiving installment payments equal to the total amount of insurance placed under the option, the payments continue until the total amount paid equals the total amount of insurance.* For example, assume that Laura has $100,000 of insurance paid to her as lifetime income under this option. If Laura dies after receiving only $10,000 in payments, the remaining $90,000 is paid in installments to another beneficiary or to her estate.

Exhibit 12.4 shows the life income-guaranteed total amount option of one insurer for each $1000 of life insurance proceeds. As noted earlier, females receive lower monthly payments because of a longer life expectancy.

**Joint-and-Survivor Income**  Under this option, income payments are paid to two persons during their lifetimes, such as a husband and wife. For example, Richard and Margo may be receiving $1200 monthly under a joint-and-survivor income annuity. If Richard dies, Margo continues to receive $1200 monthly during her lifetime. There are also variations of this option, such as a joint-and-two-thirds annuity or a joint-and-one-half annuity. Thus, the monthly income of $1200 would be reduced to $800 or $600 on the death of the first person.

Exhibit 12.5 illustrates the minimum monthly payment under the joint-and-survivor income option of one insurer for each $1000 of insurance proceeds. For example, if the insurance proceeds are $100,000, and a male and female beneficiary are both age 65, a monthly payment of $466 would be paid during the lifetime of both annuitants. However, the payments are guaranteed for 10 years.

## Advantages of Settlement Options

The major advantages of settlement options are summarized as follows:

- *Periodic income is paid to the family*. Settlement options can restore part or all of the family's share of the deceased breadwinner's earnings. The financial security of the family can then be maintained.
- *Principal and interest are guaranteed*. The insurance company guarantees both principal and interest. There are no investment worries and

**EXHIBIT 12.3**
**Life Income with Guaranteed Period**
**(minimum monthly payment per $1000 of proceeds)**

| Payee's Adjusted Age | MALE Guaranteed Period | | | | FEMALE Guaranteed Period | | | |
|---|---|---|---|---|---|---|---|---|
| | 5 Yrs | 10 Yrs | 15 Yrs | 20 Yrs | 5 Yrs | 10 Yrs | 15 Yrs | 20 Yrs |
| 60 | $5.14 | $5.08 | $4.98 | $4.84 | $4.68 | $4.85 | $4.61 | $4.54 |
| 61 | 5.25 | 5.18 | 5.07 | 4.91 | 4.76 | 4.73 | 4.68 | 4.63 |
| 62 | 5.36 | 5.28 | 5.15 | 4.97 | 4.84 | 4.81 | 4.75 | 4.67 |
| 63 | 5.48 | 5.39 | 5.24 | 5.04 | 4.93 | 4.89 | 4.83 | 4.73 |
| 64 | 5.61 | 5.50 | 5.33 | 5.10 | 5.03 | 4.99 | 4.91 | 4.80 |
| 65 | 5.75 | 5.62 | 5.42 | 5.17 | 5.13 | 5.08 | 5.00 | 4.87 |
| 66 | 5.89 | 5.75 | 5.52 | 5.23 | 5.25 | 5.19 | 5.09 | 4.94 |
| 67 | 6.05 | 5.88 | 5.62 | 5.30 | 5.36 | 5.30 | 5.18 | 5.01 |
| 68 | 6.21 | 6.02 | 5.72 | 5.36 | 5.49 | 5.41 | 5.28 | 5.08 |
| 69 | 6.39 | 6.16 | 5.82 | 5.42 | 5.63 | 5.54 | 5.38 | 5.16 |
| 70 | 6.57 | 6.31 | 5.92 | 5.48 | 5.78 | 5.67 | 5.48 | 5.23 |
| 71 | 6.77 | 6.46 | 6.02 | 5.54 | 5.94 | 5.81 | 5.59 | 5.30 |
| 72 | 6.97 | 6.62 | 6.13 | 5.60 | 6.11 | 5.95 | 5.70 | 5.37 |
| 73 | 7.19 | 6.78 | 6.23 | 5.65 | 6.29 | 6.11 | 5.81 | 5.44 |
| 74 | 7.42 | 6.95 | 6.33 | 5.69 | 6.49 | 6.27 | 5.93 | 5.50 |
| 75 | 7.66 | 7.12 | 6.42 | 5.74 | 6.70 | 6.44 | 6.04 | 5.58 |
| 76 | 7.91 | 7.29 | 6.52 | 5.78 | 6.92 | 6.61 | 6.15 | 5.62 |
| 77 | 8.18 | 7.46 | 6.60 | 5.81 | 7.16 | 6.80 | 6.27 | 5.67 |
| 78 | 8.47 | 7.84 | 6.69 | 5.84 | 7.42 | 6.98 | 6.37 | 5.72 |
| 79 | 8.77 | 7.82 | 6.77 | 5.87 | 7.69 | 7.18 | 6.48 | 5.76 |
| 80 | 9.08 | 8.00 | 6.84 | 5.90 | 7.98 | 7.37 | 6.58 | 5.80 |
| 81 | 9.41 | 8.17 | 6.91 | 5.92 | 8.29 | 7.57 | 6.67 | 5.84 |
| 82 | 9.74 | 8.34 | 6.97 | 5.94 | 8.62 | 7.77 | 6.75 | 5.87 |
| 83 | 10.10 | 8.51 | 7.03 | 5.95 | 8.96 | 7.97 | 6.83 | 5.89 |
| 84 | 10.46 | 8.67 | 7.08 | 5.96 | 9.33 | 8.16 | 6.91 | 5.92 |
| 85 & over | 10.84 | 8.82 | 7.13 | 5.97 | 9.71 | 8.34 | 6.97 | 5.94 |

NOTE: The payee's adjusted age reflects increases in longevity. To find the adjusted age, increase or decrease the payee's age at that time as follows:

| 1987–91 | 1992–98 | 1999–2006 | 2007–13 | 2014–20 | 2021–28 | 2029+ |
|---|---|---|---|---|---|---|
| +3 | +2 | +1 | 0 | −1 | −2 | −3 |

administrative problems because the funds are invested by the insurer.

- *Settlement options can be used in life insurance planning*. Life insurance can be programmed to meet the policyholder's needs and objectives.
- *An insurance windfall can create problems for the beneficiary*. The funds may be spent unwisely, bad investments may be made, and others may try to get the funds. Insurers now offer money market accounts for investment of the death proceeds so that beneficiaries are not forced to make immediate decisions concerning disposition of the funds.

## Disadvantages of Settlement Options

The major disadvantages of settlement options are summarized as follows:

- *Higher yields often can be obtained elsewhere*. Interest rates offered by other financial institutions may be considerably higher.
- *The settlement agreement may be inflexible and restrictive*. The policyholder may have a settlement agreement that is too restrictive. The beneficiary may not have withdrawal rights or the right to change options. For example, the funds may be paid over a 20-year period under the

EXHIBIT 12.4
**Life Income with Guaranteed Total Amount**
**(minimum monthly payment per $1000 of proceeds)**

| Payee's Adjusted Age | Male | Female | Payee's Adjusted Age | Male | Female |
|---|---|---|---|---|---|
| 60 | $4.93 | $4.57 | 73 | $6.47 | $5.87 |
| 61 | 5.02 | 4.64 | 74 | 6.84 | 6.01 |
| 62 | 5.11 | 4.71 | 75 | 6.81 | 6.17 |
| 63 | 5.20 | 4.79 | 76 | 7.00 | 6.34 |
| 64 | 5.30 | 4.87 | 77 | 7.19 | 6.51 |
| 65 | 5.40 | 4.96 | 78 | 7.40 | 6.70 |
| 66 | 5.52 | 5.05 | 79 | 7.62 | 6.90 |
| 67 | 5.63 | 5.14 | 80 | 7.85 | 7.11 |
| 68 | 5.75 | 5.25 | 81 | 8.09 | 7.33 |
| 69 | 5.88 | 5.36 | 82 | 8.35 | 7.57 |
| 70 | 6.02 | 5.47 | 83 | 8.61 | 7.81 |
| 71 | 6.16 | 5.60 | 84 | 8.89 | 8.07 |
| 72 | 6.31 | 5.73 | 85 & over | 9.19 | 8.35 |

NOTE: The payee's adjusted age reflects increases in longevity. To find the adjusted age, increase or decrease the payee's age at that time as follows:

| 1987–91 | 1992–98 | 1999–2006 | 2007–13 | 2014–20 | 2021–28 | 2029+ |
|---|---|---|---|---|---|---|
| +3 | +2 | +1 | 0 | −1 | −2 | −3 |

EXHIBIT 12.5
**Joint-and-Survivor Income Option 10-Year Guaranteed Period**
**(minimum monthly payment per $1000 of proceeds)**

| Male Payee's Adjusted Age | Female Payee's Adjusted Age | | | | |
|---|---|---|---|---|---|
| | 60 | 65 | 70 | 75 | 80 |
| 60 | $4.32 | $4.50 | $4.67 | $4.82 | $4.93 |
| 65 | 4.42 | 4.66 | 4.91 | 5.15 | 5.34 |
| 70 | 4.81 | 4.81 | 5.14 | 5.49 | 5.80 |
| 75 | 4.57 | 4.92 | 5.34 | 5.81 | 6.27 |
| 80 | 4.61 | 4.99 | 5.49 | 6.07 | 6.69 |

NOTE: The payee's adjusted age reflects increases in longevity. To find the adjusted age, increase or decrease the payee's age at that time as follows:

| 1987–91 | 1992–98 | 1999–2006 | 2007–13 | 2014–20 | 2021–28 | 2029+ |
|---|---|---|---|---|---|---|
| +3 | +2 | +1 | 0 | −1 | −2 | −3 |

fixed-period option with no right of withdrawal. An emergency may arise, but the beneficiary could not withdraw the funds.

- *Life income options have limited usefulness at younger ages.* Life income options should rarely be used before age 65 or 70, which restricts their usefulness at the younger ages. If a life income option is elected at a young age, the income payments are substantially reduced. Also, using a life

income option is the equivalent of purchasing a single-premium life annuity, which may be purchased at a lower cost from another insurer.

## Use of a Trust

The policy proceeds can also be paid to a trustee, such as the trust department of a commercial bank. Under certain circumstances, it may be desirable to have the policy proceeds paid to a trustee rather than disbursed under the settlement options. This would be the case if the amount of insurance is substantial; if considerable flexibility and discretion in the amount and timing of payments are needed; if there are minor children or mentally or physically challenged adults who cannot manage their own financial affairs; or if the amounts paid must be periodically changed as the beneficiary's needs and desires change. These advantages are partly offset by the payment of a trustee's fee, and the investment results cannot be guaranteed.

## ADDITIONAL LIFE INSURANCE BENEFITS

A life insurance rider can be added to a life insurance policy to provide additional benefits. Most riders require the payment of an additional premium. The following section discusses additional life insurance benefits that can be added to a life insurance policy by an appropriate rider. These benefits provide valuable protection to policyholders.

### Waiver-of-Premium Provision

A **waiver-of-premium provision** can be added to a life insurance policy. In some policies, the waiver-of-premium provision is automatically included. *Under this provision, if the insured becomes totally disabled from bodily injury or disease before some stated age, all premiums coming due during the period of disability are waived.* During the period of disability, death benefits, cash values, and dividends continue as if the premiums had been paid.

Before any premiums are waived, the insured must meet the following requirements:

- Become disabled before some stated age, such as before age 60 or 65
- Be continuously disabled for six months (Some insurers have a shorter waiting period.)
- Satisfy the definition of total disability
- Furnish proof of disability satisfactory to the insurer

The insured must be totally disabled for premiums to be waived. Total disability is defined in the policy. In many waiver-of-premium provisions, *total disability means that because of disease or bodily injury, the insured cannot do any of the essential duties of his or her job, or of any job for which he or she is suited based on schooling, training, or experience.*[5] If the insured can perform some but not all of these duties, the disability is not considered to be total, and premiums are not waived. If the insured is a minor and is going to school, premiums are waived if the minor is unable to attend school.

For example, assume that Professor Harry Crockett is a chemistry professor at a major university who has lung cancer. He cannot perform any of the essential duties of his job, which include teaching, research, and public service. As long as he remains totally disabled, all premiums are waived after a six-month elimination period. However, if he could work at another job for which he is suited based on his education, training, and experience, such as a research scientist for a chemical firm, he would not be considered totally disabled.

*Total disability can also be defined in terms of the loss of use of bodily members.* For example, if Jason loses his eyesight in an explosion, or if both legs are paralyzed from some crippling disease, he would be considered totally disabled.

Before any premiums are waived, the insured must furnish satisfactory proof of disability to the insurer. The insurer may also require continuing proof of disability once each year. If satisfactory proof of disability is not furnished, no further premiums will be waived.

Many financial planners recommend adding this provision to a life insurance policy, especially if the face amount of life insurance is large. During a period of long-term disability, premium payments can be financially burdensome. Because most persons are underinsured for disability-income benefits, waiver of premiums during a period in which income is reduced is highly desirable.

### Guaranteed Purchase Option

*The **guaranteed purchase option** gives policyholders the right to purchase additional amounts of life insurance at specified times in the future without evidence of insurability.* The guaranteed purchase option is also called the guaranteed insurability option. The purpose of the option is to guarantee the insured's future insurability. The insured may need additional life insurance in the future and may be unable to afford the additional insurance today. The guaranteed purchase option guarantees the purchase of specified amounts of life insurance in the future, even though the insured may become substandard in health or uninsurable.

**Amount of Insurance**   The typical option allows the policyholder to purchase additional amounts of life insurance every three years up to some maximum age without evidence of insurability, such as age 46. In most cases, the additional insurance increases the face amount of the original policy. However, some insurers issue a new policy for each option exercised. For example, the guaranteed purchase option of one insurer allows additional purchases of life insurance when the insured attains ages 25, 28, 31, 34, 37, 40, 43, and 46. The amount of life insurance that can be purchased at each option date is limited to the face amount of the basic policy subject to some minimum and maximum amount. For example, assume that Heather, age 22, purchases a $25,000 ordinary life policy with a guaranteed purchase option and becomes uninsurable after the policy is issued. Assuming that she elects to exercise each option, she would have the following amounts of insurance:

| | |
|---|---|
| Age 22 | $ 25,000 (basic policy) |
| | + |
| Age 25 | $ 25,000 |
| Age 28 | 25,000 |
| Age 31 | 25,000 |
| Age 34 | 25,000 |
| Age 37 | 25,000 |
| Age 40 | 25,000 |
| Age 43 | 25,000 |
| Age 46 | 25,000 |
| Total insurance at age 46 | $225,000 |

Although uninsurable, Heather has increased her insurance coverage from $25,000 to $225,000.

**Advance Purchase Privilege**   Most insurers have some type of advance purchase privilege, by which an option can be immediately exercised on the occurrence of some event. For example, if the insured marries, has a birth in the family, or legally adopts a child, an option can be immediately exercised prior to the next option

due date. Some insurers will provide automatic term insurance for 90 days if the insured marries or a child is born. The insurance expires after 90 days unless the guaranteed insurability option is exercised.

If an option is exercised under the advance purchase privilege, the number of total options is not increased. If an option is exercised early, each new purchase eliminates the next regular option date. Finally, the policyholder typically has only 30 to 60 days to exercise an option. If the option expires without being used, it cannot be exercised at some later date. This provision protects the insurer from adverse selection.

**Other Considerations**   An important consideration is whether the waiver-of-premium rider can be added to the new insurance without furnishing evidence of insurability. Insurer practices vary in this regard. The most liberal provision permits the waiver-of-premium rider to be added to the new insurance if the original policy contains such a provision. If premiums are being waived under the original policy, they are also waived for the new insurance. Thus, in our earlier example, if premiums are being waived under Heather's original policy of $25,000, the premiums for the new life insurance purchased will also be waived. A less liberal approach permits the disabled insured to purchase additional life insurance with each option, but not to waive the new premiums under the waiver-of premium rider.

### Accidental Death Benefit Rider

*The* **accidental death benefit rider** (also known as **double indemnity**) *doubles the face amount of life insurance if death occurs as a result of an accident.* In some policies, the face amount is tripled.

**Requirements for Collecting Benefits**   Before a double indemnity benefit is paid, several requirements must be satisfied:

- Death must be caused directly, and apart from any other cause, by accidental bodily injury.
- Death must occur within one year of the accident.
- Death must occur before some specified age, such as age 60, 65, or 70.

*The first requirement is that accidental injury must be the direct cause of death.* If death occurs from some other cause, such as disease, the double indemnity benefit is not paid. For example, assume that Sam is painting his two-story house. If the scaffold collapses and Sam is killed, a double indemnity benefit would be paid because the direct cause of death is an accidental bodily injury. However, if Sam died from a heart attack and fell from the scaffold, the double payment would not be made. In this case, heart disease is the direct cause of death, not accidental bodily injury.

*The second requirement is that death must occur within one year of the accident* while the rider is in effect. The purpose of this requirement is to establish the fact that accidental bodily injury is the proximate cause of death.

*Finally, the accidental death must occur before some specified age.* To limit their liability, insurers usually impose some age limitation. Coverage usually terminates on the policy anniversary date just after the insured reaches a certain age, such as 70.

Financial planners generally do not recommend purchase of the double indemnity rider. Although the cost is relatively low, there are three major objections to the rider. *First, the economic value of a human life is not doubled or tripled if death results from an accident.* Therefore, it is economically unsound to insure an accidental death more heavily than death from disease. *Second, most persons will die as a result of a disease and not from an accident.* Because most persons are underinsured, the premiums for the double indemnity rider could be better used to purchase an additional amount of life insurance, which would cover both accidental death and death from disease. *Finally, the insured may be deceived and believe that he or she has more insurance than is actually the case.* For example, a person with a $50,000 policy and a double indemnity rider may erroneously believe that he or she has $100,000 of life insurance.

## Cost-of-Living Rider

*The* **cost-of-living rider** *allows the* policyholder *to purchase one-year term insurance equal to the percentage change in the consumer price index with no evidence of insurability.* The amount of term insurance changes each year and reflects the cumulative change in the consumer price index (CPI) from the issue date of the policy. However, insurers may limit the amount of insurance that can be purchased each year, such as a maximum of 10 percent of the policy face value. The policyholder pays the entire premium for the term insurance.

For example, assume that Luis, age 28, buys a $100,000 ordinary life insurance policy and that the CPI increases 5 percent during the first year. He would be allowed to purchase $5000 of one-year term insurance, and the total amount of insurance in force would be $105,000. The term insurance can be converted to a cash-value policy with no evidence of insurability.

## Accelerated Death Benefits

Most insurers provide **accelerated death benefits** that allow part or all of the life insurance face amount to be paid to a chronically or terminally ill policyholder before he or she dies. The policy may contain provisions for accelerated benefits when the policy is purchased, or it may be added as a rider. Some insurers do not charge for the benefit. Others increase the premium by a small amount to cover the cost.

Accelerated benefits generally range from 25 percent to 95 percent of the policy face amount.[6] Some insurers pay 100 percent of the face amount, but the benefit is reduced for the loss of interest. Depending on the insurer and policy provision, certain medical conditions can trigger the payment of accelerated benefits. They include the following:[7]

- *Terminal illness.* The policyholder is terminally ill and is expected to die within 24 months.
- *Acute illness.* The policyholder has an acute illness, such as acute heart disease or AIDS, which would result in a drastically reduced life span without extensive treatment.
- *Catastrophic illness.* The policyholder has a catastrophic illness, which requires extraordinary medical treatment, such as a heart transplant or liver transplant.
- *Long term care.* The policyholder requires long term care because he or she cannot perform a certain number of daily living activities, such as eating, dressing, or bathing.
- *Nursing home confinement.* The policyholder has a condition that requires permanent confinement in an eligible institution, such as a nursing home.

The accelerated death benefits provision is a valuable provision that provides cash to terminally or chronically ill individuals who are undergoing great

---

## INSIGHT 12.3

### Accelerated Death Benefits—Real Life Example

When Jackie Blanchard's husband died at 28 with barely enough life insurance to pay for his funeral, she purchased enough coverage for herself to ensure that her young daughters, Ebony and Shanna, would be fine if something happened to her. Two years later, she was diagnosed with terminal lung cancer. Jackie used her policy's accelerated death benefit provision, which allowed her to access 75 percent of the death benefit, to finance a home and a car for her daughters, and to fund their future education. Today, Ebony, a recent college graduate, and Shanna, a high school senior, live in the home their mother purchased for them.

Source: Adaptation of "Ebony and Shanna Blanchard—A Mother's Wish, realLIFEstories, Life and Health Insurance Foundation for Education (LIFE), Arlington, VA.

---

stress. Insight 12.3 provides a real life example of how the accelerated benefits provision helped one family.

### Viatical Settlement

People who are terminally ill often need large amounts of cash for medical bills, alternative medical treatment, living expenses, and other purposes. As an alternative to the payment of accelerated benefits, terminally ill insureds may be able to sell their policies to private firms. *A **viatical settlement** is the sale of a life insurance policy by a terminally ill insured to another party, typically to investors or investor groups who hope to profit by the insured's early death.* The insured generally must have a life expectancy of 12 months or less. The policy is sold at a substantial discount, and the buyer continues to pay the premiums.

### Life Settlement

A life settlement is another version of a viatical settlement. *A **life settlement** is a financial transaction by which a policyholder who no longer needs or wants to*

---

## INSIGHT 12.4

### What Is a Life Settlement? Examples of Actual Cases

A life settlement is the sale of a life insurance policy to a third party for an amount that is greater than its cash surrender value (if any) but less than the face amount of insurance. A policyholder may no longer want or need a life insurance policy. Instead of letting a policy lapse or surrendering the policy for its cash value, the policyholder can sell the policy in a secondary market under certain conditions. Eligibility requirements vary depending on the firm. The insured generally must be age 65 or older, have a life expectancy of 15 years or less, and have deterioration in health since the policy was issued; the policy face amount must be at least $100,000; and the 2-year contestable period must have expired. The following are actual examples of life settlement cases:[a]

- *The son owned a $250,000 policy on his 79-year-old mother who was in an assisted living facility. He needed money to supplement her cost of care and was struggling to make annual premium payments of $10,844. The cash surrender value was zero. The life settlement was $80,000, or 32 percent of the death benefit.*

- *A charity owned a $500,000 universal life policy that was donated several years ago by an alumnus who is now age 82. The policy had a cash value of $79,000. Because of the continuing premium requirements and the desire to fund a current gift, the alumnus explored a life settlement arrangement. The life settlement was $210,000, or 42 percent of the death benefit and 266 percent of the cash surrender value.*

- *A corporation maintained a $500,000 term life insurance policy on a key person, age 68, who was retiring. The executive had the option of assuming ownership, but he did not need the coverage. Because the policy was term insurance, it had no cash value. The executive converted the term policy to a universal life policy and paid a conversion premium of $10,870. The executive received a life settlement of $64,400, or 13 percent of the death benefit. He was also reimbursed for the $10,870 premium to convert the policy.*

[a]Case Studies, Veris Settlement Partners at http://go2veris.com/case_studies.html (accessed April 10, 2012).

*keep a life insurance policy sells the policy to a third party for more than its cash value.* The purchaser becomes the new beneficiary and is responsible for all subsequent premium payments. Life insurance purchased years ago may no longer be needed. For example, a corporation no longer needs life insurance on a key executive because he or she has retired; a couple divorces, and life insurance is dropped; the insured can no longer afford to pay prohibitively high premiums; the children are grown; estate-tax needs have changed; or the policy may be an under-performing policy with little cash value. Insight 12.4 provides examples of actual life settlements.

Viatical settlements and life settlements have their downside. The policies are sold to parties who do not have an insurable interest in the insured's life but instead acquire a financial interest in the insured's early death. As such, there may be an incentive to murder the insured. In addition, there are numerous cases of alleged and actual fraud committed against individual investors, life insurers, and policyholders. The investment returns to investors who have purchased life settlements are often poor because insureds may live longer than expected. Finally, regulation of viatical settlement and life settlements by state insurance departments may be inadequate.

## CASE APPLICATION

Sonja, age 25, recently purchased a $100,000 ordinary life insurance policy on her life. The waiver-of-premium rider and guaranteed purchase option are attached to the policy. For each of the following situations, indicate the extent of the insurer's obligation, if any, to Sonja or to Sonja's beneficiary. Identify the appropriate policy provision or rider that applies in each case. Treat each event separately.

a. Sonja fails to pay the second annual premium due on January 1. She dies 15 days later.

b. Sonja commits suicide three years after the policy was purchased.

c. At Sonja's death, the life insurer discovers that Sonja deliberately lied about her age. Instead of being 25 years old, as she indicated, she was actually 26 years old at the time the policy was purchased.

d. Two years after the policy was purchased, Sonja is told that she has leukemia. She is uninsurable but would like to obtain additional life insurance.

e. Sonja is seriously injured in an auto accident. After six months, she is still unable to return to work. She has no income from her job, and the insurance premium payments are financially burdensome.

f. Sonja has a mentally disabled son. She wants to make certain that her son will have a continuous income after her death.

g. Sonja lets her policy lapse. After four years, she wants to reinstate the policy. Her health is fine. Point out to Sonja how she can reinstate her life insurance.

h. Sonja wants to retire and does not wish to pay the premiums on her policy. Indicate the various options that are available to her.

i. Ten years after the policy was purchased, Sonja is fired from her job. She is unemployed and is in desperate need of cash.

j. When Sonja applied for life insurance, she concealed the fact that she had high blood pressure. She dies five years later.

# SUMMARY

- The *ownership clause* states that the policyholder possesses all contractual rights in the policy while the insured is living.
- The *entire-contract clause* states that the life insurance policy and attached application constitute the entire contract between the parties.
- The *incontestable clause* states that a life insurer cannot contest the policy after it has been in force two years during the insured's lifetime.
- The *suicide clause* states that if the insured commits suicide within two years after the policy is issued, the face amount is not paid. There is only a refund of the premiums paid.
- The *grace period* allows the policyholder a period of 31 days to pay an overdue premium. Universal life and other flexible premium policies have longer grace periods, such as 61 days. The insurance remains in force during the grace period.
- There are several types of beneficiary designations. A *primary beneficiary* is the party who is first entitled to receive the policy proceeds upon the insured's death. A *contingent beneficiary* is entitled to the proceeds if the primary beneficiary dies before the insured or dies before receiving the guaranteed number of payments under an installment settlement option. A *revocable beneficiary* designation means that the policyholder can change the beneficiary without the beneficiary's consent. An *irrevocable beneficiary* designation is one that cannot be changed without the beneficiary's consent.
- Participating policies pay dividends. A *dividend* represents a refund of part of the gross premium if the experience of the company is favorable. Dividends paid to policyholders are not taxable and can be taken in several ways:

    Cash

    Reduction of premiums

    Dividend accumulations

    Paid-up additions

    Term insurance (in some companies)

- There are three *nonforfeiture* or cash-surrender options in cash-value contracts.

    Cash value

    Reduced paid-up insurance

    Extended term insurance

- The cash value can be borrowed under the *policy loan provision*. An automatic premium loan provision can

also be added to the policy, by which an overdue premium is automatically borrowed from the cash value.

- *Settlement options* are the various ways that the policy proceeds can be paid. The most common settlement options are as follows:

    Cash

    Interest option

    Fixed-period option

    Fixed-amount option

    Life income options

- A *waiver-of-premium provision* can be added to a life insurance policy, by which all premiums coming due during a period of total disability are waived. Before any premiums are waived, the insured must meet the following requirements:

    Become disabled before some stated age, such as age 60 or 65

    Be continuously disabled for six months

    Satisfy the definition of total disability

    Furnish proof of disability satisfactory to the insurer

- The *guaranteed purchase option* permits the policyholder to purchase additional amounts of life insurance at specified times without evidence of insurability. The purpose of the option is to guarantee the insured's future insurability.
- The *accidental death benefit rider (double indemnity rider)* doubles the face amount of life insurance if death occurs as a result of an accident. Consumer experts generally do not recommend purchase of the double indemnity rider.
- The *cost-of-living rider* allows the policyholder to purchase one-year term insurance equal to the percentage change in the consumer price index with no evidence of insurability.
- The accelerated benefits provision pays part or all of the life insurance death benefit to a terminally ill or chronically ill policyholder before death occurs to help pay for medical bills and other expenses.

# KEY CONCEPTS AND TERMS

Absolute assignment (236)
Accelerated death
  benefits (248)
Accidental death benefit
  rider (double
  indemnity) (247)

Automatic premium loan
  provision (237)
Aviation exclusion (236)
Change-of-plan
  provision (235)
Class beneficiary (235)

Collateral
  assignment (236)
Contingent
  beneficiary (235)
Cost-of-living rider (248)
Dividend accumulations
  option (240)
Entire-contract
  clause (232)
Extended term insurance
  option (240)
Fixed-amount (income
  of elected amount)
  option (242)
Fixed-period (income
  for elected period)
  option (242)
Grace period (233)
Guaranteed purchase
  option (246)
Incontestable clause (233)
Interest option (242)
Irrevocable
  beneficiary (235)
Life income options (243)

Life settlement (249)
Misstatement of age or sex
  clause (234)
Nonforfeiture laws (239)
Nonforfeiture options (239)
Nonparticipating
  policy (238)
Ownership clause (232)
Paid-up additions
  option (238)
Participating policy (238)
Policy loan provision (237)
Primary beneficiary (235)
Reduced paid-up insurance
  option (240)
Reinstatement
  provision (233)
Revocable beneficiary (235)
Settlement options (241)
Specific beneficiary (235)
Suicide clause (233)
Viatical settlement (249)
Waiver-of-premium
  provision (246)
War clause (236)

## REVIEW QUESTIONS

1. Briefly explain the following life insurance contractual provisions.
   a. Suicide clause
   b. Grace period
   c. Reinstatement clause

2. a. Describe the incontestable clause in a life insurance policy.
   b. What is the purpose of the incontestable clause?

3. a. Explain the requirements for reinstating a lapsed life insurance policy.
   b. What are the advantages and disadvantages of reinstating a lapsed life insurance policy?

4. Explain the following beneficiary designations.
   a. Primary and contingent beneficiary
   b. Revocable and irrevocable beneficiary
   c. Specific and class beneficiary

5. A life insurance policy is freely assignable to another party. Explain the following types of assignments:
   a. Absolute assignment
   b. Collateral assignment

6. Describe the policy loan provision that appears in a typical cash-value life insurance policy.
   a. Why is interest charged on a policy loan?
   b. List the advantages and disadvantages of a policy loan.

7. A life insurance policy that pays dividends is known as a participating policy.
   a. Identify the sources from which dividends can be paid.
   b. List the various dividend options in a typical life insurance policy.
   c. Can an insurer guarantee the payment of a dividend? Explain your answer.

8. All states have nonforfeiture laws that require the payment of a cash-surrender value when a cash-value policy is surrendered. Briefly explain the following nonforfeiture options that are found in a typical life insurance policy.
   a. Cash-value option
   b. Reduced paid-up insurance
   c. Extended term insurance

9. In addition to cash, life insurance death benefits can be paid under other settlement options. Briefly explain the following settlement options.
   a. Interest option
   b. Fixed-period option
   c. Fixed-amount option
   d. Life income options

10. Explain the definition of total disability that is found in a typical waiver-of-premium provision.

## APPLICATION QUESTIONS

1. Richard, age 35, owns an ordinary life insurance policy in the amount of $250,000. The policy is a participating policy that pays dividends. Richard has a number of financial goals and objectives. For each of the following situations, identify a dividend option that could be used to meet Richard's goals. Treat each situation separately.
   a. Richard finds the premium payments are financially burdensome. He wants to reduce his annual premium outlay.
   b. Richard has leukemia and is uninsurable. He needs additional life insurance protection.

c. Richard wants to accumulate additional cash for a comfortable retirement.

d. Richard would like to have a paid-up policy at the time of retirement.

e. Richard has substantial earned income that places him in a high marginal income-tax bracket. He wants the insurer to retain the dividends, but he does not want to pay income tax on the investment earnings.

2. Kathy, age 29, is married and has a son, age 3. She owns a $100,000 ordinary life insurance policy that contains a waiver-of-premium provision, guaranteed purchase option, and accelerated benefits rider. Kathy has several financial goals and objectives for her family. For each of the following situations, identify an appropriate contractual provision or policy benefit that will enable Kathy to meet her financial goals. Treat each situation separately.

a. If Kathy dies, she wants the policy proceeds to be paid in the form of monthly income to the family until her son attains age 18.

b. Kathy is totally disabled in an auto accident when she failed to stop at a red light. After six months, she has not recovered and remains totally disabled. As a result, she cannot return to her former job or work in any occupation based on her previous training and experience. She finds that the premium payments for life insurance are financially burdensome.

c. When she retires, Kathy would like to have the cash value in the policy paid to her in the form of life-time income. She wants the payments to continue for at least 10 years.

d. Kathy is terminally ill from a serious heart condition. Kathy's physician believes she will die within one year. Kathy has no savings and health insurance, and her medical bills are soaring. She needs $50,000 to pay all medical bills and other financial obligations.

e. Three years after the policy was issued, Kathy was diagnosed with breast cancer. As a result, she is now uninsurable. She would like to purchase additional life insurance to protect her family.

3. Jim, age 32, purchased a $300,000 five-year renewable and convertible term insurance policy. In answering the health questions, Jim told the agent that he had not visited a doctor within the last five years. However, he had visited the doctor two months earlier. The

doctor told Jim that he had a severe heart problem. Jim did not reveal this information to the agent when he applied for life insurance. Jim died three years after the policy was purchased. At that time, the life insurer discovered the heart ailment. Explain the extent of the insurer's obligation, if any, with respect to payment of the death claim.

4. Additional riders and benefits often can be added to a life insurance policy to provide greater protection to the insured. Describe each of the following riders and options:

a. Waiver-of-premium provision

b. Guaranteed purchase option

c. Double indemnity rider

d. Cost-of-living rider

e. Accelerated benefits rider

## INTERNET RESOURCES

- The **American Council of Life Insurers** represents the life insurance industry on issues dealing with legislation and regulation at the federal and state levels. The site provides consumer information on the purposes and types of life insurance. Visit the site at

  acli.com

- **Consumer Federation of America (CFA)** is a nonprofit organization that represents numerous consumer groups. This site is one of the best resources for obtaining meaningful consumer information about life insurance and other insurance products. CFA makes available a low-cost life insurance evaluation service by which individual life insurance policies can be evaluated for a small fee. Visit the site at

  consumerfed.org

- **InsWeb** provides timely information and premium quotes for life insurance as well as for homeowners, auto, and other insurance products. Visit the site at

  insweb.com

- **Insure.com** provides up-to-date information, premium quotes, and other consumer information on life insurance. Visit the site at

  insure.com

- The **Life and Health Insurance Foundation for Education (LIFE)** is a nonprofit organization that helps consumers make smart insurance decisions to protect their families.

Topics addressed include life, disability, long-term care, and health insurance. The goal is to help consumers better understand these products and the importance of insurance professionals in helping them reach these goals. Visit the site at

lifehappens.org

■ The **National Underwriter Company** publishes books and other publications on life insurance products. The company publishes the *National Underwriter,* Life & Health/Financial Services edition, a weekly trade publication that provides news about the life insurance industry. Visit the site at

nationalunderwriter.com

■ The **National Association of Insurance Commissioners (NAIC)** has a link to all state insurance departments, which provide a considerable amount of consumer information on life insurance. Click on "State and Jurisdiction Map." For starters, check out New York, Wisconsin, and California. Visit the site at

naic.org

■ **The Viatical and Life Settlement Association of America** is an organization that represents viatical settlement and life settlement brokers and funding companies. The site makes it possible to obtain the value of a life insurance policy that is no longer needed. A number of settlement plans are available. Visit the site at

mylifesettlementbroker.com

## SELECTED REFERENCES

Anderson, Buist M. *Anderson on Life Insurance.* Boston, MA: Little, Brown, 1991. See also the *September 1996 Supplement to Anderson on Life Insurance.*

Black, Kenneth, Jr., and Harold D. Skipper, Jr. *Life Insurance,* 13th ed. Upper Saddle River, NJ: Prentice-Hall, 2000, chs. 9–10.

Graves, Edward E., ed. *McGill's Life Insurance,* 8th ed. Bryn Mawr, PA: The American College, 2011, ch. 27.

Graves, Edward E., and Burke A. Christensen, eds. *McGill's Legal Aspects of Life Insurance,* 7th ed. Bryn Mawr, PA: The American College, 2010.

"The Growing Speculation in Human Lives, Through the Secondary Market for Life Insurance Policies," *The Insurance Forum,* June 2006.

"Life Insurance Companies Should Take Over the Secondary Market for Their Policies," *The Insurance Forum,* August 2006.

## NOTES

1. Edward E. Graves, ed., *McGill's Life Insurance,* 8th ed. Bryn Mawr, PA: The American College, 2011, p. 27.9.

2. InsuranceForum.com, "APR Calculator for Fractional (Modal) Premiums." See also Joseph M. Belth, ed., "Special Issue on Fractional Premiums," *Insurance Forum,* vol. 25, no. 12 (December 1998).

3. Graves, *McGill's Life Insurance,* p. 4.5.

4. Robert I. Mehr and Sandra G. Gustavson, *Life Insurance, Theory and Practice,* 4th ed. (Plano, TX: Business Publications, Inc., 1987), p. 206.

5. Graves, *McGill's Life Insurance,* pp. 27.25 and 27.26.

6. This section is based on American Council of Life Insurers, "Q & A: What You Need to Know About Accelerating Life Insurance Benefits," accessed at http://www.acli.com/Consumers/Life%20Insurance/Pages/Accelerating%20Benefits.aspx (August 8, 2012).

7. Ibid.

Students may take a self-administered test on this chapter at
**www.pearsonhighered.com/rejda**

# CHAPTER 13

# BUYING LIFE INSURANCE

*"When you buy life insurance, it's relatively easy to compare first-year premium costs. But that figure tells you nothing about what the policy will cost over the long run."*

Consumers Union

## LEARNING OBJECTIVES

**After studying this chapter, you should be able to**

◆ Explain the defects in the traditional net cost method for determining the cost of life insurance.

◆ Explain the interest-adjusted surrender cost index and net payment cost index for determining the cost of life insurance.

◆ Explain the yearly rate-of-return method for determining the annual rate of return on the saving component in a life insurance policy.

◆ Describe the suggestions to follow when purchasing life insurance.

◆ Understand how life insurance premiums are calculated.

*Ashley, age 28, is divorced with a son, age 2. She receives no child support because her former husband is disabled. Ashley earns $30,000 annually as a medical technician. Although money is tight, she would like to purchase some life insurance to protect her son. A life insurance agent recently met with Ashley and presented several proposals. However, she does not know how to evaluate the various plans. Moreover, like most insurance consumers, Ashley is unaware of the importance of performing a cost comparison of the different policies before buying life insurance.*

*This chapter is designed to answer the questions that Ashley may have concerning the purchase of life insurance. Most consumers buy life insurance without much thought. They frequently purchase life insurance from the first agent who persuades them to buy and are not aware of the huge variations in cost among insurers. As a result, they often pay more for their insurance protection than is necessary. The purchase of a high-cost policy rather than a low-cost policy can cost you thousands of dollars over your lifetime.*

*In this chapter, we discuss the fundamentals of buying life insurance. Specific topics covered include the methods for determining the cost of a life insurance policy, the rate of return on the savings component of a cash-value policy, and tips for buying life insurance. The appendix to the chapter explains how life insurance premiums are calculated.*

## DETERMINING THE COST OF LIFE INSURANCE

The cost of life insurance is a complex subject. In general, cost can be viewed as the difference between what you pay for a life insurance policy and what you get back. If you pay premiums and get nothing back, the cost of the insurance equals the premiums paid. However, if you pay premiums and later get something back, such as the cash value and dividends, your cost will be reduced. Thus, in determining the cost of life insurance, four major factors must be considered: (1) annual premiums, (2) cash values, (3) dividends, and (4) time value of money. Two cost methods that consider some or all of the preceding factors are the *traditional net cost method* and the *interest-adjusted cost method*. Although the following discussion is based on cash-value life insurance, the same cost methods can be used to determine the cost of term insurance.

### Traditional Net Cost Method

From a historical perspective, life insurers previously used the **traditional net cost method** to illustrate the net cost of life insurance. Under this method, the annual premiums for some time period are added together. Total expected dividends to be received during the same period and the cash value at the end of the period are then subtracted from the total premiums to determine the net cost of life insurance. For example, assume that the annual premium for a $10,000 ordinary life insurance policy issued to a female, age 20, is $132.10. Estimated dividends over a 20-year period are $599, and the cash surrender value at the end of the twentieth year is $2294 (see Exhibit 13.1). The average cost per year is minus $12.55 (−$1.26 per $1000).

The traditional net cost method has several defects and is misleading. *The most glaring defect is that it does not consider the time value of money.*

$$A = P\left(1 + \frac{r}{n}\right)^{nt}$$

**Exhibit 13.1**
## Traditional Net Cost Method

| | |
|---|---|
| Total premiums for 20 years | $2642 |
| Subtract dividends for 20 years | −599 |
| Net premiums for 20 years | $2043 |
| Subtract the cash value at the end of 20 years | −2294 |
| Insurance cost for 20 years | −$251 |
| Net cost per year (−$251 ÷ 20) | −$12.55 |
| Net cost per $1000 per year (−$12.55 ÷ 10) | −$1.26 |

Interest that the policyholder could have earned on the premiums by investing elsewhere is not considered. In addition, the insurance illustration often showed the insurance to be free (to have a negative cost). This is contrary to common sense, because no insurer can provide free insurance and remain in business.

### Interest-Adjusted Cost Method

The **interest-adjusted cost method** developed by the National Association of Insurance Commissioners is a more accurate measure of life insurance costs. *Under this method, the time value of money is taken into consideration by applying an interest factor to each element of cost.*

There are two principal types of interest-adjusted cost indexes, the *surrender cost index* and the *net payment cost index*. The surrender cost index is useful if you believe that you may surrender the policy at the end of 10 or 20 years, or some other time period. The net payment cost index is useful if you intend to keep your policy in force, and cash values are of secondary importance to you.

**Surrender Cost Index**   *The* surrender cost index *measures the cost of life insurance if you surrender the policy at the end of some time period, such as 10 or 20 years* (see Exhibit 13.2).

The annual premiums are accumulated at 5 percent interest, which recognizes the fact that the policyholder could have invested the premiums elsewhere. Although not shown, the annual dividends are also accumulated at 5 percent interest, which considers interest earnings on the dividends as well as the amount and timing of each dividend. Assume that the accumulated value of the dividends at the

**Exhibit 13.2**
## Surrender Cost Index

| | |
|---|---|
| Total premiums for 20 years, each accumulated at 5% | $4586 |
| Subtract dividends for 20 years, each accumulated at 5% | −824 |
| Net premiums for 20 years | $3762 |
| Subtract the cash value at the end of 20 years | −2294 |
| Insurance cost for 20 years | $1468 |
| Amount to which $1 deposited annually at the beginning of each year will accumulate to in 20 years at 5% | $34.719 |
| Interest-adjusted cost per year ($1468 ÷ $34.719) | $42.28 |
| Cost per $1000 per year ($42.28 ÷ 10) | $4.23 |

end of 20 years is $824. Using the same policy as before, the net premiums for 20 years adjusted for interest are $3762.

The next step is to subtract the cash value at the end of 20 years from the net premiums, which results in a total insurance cost of $1468. The policyholder pays this amount for the insurance protection for 20 years, after considering the time value of money.

The final step is to convert the total interest-adjusted cost for 20 years into an annual cost. This is done by dividing the total interest-adjusted cost by an *annuity due* factor of 34.719. This factor means that a $1 deposit at the *beginning* of each year at 5 percent interest will accumulate to $34.719 at the end of 20 years. By dividing the total interest-adjusted cost of $1468 by $34.719, you end up with an annual interest-adjusted cost of $42.28, or $4.23 for each $1000 of insurance. As you can see, the interest-adjusted cost is positive, which means that it costs something to own life insurance when forgone interest is considered. In this case, the average annual cost is $42.28 if the policy is surrendered after 20 years.

**Net Payment Cost Index**   *The* **net payment cost index** *measures the relative cost of a policy if death occurs at the end of some specified time period, such as 10 or 20 years. It is based on the assumption that you will not surrender the policy.* Therefore, it is the appropriate cost index to use if you intend to keep your life insurance in force.

## Exhibit 13.3
**Net Payment Cost Index**

| | |
|---|---|
| Total premiums for 20 years, each accumulated at 5% | $4586 |
| Subtract dividends for 20 years, each accumulated at 5% | −824 |
| Insurance cost for 20 years | $3762 |
| Amount to which $1 deposited annually at the beginning of each year will accumulate to in 20 years at 5% | $34.719 |
| Interest-adjusted cost per year ($3762 ÷ $34.719) | $108.36 |
| Cost per $1000 per year ($108.36 ÷ 10) | $10.84 |

The net payment cost index is calculated in a manner similar to the surrender cost index except that the cash value is not subtracted (see Exhibit 13.3).

If the policy is kept in force for 20 years, the policy has an annual cost of $108.36 ($10.84 per $1000) after interest is considered.

## Substantial Cost Variation Among Insurers

There are enormous cost variations among insurers. Exhibit 13.4 shows the 20-year historical cost performance of participating whole policies for selected insurers for a $250,000 policy issued to a preferred risk, non-smoking male, age 45. Dividends are paid in cash. The period covered is 12/31/1990 to 12/31/2010.

*In the interpretation of these indexes, the lower the number, the less costly is the policy.* Figures in the *illustrated* columns show the estimated interest-adjusted costs when the policy was first issued. Note, however, that the *actual cost* for all policies is significantly higher than the illustrated cost when the policy was first issued. The actual cost is higher than illustrated because interest rates have declined significantly during this period, which resulted in a reduction in dividends for many policyholders. As Exhibit 13.4 shows, based on actual cost, the surrender cost index over the 20-year period ranged from a low of −0.24 per $1000 for Savings Bank Life of Massachusetts to a high of $4.14 per $1000 for

## Exhibit 13.4
**Whole Life Actual Historical Performance, $250,000, Male Nonsmoker Preferred Class, Age 45**

| 20-Year Historical Performance (Policy Issued 12/31/1990. Last Day 12/31/2010) | | | Year 20 Cash Dividends* | | | |
|---|---|---|---|---|---|---|
| | | | Surrender Cost Index | | Net Payment Index | |
| Company | Leading Policy (12/31/90) | Annual Premium | Illustrated | Actual | Illustrated | Actual |
| Country Financial Life | Executive Whole Life | 4,850 | −0.99 | 2.57 | 9.78 | 13.34 |
| Guardian Life | Whole Life 100(89-Form) | 5,211 | −0.82 | 3.72 | 10.46 | 15.00 |
| Massachusetts Mutual Life | Whole Life-MM Block | 4,730 | 0.27 | 2.95 | 10.46 | 13.72 |
| Met Life | Whole Life | 4,820 | −1.73 | 2.99 | 9.10 | 13.82 |
| Mutual Trust Life | Econolife | 4,745 | −1.27 | 4.14 | 9.36 | 14.77 |
| New York Life | Whole Life | 4,710 | −2.28 | 2.02 | 8.20 | 12.50 |
| Northwestern Mutual Life | 90 Life | 5,815 | −0.24 | 1.59 | 11.26 | 13.09 |
| Penn Mutual Life | Traditional Life | 5,088 | −1.25 | 3.33 | 9.35 | 13.93 |
| Savings Bank Life of MA | Straight Life | 4,388 | −1.60 | −0.24 | 8.72 | 10.08 |
| Security Mutual Life of NY | Customizer | 4,358 | −0.76 | 3.97 | 9.36 | 14.09 |
| State Farm Life | Estate Protector | 4,708 | −0.14 | 3.69 | 9.97 | 13.81 |
| Thrivent Financial for Lutherans | Life Paid-Up at 65 (L65) | 7,235 | −3.92 | 2.42 | 13.65 | 19.99 |
| Thrivent Financial for Lutherans | Life Paid-Up at 96 (L96) | 5,103 | −1.17 | 2.82 | 10.29 | 14.29 |

*Best class at least 15% of this policy issued
SOURCE: Adapted from Roger L. Blease, "Full Disclosure Whole Report," *National Underwriter,* Life & Health Magazine, May 17, 2010.

Mutual Trust Life. Likewise, based on actual cost, the net payment cost index ranged from a low of $10.08 per $1000 for Savings Bank Life of Massachusetts to a high of $19.99 per $1000 for Thrivent Financial for Lutherans (Life Paid-Up at 65). *This wide variation in cost highlights the important point stated earlier— you can save thousands of dollars over a long period by paying careful attention to the cost index when you shop for life insurance.*

Unfortunately, most consumers do not consider interest-adjusted cost data when they buy life insurance. Instead, they use premiums as a basis for comparing costs. However, using premiums alone provides an incomplete comparison. Interest-adjusted cost data will give you more accurate information about the expected cost of a policy.

## Using Interest-Adjusted Cost Data

If you are solicited to buy life insurance, you should ask the agent to give you interest-adjusted cost data

on the policy. You should also request similar information from other insurers before you buy.

If you use interest-adjusted cost data to compare policies, keep in mind the following points:

- *Shop for a policy and not an insurer.* Some insurers have excellent low-cost policies at certain ages and coverage amounts, but they are not as competitive at other ages and coverage amounts.
- *Compare only similar plans of insurance.* You should compare policies of the same type with the same benefits. Otherwise, the comparison can be misleading.
- *Ignore small variations in the cost index numbers.* Small cost differences can be offset by other policy features or by services that you can expect to get from an agent or insurer.
- *Cost indexes apply only to a new policy.* The cost data should not be used to determine whether to replace an existing policy with a new one. Other factors should be considered as well (see Insight 13.1).

## INSIGHT 13.1

### Be Careful in Replacing an Existing Life Insurance Policy

**Life Insurance Replacement**

If you own a life insurance policy, you should be careful if you consider replacing it. Although the relative financial strength of the original company and the replacing company should be an important factor in your decision, you should consider other factors also, as described briefly below.

- *If you consider replacing a policy, your health and other items affecting eligibility should be reviewed.* You may not qualify for a new policy, or you may qualify only at high rates.
- *You should determine the cost of getting out of the original policy.* Many policies contain substantial surrender charges.
- *You should determine the cost of getting into the replacement policy.* Many policies involve substantial front-end expenses.
- *You should consider the tax implications of a replacement.* In some situations, the termination of a policy may trigger an income tax liability. It may be possible to defer the tax, but you should consult your tax adviser before you take action.
- *You should consider the incontestability clause.* If a policy is more than two years old, the company usually would be

barred from voiding the policy because of what the company considers false statements made in the application. Thus the original policy may not be contestable, while a replacement policy may be contestable for two years.

- *You should also be aware of the suicide clause. Suicide usually is excluded during the first two years of a policy.* Thus the original policy may currently cover suicide, while a replacement policy may not cover suicide for two years.

If an individual advises you to replace a policy, try to find out how much compensation he or she will receive if you follow the advice. Some individuals who recommend replacement may be acting in a professional manner and may want to help reduce your expenses or avoid the problems that may arise if your original company gets into financial trouble. However, some individuals may descend on the policyholders of a financially troubled company like sharks who detect blood in the water. The fact that an individual receives compensation for selling a replacement policy does not necessarily mean he or she is giving bad advice, but you should be on guard.

Source: Adapted from Joseph M. Belth, ed. "Life Insurance Replacement," *The Insurance Forum*, vol. 39, no. 9 (September 2012), p. 85. Used by permission of *The Insurance Forum*, Editor: Joseph M. Belth, © 2012.

■ *The type of policy you buy should not be based solely on a cost index.* You should buy the type of policy that best meets your needs, such as term, whole life, or some combination. Once you have decided on the type of policy, then compare costs.

### NAIC Policy Illustration Model Regulation

Our discussion of life insurance costs would not be complete without a brief discussion of the Life Insurance Policy Illustration Model Regulation drafted by the National Association of Insurance Commissioners (NAIC).

The majority of states have adopted the model regulation. The model act requires insurers to present certain information to applicants for life insurance. The policy illustration contains a *narrative summary* that describes the basic characteristics of the policy, including how the policy functions, underwriting class, death benefit option, payment of premiums, and any riders. The narrative summary also describes the elements of the policy that are not guaranteed, federal tax guidelines for the policy, key definitions, and interest-adjusted cost data.

In addition, the policy illustration has a *numeric summary* that shows the premium outlay, value of the accumulation account, cash-surrender values, and death benefit. Three policy values must be provided based on (1) current interest rate credited to the policy, (2) guaranteed minimum interest rate under the policy, and (3) midpoint interest rate. The illustration also shows the number of years the insurance protection will remain in force under the three sets of interest assumptions. The applicant and agent must sign the illustration and indicate they have discussed and they understand that the nonguaranteed elements in the policy are subject to change and can be higher or lower than the values shown in the illustration.

Certain deceptive sales practices are prohibited in the illustration of policy values: insurers are prohibited from using anticipated gains from improvements in mortality in the sales illustration; the term "vanishing premium" cannot be used; and the values shown in the illustration must be justified by a self-support test.

Finally, the insurer must provide an annual report on the policy and notify the policyholders when a change occurs in the dividend scale or individual pricing elements that would negatively affect the policy values. The model regulation should reduce misunderstanding of policy values by policyholders and reduce deceptive sales practices by agents.

## RATE OF RETURN ON SAVING COMPONENT

Another important consideration is the rate of return earned on the saving component of a traditional whole life insurance policy. Consumers normally do not know the annual rate of return they earn on the saving component in their policies. A consumer who buys a traditional cash-value policy with a low return can lose a considerable amount of money over the life of the policy through forgone interest. Thus, the annual rate of return you earn on the saving component is critical if you intend to invest money in a life insurance policy over a long period of time.

### Linton Yield

The **Linton yield** is one method that can be used to determine the rate of return on the saving portion of a cash-value policy. It was developed by M. Albert Linton, a well-known life insurance actuary. *In essence, the Linton yield is the average annual rate of return on a cash-value policy if it is held for a specified number of years.* It is based on the assumption that a cash-value policy can be viewed as a combination of insurance protection and a savings fund. To determine the average annual rate of return for a given period, it is first necessary to determine that part of the annual premium that is deposited in the savings fund. This amount can be determined by subtracting the cost of the insurance protection for that year from the annual premium (less any dividend). The balance of the premium is the amount that can be deposited into the savings fund. Thus, the average annual rate of return is the compound interest rate that is required to make the savings deposits grow to equal the guaranteed cash value in the policy at the end of a specified period.

Calculation of the Linton yield is complex and requires specific information. Unfortunately, current rates of return based on the Linton yield are not readily available to consumers. However, an earlier Consumer Federation of America study of 109 cash-value policies based on the Linton yield showed that the annual rates of return vary widely. Although dated, the conclusions in this study are still valid today. The study showed that the annual rates of return on cash values are negative during the early years, and consumers lose billions of dollars annually by terminating their policies early. *Average annual rates of return for the 109 policies ranged from a minus 87.9 percent the first year to 8.2 percent for the twentieth year.*[1] Linton Yields would be considerably lower today because interest rates have declined significantly in recent years. Consequently, to avoid losing money, the length of the holding period is critical. The Consumer Federation of America recommends that consumers should not purchase a cash-value policy unless they plan to hold it for at least 20 years.

As stated above, annual rates of return based on the Linton yield are usually negative during the early years of the policy. These negative returns reflect the heavy first-year acquisition and administrative expenses when the policy is first sold. An agent receives a commission, and there may be a medical examiner's fee, an inspection report, and other expenses involved in issuing the policy. As a result of these expenses, most cash-value policies have little or no cash value at the end of the first year, and the cash values remain relatively low during the early years.

Because current information on Linton Yields is not readily available, this methodology has limited usefulness as a consumer tool. We must therefore consider other methods. The yearly rate-of-return method discussed next is a simple, but valuable methodology that can enable you to calculate the annual rate of return on the saving component in your policy.

## Yearly Rate-of-Return Method

Professor Joseph M. Belth has developed the **yearly rate-of-return method** for calculating the yearly rate of return on the saving component of a cash-value policy.[2] The yearly rate of return is based on the following formula:

$$i = \frac{(CV + D) + (YPT)(DB - CV)(.001)}{(P + CVP)} - 1$$

where

$i$ = yearly rate of return on the saving component, expressed as a decimal

$CV$ = cash value at end of policy year

$D$ = annual dividend

$YPT$ = assumed yearly price per \$1000 of protection (see benchmark prices in Exhibit 13.5)

$DB$ = death benefit

$P$ = annual premium

$CVP$ = cash value at end of preceding policy year

The first expression in the numerator of the formula is the amount available in the policy at the end of the policy year. The second expression in the numerator is the assumed price of the protection component, which is determined by multiplying the amount of protection by an assumed price per \$1000 of protection. Assumed prices per \$1000 of protection for various ages are benchmarks derived from certain U.S. population death rates (see Exhibit 13.5). Finally, the expression in the denominator of the formula is the amount available in the policy at the beginning of the policy year.

For example, assume that Mark purchased a \$100,000 participating ordinary life policy at age 35. He is now age 42 at the beginning of the eighth policy year. He would like to know the yearly rate of return on the saving component for the eighth year of the policy. The annual premium is \$1500. The cash

**Exhibit 13.5**
**Benchmark Prices**

| Age | Benchmark Price |
| --- | --- |
| Under 30 | \$ 1.50 |
| 30–34 | 2.00 |
| 35–39 | 3.00 |
| 40–44 | 4.00 |
| 45–49 | 6.50 |
| 50–54 | 10.00 |
| 55–59 | 15.00 |
| 60–64 | 25.00 |
| 65–69 | 35.00 |
| 70–74 | 50.00 |
| 75–79 | 80.00 |
| 80–84 | 125.00 |

NOTE: The benchmark prices are derived from certain U.S. population death rates. The benchmark figure for each five-year age bracket is close to the death rate per \$1000 at the highest age in that bracket.

SOURCE: Adapted from Joseph M. Belth, *Life Insurance: A Consumer's Handbook*, 2nd ed. (Bloomington, IN: Indiana University Press, 1985), table 9, p. 84. Reprinted by permission of the author.

value in the policy is $7800 at the end of the seventh policy year and $9200 at the end of the eighth policy year. The eighth-year dividend is $400. Because Mark is age 42 at the beginning of the eighth policy year, the benchmark price is $4.00 per $1000 (see Exhibit 13.5).

Based on the preceding information, the yearly rate of return for the eighth policy year is calculated as follows:

$$i = \frac{(9200 + 400) + (4)(100,000 - 9200)(.001)}{(1500 + 7800)} - 1$$

$$= \frac{(9600) + (4)(90,800)(.001)}{(9300)} - 1$$

$$= \frac{9600 + 363}{9300} - 1$$

$$= \frac{9963}{9300} - 1 = 1.071 - 1 = 0.71 = 7.1\%$$

The yearly rate of return for the eighth policy year is 7.1 percent, assuming that the yearly price per $1000 of protection is $4.

The major advantage of Belth's method is simplicity—you do not need a computer. The information needed can be obtained by referring to your policy and premium notice, or by contacting your agent or insurer.

# TAXATION OF LIFE INSURANCE

Treatment of life insurance buying would be incomplete without a discussion of the taxation of life insurance. This section discusses briefly the taxation of life insurance.

## Federal Income Tax

Life insurance proceeds paid in a lump sum to a designated beneficiary are generally received income-tax free by the beneficiary. If the proceeds are periodically liquidated under a settlement option, the payments consist of both principal and interest. The principal is received income-tax free, but the interest is taxable as ordinary income.

Premiums paid for individual life insurance policies generally are not deductible for income-tax purposes. Dividends on life insurance policies generally are received income-tax free until total dividends exceed the net premiums paid for the policy. However, interest on dividends retained under the interest option is taxable to the policyholder as ordinary income. If the dividends are used to buy paid-up additions, the cash value of the paid-up additions accumulates income-tax free unless the contract is terminated with a policy gain (discussed later). Thus, compared with the interest option, the paid-up additions option provides a small tax advantage.

In addition, the annual increase in cash value under a permanent life insurance policy is presently income-tax free. However, if the policy is surrendered for its cash value, any gain is taxable as ordinary income. If the cash value exceeds the premiums paid less any dividends, the excess is taxed as ordinary income.

## Federal Estate Tax

If the insured has any ownership interest in the policy at the time of death, the entire proceeds are included in the gross estate of the insured for federal estate-tax purposes. Examples include the right to change the beneficiary, the right to borrow the cash value or surrender the policy, and the right to elect a settlement option. The proceeds are also included in the insured's gross estate if they are payable to the estate. They can be removed from the gross estate if the policyholder makes an *absolute assignment* of the policy to someone else and has no incidents of ownership in the policy at the time of death. However, if the assignment is made within three years of death, the proceeds will be included in the deceased's gross estate for federal estate-tax purposes.

A federal estate tax is payable if the decedent's taxable estate exceeds certain limits. The basic exclusion amount is $5 million, which is indexed for inflation. For 2012, the excluded amount is $5,120,000. After the taxable estate is determined, a tentative tax is calculated. The tentative tax is reduced or eliminated by a tax credit called *the unified credit*. For individuals who die in 2012, the amount of the credit is $1,772,800, which eliminates the federal estate tax completely on taxable estates of $5,120,000 or less.

To determine whether a federal estate tax is payable, the value of the gross estate must first be determined. The *gross estate* includes the value of all property in which you had an ownership interest at the time of death. The *gross estate* also includes life insurance death proceeds in which you had any incidents of ownership at the time of death, the value of certain annuities payable to your heirs or to your estate, and the value of certain property you transferred within three years of your death. The gross estate can be reduced by certain deductions in determining the *taxable estate.* Allowable deductions include funeral and administrative expenses, claims against the estate, estate settlement and probate costs, charitable bequests, and certain other deductions.

In addition, the gross estate can be reduced by the *marital deduction,* which is a deduction of the value of the property included in the gross estate but passed on to a surviving spouse. This property is taxed later, when the surviving spouse dies. For example, assume that Richard dies in 2012 and has a gross estate of $8,500,000. He leaves $3,000,000 of property outright to his spouse. Thus, the marital deduction is $3,000,000. Assume that the mortgage and debts, administrative and probate costs, and funeral expenses total $380,000. The taxable estate is $5,120,000, and the tentative federal tax is $1,772,800. However, as a result of the unified credit of $1,772,800 the federal estate tax is zero (see Exhibit 13.6).

## SHOPPING FOR LIFE INSURANCE

Developing a sound life insurance program involves seven steps, as illustrated in Exhibit 13.7 and discussed next.

### Determine Whether You Need Life Insurance

The first step is to determine whether you need life insurance. If you are married or single with one or more dependents to support, you may need a substantial amount of life insurance. You may also need life insurance if you have a temporary need, such as paying off the mortgage on your home. In addition, if you have accumulated substantial assets, large amounts of life insurance may be needed to provide estate liquidity and to pay any state or federal estate taxes.

*However, if you are single and no one is currently dependent on you for financial support, you do not need life insurance, other than a modest amount for burial purposes.* The arguments for buying life insurance when you are young to protect your future insurability are not compelling. Even if your situation

**EXHIBIT 13.6**
**Calculating Federal Estate Taxes***

| | |
|---|---|
| Gross estate | $8,500,000 |
| Less: | |
| Mortgage and debts | 300,000 |
| Administrative and probate costs | 50,000 |
| Funeral expenses | 30,000 |
| | 380,000 |
| Adjusted gross estate | $8,120,000 |
| Less: | |
| Marital deduction | −3,000,000 |
| Taxable estate | $5,120,000 |
| Tentative tax | $1,772,800 |
| Less: | |
| Unified credit | $1,772,800 |
| Federal estate tax | $          0 |

*Individual dies in 2012.

**EXHIBIT 13.7**
**Shopping for Life Insurance**

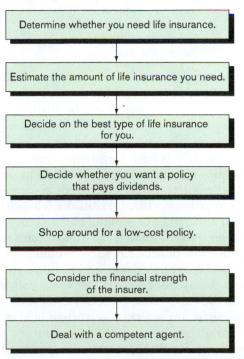

Determine whether you need life insurance.

Estimate the amount of life insurance you need.

Decide on the best type of life insurance for you.

Decide whether you want a policy that pays dividends.

Shop around for a low-cost policy.

Consider the financial strength of the insurer.

Deal with a competent agent.

should change and you need life insurance in the future, *more than nine out of ten applicants for life insurance are accepted at standard or preferred rates.* Thus, it is a waste of money to buy life insurance when it is not needed.

## Estimate the Amount of Life Insurance You Need

The needs approach is a practical method for determining the amount of life insurance to purchase. Persons with dependents often need surprisingly large amounts of life insurance. In determining the amount needed, you must consider your family's present and future financial needs, potential survivor benefits from Social Security, and other financial assets currently owned.

If you carry a sufficient amount of life insurance, it is unnecessary to purchase additional life insurance as supplemental coverage. These coverages are endless and include accidental death insurance from life insurers, accidental death and dismemberment insurance offered by commercial banks, credit life insurance on consumer loans, and life insurance sold by mail. In addition, flight insurance sold at airports is a bad buy for most consumers because commercial jets rarely crash.

## Decide on the Best Type of Life Insurance for You

The next step is to select the best type of life insurance policy for you. *The best policy is the one that best meets your financial needs.* If the amount of money you can spend on life insurance is limited, or if you have a temporary need, consider only term insurance. If you need lifetime protection, consider whole life insurance or universal life insurance. If you believe that you cannot save money without being forced to do so, also consider whole life insurance or universal life insurance as a savings vehicle. However, remember that the annual rates of return on cash-value policies can vary enormously.

Also, avoid purchasing a policy that you cannot afford. Many policyholders let their policies lapse during the early years, especially cash-value policies. Because of a surrender charge, there is little or no cash value available during the early years if the policy is surrendered. *If you drop a cash-value policy after a few months or years, you will lose a substantial amount of money. Be sure you can afford the premium.*

## Decide Whether You Want a Policy That Pays Dividends

In recent decades, participating life insurance policies that pay dividends generally have been better buys than nonparticipating policies because of high interest rates that permitted insurers to raise their dividends. However, interest rates have declined significantly in recent years, and insurers have reduced their dividends because excess interest earnings have declined. Thus, if you believe that interest rates will be higher in the future, you should consider a participating policy because excess interest has a powerful impact on dividends. However, if you believe that interest rates will remain at lower levels in the future, then consider a nonparticipating policy. Policies that do not pay dividends generally require a lower premium outlay.

You can ignore the above step if you are purchasing a variable life insurance, universal life insurance, or variable universal life insurance policy. These policies are nonparticipating and do not pay dividends.

## Shop Around for a Low-Cost Policy

One of the most important suggestions is to shop carefully for a low-cost policy. There is enormous variation in the cost of life insurance. You should not purchase a life insurance policy from the first agent who approaches you. *Instead, you should compare the interest-adjusted cost of similar policies from several insurers before you buy.* Otherwise, you may be overpaying for the insurance protection. If you make a mistake and purchase a high-cost policy, this mistake can cost you thousands of extra dollars over your lifetime.

When you shop for a low-cost policy, you should also consider no-load or **low-load life insurance**. Some life insurers sell insurance directly to the public by using telephone representatives or fee-only financial planners. The major advantage is that marketing expenses are substantially lower than for policies sold by agents to the public. Two companies that sell no-load or low-load insurance by phone are Ameritas Advisors Services (1-800-555-4655) and USAA Life Insurance (1-866-391-0347).

## Consider the Financial Strength of the Insurer

In addition to cost, you should consider the financial strength of the insurer issuing the policy. Some life insurers have become insolvent and have gone out of business. Although all states have state guaranty funds that pay the claims of insolvent life insurers, there are limits on the amount guaranteed. Although death claims are paid promptly, you may have to wait years before you can borrow or withdraw your cash value. Thus, it is important to buy life insurance only from financially sound insurers.

A number of rating organizations periodically grade and rate life insurers on their financial strength (see Exhibit 13.8). The companies are rated based on the amount of their capital and surplus, legal reserves, quality of investments, past profitability, competency of management, and numerous other factors. However, the various ratings are not always a reliable guide for consumers and can be confusing. There are wide variations in the grades given by the different rating agencies. Joseph M. Belth, a nationally known consumer expert in life insurance, recommends that an insurer should receive a high rating from at least two of the following four rating agencies before a policy is purchased. The following are considered high ratings for someone who is conservative:[3]

> Best: A++, A+, A
> Fitch: AAA, AA+, AA, AA−
> Moody's: Aaa, Aa1, Aa2, Aa3
> S&P: AAA, AA+, AA, AA−

## Deal with a Competent Agent

You should also deal with a competent agent when you buy life insurance. Selling life insurance is a tough job, and only a relatively small proportion of new life insurance agents are successful.

Most new agents receive only a minimum amount of training before they are licensed to sell life insurance. New agents also are often placed under intense pressure to sell life insurance. Even mature agents are expected to sell a certain amount of insurance. As a result, some agents have engaged in deceptive sales practices by misrepresenting the insurance to clients or by recommending policies that maximize commissions rather than meeting the client's needs.

To reduce the possibility of receiving bad advice or being sold the wrong policy, you should consider the professional qualifications of the agent. An agent who is a **Chartered Life Underwriter (CLU), Chartered Financial Consultant (ChFC), or Certified Financial Planner (CFP)** should be technically competent to give proper advice. More importantly, agents who hold the preceding professional designations are expected to abide by a code of ethics that places their clients' interests above their own. Agents who are currently studying for these professional designations should also be considered.

**EXHIBIT 13.8**

**Rating Categories for Major Rating Agencies**

| Rank Number | Ratings | | | |
|---|---|---|---|---|
| | Best | Fitch | Moody's | S&P |
| 1 | A++ | AAA | AAA | AAA |
| 2 | A+ | AA+ | AA1 | AA+ |
| 3 | A | AA | AA2 | AA |
| 4 | A− | AA− | AA3 | AA− |
| 5 | B++ | A+ | A1 | A+ |
| 6 | B+ | A | A2 | A |
| 7 | B | A− | A3 | A− |
| 8 | B− | BBB+ | BAA1 | BBB+ |
| 9 | C++ | BBB | BAA2 | BBB |
| 10 | C+ | BBB− | BAA3 | BBB− |
| 11 | C | BB+ | BA1 | BB+ |
| 12 | C− | BBBB− | BA2 | BBBB− |
| 13 | D | B+ | BA3 | B+ |
| 14 | E | B | B1 | B |
| 15 | F | B− | B2 | B− |
| 16 | S | CCC+ | B3 | CCC+ |
| 17 | | CCC | CAA1 | CCC |
| 18 | | CCC− | CAA2 | CCC− |
| 19 | | CC | CAA3 | CC |
| 20 | | C | CA | C |
| 21 | | | C | R |

NOTE: The ratings in a given rank are not necessarily equivalent to one another.

SOURCE: Joseph M. Belth, ed., "Financial Strength of Insurance Companies," *The Insurance Forum*, vol. 39, no. 9 (September 2012), p. 83. Used by permission of *The Insurance Forum*, Author: Joseph M. Belth.

## CASE APPLICATION

A participating ordinary life policy in the amount of $10,000 is sold to an individual, age 35. The following cost data are given:

| | |
|---|---:|
| Annual premium | $230 |
| Total dividends for 20 years | $1613 |
| Cash value at end of 20 years | $3620 |
| Accumulated value of the annual premiums at 5 percent for 20 years | $7985 |
| Accumulated value of the dividends at 5 percent for 20 years | $2352 |

Amount to which $1 deposited annually at the beginning of each year will accumulate in 20 years at 5 percent     $34.719

a. Based on this information, compute the annual net cost per $1000 of life insurance at the end of 20 years using the *traditional net cost method*.

b. Compute the annual *surrender cost index* per $1000 of life insurance at the end of 20 years.

c. Compute the annual *net payment cost index* per $1000 of life insurance at the end of 20 years.

## SUMMARY

- There are enormous cost variations among similar life insurance policies. Purchase of a high-cost policy can cost thousands of extra dollars over the insured's lifetime for the same amount of insurance protection.

- The traditional net cost method for determining the cost of life insurance is defective because it ignores the time value of money, and the insurance is often shown to be free.

- The interest-adjusted method is a more accurate method for determining the cost of life insurance. The time value of money is taken into consideration by applying an interest factor to each element of cost. If you are interested in surrendering the policy at the end of a certain period, the surrender cost index is the appropriate cost index to use. If you intend to keep your policy in force, the net payment cost index should be used.

- Annual rate-of-return data on the saving component in traditional cash-value life insurance policies are not readily available to consumers. However, the yearly rate-of-return method can be helpful to consumers in this regard.

- Life insurance death proceeds paid in a lump sum to a designated beneficiary are generally received income-tax free by the beneficiary. Premiums for individual life insurance are not income-tax deductible. If a policy is surrendered for its cash value, any gain is taxable as ordinary income. If the cash value exceeds the premiums paid less any dividends, the excess is taxed as ordinary income. The annual increase in cash value on a permanent life insurance policy is not taxable income to policyholders.

- If the insured has any ownership interest in the policy at the time of death, the entire proceeds are included in his or her gross estate for federal estate-tax purposes. A federal estate tax is payable if the decedent's taxable estate exceeds certain limits.

- Life insurance experts typically recommend several rules to follow when shopping for life insurance:

  Determine whether you need life insurance.

  Estimate the amount of life insurance you need.

  Decide on the best type of insurance for you.

  Decide whether you want a policy that pays dividends.

  Shop around for a low-cost policy.

  Consider the financial strength of the insurer.

  Deal with a competent agent.

## KEY CONCEPTS AND TERMS

Certified Financial Planner (CFP) (265)

Chartered Financial Consultant (ChFC) (265)

Chartered Life Underwriter (CLU) (265)

Interest-adjusted cost method (257)

Linton yield (260)

Net payment cost index (257)

No-load or low-load life insurance (264)

Surrender cost index (257)

Traditional net cost method (256)

Yearly rate-of-return method (261)

## REVIEW QUESTIONS

1. Explain the basic defect in the traditional net cost method for determining the cost of life insurance.

2. a. Why is the interest-adjusted cost method a more accurate measure of the cost of life insurance?
   b. Briefly describe the surrender cost index as a method for determining the cost of life insurance.
   c. Briefly describe the net payment cost index as a method for determining the cost of life insurance.

3. Why is the rate of return on the saving component in most cash-value policies negative during the early years of the policy?

4. Briefly explain the Linton Yield as a method for determining the rate of return on the saving component of a cash-value policy.

5. Briefly explain the yearly rate-of-return method that policyholders can use to determine the rate of return on the saving component of a cash-value policy.

6. Explain the federal income-tax treatment of a cash-value policy with respect to each of the following:
   a. Payment of premiums
   b. Annual dividends
   c. Annual increase in the cash value
   d. Payment of death proceeds to a stated beneficiary

7. Explain the federal estate-tax treatment of life insurance death proceeds.

8. Describe the suggestions that consumers should follow when life insurance is purchased.

9. The states require life insurers to disclose certain policy information to applicants for life insurance. Describe the types of information that appear on a typical disclosure statement.

10. What is a no-load or low-load life insurance policy? Explain.

## APPLICATION QUESTIONS

1. Nicole, age 25, is considering the purchase of a $20,000 participating ordinary life insurance policy. The annual premium is $248.60. Projected dividends over the first 20 years are $814. The cash value at the end of 20 years is $4314. If the premiums are invested at 5 percent interest, they will accumulate to $8631 at the end of 20 years. If the dividends are invested at 5 percent interest, they will accumulate to $1163 at the end of 20 years. A $1 deposit at the beginning of each year at 5 percent interest will accumulate to $34.719 at the end of 20 years.
   a. Based on the *traditional net cost method,* calculate the cost per $1000 per year.
   b. Based on the *surrender cost index,* calculate the cost per $1000 per year.
   c. Based on the *net payment cost index,* calculate the cost per $1000 per year.

2. Todd, age 40, is considering the purchase of a $100,000 participating ordinary life insurance policy. The annual premium is $2280. Projected dividends over the first 20 years are $15,624. The cash value at the end of 20 years is $35,260. If the premiums are invested at 5 percent interest, they will grow to $79,159 at the end of 20 years. If the dividends are invested at 5 percent interest, they will accumulate to $24,400 at the end of 20 years. A $1 deposit at the beginning of each year at 5 percent interest will accumulate to $34.719 at the end of 20 years.
   a. Based on the *traditional net cost method,* calculate the cost per $1000 per year.
   b. Based on the *surrender cost index,* calculate the cost per $1000 per year.
   c. Based on the *net payment cost index,* calculate the cost per $1000 per year.

3. John, age 52, is overweight, smokes, and had a mild heart attack five years ago. Ignoring the advice of his physician, he refuses to exercise, lose weight, and quit smoking. John owns a $25,000 participating ordinary life policy that he purchased 20 years ago. A life insurance agent approached John and proposed that he replace the older policy with a new life insurance policy. The agent claims the new policy is superior to the older policy that was purchased years ago. Despite John's health problems, the agent claims that John can get life insurance from his company. What factors should John consider before replacing the older policy with a new policy?

4. Allison is trying to complete her income-tax return. A number of questions have come up about life insurance. Explain the tax treatment of each of the following.
   a. Allison is the beneficiary named in her grandfather's life insurance policy. Her grandfather died this year and Allison received a lump-sum payment of $50,000. She wonders if she has to report the $50,000 as taxable income.

b. Allison purchased a $100,000 cash value life insurance policy on her own life six years ago. This year, the cash value increased by $380. Allison wonders if the cash-value increase must be reported as taxable income. The policy remains in force.

c. Allison's annual life insurance premium is $350. Allison itemizes her income-tax deductions. She wonders if her life insurance premium is a tax-deductible expense.

d. Allison's ordinary life insurance policy is a participating policy. This year she received a cash dividend of $120. She wonders if she is required to report the $120 as taxable income.

## INTERNET RESOURCES

■ **Ameritas Advisors Services** sells life insurance and annuities directly to consumers without traditional agents. The policies are sold without a sales load and surrender charges. Visit the site at
ameritasdirect.com

■ **Consumer Federation of America** makes available a low-cost life insurance evaluation service by which individual life insurance policies can be evaluated for a small fee. Visit the site at
consumerfed.org

■ **Insure.com** provides premium quotes on life insurance, health insurance, disability income insurance, and long-term care insurance. Visit the site at
insure.com

■ **Insurance.com** is an online independent insurance agency that provides premium quotes on life insurance, health insurance, and other insurance products. Visit the site at
insurance.com

■ **InsWeb** provides timely information and premium quotes for life insurance and other insurance products. Visit the site at
insweb.com

■ **QuickQuote** provides premium quotes on life insurance, health insurance, and numerous other insurance products. Visit the site at
quickquote.com

■ **Select Quote** monitors highly rated insurers that sell term life insurance. It claims that it makes only the strongest and most competitively priced policies available to consumers. It also represents insurers that specialize in insuring people with different risks, such as a pilot, scuba diver, or diabetic. Visit the site at
selectquote.com

■ **Term4Sale** is considered one of the best consumer sites for obtaining term insurance quotes. Visit the site at
term4sale.com

## SELECTED REFERENCES

Belth, Joseph M., ed. "Financial Strength of Insurance Companies," *The Insurance Forum,* vol. 38, no. 9 (September 2011).

Belth, Joseph M. *Life Insurance: A Consumer's Handbook,* 2nd ed. Bloomington, IN: Indiana University Press, 1985.

Black, Kenneth, Jr., and Harold D. Skipper, Jr. *Life Insurance,* 13th ed. Upper Saddle River, NJ: Prentice-Hall, 2000.

Graves, Edward E., ed. *McGill's Life Insurance,* 8th ed. Bryn Mawr, PA: The American College, 2011.

Hunt, James H. *Variable Universal Life: Worth Buying Now? And Other Types of Life Insurance.* Consumer Federation of America, November 2007.

Hunt, James H., *Miscellaneous Observations on Life Insurance: Including an Update to 2007 Paper on Variable Universal Life*, Consumer Federation of America, January 2011.

Witt, Scott J. "Variable Universal Life—Buyer Beware!" *The Insurance Forum,* Vol. 35, No. 11 (November 2008).

## NOTES

1. Consumer Federation of America, *Rates of Return on Cash-Value Policies Vary Widely,* press release, July 16, 1997.

2. This section is based on Joseph M. Belth, *Life Insurance: A Consumer's Handbook,* 2nd ed. (Bloomington, IN: Indiana University Press, 1985), pp. 89–91, 208–209.

3. Joseph M. Belth, ed., "Financial Strength of Insurance Companies," vol. 38, no. 9 (September 2011), p. 224.

 Students may take a self-administered test on this chapter at
**www.pearsonhighered.com/rejda.**

# APPENDIX

# CALCULATION OF LIFE INSURANCE PREMIUMS

Our discussion of life insurance would not be complete without a discussion of how life insurance premiums are calculated. This section discusses briefly the fundamentals of premium calculations and policy reserves of life insurers.[1]

## NET SINGLE PREMIUM

Although most life insurance policies are not purchased with a single premium, the net single premium forms the foundation for the calculation of life insurance premiums. *The* net single premium (NSP) *is defined as the present value of the future death benefit*. It is that amount, which together with compound interest, will be sufficient to pay all death claims. In calculating the NSP, only mortality and investment income are considered. A loading for expenses will be considered later, when the gross premium is calculated.

The NSP is based on three basic assumptions: (1) premiums are paid at the beginning of the policy year, (2) death claims are paid at the

end of the policy year, and (3) the death rate is uniform throughout the year.

Certain assumptions must also be made concerning the probability of death at each attained age. Although life insurers generally develop their own mortality data, we will use selected data from the 2001 Commissioners Standard Ordinary (CSO) Mortality Table for male lives in our illustration. The 2001 CSO table shows mortality data from ages 0 to 120.

Finally, since premiums are paid at the beginning of the year and death claims are paid at the end of the year, the amounts needed for death claims can be discounted for interest. It is assumed that the amounts needed for death claims can be discounted annually at 5.5 percent compound interest.

### Term Insurance

The NSP for term insurance can be easily calculated. The period of protection is only for a specified period or to a stated age. The death benefit is paid if the insured dies within the specified period, but nothing is paid if the insured dies after the period of protection expires.

**Yearly Renewable Term Insurance** The NSP for yearly renewable term insurance is considered first. Assume that a $1000 yearly renewable term insurance policy is issued to a male, age 32. *The cost of each year's insurance is determined by multiplying the amount of insurance by the probability of death, which is then multiplied by the present value of $1 for the time period the funds are held.* By referring to the 2001 CSO mortality table for males in Exhibit A1, we see that out of 9,778,587 males alive at the beginning of age 32, 11,050 males will die during the year. Therefore, the probability that a male age 32 will die during the year is 11,050/9,778,587, or 0.00113. The amount of insurance is then multiplied by this probability to determine the amount of money the insurer must have on hand from each policyholder at the end of the year to pay death claims. However, because premiums are paid in advance, and death claims are paid at the end of the year, the amount needed can be discounted for one year. From Exhibit A2, we see that the present value of $1 at 5.5 percent interest is .9479. Thus, if $1000 is multiplied by the probability of death at age 32, and the product discounted for one year's interest, the resulting net single premium is $1.07. This calculation is summarized as follows:

$$\frac{Age\ 32,\ NSP}{}$$

$$\$1000 \times \frac{11,050}{9,778,587} \times .9479 = \$1.07$$

**Exhibit A1**
**Commissioners 2001 Standard Ordinary (CSO) Table of Mortality, Male Lives (selected ages)**

| Age | Number Living at Beginning of Designated Year | Number Dying During Designated Year | Yearly Probability of Dying |
|---|---|---|---|
| 30 | 9,800,822 | 11,173 | 0.00114 |
| 31 | 9,789,650 | 11,062 | 0.00113 |
| 32 | 9,778,587 | 11,050 | 0.00113 |
| 33 | 9,767,537 | 11,233 | 0.00115 |
| 34 | 9,756,305 | 11,512 | 0.00118 |
| 35 | 9,744,792 | 11,791 | 0.00121 |
| 36 | 9,733,001 | 12,458 | 0.00128 |
| 37 | 9,720,543 | 13,026 | 0.00134 |
| 38 | 9,707,517 | 13,979 | 0.00144 |
| 39 | 9,693,539 | 14,928 | 0.00154 |
| 40 | 9,678,610 | 15,970 | 0.00165 |

SOURCE: Excerpted from 2001 CSO Composite Ultimate, Male, ANB.

**Exhibit A2**
**Present Value of $1 at 5.5% Compound Interest**

| Number of Years | 5.5% |
|---|---|
| 1 | 0.9479 |
| 2 | 0.8985 |
| 3 | 0.8516 |
| 4 | 0.8072 |
| 5 | 0.7651 |
| 6 | 0.7252 |
| 7 | 0.6874 |
| 8 | 0.6516 |
| 9 | 0.6176 |
| 10 | 0.5854 |

If $1.07 is collected in advance from each of the 9,778,587 males who are alive at age 32, this amount together with compound interest will be sufficient to pay all death claims.

**Five-Year Term Insurance** In this case, the company must pay the death claim if the insured dies any time within the five-year period. However, death claims are paid at the end of the year in which they occur and not at the end of the five-year period. Thus, the cost of each year's mortality must be computed separately and then added together to determine the net single premium.

The cost of insurance for the first year is determined exactly as before, when we calculated the net single premium for yearly term insurance. Thus, we have the following equation:

$$\frac{Age\ 32,\ NSP,}{first-year\ insurance\ cost}$$

$$\$1000 \times \frac{11,050}{9,778,587} \times .9479 = \$1.07$$

The next step is to determine the cost for the second year. Referring back to Exhibit A1, we see that at age 33, 11,233 males will die during the year. Thus, for the 9,778,587 males who are alive at age 32, the probability of dying during age 33 is 11,233/9,778,587. Note that the denominator does not change but remains the same for each probability calculation. Because the amount needed to pay second-year death claims will not be needed for two years, it can be discounted for

**EXHIBIT A3**
**Calculating the NSP for a Five-Year Term Insurance Policy, Male, Age 32**

| Age | Amount of Insurance | | Probabiity of Death | | Present Value of $1 at 5.5% | | Cost of Insurance |
|-----|--------------------|---|--------------------|---|----------------------------|---|-------------------|
| 32 | $1000 | × | $\frac{11,050}{9,778,587}$ | × | .9479 | = | $1.07 (year 1) |
| 33 | $1000 | × | $\frac{11,233}{9,778,587}$ | × | .8985 | = | 1.03 (year 2) |
| 34 | $1000 | × | $\frac{11,512}{9,778,587}$ | × | .8516 | = | 1.00 (year 3) |
| 35 | $1000 | × | $\frac{11,791}{9,778,587}$ | × | .8072 | = | 0.97 (year 4) |
| 36 | $1000 | × | $\frac{12,458}{9,778,587}$ | × | .7651 | = | 0.97 (year 5) |
| | | | | | NSP | = | $5.04 |

two years. Thus, for the second year, we have the following calculation:

$$\frac{Age\ 33,\ NSP,}{second-year\ insurance\ cost}$$

$$\$1000 \times \frac{11,233}{9,778,587} \times .8985 = \$1.03$$

For each of the remaining three years, we follow the same procedure (see Exhibit A3). If the insurer collects $5.04 in a single premium from each of the 9,778,587 males who are alive at age 32, that sum together with compound interest will be sufficient to pay all expected death claims during the five-year period.

### Ordinary Life Insurance

In calculating the NSP for an ordinary life insurance policy, the same method used earlier for the five-year term policy is used except that the calculations are carried out each year to the end of the 2001 mortality table. If the remaining calculations are performed, the NSP for a $1000 ordinary life insurance policy issued to a male, age 32, would be $109.49.[2]

# NET ANNUAL LEVEL PREMIUM

If premiums are paid annually, the net annual level premium must be the mathematical equivalent of the NSP. The net annual level premium cannot be determined by simply dividing the NSP by the number of years of premium payments. Such a division would produce an inadequate premium for two reasons. First, the NSP is based on the assumption that premiums are paid at the beginning of the period. If premiums are paid in installments, and some insureds die early, there is a loss of future premiums. Second, installment payments result in the loss of interest income because of the smaller amounts invested.

The mathematical adjustment for the loss of premiums and interest is accomplished by dividing the NSP by the present value of an appropriate life annuity due of $1. More specifically, *the **net annual level premium (NALP)*** is *determined by dividing the present value of a life annuity due of $1(PVLAD) for the premium-paying period*. Thus, we obtain the following:

$$NALP = \frac{NSP}{\text{PVLAD of \$1 for the premium–paying period}}$$

If the annual premiums are paid for life, such as in an ordinary life policy, the premium is called a *whole life annuity due*. If the annual premiums are paid for only a temporary period, such as five-year term insurance, the premium is called a *temporary life annuity due*.

### Term Insurance

Consider first the NALP for a five-year term insurance policy in the amount of $1000 issued to a male, age 32. Recall that the NSP for a five-year term insurance policy issued at age 32 is $5.04. This sum must be divided by the present value of a five-year *temporary life annuity due of $1*. For the first year, a $1 payment is due immediately. For the second year, the probability that a male age 32 will still be *alive* to pay the premium at age 33 must be determined. Referring back to Exhibit A1, 9,778,587 males are alive at age 32. Of this number, 9,767,537 are still alive at age 33. Thus, the probability of survival is 9,767,537/9,778,587. This probability is multiplied by $1 and then discounted for one year's interest. Thus, the present value of the second payment is $0.95. Similar calculations are performed for the remaining three years. The calculations are summarized as follows:

| | | |
|---|---|---|
| Age 32 | $1 due immediately | $1.00 |
| Age 33 | $\frac{9{,}767{,}537}{9{,}778{,}587} \times \$1 \times .9479 =$ | 0.95 |
| Age 34 | $\frac{9{,}756{,}305}{9{,}778{,}587} \times \$1 \times .8985 =$ | 0.90 |
| Age 35 | $\frac{9{,}744{,}792}{9{,}778{,}587} \times \$1 \times .8516 =$ | 0.85 |
| Age 36 | $\frac{9{,}773{,}001}{9{,}778{,}587} \times \$1 \times .8072 =$ | 0.81 |
| | PVLAD of $1 | = $4.51 |

The present value of a five-year temporary life annuity due of $1 at age 32 is $4.51. If the NSP of $5.04 is divided by $4.51, the net annual level premium is $1.12.

$$\text{NALP} = \frac{\text{NSP}}{\text{PVLAD of }\$1} = \frac{\$5.04}{\$4.51} = \$1.12$$

### Ordinary Life Insurance

The net annual level premium for a $1000 ordinary life insurance policy issued to a male, age 32, is calculated in a similar manner. The same procedure is used except that the calculations are carried out to the end of the mortality table. If the calculations are performed, the present value of a whole life annuity due of $1 at age 32 is $17.08.[3] The NSP ($109.49) is then divided by the present value of a whole life annuity due at age 32 ($17.08), and the NALP is $6.41.

## GROSS PREMIUM

The gross premium is determined by adding a loading allowance to the net annual level premium. The loading allowance must cover all operating expenses, provide a margin for contingencies, and, in the case of stock insurers, provide for a contribution to profits. If the policy is a participating policy, the loading must also reflect a margin for dividends.

## POLICY RESERVES

Policy reserves, also known as legal reserves, are the major liability item of life insurers.[4] Under the level-premium method for paying premiums, premiums paid during the early years are higher than necessary to pay death claims, while those paid during the later years are insufficient to pay death claims. The excess premiums must be accounted for and held for future payment to the policyholders' beneficiaries. As such, the excess premiums paid during the early years result in the creation of a policy reserve. *Policy reserves are a liability item on the insurer's balance sheet that must be offset by assets equal to that amount.* The policy reserves held by the insurer, plus future premiums and investment earnings, will enable the insurer to pay all policy benefits if the actual experience conforms to the actuarial assumptions used in calculating the reserve. Policy reserves are also called *legal reserves* because state law specifies the basis for calculating the minimum reserve required by law.

### Purposes of the Reserve

The policy reserve has two purposes. *First, it is a formal recognition of the insurer's obligation to pay future claims.* The policy reserve plus future premiums and interest earnings must be sufficient to pay all future policy benefits.

*Second, the reserve is a legal test of the insurer's solvency.* The insurer must hold assets at least equal to its legal reserves and other liabilities. This requirement is a legal test of the insurer's ability to meet its present and future obligations to policyholders. As such, policy reserves should not be viewed as a fund. Rather, they are a liability item that must be offset by assets.

### Definition of the Reserve

The policy reserve *can be defined as the difference between the present value of future benefits and the present value of future net premiums.* The net single premium is equal to the present value of future benefits. At the inception of the policy, the net single premium is also equal to the present value of future net premiums. The net single premium can be converted into a series of net level premiums without changing this relationship. However, once the first installment premium is paid, this statement is no longer true. The present value of future benefits and the present value of future net premiums are no longer equal to each other. The present value of future benefits will increase over time, because the date of death is drawing closer, while the present value of future net premiums will decline, because fewer premiums will be paid. Thus, the difference between the two is the policy reserve.

This concept can be illustrated in a simplified manner by Exhibit A4, which shows the prospective reserve (defined later) for an ordinary life policy issued to a male, age 35.

At the inception of the policy, the net single premium is equal to the present value of future benefits and the present value of future net premiums.

The present value of future benefits increases over time, while the present value of future net premiums declines, and the reserve is the difference between them. Based on the older 1980 CSO mortality table for valuing legal reserves, the reserve for an ordinary life insurance policy continues to increase until it is equal to the policy face amount at age 100. If the insured is still alive at that time, the face amount is paid to the policyholder. However, for policies issued on or after January 1, 2009, life insurers are required to use the newer 2001 CSO mortality table for the valuation of their reserves. Thus, based on the 2001 CSO mortality table, the legal reserve will steadily increase and will be equal to the policy face amount at age 121.

## Types of Reserves

The reserve can be viewed either retrospectively or prospectively. If we refer to the past experience, the reserve is known as a retrospective reserve. *The* **retrospective reserve** *represents the net premiums collected by the insurer for a particular block of policies, plus interest earnings at an assumed rate, less the assumed death claims paid out.*[5] Thus, the retrospective reserve is the excess of the net premiums accumulated at interest over the death benefits paid out.

The reserve can also be viewed prospectively when we look to the future. *The* **prospective reserve** *is the difference between the present value of future benefits and the present value of future net premiums.* The retrospective and prospective methods are the mathematical equivalent of each other. Both methods will produce the same level of reserves at the end of any given year if the same set of actuarial assumptions is used.

**EXHIBIT A4**
**Prospective Reserve—Whole Life Insurance (1980 CSO mortality table)**

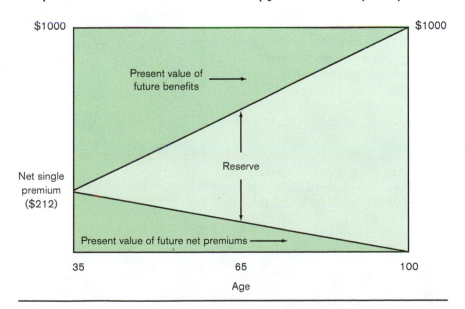

Reserves can also be classified based on the time of valuation. At the time the reserves are valued, they can be classified as terminal, initial, and mean. *A* **terminal reserve** *is the reserve at the end of any given policy year*. It is used by companies to determine cash surrender values as well as the net amount at risk for purposes of determining dividends. *The* **initial reserve** *is the reserve at the beginning of any policy year*. It is equal to the preceding terminal reserve plus the net level annual premium for the current year. The initial reserve is also used by insurers to determine dividends. Finally, *the* **mean reserve** *is the average of the terminal and initial reserves*. It is used to indicate the insurer's reserve liabilities on its annual statement.

## CASE APPLICATION

Assume that you are asked to explain how premiums for a life insurance policy are calculated. Based on the information below, answer the following questions.

a. Compute the net single premium for a five-year term insurance policy in the amount of $1000 issued to a male at age 30.

b. Compute the net annual level premium for the same policy as in part (a).

c. Is the net annual level premium the actual premium paid by the policyholder? Explain your answer.

| Age at Beginning of Year | Number Living at Beginning of Designated Year | Number Dying During Designated Year | Present Value of $1 at 5.5% | |
|---|---|---|---|---|
| | | | Year | Factor |
| 30 | 9,800,822 | 11,173 | 1 | 0.9479 |
| 31 | 9,789,650 | 11,062 | 2 | 0.8985 |
| 32 | 9,778,587 | 11,050 | 3 | 0.8516 |
| 33 | 9,767,537 | 11,233 | 4 | 0.8072 |
| 34 | 9,756,305 | 11,512 | 5 | 0.7651 |

## KEY CONCEPTS AND TERMS

Initial reserve
Mean reserve
Net annual level premium (NALP)
Net single premium (NSP)
Prospective reserve
Retrospective reserve
Terminal reserve

## NOTES

1. This section is based on Edward E. Graves, ed., *McGill's Life Insurance,* 8th ed. (Bryn Mawr, PA: The American College, 2011), chs. 11-13; and Kenneth Black, Jr. and Harold D. Skipper, Jr., *Life Insurance,* 13th ed. (Upper Saddle River, NJ: Prentice-Hall, 2000), chs. 27–28.
2. Graves, *McGill's Life Insurance,* 8th ed., p. 11.8.
3. Ibid., p. 11.21.
4. Life insurance reserves are discussed in detail in Graves, ch. 12, and Black and Skipper, ch. 29.
5. Graves, p. 12.21.

# CHAPTER 14

# ANNUITIES AND INDIVIDUAL RETIREMENT ACCOUNTS

*"Buy an annuity cheap, and make your life interesting to yourself and everybody else that watches the speculation."*

Charles Dickens

## LEARNING OBJECTIVES

**After studying this chapter, you should be able to**

◆ Show how an annuity differs from life insurance.

◆ Describe the basic characteristics of a fixed annuity and a variable annuity.

◆ Explain the major characteristics of an equity-indexed annuity.

◆ Describe the basic characteristics of a traditional tax-deductible individual retirement account (IRA).

◆ Explain the basic characteristics of a Roth IRA.

◆ Explain the income-tax treatment of a traditional IRA and a Roth IRA.

*Jennifer, age 26, recently graduated from the University of Nebraska Medical Center. She accepted a position as a registered nurse (RN) at a community hospital in Dallas, Texas. She has a number of financial goals, which include paying off her student loans and starting a saving program for a comfortable retirement. The head of the human resources department explained to Jennifer that she must be employed at the hospital for one year before she is eligible to participate in the hospital's 401(k) plan. However, the official recommended that Jennifer should sign up for a Roth individual retirement account (Roth IRA) during the interim period. She could start saving money immediately for retirement; the investment income would accumulate income-tax free; and the retirement distributions would also be income-tax free.*

*Like Jennifer, millions of workers dream of achieving financial independence and a comfortable retirement. Planning for a comfortable retirement should receive high priority in a personal risk management program. Yet current research studies show that the majority of workers are not financially prepared for retirement, and that the amounts that many workers are saving for retirement are relatively small.*

*In this chapter, we discuss the timely topic of retirement planning and how annuities and IRAs can help ensure a comfortable retirement. Two major areas are emphasized. The first part discusses the annuity concept and the different types of annuities sold today. The second part discusses the characteristics of IRAs, including the traditional tax-deductible IRA and the Roth IRA.*

## INDIVIDUAL ANNUITIES

The vast majority of American workers who retire today receive Social Security retirement benefits. Many workers also receive benefits from their employers' retirement plans. Individual annuities can also be purchased to provide additional retirement income. An annuity is a tax-deferred product. Although the premiums are paid with after-tax dollars, the investment income accumulates income-tax free and is not taxed until benefits are paid to the annuitant. The investment returns of tax-deferred compounding over long periods can be impressive.

### Annuity Principle

*An* **annuity** *can be defined as a periodic payment that continues for a fixed period or for the duration of a designated life or lives.* The person who receives the periodic payments or whose life governs the duration of payment is known as the **annuitant**.

An annuity is the opposite of life insurance. Life insurance creates an immediate estate and provides protection against dying too soon before sufficient financial assets can be accumulated. In contrast, an annuity provides protection against living too long and exhausting one's savings while the individual is still alive. Thus, *the fundamental purpose of an annuity is to provide a lifetime income that cannot be outlived.* It protects against the loss of income because of excessive longevity and the exhaustion of savings.

Annuities are possible because the risk of excessive longevity is pooled by the group. Individuals acting alone cannot be certain that their savings will be sufficient during retirement. Some will die early before exhausting their savings, whereas others will still be alive after exhausting their principal. Although the insurance company cannot predict how long any particular member of the group will live, it can determine the approximate number of annuitants who will be alive at the end of each successive year. Thus, the company can calculate the amount that each person must contribute to the pool. Interest can be earned on the funds before they are paid out to the annuitants. Also, some annuitants will die early, and their unliquidated principal can be used to provide additional payments to annuitants who survive beyond their life expectancy. Thus, annuity payments consist of three sources: (1) premium payments, (2) interest earnings, and (3) the unliquidated principal of annuitants who die early. By pooling the risk of excessive longevity, insurers can pay a lifetime income to annuitants that cannot be outlived.

Annuitants tend to be healthy individuals who generally live longer than most persons. Because of the higher life expectancy of annuitants, actuaries use special mortality tables to calculate annuity premiums.

## TYPES OF ANNUITIES

Insurers sell a wide variety of individual annuities. For the sake of convenience and understanding, the major annuities sold today can be classified as follows:

- Fixed annuity
- Variable annuity
- Equity-indexed annuity

### Fixed Annuity

A **fixed annuity** pays periodic income payments that are guaranteed and fixed in amount. During the **accumulation period** prior to retirement, premiums are credited with interest. There are typically two interest rates: a guaranteed minimum interest rate and a current interest rate. The *guaranteed rate* is the minimum interest rate that will be credited to the fixed annuity, typically 1 percent to 3 percent. The *current rate* is higher and is based on current market conditions, such as 4 percent. The current rate is guaranteed only for a limited period, typically one to five years.

As an inducement to purchase the annuity, many insurers sell *bonus annuities,* which initially increase the amount of interest credited to the annuity. For example, an investor who deposits $100,000 into an annuity with a 3 percent bonus would receive an additional $3000 of interest the first year. However, there is no such thing as a free lunch. The bonus is paid for by reduced renewal interest rates credited to the annuity in the future or by higher expense fees.

The **liquidation period** (also called the **payout period**) follows the accumulation period and refers to the period in which the funds are being paid to the annuitant. During the liquidation period, the accumulated cash can be *annuitized* or paid to the annuitant in the form of a guaranteed lifetime income. However, the periodic payments are fixed in amount and generally do not change. As a result, fixed annuities provide little or no protection against inflation.

**Payment of Benefits** A fixed annuity can be purchased so that the income payments start immediately. This type of fixed annuity is called an immediate annuity. *An* **immediate annuity** *is one where the first payment is due one payment interval from the date of purchase.* For example, if the income is paid monthly, the first payment starts one month from the purchase date, or one year from the purchase date if the income is paid annually. Immediate annuities are typically purchased in a lump sum by people near retirement. An immediate annuity has the major advantage of a guaranteed lifetime income that cannot be outlived. There are other advantages as well (see Insight 14.1).

A fixed annuity can also be purchased that defers the income payments until some later date. *A* **deferred annuity** *provides income payments at some future date.* This type of annuity is essentially a plan for accumulating a sum of money prior to retirement on a tax-deferred basis. If the annuitant dies during the accumulation period prior to retirement, a death benefit is typically paid equal to the sum of the gross premiums paid or the cash value if higher. At the maturity date of the contract, the annuitant can receive the funds in a lump sum or have them paid out under one of the settlement options (discussed later).

A fixed annuity that defers the income payments until a future date can be purchased with a lump sum, or the contract may permit flexible premium payments. A deferred annuity purchased with a lump sum is called a **single-premium deferred annuity**. In contrast, a **flexible-premium annuity** allows the annuity owner to vary the premium payments; there is no requirement that the owner must deposit a specified amount each year. Thus, the annuity owner has considerable flexibility in the payment of premiums.

## INSIGHT 14.1

### Advantages of an Immediate Annuity to Retired Workers

There are many advantages that an immediate annuity can provide to retired workers. Here is a list of just a few:

- **Security.** An immediate annuity provides stable lifetime income, which can never be outlived or which may be guaranteed for a specified period.
- **Simplicity.** The annuitant does not have to manage his or her investments, analyze markets, or report interest or dividends.
- **High Returns.** The interest rates used by insurance companies to calculate immediate annuity income are generally higher than Certificate of Deposit (CD) or Treasury rates, and because part of the principal is returned with each payment, the income received is substantially greater than would be provided by interest alone. As a result, cash flow is substantially increased.
- **Preferred Tax Treatment.** If the money used to purchase the annuity comes from a taxable account, such as a savings account, part of the income payments is received free of income taxes. A large part of each payment includes a return of principal, which is not taxable when received since it has already been taxed. Only the portion attributable to interest is taxable income.

- **Safety of Principal.** Funds are guaranteed by the insurer's assets and are not subject to the fluctuations in the financial markets.
- **No sales or administrative charges after initial purchase.** In contrast, mutual funds that provide retirement income have an annual loading for investment and administrative expenses.

Single premium immediate annuities (SPIAs) are particularly suitable for the following situations:

1. Retirement from Employment
2. Terminal Funding or Pension Terminations (including deferred commencements)
3. Retired Life Buyouts
4. Structured Settlements for Personal Injury, Estate or Divorce Cases
5. Professional Sports Contracts
6. Credit Enhancement and Loan Guarantee Transactions

SOURCE: Adapted from *Lessons in Annuities,* immediateannuity.com. Reprinted with permission of ImmediateAnnuities.com.

**Annuity Settlement Options** The annuity owner has a choice of **annuity settlement options**. Cash can be withdrawn in a lump sum or in installments, or the funds can be annuitized and paid out as life income. As a practical matter, most annuities are not annuitized.

The following settlement options are typically available:

- *Cash option.* The funds can be withdrawn in a lump sum or in installments. The taxable portion of the distribution (discussed later) is subject to federal and state income taxes. The cash option also leads to adverse selection against the insurer because those in poor health will take cash rather than annuitize the funds.
- *Life annuity (no refund).* A **life annuity (no refund)** option provides a life income to the annuitant only while the annuitant is alive. *No additional payments are made after the annuitant dies.* This type of settlement option pays the highest amount of periodic income payments

because it has no refund features. It is suitable for someone who needs maximum lifetime income and has no dependents or has provided for them through other means. However, because of the risk of forfeiting the unpaid principal if death occurs early, relatively few annuity owners elect this option.

- *Life annuity with guaranteed payments.* A **life annuity with guaranteed payments** (also called a **life annuity with period certain**) pays a life income to the annuitant with a certain number of guaranteed payments such as 5, 10, 15, or 20 years. If the annuitant dies before receiving the guaranteed number of payments, the remaining payments are paid to a designated beneficiary. This option can be used by someone who needs lifetime income but who also wishes to provide income to the beneficiary in the event of an early death. Because of the guaranteed payments, the periodic income payments are less than the income paid by a life annuity with no refund.

- *Installment refund option.* An **installment refund option** pays a life income to the annuitant. If the annuitant dies before receiving total income payments equal to the purchase price of the annuity, the payments continue to the beneficiary until they equal the purchase price. A **cash refund option** is another version of this option. If the annuitant dies before receiving total payments equal to the purchase price of the annuity, the balance is paid in a lump sum to the beneficiary.
- *Joint-and-survivor annuity.* A **joint-and-survivor annuity option** pays benefits based on the lives of two or more annuitants, such as a husband and wife or a brother and sister. The annuity income is paid until the last annuitant dies. Some contracts pay the full amount of the original income payments until the last survivor dies. Other plans pay only two-thirds or one-half of the original income after the first annuitant dies.
- *Inflation-indexed annuity option.* Many insurers offer a fixed-annuity option that provides protection against inflation. An **inflation-indexed annuity option** provides periodic payments that are adjusted for inflation. However, because of the inflation protection, the initial monthly payment is less than the payment from a traditional fixed annuity. For example, based on the rates of one insurer, a 67-year-old male in Nebraska who purchased a $250,000 immediate fixed annuity (no refund) in May 2012 would receive lifetime income of $1515 monthly. If indexed for inflation based on the Consumer Price Index (Urban), however, the initial monthly payment would be $1127 or about 26 percent less.

Exhibit 14.1 provides examples of monthly income payments for a $250,000 immediate annuity issued to a male age 67.

## Variable Annuity

A second type of annuity is a variable annuity. A **variable annuity** pays a lifetime income, but the income payments vary depending on common stock prices. *The fundamental purpose of a variable annuity is to provide an inflation hedge by maintaining the real purchasing power of the periodic payments during*

**EXHIBIT 14.1**

**Examples of Monthly Income Annuity Payments from an Immediate Annuity, $250,000 Purchase Price, Male, Age 67**

| Annuity Settlement Option | Estimated Monthly Income |
|---|---|
| Life income with no refund | $1523 |
| Life income with 5 years guaranteed payments | 1497 |
| Life income with 10 years guaranteed payments | 1461 |
| Life income with 15 years guaranteed payments | 1356 |
| Life income with 20 years guaranteed payments | 1296 |
| Joint and survivor option[a] | 1296 |
| Joint and survivor option with 20 years guaranteed | 1362 |
| Joint and survivor option with installment refund paid to beneficiaries | 1263 |

[a]Both annuitants are age 67. The survivor receives 100 percent of the monthly benefits.
SOURCE: Immediateannuities.com. Data shown are estimates for Nebraska as of May 2012. Reprinted with permission of ImmediateAnnuities.com.

*retirement.* It is based on the assumption of a positive correlation between the cost of living and common stock prices over the long run.

### Basic Characteristics of a Variable Annuity

Premiums are invested in a portfolio of common stocks or other investments that presumably will increase in value during a period of inflation. The premiums are used to purchase **accumulation units** during the period prior to retirement, and the value of each accumulation unit varies depending on common stock prices. For example, assume that the accumulation unit is initially valued at $1, and the annuitant makes a monthly premium payment of $100. During the first month, 100 accumulation units are purchased.[1] If common stock prices increase during the second month, and the accumulation unit rises to $1.10, about 91 accumulation units can be purchased. If the stock market declines during the third month, and the accumulation unit declines to $0.90, 111 accumulation units can be purchased. Thus, accumulation units are purchased over a long period of time in both rising and falling markets.

At retirement, the accumulation units are converted into **annuity units**. The number of annuity units remains constant during the liquidation period, but the value of each unit will change each month or year depending on the level of common stock prices. For example, at retirement, assume that the annuitant has 10,000 accumulation units. Assume that the accumulation units are converted into 100 annuity units.[2] As stated earlier, the number of annuity units remains constant, but the value of each unit will change over time. Assume that the annuity unit is initially valued at $10 when the annuitant retires. A monthly income of $1000 will be paid. During the second month, if the annuity unit increases in value to $10.10, the monthly income also increases to $1010. During the third month, if the annuity units decline in value to $9.90 because of a stock market decline, the monthly income is reduced to $990. Thus, the monthly income depends on the level of common stock prices.

**Guaranteed Death Benefit** Variable annuities typically provide a guaranteed death benefit that protects the principal against loss due to market declines. *If the annuitant dies during the accumulation period, the amount paid to the beneficiary will be the higher of two amounts: the account value of the annuity or the amount of total premiums paid adjusted for any withdrawals.* Thus, if the annuitant dies during a market decline, the beneficiary receives an amount at least equal to the total premiums paid (less any withdrawals).

In addition, many variable annuities go one step further and provide enhanced death benefits by the payment of an additional premium. Enhanced benefits either (1) guarantee the principal (contributions made) plus interest or (2) periodically adjust the value of the account to lock in investment gains. For example, the annuity may contain a *rising-floor death benefit* by which the death benefit is periodically reset. Thus, a 5 percent rising-floor benefit may be periodically reset so that the beneficiary will receive the principal plus 5 percent interest.

A second example is the *stepped-up benefit* by which the contract periodically locks in investment gains, such as every five years. For example, assume that $10,000 is invested in year 1, and the account is now worth $15,000 in year 5. The new death benefit is $15,000, even though the annuity owner has invested only $10,000.

Finally, an *enhanced earning benefit* is a type of death benefit that pays an additional amount for income taxes when the annuitant dies. The amount paid covers the income tax that heirs must pay on accumulated earnings in the annuity. For example, assume that $100,000 invested in a variable annuity grows to $200,000, and the annuitant dies. The designated beneficiary must pay an income tax on the $100,000 gain. The enhanced death benefit would pay an additional amount, such as 40 percent or $40,000, to help pay the income tax on the gain.

Many insurers also make available a number of additional guaranteed benefits to make variable annuities more appealing to consumers. Insight 14.2 discusses additional guaranteed benefits that can be added to a variable annuity by paying an additional premium.

**Fees and Expenses** Variable annuity owners pay a number of fees and expenses. Some fees consist of investment management and administrative fees; other fees are insurance charges that pay for the guarantees and other services provided. In addition, most variable annuities have surrender charges.

Specifically, variable annuities typically contain the following fees and expenses:

- *Investment management charge.* This charge is a payment to the investment manager and asset-management company for the brokerage services and investment advice provided in the management of the investment portfolio.
- *Administrative charge.* This charge covers the paperwork, record keeping, and periodic reports to the annuity owner.
- *Mortality and expense risk charge.* This fee, called the "M&E" fee, pays for (1) the mortality risk associated with the guaranteed death benefit and excessive longevity; (2) a guarantee that annual expenses will not exceed a certain percentage of assets after the contract is issued; and (3) an allowance for profit.
- *Surrender charge.* Most annuities have a surrender charge if the annuity is surrendered during the early years of the contract. This charge helps to pay agents and brokers who sell variable annuities. It is usually a percentage of the account value and declines over time.

## INSIGHT 14.2

### Bells and Whistles of Variable Annuities

In addition to guaranteed minimum death benefits, insurers offer a number of optional benefits to make variable annuities more appealing to consumers. They include the following:

- *Guaranteed minimum withdrawal benefits (GMWB)* This benefit guarantees that you can withdraw annually a specified percentage of the total premiums paid for the annuity until you recover your entire investment.[a] This benefit provides protection against investment losses in your account. For example, assume that Richard, age 67, has invested $100,000 in a variable annuity, but the account is now worth only $80,000 because of a bear market. If the specified percentage is 5 percent, he could withdraw $5000 each year until the entire $100,000 is recovered.

- *Guaranteed lifetime withdrawal benefits (GLWB)* Unlike the GMWB above, this benefit guarantees that your benefits will continue for life even if your initial investment is exhausted. The guaranteed withdrawal benefit is typically 4 to 5 percent of your investment in the variable annuity, which continues for life even though your investment accounts are exhausted.[b] You are not required to annuitize the principal.

- *Guaranteed minimum income benefit (GMIB)* For annuity owners who annuitize, this benefit guarantees a minimum payment regardless of the value of your account. It also provides protection against losses in your investment account. For example, the guarantee may state that if you annuitize, the minimum payment will be based on the higher of your account value or a specified percentage of the GMIB benefit base, which is equal to the amount invested compounded at a specified interest rate, such as 5 percent.[c] The higher of the two bases is used to determine your minimum income benefit. The benefit has no value for annuity owners who do not annuitize.

- *Guaranteed minimum accumulation benefit (GMAB)* This benefit guarantees that the value of the contract will be equal to a specified minimum amount after a certain number of years, such as 10 years, even though the investment portfolio has declined in value.

The guaranteed benefits are not free; additional premiums are required depending on the guarantee selected. For example, the additional annual cost of the GLWB typically ranges from 50 to 60 basis points.[d]

[a]Randy Myers, "Customizing Your Annuity: New Features Add Liquidity and Flexibility," *The Wall Street Journal,* November 14, 2007, p. D13.
[b]Ibid.
[c]George. D. Lambert, *The Cost of Variable Annuity Guarantees,* Investopedia.com.
[d]Ibid.

For example, if the surrender charge is 7 percent of the account value for the first year, it would decline one percentage point for each year until reaching zero for the eighth and later years. Most variable annuities permit partial withdrawals each year of as much as 10 percent of the account value without imposition of a surrender charge.

In addition, the annuity may have an annual contract fee, such as $25 or $50; and there may be a charge if funds are transferred from one subaccount to another. *In the aggregate, total annual fees and expenses, including the cost of riders are relatively high and can range from 3 percent to 4 percent of the total investment.[3] As a result, long-run total returns may be significantly reduced in high-cost annuities.*

### Equity-Indexed Annuity

An equity-indexed annuity offers the guarantees of a fixed annuity and limited participation in stock market gains. *An* **equity-indexed annuity** *is a fixed, deferred annuity that allows the annuity owner to participate in the growth of the stock market and also provides downside protection against the loss of principal and prior interest earnings if the annuity is held to term.* Term periods typically range from one to 15 years. The annuity value is linked to the performance of a stock market index, typically Standard and Poor's 500 Composite Stock Index. If the stock market rises, the annuity is credited with part of the gain in the index, which does not include the reinvestment of dividends. If the stock market declines, the annuity earns at least a minimum return, which typically is 3 percent on 90 percent of the principal invested.

The key elements of an equity-indexed annuity are (1) the participation rate, (2) the maximum cap rate, (3) the indexing method used, and (4) the guaranteed minimum value.

**Participation Rate** The *participation rate* is the percent of increase in the stock index credited to the contract. The insurer periodically determines the participation rate, which is subject to change. Participation rates typically range from 25 percent to 90 percent of the gain in the stock index. Investors may receive only part of the increase in the stock index (excluding the reinvestment of dividends). For example, if the participation rate is 70 percent and the stock index rises 9 percent during the measuring period, the index-linked interest rate credited to your annuity will be 6.3 percent ($9\% \times 70\% = 6.3\%$).

Instead of a participation rate, some insurers use a spread or asset fee by which a percentage is subtracted from any gain in the index. For example, if the index increased 8 percent and the spread is 3 percent, the gain credited to the annuity is only 5 percent.

**Maximum Cap Rate or Cap** Some annuities have a maximum cap rate or upper limit on the index-linked interest rate credited to your annuity. The maximum cap rate is the maximum rate of interest the annuity will earn. In the earlier example, if the annuity has a maximum cap rate of 6 percent, the interest rate credited to the annuity would be only 6 percent, not 6.3 percent. Not all annuities have a maximum cap rate.

**Indexing Method** The *indexing method* refers to the method for crediting excess interest to the annuity. Insurers use several indexing methods for crediting interest, only one of which is discussed here. Under the *annual reset method* (also known as the *ratchet method*), interest earnings are calculated based on the annual change in the stock index; the index value starting point is also reset annually. Thus, if the stock index decreases during any contract year, the decrease does not have to be recovered before any additional growth in the index will be credited to the contract.

**Guaranteed Minimum Value** Equity-indexed annuities with terms longer than one year have a guaranteed minimum value that provides downside protection against the loss of principal if the annuity is held to term. A typical minimum guarantee is 3 percent compounded on 90 percent of your initial deposit. *The result is a guaranteed minimum value at the end of the index period.* For example, if you deposit $100,000 in an equity-indexed annuity, 90 percent of that amount ($90,000) will earn a guaranteed rate of 3 percent compounded annually regardless of how the index performs. Thus, if you keep the annuity in force until the end of the index period, say seven years, you are guaranteed $110,689 in your account. However, because the minimum guarantee applies to only 90 percent of the single premium, an investor who surrenders the contract during the first three or four policy years may experience a loss of principal. If it is held to term, the principal is guaranteed against loss.

## LONGEVITY INSURANCE

Because of increased life expectancy, more people are surviving until age 90 or even beyond. There is always the risk that you will run out of money at an advanced age and are still alive. To deal with the risk of exhausting your financial assets at an advanced age, some insurers have designed longevity insurance products. **Longevity insurance** *is a generic name for a single-premium deferred annuity that begins paying benefits only at an advanced age, typically age 85.* The purpose is to provide protection against the risk of depleting your financial assets at an advanced age. For example, based on the rates of one insurer, the premium for a joint-and-survivor annuity for a married couple, both age 65, which provides a monthly income of $1500 beginning at age 85, is $49,779. In contrast, a traditional immediate annuity that provides the same income beginning at age 65 would require a single premium in excess of $300,000. Longevity insurance products are low-cost annuities because there are no cash values or death benefits in the policy. If the annuitant dies during the deferral period before payments begin, he or she will forfeit the purchase price. However, some insurers offer optional features that provide death benefits or the option of starting payments sooner, but adding these options substantially reduces the annual income the policy would pay at age 85.

Longevity insurance has both advantages and disadvantages:

- The monthly benefits kick in at an advanced age when other financial assets are likely to be exhausted.
- Compared to a traditional immediate annuity, longevity insurance is a relatively low cost annuity because the policies generally do not provide cash values or death benefits during the deferral period.
- Longevity products can be purchased with an inflation hedge, which preserves the purchasing power of the benefits that will be paid in the distant future.

On the downside, however, longevity insurance has the following disadvantages:

- Your heirs will lose money if you die during the deferral period because, as stated earlier, longevity products generally do not provide death benefits.
- Once purchased, your funds are locked up, and you do not have access to the funds in the event of an emergency.
- The risk of possible forfeiture of the purchase price if death occurs during the deferral period, or shortly after payments begin, may make the product unappealing to risks-adverse individuals.

## TAXATION OF INDIVIDUAL ANNUITIES

An individual annuity purchased from a commercial insurer is a nonqualified annuity. A *nonqualified annuity* is an annuity that does not meet the Internal Revenue Code requirements for employer benefits. As such, it does not qualify for most income-tax benefits that qualified employer retirement plans receive.

Premiums for individual annuities are not income-tax deductible and are paid with after-tax dollars. However, the investment income is tax deferred and accumulates free of current income taxes until the funds are actually distributed.

The taxable portion of any distribution is taxable as ordinary income. In addition, the taxable portion of a premature distribution before age 59½ is subject to a 10 percent penalty tax, with certain exceptions.[4]

The periodic annuity payments from an individual annuity generally are taxed according to the General Rule. Under this rule, the *net cost* of the annuity payments is recovered income-tax free over the payment period. The amount of each payment that exceeds the net cost portion is taxable as ordinary income.

An exclusion ratio must be calculated to determine the nontaxable and taxable portions of the annuity payments. The **exclusion ratio** is determined by dividing the investment in the contract by the expected return:

$$\frac{\text{Investment in the contract}}{\text{Expected return}} = \text{Exclusion ratio}$$

The *investment in the contract (basis)* is the total cost of the annuity, which generally is the total amount of premiums, contributions, or other amounts paid less certain adjustments.[5] The *expected return* is the total amount that the annuitant can expect to receive under the contract based on life expectancy. Life expectancy is obtained from actuarial tables provided by the IRS.

*Example. Assume that Ben, age 65, purchased an immediate annuity for $108,000 that pays a lifetime monthly income of $1000. The annuity has no refund features. Investment in the contract is $108,000. Based on the IRS actuarial table, Ben has a life expectancy of 20 years. Expected return is $240,000 (20 × 12 × $1000). The exclusion ratio is 0.45 ($108,000 ÷ $240,000). Each year, until the net cost is recovered, Ben receives $5400 tax free (45% × $12,000) and $6600, which is taxable. After the net cost is recovered, the total payment would be taxable.*

In summary, annuities can be attractive to investors who have made maximum contributions to other tax-advantaged plans and who wish to save additional amounts on a tax-deferred basis. Also, because of the surrender charge, the investor should expect to remain invested for 10 or more years.

However, annuities are not for everyone, especially a variable annuity. You should not purchase a variable annuity if you will need the funds before age 59½; the period of investing is less than 15 years; and you have not made maximum annual contributions to other tax-advantaged plans, such as a Section 401(k) plan and an IRA. Other considerations are important as well (see Insight 14.3).

## INDIVIDUAL RETIREMENT ACCOUNTS

An **individual retirement account (IRA)** allows workers with taxable compensation to make annual contributions to a retirement plan up to certain limits and receive favorable income-tax treatment.

---

### INSIGHT 14.3

### Ten Questions to Answer Before You Buy a Variable Annuity

Variable annuities are a valuable retirement tool if used properly. However, variable annuities are not for everyone. Before you buy an annuity, you should answer the following questions:

- *What are the annual fees and expenses?* As discussed in the text, most variable annuities have relatively high annual fees and expenses. Other investments, especially no-load index mutual funds, have significantly lower annual expense charges. Before you buy, you should shop for an annuity with relatively low annual expenses.

- *Are you willing to be locked into the annuity for at least 15 years?* Most annuities have back-end surrender charges that extend over long periods, typically seven to ten years. You will lose a substantial amount of money if you surrender the annuity during the early years. Also, the favorable income tax advantages of a variable annuity require a long holding period of at least 15 years for the tax benefits to offset the high fees and expenses.

- *Have you made maximum annual contributions to your employer's 401(k) plan or other qualified retirement plan and to an individual retirement account?* Most employers make a partial matching contribution to qualified retirement plans, and you are passing up "free money" if you don't contribute the maximum allowed. Also, an IRA may have lower annual expense charges than a variable annuity.

- *Have you considered your tolerance for risk?* The value of your annuity depends on the investment experience of the underlying subaccounts. If the premiums are invested in a stock account, the value of your annuity can decline substantially in a severe market decline. Depending on your tolerance for risk, your "comfort" level may be adversely affected.

- *Are you willing to tolerate fluctuations in monthly income?* Variable annuity retirement benefits also fluctuate with the investment experience of the underlying subaccounts. If the funds are invested in a stock market account, a substantial market decline can be financially painful. Common stocks are also sensitive to interest rates. If interest rates rise because of inflationary expectations or a change in Federal Reserve monetary policy, your variable annuity benefits may decline.

- *Will you need the funds before age 59½?* You should not buy a variable annuity if the funds will be needed before age 59½. Cash withdrawals before age 59½ generally are subject to a 10 percent federal tax penalty on the taxable portion of the distribution. You should have available cash to cover three to six months of living expenses, which reduces the need to withdraw funds from your annuity.

- *Is your combined federal and state income tax bracket at least 28 percent?* If you are in a lower tax bracket, high variable annuity fees and expenses can dilute the tax advantages of a deferred annuity.

- *Are you aware that capital gains are taxed as ordinary income when annuity distributions are made?* The taxable portion of a variable annuity distribution is taxed as ordinary income, which can be as high as 35 percent for 2012. In contrast, at the time of writing, long-term capital gains in a taxable account are taxed at a maximum capital gains rate of 15 percent (2012).

- *Are you aware that if you should die, your heirs will be taxed on the variable annuity earnings just as you would?* In contrast, mutual funds in a taxable account pass to the heirs free of income taxes because of a "stepped-up" cost basis. As a result, heirs don't pay income taxes on the accumulated gains.

- *Should you invest your IRA contributions in a variable annuity?* As a general rule, the answer is no. IRAs already receive favorable income-tax treatment. Investing IRA contributions in a variable annuity results in an unnecessary duplication of fees and expenses.

There are two basic types of IRA plans:

- Traditional IRA
- Roth IRA

## Traditional IRA

A **traditional IRA** is an IRA that allows workers to take a tax deduction for part or all of their IRA contributions. The investment income accumulates income-tax free on a tax-deferred basis, and the distributions are taxed as ordinary income.

**Eligibility Requirements**    There are two eligibility requirements for establishing a traditional tax-deductible IRA. *First, the participant must have taxable compensation during the year.* Taxable compensation includes wages and salaries, bonuses, commissions, self-employment income, and taxable alimony and separate maintenance payments. However, taxable compensation does not include interest and dividend income, pension or annuity income, Social Security, and rental income. For example, if a person receives only Social Security and investment income, he or she could not make an IRA contribution for that year.

*Second, the participant must be under age 70½.* No traditional IRA contributions are allowed for the tax year in which the participant attains age 70½ or any later year.

**Annual Contribution Limits**    Changes in the tax code have substantially increased the annual contribution limits to an IRA plan. Special catch-up rules also allow older workers to make additional contributions. The catch-up provisions are designed to help older workers who have saved little or nothing for retirement.

*For 2012, the maximum annual contribution is $5000 or 100 percent of taxable compensation, whichever is less. Older workers age 50 and over can contribute an additional $1000, or a maximum of $6000.* The annual IRA contribution limit is indexed for inflation in increments of $500.

**Income Tax Deduction of Traditional IRA Contributions**    Traditional IRA contributions may be (1) fully income-tax deductible, (2) partly deductible, or (3) not deductible at all. A full deduction is allowed in two general situations.

*First, a worker who is not an active participant in an employer's retirement plan for any part of the year can make a fully deductible IRA contribution up to the annual maximum limit.* As noted earlier, for 2012, the maximum tax-deductible IRA contribution is the lower of $5000 ($6000 if age 50 or older), or 100 percent of taxable compensation.

*Second, even if the worker is actively participating in the employer's retirement plan, the IRA contribution is fully or partly deductible if the worker's modified adjusted gross income is below certain threshold limits.* Modified adjusted gross income (AGI) generally is the adjusted gross income figure shown on your tax return without taking into account the IRA deduction and certain other items.[6] For 2012, a single person or head of household receives a full deduction if modified AGI is less than $58,000. If modified AGI is between $58,000 and $68,000, a partial deduction is allowed. No deduction is allowed if modified AGI exceeds $68,000. For 2012, married couples filing jointly receive a full deduction if modified AGI is less than $92,000 and a partial deduction if modified AGI is between $92,000 and $112,000. No deduction is allowed if modified AGI exceeds $112,000. For example, a single worker with a modified AGI less than $58,000 receives a full deduction up to the maximum contribution limit. However, a single worker with a modified AGI of $63,000 could deduct only half of the contribution. The income limits are indexed for inflation in increments of $500.

Taxpayers with incomes that exceed the phase-out limits can contribute to a traditional IRA but cannot deduct their contributions. This type of IRA is called a **nondeductible IRA**. In such cases, a Roth IRA (discussed later) should be considered.

**Spousal IRA**    In many families, a married worker is an active participant in the employer's retirement plan, but the other spouse is not an active participant. *A **spousal IRA** allows a spouse who is not in the paid labor force to make a fully deductible contribution to a traditional IRA up to the annual dollar limit even though the other spouse is covered under a retirement plan at work.* For 2012, the maximum IRA deduction for a nonworking spouse who is not an active participant is $5000 ($6000 if age 50 or older). The couple must file a joint return, and the working spouse must have sufficient earnings to cover the contribution. For 2012, a full deduction is allowed if modified AGI is less than $173,000. The tax deduction is phased out for married couples with modified AGI between $173,000 and $183,000. No deduction is allowed if modified AGI is more than $183,000.

*Example. Josh, age 35, is covered under a Section 401(k) retirement plan at work. His wife, Ashley, age 32, is a full-time homemaker. For 2012, their modified AGI is $150,000. For 2012, Ashley can make a tax-deductible IRA contribution of $5000 because she is not considered an active participant, and the couple's modified AGI is less than $173,000. However, Josh cannot make a tax-deductible contribution because his income exceeds the income threshold for active participants.*

**Tax Penalty for Early Withdrawal** With certain exceptions, distributions from a traditional IRA before age 59½ are considered to be an early withdrawal. A 10 percent tax penalty must be paid on the amount of the distribution included in gross income. However, the penalty tax does not apply to distributions that result from any of the following:

- Distributions used to pay for unreimbursed medical expenses in excess of 7½ percent of adjusted gross income (2012)
- Distributions that do not exceed the cost of your medical insurance and you lost your job and received unemployment compensation for 12 consecutive weeks because of the job loss
- Disability of the IRA owner
- Distributions to the beneficiary of a deceased IRA owner
- Distributions from a traditional IRA that are part of a series of substantially equal payments paid over your lifetime (or your life expectancy), or over the lives of you and your beneficiary (or joint life expectancies)
- Distributions that are not more than your qualified higher education expenses
- Distributions to buy, build, or rebuild a first home ($10,000 maximum)
- Distribution due to an IRS levy on the qualified plan
- Qualified reservist distributions

Distributions from a traditional IRA must start no later than April 1 of the year following the calendar year in which the individual attains age 70½. The funds can be withdrawn in a lump sum or in installments. A minimum annual distribution requirement must be met. The minimum annual distribution payment is based on the life expectancy of the individual or the joint life expectancy of the individual and his or her beneficiary. The Internal Revenue Service (IRS) has developed life expectancy tables for purposes of determining the minimum annual distribution. If the distributions are less than the amount required by law, a 50 percent excise tax is imposed on the excess accumulation. The purpose of this requirement is to force participants in traditional IRAs to have the funds paid out over a reasonable period so that the federal government can collect taxes on the tax-deferred amounts.

**Taxation of Distributions** Distributions from a traditional IRA are taxed as ordinary income, except for any nondeductible IRA contributions, which are received income-tax free. Part of the distribution is not taxable if nondeductible contributions are made. The other part is taxable and must be included in the taxpayer's income. A complex formula and an IRS worksheet must be used to compute the nontaxable and taxable portions of each distribution.

In addition, as noted earlier, a 10 percent tax penalty applies to premature distributions taken before age 59½.

**Establishing a Traditional IRA** A traditional IRA can be established with a variety of financial organizations. You can set up an IRA with a bank, mutual fund, stock brokerage firm, or life insurer. Contributions to a traditional IRA can be made anytime during the year or up to the due date for filing a tax return, not including extensions.

There are two types of traditional IRAs: (1) an individual retirement account, and (2) an individual retirement annuity.

- *Individual Retirement Account.* An individual retirement account is a trust or custodial account set up for the exclusive benefit of the account holder or beneficiaries. The trustee or custodian must be a bank, a federally insured credit union, a savings and loan institution, or an entity approved by the IRS to act as trustee or custodian. Contributions must be in cash, except for rollover contributions (discussed later) that can be in the form of property other than cash. No part of the contributions can be used to purchase a life insurance policy. Likewise, IRA assets cannot be pledged as collateral for a loan.

- *Individual Retirement Annuity.* A traditional IRA can also be established by purchasing an individual retirement annuity from a life insurer. The annuity must meet certain requirements. The annuity owner's interest in the contract must be nonforfeitable. The contract must be nontransferable by the owner. In addition, the annuity must permit flexible premiums so that if earnings change, the IRA contributions can be changed as well. Contributions cannot exceed the annual maximum limit, and the distributions must begin by April 1 of the year following the year in which the annuity owner reaches age 70½.

**IRA Investments**   IRA contributions can be invested in a variety of investments, including certificates of deposit, mutual funds, and individual stocks and bonds in a self-directed brokerage account. Contributions can also be invested in U.S. gold and silver coins and certain precious metals. However, the contributions cannot be invested in insurance contracts or collectibles, such as stamps or antiques.

**IRA Rollover Account**   A *rollover* is a tax-free distribution of cash or other property from one retirement plan, which is then deposited into another retirement plan. The amount you roll over is tax free but generally becomes taxable when the new plan pays out that amount to you or to your beneficiary. For example, if you quit your job and receive a lump-sum distribution from your employer's qualified retirement plan, the funds can be rolled over or deposited into a special **IRA rollover account.** If you receive the funds directly, the employer must withhold 20 percent for federal income taxes. The withholding can be deferred, however, if the employer transfers the funds directly into the IRA rollover account.

### Roth IRA

A **Roth IRA** is another type of IRA that provides substantial tax advantages. The annual contribution limits discussed earlier for a traditional IRA also apply to a Roth IRA.

*The annual contributions to a Roth IRA are not tax deductible. However, the investment income accumulates income-tax free, and qualified distributions are not taxable if certain requirements are met.* A qualified distribution is any distribution from a Roth IRA that (1) is made after a five-year holding period beginning with the first tax year for which a Roth contribution is made, and (2) is made for any of the following reasons:

- The individual is age 59½ or older.
- The individual is disabled.
- The distribution is paid to a beneficiary or to the estate after the individual's death.
- The distribution is used to pay qualified first-time home-buyer expenses (maximum of $10,000).

Unlike a traditional IRA, contributions to a Roth IRA can be made after age 70½ and the minimum distribution rules after attainment of age 70½ do not apply to Roth IRAs.

**Income Limits**   For 2012, for a single person or head of household, the maximum contribution to a Roth IRA is limited to workers with modified AGI under $110,000. The Roth IRA contributions are phased out if modified AGI is between $110,000 and $125,000. For 2012, for married couples filing jointly, the maximum contribution to a Roth IRA is limited to couples with modified AGI under $173,000 and is phased out for couples with a modified AGI between $173,000 and $183,000.

**Conversion to a Roth IRA**   A traditional IRA can be converted to a Roth IRA. Although the amount converted is taxed as ordinary income, qualified distributions from a Roth IRA are received income-tax free. The right to convert earlier was limited to taxpayers with annual adjusted gross incomes of $100,000 or less. However, beginning in 2010, the $100,000 income limit on converting a traditional IRA to a Roth IRA has been eliminated. As such, wealthier taxpayers can convert their traditional IRAs to a Roth IRA. Many investment firms provide interactive calculators on their Web sites to determine if conversion to a Roth IRA is financially desirable.

Based on the preceding discussion, you can see that the Roth IRA has different characteristics than a traditional IRA. Exhibit 14.2 summarizes the major differences between them.

**Exhibit 14.2**

**Comparison of a Traditional IRA with a Roth IRA**

|  | Traditional IRA | Roth IRA |
|---|---|---|
| ■ Tax status | Tax-deferred distributions | Tax-free distributions |
| ■ Eligibility | Have taxable compensation below certain annual limits (see text) | Have taxable compensation below certain annual limits (see text) |
| ■ Age limits | Be under age 70½ | No age limit |
| ■ Contribution limit | For 2012, $5000 ($6000 age 50 and older) | Same |
| ■ Tax deduction for IRA contributions | Fully deductible up to the annual contribution limit if you are not a participant in the employer's retirement plan, regardless of income; fully deductible or partially deductible up to the annual contribution limit depending on your taxable compensation, if you are a participant in the employer's retirement plan | Contributions are not deductible |
| ■ Tax on investment income | Investment income accumulates tax free | Same |
| ■ Tax on distributions | Taxed as ordinary income; no tax on nondeductible contributions | Distributions are tax-free if you meet certain conditions (see text) |
| ■ Penalty for early withdrawals | 10% federal tax on early withdrawals before age 59½ with certain exceptions | Contributions can be withdrawn tax-free. There is a 10% penalty tax on withdrawal of earnings before age 59½ with certain exceptions |
| ■ Minimum distribution requirement | Required after age 70½ | None |

## ADEQUACY OF IRA FUNDS

The IRA assets can be paid out as income when the worker retires. However, unless a life annuity is purchased, the retiree faces the risk of still being alive after the IRA account is exhausted. The duration of benefit payments, however, depends on the rate of return on the invested assets after the worker retires and withdrawal rates. Because retired workers can spend 25 or 30 years in retirement, or even longer, financial planners generally recommend that the initial withdrawal rate should be limited to 4 to 5 percent of the IRA assets. Traditionally, tables have been prepared that show how long your IRA funds will last based on average rates of return on the invested assets and annual withdrawal rates.

The problem, however, is that such tables assume that the average rate of return remains constant over the projection period. In reality, this is incorrect because actual returns will vary significantly depending on fluctuations in the stock market, bond market, and other security markets. To deal with this problem, many financial planners now use Monte Carlo simulation techniques that give a more realistic outlook of the future. These techniques simulate a wide variety of potential market outcomes that take into account fluctuations in market returns and different investment portfolios. Insight 14.4 provides an example of the Monte Carlo simulation technique of one financial planning investment firm.

## INSIGHT 14.4

### Will You Have Enough Money at Retirement? Monte Carlo Simulations Can Be Helpful

T. Rowe Price has an interactive Retirement Income Calculator on its Web site (www.troweprice.com/ric) that provides a more realistic evaluation of your retirement funds. Instead of basing calculations on a single average rate of return over the entire retirement period, the Monte Carlo technique generates 1000 computer simulations of what may happen hypothetically to your financial assets over a specified using a particular retirement planning strategy. Over the chosen time horizon, each of the 1000 simulations produces an ending balance for the portfolio based on that particular sequence of hypothetical market returns. The analysis incorporates the potential for market volatility, both positive and negative. Each of the 1000 simulations that ends with a balance of at least $1 is considered a "success." The Retirement Income Calculator combines the results of all 1000 simulations for a given strategy to determine that strategy's "simulation success rate" (i.e., the percentage of the simulations that resulted in a positive ending balance). A simulation success rate of 80% or higher is considered a good number.

Projections based on a fixed annual rate of return over the entire retirement period can result in ending balances that are substantially different from the projected ending balances based on the Monte Carlo simulations. Theoretically, an 11 percent return one year and a 7 percent return the following year will average 9 percent, but the sequence of returns you actually experience in retirement may be quite different from the averages, potentially resulting in a lower ending balance than the one you would have received using fixed annual return projections.

The box below illustrates one example of the Monte Carlo simulation technique based on the Retirement Income Calculator. It assumes a male, age 67, has $300,000 of assets with an asset allocation of 60% stocks, 30% bonds, and 10% cash before retirement and 40% stocks, 40% bonds, and 20% cash after retirement. He desires $4000 monthly (in today's dollars) to be paid over a 28-year retirement period and is planning on retiring immediately. He will receive $2000 monthly (in today's dollars) from Social Security. The simulation results indicate that the monthly retirement spending should not exceed $3,032 monthly to have a success rate of 80%.

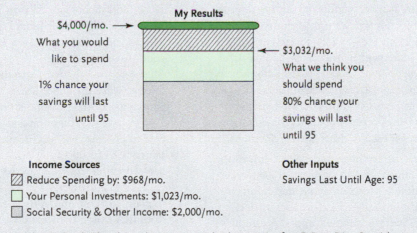

**My Results**

$4,000/mo. →
What you would like to spend

1% chance your savings will last until 95

← $3,032/mo.
What we think you should spend
80% chance your savings will last until 95

**Income Sources**

▨ Reduce Spending by: $968/mo.
☐ Your Personal Investments: $1,023/mo.
▨ Social Security & Other Income: $2,000/mo.

**Other Inputs**

Savings Last Until Age: 95

SOURCE: The graph image and the "My Results" box shown above are reprinted with permission from T. Rowe Price. Copyright 2012. Insight 14.4 above the "My Results" box was not produced by T. Rowe Price.

## CASE APPLICATION 1

Investors can invest in a wide variety of annuities and can also use different annuity settlement options to meet specific retirement needs. For each of the following retirement objectives, identify either (1) a specific annuity or (2) an annuity settlement option that can be used to meet the objective. Treat each situation separately.

a. James, age 35, is a sales representative and plans to retire at age 67. His monthly income varies. He would like to invest in an annuity that allows him to change the frequency and amount of premium payments.

b. Nancy, age 67, plans to retire in six months. She has $200,000 in a savings account. She would like to receive lifetime monthly income that is guaranteed.

c. Jennifer, age 63, plans to retire in 90 days. She has $100,000 to invest in an annuity and would like to receive lifetime monthly income to supplement her Social Security benefits. However, she is concerned that she might die before she receives back the amount invested.

d. Fred, age 70, recently retired and has $50,000 to invest for additional income. He wants the retirement benefits to be protected against the risk of inflation.

e. Mary, age 75, is a widow with no dependents who needs additional retirement income. She has $25,000 to invest in an annuity. She wants to receive the maximum amount of monthly annuity income possible.

f. Kathy, age 32, would like to invest in the stock market, but she is conservative and risk averse. She would like to participate in any stock market gains, but she also wants her principal guaranteed against loss.

## CASE APPLICATION 2

Scott and Allison are married and file a joint tax return. Scott is a graduate student who works part-time and earned $15,000 in 2012. He is not eligible to participate in his employer's retirement plan because he is a part-time worker. Allison is a high school teacher who earned $50,000 in 2012 and is an active participant in the school district's retirement plan. Assume you are a financial planner and the couple asks for your advice. Based on the preceding facts, answer each of the following questions.

a. Is Scott eligible to establish and deduct contributions to a traditional IRA? Explain your answer.

b. Is Allison eligible to establish and deduct contributions to a traditional IRA? Explain your answer.

c. Assume that Scott graduates and the couple's modified adjusted gross income is $130,000 in 2012. Both Scott and Allison participate in their employers' retirement plans. Can either Scott or Allison, or both, establish a Roth IRA? Explain your answer.

d. Allison has a baby and withdraws from the labor force to raise the child. She is no longer an active participant in the school district's retirement plan. Scott receives a promotion and continues to participate in his employer's retirement plan. His annual salary is $110,000 in 2012. Can Allison make a tax-deductible contribution to a traditional IRA? Explain your answer.

e. Explain to Scott and Allison the advantages of a Roth IRA over a traditional IRA.

# SUMMARY

- An annuity provides periodic payments to an annuitant, which continue for either a fixed period or for the duration of a designated life or lives. The fundamental purpose of a life annuity is to provide lifetime income that cannot be outlived.

- A *fixed annuity* pays periodic income payments to an annuitant that are guaranteed and fixed in amount. A fixed annuity can be purchased so that the income payments start immediately, or the payments can be deferred to some later date. Deferred annuities typically provide for flexible premiums.

- Annuity settlement options typically include the following:
  Cash
  Life income (no refund)
  Life income with guaranteed payments
  Installment refund option
  Joint-and-survivor annuity option
  Inflation-indexed annuity option

- A *variable annuity* pays a lifetime income, but the income payments vary depending on the investment experience of the subaccount in which the premiums are invested. The purpose of this type of annuity is to provide an inflation hedge by maintaining the real purchasing power of the periodic payments.

- During the *accumulation period*, variable annuity premiums purchase accumulation units, which are then converted into *annuity units* at retirement. The number of annuity units remains constant during retirement, but the value of the annuity units changes periodically so that the income payments will change over time.

- Variable annuities typically pay a guaranteed death benefit if the annuitant dies before retirement. The typical death benefit is the higher of two amounts: *the account value of the annuity or the amount of total premiums paid adjusted for any withdrawals.*

- Variable annuities have numerous fees and charges. These charges include an investment management fee, a charge for administrative expenses, a management and expense risk charge for the guaranteed death benefit and other guarantees, and a surrender charge that declines over time. In the aggregate, total fees and expenses can be substantial.

- An *equity-indexed annuity* is a fixed, deferred annuity that allows the annuity owner to participate in the growth of the stock market. It also provides downside protection against the loss of principal and prior interest earnings if the annuity is held to term.

- The key elements of an equity-indexed annuity are (1) the participation rate, (2) the maximum cap rate, (3) the indexing method used, and (4) the guaranteed minimum value.

- An *exclusion ratio* is used to determine the nontaxable and taxable portions of the periodic annuity payments. The exclusion ratio is determined by dividing the investment in the contract by the expected return.

- The major types of IRAs are (1) a traditional IRA and (2) a Roth IRA.

- A *traditional IRA* allows workers to deduct part or all of their IRA contributions. The investment income accumulates income-tax free on a tax-deferred basis, and the distributions are taxed as ordinary income.

- To be eligible for a traditional IRA, the participant must have taxable compensation and be younger than age 70½.

- For 2012, the maximum annual IRA contribution for an individual worker is limited to $5000 ($6000 if age 50 or older) or 100 percent of taxable compensation, whichever is less.

- IRA contributions to a traditional IRA are income-tax deductible if the participant (1) is not an active participant in an employer-sponsored retirement plan or (2) has taxable compensation below certain income thresholds.

- Distributions from a traditional IRA are taxed as ordinary income, except for any nondeductible IRA contributions, which are received income-tax free.

- With certain exceptions, distributions from a traditional IRA before age 59½ are considered to be a premature distribution. A 10 percent tax penalty must be paid on the amount of the distribution included in gross income.

- Distributions from a traditional IRA must start no later than April 1 of the year following the calendar year in which the individual attains age 70½.

- IRA contributions to a *Roth IRA* are not income-tax deductible. However, the investment income accumulates free of taxation, and qualified distributions are received income-tax free if certain requirements are met.

■ A qualified distribution from a Roth IRA is any distribution that (1) is made after a five-year holding period beginning with the first tax year for which a Roth contribution is made, and (2) is paid when the individual attains age 59½, becomes disabled, dies, or uses the money to pay qualified first-time home-buyer expenses. Unlike a traditional IRA, contributions to a Roth IRA can be made after age 70½, and the minimum distribution rules after attainment of age 70½ do not apply.

## KEY CONCEPTS AND TERMS

Accumulation period (277)
Accumulation unit (279)
Annuitant (276)
Annuity (276)
Annuity settlement
  options (278)
Annuity unit (280)
Cash refund option (279)
Deferred annuity (277)
Equity-indexed
  annuity (281)
Exclusion ratio (283)
Fixed annuity (277)
Flexible-premium
  annuity (277)
Immediate annuity (277)
Individual retirement
  account (IRA) (284)
Inflation-indexed annuity
  option (279)

Installment refund
  option (279)
IRA rollover account (287)
Joint-and-survivor annuity
  option (279)
Life annuity (no
  refund) (278)
Life annuity with
  guaranteed payments
  (life annuity with period
  certain) (278)
Liquidation period (277)
Longevity insurance (282)
Nondeductible IRA (285)
Roth IRA (287)
Single-premium deferred
  annuity (277)
Spousal IRA (285)
Traditional IRA (285)
Variable annuity (279)

## REVIEW QUESTIONS

1. How does an annuity differ from life insurance?

2. Describe the major characteristics of a fixed annuity.

3. Identify the annuity settlement options that are typically found in a fixed annuity.

4. Describe the basic characteristics of a variable annuity.

5. Explain the major characteristics of an equity-indexed annuity.

6. Explain the eligibility requirements for a traditional IRA.

7. What are the annual contribution limits to an IRA?

8. Explain the basic characteristics of a traditional IRA.

9. Describe the major characteristics of a Roth IRA.

10. What is an IRA rollover?

## APPLICATION QUESTIONS

1. Although both fixed and variable annuities can provide lifetime income to annuitants, they differ in important ways. Compare and contrast (1) a fixed annuity with (2) a variable annuity with respect to each of the following:
   a. Determining how the premiums are invested
   b. Stability of income payments after retirement
   c. Death benefits if the annuitant dies before retirement

2. An equity-indexed annuity and a variable annuity are both similar and different in many respects.
   a. Explain the major similarities between an equity-indexed annuity and a variable annuity.
   b. Identify the major differences between an equity-indexed annuity and a variable annuity.

3. Mario, age 65, purchased an immediate annuity for $120,000 that pays a lifetime monthly income of $1000. The annuity has no refund feature. Based on the IRS actuarial table, Mario has a life expectancy of 20 years. If Mario receives 12 monthly payments of $1000 the first year, how much taxable income must he report on his tax return?

4. Travis, age 25, graduated from college and obtained a position as a tax accountant. He is ineligible to participate in his employer's retirement plan for one year.
   a. Assume that Travis has a starting salary of $55,000 for 2012 and does not participate in the employer's retirement plan. Is Travis eligible to establish a traditional tax-deductible IRA? Explain your answer.
   b. Assume the same facts in (a). Is Travis eligible to establish a Roth IRA? Explain your answer.

5. A traditional IRA and a Roth IRA have both similarities and differences. Compare and contrast (1) a traditional IRA with (2) a Roth IRA with respect to each of the following:
   a. Income-tax treatment of IRA contributions and distributions
   b. Income limits for eligibility
   c. Determining how the IRA contributions are invested
   d. Eligibility, if any, of a spouse who is not in the paid labor force to make an IRA contribution

## INTERNET RESOURCES

- **Annuity.com** provides annuity quotes online and timely information about fixed, equity-indexed, variable, and other tax-deferred annuities. Visit the site at

  annuity.com

- **Annuityshopper.com** is an online magazine that is published twice annually. The site provides timely information on immediate annuities. Visit the site at

  annuityshopper.com

- **AnnuitySpecs.com** is a site that specializes in indexed annuities. The site provides considerable information on hundreds of indexed annuity products. Visit the site at

  AnnuitySpecs.com

- **Charles Schwab** provides informative articles and information on retirement planning, annuities, and individual retirement accounts (IRAs). Visit the site at

  schwab.com

- **Fidelity Investments** offers timely information on retirement planning, annuities, and IRAs, including interactive calculators for making IRA decisions. Visit the site at

  fidelity.com

- **ImmediateAnnuities.com** claims it is the nation's leading annuity broker. The company helps consumers purchase safe and reliable life income annuities for their retirement. Visit the site at

  immediateannuities.com

- **Insure.com** provides timely information on annuities, IRAs, and other insurance products. Visit the site at

  insure.com

- The **Roth IRA Web site** is devoted to Roth IRAs and provides a considerable amount of consumer information on this type of IRA. The site provides links to articles, books, tapes, calculators, IRS documents, and a message board on Roth IRAs. Visit the site at

  rothira.com

- **TIAA-CREF** is an excellent source of accurate information on retirement planning, annuities, and IRAs. Visit the site at

  tiaa-cref.org

- The **Vanguard Group** provides timely information on variable annuities, IRAs, and retirement planning. Visit the site at

  vanguard.com

## SELECTED REFERENCES

Graves, Edward E., ed. *McGill's Life Insurance*, 8th ed. Bryn Mawr, PA: The American College, 2011, Ch. 6.

Internal Revenue Service. *General Rule for Pensions and Annuities,* Publication 939.

Internal Revenue Service. *Individual Retirement Arrangements (IRAs)*, Publication 590.

Internal Revenue Service. *Pension and Annuity Income,* Publication 575.

Kaster, Nicholas, et al. *2012 U.S. Master Pension Guide.* Chicago, IL: CCH Inc., 2012.

Kuykendall, Lavonne. "Making the Case To Buy an Annuity," *The Wall Street Journal*, March 8, 2011, p. C15.

Myers, Randy. "A Guide to Annuities & Retirement Income," *The Wall Street Journal,* November 12, 2008, pp. D5–D11.

Myers, Randy. "Private Wealth Management, Annuities and Retirement Satisfaction," *The Wall Street Journal*, November 16, 2011, p. C7.

Scism, Leslie. "Annuity Fine Print: Guarantees Aren't Always Guaranteed," *The Wall Street Journal*, June 1, 2009, pp. Rl, R6.

Tergesen, Anne, and Leslie Scism. "Getting Smart About Annuities," *The Wall Street Journal,* April 18–19, 2009, pp. R1, R4.

## NOTES

1. A deduction for administrative expenses and sales expenses is ignored.
2. The actual number of annuity units will depend on the market value of the account, attained age of the annuitant, number of guaranteed payments, conversion rates, assumed investment return, and other factors.
3. Randy Myers, "Private Wealth Management, Annuities and Retirement Satisfaction," *The Wall Street Journal*, November 16, 2011, p. C7.
4. The 10 percent penalty tax does not apply to individuals who attain age 59½ or become totally disabled; when the distribution is received by a beneficiary or

estate after the individual dies; when the distribution is part of substantially equal payments paid over the life expectancy of the individual or individual and beneficiary; or when the distribution is from an annuity contract under a qualified personal injury settlement. Certain other exceptions also apply.

5. The procedure for determining the total cost of an annuity is horribly complex. Total cost must be reduced by (1) any refunded premiums, rebates, dividends, or unpaid loans that you received; (2) any additional premiums paid for double indemnity or disability payments; (3) any other tax-free amounts that you received; and (4) any refund features in the annuity. The IRS provides worksheets for making these calculations.

6. Modified adjusted gross income is essentially the adjusted gross income figure shown on your tax return without taking into account any IRA deductions, student loan interest deduction, foreign earned income exclusion, foreign housing exclusion or deduction, exclusion of qualified bond interest, and exclusion of employer-paid adoption expenses. For a Roth IRA, modified adjusted gross income excludes the income reported when a traditional IRA is converted to a Roth IRA.

Students may take a self-administered test on this chapter at
**www.pearsonhighered.com/rejda**

# CHAPTER 15

# HEALTH-CARE REFORM; INDIVIDUAL HEALTH INSURANCE COVERAGES

*"The supreme court's decision to uphold the Affordable Care Act ensures hard-working, middle class families will get the security they deserve and protects every American from the worst insurance company abuses."*

whitehouse.gov/healthreform

## LEARNING OBJECTIVES

**After studying this chapter, you should be able to**

◆ Explain the major health-care problems in the United States.

◆ Identify the major provisions of the Affordable Care Act that affect individuals and families.

◆ Describe the basic characteristics of individual medical expense insurance.

◆ Identify the basic characteristics of health savings accounts (HSA).

◆ Describe the key characteristics of long-term care insurance.

◆ Describe the major characteristics of disability-income insurance contracts.

*Justin, age 32, is a self-employed carpenter who was recently diagnosed with a brain tumor that required immediate surgery. The surgeon's fee, hospital expenses, other medical bills, and lost earnings totalled more than $125,000. Like many self-employed individuals, Justin had no health insurance. In addition, he could not work for six months and did not have a disability-income policy to restore his lost earnings. Because of the lack of health insurance, Justin was exposed to serious economic insecurity because of the unexpected surgery. He eventually had to declare bankruptcy.*

*As Justin's experience demonstrates, health insurance should receive high priority in a personal risk management program. If you are seriously ill or injured, you face two major problems: payment of your medical bills and the loss of earned income. A severe illness or injury can result in catastrophic medical bills. Without proper protection, you may have to pay thousands of dollars out of your own pocket for medical bills. In addition, a lengthy disability can result in the loss of substantial amounts of earned income.*

*This chapter is the first of two chapters dealing with private health insurance. This chapter is limited primarily to important individual health insurance coverages. The following chapter discusses group health insurance coverages. Although most people are covered under group plans, individual plans are still important for individuals and families who are not covered by group health insurance.*

*This chapter is divided into three major parts. The first part discusses the major health-care problems in the United States and the need for health-care reform. The second part examines the major provisions of the new Affordable Care Act that was enacted to reform the present health-care delivery system. The final part discusses several individual health insurance coverages including individual medical expense insurance, health savings accounts, long-term care insurance, and disability-income insurance.*

## HEALTH-CARE PROBLEMS IN THE UNITED STATES

The United States overall provides high-quality health care to the population. However, despite major breakthroughs in medicine, experts believe the present health-care delivery system is broken and must be reformed. Major problems that lead to enactment of the Patient Protection and Affordable Care Act in March 2010 include the following:

- Rising health-care expenditures
- Large number of uninsured in the population
- Uneven quality of medical care
- Considerable waste and inefficiency
- Defects in financing health care
- Abusive insurer practices

### Rising Health-Care Expenditures

Total health-care expenditures in the United States have increased substantially over time and are growing faster than the national economy. *According to the Centers for Medicare & Medicaid Services, estimated national health expenditures totalled just over $2.8 trillion in 2012 or 17.6 percent of the nation's gross domestic product.* Thus, more than one in six dollars of the nation's income is now spent on health care. If present trends continue, estimated national health expenditures will total $4.6 trillion in 2020, or 19.8 percent of our gross domestic product.[1]

**Comparison with Foreign Nations** The United States leads the world in total spending on health care. Per capita spending on health care in the United

States was $7598 in 2009, or 48 percent higher than the second highest spending country (Switzerland) and almost 90 percent higher than in many countries considered to be global competitors (see Insight 15.1).

According to a recent study by the Commonwealth Fund, the higher spending in the United States should not be attributed to higher incomes, an older population, or a greater supply or utilization of physicians and hospitals. Instead, the higher spending may be due to (1) higher prices paid for medical care, including prescription drugs, office visits, and higher physician and surgeon fees compared to foreign countries, (2) greater use of more expensive technology, and (3) higher obesity rates. Despite higher spending, the quality of health care in the United States shows considerable variation of performance depending on the disease being treated, and does not appear to be markedly superior to less costly systems in other industrialized countries.[2]

**Reasons for the Increase in Health-Care Expenditures**   Health-care economists have identified numerous factors that explain, at least in part, the substantial increase in health-care expenditures over time. Important factors include the following:

- *Increase in consumer demand*. Consumer demand for health-care services has increased over time because of an increase in the population, rising per capita incomes, and greater health awareness by Americans. Studies suggest that growth in average per capita income could account for 5 percent to approximately 20 percent of the growth in long-term spending on health care.[3]

- *Advances in technology*. Development of new technology and advances in existing technology are major drivers of health-care costs in the United States. Examples include magnetic resonance imaging (MRI), coronary bypass procedures, bone marrow transplants, neonatal intensive care, and renal replacement therapy for kidney failure. A Congressional Budget Office (CBO) study estimates that about half of all growth in health-care spending in the past several decades was associated with changes in medical care made possible by advances in technology.[4]

- *Cost insulation because of third-party payers*. Critics argue that consumers are insulated from the true cost of health care because they are not paying directly for the health care they receive. Most health-care costs are paid by third-party payers, such as employers, private insurers, and government, which typically pay a large part of the total cost. As a result, patients generally have little or no incentive to control cost, which encourages them to consume more health-care services than they ordinarily would. As a source of spending, government payments from Medicare, Medicaid, and other public sources, as well as payments from private health insurance, accounted for 88 percent of the nation's health-care dollars at the end of 2008. Consumers paid out-of-pocket only 12 percent of the nation's health-care dollars.[5] Because of the substantial increase in third-party payers over time, patients have less incentives to control cost.

- *Employment-based health insurance*. Most workers today obtain their health insurance coverage through an employer-sponsored group plan. Critics believe that many of the health-care problems in the United States can be traced to employment-based health insurance. This is true for several reasons. First, qualified group health insurance plans receive favorable tax treatment. Employers receive an income-tax deduction for their contributions, and the contributions are not taxable income to employees. Critics argue that, as a result of collective bargaining and the heavy tax subsidy, employers and employees often select the more costly and comprehensive types of health insurance plans, which drive up costs. Second, as stated earlier, critics argue that third-party payments for health insurance by employers insulate the employees from the true cost of health care, which reduces incentives of employees to control costs. Finally, group health insurance is temporary and not portable. Employees generally lose their group health coverage if they are laid off, fired, or retire. To deal with these problems, critics propose that individual health insurance should receive greater emphasis so that employees would still have coverage after they leave the group and also have a greater incentive to control cost.

- *State-mandated benefits*. The states require health insurers to cover certain specific diseases or groups, such as coverage of newly born infants, alcoholism and drug addiction, mental

## INSIGHT 15.1

### How Does U.S. Health-Care Spending Compare with Other Countries?

**The U.S. spends substantially more on health care than other developed countries.** The figure below shows per capita health expenditures in 2009 U.S. dollars for the Organisation for Economic Co-operation and Development (OECD) countries with above-average per capita national income. According to OECD data, health spending per capita in the United States was $7,598 in 2009. This amount was 48% higher than in the next highest spending country (Switzerland), and about 90% higher than in many other countries that we would consider global competitors. As a share of GDP, health care spending in the U.S. also exceeds spending by other industrialized nations by at least 5 percentage points (not shown). Despite this relatively high level of spending, the United States does not appear to achieve substantially better health benchmarks compared to other developed countries. *A recent study found that U.S. health-care spending is higher than that of other countries most likely because of higher prices and perhaps more readily accessible technology and greater obesity, rather than higher income, an older population, or a greater supply or utilization of hospitals and doctors.*[a]

**Per Capita Total Current Health-Care Expenditures, U.S. and Selected Countries, 2009**

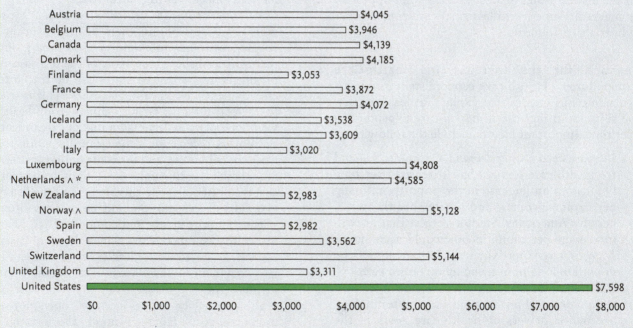

|  |  |
|---|---|
| Austria | $4,045 |
| Belgium | $3,946 |
| Canada | $4,139 |
| Denmark | $4,185 |
| Finland | $3,053 |
| France | $3,872 |
| Germany | $4,072 |
| Iceland | $3,538 |
| Ireland | $3,609 |
| Italy | $3,020 |
| Luxembourg | $4,808 |
| Netherlands ∧ * | $4,585 |
| New Zealand | $2,983 |
| Norway ∧ | $5,128 |
| Spain | $2,982 |
| Sweden | $3,562 |
| Switzerland | $5,144 |
| United Kingdom | $3,311 |
| United States | $7,598 |

∧OECD estimate.

*Break in series

Source: Organisation for Economic Co-operation and Development. "OECD Health Data: Health Expenditures and Financing", OECD Health Statistics Data from internet subscription database. http://www.oecd-ilibrary.org, data accessed on 01/10/12.

[a]David A. Squires, "Explaining High Health Care Spending in the United States: An International Comparison of Supply, Utilization, Prices, and Quality," The Commonwealth Fund, May 3, 2012.

SOURCE: Excerpted from The Henry J. Kaiser Family Foundation, *Health Care Costs, A Primer, Key Information on Health Care Costs and Their Impact,* May 2012, p. 7.

health, and coverage of chiropractors, psychologists, and physically and mentally handicapped persons. The mandated benefits increase the utilization of medical services and drive up cost.

- *Increased spending on prescription drugs.* In past years, spending on prescription drugs was not a major factor in total health-care spending. However, since the mid-1990s, spending on prescription drugs has become relatively more important as a driver of health-care costs. Prescription drugs accounted for 10 percent of total spending on health care at the end of 2008.[6]

- *Cost shifting by Medicare and Medicaid.* Medicare and Medicaid programs do not pay the full cost of providing care to patients. As a result, costs are shifted from Medicare and Medicaid to private paying patients with health insurance who must pay more for the care they receive. Experts estimate that cost shifting adds at least $1000 to the cost of a family policy each year.

- *High administrative costs.* The costs of administering private health insurance plans have also increased over time. The share of private health insurance premiums accounted for by administrative cost varies considerably by firm size. The Congressional Budget Office estimates that the average share of premiums that covers administrative costs ranges from about 7 percent of employer-sponsored plans with 1000 or more enrollees to nearly 30 percent for individuals and small firms with fewer than 25 employees.[7]

- *Rising prices in the health-care sector.* The prices of medical goods and service have increased more rapidly over time than the overall price level. Some analysts believe that rising prices in the health-care sector are another contributing factor in total health-care spending. However, a CBO study concludes that rising prices in the health-care sector account for no more than one-fifth of the long-term real increase in total health-care spending.[8]

- *Defensive medicine.* The fear of being sued for medical malpractice has forced physicians to practice defensive medicine. Defensive medicine refers to unnecessary diagnostic tests by physicians, tests with little clinical value to patients, and longer-than-necessary hospital stays. Health-care costs are higher as a result.

- *Other factors.* Other factors that drive up health-care costs include the substantial cost of emergency room treatment and inpatient hospital care for uninsured patients, and health-care fraud and abuse by health-care providers and patients.

- *In addition, contrary to popular belief, aging of the population is not a major contributing factor to the overall long-run growth in health-care spending.* According to the CBO, the percentage of aged people in the population increased during the past four decades, but the increase was too gradual and insubstantial to account for a large percentage of the total increase in per capita spending on health care. The CBO estimates that changes in the age distribution in the population from 1965 to 2005 accounted for only about 3 percent of the cumulative increase in total spending that occurred during that period.[9]

## Large Number of Uninsured Persons in the Population

The second major problem is the large number of uninsured persons in the population. *According to the 2012 Current Population Survey, 48.6 million people, or 15.7 percent of the population, had no health insurance coverage in 2011.*[10] Groups with relatively large numbers of uninsured persons include the following:

| | |
|---|---|
| Foreign born | 33.0 percent |
| Hispanic (any race) | 30.1 percent |
| Young adults (ages 19 to 25) | 27.7 percent |
| Household income under $25,000 | 25.4 percent |
| Blacks | 19.5 percent |
| Asians | 16.8 percent |

In addition, many states have a high proportion of uninsured persons. In 2011, these states include Texas (23.8 percent), New Mexico (19.6 percent), Mississippi (16.2 percent), Florida (19.8 percent), and Louisiana (20.8 percent).[11]

The problem is even more severe when the length of time an individual remains uninsured is considered. A study by The Kaiser Family Foundation showed that more than 70 percent of the people without health insurance were uninsured for more than one year, and over half were uninsured for more than three years (see Insight 15.2).

People uninsured for extended periods are exposed to great economic insecurity. According to Families USA, the consequences of being uninsured are severe. They include the following:[12]

- *The uninsured often delay or skip needed medical care because of high costs.* Uninsured adults are six times as likely as privately insured adults to go without needed medical care because of cost.
- *When the uninsured receive medical care, they frequently pay more for that care.* The uninsured

cannot negotiate discounts on hospital and physician charges that insurers obtain in their contract negotiations with health-care providers. As a result, some patients pay more than 2.5 times the charges paid by insured patients for hospital services.

- *With the exception of an emergency room, uninsured adults are less likely to have a regular source of medical care.* More than two in five uninsured adults reported that a doctor's office or clinic would not accept them as a new patient.
- *The uninsured often do not have access to regular screenings and preventive care.* As a result, uninsured adults are substantially more likely to be

---

## INSIGHT 15.2

### More Than Seventy Percent of the Uninsured Have Gone Without Health Coverage for More Than a Year

Because health insurance is primarily obtained as an employment benefit, health coverage is disrupted when people change or lose their jobs. When people are unable to obtain employer-sponsored coverage and are ineligible for Medicaid, they may be left uninsured for long periods of time if individual coverage is either unaffordable or unavailable due to their health status.

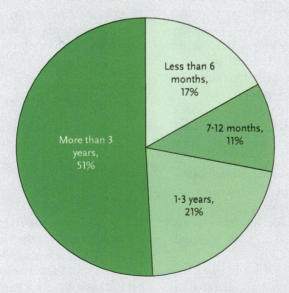

**Duration of Time Without Insurance Coverage Among the Uninsured, 2010**

Less than 6 months, 17%

7-12 months, 11%

1-3 years, 21%

More than 3 years, 51%

More than three years includes those who said they never had health insurance. Percentages are age adjusted.

SOURCE: Summary Health Statistics for the U.S. Population: National Health Interview Survey, 2010. September, 2011.

Source: Excerpted from The Henry J. Kaiser Family Foundation, *The Uninsured: A Primer, Key Facts about Americans Without Health Insurance*, October 2011, p. 8.

diagnosed with a disease in an advanced stage, such as advanced stage breast cancer.

- *The uninsured are sicker and die earlier than people with insurance.* Adults without health insurance are 25 percent more likely to die prematurely than adults with private health insurance.

## Reasons Why People Are Uninsured

Another study by National Public Radio, the Kaiser Foundation, and Harvard School of Public Health identified several reasons why adults have no health insurance.[13] The major reason cited is cost: health insurance is too expensive to purchase (37 percent). Other reasons include lack of employment or job loss (22 percent); not being eligible for coverage under an employer's plan or lack of an employer plan (11 percent); and not needing it (9 percent). Also, some people are uninsured because they have been refused coverage by insurers due to poor health, illness, or age (4 percent).

Finally, still other reasons explain why some people are uninsured. Some low-income people are eligible for coverage under the Medicaid program but fail to sign up because they are unaware they are eligible. Others with relatively high incomes do not purchase health insurance because they view spending on health insurance as a low priority. Finally, many younger people believe they are healthy, and that health insurance is unnecessary.

## Uneven Quality of Medical Care

Another problem is that the quality of medical care in the United States is uneven and varies widely depending on the physician, geographic location, and type of disease being treated. Each year, the National Committee for Quality Assurance (NCQA) examines the quality of care provided by more than 1000 commercial health-care plans across the country. The plans collectively cover two-fifths of the population in the United States. The evaluation of care is based on measures that assess how often patients receive care that conforms to evidence-based guidelines. The assessment ranges from prevention of disease to chronic disease management, which include immunizations, cancer screenings, blood pressure control, advice to quit smoking, and medication management.

NCQA concludes that, although the quality of care has improved over time, the quality of care provided for certain diseases varies widely among the states.

The quality of care provided depends on geographic location, type of health insurance plan, and disease being treated. According to the NCQA, in 2010, the top 10 states in terms of quality of care were Connecticut, Colorado, Illinois, Iowa, Massachusetts, Minnesota, New York, Oregon, Pennsylvania, and Wisconsin. The bottom 10 jurisdictions in quality include Alabama, Alaska, Arkansas, Mississippi, Montana, Louisiana, South Carolina, Utah, Wyoming, and Puerto Rico.[14]

In its 2010 report, the NCQA analyzed the health-care costs and additional lives that would be saved if all health-care plans in its survey were as good as the plans listed in the 90th percentile. The NCQA estimated that total cost savings from higher quality plans ranged from $4.6 billion to $7.4 billion. The number of preventable deaths ranged from a low of 50,657 to a high of 186,512.[15] *To put this number in perspective, and using the low estimate, the number of preventable deaths from higher quality plans exceeds the number of people who die each year in motor vehicle accidents.*

## Waste and Inefficiency

Another problem is considerable waste and inefficiency in the present system. Experts estimate that the present system wastes more than $800 billion each year, or more than one-third of total health-care spending. Wasteful spending includes the following:

- Duplication of tests because health-care records from other providers are not readily available
- Medical errors by hospitals and physicians that are largely preventable
- Unnecessary tests and treatment by physicians due to fear of malpractice lawsuits
- High administrative costs and excessive and redundant paperwork by health-care providers
- Readmissions into hospitals because of inadequate or ineffective initial treatment
- Hospitalizations for preventable conditions, such as uncontrolled diabetes, which are less costly when treated promptly
- Overuse and duplication of expensive medical technology by health-care providers, such as magnetic resonance imaging (MRI) tests

Another costly and wasteful practice is the overuse of hospital emergency rooms. For many uninsured Americans, the only available source of medical care is treatment in a hospital emergency room. As a result, emergency rooms in public hospitals provide a substantial amount of care for nonemergency treatment, which is very expensive and places severe stress on both medical personnel and physical facilities.

## Defects in Financing Health Care

Another major problem is the financing of health care in the United States. Critics argue that the financing of health care in the United States is defective and aggravates many of the problems discussed earlier. They point out the following defects:

- *Based on ability to pay.* The present system is based largely on the person's ability to pay and not on the basis of health needs. Thus, it is argued, many uninsured Americans with serious health problems do not receive needed care because they cannot pay for it.
- *Fee-for-service defects.* The traditional fee-for-service method of compensating physicians often works in a perverse way. Under this system, the more services and tests that physicians provide, the higher their incomes. Physicians are generally compensated based on the number of medical services provided and not on the medical outcomes of their patients. The fee-for-service method may encourage some physicians to prescribe unnecessary medical tests and treatment.
- *Distortions in medical care.* It is argued that the present system results in a distortion in medical care. For example, because specialists earn higher incomes, medical school graduates typically enter specialty fields and abandon general practice, which limits the supply of general practice physicians. Also, because of potentially higher incomes, some physicians prefer to practice medicine in the cities and suburbs rather than in rural areas, which exacerbates the shortage of rural physicians.

## Abusive Insurer Practices

Congressional hearings and floor debate leading to enactment of the Affordable Care Act revealed a variety of abusive insurer practices and policy limitations that harmed both policyholders and applicants for insurance. These practices included (1) exclusions for preexisting conditions, (2) rescission of insurance policies, and (3) lifetime dollar and annual limits on benefits.

- *Exclusions for preexisting conditions.* Prior to enactment of the Affordable Care Act, individual medical expense insurance policies typically contained exclusions for preexisting conditions. A **preexisting condition** is a physical or mental condition that existed during some specified time period prior to the effective date of the policy for which the insured received medical treatment. Preexisting conditions were not covered until the policy had been in force for a specified period. Depending on the policy and state, the exclusion period generally ranged from six to 18 months, unless the condition was disclosed in the application and was not excluded by a rider. If disclosed in the application, the applicant was typically charged a higher rate, or the condition was excluded by a rider to the policy. However, the House and Senate debates and congressional hearings revealed that many insurers abused the preexisting provision and denied some legitimate claims because of preexisting conditions not disclosed in the application. Examples of denied claims included the following: (1) an insured woman had a C-section in the delivery of her baby, which was considered a preexisting condition; (2) another insured woman with aggressive breast cancer had her claim denied because she did not disclose earlier treatment for acne, and (3) an insured person who experienced domestic violence was considered as having a preexisting condition. Another study by the Committee on Energy and Commerce showed that from 2007 through 2009, the four largest for-profit health insurers denied coverage to one out of every seven applicants based on a preexisting condition.[16]
- *Rescission of insurance contracts to limit benefits.* The House and Senate hearings prior to enactment of the new law revealed that some insurers rescinded individual health insurance policies to avoid paying large claims, such as claims dealing with advanced cancer or large medical bills. Rescission means insurers could

cancel an individual policy because of misrepresentation, fraud, or concealment of a preexisting condition by the insured when the policy was first issued. The time limit for contesting a claim in an individual policy in most states was two years. However, congressional hearings revealed that some insurers would collect premiums, and if the insured later submitted an expensive claim, his or her medical records would be examined to determine if the insured failed to disclose some medical condition when the policy was first issued. If any omissions or discrepancies were discovered, the insurer would refuse to pay for any additional treatment and would try to cancel the coverage retroactively. The result was that some patients with serious health problems, such as advanced breast cancer or heart disease, had their policies rescinded at the time when they were undergoing necessary and expensive treatment.

- *Lifetime or annual limits on benefits.* Prior to enactment of the Affordable Care Act, individual and group coverages typically contained lifetime and annual limits on benefits. As a result, insured patients with serious health conditions requiring treatment over an extended period often exhausted their benefits. Many policies had relatively low lifetime and annual limits. As a result, some insured patients could not pay their medical bills and were forced into bankruptcy even though they had some type of insurance policy. A national study of bankruptcies by Harvard researchers concluded that medical problems contributed to 62 percent of all bankruptcies in 2007. Three-quarters of those filing for bankruptcy had health insurance.[17]

## HEALTH-CARE REFORM

Proposals to reform health care and enact a system of national health insurance in the United States are not new. In 1912, Theodore Roosevelt included national health insurance in his presidential campaign. Since that time, numerous proposals by the Democrats in Congress to enact national health insurance have failed. In 2009, President Barack Obama introduced legislation that would overhaul and reform the health-care delivery system. Republican members of Congress strongly opposed the legislation because of

deeply held ideological and political beliefs. However, despite heated and bitter congressional debate, the legislation was enacted by Congress. On March 23, 2010, President Obama signed into law the Patient Protection and Affordable Care Act as amended by the Health Care and Education Reconciliation Act of 2010 (Affordable Care Act).

The attorneys general of 26 states immediately sued the federal government on the grounds that the new law was unconstitutional primarily because of the individual mandate provision that required most people in the United States to have coverage for health insurance or pay a financial penalty. However, on June 28, 2012, in a split and controversial decision, the Supreme Court ruled that the Affordable Care Act is constitutional, and that the individual mandate is constitutional under the taxing power of Congress.

## BASIC PROVISIONS OF THE AFFORDABLE CARE ACT

The **Affordable Care Act** extends health-care coverage to 30 million uninsured Americans, provides substantial subsidies to uninsured individuals and small business firms to make health insurance more affordable, contains provisions to lower health-care costs in the long run, and prohibits insurers from engaging in certain abusive practices. Although the full law does not become effective until January 1, 2014, many provisions are now in effect. However, the new law is complex and beyond the scope of this text to discuss in detail. Instead, we focus primarily on certain provisions that affect individual and families, employers, insurers, and health-care providers. These provisions include the following:[18]

- Individual Mandate
- Health Insurance Reforms
- Essential Health Benefits
- Affordable Insurance Exchanges
- Premium Credits to Eligible Individuals and Families
- Employer Requirements
- Premium Subsidies to Small Employers
- Early Retirement Reinsurance Program
- Expansion of Medicaid
- Preexisting Condition Insurance Plan
- Improving Quality and Lowering Costs
- Cost and Financing

## Individual Mandate

Beginning in 2014, most citizens and legal residents in the United States must have qualifying health insurance or pay a financial penalty. In 2014, the penalty will be $95 (or 1 percent of income if higher) and will gradually increase to $695 (or 2.5 percent of income) in 2016. As discussed later, the new law also provides premium tax credits so that eligible individuals can purchase affordable health insurance and comply with the law.

Certain groups are exempt from mandatory coverage. Exemptions are granted for financial hardship, religious objections, Native Americans, individuals who are uninsured for less than three months, incarcerated individuals, and undocumented immigrants. Also exempt are individuals for whom premiums for the lowest-cost plan exceed 8 percent of their income, and people with incomes below the annual thresholds for filing federal income tax returns.

The vast majority of people under age 65 will not be affected by the individual mandate and penalty provision. According to the Urban Institute, only 3 percent of the population under age 65 will be subject to penalties if they do not obtain insurance.[19] The majority of people have health insurance, are part of an exempt group, have incomes below the tax filing threshold, or can obtain coverage under the expanded Medicaid program. In addition, generous subsidies provide strong incentives for uninsured people to obtain insurance.

## Health Insurance Reforms

The new law contains numerous provisions that prohibit insurers from engaging in certain harmful practices detrimental to insurance consumers discussed earlier. Important provisions that apply to health insurers include the following:

- *Retention of coverage until age 26.* Insurers must allow young adults to remain on their parents' policies until age 26. This provision is now in effect and is especially helpful to adult children who typically lost their coverage under their parents' policy when they graduated from college or reached a limiting age of coverage.
- *Lifetime limits and annual limits prohibited.* Insurers are prohibited from imposing lifetime limits on benefits. This provision is now in effect.

Beginning in 2014, annual limits on benefits are also prohibited. Prior to 2014, annual limits can be imposed as determined by the secretary of Health and Human Services.
- *Preexisting conditions prohibited.* Insurers are prohibited from denying claims or excluding coverage for preexisting conditions for children under age 19. This provision applies to all job-related health plans as well as individual health insurance policies issued after March 23, 2010. For adults, the ban on preexisting conditions becomes effective on January 1, 2014. In addition, beginning in 2014, health insurers will no longer be able to deny coverage to women because they are pregnant or exclude maternity-related claims.
- *Rescission of insurance policies prohibited.* The new law prohibits insurers from retroactively rescinding insurance policies because of unintentional errors on the application except in cases of fraud or intentional misrepresentation of a material fact. This provision is now in effect.
- *Guaranteed access to health insurance.* Effective January 1, 2014, policies in the individual and small group markets and the Affordable Insurance Exchanges (discussed later) will be sold on a guaranteed issue basis and are guaranteed renewable. Applicants cannot be denied coverage or rated up because of their health. Variations in rating variables are allowed only for age (limited to 3 to 1 ratio), number of family members, geographical area, and tobacco use (limited to 1.5 to 1 ratio). Charging females higher premiums for coverage is prohibited.
- *Grandfathered plans.* Grandfathered plans are individual plans and employer-sponsored group plans that existed on March 23, 2010 and have not made any prohibited changes. Grandfathered plans generally can remain the same and are subject only to certain provisions of the Affordable Care Act. All health insurance plans—whether grandfathered or not—must provide certain benefits for plan years starting on or after September 23, 2010. These benefits include (1) no lifetime limits on coverage for all plans, (2) no rescissions of coverage when people get sick and have previously made an unintentional or honest mistake in the application, and (3) extension of parents' coverage to young adults under age 26.

In addition, employer-sponsored group plans must provide additional benefits, which include (1) no exclusions for preexisting conditions for children under age 19, and (2) no restricted annual limits on benefits, that is, annual dollar limits on coverage are below the amounts determined by the secretary of Health and Human Services prior to 2014.

Finally, to maintain its grandfathered status, a grandfathered plan cannot significantly cut or reduce benefits, increase coinsurance charges, significantly increase deductibles and copayment charges, significantly lower employer contributions, add or tighten any annual limit on the amount the insurer pays, and change insurers and keep a grandfathered status for the new plan.

- *Medical loss ratio.* Insurers are required to meet a minimum loss ratio of 85 percent for plans in the large group market and 80 percent for plans in the individual and small group markets. The medical loss ratio refers to the percentage of premiums paid for health insurance claims and activities that improve the quality of care. Technically, the medical loss ratio is the ratio of incurred claims plus loss adjustment expenses to earned premiums. It is a basic financial measurement used in the Affordable Care Act to encourage health plans to provide value to enrollees.

Rebates must be paid to enrollees if the loss ratios are not met because of high profits or high administrative expenses. This provision is now in effect. In 2012, insurers that did not meet the minimum loss ratio rules paid out more than $1.1 billion in rebates to nearly 13 million people, or an average rebate check of $151 per household.

In addition, the new law establishes a process for reviewing premium increases in health insurance plans and requires plans to justify premium increases. The states are required to report on trends in insurance premiums and recommend whether certain plans should be excluded from the Affordable Insurance Exchanges based on unjustified premium increases. This provision became effective in plan year 2010.

- *Limited waiting periods.* Effective January 1, 2012, waiting periods for health insurance coverage to begin are limited to a maximum 90 days.

## Essential Health Benefits

The Affordable Care Act requires insurers to offer medical expense coverages that provide essential health benefits. Effective January 1, 2014, all new medical expense policies, except stand-alone dental, vision, disability income, long-term care, and certain other policies must provide a comprehensive package of benefits and services called **essential health benefits**. This requirement applies to all new plans offered in the individual and small group markets and includes plans both in and outside of the state's Affordable Insurance Exchange. Essential health benefits must include coverage for items and medical services in the following 10 categories:

- Ambulatory patient services
- Emergency services
- Hospitalization
- Maternity and newborn care
- Mental health and substance abuse disorder services, including behavioral health treatment
- Prescription drugs
- Rehabilitative services and devices
- Laboratory services
- Preventive and wellness services and chronic disease management
- Pediatric services, including oral and vision care

Applicants will have a choice of four benefit categories that cover 60 percent to 90 percent of the benefit costs for plans that will be offered through a state exchange in the individual and small group markets. The benefit categories are as follows:

- *Bronze plan.* This plan provides essential health benefits and covers 60 percent of the benefit costs. There are annual limits on out-of-pocket payments. Out-of-pocket limits refer to deductibles, coinsurance, copayments, and other cost-sharing provisions that insureds must pay. *The cost-sharing provisions do not apply to preventive services, and out-of-pocket payments are limited to current Health Saving Account (HSA) limits ($6250 for an individual and $12,500 for a family in 2013). Without these limits, annual out-of-pocket payments could reach catastrophic levels and create substantial economic insecurity.*
- *Silver plan.* This plan provides essential health benefits and covers 70 percent of the benefit

costs. The annual out-of-pocket limits are the same as HSA limits.

- *Gold plan.* This plan provides essential health benefits and covers 80 percent of the benefit costs. The annual out-of-pocket limits are the same as HSA limits.
- *Platinum plan.* This plan provides essential health benefits and covers 90 percent of the benefit costs. The annual out-of-pocket limits are the same as HSA limits.

## Affordable Insurance Exchanges

The new law creates an **Affordable Insurance Exchange** in each state, which is a new transparent and competitive insurance marketplace where individuals and small firms with fewer than 100 employees can purchase affordable and qualified health insurance plans. Access to insurance through an exchange is limited to U.S. citizens and legal residents who are not incarcerated. The state exchanges will enable people to comparison shop for standard health insurance packages, facilitate enrollment in the various plans, and administer health insurance premium credits so that people at all income levels can purchase affordable coverage. Starting in 2014, members of Congress will also get their health insurance coverage through the exchanges.

## Health Insurance Premium Tax Credits

The new law provides premium credits to eligible individuals that will make the coverage more affordable. Eligibility for the subsidies is limited to U.S. citizens and legal immigrants who meet the income limits. Employees who have access to health insurance through an employer's plan are not eligible for the subsidies unless the employer's plan does not have an actuarial value of at least 60 percent, or the employee's share of premiums exceeds 9.5 percent of income.

- *Premium tax credits.* Refundable premium tax credits are available to eligible individuals and families with incomes between 100 percent and 400 percent of the federal poverty level (up to $44,680 for an individual and up to $92,200 for a family of four in 2012), which enables them to purchase qualified health insurance through a state Affordable Insurance Exchange. The tax credits are based on income and are designed to limit the amount spent on health insurance from 2 percent to a maximum of 9.5 percent of income, which makes the insurance affordable. The premium credits are set on a sliding scale and range from 2 percent of income for individuals with incomes between 100 percent and 133 percent of the poverty level to 9.5 percent of income for individuals with incomes between 300 percent and 400 percent of the poverty level. This provision becomes effective in 2014.

- *Cost-sharing subsidies.* Cost-sharing subsidies are also available that reduce the annual out-of-pocket payments for the deductibles, coinsurance, and other cost-sharing provisions. The cost-sharing credits, which are based on income, reduce the annual cost-sharing limits and increase the actuarial value of the basic benefit plan benefits. Cost-sharing credits are available to people with incomes between 100 percent and 400 percent of the poverty level. This provision becomes effective in 2014.

- *Employer requirements.* If an employer with at least 50 full-time equivalent employees does not offer minimum essential coverage to full-time employees and dependents, and has at least one employee receiving a tax credit or cost-sharing reduction to help pay for insurance through an exchange, the employer must pay a penalty. The fine is $2000 for each full-time employee (excluding the first 30 employees).

Employers with 50 or more full-time equivalent employees that *do provide coverage* to their employees, and have at least one full-time employee who is receiving a premium tax credit or cost-sharing reduction, will be assessed $3000 for each employee receiving the subsidy, or $2000 for each full-time employee, whichever is lower (again excluding the first 30 employees from the assessment). These provisions become effective January 1, 2014.

Finally, large employers with more than 200 employees must automatically enroll new employees in the employer's lowest-cost plan if the employee does not enroll in a plan. Employees have the choice to opt out.

## Small Employer Tax Credits

The new law contains significant tax credits for small employers to make health insurance more affordable for their employees. These provisions are summarized as follows:

- *Tax credits.* The new law provides tax credits to small employers that have fewer than 25 full-time equivalent employees and pay average annual wages of less than $50,000. This provision is now in effect. For tax years 2010 through 2013, a tax credit of up to 35 percent of the employer's contribution is available if the employer contributes at least 50 percent of the total premiums. The full tax credit is available to employers that have 10 or fewer full-time equivalent employees and pay average annual wages of less than $25,000. The maximum tax credit is phased out as the number of employees and average annual wages increase.
- *Increased tax credit in 2014.* Beginning in 2014, the tax credit for eligible small employers that purchase health insurance through a state exchange will be increased up to 50 percent of the employer's contribution if the employer contributes at least 50 percent of the total premium costs. The full credit of 50 percent will be available to small employers with 10 or fewer employees who pay average annual wages of less than $25,000. The full credit is phased out as firm size and annual average wages increase.

## Early Retirement Reinsurance Program

Many older employees under age 65 lose their health insurance if they retire early or are forced into retirement during a business recession. The new law creates a temporary reinsurance program to help employers provide health insurance to early retirees over age 55 who are ineligible for Medicare. The program reimburses employers or insurers for 80 percent of retiree claims between $15,000 and $90,000. Payments from the reinsurance program are used to reduce the costs for enrollees in the employer's plan. This provision is now in effect and applies until January 2014 when the state exchanges become fully operational. The funds, however, for this provision ran out after 14 months, and new applications are not being accepted at the time of writing.

## Expansion of Medicaid

Beginning in 2014, the Affordable Care Act expands the Medicaid program to include adults with incomes up to 133 percent of the federal poverty line ($15,415 for an individual or $26,344 for a family of three in 2012). As a result, millions of uninsured persons will be eligible for Medicaid coverage. All newly eligible adults will be guaranteed a benchmark package of essential health benefits available through the exchanges. To finance the increase in the number of recipients, the federal government will pay 100 percent of the additional costs for 2014 through 2016, 95 percent in 2017, 94 percent in 2018, 93 percent in 2019, and 90 percent in 2020 and subsequent years.

The original legislation required the states to expand their Medicaid programs to cover more uninsured people or lose existing federal funding for the Medicaid program. The Supreme Court, however, struck down this provision as unconstitutional. As stated earlier, the Supreme Court ruled that overall the Affordable Care Act is constitutional. However, the Court also ruled that a state cannot be forced into expanding its Medicaid program under the Affordable Care Act, and cannot lose existing federal funding for its Medicaid program if it fails to do so. At the time of writing, however, numerous state governors have indicated they will not expand their Medicaid programs to cover the uninsured because of funding concerns and other high priority programs.

## Preexisting Condition Insurance Plan

The new law created a temporary high-risk program, which provides affordable health insurance to individuals with preexisting conditions until the Affordable Insurance Exchanges begin operating in 2014. The program is called the Preexisting Condition Insurance Plan (PCIP) and is funded entirely by the federal government. To be eligible for coverage, an applicant must (1) be a citizen or a lawful resident of the United States, (2) be uninsured for at least six months, and (3) have a preexisting condition, or have been unable to obtain health insurance because of a medical condition.

The majority of states had high-risk pools before the new law was enacted. However, the states have the option of participating in the temporary PCIP program. If a state decides not to participate, the federal government will administer the program.

### Improving Quality and Lowering Costs

The new law has numerous provisions that will improve the quality of health care and lower costs. Some important provisions are summarized as follows:

- *Rebuilding the primary care workforce.* To strengthen the availability of primary care personnel, there are new incentives to expand the number of primary care physicians, nurses, and physician assistants. These incentives include funding for scholarships and loan repayments for primary care physicians and nurses working in underserved areas. This provision became effective in 2010.

- *Preventing disease and illness.* A new Prevention and Public Health Fund will invest in proven prevention and public health programs designed to keep Americans healthy, including programs to quit smoking and combat obesity. This provision became effective in fiscal 2010.

- *Establishing a patient-centered outcomes research institute.* The new law establishes a private non-profit institute to identify national priorities and provide research that compares the effectiveness of health-care treatments and strategies.

- *Strengthening community health centers.* The new law includes funding to support the construction of community health centers and the expansion of medical services, which will enable these centers to serve some 20 million new patients across the country. This is an important provision because community health centers are often the only affordable source of medical care to low-income and uninsured individuals. This provision became effective in 2010.

- *Cracking down on health-care fraud.* The new law requires enhanced screening procedures for health-care providers to eliminate fraud and abuse in the health-care system. Many provisions on fraud prevention are now in effect.

- *Encouraging integrated health systems.* The new law provides incentives for physicians to join together to form "accountable care organizations." In these groups, doctors can better coordinate patient care and improve the quality of care, help prevent disease and illness, and reduce unnecessary hospital admissions. If an accountable care organization provides high-quality care and reduces costs to the health-care system, it can keep some of the savings, which provides a strong financial incentive to control cost. This provision is now in effect.

- *Reducing paperwork and administrative expenses.* Health care remains one of the few industries to rely on paper records. The new law institutes a number of changes to standardize billing. It also requires health plans to begin adopting rules for the secure and confidential electronic exchange of health information. Electronic health records can reduce paperwork and administrative burdens, cut costs, reduce medical errors, and improve the quality of care.

- *Increasing Medicaid payments for primary care physicians.* Medicaid programs and health-care providers will be treating more patients in 2014, which is problematic. The new law requires the states to pay primary care physicians no less than 100 percent of Medicare payment rates in 2013 and 2014 for primary care services. The increase is fully funded by the federal government and becomes effective in January 2014. This is an important provision because many physicians and other health-care providers currently do not accept new Medicaid patients because of relatively low reimbursement rates.

- *Paying physicians based on value and not volume.* A new provision links payments to physicians to the quality of care they provide. Payments to physicians will be modified so that physicians who provide higher-value medical care will receive higher payments than those who provide lower-quality care. This provision becomes effective in 2015.

### Cost and Financing

The health-care reform legislation is expensive. In 2012, the Congressional Budget Office (CBO) projected the Affordable Care Act will cost more than $1.7 trillion in gross federal spending over the period 2012–2022, which will be partly offset by penalties and tax increases related to coverage, resulting in net spending of more than $1.2 trillion.[20] Financing the new law is complex, and funding comes from several sources:

- Savings in the Medicare and Medicaid programs by reducing fraud and abuse and unnecessary tests and procedures

- Reduced payments to Medicare Advantage plans
- New annual fees on the pharmaceutical manufacturing industry and on health insurers
- New excise tax on the sale of taxable medical devices

In addition, new taxes, fees, and penalties are imposed on the following:

- As discussed earlier, individuals who fail to maintain the required insurance coverage must pay a tax penalty. This provision becomes effective in 2014.
- Beginning in 2018, a 40 percent excise tax will be imposed on insurers and plan administrators for high-cost health insurance plans with aggregate values that exceed $10,200 for individual coverage and $27,500 for family coverage. The tax applies to the amount of premium in excess of the threshold. The thresholds are indexed for 2019 and subsequent years.
- Contributions to a flexible spending account for medical expenses are limited to $2500 yearly, which is indexed by the Consumer Price Index for subsequent years. This provision becomes effective in 2013.
- Beginning in 2013, the Medicare Hospital Insurance payroll tax will be increased 0.9 percent (from 1.45 percent to 2.35 percent) on earnings over $200,000 for single persons and $250,000 for married couples filing jointly.
- There is an additional tax of 3.8 percent on net investment income for taxpayers earning over $200,000, and for married couples earning over $250,000 who file a joint return.
- The cost of over-the-counter drugs that do not require a doctor's prescription will no longer be reimbursed by a flexible spending account or health reimbursement account. This provision becomes effective in 2013.
- The tax deduction for employers who receive Medicare Part D subsidy payments for retirees is eliminated. This provision becomes effective in 2013.
- The income threshold for deducting itemized medical expenses is increased from 7.5 percent to 10 percent of adjusted gross income. However, individuals over 65 can still deduct eligible medical expenses in excess of 7.5 percent of adjusted gross income through 2016. This provision becomes effective in 2013.

- The amount paid for indoor tanning services is subject to a 10 percent tax. This provision became effective in July 2010.

In addition, the new law contains numerous provisions that apply to the Medicare program. These provisions are designed to control rising health-care expenditures, to reduce fraud and abuse, and to make Medicare less costly and more efficient. Specific provisions dealing with Medicare are discussed in Chapter 18.

# INDIVIDUAL MEDICAL EXPENSE INSURANCE

Most people under age 65 with private health insurance have coverage under employer-sponsored group plans. Group health insurance is discussed in Chapter 16. However, individual medical expense insurance is also important in providing economic security to individuals and families who are not part of any group. Many workers quit their jobs, are laid off, or retire early and need individual protection; many unemployed workers are between jobs and need individual insurance; college students attain age 26 and are no longer eligible for coverage under their parents' plans; and a high percentage of people under age 65 are not in the paid labor force and need individual protection.

**Individual medical expense insurance** *protects an individual or family for covered medical expenses because of sickness or injury.* Consumers have a choice of numerous policy options with various deductibles, coinsurance percentages, copayments, and premiums. Most individual medical expense policies sold today typically have the following characteristics:[21]

- Major medical benefits
- Broad range of benefits
- Calendar-year deductible
- Coinsurance and copayments
- Annual out-of-pocket limits
- Exclusions

## Major Medical Benefits

Most individual medical expense plans sold today provide major medical benefits. **Major medical insurance** *is a generic term for a medical expense* *plan that pays a high percentage of covered medical expenses incurred by an insured who has a catastrophic illness or injury.* The primary purpose is to relieve the insured of the crushing financial burden of a catastrophic loss. As stated earlier, lifetime dollar limits on benefits are no longer permitted. This provision applies to both existing and new major medical plans.

## Broad Range of Benefits

Most individual medical expense policies provide a broad range of benefits. Benefits typically include the following:

- *Inpatient hospital benefits.* Covered services include the cost of a semi-private room, cardiac and intensive care units, treatment rooms and equipment, nursing care, and other services. Other covered inpatient services include charges for the operating room, surgical dressings, drugs, lab tests, X-rays, and radiology services.
- *Outpatient benefits.* Coverage for outpatient services typically includes the services listed under inpatient hospital benefits; surgery as an outpatient in a hospital or separate outpatient facility; pre-admission tests given prior to admission into the hospital as an inpatient; outpatient chemotherapy and radiation therapy; outpatient services provided in an emergency room; and other services as well.
- *Physician benefits.* Medical expense plans typically cover office visits to physicians, consultation with specialists, surgeons' fees, cost of anesthesia services, and services provided by chiropractors, physician assistants, nurse practitioners, physical therapists, and other therapists.
- *Preventive services.* Medical expense plans today cover certain preventive services with no cost-sharing provisions. To encourage prompt treatment, patients are not required to meet a deductible, coinsurance, or copayment requirements. Covered preventive services include colorectal cancer screening for adults over age 50; breast cancer mammography screening; cervical cancer screening; flu shots; and a wide variety of additional services for adults, women, and children. As stated earlier, under the new Affordable Care Act, deductibles and other cost-sharing provisions do not apply to certain preventive services, such as flu shots and pap smears. All new individual and group health plans must provide first dollar coverage for certain preventive services.
- *Outpatient prescription drugs.* Outpatient prescription drug coverage is another important benefit. There are two ways to provide coverage for prescription drugs. First, under the integrated approach, charges for prescription drugs are subject to the same deductible and coinsurance charges that apply to other covered medical expenses. Second, under a separate drug card program, prescription drugs are subject to their own deductible and copayment charges. The prescription drug program is usually administered by a third party administrator, such as a benefit pharmacy manager. A three-tier or four-tier system of pricing is commonly used. For the first tier, the copayment charge is the lowest for generic drugs. For the second tier, the copayment charge is higher for brand-name drugs on an approved list (called a formulary). For the third tier, the copayment charge is even higher for brand-name drugs that are not on the formulary. Finally, for the fourth tier, some plans may include coverage for very expensive drugs. Copayments and coinsurance charges are substantially higher for drugs in this category.

## Calendar-Year Deductible

Medical expense policies contain a deductible provision that must be satisfied before any benefits are paid. Deductibles in individual policies sold today are much higher than in policies sold in previous years. Consumers have a choice of deductibles. Typical deductibles are $1000, $1500, $2500, or some higher amount. *The purpose of the deductible is to eliminate small claims and the high administrative cost of processing them.* By eliminating small claims, insurers can provide high limits and still keep the premiums reasonable.

Most individual medical expense policies have a **calendar-year deductible,** *which is an aggregate deductible that has to be satisfied only once during the calendar year.* All covered medical expenses incurred by the insured during the calendar year can be applied toward the deductible. Once the deductible is met, no additional deductible has to be satisfied during the calendar year. To avoid paying two deductibles in a short time, a plan may have a carryover provision, which means that unreimbursed medical expenses incurred during the last three months of the calendar year and applied to that year's deductible can be carried over and applied to following year's deductible.

## Coinsurance

Individual medical expense policies contain a coinsurance provision. **Coinsurance** *is the percentage of the bill in excess of the deductible, which the insured must pay out-of-pocket up to some maximum annual dollar limit.* Insureds are typically required to pay 20 percent, 25 percent, or 30 percent of most covered medical expenses in excess of the deductible. For example, assume that an insured person has covered medical expenses of $10,000, the calendar-year deductible is $1000, and the coinsurance percentage is 20 percent. In addition to the $1000 deductible, the insured pays 20 percent of the excess, or $1800 (20% x $9000). The insurer pays the remainder, or $7200.

*The coinsurance provision has two basic purposes: (1) to reduce premiums, and (2) to prevent overutilization of plan benefits.* Coinsurance has a powerful impact on reducing premiums, and the insureds are less likely to utilize unnecessary services if they pay part of the cost.

## Copayments

Individual medical expense policies typically contain copayment provisions. **Copayment** *is a flat amount that the insured must pay for certain benefits, such as $40 for a visit to a primary care physician, or a $10 copayment for a generic drug.* Copayment should not be confused with coinsurance. Copayment is a small nominal amount paid by the insured for certain services. Coinsurance is a percentage of covered medical expenses in excess of the deductible that the insured must pay up to specified annual limits.

## Annual Out-of-Pocket Limits

Medical expense policies also contain an **annual out-of-pocket limit** (also called a **stop-loss limit**) by which 100 percent of the covered medical expenses in excess of the deductible are paid after the insured pays a certain annual amount of out-of-pocket expenses. The

purpose of the annual out-of-pocket limit is to reduce the crushing financial burden of a catastrophe loss. The insured is usually given a choice of several annual out-of-pocket limits when the policy is purchased, such as $3000, $4000, or some higher amount. Out-of-pocket limits for family policies are substantially higher.

## Exclusions

All individual major medical policies contain exclusions. Some common exclusions are as follows:

- Services determined not to be medically necessary
- Expenses caused by war
- Elective cosmetic surgery
- Eyeglasses and hearing aids
- Dental care, except as a result of an accident
- Expenses covered by workers' compensation and similar laws
- Investigative or experimental medical treatment
- Services furnished by governmental agencies unless the patient has an obligation to pay
- Expenses covered by Medicare or other government medical expense programs
- Expenses resulting from suicide or self-inflicted injury
- Pregnancy and childbirth except complications of pregnancy (maternity expenses can be covered as an optional benefit with higher premiums)

Finally, under the Affordable Care Act, beginning January 1, 2014, new individual medical expense policies sold on the Affordable Insurance Exchanges must provide benefits that meet the essential health benefits requirements discussed earlier.

## INDIVIDUAL MEDICAL EXPENSE INSURANCE AND MANAGED CARE PLANS

Most individual medical expense plans sold today are managed care plans. Managed care is a generic term for medical expense plans that provide covered medical services to the members in a cost effective manner. Cost control is heavily emphasized, and the policyholder's choice of physicians and other health-care providers may be limited to physicians, hospitals, and other health-care providers that are in the plan network.

There are different types of managed care plans. The most popular plan today is a **preferred provider organization (PPO)**. A PPO is a plan that contracts with physicians, hospitals, and other health-care providers to provide covered medical services to policyholders at discounted fees. About 83 percent of the individual medical expense policies and about 73 percent of family policies are PPO plans.[22] Under a PPO, a policyholder can elect to receive care from any physician or health-care provider. However, if a preferred provider is used, the policyholder pays lower deductible and coinsurance charges. If the policyholder receives care outside the network, he or she must pay substantially higher deductible and coinsurance charges. Managed care plans are discussed in greater detail in Chapter 16.

# HEALTH SAVINGS ACCOUNTS

Federal legislation allows all eligible persons under age 65 to establish health savings accounts and receive favorable income-tax treatment. A **health savings account (HSA)** *is a tax-exempt or custodial account established exclusively for the purpose of paying qualified medical expenses of the account beneficiary who is covered under a high-deductible health insurance plan.* Health savings accounts have two components: (1) a high-deductible health insurance policy that covers catastrophic medical bills, and (2) an investment account from which the account holder can withdraw money tax-free for medical costs. These components are discussed below.

### Eligibility Requirements

To establish a qualified HSA and receive favorable tax treatment, you must meet certain requirements. First, you must be covered by a high-deductible health plan and must not be covered by any other comprehensive health plan that is not a qualified high-deductible plan. (This requirement does not apply to accident insurance, disability insurance, dental care, vision care, long-term care insurance, auto insurance, and certain other coverages.) Second, you must not be eligible for Medicare. Finally, you must not be claimed as a dependent on another person's tax return.

### High-Deductible Health Plan

The insurance is sold with a high deductible. For 2013, the *annual deductible* must be at least $1250 for an individual and $2500 for family coverage. The family deductible applies to the entire family and not to each family member. Qualified plans with higher annual deductibles are also available with reduced premiums. The deductible does not apply to preventive services, such as mammograms, pap smears, and maternity screening. The deductible is also indexed annually for inflation.

In addition, there is a maximum limit on annual *out-of-pocket expenses*. For 2013, annual out-of-pocket expenses, including the deductible and copayments, cannot exceed $6250 for an individual and $12,500 for a family. The out-of-pocket limits are adjusted annually for inflation.

HSAs may also have a *coinsurance requirement*. Although the majority of HSA plans pay 100 percent of the cost for most covered services in excess of the deductible, some policyholders prefer a lower premium plan with coinsurance, such as 20 or 30 percent.

### Contribution Limits

HSA contributions can be made by individuals, their employers, and family members. For 2013, total contributions for individual coverage cannot exceed $3250. Total contributions for family coverage cannot exceed $6450. These amounts are adjusted annually for inflation. In addition, if you are age 55 or older, you can make an additional catch-up contribution of $1000.

### Favorable Income-Tax Treatment

The HSA investment account in a qualified plan receives favorable income-tax treatment. HSA contributions are income-tax deductible up to the annual limits described above. The tax deduction is "above the line," which means you do not have to itemize deductions on your tax return to deduct the contributions. *This means you are paying premiums with before-tax dollars.* In addition, investment earnings accumulate income-tax free, and distributions from the account are tax-free if used to pay for qualified medical expenses. However, distributions prior to age 65 for nonmedical purposes are subject to an income tax and a 10 percent tax penalty.

Once you attain age 65 or are covered under Medicare, you can no longer contribute to an HSA. However, you can still use the funds to pay for qualified medical expenses. If you are age 65 or older, you can also use the funds for nonmedical purposes, but the money used is taxable income.

## Rationale for HSAs

Proponents present numerous arguments for HSAs, which include the following:

- If consumers have to pay for health care out of pocket, they will be more sensitive to health-care costs, will avoid unnecessary services, and will shop around for health care. As a result, health-care costs can be held down.
- Health insurance will be more affordable because of lower premiums, which will reduce the number of uninsured people.
- If medical bills are not incurred, money in the HSA account can be saved for retirement.
- HSAs can be used in a group health insurance plan sponsored by an employer. Because the account belongs to the individual, it is portable. Workers will still have health insurance if they change jobs or become unemployed.

Critics of HSAs, however, present the following counterarguments:

- HSA premiums are lower only because a significant part of the initial medical bill is shifted to the insured by a high deductible.
- Low income persons and many middle-income families cannot afford to pay the high annual deductible and coinsurance payments until coverage begins. The cost-sharing provisions can aggravate the fragile financial position that many of these families now face.
- The HSA tax breaks are geared toward people with higher incomes and are of limited value to low-income persons who are currently uninsured. A dollar deposited into an HSA will save 35 cents for someone in the 35 percent tax bracket but only 10 cents for a low-income person in the 10 percent tax bracket.
- HSAs are also geared toward younger and healthier individuals who may decide not to join a traditional plan. However, unhealthy persons are more likely to remain in traditional plans. As a result, the pool of unhealthy workers may increase, which could increase premiums even more for individuals and employers who have traditional plans.
- Shopping around for less expensive health care is not practical or even possible for many sick or injured persons who require immediate medical care, and reliable cost information may not be readily available. Because of high deductible and coinsurance requirements, some insureds will postpone receiving medical care that could identify and treat a serious condition in the early stages.

## LONG-TERM CARE INSURANCE

**Long-term care insurance** is a coverage that pays a daily or monthly benefit for medical or custodial care received in a nursing facility, in a hospital, or at home. The cost of long-term care in a nursing home is staggering. The majority of long-term facilities charge $90,000 to $130,000 or even more for each year of care. The Medicare program provides only limited assistance in paying for the cost of long-term care. The patient must require medical care in a skilled nursing facility, and only up to 100 days are covered. Custodial care is excluded altogether. In addition, most elderly are not initially eligible for long-term care under the Medicaid program, which is a welfare program that imposes strict eligibility requirements and has a stringent means test. As a result, some older Americans have purchased long-term care policies to meet the crushing financial burden of an extended stay in a nursing facility.

### Chance of Entering a Nursing Home

Many older Americans will spend some time in a nursing home. According to the U.S. Department of Health and Human Services, people who reach age 65 have a 40 percent chance of entering a nursing home. About 10 percent of the people who enter a nursing home will stay there five years or more.[23]

### Basic Characteristics

Most long-term care policies sold today are tax-qualified, which meet certain standards for favorable tax treatment under the Health Insurance Portability and Accountability Act (HIPAA). Nontax-qualified policies fail to meet the HIPAA standards. Both tax-qualified and nontax-qualified policies generally have the following characteristics.[24]

**Variations in Policies**　There are several variations in the types of long-term care policies sold today. These variations can be classified as follows:

- A *facility-only policy* typically covers care in a nursing home, assisted-living facility, Alzheimer's facility, or hospice as long as the insured satisfies a benefit trigger (discussed later).
- Most insurers also make *home health-care benefits* available. Home health care provides benefits for care outside of a nursing facility or other institution and includes home health care, adult day care, and respite care. Respite care is a benefit that provides occasional full-time care to an insured who is receiving home health-care services, which allows the caregiver to take a needed break.
- A *comprehensive policy* typically covers care in a nursing home, assisted living facility, or hospice, and also has optional benefits for home health care and adult day care.

**Choice of Benefits**　Consumers have a choice of daily benefits, which typically range from $50 to $300 or more for each day of care. However, the daily benefit paid for home health care may be less than the benefits paid for nursing home care. Most policies are *reimbursement policies* which reimburse the insured for actual charges up to some specified daily limit. For example, if the daily limit is $250 and actual charges are $200, the policy would pay only $200. Some policies, however, are *per diem* policies, which pay a fixed daily benefit amount regardless of the actual charges incurred. For example, if the daily limit is $300 and actual charges are $250, the policy would pay $300.

**Elimination Period**　An **elimination period** is a waiting period during which time benefits are not paid. Most policies have elimination periods ranging from zero to 180 days. Common elimination periods are 20, 30, 60, or 90 days in duration. A longer elimination period can substantially reduce premiums. However, a longer waiting period also means higher out-of-pocket expenses, which can have a substantial financial impact unless the insured has prior savings or other sources of reimbursement. Many older retirees do not have the financial resources needed to pay for the additional out-of-pocket costs for a long-term care policy with a lengthy elimination period. For example, if the elimination period is 90 days, and the daily cost is $250, the patient incurs out-of-pocket costs of $22,500. However, with a 20-day waiting period, out-of-pocket costs would be only $5000.

**Eligibility for Benefits**　Tax-qualified policies have two **benefit triggers** that determine whether the insured is chronically ill and eligible for benefits. *The insured must meet one of the two triggers to receive benefits.* The first trigger requires the insured to be unable to perform a certain number of **activities of daily living (ADLs)**. The ADLs are eating, bathing, dressing, transferring from a bed to a chair, using the toilet, and maintaining continence. Benefits are paid if the insured cannot perform a certain number of ADLs listed in the policy without assistance from another person, such as two out of the six ADLs.

The second trigger is that the insured needs substantial supervision to be protected against threats to health and safety because of a *severe cognitive impairment*. For example, benefits can be triggered if the insured has a short- or long-term memory impairment; or becomes disoriented with respect to persons, place, time, or abstract reasoning; or has errors in judgment with respect to safety awareness. For example, someone diagnosed with Alzheimer's disease would meet this trigger.

Nontax-qualified policies often have more liberal eligibility requirements and make benefits available if a *medical necessity trigger* is met. This means that benefits can be paid if a physician certifies that long-term care is needed even if the insured does not meet any of the benefit triggers described earlier. Also, nonqualified policies may have a different list of ADLs, and the insured may have to meet a smaller number of ADLs to qualify for benefits.

**Inflation Protection**　Inflation can gradually erode the real purchasing power of the daily benefit. For example, a nursing home that charges $250 per day in 2013 might charge $450 or more for each day of care in 2023. Protection against inflation is especially important if the policy is purchased at a younger age.

Insurers use different methods to provide protection against inflation. One company allows insureds to increase the daily benefit each year based on increases in the consumer price index (CPI). Evidence of insurability is not required, but premiums are increased accordingly. For example, if the daily benefit is $200, and the CPI increases 4 percent, the new daily benefit would be $208, and a higher premium is required.

Another method is to automatically increase the initial daily benefit each year at some specified rate, such as 5 percent compound interest over the life of the policy. Adding an automatic benefit increase to the policy is expensive and can increase premiums by 20 percent to 100 percent or more.

**Guaranteed Renewable Policy**   The policies sold currently are guaranteed renewable. Once issued, the policy cannot be cancelled, but rates can be increased for the underwriting class in which the insured is placed.

**Expensive Coverage**   Long-term care insurance is expensive, especially at the older ages. For example, assume that, in Nebraska, at age 40, the annual premium is $1650 for a long-term care policy with a daily benefit of $150, three-year benefit period, 90-day elimination period, and compound interest inflation protection. If purchased at age 65, the annual premium is $2761, and if purchased at age 70, it is $4411. Some insurance agents and financial planners recommend purchase of a long-term care policy at the younger ages because premiums are lower. However, many financial planners reject that recommendation because of the lengthy period of premium payments before policy benefits may be needed. For example, if an applicant purchases a policy at age 40, he or she might pay premiums for 30 or 40 years before knowing whether the policy will be needed. In addition, other important insurance needs, such as the need for adequate life insurance or disability income, should receive higher priority at the younger ages.

**Exclusions**   Long-term care policies contain exclusions, which typically include the following:

- Certain mental and nervous disorders or diseases
- Alcoholism and drug addiction
- Illnesses caused by an act of war
- Treatment paid by the government
- Attempted suicide or self-inflicted injury

**Nonforfeiture Benefits**   Most insurers offer *nonforfeiture benefits* as an optional benefit, which provides benefits if the insured lapses the policy. The most common nonforfeiture benefits are (1) a return of premium or (2) a shortened benefit period. Under a *return of premium* benefit, the policyholder receives cash, which is a percentage of the total premiums paid (excluding interest) after the policy lapses or death occurs. Under a *shortened benefit period,* coverage continues, but the benefit period or maximum dollar amount is reduced. A nonforfeiture benefit is expensive and can increase premiums by 20 percent to 100 percent.

If the insured does not purchase an optional nonforfeiture benefit, some states require that the policy include a provision called *contingent nonforfeiture benefits upon lapse,* which gives policyholders certain options if premiums rise by a specified percentage since the policy issue date. For example, if the policy is issued at age 70, and premiums rise 40 percent above the original premium, the insured has the option of decreasing the daily benefit or of converting to a paid-up policy with a shorter duration of benefits.

**Taxation of Long-Term Care Insurance**   Long-term care insurance that meets certain requirements receives favorable income-tax treatment. The coverage can be an individual or group plan. Employer-paid premiums are deductible by the employer under a group plan and are not taxable to the employee.

Annual premiums paid by an individual for either individual or group coverage are deductible as medical expenses if the premiums paid plus other unreimbursed medical expenses exceed 10 percent of the individual's adjusted gross income. However, certain annual limits apply. For 2012, the maximum annual deduction ranged from $350 for people age 40 or below to $4240 for people over age 70. These limits are indexed for inflation.

### Long-Term Care Partnership Program

Some states have long-term care partnership programs designed to reduce Medicaid expenditures by eliminating or reducing incentives of some people to rely on Medicaid to pay for long-term care. Medicaid is a state-federal welfare program that pays for covered medical expenses of applicants who can meet a stringent means test. People who purchase qualified partnership policies from private insurers must first rely on benefits from their private policies before they are eligible for Medicaid. Financial assets cannot exceed a certain amount, typically $2000. Applicants with assets above that amount must "spend down" or deplete their assets to qualify for Medicaid. To encourage people to purchase private partnership policies and rely less on Medicaid, part or all of their assets are protected from the Medicaid spend-down requirements. For example, a person who purchases a qualified partnership policy with $300,000 of total benefits would have $300,000 of assets protected if she or he exhausts all benefits and then applies for Medicaid.

# DISABILITY-INCOME INSURANCE

**Disability-income insurance** is another important form of individual health insurance. A severe disability is a major cause of economic insecurity. In cases of long-term disability, earned income is lost, medical expenses must be paid, savings are depleted, employee benefits are lost or reduced, and someone must care for a permanently disabled person. Unless you have replacement income from disability-income insurance, income from other sources, or sufficient savings, you will be exposed to great economic insecurity. Many workers seldom think about the financial consequences of a long-term disability. However, the probability of becoming disabled before age 65 is much higher than is commonly believed. According to the Social Security Administration, a 20-year-old worker has a 3 in 10 chance of becoming disabled before reaching full retirement age.[25]

The financial impact of total disability on present savings, assets, and ability to earn an income can be devastating. In particular, the loss of earned income during an extended disability can be financially very painful. *For a single male, age 40, with annual earnings of $50,000, the present value of the lost income through age 65, increased expenses, and total financial impact is almost $1 million or 20 times annual pre-disability earnings.*[26]

Disability-income insurance provides periodic income payments when the insured is unable to work because of sickness or injury. The amount of disability insurance you can buy is related to your earnings. To prevent overinsurance and to reduce moral hazard

and malingering, most insurers limit the amount of insurance sold to no more than 60 to 70 percent of your gross earnings.

## Definitions of Total Disability

The most important policy provision in a disability income policy is the meaning of "total disability." Most policies require the worker to be totally disabled to receive benefits. Total disability can be defined in terms of the following categories:

- Inability to perform the material and substantial duties of your regular occupation
- Inability to perform the material and substantial duties of your occupation, and are not engaged in any other occupation
- Inability to perform the duties of any occupation for which you are reasonably fitted by education, training, and experience
- Inability to perform the duties of any gainful occupation
- Loss-of-income test

The most liberal definition defines total disability in terms of your own occupation. Insurers use different definitions of total disability. *In one policy,* **total disability** *means that, due solely to injury or sickness, you are unable to perform the material and substantial duties of your own occupation.* An example would be a surgeon whose hand is blown off in a hunting accident. The surgeon could no longer perform surgery and would be totally disabled under this definition. Under this definition, disability benefits would still be paid even if you were working in some other occupation so long as the disability prevents you from working in your own occupation.

Because of unfavorable claim experience, most insurers today use a *modified own occupation* definition of total disability. *Because of injury or sickness, you are unable to perform the material and substantial duties of your own occupation, and are not engaged in any other occupation.* This means if you are receiving disability income benefits and go to work in an entirely different occupation, your disability benefits will be reduced accordingly.

The third definition is often referred to as the "any occupation" definition. *Because of sickness or injury you are unable to perform the material and substantial duties or your occupation, or any occupation for which you are reasonably qualified by education, training, or experience.* Under this definition, you are considered disabled if you cannot perform the duties of your own occupation or any occupation for which you are reasonably fitted by education, training, and experience. Thus, if the surgeon who lost a hand in a hunting accident could get a job as a professor in a medical school or as a research scientist, he or she would not be considered disabled because these occupations are consistent with the surgeon's training and experience.

Another definition is often used for hazardous occupations where a disability is likely to occur. *Total disability is defined as the inability to perform the duties of any gainful occupation.* The courts generally have interpreted this definition to mean that the person is totally disabled if he or she cannot work in any gainful occupation reasonably fitted by education, training, and experience.

Finally, some insurers use a loss-of-income test to determine if the insured is disabled. *You are considered disabled if your income is reduced as a result of sickness or injury.* A disability-income policy containing this definition typically pays a percentage of the maximum monthly benefit equal to the percentage of earned income that is lost. For example, assume that Karen earns $5000 monthly and has a disability-income contract with a maximum monthly benefit of $3000. If Karen's work earnings are reduced to $2500 monthly because of the disability (50 percent), the policy pays $1500 monthly (50% x $3000).

Some insurers use a two-part definition of total disability, which combines the own occupation definition with the any occupation definition. *For some initial period of disability, such as two to five years, total disability is defined in terms of your own occupation. After the initial period of disability expires, the any occupation definition of disability is applied.* For example, Dr. Myron Pudwill is a dentist who can no longer practice because of arthritis in his hands. For the first two years, he would be considered totally disabled. However, after two years, if he could work as a research scientist or as an instructor in a dental school, he would no longer be considered disabled because he is reasonably fitted for these occupations by his education and training.

Finally, the policy may also contain a definition of *presumptive disability.* A total disability is presumed to exist if the insured suffers the total and irrecoverable loss of sight in both eyes, or the total loss or use of both hands, both feet, or one hand and one foot.

## Partial Disability

Some disability-income policies also pay partial disability benefits. **Partial disability** *means that you can perform some but not all of the duties of your occupation.* Partial disability benefits are paid at a reduced rate for a limited period, such as 50 percent for 3, 6, or 12 months. Partial disability in most policies must follow a period of total disability. For example, a person may be totally disabled in an auto accident. If the person recovers and goes back to work on a part-time basis to see if recovery is complete, partial disability benefits may be payable.

## Residual Disability

Newer policies frequently include a residual disability benefit, rather than a partial disability benefit, or this provision can be added as an additional benefit. The definition of residual disability varies among insurers. *In one policy,* **residual disability** *means that you are gainfully employed and not totally disabled but, solely because of sickness or injury, your loss of income is at least 15 percent of your prior income.* This means that a pro rata disability benefit is paid to an insured whose earned income is reduced because of sickness or injury. Earned income is compared before and after the disability, and the disability benefit paid is a specified percentage of the lost income. For example, if there is a 50 percent loss of earned income because of sickness or injury, a 50 percent disability benefit is paid.

Finally, most insurers consider a loss of earned income in excess of 75 or 80 percent to be a loss of 100 percent, in which case the full monthly benefit for total disability is paid.

One major advantage of the residual disability definition is the payment of a partial benefit if the insured returns to work but earnings are reduced. For example, Jeff is a salesperson who earns $4000 monthly. He is seriously injured in an auto accident. When he returns to work, his earnings are only $3000 monthly, or a reduction of 25 percent. If his disability-income policy pays a monthly benefit of

$2000 for total disability, a residual benefit of $500 (25 percent of $2000) is paid, and his total monthly income is $3500.

## Benefit Period

The benefit period is the length of time that disability benefits are payable after the elimination period is met. The insured has a choice of benefit periods, such as 2, 5, or 10 years, or up to age 65 or 70.

Most disabilities are relatively short. The vast majority of disabilities have durations of less than two years. However, this fact does not mean that a two-year benefit period is adequate. The longer the disability lasts, the less likely the disabled person will recover. For example, 10 percent of the people who are disabled for at least 90 days will be disabled for 5 or more years.[27] Thus, because of uncertainty concerning the duration of disability, you should elect a longer benefit period—ideally, one that pays benefits to age 65 or 70.

## Elimination Period

Individual policies normally contain an elimination period (waiting period), during which time benefits are not paid. Insurers offer a range of elimination periods, such as 30, 60, 90, 180, or 360 days. The majority of policies sold today have a 90 day elimination period. Many employers have short-term disability plans or sick leave plans that provide some income during the elimination period. One disadvantage, however, is that a group disability-income benefit is not convertible into an individual policy if the worker becomes unemployed. Thus, group insurance is not a satisfactory substitute for a high-quality disability-income policy.

High-quality disability-income policies are expensive and can cost as much as 1 to 3 percent of your annual earnings. To make disability-income insurance more affordable, some insurers sell policies with initially lower rates that gradually increase with age. This approach is similar to term life insurance rates that increase as the insured gets older.

## Waiver of Premium

Most policies automatically include a **waiver-of-premium provision**. *If the insured is totally disabled for 90 days, future premiums will be waived as long as the insured remains disabled.* In addition, there may be a refund of the premiums paid during the initial 90-day period. If the insured recovers from the disability, premium payments must be resumed.

## Rehabilitation Provision

Disability-income policies typically include a rehabilitation provision. The insurer and insured may agree on a vocational rehabilitation program. To encourage rehabilitation, part or all of the disability-income benefits are paid during the training period. At the end of training, if the insured is still totally disabled, the benefits continue as before. But if the individual is fully rehabilitated and is capable of returning to work, the benefits will terminate. The costs of rehabilitation are usually paid by the company.

## Accidental Death, Dismemberment, and Loss-of-Sight Benefits

Some disability-income policies pay accidental death, dismemberment, and loss-of-sight benefits in the event of an accident. The maximum amount paid, known as the principal sum, is based on a schedule. For example, the principal sum is paid for loss of both hands or both feet or sight in both eyes.

## Optional Disability-Income Benefits

Several optional benefits can be added to a disability-income policy. They include the following:

- *Cost-of-living rider.* Under this option, the disability benefits are periodically adjusted for increases in the cost of living, usually measured by the consumer price index. Two limitations generally apply to the cost-of-living adjustment. First, the annual increase in benefits may be limited to a certain maximum percentage (such as 5 percent per year). Second, there may be a maximum limit on the overall increase in benefits (such as a 100 percent maximum increase in benefits). The rider is expensive and can increase the basic premium by 20 to 50 percent.
- *Option to purchase additional insurance.* Your income may increase, and you may need additional disability-income benefits. Under this option, the insured has the right to purchase additional disability-income benefits at specified

times in the future with no evidence of insurability. The premium is generally based on the insured's age at the time the additional benefits are purchased.

- *Social Security rider.* Social Security disability benefits are difficult to obtain because of a strict definition of disability and stringent eligibility requirements. The Social Security rider pays you an additional amount if you are turned down for Social Security disability benefits.
- *Return of premiums.* This rider refunds part or all of the premiums if the policyholder's claim experience is favorable. There are different types of riders. For example, one rider refunds part of the premiums at specified intervals, less any claims paid. The refund typically ranges from 50 percent to 80 percent of the premiums paid, minus any claims, at the end of 5 or 10 years. The option is controversial and is not recommended. Disability-income insurance is designed to provide income protection and should not be viewed as being similar to cash-value life insurance. The option is also expensive and can increase the already high cost of a policy by 25 to 100 percent.

## INDIVIDUAL HEALTH INSURANCE CONTRACTUAL PROVISIONS

All states require certain contractual provisions to appear in individual health insurance policies, while other provisions are optional. It is beyond the scope of this text to analyze all contractual provisions in detail. Instead, attention is focused on those provisions that are relevant to insurance consumers.

### Renewal Provisions

A renewal provision refers to the length of time that an individual policy can remain in force. Renewal provisions include the following:[28]

- Guaranteed renewable
- Noncancellable
- Conditionally renewable
- Nonrenewable
- Guaranteed issue

**Guaranteed Renewable**   Most individual medical expense policies and long-term care policies are guaranteed renewable. *A **guaranteed renewable policy** is one in which the insurer guarantees to renew the policy at each anniversary date. However, the insurer has the right to increase premium rates for the underwriting class in which the insured is placed.* The policy cannot be canceled, and renewal of the policy is at the insured's sole discretion.

**Noncancellable**   Under a **noncancellable policy,** *the insurer cannot change, cancel, or refuse to renew the policy as long as premiums are paid on time. In addition, the insurer cannot change the premiums or rate structure specified in the policy.* Some disability income policies are noncancellable. As such, the insurer cannot refuse to renew, and the premiums or rate structure are guaranteed. These contracts are often referred to as "noncancellable and guaranteed renewable" policies.

In contrast, most medical expense and long-term care polices do not contain the noncancellable provision. Because premiums or the rate structure specified in the policy cannot be changed, an insurer would have no protection against inflation in medical care because rates could not be increased. As such, a noncancellable provision is seldom found in medical expense and long-term care contracts.

**Conditionally Renewable**   *Under a* **conditionally renewable policy,** *the policyholder can renew the policy until a specified age; however, the insurer has the right to decline renewal under conditions specified in the contract.* For example, the insurer may refuse to renew all policies in the state with the same form number as the policyholder's policy.

**Nonrenewable**   Some policies are **nonrenewable** and expire at the end of the protection period. These policies typically provide coverage only for a limited period, and the policyholder does not have the contractual right to renew the policy. Only the insurer has the right to renew a policy for which premiums have been paid. Examples include the following: (1) group health insurance for college students that provide coverage only during the academic year, (2) short-term, temporary health insurance for workers between jobs, for workers who are waiting for their new employers' group health insurance coverage to begin, and for recently graduated college students seeking their first job, and (3) an international travel policy that provides medical expense coverage only for a specified trip.

**Guaranteed Issue**   The Affordable Care Act has several provisions that will have a significant impact on the renewal provisions discussed above. Beginning in 2014, all new medical expense plans that offer individual and group coverage must accept all individuals and employers in the state who apply for coverage. *Thus, applicants for insurance have **guaranteed issue** of coverage and renewal and cannot be turned down.* Insurers that offer individual or group coverages must continue to renew at the option of the individual or plan sponsor. However, there are certain exceptions. Insurers can refuse to renew if the policyholder fails to pay the premium, commits fraud, or makes an intentional misrepresentation of a material fact in applying for coverage. In addition, insurers can refuse renewal of group plans under certain conditions.

### Preexisting-Conditions Exclusions

Prior to enactment of the Affordable Care Act, individual medical expense health insurance policies typically contained exclusions for preexisting conditions. As stated earlier, the Affordable Care Act now prohibits the use of preexisting conditions to deny or limit coverage for claims. For children under age 19, this provision is now in effect. For adults, the ban on preexisting conditions will become effective in 2014. As a result, health insurers will no longer be able to deny coverage to applicants because of their medical history.

### Notice of 10-Day Right to Examine Policy

If you are not satisfied with a medical expense policy, you have 10 days to return the policy after receiving it. The entire premium will be refunded, and the policy will be void.

### Claims

A number of important provisions in an individual medical expense policy deal with claims. Under the *notice of claim provision,* you are required to give notice to the insurer within 20 days after a covered loss occurs or as soon as is reasonably possible. Under the *claim forms provision,* the insurer is required to send you a claim form within 15 days after notice is received. Finally, under the *proof-of-loss provision,* you must provide proof of loss to the insurer within 90 days after a covered loss occurs. If it is not reasonably possible to provide proof of loss within 90 days, your claim will not be affected if the proof is sent as soon as possible. However, in any event, you must provide proof of loss within one year unless you are legally incapable of doing so. In most medical expense policies, health-care providers, such as physicians and hospitals, typically do the paperwork and provide insurers with the necessary information and documentation on the types of care and medical services provided.

### Grace Period

A grace period is a required provision. *The **grace period** is a 31-day period after the premium due date to pay an overdue premium.* If the premium is paid after the due date but within the grace period, coverage is still in force.

### Reinstatement

A medical expense policy has a reinstatement provision. If the premium is not paid within the grace period, the policy lapses. *The **reinstatement provision** permits the insured to reinstate a lapsed policy.* If the insured pays the premium to the insurance company or agent, and an application is not required, the policy is reinstated. However, if an application for reinstatement is required, the policy is reinstated only when the insurer approves the application. If the insurer has not previously notified the insured that the application for reinstatement has been denied, the policy is then automatically reinstated on the forty-fifth day following the date of the conditional receipt. The reinstated policy is subject to a 10-day waiting period for sickness, but accidents are covered immediately.

### Time Limit on Certain Defenses

The time limit on certain defenses is a required provision and has the same effect as the incontestable clause in life insurance. *The **time limit on certain**

**defenses** *states that after the policy has been in force for two years (three years in some states), the insurer cannot void the policy or deny a claim on the basis of misstatements in the application, except for fraudulent misstatements*. Under this provision, after two years, the insurer cannot deny a claim unless it can prove the insured made a fraudulent misstatement when the policy was first issued.

As stated earlier, the Affordable Care Act prohibits insurers from rescinding coverage unless there is fraud or an individual makes an intentional misrepresentation of a material fact. This provision applies to both individual and group coverages and is now in effect. However, the insurer can still rescind the policy if you intentionally place false or incomplete information on the application The insurer can also cancel if you fail to pay your premiums on time. If your insurer intends to rescind the policy, you must be given at least 30 days' notice to appeal the decision or to find new coverage.

---

## CASE APPLICATION

Lori, age 28, is a registered nurse who earns $4000 monthly working in a hospital. She is seriously injured in an auto accident in which she is at fault and is expected to be unable to work for at least one year. She has a guaranteed renewable disability-income policy that pays $2800 monthly up to age 65 for accidents and sickness after a 90-day elimination period. A residual disability benefit is included in the policy. Lori's policy contains the following provisions:

- Total disability means: (a) your inability during the first 24 months to perform substantially all of the important duties of your occupation; and you are not working at any gainful occupation; (b) after the first 24 months that benefits are payable, it means your inability to engage in any gainful occupation.
- Gainful occupation means: Any occupation or employment for wage or profit that is reasonably consistent with your education, training, and experience.

a. If Lori is off work for one year because of the accident, indicate the extent, if any, of the insurer's obligation to pay disability benefits.

b. Assume that Lori is disabled for one year, recovers, and returns to work part-time. If she earns $2000 monthly after returning to work, indicate the extent, if any, of the insurer's obligation to pay her disability benefits.

c. Assume that after two years, Lori is unable to return to work as a full-time hospital nurse. A drug manufacturer offers her a job as a lab technician, which she accepts. Indicate the extent, if any, of the insurer's obligation to continue paying her disability benefits.

d. Following the accident, could Lori's insurer cancel her policy or increase her premiums? Explain your answer.

---

## SUMMARY

- The health-care delivery system in the United States has several major problems:

    Rising health-care expenditures

    Large number of uninsured in the population

    Uneven quality of medical care

    Waste and inefficiency

    Defects in financing health care

    Abusive insurer practices

- The Affordable Care Act extends health-care coverage to 30 million uninsured Americans, provides substantial subsidies to uninsured individuals and small business firms to make health insurance more affordable, contains provisions to lower health-care costs in the long run, and prohibits insurers from engaging in certain abusive practices. Although the full law does not become effective until January 1, 2014, many provisions to reform health care are now in effect.

- Individual medical expense insurance is a policy that covers an individual or family for covered medical expenses due to sickness or injury. Consumers have a choice of numerous policy options with various deductibles, coinsurance, copayments, and premium amounts. Policies typically sold today have the following characteristics:

    Major medical benefits

    Broad range of benefits

Deductible

Coinsurance

Copayment

Annual out-of-pocket limit

Exclusions

- A health savings account is a high-deductible medical expense plan with an investment account that receives favorable tax treatment. The contributions go into an investment account and are income-tax deductible; the investment income builds up income-tax free; and withdrawals are also income-tax free when used to pay for qualified medical expenses.

- Long-term care insurance pays a daily or monthly benefit for medical or custodial care in a nursing facility or at home.

- Disability-income policies provide for the periodic payment of income to an individual who is totally disabled. The benefits are paid after an elimination (waiting) period is satisfied. The insured generally has a choice of benefit periods. In addition, after 90 days, all premiums are waived if the insured is totally disabled.

- The definition of disability is stated in a disability-income policy. There are various definitions of total disability. A definition often found in many policies has two parts. For some initial period, such as two years, total disability is typically defined as the inability to perform all duties of the insured's own occupation. After that time, total disability is defined as the inability to perform the duties of any occupation for which the insured is reasonably fitted by education, training, and experience.

- Health insurance policies contain certain contractual provisions. Some provisions are required by state law, while others are optional.

- A renewal provision refers to the length of time that an individual medical expense policy can remain in force. Renewal provisions include the following:

Guaranteed renewable

Noncancellable

Conditionally renewable

Nonrenewable

Guaranteed issue

- Beginning in 2014, under the Affordable Care Act, all new medical expense insurance plans that offer individual and group coverage must accept all individuals and employers in the state who apply for coverage. Thus, applicants for insurance will have guaranteed issue of coverage and renewal and cannot be turned down.

## KEY CONCEPTS AND TERMS

Activities of daily living (ADLs) (314)
Affordable Care Act (303)
Annual out-of-pocket limit (stop-loss limit) (311)
Affordable Insurance Exchange (306)
Benefit triggers (314)
Calendar-year deductible (310)
Coinsurance (311)
Conditionally renewable policy (319)
Copayment (311)
Disability-income insurance (316)
Elimination period (314)
Essential health benefits (305)
Grace period (320)
Guaranteed issue (320)
Guaranteed renewable policy (319)
Health savings accounts (HSA) (312)
Individual medical expense insurance (309)
Long-term care insurance (313)
Major medical insurance (309)
Noncancellable policy (319)
Nonrenewable policy (319)
Partial disability (317)
Preexisting-conditions clause (302)
Preferred provider organization (PPO) (312)
Reinstatement provision (320)
Residual disability (317)
Time limit on certain defenses (320)
Total disability (316)
Waiver-of-premium provision (318)

## REVIEW QUESTIONS

1. Describe briefly the major health-care problems in the United States.

2. Identify the major provisions of the Affordable Care Act that will have an impact on individuals and families.

3. a. Describe the basic characteristics of individual medical insurance.
   b. Why are deductibles and coinsurance used in medical expense policies?

4. Briefly explain the major characteristics of a health savings account (HSA).

5. Briefly explain the basic characteristics of long-term care insurance.

6. a. Explain the various definitions of disability that are found in disability-income insurance.
   b. Briefly explain the following disability-income insurance provisions:
   Residual disability
   Benefit period
   Elimination period
   Waiver of premium

7. Identify the optional benefits that can be added to a disability-income policy.

8. Explain the following renewal provisions that may appear in individual health insurance policies:
   a. Guaranteed renewable
   b. Noncancellable
   c. Conditionally renewable

9. Explain the meaning of a preexisting condition.

10. Explain the time limit on certain defenses contractual provision.

## APPLICATION QUESTIONS

1. Mark, age 28, is insured under an individual medical expense policy that is part of a preferred provider organization (PPO) network. The policy has a calendar-year deductible of $1000, 75/25 percent coinsurance, and an annual out-of-pocket limit of $2000. Mark recently had outpatient arthroscopic surgery on his knee, which he injured in a skiing accident. The surgery was performed in an outpatient surgical center. Mark incurred the following medical expenses. (Assume that the charges shown are the charges approved by Mark's insurer and that all providers are in the PPO network.)

| | |
|---|---|
| Outpatient X-rays and diagnostic tests | $800 |
| Covered charges in the surgical center | $12,000 |
| Surgeon's fee | $3000 |
| Outpatient prescription drugs | $400 |
| Physical therapy expenses | $1200 |

In addition, Mark could not work for two weeks and lost $2000 in earnings.
   a. Based on the above information, how much of the expenses will be paid by the insurance company?
   b. How much of the expenses will Mark have to pay? Explain your answer.
   c. Assume that a surgeon who is not in the PPO network actually performed the surgery. Will Mark's policy cover this fee? Explain your answer.

2. Jeff currently earns $3000 per month. He has an individual disability-income policy that will pay $2000 monthly if he is totally disabled. Disability is defined in terms of the worker's own occupation. The policy has a 30-day elimination period and also provides residual disability benefits. Benefits are payable until age 65.

   a. If Jeff is severely injured in an auto accident and cannot work for four months, how much will he collect under his policy?
   b. Assume Jeff returns to work but can only work part-time until he recovers completely. If he earns $1500 monthly, what is the amount, if any, that Jeff can collect under his policy? Explain your answer.

3. Jennifer, age 28, is divorced and has a son, age one. Six months ago, Jennifer purchased an individual medical insurance policy covering the entire family. Her son was recently diagnosed with congenital heart disease. When Jennifer submitted the medical bill for her son's treatment, the insurer attempted to deny payment on the grounds that Jennifer had concealed her son's heart condition because the condition was not disclosed in the application at the time the policy was purchased. Can the insurance company legally deny payment of the claim under the Affordable Care Act? Explain your answer.

4. Brandon, age 23, recently graduated from college. He is insured as a dependent under his father's group health insurance policy, which provided coverage for him as a student until he graduated. However, he has been unable to find a job because of a soft labor market and high unemployment in the city where he lives. He is concerned that if he should become sick or injured, he will have no health insurance to pay his bills. Identify the provision in the Affordable Care Act that will enable Brandon to keep his insurance.

## INTERNET RESOURCES

- **America's Health Insurance Plans (AHIP)** is a national trade association that represents the health insurance industry and companies that provide health insurance coverage to more than 200 million Americans. The site provides considerable information on health-care issues in the United States. Visit the site at

  ahip.org

- **Disability Income Forums** is a site for people seeking disability insurance coverage, advice, or an agent to post their questions. You will receive expert answers from some of the best disability experts in the country. Visit the site at

  disabilityinsuranceforums.com

■ **eHealthInsurance.com** provides information on major medical insurance from leading insurers. It allows you to shop privately for health insurance without sales pressure. Visit the site at

ehealthinsurance.com

■ **Families USA** works to promote high-quality affordable health for all Americans. The site provides timely information on health insurance and the problems Americans face in dealing with medical bills. Visit the site at

familiesusa.org

■ **HealthCare.gov** is the official Web site of the federal government that provides detailed information on the new health-care reform law and its implementation. Click on "Understanding the New Law" for a convenient source of information concerning the provisions of the new law. Visit the site at

healthcare.gov

■ **HealthGrades** is the leading health-care ratings organization, providing ratings and profiles of hospitals, nursing homes and physicians to consumers, corporations, health plans and hospitals. Visit the site at

healthgrades.com

■ **Insure.com** provides up-to-date information, premium quotes, and other consumer information on health insurance and other insurance products. The site also provides news releases about events that affect the insurance industry. Visit the site at

insure.com

■ The **Council for Disability Awareness** provides considerable information on the risk of long-term disability, financial impact of disability, preventing disabilities, company studies on disability, and life stories by people with disabilities. Visit this interesting site at

disabilitycanhappen.org

■ The **National Association of Health Underwriters** is a professional association of health insurance professionals who sell and service medical expense, major medical, and disability-income insurance. Visit the site at

nahu.org

■ The **National Association of Insurance Commissioners (NAIC)** has a link to all state insurance departments, which provide a considerable amount of consumer

information on the health insurance coverages discussed in this chapter. Click on "States & Jurisdiction Map." For starters, check out New York, Wisconsin, and California. Visit the site at

naic.org

## SELECTED REFERENCES

AHIP, America's Health Insurance Plans, *Guide to Individual Disability Income Insurance,* Washington, DC, 2009.

AHIP, America's Health Insurance Plans, *Guide to Long-Term Care Insurance,* Washington, DC, April 30, 2012.

AHIP, America's Health Insurance Plans, *Who Buys Long-Term Care Insurance in 2010–2011?,* Washington, DC, 2012.

AHIP Center for Policy and Research, *Individual Health Insurance 2009: A Comprehensive Survey of Premiums, Availability, and Benefits,* Washington, DC.

Blue Cross and Blue Shield Association, *Healthcare Trends in America: A Reference Guide from BCBSA (2010 Edition).*

Congressional Budget Office, *Technological Change and the Growth of Health Care Spending,* Washington, DC, January 2008.

Families USA, *Decoding Your Health Insurance: The New Summary of Benefits and Coverage,* Washington, DC, May 2012.

Families USA, *Dying for Coverage: The Deadly Consequences of Being Uninsured*, Washington, DC, June 2012.

The Henry J. Kaiser Family Foundation, *Focus on Health Reform, A Guide to the Supreme Court's Affordable Care Act Decision,* July 2012.

The Henry J. Kaiser Family Foundation, *Focus on Health Reform, Summary of New Health Reform Law,* Last Modified, April 15, 2011.

The Henry J. Kaiser Family Foundation, *Health Care Costs, A Primer, Key Information on Health Care Costs and Their Impact,* May 2012.

The Henry J. Kaiser Family Foundation, *The Uninsured: A Primer, Key Facts about Americans Without Health Insurance,* October 2011.

National Association of Insurance Commissioners, *A Shopper's Guide to Long-Term Care Insurance,* Kansas City, MO, Revised 2009.

National Committee for Quality Assurance (NCQA), *Continuous Improvement and the Expansion of Quality Measurement, the State of Health Care Quality 2011*, Washington, D.C. 2011.

O'Hare, Thomas P., and Burton T. Beam, Jr., *Individual Health Insurance Planning, Medical, Disability Income, and Long-Term Care*, 2nd ed. Bryn Mawr, PA: The American College, 2010.

U.S. Bureau of the Census, *Income, Poverty, and Health Insurance Coverage in the United States: 2011*, Washington, DC, September 2012.

## NOTES

1. Centers for Medicare & Medicaid Services, *National Health Expenditure Projections 2010-2020*, Table 1.

2. David A. Squires, "Explaining High Health Care Spending in the United States: An International Comparison of Supply, Utilization, Prices, and Quality," The Commonwealth Fund, May 3, 2012.

3. Congressional Budget Office, *Technological Change and the Growth of Health Care Spending*, January 2008, p. 9.

4. Ibid., p. 1.

5. Blue Cross and Blue Shield Association, *Healthcare Trends in America, A Reference Guide from BCBS (2010 edition)*, p. 21.

6. Ibid.

7. Congressional Budget Office, Statement of Douglas W. Elmendorf, Director, "Options for Expanding Health Insurance Coverage and Controlling Costs," Testimony before the Committee on Finance, United States Senate, February 25, 2009.

8. Congressional Budget Office, *Technological Change and the Growth of Health Care Spending*, January 2008, p. 11.

9. Ibid., p. 8.

10. U.S. Bureau of the Census, *Income, Poverty, and Health Insurance Coverage in the United States: 2011*, Washington, DC, September 2012.

11. U.S Census Bureau, Current Population Survey," Table Hl06, Health Insurance Coverage Status by State for All People: 2011," *2012 Annual Social and Economic (ASEC) Supplement*.

12. Families USA, *Dying for Coverage, The Deadly Consequences of Being Uninsured*, Washington, DC, June 2012.

13. NPR/Kaiser Foundation/Harvard School of Public Health, *Summary & Chartpack*, *The Public and the Health Care Delivery System*, April 2009.

14. National Committee for Quality Assurance (NCQA), *Continuous Improvement and the Expansion of Quality Measurement, the State of Health Care Quality 2011*, Washington, D.C., 2011.

15. National Committee for Quality Assurance (NCQA), *The State of Health Care Quality, Reform, the Quality Agenda and Resource Use*, Washington, D.C., 2010.

16. House of Representatives, Committee on Energy and Commerce, "Coverage Denials for Pre-Existing Conditions in the Individual Health Insurance Market," *Memorandum*, October 12, 2010; and "Maternity Coverage in the Individual Health Insurance Market," *Memorandum*, October 12, 2010.

17. David U. Himmelstein, Deborah Thorne, Elizabeth Warren, and Steffie Woolhandler, "Medical Bankruptcy in the United States, 2007: Results of a National Study," *American Journal of Medicine* 122, no. 8 (August 2009): 741–746.

18. This section is based on "The Health Care Law & You," HealthCare.gov, and Henry J. Kaiser Family Foundation, *Focus on Health Reform, Summary of New Health Reform Law*, Last Modified, April 15, 2011.

19. Linda J. Blumberg, Matthew Buettgens, Judy Feder, "The Individual Mandate in Perspective, Timely Analysis of Immediate Health Policy Issues," Urban Institute, March 2012.

20. "Patient Protection and Affordable Care Act," *Wikipedia Free Encyclopedia*.

21. This section is based on AHIP Center for Policy and Research, *Individual Health Insurance 2009: A Comprehensive Survey of Premiums, Availability, and Benefits*, October 2009; and Thomas P. O'Hare and Burton T. Beam, Jr., *Individual Health Insurance Planning: Medical, Disability Income, and Long-Term Care*, 2nd ed. (Bryn Mawr, PA: The American College, 2010).

22. AHIP Center for Policy and Research, *Individual Health Insurance 2009: A Comprehensive Survey of Premiums, Availability, and Benefits*, October 2009.

23. "Long-term Care," Medicare.gov.

24. This section is based on National Association of Insurance Commissioners, *A Shopper's Guide to Long-Term Care Insurance*, Revised 2009; and

Thomas P. O'Hare and Burton T. Beam, Jr., *Individual Health Insurance Planning: Medical, Disability Income, and Long-Term Care*, 2nd ed. (Bryn Mawr, PA: The American College, 2010), Ch. 19.

25. "Disability Benefits," SSA Publication No. 05-10029, June 2012.

26. America's Health Insurance Plans, Press Release, "Financial Impact on Disabled Individuals Can Be Staggering, Says New Study," May 15, 2009.

27. O'Hare and Beam, *Individual Health Insurance Planning: Medical, Disability Income, and Long-Term Care*, p. 12.3.

28. Ibid., pp. 3.21–3.24.

# CHAPTER 16

# EMPLOYEE BENEFITS: GROUP LIFE AND HEALTH INSURANCE

*"Employee benefits are an extremely important part of an employee's financial security."*

Jerry S. Rosenbloom, *The Handbook of Employee Benefits*

## LEARNING OBJECTIVES

**After studying this chapter, you should be able to**

◆ Explain the underwriting principles followed in group insurance.

◆ Describe the basic characteristics of group term life insurance.

◆ Describe the major characteristics of the following managed care plans:
   Health maintenance organizations (HMOs)
   Preferred provider organizations (PPOs)
   Point of service plans (POS)

◆ Understand how the new Affordable Care Act affects group medical expense insurance.

◆ Explain the basic characteristics of consumer-directed health plans.

◆ Explain the basic characteristics of group dental insurance plans.

◆ Describe the important characteristics of group short-term and group long-term disability-income plans.

*Employee benefits play an important role in the personal risk-management programs of workers and their families. The various benefits provide considerable economic security to employees and their families. The benefits are also important in calculating total employee compensation. Employer-sponsored benefits generally can increase the total wage package by 20 percent to 40 percent. For example, Jennifer, age 24, is an English major who recently graduated from a large southern university. She interviewed for a job with a nonprofit charitable organization. The director explained to Jennifer that the charity sponsors a number of employee benefit plans, which include group life and health insurance, a 401(k) plan, and paid holidays and vacation. When added to the starting salary, the total wage package became more appealing, and Jennifer accepted the job offer.*

*This chapter is the first of two chapters dealing with employee benefit plans. In this chapter, we limit our discussion to group life insurance and group health insurance plans. Retirement plans are covered in Chapter 17. Important topics discussed in this chapter include group life insurance, group medical expense insurance, group dental insurance, group disability-income plans, and the impact of the new Affordable Care Act on group health insurance coverages. The chapter concludes with a discussion of cafeteria plans.*

## MEANING OF EMPLOYEE BENEFITS

**Employee benefits** *are employer-sponsored benefits other than wages, which enhance the economic security of individuals and families and are partly or fully paid for by employers.* These benefits include group life insurance, group medical expense and dental insurance plans, group short-term and long-term disability plans, paid holidays and vacations, paid family and medical leaves, wellness programs, employee assistance programs, educational assistance, employee discounts, and numerous other benefits. Employee benefits also include the employer contributions to Social Security and Medicare, state unemployment compensation programs, workers' compensation, and temporary disability insurance. However, it is beyond the scope of this chapter to analyze all employee benefits in detail. Instead, we focus our attention largely on group life insurance and group health insurance plans.

## FUNDAMENTALS OF GROUP INSURANCE

Group insurance is based on certain fundamentals. The following section discusses the major differences between group and individual insurance, basic group underwriting principles, and eligibility requirements for group insurance benefits.

### Differences between Group Insurance and Individual Insurance

Group insurance differs from individual insurance in several respects. *A distinct characteristic is the coverage of many persons under one contract.* A **master contract** is formed between the group policyholder and insurer for the benefit of the individual members. In most plans, the group policyholder and the insurer are the two parties to the contract. Employees are not a party to the contract. Instead, they receive a certificate of insurance that shows they are insured and the benefits provided.

*A second characteristic is that group insurance usually costs less than comparable insurance purchased individually.* Employers usually pay part or all of the cost, which reduces or eliminates premium payments by the employees. In addition, administrative and marketing expenses are reduced as a result of mass distribution methods.

*A third characteristic is that individual evidence of insurability is usually not required.* Group selection of risks is used, not individual selection. The insurer is concerned with the insurability of the group as a whole rather than with the insurability of any single member within the group.

*Finally,* **experience rating** *is used in group insurance plans.* If the group is sufficiently large, the actual loss experience of the group is a major factor in determining the premiums charged.

## Basic Underwriting Principles

Group insurers follow certain basic underwriting principles so that the loss experience of the group overall is favorable. The basic underwriting principles used in group life insurance include the following:[1]

- Insurance incidental to the group
- Flow of persons through the group
- Automatic determination of benefits
- Minimum participation requirements
- Third-party sharing of cost
- Simple and efficient administration

**Insurance Incidental to the Group**   Insurance should be incidental to the group, which means the group should not be formed for the sole purpose of obtaining insurance. The purpose of this requirement is to reduce adverse selection against the insurer. If the group is formed for the specific purpose of obtaining insurance, a disproportionate number of unhealthy persons would join the group to obtain low-cost insurance, and the loss experience would be unfavorable.

**Flow of Persons Through the Group**   Ideally, in group life insurance, there should be a flow of younger persons into the group and a flow of older persons out of the group. Without a flow of younger persons into the group, the average age of the

group will increase, and premium rates will likewise increase. Higher premiums may cause some younger and healthier members to drop out of the plan, while the older and unhealthy members will still remain, which would lead to still higher losses and increased rates.

**Automatic Determination of Benefits**   Benefits should be automatically determined by some formula that precludes individual selection of insurance amounts. The amount of group life insurance can be based on earnings, position, length of service, or some combination of these factors. *The purpose of this requirement is to reduce adverse selection against the insurer.* If individual members were permitted to select unlimited amounts of insurance, unhealthy persons would likely select larger amounts, while healthier persons would likely select smaller amounts. The result would be a disproportionate amount of insurance on the impaired lives. However, many group life insurance plans today allow employees to select their own benefit levels up to certain maximum limits. If additional amounts of insurance are desired above the maximum allowed, evidence of insurability is required.

**Minimum Participation Requirements**   A minimum percentage of the eligible employees must participate in the plan. If the plan is a **noncontributory plan**, the premiums are paid entirely by the employer and 100 percent of the eligible employees must be covered. If the plan is a **contributory plan**, the employee pays part or all of the cost and a large proportion of the eligible employees must elect to participate in the plan. In a contributory plan, it may be difficult to get 100 percent participation, so a lower percentage such as 50 to 75 percent is typically required.

There are two reasons for the minimum participation requirement. First, if a large proportion of eligible employees participate, adverse selection is reduced because the possibility of insuring a large proportion of unhealthy lives is reduced. Second, if a high proportion of eligible members participate, the expense rate per insured member or per unit of insurance can be reduced.

**Third-Party Sharing of Cost**   Ideally, individual members should not pay the entire cost of their protection. In most groups, the employer pays part of the cost.

A third-party sharing of cost avoids the problem of a substantial increase in premiums for older members. In a plan in which the members pay the entire cost, younger persons help pay for the insurance provided to older persons. Once they become aware of this fact, some younger persons may drop out of the plan and obtain their insurance at lower cost elsewhere. Older unhealthy members will still remain, causing premiums to increase even more. However, if the employer absorbs any increase in premiums because of adverse mortality experience, premiums paid by the employees can be kept fairly stable. In addition, a third-party sharing of cost makes the plan financially more attractive to individual members and encourages greater participation in the plan.

**Simple and Efficient Administration** The group plan should be simple and efficiently administered. Premiums are collected from the employees by payroll deduction, which reduces the insurer's administrative expenses and keeps participation in the plan high.

### Eligibility Requirements in Group Insurance

Insurers typically require that certain eligibility requirements must be satisfied before the insurance is in force. The eligibility requirements generally are designed to reduce adverse selection against the insurer.

**Eligible Groups** Eligible groups are determined by insurance company policy and state law. Eligible groups include individual employer groups, multiple-employer groups, labor unions, creditor-debtor groups, and miscellaneous groups, such as fraternities, sororities, and alumni groups.

Group insurers usually require the group to be a certain size before the group is insured. Traditionally, this size was 10 members, but some insurers now insure groups with as few as 2 or 3 members. There are two reasons for a minimum-size requirement. First, the insurer has some protection against insuring a group that consists largely of substandard individuals, so that the financial impact of one impaired life on the loss experience of the group is reduced. Second, certain fixed expenses must be met regardless of the size of the group. The larger the group, the broader the base over which these expenses can be spread, and the lower the expense rate per unit of insurance.

**Eligibility Requirements** Before employees can participate in a group insurance plan, they must meet certain eligibility requirements, including the following:

- Be a full-time employee
- Satisfy a probationary period
- Apply for insurance during the eligibility period
- Be actively at work when insurance becomes effective

Employers generally require the workers to be employed full-time before they can participate in the plan. A *full-time worker* is one who works the required number of hours established by the employer as a normal work week, which is at least 30 hours. However, some group plans today permit part-time workers to be covered.

Some group plans require new employees to satisfy a **probationary period**, which generally is a period of one to three months, before they can participate in the plan. The purpose is to screen out employees who work for the firm only a short time. It is costly to insure workers and maintain records where there is considerable labor turnover.

After the probationary period (if any) expires, the employee is eligible to participate in the plan. However, if the plan is contributory, the employee must request coverage either before or during the eligibility period. The **eligibility period** is a short period of time—typically 31 days—during which the employee can sign up for the insurance without furnishing evidence of insurability.

Finally, for group life insurance, employees typically must be actively at work on the day the insurance becomes effective. Some employees may be sick or injured on the date their group life insurance becomes effective. Coverage begins when the employee returns to work.

## GROUP LIFE INSURANCE PLANS

Group life insurance is a popular and relatively inexpensive employee benefit. In 2010, group insurance accounted for 42 percent of the face amount of life insurance in force in the United States.[2] Group life insurance plans include the following:

- Group term life insurance
- Group universal life insurance

- Group accidental death and dismemberment insurance (AD&D)
- Worksite marketing programs

## Group Term Life Insurance

**Group term life insurance** is the most important form of group life insurance. Most group life insurance in force today is group term life insurance.

**Basic Characteristics** Group term insurance has several basic characteristics. First, the insurance provided is *yearly renewable term insurance,* which provides low-cost protection to the employees during their working years, especially to younger employees.

Second, the amount of term insurance on an employee's life can be based on the worker's earnings, position, or it can be a flat amount for all. The amount of insurance is typically some multiple of the employee's salary or earnings, such as one to three times earnings. The term insurance remains in force as long as the employee is part of the group.

Third, if employees leave the group because of termination of employment or retirement, they can convert their term insurance to an individual cash-value policy within 31 days without evidence of insurability. As a practical matter, relatively few employees convert their group insurance because of substantially higher premiums. Those who do convert are usually substandard in health or uninsurable, which results in strong adverse selection against the insurer.

Fourth, most group plans allow a modest amount of life insurance to be written on the employee's spouse and dependent children. Because of state law and tax considerations, the amount of dependent life insurance is relatively low. The insurance on the spouse's life can be converted to an individual cash-value policy. Some states require that the conversion option also applies to insurance on the children.

In addition, some employers provide a reduced amount of term insurance on retired employees. The amount of insurance may be a flat amount, such as $10,000, or it may be a percentage of the amount of insurance at the date of retirement, such as 50 percent.

Finally, group term life insurance is used by commercial banks and other lending institutions to insure the lives of debtors. Credit life insurance provides for the cancellation of any outstanding debt if the borrower dies. The lending institution is both the policyholder and beneficiary. The unpaid balance of the loan is paid to the creditor at the debtor's death. Many financial planners do not recommend the purchase of credit life insurance because of excessive rates. Although the rates are regulated by the states, many debtors are overcharged for their protection.

**Types of Group Term Coverages** There are several types of group term insurance coverages used today:

- *Basic amount of term insurance.* Employers typically provide a basic amount of term insurance on covered employees, which is usually some multiple of salary or earnings, such as one to three times the worker's base salary. The insurance does not require evidence of insurability, and the employer pays part or all of the premiums. Premiums paid by the employer on the first $50,000 of coverage are not taxed as income to the employee.

- *Supplemental term insurance.* Group life insurance plans typically include **supplemental term insurance.** This is a voluntary coverage paid entirely by the employee. Employers offer this coverage to supplement employer-paid basic term insurance. Under a supplemental plan, covered employees can purchase additional amounts of life insurance without evidence of insurability up to certain limits to meet their personal financial needs. If the additional insurance requested exceeds these limits, the employee must provide evidence of insurability.

- *Portable term insurance.* Some group plans have a **portable term insurance** option that allows employees to continue their term insurance protection if they lose their eligibility for group coverage, such as termination of employment or retirement. Under this plan, employees can take their term coverage with them if they are no longer eligible for group insurance. Employees generally have 31 days to elect portable coverage when their group term insurance benefits are terminated. The amount of portable insurance is the same amount the employee had at the time of coverage termination, or a lesser amount. The portable coverage continues until age 70, or until age 80 at a reduced amount in some insurers.

### Group Accidental Death and Dismemberment (AD&D) Insurance

Most group life insurance plans also provide **group accidental death and dismemberment (AD&D) insurance** that pays additional benefits if the employee dies in an accident or incurs certain types of bodily injury. The AD&D benefit is some multiple of the group life insurance benefit, such as one or two times the insurance on the employee's life. The full AD&D benefit, called the *principal sum,* is paid if the employee dies in an accident. In addition, a percentage of the principal sum is paid for certain types of dismemberments, such as one-half the principal sum for the loss of a hand, foot, or eye because of accidental bodily injury.

### Group Universal Life Insurance

**Group universal life insurance** is a voluntary life insurance product paid entirely by the employee through payroll deduction. This type of insurance combines the benefits of term insurance and whole life insurance. Under one approach, there is only one plan.[3] The employee who wants term insurance pays only the mortality and expense charges for term insurance. The employee who wants to accumulate cash values must pay substantially higher premiums into a cash value account. Under a second approach, two plans are used—term insurance and universal life insurance. The employee who wants only term insurance pays into the term insurance plan. The employee who wants universal life insurance must pay higher premiums so that cash values are accumulated. The employee may be required to pay initial premiums equal to two or three times the cost of the pure insurance protection. If the employee leaves the group, he or she can keep the group universal policy in force by paying premiums directly to the insurer.

Group universal life insurance has characteristics similar to individual universal life insurance. These characteristics have already been discussed in Chapter 11, so additional treatment is not needed here.

### Worksite Marketing Programs

Many group insurers have **worksite marketing programs,** which allow an insurer to offer its insurance products to interested employees. Under this system, individual producers contact business firms, and, with the approval of the firm, conduct sales interviews on site with employees interested in purchasing individual life insurance or annuities. Depending on the insurer, employees can buy individual whole life insurance, universal life insurance, variable universal life insurance, voluntary accidental death and dismemberment insurance, fixed and variable annuities, and other insurance products as well. Premiums are paid by payroll deduction, and employees can keep their policies even if they leave the company.

## GROUP MEDICAL EXPENSE INSURANCE

**Group medical expense insurance** is an employee benefit that pays the cost of hospital care, physicians' and surgeons' fees, prescription drugs, and related medical expenses. These plans are extremely important in providing economic security to employees and their families. Most insured workers obtain their coverage through employer-sponsored medical expense plans.

Group medical expense coverage is available from several providers including the following:

- Commercial insurers
- Blue Cross and Blue Shield plans
- Managed care organizations
- Self-insured employer plans

### Commercial Insurers

Commercial life and health insurers sell both individual and group medical expense plans. Some property and casualty insurers also issue various types of health insurance. Most individuals and families insured by commercial insurers are covered under group plans. The business is highly concentrated, and a relatively small number of health insurers dominate the market. *According to a 2011 study by the American Medical Association (AMA), in 96 percent of the metropolitan markets, one insurer controlled at least 30 percent of the market for HMO and PPO coverages. In nearly half of the metropolitan areas, one insurer controlled 50 percent or more of the commercial market.*[4] As a result, the AMA believes physicians are usually at a competitive disadvantage in negotiating rates with health insurers since almost half of the physicians work in practices with fewer than five physicians.[5]

## Blue Cross and Blue Shield Plans

**Blue Cross and Blue Shield plans** are medical expense plans that cover hospital expenses, physician and surgeon fees, ancillary charges, and other medical expenses.

Blue Cross plans cover hospitalization and related expenses. The plans typically provide service benefits rather than cash benefits to the insured, and payment is made directly to the hospital rather than to the insured.

Blue Shield plans cover physicians' and surgeons' fees and related medical expenses. Most plans today include both Blue Cross and Blue Shield coverage. The joint plans offer both basic medical expense benefits and major medical insurance. Finally, like commercial insurers, Blue Cross and Blue Shield plans also sponsor managed care plans, including HMOs and PPOs.

In the majority of states, Blue Cross and Blue Shield plans are nonprofit organizations that receive favorable tax treatment and are regulated under special legislation. However, in order to raise capital and become more competitive, several Blue Cross and Blue Shield plans have converted to a for-profit status, with stockholders and a board of directors. In addition, many nonprofit plans own for-profit affiliates.

Blue Cross Blue Shield plans dominate the HMO and PPO markets, especially in certain states and metropolitan areas. *In 2010, the AMA study showed that Blue Cross and Blue Shield of Alabama had a market share of 93 percent of the PPO and HMO combined market in Alabama. In six large metropolitan service areas (Chicago, Dallas, Philadelphia, Boston, Houston, and Seattle), Blue Cross and Blue Shield plans had a market share of 39 percent to 79 percent for the combined HMO and PPO market.*[6]

## Managed Care Organizations

Managed care organizations are another source of group medical expense benefits. These organizations generally are for-profit organizations that offer managed care plans to employers. As stated earlier, managed care is a generic term for medical expense benefits that are provided to covered employees in a cost-effective manner. There is great emphasis on controlling costs, and the medical care provided by physicians is carefully monitored. Managed care is discussed in greater detail later in the chapter.

## Self-Insured Plans by Employers

Many employers self-insure part or all of the benefits provided to their employees. **Self-insurance** (also called **self-funding**) means that the employer pays part or all of the cost of providing health insurance to the employees. In 2011, 60 percent of covered workers were enrolled in plans that were partially or completely self-funded (see Exhibit 16.1).

Many self-insured plans also have stop-loss insurance in force. *Stop-loss insurance means that a commercial insurer will pay claims that exceed a certain dollar amount overall, or for a particular participant.* In addition, many employers have administrative services only (ASO) contracts with commercial insurers. *An ASO contract is a contract between the employer and commercial insurer (or other third party) in which the insurer provides administrative services only,* such as plan design, claims processing, actuarial support, and record keeping.

Employers self-insure their medical expense plans for several reasons, including the following:

- Under the Employee Retirement Income Security Act of 1974 (ERISA), self-insured plans generally are not subject to state regulation. Thus, a national employer does not have to comply with laws in 51 jurisdictions.
- Costs may be reduced or increased less rapidly because of savings in state premium taxes, commissions, and the insurer's profit.
- The employer retains part or all of the funds needed to pay claims and earns interest until the claims are paid.
- Self-insured plans are exempt from state laws that require insured plans to offer certain state-mandated benefits.

# TRADITIONAL INDEMNITY PLANS

Group medical expense plans have changed dramatically over time. Older plans generally were indemnity plans while newer ones are managed care plans. Older plans were called **indemnity plans** or **fee-for-service plans**. Physicians were paid a fee for each covered service and were reimbursed on the basis of reasonable and customary charges up to some maximum limit. Applicants had considerable

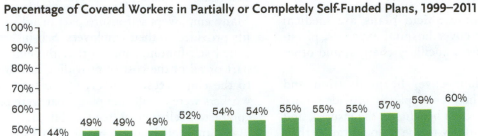

EXHIBIT 16.1
**Percentage of Covered Workers in Partially or Completely Self-Funded Plans, 1999–2011**

*Tests found no statistical difference from estimate for the previous year shown (p<.05).
No statistical tests are conducted for years prior to 1999.

SOURCE: Kaiser/HRET Survey of Employer-Sponsored Health Benefits, 1999–2011

freedom in selecting physicians and other health-care providers; the plans paid cash indemnity benefits for covered services up to certain limits; and cost containment was not heavily stressed. Physicians could bill patients for amounts in excess of the amount paid by the insurer.

Because of the rapid growth in managed care plans, traditional indemnity plans have declined in importance over time and covered only 1 percent of all covered employees in 2011. Today, managed care plans dominate both the individual and group medical expense markets.

## MANAGED CARE PLANS

The vast majority of covered employees are in managed care plans. **Managed care** is a generic name for medical expense plans that provide covered services to the members in a cost-effective manner. Under managed care plans, the employee's choice of physicians and hospitals may be limited to certain health-care providers; cost control and reduction are heavily emphasized; utilization review is done at all levels; the quality of the care provided by physicians is carefully monitored and evaluated; health-care providers may share in the financial results through

incentive payment programs that meet budgeted costs and utilization levels; and preventive care and healthy lifestyles are emphasized.

There are several types of managed care plans. The most important include the following:

- Health maintenance organizations (HMOs)
- Preferred provider organizations (PPOs)
- Point-of-service (POS) plans

### Health Maintenance Organizations (HMOs)

A **health maintenance organization (HMO)** *is an organized system of health care that provides comprehensive medical services to its members on a prepaid basis.*

**Basic Characteristics**   HMOs have a number of basic characteristics, including the following:

- *Organized health-care plan.* HMOs have the responsibility of organizing and delivering comprehensive health services to their members. HMOs negotiate rates and enter into agreements with hospitals and physicians to provide medical services, hire ancillary personnel, and have general managerial control over the various medical services provided.

- *Broad, comprehensive medical services.* HMOs provide broad, comprehensive health services to their members. Covered services typically include hospital care, surgeons' and physicians' fees, maternity care, laboratory and X-ray services, outpatient services, special-duty nursing, and numerous other medical services. Office visits to HMO physicians are also covered, either in full or at a nominal charge for each visit.

- *Restrictions on the choice of health-care providers.* Traditional HMOs typically limit the choice of physicians and other health-care providers who are part of the HMO network. However, many HMOs now allow enrollees to select physicians outside the network by paying substantially higher deductibles and coinsurance amounts. In addition, because HMOs operate in a limited geographical area, there may be limited coverage for treatment received outside of the area. Most HMOs generally provide only emergency medical treatment outside of the geographical area of the HMO.

- *Payment of fixed premiums and cost-sharing provisions.* HMO members typically pay a fixed prepaid fee (usually paid monthly) for the medical care provided. However, many HMOs also have cost-sharing provisions. In previous years, HMOs did not emphasize deductibles or coinsurance to any great extent. In recent years, however, employers have been faced with sizable premium increases. To hold down costs, many HMOs now require enrollees to meet an annual deductible. Some HMOs impose an inpatient deductible or copayment charge for a hospital stay. Employees also have copayments for certain services, such as $30 for an office visit or $10 for a generic drug.

- *Heavy emphasis on controlling cost.* HMOs place heavy emphasis on controlling costs. There are different methods for compensating physicians, hospitals, and other health-care providers to control cost. First, a common method used to pay network physicians is called a *modified fee-for-service method.*[7] HMOs typically enter into contracts with physicians, hospitals, and other health-care providers to provide covered medical services based on negotiated fees, which typically are discounted fees. Providers are free to set their own fees. However, the maximum amount paid for a covered procedure is based on a negotiated fee schedule, which lists the maximum amount paid for each covered service. Hospitals in the network generally are paid a negotiated fee for each day a plan member is hospitalized regardless of the hospital's actual cost. Second, some HMOs reimburse physicians or medical groups based on a **capitation fee**, which is a fixed annual amount for each plan member regardless of the number of medical services provided. Third, some employers, especially smaller employers, have banded together to form purchasing cooperatives to obtain more favorable prices from health-care providers. Finally, HMOs typically emphasize preventive care and healthy lifestyles, which also hold down costs in the long run.

Other techniques for holding down costs include (1) pre-certification and approval for nonemergency admission into a hospital as an inpatient; (2) certain types of surgery are performed on an outpatient basis; and (3) many HMOs require patients to obtain the approval of a gatekeeper physician to see a specialist. A **gatekeeper physician** is a primary care physician who determines whether medical care from a specialist is necessary.

### Types of HMOs

There are several types of HMOs:

- *Staff model.* Under a staff model, physicians are employees of the HMO and are paid a salary and possibly an incentive bonus to hold down costs. The HMO may own its own hospitals, laboratories, or pharmaceutical firms, or enter into contracts with other providers for such services.

- *Group model.* Under a group model, physicians are employees of another group that has a contract with the HMO to provide medical services to HMO members. The HMO may pay the group of physicians a monthly or annual capitation fee for each member. As stated earlier, a capitation fee is a fixed amount for each member regardless of the number of services provided. In return, the group agrees to provide all covered services to members during the year. The group model typically has a closed panel of physicians that requires HMO members to use physicians affiliated with the HMO.

- *Network model*. Under a network model, the HMO contracts with two or more independent group practices to provide medical services to covered members. The HMO pays a fixed monthly fee for each member to the medical group.
- *Individual practice association plan*. A final type of HMO is an **individual practice association (IPA) plan**. An IPA is an open panel of physicians who work out of their own offices and treat patients on a fee-for-service basis. However, the individual physicians agree to treat HMO members at reduced fees, either a capitation fee for each member or a reduced fee for each HMO patient treated. In addition, to encourage cost containment, IPAs could have risk-sharing agreements with the participating physicians, and payments might be reduced if the plan experience is poor. A bonus is paid if the plan experience is better than expected.

### Preferred Provider Organizations (PPOs)

Another type of managed care plan is a preferred provider organization. *A* **preferred provider organization (PPO)** *is a plan that contracts with health-care providers to provide certain medical services to the plan members at discounted fees.* To encourage patients to use PPO providers, deductibles and coinsurance charges are reduced.

PPOs should not be confused with HMOs. There are important differences between them.[8] First, PPO providers typically do not provide medical care on a prepaid basis, but are paid on a fee-for-service basis as their services are used. However, the fees charged are negotiated fees that are typically below the provider's regular fee.

Second, unlike an HMO, patients are not required to use a preferred provider but have freedom of choice every time they need care. However, the patients have a financial incentive to use a preferred provider because of lower deductible and coinsurance charges.

Third, if the health-care provider's actual charge exceeds the negotiated fee, the provider absorbs the excess amount. In such cases, savings to the patient are substantial. For example, assume that a surgeon who participates in a PPO charges a regular fee of $5000 for a knee operation. If the negotiated fee is $3000, the patient does not pay the additional $2000. The surgeon absorbs this amount.

Finally, PPOs generally do not have a gatekeeper physician, and employees do not have to get permission from a primary care physician to see a specialist. In contrast, to control costs, many HMOs require members to obtain permission from their primary care physician to see a specialist. In contrast, patients in a PPO can visit a specialist directly without first getting approval from the primary care physician.

PPOs have the major advantage of controlling health-care costs because provider fees are negotiated at a discount. PPOs also help physicians to build up their practice. Patients also benefit because they pay substantially less for their medical care.

### Point-of-Service (POS) Plans

A **point-of-service (POS) plan** is another managed care plan that combines the characteristics of both HMOs and PPOs, but members have the option to elect care outside the network. The POS plan establishes a network of preferred providers. At the time medical care is needed (point of service), a plan member has the option to elect care within the network or go outside the network. *If patients receive care from network providers, they pay substantially lower out-of-pocket expenses, which is similar to an HMO or PPO. However, if patients elect to receive care outside the network, the care is covered, but the patients must pay substantially higher deductibles and coinsurance charges.*

The POS plan has the major advantage of preserving freedom of choice for policyholders; it eliminates the fear that policyholders cannot see a physician or specialist of their choice. The major disadvantage is the substantially higher cost for care outside the network.

## KEY FEATURES OF GROUP MEDICAL EXPENSE INSURANCE

Employers have a choice of dozens of group medical expense plans with various deductibles, coinsurance percentages, copayment amounts, and premiums. New group medical expense plans sold today generally have the following features:

- *Comprehensive benefits*. Most new plans provide comprehensive benefits to covered employees with no lifetime limits and, beginning in 2014, no annual limits on benefits. Typical benefits include coverage for primary care physicians, surgeons, specialists, chiropractors, and other providers; inpatient hospital costs, outpatient diagnostic tests, outpatient surgery, emergency room fees, prescription drugs, maternity and baby benefits, mental illness and substance abuse, and numerous other benefits.

- *Calendar-year deductible.* Group plans typically have a **calendar-year deductible** that must be satisfied before benefits are paid. The deductible can be either an individual deductible or **family deductible** in which covered medical expenses of family members can be applied to the deductible. The majority of PPOs typically have calendar-year deductibles. In many PPO plans, the annual deductible is at least $1000, especially for smaller firms. However, at the present time, only a relatively small percentage of HMOs require covered employees to meet an annual deductible. According to a survey by the Kaiser Family Foundation and Health Research & Education Trust, only 29 percent of the workers enrolled in HMOs had to meet an annual deductible in 2011.[9]

- *Coinsurance requirements.* Most plans also have coinsurance requirements in which the employee must pay a certain percentage of covered expenses in excess of the annual deductible up to some maximum annual limit, such as 20, 25 percent, or 30 percent. The coinsurance percentage is substantially higher if care is received outside the network, such as 40 percent.

- *Copayments.* Most covered workers in HMOs, PPOs, and POS plans face copayments for certain expenses, such as an office visit to a primary care physician or specialist, or purchase of a prescription drug.

- *Annual limit on out-of-pocket expenses.* Most plans have **annual limits on out-of-pocket expenses**, such as $3000 for individual coverage and $6000 for family coverage. The plans specify the medical expenses that can be counted towards meeting the annual limit. Not all medical expenses can be applied to the annual limit. The majority of plans allow the deductible and coinsurance amounts to be counted. However, most plans do not count copayment charges for physician office visits, prescription drugs, and certain other charges in determining whether the annual limit has been reached.[10]

- *No cost-sharing for certain preventive services.* Certain routine and preventive services are not subject to cost-sharing provisions (deductibles, coinsurance, and copayments). If care is received from a network provider, there is 100 percent reimbursement. If care is received outside the network, the cost is subject to substantially higher deductible and coinsurance charges. Examples of preventive services include mammograms and pap smears; immunizations, such as flu shots and vaccinations for children; screening for colorectal cancer; cardiac stress tests; and hearing and vision exams.

- *Noncovered services.* All group medical expense plans have exclusions and limitations on certain services. Depending on the plan, excluded services can include services for injury or sickness arising out of and in the course of employment; services for illness or injury sustained while performing military service; services considered to be experimental or investigative; eyeglasses and hearing aids; and services, drugs, and supplies considered not to be cost effective when compared to standard alternatives.

# AFFORDABLE CARE ACT REQUIREMENTS AND GROUP MEDICAL EXPENSE INSURANCE

The Affordable Care Act will be phased in from 2010 through 2018. Many provisions that affect group medical expense plans are now in effect. Although most provisions have already been discussed in Chapter 15, certain provisions are repeated here because of their importance and direct impact on group medical expense plans. Unless otherwise noted, the provisions discussed below are now in effect:

- *Retention of coverage until age 26.* Insurers must allow young adults to remain on their parents' policies until age 26.

- *Lifetime limits and annual limits prohibited.* Insurers are prohibited from imposing lifetime limits on benefits. Beginning in 2014, annual limits on benefits are also prohibited. Prior to that time, annual limits cannot be less than the amounts determined by the secretary of Health and Human Services.

- *Preexisting conditions prohibited.* Preexisting condition exclusions or limitations are prohibited for children under age 19. For adults, the ban on preexisting conditions becomes effective on January 1, 2014.
- *Small employer tax credits.* Tax credits are available to small employers that have fewer than 25 full-time equivalent employees and pay average annual wages of less than $50,000. A tax credit of up to 35 percent of the employer's contribution is available if the employer contributes at least 50 percent of total premium costs. In 2014, the tax credit will increase up to 50 percent.
- *No cost sharing for certain preventive services.* As stated earlier, certain routine and preventive services are not subject to cost-sharing provisions.
- *Required minimum medical loss ratio.* Insurers must meet a minimum medical loss ratio of 85 percent for plans in the large group market and 80 percent for plans in the individual and small group markets. Rebates must be paid to enrollees if the loss ratios are not met.
- *Grandfathered plans.* Grandfathered plans are individual plans and employer-sponsored group plans that existed on March 23, 2010 and have not made any prohibited changes. Grandfathered plans generally can remain the same and are subject only to certain provisions of the Affordable Care Act. These provisions have already been discussed in Chapter 15, and additional treatment is not needed here.
- *Flexible spending account limits.* Contributions to a flexible spending account for unreimbursed medical expenses, such as deductibles, coinsurance, copayments, and certain other expenses, are limited to $2500 yearly (indexed for inflation).
- *Out-of-network claim payments for emergency room visits.* Claim payments for emergency room visits outside the network must be the same payment amount as the amount paid for a visit to an emergency room inside the network. A requirement for prior approval of a visit to an emergency room is prohibited.
- *Uniform coverage documents.* Health plans must describe the coverage in a uniform format and give it to participants upon enrollment and renewal. The document cannot exceed four pages and must include definitions and examples.
- *Employer W-2 reporting obligations.* Employers must disclose the aggregate value of plan benefits on W-2 forms to employees. The amount reported is not taxable to the employee but is designed to be informational and provide greater transparency on the cost of health care.

The full law generally becomes operational on January 1, 2014. Provisions that will affect group medical expense plans at that time and later include the following:

- *Guaranteed issue.* Applicants for insurance have guaranteed issue and availability of coverage and cannot be turned down or rated up regardless of their health and medical condition.
- *Individual mandate.* Most Americans must have health insurance that meets certain minimum standards or pay a financial penalty.
- *Affordable Insurance Exchanges.* Individuals and small employers can purchase medical expense policies and apply for premium subsidies through state-based insurance exchanges. When fully operational, the new law extends health insurance coverage to an additional 30 million uninsured people in the United States. As a result, the devastating financial consequences of being uninsured over an extended period will be dramatically reduced. Insight 16.1 discusses in greater detail the financial implications of the lack of coverage by the uninsured.
- *Employer requirements.* If an employer with at least 50 full-time equivalent employees does not offer minimum essential coverage to full-time employees and dependents, and has at least one employee receiving a tax credit or cost-sharing reduction to help pay for insurance through an exchange, the employer must pay a penalty. The fine is $2000 for each full-time employee (excluding the first 30 employees).
- *Tax on high-value policies.* In 2018, a 40 percent excise tax will be levied on insurers and plan administrators for high-cost health insurance plans with aggregate values that exceed $10,200 for individual coverage and $27,500 for family coverage. The tax applies to the amount of premium in excess of the threshold.

## INSIGHT 16.1

## What Are the Financial Implications of Lack of Coverage?

For many of the uninsured, the costs of health insurance and medical care are weighed against equally essential needs. When the uninsured do receive health care, they may be charged for the full cost of that care, which can strain family finances and lead to medical debt. The uninsured are more likely to report problems with high medical bills than those with insurance. Low-income individuals, who comprise a large share of the uninsured, were three times as likely as those with higher incomes to report having difficulty paying basic monthly expenses such as rent, food, and utilities.[a]

- *Most of the uninsured do not receive health services for free or at reduced charge.* Hospitals frequently charge uninsured patients two to four times what health insurers and public programs actually pay for hospital services.[b] Slightly less than half of the uninsured know of a provider in their community who charges less to patients without insurance.[c] More than half of uninsured adults paid full price for their usual source of care, with 82% of uninsured adults who used any medical services in the previous year paying some amount out-of-pocket for health care.[d]

- *The uninsured are increasingly paying "up front" before services will be rendered.* When the uninsured are unable to pay the full medical bill in cash at the time of service, they can sometimes negotiate a payment schedule with a provider, pay with credit cards (typically with high interest rates), or can be turned away.[e]

- *The uninsured spend less than half of what the insured spend on health care, but pay for a larger portion of their care out-of-pocket.* In 2008, the average person who was uninsured for a full-year incurred $1686 in total health care costs compared to $4463 for the nonelderly with coverage.[f] The uninsured pay for about a third of this care out-of-pocket, totaling $30 billion in 2008. This included the health-care costs for those uninsured all year and the costs incurred during the months the part-year uninsured have no health coverage.

- *Being uninsured leaves individuals at an increased risk of amassing unaffordable medical bills.* Uninsured adults are three times as likely as the insured to have been unable to pay for basic necessities such as housing or food due to medical bills. Medical bills may also force uninsured adults to exhaust their savings. In 2010, 27% of uninsured adults used up all or most of their savings paying medical bills.

- *Most of the uninsured have few, if any, savings and assets they can easily use to pay health care costs.* Half of uninsured households had $600 or less in total assets (not including their house and cars) in 2004, compared to median assets of $5500 for insured households.[g] Moreover, after households' debts are subtracted from assets, the median net worth of uninsured households drops to zero—leaving many of the uninsured with no financial reserves to pay unexpected medical bills.

- *Unprotected from medical costs and with few assets, the uninsured are at risk of being unable to pay off medical debt.* Like any bill, when medical bills are not paid or paid off too slowly, they are turned over to a collection agency, and a person's ability to get further credit is significantly limited. In 2010, one-third of uninsured adults reported that a collection agency contacted them about unpaid medical bills in the previous year.

[a]Collins et al., 2011, "Help on the Horizon: How the Recession Had Left Millions of Workers Without Health Insurance, and How Health Reform Will Bring Relief" The Commonwealth Fund. Available at: http://www.commonwealthfund.org/Surveys/2011/Mar/2010-Biennial-Health-Insurance-Survey.aspx

[b]Anderson G. 2007. "From 'Soak The Rich' To 'Soak The Poor': Recent Trends In Hospital Pricing." *Health Affairs* 26(4): 780–789.

[c]Cunningham P., Hadley J., Kenney G., and Davidoff A. 2007. "Identifying Affordable Sources of Medical Care among Uninsured Persons." *Health Services Research* 42(1p1), 265–285.

[d]Carrier E., Yee T., and Garfield R. 2011. "The Uninsured and Their Health Care Needs: How Have They Changed Since the Recession?" Kaiser Commission on Medicaid and the Uninsured. (Forthcoming)

[e]Asplin B., et al., 2005. "Insurance Status and Access to Urgent Ambulatory Care Follow-up Appointments." *JAMA* 294(10): 1248–54.

[f]Hadley J., Holahan J., Coughlin T., and Miller D. 2008. "Covering the Uninsured in 2008: Current Costs, Sources of Payment, and Incremental Costs." *Health Affairs* 27(5): w399–415.

[g]Jacobs P. and Claxton G. 2008 "Comparing the Assets of Uninsured Households to Cost Sharing Under High Deductible Health Plans," *Health Affairs* 27(3): w214–21 (published online April 15, 2008).

SOURCE: Adapted from The Henry J. Kaiser Family Foundation, *The Uninsured: A Primer, Key Facts about Americans Without Health Insurance*, October 2011, pp. 14–15.

## CONSUMER-DIRECTED HEALTH PLANS

Consumer-directed health plans are becoming increasingly popular with both employers and employees in the group medical expense market. *A* **consumer-directed health plan (CDHP)** *is a generic term for a plan that combines a high-deductible health plan with a health savings account (HSA) or health reimbursement arrangement (HRA).*These plans are designed to make employees more sensitive to health-care costs, to provide a financial incentive to avoid unnecessary care, and to seek out low-cost providers.

### High-Deductible Health Plans

A **high-deductible health plan** is a medical expense plan with an annual deductible that is substantially higher than deductibles in traditional medical expense plans and generally ranges from at least $1200 to $5000 or some higher amount. A high-deductible plan that meets certain federal requirements for a qualified health savings account (HSA) is called an *HSA-qualified high-deductible health plan (HDHP)*. To receive favorable tax treatment, the account holder must meet the following requirements: (1) be covered under a qualified high-deductible plan, (2) have no other first-dollar medical coverage (certain exceptions apply), (3) not be enrolled in Medicare, and (4) not claimed as a dependent on another person's tax return.

In addition, the high-deductible plan must meet certain requirements. Dollar amounts are indexed for inflation. For 2013, the minimum annual deductible must be at least $1250 for individual coverage and $2500 for family coverage. The employer, employee, or both can contribute to the HSA account; however, HSA contributions cannot exceed $3250 for individual coverage and $6450 for family coverage.

The plan may also contain a coinsurance requirement. Many high-deductible plans pay 100 percent of covered medical expenses in excess of the deductible. However, other high-deductible plans have a coinsurance requirement that applies to covered charges in excess of the deductible. The coinsurance percentage is typically 20 or 30 percent of covered expenses in excess of the deductible up to some maximum annual out-of-pocket limit. The coinsurance percentage is significantly higher if care is received outside the network. Certain basic preventive services, however, are not subject to cost-sharing provisions. For 2013, maximum out-of-pocket expenses (deductible, copayments, other amounts, but not premiums) cannot exceed $6250 for individual coverage and $12,500 for family coverage.

A qualified HSA plan has substantial tax advantages. Employer contributions to an HSA are not taxable as income to the employees; employee contributions are made with before-tax dollars; investment earnings accumulate income-tax free; and distributions from the HSA account are free from taxation if used to pay for qualified medical expenses.

### Health Reimbursement Arrangements

A high-deductible plan can also be combined with a health reimbursement account. *A* **health reimbursement arrangement (HRA)** *is an employer-funded plan with favorable tax advantages, which reimburse employees for medical expenses not covered by the employer's standard insurance plan.* HRAs are 100 percent employer-funded and controlled. The employer specifies the out-of-pocket expenses that are covered. For example, an HRA can reimburse covered employees for deductibles, coinsurance, copayments, and services not covered under the employer's plan. The employer receives a tax deduction for the amounts contributed, and the contributions are not taxable as income to the employees. Amounts in the employee's account at the end of the year can be rolled over to the next year.

## RECENT DEVELOPMENTS IN EMPLOYER-SPONSORED HEALTH PLANS

Most of the recent developments in employer-sponsored health plans focus on holding down rising health-care costs to employers. These developments include the following:

- *Continued escalation in health insurance premiums.* Group health insurance premiums continue to rise. In 2011, average annual premiums for employer-sponsored health plans reached $5429 for single coverage and $15,073 for family coverage (see Exhibit 16.2). The rise in premiums has substantially exceeded the growth in workers' wages and general inflation.

As a result, the financial burden of rising premiums on workers has been increasingly painful.

- *Higher deductibles for employees.* In response to rising costs, employers continue to shift costs to their employees by higher cost-sharing provisions. In addition to higher premiums, a growing number of employees face significantly higher annual deductibles in their employers' plans. In 2011, the average annual deductible for single coverage was $675 for workers in PPOs, $911 for workers in HMOs, $928 for workers in POS plans, and $1908 for workers in high-deductible health plans with a savings option. *Overall, for single coverage, almost one in three covered workers now face annual deductibles of $1000 or more. At smaller firms, half of the workers face annual deductibles of $1000 or more, while one* in four covered workers have annual deductibles of $2000 or more.[11]

- *Dominance of PPOs.* Preferred provider organizations continue to dominate group health insurance markets. In 2011, 55 percent of covered workers were enrolled in PPOs (see Exhibit 16.3).

- *Continued growth of high-deductible health plans with a savings option (HDHP-SO).* In 2011, 17 percent of covered workers in employer-sponsored health plans were enrolled in HDHP-SO plans, up sharply from 4 percent in 2006. (See Exhibit 16.3.) These plans have a deductible of at least $1000 for single coverage and $2000 for family coverage. High-deductible plans combined with a Health Reimbursement Arrangement (HRA) are referred to as HDHP/HRA plans. These plans are appealing to both

**Exhibit 16.2**

**Average Annual Premiums for Single and Family Coverage, 1999–2011**

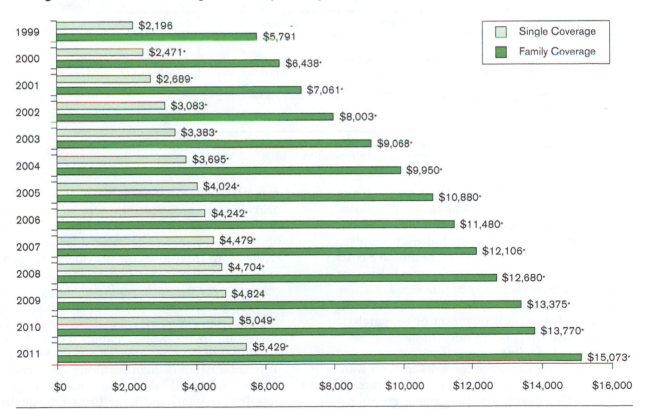

*Estimate is statistically different from estimate for the previous year shown (p<.05).

SOURCE: Kaiser/HRET Survey of Employer-Sponsored Health Benefits, 1999–2011.

**EXHIBIT 16.3**

**Distribution of Health Plan Enrollment for Covered Workers, by Plan Type, 1988–2011**

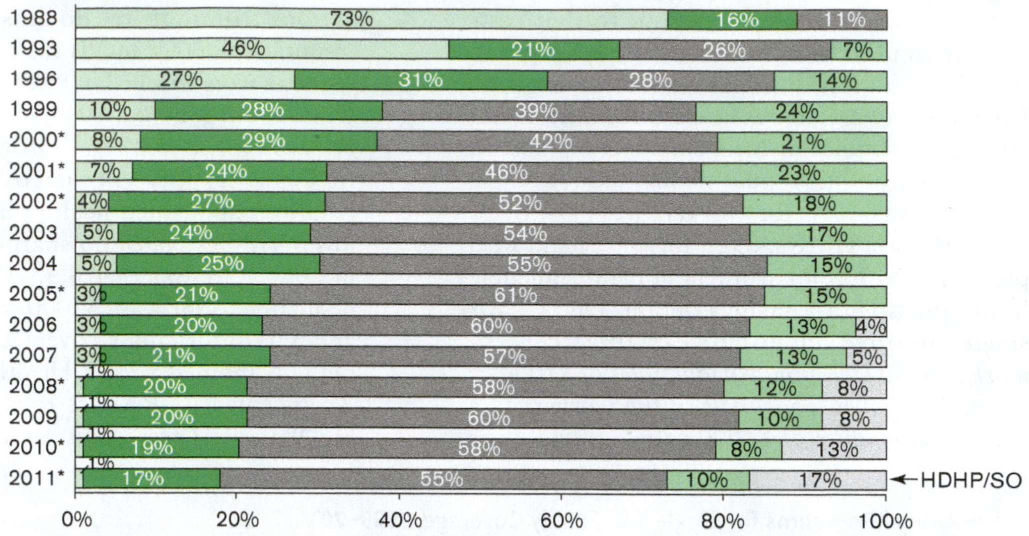

*Distribution is statistically different from the previous year shown (p<.05).
No statistical tests were conducted for years prior to 1999. No statistical tests were conducted for 2005 and 2006 due to the addition of HDHP/SO as a new plan type in 2006.

Note: Information was not obtained for POS plans in 1988. A portion of the change in plan type enrollment for 2005 is likely attributable to incorporating more recent Census Bureau estimates of the number of state and local government workers and removing federal workers from the weights. See the Survey Design and Methods section from the 2005 Kaiser/HRET Survey of Employer-Sponsored Health Benefits for additional information.

SOURCE: Kaiser/HRET Survey of Employer-Sponsored Health Benefits, 1999–2011; KPMG Survey of Employer-Sponsored Health Benefits, 1993, 1996; The Health Insurance Association of America (HIAA), 1988.

employers and employees. Employers have an effective tool for controlling health-care costs, and employees pay lower premiums. There is also some evidence that high-deductible plans are effective in holding down health-care costs for employers. However, some critics believe the quality of health care may be threatened. Because of a high deductible, some employees may postpone needed medical treatment or the purchase of life-enhancing prescription drugs.

- *Continued decline in medical coverage for early retirees.* Coverage for workers who want to retire early is becoming increasingly rare. *In 2011, only 24 percent of large employers offered health insurance coverage to retirees under age 65, down sharply from 46 percent in 1993.*[12]
- *Tiered or high-performance networks.* To hold down cost, some plans have established tiered or

high-performance networks in which health-care providers are grouped into tiers based on the quality and cost of medical care provided. The objective is to encourage covered employees to receive care from low-cost providers that provide high-quality care. *This is done either by restricting the network to efficient providers or by having different copayment or coinsurance charges for different tiers in the network.* According to the Kaiser Family Foundation, 20 percent of the firms offering coverage in 2011 included a tiered or high-performance provider network in their health plans with the largest enrollment. Small and large firms are equally likely to have a plan that includes a tiered or high performance network.[13]

- *Tiered pricing for prescription drugs.* To hold down increases in prescription drug costs, many employers have also adopted a tiered pricing system for prescription drugs. The vast majority of employees now face a three-tier or four-tier pricing system for prescription drugs. Copayment charges vary depending on the drug used. In 2011, the average copayment for first-tier drugs (generic drugs) was $10. For second-tier drugs (brand-name drugs listed on a formulary), the average copayment was $29; for third-tier drugs (brand-name drugs not on the formulary), the average copayment was $49; and for fourth-tier drugs (special-ity drugs), the average copayment was $91.[14] Fourth-tier drugs generally are costly biological agents and drugs.

- *Wellness benefits.* Many employers have designed voluntary wellness programs for their employees. These include weight-loss programs, gym membership discounts, onsite exercise facilities, smoking cessation programs, nutrition programs, newsletters, Web sites that encourage healthy living, and similar programs. Many large employers provide financial incentives to their employees to encourage them to participate in health management or wellness programs. Beginning in 2014, the Affordable Care Act allows employers to give a wellness discount of up to 30 percent of the premiums paid by an employee.

- *Health risk assessments.* Large employers increasingly are using health risk assessments to learn about their employees' health habits. A *health risk assessment (HRA)* is an evaluation of the employee's health status based on information provided by the employee, such as health history and current medical condition. HRAs identify employees who might benefit from disease management programs, such as counselling and preventive services for asthma, diabetes, heart disease, and other diseases.

- *Onsite health clinics.* Many large employers (1000 employees or more) have onsite health clinics for employees at one or more locations. Employees can receive treatment for nonoccupational diseases or injury at these locations. Employers with onsite facilities believe it is less expensive to provide onsite coverage for routine medical expenses rather than through traditional health-care channels.

## GROUP MEDICAL EXPENSE CONTRACTUAL PROVISIONS

Group medical expense insurance plans contain numerous contractual provisions that can have a significant financial impact on the insured. Three important provisions deal with (1) preexisting conditions, (2) coordination of benefits, and (3) continuation of group health insurance.

### Preexisting Conditions

In 1996, Congress enacted the **Health Insurance Portability and Accountability Act** (**HIPAA**), which placed restrictions on the right of insurers and employers to deny or limit coverage for preexisting conditions. Under HIPAA, employer-sponsored group health insurance plans could not exclude or limit coverage for a preexisting condition for more than 12 months (18 months for late enrollees). A **preexisting condition** *was defined as a medical condition diagnosed or treated during the previous six months.* After the initial 12-month period expired, no new preexisting condition period could be imposed on workers who maintained continuous coverage with no more than a 63-day gap in coverage, even if the workers changed jobs or health-care plans.

In addition, insurers and employers had to give credit for previous coverage of less than 12 months with respect to any preexisting condition exclusion found in the new health plan. For example, a worker with a pre-existing condition who was previously insured for eight months under a group plan when he or she changed jobs would face an additional exclusion of only four months, rather than the normal 12 months.

The Affordable Care Act substantially changed the preexisting conditions under HIPAA just discussed. They include the following:

- Individual policies and job-based health insurance plans cannot exclude coverage for preexisting conditions or disabilities in children under age 19. This provision is now in effect and has a major beneficial impact on dependents under age 19 who are disabled or have a preexisting condition when the employee changes jobs.

- Beginning in 2014, insurers are prohibited from denying or limiting coverage for preexisting conditions to adults as well. Prior to 2014, adults with preexisting conditions, such as cancer or heart disease, have some protection under the HIPAA provisions just discussed.

## Coordination of Benefits

Group medical insurance plans typically contain a **coordination-of-benefits provision**, which specifies the order of payment when an insured is covered under two or more group health insurance plans. Total recovery under all plans is limited to 100 percent of covered expenses. The purpose is to prevent overinsurance and duplication of benefits if an insured is covered by more than one health plan.

The coordination-of-benefit provisions in most group plans are based on rules developed by the National Association of Insurance Commissioners (NAIC). These rules are complex and are beyond the scope of this text to discuss in detail. The following summarizes the major provisions based on the NAIC rules.

- *Coverage as an employee is usually primary to coverage as a dependent.* For example, Karen and Chris Swift both work, and each is insured as a dependent under the other's group medical insurance plan. If Karen incurs covered medical expenses, her plan pays first. She then submits any unreimbursed expenses (such as the deductible and coinsurance payments) to Chris's insurer for payment. No more than 100 percent of the eligible medical expenses are paid under both plans.
- With respect to dependent children, if the parents are married or are not separated, *the plan of the parent whose birthday occurs first during the year is primary; the plan of the parent with the later birthday is secondary.* For example, if Karen's birthday is in January and Chris's birthday is in July, Karen's plan would pay first if their son is hospitalized. Chris's plan would be secondary.
- If the parents of dependent children are not married, or are separated (regardless of whether they have ever been married), or are divorced, and there is no court decree specifying who is responsible for the child's health-care expenses, the following rules apply:
  - The plan of the parent who is awarded custody pays first.
  - The plan of the step-parent who is the spouse of the parent awarded custody pays second.
  - The plan of the parent without custody pays third.
  - The plan of the step-parent who is the spouse of the parent without custody pays last.

## Continuation of Group Medical Expense Insurance

Employees often quit their jobs, are laid off, or are fired. If a qualifying event occurs that results in a loss of coverage, employees and covered dependents can elect to remain in the employer's group health insurance plan for a limited period under the Consolidated Omnibus Budget Reconciliation Act of 1985 (also known as COBRA). The **COBRA law** applies to firms with 20 or more employees. *A qualifying event includes termination of employment for any reason (except gross misconduct), divorce or legal separation, death of the employee, and attainment of a maximum age by dependent children.* If the worker loses his or her job or no longer works the required number of hours, the terminated worker and his or her covered dependents can elect to remain in the employer's plan for as long as 18 months. If the worker dies or is divorced or legally separated or has a child who is no longer eligible for coverage, covered dependents have the right to remain in the group plan for up to three years. Workers and dependents who elect to remain in the employer's plan under COBRA are required to pay 102 percent of the group insurance rate.

# GROUP DENTAL INSURANCE

**Group dental insurance** helps pay the cost of normal dental care and also covers damage to teeth from an accident. Dental insurance has the principal advantage of helping employees meet the costs of regular dental care. It also encourages insureds to see their dentists on a regular basis, thereby preventing or detecting dental problems before they become serious.

## Benefits

Employers have a choice of dental plans with various benefits, deductibles, and coinsurance requirements. Group dental insurance plans typically cover a wide variety of dental services, including X-rays, cleaning, fillings, extractions, inlays, bridgework and dentures, oral surgery, root canals, and orthodontia. In some plans, orthodontia benefits are excluded. A small number of plans are indemnity plans (also called fee-for-service plans). Dentists are reimbursed on the basis of their reasonable and customary charges subject to any limitations on benefits stated in the plan. However, the majority of dental plans today are managed care plans, such PPO dental plans or HMO dental plans. In particular, PPO dental plans are becoming increasingly popular with both employers and employees. Under these plans, dentists are reimbursed for covered services based on negotiated fees.

### Calendar-Year Deductible

A covered employee must satisfy an individual deductible each calendar year. If the employee elects family coverage, a family deductible must be met. However, the plan may permit family members to combine their covered expenses to meet the required deductible amount. To promote loss prevention and encourage routine dental care, the deductible may not apply to certain diagnostic and preventive services, such as two oral examinations each year, teeth cleaning and dental X-rays.

### Coinsurance

After the calendar deductible is met, the employee must meet a coinsurance requirement and pay a certain percentage of charges in excess of the deductible. Dental services are typically grouped into different levels, with varying coinsurance requirements. To encourage regular visits to a dentist, some plans do not impose any coinsurance requirement for one or two routine dental examinations each year. However, fillings and oral surgery may be paid only at a rate of 80 percent, while the cost of orthodontia or dentures may be paid at a lower rate of 50 percent.

The following is an example of the classification of benefits and the reimbursement levels:[15]

- Type I. Diagnostic and preventive services: 100 percent
- Type II. Basic services, including anaesthesia and basic restoration: 75 percent
- Type III. Major restoration, including endodontic, oral surgery, periodontics, and prosthodontics: 50 percent
- Type IV. Orthodontics: 50 percent

### Calendar-Year Maximum Benefits

In addition to deductibles and coinsurance, most plans have a maximum limit on benefits paid during the calendar year, such as $1000, or $2000. After maximum benefits are paid, additional dental services are not covered for the remainder of the calendar year.

### Noncovered Services

To control costs, certain dental services are not covered. Excluded services may include services provided primarily for cosmetic purposes; services considered to be investigative or not medically necessary; injectable drugs or drugs dispensed in a provider's office; services provided with respect to congenital malformations (e.g., missing teeth); and replacement of third molars with prostheses.

### Predetermination-of-Benefits Provision

A *predetermination-of-benefits provision* is also used to control costs. Although this provision is usually not mandatory, it provides useful information to both the dentist and patient on the amount that will be paid. Under this provision, if the cost of dental treatment exceeds a certain amount, such as $300, the dentist submits a plan of treatment to the insurer. The insurer reviews the treatment plan and determines the amount that will be paid. The employee is informed of the cost then makes a decision on whether to proceed with the proposed plan.

## GROUP DISABILITY-INCOME INSURANCE

**Group disability-income insurance** pays weekly or monthly cash payments to employees who are disabled from accidents or illness. There are two basic types of plans: (1) short-term plans and (2) long-term plans.

### Short-Term Plans

Many employers have short-term plans that pay disability benefits for relatively short periods that generally range from 13 weeks to 52 weeks. The majority of short-term plans pay benefits for a maximum period of 13 or 26 weeks. In addition, most plans have a short elimination period of one to seven days for sickness, while accidents are typically covered from the first day of disability. Some plans have elimination periods that apply to both accidents and sickness.

A few plans have no elimination period, especially if the employee is hospitalized. The elimination period reduces nuisance claims, holds down costs, and discourages malingering and excessive absenteeism.

Most short-term plans cover only **nonoccupational disability,** which means that an accident or illness must occur off the job. *Disability is usually defined in terms of the worker's own occupation. You are considered totally disabled if you are unable to perform each and every duty of your regular occupation.* Short-term plans generally do not cover partial disability; you must be totally disabled to qualify. However, a few plans provide partial disability benefits to participants.

The amount of disability-income benefits is related to the worker's normal earnings and is typically equal to some percentage of weekly earnings, such as 50 to 70 percent. Thus, if Amy's weekly earnings are $600 and the plan replaces 70 percent of earnings, she would collect a maximum weekly benefit of $420 if she becomes disabled.

### Long-Term Plans

Many employers also have long-term plans that pay benefits for longer periods, typically ranging from two years to age 65. However, if the disability occurs beyond age 65, benefits are paid for a limited period. For example, under the plan of one disability insurer, if the worker is younger than 60 at the time of disability, the maximum benefit period is to age 65. However, if a worker age 66 becomes disabled, the maximum benefit period is only 21 months.

A dual definition of disability is typically used to determine whether a worker is totally disabled. *For the first two years, you are considered disabled if you are unable to perform all of the material duties of your own occupation. After two years, you are still considered disabled if you are unable to work in any occupation for which you are reasonably fitted by education, training, and experience.* In addition, in contrast to short-term plans, long-term plans typically cover both occupational and nonoccupational disability.

The disability-income benefits are usually paid monthly and the maximum monthly benefits are substantially higher than the benefits paid by short-term plans. The maximum monthly benefit is generally limited to 50 to 70 percent of the employee's normal earnings. Most plans commonly pay maximum monthly benefits of $2000, $3000, $4000, or some higher amount. A waiting period of three months or six months is typically required before the benefits are payable.

To reduce malingering and moral hazard, other disability-income benefits are taken into consideration. If the disabled worker is also receiving Social Security or workers compensation benefits, the long-term disability benefit is reduced accordingly. However, many plans limit the reduction only to the amount of the initial Social Security disability benefit. Thus, if Social Security disability benefits are increased because of increases in the cost of living, the long-term disability-income benefit is not reduced further.

Some long-term plans have additional supplemental benefits. Under the *cost-of-living adjustment,* benefits paid to disabled employees are adjusted annually for increases in the cost of living. However, there may be a maximum limit on the percentage increase in benefits.

Under the *pension accrual benefit,* the plan makes a pension contribution so that the disabled employee's pension benefit remains intact. For example, if both Carlos and his employer contribute 6 percent of his salary into a retirement plan, and Carlos becomes disabled, the plan would pay an amount equal to 12 percent of his monthly salary into the company's retirement plan for as long as he remains disabled. Thus, Carlos would still receive retirement benefits at the normal retirement age.

Finally, if the disabled worker dies, the plan may pay monthly *survivor income benefits* to an eligible surviving spouse or children for a limited period—such as two years—following the disabled worker's death.

## CAFETERIA PLANS

The final part of this chapter deals with cafeteria plans. **Cafeteria plans** *allow employees to select those employee benefits that best meet their specific needs.* Instead of a single benefits package that applies to all employees, cafeteria plans allow employees to select among the various group life, medical expense, disability, dental, and other plans that are offered. Cafeteria plans also allow employers to introduce new benefits to meet the specific needs of certain employees.

Cafeteria plans take several forms. The most common are (1) full choice plans, (2) premium conversion plans, and (3) flexible spending accounts. Although these categories are not mutually exclusive, cafeteria plans share certain common characteristics.

- *Full choice plans.* These plans are also called "full flex plans." This type of plan allows employees to select a full range of benefits. There is typically a core plan that offers a basic core of benefits to all participating employees. In addition, there may be a second layer of optional benefits from which employees can choose. The employer gives each employee a certain number of dollars or credits that can be spent on the different benefits or taken as cash. If taken as cash, the employer's credits are taxed as income to the employee.
- *Premium conversion plans.* Many cafeteria plans are premium conversion plans, which is a generic name for a plan that allows employees to make their premium contributions for plan benefits with before-tax dollars. Premium-conversion plans are commonly used for group health and dental insurance. Employees elect to reduce their salaries, and the salary reduction is used to pay for plan benefits. In effect, employee premium contributions are paid with before-tax dollars.
- *Flexible spending accounts.* Many cafeteria plans are flexible spending accounts. *A **flexible spending account** is an arrangement that permits employees to pay for certain unreimbursed medical expenses with before-tax dollars.* The employee agrees to a salary reduction, which is used to pay for certain expenses permitted by the Internal Revenue Code with before-tax dollars. These expenses include unreimbursed medical and dental expenses, plan deductibles, coinsurance charges, eyeglasses, hearing aids, cosmetic surgery, and other expenses not covered under a typical group plan. Under the Affordable Care Act, beginning in 2013, employee contributions to a flexible spending account are limited to a maximum of $1250 each year. Any unused amounts in the flexible spending account at the end of the year are forfeited to the employer. However, the Internal Revenue Service has ruled that employers could allow employees a grace period of up to 2½ months to spend the unused balances. The plan must be specifically designed to include this feature.

Many employers provide debit cards that employees can use to pay for unreimbursed expenses out of their account balances. The debit card allows employees to be reimbursed immediately for their uncovered out-of-pocket expenses.

Finally, if the cafeteria plan meets certain requirements specified in the Internal Revenue Code, the employer's credits are not currently taxable to the employee.

Cafeteria plans have certain advantages, including the following:

- Employees can select those benefits that best meet their specific needs.
- Employees generally pay their share of the cost of benefits with before-tax dollars. As a result, take-home pay declines by less than the reduction in salary.
- Employers can more easily control rising employee benefit costs. For example, an employer may limit the number of benefit dollars or credits given to each employee or offer the employees a medical expense plan with a higher deductible.

Cafeteria plans also have certain disadvantages, including the following:

- The employer may incur higher initial development and administrative costs in establishing and managing a cafeteria plan rather than a traditional employee benefits plan.
- Administrative complexity is increased. The employee benefits manager must have knowledge of the details of a large number of plans and must be able to answer the specific questions of employees concerning these plans.

---

## CASE APPLICATION

Karen Swift is president of an accounting firm that has 10 employees. The only employee benefit provided by the firm is a paid two-week vacation for employees with one or more years of service. The firm's profits have substantially increased, and Karen would like to provide some additional benefits to the employees. Karen needs advice concerning the types of benefits to provide. Assume you are an employee benefits consultant. Based on the following considerations, answer the following questions:

a. Karen would like to provide health insurance benefits to the employees. Describe briefly the major types of managed care plans that she might consider.

b. Assume that Karen is considering both a preferred provider organization (PPO) and a health maintenance organization plan (HMO). Explain the major differences between these two plans to Karen.

c. Are there any other group health insurance benefits that Karen might consider? Explain your answer.

d. Karen is concerned that rising health-care costs may result in an increased financial burden to the firm. Describe a group health-care plan that Karen might consider to deal with the problem of rising health-care costs.

---

## SUMMARY

- Group insurance provides benefits to a number of persons under a single master contract. Low-cost protection is provided, because the employer pays part or all of the premiums. Evidence of insurability is usually not required. Larger groups are subject to experience rating, by which the group's loss experience determines the premiums charged.

- Certain underwriting principles are followed in group insurance to obtain favorable loss experience:

  Insurance should be incidental to the group.

  There should be a flow of persons through the group.

  The benefits should be determined by some formula that precludes individual selection of insurance amounts.

  A minimum percentage of eligible employees should participate in the plan.

  There should be third-party sharing of costs.

  There should be simple and efficient administration of the plan.

- Most groups today are eligible for group insurance benefits. However, employees must meet certain eligibility requirements:

  Be full-time employees.

  Satisfy a probationary period in some plans.

  Apply for insurance during the eligibility period.

  Be actively at work when the insurance becomes effective.

- There are several types of group life insurance plans:

  Group term life insurance

  Group accidental death and dismemberment (AD&D) insurance

  Group universal life insurance

  Worksite marketing programs

- Group medical expense plans are available from a number of sources, including the following:

  Commercial insurers

  Blue Cross and Blue Shield

  Health maintenance organizations (HMOs)

  Self-insured plans by employers

- Managed care is a generic name for a medical expense plan that provides necessary medical care in a cost-effective manner. Major types of managed care plans are HMOs, PPOs, and POS plans.

- A health maintenance organization (HMO) is a managed care plan that provides broad, comprehensive services to its members for a fixed, prepaid fee. A typical HMO has the following characteristics:

  Organized plan to deliver health services to the members

  Broad, comprehensive health services

  Restrictions on the choice of health-care providers

  Payment of fixed premiums and cost-sharing provisions

  Heavy emphasis on controlling costs

- A preferred provider organization (PPO) is a plan that contracts with health-care providers to provide certain medical services to its members at discounted fees. Members pay lower deductibles and coinsurance charges if preferred providers are used.

- A point-of-service (POS) plan is a managed care plan that allows members to receive medical care outside the network of preferred providers. However, the patient must pay substantially higher deductible and copayment charges.

- Group medical expense plans have a number of common characteristics: payment of comprehensive benefits, calendar-year deductible, coinsurance requirements, copayments, no cost sharing for preventive services, and exclusions or limitations of certain services.

- The Affordable Care Act will have a significant impact on group medical expense plans. The new law will be phased in from 2010 through 2018. However, many provisions that affect group medical expense plans are now in effect. The full law generally will become effective on January 1, 2014.

- A consumer-directed health plan (CDHP) is a generic term for a plan that combines a high-deductible health plan with a health savings account (HSA) or health reimbursement arrangement (HRA). These plans are designed to make employees more sensitive to health-care costs, to provide a financial incentive to avoid unnecessary care, and to seek out low-cost providers.

- Under the Affordable Care Act, group medical expense plans cannot exclude coverage for preexisting conditions or disabilities in children under age 19. Beginning in 2014, insurers are prohibited from denying or limiting coverage for preexisting conditions to adults as well.

- Group medical expense plans usually contain a coordination-of-benefits provision, which specifies the order of payment when an insured is covered under two or more group medical expense plans. Total recovery under all plans is limited to 100 percent of covered expenses.

- Under the COBRA law, if a qualifying event occurs that results in a loss of coverage, employees and covered dependents can elect to remain in the employer's health insurance plan for a limited period. The terminated employee must pay 102 percent of the total group premium.

- Group dental insurance plans typically cover a wide variety of dental services. Dental services are typically grouped into different levels with varying coinsurance requirements. In many plans, coinsurance does not apply to diagnostic and preventive services, such as cleaning of teeth, or the coinsurance percentage is lower.

- Many employers provide disability-income benefits to covered employees. There are two basic types of plans:

  Short-term disability-income plans
  Long-term disability-income plans

- Cafeteria plans allow employees to select those benefits that best meet their specific needs. Flexible spending accounts in a cafeteria plan allow employees to pay for the benefits with before-tax dollars.

## KEY CONCEPTS AND TERMS

Annual limits on out-of-pocket expenses (337)
Blue Cross and Blue Shield plans (333)
Cafeteria plans (346)
Calendar-year deductible (337)
Capitation fee (335)
COBRA law (344)
Coinsurance provision
Consumer-directed health plans (CDHP) (340)
Contributory plan (329)
Coordination-of-benefits provision (344)
Eligibility period (330)
Employee benefits (328)
Experience rating (329)
Family deductible (337)
Fee-for-service plans (333)
Flexible spending account (347)
Gatekeeper physician (335)
Group accidental death and dismemberment (AD&D) insurance (332)
Group dental insurance (344)
Group disability-income insurance (345)
Group medical expense insurance (332)
Group term life insurance (331)
Group universal life insurance (332)
Health Insurance Portability and Accountability Act (HIPAA) (343)
Health maintenance organization (HMO) (334)
Health reimbursement arrangement (HRA) (340)
High-deductible health plan (340)
Indemnity plans (333)
Individual practice association (IPA) plan (336)
Managed care (334)
Master contract (328)
Noncontributory plan (329)
Nonoccupational disability (346)
Point-of-service (POS) plan (336)
Portable term insurance (331)
Pre-existing condition (343)
Preferred provider organization (PPO) (336)
Probationary period (330)
Self-insurance (self-funding) (333)
Supplemental term insurance (331)
Worksite marketing programs (332)

## REVIEW QUESTIONS

1. Describe the basic underwriting principles that are followed in group insurance.

2. Explain the typical eligibility requirements that employees must meet in group insurance plans.

3. Briefly describe the following types of group life insurance plans:
   a. Group term life insurance
   b. Group accidental death and dismemberment insurance (AD&D)
   c. Group universal life insurance
   d. Worksite marketing programs

4. a. Describe the major characteristics of Blue Cross and Blue Shield plans.
   b. Why do many employers self-insure (self-fund) their group medical expense plans?

5. a. Briefly explain the basic characteristics of the following types of managed care plans:
      1. Health maintenance organizations (HMOs)
      2. Preferred provider organizations (PPOs)
      3. Point-of-service (POS) plans
   b. Identify the features of group medical expense plans.

6. What is a consumer-directed health plan (CDHP)?

7. Identify the major provisions of the Affordable Care Act that affect individuals, families, and employers.

8. Briefly explain each of the following group medical expense provisions:
   a. Coordination of benefits
   b. Continuation of group health insurance under the COBRA law

9. Briefly explain the basic characteristics of group dental insurance plans.

10. Briefly describe the major characteristics of the following group disability-income plans:
    a. Short-term disability-income plans
    b. Long-term disability-income plans

11. Describe the basic characteristics of cafeteria plans in an employee benefits program.

## APPLICATION QUESTIONS

1. Group term life insurance and group universal life insurance have different characteristics and objectives. Compare (1) group term insurance with (2) group universal life insurance with respect to each of the following:
   a. Period of protection provided
   b. Right to continue the coverage after termination of employment
   c. Availability of employer contributions

2. Margo, age 35, was severely injured in an auto accident. She is covered under her employer's preferred provider organization (PPO) plan. The plan has a $1000 calendar-year deductible, 80/20 percent coinsurance, and an annual out-of-pocket limit of $3000. As a result of the accident, Margo incurred the following medical expenses:

| | |
|---|---|
| Cost of ambulance to the hospital | $500 |
| Hospital bill for a three-day stay | $24,000 |
| Surgery for broken leg | $5000 |
| Prescription drugs outside the hospital | $300 |
| Physical therapy for the broken leg | $1200 |

In addition, Margo could not work for one month and lost $4000 in earnings.
   a. Based on this information, how much will Margo collect for her injury if she receives medical care from health care providers who are part of the PPO network? (Assume that all charges shown are the allowable or approved charges by the insurer and all providers are in the PPO network.)
   b. Assume that Margo's broken leg does not heal properly, and she needs another surgical operation. Margo would like a different surgeon with an outstanding professional reputation to perform the operation. The surgeon is not a member of the PPO network. Will Margo's plan pay for the surgery? Explain your answer.

3. Doug, age 40, is the owner of a small firm that sells window blinds and cleans carpets. The company provides health insurance for seven employees. The wife of one employee has breast cancer and has incurred substantial medical bills, which resulted in a 40 percent increase in health insurance premiums for the company. Doug is not certain that the company can continue to provide health insurance for the employees because of the substantial increase in premiums. Explain the provision in the Affordable Care Act that will enable Doug to provide affordable health insurance to his employees.

4. Ken, age 52, works only part-time and has no health insurance. The cartilage in both his knees is severely eroded from osteoarthritis, which causes severe pain during his daily activities. As a result, Ken requires major surgery and a total knee replacement for both knees. He has been unable to obtain health insurance because of this condition. Explain one or more provisions in the new Affordable Care Act that will enable Ken to obtain health insurance.

5. Jane, age 28, and John, age 30, are married and have a son, age one. Jane is covered under her employer's group medical expense plan as an employee. Jane is also covered under John's plan as a dependent. The son is covered under both plans as a dependent. Jane's birthday is January 10, while John's birthday is November 15. Both plans have the same coordination-of-benefits provision.

   a. If Jane is hospitalized, which plan is primary? Which plan is excess?
   b. If the son is hospitalized, which plan is primary? Which plan is excess?
   c. Assume that the couple gets a divorce, and Jane is awarded custody of her son. A court decree states that John must provide health insurance on his son. If the son is hospitalized after the divorce, which plan is primary? Which plan is excess?

6. Many employers have both group short-term and long-term disability-income plans. Compare (1) short-term plans with (2) long-term plans with respect to each of the following:

   a. Definition of disability under the plan
   b. Elimination period
   c. Length of the benefit period
   d. Offsets if other disability-income benefits are received

## INTERNET RESOURCES

- **America's Health Insurance Plans (AHIP)** is a national trade association that represents companies that provide health insurance coverage to more than 200 million Americans. The site provides considerable information on health-care issues in the United States. Visit the site at

  ahip.org

- **Blue Cross and Blue Shield** plans are nonprofit corporations that provide medical, hospital, and surgical benefits to plan members in specific geographical areas. The various plans account for a substantial portion of the group health insurance market. Visit the site at

  bcbs.com

- The **Employee Benefit Research Institute (EBRI)** is a nonprofit organization devoted exclusively to the dissemination of data, policy research, and educational material on economic security and employee benefits. EBRI has an online data book that provides ongoing statistics on employee benefits. Visit the site at

  ebri.org

- **HealthCare.gov** is the official Web site of the federal government that provides detailed information on the new health-care reform law and its implementation. Click on "Understanding the New Law" for a convenient source of information concerning the provisions of the new law. Visit the site at

  healthcare.gov

- **Healthgrades.com** uses a star system to rate hundreds of hospitals based on specific procedures. The stars range from a high of five to a low of one. Hospitals that have fewer complications for a specific procedure receive a higher grade. Information on physicians and nursing homes is also available. Visit the site at

  healthgrades.com

- The **International Foundation of Employee Benefit Plans** is a nonprofit educational organization that provides programs, publications, and research studies to individuals in the employee benefits field. The organization cosponsors the Certified Employee Benefit Specialist (CEBS) program. Visit the site at

  ifebp.org

- The **Centers for Disease Control and Prevention (CDC)** is the leading federal agency for protecting the health and safety of people in the United States and abroad. CDC provides credible statistics to enhance health decisions and to promote good health. The CDC serves as the national focus for disease prevention and control, environmental health, and educational activities to improve health. Visit the site at

  cdc.gov/nchs

- The **National Committee for Quality Assurance (NCQA)** provides information to employers and consumers on the quality of their health-care plans. NCQA issues a report card on the quality of care provided and has an accreditation program for health-care plans. Visit the site at

ncqa.org

## SELECTED REFERENCES

AHIP, *An Employer's Guide to Income Insurance,* Washington, DC, 2009.

Bikoff, Lauren, et al., *2012 U.S. Master Employee Benefits Guide.* Chicago, IL: CCH Incorporated, 2012.

Blue Cross and Blue Shield Association, *Healthcare Trends in America: A Reference Guide from BCBSA (2010 Edition).*

The Henry J. Kaiser Family Foundation, *Focus on Health Reform, Summary of New Health Reform Law,* last modified April 15, 2011.

The Kaiser Family Foundation and Health Research and Educational Trust, *Employer Health Benefits 2011 Summary of Findings.*

The Kaiser Family Foundation and Health Research and Educational Trust, *Employer Health Benefits 2011 Annual Survey,* September 2011.

National Committee for Quality Assurance (NCQA), *Continuous Improvement and the Expansion of Quality Measurement, the State of Health Care Quality 2011,* Washington, D.C. 2011.

New York Department of Insurance, *New York Consumer Guide to Health Insurers,* 2010.

Rosenbloom, Jerry S., *The Handbook of Employee Benefits,* 7th ed. New York: McGraw-Hill, 2011.

York, Juliana H. and Burton T. Beam, Jr., *Group Benefits: Basic Concepts and Alternatives,* 13th ed. Bryn Mawr, PA: The American College Press, 2012.

## NOTES

1. Davis W. Gregg, "Fundamental Characteristics of Group Insurance," in Davis W. Gregg and Vane B. Lucas, eds., *Life and Health Insurance Handbook,* 3rd, ed. (Homewood, IL: Richard D. Irwin, Inc., 1973), pp. 362–363, and Juliana H. York, and Burton T. Beam, Jr., *Group Benefits: Basic Concepts and Alternatives,* 13th ed. (Bryn Mawr, PA: The American College Press, 2012), ch.2.

2. *Life Insurers Fact Book 2011,* (Washington, DC: American Council of Life Insurers, 2011), Table 7.1, p.66.

3. York and Beam, pp. 5.5–5.6.

4. Emily Berry, "Few physicians can avoid dominant health insurers," amednews.com,

5. Ibid.

6. Ibid.

7. York and Beam, p. 9.16.

8. York and Beam, pp. 9.37–9.38.

9. The Kaiser Family Foundation and Health Research and Educational Trust, *Employer Health Benefits, 2011 Summary of Findings,* 2011.

10. Ibid.

11. Ibid.

12. Mercer Press Release, "Employers accelerate efforts to bring health benefit costs under control," November 16, 2011.

13. The Kaiser Family Foundation and Health Research and Educational Trust, *Employer Health Benefits 2011 Summary of Findings,* 2011.

14. Ibid.

15. Ronald L. Huling, "Dental Plan Design," in Jerry S. Rosenbloom, ed., *The Handbook of Employee Benefits,* 7th ed. (New York, NY: McGraw-Hill, 2011), p. 326.

Students may take a self-administered test on this chapter at
**www.pearsonhighered.com/rejda**

# CHAPTER 17

# EMPLOYEE BENEFITS: RETIREMENT PLANS

*"Retirement at age 65 is ridiculous. When I was 65, I still had pimples."*

George Burns

*"When some fellers decide to retire, nobody knows the difference."*

Kin Hubbard

## LEARNING OBJECTIVES

**After studying this chapter, you should be able to**

◆ Explain the basic features of private retirement plans, including:

   Minimum age and service requirements
   Retirement ages
   Vesting rules

◆ Distinguish between defined-contribution and defined-benefit retirement plans.

◆ Describe the basic characteristics of Section 401(k) plans.

◆ Explain the major features of profit-sharing plans.

◆ Describe the basic characteristics of Keogh plans for the self-employed.

◆ Identify the major features of SIMPLE retirement plans for small employers.

*Tiffany, age 28, is a pharmacist who is employed by a large national retail chain. The company recently installed a new 401(k) plan that replaced an older defined-benefit pension plan that the company plans to phase out. Eligible employees are automatically enrolled in the new plan. Tiffany has several questions, including the amount she can contribute, the amount contributed by the firm, the retirement age, and investment options. She also wants to know if she will receive the employer's contributions if she leaves the company.*

*Like Tiffany, many employees are bewildered by the complexities of private retirement plans. This chapter deals with the questions that Tiffany and others may have concerning the characteristics of 401(k) plans and other qualified retirement plans. Although private retirement plans are complicated, they are extremely important in maintaining your economic security during retirement. When added to Social Security benefits, additional benefits from your retirement plan will enable you to attain a higher standard of living during retirement.*

*In this chapter, we discuss the fundamentals of private retirement plans. The chapter is divided into several parts. The first part discusses the fundamentals of private retirement plans, which include eligibility requirements, retirement ages, and vesting rules. The second part explains the major types of retirement plans, which include defined-benefit and defined-contribution plans, 401(k) plans, profit-sharing plans, and retirement plans for the self-employed. The final part discusses several current problems and issues in tax-deferred retirement plans.*

## FUNDAMENTALS OF PRIVATE RETIREMENT PLANS

Millions of workers participate in private retirement plans. These plans have an enormous social and economic impact on the nation. Retirement benefits increase the economic security of both individuals and families during retirement. Retirement contributions are also an important source of capital funds to the financial markets. These funds are invested in new plants, machinery, equipment, housing developments, shopping centers, and other worthwhile economic investments.

Federal legislation and the Internal Revenue Code have had a great influence on the design and growth of private retirement plans. The **Employee Retirement Income Security Act of 1974 (ERISA)** established minimum pension standards to protect the rights of covered workers.

More recently, the **Pension Protection Act of 2006** increases the funding obligations of employers,

makes permanent the higher contribution limits that were scheduled to expire at the end of 2010, encourages automatic enrollment of employees in Section 401(k)plans and defined-contribution plans, and contains numerous additional provisions that affect the design of private retirement plans.

The Internal Revenue Service (IRS) also exerts a significant influence on private retirement plans. The IRS continuously issues new rules and regulations that affect the design and growth of private retirement plans. The following discussion is based on current IRS requirements at the time of this writing.[1]

### Favorable Income Tax Treatment

Private retirement plans that meet certain IRS requirements are called **qualified plans** and receive favorable income tax treatment. The employer's contributions are tax deductible up to certain limits as an ordinary business expense; the employer's contributions are not considered taxable income to the employees; the investment earnings on plan assets accumulate on a tax-deferred basis; and the pension benefits attributable to the employer's contributions are not taxed until the employee retires or receives the funds. The tax advantages of qualified plans to employees are substantial, especially if the employee starts early.

## Minimum Coverage Requirements

A qualified plan must benefit workers in general and not only **highly compensated employees**.[2] Certain **minimum coverage requirements** must be satisfied to receive favorable tax treatment. The coverage rules are complex and beyond the scope of the text to discuss in detail. However, to reduce discrimination in favor of highly compensated employees, a qualified retirement plan must meet one of the following tests:

- *Ratio percentage test.* Under this test, the percentage of non-highly compensated employees covered under the plan must be at least 70 percent of the percentage of highly compensated employees who are covered.

    *Example. For the current plan year, the retirement plan for the Swift Corporation covers 90 percent of the highly compensated employees and 63 percent of the non-highly compensated employees. The ratio percentage is 70 percent (63 percent / 90 percent), and the plan meets the ratio percentage test.*

- *Average benefits test.* Under this test, two requirements must be met: (1) the plan must benefit a reasonable classification of employees and must not discriminate in favor of highly compensated employees, and (2) the average benefit for the non-highly compensated employees must be at least 70 percent of the average benefit provided to all highly compensated employees.

The minimum coverage tests typically come into play when an employer establishes a retirement plan for employees in one location (e.g., the Philadelphia office) but not in another location (e.g., the Boston office). The coverage tests are also important if an employer establishes a retirement plan for some workers based on the job classification but not location.

## Minimum Age and Service Requirements

Most pension plans have a **minimum age and service requirement** that must be met before employees can participate in the plan. *Under present law, all eligible employees who have attained age 21 and have completed one year of service must be allowed to participate in the plan.* The plan can require two years of service, however, if there is 100 percent immediate vesting (discussed later) upon entry into the plan.

For purposes of determining eligibility, a worker who works at least 1000 hours during an initial 12-month period after being hired earns one year of service. An hour of service is any hour the employee works or for which he or she is entitled to be paid.

## Retirement Ages

A typical pension plan has three retirement ages:

- Normal retirement age
- Early retirement age
- Deferred retirement age

**Normal Retirement Age**  The **normal retirement age** is the age that a worker can retire and receive full, unreduced pension benefits. Age 65 is the normal retirement age in most plans. However, as a result of an amendment to the Age Discrimination in Employment Act, most employees cannot be forced to retire at some stated mandatory retirement age. To remain qualified, with certain exceptions, private pension plans cannot impose a mandatory retirement age.

**Early Retirement Age**  An **early retirement age** is the earliest age that workers can retire and receive a retirement benefit. The majority of employees currently retire before age 65. For example, a typical plan may permit a worker with 10 years of service to retire at age 55.

In a defined-benefit plan (discussed later), the retirement benefit is actuarially reduced for early retirement. The actuarial reduction is necessary for three reasons: (1) the worker's full benefit will not have accrued by the early retirement date; (2) the retirement benefit is paid over a longer period of time; and (3) early retirement benefits are paid to some workers who would have died before reaching the normal retirement age.

**Deferred Retirement Age**   The **deferred retirement age** is any age beyond the normal retirement age. Some older employees continue working beyond the normal retirement age. However, under current law with certain exceptions, workers can defer retiring with no maximum age limit as long as they can do their jobs. Employees who continue working beyond the normal retirement age continue to accrue benefits under the plan.

## Vesting Provisions

**Vesting** *refers to the employee's right to the employer's contributions or benefits attributable to the contributions if employment terminates prior to retirement.* The employee is always entitled to the contributions he or she makes to the plan if employment terminates prior to retirement. However, the right to the employer's contributions, or benefits attributable to the contributions, depends on the extent to which vesting has been attained.

**Defined-Benefit Plans**   Qualified defined-benefit plans must meet one of the following **minimum vesting standards:**

- *Five-year cliff vesting.* Under this rule, the employee must be 100 percent vested after five years of service.
- *Seven-year graded vesting.* Under this rule, the rate of vesting must meet or exceed the following minimum standard:

| Years of Service | Percentage Vested |
| --- | --- |
| 3 | 20% |
| 4 | 40 |
| 5 | 60 |
| 6 | 80 |
| 7 | 100 |

**Defined-Contributions Plans**   Employer contributions to a qualified defined-contribution or profit-sharing plan must vest at a faster rate. Faster vesting is designed to encourage greater participation by lower- and middle-income employees.

Defined-contribution and profit-sharing plans must meet one of the following minimum vesting schedules:

- *Three-year cliff vesting.* Employer contributions must be 100 percent vested after three years.

- *Six-year graded vesting.* Employer contributions must meet or exceed the following vesting schedule:

| Years of Service | Percentage Vested |
| --- | --- |
| 1 | 0% |
| 2 | 20 |
| 3 | 40 |
| 4 | 60 |
| 5 | 80 |
| 6 | 100 |

From the employer's viewpoint, the basic purpose of vesting is to reduce labor turnover. Employees have an incentive to remain with the firm until a vested status has been attained. In a defined-benefit plan, if employees terminate their employment before full vesting is attained, the forfeitures generally are used to reduce the employer's future pension contributions. However, in a defined-contribution plan, forfeitures can either be reallocated to the accounts of the remaining participants or used to reduce future employer contributions.

## Early Distribution Penalty

A 10 percent penalty tax applies to funds withdrawn from a qualified plan before age 59½. The 10 percent penalty tax applies to the amount included in gross income. However, there are exceptions to this rule. The early distribution penalty does not apply to any of the following distributions:

- Made to a beneficiary or to the employee's estate on or after the death of the employee
- Made because the employee has a qualifying disability
- Made as part of a series of substantially equal payments beginning after separation from service, and paid at least annually over the employee's life expectancy, or over the joint lives or joint life expectancy of the employee and designated beneficiary
- Made to an employee after attaining age 55 and separation from service
- Made to an alternate payee under a qualified domestic relations order
- Made to an employee for medical care up to the amount allowable as a medical expense

deduction (determined without regard to the itemizing of deductions)

- Made because of an IRS levy
- Made as a qualified reservist distribution

### Minimum Distribution Requirements

Pension contributions cannot remain in the plan indefinitely. Plan distributions must start no later than April 1 of the calendar year following the year in which the individual attains age 70½. However, participants older than 70½ who are still working can delay receiving minimum distributions from a qualified retirement plan. The required beginning date of a participant who is still employed after age 70½ is April 1 of the calendar year that follows the calendar year in which he or she retires. *The preceding rule does not apply to individual retirement accounts (IRAs) and certain other qualified plans.*

Finally, the minimum distribution rules do not apply to Roth IRAs.

### Integration with Social Security

Many qualified retirement plans are integrated with Social Security. Employers pay half of the OASDI payroll tax and argue that Social Security benefits should be taken into consideration in the calculation of private retirement benefits. As a result, pension costs can be reduced. Integration also permits employers to increase the pension contributions for highly compensated employees who have earnings above the integration level without violating the anti-discrimination rules that prohibit employers from discriminating in favor of highly paid employees.

The integration level can be any amount up to the maximum taxable Social Security wage base for the plan year ($110,100 for 2012). The integration level can be set lower, but this generally reduces the maximum excess contribution. The Internal Revenue Service (IRS) has prescribed complex integration rules (called permitted disparity rules) that limit the employer's contributions made on behalf of highly compensated employees. It is beyond the scope of the text to discuss these rules in detail. However, the rules are designed to limit the pension contributions the employer can make on behalf of highly compensated employees with earnings above the integration

level. For example, assume that a money purchase plan has a contribution rate of 6 percent of compensation up to the Social Security taxable wage base ($110,100 for 2012) and 11.5 percent of compensation in excess of the taxable wage base. In this case, the excess contribution percentage does not exceed the permitted disparity limits.[3]

### Top-Heavy Plans

Special rules apply to top-heavy plans. A **top-heavy plan** is a retirement plan in which more than 60 percent of the plan assets are in accounts attributed to key employees. A plan is considered top-heavy if the present value of the cumulative accrued benefits for the key employees exceeds 60 percent of the present value of the cumulative accrued benefits under the plan for all covered employees.

A top-heavy plan must meet certain additional requirements to retain its qualified status. These requirements include the following:

- A special rapid vesting schedule must be used for nonkey employees (100 percent vesting after three years, or 20 percent after two years and 20 percent for each year thereafter).
- Certain minimum benefits or contributions must be provided for nonkey employees.

## TYPES OF QUALIFIED RETIREMENT PLANS

A wide variety of qualified retirement plans are available today to meet the specific needs of employers. There are two basic types of qualified retirement plans: (1) defined-benefit plans and (2) defined-contribution plans. Different rules apply to each type of plan. The most important retirement plans include the following:

- Defined-benefit plans
- Defined-contribution plans
  - Money purchase plan
  - Section 401(k) plans
  - Section 403(b) plans
  - Profit sharing plans
  - Keogh plans for the self-employed
  - Simplified employee pension (SEP) plans
  - SIMPLE retirement plans

# DEFINED-BENEFIT PLANS

## Traditional Defined-Benefits Plans

From a historical perspective, employers typically established defined-benefit plans that paid guaranteed benefits to retired workers. In a **defined-benefit plan,** *the retirement benefit is known in advance, but the contributions will vary depending on the amount needed to fund the desired benefit.* For example, assume that James, age 50, is entitled to a retirement benefit at the normal retirement age equal to 50 percent of average pay for the highest three consecutive years of earnings. An actuary then determines the amount that must be contributed to produce the desired benefit.

In a defined-benefit plan, the benefit amount can be based on **career-average earnings**, which is an average of the worker's earnings while participating in the plan, or it can be based on **final average pay**, which generally is an average of the worker's earnings over a three- to five-year period just prior to retirement.

When a new defined-benefit pension plan is installed, some older workers may be close to retirement. To pay more adequate retirement benefits, defined-benefit plans may give credit for service with the firm prior to the installation of the plan. The **past-service credits** provide additional pension benefits. The actual amount paid, however, will depend on the benefit formula used to determine benefits.

## Limits on Benefits

Defined-benefit plans have annual limits on pension benefits that can be funded. For 2012, under a defined-benefit plan, the maximum annual benefit is limited to 100 percent of the worker's average compensation for the three highest consecutive years of compensation, or $200,000, whichever is lower. This latter figure is indexed for inflation.

There is also a maximum limit on the annual compensation that can be counted in determining benefits. For 2012, the maximum annual compensation that can be counted in the benefit formula is $250,000 (indexed for inflation).

## Defined-Benefit Formulas

Retirement benefits in defined-benefit plans are based on formulas that, combined with Social Security, will generally replace 50 percent to 60 percent of the worker's gross earnings prior to retirement. They include the following:

- *Unit-benefit formula.* Under this formula, both earnings and years of service are considered. For example, the plan may pay a retirement benefit equal to 1 percent of the worker's final average pay multiplied by the number of years of service. Thus, a worker with a final average monthly salary of $4000 and 30 years of service would receive a monthly retirement benefit of $1200.
- *Flat percentage of annual earnings.* Under this formula, the retirement benefit is a fixed percentage of the worker's earnings, such as 25 to 50 percent. The benefit may be based on career-average earnings or on an average of final pay. This formula sometimes lowers the amount provided if the employee does not have the required amount of service. For example, a plan may provide benefits equal to 50 percent of average final pay if the employee has 30 years of service. However, if the employee has only 20 years of service, he or she will receive only two-thirds of the benefit.
- *Flat dollar amount for each year of service.* Under this formula, a flat dollar amount is paid for each year of credited service. For example, the plan may pay $40 monthly at the normal retirement age for each year of credited service. If the employee has 30 years of credited service, the monthly pension is $1200. This formula is not widely used except in union-negotiated retirement plans.
- *Flat dollar amount for all employees.* This formula is sometimes used in collective bargaining plans by which a flat dollar amount is paid to all employees regardless of their earnings or years of service. Thus, the plan may pay $800 monthly to each worker who retires.

Years of service are extremely important in determining the total pension benefit. Frequent job changes and withdrawal from the labor force for extended periods can significantly reduce the size of the pension benefit. This is especially true for women who often have prolonged breaks in employment due to family considerations.

## Pension Benefit Guaranty Corporation

Participants in defined-benefit plans are protected against the loss of pension benefits up to certain limits if the pension plan should terminate. The **Pension Benefit**

Guaranty Corporation (PBGC) is a federal corporation that guarantees the payment of vested or nonforfeitable benefits up to certain limits if a private pension plan is terminated. For plans terminated in 2012, the maximum guaranteed pension at age 65 for a straight-life annuity (no survivor benefits) is $4,653.41 per month ($55,840.92 annually). The maximum monthly payment is lower for those who elect survivor benefits.

## Advantages of Defined-Benefit Plans

Defined-benefit retirement plans have the major advantages of guaranteeing the worker's retirement benefit; the retirement benefits reflect more accurately the effects of inflation because the benefits are usually based on a final-pay formula; the plans are usually noncontributory, which means that only the employer contributes to the plan; and the investment risk falls directly on the employer, not the employee.

In addition, defined-benefit plans favor workers who enter the plan at older ages because the employer must contribute a relatively larger amount for older workers than for younger workers.

## Disadvantages of Defined-Benefit Plans

Defined-benefit plans have declined in relative importance over the years. Because of actuarial considerations, defined-benefit plans are more complex and expensive to administer than defined-contribution plans. Also, many defined-benefit plans have large unfunded past-service liabilities that are expensive to fund. Because of cost and complexity, many corporations have frozen or have terminated their defined-benefit plans. As a substitute, many companies have replaced their defined-benefit plan with a defined-contribution plan, which is less costly and easier to administer.

## Cash-Balance Plans

To reduce pension costs, many employers have converted their traditional defined-benefit plans to a cash-balance plan. *A* **cash-balance plan** *is a defined-benefit plan in which the benefits are defined in terms of a hypothetical account balance; actual retirement benefits will depend on the value of the participant's account at retirement.*

In a typical cash-balance plan, the employer establishes "hypothetical accounts" for plan participants.

The accounts are hypothetical because the contributions and interest credits are bookkeeping credits. Actual contributions are not allocated to the participants' accounts, and the accounts do not reflect actual investment gains or losses. The investment credits are also hypothetical and are based on an interest rate stated in the plan or on some external index.

Each year, the participants' accounts are credited with (1) a *pay credit,* such as 4 percent of compensation, and (2) an *interest credit,* such as 5 percent on the account balance. The interest credit can be based on a fixed rate or on a variable rate pegged to some index, such as a one-year Treasury bill rate. Investment gains and losses on the plan's assets do not directly affect the benefits promised to the participants. Thus, the employer bears the investment risks and realizes any investment gains. For example, assume that the employer makes a contribution of 4 percent of pay each year to the participants' accounts. If James earns $50,000 annually, his "account" is credited with $2000. Each year, his account balance will be credited with a stated interest rate, such as 5 percent. At retirement, James can elect to receive a life annuity that will pay him a life income. Instead of an annuity, the cash-balance plan may allow him to elect a lump-sum payment equal to the account balance, which can then be rolled over into an IRA.

Many employers have converted traditional defined-benefit plans into cash-balance plans in an effort to hold down pension costs. Also, younger workers benefit because they can understand the plan better; benefits accrue at a faster pace than under a traditional defined-benefit plan; and the benefits are portable for workers who leave before retirement age.

On the downside, however, critics argue that the switch to a cash-balance plan can reduce expected benefits for older workers by 20 to 40 percent. When the conversion occurs, plan benefits are "frozen," which means that earned benefits do not continue to grow. However, under a defined-benefit plan, a large part of the initial retirement benefit is earned during the last three to five years prior to retirement. When benefits are frozen, the worker's pension grows only from the annual interest and wage credits under the cash-balance plan. As a result, the initial retirement benefit for an older worker may be substantially less than if the defined-benefit formula had remained in place.

# DEFINED-CONTRIBUTION PLANS

Most newly installed qualified retirement plans are defined-contribution plans. In a **defined-contribution plan**, *the contribution rate is fixed, but the actual retirement benefit varies*. For example, both the employer and employee may each contribute 6 percent of the employee's pay into the plan. The actual retirement benefit, however, depends on the age of entry into the plan, the contribution rate, the types of investments and investment returns, and the age of retirement. As such, retirement benefits can only be estimated.

## Money Purchase Plans

One type of defined-contribution plan is a money purchase plan. *A* **money purchase plan** *is a plan in which each participant has an individual account, and the employer's contribution is a fixed percentage of the participant's compensation*. For example, the money purchase formula may specify an annual contribution by the employer of 10 percent of base pay into the plan. If the plan is contributory, both the employee and employer may contribute at the same rate, such as 5 percent, or the plan may specify a higher employer contribution rate, such as 6 percent for the employer and 4 percent for the employee.

Each employee has an individual account, and the retirement contributions and investment income are credited to the account. The employee receives periodic statements that show the account value and investment income and contributions credited to the account. Amounts forfeited by employees who terminate their employment before they attain full vesting are used to reduce future employer contributions or are reallocated to the accounts of the remaining employees.

## Limits on Contributions

Defined-contribution plans have annual limits on the amounts that can be contributed into the plan. For 2012, under a defined-contribution plan, the maximum annual addition that can be credited to an employee's account is 100 percent of compensation, or $50,000, whichever is lower. Workers age 50 and older can make an additional catch-up contribution of $5500. Annual additions include both employer and employee contributions and any forfeitures allocated to the employee's account.

There is also a maximum limit on the annual compensation that can be counted in determining the amount that can be contributed each year. For 2012, the maximum annual compensation that can be counted in the benefit formula is $250,000 (indexed for inflation).

Defined-contribution plans are widely used by business firms today. One financial advantage to the firm is that past-service credits are not granted for service prior to the plan's inception date, which reduces the employer's cost. Defined-contribution plans are also widely used by nonprofit organizations and state and local governments, where pension costs must be budgeted as a percentage of payroll.

However, from the employee's perspective, a defined-contribution plan has several disadvantages. Retirement benefits can only be estimated, and the benefit formula may produce an inadequate benefit if the worker enters the plan at an advanced age. In addition, some employees do not understand the factors to consider in choosing a particular investment, such as a stock fund, bond fund, money market fund, and other investment options. Finally, investment losses fall directly on participating employees. In the severe 2007–2009 economic downswing, the economy experienced a massive financial meltdown and brutal stock market crash that substantially reduced the life savings of most workers in defined-contribution plans.

# SECTION 401(k) PLANS

Another important defined-contribution plan is a Section 401(k) plan.

*A* **Section 401(k) plan** *is a qualified cash or deferred arrangement (CODA) that allows eligible employees the option of putting money into the plan or receiving the funds as cash*. Employer contributions are not currently taxable as income to plan participants.

A Section 401(k) plan can be a qualified profit-sharing plan, savings or thrift plan, or stock bonus plan. A plan can be established that includes both employer and employee contributions or employee contributions alone.

In a typical plan, both the employer and employees contribute, and the employer matches part or all of the employee's contributions. For example, for each dollar contributed by the employee, the employer may contribute 25 or 50 cents, or some higher amount.

Most plans allow the employees to determine how the funds are invested. Employees typically have a choice of investments, such as a common stock mutual fund, bond fund, fixed-income fund, and numerous other funds. Many employees, however, make some common mistakes when they invest their 401(k)

contributions, which ultimately reduce the amounts accumulated for retirement (see Insight 17.1).

### Annual Limit on Elective Deferrals

Eligible employees can voluntarily elect to have their salaries reduced if they participate in a Section 401(k) plan. The salary reduction is technically called an "elective deferral." The amount of salary

---

## INSIGHT 17.1

### Six Common 401(k) Mistakes

For the vast majority of people, having a 401(k) retirement plan is essential to their future financial health. As a matter of fact, a 401(k) is so vital to a comfortable retirement that possibly the most important thing for most people who are eligible to invest in such plans is to know what mistakes they should avoid making. Listed here are six of the most common 401(k) mistakes that people make. Don't repeat them in your investment program.

- **The first (and possibly worst) mistake:** *investing in volatile securities (such as* stocks), *then selling in a panic if their prices decline.* In other words, the worst mistake is for a novice to make an investment which is suitable only for sophisticated investors. Stocks can be great investments—for those who are experienced in the stock market and are equipped with the proper risk tolerance.

- **The second (and also quite expensive) mistake:** *not taking advantage of a 401(k) plan when one is available.* Many millions of eligible Americans have not elected to participate in their employer-sponsored plans. This represents a golden opportunity to procure help in building a substantial retirement fund, an opportunity that daily slips further away from those that may need it the most. Studies have shown that the well-to-do are as likely to participate in salary-deferral plans as the less well-to-do, who would probably benefit more.

- **The third mistake:** *not taking advantage of employers' contributions.* Many companies match their employees' contributions up to a certain amount. For instance, if the employee contributes 3 percent of his or her salary to the 401(k) plan, the employer may match that contribution by adding an extra 1.5 percent to the employee's account. That's an immediate *fifty percent* return on the invested money, and it's free! Not to mention the fact that the matching funds compound right along with the employee's contributions. Yet many people don't even put the minimum amount of money into their 401(k) plans that would be matched by their employers.

- **Mistake number four:** *not putting away more money.* Studies have found that only about one-third of active participants contributed the maximum annual amounts (the maximum amount can change yearly in line with inflation). The least that a savvy employee should contribute is the amount that will be matched by his or her employer's contribution. Again, it's senseless to turn down free money.

- **The fifth mistake:** *not putting enough money into the stock market.* Yes, mistake number one above warned of investing in the stock market. It's volatile; it can rise and fall with alarming quickness. It can drop in value and remain down for extended periods of time. Yet, over the years, the stock market has rewarded investors more generously than fixed-income investments (bonds), cash equivalents (such as money market funds), precious metals, antiques and collectibles, and most other investments. To be invested exclusively in the safest assets available will only serve to guarantee that the employee will earn much lower returns than if his or her portfolio were properly allocated to include at least some riskier investment options.

- **And, mistake number six:** *putting too much money into the employer's stock.* Actually, the real mistake here is not being fully *diversified*—not having enough money in a variety of different investments. The company may be a fantastic place to work; fair, generous, and a home away from home. It may be a thriving enterprise, making huge profits; the stock may even be selling for less than it should. Regardless, it's still a bad idea—and goes against one of the first tenets of prudent investing—to have one stock dominating the investing portfolio, even if that stock can be bought cheaply.

SOURCE: Adaptation of "Six Common 401(k) Mistakes," Financial Web at finweb.com. Reprinted by permission from Internet Brands, Inc.

deferred is then invested in the employer's Section 401(k) plan. The amounts deferred accumulate free of current income taxes until the funds are withdrawn. However, Social Security taxes must be paid on the contributions to the plan. The funds are taxed as ordinary income when withdrawals are made.

For 2012, the maximum limit on elective deferrals in a Section 401(k) plan is $17,000 for workers under age 50. Workers who are age 50 or older before the end of the plan year can make an additional catch-up contribution of $5500. The maximum dollar limits are indexed for inflation in increments of $500.

### Actual Deferral Percentage Test

To prevent discrimination in favor of highly compensated employees in a Section 401(k) plan, an **actual deferral percentage (ADP) test** must be satisfied. That is, the actual percentage of salary deferred for highly compensated employees is subject to certain limitations. In general, the eligible employees are divided into two groups: (1) highly compensated employees, and (2) other eligible employees. The percentage of salary deferred for each employee is totaled and then averaged to get an ADP for each group. The ADPs of both groups are then compared. For example, if the non-highly compensated group has an ADP of 6 percent, the maximum ADP for the highly compensated group is limited to 8 percent for favorable tax treatment.[4]

### Limitations on Distributions

As noted earlier, a 10 percent penalty tax applies to an early distribution of funds before age 59½ with certain exceptions that were discussed earlier.

The plan may also permit the withdrawal of funds for a hardship. The IRS recognizes the following as a hardship withdrawal:

- Payments to prevent eviction or foreclosure on your home
- Certain nonreimbursable medical expenses
- Purchase of a primary residence
- Payments for post-secondary education expenses
- Burial or funeral expenses
- Certain expenses incurred for the repair or damage to the employee's principal residence, which would qualify as a deductible casualty expense

The 10 percent penalty tax still applies to a hardship withdrawal. However, Section 401(k) plans typically have a *loan provision* that allows funds to be borrowed without a tax penalty.

Despite the substantial tax penalties for a premature distribution, many employees often use their 401(k) funds and other retirement funds for purposes other than retirement, such as spending the funds outright, paying off debts, or buying a home. Employees who take money out of their retirement plans early will receive a substantially lower amount of income during retirement. As a result, they may be exposed to serious economic insecurity during retirement.

### Roth 401(k) Plan

Employers have the option of allowing employees to invest in a Roth 401(k) plan. In a traditional 401(k) plan, you make contributions with before-tax dollars, and distributions are taxed as ordinary income. In a **Roth 401(k) plan,** *you make contributions with after-tax dollars, and qualified distributions at retirement are received income-tax free.* Investment earnings also accumulate on a tax-free basis. Distributions from the Roth 401(k) are income-tax free if you are at least age 59½, and the account is held for at least five years. However, with certain exceptions, there is a 10 percent tax penalty under both plans if you withdraw funds before age 59½.

There are no income limitations. Employees at all income levels can contribute to a Roth 401(k). For 2012, if you are under age 50, you can contribute a maximum of $17,000 into the plan. If you are age 50 or older, you can contribute an additional $5500. You can split the contributions between a traditional 401(k) and a Roth 401(k), but your contributions to both accounts cannot exceed the maximum annual limits. If your employer makes a matching contribution, it is made with before-tax money and must go into the traditional 401(k) plan.

Another advantage is that funds in a Roth 401(k) can be rolled over into a Roth IRA, which has no minimum distribution requirements at age 70½. As a result, larger sums can be bequeathed to heirs on a tax-free basis.

### Individual 401(k) Retirement Plan

An individual 401(k) retirement plan provides attractive tax advantages to self-employed individuals. The **individual 401(k) retirement plan** is a plan that combines a profit-sharing plan with a 401(k) plan. The plan is limited to self-employed individuals or business owners with no employees other than a spouse, which include sole proprietors, partnerships, corporations, and "S" corporations. Taxable income is reduced by contributions into the plan, and investment income accumulates income-tax free. For 2012, an individual 401(k) plan allows a maximum annual contribution of 25 percent of compensation (20 percent of net self-employment income for the business owner) into the plan. In addition, for 2012, the business owner can elect a salary deferral up to $17,000, which also reduces taxable income. Older workers age 50 and over can make an additional catch-up contribution of $5500. However, for 2012, total profit-sharing contributions and salary deferral for an individual under age 50 cannot exceed $50,000. The tax savings are substantial.

*Example. Brandon, age 35, is a finance professor who has self-employment income from part-time consulting. In 2012, after deducting allowable expenses and one-half of the Social Security payroll tax, Brandon has a net income of $50,000. He can elect a maximum salary deferral of $17,000. He can also contribute 20 percent or $10,000 into his 401(k) plan. As a result, his taxable income from consulting is reduced from $50,000 to $23,000. Brandon has tax sheltered 54 percent of his net earnings.*

### Section 403(b) Plans

**Section 403(b) plans** are retirement plans designed for employees of public educational systems and tax-exempt organizations, such as hospitals, non-profit groups, and churches. These plans are also known as **tax-sheltered annuities (TSAs)**. Under the plan, eligible employees voluntarily elect to reduce their salaries by a fixed amount. The salary reduction is called an "elective deferral," which is then invested in the 403(b) plan. Employers may make a matching contribution, such as 50 cents for each dollar contributed by the employee by salary reduction. For example, if Kathy earns $3000 monthly and elects to defer $300 monthly, only $2700 is subject to income taxes. The $300 salary reduction plus any employer contributions are then invested in the 403(b) plan.

A 403(b) plan can be funded by purchasing an annuity from an insurance company or by investing in mutual funds. If an annuity is used, the employer must purchase the annuity, and the employee's rights under the contract must be nonforfeitable. *Nonforfeitable* means that the amounts contributed by the employer cannot be taken away from the employee. Employee salary reductions are always nonforfeitable. In addition, the annuity must be nontransferable. *Nontransferable* means the annuity contract cannot be sold, assigned, or pledged as collateral for a loan.

Current law places a maximum annual dollar limit on elective deferrals under a 403(b) plan. For 2012, the maximum limit on elective deferrals for workers under age 50 is $17,000. Employees age 50 and older can make an additional catch-up contribution of $5500. The above limits are adjusted for increases in the cost-of-living.

Finally, employers have the option of allowing employees to invest in a **Roth 403(b) plan**. A Roth 403(b) plan is similar to the Roth 401(k) plan discussed earlier. Contributions to the plan are made with after-tax dollars; investment earnings accumulate on a tax-free basis; and qualified distributions at retirement are received income-tax free.

## PROFIT-SHARING PLANS

Many employers have profit-sharing plans to provide retirement income to eligible employees. A **profit-sharing plan** *is a defined-contribution plan in which the employer's contributions are typically based on the firm's profits.* However, there is no requirement that the employer must actually earn a profit to contribute to the plan.

Employers establish profit-sharing plans for several reasons. Eligible employees are encouraged to work more efficiently; the employer's cost is not affected by the age or number of employees; and there is greater flexibility in employer contributions. If there are no profits, there are no contributions.

The profit-sharing contributions can be discretionary—based on an amount determined annually by the board of directors—or they can be based on a formula, such as a certain percentage of profits above a certain level. There are annual limits, however, on the amount that can be contributed into an employee's profit sharing account. For 2012, the maximum employer tax-deductible contribution is limited to 25 percent of the employee's compensation or $50,000, whichever is less.

The profit-sharing funds are typically distributed to the employees at retirement, death, disability, or termination of employment (only the vested portion), or after a fixed number of years (at least two years). Amounts forfeited by employees who leave the company before they attain full vesting are reallocated to the accounts of the remaining participants.

A 10 percent tax penalty applies to a distribution to a participant younger than age 59½. To avoid the tax penalty, many plans have loan provisions that permit employees to borrow from their accounts.

## KEOGH PLANS FOR THE SELF EMPLOYED

Sole proprietors and partners can establish qualified retirement plans and enjoy most of the favorable tax advantages now available to participants in qualified corporate pension plans. Retirement plans for the owners of unincorporated business firms are commonly called **Keogh plans**. The contributions to the plan are income-tax deductible up to certain limits, and the investment income accumulates on a tax-deferred basis. The amounts deposited and the investment earnings are not taxed until the funds are distributed.

With certain exceptions, the same rules that apply to qualified corporate pension plans now apply to retirement plans for the self-employed.

**Limits on Contributions and Benefits**   A Keogh plan can be either a defined-contribution plan or a defined-benefit plan. For 2012, if the Keogh plan is a *defined-contribution plan*, the maximum annual contribution on behalf of eligible employees cannot exceed 25 percent of compensation or $50,000, whichever is less. Older participants age 50 or older can make additional catch-up contributions up to $5500.

However, for self-employed individuals, certain adjustments to net earnings must be made to determine the maximum deduction. Net earnings must be reduced by the deductible part of the Social Security self-employment tax and the deduction for contributions by the self-employed individual into the plan. Fortunately, the Internal Revenue Service has prepared a worksheet to help you make the correct calculation. *For 2012, after making these adjustments, the maximum annual contribution is limited to 20 percent of net earnings but not to exceed $50,000.* Older self-employed individuals age 50 or older can make additional catch-up contributions as noted above.

For example, after the above adjustments are made, assume that Shannon has net self-employment earnings of $50,000. She can make a maximum tax-deductible contribution of $10,000 into the plan, which reduces her taxable earnings to $40,000. This amount is exactly equal to 25 percent of her net income after the contribution is made ($10,000/$40,000 = 25%).

For 2012, if the Keogh plan is *a defined-benefit plan*, a self-employed individual can fund for a maximum annual benefit equal to 100 percent of average compensation for the three highest consecutive years of compensation, or $200,000, whichever is lower. This latter figure is indexed for inflation.

For example, assume that Nancy, age 50, establishes a defined-benefit plan that will provide a retirement benefit equal to 50 percent of her net income at age 65. If average net income for the three highest consecutive years is $50,000, she can fund for a maximum annual benefit of $25,000. An actuary then determines the amount that she can contribute annually into the plan to reach that goal. In this case, based on 7 percent investment return and certain actuarial assumptions, Nancy could contribute $10,847 annually into the plan.

### Other Requirements

Certain other requirements must also be met, including the following:

- All employees at least age 21 and with one year of service must be included in the plan. A two-year waiting period can be required if the plan provides for full and immediate vesting upon entry.
- Certain annual reports must be filed with the IRS.
- A 10 percent tax penalty applies to the withdrawal of funds prior to age 59½ (except for certain distributions as noted earlier).
- Plan distributions must start no later than April 1 of the year following the calendar year in which the self-employed person attains age 70½.
- If the plan is top-heavy, the special top-heavy rules discussed earlier must also be met.

## SIMPLIFIED EMPLOYEE PENSION

A **simplified employee pension (SEP)** is a retirement plan in which the employer contributes to an IRA established for each eligible employee; however, the annual contribution limits are substantially higher. SEP plans are popular with smaller employers because the amount of required paperwork is minimal.

In one type of plan, called a **SEP-IRA**, the employer contributes to an IRA owned by each employee. The SEP-IRA must cover all qualifying employees who are at least age 21, have worked for the employer in at least three of the immediately preceding five years, and have received at least $550 (indexed limit for 2012) from the employer in compensation during the tax year.

For 2012, the maximum annual tax-deductible employer contribution to a SEP-IRA is limited to 25 percent of the employee's compensation, or $50,000, whichever is less. A SEP-IRA is funded only by employer contributions. Employees cannot contribute to the plan. There is full and immediate vesting of all employer contributions under the plan.

## SIMPLE RETIREMENT PLANS

Smaller employers are eligible to establish a Savings Incentive Match Plan for Employees, or SIMPLE for short. The **SIMPLE retirement plan** is limited to employers that employ 100 or fewer eligible employees and do not maintain another qualified plan. Under a SIMPLE plan, smaller employers are exempt from most nondiscrimination and administrative rules that apply to qualified plans. A SIMPLE plan can be structured either as an IRA or as a 401(k) plan. Only the IRA arrangement is discussed here (SIMPLE-IRA).

### Eligible Employees

All employees who have earned at least $5000 from the employer during any two previous years and who are reasonably expected to earn at least $5000 during the current year must be allowed to participate in a SIMPLE plan. Self-employed individuals can also participate.

### Employee Contributions

For 2012, eligible employees can elect to make before-tax contributions to an IRA of up to $11,500. Participants age 50 and older in 2012 can elect an additional catch-up contribution of $2500.

### Employer Contributions

Employers can choose between two options and can switch options each year if certain notification requirements are met:

- *Matching option.* The employer matches the employee's contributions on a dollar-for-dollar basis up to 3 percent of the employee's compensation but not to exceed $11,500 for 2012.
- *Nonelective contribution option.* The employer must contribute 2 percent of compensation for each eligible employee who has earned at least $5000 for 2012. (For 2012, the maximum compensation for determining contributions is $250,000.) The contribution must be made regardless of whether the employee participates or not.

All contributions go into an IRA account and are fully and immediately vested. Withdrawals of funds by SIMPLE participants under age 59½ are subject to a 10 percent tax penalty with certain exceptions. However, withdrawals during the first two years of participation are subject to a stiff 25 percent tax penalty.

## FUNDING AGENCY AND FUNDING INSTRUMENTS

An employer must select a funding agency when a pension plan is established. *A **funding agency** is a financial institution that provides for the accumulation or administration of the funds that will be used to pay pension benefits.* If the funding agency is a commercial bank or individual trustee, the plan is called a *trust-fund plan.* If the funding agency is a life insurer, the plan is called an *insured plan.* If both funding agencies are used, the plan is called a *split-funded combination plan.*

The employer must also select a funding instrument to fund the pension plan. *A **funding**

**instrument** *is a trust agreement or insurance contract that states the terms under which the funding agency will accumulate, administer, and disburse the pension funds.* Funding instruments that are widely used today include the following:[5]

- Trust-fund plan
- Separate investment account
- Guaranteed investment contract (GIC)

### Trust-Fund Plan

Most private pension plan assets are invested in trust-fund plans. Under a **trust-fund plan**, all contributions are deposited with a trustee, who invests the funds according to the trust agreement between the employer and trustee. The trustee can be a commercial bank or individual trustee. Annuities are not purchased when the employees retire, and the pension benefits are paid directly out of the fund. The trustee does not guarantee the adequacy of the fund. In addition, there are no guarantees of principal and interest rates when a defined-benefit plan is used. A consulting actuary periodically determines the adequacy of the fund.

### Separate Investment Account

A separate investment account is a group pension product with a life insurance company. Under a **separate investment account**, the plan administrator can invest in one or more of the separate accounts offered by the insurer. The pension contributions can be invested in stock funds, bond funds, and similar investments. The assets in the separate account are segregated from the insurer's general investment account and are not subject to claims by the insurer's creditors. Separate accounts are popular because they permit the plan administrator to invest in a wide variety of investments, including common stocks.

### Guaranteed Investment Contract

A **guaranteed investment contract (GIC)** is an arrangement in which the insurer guarantees the interest rate for a number of years on a lump-sum deposit. The insurer also guarantees the principal against loss. Guaranteed investment contracts are popular with employers because of interest rate guarantees and protection against the loss of principal. Guaranteed investment contracts are sometimes used to fund the fixed-income option in a defined-contribution retirement plan, such as a 401(k) plan. In addition, most guaranteed investment contracts make annuity options available at retirement, but employers are not required to use these options.

## PROBLEMS AND ISSUES IN TAX-DEFERRED RETIREMENT PLANS

Although tax-deferred retirement plans have great potential in reducing economic insecurity during retirement, several serious problems must be resolved. They include the following:[6]

- *Inadequate 401(k) account balances.* The majority of households nearing retirement have 401(k) plans. Most participants, however, have inadequate assets in their 401(k) accounts for a comfortable retirement. According to the Center for Retirement Research, the median 401(k) account balance, including plans from previous employment, was only $149,400 in 2010. *This amount would provide only $9073 annually, or less than one-fourth of the additional amount needed to supplement Social Security and other pension income for a comfortable retirement.*[7]
- *Incomplete coverage of the labor force.* Coverage of the labor force is incomplete. *In March 2011, 64 percent of private industry employees had access to retirement benefits, and only 49 percent actually participated in the plans.*[8] This is due to several factors. Retirement plans are expensive, and many small firms cannot afford them. Also, membership in labor unions, which historically have bargained aggressively for pensions, has declined significantly over time. In addition, to reduce labor costs, an increasing number of firms employ part-time employees and independent contractors who generally are ineligible to participate. Finally, employment in the

services industry has increased substantially over time; service firms generally are financially weaker and less inclined to install retirement plans than larger manufacturing firms.

- *Lower benefits for women.* Women are more likely to receive lower retirement benefits than men. *According to the Employee Benefit Research Institute (EBRI), in 2010, the median annual retirement benefit from employment-based pension plans and retirement annuities for people age 65 and over was $15,000 for males and only $8400 for females.*[9] Pension payments are lower because women enter and leave the labor force more frequently than men because of family obligations, and pension contributions and benefits are lower as a result. Also, women generally are paid less than men, which results in lower pension benefits. Finally, women are more likely to work in part-time jobs where employer-sponsored pension plans may not be available.

- *Limited protection against inflation.* Most participants in employer-sponsored retirement plans are in defined-contribution plans where the benefit amount depends on the value of the employee's account at retirement. Most retired workers do not annuitize their account balances in the form of lifetime income from an insurer but invest the funds on their own. Many retired workers are risk adverse and invest a large part of their retirement assets in fixed income investments, which provide only limited protection against inflation. Likewise, if an immediate annuity is purchased, the annuity typically pays fixed benefits, which also does not provide an inflation hedge unless an option that indexes benefits to inflation is available. If the index option is elected, initial payments are significantly lower than a traditional fixed-income annuity, typically 25 percent to 30 percent lower. Finally, some retired workers receive benefits from defined-benefit pension plans, and most defined-benefit plans do not adjust benefits annually for inflation. As such, the real purchasing power of the benefits declines over time.

- *Spending lump-sum pension distributions.* Millions of workers change jobs each year and often receive lump-sum distributions from their employers' retirement plans. Part or all of the distributions are spent rather than saved for retirement. According to EBRI, 16.2 million workers received lump-sum distributions of retirement assets from 2004 through 2006. The median amount was relatively small ($10,000). *Only 47 percent of those taking a lump-sum distribution reinvested part or all of the money into tax-qualified savings, such as another employment-based plan, IRA, or annuity.*[10] Many workers used part or all of the funds for consumption needs, home purchases, paying down debt, starting a business, education expenses, or expenses in changing jobs. Spending a lump-sum distribution reduces economic security during retirement because the cash is spent, and retirement benefits, if any, are lower. There are also substantial tax penalties for premature distributions before age 59½. A lump-sum distribution is taxed as ordinary income, and, with certain exceptions, a 10 percent penalty tax also applies. Finally, the benefits of compound interest on a tax-deferred basis are lost.

- *Investment mistakes by participants that jeopardize economic security.* Three mistakes are worth noting. First, many eligible workers do not participate in their employers' plans, or if they do, they contribute less than the maximum allowed; as a result, employees who do not participate are passing up "free money" from the matching contributions of employers. Second, many older workers near retirement are too heavily invested in common stock, which can result in substantial losses during market declines. An EBRI study showed that older workers (ages 56–65) experienced losses of 25 percent or more in their 401(k) plans in 2008 when the stock market declined sharply. *One in four participants, ages 56–65, had more than 90 percent of their account balances invested in equities.*[11] Finally, some employees continue to invest heavily in company stock, which can result in significant losses if the company experiences financial problems.

## CASE APPLICATION

Richard, age 40, is the owner of Auto Repair, Inc. In addition to Richard, the company has five employees. Richard wants to establish a retirement plan for his employees. He is considering two plans: (1) a *Section 401(k) plan* and (2) a *SEP-IRA*. Assume you are a financial planner and Richard asks for your advice. Answer the following questions.

a. Explain to Richard the advantages and disadvantages of each plan.

b. Assume that Auto Repair establishes a 401(k) plan. Employees can elect a salary deferral of up to 6 percent of compensation but not to exceed

$17,000 (2012 limit for participants under age 50). The company makes a matching contribution of 50 cents for each dollar contributed. James, age 25, is a mechanic who has decided to defer only 3 percent of his wages because of substantial personal expenses. What advice would you give to James?

c. Susan, age 28, is the company's office manager and earns $35,000. She has worked for the company for three years. Can Richard exclude her from participating in the 401(k) plan to hold down retirement contributions? Explain your answer.

## SUMMARY

- Qualified retirement plans receive favorable income-tax treatment. Employer contributions are tax-deductible and not considered taxable income to the employees; investment earnings accumulate income-tax free; and pension benefits attributable to the employer's contributions are not taxed until the employee retires or receives the funds.

- Under the tax law, qualified pension plans must meet certain minimum coverage requirements, which are designed to reduce discrimination in favor of highly compensated employees.

- To meet the minimum coverage requirement, a qualified retirement plan must satisfy one of the following tests:

   Ratio percentage test

   Average benefit test

- All employees who are at least age 21 and have one year of service must be allowed to participate in a qualified retirement plan.

- A retirement plan has a normal retirement age, an early retirement age, and a deferred retirement age. Most employees cannot be forced to retire at some mandatory retirement age. Benefits generally continue to accrue for employees who work beyond the normal retirement age.

- The benefits in a defined-benefit plan are typically based on the following benefit formulas:

   Unit-benefit formula

   Flat percentage of annual earnings

   Flat dollar amount for each year of service

   Flat dollar amount for all employees

- Vesting refers to the employee's right to the employer's contributions or benefits attributable to the contributions if employment terminates prior to retirement. Qualified retirement plans must meet certain minimum vesting standards.

- A *defined-benefit plan* is a retirement plan in which the retirement benefit is known in advance, but the contributions vary depending on the amount needed to fund the desired benefit.

- For 2012, the maximum annual benefit is limited to 100 percent of the worker's average compensation for the three highest consecutive years of compensation, or $200,000, whichever is lower.

- A *cash-balance plan* is a defined-benefit plan in which the benefits are defined in terms of a hypothetical account balance. The participant's account is credited with a pay credit and an interest credit. Actual retirement benefits will depend on the value of the participant's account at retirement.

- A *defined-contribution plan* is a retirement plan in which the contribution rate is fixed, but the actual retirement benefit varies depending on the age of entry into the plan, contribution rate, investment returns, and age of retirement. For 2012, the maximum annual addition that can be credited to an employee's account is 100 percent of compensation, or $50,000, whichever is lower.

- A *money purchase plan* is a defined-contribution plan in which each participant has an individual account, and the employer's contribution is a fixed percentage of the participant's compensation.

- A *Section 401(k) plan* is a qualified cash or deferred arrangement (CODA) that allows eligible employees the option of putting money into the plan or receiving the funds as cash. The employee typically agrees to a salary reduction, which reduces the employee's taxable income. For 2012, the maximum salary reduction is limited to $17,000 for participants under age 50. Participants age 50 and older can make a catch-up contribution of $5500. These limits are indexed for inflation. The contributions deposited in the plan accumulate income-tax free until the funds are withdrawn.

- A *Section 403(b) plan* is a retirement plan for employees of public schools and tax-exempt organizations. This plan is also called a *tax-sheltered annuity.* Eligible employees can voluntarily elect to reduce their salaries by a fixed amount, which is then invested in the plan. For 2012, the maximum elective deferral for workers under age 50 is $17,000. Participants age 50 and older can make a catch-up contribution of $5500.

- A *profit-sharing plan* is a defined-contribution plan in which the employer's contributions are typically based on the firm's profits.

- A self-employed individual can establish a *Keogh plan* and receive favorable federal income-tax treatment. The contributions to the plan are income-tax deductible, and the investment income accumulates on a tax-deferred basis.

- A *simplified employee pension (SEP)* is a retirement plan in which the employer contributes to an individual retirement account (IRA) established for each eligible employee. For 2012, the maximum annual tax-deductible employer contribution to a SEP-IRA is limited to 25 percent of the employee's compensation, or $50,000, whichever is less. There is full and immediate vesting of all employer contributions under the plan.

- Under a *SIMPLE plan,* for 2012, eligible employees can elect to contribute up to $11,500. Employees age 50 and older can make an additional catch-up contribution of $2500. The maximum annual contribution limit will increase in the future. The employer has the option of either matching the employee's contributions on a dollar-for-dollar basis up to 3 percent of compensation, or making a nonelective contribution of 2 percent of compensation for all eligible employees.

- The major types of funding instruments to fund a pension plan include the following:

  Trust-fund plan

  Separate investment account

  Guaranteed investment contract (GIC)

- Tax-deferred retirement plans have a number of current problems and issues, which include the following:

  Inadequate 401(k) account balances

  Incomplete coverage of the labor force

  Lower benefits for women

  Limited protection against inflation

  Spending lump-sum pension distributions

  Investment mistakes by participants that jeopardize economic security

## KEY CONCEPTS AND TERMS

Actual deferral percentage (ADP) test (362)
Career-average earnings (358)
Cash-balance plan (359)
Deferred retirement age (356)
Defined-benefit plan (358)
Defined-contribution plan (360)
Early retirement age (355)
Employee Retirement Income Security Act of 1974 (ERISA) (354)
Final average pay (358)
Funding agency (365)
Funding instrument (366)
Guaranteed investment contract (GIC) (366)
Highly compensated employees (355)
Individual 401(k) retirement plan (362)
Keogh plans (364)
Minimum age and service requirement (355)
Minimum coverage requirements (355)
Minimum vesting standards (356)

Money purchase plan (360)
Normal retirement age (355)
Past-service credits (358)
Pension Benefit Guaranty Corporation (PBGC) (359)
Pension Protection Act of 2006 (354)
Profit-sharing plan (363)
Qualified plan (354)
Roth 401(k) plan (362)
Roth 403(b) plan (363)
Section 401(k) plan (360)
Section 403(b) plan (363)
Separate investment account (366)
SEP-IRA (365)
SIMPLE retirement plan (365)
Simplified employee pension (SEP) (365)
Tax-sheltered annuities (TSAs) (363)
Top-heavy plan (357)
Trust-fund plans (366)
Vesting (356)

## REVIEW QUESTIONS

1. a. What are the federal income-tax advantages to employers in a qualified retirement plan?
   b. What are the federal income-tax advantages to employees in a qualified retirement plan?

2. A qualified retirement plan must meet certain minimum coverage requirements to receive favorable income-tax treatment. Explain the ratio percentage test.

3. Explain the following retirement ages in a typical qualified retirement plan:
   a. Early retirement age
   b. Normal retirement age
   c. Deferred retirement age

4. a. Briefly explain the basic characteristics of a traditional defined-benefit retirement plan.
   b. What is a cash-balance retirement plan?

5. a. Briefly explain the basic characteristics of a defined-contribution retirement plan.
   b. What is a money purchase plan?

6. a. Describe the basic characteristics of a Section 401(k) plan.
   b. What is a Roth 401(k) plan?
   c. Describe the basic characteristics of a Section 403(b) plan (also called a tax-sheltered annuity).

7. Explain the major characteristics of a profit-sharing plan.

8. Describe the basic features of a Keogh plan for the self-employed.

9. Briefly explain the major characteristics of a simplified employee pension (SEP).

10. a. Briefly explain the basic characteristics of a SIMPLE retirement plan.
    b. Identify the major problems that are currently present in tax-deferred retirement plans.

## APPLICATION QUESTIONS

1. Qualified retirement plans must meet certain requirements to receive favorable federal income-tax treatment. Briefly explain each of the following:
   a. Minimum age and service requirements
   b. Vesting provisions
   c. Limitations on contributions and benefits
   d. Early distribution tax penalty

2. A national labor union representing pipeline construction workers has a defined-benefit pension plan for its members. Ron, age 65, is a heavy equipment operator who wants to retire. He has been a member of the union for 30 years. The pension plan has a unit-benefit formula, which provides a retirement benefit equal to 1.5 percent of the worker's final average compensation for each year of credited service. Final average compensation is based on the worker's three highest consecutive years of earnings prior to retirement. Ron's final average compensation is $70,000. How much will Ron receive each month when he retires?

3. Brandon, age 26, is a self-employed plumber. One month ago, Brandon hired his brother, age 20, to help in the business. Brandon wants to accumulate a retirement fund and decides to adopt a Keogh plan to fund his retirement. Brandon's net earnings (after certain adjustments) are $80,000.
   a. What is the maximum tax-deductible contribution Brandon can make to the Keogh plan?
   b. Does Brandon have to include his brother in his Keogh plan? Explain your answer.

4. An employer must select a funding agency and a funding instrument when a pension plan is established.
   a. What is a funding agency?
   b. Briefly describe each of the following funding instruments:
      1. Trust-fund plan
      2. Guaranteed investment contract

## INTERNET RESOURCES

- The **American Benefits Council** is an organization that represents plan sponsors and technical professionals in the employee benefits field. The site provides an analysis of proposed legislation affecting private pension plans and other employee benefits. Visit the site at

  **appwp.org**

- The **Employee Benefit Research Institute (EBRI)** is a nonprofit organization that makes available research studies and notes on qualified retirement plans. Visit the site at

  **ebri.org**

- The **Employee Benefits Security Administration (EBSA)** is an agency of the U.S. Department of Labor that provides information and statistics on qualified retirement plans. Visit the site at

  **dol.gov/ebsa**

- **Charles Schwab** provides informative articles and information on retirement planning, annuities, and individual retirement accounts (IRAs). Visit the site at

  **schwab.com**

- **Fidelity Investments** provides a substantial amount of timely information on retirement planning and qualified retirement plans, including 401(k) plans. Visit the site at

  **fidelity.com**

- **The Roth 401(k) Web Site** provides technical and planning information on the Roth 401(k) plan to practitioners and consumers. Visit the site at

  roth401k.com

- **The Pension Benefit Guaranty Corporation** is a federal corporation that protects the retirement benefits of workers in defined-benefit pension plans. The site provides timely information on defined-benefit pension plans. Visit the site at

  pbgc.gov

- **The Vanguard Group** provides timely information on retirement planning, variable annuities, and IRAs. Visit the site at

  vanguard.com

- **TIAA-CREF** has an excellent site that provides a considerable amount of information on retirement planning and retirement options. Visit the site at

  tiaa-cref.org

## SELECTED REFERENCES

Browning, E.S. "Retiring Boomers Find 401(k) Plans Fall Short," *The Wall Street Journal,* February 19–20, 2011, pp. A1, A11.

Bureau of Labor Statistics, "Employee Benefits in the United States—March 2011," News Release, July 26, 2011.

Employee Benefit Research Institute, *The Impact of the Recent Financial Crisis on 401(k) Account Balances, EBRI Issue Brief, No. 326,* February 2009.

Employee Benefit Research Institute, "More Detail on Lump-Sum Distributions of Workers Who have Left a Job," *Notes,* Vol. 30, No. 7, July 2009.

Employee Benefits Research Institute, *EBRI Data Book on Employee Benefits,* Chapter 8, updated October 11, 2011.

Employee Benefit Research Institute, "EBRI's 2012 Retirement Confidence Survey: Job Insecurity, Debt, Weigh on Retirement Confidence, Savings," *EBRI Issue Brief, No. 362,* March 13, 2012.

Internal Revenue Service, *Publication 4222, 401(k) Plans for Small Businesses,* December 2011.

Internal Revenue Service, *Publication 571, Tax-Sheltered Annuity Plans (403(b) Plans),* 2011.

Internal Revenue Service, *Publication 560, Retirement Plans for Small Business (SEP, SIMPLE, and Qualified Plans),* February 7, 2012.

Kaster, Nicholas, et al., *2012 U.S. Master Pension Guide,* Chicago, IL: CCH Inc., 2012.

Rosenbloom, Jerry S., ed. *The Handbook of Employee Benefits,: Health and Group Benefits* 7th ed. The McGraw-Hill Companies, New York: McGraw-Hill, 2011.

Society of Actuaries. *Managing Post-Retirement Risks, A Guide to Retirement Planning,* October 2011.

## NOTES

1. This chapter is based on Internal Revenue Service Publications 560, 571, and 4222; and Nicholas Kaster, et al., *2012 U.S. Master Pension Guide* (Chicago, IL: CCH Inc., 2012).

2. For 2012, highly compensated employees are employees who (1) owned 5 percent of the company at any time during the year or preceding year or (2) had compensation from the employer in excess of $115,000 (indexed for inflation), or if the employer elects, were in the highest 20 percent of employees based on compensation for the preceding year.

3. For details, see Nicholas Kaster, et al., *2012 U.S. Master Pension Guide* (Chicago, IL: CCH, Inc., 2012), pp. 327–328.

4. Nicholas Kaster, et al., *2012 U.S. Master Pension Guide* (Chicago, IL: CCH Inc., 2012), p. 1052.

5. David A. Littell and Kenn Beam Tacchino, *Planning for Retirement Needs,* 9th ed. (Bryn Mawr, PA: The American College, 2007), ch. 12.

6. George E. Rejda, *Social Insurance and Economic Security,* 7th ed. Armonk, New York: M.E. Sharpe, 2012, pp. 82–86.

7. E.S. Browning, "Retiring Boomers Find 401(k) Plans Fall Short," *The Wall Street Journal,* February 19–20, 2011, p. A11.

8. Bureau of Labor Statistics, "Employee Benefits in the United States—March 2011," News Release, July 26, 2011, Table 1.

9. Employee Benefits Research Institute, *EBRI Data Book on Employee Benefits,* Chapter 8, Tables 8.1 and 8.2, updated October 11, 2011.

10. Employee Benefit Research Institute, "More Detail on Lump-Sum Distributions of Workers Who have Left a Job," *Notes,* July 2009, Vol. 30, No. 7, Figure 5.

11. Employee Benefit Research Institute, "The Impact of the Recent Financial Crisis on 401(k) Account Balances," *EBRI Issue Brief No. 326,* February 2009.

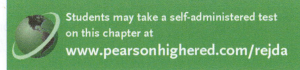

Students may take a self-administered test on this chapter at
**www.pearsonhighered.com/rejda**

# CHAPTER 18

# SOCIAL INSURANCE

*"Economic security is one of the unfulfilled needs of humans. Social security programs have been designed to aid people in their quest for economic security."*

Robert J. Myers
*Social Security*, 4th ed.

*Social insurance programs are compulsory government insurance programs with certain characteristics that distinguish them from private insurance and other government insurance programs. The various programs provide a safety net against economic insecurity that can result from old age, premature death, poor health, unemployment, and job-related disabilities. For example, Andrew, age 29, died instantly in a motorcycle accident in early 2013. He left behind a wife and two children, ages one and three. At the time of his death, Andrew qualified for Social Security survivor benefits. Based on his covered earnings, his family is currently receiving monthly benefits of approximately $2140, which enables them to maintain at least a minimum standard of living.*

*In this chapter, we discuss the major social insurance programs in the United States. Programs discussed include Social Security (OASDI) and Medicare, state unemployment compensation programs, and workers compensation programs.*

## SOCIAL INSURANCE

### Reasons for Social Insurance

Although the United States has a highly developed system of private insurance, social insurance programs are necessary for several reasons.

- *Social insurance programs are enacted to solve complex social problems.* A social problem affects most or all of society and is so serious that direct government intervention is necessary. For example, the Social Security program came into existence because of the Great Depression of the 1930s, when massive unemployment required a direct government attack on economic insecurity.
- *Social insurance programs are necessary because certain risks are difficult to insure privately.* For example, unemployment is difficult to insure privately because it does not completely meet the requirements of an insurable risk. However, the risk of unemployment can be insured by state unemployment insurance programs.

- *Social insurance programs provide a base of economic security to the population.* Social insurance programs provide a layer of financial protection to most persons against the long-term financial consequences of premature death, old age, occupational and nonoccupational disability, and unemployment.

### Basic Characteristics of Social Insurance

Social insurance programs in the United States have certain characteristics that distinguish them from other government insurance programs:[1]

- Compulsory programs
- Floor of income
- Emphasis on social adequacy rather than individual equity
- Benefits loosely related to earnings
- Benefits prescribed by law
- No means test
- Full funding unnecessary
- Financially self-supporting

**Compulsory Programs**   With few exceptions, social insurance programs are compulsory. A compulsory program has three major advantages. First, the goal of providing a floor of income to the population can be achieved more easily. Second, adverse selection is reduced, because both healthy and unhealthy lives are covered. Finally, in a large program that is compulsory, fewer random or accidental fluctuations in loss experience are likely to occur, and the necessity of providing margins in contingency reserves is reduced.

**Floor of Income**   Social insurance programs are generally designed to provide only a floor of income with respect to the risks that are covered. Most persons are expected to supplement social insurance benefits with their own personal program of savings, investments, and private insurance.

The concept of a floor of income is difficult to define. One extreme view is that the floor of income should be so low as to be virtually nonexistent. Another extreme view is that the social insurance benefit by itself should be high enough to provide a comfortable standard of living, so that private insurance benefits would be unnecessary. A more realistic view is that social insurance benefits, when combined with other income and financial assets, should be sufficient for most persons to maintain a reasonable standard of living. Any group whose basic needs are still unmet would be provided for by supplemental public assistance (welfare) benefits.

**Social Adequacy Rather Than Individual Equity**   Social insurance programs pay benefits based largely on social adequacy rather than on individual equity. **Social adequacy** *means that the benefits paid should provide a certain standard of living to all contributors. This means that the benefits paid are heavily weighted in favor of certain groups, such as low-income persons, large families, and the presently retired aged.* In technical terms, the actuarial value of the benefits received by these groups exceeds the actuarial value of their contributions. In contrast, the individual equity principle is followed in private insurance. **Individual equity** *means that contributors receive benefits directly related to their contributions; the actuarial value of the benefits is closely related to the actuarial value of the contributions.*

The basic purpose of the social adequacy principle is to provide a floor of income to all covered persons. If low-income persons received social insurance benefits actuarially equal to the value of their tax contributions (individual equity principle), the benefits paid would be so low that the basic objective of providing a floor of income to everyone would not be achieved.

**Benefits Loosely Related to Earnings**   Social insurance benefits are loosely related to the worker's earnings. The higher the worker's covered earnings, the greater will be the benefits. The relationship between higher earnings and higher benefits is loose and disproportionate, but it does exist. Thus, some consideration is given to individual equity.

**Benefits Prescribed by Law**   Social insurance programs are prescribed by law. The benefits or benefit formulas, as well as the eligibility requirements, are established by law. In addition, the administration or supervision of the program is performed by government.

**No Means Test**   Social insurance benefits are paid as a matter of right without any demonstration of need. A formal means test is not required. A **means test** is used in public assistance; welfare applicants must show that their income and financial assets are below certain levels as a condition of benefit eligibility. By contrast, applicants for social insurance benefits have a statutory right to the benefits if they fulfill certain eligibility requirements.

**Full Funding Unnecessary**   For example, the Social Security program is not fully funded. A **fully funded program** means that the accumulated OASDI trust fund assets plus the present value of future contributions will be sufficient to discharge all liabilities over the valuation period. Social Security actuaries make cost estimates over a 75-year projection period and even beyond. According to the 2012 Board of Trustees report, the present value of the unfunded obligations over the 75-year period from 2012 through 2086 is $8.6 trillion. The present value of the unfunded obligations from 2012 through the infinite horizon is $20.5 trillion. (Infinite horizon means that the current OASDI program and the demographic and most economic trends used for the 75-year projection period continue indefinitely.) However, the combined OASDI trust fund balance at the end of 2011 totaled only $2.7 trillion.[2] To be fully funded, a substantially higher trust fund balance would be required.

A fully funded Social Security program is unnecessary for several reasons. First, because the program will operate indefinitely and not terminate in the predictable future, full funding is unnecessary. Second, because the Social Security program is compulsory, new workers will always enter the program and pay taxes to support it. Third, the federal government can use its taxing and borrowing powers to raise additional revenues if the program has financial problems. Finally, from an economic viewpoint, full funding would require substantially higher Social Security taxes, which would be deflationary and cause substantial unemployment. In contrast, private pension plans must emphasize full funding because private pension plans can terminate.

**Financially Self-Supporting**  Social insurance programs in the United States are designed to be financially self-supporting. This means the programs should be almost completely financed from the earmarked contributions of covered employees, employers, the self-employed, and interest on the trust-fund investments.

## OLD-AGE, SURVIVORS, AND DISABILITY INSURANCE

The Old-Age, Survivors, and Disability Insurance (OASDI) program, commonly known as **Social Security,** is the most important social insurance program in the United States. Social Security was enacted into law as a result of the Social Security Act of 1935. More than nine out of ten workers are working in occupations covered by Social Security, and about one in six persons receives a monthly cash benefit.

### Covered Occupations

Virtually all private-sector employees are covered under Social Security at the present time. Federal civilian employees hired after 1983 are also covered on a compulsory basis. In addition, state and local government employees can be covered by a voluntary agreement between the state and federal government. The majority of state and local government employees are now covered.

### Determination of Insured Status

Before you or your family can receive benefits, you must have credit for a certain amount of work in covered employment. Credits can be earned anytime during the year. For 2013, you receive one **credit** (also called a **quarter of coverage**) for each $1160 of covered earnings. A maximum of four credits can be earned each year. The amount of covered earnings required to earn one credit will automatically increase each year as average wages in the national economy rise.

To become eligible for the various benefits, you must attain an insured status. There are three types of insured status:

- Fully insured
- Currently insured
- Disability insured

Retirement benefits require a fully insured status. Survivor benefits require either a fully insured or currently insured status, although certain survivor benefits require a fully insured status. Disability benefits require a disability-insured status.

**Fully Insured**  To be eligible for retirement benefits, you must be fully insured. You are **fully insured** for retirement benefits if you have 40 credits. However, for people born before 1929, fewer credits are required.

**Currently Insured**  You are **currently insured** if you have earned at least six credits during the last 13 calendar quarters ending with the quarter of death, disability, or entitlement to retirement benefits.

**Disability Insured**  You must meet two work tests to be **disability insured:** (1) a recent work test and (2) a duration of work test. The number of credits required to meet the *recent work test* depends on your age when you become disabled. The following rules apply:

- If you become disabled before age 24, you need one and a half years of work (six credits) in the three years before you became disabled.
- For ages 24 through 30, you need credits for half of the time between age 21 and the time you became disabled. For example, a worker disabled at age 27 needs credit for three years of work out of the past six years.
- If you become disabled at age 31 or older, you need at least five years of work out of the past 10 years immediately before you became disabled.

A *duration of work test must* also be satisfied. The work, however, does not have to occur within a certain period of time. The following table shows how many credits you would need at selected ages to meet the duration of work test:

| If you become disabled: | Then you generally need: |
|---|---|
| Before age 28 | 1.5 years of work |
| 30 | 2 years |
| 34 | 3 years |
| 38 | 4 years |
| 42 | 5 years |
| 44 | 5.5 years |
| 46 | 6 years |
| 48 | 6.5 years |
| 50 | 7 years |
| 52 | 7.5 years |
| 54 | 8 years |
| 56 | 8.5 years |
| 58 | 9 years |
| 60 | 9.5 years |

Finally, blind persons are required only to have a fully insured status. They are not required to meet the recent-work test requirement that applies to other disability applicants.

## TYPES OF BENEFITS

The total program consists of Social Security (OASDI) and Medicare. The OASDI program pays monthly retirement, survivor, and disability benefits to eligible beneficiaries. The Medicare program covers the medical expenses of almost all persons aged 65 and older and certain disabled beneficiaries younger than age 65. We discuss only OASDI cash benefits at this point; Medicare is covered later in the chapter.

### Retirement Benefits

Social Security retirement benefits are an important source of income for most retired workers. Without these benefits, poverty and economic insecurity among the aged would be substantially increased.

**Full Retirement Age**   For persons born in 1937 or earlier, the **full retirement age** for unreduced benefits is age 65. For persons born between 1943–1954, the full retirement age is 66. The full retirement age will gradually increase in the future to age 67 to improve the financial solvency of the OASDI program and to allow for the increase in life expectancy (see Exhibit 18.1).

**Exhibit 18.1**
**Social Security Full Retirement Age and Reduction in Benefits by Age**

*No matter what your full retirement age (also called "normal retirement age") is, you may start receiving benefits as early as age 62.*

| Year of Birth[a] | Full Retirement Age | Age 62 Reduction Months[b] | Monthly % Reduction | Total % Reduction at Age 62 |
|---|---|---|---|---|
| 1937 or earlier | 65 | 36 | .555 | 20.00 |
| 1938 | 65 and 2 months | 38 | .548 | 20.83 |
| 1939 | 65 and 4 months | 40 | .541 | 21.67 |
| 1940 | 65 and 6 months | 42 | .535 | 22.50 |
| 1941 | 65 and 8 months | 44 | .530 | 23.33 |
| 1942 | 65 and 10 months | 46 | .525 | 24.17 |
| 1943–1954 | 66 | 48 | .520 | 25.00 |
| 1955 | 66 and 2 months | 50 | .516 | 25.84 |
| 1956 | 66 and 4 months | 52 | .512 | 26.66 |
| 1957 | 66 and 6 months | 54 | .509 | 27.50 |
| 1958 | 66 and 8 months | 56 | .505 | 28.33 |
| 1959 | 66 and 10 months | 58 | .502 | 29.17 |
| 1960 and later | 67 | 60 | .500 | 30.00 |

[a]If you were born on January 1, you should refer to the previous year.
[b]If you were born on the first of the month, the benefit is figured as if your birthday were in the previous month.
SOURCE: Social Security Administration.

**Early Retirement Age** Workers and their spouses can retire as early as age 62 with actuarially reduced benefits (see Exhibit 18.1).

The actuarial reduction in benefits for early retirement at age 62 will gradually increase to 30 percent in the future when the higher full retirement age provisions become fully effective.

**Monthly Retirement Benefits** Monthly retirement benefits can be paid to retired workers and their dependents. Eligible persons include the following:

- *Retired worker.* Monthly retirement benefits can be paid at the full retirement age to a fully insured worker. Reduced benefits can be paid as early as age 62.
- *Spouse of a retired worker.* The spouse of a retired worker can also receive monthly benefits if she or he is at least age 62 and has been married to the retired worker for at least one year. A divorced spouse is also eligible for benefits based on the retired worker's earnings if she or he is at least age 62 and the marriage lasted at least 10 years.
- *Unmarried children younger than age 18.* Monthly benefits can also be paid to unmarried children of a retired worker who are younger than age 18 (or 19 if full-time elementary or high school students).
- *Unmarried disabled children.* Unmarried disabled children age 18 or older are also eligible for benefits based on the retired worker's earnings if they were severely disabled before age 22 and continue to remain disabled.
- *Spouse with dependent children younger than age 16.* A spouse at any age can receive a monthly benefit if the spouse is caring for an eligible child younger than age 16 (or is caring for a child of any age who was disabled before age 22) who is receiving a benefit based on the retired worker's earnings. The mother's or father's benefit terminates when the youngest child attains age 16 (unless the mother or father is caring for a child disabled before age 22).

**Retirement Benefit Amount** The monthly retirement benefit is based on the worker's **primary insurance amount (PIA)**, which is the monthly amount paid to a retired worker at the full retirement age or to a disabled worker. The PIA, in turn, is based on the worker's **average indexed monthly earnings (AIME)**, which is a method that updates the worker's past earnings based on increases in the average wage in the national economy. A worker's past earnings are adjusted by changes in the average wage index, which brings them up to their approximate equivalent value at the time of retirement or eligibility for other benefits. The indexing of covered wages results in a relatively constant replacement rate so that workers retiring today and in the future will have about the same proportion of their work earnings replaced by OASDI benefits.

For persons born after 1928, the highest 35 years of indexed earnings are used to calculate the worker's AIME for retirement benefits. (For those born earlier, fewer years are counted.) The AIME is then used to determine the worker's primary insurance amount. A weighted benefit formula is used, which weights the benefits heavily in favor of low-income groups. This weighting reflects the social adequacy principle discussed earlier.

Exhibit 18.2 shows estimated annual retirement benefits in constant dollars for various income levels, and the percent of earnings replaced by retirement benefits, from 2012 to 2090. For 2012, Social Security retirement benefits replaced about 58 percent of earnings for low-income workers, about 43 percent for medium-income workers, about 36 percent for high-income earners, and about 29 percent for high-income workers with steady maximum earnings.

As you can see, the social adequacy principle explained earlier is clearly evident. Low-income workers have a much higher percentage of their career-average earnings replaced by Social Security than workers at higher income levels. In addition, the floor-of-income principle discussed earlier is also evident. Social Security benefits provide only a floor or a base of income, rather than full replacement of your earnings.

**Delayed Retirement** Some workers delay their retirement and work beyond the full retirement age. If you continue working, you can increase your future Social Security benefits in two ways. First, each additional year of work adds another year of earnings to your Social Security earnings record. Higher lifetime earnings may result in higher benefits when you retire.

Second, a **delayed retirement credit** is available if you delay receiving retirement benefits beyond the full retirement age. Your primary insurance amount will be increased by a certain percentage from the time you reach the full retirement age until you start receiving benefits, or until you reach age 70. The percentage increase varies depending on the year of

EXHIBIT 18.2

Annuul Scheduled Benefit Amounts[a] for Retired Workers with Various Pre-Retirement Earnings Patterns, Based on Intermediate Assumptions, Calender Years (2012-2090)

| Year attain age 65[b] | Retirement at full retirement age | | |
|---|---|---|---|
| | Age at retirement | CPI-indexed 2012 dollars[c] | Percent of earnings replaced |
| **Scaled Low earnings[d]** | | | |
| 2012.......... | 66:0 | $11,390 | 57.8 |
| 2015.......... | 66:0 | 11,327 | 53.7 |
| 2020.......... | 66:2 | 12,481 | 53.9 |
| 2025.......... | 67:0 | 13,643 | 55.5 |
| 2030.......... | 67:0 | 14,347 | 55.3 |
| 2035.......... | 67:0 | 15,161 | 55.2 |
| 2040.......... | 67:0 | 16,042 | 55.1 |
| 2045.......... | 67:0 | 16,988 | 55.3 |
| 2050.......... | 67:0 | 17,960 | 55.3 |
| 2055.......... | 67:0 | 18,958 | 55.4 |
| 2060.......... | 67:0 | 20,001 | 55.4 |
| 2065.......... | 67:0 | 21,084 | 55.4 |
| 2070.......... | 67:0 | 22,228 | 55.4 |
| 2075.......... | 67:0 | 23,428 | 55.4 |
| 2080.......... | 67:0 | 24,710 | 55.4 |
| 2085.......... | 67:0 | 26,079 | 55.3 |
| 2090.......... | 67:0 | 27,551 | 55.3 |
| **Scaled Medium earnings[e]** | | | |
| 2012.......... | 66:0 | 18,771 | 42.9 |
| 2015.......... | 66:0 | 18,667 | 39.8 |
| 2020.......... | 66:2 | 20,575 | 40.0 |
| 2025.......... | 67:0 | 22,498 | 41.2 |
| 2030.......... | 67:0 | 23,644 | 41.0 |
| 2035.......... | 67:0 | 24,987 | 40.9 |
| 2040.......... | 67:0 | 26,444 | 40.9 |
| 2045.......... | 67:0 | 27,999 | 41.0 |
| 2050.......... | 67:0 | 29,603 | 41.1 |
| 2055.......... | 67:0 | 31,244 | 41.1 |
| 2060.......... | 67:0 | 32,958 | 41.1 |
| 2065.......... | 67:0 | 34,745 | 41.1 |
| 2070.......... | 67:0 | 36,632 | 41.1 |
| 2075.......... | 67:0 | 38,607 | 41.1 |
| 2080.......... | 67:0 | 40,719 | 41.0 |
| 2085.......... | 67:0 | 42,979 | 41.0 |
| 2090.......... | 67:0 | 45,403 | 41.0 |
| **Scaled High earnings[f]** | | | |
| 2012.......... | 66:0 | $24,891 | 35.5 |
| 2015.......... | 66:0 | 24,745 | 33.0 |
| 2020.......... | 66:2 | 27,252 | 33.1 |

| Year attain age 65[b] | Retirement at full retirement age | | |
|---|---|---|---|
| | Age at retirement | CPI-indexed 2012 dollars[c] | Percent of earnings replaced |
| 2025........... | 67:0 | 29,817 | 34.1 |
| 2030........... | 67:0 | 31,337 | 34.0 |
| 2035........... | 67:0 | 33,110 | 33.9 |
| 2040........... | 67:0 | 35,041 | 33.9 |
| 2045........... | 67:0 | 37,101 | 33.9 |
| 2050........... | 67:0 | 39,227 | 34.0 |
| 2055........... | 67:0 | 41,404 | 34.0 |
| 2060........... | 67:0 | 43,675 | 34.0 |
| 2065........... | 67:0 | 46,045 | 34.0 |
| 2070........... | 67:0 | 48,543 | 34.1 |
| 2075........... | 67:0 | 51,160 | 34.0 |
| 2080........... | 67:0 | 53,957 | 34.0 |
| 2085........... | 67:0 | 56,951 | 34.0 |
| 2090........... | 67:0 | 60,163 | 33.9 |
| **Steady maximum earnings[g]** | | | |
| 2012........... | 66:0 | 29,902 | 28.7 |
| 2015........... | 66:0 | 30,115 | 26.5 |
| 2020........... | 66:2 | 33,338 | 26.5 |
| 2025........... | 67:0 | 36,667 | 27.3 |
| 2030........... | 67:0 | 38,600 | 27.2 |
| 2035........... | 67:0 | 40,803 | 27.1 |
| 2040........... | 67:0 | 43,148 | 27.1 |
| 2045........... | 67:0 | 45,697 | 27.1 |
| 2050........... | 67:0 | 48,251 | 27.2 |
| 2055........... | 67:0 | 50,820 | 27.3 |
| 2060........... | 67:0 | 53,607 | 27.3 |
| 2065........... | 67:0 | 56,521 | 27.3 |
| 2070........... | 67:0 | 59,582 | 27.3 |
| 2075........... | 67:0 | 62,798 | 27.3 |
| 2080........... | 67:0 | 66,237 | 27.3 |
| 2085........... | 67:0 | 69,911 | 27.3 |
| 2090........... | 67:0 | 73,854 | 27.2 |

[a]Annual amounts are the total for the 12-month period starting with the month of retirement.
[b]Attain age 65 on January 1 of the year.
[c]CPI-indexed dollar adjustment uses the adjusted CPI indexing series shown in table VI.F6.
[d]Career-average earnings at about 45 percent of the national average wage index (AWI).
[e]Career-average earnings at about 100 percent of the AWI.
[f]Career-average earnings at about 160 percent of the AWI.
[g]Earnings for each year at or the contribution and benefit base.

SOURCE: Adapted from *The 2012 Annual Report of the Board of Trustees of the Federal Old-Age and Survivors Insurance and Disability Insurance Trust Funds*, Washington, DC: U.S. Government Printing Office, 2012, Table V.C 7, pp. 142–143.

birth. For workers born in 1943 or later, the primary insurance amount is increased 8 percent per year (prorated monthly) for each year of delay beyond the full retirement age.

About half of the OASDI beneficiaries apply for retirement benefits during the first year they become eligible (age 62) and receive actuarially reduced benefits. However, if you delay retiring until you reach the full retirement age, or attain age 70, your benefits will be substantially higher. The higher returns from delayed retirement are impressive. For example, assume your full retirement age is age 66. If *you retire at age 70 instead of age 62, your monthly benefit will be 76 percent higher. Even if you retire at the full retirement age (currently age 66 in 2012), your monthly benefit will be 33 percent higher. In contrast, if you retire early at age 62, your monthly benefit will be 25 percent lower than the amount payable at the full retirement age.*[3] The actuarial reduction will gradually increase to 30 percent of the PIA in the future.

Is it desirable to receive Social Security benefits early? This is a complex question to answer and depends on your need for retirement income, state of health, life expectancy, whether you are still working in the labor force, and whether you have other financial assets that yield income. Insight 18.1 discusses this issue in greater detail.

**Automatic Cost-of-Living Adjustment**  The cash benefits are automatically adjusted each year for changes in the cost of living, which maintains the real purchasing power of the monthly benefits during periods of inflation. Whenever the consumer price index for all urban wage earners and clerical workers on a quarterly basis increases from the third quarter of the previous year to the third quarter of the present year, the benefits are automatically increased by the same percentage for the December benefits (payable in January). The cost-of-living increase for benefits payable in January 2013 was 1.7 percent.

**Earnings Test**  The OASDI program has an **earnings test (retirement test)** that can result in a reduction or loss of monthly benefits for workers with earned incomes above certain annual limits. The earnings test applies to the following:

- *Beneficiary under the full retirement age.* If a beneficiary is under the full retirement age for the entire year, $1 in benefits will be deducted for each $2 of earnings in excess of the annual limit. For 2013, the annual limit is $15,120. The annual limit is increased annually based on increases in average wages in the national economy.

- *Calendar year in which the beneficiary attains the full retirement age.* The earnings test is liberalized for this age group. In the calendar year in which the beneficiary attains the full retirement age, $1 in benefits will be deducted for each $3 of earnings above the annual limit. For 2013, the annual limit is $40,080. *However, only earnings before the month in which the beneficiary attains the full retirement age are counted.* For example, assume that Jason attains the full retirement age in July 2013. During the first six months of 2013, Jason earned $43,080. Because his earnings are $3000 over the annual limit, he will lose $1000 in benefits.

  The annual limit for this age group will increase in the future based on increases in average wages in the national economy.

- *Earnings test eliminated after attainment of the full retirement age.* The earnings test does not apply in and after the month the beneficiary attains the full retirement age. *Beneficiaries who have attained the full retirement age or beyond can earn any amount and receive full OASDI benefits.* As an alternative, beneficiaries who continue working beyond the full retirement age can elect to receive a delayed retirement credit instead of monthly cash benefits.

The earnings test does not apply to investment income, dividends, interest, rents, or annuity payments. The purpose of this exception is to encourage private savings and investments to supplement OASDI benefits.

## Survivor Benefits

Survivor benefits can be paid to the dependents of a deceased worker who is either fully or currently insured. For certain survivor benefits, a fully insured status is required.

Social Security survivor benefits provide a substantial amount of financial protection to families in terms of private life insurance equivalents. Survivor benefits are especially valuable for younger families with children. For example, assume that a worker,

## INSIGHT 18.1

### Taking Social Security: Sooner Might Not Be Better

The thought of receiving Social Security benefits early can be enticing. If you can start getting payments as soon as age 62, why wait until you reach full retirement age at 66 or 67?

The answer is simple: Waiting could mean putting more money in your pocket over the long term. If you start collecting Social Security before full retirement, you could get less each month than if you wait just a few years.

#### How much less will you get?

The amount of the reduction depends on how many months before your full retirement age you start taking benefits. The earlier you start, the bigger the cut.

Your birth year determines your full retirement age. If you were born between 1943 and 1954, it's age 66—increasing incrementally until it reaches the maximum age of 67 for people born in 1960 and after.

According to the Social Security Administration, older baby boomers who started taking benefits at age 62 will see a lifelong reduction of 25% in monthly payments compared with what they would have gotten by waiting until full retirement age. The percentage increases to 30% if your birth year is after 1959. Spouses also will see at least a 30% drop in the benefit amount they receive, and those born after 1959 face a 35% drop.

While you can collect benefits before full retirement age and continue working, you might get hit with an earned-income penalty. The Social Security Administration deducts $1 from your payments for every $2 you earn above an income threshold ($14,640 for 2012). The year you reach full retirement age, the deduction changes to $1 for every $3 you earn (up to $38,880 in 2012) until you reach your birth month—after that, the earned-income penalty no longer applies.

Your actual benefit amount is based on the income you earned during your working life. If you're under age 60, you won't get an earned income estimate from Social Security mailed to you; however, you can check this information—and confirm it's correct—at ssa.gov.

#### Consider waiting to file for benefits

Given the downsides of taking benefits early, you may want to think about waiting until you reach your full retirement age, suggests John Ameriks of Vanguard Investment Counseling & Research.

"If you don't have an immediate need for Social Security, it may be best to delay taking the benefit," Mr. Ameriks said.

For example, if you were born in 1946 and put off taking benefits until age 70 (in 2016), you'd see a 32% increase in monthly payment amount over what you would have received by starting this year. That's because you get an increase (two-thirds of 1%) for each month you delay beyond full retirement age.

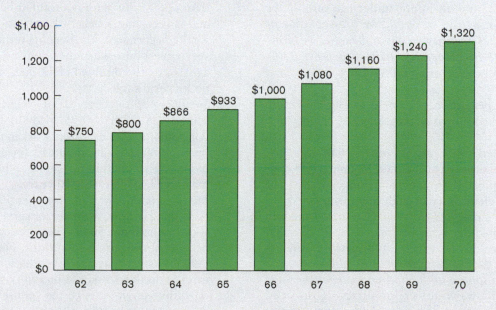

Monthly payment by age you choose to receive benefits

*(Continued)*

## INSIGHT 18.1    (Continued)

The sample benefits used in this chart are based on Social Security Administration estimates for a person who qualifies to receive a starting monthly benefit payment of $1,000 at the full retirement age of 66. All amounts are in today's dollars and don't include potential earnings from reinvestment. Actual income will include any increases in benefits based on inflation.

Of course, if you need to take Social Security to help meet your current spending needs, you should feel free to do so, Mr. Ameriks added. And because there's no advantage to waiting past age 70 to apply for benefits, don't hold out any longer than that.

### A method to maximize benefits when you're married

If your spouse also qualifies to receive benefits based on his or her employment history, there's a strategy generally called restricted application that could help you maximize how much your household gets from Social Security.

Here's how it works: The lower-earning spouse applies for benefits at age 62 and receives the reduced amount. The higher-earning spouse files for spousal benefits *only* at age 66, collecting half of the lower-earning spouse's full benefits while postponing his or her own full benefits until age 70—so that they'll continue to increase.

While the dollar amounts will vary based on your situation, here's an example: The lower-earning spouse qualifies for a $1,000 full benefit but takes a lower benefit of $750 at age 62. The higher-earning spouse gets $500 when filing for spousal benefits only. The addition of the spousal benefit can give you $6,000 more in Social Security income each year.

Another advantage of this method: The lower-earning spouse will get a higher survivor benefit if he or she survives the higher earner.

### Plan for a longer life expectancy

Your expected longevity is another important factor to consider in this decision, Mr. Ameriks said. Americans' life expectancy is on the rise, with a quarter of today's 65-year-olds projected to live past age 90—and 1 out of 10 to live past age 95—according to the Social Security Administration.

Of course, you can't predict exactly how long you'll live, but your health status and family history can give an indication. If you're concerned your life span will be shorter, you may want to start collecting benefits at age 62. Your monthly payments will be reduced, but you could receive a higher lifetime amount because you started taking benefits sooner.

However, if you expect to be one of those longer-living people—or you're concerned about the risk of outliving your assets—you might consider waiting to receive benefits until age 70 to boost your future monthly payments.

SOURCE: Excerpted from "Taking Social Security: Sooner Might Not Be Better," The Vanguard Group. April 24, 2012.

---

age 30, with average earnings, has a spouse, age 28, a child, age 2, and an infant under age one. *If the worker died at age 30 in 2008, the present value of expected Social Security survivor benefits in terms of private life insurance equivalents is $476,000.*[4] However, the benefits are paid monthly and not in a lump sum.

Survivor benefits can be paid to eligible family members in the following categories:

- *Unmarried children younger than age 18.* Survivor benefits can be paid to unmarried children younger than age 18 (younger than 19 if full-time elementary or high school students).
- *Unmarried disabled children.* Unmarried children age 18 or older who become severely disabled before age 22 are eligible for survivor benefits based on the deceased parent's earnings.
- *Surviving spouse with children younger than age 16.* A widow, widower, or surviving divorced spouse is entitled to a monthly benefit if she or he is caring for an eligible child who is younger than age 16 (or who is disabled before age 22) and is receiving a benefit based on the deceased worker's earnings. The benefits terminate for the surviving spouse when the youngest child reaches age 16, or the disabled child dies, marries, or is no longer disabled.
- *Surviving spouse age 60 or older.* A surviving spouse age 60 or older is also eligible for survivor benefits. The deceased worker must be fully insured. A surviving divorced spouse age 60 or older is also eligible for survivor benefits if the marriage lasted at least 10 years.
- *Disabled widow or widower ages 50 through 59.* A disabled widow, widower, or surviving divorced spouse who is age 50 or older can receive survivor benefits under certain conditions. The benefits can be paid as early as age 50 if the widow or widower is disabled, and the disability started before or within seven years of the spouse's death. The deceased must be fully insured.

- *Dependent parents.* Dependent parents age 62 and older can also receive survivor benefits based on the deceased's earnings. The deceased worker must be fully insured.
- *Lump-sum death benefit.* A lump-sum death benefit of $255 can be paid when a worker dies. The benefit, however, can be paid only if there is an eligible surviving widow, widower, or entitled child.

## Disability Benefits

Disability-income benefits can be paid to disabled workers who meet certain eligibility requirements. The insurance value of the protection provided is substantial. *Referring back to the previous example, the present value of expected disability-income benefits for a worker entitled to disability benefits at age 30 is $465,000.*[5] This amount represents (1) the present value of expected benefits paid to the disabled worker and his/her dependents while the disabled worker is alive, and (2) the present value of the benefits paid to the survivors after the disabled worker's death, or after reaching the disability conversion age (age at which disability benefits are converted to retirement benefits).

To be eligible for benefits, a disabled worker must meet the following eligibility requirements:

- Be disability insured
- Meet a five-month waiting period
- Satisfy the definition of disability

A disabled worker must be disability insured and must also satisfy a five-month waiting period. Benefits begin after a waiting period of five full calendar months. Therefore, the first payment is for the sixth full month of disability.

The definition of disability stated in the law must also be met. A strict definition of disability is used in the program: *The worker must have a physical or mental condition that prevents him or her from doing any substantial gainful activity and is expected to last (or has lasted) at least 12 months or is expected to result in death.* The impairment must be so severe that the worker is prevented from doing any substantial gainful work in the national economy. In determining whether a person can do substantial gainful work, his or her age, education, training, and work experience can be taken into consideration. If the disabled person cannot work at his or her own occupation but can

engage in other substantial gainful work, the disability claim will not be allowed.

The major groups eligible to receive OASDI disability-income benefits are as follows:

- *Disabled worker.* A disabled worker under the full retirement age receives a benefit equal to 100 percent of the primary insurance amount. The worker must meet the definition of disability, be disability insured, and satisfy a full five-month waiting period.
- *Spouse of a disabled worker.* Benefits can be paid to the spouse of a disabled worker at any age if she or he is caring for a child younger than age 16 or a child who became disabled before age 22 and is receiving benefits based on the disabled worker's earnings. If no eligible children are present, the spouse must be at least age 62 to receive benefits.
- *Unmarried children younger than age 18.* Disability benefits can be paid to unmarried children younger than age 18 (or younger than 19 if a full-time elementary or high school student).
- *Unmarried disabled children.* Unmarried children age 18 or older who became severely disabled before age 22 are also eligible for benefits, based on the disabled worker's earnings.

## Taxation of OASDI Benefits

Some beneficiaries who receive monthly cash benefits must pay an income tax on part of the benefits. The amount of benefits subject to taxation depends on your combined income. *Combined income* is the sum of your adjusted gross income, plus tax-free interest, plus one-half of your Social Security benefits. If your combined income exceeds certain dollar thresholds, some benefits are taxable.

- If you file a federal tax return as an individual and your combined income is between $25,000 and $34,000, up to 50 percent of the benefits are subject to taxation. If your combined income exceeds $34,000, up to 85 percent of your benefits are subject to taxation.
- If you are married and file a joint tax return and have a combined income between $32,000 and $44,000, up to 50 percent of the benefits are subject to taxation. If your combined income exceeds $44,000, up to 85 percent of the benefits are subject to taxation.

■ For married taxpayers who file separate tax returns and have lived together anytime during the year, the dollar threshold is zero. If not living together, you are considered to be a single person.

The Social Security Administration will send you a form each year that shows the amount of Social Security benefits received. The Internal Revenue Service has prepared a detailed worksheet to determine the amount of benefits, if any, to include in your taxable income.

### Financing Social Security Benefits

Social Security benefits are financed by a payroll tax paid by employees, employers, and the self-employed; interest income on the trust fund investments; and revenues derived from the taxation of part of the monthly cash benefits.

In 2012, the combined payroll tax rate for both OASDI and Medicare is 7.65 percent, which is paid by both the employee and employer. The Social Security portion (OASDI) is 6.2 percent on covered earnings up to a maximum of $110,100. In 2012, the Medicare portion (HI) is 1.45 percent on all earned income, including income that exceeds the maximum taxable earnings base. However, in 2011 and 2012, the OASDI payroll tax rate paid by workers was reduced 2 percentage points to 4.2 percent for workers to help stimulate the economy and reduce the unemployment rate. The temporary reduction of 2 percent in the OASDI payroll tax rate expired at the end of 2012. The maximum taxable earnings base for OASDI ($110,100 in 2012) will automatically increase in the future if wages in the national economy increase. In 2013, the maximum taxable wage base increased to $113,700.

## MEDICARE

Medicare is an important part of the total Social Security program that covers the medical expenses of most persons age 65 and older. Medicare also covers disabled persons younger than age 65 who have been entitled to disability benefits for at least 24 months. In addition, the program covers persons younger than age 65 who need long-term kidney dialysis treatment or a kidney transplant.

The Medicare program is complex and controversial. The present program also includes prescription

drug plans and health-care plans of private insurers. Medicare currently has a bewildering array of plans, which include the following:

■ The Original Medicare Plan
■ Medicare Advantage Plans
■ Other Medicare Health Plans
■ Medicare Prescription Drug Plans

The following section discusses the major provisions in each of these plans.[6]

### The Original Medicare Plan

Beneficiaries can elect the Original Medicare Plan, which is the traditional plan run by the federal government that provides Part A and Part B benefits. Beneficiaries can elect any provider that accepts Medicare patients. Medicare pays its share of the bill, and the beneficiary pays the balance. Some services are not covered.

**Hospital Insurance** Hospital Insurance (also called **Medicare Part A**) provides coverage for inpatient hospital stays and other benefits as well. Part A benefits include the following:

■ *Inpatient hospital care.* Inpatient care in a hospital is covered for up to 90 days for each benefit period. A *benefit period* starts when the patient first enters the hospital and ends when the patient has been out of the hospital or skilled nursing facility for 60 consecutive days. For the first 60 days, Medicare pays all covered costs except for an initial inpatient hospital deductible ($1184 in 2013). The deductible is paid only once during the benefit period no matter how many times the patient is hospitalized. For the 61st through 90th day, Medicare pays all covered costs except for a daily coinsurance charge ($296 in 2013). If the patient is still hospitalized after 90 days, a *lifetime reserve* of 60 additional days is available. Lifetime reserve days are subject to a daily coinsurance charge ($592 in 2013). The inpatient hospital deductible and coinsurance charges are adjusted annually to reflect changes in hospital costs.

■ *Skilled nursing facility care.* Inpatient care in a skilled nursing facility is covered up to a maximum of 100 days in a benefit period. The first 20 days of covered services are paid in full. For the next 80 days, the patient must pay a daily coinsurance charge ($148 in 2013). No benefits are available after 100 days of care in a benefit period. To be eligible for coverage, the patient must be hospitalized first for at least three days and must require skilled nursing care. Intermediate care and custodial care are not covered.

■ *Home health care.* Health-care services in the patient's home are covered if the patient requires skilled care and meets certain conditions. Covered services include part-time or intermittent skilled nursing care, home health-aide services, physical therapy, occupational therapy, and speech-language services that are ordered by the patient's doctor and provided by a Medicare-certified home health-care agency. Also covered are medical social services, durable medical equipment, medical supplies, and other services. The patient must be homebound, which means that leaving home requires considerable effort.

No cost-sharing provisions apply to covered services, but the patient must pay 20 percent of the Medicare-approved amount for durable medical equipment.

■ *Hospice care.* Hospice care is available for beneficiaries with a terminal illness. Benefits include drugs for pain relief and symptom control, medical and support services from a Medicare-approved hospice, and other services not otherwise covered by Medicare. Hospice care is usually given in the patient's home. However, short-term hospital and inpatient respite care are covered when necessary. Respite care is care given to a hospice patient so that the usual caregiver can rest for a short period.

■ *Blood transfusions.* Part A also pays for the cost of inpatient blood transfusions in a hospital or skilled nursing facility during a covered stay. If the hospital obtains blood from a blood bank at no charge, the patient does not have to pay for the blood or replace it. However, if the hospital buys blood for the patient, he or she must pay the hospital's cost for the first three units of blood received in a calendar year, or the patient or some other person must donate the blood.

**Payments to Hospitals**  Hospitals are reimbursed for inpatient services under a prospective payment system. Hospital care is classified into **diagnosis-related groups (DRGs)** and a flat amount is paid for each type of care depending on the diagnosis group

in which the case is placed. Thus, a flat, uniform amount is paid to each hospital for the same type of care or treatment. However, the amount paid varies among different geographical locations and by urban and rural facilities.

The purpose of the DRG system is to create a financial incentive to encourage hospitals to operate more efficiently. Hospitals can keep the payment amounts that exceed their costs, but they must absorb any costs in excess of the DRG flat amounts.

**Medical Insurance**  Medical Insurance (also called **Medicare Part B**) is a voluntary program that covers physicians' fees and related medical services. Beneficiaries who are covered under Part A on the basis of their covered earnings are automatically covered under Part B unless they voluntarily decline the coverage.

Part B pays for certain services that are medically necessary. There are two broad categories of covered services under Part B: (1) medically necessary services and supplies, and (2) preventive services. Examples of medically necessary services include physician services, such as diagnosis, treatment, and surgery; outpatient care; home health services; durable medical equipment; and other medical services.

A wide variety of preventive services are also covered. They include flu shots, pap smears, breast exams, screening colonoscopies to detect colon cancer, diabetes screenings, prostrate cancer screenings, and smoking cessation. Beneficiaries pay nothing for most preventive services if the care is provided by a physician or other health-care provider who accepts an assignment. However, some preventive services require beneficiaries to pay a deductible or coinsurance or both.

Medicare Part A and Part B have numerous exclusions. They include long-term care in a skilled nursing facility beyond the first 100 days, routine dental care, dentures, cosmetic surgery, acupuncture, hearing aids, and exams for fitting hearing aids.

**Amount Paid by Part B**  The beneficiary must meet an annual Part B deductible ($147 in 2013), which is indexed to the growth in Part B spending. *Part B then pays 80 percent of the Medicare-approved amount for most covered services, including physicians' services, outpatient hospital services,* *outpatient surgery, diagnostic tests, and other services.* For outpatient mental health care, beneficiaries generally pay 35 percent of the Medicare approved amount. The coinsurance percentage will decrease to 20 percent in 2014. However, there is no charge for home health-care services and certain preventive services, such as flu shots.

Medical payments to physicians are made on an assigned or nonassigned basis. By accepting an assignment, a physician agrees to accept the Medicare-approved amount as payment in full. The patient is not liable for any additional out-of-pocket costs other than the calendar-year deductible and coinsurance payments. However, physicians who do not accept an assignment of a Medicare claim cannot charge more than 15 percent above the allowable charge. Many physicians refuse to accept new Medicare patients because the Medicare-approved payments are often less than the physician's actual cost of treatment.

**Part B Monthly Premiums**  Beneficiaries with Part B coverage pay monthly premiums, which are supplemented by the federal government out of its general revenues. Under previous law, all Part B beneficiaries paid only 25 percent of the cost of the program, and the federal government paid the rest. Part B premiums are now means tested based on modified adjusted gross income. Upper-income beneficiaries pay substantially more than 25 percent of the cost. The income reported two years earlier on the beneficiary's federal income tax return determines the Part B premiums paid. In 2013, the standard monthly premium for most beneficiaries is $104.90. However, some beneficiaries must pay higher premiums because their modified adjusted gross income exceeds certain thresholds.

## Financing of Medicare

Hospital Insurance (Part A) is financed by a payroll tax paid by covered employees, employers, and the self-employed, plus a relatively small amount of general revenues. As stated earlier, the payroll tax for covered employees and employers is 1.45 percent on all covered earnings, even those that exceed the maximum Social Security taxable wage base. Beginning in 2013, the Hospital Insurance payroll tax will be increased from 1.45 percent to 2.35 percent for single

persons with earnings over $200,000 and for married couples with incomes over $250,000 filing jointly. The additional payroll tax on high wage earners is part of the financing provisions under the new Patient Protection and Affordable Care Act.

As stated earlier, Medical Insurance (Part B) is financed by monthly premiums and the general revenues of the federal government.

## Medicare Advantage Plans

**Medicare Advantage Plans (Part C)** are private health insurance plans that are part of the Medicare program. Beneficiaries can elect to be covered under such plans instead of the Original Medicare Plan. Medicare Advantage Plans must cover all services that Original Medicare covers except hospice care. Original Medicare covers hospice care. Medicare Advantage Plans generally include additional benefits, such as prescription drugs, vision benefits, and dental care, and health and wellness programs. Most Medicare Advantage Plans include Medicare prescription drug coverage. In most plans, members generally must use plan physicians, hospitals, and other providers or else pay more or all of the costs. In addition, plan members usually pay a monthly premium (in addition to the Part B premium) and copayment or coinsurance charges for covered services.

Medicare Advantage Plans include the following:

- Health maintenance organization (HMO)
- Preferred provider organization (PPO)
- Private fee-for-service plans (PFFS)
- Special needs plans (SNP)
- Medical savings accounts (MSA)

**Health Maintenance Organization (HMO)**  Medicare HMOs are managed care plans operated by private insurers. Managed care is a generic term to describe a plan where health care is carefully monitored, and there is great emphasis on controlling costs. Patients generally must receive care from physicians and hospitals that are part of the network. However, beneficiaries are covered for emergency or urgently needed care outside of the service area of the HMO. Some Medicare HMOs have a point-of-service option that allows patients to see providers who are not part of the plan network, but they must pay higher out-of-pocket costs for the services provided.

**Preferred Provider Organization (PPO)** Beneficiaries have the option of receiving care from a Medicare PPO. In addition to covered Medicare services, the PPO may provide additional benefits, such as coverage for prescription drugs or vision care.

There are two types of PPOs: (1) regional PPOs, which serve one of 26 regions established by Medicare, and (2) local PPOs, which service the counties that the PPO plan elects to include in its service area. PPO members can see any doctor or health-care provider that belongs to the plan network. Members can also receive care for covered services outside the network, but they must pay higher out-of-pocket costs. Plan members do not have to choose a primary care physician, and a referral from a primary care physician to see a specialist is not required.

**Private Fee-for-Service Plans (PFFS)** These plans are fee-for-service plans offered by private companies. A fee is charged for each service provided. *A distinctive feature is that the private company, rather than Medicare, decides how much it will pay and the amounts members must pay for the services provided.* Members can go to any Medicare-approved doctor or hospital that accepts the terms of the plan's payments. Not all providers will accept the patient.

**Special Needs Plans (SNP)** This is a special type of plan that provides more focused care for specific groups of people, such as those who reside in nursing homes, or those who are covered under both Medicare and Medicaid, or those with certain chronic or disabling conditions. For example, a special needs plan may exist for beneficiaries with diabetes that has health-care providers with experience in treating diabetes; the plan may also provide education, nutrition, and exercise programs to control diabetes.

**Medical Savings Accounts (MSA)** Medical savings accounts have two components—a high-deductible health plan and a bank account. Medicare gives the plan a yearly amount for the member's health care, and the plan deposits part of this money into the member's account. The money in the account and any interest accrued are not taxable if the money is used for health-care costs. The amount deposited is usually less than the deductible amount, so the member has to pay an out-of-pocket amount before coverage begins. After the deductible is met, the plan provides Medicare-covered services.

**Other Medicare Health Plans** Some Medicare health plans are not considered Medicare Advantage plans but are still part of the overall Medicare program. Some plans provide coverage for both Part A (Hospital Insurance) and Part B (Medical Insurance), while most other plans provide coverage only for Part B. In addition, some plans provide Part D prescription drug coverage. These plans include the following:

1. **Medicare Cost Plans.** Medicare Cost Plans are available in certain parts of the country. You can join even if you have only Part B. If you have coverage for both Part A and Part B and receive care from a non-network provider, the services are covered under Original Medicare. However, you must pay the Part A and Part B deductibles and coinsurance. In addition, you can join anytime the plan is accepting new members and can leave anytime and return to Original Medicare.

   Another type of Medicare Cost Plan provides coverage only for Part B services. These plans never include coverage for Part D (prescription drugs), and Part A services are provided by Original Medicare. These plans are sponsored by employers and labor unions or by companies that do not provide Part A services.

2. **Demonstration and Pilot Programs.** Medicare also has a number of demonstration and pilot programs that test and evaluate recommendations for improving Medicare. These programs usually operate only for a limited period for a specific group of people or are offered only in specific areas.

3. **PACE programs.** PACE programs (programs of all-inclusive care for the elderly) are programs designed to help elderly and disabled individuals who need a nursing home level of care to remain in the community. PACE programs combine medical, social, and long-term care services, and prescription drug coverage for frail elderly and people with disabilities. As a result, sick and disabled elderly can live safely in the community with the help of PACE services.

## Medicare Prescription Drug Coverage

**Medicare Prescription Drug Coverage (Part D)** is available to all Medicare beneficiaries. To obtain coverage, you must belong to a private plan run by an insurance company or other private company approved by Medicare. There are numerous plans available today, and the plans vary in cost and the types of drugs covered. Beneficiaries must select a specific drug plan and pay monthly premiums. Premiums and deductibles are waived for beneficiaries with limited incomes and resources (called "extra help"). The monthly premium is not affected by health status or the number of prescriptions used.

Beneficiaries who are covered under the Original Medicare Plan can add prescription drug coverage to their benefits by joining a stand-alone Medicare Prescription Drug Plan that covers only prescription drugs. Alternatively, beneficiaries can join a Medicare Advantage Plan or other Medicare health plan that provides prescription drug coverage in addition to covered Medicare services. Beneficiaries who are now covered for prescription drugs under the group plans of former employers or labor unions can elect to remain in their present plan.

**Cost of Prescription Drug Coverage**    Beneficiaries pay part of the cost, and Medicare pays part of the cost. Monthly premiums vary depending on the plan selected. In 2013, the average monthly premium for standard Part D coverage is an estimated $30.

All prescription drug plans must provide at least standard coverage, which Medicare has established. The cost-sharing provisions for the various plans are complex and are summarized below:

- *Annual deductible.* You must meet an annual deductible. For 2013, no plan can have a deductible that exceeds $325. The deductible changes each year.
- *Copayment or coinsurance charge.* After the annual deductible is met, you must meet a copayment or coinsurance charge. This is the amount you must pay for your prescription after meeting the deductible. In some plans, you pay the same copayment amount (fixed amount) or coinsurance charge (a percentage of the cost) for each prescription filled. In other plans, there may be different levels or tiers with different costs, such as generic drugs that cost less than brand names. Some brand names may also have a lower copayment charge than other brand names. For 2013, maximum copayment or coinsurance charges for all prescription drugs (including the deductible) are limited to $2970. This limit also changes each year.
- *Coverage gap.* Most Medicare drug plans have a coverage gap (also called a "donut hole"). This means that after you and your plan spend a certain amount for covered drugs, you must pay out-of-pocket your entire drug costs until you reach a maximum limit. The annual deductible, coinsurance or copayments, and the amount you pay while in the coverage gap all count toward the out-of-pocket limit. The limit does not include the monthly premium.

  In 2013, once you and your plan spend $2970 for covered drugs (including the deductible), you are in the coverage gap. In 2013, under the new Affordable Care Act, you receive a 47.5 percent discount on covered brand-name prescription drugs, and you pay 79 percent of the cost for covered generic drugs. You must pay all of your drug costs until you have spent $4750 out of pocket. If you are a low-income beneficiary, you will not have a coverage gap.
- *Catastrophic coverage.* In 2013, once you have spent $4750 out-of-pocket for the year, your coverage gap ends, and you have catastrophic coverage. At this point, you pay only a small coinsurance amount or copayment (such as $6) for each covered drug for the remainder of the year.

For 2013, Exhibit 18.3 shows how these provisions work under current law.

**Financial Help for Low-Income Beneficiaries**    The Medicare prescription program provides financial help for beneficiaries with limited incomes and financial resources. Depending on the amount of annual income and financial resources, the monthly premiums and yearly deductible are reduced or waived. However, low-income beneficiaries must pay a small copayment charge for each prescription filled.

Exhibit 18.3
**Example of Cost-Sharing Provisions Under Medicare Prescription Drug Coverage**

| Monthly Premium—Ms. Smith pays a monthly premium throughout the year. | | | |
|---|---|---|---|
| **1. Yearly Deductible** | **2. Copayment or Coinsurance (What you pay at the pharmacy)** → | **3. Coverage Gap** → | **4. Catastrophic Coverage** → |
| Ms. Smith pays the first $325 of her drug costs before her plan starts to pay its share. | Ms. Smith pays a **copayment**, and her plan pays its share for each covered drug until their **combined** amount (plus the **deductible**) reaches $2970. | Once Ms. Smith and her plan have spent $2970 for covered drugs, she is in the coverage gap. In 2013, she gets a 47.5% discount on covered brand-name prescription drugs and she pays 79% of the plan's cost for covered generic drugs. What she pays (and the discount paid by the drug company) counts as out-of-pocket spending, and helps her get out of the coverage gap. | Once Ms. Smith has spent $4750 out-of-pocket for the year, her coverage gap ends. Now she only pays a small **coinsurance** or copayment for each drug until the end of the year. |

Source: Centers for Medicare & Medicaid Services, *Medicare & You, 2013*, p. 87.

## Medigap Insurance

Because of numerous exclusions, deductibles, cost-sharing provisions, and limitations on approved charges, Medicare does not pay all medical expenses. As a result, most Medicare beneficiaries either have post-retirement health benefits from their former employers or have purchased a Medigap policy or Medicare supplement policy that pays part or all of the covered charges not paid by Medicare.

Medigap policies are sold by private insurers and are strictly regulated by federal law. There are 10 standard policies, each of which offers a different combination of benefits. Each policy has a letter designation ranging from A through N. Insurers are not allowed to change the various combinations of benefits or the letter designations. Plans E, H, I, and J sold earlier are no longer available, but policyholders who purchased these plans can keep them.

Some states make available another type of supplemental plan called Medicare SELECT, which requires the policyholder to use specific hospitals, and in some cases, certain physicians and health-care providers to receive full coverage.

## IMPACT OF THE AFFORDABLE CARE ACT ON MEDICARE

The Affordable Care Act contains numerous provisions that have a significant impact on the benefits provided, quality of care, reduction of costs, and financing of the Medicare program. They include the following:[7]

- *Rebates for the Part D coverage gap (donut hole).* An estimated 4 million beneficiaries reached the prescription coverage gap (donut hole) under Part D in 2010. Beneficiaries entering the coverage gap received a $250 rebate check. In 2011, seniors in the coverage gap received a 50 percent discount on covered brand-name prescription drugs. Over the next 10 years, seniors will receive additional savings on brand-name and generic drugs, so that the donut hole is completely eliminated by 2020.
- *Cracking down on health-care fraud.* Current efforts to fight Medicare fraud have resulted in savings of more than $2.5 billion. The new law provides additional funds to combat fraud and requires providers to use new screening procedures to detect fraud and waste in Medicare, Medicaid, and the Children's Health Insurance Program (CHIP).
- *Providing free preventive care for seniors.* As stated earlier, the new law provides certain free preventive services, including annual wellness visits and personalized prevention plans to seniors on Medicare.
- *Reducing overpayments to Medicare Advantage Plans.* The new law gradually reduces overpayments to private insurers that sell Medicare Advantage Plans. In 2010, Medicare paid private insurers, on average, more than $1100 more per enrollee for Medicare Advantage Plans than it spent on Original Medicare. As a result, premiums have increased for all Medicare beneficiaries.
- *Improving health-care quality and efficiency.* The new law creates a Center for Medicare & Medicaid Services that will test new ways of delivering health care to patients and is expected to improve the quality of care while slowing the rate of growth in Medicare costs.
- *Reducing unnecessary hospital readmissions.* Care for seniors will be improved to reduce or avoid unnecessary hospital readmissions. The Community Care Transitions Program will help high-risk Medicare beneficiaries who are hospitalized avoid unnecessary readmission to a hospital by better coordination of care and by connecting patients to services in their communities.
- *Innovations to hold down Medicare costs.* The Independent Payment Advisory Board will begin operations to develop and submit proposals to Congress and the president to extend the life of the Medicare Trust Fund. The board will focus on the reduction of waste and recommend ways to reduce costs, improve health outcomes for patients, and expand access to high-quality care.
- *Linking payments to quality outcomes.* The new law establishes a hospital Value-Based Purchasing program (VBP) in the Original Medicare Plan, which provides financial incentives to hospitals to improve their quality of care. Hospital performance will be reported publically, beginning with measures relating to heart attacks, heart failure, pneumonia, surgical care, hospital infections, and patient perceptions.
- *Bundling of payments.* The new law establishes pilot programs to encourage the bundling of payments to health-care providers to improve the coordination and quality of patient care. Under the bundling of payments, physicians, hospitals, and other health-care providers are paid a flat rate for an episode of care rather than under the present system in which each test or service, or bundles of items or services, are billed separately to Medicare. For example, under the present system, a surgical procedure generates multiple claims from multiple providers. Under the proposed system, the entire team would be compensated with a bundled payment that provides incentives to deliver health-care services more efficiently while maintaining or improving the quality. Any savings would be shared with the providers and Medicare.

## PROBLEMS AND ISSUES

Social Security and Medicare are currently faced with serious financial problems and issues. Two timely issues that merit discussion are the following:

- Long-range OASDI actuarial deficit
- Medicare financial crisis

### Long-Range OASDI Actuarial Deficit

It has always been the intent of Congress that the OASDI program should be actuarially sound. Although the present program is currently running an annual surplus, the program will experience a serious long-range actuarial deficit in the years ahead. The 2012 Board of Trustees report made the following conclusions:[8]

- The combined OASDI trust funds will be exhausted in 2033, which is three years sooner than projected in the 2011 report. *In 2033, non-interest income will be sufficient to pay only about 75 percent of scheduled benefits.*
- The projected actuarial deficit over the 75-year long-range period (2012-2086) is 2.67 percent of taxable payroll, which is 0.44 percentage points higher than projected in the 2011 report.
- To pay all scheduled benefits, over the 75-year period, the trust funds require additional revenue equivalent to $8.6 trillion in present value dollars.
- The Disability Insurance (DI) Trust Fund is projected to be exhausted in 2016, two years sooner than projected in the 2011 report.

## Reducing the Long-Range Deficit

Reducing the long-range deficit will require some hard choices. The deficit can be reduced or eliminated by (1) increasing payroll taxes, (2) decreasing benefits, (3) using general revenues of the federal government to pay benefits, or (4) by some combination of each. Proposed changes include the following:

- Use "progressive indexing" to determine benefits. For purposes of determining the worker's average monthly indexed earnings, a price index rather than a wage index would be used, which results in substantial cost savings. However, the indexing method for lower income groups would still be based on a wage index, as is now the case. As covered earnings increase, a combination of wage and price indexing would be used. For upper income groups, the indexing method would be based largely on a price index. The overall result would be a substantial reduction in the long-range deficit.
- Increase the Social Security payroll tax for both employers and employees.
- Move up scheduled increases in the full retirement age, or increase the age beyond age 67.
- Reduce benefits for future retirees across the board.
- Increase the OASDI taxable wage earnings base to cover a larger percentage of earnings.

- All OASDI benefits would be subject to the federal income tax (instead of a maximum of 85 percent as is now the case).
- Extend OASDI coverage on a compulsory basis to all new state and local government employees.
- Increase the number of years used in calculating retirement benefits from 35 to 38.
- Invest part of the trust fund assets in private investments, such as common stock.

In addition, the general revenues of the federal government could be used to fund part of the program. However, the federal budget is experiencing huge deficits at the present time. Thus, increased reliance on general revenue financing to reduce the long-range deficit is unlikely.

The American Academy of Actuaries has designed a Social Security game that allows you to make hypothetical changes in the Social Security program and see the impact of your proposed changes on the long-range actuarial deficit. A major advantage of the game is that it reflects your proposed changes to OASDI based on your political and ideological beliefs (see Insight 18.2).

## Medicare Financial Crisis

Medicare Part A also has serious financial problems. *According to the 2012 Board of Trustees report, the projected 75-year actual deficit in the Hospital Insurance (HI) Trust Fund is 1.35 percent of taxable payroll, up from 0.79 percent projected the previous year.* The actuarial imbalance over 75 years amounts to 36 percent of tax receipts or 26 percent of program costs. *In addition, the Hospital Insurance (HI) trust fund will be exhausted in 2024, the same date projected in the previous report, at which time dedicated revenues will be sufficient to pay only 87 percent of program costs. The share of HI expenditures that can be financed with HI dedicated revenues will continue to decline slowly until it reaches 67 percent in 2045.*[9]

The unsatisfactory financial condition is due to several factors, including higher prices for medical services, increased volume and complexity of medical services, aging of the population and increased Medicare enrollments, overpayments to private insurers that sell Medicare Advantage Plans (Part B), and increased expenditures from prescription drugs.

## INSIGHT 18.2

### What Are Your Solutions for Reforming Social Security?

There are no easy solutions for reforming Social Security. The long-range actuarial deficit can be eliminated by increasing revenues, reducing benefits, or both. The American Academy of Actuaries has an interactive program on its Web site (www.actuary.org/socialsecurity/game.html) that allows you to make hypothetical changes in the Social Security program. The program then shows the estimated change in the long-range actuarial deficit based on the Board of Trustees Reports. Also shown are arguments for and against the proposed change. One major advantage is that you can propose changes that are consistent with your political, economic, and ideological beliefs. The following are examples of the proposed changes:

| | Reduction in Long-Range Deficit |
|---|---|
| **Benefit Reductions** | |
| • Gradually increase the retirement age for full benefits. | 31% |
| • Reduce the cost-of-living adjustment (COLA) by 1/2 percentage point. | 40% |
| • Reduce benefits by 5 percent for future retirees. | 31% |
| • Use progressive indexing to reduce benefits for future retirees. | 43% |
| **Revenue Increases** | |
| • Raise the payroll tax from 6.2% to 6.7%, both for workers and employers. | 48% |
| • Increase wages subject to the Social Security tax. | 37% |
| • Tax Social Security benefits like pension benefits. | 14% |
| • Include new state and local government workers. | 9% |

Source: Adapted and modified by the author based upon a portion of an earlier version of *The Social Security Game* created by the American Academy of Actuaries, which has been revised and updated and is posted at the Academy Web site at http://www.actuary.org/socialsecurity/game.html.

Additional factors include inflation in hospital costs exceeding the overall rate of inflation, fraud and abuse by health-care providers, increased home health-care costs, and an inefficient and inflationary fee-for-service method of reimbursement.

To hold down Medicare costs, Congress earlier reduced payments to hospitals and physicians, placed spending limits on specified services, placed limits on fee increases paid to physicians, implemented the diagnosis-related group method in which flat amounts are paid to hospitals for each specific case, and introduced other cost-reduction measures as well. Despite these earlier efforts, however, Medicare costs continued to increase. More recently, as discussed earlier, the new Affordable Care Act contains several cost-containment provisions to slow the growth in Medicare costs. Some provisions are now in force, while others will become effective in the future. Some experts, however, believe that, until the health-care delivery system is significantly reformed, the cost-containment provisions will have only a limited impact on Medicare costs.

## UNEMPLOYMENT INSURANCE

**Unemployment insurance** *programs are federal-state programs that pay weekly cash benefits to workers who are involuntarily unemployed.* Each state has its own unemployment insurance program. The various state programs arose out of the unemployment insurance provisions of the Social Security Act of 1935.

Unemployment insurance has several basic objectives:

- Provide cash income during involuntary unemployment
- Help unemployed workers find jobs
- Encourage employers to stabilize employment
- Help stabilize the economy

Weekly cash benefits are paid to unemployed workers during periods of **short-term involuntary unemployment,** thus helping them maintain their economic security. A second objective is to help unemployed workers find jobs; applicants for benefits must register for work at local employment offices, and officials provide assistance in finding suitable jobs. A third objective is to encourage employers to stabilize their employment through experience rating (discussed later). Finally, unemployment benefits help stabilize the economy during recessionary periods.

## Coverage

Most private firms, state and local governments, and nonprofit organizations are covered for unemployment benefits. A *private firm* is subject to the federal unemployment tax if it employs one or more employees in each of at least 20 weeks during the calendar year (or preceding calendar year), or it pays wages of $1500 or more during a calendar quarter of either year.

Most jobs in *state and local government* are also covered for unemployment insurance benefits. However, state and local governments are not required to pay the federal unemployment tax but instead may elect to reimburse the system for the benefits paid to government employees.

In addition, *nonprofit charitable, educational, or religious organizations* are covered if they employ four or more workers for at least one day in each of 20 different weeks during the current or prior year. A nonprofit organization has the right either to pay the unemployment tax or to reimburse the states for the benefits paid.

## Eligibility Requirements

An unemployed worker must meet the following *monetary eligibility requirements* to receive benefits:

- Earn qualifying wages and employment during the base year
- Be able to work and available for work
- Actively seek work
- Meet a waiting period

*The applicant must earn qualifying wages of a specified amount during his or her base period.* In most states, the base period is the first four of the last five calendar quarters preceding the unemployed worker's claim for benefits. Most states also require employment in at least two calendar quarters during the base period. The purpose of this requirement is to limit benefits to workers with a current attachment to the labor force.

*The applicant must be able to work and must be available for work.* This means the applicant is capable of working and is ready, willing, and otherwise prepared to work. *The applicant must also actively seek work.* He or she must register for work at a public employment office and actively seek work or make a reasonable effort to obtain work. An unemployed worker is not required to take any job. However, if an applicant refuses suitable work without good cause, he or she can be disqualified for benefits. Suitable work generally is work in the applicant's customary occupation that meets certain health, safety, moral, and labor standards.

*Finally, a one-week waiting period must be satisfied in most states.* The waiting period eliminates short-term claims, holds down costs, and provides time to process the claim.

Applicants must also meet certain *nonmonetary eligibility requirements*, which refer to provisions in the law that disqualify certain weeks of unemployment because of actions by the workers who filed the claims. These actions include (1) voluntarily quitting work without good cause, (2) refusal of suitable work without good cause, (3) discharge for misconduct related to the job, (4) inability or unwillingness to accept full-time work, and (5) unemployment because of participation in a labor dispute. Depending on state law and the reason for disqualification, benefits can be postponed for a certain number of weeks or for the entire duration of unemployment until the worker again qualifies for benefits or benefits otherwise payable may be reduced in amount.

## Benefits

Unemployment insurance benefits fall into several categories—regular state benefits, extended benefits, and temporary emergency unemployment benefits.

- *Regular State Benefits.* Each state has its own program. A weekly cash benefit is paid for each week of total unemployment. The benefit paid varies with the worker's past wages, within certain minimum and maximum dollar amounts. The majority of states use a formula that pays weekly benefits based on a fraction of the worker's high quarter wages. For example, a fraction of 1/26 results in the payment of benefits equal to 50 percent of the worker's full-time wage in the highest quarter (subject to minimum and maximum amounts). For instance, assume that Jennifer earns $500 weekly or $6500 during her highest quarter. Applying the fraction of 1/26 to this amount produces a weekly unemployment benefit of $250, or 50 percent of her full-time weekly wage. Several states also pay a dependent's allowance for certain dependents. In March 2012, the average weekly benefit in the United States was $305.[10] In most states, the maximum duration of regular benefits is 26 weeks.

- *Extended Benefits.* Extended benefits are also available to workers who exhaust their regular benefits in states with high unemployment. The basic **extended benefits (EB) program** provides up to 13 additional weeks of benefits in states with high unemployment. Some states have also enacted voluntary programs by which seven additional weeks of extended benefits (20 weeks maximum) can be paid during periods of extremely high unemployment. The weekly benefit amount of extended benefits is the same as the regular unemployment compensation benefit.

- *Emergency Unemployment Compensation.* During recessions, millions of unemployed workers exhaust their regular state benefits. In addition, many unemployed workers who exhausted their regular benefits live in states where the unemployment rate is not high enough to trigger additional weeks of benefits under the permanent EB program. To deal with the exhaustion of benefits, Congress on numerous occasions has enacted temporary emergency programs that provided additional weeks of benefits to unemployed workers. In 2008, Congress enacted the Emergency Unemployment Compensation (EUC) program, which is a 100 percent federally funded program that provides additional weeks of benefits to eligible claimants who have exhausted their regular state benefits. The EUC program has been modified several times. The Middle Class Tax Relief and Job Creation Act of 2012 extended the expiration date of the EUC program to January 2, 2013 and made several changes to the program. However, at the end of 2012, Congress again extended the payment of temporary EUC benefits for one additional year through 2013.

## Financing

State unemployment insurance programs are financed largely by payroll taxes paid by employers on the covered wages of employees. Three states also require minimal employee contributions. All tax contributions are deposited in the Federal Unemployment Trust Fund. Each state has a separate account, which is credited with the unemployment-tax contributions and the state's share of investment income. Unemployment benefits are paid out of each state's account.

For 2012, covered employers paid a federal payroll tax of 6.0 percent on the first $7000 of annual wages paid to each covered employee. Employers can credit toward the federal tax any contributions paid under an approved unemployment insurance program and any tax savings under an approved experience-rating plan. The total employer credit is limited to a maximum of 5.4 percent. The remaining 0.6 percent is paid to the federal government and used for state and federal administrative expenses, for financing the federal government's share of the extended-benefits program, and for maintaining a loan fund from which states can temporarily borrow when their accounts are depleted.

Because of a desire to strengthen their unemployment reserves and maintain fund solvency, the majority of states have a taxable wage base that exceeds $7000. In 2012, the higher taxable wage base ranged from $7700 in Louisiana to $38,800 in Hawaii.

**Experience rating** is also used, by which firms with favorable employment records pay reduced tax rates. The major argument in support of experience rating is that firms have a financial incentive to stabilize their employment.

## Problems and Issues

State unemployment compensation programs have numerous problems and issues. Some important problems are summarized as follows:

- *Small proportion receiving benefits.* State unemployment compensation programs do not cover all unemployed persons. There are various methods for measuring the proportion of the unemployed who receive regular state benefits. One common measure is the recipiency rate, which represents the insured unemployed in regular state programs as a percentage of the total unemployed. *For 2011, a year of high unemployment, the recipiency rate ranged from a high of 47 percent in Arkansas to a low of 17 percent in South Dakota. The recipiency rate for the nation was only 26 percent.*[11]

The low recipiency rates are due to several factors. The states have adopted tighter eligibility requirements and more restrictive policy changes; many unemployed are temporarily denied benefits because of the initial waiting period; many unemployed are re-entrants or new entrants into the labor force and have not earned qualifying wages; some unemployed workers had jobs in noncovered occupations; others are disqualified for various reasons; many remain unemployed after they exhaust their benefits; and many unemployed fail to file for benefits. Thus, the effectiveness of present state unemployment insurance programs as a primary defense against short-term unemployment can be seriously questioned.

- *Inadequate financing.* Many states have relatively low trust fund balances, which has forced them to borrow from their federal unemployment accounts during business recessions. One measure of the adequacy of financing is the *average high-cost multiple*, which indicates how long a state can pay benefits if it paid benefits equivalent to the average amount paid out during the three highest-cost 12-month periods during the previous 20 years, without collecting any additional revenue. Labor experts recommend an average high-cost multiple of 1.5, which means a state would have enough money to pay benefits for 1.5 years at a rate equivalent to the average amount paid out during the previous three worst 12-month periods without the benefit of any revenue inflow. *However, in the first quarter of 2009, a period of severe unemployment in the nation, only 12 states had a high-cost multiple of 1.0 or higher.*[12] As a result, the majority of states depleted their trust fund reserves and had to borrow from the federal government to continue paying benefits.

- *High exhaustion rates during recessions.* Another important problem is the relatively high percentage of claimants who exhaust their regular state unemployment benefits during business recessions. *At the end of calendar 2009, a recession year with historically high unemployment,* *the exhaustion rate was 55 percent.* Since that time, the exhaustion rate declined slightly but still remains at a high level. At the end of March 2012, the exhaustion rate for the United States was about 48 percent.[13] Because of the limited duration of unemployment benefits, many claimants exhaust their regular benefits during business recessions and are still unemployed.

## WORKERS COMPENSATION

**Workers compensation** *is a social insurance program that provides medical care, cash benefits, and rehabilitation services to workers who are injured or sick from job-related accidents or disease.* The benefits are extremely important in reducing the economic insecurity that may result from a job-related disability.

### Development of Workers Compensation

Under the *common law of industrial accidents*, dating back to 1837, workers injured on the job had to sue their employers and prove negligence before they could collect damages. However, an employer could use three common law defenses to defeat lawsuits from injured workers:

- Contributory negligence doctrine
- Fellow-servant doctrine
- Assumption-of-risk doctrine

Under the **contributory negligence doctrine**, an injured worker could not collect damages from the employer if he or she contributed in any way to the injury. Under the **fellow-servant doctrine**, the injured worker could not collect if the injury resulted from the negligence of a fellow worker. And under the **assumption-of-risk doctrine**, the injured worker could not collect if he or she had advance knowledge of the dangers inherent in a particular occupation and still chose to work in that occupation. As a result of the harsh common law, relatively few disabled workers collected adequate amounts for their injuries.

The enactment of *employer liability laws* between 1885 and 1910 was the next step in the development of workers compensation. These laws reduced the effectiveness of the common law defenses, improved the legal position of injured workers, and required employers to provide safe working conditions for their employees. However, injured workers were still required to sue their employers and prove negligence before they could collect for their injuries.

Finally, the states passed *workers compensation laws* as a solution to the growing problem of work-related accidents. In 1908, the federal government passed a workers compensation law covering certain federal employees, and by 1920, most states had passed similar laws. All states today have workers compensation laws.

Workers compensation is based on the fundamental principle of **liability without fault.** *The employer is held absolutely liable for job-related injuries or disease suffered by the workers, regardless of who is at fault.* Disabled workers are paid for their injuries according to a schedule of benefits established by law. The workers are not required to sue their employers to collect benefits. The laws provide for the prompt payment of benefits to disabled workers regardless of fault and with a minimum of legal formality. The costs of workers compensation benefits are therefore considered to be a normal cost of production, which is included in the price of the product.

## Objectives of Workers Compensation

State workers compensation laws have several basic objectives:

- Broad coverage of employees for job-related accidents and disease
- Substantial protection against the loss of income
- Sufficient medical care and rehabilitation services
- Encouragement of safety
- Reduction in litigation

*A fundamental objective is to provide broad coverage of employees for job-related accidents and disease.* That is, workers compensation laws should cover the vast majority of occupations or job-related accidents and disease.

*A second objective is to provide substantial protection against the loss of income.* The cash benefits are designed to restore a substantial proportion of the disabled worker's lost earnings, so that the disabled worker's previous standard of living can be maintained.

*A third objective is to provide sufficient medical care and rehabilitation services to injured workers.* Workers compensation laws require employers to pay hospital, surgical, and other medical costs incurred by injured workers. Also, the laws provide for rehabilitation services to disabled employees so they can be restored to productive employment.

*Another objective is to encourage firms to reduce job-related accidents and to develop effective safety programs.* Experience rating is used to encourage firms to reduce job-related accidents and disease, because firms with superior accident records pay relatively lower workers compensation premiums.

*Finally, workers compensation laws are designed to reduce litigation.* The benefits are paid promptly to disabled workers without requiring them to sue their employers. The objective is to reduce or eliminate the payment of legal fees to attorneys, and time-consuming and expensive trials and appeals.

## Complying with the Law

Employers can comply with state law by purchasing a workers compensation policy, by self-insuring, or by obtaining insurance from a monopoly or competitive state fund.

Most firms purchase a workers compensation policy from private insurers. The policy pays the benefits that the employer must legally provide to workers who have a job-related accident or disease.

Self-insurance is allowed in most states. Many large firms self-insure their workers compensation losses to save money. In addition, group self-insurance is often available to smaller firms that pool their risks and liabilities.

Finally, workers compensation insurance can be purchased from a state fund in certain states. In some states, covered employers generally must purchase workers compensation insurance from a **monopoly state fund** or self-insure the risk. Other states have a **competitive state fund** that competes with private insurers.[14]

## Covered Occupations

Although most occupations are covered by workers compensation laws, certain occupations are excluded or have incomplete coverage. Because of the nature of the work, most states exclude or provide incomplete coverage for farm workers, domestic servants, and casual employees. Some states have numerical exemptions, by which small firms with fewer than a specified number of employees (typically three to five) are not required to provide workers compensation benefits. However, employers can voluntarily cover employees in an exempted class.

## Eligibility Requirements

Two principal eligibility requirements must be met to receive workers compensation benefits. First, the disabled person must work in a covered occupation. Second, the worker must have a job-related accident or disease. *This means the injury or disease must arise out of and in the course of employment.* The courts have gradually broadened the meaning of this term over time. The following situations are usually covered under a typical workers compensation law:

- An employee who travels is injured while engaging in activities that benefit the employer.
- The employee is injured while performing specified duties at a specified location.
- The employee is on the premises and is injured going to the work area.
- The employee has a heart attack while lifting some heavy materials while at work.

## Workers Compensation Benefits

Workers compensation laws provide four principal benefits:

- Unlimited medical care
- Disability income
- Death benefits
- Rehabilitation services

**Unlimited Medical Care**   Medical care generally is covered in full in virtually all states with no time or monetary limitations. However, some states have special provisions that limit the amounts paid for certain medical procedures. In addition, to save costs, the majority of states provide for optional deductibles in medical care.

Medical care is expensive. To hold down medical costs, many states allow employers to use managed care arrangements to treat injured employees. The use of health maintenance organizations (HMOs) and preferred provider organizations (PPOs) has also increased over time.

**Disability Income**   Disability-income benefits can be paid after the disabled worker satisfies a waiting period that usually ranges from three to seven days. If the injured worker is still disabled after a certain number of days or weeks, most states pay disability benefits retroactively to the date of injury.

The weekly cash benefit is based on a percentage of the injured worker's average weekly wage, typically two-thirds, and the degree of disability. There are four classifications of disability: (1) temporary total, (2) permanent total, (3) temporary partial, and (4) permanent partial. Temporary total disability claims are the most common and account for the majority of all cash claims.

**Death Benefits**   Death benefits can be paid to eligible survivors if the worker dies as a result of a job-related accident or disease. Two types of benefits are paid. First, a burial allowance is paid. Second, weekly income benefits can be paid to eligible surviving dependents. The weekly benefit is based on a proportion of the deceased worker's wages (typically two-thirds) and is usually paid to a surviving spouse for life or until she or he remarries. Upon remarriage, the widow or widower typically gets one or two years of payments in a lump sum. A weekly benefit can also be paid to each dependent child until a specified age, such as age 18 or later.

**Rehabilitation Services**   All states provide rehabilitation services to restore disabled workers to productive employment. In addition to weekly disability benefits, workers who are being rehabilitated are compensated for board and room, travel, books, and equipment. Training allowances may also be paid in some states.

## Problems and Issues

Workers compensation programs face a number of problems and issues in their daily operations. Three problems that merit a brief discussion include the following:

- Rising share of medical costs to total benefits
- Fraud and abuse
- Impact of an aging workforce on workers compensation costs

## Rising Share of Medical Costs to Total Benefits

Medical costs as a percentage of total costs have risen significantly over time. Workers compensation claims have two components: (1) payments for lost income (called indemnity payments), and (2) payments for medical care. In the past, indemnity payments have accounted for a larger proportion of total costs than medical care. However, this relationship has changed. According to the National Council on Compensation Insurance medical costs comprised 58 percent of total losses in NCCI states in 2009 compared with only 47 percent in 1989.[15] The rising share of medical costs can be partly explained by differences in the rate of growth in medical care and wages. Medical costs are rising more rapidly than wages. As a result, medical costs account for a larger proportion of total costs than indemnity payments, which are based on wages. In addition, medical utilization has increased in recent years. Utilization refers to the number of medical tests and treatments per claim. In recent years, the number of billed treatments per claim has increased, which also helps to explain the rising share of medical costs.

## Fraud and Abuse

Fraud and abuse in workers' compensation continues to be an important problem. According to the Insurance Information Institute, fraud accounts for 10 percent of all incurred losses and loss adjustment expenses in the property and casualty industry, or about $30 billion yearly. Of that amount, workers compensation fraud accounts for approximately 25 percent, or $7.2 billion yearly, according to the National Insurance Crime Bureau.[16]

Several types of fraud and abuse practices have been identified. They include the following:

- *Misclassification of employees.* Unethical employers often hire new workers and classify them as independent contractors rather than employees. Another scheme is to pay workers off the books to reduce the number of employees on the payroll. As a result, unethical employers avoid paying workers compensation premiums for these employees.
- *Phony claims.* Some workers fake or exaggerate their injuries and submit phony claims. Examples of phony claims are claims submitted by workers who are injured off the job but allege they were injured at work so that workers compensation pays the bill; the faking of soft-tissue injuries in the lower back or neck that are difficult to disprove; and workers who inflate their injuries, such as a worker who has a minor back injury but claims that his or her back is badly strained in order to receive benefits for a longer period.
- *Premium fraud by employers.* Dishonest techniques include misrepresentation and underreporting of payroll; false information about the jobs performed by employees, which produces a lower classification rate; and declaring employees as independent contractors rather than employees, as stated earlier.
- *Fraud and abuse by physicians, health-care providers, and attorneys.* Many physicians and chiropractors abuse the system by overcharging for medical services, by billing for services never provided, or by referring patients to a physician-owned lab where unnecessary tests are performed. Some attorneys and physicians have organized fraudulent claim rings and have actively solicited and colluded on claims. Other physicians have shifted nonreimbursed costs from Medicare and Medicaid to workers compensation insurers by overcharging for the medical services provided.

## Workers Compensation Costs and an Aging Workforce

Many experts believe that an aging workforce has a potentially adverse impact on workers compensation costs.[17] The proportion of older workers ages 55 to 64 in the labor force has grown steadily, and the proportion of workers ages 45 to 54 has also increased but at a slower rate. In contrast, the proportion of younger workers ages 35 to 44 has decreased.

In the evaluation of loss costs, both the severity and frequency of claims must be considered. A study by the National Council on Compensation Insurance (NCCI) concluded that claims of older workers cost more than younger workers, and that differences in injury rates between the two groups have largely disappeared. Therefore, differences in loss costs between the two groups in recent years are due largely to differences in severity since differences in frequency by age have largely disappeared.[18] The NCCI study also concluded that there are major differences in the types of injuries between the two groups. Older workers tend to have more rotator cuff and knee injuries, while younger workers tend to have more back and ankle sprains. In addition, older workers generally tend to be paid higher wages and benefits than younger workers. The NCCI study has two major conclusions: (1) older workers may be paid higher wages, which result in higher indemnity payments, and (2) medical costs are also higher because injuries to older workers result in more medical care per claim. There are a greater number of billed medical treatments per claim for older workers.[19] The overall result is higher claim costs for older workers.

## CASE APPLICATION

Sam, age 35, and Kathy, age 33, are married and have a son, age 1. Sam is employed as an accountant and earns $75,000 annually. Kathy is professor of finance at a large state university and earns $150,000 annually. Both are currently and fully insured under the OASDI program. Assume you are a financial planner who is asked to give them advice concerning OASDI and other social insurance programs. Answer each of the following questions based on the following situations. Treat each situation separately.

a. Sam is killed instantly in an auto accident. To what extent, if any, would the surviving family members be eligible to receive OASDI survivor benefits?

b. Kathy has laryngitis that damaged her vocal cords. As a result, she can no longer teach. She is offered a research position in the business research bureau of the university where she is employed. To what extent, if any, would Kathy be eligible to receive OASDI disability benefits?

c. A deranged student fired a pistol at Kathy because she gave him a grade of D. As a result, Kathy was seriously injured and is expected to be off work for at least one year while she is recovering. To what extent, if any, would existing social insurance programs in the United States provide income during the period of temporary disability?

d. Sam would like to retire at age 62 and still work part-time as an accountant. He has been informed that the OASDI earnings test would be relevant in his case. Explain how the earnings test might affect his decision to work part-time after retirement.

e. Sam resigned from his job to find a higher-paying position. Explain whether Sam could receive unemployment insurance benefits during the period of temporary unemployment before he finds a new job.

## SUMMARY

- Social insurance programs are compulsory insurance programs with certain characteristics that distinguish them from other government insurance programs. Social insurance programs in the United States have the following characteristics:

  Compulsory programs

  Floor of income

  Emphasis on social adequacy rather than individual equity

  Benefits loosely related to earnings

  Benefits prescribed by law

  No means test

  Full funding unnecessary

  Financially self-supporting

- The Old-Age, Survivors, and Disability Insurance (OASDI) program, commonly called Social Security, is the most important social insurance program in the United States. The program pays monthly cash benefits to eligible beneficiaries who retire or become disabled. The program also pays survivor benefits to eligible surviving family members.

- Medicare currently has numerous plans, which include (1) the Original Medicare Plan, (2) Medicare Advantage Plans, (3) Other Medicare Health Plans, and (4) Medicare Prescription Drug Plans.

- Unemployment insurance programs are federal-state programs that pay weekly cash benefits to workers who are involuntarily unemployed. Unemployment insurance programs have several objectives:

  Provide cash income to unemployed workers during periods of involuntary unemployment

Help unemployed workers find jobs

Encourage employers to stabilize employment

Help stabilize the economy

■ Unemployed workers must meet certain monetary eligibility requirements to receive weekly cash benefits:

Earn qualifying wages and employment during the base year

Be able to work and available for work

Actively seek work

Meet a waiting period

■ Unemployed workers must also meet nonmonetary eligibility requirements to receive unemployment benefits, which refer to certain disqualifying acts that can result in the postponement or denial of benefits. They include voluntarily quitting work without good cause, refusal of suitable work without good cause, discharge for misconduct related to the job, inability or unwillingness to accept full-time work, and unemployment because of a labor dispute.

■ Workers compensation is a social insurance program that provides medical care, cash benefits, and rehabilitation services to workers who become disabled from job-related accidents or disease. Workers compensation laws have the following objectives:

Broad coverage of employees for job-related injuries and disease

Substantial protection against the loss of income

Sufficient medical care and rehabilitation services

Encouragement of safety

Reduction in litigation

■ Workers compensation laws typically pay the following benefits:

Unlimited medical care

Weekly disability-income benefits

Death benefits to survivors

Rehabilitation services

## KEY CONCEPTS AND TERMS

Assumption-of-risk doctrine (395)

Average indexed monthly earnings (AIME) (377)

Competitive state fund (396)

Contributory negligence doctrine (395)

Credit (quarter of coverage) (375)

Currently insured (375)

Delayed retirement credit (377)

Diagnosis-related groups (DRGs) (385)

Disability insured (375)

Earnings test (retirement test) (380)

Experience rating (394)

Extended benefits program (394)

Fellow-servant doctrine (395)

Full retirement age (376)

Fully funded program (374)

Fully insured (375)

Hospital Insurance (Medicare Part A) (384)

Individual equity (374)

Liability without fault (396)

Means test (374)

Medical Insurance (Medicare Part B) (385)

Medicare Advantage Plans (Part C) (386)

Medicare Prescription Drug Coverage (Part D) (388)

Monopoly state fund (396)

Primary insurance amount (PIA) (377)

Short-term involuntary unemployment (392)

Social adequacy (374)

Social Security (375)

Unemployment insurance (392)

Workers compensation (395)

## REVIEW QUESTIONS

1. Explain the reasons for social insurance programs in the United States.

2. Describe the basic characteristics of social insurance programs.

3. The OASDI program has several types of insured status. Briefly explain the meaning of the following:
   a. Fully insured
   b. Currently insured
   c. Disability insured

4. The OASDI program provides several major benefits. Briefly describe each of the following:
   a. Retirement benefits
   b. Survivor benefits
   c. Disability benefits

5. Explain the definition of disability used in the OASDI program.

6. a. The Original Medicare Plan provides several benefits. Identify the major benefits that are available under each of the following:
      1. Hospital Insurance (Medicare Part A)
      2. Medical Insurance (Medicare Part B)
   b. Briefly describe the major choices available to Medicare beneficiaries under Medicare Advantage Plans.
   c. Briefly describe the Medicare Prescription Drug Coverage program

7. Explain the basic objectives of state unemployment compensation programs.

8. Explain the eligibility requirements for receiving unemployment compensation benefits.

9. Describe the basic objectives of workers compensation laws.

10. Identify the major benefits provided under a typical workers compensation law.

## APPLICATION QUESTIONS

1. The Social Security Administration has several benefit calculators available on its Web site. The "Quick Calculator" will give you a rough estimate of your retirement benefits. Benefit estimates depend on your date of birth and earnings history. For security purposes, the calculator will not access your actual earnings record to obtain your past earnings. Instead, the calculator will estimate your earnings based on the information you provide. Although the calculator makes an initial assumption about your past earnings, you can change the assumed earnings after you complete and submit the form. You must enter the day of your birth, actual or estimated earnings for the current year, and your future retirement date (optional). The site can be accessed at socialsecurity.gov/OACT/quickcalc/. Using the "Quick Calculator," estimate your Social Security retirement benefits.

2. The OASDI program provides retirement benefits to covered employees and their dependents. Explain whether each of the following persons would be eligible for OASDI retirement benefits based on the retired worker's earnings record. Treat each situation separately.
   a. A retired worker's unmarried son, age 25, who became totally disabled at age 15 because of an auto accident.
   b. A spouse, age 63, of a retired worker who is no longer caring for an unmarried child under age 18.
   c. A retired worker's spouse, age 45, who is caring for the 12-year-old daughter of the retired worker.
   d. A divorced spouse, age 55, who was married to a retired worker for six years.

3. The OASDI program pays survivor benefits to eligible family members based on the deceased worker's earnings record. Explain whether each of the following persons would be eligible for OASDI survivor benefits based on the deceased worker's earnings record. Treat each situation separately.

   a. A surviving spouse, age 35, who is caring for an unmarried child under age 16.
   b. A son, age 19, who is attending college full-time.
   c. A surviving spouse, age 55, who has no children under age 16 in her care.
   d. A surviving spouse, age 60, who has been out of the labor force for several years.

4. The OASDI program pays disability benefits to a disabled worker and eligible family members. Explain whether each of the following persons would be eligible for disability-income benefits. In each case, assume that the disabled worker is disability-insured. Treat each situation separately.
   a. A worker, age 22, who is injured in an auto accident and is expected to return to work within three months.
   b. The disabled worker's spouse, age 35, who is caring for a dependent child under age 16; the disabled worker is currently receiving benefits.
   c. The disabled worker's daughter, age 16, who is attending high school full-time.
   d. A chemistry professor, age 50, who can no longer teach because of chronic laryngitis but can work as a research scientist for a drug company.
   e. A worker, age 40, with a crushed foot who expects to be off work for at least one year.

5. The Original Medicare Plan consists of Hospital Insurance (Medicare Part A) and Medical Insurance (Medicare Part B). For each of the following losses, indicate whether the loss is covered under Medicare Part A or Medicare Part B. (Ignore any deductible or coinsurance requirements. Treat each situation separately.)
   a. Mary, age 66, is hospitalized for five days because of a heart attack.
   b. John, age 62, has prostate cancer and visits his family doctor for treatment.
   c. Marion, age 80, is a patient in a skilled nursing facility. She has been confined to the nursing home for more than two years.
   d. Don, age 72, has a hearing impairment and obtains a hearing aid from a local firm.
   e. Sarah, age 68, has a speech impairment and is confined to her home because of a stroke. A licensed speech therapist visits her in the home and provides services to restore her speech.
   f. Fred, age 78, has an arthritic hip that makes it painful to walk and needs surgery to have the hip replaced.

g. Michael, age 65, is covered under the Original Medicare Plan. His spouse, age 62, has cancer and requires chemotherapy.

6. A critic of state unemployment insurance programs stated that "unemployment insurance programs are designed to maintain economic security for unemployed workers, but several critical problems must be resolved."
   a. What type of unemployment is covered under a typical state unemployment insurance program?
   b. Describe some actions that may disqualify a worker for unemployment benefits.
   c. Why is the fraction of unemployed workers who receive unemployment benefits relatively low?

7. Workers compensation laws provide considerable financial protection to workers who have a job-related accident or disease.
   a. Explain the fundamental legal principles on which workers compensation laws are based.
   b. List the various ways that covered employers can comply with the state's workers compensation law.
   c. Explain the eligibility requirements for collecting workers compensation benefits.

## INTERNET RESOURCES

- The **Center for Retirement Research** at **Boston College** provides cutting-edge research studies on retirement issues, Social Security, and other topics dealing with economic security. The goals of the center are to promote research on retirement issues, to transmit new findings to the policy community and the public, to help train new scholars, and to broaden access to valuable data sources. Visit the site at

  crr.bc.edu

- The **Employment and Training Administration (ETA)** is a federal agency in the U.S. Department of Labor that provides detailed information and data on state unemployment compensation programs. Visit the site at

  doleta.gov

- The **Centers for Medicare & Medicaid Services (CMS)**, which is part of the U.S. Department of Health and Human Services, administers the Medicare program. CMS provides timely information and data on the Medicare program to consumers, health-care professionals, and the media, including actuarial cost estimates for the program. Visit the site at

  cms.gov

- **Medicare.gov** is the official government site for people on Medicare. The site provides information on the basics of Medicare, nursing homes, participating physicians, Medicare publications, and prescription drug assistance programs. Visit the site at

  medicare.gov

- The **National Academy of Social Insurance** is a professional organization that attempts to improve public understanding of social insurance programs. It publishes timely and important research studies on Social Security and Medicare. Visit the site at

  nasi.org

- The **National Commission to Preserve Social Security** has the goal to protect, preserve, promote, and ensure the financial security, health, and well-being of current and future generations of older Americans. The organization issues timely articles and studies on the current Social Security and Medicare programs. Visit the site at

  ncpssm.org/

- The **National Council on Compensation Insurance Holdings, Inc.** develops and administers rating plans and systems for workers compensation insurance. Visit the site at

  ncci.com

- The **Office of the Chief Actuary** in the Social Security Administration provides actuarial cost estimates of the OASDI program and determines the annual cost-of-living adjustments in benefits. The site provides a number of timely publications. Visit the site at

  socialsecurity.gov/OACT

- **Social Security Online** is the official Web site for the Social Security Administration, which administers the Social Security (OASDI) program in the United States. The site provides updated information on retirement, survivor, and disability benefits and recent changes in the program. Visit the site at

  socialsecurity.gov

- The **Social Security Advisory Board** is an independent, bipartisan board that advises the president and members of Congress on matters relating to Social Security. Its Web site provides timely and relevant reports dealing with Social Security. Visit the site at

  ssab.gov

- The **Workers Compensation Research Institute** is an independent, nonprofit research organization providing high-quality, objective information about public policy issues involving workers compensation systems. Visit the site at

wcrinet.org/

## SELECTED REFERENCES

American Academy of Actuaries, *A Guide to Analyzing the Issues: Social Security Reform,* 2012.

The Board of Trustees, Federal Old-Age and Survivors Insurance and Disability Insurance Trust Funds, *The 2012 Annual Report of the Board of Trustees of the Federal Old-Age and Survivors Insurance and Federal Disability Insurance Trust Funds.* Washington, DC: U.S. Government Printing Office, 2012.

The Boards of Trustees, Federal Hospital Insurance and Federal Supplementary Medical Insurance Trust Funds, *2012 Annual Report of the Boards of Trustees of the Federal Hospital Insurance and Federal Supplementary Medical Insurance Trust Funds.* Washington, DC: U.S. Government Printing Office, 2012.

Congressional Budget Office, *Social Security Policy Options.* Publication no. 4140, Washington, DC, July 2010.

Insurance Information Institute. "Workers Compensation," *Issues Updates,* May 2012. This source is periodically updated.

Mealy, Dennis C. "2011 State of the Line, Analysis of Workers Compensation Results," National Council on Compensation Insurance, 2011.

*Medicare & You 2013.* Baltimore, Maryland: Centers for Medicare & Medicaid Services, September 2012.

National Academy of Social Insurance, "The Role of Benefits in Income and Poverty." Social Security at nasi.org.

National Council of Compensation Insurance, *Issues Report, Workers Compensation, 2012.* Available at https://www.ncci.com/Documents/IR_2012.pdf (accessed August 22, 2012).

Nichols, Orlo R., Office of Chief Actuary, Social Security Administration, "The Insurance Value of Potential Survivor and Disability Benefits for an Illustrative Worker," Memorandum, August 15, 2008.

Rejda, George E. *Social Insurance and Economic Security,* 7th ed., Armonk, New York: M.E. Sharpe, 2012.

Reno, Virginia P., and Joni I. Lavery, National Academy of Social Insurance, "When to Take Social Security Benefits: Questions to Consider," *Social Security Brief,* No. 31, January 2010.

Social Security and Medicare Boards of Trustees, *Status of the Social Security and Medicare Programs: A Summary of the 2012 Annual Reports.* Washington, DC, 2012.

Vroman, Wayne, National Academy of Social Insurance, "Unemployment Insurance: Problems and Prospects," *Unemployment Insurance Brief,* No. 2, October 2011.

Woodbury, Stephen A., and Margaret C. Simms, National Academy of Social Insurance, "Strengthening Unemployment Insurance for the 21st Century: An Agenda for Future Research,"*Unemployment Insurance Brief,* No. 1, January 2011.

Workers Compensation Research Institute. *Workers' Compensation Laws as of January 2012,* Cambridge, MA.

## NOTES

1. George E. Rejda, *Social Insurance and Economic Security,* 7th ed. (Armonk, New York: M.E. Sharpe, 2012), pp. 24–30, chs. 5–7.

2. *The 2012 Annual Report of the Board of Trustees of the Federal Old-Age and Survivors Insurance and Disability Insurance Trust Funds.* (Washington DC: U.S. Government Printing Office, 2012), Table II.B1, p. 6; Table IV.B6, p. 65.

3. Social Security Online, Office of the Chief Actuary, "Social Security Benefits, Effect of Early or Delayed Retirement on Retirement Benefits." Available at www.ssa.gov/oact/ProgData/ar_drc.html (accessed August 22, 2012).

4. Orlo R. Nichols, Office of Chief Actuary, Social Security Administration, "The Insurance Value of Potential Survivor and Disability Benefits for an Illustrative Worker," Memorandum, August 15, 2008.

5. Ibid.

6. This section is based on *Medicare & You, 2012,* Centers for Medicare & Medicaid Services, U.S. Department of Health and Human Services.

7. This section is based on Henry J. Kaiser Family Foundation, "Summary of New Health Care Reform Law," last modified April 15, 2011.

8. SSA Press Office, "Social Security Board of Trustees: Projected Trust Fund Exhaustion Three Years Sooner Than Last Year," News Release, April 23, 2012, and Social Security and Medicare Board of Trustees, *Status of Social Security and Medicare Programs, A Summary of the 2012 Annual Reports,* 2012.

9. Social Security and Medicare Board of Trustees, *Status of Social Security and Medicare Programs, A Summary of the 2012 Annual Reports,* 2012.

10. U.S. Department of Labor, Employment and Training Administration, "Monthly Program and Financial Data." Available at www.ows.doleta.gov/unemploy/claimssum.asp (accessed August 22, 2012).

11. U.S. Department of Labor, Employment and Training Administration, "Recipiency Rates by States," in *Unemployment Insurance Chartbook*. Available at www.doleta.gov/unemploy/chartbook.cfm (accessed August 22, 2012).

12. U.S. Department of Labor, Employment and Training Administration,"Unemployment Insurance Data Summary," First Quarter, 2009. Available at www.ows.doleta.gov/unemploy/content/data.asp (accessed August 22, 2012).

13. U.S. Department of Labor, Employment and Training Administration, "Exhaustion Rates, Regular State UI Final Payments as a Percent of First Payments*" in Unemployment Insurance Chartbook*. Available at www.doleta.gov/unemploy/chartbook.cfm (accessed August 22, 2012).

14. Exclusive or monopoly funds exist in North Dakota, Ohio, Washington, and Wyoming. Competitive state funds exist in Arizona, California, Colorado, Hawaii, Idaho, Kentucky, Louisiana, Maine, Maryland, Minnesota, Missouri, Montana, New Mexico, New York, Oklahoma, Oregon, Pennsylvania, Texas, Utah, and West Virginia. Arizona is scheduled to be a privatized by 2013. Wyoming is compulsory only for extra hazardous occupations. Employers in non-hazardous operations may elect to insure with the state fund or opt to go without coverage. See Insurance Information Institute, "Workers Compensation," *Issues Updates*, May 2012. This source is periodically updated.

15. Dennis C. Mealy, National Council on Compensation Insurance, "Annual Issues Symposium 2010, State of the Line," May 6, 2010, Orlando, Florida, NCCI Holdings Available at https://www.ncci.com/Documents/AIS-2010-SOL-Presentation.pdf (accessed August 22, 2012).

16. Travelers Insurance, "Risk Control: Managing Workers Compensation Fraud," 2008.

17. This section is based on Tanya Restrepo, and Harry Shuford, "Workers Compensation and the Aging Workforce," in National Council on Compensation Insurance, *Issues Report, Workers Compensation 2012* pp. 32–36.

18. Ibid.

19. Ibid.

# CHAPTER 19

# THE LIABILITY RISK

*"I was never ruined but twice, once when I lost a lawsuit and once when I won one."*

Voltaire

## LEARNING OBJECTIVES

**After studying this chapter, you should be able to**

◆ Define negligence and explain the elements of negligence.

◆ Explain the following legal defenses that can be used in a lawsuit:

Contributory negligence
Comparative negligence
Assumption of risk
Last clear chance rule

◆ Apply the law of negligence to specific liability situations.

◆ Explain the defects in the current tort liability system and the proposals for tort reform.

◆ Explain the following tort liability problems:

Defective tort liability system
Medical malpractice
Corporate governance and financial sector issues

*Garrett purchased a pit bull dog that he kept in his backyard. Although there was a fence around the yard, the fence was not well maintained. One evening, Garrett's neighbor decided to take his dog for a walk. Garrett's dog was able to get under the backyard fence and attack the neighbor's dog. When the neighbor attempted to separate the dogs, the pit bull attacked him. The neighbor suffered severe bites to his legs, arms, and face. The neighbor's dog had to be euthanized because of the injuries inflicted by Garrett's dog. The neighbor sued Garrett. During the trial, it was revealed that Garrett had previously been fined by the city when his dog escaped from the yard and attacked a mail carrier. The court ordered Garrett to pay the neighbor $250,000 in damages.*

*Garrett experienced the legal impact of being negligent in a financially painful manner. Like Garrett, other people often face similar liability situations. Motorists are sued because of the negligent operation of their vehicles. Corporations are sued because of defective products that cause injuries, aggressive accounting practices and fraud that result in investor losses, violation of securities laws, insider trading, inadequate oversight of management, and for numerous other reasons. Physicians, attorneys, accountants, engineers, and other professionals are sued for malpractice, negligence, and incompetence. Likewise, government entities and charities are sued because they no longer enjoy complete immunity against lawsuits. Thus, the liability risk is extremely important to people who wish to avoid or minimize potential losses.*

*In this chapter, we discuss the law of negligence and the tort liability system in the United States. This knowledge forms the foundation for an understanding of personal and business liability insurance discussed later in the text. Specific topics discussed include the law of negligence, elements of negligence, application of the law of negligence to specific liability situations, current tort liability problems, and tort reform.*

## BASIS OF LEGAL LIABILITY

Each person has certain legal rights. A **legal wrong** is a violation of a person's legal rights, or a failure to perform a legal duty owed to a certain person or to society as a whole.

There are three broad classes of legal wrongs. A *crime* is a legal wrong against society that is punishable by fines, imprisonment, or death. A *breach of contract* is another class of legal wrongs. Finally, a **tort** is a legal wrong for which the law allows a remedy in the form of money damages. The person who is injured or harmed (called the **plaintiff** or *claimant* in a legal action) by the actions of another person (the **tortfeasor [alleged wrongdoer]** or *defendant* in a legal action) can sue for damages.

Torts generally can be classified into three categories:

- Intentional torts
- Strict liability (absolute liability)
- Negligence

### Intentional Torts

Legal liability can arise from an intentional act or omission that results in harm or injury to another person or damage to the person's property. Examples of intentional torts include assault, battery, trespass, false imprisonment, fraud, libel, slander, and patent or copyright infringement.

## Strict Liability

Because the potential harm to an individual or society is so great, some people may be held liable for the harm or injury done to others even though negligence cannot be proven. **Strict liability** *means that liability is imposed regardless of negligence or fault.* Strict liability is also referred to as **absolute liability**. Some common situations in which strict liability applies include the following:

- Blasting operations
- Manufacturing of explosives
- Owning wild or dangerous animals
- Crop spraying from airplanes
- Occupational injury and disease of employees under a workers compensation law

## Negligence

Negligence is another type of tort that can result in substantial liability. Because negligence is so important in liability insurance, it merits special attention.

# LAW OF NEGLIGENCE

**Negligence** *typically is defined as the failure to exercise the standard of care required by law to protect others from an unreasonable risk of harm.* The meaning of the term "standard of care" is based on the care required of a reasonably prudent person. In other words, your actions are compared with the actions of a reasonably prudent person under the same circumstances. If your conduct and behavior are below the standard of care required of a reasonably prudent person, you may be found negligent.

The standard of care required by law is not the same for each wrongful act. Its meaning is complex and depends on the age and knowledge of the parties involved; court interpretations over time; skill, knowledge, and judgment of the claimant and tortfeasor; seriousness of the harm; and a host of additional factors.

## Elements of Negligence

To collect damages, the injured person must show that the tortfeasor is guilty of negligence. There are four essential **elements of negligence**.

- Existence of a legal duty
- Failure to perform that duty
- Damage or injury to the claimant
- Proximate cause relationship between the negligent act and the infliction of damage

**Existence of a Legal Duty**    *The first requirement is the existence of a legal duty to protect others from harm.* For example, a motorist has a legal duty to stop at a red light and to drive an auto safely within the speed limits. A manufacturer has a legal duty to produce a safe product. A physician has a legal duty to inquire about allergies before prescribing a drug.

If there is no legal duty imposed by law, you cannot be held liable. For example, you may be a champion swimmer, but you have no legal obligation to dive into a swimming pool to save a two-year-old child from drowning. Nor do you have a legal obligation to stop and pick up a hitchhiker at night when the temperature is 10 degrees below zero. To be guilty of negligence, there must first be a legal duty or obligation to protect others from harm.

**Failure to Perform That Duty**    *The second requirement is the failure to perform the legal duty required by law;* that is, you fail to comply with the standard of care to protect others from harm. Your actions would be compared with the actions of a reasonably prudent person under similar circumstances. If your conduct falls short of this standard, the second requirement would be satisfied.

The defendant's conduct can be either a positive or negative act. Driving at high speeds in a residential area or running a red light are examples of positive acts that a reasonably prudent person would not do. A negative act is simply the failure to act: you fail to do something that a reasonably prudent person would have done. For example, if you injure someone because you failed to repair the faulty brakes on your car, you could be found guilty of negligence.

**Damage or Injury**    *The third requirement is damage or injury to the claimant.* The injured person must show damage or injury as a result of the action or inaction of the alleged tortfeasor. For example, a speeding motorist may run a red light, smash into your car, and seriously injure you. Because you are injured and your car is damaged, the third requirement of negligence has been satisfied.

The dollar amount of damages the claimant is entitled to recover from the negligent party depends on several factors. The law recognizes different types of damages, which are expressed in monetary terms (see Exhibit 19.1).

**Compensatory damages** are awards that compensate injured victims for the losses actually incurred. Compensatory damages include both special damages and general damages. **Special damages** are awards for losses that can be determined and documented, such as medical expenses, lost earnings, or property damage. **General damages** are awards for losses that cannot be specifically measured or itemized, such as compensation for pain and suffering, disfigurement, or loss of companionship of a spouse.

**Punitive damages** are awards designed to punish people and organizations for egregious acts so that others are deterred from committing the same wrongful act. Awards for punitive damages are often several times the amount awarded for compensatory damages.

**Proximate Cause Relationship**   The final requirement is that a proximate cause relationship must exist. *A **proximate cause** is a cause unbroken by any new and independent cause, which produces an event that otherwise would not have occurred.* That is, there must be an unbroken chain of events between the negligent act and the injury or harm that occurs. For example, a drunk driver who runs a red light and kills another motorist would meet the proximate cause requirement.

## Defenses Against Negligence

Certain legal defenses can defeat a claim of negligence. Some important legal defenses include the following:

- Contributory negligence
- Comparative negligence
- Last clear chance rule
- Assumption of risk

**Contributory Negligence**   A few jurisdictions have contributory negligence laws.[1] **Contributory negligence** *means that if the injured person's conduct falls below the standard of care required for his or her protection, and such conduct contributed to the injury, the injured person cannot collect damages.* Thus, under strict application of common law, if you contributed in any way to your own injury, you cannot collect damages. For example, if a motorist on an expressway suddenly slows down without signaling and is rear-ended by another driver, the failure to signal could constitute contributory negligence. The first motorist cannot collect damages for injuries if contributory negligence is established.

**Comparative Negligence**   Because of the harshness of contributory negligence laws if rigorously applied, most states have enacted some type of comparative negligence law. Such laws allow an injured person to recover damages even though he or she has contributed to the injury. Under a **comparative negligence law**, if both the plaintiff (injured person) and the defendant (party accused of negligence) contribute to the plaintiff's injury, the financial burden of the injury is shared by both parties according to their respective degrees of fault.

Comparative negligence laws are not uniform among the states. The major types of comparative negligence laws can be classified as follows:[2]

- Pure rule
- 50 percent rule
- 51 percent rule

### Exhibit 19.1
**Types of Damages**

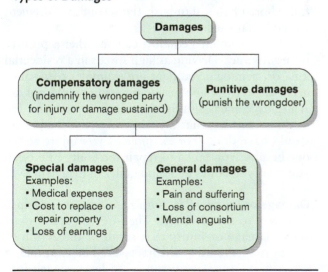

SOURCE: Donald S. Malecki, Arthur L. Flitner, and Jerome Trupin, *Commercial Liability Risk Management and Insurance*, 7th ed. (Malvern, PA: American Institute for Chartered Property Casualty Underwriters/Insurance Institute of America, 2008), Exhibit 1-3, p. 1.10.

Thirteen states recognize the pure rule.[3] Under the *pure rule,* you can collect damages for your injury even if you are negligent, but your award is reduced proportionately. For example, if you are 60 percent at fault in an auto accident and your actual damages are $10,000, your award is reduced by 60 percent to $4000.

Twelve states follow the 50 percent rule.[4] Under the *50 percent rule,* you cannot recover if you are 50 percent or more at fault. However, if you are 49 percent or less at fault, you can recover from the other party, but your award will be reduced. For example, assume you are in an auto accident, and you are 50 percent or more at fault. You would recover nothing. However, if you were only 49 percent at fault, and your actual damages are $10,000, you would be able to recover, but the damage award would be reduced 49 percent to $5100.

Twenty-one states follow the 51 percent rule.[5] Under the *51 percent rule,* you cannot recover if you are 51 percent or more at fault. However, you can recover if you are 50 percent or less at fault, but the damage award will be reduced. For example, assume you are in an auto accident and your actual damages are $100,000. If you are 51 percent at fault, you would recover nothing. However, if you were only 50 percent at fault, you could recover, but your award would be reduced to $50,000.

**Last Clear Chance Rule**    Another statutory modification of the contributory negligence doctrine is known as the **last clear chance rule,** *which states that a plaintiff who is endangered by his or her own negligence can still recover damages from the defendant if the defendant has a last clear chance to avoid the accident but fails to do so.* For example, a jaywalker who crosses the street against a red light is breaking the law. But if a motorist has a last clear chance to avoid hitting the jaywalker and fails to do so, the injured jaywalker can recover damages for the injury.

**Assumption of Risk**    The **assumption of risk** doctrine is another defense that can be used to defeat a claim for damages. *Under this doctrine, a person who understands and recognizes the danger inherent in a particular activity cannot recover damages in the event of an injury.* In effect, the assumption of risk bars recovery for damages even though another person's negligence causes the injury. For example, assume you are teaching a friend with a severe vision impairment to

drive a car, and he negligently crashes into a telephone pole and injures you. He could use the assumption of risk doctrine as a legal defense if you sue for damages.

Many states have eliminated assumption of risk as a separate defense. Formerly, assumption of risk was an affirmative defense available to defendants. However, in most jurisdictions currently, assumption of risk has been subsumed or incorporated within the state's comparative negligence or contributory negligence law.

## IMPUTED NEGLIGENCE

**Imputed negligence** *means that under certain conditions, the negligence of one person can be attributed to another.* Several examples can illustrate this principle. First, an *employer–employee relationship* may exist where the employee is acting on behalf of the employer. The negligent act of an employee can be imputed to the employer. Therefore, if you are driving a car to deliver a package for your employer and negligently injure another motorist, your employer could be held liable for your actions.

Second, many states have some type of **vicarious liability law,** by which a motorist's negligence is imputed to the vehicle's owner. For example, if the driver is acting as an agent for the owner of the vehicle, the owner can be held legally liable. Thus, if Jeff drives Lisa's car to a dry cleaner to pick up her garment, Lisa could be held legally liable if Jeff injures someone while driving the car.

Third, under the **family purpose doctrine,** the owner of an automobile can be held liable for the negligent acts committed by immediate family members while they are operating the family car. Thus, if Shannon, age 16, negligently injures another motorist while driving her father's car and is sued for $100,000, her father could be held liable.

In addition, imputed negligence may arise out of a *joint business venture.* For example, two brothers may be partners in a business. One brother may negligently injure a customer with a company car, and the injured person sues for damages. Both partners could be held liable for the injury.

A **dram shop law** is a final example of imputed negligence. Under such a law, a business that sells liquor can be held liable for damages that may result from the sale of liquor. For example, assume that a bar owner continues to serve a customer who is drunk, and that after the bar closes, the customer injures three people while driving home. The bar owner could be held legally liable for the injuries.

## RES IPSA LOQUITUR

An important modification of the law of negligence is the doctrine of **res ipsa loquitur**, meaning "the thing speaks for itself." *Under this doctrine, the very fact that the injury or damage occurred establishes a presumption of negligence on behalf of the defendant. It is then up to the defendant to refute the presumption of negligence.* That is, the accident or injury normally would not have occurred if the defendant had not been careless. Examples of the doctrine of *res ipsa loquitur* include the following:

- A dentist extracts the wrong tooth.
- A surgeon leaves a surgical sponge in the patient's abdomen.
- An operation is performed on the wrong patient or wrong limb.

To apply the doctrine of *res ipsa loquitur*, the following requirements must be met:

- The event is one that normally does not occur in the absence of negligence.
- The defendant has exclusive control over the instrumentality causing the accident.
- The injured party has not contributed to the accident in any way.

## SPECIFIC APPLICATIONS OF THE LAW OF NEGLIGENCE

### Property Owners

Property owners have a legal obligation to protect others from harm. However, the standard of care owed to others depends upon the situation. Three groups traditionally have been recognized: (1) trespasser, (2) licensee, and (3) invitee.[6] However, as will be discussed later, a number of jurisdictions have abolished or modified these common law classifications.

**Trespasser**    *A* **trespasser** *is a person who enters or remains on the owner's property without the owner's consent.* In general, the trespasser takes the property as he or she finds it. The property owner does not have any obligation to the trespasser to keep the land in reasonably safe condition. However, the property owner cannot deliberately injure the trespasser or set a trap that would injure the trespasser. The duty to refrain from injuring the trespasser or from setting a trap to injure that person is sometimes referred to as the *duty of slight care.*

**Licensee**    *A* **licensee** *is a person who enters or remains on the premises with the occupant's expressed or implied permission.* Examples of licensees include door-to-door salespersons, solicitors for charitable or religious organizations, police officers and firefighters when they are on the property to perform their duties, and social guests in most jurisdictions. A licensee takes the premises as he or she finds them. However, the property owner or occupant is required to warn the licensee of any unsafe condition or activity on the premises that is not apparent, but there is no obligation to inspect the premises for the benefit of the licensee.

**Invitee**    *An* **invitee** *is a person who is invited onto the premises for the benefit of the occupant.* Examples of invitees include business customers in a store, mail carriers, and garbage collectors. In addition to warning the invitee of any dangerous condition, the occupant has an obligation to inspect the premises and to eliminate any dangerous condition revealed by the inspection. For example, a store escalator may be faulty. The customers must be warned about the unsafe escalator (perhaps by a sign) and prevented from using it. The faulty escalator must be repaired; otherwise, customers in the store could be injured, and the owner would be liable.

Many jurisdictions have abolished either partly or completely the preceding common law classifications with respect to the degree of care owed to visitors. According to the Nebraska Supreme Court, the majority of states and the District of Columbia have either reconsidered the traditional common law classification scheme or have abolished some or all of the categories.[7]

### Attractive Nuisance Doctrine

*An* **attractive nuisance** *is a condition that can attract and injure children.* Under the attractive nuisance doctrine, the occupants of land are liable for the injuries of children who may be attracted by some dangerous condition, feature, or article. This doctrine is based on the principles that children may not be able to recognize the inherent danger that may be present and may be injured, and that it is in the best interest of society to protect them rather than to protect the owner's right to the land. Thus, the possessor of the land must keep the premises in a safe condition and use ordinary care to protect the trespassing children from harm.[8]

Several examples can illustrate the attractive nuisance doctrine, by which the occupant or owner can be held liable:

- A homeowner carelessly leaves a ladder standing on the side of the house. A small child climbs the ladder and falls off the roof, breaking both legs.
- A homeowner has a miniature house for the children. A neighbor's child attempts to enter through an unlocked window, which falls on her neck and strangles her.
- A building contractor carelessly leaves the keys in a tractor. While driving the tractor, two small boys are seriously injured when the tractor overturns.

## Owners and Operators of Automobiles

The owner of an automobile who drives in a careless and irresponsible manner can be held liable for property damage or bodily injury sustained by another person. There is no single rule of law that can be applied in this situation. The legal liability of the owner who is also the operator has been modified over time by court decisions, comparative negligence laws, the last clear chance rule, no-fault auto insurance laws (see Chapter 23), and a host of additional factors. However, the laws in all states clearly require the owner of an automobile to exercise reasonable care while operating the automobile.

With respect to the liability of the owner who is not the operator, the general rule is that the owner is not liable for the negligent acts of operators. But there are exceptions to this general principle. In all states the owner can be held liable for an operator's negligence if an *agency relationship* exists. As stated earlier, if your friend drives your car on a business errand for you and injures someone, you can be held liable. In addition, under the family purpose doctrine

discussed earlier, the owner of an automobile can be held liable for the negligent operation of the vehicle by an immediate family member.

## Government Entities

Based on the common law, federal, state, and local governments could not be sued unless the government gave its consent. The immunity from lawsuits was based on the doctrine of **sovereign immunity**, meaning that the king or queen can do no wrong. This doctrine, however, has been significantly modified over time by both statutory law and court decisions.

A governmental unit can be held liable if it is negligent in the performance of a **proprietary function**. Proprietary functions of government typically include the operation of water plants; electrical, transportation, and telephone systems; municipal auditoriums; and similar money-making activities. Thus, if some seats collapse at a concert in a city auditorium, the city can be sued and held liable for injuries to spectators. With respect to **governmental functions**—for example, the planning of a sewer system—immunity from lawsuits also has eroded over time. Today, government entities can be sued in almost every aspect of governmental activity, including false arrest, failure to meet certain standards of care, and failure to arrest.

## Charitable Institutions

At one time, charitable institutions were generally immune from lawsuits. This immunity has gradually been eliminated by state law and court decisions. The trend today is to hold charities responsible for acts of negligence. This is particularly true with respect to commercial activities. For example, a hospital operated by a religious group can be sued for malpractice, and a church sponsoring a dance, carnival, or bingo game can be held liable for injuries to participants.

## Employer and Employee Relationships

Under the doctrine of *respondeat superior*, an employer can be held liable for the negligent acts of employees while they are acting on the employer's behalf. Thus, if a sales clerk in a sporting goods store carelessly drops a barbell on a customer's toe, the owner of the store can be held liable.

For an employer to be held liable for the negligent acts of the employees, two requirements must be fulfilled. *First, the worker's legal status must be that of an employee.* A person typically is considered an employee if he or she is given detailed instructions on how to do a job, is furnished tools or supplies by the employer, and is paid a wage or salary at regular intervals. *Second, the employee must be acting within the scope of employment when the negligent act occurred.* That is, the employee must be engaged in the type of work that he or she is employed to perform. There is no simple test to determine whether the tort is committed within the scope of employment. Numerous factors are considered, including whether the act is authorized by the employer, whether the act is one commonly performed by the employee, and whether the act is intended to advance the employer's interests.[9]

### Parents and Children

Under the earlier common law, parents usually were not responsible for their children's torts. Children who reached the age of reason were responsible for their own wrongful acts. However, there are several exceptions to this general principle. *First, a parent can be held liable if a child uses a dangerous weapon, such as a gun or knife, to injure someone.* For example, if a 10-year-old child is permitted to play with a loaded revolver, and someone is thereby injured or killed, the parents can be held responsible. *Second, the parents can be legally liable if the child is acting as an agent for the parents.* For example, if a son or daughter is employed in the family business, the parents can be held liable for any injury to a customer caused by the child's actions. *Third, if a family car is operated by a minor child, the parents can be held liable under the family purpose doctrine discussed earlier.* In addition, property damage and vandalism by children have increased over time, especially by teenagers. *Most states have passed laws that hold the parents liable for the willful and malicious acts of children that result in property damage to others.* For example, Nebraska has a parental liability law that holds the parents liable for the willful and intentional destruction of property by minor children.

### Animals

Owners of wild animals are held strictly liable (absolutely liable) for the injuries of others even if the animals are domesticated. For example, an owner of an exotic pet such as a tiger is strictly liable if the pet escapes and injures someone even if the owner uses due care in keeping the animal restrained.

In addition, depending on the state, strict liability may also be imposed on the owners of ordinary pets, such as dogs. Until recently, dog owners were liable for dog bites and other injuries only if the injured person could prove that the owner knew the dog was dangerous. If the dog had never bitten anyone previously, the dog owner usually was not liable. *However, in about one-third of the states and the District of Columbia, the injured person has to show only that the dog caused the injury; in such cases, the dog owner is liable based on the doctrine of strict liability.*[10]

## CURRENT TORT LIABILITY PROBLEMS

The tort liability system has numerous problems at the present time. It is beyond the scope of the text to discuss all tort problems in detail. However, three timely problem areas merit a brief discussion:

- Defective tort liability system
- Medical malpractice
- Corporate governance and the financial sector

### Defective Tort Liability System

Critics maintain that the present tort system has numerous defects that reduce its effectiveness in compensating injured victims. Major defects include the following:

- Rising tort liability costs
- Inefficiency in compensating injured victims
- Uncertainty of legal outcomes
- High jury awards
- Long delays in settling lawsuits

**Rising Tort Liability Costs**    Critics claim that the tort system in the United States is costly and that the legal costs of settling lawsuits are enormous. Although the increase in tort costs has moderated in recent years, total tort costs are substantial. A Towers Watson study showed that tort costs totaled $264.6 billion in 2010, which was 5.1 percent higher than 2009. This figure, the highest annual estimated tort cost of U.S. history, is equivalent to a tax of $857 per person (see Exhibit 19.2).[11] These costs include benefits paid or expected to be paid to third parties, defense costs, and administrative costs. Total tort costs include: (1) insured costs excluding medical malpractice, (2) self-insured costs excluding medical malpractice, and (3) medical malpractice costs.[12] The 2010 total includes an estimated $19 billion in tort costs incurred by BP (British Petroleum) because of the Deepwater Horizon oil spill.

Exhibit 19.2 also shows that tort costs are a relatively heavy burden on the economy. Tort costs have increased faster than growth in the American economy over time. In recent years (2006–2010), tort costs as a percentage of Gross Domestic Product (GDP) have ranged from 1.78 percent of GDP to a high of 1.85 percent. Although tort costs as a percentage of GDP have declined significantly since 2002, tort costs are substantially higher in the United States than in other industrialized countries, which makes it more difficult for American companies to compete in global markets.

Several factors help explain the substantial increase in tort costs over time.[13] These factors include the following:

- *Social inflation that results in juries and judges being desensitized to the value of the dollar when damages are awarded*
- *Aggressive and creative litigation strategies by plaintiffs' attorneys to maximize awards*
- *Rising medical costs that increase the costs of personal injury claims*
- *Abuses in class-action lawsuits and the definition of a "class"*
- *Actions by the states in striking down portions of state tort reform legislation*
- *An increase in the number and size of stockholder lawsuits against boards of directors and company officials because of corporate fraud, greed, illegal manipulation of earnings, and accounting scandals*
- *A deep pocket syndrome in which some plaintiffs' attorneys go after defendants who can pay large settlements*
- *Exploitation of high-verdict cases by the media*

**Future Tort Costs**    Excluding the impact of the BP claims paid in 2010, tort costs were expected to rise 3 percent in 2011 and 4 percent in 2012.[14] Some experts believe litigation will increase in the future because of adverse events that impacted the U.S. economy, as well as other causes. Lawsuits may increase because of the following:

- The credit crunch following the collapse of the mortgage and housing markets
- Employment practices litigation alleging gender discrimination in pay, promotion, and work assignments
- Environmental claims, including alleged water contamination caused by the new natural gas drilling method "fracking"
- Claims from same-sex couples alleging discrimination
- High unemployment that occurred during and after the financial crisis

**EXHIBIT 19.2**
**Tort Costs Relative to GDP ($billions)**

| Year | U.S. Tort Costs | U.S. GDP | Tort Costs as % of GDP |
|------|------|------|------|
| 1950 | $ 1.8 | $ 294 | 0.62% |
| 1960 | 5.4 | 526 | 1.03 |
| 1970 | 13.9 | 1,039 | 1.34 |
| 1980 | 42.7 | 2,790 | 1.53 |
| 1990 | 130.2 | 5,803 | 2.24 |
| 2000 | 179.1 | 9,817 | 1.82 |
| 2001 | 205.4 | 10,128 | 2.03 |
| 2002 | 232.9 | 10,470 | 2.22 |
| 2003 | 245.7 | 11,142 | 2.21 |
| 2004 | 260.3 | 11,853 | 2.20 |
| 2005 | 261.4 | 12,623 | 2.07 |
| 2006 | 246.9 | 13,377 | 1.85 |
| 2007 | 252.0 | 14,029 | 1.80 |
| 2008 | 254.9 | 14,292 | 1.78 |
| 2009 | 251.8 | 13,939 | 1.81 |
| 2010 | 264.6 | 14,527 | 1.82 |

SOURCE: Towers Watson, 2011 *Update on U.S. Tort Cost Trends* (2011), Table 2. Reprinted by permission of Towers Watson.

- Investment schemes that defrauded investors of billions of dollars
- Claims arising from the toxic side-effects of nanotechnology[15]
- Unprecedented intervention by the federal government into the economy, with billions of dollars of taxpayer funds given to large commercial banks, insurance companies, financial institutions, and other organizations without proper oversight and accounting

### Inefficiency in Compensating Injured Victims

Another criticism is that the present system is inefficient in compensating injured victims. The number of class-action lawsuits has increased over time. However, critics charge that plaintiffs often receive relatively small amounts for their injuries or doubtful benefits (such as coupons or discounts to buy the defendant's products), while attorneys receive a large and disproportionate share of the settlement.

In addition, *critics argue that the present system is inefficient because injured victims receive less than half of each tort dollar paid.* An earlier Tillinghast study found that out of each dollar spent on liability claims, injured victims received only 22 cents for their actual economic loss (such as payment for medical bills and lost wages) and another 24 cents for noneconomic loss (such as pain and suffering). The remaining 54 cents is paid for claimants' attorneys, defense costs, and administrative costs.[16]

**Uncertainty of Legal Outcomes**  Critics also argue that because of changing legal doctrines, there is considerable uncertainty in predicting legal outcomes. The result is confusion for insurers, employers, risk managers, government officials, and taxpayers.

For example, an injured party at one time had to prove that the other party was at fault to collect damages. Today, emphasis is on providing the injured party with some form of legal redress, regardless of blame. Thus, critics argue that the ability to pay is more important today than determining who is at fault, and that the burden of paying injured persons falls heavily on insurers, wealthy people, corporations, and others with "deep pockets."

As a result of the uncertainty in legal outcomes, liability insurers often must pay tort liability claims that they did not envision paying when the liability coverage was first written.

**High Jury Awards**  Critics also argue that jury awards for certain types of lawsuits continue to increase. These cases include motor vehicle liability, premises liability, wrongful death, medical malpractice, and products liability. Exhibit 19.3 shows the increase in both median and average jury awards between 2000 and 2009. Higher jury awards and out-of-court settlements result in the need to purchase higher liability insurance limits, which increases the cost of doing business. This cost, in turn, is passed on to consumers through increases in the cost of goods and services.

Finally, the likelihood of a catastrophic award varies drastically by venue. Some states are perceived to treat defendants fairly and equitably, whereas others are perceived to be unfair to defendants. According to the American Tort Reform Association (ATRA), some states and counties are so unfair to defendants that they are labeled "judicial hellholes." ATRA believes that judges in certain areas systematically apply laws and procedures in an unfair manner, generally against defendants in civil lawsuits. ATRA issues an annual report that identifies the areas considered to be judicial hellholes (see Insight 19.1).

**Long Delays in Settling Lawsuits**  The tort system is also marred by long delays in settling lawsuits. Cases take months or years to settle. In 1950, only 20 civil trials in the federal courts lasted longer than 20 days. By 1981, the number of comparable lengthy trials had increased nine-fold. More recent studies show that lengthy delays are still a problem. The National Center for State Courts found that the median processing time in 1989 for all tort cases in 25 urban trial courts studied was 441 days. According to Jury Verdict Research, between 1997 and 2003, it took an average of 38 months from the time of the incident for a trial to begin in motor vehicle accidents and 52 months in medical malpractice cases.[17]

A considerable amount of time involves a pre-trial examination of the facts, such as interviews, depositions, and requests for documents. Repeated requests for documents can be time-consuming and expensive during the discovery stage of a suit. Moreover, attorneys frequently use delaying tactics during the discovery stage as an economic weapon against opponents. The overall result is a substantial increase in delay and cost.

**Exhibit 19.3**

**Median[1] and Average Personal Injury Jury Awards, 2000 and 2009 (000 omitted)**

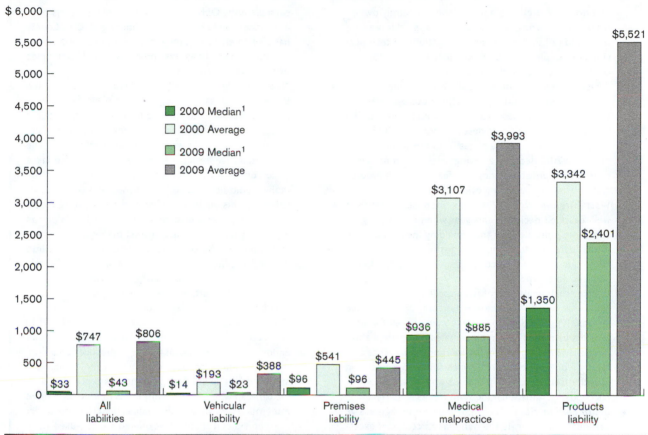

Legend:
- 2000 Median[1]
- 2000 Average
- 2009 Median[1]
- 2009 Average

Data:

| Category | 2000 Median | 2000 Average | 2009 Median | 2009 Average |
|---|---|---|---|---|
| All liabilities | $33 | $747 | $43 | $806 |
| Vehicular liability | $14 | $193 | $23 | $388 |
| Premises liability | $96 | $541 | $96 | $445 |
| Medical malpractice | $936 | $3,107 | $885 | $3,993 |
| Products liability | $1,350 | $3,342 | $2,401 | $5,521 |

[1]Represents the midpoint jury award. Half of awards are above the median and half are below.

SOURCE: Insurance Information Institute, *The Insurance Fact Book 2009*, P. 166 and *The Insurance Fact Book 2012*, P. 182. Reprinted with permission from *Current Award Trends in Personal Injury*. Copyright 2008 by LRP Publications, 747 Dresher Road, P.O. Box 980, Horsham, PA 19044-0980. All rights reserved.

## INSIGHT 19.1

### Judicial Hellholes 2011–2012

Judicial hellholes are places where judges systematically apply laws and court procedures in an inequitable manner, generally against defendants in civil lawsuits. Eight areas of the country have developed reputations for uneven justice:

- **Philadelphia**. Philadelphia hosts a disproportionate share of Pennsylvania's lawsuits and, as demonstrated by this report, forum shopping for plaintiff-friendly courts within the state is primarily a "Philly phenomenon." Of greatest concern is the Complex Litigation Center (CLC) in Philadelphia, where judges have actively sought to attract personal injury lawyers from across the state and the

country. Plaintiff-friendly law, expedited procedures, a reputation for a high plaintiff-win rate and generous awards contribute to Philadelphia's status as a venue of choice. Success in addressing the flow of medical liability cases to Philadelphia and the legislature's recent limiting of a defendant's liability to its share of fault provide some hope for the future.

- **California.** While Los Angeles historically earned a reputation as the most plaintiff-friendly jurisdiction in the Golden State, small business-destroying lawsuits filed by professional plaintiffs have spread throughout California. These individuals have filed thousands

*(Continued)*

of extortionate claims against popular family-owned restaurants, book stores and salons, demanding thousands of dollars to settle allegations of technical violations of disabled access standards, and California's courts have enabled the extortion. Recent court decisions demonstrate that California remains friendly to consumer lawsuits (even after voters attempted to rein in abuse), class actions, and high awards. The California Supreme Court deserves praise for its recent rejection of "phantom damages," but the adverse effect of its late 2010 decision allowing local government officials to hire private contingency-fee lawyers to enforce state law is now becoming evident.

- **West Virginia.** West Virginia's high court reached well-reasoned decisions this year when interpreting its consumer protection law and upholding the limit on subjective pain and suffering damages in lawsuits against healthcare providers. Such rulings, while helpful, do not address core problems in West Virginia's civil justice system, such as its lack of full appellate review, liability rules that are out of the mainstream, and excessive awards. West Virginia continues to be a haven for weak lawsuits by plaintiffs from other states. The state's attorney general remains under fire for running his office as if it were a private personal injury law firm and distributing litigation settlements to programs and organizations of his choosing, rather than the state and its taxpayers.

- **South Florida.** South Florida, known for its aggressive personal injury bar, is the national epicenter of excessive and fraudulent automobile insurance litigation and tobacco lawsuits. The state's insufficiently rigorous standard for admission of expert testimony contributes to its reputation as a judicial hellhole. While the state legislature has made steady progress in reasonably limiting liability in certain areas, the Florida Supreme Court's record of striking down such legislative efforts leaves observers cautiously optimistic at best.

- **Madison and St. Clair Counties, Illinois.** These two counties in the Metro East have come a long way since hitting rock bottom, but there are concerns of a relapse. For instance, this year the Illinois Supreme Court reversed a Madison County ruling that, after a one-sided trial that favored the plaintiff, would have imposed new liability on manufacturers. Mid-level appellate courts threw out two class actions certified by Madison County judges. A tobacco lawsuit that had resulted in a $10.1 billion verdict may be back on the Madison County docket. Similarly, after significantly culling its asbestos docket in recent years, Madison County is again the national epicenter for

such lawsuits. Only about 1 in 10 asbestos claims have any connection to the area. Neighboring St. Clair County has also emerged as a magnet for mesothelioma claims and hosts lawsuits against pharmaceutical companies from around the country.

- **New York City and Albany, New York.** The mayor of the Big Apple and its chief legal officer plead for reforms that would reduce the massive liability payouts that cost taxpayers over $500 million annually, but state legislators in Albany remain wedded to the plaintiffs' bar. The same expansive liability that burdens the city also takes its toll on New York's businesses, such as the photography studio being sued by a groom who was not satisfied with his wedding album and sought to re-create the wedding after a divorce, or the White Castle patron who brought a federal case against the restaurant when, at 290 pounds, he could no longer comfortably fit into its booths. Offering a minor dose of sanity, New York's highest court upheld dismissal of a lawsuit, featured in the 2010-2011 report, wherein one golf pal sued another after being struck by a bad shot.

- **Clark County, Nevada.** Since Clark County's May 2010 verdict that pinned a half-billion dollars in liability for an endoscopy clinic's unsanitary, illegal practices on a drug maker, the hits just keep on coming. Even as separate state and federal criminal prosecutions proceed against the clinic's owner, Clark County juries returned two more multimillion-dollar awards against the company under the theory that it should have offered a widely-used anesthetic solely in smaller vials to limit the potential for reuse, despite a clear warning on the label against use for multiple patients. Some Clark County judges have kept jurors from learning the full scope of the clinic's role in the resulting hepatitis outbreak when considering the drug maker's responsibility.

- **McLean County, Illinois.** After a year of observation on the "Watch List," McLean County advances to a judicial hellhole due to its unique practice of allowing lawsuits that seek compensation for asbestos-related injuries, even when the plaintiff did not come in contact with the named defendant's products. These "civil conspiracy" lawsuits target deep-pocket companies with allegations that they had some role in concealing the dangers of asbestos from the public decades ago. One such McLean case recently resulted in a stunning $90 million verdict.

SOURCE: Adapted from "Executive Summary," *Judicial Hellholes 2011-2012,* American Tort Reform Association (2012). Reprinted with permission from the American Tort Reform Association (ATRA).

**Reforming the Tort System**    Most states have enacted or are considering tort-reform legislation to deal with the problems discussed earlier. Some important state tort reforms include the following:[18]

- *Capping noneconomic damages, such as pain and suffering.* Many states have enacted legislation that places a maximum limit on noneconomic damages, such as compensation for pain and suffering. Reform measures may include all tort suits or only specific suits, such as medical malpractice.
- *Reinstating the state-of-the-art defense.* This proposal has relevance with respect to products liability suits. If the product conformed to the prevailing state of technology or industry and government standards at the time the product was manufactured, it would not be considered a defective product today.
- *Restricting punitive damages.* Punitive damages were originally intended to punish defendants for egregious conduct and to deter others from engaging in the same behavior. However, in many cases, awards for punitive damages are so large that they bear little relationship to the compensatory damages awarded by the courts. More than half of the states have passed laws that limit the imposition of punitive damages. Other states are considering legislation that would limit the maximum amount that could be paid for punitive damages or restrict the imposition of punitive damages to certain types of cases.
- *Modifying the collateral source rule.* Under the **collateral source rule,** *the defendant cannot introduce any evidence that shows the injured party has received compensation from other collateral sources.* For example, a delivery driver who is injured in a rear-end collision may be able to collect medical expenses from the negligent driver. However, job-related medical expenses are also covered under a state's workers compensation law. Therefore, the injured driver might "double dip" and receive a total amount that exceeds the medical bills. The collateral source rule would be modified so that recovery from other sources could be considered in determining the amount of damages. About one-third of the states have enacted laws that would alter this rule. The effect would be to reduce the size of the damages awarded.

- *Modifying the joint and several liability rule.* Under the **joint and several liability rule,** *several people may be responsible for the injury, but a defendant who is only slightly responsible may be required to pay the full amount of damages.* This could happen if one defendant had substantial financial assets ("deep pockets"), and the other defendants had few or no assets. Under tort reform, the joint and several liability rule would be modified. For example, many states now prohibit application of the joint and several liability rule to noneconomic damages, such as pain and suffering.
- *Alternative dispute resolution (ADR) techniques.* An **alternative dispute resolution (ADR)** *is a technique for resolving a legal dispute without litigation.* For example, **arbitration** is a technique by which parties in a dispute agree to be bound by the decision of an independent third party. **Mediation** is a technique by which a neutral third party tries to arrange a settlement without resorting to litigation. To reduce lawsuits between insurers and consumers over claims, many states now use binding arbitration or formal mediation to resolve disputes.

**Effectiveness of State Tort Reform Proposals**    To determine the effectiveness of tort reform legislation, the Congressional Budget Office (CBO) reviewed nine empirical research studies dealing with tort reform. The studies analyzed the effects of tort reform legislation, including caps on damages, modifications to joint-and-several liability, and changes in the collateral-source rule. Some major conclusions are the following:[19]

- The most consistent finding in the studies reviewed was that caps on damages reduced the number of lawsuits filed, the value of the awards, and insurance costs.
- Four studies examined the effects of modifying the joint-and-several liability rule. The results were mixed. One study found no effect. Another study found no effect on the number of lawsuits filed after enactment of the reform but a significant surge in cases before the reform took effect. A third study found an increase in the value of noneconomic awards but found no other significant effects. The final study provided evidence

that joint-and-several liability reform was a factor in reducing insurers' losses in the mid-1980s.

■ Two studies separately analyzed the impact of reform of the collateral-source rule. One study found that both economic and noneconomic damages were reduced. The other study found that discretionary collateral-rule offsets (considered by the judge's discretion) led to increased profitability for insurers.

The CBO, however, urged caution in interpreting the above results. First, data were limited, and the findings were not sufficiently consistent to be considered conclusive. Second, some studies were limited because they analyzed only specific types of torts, such as bodily injury claims in auto accidents, which made generalizations difficult. Finally, various tort reform measures may be enacted as a package, which makes it difficult for policymakers to separate the effects of the different types of tort reform.

## Medical Malpractice

Although medical malpractice costs have moderated in recent years, medical malpractice remains an important liability issue. Medical malpractice occurs when a negligent act or omission by a physician or other health-care professional results in injury or harm to the patient. A study of a large sample of physicians found that each year during the period studied (1991-2005), 7.4 percent of the physicians had a malpractice claim with 1.6 percent of the claims resulting in a payment. The mean malpractice award was $274,887 and the median was $111,749. Higher-risk specialties (e.g., neurosurgery) had a higher incidence of claims than lower-risk specialties (e.g., family practice).[20]

An unfavorable medical outcome alone does not necessarily mean the physician is negligent. To determine liability, the patient must show that the doctor deviated from the generally accepted standards of practice in this particular case. In addition, if the standard of care was not followed, the patient must show that this failure caused the injury. The physician's negligence must cause injury or harm to the patient. Even if the physician makes the wrong diagnosis, fails to treat the illness or injury properly, or prescribes the wrong drug, there is no case unless the negligence actually caused the injury or worsened the condition.

**Medical Malpractice Tort Costs**　The Towers Watson study of tort costs shows that medical malpractice tort costs have decreased in inflation-adjusted dollars since 2004. Tort reforms in several states have contributed to this result.[21] Medical malpractice claims, however, remain an important component of total tort costs. In 2010, medical malpractice costs totaled $29.8 billion, or 11 percent of total tort costs for that year.[22] This figure suggests that Americans still maintain an increased willingness to sue physicians and other health-care providers for alleged or actual acts of malpractice.

**Medical Errors and Malpractice Costs**　Many medical malpractice suits are due to medical errors by health-care providers, especially errors in hospitals that result in the death of patients. Medical errors occur for several reasons, including inexperienced physicians; complex new technology; new medical and surgical procedures for treating patients; poor communication among health-care providers; sleep deprivation of interns; drugs with similar names; improper documentation and illegible writing; inadequate nurse-to-patient ratios; and numerous other reasons. These errors include performing surgery on the wrong patient, performing the wrong procedure, and performing the surgery on the wrong area (wrong site/wrong side). Such incidents occur more often than expected.

Although most medical errors are preventable, they do occur, and the cost to society is substantial. A widely cited study by the Institute of Medicine estimates that medical errors may cause 44,000 to 98,000 deaths each year. Another study by HealthGrades estimates that an average of 195,000 people in the United States died from preventable hospital errors in each of the years 2000, 2001, and 2002.[23]

**Why Do Patients Sue Physicians?**　In addition to medical errors, other reasons help explain why patients often sue physicians and other health-care providers. These reasons are summarized as follows:

■ The intimate relationship between patients and physicians that existed in the past has been lost.
■ People are more litigious than in the past.
■ Physicians and other medical experts will now testify against physicians in malpractice cases.
■ The media has made more people aware of the vulnerability of physicians to malpractice suits.

- Physicians accuse attorneys of filing malpractice suits because of the high fees that attorneys may collect if they win.
- There is a growing resentment against large for-profit health-care firms and managed care plans.

Regardless of the reason, the majority of medical malpractice plaintiffs lose if the case goes to a jury. In the study cited earlier, 78 percent of the claims did not result in a payment to the claimant.[24] In addition, a 2007 study of medical malpractice claims closed in seven large states by the U.S. Department of Justice showed that most claims were closed without payment.[25]

**Reducing Medical Malpractice Costs** Health-care providers are now using a number of newer methods to reduce medical malpractice costs. They include the following:

- *Not charging for "never events"* Many hospitals are now adopting policies that require them to forsake charges for treatment that involve medical errors called "never events." As a result, patient safety is improved, and medical malpractice claims may decline. "Never events" are medical errors that are clearly identifiable and preventable and should never occur. *However, one risk management firm believes that "never events" account for one in six medical malpractice claims.*[26] Examples include surgery on the wrong person or wrong body part, foreign objects left in a patient after surgery, mismatched blood transfusions, major medication errors, severe "pressure ulcers" acquired in the hospital, and preventable post-operative deaths. In addition, Medicare recently announced it will no longer pay for eight types of serious medical errors, which include surgery on the wrong person or wrong site.
- *Laws allowing physicians to apologize* More than half the states have passed laws that allow physicians to apologize for their medical errors without allowing the admission to be used against them in court. These laws are also called "I'm sorry laws." Studies have shown that an upfront apology by the physician for a medical error can relieve the patient's anger and frustration, which

may result in a quicker settlement rather than lengthy and costly litigation.[27]
- *Prompt disclosure of medical errors* Prompt disclosure of medical errors and open communication between patients and health-care providers can lead to fewer lawsuits, quicker settlements, and reduced litigation costs. Many states now have laws that mandate the reporting of medical errors.
- *Problem physicians* Action would be taken against the small proportion of physicians who have multiple judgments against them. For example, to retain their license, problem physicians could be required to take training programs to reduce medical errors.
- *Emphasize risk management principles* For example, anaesthesiologists earlier developed certain practice standards to reduce malpractice claims. The causes of most claims were identified, and practice standards were developed to avoid them. As a result, malpractice claims declined. Other risk management suggestions include the study of medical malpractice prevention as part of the licensing requirement; the use of new technology to reduce medical errors, such as writing prescriptions with electronic equipment; and mandatory reporting of medical errors.

## Corporate Governance and the Financial Sector

Corporate governance and the financial sector continue to be problem areas. In the 1990s, several large corporations used dishonest or aggressive accounting practices to inflate stated earnings and profits; while other companies concealed or misstated accounting transactions. When earnings were revised downward, stockholders lost millions of dollars. Because of class action suits by angry stockholders, employees, and other investors, several large corporations were forced into bankruptcy. Thousands of employees lost their jobs and a large part of their retirement savings. The Securities and Exchange Commission indicted numerous company officials in different industries for securities fraud, illegal accounting practices, destruction of company records, and obstruction of justice. Some company officials pleaded guilty and are serving lengthy federal prison sentences.

More recently, during the severe economic downturn between 2008 and 2011, many large corporations had defective financial risk management programs in which major financial risks were poorly assessed and managed. As a result, large corporations lost billions of dollars because of improper management of financial loss exposures. Many econometric models were flawed, assuming that housing prices would increase indefinitely. This assumption led some lenders to extend loans to individuals who normally would not qualify for the loan (sub-prime mortgages) and who later defaulted.

Boards of directors have been criticized for lax corporate governance and inadequate oversight of management. Boards are criticized because of the disconnect between the boards and audit committees, poor internal controls and accountability, excessive executive salaries, undisclosed CEO and director financial arrangements, compromising of auditors and lawyers, and unclear disclosure of complex financial transactions (such as off-balance-sheet transactions and the use of derivatives). Critics claim that many board members are mere figureheads who are on the board because of their names or national visibility, that board members may not understand complex financial transactions, and that board members often serve on multiple boards and cannot devote the time necessary to understand and scrutinize the actions of management.

Promises of high investment returns enticed some investors to place money with fraudulent organizations. For example, Bernard Madoff was convicted in 2009 of defrauding investors of billions of dollars in a Ponzi scheme and Allen Stanford, Chairman of the Stanford Financial Group, was convicted in 2012 of leading a $7 billion investment fraud. These and other investment scams triggered lawsuits from the defrauded investors.

These problems led to Congressional action. In 2002, Congress enacted the *Sarbanes-Oxley Act* corporate accountability law. The law is designed to expose and punish acts of corruption, restore confidence in corporate America, and protect investors. The law requires the company's CEO and CFO to swear to the accuracy of the quarterly and annual financial reports, makes it generally unlawful for an accounting firm to provide major nonaudit services to a company while auditing the company, and prohibits companies from retaliating against stock market analysts who criticize them. In 2010, Congress passed the *Dodd-Frank Wall Street Reform and Consumer Protection Act*. This wide-ranging law addresses many aspects of the financial sector, including financial disclosure, liquidation of financial institutions, regulation of credit ratings agencies, and predatory lending practices.

## CASE APPLICATION

Michael went deer hunting with Ed. After seeing bushes move, Michael quickly fired his rifle at what he thought was a deer. However, Ed caused the movement in the bushes and was seriously injured by the bullet. Ed survived and later sued Michael on the grounds that "Michael's negligence was the proximate cause of the injury."

a. Based on the above facts, is Michael guilty of negligence? Your answer must include a definition of negligence and the essential elements of negligence.

b. Michael's attorney believes that if contributory negligence could be established, it would greatly influence the outcome of the case. Do you agree with Michael's attorney? Your answer must include a definition of contributory negligence.

c. If Michael can establish comparative negligence on the part of Ed, would the outcome of the case be changed? Explain your answer.

d. Assume that Michael and Ed are hunting on farmland without obtaining permission from the owner. If Michael fell into a marshy pond covered by weeds and injured his back, would the property owner be liable for damages? Explain your answer.

# SUMMARY

- A tort is a legal wrong for which the law allows a remedy in the form of money damages. There are three categories of torts: intentional torts, strict liability, and negligence.

- Negligence is defined as the failure to exercise the standard of care required by law to protect others from an unreasonable risk of harm. There are four elements of negligence:

   Existence of a legal duty

   Failure to perform that duty

   Damages or injury to the claimant

   Proximate cause relationship

- *Contributory negligence* means that if the injured person's conduct falls below the standard of care required for his or her protection, and such conduct contributed to the injury, the injured person cannot collect damages. Under a *comparative negligence law,* the injured person can collect damages, but the award is reduced. Under the *last clear chance rule,* a plaintiff who is endangered by his or her own negligence can still recover damages from the defendant if the defendant has a last clear chance to avoid the accident but fails to do so. Under the *assumption of risk doctrine,* a person who understands and recognizes the danger inherent in a particular activity cannot recover damages in the event of injury.

- Under certain conditions, the negligence of one person can be imputed to another. Imputed negligence may arise from an employer–employee relationship, vicarious liability law, family purpose doctrine, joint business venture, or a dram shop law.

- Under the doctrine of *res ipsa loquitur* (the thing speaks for itself), the very fact that the injury or damage occurs establishes a presumption of negligence on behalf of the defendant.

- The standard of care required by law varies with the situation. Specific liability situations can involve property owners, attractive nuisances, owners and operators of automobiles, governmental units and charitable institutions, employers and employees, parents and children, and the owners of animals.

- Tort reform advocates claim that the present tort liability system in the United States has the following defects:

   Rising tort liability costs

   Inefficiency in compensating injured victims

   Uncertainty of legal outcomes

   Higher jury awards

   Long delays in settling lawsuits

- Some state tort reform proposals include the following:

   Capping noneconomic damages, such as pain and suffering

   Reinstating the state-of-the art defense

   Restricting punitive damage awards

   Modifying the collateral source rule

   Modifying the joint and several liability rule

   Alternative dispute resolution (ADR) techniques

- The medical malpractice problem is due to several factors. These causes include medical errors by healthcare providers, increased willingness of patients to sue physicians, exploitation of malpractice suits by the media, loss of the intimate relationship between physicians and patients that existed in the past, increased willingness of physicians and medical experts to testify against other physicians, increased tendency for attorneys to file malpractice suits because of potentially high fees, and the ineffectiveness or reluctance of some state medical boards to discipline physicians.

- Problems with corporate governance and the financial sector continue to give rise to liability claims. Corporations have been sued because of dishonest accounting practices, defective financial risk management programs, and ineffective boards leading to lax corporate governance and inadequate oversight of management. In addition, fraudulent investment schemes, predatory lending, and similar practices led to Congressional action.

# KEY CONCEPTS AND TERMS

Alternative dispute
 resolution (ADR) (417)
Arbitration (417)
Assumption of risk (409)
Attractive nuisance (410)
Collateral source rule (417)
Comparative negligence
 law (408)
Compensatory
 damages (408)
Contributory
 negligence (408)

Dram shop law (409)
Elements of negligence (407)
Family purpose
 doctrine (409)
General damages (408)
Governmental
 function (411)
Imputed negligence (409)
Invitee (410)
Joint and several liability
 rule (417)
Last clear chance rule (409)

Legal wrong (406)
Licensee (410)
Mediation (417)
Negligence (407)
Plaintiff (406)
Proprietary function (411)
Proximate cause (408)
Punitive damages (408)
*Res ipsa loquitur* (410)
*Respondeat superior* (411)

Sovereign immunity (411)
Special damages (408)
Strict liability (absolute
    liability) (407)
Tort (406)
Tortfeasor (alleged
    wrongdoer) (406)
Trespasser (410)
Vicarious liability
    law (409)

## REVIEW QUESTIONS

1. a. What is negligence?
   b. Explain the four elements of negligence.

2. What is the meaning of strict liability?

3. Explain the following types of damages:
   a. Compensatory damages (special damages and general damages)
   b. Punitive damages

4. Describe the following legal defenses that can be used by defendants who are accused of negligence:
   a. Contributory negligence
   b. Comparative negligence
   c. Last clear chance rule
   d. Assumption of risk doctrine

5. Explain the meaning of imputed negligence.

6. Explain the meaning of *res ipsa loquitur.*

7. Briefly describe the standard of care to protect others from harm for each of the following liability situations:
   a. Property owners
   b. An attractive nuisance
   c. Owners and operators of automobiles
   d. Governmental units and charitable institutions
   e. Employers and employees
   f. Parents and children
   g. Owners of animals

8. a. Explain the major defects in the tort liability system in the United States.
   b. Identify several proposals for tort reform in the United States.

9. a. Explain the reasons for the medical malpractice problem in the United States.
   b. Identify several methods for reducing medical malpractice costs.

10. Briefly describe the problems with corporate governance and the financial sector which have led to increased litigation.

## APPLICATION QUESTIONS

1. Smith Construction is building a warehouse for Raymond. The construction firm routinely leaves certain construction equipment at the building site overnight and on weekends. Late one night, Fred, age 10, began playing on some of Smith's construction equipment. Fred accidentally released the brakes of a tractor on which he was playing, and the tractor rolled down a hill and smashed into the building under construction. Fred was severely injured in the accident. Fred's parents sued both Smith Construction and Raymond for the injury.
   a. Based on the elements of negligence, describe the requirements that must be met for Smith Construction to be held liable for negligence.
   b. Describe the various classes of persons that are recognized by the law with respect to entering upon the property of another. In which class of persons would Fred belong?
   c. What other legal doctrine is applicable in this case because of Fred's age? Explain your answer.

2. a. Parkway Distributors is a wholesale firm that employs several outside salespersons. Emily, a salesperson employed by Parkway Distributors, was involved in an accident with another motorist while she was using her car to make regular sales calls for Parkway Distributors. Emily and the motorist are seriously injured in the accident. The motorist sues both Emily and Parkway Distributors for the injury based on negligence.
   1. Describe the requirements that the motorist must establish to show that Emily is guilty of negligence.
   2. On what legal basis might Parkway Distributors be held legally liable for the injury to the motorist? Explain your answer.
   b. Tom asks his girlfriend, Megan, to go to a supermarket and purchase some steaks for dinner. While driving Tom's car to the supermarket, Megan failed to stop at a red light and seriously injured a pedestrian. Does Tom have any legal liability for the injury? Explain your answer.

3. Whirlwind Mowers manufactures and sells power lawn mowers to the public and distributes the products through its own dealers. Andrew is a homeowner who has purchased a power mower from an authorized dealer on the basis of the dealer's recommendation that "the mower is the best one available to do the job." Andrew was cutting his lawn when the mower blade flew off and seriously injured his leg.

   a. Andrew sues Whirlwind Mowers and asks for damages based on negligence in producing the power mower. Is Whirlwind Mowers guilty of negligence? Explain your answer.

   b. The doctrine of *res ipsa loquitur* can often be applied to cases of this type. Show how this doctrine can be applied to this case. Your answer must include a definition of *res ipsa loquitur*.

   c. Explain the various types of damages that Andrew might receive if Whirlwind Mowers is found guilty of negligence.

4. Matthew was involved in an auto accident. He was judged to be 40 percent at fault in the accident, and the other party was judged to be 60 percent at fault. Matthew's actual damages were $50,000. Under a pure comparative negligence law, how much, if anything, will Matthew receive for his injury?

5. Dr. Jones is an orthopedic surgeon. One patient required arthroscopic surgery on his right knee because of cartilage damage. When the patient awoke from surgery, he was surprised to see bandages on both knees. He was told that Dr. Jones made an incision on the wrong knee, realized his mistake, and then proceeded with the surgery on the correct knee. In this case, Dr. Jones is presumed to be negligent under which legal doctrine?

6. Sarah is a college student who was late for class. She tried to cross the street in the middle of the block instead of at the intersection corner where a traffic light was in operation. A motorist hit her. Although Sarah placed herself in danger, she may be able to collect for her injuries if she can show that the motorist had an opportunity to avoid hitting her but failed to do so. Identify the legal rule that might apply in Sarah's case.

7. Elizabeth was injured in a work-related auto accident. She sued the other driver for her injuries, and the case went to court. While questioning Elizabeth, the defendant's attorney asked her if her injuries were paid under the company's group health insurance plan. Elizabeth's attorney immediately objected to the question. The judge ruled that the question was improper and instructed the jury to disregard the question. Based on the judge's reaction to the question, identify the legal rule that is in force in the jurisdiction where the trial took place.

8. Daniel believes that a chemical company is responsible for contaminating some land that he owns. He files suit against the chemical company. Rather than have the case go to court, the chemical company's attorney suggests arbitration to resolve the legal dispute. Explain how arbitration would work in this case.

# INTERNET RESOURCES

- **American Tort Reform Association (ATRA)** ATRA is a national organization devoted exclusively to repairing the civil justice system by advocating tort reform. ATRA fights in Congress and state legislatures to make the system fairer. Visit the site at

  atra.org/

- **FreeAdvice.com** is a leading legal site for consumers and small businesses. The site provides general legal information to help people understand their legal rights on numerous legal topics and insurance topics. Visit the site at

  freeadvice.com

- **Nolo.com** is a leading source of self-help legal information for consumers, including topics dealing with personal injury law. Visit the site at

  nolo.com

- The **Legal Information Institute** of Cornell Law School provides detailed information on torts, personal injury, and products liability law. Hot links are provided for federal laws, the Constitution, and other headings. A helpful link is "State Statutes by Topic," which provides an alphabetical listing of topics. Visit the site at

  law.cornell.edu

- The **RAND Institute for Civil Justice** publishes numerous high-quality research studies that make recommendations for improving the civil justice system in the United States. Several studies examine many of the liability issues discussed in this chapter. Visit the site at

  rand.org/icj/

## SELECTED REFERENCES

Congress of the United States, Congressional Budget Office, *The Effects of Tort Reform: Evidence from the States,* June 2004, and 2009 letter addressing effects of proposals to limit costs related to medical malpractice.

Dial, David, et al., *Tort Excess 2005: The Necessity for Reform from a Policy, Legal and Risk Management Perspective,* Insurance Information Institute, 2005.

Hartwig, Robert P., *Medical Malpractice Insurance & the Insurance Cycle,* Insurance Information Institute, May 15, 2008.

Hartwig, Robert P. and James Lynch, *Tort Inflation 2012: Stability Today, but for How Long?* Insurance Information Institute, June 2010.

*The I.I.I. Insurance Fact Book 2012,* New York: Insurance Information Institute, 2012.

Jury Verdict Research, *Jury Verdict Research Releases Medical Malpractice Study: Yearly Analyses Show an Upward Trend in Median Awards for Personal Injury Cases,* JVR News Release, June 22, 2005.

"Liability System," *Issues Updates,* Insurance Information Institute, March 2012. This source is periodically updated.

"Medical Malpractice," *Issues Updates,* Insurance Information Institute, March 2012. This source is periodically updated.

Towers Watson, *U.S. Tort Cost Trends, 2011 Update.*

## NOTES

1. Alabama, the District of Columbia, Maryland, North Carolina, and Virginia.
2. This section is based on *Comparative Fault Systems in All 51 Jurisdictions,* Matthiesen, Wickert & Lehrer, S.C., Attorneys at Law, Hartford, WI.
3. Alaska, Arizona, California, Florida, Kentucky, Louisiana, Mississippi, Missouri, New Mexico, New York, Rhode Island, South Dakota, and Washington.
4. Arkansas, Colorado, Georgia, Idaho, Kansas, Maine, Nebraska, North Dakota, Oklahoma, Tennessee, Utah, and West Virginia.
5. Connecticut, Delaware, Hawaii, Illinois, Indiana, Iowa, Massachusetts, Michigan, Minnesota, Montana, Nevada, New Hampshire, New Jersey, Ohio, Oregon, Pennsylvania, South Carolina, Texas, Vermont, Wisconsin, and Wyoming.
6. This section is based on Donald J. Hirsch, *Casualty Claim Practice,* 6th ed. (Burr Ridge, IL: Irwin, 1996), pp. 58–62.
7. *Opinion of the Supreme Court of Nebraska, Case Title, Roger W. Heins, Appellant, v. Webster County, Nebraska, doing business as Webster County Hospital, Appellee.* Filed August 23, 1996, No. S-94-713.
8. James J. Lorimer, et al., *The Legal Environment of Insurance,* 4th ed., vol. 2 (Malvern, PA: American Institute for Chartered Property Casualty Underwriters, 1993), pp. 18–19.
9. Ibid., p. 132.
10. Insurance Information Institute. "Dog Bite Liability," *Issues Updates,* June 2012.
11. These figures were taken from Towers Watson's, "U.S. Tort Cost Trends, 2011 Update."
12. Although Towers Watson (previously Towers Perrin) has been studying tort costs since 1985, not everyone agrees with its method of counting tort costs. Several sources believe they overstate costs. See, for example, "Towers Perrin: 'Grade F' for Fantastically Inflated 'Tort Cost' Report," J. Robert Hunter and Joanne Doroshow, Americans for Insurance Reform, January 28, 2010.
13. David Dial et al., *Tort Excess 2005: The Necessity for Reform from a Policy, Legal and Risk Management Perspective,* Insurance Information Institute, 2005.
14. U.S. Tort Cost Trends, 2011 Update, Towers Watson.
15. The use of tiny, nano-sized, particles is increasing in many products (medicine, cosmetics, paint, antiseptics, coatings, etc.). There is concern that nano particles may have side-effects similar to asbestos. See "Nanotechnology: Brave New World for Civil Tort Plaintiffs," by Ishna Neamatullah, published in the SciTech Lawyer, Vol. 6 (2009); and "The Nanotechnology Revolution: Ushering in a New Wave of Toxic Torts?" December 2009, www.gordonrees.com/publications
16. These results from Tillinghast were reported in *The III Fact Book, 2005,* p. 131.
17. Insurance Information Institute, "Liability System," *Hot Topics & Issues Updates,* November 2005.
18. This section is based on Insurance Information Institute, "Liability System," *Issues Update,* March 2012. This source is periodically updated. See also David Dial, et al., *Tort Excess 2005: The Necessity for Reform from a Policy, Legal and Risk Management Perspective,* Insurance Information Institute, 2005.

19. Congress of the United States, Congressional Budget Office, *The Effects of Tort Reform: Evidence from the States,* June 2004.

20. See "Malpractice Risk According to Specialty," by Anumpa Jena, Seth Seabury, Darius Lakdawalla, and Smitabh Chandra, *The New England Journal of Medicine*, August 2011.

21. Towers Watson, "U.S. Tort Cost Trends, 2011 Update."

22. Ibid.

23. HealthGrades, *In-Hospital Deaths from Medical Errors at 195,000 per Year, HealthGrades Study Finds,* Press Release, July 27, 2004.

24. "Malpractice Risk According to Specialty," by Anumpa Jena, Seth Seabury, Darius Lakdawalla, and Smitabh Chandra, *The New England Journal of Medicine*, August 2011.

25. Insurance Information Institute, "Medical Malpractice," *Issues Updates,* August 2009. This source is periodically updated.

26. Insurance Information Institute, "Medical Malpractice," *Issues Updates,* August 2009.

27. Flauren Fagadau Bender. "'I'm Sorry' Laws and Medical Liability," *Virtual Mentor,* April 2007, Vol. 9, No. 4: 300–304.

# CHAPTER 20

# HOMEOWNERS INSURANCE, SECTION I

*"There's no place like home, after the other places close."*

English Proverb

## LEARNING OBJECTIVES

**After studying this chapter, you should be able to**

◆ Identify the major homeowners policies for homeowners, condominium owners, and renters.

◆ Explain the major provisions in Section I of the Homeowners 3 policy, including
 Section I property coverages
 Section I perils insured against
 Section I exclusions

◆ Given a specific property loss situation, explain whether the Homeowners 3 policy would cover the loss.

◆ Explain the insured's duties after a loss occurs.

◆ Explain and give an illustration of the loss settlement provisions in the Homeowners 3 policy.

*"At least everyone is safe," a glassy-eyed, shell-shocked, Nora Franklin said to the news reporter, "That's what is important." Nora and her husband were surveying what used to be their home. A tornado had leveled the home and destroyed most of the contents. Nora, her husband, and their two young children took refuge in the basement of the home as the storm hit. A claims adjuster from the Franklin's insurance company arrived after the reporter left. The Franklins were relieved to learn that under their homeowners insurance policy there is coverage for their destroyed home, their personal property, and a detached garage that was also destroyed. As an insured peril made their home uninhabitable, their stay at a local motel while the home is being rebuilt will also be covered.*

*A home is the most valuable physical asset most families will ever own. The above example shows clearly how a homeowners policy provides economic security to a family. In this chapter, we discuss the major homeowners policies that are sold today to insure homes, condominium units, and personal property. We also discuss the various limitations and exclusions that appear in current homeowners and renters policies.*

*Each homeowners policy is divided into two major sections. Section I covers the property of the insured, which can include a home or condominium, other structures, personal property, and loss of use. Section II provides personal liability insurance and also covers medical payments to others. This chapter discusses the Section I provisions. The Section II provisions are discussed in Chapter 21.*

## HOMEOWNERS INSURANCE

Homeowners insurance contracts were first introduced in the 1950s. Since that time, they have been revised several times. In this chapter, we discuss the homeowners forms drafted by the Insurance Services Office (ISO). In 2010, ISO released a new edition of the homeowners policy for use beginning in 2011. A copy of the new edition of the ISO Homeowners 3 form, which will be examined in greater detail in this chapter, is provided in Appendix A at the end of the text.[1]

ISO forms are widely used throughout the United States. Some insurers, however, use the homeowners forms designed by the American Association of Insurance Services (AAIS), which is an advisory organization similar to ISO. Other insurers use their own forms, which differ slightly from the ISO forms.

### Eligible Dwellings

A homeowners policy on a private dwelling is designed for the owner-occupants of a one-, two-, three-, or four-family dwelling used exclusively for private residential purposes (although certain business occupancies are permitted, such as a home day care business and offices for business or professional purposes). A one-family dwelling may not be occupied by more than one additional family or more than two roomers or boarders. Separate homeowners forms are written for renters and condominium unit owners.

### Overview of Homeowners Policies

The following forms are used in the current ISO homeowners (HO) program:

- HO-2 (broad form)
- HO-3 (special form)
- HO-4 (contents broad form)
- HO-5 (comprehensive form)
- HO-6 (unit-owners form)
- HO-8 (modified coverage form)

**Homeowners 2 (Broad Form)**  Homeowners 2 *is a named-perils policy that insures the dwelling, other structures (e.g., a detached garage or tool* *shed), and personal property against loss from certain listed perils.* Covered perils include fire, lightning, windstorm, hail, explosion, and other perils. A complete list of covered perils can be found in Exhibit 20.1. The HO-2 also covers the additional living expenses or fair rental value in the event a covered loss makes the dwelling uninhabitable.

**Homeowners 3 (Special Form)**   Homeowners 3 *insures the dwelling and other structures against direct physical loss to property.* This means that all direct physical losses to the dwelling and other structures are covered, except those losses specifically excluded. Losses to the dwelling and other structures are paid on the basis of full replacement cost with no deduction for depreciation if certain conditions (discussed later) are met. Personal property is covered for the same broad form perils listed for the HO-2 policy.

**Homeowners 4 (Contents Broad Form)**   Homeowners 4 *is designed for tenants who rent apartments, houses, or rooms.* Homeowners 4 covers the tenant's personal property against loss or damage and also provides personal liability insurance. Personal property is covered for the same named perils listed in Homeowners 2. In addition, 10 percent of the insurance on personal property can be applied to cover any additions or alterations to the building made by the insured.

Although most renters need a homeowners policy, the majority of tenants are uninsured. A Homeowners 4 policy, however, is especially valuable if a total loss occurs, especially in the case of a fire in which all of your belongings are totally destroyed. The cost of replacing your furniture, clothes, books, laptop computer and other electronic equipment, television, cosmetics, food, and other personal property can easily exceed $15,000. Additional living expenses are paid if an insured peril renders the rented apartment or home uninhabitable. The HO-4 also provides a minimum of $100,000 of personal liability insurance that covers most personal activities. The annual premium generally is less than $175. Insight 20.1 discusses the value of a homeowners policy to one tenant who incurred a major loss in an apartment fire.

**Homeowners 5 (Comprehensive Form)**   *The Homeowners 5 form insures the dwelling, other structures, and personal property against direct physical loss to property.* This provision means that all direct physical losses are covered except those losses specifically excluded. Unlike the other homeowners forms that cover personal property only for certain named perils, HO-5 insures personal property for all direct physical losses except those losses specifically excluded.

**Homeowners 6 (Unit-Owners Form)**   Homeowners 6 *is designed for the owners of condominium units and cooperative apartments.* The condominium association carries insurance on the building and other property owned in common by the owners of the different units. Homeowners 6 covers the personal property of the unit owner for the same named perils listed in Homeowners 2. In addition, there is a minimum of $5000 of insurance on the condominium unit that covers certain property, such as built-in appliances, carpets, additional kitchen cabinets, and wallpaper.

**Homeowners 8 (Modified Coverage Form)** Homeowners 8 *is a modified coverage form that covers loss to the dwelling and other structures on the basis of repair cost, which is the amount required to repair or replace damaged property using common construction materials and methods.* Payment is not based on replacement cost. In some states, actual cash value is used to determine the amount payable.

The HO-8 policy is designed for an older home whose replacement cost substantially exceeds its market value. For example, an older home with a replacement cost of $300,000 may have a market value of only $200,000. Insurers will not insure a home for replacement cost when its current market value is substantially lower. Thus, to make homeowners coverage available for older homes and to reduce moral hazard, the HO-8 form was developed.

The HO-8 policy provides only limited coverage for the theft of personal property. Theft coverage is limited to a maximum of $1000 per occurrence and applies only to losses that occur on the residence premises.

Exhibit 20.1 compares the various homeowners forms, basic coverages, and insured perils.

**EXHIBIT 20.1**

**Comparison of ISO Homeowners Coverages**

| Coverage | HO-2 (broad form) | HO-3 (special form) | HO-4 (contents broad form) |
|---|---|---|---|
| | Section I Coverages | | |
| A. Dwelling | Minimum varies by company. | Minimum varies by company. | Not applicable |
| B. Other structures | 10% of A | 10% of A | Not applicable |
| C. Personal property | 50% of A | 50% of A | Minimum amount varies. |
| D. Loss of use | 30% of A | 30% of A | 30% of C |
| Covered perils | Fire or lightning<br>Windstorm or hail<br>Explosion<br>Riot or civil commotion<br>Aircraft<br>Vehicles<br>Smoke<br>Vandalism or malicious mischief<br>Theft<br>Falling objects<br>Weight of ice, snow, or sleet<br>Accidental discharge or overflow of water or steam<br>Sudden and accidental tearing apart, cracking, burning, or bulging of a steam, hot water, air conditioning, or automatic fire protective sprinkler system, or from within a household appliance<br>Freezing of a plumbing, heating, air conditioning, or automatic fire sprinkler system, or of a household appliance<br>Sudden and accidental damage from artificially generated electrical current<br>Volcanic eruption | Dwelling and other structures are covered against direct physical loss to property.<br><br>All direct physical losses are covered except those losses specifically excluded.<br><br>Personal property is covered for the same perils as HO-2. | Same perils as HO-2 for personal property |
| | Section II Coverages[a] | | |
| E. Personal liability | $100,000 | $100,000 | $100,000 |
| F. Medical payments to others | $1000 per person | $1000 per person | $1000 per person |

[a]Minimum amounts can be increased.

(Continued)

EXHIBIT 20.1 (continued)
**Comparison of ISO Homeowners Coverages**

| HO-5 (comprehensive form) | HO-6 (unit-owners form) | HO-8 (modified coverage form) |
|---|---|---|
| | Section I Coverages | |
| Minimum varies by company. | $5000 minimum. | Minimum varies by company. |
| 10% of A | Included in Coverage A | 10% of A |
| 50% of A | Minimum amount varies. | 50% of A |
| 30% of A | 50% of C | 10% of A |
| Dwelling and other structures are covered against direct physical loss to property. All direct physical losses are covered except those losses specifically excluded. Personal property is covered against direct physical loss to property. All direct physical losses are covered except those losses specifically excluded. | Same perils as HO-2 for personal property. | Fire or lightning<br>Windstorm or hail<br>Explosion<br>Riot or civil commotion<br>Aircraft<br>Vehicles<br>Smoke<br>Vandalism or malicious mischief<br>Theft (applies only to loss on the residence premises up to a maximum of $1000)<br>Volcanic eruption |
| | Section II Coverages[a] | |
| $100,000 | $100,000 | $100,000 |
| $1000 per person | $1000 per person | $1000 per person |

[a]Minimum amounts can be increased.

## INSIGHT 20.1

### Lesson to Be Learned from Apartment Fire

The insurance industry could hardly ask for a more effective illustration of the value of renter's insurance than the fire at Thomasbrook Apartments a week ago. Apartment residents who haven't gotten around to getting a policy should use the example as motivation to explore that option.

Michael R. Adams was glad he had taken that step after a fire swept through the building and forced tenants from 23 apartments. The blaze started when a tenant discarded a cigarette in a plastic coffee container on a balcony.

"I'm just glad I decided to get insurance," said Adams, age 23. Because he paid $110 for a policy, he had coverage to get a hotel room and to buy food, even though he fled the apartment so fast he left his wallet behind.

Alicia Harms had just moved in recently and had not yet found coverage.

"I grabbed my laptop and purse and ran. I lost everything," she said.

Ten of 23 apartments vacated as a result of the fire had no renter's insurance, according to Bob Kelley of the Red Cross.

That percentage actually is better than the national statistics. A 2006 survey by the Insurance Research Council found that 43 percent of tenants had no renter's insurance.

## ANALYSIS OF HOMEOWNERS 3 POLICY (SPECIAL FORM)

In the remainder of this chapter, we examine the major provisions that appear in Section I in the Homeowners 3 policy (special form). As you study this section, you may find it helpful to refer to the Homeowners 3 policy in Appendix A at the end of this text.

### Persons Insured

Certain words and phrases are defined in the policy. One of the most important is the meaning of the term "insured." The following persons are considered insureds under the policy:

- *Named insured and residents of the household who are your relatives.* The named insured is the person or persons named in the declarations page of the policy. The named insured under the policy is also referred to as "you." Coverage also applies to the spouse of the named insured if she or he is a resident of the same household. Children and other relatives residing in the named insured's household are covered.
- *Other persons under age 21.* Other persons under age 21 who are in the care of the named insured or the care of a household resident who is a relative. Examples are a foster child, a ward of the court, or a foreign exchange student.
- *Full-time student away from home.* The definition of "insured" includes a full-time student away from home who was a resident of the named insured's household before moving out to attend school, provided the student is under age 24 and a relative of the named insured, or is under age 21 and in the care of the named insured or the care of a household resident who is your relative.

In addition to the above, the definition of "insured" includes the following persons under the Section II coverages:

- *Any person legally responsible for covered animals or watercraft.* For example, if you leave your dog with a neighbor, and the dog bites someone, the neighbor has liability coverage under your policy. However, coverage does not apply to a person or organization having custody of animals or watercraft for business purposes, such as an operator of a dog kennel or boat marina.
- *With respect to a motor vehicle covered by the policy, coverage applies to persons employed by the named insured or by other insureds as defined above while working for the insured.*

For example, if an employee mows your lawn with a riding mower that you own and someone is injured, he or she has liability coverage under your policy.

# SECTION I COVERAGES

There are four basic coverages and several additional coverages in Section I of the Homeowners 3 policy:

- Coverage A: Dwelling
- Coverage B: Other structures
- Coverage C: Personal property
- Coverage D: Loss of use
- Additional coverages

## Coverage A: Dwelling

Coverage A covers the dwelling on the residence premises as well as any structure attached to the dwelling. Thus, the home and an attached garage or carport would be insured under this section. Materials and supplies intended for construction or repair of the dwelling or other structures are also covered.

Coverage A specifically excludes land. Thus, if the land on which the dwelling is located is damaged from an insured peril—such as an airplane crash—the land is not covered.

## Coverage B: Other Structures

Coverage B insures other structures on the residence premises that are separated from the dwelling by clear space. This coverage includes a detached garage, tool shed, or horse stable. Structures connected to the dwelling only by a fence, utility line, or other similar connections are considered to be "other structures."

The amount of insurance under Coverage B is based on the amount of insurance on the dwelling (Coverage A). Under the HO-3 policy, 10 percent of the insurance on the dwelling applies as additional insurance to the other structures. For example, if the home is insured for $300,000, the other structures are covered for $30,000.

Coverage B has several important exclusions. Land damage is excluded. Also, with the exception of a private garage, there is no coverage if the other structure is rented to someone who is not a tenant of the dwelling. For example, assume that Todd owns and occupies a home that has a horse stable on the premises. If Todd rents the horse stable to another person, he would have no coverage if the stable burns in a fire.

In addition, other structures from which a business is conducted are not covered. Thus, if Charles operates an auto repair business in a detached garage, the garage is not covered if it is damaged in a tornado.

Finally, other structures used to store business property are excluded. However, the current form covers a structure that contains business property owned by the insured or tenant of the dwelling, provided such property does not include gaseous or liquid fuel, other than fuel in a permanently installed fuel tank in a vehicle parked in the structure. For example, if a professional painter stores ladders in a storage shed on his own premises, the shed would be covered as long as it does not contain gaseous or liquid fuel (other than fuel in the tank of a parked vehicle).

## Coverage C: Personal Property

Personal property owned or used by an insured is covered anywhere in the world. This provision also includes borrowed property. In addition, after a loss and at the named insured's request, the insurance can be extended to cover the personal property of a guest or resident employee while the property is in any residence occupied by an insured. For example, if you invite a guest to dinner in your home and the guest's coat burns in a fire, the loss can be covered under your policy.

The amount of insurance on personal property is equal to 50 percent of the amount of insurance on the dwelling, which can be increased if desired. The insurance on personal property covers you both on and off the premises. For example, Claire, age 20, is a college student who is temporarily away from her parents' home during the academic year. If a thief breaks into her dormitory room and steals a laptop computer, the loss is covered under her parents' policy.

An important limitation applies to personal property away from the premises if the property is usually located at another residence, such as personal property in a vacation home or cabin. *In such cases, the off-premises coverage is limited to 10 percent of Coverage C, or $1000, whichever is greater.*

For example, assume that Eric has $150,000 of insurance on his personal property. He could take that property on an extended trip to Europe and have coverage up to a maximum of $150,000 while it is off the premises. Assume by contrast that Eric owns a cabin or summer home on a river, and that furniture and fishing gear are normally kept there the entire year. In this case, a maximum of $15,000 (10 percent of $150,000) would apply to the loss of personal property at that location.

The 10 percent limitation does not apply to personal property that is moved from the residence premises because the residence premises is being repaired or remodeled and is not a fit place in which to live or store property. For example, the 10 percent limitation does not apply to personal property located at a residence temporarily occupied by an insured while the residence premises is undergoing repair or remodeling and is not a fit place in which to live.

The limitation also does not apply to personal property in a newly acquired principal residence for 30 days from the time the named insured begins to move the property there. The amount of insurance under Coverage C applies in full to such personal property during the 30-day period. However, the insurer must be notified within 30 days for full protection to continue.

The "new" policy form specifically addresses personal property in self-storage facilities. This property is covered for up to 10 percent of the Coverage C limit, or $1000; whichever is greater. These limits do not apply to property put in storage while the residence premises is being repaired or rebuilt, or because the residence premises is not fit for habitation or storage of property. These limits also do not apply if the property is usually kept at an insured's residence other than the residence premises.

**Special Limits of Liability** Because of moral hazard and loss-adjustment problems, and a desire by the insurer to limit its liability, certain types of property have maximum dollar limits on the amount paid for any loss (see Exhibit 20.2).

The $200 limit on money includes coin collections. If you have a valuable coin collection, it should be scheduled and insured for a specific amount of insurance. A **schedule** *is a list of covered property with specific amounts of insurance.* A valuable stamp collection should also be insured separately because there is a $1500 limit on stamps.

Coverage on watercraft of all types is limited to $1500, including trailers, furnishings, equipment, and outboard motors. A boat with a value in excess of this limit should be insured separately.

The theft of jewelry and furs is limited to a maximum of $1500. Expensive jewelry and furs should be scheduled and specifically insured. In addition, there is a $2500 limit on the theft of firearms and a $2500 limit on the theft of silverware, goldware, platinumware, and pewterware. Thus, a valuable set of silverware should be specifically insured based on the current value of the set. Note that the limits on jewelry, furs, guns, silverware, and goldware apply only to the theft peril. The full amount of insurance applies to losses from other covered perils.

Property used primarily for business purposes is limited to $2500 on the premises. There's a $1500 limit on property used for business purposes when it is away from the residence. This limit does not apply to antennas, tapes, wires, disks and other media used with electronic equipment that reproduces, receives, or transits audio, visual, or data signals and is in or upon a motor vehicle.

The homeowners policy provides $1500 of coverage on portable electronic equipment that reproduces receives or transmits audio, visual or data signals and is designed to be operated by more than one power source, one of which is a motor vehicle's electrical system. This limit applies to equipment used for personal or business use while the equipment is in or upon a motor vehicle.

*Finally, there is a $250 limit for antennas, tapes, wires, records, disks, and other media used with electronic equipment that reproduces, receives, or transmits audio, visual, or data signals and is in or upon a motor vehicle.*

**Property Not Covered** Certain types of property are excluded under Coverage C. The following property is not covered.

EXHIBIT 20.2
**Special Limits of Liability**

| Type of Property | Amount |
|---|---|
| 1. Money, bank notes, bullion, gold, silver, platinum, coins, medals, stored value cards, and smart cards | $200 |
| 2. Securities, valuable papers, manuscripts, personal records, passports, tickets, and stamps | $1500 |
| 3. Watercraft of all types | $1500 |
| 4. Trailers not used with watercraft of all types | $1500 |
| 5. Theft of jewelry, watches, furs, and precious and semiprecious stones | $1500 |
| 6. Theft of firearms and related equipment | $2500 |
| 7. Theft of silverware, goldware, platinumware, and pewterware | $2500 |
| 8. Property on the residence premises used primarily for business purposes | $2500 |
| 9. Property away from the residence premises used primarily for business purposes. The limit does not apply to antennas, tapes, wires, records, disks, and other media that are (1) used with electronic equipment that reproduces, receives, or transmits audio, visual, or data signals; and (2) is in or upon a motor vehicle. | $1500 |
| 10. Portable electronic equipment that (1) reproduces, receives, or transmits audio, visual, or data signals; (2) is designed to be operated by more than one power source, one of which is the motor vehicle's electrical system; and (3) is on or upon a motor vehicle. | $1500 |
| 11. Antennas, tapes, wires, records, disks, and other media that are used with electronic equipment that reproduces, receives, or transmits audio or visual signals and is in or upon a motor vehicle. | $250 |

1. *Articles separately described and specifically insured*. Coverage C does not cover articles separately described and specifically insured under either the homeowners policy or some other policy. The intent here is to avoid duplicate coverage. Thus, if jewelry or furs are specifically insured, Coverage C of the homeowners policy will not contribute toward the loss.

2. *Animals, birds, and fish*. Pets are excluded because they are difficult to value. Specialized coverages can be used to cover high-value animals, such as thoroughbred horses and pedigreed dogs.

3. *Motor vehicles*. Motor vehicles and their accessories and equipment are specifically excluded. Thus, cars, motorcycles, and motorscooters are excluded under the policy. Likewise, the theft of a car battery or wheel covers from a car would not be covered.

The exclusion does not apply to portable electronic equipment that reproduces, receives, or transmits audio, visual, or data signals and is designed so that it may be operated from a power source other than the vehicle's electrical system.

Motor vehicles not required to be registered for use on public roads that are used solely to service the insured residence or designed to assist the handicapped are exempt from the exclusion. Thus, a garden tractor, riding lawn mower, or electric wheelchair would normally be covered under the policy.

4. *Aircraft and parts*. Aircraft and parts are specifically excluded. However, the policy does cover hobby or model aircraft not used or designed to carry people or cargo.

5. *Hovercraft and parts*. Hovercraft and parts are also excluded. A hovercraft is a self-propelled vehicle that generates a cushion of air on which to move.

6. *Property of roomers, boarders, and other tenants.* Property of roomers and boarders who are not related to an insured is excluded. Thus, if the insured rents a room to a student, the student's property is not covered under the insured's homeowners policy. However, the property of roomers, boarders, and tenants related to an insured is covered.

7. *Property in a regularly rented apartment.* Property in an apartment regularly rented or being held for rental to others by an insured is specifically excluded. However, as discussed later, the homeowners policy provides some coverage for landlord's furnishings in an apartment on the residence premises that is regularly rented or held for rental.

8. *Property rented or held for rental to others off the residence premises.* Property away from the residence premises that is rented to others is specifically excluded. For example, if Jennifer owns a bike rental business, the bicycles are not covered under Jennifer's homeowners policy.

9. *Business data.* The homeowners policy excludes business data stored in books of account, drawings or other paper records, or in computers and related equipment. The overall effect of this exclusion is to eliminate coverage for the expense of reproducing business records.

10. *Credit cards, electronic fund transfer cards, or access devices.* Coverage of personal property does not include credit cards, electronic fund transfer cards, or access devices. There is some coverage for the unauthorized use of such cards under Additional Coverages (discussed later).

11. *Water or steam.* The homeowners policy excludes coverage of water or steam as personal property. Thus, water or steam delivered through a public water main or from the insured's own well is excluded. Also, water in a swimming pool is not covered.

## Coverage D: Loss of Use

Coverage D provides protection when the residence premises cannot be used because of a covered loss. The amount of additional insurance under this coverage is 30 percent of the amount of insurance on the

dwelling (Coverage A). Three benefits are provided: *additional living expense, fair rental value, and prohibited use.*

**Additional Living Expense**    If a covered loss makes the residence premises not fit to live in, the insurer pays the additional living expenses that the insured may incur as a result of the loss. **Additional living expense** *is the increase in living expenses actually incurred by the insured to maintain the family's normal standard of living.* For example, assume that Heather's home is damaged by a fire. If she rents a furnished apartment for three months at $800 per month, the additional living expense of $2400 would be covered.

**Fair Rental Value**    The fair rental value is also paid when part of the premises is rented to others. **Fair rental value** *means the rental value of that part of the residence premises rented to others or held for rental less any expenses that do not continue while the premises are not fit to live in.* For example, Heather may rent a room to a student for $200 per month. If the home is uninhabitable after a fire, and it takes three months to rebuild, Heather would receive $600 for the loss of rents (less any expenses that do not continue). This payment would be in addition to the payment under the additional living expense coverage described earlier.

**Prohibited Use**    Loss-of-use coverage also includes prohibited use losses. Even if the covered home is not damaged, a civil authority may prohibit the insured from using the premises because of direct damage to neighboring premises from an insured peril. The additional living expenses and fair rental value can be paid for up to two weeks. For example, Heather may be ordered out of her home by a fire marshal because the house next door is unstable after an explosion occurred. Her additional living expenses and fair rental value loss would be covered for up to two weeks.

## Additional Coverages

In addition to basic Coverages A, B, C, and D, the HO-3 policy provides several additional coverages.

**Debris Removal**    The homeowners policy pays the reasonable expense of removing the debris of covered property damaged by an insured peril. Debris removal also pays the cost of removing volcanic ash or dust from a volcanic eruption that causes a direct loss to a building or property inside a building.

The cost of removing debris is included in the policy limit that applies to the damaged property. However, if the actual damage plus the cost of removal exceed the policy limit, an additional 5 percent of the amount of insurance is available for debris removal. For example, assume that a detached garage is covered for $30,000, and a total loss from a fire occurs. If the entire $30,000 is needed to rebuild the garage, up to an additional $1500 is also available for debris removal.

In addition, the homeowners policy covers the removal of trees owned by the named insured felled by windstorm or hail, or by the weight of ice, snow, or sleet. Coverage also applies to the removal of a neighbor's tree felled by a Coverage C peril. Coverage applies provided the tree (1) damages a covered structure, or (2) blocks a driveway and prevents a motor vehicle required to be registered for road use from entering or leaving the residence premises, or (3) blocks and prevents use of a ramp or access fixture designed to assist a handicapped person to enter and leave the dwelling. The maximum paid is limited to $1000 regardless of the number of fallen trees. No more than $500 of that limit is paid for the removal of any one tree. This coverage is additional insurance.

**Reasonable Repairs**   The policy pays the reasonable cost of necessary repairs incurred by the insured to protect the property from further damage after a covered loss occurs. For example, a broken window may have to be temporarily boarded up immediately after a severe windstorm to protect personal property from further damage. This coverage does not increase the limit of insurance that applies to covered property.

**Trees, Shrubs, and Other Plants**   The homeowners policy covers trees, shrubs, plants, or lawns on the residence premises against loss from a limited number of perils. *Coverage is provided only for fire, lightning, explosion, riot, civil commotion, aircraft, vehicles not owned or operated by a resident of the premises, vandalism, malicious mischief, or theft.* Note that *windstorm* is not listed. If an expensive tree is blown over in a severe windstorm, the cost of replacing the tree is not covered.

The maximum limit for a loss under this coverage is 5 percent of the insurance that covers the dwelling. However, no more than $500 of that limit can be applied to any single tree, plant, or shrub. This coverage is additional insurance.

**Fire Department Service Charge**   The insurer will pay up to $500 if the named insured is liable by a contract or agreement for a fire department charge when firefighters from another municipality are called to protect covered property from an insured peril. This coverage is additional insurance. No deductible applies to this coverage.

**Property Removal**   If property is removed from the premises because it is endangered by an insured peril, direct loss from any cause is covered for a maximum of 30 days while the property is removed. Thus, furniture being moved and stored in a warehouse because of a fire in the home is covered for a direct loss from any cause for a maximum of 30 days. For example, if an earthquake occurred and damaged the furniture stored in a warehouse after the fire, the loss caused by the otherwise excluded earthquake would be covered. This coverage does not increase the limit of insurance that applies to the property being removed.

**Credit Card, Electronic Fund Transfer Card or Access Device, Forgery, and Counterfeit Money**   If credit cards are stolen or lost and used in an unauthorized manner, any loss to the insured is covered up to a maximum of $500. Likewise, loss that results from the theft or unauthorized use of an insured's electronic fund transfer card is covered. If a forged or altered check results in a loss to the insured, it is also covered. If the insured accepts counterfeit money in good faith, that loss is covered, too. This coverage is additional insurance. No deductible applies to this coverage.

**Loss Assessment**   The insurer pays up to $1000 for any loss assessment charged against the named insured by a corporation or association of property owners because of the direct loss to property collectively owned by all members. For example, property owners in a subdivision may belong to a homeowners association that collectively owns a clubhouse, swimming pool, tennis courts, fences, and a sign at the entrance to the subdivision. Assume that a tornado completely destroys the clubhouse. If the homeowners association insurance policy does not cover the entire loss, each property owner may be assessed his or her share of the loss. HO-3 will pay up to $1000 for any loss assessment charge that otherwise the property owner would have to pay. This coverage is additional insurance.

**Collapse**   Collapse of a building is covered as an additional coverage. The policy defines collapse as an abrupt falling down or caving in of a building or any part of a building with the result that the building or part of the building cannot be occupied for its intended use.[2]

Collapse of a building (or any part of a building) is covered only if the loss is caused by any of the following:

- Perils insured against in Coverage C
- Hidden decay, unless known to the insured prior to collapse
- Hidden insect or vermin damage, unless known to the insured prior to collapse
- Weight of contents, equipment, animals, or people
- Weight of rain that collects on a roof
- Use of defective materials or methods in construction, remodeling, or renovation if the collapse occurs during the course of construction, remodeling, or renovation

**Glass or Safety Glazing Material**   The policy covers the breakage of glass or safety glazing material that is part of a covered building, storm door, or storm window. Damage to covered property from the glass or safety glazing material is also covered. For example, if a baseball breaks a storm window, the glass damage is covered. If the shattering of glass causes damage to a lamp near the window, damage to the lamp is also covered. This coverage does not increase the limit of insurance that applies to the damaged property.

**Landlord's Furnishings**   The homeowners policy will pay up to $2500 for loss to the named insured's appliances, carpets, and other household furnishings in each apartment on the residence premises that is regularly rented out or held for rental by an insured. The coverage applies to all losses caused by the perils insured against (Coverage C perils), with the exception of theft. For example, Susan has a furnished apartment on the second floor of her house that is rented to students. The appliances, carpets, and furniture inside

the apartment are covered up to $2500. This coverage does not increase the limit of insurance that applies to the damaged property.

**Ordinance or Law**   Many communities have building codes that may increase the cost of repairing or reconstructing a damaged building. For example, a new ordinance may require the use of copper pipes rather than galvanized or plastic pipes when the pipes must be replaced after a loss.

The named insured can apply up to 10 percent of the amount of insurance under Coverage A to cover the increased costs of construction or repair because of some ordinance or law. If higher amounts of insurance are desired, an endorsement can be added to the policy. The coverage provided is additional insurance.

**Grave Markers**   Grave markers, including mausoleums, are covered for up to $5000 for loss caused by a peril insured against under Coverage C. This coverage does not increase the limit of insurance that applies to the damaged property.

## SECTION I PERILS INSURED AGAINST

In this section, we discuss the various perils, or causes of loss, to covered property. Hopefully after reading this section you will be well-informed about covered causes of loss under the homeowners policy.

### Dwelling and Other Structures (Coverage A and B)

The dwelling and other structures are insured against "direct physical loss to property." *This means that direct physical losses are covered except certain losses specifically excluded.* If a loss to the dwelling or other structure is not excluded, the loss is covered under the policy.

**Excluded Losses**   Certain types of losses to the dwelling and other structures, however, are specifically excluded. They include the following:

1. *Collapse.* Losses involving collapse are specifically excluded, except those collapse losses covered under "additional coverages" discussed earlier.
2. *Freezing.* Freezing of a plumbing, heating, air conditioning, or automatic fire protection sprinkler

system, or household appliance is not covered unless the named insured uses reasonable care to maintain heat in the building, or the water supply is shut off and drained.

However, if the building has an automatic sprinkler system, the insured is required to use reasonable care to continue the water supply and maintain heat in the building for the coverage to apply.

3. *Fences, pavement, patio, and similar structures.* Damage to a fence, pavement, patio, swimming pool, foundation, and similar structures is not covered if the damage is caused by freezing and thawing, or from the pressure or weight of water or ice.

4. *Dwelling under construction.* Theft to a dwelling under construction, or of materials and supplies used in construction, is not covered until the dwelling is both completed and occupied.

5. *Vandalism and malicious mischief.* Damage from vandalism, malicious mischief, or the breakage of glass and safety-glazing materials is not covered if the dwelling is vacant for more than 60 consecutive days immediately before the loss.

6. *Mold, fungus, or dry rot.* Loss to the dwelling or other structures from mold, fungus, or dry rot is excluded. However, an undetected loss—mold, fungus, or dry rot within the walls, ceilings, or beneath the floor caused by the accidental discharge of water or steam from a plumbing, heating, air conditioning, household appliance, or fire sprinkler system—is covered under the policy. In addition, loss from the discharge or overflow of water or steam from a storm drain, or water, steam, or sewer pipes off the residence premises is covered as well.

7. *Other exclusions.* The following causes of loss are also excluded:
   - Wear and tear, marring, deterioration
   - Mechanical breakdown, latent defect, inherent vice (tendency of property to decompose)
   - Smog, rust or other corrosion, or dry rot
   - Smoke from agricultural smudging or industrial operations
   - Discharge, seepage, or release or escape of pollutants unless the discharge or release is caused by a Coverage C peril
   - Settling, cracking, shrinking, bulging, or expansion of pavements, patios, foundations, walls, floors, roofs, or ceilings

   - Animals owned or kept by an insured
   - Birds, rodents, or insects[3]
   - Nesting or infestation, or discharge or release of waste or secretions by animals

## Personal Property

Personal property (Coverage C) is covered on a named-perils basis. The policy pays for direct physical loss to personal property from the perils discussed in the following section.

**Fire or Lightning** The homeowners policy covers a direct physical loss to property from fire or lightning. Direct physical loss means that fire or lightning is the proximate cause of the loss. **Proximate cause** *means there is an unbroken chain of events between the occurrence of a covered peril and damage or destruction of the property.* For example, assume a fire starts in the bedroom of your home. Firefighters spray water in the other rooms to keep the fire from spreading, and the water causes considerable damage to your books, furniture, and drapes. The entire loss is covered, including the water damage, because fire is the proximate cause of loss.

What is a fire? The homeowners policy does not define a fire; however, various court decisions have clarified its meaning. Two requirements generally must be met. *First, there must be combustion or rapid oxidation that causes a flame or at least a glow.* Thus, scorching, heating, and charring that occur without a flame or glow are not covered. For example, a garment accidentally scorched by an iron is not covered because there is no flame or glow. *Second, the fire must be hostile or unfriendly.* A hostile fire is outside its normal confines. A friendly fire is intentionally started and is exactly where it is supposed to be. The courts generally have ruled that if a property insurance policy is written on a named perils basis, damage from a friendly fire is not covered. However, if the policy is written on an "all risks" (open-perils) basis, damage from a friendly fire is covered since there is no exclusion for such damage.[4]

**Windstorm or Hail** Windstorm or hail damage is also covered. However, damage to the interior of the building and its contents because of rain, snow, sand, or dust is not covered unless there is an opening in the roof or wall caused by wind or hail that allows the elements to enter. For example, if a window is left open, rain damage to a sofa is not covered under the HO-3 policy. But if the wind or hail breaks the window, allowing rain to enter through the opening, the water damage to personal property inside the room would be covered.

An important exclusion applies to boats. Boats and related equipment are covered only while inside a fully enclosed building. For example, if a boat is stored in the driveway of the home and is damaged by a windstorm, the loss is not covered.

**Explosion** Broad coverage is provided for damage caused by an explosion. Any type of explosion loss is covered, such as a furnace explosion that damages personal property.

**Riot or Civil Commotion** Damage to personal property from a riot or civil commotion is covered. Each state defines the meaning of a riot. It is usually defined as an assembly of three or more persons who commit a lawful or unlawful act in a violent or tumultuous manner, to the terror or disturbance of others. Civil commotion is a large or sustained riot that involves an uprising of the citizens.

**Aircraft** Aircraft damage, including damage from self-propelled missiles and spacecraft, is covered. For example, if a commercial jet crashes into your residence, damage to your personal property is covered. Likewise, if a self-propelled missile from a nearby military base goes astray, and damages your personal property, the loss is covered.

**Vehicles** Property damage from vehicles is covered. For example, if your suitcase, clothes, and camera are damaged in an auto accident, the loss is covered. Likewise, if you carelessly back out of the garage and run over your bicycle, the loss is covered.

**Smoke** Sudden and accidental damage from smoke is covered, including emissions of smoke or fumes from a furnace or related equipment. For example, if the fireplace malfunctions and smoke pours into the family room, any smoke damage to the furniture, rugs, or drapes is covered. However, smoke damage from agricultural smudging or industrial operations is specifically excluded.

**Vandalism or Malicious Mischief** If someone intentionally damages your personal property, the loss is covered.

**Theft** Theft losses are covered, including the attempted theft and the loss of property when it is likely that the property has been stolen. Although coverage of theft is fairly broad, there are several exclusions. They include the following:

1. *Theft by an insured is excluded.* For example, if Danielle, age 16, steals $100 from her mother's purse before running away from home, the theft is not covered.
2. *Theft in or to a dwelling under construction,* or of materials and supplies used in the construction of a dwelling, is not covered until the dwelling is completed and occupied.
3. *Theft from any part of the premises rented to someone other than an insured is not covered.* For example, if the insured rents a room to a student, the theft of a radio owned by the insured and located inside the room would not be covered.

Several important exclusions apply when the theft occurs away from the residence premises. They include the following:

1. *Temporary residence.* If property is located at any other residence owned, rented to, or occupied by an insured, the loss is not covered unless an insured is temporarily residing there. For example, Brian owns a cabin on the river. Theft of property inside the cabin is not covered unless Brian is temporarily residing there. He is not required to be physically present at the residence at the time of loss, but he must be temporarily living or residing there. For example, if he is fishing at the river when the theft occurs, the loss would be covered.

In addition, *theft of personal property of an insured student while at a residence away from home is covered if the student has been there any time during the 90 days immediately preceding the loss.* For example, assume you are attending college and are temporarily living away from home. If your television is stolen from your college residence, the loss is covered by your parent's HO-3 policy if you have been there any time during the 90-day period preceding the loss.[5]

2. *Watercraft.* Theft of a boat, its furnishings, equipment, and outboard motor is excluded if the theft occurs away from the premises.
3. *Trailers, semitrailers, and campers.* Theft of trailers, semitrailers, or campers away from the premises is not covered. Trailers and campers can be covered under the personal auto policy, which is discussed in Chapter 22.

**Falling Objects**   Damage to personal property from falling objects is covered. However, loss to property inside the building is not covered unless the roof or outside wall of the building is first damaged by the falling object. For example, if a mirror on a stand falls and breaks, the loss is not covered. But if the mirror falls and breaks because the exterior of the dwelling is first damaged by a falling tree, the loss would be covered.

**Weight of Ice, Snow, or Sleet**   Damage to indoor personal property resulting from the weight of ice, snow, or sleet is covered. For example, if the weight of snow causes the roof to sag, any damage to the personal property inside the dwelling would be covered.

**Accidental Discharge or Overflow of Water or Steam**   If loss results from an accidental discharge or overflow of water or steam from a plumbing, heating, air conditioning, or automatic fire protective sprinkler system, or from a household appliance, the property damage is covered. For example, if an automatic dishwasher malfunctions and floods the kitchen, water damage to personal property, such as an area rug, would be covered. However, the cost of repairing the system or appliance from which the water or steam escapes is not covered.

**Sudden and Accidental Tearing Apart, Cracking, Burning, or Bulging of a Steam, Hot Water, Air Conditioning, or Automatic Fire Protective Sprinkler System, or Appliance for Heating Water**   If any of these perils cause damage to personal property, the loss is covered. For example, damage to personal property from a hot water heater that suddenly cracks is covered.

**Freezing of a Plumbing, Heating, Air Conditioning, or Automatic Fire Protective Sprinkler System, or Household Appliance**   Freezing is not covered unless the insured used reasonable care to maintain heat in the building, or shuts off the water supply and drains the system. However, if there is an automatic sprinkler system in the building, the insured must use reasonable care to continue the water supply and maintain heat for coverage to apply.

**Sudden and Accidental Damage from an Artificially Generated Electrical Current**   For example, an electrical power surge that causes an electric clothes dryer to burn out would be covered. However, loss to tubes, transistors, or electronic components that are part of appliances, computers, or home entertainment units is specifically excluded. Thus, a television picture tube that burns out is not covered.

**Volcanic Eruption**   Loss resulting from a volcanic eruption is also covered. However, losses caused by earthquakes, land shock waves, or tremors are excluded.

## SECTION I EXCLUSIONS

In addition to the specific exclusions previously discussed, several general exclusions appear in the policy.

**Concurrent Causation Losses**   The homeowners policy contains language that excludes concurrent causation losses. *The exclusion means that if a single loss is caused by two or more perils that occur concurrently or in any sequence, and one peril is covered under the policy (e.g., windstorm) and the other peril is excluded (e.g., flood), the entire loss is excluded.* The concurrent causation exclusion created serious loss adjustment problems when Hurricane Katrina occurred in 2005. Thousands of homes were damaged or destroyed by both windstorm and flood. Many insurers took the position that such losses were concurrent causation losses, and therefore, the loss was not covered. Other insurers paid for the wind damage but excluded damage from flood. In many cases, policyholders viewed the loss payments for any windstorm damage as inadequate. In class-action lawsuits that followed, the courts generally took the position that concurrent causation exclusions are valid.

### Ordinance or Law

With the exception of the ordinance or law coverage described earlier under the additional coverages section, and glass replacement as required by law, the policy excludes loss due to any ordinance or law. However, as noted earlier, if the amount of insurance provided under the additional coverages section is inadequate, higher amounts can be obtained by an endorsement to the policy.

### Earth Movement

Property damage from earth movement is excluded. This includes damage from an earthquake, shock waves from a volcanic eruption, landslide, mudslide or mudflow, subsidence or sinkholes, or earth rising, sinking, or shifting. However, an ensuing direct loss caused by fire, explosion, or theft is covered. An earthquake endorsement can be added to the policy.

### Water Damage

Property damage from certain water losses is specifically excluded. The following types of water damage losses are not covered:

- Floods, surface water, waves (including tidal and tsunami), tides, tidal water, and overflow or spray from a body of water whether or not driven by wind, including storm surge
- Water that backs up through sewers or drains or overflows from a sump pump
- Water below the surface of the ground that exerts pressure on or seeps through a building, sidewalk, driveway, foundation, swimming pool, or other structure
- Waterborne material carried or moved by any of the above

The revised policy states that these water losses are excluded regardless of whether they are caused by an act of nature or another cause. It goes on to state that the water exclusion applies to, but is not limited to; escape, overflow or discharge of water from a levee, dam, seawall, or any containment system.

### Power Failure

There is no coverage for loss caused by the failure of power or other utility service if the failure takes place off the residence premises. For example, if the contents of a freezer thaw and spoil because of the failure of an electrical power plant 15 miles away, the loss is not covered. However, if the

power failure is caused by an insured peril on the residence premises, any resulting loss is covered. Thus, if lightning strikes the home and power is interrupted on the premises, the spoilage of food in a freezer is covered.

### Neglect

If the insured neglects to use all reasonable means to save and preserve the property at or after the time of loss, the loss is not covered. For example, a broken window may have to be boarded up after a windstorm to protect personal property in the room from wind or rain damage.

### War

Property damage from war is specifically excluded. War is excluded in nearly all property insurance contracts.

### Nuclear Hazard

Nuclear hazard losses are excluded, including nuclear reaction, radiation, or radioactive contamination. For example, if a radiation leak from a nuclear power plant contaminates your property, the loss is not covered.

### Intentional Loss

An intentional loss is excluded. An intentional loss is a loss arising out of any act the insured commits or conspires to commit with the intent to cause a loss. For example, if the insured arranges to have his home burned to collect the claim payment, the loss is not covered.

### Governmental Action

Loss due to governmental action is also excluded. Governmental action refers to the destruction, confiscation, or seizure of property by any governmental or public authority. For example, if the house and cash of a drug dealer are seized by drug enforcement officials, the loss would not be covered. However, the exclusion does not apply to acts ordered by a government or public authority to prevent the spread of a fire.

### Weather Conditions

This exclusion applies only to weather conditions that contribute to a loss that would otherwise be excluded. For example, landslide damage caused by excessive rain and heavy winds is excluded under this provision. Likewise, flooding or earth movement caused by excessive rain is excluded. However, damage to a house caused solely by windstorm or hail would be covered.

### Acts or Decisions

This exclusion applies to losses that result from the failure to act by any person, group, organization, or government body. For example, if a governmental unit fails to develop a plan to control flood losses, property damage from a flood that resulted from failure to develop a plan would not be covered.

### Faulty, Inadequate, or Defective Planning and Design

Also excluded are losses that result from faulty or defective planning, zoning, design, workmanship, materials, or maintenance. For example, a completed house that pulls away from the foundation because of faulty design would not be covered.

## SECTION I CONDITIONS

Section I of the homeowners policy contains numerous conditions. The most important are discussed here.

### Insurable Interest and Limit of Liability

If more than one party has an insurable interest in the property, the insurer's liability for any one loss is limited to each insured's insurable interest at the time of loss but not to exceed the maximum amount of insurance.

### Deductible

The deductible shown in the declarations applies to each covered loss.[6] The deductible can be increased to reduce premiums. For example, if the insured increases

a $250 deductible to $500, it can reduce premiums by up to 12 percent; and raising the deductible to $1000 can reduce premiums by up to 25 percent. The deductible does not apply to a fire department service charge or to losses involving credit cards, ATM cards, forgery, or counterfeit money.

In states that are vulnerable to catastrophes, insurers can use *percentage deductibles* rather than dollar deductibles to limit their exposure to catastrophe losses from natural disasters. Eighteen states and the District of Columbia have hurricane deductibles.[7] *Depending on the state and insurer, percentage deductibles for windstorm and hail losses, may be mandatory in some coastal areas. These deductibles vary from 1 percent to 15 percent of the limit of insurance on the dwelling.* For example, if a house is insured for $200,000 with a 2 percent windstorm deductible, the first $4000 of loss must be paid by the policyholder. Depending on the state, policyholders may be given a "buy back option," which requires payment of a higher premium to have a traditional dollar deductible. Percentage deductibles are common when earthquake coverage is added through an endorsement.

### Duties After a Loss

The insured must perform certain duties after a loss occurs. The insurer has the right to deny coverage for a loss if the insured does not comply with his or her duties and such failure is prejudicial to the insurer. The following duties are required:

- *Give prompt notice.* The insured must give prompt notice to the insurer or an agent of the insurer. In case of a theft, the police must be notified as well. The credit card company or bank must also be notified in case of loss or theft of a credit or ATM card.
- *Protect the property.* The insured must protect the property from further damage, make reasonable and necessary repairs to protect the property, and keep an accurate record of the repair expenses.
- *Prepare an inventory of damaged personal property.* The inventory must show in detail the quantity, description, actual cash value, and the amount of loss. Taking an inventory of your property before a loss occurs is highly advisable (see Insight 20.2).

## INSIGHT 20.2

### How Do I Take a Home Inventory and Why?

Would you be able to remember all the possessions you've accumulated over the years if they were destroyed by a fire? Having an up-to-date home inventory will help you get your insurance claim settled faster, verify losses for your income tax return and help you purchase the correct amount of insurance.

Start by making a list of your possessions, describing each item and noting where you bought it and its make and model. Clip to your list any sales receipts, purchase contracts, and appraisals you have. For clothing, count the items you own by category—pants, coats, shoes, for example—making notes about those that are especially valuable. For major appliance and electronic equipment, record their serial numbers, usually found on the back or bottom.

- **Don't be put off!** If you are just setting up a household, starting an inventory list can be relatively simple. If you've been living in the same house for many years, however, the task of creating a list can be daunting. Still, it's better to have an incomplete inventory than nothing at all. Start with recent purchases and then try to remember what you can about older possessions.
- **Big ticket items.** Valuable items like jewelry, art work and collectibles may have increased in value since you

received them. Check with your agent to make sure that you have adequate insurance for these items. They may need to be insured separately.

- **Take a picture.** Besides the list, you can take pictures of rooms and important individual items. On the back of the photos, note what is shown and where you bought it or the make. Don't forget things that are in closets or drawers.
- **Videotape it.** Walk through your house or apartment videotaping and describing the contents. Or do the same thing using a tape recorder.
- **Use a personal computer.** Use your PC to make your inventory list. Personal finance software packages often include a homeowners room-by-room inventory program.
- **Storing the list, photos and tapes.** Regardless of how you do it (written list, disk, photos, videotape or audio tape), keep your inventory along with receipts in your safe deposit box or at a friend's or relative's home. That way you'll be sure to have something to give your insurance representative if your home is damaged. When you make a significant purchase, add the information to your inventory while the details are fresh in your mind.

SOURCE: Reprinted by permission from the Insurance Information Institute.

- *Exhibit the damaged property.* The insured may be required to show the damaged property to the insurer as often as is reasonably required. The insured may also be required to submit to questions under oath without any other insured being present and sign a sworn statement.
- *File a proof of loss within 60 days after the insurer's request.* The proof of loss must include the time and cause of loss, interest of the insured and all others in the property, all liens on the property, other insurance covering the loss, and other relevant information.

### Loss Settlement

This section of the homeowners policy deals with the payment of losses. You should know how losses are settled under a homeowners policy.

**Personal Property**   Covered losses to personal property are settled on the basis of *actual cash value* at the time of loss but not to exceed the amount necessary to repair or replace the property. Losses to carpets, domestic appliances, awnings, and outdoor antennas and outdoor equipment are also paid on an actual cash value basis. In addition, losses to structures that are not buildings, as well as grave markers, are paid on an actual cash value basis.

Personal property can be insured for replacement cost by adding a replacement cost endorsement to the policy. Under this endorsement, there is no deduction for depreciation in determining the amount paid for a loss to personal property. You should consider insuring your personal property on the basis of replacement cost. Otherwise, if a loss occurs, you could pay a substantial amount of money out of pocket (see Insight 20.3).

## INSIGHT 20.3

### The Big Gap Between Replacement Cost and Actual Cash Value Can Empty Your Wallet

If you own personal property, you should consider the big gap between replacement cost and actual cash value. *You could pay a large amount out of pocket because of depreciation if the loss payment is based on actual cash value.* The table below, based on the depreciation schedule of a large property and

casualty insurer, shows that the insured would receive $7790 (less the deductible) based on *replacement cost* compared with only $3967 based on *actual cash value*. Actual cash value is replacement cost less depreciation.

| Item | Age | Replacement Cost | Depreciation | Actual Cash Value |
|------|-----|------------------|--------------|-------------------|
| Television | 5 years | $ 900 | $ 450 | $ 450 |
| Sofa | 4 years | 1500 | 600 | 900 |
| Draperies | 2 years | 2000 | 400 | 1600 |
| 5 women's dresses | 4 years | 500 | 400 | 100 |
| 3 pairs of men's shoes | 2 years | 200 | 133 | 67 |
| 3 end tables | 15 years | 1200 | 900 | 300 |
| Refrigerator | 10 years | 800 | 560 | 240 |
| Area rug | New | 200 | 0 | 200 |
| Cosmetics | 6 months | 200 | 180 | 20 |
| Kitchen dishes | 4 years | 250 | 200 | 50 |
| 30 cans food | New | 40 | 0 | 40 |
| Total | | $7790 | $3823 | $3967 |

NOTE: The above hypothetical losses show the effect of depreciation, which is based on age and condition of the property; the older the item, the greater is the amount of depreciation.

**Dwelling and Other Structures**   Covered losses to the dwelling and other structures are paid on the basis of replacement cost with no deduction for depreciation. Replacement cost insurance on the dwelling is one of the most valuable features in a homeowners policy. If the amount of insurance carried is equal to at least 80 percent of the replacement cost of the damaged building at the time of loss, full replacement cost is paid up to the limits of the policy with no deduction for depreciation. **Replacement cost** *is the amount necessary to repair or replace the dwelling with material of like kind and quality at current prices.* For example, assume that a home has a current replacement value of $250,000 and is insured for $200,000. If the home is damaged by a tornado, and repairs cost $50,000, the full $50,000 is paid with no

deduction for depreciation. If the home is totally destroyed, however, the maximum amount paid for the damage to the building is the face amount of the policy—in this case, $200,000.

A different set of rules applies if the amount of insurance carried is less than 80 percent of the replacement cost at the time of loss. Stated simply, if the insurance carried is less than 80 percent of the replacement cost, the insured receives the *larger* of the following two amounts:

(1) Actual cash value of that part of the building damaged

or

(2) $\dfrac{\text{Amount of insurance carried}}{80\% \times \text{Replacement cost}} \times \text{Loss}$

For example, assume that a dwelling has a replacement cost of $250,000, but is insured for only $150,000. The roof of the house is 10 years old and has a useful life of 20 years, so it is 50 percent depreciated. Assume that the roof is severely damaged by a tornado, and the replacement cost of a new roof is $20,000. Ignoring the deductible, the insured receives the larger of the following two amounts:

(1)  Actual cash value = $20,000 − $10,000

$$= \$10,000$$

(2)  $\dfrac{\$150,000}{80\% \times \$250,00} \times \$20,000 = \$15,000$

The insured receives $15,000 for the loss. The entire loss would have been paid if the insured had carried at least $200,000 of insurance.

With the exception of losses that are both less than 5 percent of the amount of insurance and less than $2500, the insured must actually repair or replace the property to receive full replacement cost. Otherwise, the loss is paid on the basis of actual cash value. However, the insured can submit a claim for the actual cash value and then collect an additional amount when the actual repair or replacement is completed, provided the additional claim is made within 180 days after the loss.

**Extended and Guaranteed Replacement Cost**   A home may be damaged beyond repair by a major catastrophe, such as a hurricane or tornado. Also, there may be a shortage of lumber and other building materials after a catastrophe occurs, which can substantially increase the cost of rebuilding. Insuring your home for only 80 percent of replacement cost will not provide complete protection. Some insurers make available an **extended replacement cost endorsement**, which pays up to an extra 20 percent or more above the policy limits, depending on the insurer. The insured agrees to insure the dwelling for full replacement cost and must also notify the insurer if alterations or remodeling increase the value of the dwelling.

A few insurers offer **guaranteed replacement cost** coverage. The insured agrees to insure the home to 100 percent of its estimated replacement cost rather than 80 percent. *If a total loss occurs, the insurer agrees to replace the home exactly as it was before the loss even if the replacement cost exceeds the*

*amount of insurance stated in the policy.* For example, if the home is insured for $400,000 and it costs $500,000 to restore the home to its previous condition, the insurer will pay $500,000. Because of underappraising the value of the home by some insurance agents, price gouging by some contractors because of a shortage of building materials, inflation, and fraud in some cases, guaranteed replacement cost policies are rapidly disappearing.

### Loss to a Pair or Set

In the event of **loss to a pair or set**, the insurer can elect either (1) to repair or replace any part so that the pair or set is restored to its value before the loss occurred, or (2) pay the difference in actual cash value of the property before and after the loss. For example, Kathy has three matching wall decorations hanging on a wall in her living room, and one is badly damaged in a fire. The insurer can elect either to repair or replace the damaged wall decoration so that the set is restored to its value before the loss, or pay the difference in actual cash value of the entire set before and after the loss.

### Appraisal Clause

*The* **appraisal clause** *is used when the insured and insurer agree that the loss is covered, but the amount of the loss is in dispute.* Either party can demand that the dispute be resolved by an appraisal. Each party selects a competent and impartial appraiser. The appraisers then select an umpire. If they cannot agree on an umpire after 15 days, a judge in a court of record will appoint one. If the appraisers fail to agree on the amount of the loss, only their differences are submitted to the umpire. An agreement in writing by any two of the three is then binding on both parties. Each party pays the fee of his or her appraiser, and the umpire's fee is shared equally by both parties.

### Other Insurance and Service Agreements

If other insurance covers a Section I loss, the insurer will pay only the proportion of the loss that its limit of liability bears to the total amount of insurance covering the loss. The pro rata liability clause was explained in Chapter 10.

The pro rata liability clause does not apply to articles of personal property that are separately described and specifically insured by other insurance. In such cases, as stated in Coverage C (Property Not Covered), personal property that is separately described and specifically insured is not covered by the homeowners policy.

Finally, many homeowners purchase home warranty contracts or appliance service agreements that guarantee the repair or replacement of defective parts if certain conditions are met. The homeowners policy is excess over any amount payable under a home warranty or service agreement.

### Suit Against the Insurer

No legal action can be brought against the insurer unless all policy provisions have been complied with, and legal action is started within two years after the loss occurs.

### Insurer's Option

After giving written notice to the insured, the insurer has the right to repair or replace any part of the damaged property with like property. For example, assume that a television set is stolen. By giving written notice, the insurer can replace the stolen TV with a similar item rather than paying cash. Insurers often can purchase televisions, stereos, and other types of property from wholesale distributors at a lower cost than the insured would pay in the retail market. By exercising the replacement option, an insurer can meet its contractual obligation for a covered loss, and its loss settlement costs can be reduced.

### Loss Payment

The insurer is required to make a loss payment directly to the named insured unless some other person is named in the policy or is legally entitled to receive the loss payment. In many homeowners contracts, a mortgagee (lender) is named in the policy, which allows the mortgagee to receive a loss payment to the extent of its insurable interest. A legal representative of the insured is also entitled to receive a loss payment. For example, if Angela dies before receiving payment for a covered loss, the loss payment is made to the executor of her estate.

### Abandonment of Property

The insurer is not obligated to accept any property abandoned by the insured after a loss occurs. The insurer has the option of paying for the damaged property in full and then taking the damaged property as salvage, or the insurer can elect to have the property repaired. However, the decision to exercise these options belongs to the insurer. For example, assume your personal property is insured for $50,000. A fire occurs, and the salvage value of the property after the loss is $10,000. The insurer can pay you $40,000, or it can take the damaged property and pay you $50,000. However, you cannot abandon the property to the insurer and demand payment of $50,000.

### Mortgage Clause

The **mortgage clause** is designed to protect the mortgagee's insurable interest. The mortgagee usually is a savings and loan institution, commercial bank, or other lending institution that makes a loan to the mortgagor (home buyer) so that the property can be purchased. The property serves as collateral for the mortgage loan. If the property is damaged or destroyed, the collateral securing the loan is impaired, and the loan might not be repaid.

The mortgagee's insurable interest in the property can be protected by the mortgage clause that is part of the homeowner policy. *Under this provision, if the mortgagee is named in the policy, the mortgagee is entitled to receive a loss payment from the insurer to the extent of its interest, regardless of any policy violation by the insured.* For example, if Troy intentionally sets fire to his house, the loss is not covered because the fire is intentional. However, the mortgagee's insurable interest in the property is still protected. The loss payment would be paid to the mortgagee to the extent of the mortgagee's interest. The mortgagee is also entitled to a 10-day cancellation notice if the insurer decides to cancel the coverage.

In exchange for the guarantee of payment, the mortgage clause imposes certain obligations on the mortgagee. They are as follows:

- To notify the insurer of any change in ownership, occupancy, or substantial change in risk of which the mortgagee is aware

- To pay any premium due if the insured neglects to pay the premium
- To provide a proof-of-loss statement if the insured fails to do so
- To give subrogation rights to the insurer in those cases where the insurer denies liability to the insured but must make a loss payment to the mortgagee

## Policy Period

The policy period begins and ends at 12:01 a.m. standard time on the dates specified in the policy period. Only losses that occur during the policy period are covered.

## Concealment or Fraud

The policy states that no insured is covered if any insured intentionally conceals or misrepresents any material fact, engages in fraudulent conduct, or makes false statements relating to the insurance. The provision applies both before and after a loss.

# SECTION I AND II CONDITIONS

The homeowners policy contains several common conditions that apply to both Sections I and II.[8] They are summarized as follows:

- *Liberalization Clause.* If the insurer broadens the coverage it offers without charging a higher premium within 60 days before inception of the policy or during the policy period, the broadened coverage applies immediately to the present policy. However, the liberalization clause does not apply to changes that are implemented with a general program revision that includes both a broadening and restriction of coverage.
- *Waiver or Change of Policy Provisions.* A waiver or change in any policy provision must be approved in writing by the insurer to be valid.
- *Cancellation.* The insured can cancel at any time by returning the policy or by notifying the insurer in writing when the cancellation is to become effective.

  The insurer can cancel under the following conditions:

1. The premium is not paid. The insured must be given at least 10 days' written notice of cancellation.

2. A new policy can be canceled for any reason if it has been in force for less than 60 days and is not a renewal policy. The insured must be given at least 10 days' notice of cancellation.

3. If the policy has been in force for 60 or more days or is a renewal policy, the insurer can cancel if there is a material misrepresentation of fact that would have caused the insurer not to issue the policy, or if the risk has increased substantially after the policy was issued. The insured must be given at least 30 days' notice of cancellation.

4. If the policy is written for a period longer than one year, it can be canceled for any reason on the anniversary date by giving the insured at least 30 days' notice of cancellation.

   State law may specify the conditions under which insurers can cancel or non-renew a policy. Whenever there is a conflict between state law and any policy provision, state law has priority over the policy provision. This is handled by an amendatory endorsement to the policy that makes the policy conform to state law.

- *Nonrenewal of the Policy.* The insurer has the right not to renew the policy when it expires. The insured must be given at least 30 days' notice before the expiration date if the policy is not renewed.
- *Assignment of the Policy.* The homeowners policy cannot be assigned to another party without the insurer's written consent. Thus, if Paul sells his home to Susan, he cannot validly assign his homeowners policy to Susan unless the insurer agrees to the assignment. As a practical matter, the new owner usually buys his or her own policy. The homeowners policy is a personal contract between the insured and insurer. The assignment provision allows the insurer to select its own insureds and provides some protection against moral hazard and adverse selection. However, after a loss occurs, the loss payment can be freely assigned to another party without the insurer's consent. The party who receives the payment does not become a new insured, and the risk to the insurer is not increased.
- *Subrogation.* A general principle is that an insured cannot unilaterally waive the insurer's right of subrogation against a third party who caused the loss without jeopardizing coverage under the policy. However, the homeowners

policy contains an important exception to this general principle. The subrogation clause allows the insured to waive in writing, before a loss occurs, all rights of recovery against any person. For example, assume that Jerome lives in one unit of a duplex and rents out the other unit. The lease may state that Jerome as landlord waives his right of recovery against the tenant if the tenant should negligently cause a loss (such as a fire). The waiver would protect the tenant against a subrogation recovery by Jerome's insurer if the tenant should cause a loss. To be effective, however, the waiver must be in writing before a loss occurs.

If the right of recovery is not waived, the insurer may require the insured to assign all rights of recovery against a third party to the extent of the loss payment. This provision allows the insurer to exercise its subrogation rights against a negligent third party who caused the loss.

- *Death of Named Insured or Spouse.* If the named insured or resident spouse dies, coverage is extended to the legal representative of the deceased but only with respect to the premises and property of the deceased. Coverage also continues for resident relatives who are insured under the policy at the time of the named insured or spouse's death.

## CASE APPLICATION

Jack and Jane are married and own a home insured for $150,000 under an unendorsed HO-3 policy. The replacement cost of the home is $250,000. Personal property is insured for $75,000. Jane has jewelry valued at $10,000. Jack has a coin collection valued at $15,000 and a motorboat valued at $20,000.

a. Assume you are a financial planner who is asked to evaluate the couple's HO-3 policy. Based on the above facts, do you believe that their present coverages are adequate? If not, make several recommendations for improving the coverage.

b. A fire damaged one bedroom of the home. The actual cash value of the loss is $10,000. The cost of repairs is $16,000. How much will the insurer pay for the loss?

c. A burglar broke into the home and stole a new television, jewelry, and several paintings. The

actual cash value of the stolen property is $4000. The cost of replacing the property is $9000. In addition, the coin collection was taken. Indicate the extent, if any, to which an unendorsed HO-3 policy will cover these losses.

d. Assume that Jack and Jane have a disagreement with their insurer concerning the value of the above losses. How would the dispute be resolved under their HO-3 policy?

e. Assume that Jane operates an accounting business from her home. Her home business office contains a computer used solely for business, office furniture, file cabinets, and other business personal property. Explain whether her HO-3 policy would cover business personal property used in a home business.

## SUMMARY

- The homeowners policy can be used to cover the dwelling, other structures, personal property, additional living expenses, personal liability claims, and medical payments to others.

- Section I provides coverage on the dwelling, other structures, personal property, loss-of-use benefits, and additional coverages. Section II provides personal liability insurance to the insured and also covers the medical

expenses of others who may be injured while on the insured premises or by some act of the insured or by an animal owned by the insured.

- The HO-2 policy (broad form) covers the dwelling, other structures, and personal property against loss on a named-perils basis.

- The HO-3 policy (special form) covers the dwelling and other structures against direct physical loss to the described property. All losses to the dwelling and other structures are covered except those losses specifically excluded. Personal property is covered on a named-perils basis.

■ The HO-4 policy (contents broad form) is designed for renters. HO-4 covers the personal property of tenants on a named-perils basis and also provides personal liability insurance.

■ The HO-5 policy (comprehensive form) insures the dwelling, other structures, and personal property against direct physical loss to property. All direct physical losses are covered except those losses specifically excluded.

■ The HO-6 policy (unit-owners form) is designed for residential condominium unit owners. HO-6 covers the personal property of the insured on a named-perils basis. There is also a minimum of $5000 of insurance on the condominium unit that covers certain property, such as alterations, fixtures, and improvements.

■ The HO-8 policy (modified coverage form) is designed for some older homes. Losses to the dwelling and other structures are paid on the basis of repair cost, which is the amount required to repair or replace the property using common construction materials and methods. Losses are not paid based on replacement cost.

■ The conditions section imposes certain duties on the insured after a loss to covered property occurs. The insured must give immediate notice of the loss; the property must be protected from further damage; the insured must prepare an inventory of the damaged personal property and may be required to show the damaged property to the insurer as often as is reasonably required; and proof of loss must be filed within 60 days after the insurer's request.

■ The replacement cost provision is one of the most valuable features of the homeowners policy. Losses to the dwelling and other structures are paid on the basis of replacement cost if the insured carries insurance at least equal to 80 percent of the replacement cost at the time of loss. Losses to personal property are paid on the basis of actual cash value. However, an endorsement can be added to cover personal property on a replacement cost basis.

■ A deductible applies to most Section I losses. A straight deductible is common; a percentage of value deductible may also be used.

■ The mortgage clause provides protection to the mortgagee. The mortgagee (e.g., a bank) is entitled to receive a loss payment from the insurer regardless of any policy violation by the insured.

## KEY CONCEPTS AND TERMS

Additional living expense (435)
Appraisal clause (445)
Extended replacement cost endorsement (445)
Fair rental value (435)
Guaranteed replacement cost (445)
Homeowners 2 (broad form) (427)
Homeowners 3 (special form) (428)
Homeowners 4 (contents broad form) (428)
Homeowners 5 (comprehensive form) (428)
Homeowners 6 (unit-owners form) (428)
Homeowners 8 (modified coverage form) (428)
Loss to a pair or set (445)
Mortgage clause (446)
Proximate cause (438)
Replacement cost (444)
Schedule (433)

## REVIEW QUESTIONS

1. Identify the basic types of homeowners policies that are used today.

2. Identify the persons who are insured under a homeowners policy.

3. The Section I property coverages provide different types of coverages to an insured. For each of the following coverages, briefly describe the type of coverage provided, and give an example of a loss that would be covered.
   a. Coverage A—Dwelling
   b. Coverage B—Other Structures
   c. Coverage C—Personal Property
   d. Coverage D—Loss of Use
   e. Additional Coverages

4. a. Briefly describe the special limits of liability that apply to certain types of personal property.
   b. Why are these special limits used?

5. a. Coverage A and Coverage B under a Homeowners 3 policy insure the dwelling and other structures against "direct physical loss." Explain the meaning of this phrase.
   b. Coverage C under a Homeowners 3 policy covers personal property on a named-perils basis. List the various perils that are covered.

6. List the major exclusions that are found in Section I of the Homeowners 3 policy.

7. Briefly describe the duties imposed on the insured under a homeowners policy after a property loss occurs.

8. The Section I Conditions section of the Homeowners 3 policy deals with the payment of losses to an insured.

a. How is the amount paid for a covered loss to personal property determined?

b. How is the amount paid for a covered loss to the dwelling and other structures determined?

9. a. Describe the extended replacement cost endorsement that can be added to a Homeowners 3 policy.

b. What is a guaranteed replacement cost policy?

10. A home buyer may obtain a mortgage loan to purchase a house. Explain briefly how the mortgage clause protects the insurable interest of the lending institution (mortgagee).

## APPLICATION QUESTIONS

1. Heather owns a home with a replacement cost of $400,000 that is insured under a Homeowners 3 policy for $280,000. The roof was badly damaged in a severe windstorm, and it will cost $20,000 to repair the roof. The actual cash value of the loss is $10,000. Ignoring any deductible, how much will Heather collect from the insurer?

2. Michelle purchased a Homeowners 3 policy with no special endorsements to cover her home and personal property. A fire occurred and destroyed a big screen television. Michelle paid $4000 for the TV new, and it was 25 percent depreciated when the fire occurred. The replacement cost of a similar television is $3800. Ignoring any deductible, how much will Michelle collect for the loss?

3. Tom and Cindy Jones insured their home and personal property under an unendorsed Homeowners 3 policy. The home has a current replacement cost of $300,000. The policy contains the following limits:

| | |
|---|---|
| Coverage A | $240,000 |
| Coverage B | 24,000 |
| Coverage C | 120,000 |
| Coverage D | 72,000 |

The home was badly damaged in a fire, and the family was forced to live in a motel for 60 days while their home was being rebuilt. Undamaged personal property was stored in a rental unit during the period of reconstruction. What dollar amount, if any, is payable under their Homeowners 3 policy for the following (ignore any deductible)?

a. Three bedrooms were totally destroyed in the fire. The replacement cost of restoring the bedrooms is $80,000. The actual cash value of the loss is $50,000.

b. Monthly mortgage payment of $1500 on their home

c. Rental of motel room at $100 daily for 60 days

d. Meals eaten in the motel restaurant for 60 days at an average cost of $60 daily (food costs at home average $20 daily)

e. Rent for storing undamaged furniture in a rental unit while the home is being rebuilt, $200 monthly

4. Megan has her home and personal property insured under an unendorsed Homeowners 3 (special form) policy. Indicate whether each of the following losses is covered. If the loss is not covered, explain why it is not covered.

a. Megan carelessly spills a can of paint while painting a bedroom. A wall-to-wall carpet that is part of the bedroom is badly damaged and must be replaced.

b. Water backs up from a clogged drainpipe, floods the basement, and damages some books stored in a box.

c. Megan's house is totally destroyed by a tornado. Her valuable doberman pinscher dog is killed by the tornado.

d. During a frost warning, smudge pots from a nearby orange grove emit dense smoke that settles on Megan's freshly painted house.

e. Megan is on vacation, and a thief breaks into her hotel room and steals a suitcase containing jewelry, money, clothes, and an airline ticket.

f. Megan's son is playing baseball in the yard. A line drive shatters the living room window.

g. A garbage truck accidentally backs into the garage door and damages it.

h. Defective wiring causes a fire in the attic. Damage to the house is extensive. Megan is forced to move into a furnished apartment for three months while the house is being rebuilt.

i. Megan's son, age 20, is attending college but is home for Christmas. A stereo set is stolen from his dormitory room during his absence.

j. During the winter, heavy snow damages part of the front lawn, and the sod must be replaced.

k. During a windstorm, an elm tree in Megan's yard is blown over.

l. The home is badly damaged in a severe earthquake. As a result of the earthquake, the front lawn has a 3-foot crack and is now uneven.

m. An icemaker in the refrigerator breaks and water seeps into the flooring and carpets, causing considerable damage to the dwelling.

5. James has his home and personal property insured under a Homeowners 3 (special form) policy. The dwelling is insured for $120,000. The replacement cost of the home is $200,000. Indicate the extent to which each of the following losses would be covered under James's Homeowners 3 policy. (Ignore the deductible.)

   a. Lightning strikes the roof of the house and severely damages it. The actual cash value of the damaged roof is $10,000, and it will cost $16,000 to replace the damaged portion.

   b. A living room window is broken in a hailstorm. The drapes are water stained and must be replaced. The actual cash value of the damaged drapes is $400. Replacement cost is $600.

   c. The water heater explodes and damages some household contents. The actual cash value of the damaged property is $2000, and the cost of replacing the property is $3200.

6. Sarah owns a valuable diamond ring that has been in her family for generations. She is told by an appraiser that the ring has a current market value of $50,000. She feels that the ring is adequately insured because she purchased a Homeowners 3 (special form) policy. Is Sarah correct in her thinking? If not, what would you advise her concerning proper protection of the ring?

7. Paul has his home and its contents insured under a Homeowners 3 (special form) policy. He carries $160,000 of insurance on the home, which has a replacement cost of $200,000. Explain the extent to which each of the following losses is covered. (Ignore the deductible.) If Paul's policy does not cover the loss or inadequately covers any of these losses, show how full coverage can be obtained.

   a. Paul's stamp collection, which is valued at $5000, is stolen from his home.

   b. Teenage vandals break into Paul's home and destroy a painting that has a market value of $1000.

   c. A motorboat stored in the driveway of Paul's home is badly damaged during a hailstorm. The actual cash value of the damaged portion is $8000, and its replacement cost is $20,000.

8. Craig owns a home with a replacement cost of $200,000 that is subject to a $100,000 mortgage held by First Federal as the mortgagee. Craig has the home insured for $160,000 under the HO-3 policy, and First Federal is named as mortgagee under the Mortgage Clause. Assume there is a covered fire loss to the dwelling in the amount of $50,000. To whom would the loss be paid? Explain your answer.

## INTERNET RESOURCES

- The **Insurance Information Institute** provides timely information on homeowners insurance and other personal property insurance coverages. Articles on homeowners insurance and other property and liability coverages can be accessed directly online. Visit the site at

  iii.org

- **Insure.com** provides up-to-date information, premium quotes, and other consumer information on homeowners insurance. Visit the site at

  insure.com

- **Insurance.com** provides premium quotes on a variety of insurance products, including homeowners and renters insurance, auto insurance, life insurance, and health insurance. Visit the site at

  insurance.com

- **InsWeb** provides premium quotes on homeowners, auto, and other insurance products. You can comparison shop from your computer. The site also has a learning center that provides consumer information on the different types of insurance. Visit the site at

  insweb.com

- The **International Risk Management Institute (IRMI)** is an online source that provides valuable information about personal lines and commercial lines. The site provides timely articles on a wide range of risk management and insurance topics and offers a number of free e-mail newsletters. Visit the site at

  irmi.com

- The **National Association of Insurance Commissioners (NAIC)** has a link to all state insurance departments, which provide a considerable amount of consumer information on homeowners insurance. Click on the "States & Jurisdictions Map" link. Then you can click on specific states. For starters, check out New York, Wisconsin, California, and Texas. Visit the site at

  naic.org

## SELECTED REFERENCES

"Catastrophes: Insurance Issues," Issues Updates, Insurance Information Institutes, July 2012. This source is periodically updated.

*Fire, Casualty & Surety Bulletins,* Personal Lines volume, Dwelling section. Erlanger, KY: National Underwriter Company. The bulletins are updated monthly.

International Risk Management Institute (IRMI). *Personal Lines Pilot,* various issues.

"ISO Announced the Filing of its New 2011 Countrywide Homeowners Program,"Alliance Insurance Agents of Texas, May 12, 2010.

Nyce, Charles, *Personal Insurance*, 2nd ed. Malvern, PA: American Institute for Charted Property and Casualty Underwriters/Insurance Institute of America, 2008.

Richardson, Diane W. *Homeowners Coverage Guide,* 4th ed. Cincinnati, OH: The National Underwriter Company, 2011.

## NOTES

1. The discussion of homeowners insurance in this chapter is based on the *Fire, Casualty & Surety Bulletins,* Personal Lines volume, Dwelling section (Erlanger, KY: National Underwriter Company); Personal Lines Pilot, International Risk Management Institute (IRMI); *Homeowners Coverage Guide*, 4th Edition, by Diane Richardson; and the copyrighted homeowners forms drafted by the Insurance Services Office (ISO).

2. The revised HO-3 explicitly states that "direct physical damage" must occur from an abrupt collapse for there to be coverage. Wording in the previous form created ambiguity over whether a building that was damaged but had not collapsed or that collapsed over time was covered. This form makes it clear that damage must occur and that the collapse must be "abrupt."

3. "Vermin" was listed previously in this exclusion, but that term was eliminated in the revised form. The following exclusion (nesting / infestation / release of waste) is new to this form.

4. International Risk Management Institute, *Personal Lines Pilot #53*, December 14, 2007.

5. In the previous form, it was 60 days. The "new" form increases the time to 90 days.

6. In the previous version of the ISO HO-3 policy, the Deductible section followed the definitions and preceded the Section I coverage discussion. In the revised policy, the Deductible section was moved to Section I conditions, clarifying that the deductible applies to the property coverage, not to Section II claims.

7. See "The 2012 Hurricane Season has Begun: Do You Understand Your Hurricane Deductible?" Insurance Information Institute, June 7, 2012.

8. There are three sets of conditions for the two sections. One set of conditions applies to Section I and II. The second set applies to Section I only. These two sets are discussed in this chapter. The third set, which applies to Section II only, is discussed in the following chapter.

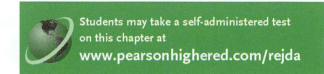

Students may take a self-administered test on this chapter at
www.pearsonhighered.com/rejda

# CHAPTER 21

# HOMEOWNERS INSURANCE, SECTION II

*"How to win in court: If the law is on your side, pound on the law; if the facts are on your side, pound on the facts; if neither is on your side, pound on the table."*

Unknown

## LEARNING OBJECTIVES

**After studying this chapter, you should be able to**

◆ Explain the personal liability coverage found in Section II of the homeowners policy.

◆ Explain the medical payments to others coverage found in Section II of the homeowners policy.

◆ Identify the major exclusions that apply to the Section II coverages in the homeowners policy.

◆ Discuss important conditions that apply to the Section II coverages in the homeowners policy.

◆ Explain the following endorsements that can be added to a homeowners policy:
   Inflation guard endorsement
   Personal property replacement cost endorsement

◆ Explain the suggestions that consumers should follow when shopping for a homeowners policy.

*Tom and Stacy Green invited their neighbors over for a cookout. Tom used an old grill with charcoal briquettes to prepare some hamburgers on the wooden deck of the home. After dinner, Tom and Stacy did not think about checking the grill before they went to bed. During the night, a strong wind knocked over the grill. Some of the charcoal was still hot, and it set the deck on fire. Given dry conditions in the area, the fire also spread to the home next door to the Greens. The fire department was called, and they were able to extinguish the fire. The Greens suffered minor damage to their home. The neighbor's home, however, sustained $50,000 in damage. The neighbors are upset with the Greens and have threatened to sue them for the damage to their property and for their living expenses while their home is being repaired.*

*Fortunately, the Greens are protected by an ISO Homeowners 3 policy. In the previous chapter, we learned how Section I of the policy protects against property losses—losses to the dwelling, other structures, personal property, and loss of use. In this chapter, we will examine Section II of the policy. This part of the policy provides personal liability insurance and coverage for medical payments to others. We will also discuss some important endorsements that can be added to the homeowners policy to broaden the coverage and some tips that you should follow when shopping for a homeowners policy.*

## PERSONAL LIABILITY INSURANCE

Personal liability insurance protects the named insured and family members against legal liability arising out of their personal acts. The insurer will provide a legal defense and pay those sums that an insured is legally obligated to pay up to the policy limit.[1] With the major exceptions of legal liability arising out of the negligent operation of an automobile, and business and professional liability, most personal acts are covered.

The Section II coverages in the various homeowner forms designed by the Insurance Services Office (ISO) are identical. The ISO Homeowners 3 policy is provided in Appendix A at the end of the text. The following section discusses the major provisions in Section II.

### Insuring Agreements

The Section II liability coverages in the homeowners policy provide the following two coverages:

- Coverage E: Personal liability, $100,000 per occurrence

- Coverage F: Medical payments to others, $1000 per person

Higher limits are available for a small additional premium.

**Coverage E: Personal Liability** *Personal liability insurance protects an insured when a claim or suit for damages is brought because of bodily injury or property damage allegedly caused by an insured's negligence.* If you are liable for damages, the insurer will pay up to the policy limits those sums that you are legally obligated to pay. Damages also include any prejudgment interest awarded against you.

The minimum amount of liability insurance is $100,000 for each occurrence. The insurance amount is a single limit that applies to both bodily injury and property damage liability on a per-occurrence basis. **Occurrence** *is defined as an accident, including continuous or repeated exposure to substantially the same general harmful conditions, which results in bodily injury or property damage during the policy period.* An occurrence can be a sudden accident, or it can be a gradual series of incidents that occur over time.

The insurer also agrees to provide a legal defense even if the suit is groundless, false, or fraudulent. The insurer has the right to investigate and settle the claim or suit either by defending you in a court of law or by settling out of court. As a practical matter, most personal liability suits are settled out of court. The insurer must defend you and cannot offer or tender its policy limits to be relieved of its duty to defend. Unless the claim is settled for a lesser amount, defense coverage continues until the policy limits are exhausted by payment of a judgment or settlement.

Personal liability coverage is broad. The following examples illustrate the types of losses covered:

- Your dog bites a small child; dog bites account for a large percentage of all homeowners liability claims.[2] (see Insight 21.1)

- While burning leaves in the yard, you accidentally set fire to your neighbor's house.
- A guest in your home trips on a torn carpet and sues you for bodily injury.
- You are shopping and carelessly break an expensive vase.

Personal liability insurance is based on legal liability. Before the insurer will pay any sums for damages, you must be legally liable. In contrast, medical payments to others, discussed next, is not based on negligence or legal liability.

**Coverage F: Medical Payments to Others**  This coverage is a mini-accident policy that is part of a homeowners policy. *Medical payments to others is not based on legal liability. The insured is not*

---

## INSIGHT 21.1

### Dog Bites Hurt, So Do Lawsuits

Sixty-two percent of U.S. households, or 72.9 million homes, own a pet, according to a 2011 survey from by the American Pet Products Association.

Over the years, many states have passed laws with stiff penalties for owners of dogs that cause serious injuries or deaths. In about one-third of states, owners are "strictly liable" for their dogs' behavior, while in the rest of the country they are liable only if they knew or should have known their dogs had a propensity to bite (known as the "one free bite" principle).

- *Claims:* Dog bites accounted for more than one-third of all homeowners insurance liability claims paid out in 2011, costing nearly $479 million, according to the Insurance Information Institute (I.I.I.). State Farm Mutual Automobile Insurance Company, the largest writer of homeowners insurance in the U.S., paid out more than $109 million as a result of its nearly 3,800 dog bite claims in 2011. An analysis of homeowners insurance data by the I.I.I. found that the average cost paid out for dog bite claims was $29,396 in 2011, up 12.3 percent from $26,166 in 2010. From 2003 to 2011 the cost of the average dog bite claim increased by 53.4 percent. The number of claims rose 3.3 percent from 15,770 in 2010 to 16,292 in 2011.
- *Insurers are Limiting their Exposure:* Homeowners and renters insurance policies typically cover dog bite liability. Most policies provide $100,000 to $300,000 in

liability coverage. If the claim exceeds the limit, the dog owner is responsible for all damages above that amount, including legal expenses. Most insurance companies insure homeowners with dogs. However, once a dog has bitten someone, it poses an increased risk. In that instance, the insurance company may suggest that the homeowner find the dog a new home, or it may charge a higher premium, nonrenew the homeowner's insurance policy, or exclude the dog from coverage.

Many insurers are taking steps to limit their exposure to such losses. Some companies require dog owners to sign liability waivers for dog bites, while others charge more for owners of biting breeds such as pit bulls and Rottweilers and others are not offering insurance to dog owners at all. Some will cover a pet if the owner takes the dog to classes aimed at modifying its behavior or if the dog is restrained with a muzzle, chain, or cage. It is unlikely that insurers will begin offering specialty insurance policies just for dog bites since the cost of such policies would be prohibitive.

- *Dog Owners' Liability:* Dog owners are liable for injuries their pets cause if the owner knew the dog had a tendency to cause that kind of injury; if a state statute makes the owner liable, whether or not the owner knew the dog had a tendency to cause that kind of injury; or if the injury was caused by unreasonable carelessness on the part of the owner.

*(Continued)*

**INSIGHT 21.1** (Continued)

There are three kinds of law that impose liability on owners:

1. *A dog-bite statute:* where the dog owner is automatically liable for any injury or property damage the dog causes without provocation.
2. *The one-bite rule:* where the dog owner is responsible for an injury caused by a dog if the owner knew the dog was likely to cause that type of injury—in this case, the victim must prove the owner knew the dog was dangerous.
3. *Negligence laws:* where the dog owner is liable if the injury occurred because the dog owner was unreasonably careless (negligent) in controlling the dog.

In most states, dog owners aren't liable to trespassers who are injured by a dog. A dog owner who is legally responsible for an injury to a person or property may be responsible for reimbursing the injured person for medical bills, time off work, pain and suffering, and property damage.

*Source:* Adapted from "Dog Bite Liability," Insurance Information Institute, *Issues Updates,* June 2012, October 2009, Reprinted by permission from the Insurance Information Institute.

---

*required to be legally liable for coverage to apply.* In contrast, personal liability coverage, discussed earlier, requires the insured to be legally liable for the coverage to apply.

**Medical payments to others** *pays the reasonable medical expenses of another person who is accidentally injured while on an insured location, or by the activities of an insured, resident employee, or animal owned by or in the care of an insured.* This coverage can be illustrated by the following examples:

- A guest slips in your home and breaks an arm. Reasonable medical expenses are paid up to the policy limit.
- A neighbor's child falls off a swing in your backyard and is injured. The child's medical expenses are covered up to the policy limit.
- You are playing golf and accidentally injure another golfer.
- Your dog bites a neighbor. The neighbor's medical expenses are paid up to the policy limit.

The insurer will pay for necessary medical expenses incurred or medically ascertained within three years from the date of the accident. The medical expenses covered are the reasonable charges for medical and surgical procedures, X-rays, dental care, ambulances, hospital stays, professional nursing, prosthetic devices, and funeral services.

*Medical payments coverage does not apply to you or to regular residents of your household, other than a residence employee.* For example, if a swing set in your backyard collapses, and your daughter and a neighbor's child are injured, only the medical expenses of the neighbor's child are covered.

An exception is a residence employee who is injured on the premises. For example, if a babysitter burns her hand while cooking lunch for your children, her medical expenses are covered under the policy, unless a state's workers compensation law applies to the loss.

*With respect to the medical expenses of others, the policy states the situations under which coverage applies.* Medical payments to others applies only to the following persons and situations:

- A person on the insured location (discussed later) with the permission of an insured
- A person off the insured location, if the bodily injury

  - Arises out of a condition on the insured location or the ways immediately adjoining
  - Is caused by activities of an insured
  - Is caused by a residence employee in the course of employment by an insured
  - Is caused by an animal owned by or in the care of an insured

Medical payments to others cover the medical expenses of a person who is accidentally injured while on an insured location with the permission of an insured. *Insured locations* include the following:

- Residence premises shown in the declarations
- Any other residence acquired during the policy period, such as a summer home
- Rented garage or storage unit
- Nonowned premises where an insured is temporarily residing, such as a motel room
- Vacant land other than farmland

- Land owned or rented to an insured on which a residence is being built for an insured
- Cemetery plots or burial plots
- Part of a premises occasionally rented to an insured for nonbusiness purposes, such as a hall rented for a wedding reception

Medical payments to others also covers injuries away from an insured location if the injury arises out of a condition on the insured location or ways immediately adjoining, or is caused by activities of an insured, by a resident employee in the course of employment by an insured, or by an animal owned or in the care of an insured. For example, coverage applies to a pedestrian who trips or falls on an icy sidewalk or street adjacent to the premises. Coverage also applies if an insured accidentally injures another player while playing basketball. Likewise, if a baby-sitter takes your children to a public park and accidentally injures another child, coverage applies.

# SECTION II EXCLUSIONS

The Section II coverages contain numerous exclusions. Some exclusions apply to both personal liability (Coverage E) and medical payments to others (Coverage F). Other exclusions apply separately to Coverage E and to Coverage F.

### Exclusions That Apply to Both Coverage E and Coverage F

The following section discusses several exclusions that apply to both Coverage E and Coverage F.

**Motor Vehicle Liability**   Legal liability arising out of motor vehicles is not covered if the involved vehicle is:

- Registered for use on public roads or property
- Not registered for use on public roads or property but such registration is required by law or government regulation
- Used in an organized race or speed contest
- Rented to others
- Used to carry persons or cargo for a charge
- Used for any business purpose, except for a motorized golf cart while on a golfing facility

*Thus, liability arising out of cars, trucks, motorcycles, mopeds, and motorbikes is not covered.*

In addition, if you are towing a boat trailer, horse trailer, or rental trailer, coverage does not apply. Coverage can be obtained by purchasing an auto insurance policy.

Certain vehicles, however, are exceptions to the preceding exclusion, and therefore, coverage applies. The preceding exclusion of motor vehicles does not apply to the following:

- *The vehicle is in dead storage on an insured location.* For example, an unlicensed car may be on blocks in the insured's garage. A liability claim arising out of dead storage of the car is covered if the car is not subject to motor vehicle registration.
- *The vehicle is used solely to service a residence.*[3] For example, if a riding lawn mower is used solely to mow the insured's lawn at the residence, coverage applies if an insured injures someone while using the mower.
- *The vehicle is designed to assist the handicapped.* For example, if a handicapped person injures someone while operating a motorized wheelchair, coverage applies.
- *The vehicle is designed for recreational use off public roads and is not owned by the insured; or it is owned by the insured and the occurrence takes place on an insured location; or the vehicle is owned by the insured and the occurrence takes place off an insured location; or the vehicle is designed for use as a toy by children under seven years of age, is battery-powered, or is not built to travel at a speed exceeding five miles per hour on level ground.* For example, property damage caused by the insured while operating a rented all-terrain vehicle (ATV) would be covered, as would an owned ATV used on an insured location. Liability arising from a toy car owned by the insured used at a park would also be covered.[4]
- *Liability arising out of the use of a motorized golf cart owned by an insured is also covered.* The golf cart must be designed to carry no more than four people and must have a maximum speed of no more than 25 miles per hour. Coverage applies if the cart is on a golfing facility and is used to play golf or some other recreational activity allowed by the facility. Coverage also applies if the cart is used to travel to and from an area where motor vehicles or golf carts are parked or stored, or is

used to cross public roads at designated points to access the facility. Finally, coverage applies at a private residential community, including its roads upon which a motorized golf cart can legally travel, which is subject to the authority of property owner's association and contains the insured's residence. Thus, if an insured has a home in a private residential community that has a golf course and the insured injures someone while driving the golf cart to the facility, coverage would apply.

**Watercraft Liability**  The Section II coverages exclude watercraft liability if the boat is used in an organized race or speed contest (except sailboats or a predicted log cruise), rented to others, used to carry people or cargo for a fee, or used for any business purpose.

Certain watercraft are exceptions to the preceding exclusion, and therefore coverage applies.

**Aircraft Liability**  The Section II coverages exclude aircraft liability. An aircraft is any device used or designed to carry people or cargo in flight, such as an airplane, helicopter, glider, or hot air balloon. However, the exclusion does not apply to model or hobby aircraft not used or designed to carry people or cargo.

**Hovercraft Liability**  The homeowners policy excludes coverage for hovercraft liability. A hovercraft is defined as a self-propelled motorized ground effect vehicle and includes flarecraft and air cushion vehicles.

**Expected or Intentional Injury**  The Section II coverages do not apply to bodily injury or property damage that is expected or intended by an insured. For example, suppose a softball player intentionally hits the umpire with a bat, and it is clear that the player intended to injure the umpire. Any claim or suit for damages would not be covered.

The exclusion does not apply to bodily injury or property damage that results from the use of reasonable force by an insured to protect persons or property. Thus, if Mark injures a mugger who is trying to rob him, any resulting suit for damages would be covered.

**Business Activities**  Liability arising out of a business activity is excluded. A business is defined as a trade, profession, or occupation that the insured engages in on a full-time, part-time, or occasional basis. It also includes any other activity engaged in for money or other compensation. For example, if you operate a beauty shop in your home and carelessly burn a customer with a hair dryer, a lawsuit by the customer is not covered.

Certain activities, however, are not subject to the business exclusion:[5]

- Activities for which no insured received more than $2000 in total compensation for the 12 months prior to the policy period
- Volunteer activities for which no money is received except for expenses
- Providing home care services without compensation, other than the mutual exchange of such services
- Providing home day care services to a relative

For example, a garage sale not conducted as a regular business, volunteer work for a local church, and babysitting by a grandmother for her grandchildren would be covered.

In addition, legal liability arising out of the rental of any part of the premises is excluded. There are several exceptions to the rental exclusion. First, if a house is occasionally rented and used only as a residence, coverage applies. For example, if a professor rents out his or her home over homecoming or graduation weekend, coverage will still apply.

Coverage also applies if part of the residence is rented to others. For example, assume that you live in a duplex and rent the other unit to a single family. Liability coverage still applies if the renting family does not take in more than two roomers or boarders.

Coverage also applies if part of the insured residence is rented and used as an office, school, studio, or private garage. For example, if a room above a garage is rented to an artist who uses the room as a studio, an insured still has coverage for claims arising out of the rental.

Finally, coverage also applies to an insured under age 21 who is involved in a part-time or occasional self-employed business with no employees. For example, teenagers are covered while delivering newspapers on a bicycle, washing cars, or babysitting.

**Professional Services**   Legal liability arising out of professional services is excluded. Physicians and dentists are not covered for malpractice claims under the homeowners policy. Also, attorneys, accountants, nurses, architects, engineers, and other professionals are not covered for legal liability for rendering or failing to render professional services. The loss exposures involving professional activities are substantially different from those faced by the typical homeowner. For this reason, a professional liability policy is necessary to cover professional activities. Professional liability insurance is examined in greater detail in Chapter 26.

**Uninsured Locations**   Liability arising out of the ownership or rental of a premises that is not an "insured location" is also excluded. The meaning of "insured location" has already been explained. Examples of uninsured locations would be farmland owned or rented by an insured, a principal or secondary residence owned by an insured other than the named insured or spouse, and land owned by an insured on which a 12-unit apartment is being built.

**War**   Section II coverages exclude war, undeclared war, civil war, insurrection, rebellion, and other hostile military acts. The homeowners contracts also exclude liability arising out of the discharge of a nuclear weapon even if accidental.

**Communicable Disease Exclusion**   Liability arising out of the transmission of a communicable disease by an insured is excluded under both personal liability insurance and medical payments to others. The exclusion applies to all communicable diseases and is not limited to sexually transmitted diseases.

**Sexual Molestation, Corporal Punishment, or Physical or Mental Abuse**   The homeowners policy excludes bodily injury or property damage liability arising out of sexual molestation, corporal punishment, or physical or mental abuse.

**Controlled Substance Exclusion**   Liability arising out of the use, sale, manufacture, delivery, transfer, or possession of a controlled substance is specifically excluded. Controlled substances include methamphetamine, cocaine, LSD, marijuana, and all narcotic drugs. The exclusion does not apply to the legitimate use of prescription drugs by a person who is following the orders of a licensed health-care professional.[6]

### Exclusions That Apply Only to Coverage E

Several exclusions apply only to Coverage E (personal liability).

**Contractual Liability**   Contractual liability *means that an insured agrees to assume the legal liability of another party by a written or oral contract.* The policy excludes the following contractual liability exposures:

- *Liability for any loss assessment* charged against the named insured as a member of any association, corporation, or community of property owners. However, an additional coverage (discussed later) provides $1000 of coverage for a loss assessment if certain conditions are met.
- *Liability under any contract or agreement is excluded.* However, the exclusion does not apply to written contracts that (1) directly relate to the ownership, maintenance, or use of an insured location, or (2) where the liability of others is assumed by the named insured prior to an occurrence. Thus, there would be coverage for liability assumed under a written lease, an equipment rental agreement if the equipment is used to maintain the residence premises, or other written contracts where legal liability of a nonbusiness nature is assumed by an insured prior to an occurrence.

**Property Owned by an Insured**   *Property damage to property owned by an insured is also excluded.* Thus, if a teenage son accidentally breaks some furniture, the parents' claim for damages against their son would not be covered.

**Property in the Care of an Insured**   *Damage to property rented to, occupied or used by, or in the care of an insured is not covered.* For example, if you damage an apartment that you are renting, a lawsuit by the landlord seeking reimbursement for the damage would not be covered.

The exclusion does not apply to property damage caused by fire, smoke, or explosion. For example, if you rent an apartment and carelessly start a fire, you can be held liable for the damage. In such a case, the homeowners policy would cover the property damage to the apartment building up to the policy's liability limit.

**Workers Compensation** *There is no coverage for bodily injury to any person who is eligible to receive benefits provided an insured under a workers compensation, nonoccupational disability, or occupational disease law.* This is true if the workers compensation benefits are either mandatory or voluntary. In some states, domestic workers must be covered for workers compensation benefits by their employers; in other states, the coverage is voluntary.

**Nuclear Energy** *The homeowners policy excludes liability arising out of nuclear energy.* If an insured is involved in a nuclear incident, any resulting liability is not covered by the homeowners policy.

**Bodily Injury to an Insured** *There is no coverage for bodily injury to the named insured or to an insured as defined in the policy.* For example, if one spouse accidentally trips and injures the other spouse, the injured spouse cannot collect damages.

### Exclusions That Apply Only to Coverage F

A final set of exclusions applies only to Coverage F (medical payments to others).

**Injury to a Residence Employee Off an Insured Location** *If an injury to a residence employee occurs off an insured location and does not arise out of or in the course of employment by an insured, medical payments coverage does not apply.* For example, Tanya is employed by the named insured as a cook. While walking home after work, she falls and injures her back. Because the injury does not arise out of employment, medical payments coverage does not apply.

**Workers Compensation** This exclusion is similar to the workers compensation exclusion discussed earlier under personal liability insurance. *Medical payments coverage does not apply to any person who is eligible to receive benefits under a workers compensation, nonoccupational disability, or occupational disease law.* If the law requires workers compensation coverage, the medical payments exclusion applies.

**Nuclear Energy** Medical payments coverage does not cover any person for bodily injury that results from nuclear reaction, radiation, or radioactive contamination.

**Persons Regularly Residing on the Insured Location** *Medical payments coverage does not cover injury to any person (other than a residence employee of an insured) who regularly resides on any part of the insured location.* Thus, a tenant injured in a household accident cannot receive payment for medical expenses. The intent here is to minimize collusion among household members.

## SECTION II ADDITIONAL COVERAGES

A homeowners policy automatically includes several additional coverages, including coverage for claim expenses, first-aid expenses, damage to property of others, and loss-assessment charges.

### Claim Expenses

**Claim expenses** are paid as an additional coverage. The insurer pays the court costs, attorney fees, and other legal expenses incurred in providing a legal defense. The claim expenses are paid in addition to the policy limits for liability damages.

The insurer also pays the premiums on bonds required in a suit defended by the insurer. For example, a judgment may be appealed, and if an appeal bond is required, the insurer pays the premium.

Reasonable expenses incurred by the insured at the insurer's request to assist in the investigation and defense of a claim or suit are also paid. This obligation includes payment for the actual loss of earnings up to $250 per day. Finally, interest on a judgment that accrues after the judgment is awarded, but before payment is made, is also paid by the insurer.

### First-Aid Expenses

The insurer pays any **first-aid expenses** incurred by the insured for bodily injury covered under the policy. For example, a guest may slip in your home and break a leg. If you call an ambulance to take the injured person to the hospital and are later billed for

$600 by the ambulance company, this amount would be paid as a first-aid expense.

## Damage to Property of Others

**Damage to property of others** *pays up to $1000 per occurrence for property damage caused by an insured.* The damaged property is valued on the basis of replacement cost. This coverage can be illustrated by the following examples:

- A son, age 10, accidentally breaks a neighbor's window while playing softball.
- While attending a party at a friend's home, you carelessly burn a hole in your friend's carpet with your cigarette.
- You borrow your neighbor's lawn mower and accidentally damage the blade by striking a rock.

The insured is not required to be legally liable for coverage to apply. The loss is paid even when there is no legal obligation to do so.

The purpose of this coverage is to preserve personal friendships and keep peace in the neighborhood. Also, in many states, the parents are held responsible for the property damage caused by a young child. If this coverage were not provided, the person whose property is damaged would have to file a claim for damages against the insured who caused the damage.

A maximum of $1000 is paid under this coverage. Amounts in excess of this limit are paid only by proving negligence and legal liability by the person who caused the damage.

Damage to property of others also contains a specific set of exclusions. The major ones are summarized as follows:

- *Property Covered Under Section I.* Property damage is excluded to the extent of any amount recoverable under Section I of the policy.
- *Intentional Property Damage by an Insured Age 13 or Older.* If the property damage is intentionally caused by an insured, age 13 or older, coverage does not apply. This exclusion is relevant to teenage vandalism, which is a serious national problem. Thus, if a teenager damages a plate-glass window with a slingshot, deliberately knocks over a mailbox, or maliciously damages a tree, the parents' policy will not cover the property damage.

- *Property Owned by an Insured.* Property damage to property owned by an insured is also excluded. For example, if a son damages some power tools owned by his parents, the damage would not be covered. However, coverage does apply if the property is rented. Thus, if you rent a television and accidentally drop it, the damage is covered.
- *Property Owned by or Rented to a Tenant.* Coverage does not apply to property owned by or rented to a tenant of an insured or to a resident in the named insured's household.
- *Business Liability.* Property damage arising out of a business engaged in by an insured is excluded. Thus, if you operate a lawn-maintenance business and accidentally cut down a shrub while mowing a customer's lawn, the damage is not covered.
- *Act or Omission in Connection with the Premises.* Property damage caused by an act or omission in connection with a premises owned, rented, or controlled by an insured, other than an insured location, is not covered. For example, without an endorsement, farmland is not covered under the homeowners policy. Thus, if an insured accidentally damages the tractor of the tenant who is farming the land, coverage does not apply.
- *Motor Vehicles, Aircraft, Watercraft, or Hovercraft.* Property damage that results from the ownership, maintenance, or use of a motor vehicle, aircraft, watercraft, or hovercraft is not covered. For example, if you run over a neighbor's 10-speed bicycle with your auto, the loss is not covered.

## Loss Assessment

The homeowners policy provides coverage of $1000 for certain loss assessments. Higher limits are available by endorsement. For example, assume that a small child drowns in the swimming pool owned by the homeowners association and that the association must pay a liability judgement of $1,100,000. If the association's liability policy had a policy limit of $1 million, the $100,000 balance will be split among the association members and each member would be assessed a portion of the $100,000 balance. The homeowners policy would pay your loss-assessment charge up to $1000. This amount can be increased by an endorsement.

## SECTION II CONDITIONS

In the previous chapter, some important conditions that apply to Section I and to both Sections I and II were discussed. Some important conditions that apply to Section II only are discussed here.

### Limit of Liability

The insurer's total liability under Coverage E for all damages arising from one occurrence will not be more than the limit shown in the declarations. The liability limit is the same regardless of the number of insureds, claims made, or people injured. The insurer's total liability for medical expenses for bodily injury to one person resulting from an accident will not exceed the Coverage F limit shown in the declarations.

### Duties after an "Occurrence"

Written notice of the event must be provided to the insurer, including the time, place, circumstances, and names of any claimants and witnesses. The insured must cooperate with the insurer in investigating and settling the claim, and forward to the insurer any notice, demand, summons, or other document relating to the occurrence.

### Duties of an Injured Person under Coverage F

The injured person (or his/her representative) must provide written proof of claim and authorize the insurer to obtain copies of medical records. The injured person must also submit to a physical examination by a doctor selected by the insurer.

### No Suit against Insurer

An insured may not sue the insurer unless the insured has complied with the conditions required in Section II. No action can be brought against the insurer with respect to Coverage E until the obligation of the insured has been determined by final judgment or by an agreement signed by the insurer.

### Other Insurance

This insurance is excess over other valid and collectible insurance except where the other insurance was written specifically as excess coverage over the limits that apply in this policy.

### Concealment and Fraud

No coverage is provided to an insured who before or after a loss concealed or misrepresented any circumstance or material fact, engaged in fraudulent conduct, or made false statements about the insurance.

## ENDORSEMENTS TO A HOMEOWNERS POLICY

Some property owners have special needs or desire broader coverage than that provided by a standard homeowners policy. Numerous endorsements can be added to a homeowners policy to meet individual needs, including the following:

- Inflation guard endorsement
- Earthquake endorsement
- Personal property replacement cost loss settlement endorsement
- Scheduled personal property endorsement (with agreed value loss settlement)
- Personal injury endorsement
- Watercraft endorsement
- Home business insurance coverage endorsement
- Identity theft endorsement

### Inflation Guard Endorsement

Many homeowners are underinsured because inflation has increased the replacement cost of their home. If a loss occurs and you do not carry insurance at least equal to 80 percent of the replacement cost of the dwelling, you will be penalized because the full replacement cost will not be paid. Unfortunately, some homeowners do not discover they are underinsured until after a loss has occurred.

To deal with inflation, you should add an **inflation guard endorsement** to your homeowners policy if it is not included by your insurer. The inflation guard endorsement is designed for use with the ISO homeowner forms and provides for an annual pro rata increase in the limits of insurance under Coverages A, B, C, and D. The percentage increase is selected by the insured, such as 3 percent or 5 percent. For example, if the policyholder selects a 3 percent inflation guard endorsement, the various limits are increased by 3 percent annually. This specified annual percentage increase is prorated throughout the policy year. Thus, a house originally insured for $300,000 would be covered for $304,500 at the end of six months.

### Earthquake Endorsement

An **earthquake endorsement** can be added that covers direct physical loss to property covered under Section I caused by an earthquake. This coverage includes shock waves and tremors related to a volcanic eruption. A single earthquake is defined as all earthquake shocks that occur within a 72-hour period. A deductible must be satisfied. The base deductible is a percentage of the limit stated in the declarations that applies *either* to the dwelling (Coverage A) or to personal property (Coverage C), whichever is greater. There is a minimum deductible of $500. The deductible can be increased with a reduction in premiums. There is no other deductible that applies to an earthquake loss. The deductible does not apply to Coverage D (loss of use) and to additional coverages. In some states where earthquakes occur frequently, or the risk of an earthquake is high, deductibles of 10 to 20 percent are typically used.

Although earthquakes can cause catastrophic losses, most property owners in earthquake zones do not have earthquake insurance. Insurers in California selling homeowners insurance must offer earthquake insurance on new policies, but the majority of homeowners do not carry earthquake insurance. The major reasons for their reluctance to purchase earthquake coverage are high cost, high deductibles, a mistaken belief that earthquakes will not occur, and the belief that the federal government will provide disaster relief.

In California, earthquake coverage is also available through the California Earthquake Authority (CEA). The CEA is a privately financed, publicly managed entity that offers residential earthquake insurance to California homeowners, renters, condominium unit owners, and mobilehome owners. Seventeen private insurers participate in the arrangement. Structural damage to a home is subject to a deductible of 15 percent of the amount of insurance on the dwelling; however, a 10 percent deductible is available if the homeowner pays a higher premium. As stated earlier, most homeowners do not carry earthquake coverage. According to the Insurance Information Institute, only about 12 percent of Californians purchase earthquake insurance.[7]

### Personal Property Replacement Cost Loss Settlement Endorsement

An unendorsed homeowners policy covers losses to personal property on the basis of actual cash value. However, a **personal property replacement cost loss settlement endorsement** can be added to the policy. *Under the endorsement, claims are paid on the basis of replacement cost with no deduction for depreciation.* The endorsement applies to personal property, awnings, carpets, domestic appliances, and outdoor equipment.

The replacement cost endorsement for personal property has several important limitations. The amount paid is limited to the *smallest* of the following amounts:

- Replacement cost at the time of loss
- Full repair cost
- Coverage C limit, if applicable
- Any special dollar limits in the policy (such as theft limits on jewelry, furs, and silverware)
- For loss to any item, the limit of liability that applies to the item

If the cost to repair or replace exceeds $500, the property must actually be repaired or replaced to receive replacement cost. Otherwise, only the actual cash value is paid.

The replacement cost endorsement excludes certain types of property, such as antiques, fine arts, and similar property; collector's items and souvenirs; property that is not in good or working condition; and obsolete property stored or not used.

As a general rule, you should consider adding the replacement cost endorsement for personal property to your homeowners policy. You usually cannot find used property that replaces exactly the property lost. Also, because of depreciation, the amount paid for a loss based on an actual cash value policy is substantially less than that payable based on replacement cost. Most insureds typically are unaware of the big difference between replacement cost and actual cash value.

### Scheduled Personal Property Endorsement (with Agreed Value Loss Settlement)

The homeowners policy has limits on the amounts paid for certain personal property losses, such as theft of jewelry and firearms. Also, insureds may desire broader coverage than the homeowners policy provides. If you own valuable jewelry, furs, silverware, cameras, musical instruments, fine arts, antiques, or a stamp or coin collection, you can list the property in a schedule and insure it for a specific amount agreed to by the insurer.

The **scheduled personal property endorsement (with agreed value loss settlement)** provides additional coverage for nine classes of property. Depending on the needs of an insured, individual items are scheduled and insured for a specific amount. The categories are as follows:

1. Jewelry
2. Furs
3. Cameras
4. Musical instruments
5. Silverware
6. Golfer's equipment
7. Fine arts
8. Postage stamps
9. Rare and current coins

The endorsement insures property against direct physical loss, which means the property is insured on an open-perils basis. *All direct physical losses to scheduled property are covered except those losses specifically excluded.* For example, if a diamond ring insured for $25,000 is stolen, the amount paid is $25,000.

## Personal Injury Endorsement

The homeowners policy only covers legal liability arising out of bodily injury or property damage to someone else. Personal injury coverage, which should not be confused with bodily injury coverage, can be added to the homeowners policy through an endorsement.

**Personal injury** means legal liability arising out of the following:

- False arrest, detention, or imprisonment
- Malicious prosecution
- Wrongful eviction, wrongful entry, or invasion of the right of private occupancy of a room, dwelling, or premises
- Any manner of oral or written publication of material that slanders or libels a person or organization, or an organization's products or services[8]
- Oral or written publication of material that violates a person's right to privacy

For example, if you have a person arrested who is later found innocent, or if you make false statements that damage a person's reputation, you may be liable for damages. These losses are not covered under a homeowners policy but would be covered by the personal injury endorsement.

## Watercraft Endorsement

The **watercraft endorsement** covers watercraft that are otherwise excluded under the homeowners policy. The endorsement provides liability and medical payments coverage on any inboard or inboard-outdrive powered watercraft; sailing vessels 26 feet or more in length; and watercraft powered by one or more outboard motors exceeding 25 total horsepower.

## Home Business Insurance Coverage Endorsement

A growing number of homeowners operate a business out of their homes. A standard homeowners policy provides only limited coverage on business property, and legal liability arising out of a business operation is excluded. A **home business insurance coverage endorsement** can be added that covers both business property and legal liability arising out of a home-based business. This type of endorsement increases the coverage on business property on the residence premises from $2500 to the Coverage C limit on personal property. Coverage on business property away from the premises is increased from $1500 to a higher amount. The endorsement also provides coverage for accounts receivable, valuable papers and records, and the loss of business income and extra expenses when loss from an insured peril causes the business to be suspended.

The home business insurance endorsement covers business liability loss exposures that are normally found in a commercial package policy for a business firm. Liability coverage includes (1) bodily injury and property damage liability, (2) personal and advertising injury, and (3) products and completed operations exposures associated with the home business. These coverages are discussed in Chapter 26.

## Identity Theft Endorsement

Identity theft is a serious problem in the United States. Identity theft occurs when a thief uses your name, driver's license, ATM account number, credit card number, laptop computer, or other identification for fraudulent purposes. The Bureau of Justice Statistics reported that 8.6 million U.S. households were victimized by identity theft in 2010, up from 6.4 million households in 2005. The estimated direct loss to households in 2010 was $13.3 billion, an average of $2200 for each household that experienced a loss.[9] Losses occurred because of criminal use of stolen credit cards and ATM cards and fraudulently using someone else's personal information to obtain a new credit card or to open some other type of account, such as a utility account.

Victims of identity theft must spend time and trouble attempting to correct or re-establish their credit history. In addition to direct costs, out-of-pocket expenses, and the time spent in resolving credit problems, a large percentage of victims often experience more severe problems. Many victims experience harassment by bill collectors, denial of new credit, inability to use existing credit cards, inability to obtain loans, arrest, termination of their utility service, criminal investigation or civil suit, and difficulty in accessing their bank accounts.

An **identity theft endorsement** can be added to a homeowners policy. The endorsement reimburses crime victims for the cost of restoring their identity and cleaning up their credit report. To illustrate, one insurer provides expense reimbursement limits from $500 to $25,000 per covered person to restore the victim's credit history. The following expenses are covered:

- Lost wages up to a certain limit because of time off to deal with identity theft
- Loan reapplication fees to reapply for loans turned down because of erroneous credit information that reflects the identity theft
- Phone charges for calling financial institutions, business firms, and law enforcement agencies to discuss the identity theft
- Certified mail and notary costs for completing and delivering fraud affidavits
- Attorney fees incurred with the insurer's prior consent because of the cost of defending suits brought incorrectly by business firms and collection agencies, removing criminal or civil judgments wrongly entered against the insured, and challenging information on a credit report

Finally, it should be noted that identity theft insurance covers only expenses incurred and not any dollar amount that the thief may steal.

# COST OF HOMEOWNERS INSURANCE

As an informed consumer, you should understand how the cost of a homeowners policy is determined. Also, certain underwriting factors determine if an applicant for a homeowners policy is acceptable. Major rating and underwriting factors include the following:

- Construction
- Location
- Fire-protection class
- Construction costs
- Age of the home
- Type of policy
- Deductible amount
- Insurance score
- Loss history report

## Construction

Construction of the home is an extremely important rating factor. The more fire-resistant the home is, the lower the rate. Thus, wooden homes cost more to insure than brick homes. However, earthquake insurance costs are substantially less for wooden homes.

## Location

Location of the home is another important rating factor. For rating purposes, the loss experience of each rating territory is determined. Insureds who reside in territories with high losses from fires, storms, natural disasters, or crime must pay higher rates than insureds who reside in low-loss territories.

## Fire-Protection Class

The fire-protection class affects the rates charged. The Insurance Services Office (ISO) rates the quality of public fire departments from one to ten. A lower number results in a lower rate. Accessibility of the home to the fire department and water supply (e.g., fire hydrants) is also important. Homes in rural areas generally have higher rates than homes in large cities.

## Construction Costs

Construction costs have a significant effect on rates. The costs of labor and materials vary widely in the United States. The higher the cost of repairing or rebuilding your home, the higher your premium is likely to be.

### Age of the Home

The age of the home also affects the rate charged. Insurers charge less to insure newer homes than older homes. Older homes may be more susceptible to damage from fires and storms, have older wiring, and may have been constructed when the building code was less stringent.

### Type of Policy

The type of policy is extremely important in determining the total premium. The Homeowners 3 policy (special form) is more expensive than the Homeowners 2 policy (broad form) because the coverage is broader. The Homeowners 5 policy (comprehensive form) is the most expensive contract because the dwelling, other structures, and personal property are covered on an "all risks" or "open perils" basis. All direct physical damage losses are covered except those losses specifically excluded.

### Deductible Amount

The deductible amount has an important effect on cost. The higher the deductible, the lower the premium. The deductible can be increased with a reduction in premiums. The deductible does not apply to a fire department service charge, coverage for credit or ATM cards, scheduled property that is specifically insured, and the personal liability coverages under Section II.

### Insurance Score

Many insurers also use the applicant's credit record for purposes of underwriting and rating. The applicant's credit record is used to determine an insurance score. An **insurance score** *is a credit-based score that is highly predictive of future claim costs.* Insurance scores predict the average claim behavior for a group of insureds with essentially the same credit history. Insureds as a group with poor credit records and low insurance scores generally file more homeowners claims than insureds with good credit and higher insurance scores.

Several credit organizations calculate insurance scores for insurers. One of the most important is the Fair Isaac Corporation (FICO), which calculates insurance scores for insurers. The majority of consumers have good credit records.

Insurers claim there is a strong and statistically significant relationship between insurance scores and underwriting experience. The lower the insurance score, the more likely insureds as a group are likely to file homeowners claims. Actuarial studies generally support this conclusion.

### Loss History Report

For underwriting and rating purposes, insurers also use a **loss history report** that reveals the prior claim history of a home. The most widely used loss history report is the Comprehensive Loss Underwriting Exchange (CLUE) report available from LexisNexis.[10] CLUE reports provide data for up to seven years on a property, including the date of any loss, the type of loss, and the amount the insurer paid. More than 90 percent of insurers writing homeowners insurance contribute claim data to the CLUE database. The Insurance Services Office (ISO) also has a loss history database. ISO's A-PLUS (Automobile-Property Loss Underwriting Service) aggregates claims data from insurers that can be used by underwriters.

The use of loss history reports is controversial. Critics claim that insurers are concerned about mold claims and water damage and do not wish to insure homes that have experienced such losses. Some homebuyers have found it difficult to obtain homeowners insurance because the loss history report indicated a history of previous claims on the home they would like to purchase. Likewise, some homeowners selling their homes may not get the best price if the home has been rejected by several insurers because of previous claims.

However, in rebuttal, insurers claim they can rate coverage more accurately by using loss history reports in their underwriting. Also, insurers can detect fraudulent claims more easily.

### Suggestions for Buying a Homeowners Policy

As a careful insurance consumer, you should remember certain suggestions when purchasing a homeowners policy (see Exhibit 21.1).

**EXHIBIT 21.1**
**Tips for Buying a Homeowners Policy**

**Carry Adequate Insurance**   The first suggestion is to carry adequate amounts of property insurance on both your home and personal property. This consideration is particularly important if a room is added or home improvements are made because the value of the home may be substantially increased. The home must be insured for at least 80 percent of its replacement cost to avoid a penalty if a partial loss to the dwelling occurs. *However, you should seriously consider insuring your home for 100 percent of its replacement cost.* Few homeowners can afford an additional out-of-pocket payment equal to 20 percent of replacement cost if a total loss occurs.

**Add Necessary Endorsements**   Certain endorsements may be necessary depending on your needs, local property conditions, or high values for certain types of personal property. To deal with inflation, you should add an *inflation guard endorsement* to your homeowners policy if your insurer does not include it. An *earthquake endorsement* is desirable if you live in an earthquake zone. The *personal property replacement cost endorsement* is also desirable because you are indemnified on the basis of replacement cost with no deduction for depreciation. In addition, if you own valuable property, such as

jewelry, furs, fine art, or a valuable coin or stamp collection, you should add the *scheduled personal property endorsement* to your policy. Each item is listed and specifically insured for a certain amount.

**Shop Around for a Homeowners Policy**   Another important suggestion is to shop around for a homeowners policy. Because considerable price variation occurs among insurers, you can often reduce your homeowners premium by shopping around. Consequently, it pays to get a premium quote from several insurers before you buy a homeowners policy. Several Internet sites provide premium quotes (see Internet Resources). Some states also publish shoppers' guides to assist consumers who purchase homeowners policies. These guides indicate the wide variation in premiums charged by insurers. For example, the Arizona Department of Insurance surveyed 59 insurers in selected cities in Arizona to determine the cost of homeowners insurance. Exhibit 21.2 provides premium data for a $300,000 homeowners policy in five cities in Arizona. *The cost difference between the lowest- and highest-cost policy on a masonry dwelling in Phoenix, Arizona, was $3211 ($473 vs. $3684).* Clearly, it pays to shop around.

**EXHIBIT 21.2**
**Examples of Wide Variation in Annual Homeowners Premiums in Five Cities in Arizona**

COVERAGES: Dwelling: $300,000; Other Structures Coverage: $30,000; Contents Coverage: $225,000; Additional Living Expense Coverage: $60,000; Personal Liability Coverage: $300,000; Medical Payments Coverage: $1,000; $500 Flat Deductible.
CHARACTERISTICS: A two story, single family dwelling with single-cylinder dead-bolt locks, one fire extinguisher, and two smoke detectors. Excellent condition, masonry or frame (composition roof), built in January, 2011.

Premiums shown are annual premiums as of March 1, 2012.

| NAME OF INSURER | I PHOENIX MASONRY | I PHOENIX FRAME | II MESA MASONRY | II MESA FRAME | III PEORIA MASONRY | III PEORIA FRAME | IV FLAGSTAFF MASONRY | IV FLAGSTAFF FRAME | V TUCSON MASONRY | V TUCSON FRAME | # of Complaints (C) | Exposures (E) × 1000 | Complaint Ratio CR |
|---|---|---|---|---|---|---|---|---|---|---|---|---|---|
| American National P&C Co | $473 | $497 | $452 | $475 | $451 | $474 | $381 | $402 | $388 | $408 | 2 | 7,381 | 0.271 |
| LM Ins Corp | 483 | 479 | 465 | 462 | 474 | 471 | 419 | 418 | 460 | 457 | 0 | 2,490 | 0.000 |
| United Services Automobile Assoc | 501 | 529 | 528 | 558 | 455 | 482 | 515 | 543 | 471 | 501 | 4 | 69,981 | 0.057 |
| Pekin IC | 568 | 568 | 550 | 550 | 560 | 560 | 522 | 522 | 396 | 396 | 0 | 38 | 0.000 |
| American Strategic Ins Corp | 578 | 608 | 517 | 543 | 489 | 513 | 479 | 501 | 457 | 479 | 3 | 19,897 | 0.151 |
| Travelers Home and Marine IC | 617 | 631 | 619 | 630 | 659 | 674 | 596 | 604 | 466 | 468 | 8 | 71,598 | 0.112 |
| Arizona Home IC | 622 | 622 | 568 | 568 | 538 | 538 | 673 | 673 | 568 | 568 | 8 | 13,679 | 0.585 |
| Balboa IC | 665 | 671 | 539 | 545 | 461 | 469 | 477 | 487 | 415 | 419 | 5 | 11,870 | 0.421 |
| Farmers Ins Exchange | 679 | 692 | 610 | 616 | 711 | 726 | 434 | 439 | 418 | 423 | 18 | 98,916 | 0.182 |
| Pharmacists Mutual IC | 701 | 677 | 617 | 670 | 607 | 677 | 646 | 718 | 646 | 718 | 0 | 740 | 0.000 |
| Amica Mutual IC | 756 | 756 | 638 | 638 | 611 | 611 | 553 | 553 | 596 | 596 | 2 | 8,721 | 0.229 |
| Kemper Independence IC | 772 | 795 | 752 | 774 | 779 | 802 | 728 | 749 | 617 | 634 | 2 | 13,111 | 0.153 |
| Fidelity National IC | 789 | 843 | 593 | 631 | 543 | 576 | 673 | 717 | 615 | 657 | 19 | 17,934 | 1.059 |
| Metropolitan P&C IC | 799 | 853 | 563 | 599 | 443 | 471 | 673 | 719 | 517 | 550 | 10 | 36,499 | 0.274 |
| American Commerce IC | 808 | 914 | 603 | 668 | 590 | 673 | 496 | 573 | 434 | 492 | 0 | 5,219 | 0.000 |
| State Farm Fire and Cas Co | 815 | 904 | 783 | 867 | 496 | 549 | 595 | 659 | 635 | 705 | 98 | 453,490 | 0.216 |
| Unigard IC | 826 | 848 | 863 | 888 | 891 | 914 | 720 | 747 | 800 | 824 | 0 | 2,255 | 0.000 |
| Mercury Cas Co | 832 | 859 | 832 | 855 | 871 | 897 | 780 | 797 | 582 | 588 | 0 | 3,769 | 0.000 |
| Armed Forces Ins Exchange | 837 | 868 | 718 | 744 | 634 | 655 | 766 | 794 | 634 | 655 | 1 | 1,622 | 0.617 |

Complaint Ratio (CR) = # of Complaints (C) divided by # of Exposures (E) × 1000 = Complaint Ratio

**EXHIBIT 21.2**
**Examples of Wide Variation in Annual Homeowners Premiums in Five Cities in Arizona**

| NAME OF INSURER | I PHOENIX | | II MESA | | III PEORIA | | IV FLAGSTAFF | | V TUCSON | | Complaint Ratio (CR) # of Complaints (C) divided by # of Exposures (E) × 1000 = Complaint Ratio | | |
|---|---|---|---|---|---|---|---|---|---|---|---|---|---|
| | MASONRY | FRAME | MASONRY | FRAME | MASONRY | FRAME | MASONRY | FRAME | MASONRY | FRAME | C | E | CR |
| Horace Mann IC | 842 | 866 | 718 | 740 | 790 | 813 | 673 | 693 | 814 | 838 | 1 | 974 | 1.027 |
| IDS Property Cas IC | 859 | 859 | 824 | 824 | 547 | 547 | 597 | 597 | 580 | 580 | 7 | 23,089 | 0.303 |
| Central Mutual IC | 861 | 954 | 766 | 848 | 766 | 848 | 658 | 729 | 690 | 763 | 1 | 7,155 | 0.140 |
| SECURA Supreme IC | 885 | 930 | 582 | 612 | 704 | 740 | 607 | 639 | 495 | 520 | 0 | 2,090 | 0.000 |
| Great Northwest IC | 886 | 886 | 663 | 663 | 695 | 695 | 631 | 631 | 728 | 718 | 0 | 531 | 0.000 |
| Badger Mutual IC | 894 | 968 | 727 | 783 | 581 | 622 | 581 | 622 | 581 | 622 | 1 | 4,521 | 0.221 |
| Nationwide IC of America | 938 | 911 | 922 | 893 | 776 | 754 | 1,016 | 994 | 765 | 743 | 1 | 10,487 | 0.095 |
| Universal North America IC | 956 | 956 | 559 | 559 | 561 | 561 | 662 | 662 | 584 | 584 | 0 | 7,369 | 0.000 |
| American Automobile IC | 958 | 958 | 762 | 762 | 1,044 | 1,044 | 849 | 849 | 791 | 791 | 0 | 2,319 | 0.000 |
| Austin Mutual IC | 963 | 1,174 | 731 | 891 | 731 | 891 | 665 | 808 | 704 | 858 | 3 | 7,471 | 0.402 |
| Pacific Specialty IC | 971 | 1,056 | 852 | 954 | 728 | 809 | 704 | 782 | 704 | 782 | 44 | 11,201 | 3.928 |
| Trumbull IC | 988 | 965 | 956 | 932 | 890 | 872 | 955 | 936 | 835 | 821 | 1 | 3,121 | 0.320 |
| Merastar IC | 1,001 | 1,001 | 798 | 798 | 768 | 768 | 708 | 708 | 678 | 678 | 0 | 57 | 0.000 |
| Praetorian IC | 1,016 | 1,016 | 931 | 913 | 916 | 916 | 876 | 876 | 842 | 842 | 0 | 2,663 | 0.000 |
| Civil Service Employees IC | 1,047 | 1,140 | 811 | 882 | 865 | 942 | 736 | 799 | 758 | 826 | 0 | 1,009 | 0.000 |
| Empire Fire & Marine IC | 1,063 | 1,063 | 954 | 954 | 958 | 958 | 888 | 888 | 879 | 879 | 1 | 5,417 | 0.185 |
| Homesite Ind Co | 1,065 | 1,161 | 871 | 948 | 849 | 923 | 801 | 872 | 812 | 884 | 35 | 45,410 | 0.771 |
| ACA IC | 1,079 | 1,079 | 746 | 746 | 763 | 763 | 713 | 713 | 673 | 673 | 16 | 46,693 | 0.343 |
| Electric IC | 1,080 | 1,080 | 918 | 918 | 914 | 914 | 783 | 783 | 799 | 799 | 2 | 3,512 | 0.569 |
| Country Mutual IC | 1,082 | 1,082 | 941 | 941 | 907 | 907 | 907 | 907 | 782 | 782 | 4 | 27,138 | 0.147 |
| Allstate P&C IC | 1,085 | 1,132 | 1,021 | 1,065 | 1,010 | 1,053 | 953 | 985 | 868 | 889 | 11 | 100,381 | 0.110 |
| ACUITY, A Mutual IC | 1,100 | 1,100 | 1,104 | 1,104 | 981 | 981 | 822 | 822 | 893 | 893 | 3 | 8,913 | 0.337 |
| First American P&C IC | 1,109 | 1,109 | 760 | 760 | 840 | 840 | 665 | 665 | 766 | 766 | 7 | 13,754 | 0.509 |

Premiums shown are annual premiums as of March 1, 2012.

(Continued)

**Exhibit 21.2 (Continued)**
**Examples of Wide Variation in Annual Homeowners Premiums in Five Cities in Arizona**

Premiums shown are annual premiums as of March 1, 2012.

| NAME OF INSURER | I PHOENIX | | II MESA | | III PEORIA | | IV FLAGSTAFF | | V TUCSON | | Complaint Ratio (CR) # of Complaints (C) divided by # of Exposures (E) × 1000 = Complaint Ratio | | |
|---|---|---|---|---|---|---|---|---|---|---|---|---|---|
| | MASONRY | FRAME | MASONRY | FRAME | MASONRY | FRAME | MASONRY | FRAME | MASONRY | FRAME | C | E | CR |
| Wilshire IC | 1,126 | 1,126 | 1,126 | 1,126 | 1,126 | 1,126 | 1,126 | 1,126 | 1,126 | 1,126 | 0 | 793 | 0.000 |
| Milbank IC | 1,129 | 1,323 | 849 | 992 | 815 | 953 | 743 | 869 | 705 | 824 | 2 | 8,110 | 0.247 |
| Safeco IC of America | 1,132 | 1,098 | 894 | 867 | 840 | 816 | 887 | 887 | 807 | 782 | 6 | 29,847 | 0.201 |
| Sentry Ins a Mutual Co | 1,155 | 1,210 | 1,103 | 1,155 | 1,097 | 1,148 | 1,006 | 1,053 | 722 | 754 | 0 | 6,147 | 0.000 |
| California Cas Ind Exchange | 1,157 | 1,205 | 1,103 | 1,140 | 1,022 | 1,059 | 869 | 895 | 895 | 933 | 1 | 5,162 | 0.194 |
| Union IC of Providence | 1,169 | 1,169 | 988 | 988 | 1,007 | 1,007 | 812 | 812 | 1,025 | 1,025 | 2 | 1,689 | 1.184 |
| American Family Mutual IC | 1,184 | 1,208 | 975 | 995 | 1,007 | 1,028 | 892 | 910 | 896 | 914 | 56 | 146,144 | 0.383 |
| American Summit IC | 1,204 | 1,300 | 1,085 | 1,169 | 915 | 982 | 883 | 947 | 986 | 1,059 | 8 | 2,928 | 2.732 |
| Farm Bureau P&C IC | 1,211 | 1,262 | 961 | 977 | 934 | 971 | 787 | 817 | 939 | 977 | 3 | 15,980 | 0.188 |
| Century-National IC | 1,269 | 1,269 | 912 | 912 | 912 | 912 | 1,085 | 1,085 | 912 | 912 | 0 | 4,305 | 0.000 |
| Encompass P&C Co | 1,303 | 1,365 | 930 | 971 | 999 | 1,046 | 828 | 863 | 796 | 827 | 1 | 4,996 | 0.200 |
| Cincinnati IC | 1,431 | 1,510 | 961 | 1,014 | 976 | 1,030 | 939 | 991 | 800 | 844 | 0 | 2,775 | 0.000 |
| American Security IC | 1,465 | 1,465 | 1,465 | 1,465 | 1,465 | 1,465 | 1,335 | 1,335 | 1,465 | 1,465 | 2 | 687 | 2.911 |
| Owners IC | 1,537 | 1,624 | 1,463 | 1,518 | 969 | 1,005 | 1,059 | 1,117 | 999 | 1,054 | 5 | 15,299 | 0.327 |
| Pacific Ind Co | 1,739 | 1,739 | 1,621 | 1,621 | 1,667 | 1,667 | 1,496 | 1,496 | 1,272 | 1,272 | 0 | 457 | 0.000 |
| American Modern Select IC | 2,991 | 2,991 | 2,991 | 2,991 | 2,991 | 2,991 | 2,991 | 2,991 | 2,991 | 2,991 | 1 | 362 | 2.762 |
| Scottsdale IC | 3,684 | 3,684 | 3,684 | 3,684 | 3,684 | 3,684 | 3,684 | 3,684 | 3,684 | 3,684 | 4 | 2,861 | 1.398 |

Source: Excerpted from Arizona Department of Insurance, 2012 Consumer Guide and Premium Comparison for Homeowners Insurance.

### Consider a Higher Property Insurance Deductible

Another suggestion for reducing premiums is to purchase a policy with a higher deductible for property insurance. The standard homeowners deductible is $500. *A higher deductible can substantially reduce your premiums.* You can usually get a discount of 20 to 30 percent discount with a $1000 deductible. For example, Patrick has a $1000 deductible in his homeowners policy instead of the standard $500, which saves him $120 annually. In other words, Patrick saves $120 each year but loses only $500 in coverage. That additional $500 is very expensive coverage.

### Take Advantage of Discounts

When you shop for a homeowners policy, you should inquire whether you are eligible for any discounts or credits, which can further reduce your premiums. Insurers offer a wide variety of discounts based on numerous factors, including age of the home, fire and smoke alarms, sprinkler system, dead-bolt locks, and fire extinguishers.

The appendix to this chapter, provided on the companion website (www.pearsonhighered.com/rejda), provides additional suggestions for reducing the cost of a homeowners policy.

### Don't Ignore Floods and Earthquakes

The homeowners policy covers hurricanes, tornadoes, windstorms, and fire losses. However, floods and earthquakes are specifically excluded. Although federal flood insurance is available and an earthquake endorsement can be added to the homeowners policy, most property owners are not insured against these two perils. If you reside in a flood or earthquake zone, you should seriously consider covering such perils in your personal risk management program. Otherwise, you stand to lose a substantial amount of money if a flood or earthquake occurs. For example, in 2005, Hurricane Katrina caused flooding in more than 80 percent of the city of New Orleans, which resulted in billions of property damage losses. Most homeowners did not carry flood insurance and experienced severe financial problems as a result.

### Improve Your Credit Record

Another important suggestion is to improve your credit record. As noted earlier, many insurers use an applicant's credit record and insurance score for purposes of underwriting and rating. Applicants with good or superior credit records may be able to purchase a homeowners policy less expensively than applicants with poor credit records. A good credit record can also result in lower interest rates on mortgage loans, auto loans, and credit cards. A poor credit record can be improved over time.

### Consider Purchasing a Personal Umbrella Policy

**A personal umbrella policy** provides an additional $1 million to $10 million of liability insurance after the underlying coverage is exhausted. It also covers liability arising out of personal injury, including coverage for libel, slander, and defamation of character. The homeowners policy does not cover personal injury without an endorsement. Also, in addition to coverage on your home and personal activities, the personal umbrella policy provides excess liability insurance on your cars, boats, and recreational vehicles. The personal umbrella policy is explained in greater detail in Chapter 24.

Finally, at the time of this writing, the United States has begun to recover from one of the most severe recessions in its history. Some policyholders who have lost their jobs and are strapped for cash may be tempted to drop certain insurance coverages to save money. The Insurance Information Institute (I.I.I.) warns that dropping or substantially modifying existing coverages may leave you dangerously underinsured. Insight 21.2 identifies five mistakes consumers should avoid in a struggling economy. The online appendix to this chapter (pearsonhighered.com/rejda) provides additional suggestions on how to save money on homeowners insurance.

## INSIGHT 21.2

### Trying to Save Money? Avoid the Five Biggest Insurance Mistakes!

With nearly one in 10 Americans out of work, and others forced to make ends meet with less money, many people are looking for ways to cut costs. There are smart ways to save on home and auto insurance; however, there are also mistakes that can result in being dangerously underinsured, according to the Insurance Information Institute (I.I.I.).

"When money is tight, it is extremely important to be financially protected against a catastrophe with the right amount and type of insurance," said Jeanne M. Salvatore, senior vice president and consumer spokesperson for the I.I.I. "By taking a few simple steps, it is possible to cut costs and still be protected should disaster strike."

*(Continued)*

## INSIGHT 21.2    (Continued)

Following are five of the biggest insurance mistakes that consumers should look out for:

1. **Insuring a home for its real estate value rather than for the cost of rebuilding**
   When real estate prices go down, some homeowners may think they can reduce the amount of insurance on their home. But insurance is designed to cover the cost of rebuilding, not the sales price of the home. You should make sure that you have enough coverage to completely rebuild your home and replace your belongings.
   *A better way to save*: Raise your deductible. An increase from $500 to $1,000 could save up to 25 percent on your premium payments.

2. **Selecting an insurance company by price alone**
   It is important to choose a company with competitive prices but also one that is financially sound and provides good customer service.
   *A better way to save*: Check the financial health of a company with independent rating agencies and ask friends and family for recommendations. You should select an insurance company that will respond to your needs and handle claims fairly and efficiently.

3. **Dropping flood insurance**
   Damage from flooding is not covered under standard homeowners and renters insurance policies. Coverage is available from the National Flood Insurance Program (NFIP), as well as from some private insurance companies. Many homeowners are unaware they are at risk for flooding, but in fact 25 percent of all flood losses occur in low risk areas.
   *A better way to save*: Before purchasing a home, check with the NFIP to check whether it is in a flood zone; if so, consider a less risky area. If you are already living in a flood zone area, look at mitigation efforts that can reduce your risk of flood damage and consider purchasing flood insurance.

4. **Only purchasing the legally required amount of liability for your car**
   In today's litigious society, buying only the minimum amount of liability means you are likely to pay more out-of-pocket—and those costs may be steep.
   *A better way to save*: Consider dropping collision and/or comprehensive coverage on older cars worth less than $1,000. The insurance industry and consumer groups generally recommend a minimum of $100,000 of bodily injury protection per person and $300,000 per accident.

5. **Neglecting to buy renters insurance**
   A renters policy covers your possessions and additional living expenses if you have to move out due to a disaster. Equally important, it provides liability protection in the event someone is injured in your home and decides to sue.
   *A better way to save*: Look into multi-policy discounts. Buying several policies with the same insurer, such as renters, auto, and life will generally provide savings.

SOURCE: Insurance Information Institute, "Trying to Save Money? Avoid the Five Biggest Insurance Mistakes!" Press release, October 25, 2010.

## CASE APPLICATION

James and Megan Webb recently purchased a home for $300,000. The home is insured under an HO-3 policy for $250,000 with no endorsements attached. Megan collects antiques for a hobby. James has a stamp collection that contains several rare stamps. The couple also owns a 30-foot sailboat that they use on weekends.

a. Assume you are a risk management consultant who has been asked to evaluate the couple's HO-3 policy. Identify three endorsements that James and Megan may wish to purchase to modify their HO-3 policy.

b. Explain how the above HO-3 policy would be modified by each endorsement identified in your answer to (a) above.

c. For each of the following losses, indicate whether Section II of the homeowners policy would provide full coverage for the loss. If full coverage would not be provided, explain why.

1. Megan entertains members of a local garden club in her home and serves the guests a buffet luncheon. Two guests become seriously ill and sue Megan, alleging she had served them contaminated food. The court awards each guest damages of $60,000.

2. James is an architect. The roof of a new addition to a client's home collapses. The client alleges that the roof collapsed because of faulty design. The cost of rebuilding is $40,000. The client seeks to recover that amount from James.

3. During a visit to a friend's home, Megan accidentally breaks a figurine that she picked up to admire. The figurine has a value of $475. The friend is seeking damages from Megan.

## SUMMARY

- Section II of the homeowners policy protects the named insured, resident relatives, and other persons for legal liability arising out of their personal acts.

- Insured locations include the residence premises described in the declarations, other residences acquired during the policy period, a residence where an insured is temporarily residing, vacant land other than farmland, cemetery or burial plots, land on which a residence is being built, and occasional rental of a premises for other than business purposes.

- Personal liability insurance (Coverage E) protects an insured against a claim or suit for damages because of bodily injury or property damage caused by negligence. The company will provide a legal defense and pay those sums that the insured is legally obligated to pay up to the policy limits.

- Medical payments to others (Coverage F) pays the reasonable medical expenses of another person who may be accidentally injured on the premises, or by the actions of an insured, resident employee, or animal owned by or in the care of an insured. It is not necessary to prove negligence and establish legal liability before the medical expenses are paid. The coverage does not apply to injuries of the named insured and regular residents of the household, other than residence employees.

- Section II provides four additional coverages: (1) claim expenses, (2) first-aid expenses, (3) damage to property of others, and (4) coverage for a loss-assessment charge.

- Numerous endorsements can be added to a homeowners policy to meet individual needs, including the following:

  Inflation guard endorsement

  Earthquake endorsement

  Personal property replacement cost loss settlement endorsement

  Scheduled personal property endorsement (with agreed value loss settlement)

  Personal injury endorsement

  Watercraft endorsement

  Home business insurance coverage endorsement

  Identity theft endorsement

- The cost of a homeowners policy depends on numerous factors. These include construction, location, fire-protection class, construction costs, age of the home, type of policy, deductible amount, insurer, insurance score, and loss history report.

- Certain suggestions should be followed when shopping for a homeowners policy:

  Carry adequate insurance.

  Add necessary endorsements.

  Shop around for a homeowners policy.

  Consider a higher property insurance deductible.

  Take advantage of discounts.

  Don't ignore the perils of flood and earthquake.

  Improve your credit record.

  Consider purchasing a personal umbrella policy.

## KEY CONCEPTS AND TERMS

Claim expenses (460)
Contractual liability (459)
Damage to property of others (461)
Earthquake endorsement (463)
First-aid expenses (460)
Home business insurance coverage endorsement (464)
Identity theft endorsement (465)
Inflation guard endorsement (462)
Insurance score (466)
Loss history report (466)
Medical payments to others (456)
Occurrence (454)
Personal injury (464)
Personal liability (454)
Personal property replacement cost loss settlement endorsement (463)
Personal umbrella policy (471)
Scheduled personal property endorsement (with agreed value loss settlement) (464)
Watercraft endorsement (464)

## REVIEW QUESTIONS

1. What is the meaning of *occurrence* under Section II of the homeowners policy?

2. Briefly explain the personal liability coverage (Coverage E) in Section II of the homeowners policy.

3. a. Briefly explain the coverage for medical payments to others (Coverage F) in Section II of the homeowners policy.

   b. Identify the people who are covered for medical payments to others (Coverage F) in the homeowners policy.

4. Personal liability (Coverage E) and medical payments to others (Coverage F) provide protection to insureds at various insured locations. Identify the insured locations under Section II in the homeowners policy.

5. List the major exclusions that apply to personal liability (Coverage E) and medical payments to others (Coverage F) in the homeowners policy.

6. Section II of the homeowners policy provides several additional coverages. One additional coverage is called *damage to the property of others*. Briefly describe this coverage.

7. Briefly describe the following endorsements that can be added to a homeowners policy:
   a. Earthquake endorsement
   b. Inflation guard endorsement
   c. Personal property replacement cost loss settlement endorsement.
   d. Scheduled personal property endorsement (with agreed value loss settlement)
   e. Identity theft endorsement

8. Homeowners insurance premiums are based on a number of factors. Identify the major factors that determine the cost of a homeowners policy.

9. Many insurers now use insurance scores in the underwriting and rating of a homeowners policy.
   a. What is an insurance score?
   b. Why do insurers use insurance scores in underwriting and rating?

10. Briefly explain the suggestions that consumers should follow when shopping for a homeowners policy.

# APPLICATION QUESTIONS

1. Indicate whether the following losses are covered under Section II of the homeowners policy. Assume there are no special endorsements. Give reasons for your answers.
   a. The named insured's dog bites a neighbor's child and also chews up the neighbor's coat.
   b. A son living at home accidentally injures another player while playing softball.
   c. A guest slips on a waxed kitchen floor and breaks an arm.
   d. A neighbor's child falls off a swing in the named insured's yard and breaks an arm.
   e. The named insured accidentally falls on an icy sidewalk and breaks a leg.
   f. While driving to the supermarket, the named insured injures another motorist with the automobile.
   g. A ward of the court, age 10, in the care of an insured, deliberately breaks a neighbor's window.

   h. The named insured paints houses for a living. A can of paint accidentally spills onto a customer's roof and discolors it.
   i. The named insured falls asleep while smoking a cigarette in a rented hotel room, and the room is badly damaged by the fire.
   j. The named insured borrows a camera, and it is stolen from a motel room while the insured is on vacation.

2. Joseph is the named insured under a Homeowners 3 policy (special form) with a liability limit of $100,000 per occurrence and a $1000 limit for medical payments to others. For each of the following situations, explain whether the loss is covered under Section II of Joseph's homeowners policy.
   a. Joseph is a self-employed accountant who works out of his home. One of Joseph's clients sues him for negligence in the preparation of a tax return and is awarded a $3000 judgment against him.
   b. Joseph's 25-year-old son, who recently married and now lives in his own apartment, negligently kills another hunter in a hunting accident. The son is sued for $1 million in a wrongful-death lawsuit.

3. Martha rents an apartment and is the named insured under a Homeowners 4 policy (contents broad form) with a liability limit of $100,000 per occurrence and $1000 medical payments. For each of the following situations, indicate to what extent, if any, the loss is covered under Section II of Martha's homeowners policy. Assume there are no special endorsements, and each situation is an independent event.
   a. Martha attends a party at a friend's house. She accidentally burns a hole in a couch with her cigarette. It will cost $500 to repair the damaged couch.
   b. Martha rents a snowmobile at a ski resort and accidentally collides with a skier. Martha is sued for $200,000 by the injured skier.

4. Explain whether each of the following losses would be covered under Section II in the homeowners policy. If the loss is not covered, explain how coverage can be obtained.
   a. The insured owns a restaurant in a large city. The insured is sued by several customers who allege they became seriously ill from a contaminated banana cream pie served at the restaurant.
   b. While operating a 30-foot sailboat, the insured injures a swimmer.
   c. The named insured is sued by his ex-wife, who alleges her reputation has been ruined because the insured lied about her relationship with another man.

5. Jerry and Lois Gower own and operate the Gower Painting Co. The couple is insured under a Homeowners 3 policy with no special endorsements. The policy has a $100,000 per occurrence limit for personal liability and a $1000 limit for medical payments to others. For each of the following situations, indicate to what extent, if any, the loss is covered under Section II of their homeowners policy.

   a. Jerry left a ladder standing against a house that he was painting. When Jerry went to lunch, a child, age 7, climbed the ladder and was seriously injured when the ladder collapsed. Jerry is sued by the child's parents for $200,000.

   b. Lois accidentally fell off the roof of a house that she was painting and injured her leg. She incurred medical expenses of $3000.

   c. The couple's daughter, Jennifer, age 22, attends college at a large Midwestern university. While playing softball, Jennifer made a hard slide into second base and accidentally injured the opposing player. The injured player claims Jennifer intended to injure her and sues Jennifer for $50,000.

   d. Lois has a pet basset hound, Huey. Huey is a friendly, docile dog and loves people. One morning, Lois carelessly left the backyard gate open, and Huey escaped from the fenced yard. A neighbor tried to catch the dog, and Huey bit him on the hand and leg. The neighbor incurred medical bills of $800. Lois is later sued by the neighbor for $50,000 when the dog bite became infected and did not heal.

   e. Jerry is playing golf with a friend who is riding in a golf cart that he is operating. The cart overturned when Jerry carelessly drove the cart off the fairway and hit a tree. Jerry's friend is seriously injured and sues Jerry for $150,000.

## INTERNET RESOURCES

- The **Insurance Information Institute** provides timely information on homeowners insurance and other personal property and liability insurance coverages. Articles on homeowners insurance and other property and liability coverages can be accessed directly online. Visit the site at

  iii.org

- **Insurancesavenow.com** provides premium quotes on a variety of insurance products, including homeowners and renters insurance, auto insurance, life insurance, and health insurance. Visit the site at

  insurancesavenow.com

- **Insure.com** provides news, premium quotes, and other consumer information on homeowners insurance. Visit the site at

  insure.com

- **InsWeb** provides premium quotes on homeowners, auto, and other insurance products. You can comparison shop from your computer. Visit the site at

  insweb.com

- The **International Risk Management Institute (IRMI)** is an online source that provides valuable information about personal lines and commercial lines. The site provides timely articles on a wide range of risk management and insurance topics and offers a number of free e-mail newsletters. Visit the site at

  irmi.com

## SELECTED REFERENCES

"Catastrophes: Insurance Issues," *Issues Updates,* Insurance Information Institute, July 2012. This source is periodically updated.

"Earthquakes: Risk and Insurance Issues," *Issues Updates,* Insurance Information Institute, April 2012. This source is periodically updated.

Fair Isaac Corporation. *Predictiveness of Credit History for Insurance Loss Relativities.* A Fair Isaac Paper, October 1999.

Hartwig, Robert P. and Claire Wilkinson. *The Use of Credit Information in Personal Lines Insurance Underwriting.* New York: Insurance Information Institute, Insurance Issues Series, vol. 1, no. 2, June 2003.

"Home Buyers Insurance Checklist," Insurance Information Institute.

Lee, Diana, et al. "Give Us Some Credit: The Use of Credit Information in Insurance Underwriting and Rating," *Risk Management* & *Insurance Review,* vol. 8, no. 1, Spring 2005.

Nyce, Charles, ed. *Personal Insurance,* 2nd ed. Malvern, PA.: American Institute for Chartered Property Casualty Underwriters/Insurance Institute of America, 2008.

Richardson, Diane W. *Homeowners Coverage Guide,* 4th ed. Cincinnati, OH: The National Underwriter Company, 2011.

"What Types of Disasters are Covered by Homeowners Insurance," Insurance Information Institute.

## NOTES

1. The discussion of Section II coverages in this chapter is based largely on the *Fire, Casualty & Surety Bulletins*, Personal Lines volume, Dwelling section (Erlanger, KY: National Underwriter Company); National Underwriter Company's *Homeowners Coverage Guide*, 4th Edition, Personal Lines Pilot newsletters from the International Risk Management Institute (IRMI); and the HO-3 policy drafted by the Insurance Services Office (ISO).

2. The 2011 revision of ISO's homeowners forms makes available an endorsement that excludes canine liability.

3. The previous ISO form stated "an insured's residence." The new form simply states "a residence," so coverage would apply, for example, while mowing a neighbor's lawn.

4. This coverage for toy cars that young children can ride in or on was added in the latest revision of the homeowners form.

5. These activities are not listed in Section II of the policy. In the definitions section, "Business" is defined and these activities are listed as exceptions to the definition.

6. The previous policy version stated "licensed physician." Coverage was broadened to "health care professional" in the revision.

7. "Earthquakes: Risk and Insurance Issues," *Issues Updates*, Insurance Information Institute, April 2012. This topic is periodically updated.

8. The wording "in any manner" was added to the Personal Injury endorsement to extend coverage for Internet-related loss exposures. An endorsement with an aggregate limit for personal injury losses is also available.

9. These statistics were obtained from "Identity Theft Reported by Households Rose 33 Percent from 2005 to 2010," as reported in a press release issued by the Bureau of Justice Statistics, Nov. 30, 2011.

10. CLUE Reports were originally prepared by a company called ChoicePoint. ChoicePoint was purchased by Reed Elsevier, the parent company of LexisNexis, in 2008.

Students may take a self-administered test on this chapter at
**www.pearsonhighered.com/rejda**

# CHAPTER 22

# AUTO INSURANCE

*"A careful driver is one who honks his horn when he goes through a red light."*

Henry Morgan

## LEARNING OBJECTIVES

**After studying this chapter, you should be able to**

◆ Identify the parties that are insured for liability coverage under the Personal Auto Policy (PAP).

◆ Describe the liability coverage in the PAP.

◆ Explain the medical payments coverage in the PAP.

◆ Describe the uninsured motorists coverage in the PAP.

◆ Explain the coverage for damage to your auto in the PAP.

◆ Explain the duties imposed on the insured after an accident or loss.

*As Beth pulled out of her driveway, she knew that she was late for work. Her boss had warned her that the next time she was late, she would be fired. As Beth sped along, she thought about calling a co-worker on her cell phone to ask him to cover for her until she arrived. Unfortunately, Beth did not notice that the car ahead of her had stopped for a pedestrian in the crosswalk. She could not avoid the stopped car and ran into it. The driver of the car sustained severe injuries and his car was extensively damaged. Beth sustained minor injuries and the front end of her car was heavily damaged.*

*Fortunately, Beth's auto insurance policy protected her against the financial consequences of her careless driving. Her insurer covered her legal liability as well as her medical bills and the cost of repairing her car, less a modest deductible. Auto insurance provides similar protection to millions of motorists. It is one of the most important coverages to emphasize in a personal risk management program. Legal liability arising out of an auto accident can reach catastrophic levels; medical bills and physical damage to an expensive car can be substantial; and noneconomic costs may also be incurred, including pain and suffering and the unexpected death of a family member.*

*In this chapter, we discuss the major provisions of the Personal Auto Policy (PAP) drafted by the Insurance Services Office (ISO). The PAP form is widely used throughout the United States. Some insurers, such as State Farm and Allstate, have developed their own forms that differ somewhat from the PAP form, but the differences are relatively minor.*

## OVERVIEW OF PERSONAL AUTO POLICY

In this section, we discuss the major provisions of the 2005 Personal Auto Policy (PAP) drafted by the Insurance Services Office (ISO).[1] The 2005 PAP is widely used throughout the United States and replaces the older 1998 form. A copy of this policy is provided in Appendix B at the end of the text.

### Eligible Vehicles

Only certain types of vehicles are eligible for coverage under the PAP. An eligible vehicle is a four-wheeled motor vehicle owned by the insured or leased by the insured for at least six continuous months. Thus, a private passenger auto, station wagon, or sport utility vehicle owned by the insured is eligible for coverage. Also, as explained later, a van or pickup can be insured under the PAP if certain requirements are met.

### Your Covered Auto

An extremely important provision is the definition of **your covered auto**. Four classes of vehicles are considered to be covered autos:

- Any vehicle shown in the declarations
- A newly acquired auto
- A trailer owned by the named insured
- A temporary substitute vehicle

**Any Vehicle Shown in the Declarations** Any vehicle shown on the declarations page is a covered auto. Covered autos include a private passenger auto, station wagon, sport utility vehicle, pickup, or van owned by the named insured. A pickup or van must (1) have a Gross Vehicle Weight Rating of 10,000 pounds or less, and (2) must not be used to transport business materials unless the materials are incidental to the named insured's business, and that business is installing, maintaining, or repairing furnishings or equipment, or is used in farming or ranching. For example, plumbers and electricians can transport their tools and materials in their vans or pickups and still have coverage under the personal auto policy. A vehicle listed in the declarations that is leased for at least six months is a covered auto as well.

**Newly Acquired Auto**   A newly acquired private passenger auto, pickup, or van is a covered auto if it is acquired by the named insured during the policy period.

- *With respect to liability coverage, medical payments coverage, and uninsured motorists coverage,* coverage begins automatically on the date you become the owner. If the coverages on all listed vehicles are not the same, you receive the broadest coverage provided for any vehicle shown in the declarations.

  If the vehicle you acquire is an *additional vehicle,* you are automatically covered for 14 days, but you must notify the insurer within 14 days after you become the owner for coverage to continue.

  If the vehicle you acquire is a *replacement vehicle,* you are automatically covered until the policy expires; you are not required to notify the insurer. A replacement vehicle is one that replaces a vehicle shown in the declarations. As a result, liability coverage, medical payments coverage, and uninsured motorists coverage apply automatically to a replacement vehicle without first having to notify the insurer.

- *With respect to coverage for damage to your auto,* however, a different set of rules applies. The PAP contains notification provisions that apply separately to collision coverage and other-than-collision coverage. *If the declarations page indicates that collision coverage applies to at least one auto, the newly acquired auto is automatically covered on the date of ownership, but you must notify the insurer within 14 days after you become the owner for collision coverage to continue.* The lowest deductible on any vehicle shown in the declarations applies to the newly acquired auto. A similar notification provision applies separately to other-than-collision coverage.

- The time requirement for notifying the insurer is shorter if there is no collision coverage on any vehicle. *If the declarations page does not indicate collision coverage for at least one auto,*

*a newly acquired auto is automatically insured for collision coverage for only four days.* You must notify the insurer within four days after you become the owner for collision coverage to continue. If a loss occurs before you notify the insurer, a $500 collision deductible must be met. A similar notification provision applies separately to other-than-collision coverage.

**Trailer Owned by the Named Insured**   A trailer owned by the named insured is also a covered auto. A trailer is a vehicle designed to be pulled by a private passenger auto, pickup, or van and also includes a farm wagon or farm implement while being towed by such vehicles. For example, you may be pulling a boat trailer that overturns and injures another motorist. The liability coverage in the PAP would cover the loss.

**Temporary Substitute Vehicle**   A temporary substitute vehicle is also a covered auto. A **temporary substitute vehicle** is a nonowned auto or trailer that you are temporarily using because of mechanical breakdown, repair, servicing, loss, or destruction of a covered vehicle. For example, if you drive a loaner car furnished by a repair shop or drive a friend's car while your car is in the garage for repairs, your PAP covers liability arising out of use of the loaner car.

### Summary of PAP Coverages

The PAP consists of a declarations page, a definitions section, and the following six parts:

- Part A:   Liability Coverage
- Part B:   Medical Payments Coverage
- Part C:   Uninsured Motorists Coverage
- Part D:   Coverage for Damage to Your Auto
- Part E:   Duties after an Accident or Loss
- Part F:   General Provisions

## PART A: LIABILITY COVERAGE

Liability coverage (Part A) is the most important part of the PAP as legal liability arising from negligent use of an auto can be quite large. Liability coverage protects a covered person against a lawsuit or claim arising out of the ownership or operation of a covered vehicle.

## Insuring Agreement

In the insuring agreement, the insurer agrees to pay any damages for bodily injury or property damage for which any insured is legally responsible because of an auto accident. The PAP is typically written with split limits. Split limits *mean that the amounts of insurance for bodily injury liability and property damage liability are stated separately.* For example, split limits of $250,000/$500,000/$100,000 mean that you have bodily injury liability coverage of $250,000 for each injured person and a maximum of $500,000 of bodily injury coverage for each accident. You also have $100,000 of property damage liability coverage. (Practitioners frequently refer to such limits as 250/500/100.)

Liability coverage can also be written with a single limit by adding an appropriate endorsement to the policy. A single limit *applies to both bodily injury and property damage liability: the total amount of insurance applies to the entire accident without a separate limit for each injured person.* For example, a single limit of $500,000 would apply to both bodily injury and property damage liability.

The amount paid as damages includes any prejudgment interest awarded against the insured. Many states allow plaintiffs (injured persons) to receive interest on the judgment from the time the lawsuit is entered to the time the judgment is determined. Any prejudgment interest is part of the damages awarded and is subject to the policy limit of liability.

The insurer also agrees to defend you and pay all legal defense costs. The defense costs are paid in addition to the policy limits. *However, the insurer's duty to settle or defend the claim ends when the limit of liability has been exhausted by payment of a judgment or settlement.* This provision means that the insurer cannot deposit the policy limits into an escrow account and walk away without first defending the insured. The obligation to defend ends when the policy limits are exhausted by payment of a judgment against the insured or settlement with a claimant. The duty to defend also ends if the claim is settled for less than the policy limits.

In addition, the insurer has no obligation to defend any claim not covered by the policy. For example, if you intentionally cause bodily injury or property damage while driving the covered auto and you are sued, the insurer has no obligation to defend you because intentional acts are specifically excluded.

## Insured Persons

The following four groups are insured parties under the liability section of the PAP:

- The named insured and any resident family member
- Any person using the named insured's covered auto with permission
- Any person or organization legally responsible for any insured's use of a covered auto on behalf of that person or organization
- Any person or organization legally responsible for the named insured's or family members' use of any auto or trailer (other than a covered auto or one owned by that person or organization)

*First, the named insured and resident family members are insured for liability coverage.* Coverage also applies to a spouse if a resident of the same household. In recognition of widespread divorce and separation found today, the PAP provides coverage for 90 days to a spouse who no longer resides in the named insured's household and is not listed as a named insured in the policy. If a spouse ceases to be a resident of the same household and is not listed as a named insured, the spouse is covered for 90 days following the change in residency, or until the spouse obtains a separate PAP or the policy period ends, whichever occurs first. If both spouses are named in the declarations as named insureds in the same PAP, the policy covers both spouses even though one spouse no longer resides in the same residence.

For example, Jennifer and James are married and live in the same residence. Jennifer is the named insured under her PAP policy. Assume that James is not listed as a named insured in her policy. He is still considered a named insured because he is Jennifer's husband. If the couple separates and James moves into another apartment, he is covered for 90 days under Jennifer's policy, or until he purchases his own policy, if earlier. However, if both were named insureds under the same PAP, James would continue to be covered as a named insured until the policy expires, or until he purchases his own policy, if earlier.

A family member is a person related to the named insured by blood, marriage, or adoption who resides in the same household, including a ward of the court or foster child. *Thus, the husband, wife, and children are covered while using any auto, owned or nonowned*. If the children are attending college and are temporarily away from home, they are still covered under their parents' policy.

*Second, any other person using the named insured's covered auto is also insured provided that person can establish a reasonable belief that permission to use the covered auto exists*. For example, John may have permitted his girlfriend, Susan, to drive his car several times over the past six months. If Susan uses John's car without his express permission, she is covered under his policy as long as she can show a reasonable belief that John would have given her permission to use the car.

*Third, coverage also applies to any person or organization legally responsible for any insured's use of a covered auto on behalf of that person or organization*. For example, assume that Mark drives his car on an errand for his employer and negligently injures another motorist. If the injured motorist sues Mark's employer, the employer has coverage under Mark's PAP.

*Finally, coverage applies to any person or organization legally responsible for the named insured's or family members' use of any auto or trailer (other than a covered auto or one owned by the person or organization)*. For example, assume that Mark borrows the car of a fellow worker to mail a package for his employer. If Mark negligently injures someone while using that car and the injured person sues Mark's employer, the employer has coverage under Mark's PAP. However, the PAP does not extend coverage to the employer when the named insured is using an auto owned by the employer. So if Mark is driving to the post office in a company car, the employer is not insured under Mark's PAP.

### Supplementary Payments

In addition to the policy limits and a legal defense, certain **supplementary payments** can be paid. They include the following:

- Up to $250 for the cost of a bail bond
- Premiums on appeal bonds and bonds to release attachments
- Interest accruing after a judgment
- Up to $200 daily for the loss of earnings
- Other reasonable expenses

Premiums on a bail bond can be paid up to $250 because of an auto accident that results in property damage or bodily injury. However, payment is not made for a traffic violation such as a speeding ticket except if an accident occurs. For example, assume Tyler is drunk and injures another motorist in an auto accident. If he is arrested, and bail is set at $2500, the insurer will pay the bail bond premium up to a maximum of $250.

Premiums on an appeal bond and a bond to release an attachment of property in any suit defended by the insurer are also paid as supplementary payments.

If interest accrues after a judgment is awarded, the interest is paid as a supplementary payment. Any prejudgment interest, however, is part of the liability limits.

The insurer will also pay up to $200 daily for the loss of earnings (but not other income) due to attendance at a hearing or trial at the insurer's request.

Finally, other reasonable expenses incurred at the insurer's request are paid. For example, you may be a defendant in a trial and the insurer may request that you testify. If you have meal or transportation expenses, they would be paid as a supplemental payment.

### Exclusions

A lengthy list of exclusions applies to the liability coverage under the PAP. They are summarized as follows:

1. *Intentional injury or damage.* Intentional bodily injury or property damage is specifically excluded. For example, a driver changes lanes suddenly without signaling and cuts sharply in front of Richard's car. Richard is enraged and deliberately rams the vehicle. The intentional property damage to the other driver's car is not covered by Richard's PAP. Unfortunately, "road rage" is widespread nationally and is responsible for numerous motor vehicle deaths.

2. *Property owned or transported.* Liability coverage is not provided to any person for damage to property owned or being transported by that person. For example, the suitcase and camera belonging to a friend may be damaged in an auto accident while you and your friend are on vacation together. The damage would not be covered by your PAP.

3. *Property rented, used, or in the insured's care.* Damage to property rented to, used by, or in the care of the insured is not covered. For example, if you rent some skis that are damaged in an auto accident, the property damage is not covered. The exclusion, however, does not apply to property damage to a residence or private garage. For example, if you rent a house and carelessly back into a partly opened garage door, the property damage to the door would be covered.

4. *Bodily injury to an employee.* Bodily injury to an employee of the insured who is injured during the course of employment is also excluded. The intent here is to cover the employee's injury under a workers compensation law. However, a domestic employee injured during the course of employment would be covered if workers compensation benefits are not required or available.

5. *Use as a public or livery conveyance.* Another exclusion is liability arising out of the ownership or operation of a vehicle while it is being used as a public or livery conveyance. The intent here is to exclude coverage if the insured makes the vehicle available for hire to the general public. For example, if you use your car as a public taxi, the exclusion applies. However, the exclusion does not apply to a share-the-expense carpool.

6. *Vehicles used in the auto business.* If a person is employed or engaged in the auto business, liability arising out of the operation of vehicles in the auto business is excluded. The auto business refers to the selling, repairing, servicing, storing, or parking of vehicles designed for use mainly on public highways. It also includes road testing and delivery. For example, assume you take your car to a garage for repairs. If a mechanic has an accident and injures someone while road testing your car, your PAP liability coverage does not protect the mechanic. However, if you are sued because you are the car owner, you are covered. The intent is to exclude loss exposures that should be covered under the auto repair firm's liability insurance.

The preceding exclusion does not apply to the operation, ownership, or use of a covered auto by the named insured, by any resident family member, or by any partner, agent, or employee of the named insured or family member. For example, if an auto mechanic has

an accident while driving his or her own car to pick up a repair part, the mechanic's PAP would cover the loss.

7. *Other business vehicles.* Liability coverage does not apply to any vehicle maintained or used in any other business (other than farming or ranching). This exclusion is similar to the preceding auto business exclusion except it applies to all other business use with certain exceptions. The intent here is to exclude liability coverage for commercial vehicles and trucks that are used in a business. For example, if you drive a city bus or operate a large cement truck, your PAP liability coverage does not apply.

The exclusion does not apply to an owned or nonowned private passenger auto, pickup, or van. Thus, you are covered if you drive your car on company business.

8. *Using a vehicle without reasonable belief of permission.* If a person uses a vehicle without a reasonable belief that he or she has permission to do so, the liability coverage does not apply. The exclusion does not apply to a family member who is using a covered auto owned by the named insured.

9. *Nuclear energy exclusion.* Liability of insureds who are covered under special nuclear energy contracts is also excluded.

10. *Vehicle with fewer than four wheels.* Liability coverage does not apply to any vehicle that has fewer than four wheels or is designed for use mainly off public roads. Thus, motorcycles, mopeds, motorscooters, minibikes, and trail bikes are excluded. However, the exclusion does not apply if the vehicle is being used in a medical emergency or to any *nonowned* golf cart. For example, if you rent a golf cart and injure another golfer, liability coverage applies.

11. *Vehicle furnished or made available for the named insured's regular use.* Liability coverage excludes a vehicle other than a covered auto that is owned by, furnished to, or made available for the named insured's regular use. You can occasionally drive another person's car and still have coverage under your policy. *However, if the nonowned auto is driven regularly or is furnished or made available for your regular use, your PAP liability coverage does not apply.* For example, if your employer furnishes you with a car, or if a

car is available for your regular use in a company carpool, the liability coverage does not apply. The key point is not how frequently you drive someone else's car, but whether it is furnished or made available for your regular use.

For an additional premium, the **extended nonowned coverage endorsement** can be added to the PAP that covers the insured while operating a nonowned auto on a regular basis.

12. *Vehicle owned by, furnished, or made available for the regular use of any family member.* This exclusion is similar to the preceding exclusion. However, it does not apply to the named insured and spouse. For example, if Mary borrows a car owned and insured by her son who lives with her, the liability coverage under Mary's PAP would cover her while driving the son's car.

13. *Racing vehicle.* Liability coverage does not apply to any vehicle while it is located inside a racing facility for the purpose of competing in or preparing for a prearranged racing or speed contest.

## Limit of Liability

As noted earlier, the PAP is typically written with split limits. That is, the amounts of insurance for bodily injury liability and property damage liability are stated separately. The maximum amount paid for bodily injury to each person is the amount shown in the declarations. Subject to that limit for each person, the maximum amount paid for bodily injury to all persons resulting from any one auto accident is the amount shown in the declarations. The maximum amount paid for property damage resulting from any one auto accident is also shown in the declarations.

## Out-of-State Coverage

An important provision applies if an accident occurs in a state other than where the covered auto is principally garaged. If the accident occurs in a state that has a financial responsibility law with higher liability limits than the limits shown in the declarations, the PAP automatically provides the higher specified limits.

Likewise, if the state has a compulsory insurance or similar law that requires a nonresident to have insurance whenever he or she uses a vehicle in

### Exhibit 22.1
**Primary and Excess Insurance**

Ken is the named insured and borrows Karen's car with her permission. Ken has $50,000 of liability insurance and Karen has a $100,000 limit. Both policies will cover any loss. Ken negligently injures another motorist and must pay damages of $125,000. *The rule is that insurance on the borrowed car is primary, and other insurance is excess.*

Each company pays as follows:

| | |
|---|---|
| Karen's insurer (primary) | $100,000 |
| Ken's insurer (excess) | $25,000 |
| Total | $125,000 |

that state, the PAP provides the required minimum amounts and types of coverage.

## Other Insurance

In some cases, more than one liability policy covers a loss. If other applicable liability insurance applies to an *owned vehicle*, the insurer pays only its pro rata share of the loss. The insurer's share is the proportion that its limit of liability bears to the total applicable limits of liability under all policies. However, if the insurance applies to a *nonowned vehicle*, the insurer's insurance is excess over any other collectible insurance (see Exhibit 22.1).

# PART B: MEDICAL PAYMENTS COVERAGE

**Medical payments coverage** is frequently included in the PAP. Medical payments are paid without regard to fault.

## Insuring Agreement

Under this provision, the company will pay all reasonable medical and funeral expenses incurred by an insured for services rendered within three years from the date of the accident. Covered expenses include medical, surgical, X-ray, dental, and funeral expenses. The benefit limits typically range from $1000 to $10,000 per person and apply to each insured who is injured in the accident.

Medical payments coverage is not based on fault. Thus, if you are injured in an auto accident and are at fault, medical payments can still be paid to you and to other injured passengers in the car.

### Insured Persons

Two groups are insured for medical payments coverage:

- Named insured and family members
- Other persons while occupying a covered auto

*The named insured and family members are covered if they are injured while occupying any motor vehicle or are injured as pedestrians when struck by a motor vehicle designed for use mainly on public roads.* For example, if the parents and children are injured in an auto accident while on vacation, their medical expenses are covered up to the policy limits. If the named insured or any family member is struck by a motor vehicle or trailer while walking, his or her medical expenses are also paid. However, if you are injured by a farm tractor, snowmobile, or bulldozer, your injuries are not covered because these vehicles are not designed for use mainly on public roads.

*Other persons are also covered for their medical expenses while occupying your covered auto.* For example, if you own your car and are the named insured, all passengers in your car are covered for their medical expenses under your policy. However, if you are operating a vehicle you do not own, other passengers in the car (other than family members) are not covered for their medical expenses under your policy. The intent here is to have other passengers in the nonowned vehicle seek protection under their own insurance or under the medical expense coverage that applies to the nonowned vehicle.

### Exclusions

Medical payments coverage has numerous exclusions. They are summarized as follows:

1. *Motorized vehicle with fewer than four wheels.* Bodily injury while occupying a motorized vehicle with fewer than four wheels is excluded. Occupying is defined in the policy as "in, upon, or getting in, on, out or off."
2. *Public or livery conveyance.* When a covered auto is used as a public or livery conveyance, the

medical payments coverage does not apply. The exclusion does not apply to a share-the-expense car pool.
3. *Using the vehicle as a residence.* Coverage does not apply if the injury occurs while the vehicle is being used as a residence or premises. For example, if you own and occupy a camper trailer as a residence in a campground while on vacation, medical expense coverage does not apply if you burn yourself while cooking on a stove in the trailer.
4. *Injury occurring during course of employment.* Coverage does not apply if the injury occurs during the course of employment and workers compensation benefits are required or available.
5. *Vehicle furnished or made available for the named insured's regular use.* Coverage does not apply to any injury sustained while occupying or when struck by a vehicle (other than a covered auto) that is owned by the named insured or is furnished or made available for the named insured's regular use. The intent here is to avoid providing "free" medical payments coverage on an owned or regularly used car not described in the policy.
6. *Vehicle furnished or made available for the regular use of any family member.* A similar exclusion applies to any vehicle (other than a covered auto) that is owned by any family member or is furnished or made available for the regular use of any family member. The exclusion does not apply to the named insured and spouse. For example, if a son living at home owns a car that is not insured for medical payments coverage, and the parents are injured while occupying the son's car, the parents' medical expenses would be covered under their policy.
7. *Using a vehicle without a reasonable belief of permission.* Coverage does not apply if the injury occurs while occupying a vehicle without a reasonable belief of being entitled to do so. The exclusion does not apply to a family member who is using a covered auto owned by the named insured.
8. *Vehicle used in the business of an insured.* Coverage does not apply to any injury sustained while occupying a vehicle when it is being used in the business of an insured. The intent here is to exclude medical payments coverage for

nonowned trucks and commercial vehicles used in the business of an insured person. The exclusion does not apply to a private passenger auto, to a pickup or van, or to a trailer used with any of the preceding vehicles.

9. *Nuclear weapon, radiation, or war.* Bodily injury from a nuclear weapon, nuclear radiation, or war is not covered.

10. *Racing vehicle.* Coverage does not apply to a bodily injury sustained while occupying a vehicle located inside a racing facility for the purpose of competing in or preparing for a prearranged racing or speed contest.

### Other Insurance

If other auto medical payments insurance applies to an *owned vehicle,* the insurer pays its pro rata share of the loss based on the proportion that its limits bear to the total applicable limits.

However, medical payments coverage is excess with respect to a *nonowned vehicle.* For example, assume that Kim is driving her car and picks up Patti for lunch. Kim loses control of the car and hits a tree, and Patti is injured. Patti's medical bills are $6000. Kim has $5000 of medical expenses coverage, and Patti has $10,000. Kim's insurer pays the first $5000 as primary insurer, and Patti's insurer pays the remaining $1000 as excess insurance.

## PART C: UNINSURED MOTORISTS COVERAGE

Some motorists are irresponsible and drive without liability insurance. Across the United States, if someone is injured in an auto accident, the chances are about one in seven that the at-fault driver is uninsured. According to the Insurance Research Council (IRC), the estimated percentage of uninsured motorists in the United States in 2009 was 13.8 percent. That number is down from 14.3 percent in 2008. The recession had an impact on the number of uninsured drivers, but the IRC study found that impact had declined in the last year analyzed (see Insight 22.1).

---

### INSIGHT 22.1

#### Recession Marked by Bump in Uninsured Motorists

*Approximately one in seven drivers across the United States may be driving uninsured, according to a recent study by the Insurance Research Council. The estimated percentage of uninsured drivers decreased for four straight years before increasing to 14.3 percent in 2008, and then dropping to 13.8 percent in 2009. The increasing percentage of uninsured drivers was attributable to the recession, according to the IRC.*

The study, *Uninsured Motorists, 2011 Edition,* estimates the percentage of uninsured drivers countrywide and by state for 2008 and 2009. The IRC estimates the uninsured driver population using a ratio of insurance claims made by individuals who were injured by uninsured drivers to claims made by individuals who were injured by insured drivers. The study contains recent statistics by state on uninsured motorists claim frequency, bodily injury liability claim frequency, and the ratio of uninsured motorists to bodily injury claim frequencies.

The magnitude of the uninsured motorists problem varied widely from state to state. In 2009, the five states with the highest uninsured driver estimates were Mississippi (28 percent), New Mexico (26 percent), Tennessee (24 percent), Oklahoma (24 percent), and Florida (24 percent). The five states with the lowest uninsured driver estimates were Massachusetts (4 percent), Maine (4 percent), New York (5 percent), Pennsylvania (7 percent), and Vermont (7 percent).

The report found a strong correlation between the percent of uninsured motorists and the unemployment rate; however, the impact leveled-off in the most recent year. "The percent of uninsured motorists is an unfortunate consequence of the economic downturn and illustrates how virtually everyone is affected by recent economic developments," said Elizabeth Sprinkel, Senior Vice President of the IRC. "Despite laws in many states requiring drivers to maintain insurance, about one in seven motorists remain uninsured. This forces responsible drivers who carry insurance to bear the burden of paying for injuries caused by drivers who carry no insurance at all."

The IRC study examined data collected from nine insurers, representing approximately 50 percent of the private passenger auto insurance market in the U.S.

SOURCE: Insurance Research Council, *Recession Marked by Bump in Uninsured Motorists,* News Release, April 21, 2011. Reprinted with permission.

There is wide variation in the percentage of uninsured drivers among the states. The IRC study showed that the estimated percentage of uninsured drivers ranged from a high of 28 percent in Mississippi to a low of 4 percent in Massachusetts and Maine (see Exhibit 22.2).

**Uninsured motorists coverage** pays for bodily injury (and property damage in some states) caused by an uninsured motorist, by a hit-and-run driver, or by a negligent driver whose insurance company is insolvent.

### Insuring Agreement

The insurer agrees to pay compensatory damages that an insured is legally entitled to receive from the owner or operator of an uninsured motor vehicle because of bodily injury caused by an accident. Damages include medical bills, lost wages, and compensation for a permanent disfigurement resulting from the accident. Several important points must be emphasized with respect to this coverage.

1. *The coverage applies only if the uninsured motorist is legally liable.* If the uninsured motorist is not liable, the insurer will not pay for the bodily injury.
2. *The insurer's maximum limit of liability for any single accident is the amount shown in the declarations.* You cannot receive duplicate payments for the same elements of loss under the uninsured motorists coverage and Part A (liability coverage) or Part B (medical payments coverage) of the policy, or any underinsured motorists coverage provided by the policy. Also, you cannot receive a duplicate payment for any element of loss for which payment has been made by or on behalf of persons or organizations legally responsible for the accident. Finally, the insurer will not pay you for any part of a loss if you are entitled to be paid for that part of the loss under a workers compensation or disability benefits law.
3. *The claim is subject to arbitration if the insured and insurer disagree over the amount of damages or whether the insured is entitled*

### Exhibit 22.2
**Estimated Percentage of Uninsured Motorists in the United States in 2009**

| State | Uninsured | State | Uninsured | State | Uninsured |
|---|---|---|---|---|---|
| Mississippi | 28% | Maryland | 15% | Virginia | 11% |
| New Mexico | 26% | Texas | 15% | Delaware | 11% |
| Tennessee | 24% | Illinois | 15% | South Carolina | 11% |
| Oklahoma | 24% | Wisconsin | 15% | Wyoming | 10% |
| Florida | 24% | Missouri | 14% | Oregon | 10% |
| Alabama | 22% | North Carolina | 14% | Kansas | 10% |
| Michigan | 19% | Nevada | 13% | Connecticut | 10% |
| Kentucky | 18% | Minnesota | 13% | North Dakota | 9% |
| Rhode Island | 18% | Alaska | 13% | South Dakota | 9% |
| Indiana | 16% | Louisiana | 13% | Utah | 8% |
| Washington | 16% | Arizona | 12% | Idaho | 8% |
| Arkansas | 16% | Iowa | 11% | Nebraska | 8% |
| Ohio | 16% | Montana | 11% | Vermont | 7% |
| Georgia | 16% | Hawaii | 11% | Pennsylvania | 7% |
| District of Columbia | 15% | New Jersey | 11% | New York | 5% |
| Colorado | 15% | New Hampshire | 11% | Maine | 4% |
| California | 15% | West Virginia | 11% | Massachusetts | 4% |

SOURCE: Insurance Research Council, *Recession Marked by Bump in Uninsured Motorists*, News Release, April 21, 2011. Reprinted with permission.

*to receive any damages*. However, both the insured and insurer must agree to arbitration. Under this provision, each party selects an arbitrator. The two arbitrators select a third arbitrator. A decision by two of the three arbitrators is binding on all parties. However, the decision is binding only if the damages awarded do not exceed the state's minimum financial responsibility law limits.

4. *Some states also include coverage for property damage from an uninsured motorist in their uninsured motorists law*. In these states, if an uninsured driver runs a red light and smashes into your car, the property damage to the car would be covered under your uninsured motorists coverage, subject to any applicable deductible.

There is considerable variation among the states that include property damage coverage in their uninsured motorists law. In some states, property damage coverage is an optional coverage that is purchased separately from the regular uninsured motorists coverage. In other states, both bodily injury and property damage coverages are included together in the uninsured motorists coverage; however, the insured may have the option of waiving the coverage if it is not desired. Finally, the property damage is subject to a deductible.

## Insured Persons

Three groups are covered under the uninsured motorists coverage:

- The named insured and his or her family members
- Any other person while occupying a covered auto
- Any person legally entitled to recover damages because of bodily injury to a person described previously

First, the named insured and his or her family members are covered if they are injured by an uninsured motorist. Second, any other person who is injured while occupying a covered auto is also an insured; the coverage applies only if the individual is occupying a covered auto. Finally, any person legally entitled to recover damages because of bodily injury or death to a previously described person is also insured. An individual may not be physically involved in the accident but may be

entitled to recover damages from the person or organization legally responsible for the bodily injury of the insured person. For example, if the named insured is killed by an uninsured motorist, the surviving spouse could collect damages under the uninsured motorists coverage.

## Uninsured Vehicles

An extremely important provision defines an uninsured motor vehicle. Four groups of vehicles are considered to be uninsured vehicles:

1. An uninsured vehicle is a motor vehicle or trailer for which no bodily injury liability insurance policy applies at the time of the accident.
2. A bodily injury liability policy may be in force on a vehicle. However, the amount of insurance on that vehicle may be less than the amount required by the state's financial responsibility law in the state where the named insured's covered auto is principally garaged. This vehicle is also considered to be an uninsured motor vehicle.
3. A hit-and-run vehicle is also considered to be an uninsured vehicle. Thus, if the named insured or any family member is struck by a hit-and-run driver while occupying a covered auto or a nonowned auto, or while walking, the uninsured motorists coverage will pay for the injury.
4. Another uninsured vehicle is one to which a bodily injury liability policy applies at the time of the accident, but the insurer denies coverage or becomes insolvent. For example, assume that you are involved in an auto accident, and the other driver is at-fault. If the negligent driver's insurer denies coverage, you can file a claim under the uninsured motorist coverage in your own policy. Likewise, if you have a valid claim against a negligent driver, but his or her insurer becomes insolvent before the claim is paid, your uninsured motorists coverage would pay the claim.

## Exclusions

Uninsured motorists coverage has several general exclusions, summarized as follows:

1. *No uninsured motorists coverage on vehicle*. Coverage does not apply to an insured while

occupying or when struck by a motor vehicle owned by that insured, which is not insured for this coverage under the policy.

2. *Primary coverage under another policy.* Family members are not covered while they are occupying a vehicle owned by the named insured, which is insured for uninsured motorists' coverage on a primary basis under another policy. The intent here is to have such family members seek protection under the policy insuring the vehicle that they are occupying.

3. *Settling a claim without the insurer's consent.* If an insured or legal representative settles a bodily injury claim without the insurer's consent, and the settlement jeopardizes the insurer's right to recover a loss payment, the uninsured motorists coverage does not apply. The purpose of this exclusion is to protect the insurer's subrogation rights.

4. *Using the vehicle as a public or livery conveyance.* If an insured occupies a covered auto when it is being used as a public or livery conveyance, coverage does not apply. The exclusion does not apply to a share-the-expense car pool.

5. *No reasonable belief of permission.* Coverage does not apply to any insured who is using a vehicle without a reasonable belief that he or she is entitled to do so. This exclusion does not apply to a family member who is using a covered auto owned by the named insured.

6. *No benefit to workers compensation insurer.* The uninsured motorists coverage cannot directly or indirectly benefit a workers compensation insurer or self-insurer. A workers compensation insurer may have a legal right of action against a third party who has injured an employee. If an uninsured driver injures an employee who receives workers compensation benefits, the workers compensation insurer could sue the uninsured driver or attempt to make a claim under the injured employee's uninsured motorists coverage. This exclusion prevents the uninsured motorists coverage from providing benefits to the workers compensation insurer.

7. *No punitive damages.* The PAP excludes payment for punitive or exemplary damages under the uninsured motorists coverage.

### Other Insurance

The PAP contains a number of complex provisions that apply when more than one uninsured motorist coverage applies to the loss. These provisions are summarized as follows:

- The maximum amount paid is limited to the highest limit of any of the policies that provide uninsured motorists coverage.
- If an insurer provides uninsured motorists coverage on a *vehicle not owned by the named insured, the insurance provided is excess over any collectible insurance providing insurance on a primary basis.* For example, Jeffrey has an uninsured motorists coverage limit of $25,000, and Ashley has an uninsured motorists coverage limit of $50,000. If Jeffrey is injured by an uninsured driver while occupying Ashley's car and has bodily injuries of $60,000, Ashley's policy is primary and pays $50,000. Jeffrey's insurer pays the remaining $10,000 as excess insurance.
- When the named insured's policy and the other policy provide uninsured motorists coverage on a *primary basis,* each policy pays its pro rata share of the loss. Each insurer's share is the proportion that its limit of liability bears to the total of all applicable limits of liability for coverage provided on a primary basis.
- When the named insured's policy and the other policy provide uninsured motorists coverage on an *excess basis,* each policy also pays its pro rata share of the loss. Each insurer's share is the proportion that its limit of liability bears to the total of all applicable limits of liability for coverage provided on an excess basis.

### Underinsured Motorists Coverage

**Underinsured motorists coverage** can be added to the PAP to provide more complete protection. Underinsured motorists coverage applies when a negligent third-party driver carries liability insurance, but the limits carried are less than the insured's actual damages for bodily injury.

An underinsured vehicle is defined as a vehicle to which a liability policy applies at the time of the accident, but the liability limits carried are less than the limits provided by the insured's underinsured motorists coverage. The maximum amount paid for bodily injury under the coverage varies among the states. *In general, the maximum amount paid is the underinsured motorists coverage limit stated in the policy less the amount paid by the negligent driver's insurer.* For example, assume that Kristen adds underinsured motorists coverage to her policy in the amount of $100,000. She is injured by a negligent driver who has liability limits of $25,000/$50,000, which satisfy the state's minimum required bodily injury limits. If her bodily injury damages are $100,000, she would receive only $25,000 from the negligent driver's insurer, because that amount is the driver's applicable limit of liability. However, she would receive another $75,000 from her insurer under her underinsured motorists coverage.

However, assume that Kristen's bodily injury damages are $125,000. The maximum amount she would collect under the underinsured motorists coverage is still only $75,000, which is the difference between the $100,000 limit under her underinsured motorists coverage and the $25,000 collected from the negligent driver's insurer (see preceding rule). To collect the full amount of her injury, Kristen should have carried limits of at least $125,000.

Underinsured motorists coverage endorsements are not uniform among the states. In some states, underinsured motorists coverage can be added as an endorsement to the PAP to complement the coverage provided by the uninsured motorists coverage. In other states, a single endorsement provides both uninsured and underinsured coverage and replaces uninsured motorists coverage that is part of the standard PAP. In addition, some states make the underinsured motorists coverage mandatory, while other states make it optional. Finally, the available or required limits for underinsured motorists coverage also vary by state.

## PART D: COVERAGE FOR DAMAGE TO YOUR AUTO

Part D (**coverage for damage to your auto**) provides coverage for damage or theft of an auto.

### Insuring Agreement

The insurer agrees to pay for any direct and accidental loss to a covered auto or any nonowned auto as defined in the insuring agreement, including their

equipment, less any deductible. If two autos insured under the same policy are damaged in the same accident, only one deductible must be met. If the deductible amounts are different, the higher deductible will apply. *Two optional coverages are available: (1) collision coverage and (2) other-than-collision coverage (also called comprehensive).* A collision loss is covered only if the declarations page indicates that collision coverage is provided for that auto. Likewise, coverage for an other-than-collision loss is in force only if the declarations page indicates that other-than-collision coverage is provided for that auto.

**Collision Loss**   **Collision** *is defined as the upset of your covered auto or nonowned auto or its impact with another vehicle or object.* The following are examples of a collision loss:

- You lose control of your car on an icy road, and it overturns.
- Your car hits another car, a telephone pole, a tree, or a building.
- Your car is parked, and you find the rear fender dented when you return.
- You open your car door in a parking lot, and the door is damaged when it hits the vehicle parked next to you.

*Collision losses are paid regardless of fault.* If you cause the accident, your insurer will pay for the damage to your car, less any deductible. If the other driver damages your car, you can either collect from the negligent driver (or from his or her insurer), or look to your insurer to pay the claim. If you collect from your own insurer, you must give up subrogation rights to your insurer, who will then attempt to collect from the negligent party who caused the accident. If the entire amount of the loss is recovered, your insurer will refund the deductible.

**Other-Than-Collision Loss**   The PAP can be written to cover an **other-than-collision loss**. The PAP distinguishes between a collision and an other-than-collision loss. This distinction is important because some car owners do not wish to pay for collision coverage on their cars. Also, the deductibles under the two coverages may be different. Other-than-collision coverage is frequently written with a lower deductible.

Loss from any of the following perils is considered to be an other-than-collision loss:

- Missiles or falling objects
- Fire
- Theft or larceny
- Explosion or earthquake
- Windstorm
- Hail, water, or flood
- Malicious mischief or vandalism
- Riot or civil commotion
- Contact with a bird or animal
- Glass breakage.

These perils are self-explanatory, but a few comments are in order. Theft of the vehicle is covered, including the theft of equipment, such as wheel covers, tires, or a stereo. Theft of an air bag from a covered vehicle parked on the street is also covered.

Colliding with a bird or animal is not a collision loss. Thus, if you hit a bird or deer with your car, the physical damage to the car is considered to be an other-than-collision loss.

Finally, if glass breakage is caused by a collision, you can elect to have it covered as a collision loss. This distinction is important because both coverages (collision loss and other-than-collision loss) are written with deductibles. Without this qualification, you would have to pay two deductibles if the car has both body damage and glass breakage in the same accident. By treating glass breakage as part of the collision loss, only the collision deductible must be satisfied.

**Nonowned Auto** The Part D coverages also apply to a nonowned auto. As defined in Part D, a **nonowned auto** *is a private passenger auto, pickup, van, or trailer not owned by or furnished or made available for the regular use of the named insured or family member, while it is in the custody of or is being operated by the named insured or family member.* For example, if Tom borrows Mike's car, Tom's collision coverage and other-than-collision coverage on his car apply to the borrowed car. However, Tom's insurance is excess over any physical damage insurance on the borrowed car.

Part D coverages apply only if the nonowned auto is not furnished or made available for the regular use of the named insured or family members. The courts generally have ruled that a vehicle is not furnished or made available for your regular use if you must ask permission every time you use the vehicle. Thus, you can occasionally drive a nonowned vehicle with permission, and your Part D coverages will apply to the borrowed vehicle. *However, if the vehicle is driven on a regular basis or is furnished or made available for your regular use, the Part D coverages do not apply.* The key point here is not how frequently you drive a nonowned auto, but whether the vehicle is furnished or made available for your regular use.

The Part D coverages also apply to a temporary substitute vehicle, which is also considered in Part D to be a nonowned auto. A temporary substitute vehicle is a nonowned auto or trailer that is used as a temporary replacement for a covered auto that is out of normal use because of its breakdown, repair, servicing, loss, or destruction. *Thus, the Part D coverages that apply to a covered auto also apply to a temporary substitute vehicle.* For example, if your car is in the shop for repairs, and you are furnished a loaner car, your physical damage insurance also applies to the loaner car.

If you have an accident while operating a nonowned auto, the PAP provides the broadest physical damage coverage applicable to any covered auto shown in the declarations. For example, assume that you own two cars. One vehicle is insured for both collision and other-than-collision, and the other is insured only for other-than-collision. If you drive a nonowned auto, the borrowed vehicle is covered for both collision and other-than-collision losses.

**Collision Damage Waiver on Rental Cars** Our discussion of collision insurance on nonowned cars would not be complete without a brief discussion of the collision damage waiver (CDW) on rental cars. This coverage is sometimes called a loss damage waiver (LDW). When you rent a car and check the CDW box, you are relieved of financial responsibility if the rental car is damaged or stolen. However, the rental agreement contains numerous restrictions. The CDW may be void even when checked if you cause an accident by speeding, driving while intoxicated, or driving on unpaved roads. The CDW is expensive and can easily increase the daily rental cost by $15, $20, or some higher amount.

Should you purchase the CDW if you rent a car? Many consumer experts say the CDW is not needed if (1) you carry collision and comprehensive insurance on your own car because the coverages also apply to the rental car, and (2) certain credit cards cover the physical damage or theft of a rental car on an excess basis if the card is used to rent the car.

The preceding view that the CDW may be unnecessary is not uniform among all financial advisors. In particular, the Independent Insurance Agents & Brokers of America, an association of independent property/casualty insurance agents and brokers, says consumers in general should purchase the CDW, at least for short-term rentals. Because of numerous restrictive provisions in the rental agreement, incomplete protection under the PAP, and credit card limitations, the organization believes consumers generally should buy the CDW even if it is costly (see Insight 22.2).

**Deductible**   The collision coverage is typically written with a straight deductible of $250, $500, or some higher amount. Coverage for other-than-collision losses is also normally written with a deductible. Deductibles are designed to prevent small claims, hold down premiums, and encourage the insured to be careful in protecting the car from damage or theft.

### Transportation Expenses

Part D also pays for temporary transportation expenses. The insurer will pay, without application of a deductible, up to $20 daily to a maximum of $600 for temporary transportation expenses incurred by the insured because of loss to a covered auto. Payments can be made for a train, bus, taxi, rental car, or other transportation expense. *Transportation*

---

## INSIGHT 22.2

### Top 10 Reasons to Purchase the Rental Car Damage Waiver

Although most collision damage waiver (CDW) or loss damage waiver (LDW) fees are considered outrageous, the insured is best advised to purchase the CDW/LDW for short-term rentals. This is not only in the best interest of the insured, but also the agent since an inadequately covered loss may result in the loss of an account or worse, an E&O claim. This is becoming increasingly the case as rental car companies charge ever-higher fees and penalties for occurrences not covered by most auto policies.

- *Loss Valuation.* The value of a rental car, according to virtually all rental agreements, is determined solely at the discretion of the rental company and may be significantly different from the "ACV" basis used by most auto policies. The ISO Personal Auto Policy (PAP) covers the lesser of the "actual cash value" of the vehicle or the amount "necessary" to repair or replace the damaged property. The rental agreement may very well contractually obligate the insured to reimburse the lessor for the "full value" (whatever that is) of the vehicle. Under the current PAP, the "betterment" clause may result in the insured being significantly underinsured relative to his/her obligations under the rental agreement.
- *Loss Settlement.* As implied above, there may very well be disagreement over the value of the vehicle or the amount charged for labor and materials to repair the property—depending on the PAP edition, the Appraisal clause may

be invoked by the insurer with its accompanying costs covered partially by the insured. More importantly, the PAP insurer has the right to "*inspect and appraise the damaged property before its repair or disposal*"—the rental company may choose to effect the repairs immediately, potentially resulting in a lack of PAP coverage because of failure to comply with the condition cited above. In a recent claim involving farm equipment under a similar policy provision, the insurer denied coverage when the farmer had the property repaired immediately in order to minimize lost production and the insurer never had the opportunity to appraise the damage.

- *Loss Payment.* The rental agreement may require immediate reimbursement for damages, and it is not uncommon for the rental company to charge the insured's credit card. This can create a significant debt, "max" out the card's credit limit (perhaps shortening a vacation or business trip), result in litigation, etc.
- *Loss Damage Waivers (LDW).* The rental agreement usually requires reimbursement for more than collision, making the insured responsible for ANY "loss" in value beyond normal wear and tear regardless of fault. Obviously, the PAP must include collision coverage on at least one insured owned vehicle for collision coverage to transfer to the nonowned auto. If the rental agreement includes a Loss (not just Collision) Damage Waiver (LDW), the policy must also include comprehensive

*(Continued)*

## INSIGHT 22.2   (Continued)

coverage to protect the insured. Even so, keep in mind that the insured's contractual liability under the rental agreement may be almost absolute, so it's possible the PAP may not respond to all losses. *(Note: Likewise, the PAP might respond to losses not covered by the LDW such as use off paved roads, use while intoxicated, use by unlisted drivers such as valet parking (see below), etc. Therefore, it is important to have BOTH PAP and LDW coverage.)*

- **Indirect Losses.** The insured most likely will be responsible for the rental company's loss of rental income on the damaged unit. The PAP has, at best, daily and maximum caps for this indirect loss and, depending on the edition date, an unendorsed policy or proprietary company form may pay only for loss of income resulting from theft. In addition, many rental companies will not divulge their fleet utilization logs for competitive reasons, or their rental agreements may make the renter responsible for loss of use without regard to fleet utilization rates. If so, the renter may be charged even though unused rental vehicles are sitting on the lot. In one case, a renter was hit with a $2000 loss of use charge, far more than what her PAP covered.

  In addition, rental car companies are increasingly inclined to charge for "diminution of value," an indirect loss that is not covered by the PAP's physical damage section (nor by most credit card coverages). We have seen documented examples of these charges for amounts of $5000 and almost $8000 and heard of one that was allegedly $15,000 on an upscale SUV rental.

- **Administrative Expenses.** The rental contract may make the insured liable for various "administrative" or loss-related expenses such as towing (e.g., one insured was charged for a 230-mile tow), storage, appraisal, claims adjustment, etc. None of these expenses are typically covered by the PAP.

- **Other Insurance.** The PAP says it is excess over: (1) any coverage provided by the owner of the auto (does "coverage" include rental car company self-insured plans?), (2) any other applicable physical damage insurance, and (3) any other source of recovery applicable to the loss—CDW/LDW, travel policies, credit card coverages, etc. (what if the credit card coverage says it's excess over the auto policy?). The potential controversy over who pays what is obvious and can result in litigation. In addition, keep in mind that many states (e.g., MD, MN, NY, TN) have statutes, proprietary forms, and/or case law precedents that may govern this and other rental car exposures. For example, the

PAP is primary rather than excess for nonowned autos loaned or rented by a dealer, but not rental agencies. Another state makes the PAP primary only if the auto is rented without purchasing a damage waiver. Another state only modifies the PAP with regard to liability for rental cars, not physical damage. Another state makes no exceptions for any nonowned autos including rentals. Needless to say, since the PAP Out of State condition says the policy will comply with state laws, it can become virtually impossible to know whether the PAP will respond on a primary or excess basis in a given state while on a trip . . . yet another reason to rely on the rental company's damage waiver.

- **Excluded Vehicles & Territories.** The PAP normally does not provide physical damage coverage for motorcycles or other non-auto/pickup/van vehicles (e.g., motorhomes) and use of covered vehicles is limited to the U.S., its territories and possessions, Puerto Rico, and Canada (the rental agreement may also exclude operation outside a specific geographical area, in which case the PAP could provide coverage not provided for under an LDW). In addition, if the insured is renting a trailer (U-Haul, camper trailer, etc.), PAP coverage is typically limited to only $500–$1,500. The insured usually has no choice but to rely on the rental company's damage waiver for coverage under these circumstances.

- **Excluded Uses and Drivers.** The PAP may have limitations on use of vehicles that are not otherwise excluded by the rental agreement damage waiver—for example, some older editions of the PAP (and perhaps some proprietary company forms) provide no physical damage coverage for the business use of nonowned pickup trucks or vans. Also, the PAP may include an exclusionary endorsement for certain individuals or may apply only to designated individuals that can be covered by listing them on the rental agreement. In contrast, the damage waiver usually only applies to designated individuals (with certain omnibus "insureds" such as spouses), so having both a PAP and the damage waiver can again be advantageous.

- **Additional and/or Future Costs.** The PAP will most certainly include a deductible in the range of $100–$500 or more. In addition, payment for damage to a rental car may result in a significant premium increase (if not nonrenewal) via surcharges or loss of credits.

SOURCE: *Adaptation of Top 10 Reasons to Purchase the Rental Car Damage Waiver*, Virtual University, Independent Insurance Agents & Brokers of America, Inc., 2009.

*expenses resulting from a collision loss are paid if the auto is covered by collision coverage. Likewise, transportation expenses resulting from an other-than-collision loss are paid if the auto is covered by other-than-collision loss coverage.*

The coverage also includes payment of any expenses for which the insured is legally responsible because of loss to a nonowned auto, such as the loss of daily rent on a rental car.

Finally, if the loss is caused by the theft of a covered auto or nonowned auto, expenses incurred during the first 48 hours after the theft occurred are not covered. If the loss is caused by a peril other than theft, expenses incurred during the first 24 hours after the auto has been withdrawn from use are not covered.

Coverage for *towing and labor costs* can be added by an endorsement. This coverage pays for towing and labor costs if a covered auto or nonowned auto breaks down, provided the labor is performed at the place of breakdown. The breakdown can be for any reason, and the amount paid is the amount shown in the endorsement. For example, if you call a repair truck because your car fails to start, the labor costs and any towing costs will be paid up to the policy limits. Labor costs, however, are covered only for work done at the place of the breakdown. Charges for gasoline or a battery provided at the breakdown site are not covered. Also, the cost of repairs at a service station or garage is not covered.

## Exclusions

Numerous exclusions apply to the Part D coverages, summarized as follows:

1. *Use as a public or livery conveyance.* Loss to a covered auto or any nonowned auto is excluded while the vehicle is being used as a public or livery conveyance. For example, if you use your car as a public taxi, the exclusion applies. Again, the exclusion does not apply to a share-the-expense carpool.
2. *Damage from wear and tear, freezing, and mechanical or electrical breakdown.* There is no coverage for any damage due to wear and tear, freezing, mechanical or electrical breakdown, or road damage to tires. The intent here is to exclude the normal maintenance cost of operating an auto. However, the exclusion does

not apply to the theft of a covered auto or any nonowned auto. For example, if a stolen car is recovered but the electrical system is damaged by a thief who hot-wired the car, the loss is covered.

3. *Radioactive contamination or war.* Damage from radioactive contamination or war is excluded.
4. *Electronic equipment.* The PAP expands coverage of certain types of electronic equipment. New cars often include electronic equipment such as navigational systems, video entertainment systems, and Internet access systems. Because the electronic equipment is permanently attached to the vehicle, insureds expect that the PAP will cover such equipment.

Coverage of electronic equipment is somewhat complicated. The PAP first excludes loss to electronic equipment that reproduces, receives, or transmits audio, visual, or data signals. The policy provides examples of excluded equipment, including but not limited, to the following:

- Radios and stereos
- Tape decks
- Compact disc systems
- Navigation systems
- Internet access systems
- Personal computer
- Video entertainment systems
- Telephones
- Televisions
- Two-way mobile radios
- Scanners
- Citizens band radios

*However, the above exclusion does not apply to electronic equipment that is permanently installed in a covered auto or nonowned auto. Thus, there is coverage of such equipment if the equipment is permanently installed in the vehicle.* Note that a car telephone must be permanently installed for coverage to apply. Thus, a portable cell phone that many people keep in their cars would not be covered.

Mounting evidence indicates that using a cell phone or texting while driving can be extremely dangerous. According to the National Highway Traffic Safety Administration, more than 3000 people died in 2010 because of "distracted driving."[2] Survey results released by State Farm in 2012 found that only 43 percent of drivers 16 and 17 years old said they had never texted while driving, while 64 percent of drivers aged 18 to 29 said they had texted while driving.[3] A 2009 study by the Virginia Tech Transportation Institute found that the collision risk became 23 times higher when the drivers were texting.[4] A University of Utah study found that drivers using cell phones also contribute to traffic congestion because they drive more slowly and are less likely to pass slow-moving vehicles.[5] Problems caused by using cell phones and texting while driving led to the National Transportation Safety Board to call for banning their use while driving (see Insight 22.3).

5. *Tapes, records, and discs.* Loss to stereo tapes, records, discs, or other media designed for use with the electronic equipment described previously is also excluded. An endorsement can be added to the PAP to cover excluded tapes, records, and discs.

6. *Government destruction or confiscation.* The PAP excludes total loss to a covered auto or non-owned auto due to destruction or confiscation by a governmental or civil authority. For example, if a federal drug agency confiscates a drug dealer's car, the loss would not be covered.

7. *Trailer, camper body, or motor home.* The PAP excludes loss to a trailer, camper body, or motor home not shown in the declarations. This exclusion also applies to facilities and equipment, such as cooking, dining, plumbing or refrigeration equipment, and awnings or cabanas.

## INSIGHT 22.3

### No Call, No Text, No Update Behind the Wheel: NTSB Calls for Nationwide Ban on PEDs while Driving

DECEMBER 13, 2011

Following today's Board meeting on the 2010 multi-vehicle highway accident in Gray Summit, Missouri, the National Transportation Safety Board (NTSB) called for the first-ever nationwide ban on driver use of **portable electronic devices (PEDs)** while operating a motor vehicle.

The safety recommendation specifically calls for the 50 states and the District of Columbia to ban the nonemergency use of portable electronic devices (other than those designed to support the driving task) for all drivers. The safety recommendation also urges use of the NHTSA model of high-visibility enforcement to support these bans and implementation of targeted communication campaigns to inform motorists of the new law and heightened enforcement.

"According to NHTSA, more than 3,000 people lost their lives last year in distraction-related accidents", said Chairman Deborah A.P. Hersman. "It is time for all of us to stand up for safety by turning off electronic devices when driving."

"No call, no text, no update, is worth a human life."

On August 5, 2010, on a section of Interstate 44 in Gray Summit, Missouri, a pickup truck ran into the back of a truck-tractor that had slowed due to an active construction zone. The pickup truck, in turn, was struck from behind by a school bus. That school bus was then hit by a second school bus that had been following. As a result, two people died and 38 others were injured.

The NTSB's investigation revealed that the pickup driver sent and received 11 text messages in the 11 minutes preceding the accident. The last text was received moments before the pickup struck the truck-tractor.

The Missouri accident is the most recent distraction accident the NTSB has investigated. However, the first investigation involving distraction from a wireless electronic device occurred in 2002, when a novice driver, distracted by a conversation on her cell phone, veered off the roadway in Largo, Maryland, crossed the median, flipped the car over, and killed five people.

Since then, the NTSB has seen the deadliness of distraction across all modes of transportation.

- In 2004, an experienced motorcoach driver, distracted on his hands-free cell phone, failed to move to the center lane and struck the underside of an arched stone bridge on the George Washington Parkway in Alexandria, Virginia. Eleven of the 27 high school students were injured.
- In the 2008 collision of a commuter train with a freight train in Chatsworth, California, the commuter train engineer, who had a history of using his cell phone for personal communications while on duty, ran a red signal while texting. That train collided head-on with a freight train—killing 25 and injuring dozens.
- In 2009, two airline pilots were out of radio communication with air traffic control for more than an hour because they were distracted by their personal laptops. They overflew their destination by more than 100 miles, only realizing their error when a flight attendant inquired about preparing for arrival.

- In Philadelphia in 2010, a barge being towed by a tugboat ran over an amphibious "duck" boat in the Delaware River, killing two Hungarian tourists. The tugboat mate failed to maintain a proper lookout due to repeated use of a cell-phone and laptop computer.
- In 2010, near Munfordville, Kentucky, a truck-tractor in combination with a 53-foot-long trailer, left its lane, crossed the median and collided with a 15-passenger van. The truck driver failed to maintain control of his vehicle because he was distracted by use of his cell-phone. The accident resulted in 11 fatalities.

In the last two decades, there has been exponential growth in the use of cell-phone and portable electronic devices. Globally, there are 5.3 billion mobile phone subscribers or 77 percent of the world population. In the United States, that percentage is even higher—it exceeds 100 percent.

Further, a Virginia Tech Transportation Institute study of commercial drivers found that a safety-critical event is 163 times more likely if a driver is texting, e-mailing, or accessing the Internet.

"The data is clear; the time to act is now. How many more lives will be lost before we, as a society, change our attitudes about the deadliness of distractions?" Hersman said.

A synopsis of the NTSB report, including the probable cause, findings, and a complete list of the safety recommendations, will be available online after the meeting.

The NTSB's full report will be available on the website in several weeks.

SOURCE: NTSB Press Release, Dec. 13, 2011.

---

For example, damage to a stove or refrigerator is not covered.

The exclusion does not apply to a nonowned trailer. Likewise, it does not apply to a trailer or camper body acquired during the policy period provided that you notify the insurer within 14 days after you become the owner.

8. *Loss to a nonowned auto used without reasonable belief of permission.* Loss to a nonowned auto is not covered when it is used by the named insured or his or her family member without a reasonable belief of permission.

9. *Radar detection equipment.* Equipment for the detection or location of radar or laser is excluded. This exclusion is justified on the basis that radar detection equipment circumvents state and local speed laws.

10. *Custom furnishings or equipment.* Loss to customized furnishings or equipment in or upon a pickup or van is not covered. Such furnishings or equipment include special carpeting, furniture or bars, height-extending roofs, and custom murals or paintings.

In 2009, ISO introduced an optional endorsement that insurers can use, which replaces this exclusion. The present exclusion of custom furnishings or equipment applies only to pickups and vans. The new endorsement redefines custom equipment and now applies to all vehicles. However, the endorsement provides $1500 of coverage for items that qualify as custom equipment.[6]

11. *Nonowned auto used in the auto business.* Loss to a nonowned auto maintained or used by someone engaged in the business of selling, repairing, servicing, storing, or parking vehicles designed for use on public highways is specifically excluded. For example, if the insured is a mechanic who damages a customer's car while road testing it, the loss is not covered under the mechanic's PAP. Instead, this business loss exposure should be covered under a commercial garage policy.

12. *Racing vehicle.* Loss to a covered auto or non-owned auto is not covered while it is located inside a racing facility for the purpose of competing in or preparing for a prearranged racing or speed contest.

13. *Rental car.* Loss to or loss of use of a vehicle rented by the named insured or family member is not covered if a state law or rental agreement precludes the car rental agency from recovering from the named insured or family member.

## Limit of Liability

The amount paid for a physical damage loss to a covered vehicle is the lower of (1) actual cash value of the damaged or stolen property, or (2) amount necessary to replace the property with other property of like kind and quality. If the cost of repairs exceeds the vehicle's actual cash value, the vehicle may be declared a constructive total loss, and the amount paid is the actual cash value less the deductible. In practice, insurers declare a vehicle to be a total loss if the estimated cost of repairs plus the salvage value exceeds the actual cash value of the car.

For a partial loss, such as a smashed fender, only the amount necessary to repair or replace the damaged property with property of like kind and quality will be paid. A car can be repaired with parts manufactured by the original equipment manufacturer (*OEM*) or with generic auto parts (also called *after market parts*). Some policyholders believe that generic auto parts are of lower quality than OEM parts, which has resulted in a number of lawsuits against auto insurers. However, in 2005, the Illinois Supreme Court ruled that insurers are free to use less expensive generic auto parts to repair damaged cars and trucks.

Most states now require insurers to notify policyholders when generic auto parts are used to repair the vehicle. Insurance company practices differ in this regard. In some cases, policyholders can pay the difference between OEM parts and generic parts and have the vehicle repaired with OEM parts. Some auto insurers offer policyholders a choice between OEM parts and generic parts by an endorsement to the policy. Some insurers always use OEM parts, while others use OEM parts for repairing new or late model cars. You should contact your agent and inquire about the claim settlement practices of your company so you know what to expect if your car is damaged.

The PAP also has limits on the amount paid for certain losses. Loss to a nonowned trailer is limited to $1500. Loss to equipment designed for the reproduction of sound, which is installed in locations not used by the auto manufacturer for such equipment, is limited to $1000.

**Betterment**    If the value of the vehicle is increased after repairs are completed (such as repainting the entire car when only one fender and door are damaged), the insurer will not pay for the **betterment** or increase in value.

**Diminution in Value**    A car damaged in an auto accident may have a reduced market or resale value. In recent years, many insureds have requested payment for the loss in market value. The Insurance Services Office has prepared a clarifying endorsement that insurers can add to the policy. The endorsement states that any loss in market or resale value (also called **diminution in value**) from a direct and accidental physical damage loss to a covered auto is not covered.

Finally, many consumers finance the purchase of a new car by a bank loan or lease the car for a specified period. The value of a new car declines substantially during the first year because of depreciation. Also, the collision deductible on a leased car may be $500 or higher. If a new car is totaled in an accident shortly after purchase, the amount paid by the insurer may be substantially less than the payoff amount of the loan or lease. As a result, you could owe a bank or other financial institution hundreds or thousands of dollars. This risk can be handled by **gap insurance,** *which pays the difference between the amount your insurer pays for a totaled car and the amount owed on the loan or lease.*

You normally do not buy a gap policy when you lease a car. The dealer typically buys a master policy from an insurer and includes the cost in the monthly lease payment. You should check with the car dealer before you buy or lease a car.

ISO also has an endorsement that can be added to the PAP that bridges the gap between the amount paid by Part D and the amount owed to the lessor or lender.

## Payment of Loss

The insurer has the option of paying for a physical damage loss in money (including any sales tax) or repairing or replacing the damaged or stolen property. If the car or its equipment is stolen and recovered later, the insurer will pay the expense of returning the stolen car to the named insured and will also pay for any damage resulting from the theft. The insurer also has the right to keep all or part of the recovered stolen property at an agreed or appraised value.

In addition, insurers can recover part of their loss payments by salvage. When a vehicle is considered a constructive total loss, it can be repaired, but it is not cost effective to do so. In such cases, the insurer takes the car and sells it to a salvage dealer, which allows the insurer to recover part of the loss payment.

## Other Sources of Recovery

If other insurance covers a physical damage loss, the insurer pays only its pro rata share. The insurer's share is the proportion that its limit of liability bears to the total of all applicable limits.

With respect to a nonowned auto (including a temporary substitute), the Part D coverages are excess over any other collectible source of recovery. *Thus, any physical damage insurance on the borrowed car is primary, and your physical damage insurance is excess.* If you borrow a car and damage it, the owner's physical damage insurance (if any) applies first, and your collision insurance is excess, subject to any deductible. For example, assume that you borrow a friend's car and damage it in an accident. The owner's collision deductible is $500, and your collision deductible is $250. If repairs to the borrowed car are $2000, the owner's PAP pays $1500 ($2000 − $500), and your PAP pays $250 ($500 − $250). The remaining $250 of loss would have to be paid either by the owner or by you. In short, if the owner's collision deductible is larger than your deductible, your insurer pays the difference between the two deductibles.

### Appraisal Provision

The PAP contains an **appraisal provision** for handling disputes over the amount of a physical damage loss. This provision is particularly important in the case of damage to a low-mileage car or to a car in above-average condition. The insured may claim that the car is worth more than the amounts stated in various sources listing auto values.[7] To resolve the dispute, either party can demand an appraisal of the loss. Each party selects a competent and impartial appraiser. The two appraisers then select an umpire. Each appraiser states separately the actual cash value of the car and the amount of the loss. If the appraisers fail to agree, they submit their differences to the umpire. A decision by any two parties is binding on all. Each party pays his or her appraiser, and the umpire's expenses are shared equally. Finally, by agreeing to an appraisal, the insurer does not waive any rights under the policy.

## PART E: DUTIES AFTER AN ACCIDENT OR LOSS

You should know what to do if you have an accident or loss. Some obligations are based on common sense, while others are required by law and by the provisions of the PAP. You should first determine if anyone is hurt. If someone is injured, an ambulance should be called immediately. If there are bodily injuries, or the property damage exceeds a certain amount (such as $200), you must notify the police in most jurisdictions. You should give the other driver your name, address, and the name of your agent and insurer and request the same information from him or her. You should also get the name and address of any witnesses.

You should not admit fault. The question of who caused the accident will be determined by the insurers involved or by a court of law.

After the accident occurs, the PAP requires you to perform certain duties. The PAP states specifically that the insurer has no duty to provide coverage if you fail to comply with certain listed duties. However, the insurer can deny coverage only if failure to comply is prejudicial (harmful) to the insurer. Many courts have held that the insured's failure to comply with every duty may not harm the insurer's position or interest. The PAP recognizes this principle and states that the insurer is relieved of its obligation to provide coverage only if failure to comply with the listed duties is prejudicial to the insurer.

You are required to notify your company or agent promptly of the accident. Failure to report the accident promptly to your insurer could jeopardize your coverage if you are later sued by the other driver. In addition, you must cooperate with the insurer in the investigation and settlement of a claim. You must send to the insurer copies of any legal papers or notices received in connection with the accident. If you are claiming benefits under the uninsured motorists, underinsured motorists, or medical payments coverages, you may be required to take a physical examination at the insurer's expense. You must also authorize your insurer to obtain medical reports and other pertinent records. Finally, you must submit a proof of loss at the insurer's request.

Some additional duties are imposed on you if you are seeking benefits under the uninsured motorists coverage. The police must be notified if a hit-and-run driver is involved. Also, if you bring a lawsuit against the uninsured driver, you must send copies of the legal papers to your insurer.

If your car is damaged, and you are seeking indemnification under Coverage D, other duties are imposed on you. You must take reasonable steps to protect the vehicle from further damage; your insurer will pay for any expense involved. You must also permit the insurer to inspect and appraise the car before it is repaired.

# PART F: GENERAL PROVISIONS

This section contains a number of general provisions. Only two of them are discussed here.

## Policy Period and Territory

The PAP provides coverage only in the United States, its territories or possessions, Puerto Rico, and Canada. The policy also provides coverage while a covered auto is being transported between the ports of the United States, Puerto Rico, or Canada. For example, if you rent a car while vacationing in England, Germany, or Mexico, you are not covered. Additional auto insurance must be purchased to be covered while driving in foreign countries. If you intend to drive in Mexico, you should first obtain liability insurance from a Mexican insurer. A motorist from the United States who has not purchased insurance from a Mexican insurer could be detained in jail after an accident, have his or her automobile impounded, and be subject to other penalties as well.

## Termination

An important provision applies to termination of the insurance by either the insured or insurer. There are four parts to this provision:

- Cancellation
- Nonrenewal
- Automatic termination
- Other termination provisions

All states place restrictions on the insurer's right to cancel or nonrenew an auto insurance policy. Many states, however, have laws that differ from the termination provisions contained in the PAP. In such cases, an endorsement is added to the PAP to make the auto policy conform to state law.

**Cancellation**   The named insured can cancel at any time by returning the policy to the insurer or by giving advance written notice of the effective date of **cancellation**.

The insurer also has the right of cancellation. If the policy has been in force for *fewer than 60 days*, the insurer can cancel by sending a cancellation notice to the named insured. At least 10 days' notice must be given if the cancellation is for nonpayment of premiums and at least 20 days' notice is required in all other cases. Thus, the insurer has 60 days to investigate a new insured to determine whether he or she is acceptable.

After the policy has been in force for 60 days, or it is a renewal or continuation policy, the insurer can cancel for only three reasons: (1) the premium has not been paid, (2) the driver's license of any insured has been suspended or revoked during the policy period, or (3) the policy was obtained through material misrepresentation.

**Nonrenewal**   The insurer may also discontinue coverage through **nonrenewal** of the policy at the end of the coverage period. If the insurer decides not to renew the policy, the named insured must be given at least 20 days' notice before the end of the policy period.

**Automatic Termination**   If the insurer decides to renew the policy, an automatic termination provision becomes effective. This means that if the named insured does not accept the insurer's offer to renew, the policy automatically terminates at the end of the current policy period. Thus, once the insurer bills the named insured for another period, the insured must pay the premium, or the policy automatically terminates on its expiration date. However, some insurers may provide a short grace period to pay an overdue renewal premium.

Finally, if other insurance is obtained on a covered auto, the PAP insurance on that auto automatically terminates on the day the other insurance becomes effective.

**Other Termination Provisions**   Many states place additional restrictions on the insurer's right to cancel or not renew an auto insurance policy. If state law requires a longer period of advance notice to the named insured or modifies any termination provision, the PAP is modified to comply with those requirements. Also, if the policy is canceled, the named insured is entitled to any premium refund; however, making or offering to make a premium refund is not a condition for cancellation. Finally, the effective date of cancellation stated in the cancellation notice is the end of the policy period.

# INSURING MOTORCYCLES AND OTHER VEHICLES

The PAP excludes coverage for motorcycles, mopeds, and similar vehicles. However, a **miscellaneous-type vehicle endorsement** can be added to the PAP to insure motorcycles, mopeds, motorscooters, golf carts, motor homes, dune buggies, and similar vehicles. One exception is a snowmobile, which requires a separate endorsement to the PAP. The miscellaneous-type vehicle endorsement can be used to provide the same coverages found in the PAP.

You should be aware of several points if the miscellaneous-type vehicle endorsement is added to the PAP. First, the liability coverage does not apply to a nonowned vehicle. Although other persons are covered while operating your motorcycle with your permission, the liability coverage does not apply if you operate a nonowned motorcycle (other than as a temporary substitute vehicle).

Second, a passenger hazard exclusion can be elected, which excludes liability for bodily injury to any passenger on the motorcycle. When the exclusion is used, the insured pays a lower premium; however, if a passenger on your motorcycle is thrown off and is injured, the liability coverage on the motorcycle does not apply.

Finally, the amount paid for any physical damage losses to the motorcycle is limited to the lowest of (1) the stated amount shown in the endorsement, (2) the actual cash value, or (3) the amount necessary to repair or replace the property (less any deductible).

---

## CASE APPLICATION

Kim, age 20, is a college student who recently purchased her first car from a friend who had financial problems. The vehicle is a high mileage, 2001 Toyota Corolla with a current market value of $2000. Assume you are a financial planner and Kim asks your advice concerning the various coverages in the PAP.

a. Briefly describe the major coverages that are available in the PAP.

b. Which of the available coverages in (a) should Kim purchase? Justify your answer.

c. Which of the available coverages in (a) should Kim not purchase? Justify your answer.

d. Assume that Kim purchases the PAP coverages that you have recommended. To what extent, if any, would Kim's insurance cover the following situations?

   1. Danielle, Kim's roommate, borrows Kim's car with her permission and injures another motorist. Danielle is at fault.

   2. Kim is driving under the influence of alcohol and is involved in an accident where another motorist is seriously injured.

   3. During the football season, Kim charges a fee to transport fans from a local bar to the football stadium. Several passengers are injured when Kim suddenly changes lanes without signaling and hits another car.

   4. Kim drives her boyfriend's car on a regular basis. While driving the boyfriend's car, she is involved in an accident in which another motorist is injured. Kim is at fault.

   5. Kim rents a car in England where she is participating in a summer study program. The car is stolen from a dormitory parking lot.

e. Kim also owns a motorcycle. To what extent, if any, does Kim's PAP cover the motorcycle?

## SUMMARY

- The Personal Auto Policy (PAP) consists of a declarations page, a definitions section, and six major parts:

    | | |
    |---|---|
    | Part A: | Liability Coverage |
    | Part B: | Medical Payments Coverage |
    | Part C: | Uninsured Motorists Coverage |
    | Part D: | Coverage for Damage to Your Auto |
    | Part E: | Duties After an Accident or Loss |
    | Part F: | General Provisions |

- Liability coverage protects the insured from bodily injury and property damage liability arising out of the negligent operation of an auto or trailer. The insurer also pays legal defense costs.

- A covered auto includes any vehicle shown in the declarations; newly acquired vehicles; a trailer owned by the insured; and a temporary substitute auto.

- Insured persons include the named insured and spouse, resident family members, other persons using a covered auto if a reasonable belief that permission to use the vehicle exists, and any person or organization legally responsible for the acts of a covered person.

- Medical payments coverage pays all reasonable medical, dental, and funeral expenses incurred by an insured person for services rendered within three years from the date of the accident.

- Uninsured motorists coverage pays for the bodily injury of a covered person caused by an uninsured motorist, a hit-and-run driver, or a negligent driver whose insurer is insolvent.

- Underinsured motorists coverage can be added as an endorsement to the PAP. The coverage applies when a negligent driver carries liability insurance, but the liability limits carried are less than the limit provided by the underinsured motorists coverage.

- Coverage for damage to your auto pays for a direct physical loss to a covered auto or nonowned auto less any deductible. A collision loss or other-than-collision loss is covered only if the declarations page indicates that these coverages are in effect.

- Certain duties are imposed on the insured after an accident occurs. A person seeking coverage must cooperate with the insurer in the investigation and settlement of a claim and send to the insurer copies of any legal papers or notices received in connection with the accident.

- After the policy has been in force for 60 days, or it is a renewal or continuation policy, the insurer can cancel the policy only if the premium has not been paid, the driver's license of an insured has been suspended or revoked during the policy period, or the policy was obtained through material misrepresentation. The insurer can also discontinue coverage by not renewing the policy. If the insurer decides not to renew the policy when it comes up for renewal, the named insured must be given at least 20 days' notice of its intention not to renew. The renewal and cancellation provisions may be modified to comply with state law.

- Motorcycles and mopeds can be insured by adding the miscellaneous-type vehicle endorsement to the personal auto policy.

## KEY CONCEPTS AND TERMS

Appraisal provision (497)
Betterment (496)
Cancellation (498)
Collision (489)
Coverage for damage to your auto (489)
Diminution in value (496)
Extended nonowned coverage endorsement (483)
Gap insurance (496)
Liability coverage (479)
Medical payments coverage (483)
Miscellaneous-type vehicle endorsement (499)
Nonowned auto (490)
Nonrenewal (498)
Other-than-collision loss (489)
Single limit (480)
Split limits (479)
Supplementary payments (481)
Temporary substitute vehicle (479)
Underinsured motorists coverage (488)
Uninsured motorists coverage (486)
Your covered auto (478)

## REVIEW QUESTIONS

1. The Personal Auto Policy (PAP) contains several coverages that meet the insurance needs of typical insureds. For each of the following coverages, briefly describe the type of coverage provided, and give an example of a loss that would be covered.
    a. Part A: Liability Coverage
    b. Part B: Medical Payments Coverage
    c. Part C: Uninsured Motorists Coverage
    d. Part D: Coverage for Damage to Your Auto

2. The PAP provides coverage for *your covered auto*. Identify the four classes of vehicles that are considered to be covered autos.

3. The PAP provides liability coverage to four groups. Identify the four groups of persons or parties who can be insured under the PAP.

4. In addition to the policy limits and a legal defense, the PAP provides for certain supplementary payments. Briefly describe the supplementary payments that can be paid under the liability section of the PAP.

5. a. List the major exclusions that apply to liability coverage (Part A) in the PAP.
   b. List the major exclusions that apply to medical payments coverage (Part B) in the PAP.

6. Describe the major features of uninsured motorists coverage (Part C) in the PAP.

7. Coverage for Damage to Your Auto (Part D) in the PAP provides for two optional coverages: (1) collision coverage, and (2) other-than-collision coverage.
   a. What is a collision loss? Explain your answer.
   b. What is an other-than-collision loss? Explain your answer.
   c. List the major exclusions that apply to Coverage for Damage to Your Auto (Part D).

8. Coverage for Damage to Your Auto (Part D) in the PAP also covers the insured while driving a nonowned auto.
   a. Define the meaning of a nonowned auto.
   b. If the insured drives a nonowned auto on a regular basis, does the insured's PAP provide coverage? Explain your answer.

9. Explain the duties imposed on the insured after an accident or loss occurs.

10. Does the PAP cover you if you are driving a vehicle in a foreign country? Explain your answer.

## APPLICATION QUESTIONS

1. Fred has a PAP with the following coverages:
   Liability coverages: $100,000/$300,000/$50,000
   Medical payments coverage: $5000 each person
   Uninsured motorists coverage: $25,000 each person
   Collision loss: $250 deductible
   Other-than-collision loss: $100 deductible

   With respect to each of the following situations, indicate whether the loss is covered and the amount payable, if any, under the policy. Assume that each situation is a separate event.
   a. Fred's son, age 16, is driving a family car, runs a red light, and kills a pedestrian. The family of the deceased pedestrian sues and damages are awarded in the amount of $500,000.
   b. Fred borrows a friend's car to go to the supermarket. He fails to stop at a red light and negligently smashes into another motorist. The other driver's car, valued at $15,000, is totally destroyed. In addition, repairs to the friend's car are $5000.
   c. Fred's daughter, Heather, attends college in another state and drives a family auto. Heather lets her boyfriend drive the car, and he negligently injures another motorist. The boyfriend is sued for $50,000.
   d. Fred's wife is driving a family car in a snowstorm. She loses control of the car on an icy street and smashes into the foundation of a house. The property damage to the house is $30,000. The damage to the family car is $8000. Fred's wife has medical expenses of $5000.
   e. Fred is walking across a street and is struck by a motorist who fails to stop. He has bodily injuries in the amount of $15,000.
   f. Fred's car is being repaired for faulty brakes. While road testing the car, a mechanic injures another motorist and is sued for $50,000.
   g. Fred's car hits a cow crossing a highway. The cost of repairing the car is $2500.
   h. A thief breaks a car window and steals a camera and golf clubs locked in the car. It will cost $400 to replace the damaged window. The stolen property is valued at $500.
   i. Fred's wife goes shopping at a supermarket. When she returns, she finds that the left rear fender has been damaged by another driver who did not leave a name. The cost of repairing the car is $2000.
   j. Fred works for a construction company. While driving a large cement truck, he negligently injures another motorist. The injured motorist sues Fred for $25,000.
   k. Fred's son drives a family car on a date. He gets drunk, and his girlfriend drives him home. The girlfriend negligently injures another motorist, who has bodily injuries in the amount of $200,000.
   l. Compact discs (CDs) valued at $500 are stolen from Fred's car. The car was locked when the theft occurred.
   m. While driving a rented golf cart, Fred accidentally injures another golfer with the cart.

2. Karen is the named insured under a PAP that provides coverage for bodily injury and property damage liability, medical payments, and uninsured motorists

coverage. For each of the following situations, briefly explain whether the claim is covered by Karen's PAP.

a. Karen ran into a telephone pole and submitted a medical expense claim for Jason, a passenger in Karen's car at the time of the accident.

b. Karen allowed Scott to use her car. While operating Karen's car, Scott damaged Gray's car in an accident caused by Scott's negligence. Karen is sued by Gray for damages.

c. Karen's husband ran over a bicycle while driving a friend's car. The owner of the bicycle demands that Karen's husband pay for the damage.

d. In a fit of anger, Karen deliberately ran over the wagon of a neighbor's child that had been left in Karen's driveway after repeated requests that the wagon be left elsewhere. The child's parents seek reimbursement.

3. Janet has a PAP with the following coverages:
Liability coverages: $100,000/$300,000/$50,000
Medical payments coverage: $5000 each person
Uninsured motorists coverage: $25,000 each person
Collision loss: $250 deductible
Other-than-collision loss: $100 deductible
Towing and labor cost coverage: $75 each disablement

To what extent, if any, is each of the following losses covered under Janet's PAP? Treat each event separately.

a. Janet rents a car while on vacation. She is involved in an accident with another motorist when she fails to yield the right of way. The injured motorist is awarded a judgment of $100,000. The rental agency carries only liability limits of $30,000 on the rental car. The rental agency carries no collision insurance on its cars and is seeking $15,000 from Janet for repairs to the rental car.

b. Janet borrows her friend's car with permission. Janet is in an accident with another motorist in which she is at fault. The cost of repairing the friend's car is $5000. The friend's auto policy has a $500 deductible for collision losses and $100 for other-than-collision losses.

c. Janet is employed as a salesperson and is furnished a company car. She is involved in an accident with another motorist while driving the company car during business hours. The injured motorist claims Janet is at fault and sues her for $100,000. Damage to the company car amounts to $5000.

d. Janet's car will not start because of a defective battery. A tow truck brings the car to a service station where the battery is replaced. Towing charges are $60. The cost of replacing the battery is $100.

4. Michael was driving a neighbor's pickup truck to get a load of firewood. A child darted out between two parked cars and ran into the street in front of the truck. In an unsuccessful attempt to avoid hitting the child, Michael lost control of the vehicle and hit a telephone pole. The child was critically injured, the pickup truck was badly damaged, and the telephone pole collapsed. Michael has liability coverage and collision coverage under his PAP. The neighbor also has a PAP with liability coverage and collision coverage on the pickup.

a. If Michael is found guilty of negligence, which insurer will pay first for the bodily injuries to the child and the property damage to the telephone pole? Explain.

b. Which insurer will pay for the physical damage to the neighbor's pickup? Explain.

5. Pablo traded in his 2000 Ford for a new Ford. One week later, he hit an oily spot in the road on his way to work and skidded into a parked car. The 2000 Ford was insured under the PAP with full coverage, including a $250 deductible for a collision loss. At the time of the accident, Pablo had not notified his insurer of the trade-in. The physical damage to the parked car was $8000. Damage to Pablo's car was $5000. Will Pablo's PAP cover either or both of these losses? Explain.

6. James, age 18, lives at home and occasionally drives the car of his friend, Mary. Mary carries $300,000 of liability insurance on her car under a PAP. James is also insured under his mother's PAP, which provides $500,000 of liability coverage. Assume that James has an accident while using Mary's car and is found to be legally liable in the amount of $400,000. How much, if any, will each policy pay? Explain your answer.

7. Patrick has a PAP with liability limits of $50,000/$100,000/$25,000. Patrick failed to stop at a red light and hit a van. The van sustained damages of $15,000. Three passengers in the van were injured and incurred the following bodily injuries:
Passenger A, $15,000
Passenger B, $60,000
Passenger C, $10,000

Patrick was also injured and incurred medical bills of $10,000. His car sustained damages of $10,000. Because of his injury, Patrick was unable to work and lost $5000 in wages. How much will Patrick's insurer pay under the liability coverage (Part A) section of his PAP? Explain your answer.

## INTERNET RESOURCES

- **Carinsurance.com** allows shoppers to compare rates from multiple-insurance companies. Shoppers enter information on a quote form. Then, Carinsurance.com contacts the companies directly to provide an immediate comparison of rates. Visit the site at

  carinsurance.com

- The **Insurance Research Council (IRC),** a division of The Institutes (the American Institute for CPCU), provides the insurance industry and the public with timely research studies that are relevant to public policy issues dealing with risk and insurance. Visit the site at

  http://www.insurance-research.org/

- The **RAND Institute for Civil Justice** is a RAND Law, Business, and Regulation Center within the RAND Corporation. The Institute conducts independent, objective research and analysis concerning the civil justice system. Many research studies deal with auto insurance and the insurance industry. Visit the site at

  rand.org/law-business-regulation/centers/civil-justice.html

- **GEICO** sells auto insurance directly over the phone (800-861-8380). The company claims that a 15-minute call can save you 15 percent or more on auto insurance rates. GEICO also has a Web site that provides similar premium quotes online. Visit the site at

  geico.com

- The **Insurance Information Institute** provides timely information on auto insurance and other personal property insurance coverages. Numerous consumer brochures and articles on auto insurance and other property and liability coverages can be accessed directly online. Visit the site at

  iii.org

- **InsWeb** provides premium quotes for auto, homeowners, and other insurance products. In addition, the site has a learning center and provides insurance information and articles to consumers. Visit the site at

  insweb.com

- The **International Risk Management Institute (IRMI)** is an online source that provides valuable information about personal lines and commercial lines. The site provides timely articles on a wide range of risk management and insurance topics and offers a number of free e-mail newsletters. Visit the site at

  irmi.com

- The **Progressive Casualty Insurance Company** has a user-friendly site that gives auto insurance quotes for most states. Progressive claims its rates are highly competitive. Progressive also provides comparison rates from other insurers. Visit the site at

  progressive.com

- The **National Association of Insurance Commissioners (NAIC)** has a link to all state insurance departments, which provide a considerable amount of consumer information on auto insurance. Visit the site at

  naic.org

## SELECTED REFERENCES

"A Consumer's Guide to: Auto Insurance; Choosing and Using Your Auto Insurance Coverage," Washington State Office of the Insurance Commissioner, 2012.

"Cellphones and Driving," *Issues Updates,* Insurance Information Institute, June 2012. This source is periodically updated.

*Fire, Casualty & Surety Bulletins,* Personal Lines volume, Personal Auto section. Erlanger, KY: National Underwriter Company. The bulletins are updated monthly.

"Generic Auto Crash Parts," *Issues Updates*, Insurance Information Institute, February, 2012.

Nyce, Charles, ed. *Personal Insurance,* 2nd ed. Malvern, PA.: American Institute for Chartered Property Casualty Underwriters/Insurance Institute of America, 2008.

Wiening, Eric A. and David D. Thamann. *Personal Auto,* 2nd ed., second printing. Erlanger, KY: The National Underwriter Company, 2009.

## NOTES

1. The material in this chapter is based on *Fire, Casualty & Surety Bulletins*, Personal Lines volume, Personal Auto section (Erlanger, KY: National Underwriter Company); and the 2005 edition of the Personal Auto Policy prepared by the Insurance Services Office.
2. "Cellphones and Driving," Insurance Information Institute, *Issues Updates,* June, 2012. This source is periodically updated.
3. Ibid.
4. "Cellphones and Driving," Insurance Information Institute, *Issues Updates,* June 2012.
5. "Drivers on Cell Phones Clog Traffic, Longer Commutes Due to Fewer Lane Changes, Slower Speed," News Release, University of Utah, January 2, 2008.
6. Eric A. Wiening and David D. Thamann. *Personal Auto, Personal Lines Coverage Guide*, 2nd ed., second printing. Erlanger, KY: The National Underwriter Company, 2009.
7. A popular Web site for estimated vehicle values is Kelly Blue Book. By entering the year the car was manufactured, the make (e.g., Honda) and model (e.g., Civic) and other information (e.g., engine size, two-door vs. four-door, etc.), an estimated value is provided. Visit the Web site at: kbb.com.

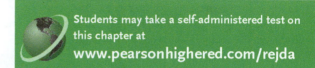

Students may take a self-administered test on this chapter at

**www.pearsonhighered.com/rejda**

# CHAPTER 23

# AUTO INSURANCE AND SOCIETY

*"The current system of paying for auto injuries suffers from two fundamental problems: premiums are too high and victims with serious injuries rarely receive full compensation."*

Joint Economic Committee, 105th Congress

## LEARNING OBJECTIVES

**After studying this chapter, you should be able to**

◆ Describe each of the following approaches for compensating auto accident victims:
 Financial responsibility laws
 Compulsory insurance laws
 Unsatisfied judgment fund
 Uninsured motorists coverage
 Low-cost auto insurance
 "No pay, no play" laws

◆ Explain the meaning of no-fault auto insurance and the rationale for no-fault insurance laws.

◆ Describe each of the following methods for providing auto insurance to high-risk drivers:
 Auto insurance plan
 Joint underwriting association (JUA)
 Reinsurance facility
 Specialty insurers

◆ Identify the major factors that determine the cost of auto insurance to consumers.

◆ Explain the suggestions that consumers should follow when shopping for auto insurance.

*Steve was convicted for his second driving under the influence of alcohol offense after he ran off the road and hit a tree. His drivers license was suspended for two years. After serving the suspension, Steve took the driving test and his license was reinstated. When he tried to buy auto insurance, however, none of the companies were willing to insure him. "What kind of a system is this?" Steve said, "The state says I have to have liability insurance to drive, but no one will insure me. That doesn't make any sense. And all I really need is collision insurance, like for when I hit the tree. Why am I being forced to buy liability insurance?"*

*While Steve has regained his driving privileges, his state requires him to be able to compensate people who he may injure while operating a motor vehicle. Given his driving history, it's not surprising that insurers are reluctant to insure him. Each year, over one million motorists are injured or killed in auto accidents in the United States. Society then has the problem of compensating these victims for their bodily injuries and property damage caused by negligent drivers. Society also has the burden of providing auto insurance to irresponsible drivers, including drunk drivers, high-risk drivers, and drivers who habitually break traffic laws. Society must also deal with the problem of compensating innocent accident victims who are injured by uninsured drivers.*

*In this chapter, we discuss the preceding problems in some depth. Four areas are emphasized: (1) the various approaches for compensating auto accident victims, (2) no-fault auto insurance as an alternative to the tort liability system, (3) methods for providing auto insurance to high-risk drivers, and (4) suggestions for buying auto insurance.*

## APPROACHES FOR COMPENSATING AUTO ACCIDENT VICTIMS

In many cases, innocent people who have been injured in auto accidents are unable to recover financial damages from the negligent motorists who injured them. Although accident victims may have bodily injuries or suffer property damage, they may recover nothing or receive less than full indemnification. To deal with this problem, states use a number of approaches to provide some protection to accident victims from irresponsible and reckless drivers. They include the following:[1]

- Financial responsibility laws
- Compulsory insurance laws
- Unsatisfied judgment funds
- Uninsured motorists coverage
- Low-cost auto insurance
- "No pay, no play" laws
- No-fault auto insurance

### Financial Responsibility Laws

All states have enacted some type of financial responsibility law or compulsory insurance law that requires motorists to furnish proof of financial responsibility up to certain minimum dollar limits. A **financial responsibility law** *does not require proof of financial responsibility until after the driver has his or her first accident or until after conviction for certain offenses, such as driving under the influence of alcohol.* Proof of financial responsibility is typically required under the following circumstances:

- After an accident involving bodily injury or property damage over a certain amount
- Upon failure to pay a final judgment resulting from an auto accident
- Following a conviction for certain offenses, such as drunk driving or reckless driving

Under these conditions, if a motorist cannot demonstrate that he or she meets the state's financial responsibility law requirements, the state can revoke or suspend the motorist's driving privileges.

Evidence of financial responsibility can be provided by producing evidence of an auto insurance policy with at least certain minimum liability limits, such as $25,000/$50,000/$25,000.[2] Other ways in which the financial responsibility law can be satisfied are by posting a bond, by depositing securities or money in the amount required by law, or by showing that the person is a qualified self-insurer. Exhibit 23.1 shows the minimum auto liability insurance limits for the various states. The first two figures refer to

bodily injury liability, and the third figure refers to property damage liability. For example, 20/40/10 means bodily injury liability coverage of $20,000 per person, $40,000 per accident, and $10,000 for property damage liability.

Although financial responsibility laws provide some protection against irresponsible motorists, they have two major defects:

- *There is no guarantee that all accident victims will be paid.* Financial responsibility must be demonstrated after an accident. The accident victim may not be paid if he or she is injured by an uninsured

**EXHIBIT 23.1**
## Automobile Financial Responsibility Limits by State

The chart below shows mandatory requirements for bodily injury (BI) liability, physical damage (PD) liability, no-fault personal injury protection (PIP), and uninsured (UM) and underinsured (UIM) motorists coverage. It also indicates which states only have financial responsibility (FR) laws.

### AUTOMOBILE FINANCIAL RESPONSIBILITY LIMITS BY STATE

| State | Insurance Required | Minimum Liability Limits[1] |
| --- | --- | --- |
| Alabama | BI & PD Liab | 25/50/25 |
| Alaska | BI & PD Liab | 50/100/25 |
| Arizona | BI & PD Liab | 15/30/10 |
| Arkansas | BI & PD Liab, PIP | 25/50/25 |
| California | BI & PD Liab | 15/30/5[2] |
| Colorado | BI & PD Liab | 25/50/15 |
| Connecticut | BI & PD Liab | 20/40/10 |
| Delaware | BI & PD Liab, PIP | 15/30/10 |
| D.C. | BI & PD Liab, UM | 25/50/10 |
| Florida | PD Liab, PIP | 10/20/10[3] |
| Georgia | BI & PD Liab | 25/50/25 |
| Hawaii | BI & PD Liab, PIP | 20/40/10 |
| Idaho | BI & PD Liab | 25/50/15 |
| Illinois | BI & PD Liab, UM | 20/40/15 |
| Indiana | BI & PD Liab | 25/50/10 |
| Iowa | BI & PD Liab | 20/40/15 |
| Kansas | BI & PD Liab, PIP, UM | 25/50/10 |
| Kentucky | BI & PD Liab, PIP | 25/50/10 |
| Maine | BI & PD Liab, UM, UIM | 50/100/25[4] |
| Maryland | BI & PD Liab, PIP[5], UM, UIM | 30/60/15 |
| Massachusetts | BI & PD Liab, PIP, UM, UIM | 20/40/5 |

*(Continued)*

**Exhibit 23.1 (continued)**
**Automobile Financial Responsibility Limits by State**

| State | Insurance Required | Minimum Liability Limits |
|-------|-------------------|-------------------------|
| Michigan | BI & PD Liab, PIP | 20/40/10 |
| Minnesota | BI & PD Liab, PIP, UM, UIM | 30/60/10 |
| Mississippi | BI & PD Liab | 25/50/25 |
| Missouri | BI & PD Liab, UM | 25/50/10 |
| Montana | BI & PD Liab | 25/50/10 |
| Nebraska | BI & PD Liab, UM, UIM | 25/50/25 |
| Nevada | BI & PD Liab | 15/30/10 |
| New Hampshire | FR only, UM | 25/50/25[4] |
| New Jersey | BI & PD Liab, PIP, UM, UIM | 15/30/5[6] |
| New Mexico | BI & PD Liab | 25/50/10 |
| New York | BI & PD Liab, PIP, UM | 25/50/10[7] |
| North Carolina | BI & PD Liab, UIM[8] | 30/60/25 |
| North Dakota | BI & PD Liab, PIP, UM, UIM | 25/50/25 |
| Ohio | BI & PD Liab | 12.5/25/7.5 |
| Oklahoma | BI & PD Liab | 25/50/25 |
| Oregon | BI & PD Liab, PIP, UM, UIM[9] | 25/50/20 |
| Pennsylvania | BI & PD Liab, PIP | 15/30/5 |
| Rhode Island | BI & PD Liab | 25/50/25[3] |
| South Carolina | BI & PD Liab, UM | 25/50/25 |
| South Dakota | BI & PD Liab, UM, UIM | 25/50/25 |
| Tennessee | BI & PD Liab | 25/50/15[3] |
| Texas | BI & PD Liab | 30/60/25 |
| Utah | BI & PD Liab, PIP | 25/65/15[3] |
| Vermont | BI & PD Liab, UM, UIM | 25/50/10 |
| Virginia | BI & PD Liab[10], UM, UIM | 25/50/20 |
| Washington | BI & PD Liab | 25/50/10 |
| West Virginia | BI & PD Liab, UM | 20/40/10 |
| Wisconsin | BI & PD Liab, UM, UIM | 25/50/10 |
| Wyoming | BI & PD Liab | 25/50/20 |

[1]The first two numbers refer to bodily injury liability limits and the third number to property liability. For example, 20/40/10 means coverage up to $40,000 for all persons injured in an accident, subject to a limit of $20,000 for one individual, and $10,000 coverage for property damage.

[2]Low-cost policy limits for low-income drivers in the California Automobile Assigned Risk Plan are 10/20/3.

[3]Instead of policy limits, policyholders can satisfy the requirement with a combined single limit policy. Amounts vary by state.

[4]In addition, policyholders must also carry at least $2000 for medical payments.

[5]May be waived for the policyholder but is compulsory for passengers.

[6]Basic policy (optional) limits are 10/10/5. Uninsured and underinsured motorist coverage not available under the basic policy but uninsured motorist coverage is required under the standard policy.

[7]In addition, policyholders must have 50/100 for wrongful death coverage.

[8]Mandatory in policies with UM limits exceeding 30/60.

[9]Mandatory when UM liability limit is greater than required FR.

[10]Compulsory to buy insurance or pay an Uninsured Motorists Vehicle (UMV) fee to the state department of motor vehicles.

Note: Data are from Property Casualty Insurers Association of America; state departments of insurance.

Source: *The Insurance Fact Book 2012,* New York: Insurance Information Institute, pp. 74–76. Reprinted by permission from the Insurance Information Institute.

driver, hit-and-run driver, or the driver of a stolen car. An irresponsible motorist often drives without a license, so the law fails to achieve the objective of getting the irresponsible driver off the road.

- *Accident victims may not be fully indemnified for their injuries.* Most financial responsibility laws require only minimum liability insurance limits, which are relatively low. If the bodily injury exceeds the minimum limit, the accident victim may not be fully compensated.

### Compulsory Insurance Laws

Liability insurance is compulsory in most states and the District of Columbia. *A* **compulsory insurance law** *requires motorists to carry at least a minimum amount of liability insurance before the vehicle can be licensed or registered.*

Some people believe that compulsory insurance laws provide greater protection than financial responsibility laws because motorists must provide evidence of financial responsibility before an accident occurs. However, studies by various groups conclude that compulsory insurance laws generally are ineffective in reducing the percentage of uninsured drivers.

- *In general, there is no correlation between compulsory insurances laws and the number of uninsured vehicles on the highway.* There will always be part of the population that chooses to drive without insurance. That percentage is not precisely known and varies among the states. This group either takes a chance or pursues fraudulent compliance measures.[3]
- *According to the Property Casualty Insurers Association of America, mandatory auto insurance does not reduce the number of uninsured drivers.* Unlicensed and uninsured drivers are involved in more than 20 percent of the fatal crashes on America's highways. Compulsory insurance laws do not prevent drivers from owning or operating a vehicle.[4]
- *Some states have employed computer databases to attempt to track uninsured motorists. Evidence suggests that such reporting systems have not effectively met their major objective of identifying and tracking uninsured drivers.* Reporting programs are costly, difficult to implement, hard to maintain, and have experienced problems with data consistency.[5]

Finally, you may be involved in an auto accident where the other driver is at fault but is in compliance with the state's compulsory insurance law. You can file a claim against the negligent driver or his or her insurer for any bodily injury or physical damage to your car. These claims are called "third-party" claims. A third-party claim against another driver's insurer is a common source of complaint to state insurance departments. Insight 23.1, prepared by the Utah Department of Insurance, discusses some common questions and answers about third-party claims. Although some answers refer specifically to Utah law, they may be relevant to drivers in other states as well.

### Unsatisfied Judgment Funds

A few states[6] have established unsatisfied judgment funds for compensating innocent accident victims. *An* **unsatisfied judgment fund** *is a state fund for compensating auto accident victims who have exhausted all other means of recovery.* These funds have certain common characteristics:[7]

- The accident victim must obtain a judgment against the negligent motorist and must show that the judgment cannot be collected.
- The maximum amount paid by the fund generally is limited to the limits specified in the state's compulsory insurance law. The amount paid may also be reduced by collateral sources of recovery, such as workers compensation benefits.
- The negligent driver is not relieved of legal responsibility when the fund makes a payment to the accident victim. Negligent drivers must repay the fund or lose their driver's license until the fund is reimbursed for the payments.

The method of financing benefits varies from state to state. Funds can be obtained by charging a fee to each motorist, by assessing insurers based on the amount of auto liability insurance written in the state, by assessing the uninsured motorists in the state, and by surcharging drivers with convictions for moving vehicle violations.

### Uninsured Motorists Coverage

**Uninsured motorists coverage** is another approach for compensating injured auto accident victims. The injured person's insurer agrees to pay the

## INSIGHT 23.1

### Filing an Auto Claim with the Other Party's Insurance Company

After an auto accident, one of the first things you may have to do is file an insurance claim for damages. When these accidents occur, you have the option to file the claim with either your own insurance company, if you have the appropriate coverages (a "first-party" claim), or with the other driver's insurance company (a "third-party" claim).

Insurance laws differ with regard to first and third party claims, so it is important that you understand your rights and duties in both cases. In a first-party claim, you have a direct contract that requires your insurance company to fulfill all the conditions stated in your policy. In a third-party claim, you do not have a direct contract with the insurance company and their primary obligation is to their own policyholder. This fact sheet discusses your rights and duties in Utah when you file a third-party claim with another driver's insurance company.

#### How Much Insurance Must the Other Driver Have?

Utah law requires motorists to carry bodily injury and property damage liability insurance to help pay for damages they cause in an auto accident. The minimum amounts drivers are required to carry are: $25,000 per person and $65,000 for two or more persons for bodily injury liability and $15,000 for property damage liability. Typically this is shown on your policy as 25/65/15.

#### What Happens After I File a Claim?

Utah State Law requires that any person in your vehicle who incurs bodily injuries will first have to submit their claim to the insurance company covering your vehicle. For each person injured, the first $3000 in medical expenses will be covered by your policy under Personal Injury Protection before you can file a claim with the responsible insurer.

After you file a claim with the other driver's insurance company, they will investigate the claim and offer a settlement if they determine their insured is legally responsible for your injuries or damages. In most cases, an insurance company will not settle a claim for bodily injury liability until such time as you have completed all medical treatment(s) for your injuries. This could mean an extended period of time may pass before any settlement occurs should these injuries require extensive medical care. At the time you are ready to settle your bodily injury claim, the insurance company will require you to sign a "release for damages." This means you agree that the amount offered is the only amount you will ever receive from the other driver and their insurance company. Be sure you are ready to accept a final amount before you cash the check or sign the release.

In case of property damage to your vehicle, in addition to your injuries, you and the insurance company may readily agree on the amount of damage, but you may not be ready to settle the bodily injury claim because of ongoing medical bills. An insurance company may not refuse to pay your agreed-upon property damage claim because the bodily injury claim is still outstanding.

#### Who Decides Fault and How Much They Owe?

Utah has a "comparative negligence" law which means that more than one person can be at fault in an accident. Under this law, you can collect damages only if you are less than 50% at fault for the accident. The settlement can then be reduced by your percentage of fault.

As an example, if the other driver is 80% at-fault and you are 20% at fault, you can collect for your damages because you were less that 50% at fault. However, the other driver's insurance company might only offer to pay for 80% of your damages.

#### When Will the Insurance Company Contact Me?

Utah insurance rules (R590-190, 191 or 192) require a company to provide a substantive response to a claimant within 15 days of a request for response. The rules further states the insurer has a 30-day time frame to accept or deny your claim. However, if the investigation cannot be completed within that time, the company is allowed additional time to complete their investigation.

#### What Kind of Information Must I Provide?

There is no law that sets forth the information you must provide. However, the insurance company will need to determine:

- whether their insured is legally responsible for the accident and to what extent;
- the amount of your damages or bodily injury; and
- whether your damages or injuries are directly related to the accident.

Therefore, it is in your best interest to provide as much information as possible to substantiate your claim. In addition, if you fail to cooperate fully, the company could deny your claim altogether.

#### How Many Repair Estimates Must I Submit?

The other insurance company may ask for several estimates. There is no law that states how many estimates you must submit or that limits the number the company may ask for.

#### May I Choose My Own Repair Shop?

Yes. You are not required to use a repair shop suggested by the insurance company. However, if the repair shop you have selected charges more than the company's suggested shop, you may have to pay the difference.

## INSIGHT 23.1

### Can the Insurance Company Deduct for "Betterment"?

Yes. If your vehicle is being repaired with newer parts, the company may not have to pay for the "betterment." There is no law, or contractual agreements, requiring "replacement coverage" using new parts. However, any deductions for betterment must be itemized on a written explanation of those repairs.

An example of "betterment" could be the replacement of your vehicle's damaged five-year old muffler. The insurance company could have it repaired by replacing it with another five-year old muffler. If a five-year old muffler can't be found, the repair shop could use a new muffler, but you may have to pay the difference.

### Can the Insurance Company Deduct for Things Like Un-repaired Damage or Rust?

Yes. The insurance company may deduct a reasonable amount from the values if your vehicle has old, un-repaired collision damages. The company should itemize and specify the dollar amount of any such deductions.

### What Are My Rights Concerning Replacement Crash Parts?

Insurance companies are not required to use original equipment manufacturer (OEM) replacement parts, such as GM or Ford. However, Utah law states that any insurance company who uses non-original manufacturers, or after-market parts, must disclose their use to a consumer in writing on the estimate, identifying each non-OEM part to be replaced.

### May I Rent a Car?

Utah insurance regulations require an at-fault driver's insurance company to provide payment for the "reasonably incurred cost of transportation" or for the "reasonably incurred rental cost of a substitute vehicle" during the time your damaged vehicle is being repaired. The insurer is obligated to pay for loss of use only if they accept liability. If your vehicle is a total loss, that payment would be from the date of the accident, which has been timely reported, until the time a reasonable settlement offer is made by the insurance company.

Most companies will pay a flat amount, for example, $20 per day. Neither insurance contracts nor insurance law specifies the type of vehicle you may rent. However if there are special circumstances that require a vehicle similar to your damaged vehicle, let the insurance company know of those needs to see whether or not they will cover those costs.

### What About Personal Property that Was in My Vehicle?

The property damage liability portion of the other driver's policy will most likely cover damage to personal property in your vehicle.

### Do I Have to Pay a Deductible?

When you file a claim with another driver's insurance company, you do not have to pay a deductible.

### What if the Insurance Company Denies My Claim or I Disagree with Their Settlement Offer?

If the other driver's insurance company denies your claim or you disagree with their offer, there is no additional appraisal requirement. Your only recourse is to:

- Make a claim under your own policy if you have the appropriate coverage.
- File suit against the at-fault driver in small claims court, if your damages fall within the $10,000 limit for small claims suits; or
- Seek other appropriate legal counsel.

Only a judge or jury can ultimately decide who was at fault in an accident or how much another person owes you for your damages.

### Must I Conclude My Claim within a Certain Time Frame?

Yes. You must either accept a final settlement offer, or file a lawsuit, within the time periods required by the appropriate statutes of limitations:

- For Bodily Injury claims — Within 4 years from the date of the accident.
- For Property Damage claims — Within 3 years from the date of the accident.
- For bodily injury or property damage caused by an accident with a government entity — Within the appropriate time period imposed by the statute of limitation for that particular entity of government.

If you fail to accept a final settlement offer or file a suit before the statute of limitations ends, you may jeopardize your right to receive any settlement at all.

SOURCE: Utah Department of Insurance.

accident victim who has a bodily injury (or property damage in some states) caused by an uninsured motorist, by a hit-and-run driver, or by a negligent driver whose insurer is insolvent. Uninsured motorists coverage is discussed in greater detail in Chapter 22.

Uninsured motorists coverage has the following advantages.

- *Motorists have some protection against an uninsured driver.* Many states require the coverage to be mandatorily included in all auto liability insurance policies sold within the state. In other states, coverage is included in the policy unless the insured voluntarily declines the protection by signing a written waiver.

■ *Claim settlement is faster and more efficient than a tort liability lawsuit.* Although the accident victim must establish negligence by the uninsured driver, it is not necessary to sue the negligent driver and win a judgment.

Uninsured motorist's coverage, however, has several defects as a technique for compensating injured auto accident victims. They include the following:

■ *Unless higher limits are purchased, the maximum amount paid is limited to the limits specified in the state's financial responsibility or compulsory insurance law requirement.* The minimum limits are relatively low. Thus, the accident victim may not be fully compensated for his or her loss.

■ *The injured person must establish that the uninsured motorist is legally liable for the accident.* This task may be difficult in some cases and expensive if an attorney must be hired.

■ *Property damage is not covered in most states.* Unless you have collision coverage, you would collect nothing for any property damage to your car caused by an uninsured motorist in those states.

### Low-Cost Auto Insurance

As stated earlier, compulsory insurance laws generally have not been effective in reducing the number of uninsured drivers. A few states have enacted new laws to deal with the problem. Many drivers are uninsured because of the high cost of auto insurance. **Low-cost auto insurance** provides minimum amounts of liability insurance at reduced rates to motorists who cannot afford regular insurance or have limited financial assets to protect. For example, in New Jersey a standard and a basic low-cost policy are available. The basic policy provides $15,000 per person per accident, up to $250,000 for catastrophic medical injuries and $5000 for property damage liability. Bodily injury liability ($10,000 for all persons per accident) is available as an option. Uninsured motorists and physical damage coverage are not offered under the plan. New Jersey also offers a "Special Auto Insurance Policy" (SAIP) through which

Medicaid-eligible drivers can get a medical care-only policy for $365. The SAIP covers emergency medical treatment following an accident and brain and spinal cord injuries up to $250,000. It does not provide liability coverage or physical damage coverage.[8]

California's low-cost plan is available to low-income drivers over the age of 19 who have a good driving record. Rates are determined on a county basis, and drivers may purchase up to $10,000 per person in liability coverage with $20,000 available per accident. Uninsured and underinsured motorists coverages are available, and premiums can be paid through installments. The program was introduced in 1999 and at year-end 2011, fewer than 12,000 policies were in force statewide.[9]

### "No Pay, No Play" Laws

Another approach is enactment of **"no pay, no play" laws**, which restrict uninsured motorists from suing negligent drivers for noneconomic damages, such as compensation for pain and suffering. Some states are considering the proposal as a method for reducing the number of uninsured drivers.[10] Ten states have enacted such laws. In Michigan, for example, uninsured drivers who are 50 percent or more at fault cannot collect noneconomic damages after an auto accident. Louisiana requires uninsured drivers to pay the first $10,000 of out-of-pocket medical expenses and the first $10,000 in property damage before they can sue for damages. Oklahoma's law prohibits uninsured drivers to be compensated for noneconomic damages, such as pain and suffering. New Jersey prohibits uninsured drivers, drunk drivers, and motorists who commit intentional acts from filing lawsuits for economic and noneconomic damages.

### No-Fault Auto Insurance

No-fault auto insurance is another method for compensating injured accident victims. Because of dissatisfaction and defects in the traditional tort liability system, about half of the states, the District of Columbia, and Puerto Rico currently have some type of no-fault law in effect.

**Definition of No-Fault Insurance** No-fault auto insurance *means that after an auto accident involving bodily injury, each party collects from his or her*

*own insurer regardless of fault.* It is not necessary to determine who is at fault and prove negligence before a loss payment is made. Regardless of who caused the accident, each party collects from his or her own insurer.

In addition, most no-fault laws place some restriction on the right to sue the negligent driver who caused the accident. If a bodily injury claim is below a certain **monetary threshold** (such as $5000), an injured motorist is not be permitted to sue but instead would collect from his or her own insurer. However, if the bodily injury claim exceeds the threshold amount, the injured person has the right to sue the negligent driver for damages. If the negligent driver is insured, the negligent driver's insurance company will usually cover the loss.

In some states, a verbal rather than monetary threshold is used. *A* **verbal threshold** *means that a suit for damages is allowed only in serious cases, such as those involving death, dismemberment, disfigurement, or permanent loss of a bodily member or function.* Thus, if the injured person has a less severe injury than those listed, the injured person would not be permitted to sue but instead would collect from his or her insurer.

**Basic Characteristics of No-Fault Plans**    No-fault plans vary widely among the states with respect to the type of law, benefits provided, and restrictions on the right to sue.[11]

1.  *Types of no-fault plans.* Several types of no-fault plans and proposals exist. They include the following:

    - Pure no-fault plan
    - Modified no-fault plan
    - Add-on plan
    - Choice no-fault plan

    Under a **pure no-fault plan,** *accident victims could not sue at all, regardless of the amount of the claim, and no payments would be made for pain and suffering.* In effect, the tort liability system would be abolished, because accident victims could not sue for damages. Instead, injured persons would receive unlimited medical benefits and lost wages from their insurers. No state has enacted a pure no-fault plan at this time.

    Under a **modified no-fault plan,** *an injured person has the right to sue a negligent driver only*

    *if the bodily injury claim exceeds the dollar or verbal threshold.* Otherwise, the accident victim collects from his or her own insurer. Thus, modified no-fault plans only partially restrict the right to sue.

    An **add-on plan** *pays benefits to an accident victim without regard to fault, and the injured person still has the right to sue the negligent driver who caused the accident.* This plan also includes the right to sue for pain and suffering. Because the injured person retains the right to sue, add-on plans are not true no-fault laws.

    Three states (Kentucky, New Jersey, and Pennsylvania) have **choice no-fault plans.** Under such laws, motorists can elect to be covered under the state's no-fault law and pay lower premiums, or they can retain the right to sue under the tort liability system and pay higher premiums.

    Slightly more than half of the jurisdictions with no-fault laws have enacted modified plans where restrictions are placed on the right to sue. The remainder have add-on plans or choice no-fault laws. As noted earlier, no state has enacted a pure no-fault plan, and three states have choice no-fault laws.

2.  *No-fault benefits.* No-fault benefits are provided by adding an endorsement to an auto insurance policy. The endorsement is typically called "personal injury protection coverage (PIP)" which describes the no-fault benefits. Benefits are restricted to the injured person's economic loss, such as medical expenses, a percentage of lost wages, and certain other expenses. The injured person can sue for *noneconomic loss* (such as pain and suffering and inconvenience) only if the dollar threshold is exceeded or the verbal threshold is met.

    The following benefits are typically provided:

    - Medical expenses
    - Loss of earnings
    - Essential services expenses
    - Funeral expenses
    - Survivors' loss benefits

    *Medical expenses are paid usually up to some maximum limit.* Michigan has no dollar limit on medical benefits. Rehabilitation expenses incurred by an injured accident victim are also paid.

    *Payments are made for the loss of earnings.* The no-fault benefits are typically limited to a stated percentage of the disabled person's weekly or monthly earnings, with a maximum limit in terms of dollar amount and duration.

*Benefits are also paid for* **essential services expenses** *ordinarily performed by the injured person.* Examples include housework, cooking, lawn mowing, and house repairs.

*Funeral expenses are paid up to some dollar limit.* In some states, funeral expenses are included as part of the medical expense limit. In other states, funeral expenses are a separate benefit.

**Survivors' loss benefits** *are payable to eligible survivors, such as a surviving spouse and dependent children.* The survivors typically receive periodic income payments or a lump sum to compensate them for the death of a covered person.

A number of states also require that **optional no-fault benefits** above the prescribed minimums be made available. Likewise, many states require insurers to offer **optional deductibles** that may be used to restrict or eliminate certain no-fault coverages.

3. *Right to sue.* In those states with add-on plans, there are no restrictions on the right to sue. The accident victim can receive first-party no-fault benefits from his or her insurer and still sue the negligent driver for damages.

All states permit a lawsuit in the event of a serious injury. A serious injury typically is an injury that results in death, dismemberment, disfigurement, bone fracture, permanent loss of a bodily function or organ, or permanent disability. Under these circumstances, the injured person can sue for damages, including payment for pain and suffering.

In those states with modified no-fault laws, the right to sue is restricted. In general, the accident victim can sue the negligent driver for general damages, including pain and suffering, only if a dollar or verbal threshold is met.

Finally, the three states with choice no-fault laws allow motorists to elect coverage under the state's no-fault law with lower premiums and restrictions on lawsuits or, alternatively, to retain the right to sue under the tort liability system with higher premiums.

4. *Exclusion of property damage.* With the exception of Michigan, no-fault laws cover only bodily injury and not property damage.

Thus, if a negligent driver smashed into your car, you would still be permitted to sue for the property damage to your car. It is argued that a lawsuit for property damage does not normally result in long court delays, expensive legal fees, and defects similar to those now found in bodily injury lawsuits. Also, the size of a property damage claim settlement is relatively small when compared to bodily injury liability settlements.

**Arguments for No-Fault Laws**   Proponents of no-fault laws argue that an alternative system is needed because of defects in the liability system. These defects include the following:

- *Difficulty in determining fault.* Critics argue that auto accidents occur suddenly and unexpectedly, and determination of fault is often difficult. Under a no-fault law, it is not necessary to determine fault. Each party collects from his or her insurer if the bodily injury claim is below a certain dollar threshold or does not meet the description of a verbal threshold.

- *Inequity in claim payments.* Under the present tort system, small claims are often overpaid, whereas serious claims may be underpaid. As a result, auto accident victims with serious injuries often recover less than the full amount of their economic losses.

- *High transactions costs and attorney fees.* Critics also argue that the present tort system incurs high transactions costs and attorney fees. More than half of the tort dollars moving through the traditional tort system never reach injured victims. As noted in Chapter 19, attorney fees, legal defense costs, and administrative costs account for over half of each dollar paid. Thus, the present system is flawed by high transactions costs and attorney fees.

- *Fraudulent and inflated claims.* The present system is flawed because of fraudulent and inflated claims. Two types of abuse are present. First, explicit fraud occurs, including staged auto accidents, fake claims, and collusion among doctors, attorneys, and chiropractors. Second, the tort system encourages injured victims to inflate their claims above their actual losses to increase their damage awards. Because payments for noneconomic losses (pain and suffering) are difficult to calculate, one rule of thumb is to calculate such losses as two to three times the claimant's economic losses (medical bills and lost wages). *When pain and suffering awards are based on a multiple of medical expenses and wage loss, claimants have a powerful incentive to inflate their claims.*

■ *Delay in payments.* Under the present tort system, many claims are not paid promptly because of the time consumed by investigation, negotiation, and waiting for a court date. Moreover, hiring an attorney does not necessarily speed up payment. An Insurance Research Council (IRC) study of auto accident victims showed that claimants without attorneys received payments significantly more quickly than claimants with attorneys. *Among claimants without an attorney, 62 percent of those who filed with their own insurer, and 40 percent of those who filed with another insurer, settled their claims within three months. In contrast, among claimants who hired an attorney, only 29 percent of those who filed with their own insurer, and 8 percent of those who filed with another insurer, settled their claims in less than three months.*[12]

### Arguments Against No-Fault Laws

Supporters of the tort system argue that no-fault laws are also defective. Major arguments against no-fault laws include the following:

■ *Defects of the negligence system are exaggerated.* A large proportion of fatal crashes and serious accidents involve alcohol where fault can usually be determined without difficulty. Also, the fact that most claims are settled out of court suggests that the present system is working fairly well.

■ *Claims of efficiency and premium savings are exaggerated.* Predictions of greater efficiency and premium savings from no-fault laws are exaggerated and unreliable. In many states with no-fault laws, premiums have increased more rapidly than in tort liability states.

■ *Court delays are not universal.* Court delays are a problem only in certain large metropolitan areas, and delays can be reduced by providing more adequate courts and improved procedures. The courts are burdened because of an increase

in the number of divorce cases, drug and other criminal cases, and other types of civil suits.

■ *Safe drivers may be penalized.* A no-fault plan may penalize safe drivers and provide a bonus for irresponsible motorists who cause accidents. The rating system may inequitably allocate accident costs to the drivers who are not at fault, and their premiums may go up as a result.

■ *There is no payment for pain and suffering.* Plaintiff attorneys argue that the true cost to the accident victim cannot be measured only by the actual dollar amount of medical expenses and loss of wages. Pain and suffering should also be considered in determining the amount of damages.

■ *The tort liability system needs only to be reformed.* This reform could be accomplished by increasing the number of judges and courtrooms, limiting the fees of attorneys, and using arbitration rather than the courts to settle small cases.

### Evaluation of No-Fault Laws

Some states have repealed their no-fault laws because relatively low monetary thresholds increased the number of lawsuits and costs. Other states have changed their plans over time. A recent study of no-fault plans by RAND's Institute for Civil Justice[13] provides valuable information concerning the declining popularity of no-fault plans. The two major findings of the study are:

■ *No-fault plans initially reduced litigation in claims settlement, but that advantage has declined over time.* Today the two systems, tort and the various forms of no-fault, are largely the same in terms of accident victims seeking legal remedies and noneconomic damage awards.

■ *Auto liability insurance premiums are significantly higher in no-fault states than in tort states. In three states that repealed their no-fault law during the period examined, liability insurance premiums dropped by 10 to 30 percent.* Two explanations were offered for the high cost of no-fault insurance relative to the cost of coverage under the traditional tort system. First, as noted at the beginning of this section, *no-fault systems offer a broader range of benefits than the benefits offered under traditional medical payments coverage in tort system states.* Second, *auto insurers pay more for the same medical services in no-fault states than in tort-system states.* The authors of the study offered several possible explanations for this second phenomenon.[14] In no-fault states, auto insurers become primary health-care insurers for benefits paid under no-fault's PIP coverage. Traditional health insurers have greater expertise than auto insurers. Second, traditional health insurers are better at designing medical insurance contracts that assist in cost containment. Third, fear of bad-faith claims actions against auto insurers prevents them from being more aggressive in investigating medical claims of their policyholders.

## AUTO INSURANCE FOR HIGH-RISK DRIVERS

Some drivers have difficulty obtaining auto insurance through normal market channels. This group includes younger drivers who account for a disproportionate number of auto accidents, drivers with poor driving records, and drivers with one or more convictions for drunk driving. These drivers can obtain auto insurance in the **shared market (also called the residual market)**. The shared market refers to plans in which auto insurers participate to make insurance available to drivers who are unable to obtain coverage in the standard markets.

High-risk drivers who have difficulty in obtaining auto insurance in the standard markets can purchase the insurance from a number of sources. They include the following:

- Automobile insurance plan
- Joint underwriting association (JUA)
- Reinsurance facility
- Maryland Automobile Insurance Fund
- Specialty insurers

### Automobile Insurance Plan

Most states have an **automobile insurance plan (also called an assigned risk plan)** that makes auto insurance available to drivers who are unable to obtain insurance in the voluntary market. Under such a plan, all auto insurers in the state are assigned their proportionate share of high-risk drivers based on the total volume of auto insurance premiums written in the state. For example, if Insurer A writes 5 percent of the auto insurance premiums in the state, Insurer

A must accept 5 percent of the high-risk applicants in the automobile insurance plan (see Exhibit 23.2). The premiums charged, however, are substantially higher than those charged in the voluntary markets. It is not uncommon for high-risk drivers to pay two or three times the standard premium.

The major advantage of automobile insurance plans is that a high-risk driver generally has at least one source for obtaining liability insurance. Thus, the social objective of protecting innocent accident victims is at least partially met. Nevertheless, such plans have several disadvantages, which include the following:

- *Despite higher premiums paid by high-risk drivers, auto insurance plans have incurred substantial underwriting losses.* Thus, good drivers in the voluntary markets are subsidizing the substandard drivers.
- *High premiums may cause many high-risk drivers to go uninsured.* This effect is the exact opposite of what the plans are intended to accomplish.

**EXHIBIT 23.2**

**Example of an Automobile Insurance Plan (Generalized)**

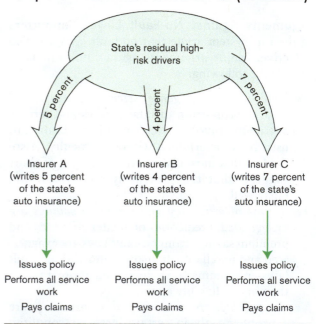

SOURCE: Adapted from Karen L. Hamilton and Cheryl L. Ferguson, *Personal Risk Management and Property-Liability Insurance,* 1st ed. (Malvern, PA: American Institute for Chartered Property Casualty Underwriters/Insurance Institute of America, 2002), Exhibit 9-5, p. 9.37.

- *Many drivers who are "clean risks" with no driving convictions are often arbitrarily placed in the plans.* This can happen when poor territorial loss experience or inadequate rate increases granted by regulatory officials cause insurers to restrict the writing of auto insurance in a given territory or state in the standard markets.

## Joint Underwriting Association

A few states have established joint underwriting associations to make auto insurance available to high-risk drivers. A **joint underwriting association (JUA)** is an organization of auto insurers operating in the state in which high-risk business is placed in a common pool, and each company pays its pro rata share of pool losses and expenses. The JUA influences the design of the high-risk auto policy and sets the rates that are charged. All underwriting losses are proportionately shared by the companies based on premiums written in the state.

A limited number of insurance companies are designated as servicing insurers to administer the high-risk JUA business. Each agent or broker is assigned a company that provides claim services and other services to the policyholders. Although only a limited number of large insurers are servicing insurers, all insurers share in the underwriting losses, as noted earlier.

## Reinsurance Facility

A few states have established a **reinsurance facility (or pool)** for placing high-risk drivers. Under this arrangement, the insurance company must accept all applicants for insurance, both good and bad drivers. If the applicant is considered a high-risk driver, the insurer has the option of placing the driver in the reinsurance pool. Although the high-risk driver is in the reinsurance pool, the original insurer services the policy. Underwriting losses in the reinsurance facility are shared by all auto insurers in the state.

## Maryland Automobile Insurance Fund

The **Maryland Automobile Insurance Fund** is a state fund that makes auto insurance available to Maryland motorists who are unable to obtain insurance in the voluntary markets. The state fund came into existence in 1972 because of high rates charged by private insurers, large numbers of motorists who had been placed in the assigned risk plan, and difficulties experienced by high-risk drivers in obtaining insurance. The fund provides insurance to drivers who have been canceled or refused insurance by private insurers.

## Specialty Insurers

**Specialty insurers** are insurers that specialize in insuring motorists with poor driving records. These insurers typically insure drivers who have been canceled or refused insurance, teenage drivers, and drivers convicted of drunk driving. The premiums are substantially higher than premiums charged in the standard market. The actual premium paid is based on the individual's driving record, typically over the past three years. The higher the number of chargeable accidents or moving vehicle traffic violations, the higher the premium charged. The liability insurance limits are at least equal to the financial responsibility law requirement in the state, and many insurers offer higher limits on an optional basis. In addition, because the drivers have a relatively high probability of being involved in an accident, medical payments coverage often has relatively low limits, and collision insurance may require a high deductible.

# COST OF AUTO INSURANCE

Auto insurance is expensive. Auto insurers have substantially increased their rates over time because of rising medical costs, higher motor vehicle repair costs, soaring jury awards in motor vehicle liability cases, and insurance fraud and abuse. You should be aware of the factors that determine auto insurance premiums and what you can do to reduce your premiums.

The major rating factors for determining private passenger auto premiums are as follows:

- Territory
- Age, gender, and marital status
- Use of the auto
- Driver education
- Good student discount
- Number and types of cars
- Individual driving record
- Insurance score

## Territory

A base rate for liability insurance is first established, determined largely by the territory where the auto is principally used and garaged. Each state is divided into rating territories—for example, a large city, a part of a city, a suburb, or a rural area. Claims data are compiled for each territory in determining the basic rate. Thus, a city driver normally pays a higher rate than a rural driver because of the higher number of auto accidents in congested cities. In particular, auto insurance premiums are substantially higher in certain large cities because of factors such as higher density of traffic, increased likelihood of theft and vandalism, and higher incidence of fraud. Exhibit 23.3 shows average auto insurance premiums for the 10 most expensive and 10 least expensive cities as of August 2011.

## Age, Gender, and Marital Status

Age, gender, and marital status are important in determining the total premium. Most states permit these factors to be used in determining premiums.

Age is an extremely important rating factor because young drivers are involved in a disproportionate number of auto accidents. In 2009, licensed drivers under age 20 accounted for 6.4 percent of all licensed drivers. However, this group accounted for 1,473,000 motor vehicle crashes in 2009, or 15.3 percent of the drivers in all crashes (see Exhibit 23.4).

Gender is also important in determining the total premiums. Male drivers typically are involved in a higher proportion of both total accidents and fatal auto accidents than female drivers.[15] As a result of higher accident rates, males generally pay more for auto insurance than females.

Marital status is also important for some age groups, because young married male drivers tend to have relatively fewer accidents than unmarried male drivers in the same age category.

Certain credits and rate discounts may be allowed with respect to the rating factor of age. A premium credit may be given if a youthful driver of a family car is attending a school or college more than 100 miles away from home and does not have a car at school. Also, female drivers ages 30 through 64 may be eligible for a rate discount if they are the only drivers in their households. Older drivers are also eligible for rate discounts from many insurers.

**Exhibit 23.3**
**Top Ten Most Expensive and Least Expensive Cities for Automobile Insurance, 2011[1]**

| Rank | Most Expensive Cities | Average Annual Auto Premiums | Rank | Least Expensive Cities | Average Annual Auto Premiums |
|---|---|---|---|---|---|
| 1 | Detroit, MI | $5,941 | 1 | Roanoke, VA | $937 |
| 2 | Philadelphia, PA | $4,076 | 2 | Green Bay, WI | $999 |
| 3 | New Orleans, LA | $3,599 | 3 | Wapakoneta, OH | $1,008 |
| 4 | Miami, FL | $3,388 | 4 | Portland, ME | $1,053 |
| 5 | Newark, NJ | $2,867 | 5 | Boise, ID | $1,065 |
| 6 | Baltimore, MD | $2,851 | 6 | Richmond, VA | $1,109 |
| 7 | Tampa, FL | $2,796 | 7 | Fairfield, OH | $1,111 |
| 8 | Providence, RI | $2,711 | 8 | Charlotte, NC | $1,134 |
| 9 | Los Angeles, CA | $2,664 | 9 | Lafayette, IN | $1,140 |
| 10 | Las Vegas, NV | $2,651 | 10 | Pocatello, ID | $1,143 |

[1]As of August, 2011. Based on business driving for a 2012 Chevrolet Malibu LS with $100,000/$300,000/$50,000 liability limits, collision and comprehensive with $500 deductibles, and $100,000/$300,000 uninsured motorists coverage.

NOTE: Data are from Runzheimer International.

SOURCE: *The Insurance Information Fact Book 2012*, New York: Insurance Information Institute, p. 65.

**Exhibit 23.4**
**Drivers in Motor Vehicle Crashes by Age, 2009**

| Age Group | Number of Licensed Drivers | Percent of Total | Drivers in Fatal Crashes | Involvement Rate[1] | Drivers in all Crashes | Involvement Rate[1] |
|---|---|---|---|---|---|---|
| Under 16 | 409,526 | 0.2% | 181 | NA | 148,000 | NA |
| 16 to 20 | 12,913,024 | 6.2 | 5,051 | 39.12 | 1,325,000 | 10,261 |
| 21 to 24 | 14,053,321 | 6.7 | 4,597 | 32.71 | 1,146,000 | 8,155 |
| 25 to 34 | 36,326,817 | 17.3 | 8,610 | 23.70 | 1,908,000 | 5,252 |
| 35 to 44 | 38,158,133 | 18.2 | 7,757 | 20.33 | 1,694,000 | 4,439 |
| 45 to 54 | 41,665,892 | 19.9 | 7,664 | 18.39 | 1,603,000 | 3,847 |
| 55 to 64 | 33,156,841 | 15.8 | 5,276 | 15.91 | 994,000 | 2,998 |
| 65 to 74 | 19,124,755 | 9.1 | 2,868 | 15.00 | 480,000 | 2,510 |
| Over 74 | 13,810,077 | 6.6 | 2,550 | 18.46 | 315,000 | 2,281 |
| Total | 209,618,386 | 100% | 45,230[2] | 21.58 | 9,614,000 | 4,586 |

[1] Per 100,000 licensed drivers.
[2] Includes drivers of unknown age.

NA=Not applicable.

NOTE: Data are from U.S. Department of Transportation, National Highway Traffic Safety Administration; Federal Highway Administration.

SOURCE: *The Insurance Fact Book 2012*: New York: Insurance Information Institute, p. 154.

When teenagers are added to the parent's policy, auto insurance premiums soar. Discounts are especially important in such cases, especially discounts for an approved safe-driver course and for being a good student. Some tips for insuring teen drivers are offered in Insight 23.2.

## Use of the Auto

Use of the auto is another important rating factor. Insurers classify vehicles on the basis of how the car is driven, such as the following:

- Pleasure use—not used in business or customarily driven to work, unless the one-way mileage to work is under 3 miles
- Drive to work—not used in business, but is driven 3 to 15 miles to work each day
- Drive to work—not used in business, but is driven 15 or more miles each way
- Business use—customarily used in business or professional pursuits
- Farm use—principally garaged on a farm or ranch, and not used in any other business or driven to school or work

A car classified for farm use has the lowest rating factor, followed next by pleasure use of the car. Driving the car to work or using it for business purposes requires a higher rating factor.

Some insurers are using technology, rather than general classifications, to better track vehicle use. California permits insurers to use actual mileage as a rating factor, with the mileage monitored by OnStar or a similar service. Some insurers are experimenting with data recorders to more closely track the use of a vehicle. *A **data recorder** is an electronic device that can be installed in a vehicle to track certain driving behaviors.* For example, an insurer may wish to know how quickly a vehicle accelerates, how hard brakes are applied, how far it is driven, and whether it is driven in the daytime or at night. Progressive Insurance Company launched a voluntary program in 2011 through which their policyholders could elect to have a data recorder installed in their vehicle in hopes of lowering premiums. Use of data recorders raises privacy issues, as well as questions regarding who owns the data and how the data may be used.

## Driver Education

If a youthful operator successfully completes an approved driver education course, he or she can receive a driver training credit, such as 10 or 15 percent. The rate credit is based on the premise that driver education courses for teenage drivers can reduce accidents.

## Good Student Discount

A **good student discount** can also reduce premiums. The cost reduction is based on the premise that good students are better drivers; the psychological makeup and intellectual capacity of superior students also contribute to the safer operation of an auto. Good students generally are cautious and risk adverse. This risk aversion may also be reflected in their driving habits, which make them better drivers.

To qualify for the discount, typically the individual must be a full-time student in high school or college, be at least age 16, and meet one of the following:

- Rank in the upper 20 percent of the class
- Have a B or better average, or the equivalent
- Have at least a 3.0 average
- Be on the dean's list or honor roll

---

## INSIGHT 23.2

### Protect Yourself: Insuring Your Teen Driver

*Insuring a teen driver is often an additional cost for many parents. Many companies consider drivers under the age of 25 a higher risk, and this often translates into higher premiums. Here are some tips from the National Association of Insurance Commissioners (NAIC) to help you get the best value for your auto insurance dollar.*

**1. Teen Driver Facts**

According to the American Academy of Pediatrics, one-third of deaths of people ages 16 to 20 are due to motor-vehicle accidents. That's more than 5000 teens a year. Faced with those statistics, it's important to view teen driving as a privilege, not a right.

**2. Lay the Ground Rules**

Insuring a teen driver will result in additional costs for you, no matter which insurance policy you choose. However, how well your teen respects the privilege of driving is a factor you can control. Lay some ground rules for safe driving before your teen ever gets in the driver's seat. Set up driving rules, including:

- Hours during which the teen can and cannot drive
- Number of friends allowed in the car at one time
- Number of miles teen is allowed to drive per day or week

You may also want to consider setting up a driving contract with your teen. The contract should clearly list the teen's duties and responsibilities when driving and caring for the vehicle and should be signed by both of you.

**3. Purchase a Vehicle or Add a Driver?**

You may not want to purchase a car specifically for your teenager, but adding another driver to your policy can be costly. For example, if you drive a newer, expensive sports car, adding a teen driver may considerably raise your premiums. However, a modestly priced economy car with liability coverage may be more appropriate for your teen. Make sure you discuss options with your insurance agent.

**4. Give Complete, Correct Information**

When you call for a quote or fill out an application, give complete and correct information, such as make, model and year of the car the teen will be driving. Since your premium quote will be based on this information, it is very important that your information be as accurate and complete as possible.

**5. Shop Around**

It pays to shop around before buying insurance. Different companies can offer noticeably different premiums. For example, if your child is an honor roll student, passed a driver's education course or has a job, some companies may offer a reduced premium. Some discounts include:

- Two or more cars on a policy
- Participation in driver education courses
- Good student driver under age 25
- Airbags or other safety equipment
- Anti-theft devices
- Auto/home insurance on same policy or with same company

**6. Consider Revising Coverage, Deductibles**

You may reduce your auto insurance costs by raising the deductibles on physical damage (collision and comprehensive) coverages. Be sure to review your current deductibles to determine whether you can afford to absorb a larger portion of your loss in the event of an accident. Also, consider lowering or eliminating physical damage coverages on older vehicles—unless a lienholder, such as a bank, requires it.

**7. Regularly Review Your Policy; Update Accordingly**

Regularly review your policy to make sure the basis for your premium is as accurate as possible. Here are some things that can affect your premium:

- Adding or removing a vehicle from your policy
- Teen graduates from high school or reaches the age 18

**8. Get More Information**

For more information, contact your state insurance department. You can link to your insurance department's Web site by visiting www.naic.org. Click on "State Insurance Web Sites," then click on your state.

Source: The National Association of Insurance Commissioners (NAIC), *Consumer Alert*.

A school official must sign a form indicating that the student has met one of the scholastic requirements.

## Number and Types of Cars

A **multicar discount** is available if the insured owns two or more cars. This discount is based on the assumption that two cars owned by the same person will be driven more than one car, but not twice as much.

The year, make, and model also affect the cost of physical damage insurance on the car. As the car gets older, premiums for physical damage insurance decline.

Also, the cost of repairs is an important rating factor for physical damage insurance. New cars are rated based on susceptibility to damage and cost of repairs. Cars that are damage-resistant and relatively easy to repair generally have lower rates.

## Individual Driving Record

Many insurers have **safe driver plans** where the premiums paid are based in large part on the individual driving records of the insured and vehicle operators who live with the insured. Drivers who have clean driving records qualify for lower rates than drivers who have poor records. A clean driving record means that the driver has not been involved in any accident where he or she is at fault and has not been convicted of a serious traffic violation in the last three years.

Points are assessed for accidents and traffic violations, and rate surcharges are applied accordingly. Points are charged for a conviction of drunk driving, failure to stop and report an accident, homicide or assault involving an auto, driving on a suspended or revoked driver's license, and other offenses. The actual premium paid is based on the total number of accumulated points.

Most insurers impose a surcharge for a chargeable accident that exceeds a given amount, such as $500. The surcharge generally lasts three to six years. For example, the base premium may be surcharged 10 percent for the first accident and 25 percent for the second.

## Insurance Score

Another important rating factor is an insurance score based on the applicant's credit record. *An insurance score is a credit-based score that proponents claim is highly predictive of future claim costs.* They believe that individuals who are careful with credit usage will also exercise care in other areas, such as driving behavior. An insurance score is a statistical analysis of an individual's credit record that insurers believe helps to predict the likelihood of filing an insurance claim within a specified future time period. The insurance score is based on an individual's credit history and is combined with other rating factors for purposes of underwriting and rating. Insurers claim there is a high inverse correlation between insurance scores and the likelihood of an auto accident. As a group, drivers with poor credit tend to file relatively more claims than drivers with good credit; conversely, drivers with good credit tend to file relatively fewer claims. Actuarial studies generally support this conclusion.

Credit organizations, such as Fair Isaac Company (FICO) and ChoicePoint, calculate insurance scores for auto insurers based on the applicant's credit history. A mathematical formula assigns weights to various credit factors and then summarizes the results in a three digit number. The formulas used to calculate insurance scores are proprietary, but typically include late payments, outstanding debt, past due amounts, public records, payment patterns, and similar credit factors.

## SHOPPING FOR AUTO INSURANCE

As a careful insurance consumer, you should remember certain suggestions when you buy auto insurance (see Exhibit 23.5).

### Carry Adequate Liability Insurance

The most important rule in purchasing auto insurance is to carry adequate liability insurance. If you carry minimum limits to satisfy the state's financial or compulsory insurance law, such as $25,000/$50,000/$25,000, you are seriously underinsured. Even if you carry higher limits of $100,000/$300,000/$50,000, you are still underinsured if a bad accident occurs and you are at fault. A negligent driver who is underinsured could have a deficiency judgment filed against him or her, under which both present and future income and assets could be attached to satisfy the judgment. You can avoid this problem by carrying adequate liability limits.

You should also consider purchasing a personal umbrella policy, which will provide another $1 million to $10 million of liability insurance on an excess basis after the underlying auto insurance liability limit is exhausted. The personal umbrella policy is discussed in Chapter 24.

### Carry Higher Deductibles

Another important suggestion is to carry higher deductibles for collision and other-than-collision losses (also called comprehensive). Many insureds have $250 deductibles. Increasing the deductible from $250 to $500, however, will reduce your collision and comprehensive cost by 15 to 30 percent. If you can afford to fund a higher deductible, you might even consider a $1000 collision deductible.

**EXHIBIT 23.5**
**Tips for Buying Auto Insurance**

Insight 23.3 discusses the important factors you should consider before you increase the collision deductible.

### Drop Collision Insurance on Older Vehicles

You should consider dropping collision insurance on your car if it is an older model with a low market value. The cost of repairs after an accident will often exceed the value of an older car, but the insurer will pay no more than its current market value (less the deductible). One rough rule of thumb is that when a standard auto (such as a Chevrolet, Ford, or Dodge) is more than six years old, you should drop the collision coverage on the car.

### Shop Around for Auto Insurance

Another important suggestion is to shop carefully for auto insurance. There is intense price competition among insurers, and there may be significant differences in premiums.[16] Contact several insurers

---

## INSIGHT 23.3

### Increasing the Collision Deductible to Save Money—Some Important Considerations

Financial advisors commonly recommend a higher collision deductible to save money. Typical ads claim annual premium savings of 10 percent to 40 percent. However, a higher collision deductible may not always be the best option for all insureds. Other factors must be considered to justify a higher deductible.

- *Ability to fund a higher deductible.* A higher deductible should not be selected if you have limited savings and cannot pay a higher deductible if a loss occurs. For example, if you increase the deductible from $250 to $1000, your out-of-pocket expense will increase $750 if an at-fault accident occurs. Most insureds probably will use a credit card to finance the deductible. If the deductible is financed by monthly payments, relatively high interest payments over time will wipe out part or all of the premium savings, especially if an early loss occurs.

- *Premium savings from a higher deductible.* A key consideration is the premium savings that result from a higher deductible. You should not select a higher deductible if the premium savings are minimal. There is no single rule here, but one rule, by the International Risk Management Institute (IRMI), makes some sense. *IRMI recommends a higher deductible if the premium savings over the next two years equal or exceed the difference between the two deductibles.* For example, assume that a $250 deductible requires an annual collision premium of $1000, and that a $500 deductible reduces the premium to $800, for an annual savings of $200. Total premium savings over the two-year period are $400, which exceed the difference between the two deductibles ($250).[1] The higher deductible is justified. In effect, if a loss occurs, you would be funding the difference in deductibles over a two-year period.

Next, consider an actual case where the premium savings are minimal. Kevin, age 34, increased the collision deductible from $100 to $1000 with an annual savings of $324. Total premium savings over the two-year period are $648, which is less than the difference between the two deductibles ($900). Based on the IRMI rule, the higher deductible is not justified.

- *Insured's driving record.* The insured's driving record is critical to the financial success of a high-deductible policy. You should not select a higher deductible if your driving record is poor. At-fault accidents will wipe out any premium savings from the higher deductible, especially if several accidents occur during a relatively short period. Higher deductibles, however, benefit insureds with good driving records since the cumulative savings in annual premiums will be substantial over a long period of time if no losses occur.

- *Collision insurance on older cars.* Collision insurance on older cars with a relatively low market value (e.g., $2000 to $3000) generally should not be purchased. If an at-fault collision loss occurs, you will receive the actual cash value of the loss minus a deductible. The cost of repairs after the accident will often exceed the value of an older car, but the insurer will not pay more than its actual cash value. Retaining the physical damage loss exposure for an older car generally is less expensive than paying the higher premiums for collision coverage and absorbing a deductible after a loss occurs. Moreover, if you are at fault in an accident, insurers typically impose a premium surcharge for three to six years. Total collision and surcharged premiums, plus the deductible that must be paid if an at-fault accident occurs, may exceed the value of the older car during this same period.

[1]"Personal Lines Beat: Selling Higher Deductibles," *Personal Lines Pilot*, IRMI e-mail newsletter, Issue #51, October 12, 2007.

and compare premiums. Many state insurance departments publish shoppers' guides to help insurance consumers make better purchase decisions. State insurance departments also have Web sites that provide information on auto insurance rates in different cities within the state. For example, Exhibit 23.6 compares the rates of 14 insurers that write a large part of the coverage in Nebraska for six different classes of drivers in southeast and southwest Omaha. As you can see, rates among insurers vary widely for the same coverages. Although the savings by shopping around and comparing rates can be substantial, remember that the premium is not the only factor to consider.

**Exhibit 23.6**
**Wide Variation in Auto Insurance Premiums for Omaha, Nebraska (Six-Month Premiums: August 1, 2010 Rates)**

| | Type of Car and Coverage Limits | |
|---|---|---|
| | *2009 Toyota Camry LE 4-Door* | |
| Liability Limits of: | $100,000/$300,000 | Bodily Injury |
| | $100,000 | Property Damage |
| | $5,000 | Medical Payments |
| | $100,000/$300,000 | Underinsured Motorist |
| | $100,000/$300,000 | Uninsured Motorist |
| | $250 | Collision Deductible |
| | $100 | Comprehensive Deductible |

*Hypothetical Drivers*

Example 1: 17-year-old single male, principal driver, pleasure use, driving fewer than 12,000 miles annually, lives with parents. No violations or accidents in the last three years.

Example 2: 17-year-old single female, principal driver, pleasure use, driving fewer than 12,000 miles annually, lives with parents. No violations or accidents in the last three years.

Example 3: 21-year-old single male, principal driver, pleasure use, driving fewer than 12,000 miles annually, student, rents apartment. No violations or accidents in the last three years.

Example 4: 21-year-old single female, principal driver, pleasure use, driving fewer than 12,000 miles annually, student, rents apartment. No violations or accidents in the last three years.

Example 5: 44-year-old married female, principal driver, pleasure use, driving fewer than 12,000 miles annually, employed 10+ years, owns home 15+ years. No violations or accidents in the last three years.

Example 6: 65-year-old married male, principal driver, pleasure use, driving fewer than 12,000 miles annually, employed 10+ years, owns home 15+ years. No violations or accidents in the last three years.

| | Premiums: Southeast Omaha | | | | | |
|---|---|---|---|---|---|---|
| | *Example 1* | *Example 2* | *Example 3* | *Example 4* | *Example 5* | *Example 6* |
| Company | *17-yr-old Single Male* | *17-yr-old Single Female* | *21-yr-old Single Male* | *21-yr-old Single Female* | *44-yr-old Married Female* | *65-yr-old Married Male* |
| Allstate Fire & Casualty Ins. Co. | 2,024 | 1,489 | 1,173 | 980 | 665 | 640 |
| American Family Mutual Ins. Co. | 1,875 | 1,232 | 996 | 875 | 454 | 417 |
| Farm Bureau Mutual Ins. Co | 2,325 | 1,889 | 1,195 | 1,160 | 804 | 686 |

**EXHIBIT 23.6**
**Wide Variation in Auto Insurance Premiums for Omaha, Nebraska (Six-Month Premiums: August 1, 2010 Rates)**

| Company | Premiums: Southeast Omaha | | | | | |
|---|---|---|---|---|---|---|
| | Example 1 | Example 2 | Example 3 | Example 4 | Example 5 | Example 6 |
| | 17-yr-old Single Male | 17-yr-old Single Female | 21-yr-old Single Male | 21-yr-old Single Female | 44-yr-old Married Female | 65-yr-old Married Male |
| Farmers Ins. Exchange | 703 | 683 | 692 | 598 | 413 | 399 |
| Farmers Mutual Ins. Co. of Nebr. | 1,859 | 1,307 | 1,213 | 914 | 494 | 457 |
| GEICO General Insurance Co. | 1,612 | 1,196 | 768 | 738 | 834 | 348 |
| Motor Club Insurance Association | 3,641 | 2,605 | 2,218 | 1,609 | 767 | 693 |
| Nationwide Agribusiness Ins. Co. | 1,590 | 1,191 | 1,059 | 838 | 423 | 367 |
| Progressive Northern Ins. Co. | 3,644 | 3,012 | 1,253 | 948 | 569 | 543 |
| Progressive Universal Ins. Co. | 3,066 | 2,547 | 1,083 | 810 | 584 | 561 |
| Shelter Mutual Insurance Co. | 2,558 | 1,693 | 1,550 | 1,161 | 684 | 538 |
| State Farm Fire & Casualty Co. | 3,055 | 2,258 | 1,775 | 1,406 | 722 | 641 |
| State Farm Mutual Auto Ins. Co. | 2,662 | 1,967 | 1,547 | 1,225 | 630 | 559 |
| United Services Automobile Ass'n | 1,160 | 994 | 559 | 485 | 322 | 330 |

| Company | Premiums: Southwest Omaha | | | | | |
|---|---|---|---|---|---|---|
| | Example 1 | Example 2 | Example 3 | Example 4 | Example 5 | Example 6 |
| | 17-yr-old Single Male | 17-yr-old Single Female | 21-yr-old Single Male | 21-yr-old Single Female | 44-yr-old Married Female | 65-yr-old Married Male |
| Allstate Fire & Casualty Ins. Co. | 1,666 | 1,234 | 967 | 811 | 554 | 534 |
| American Family Mutual Ins. Co. | 1,875 | 1,232 | 996 | 875 | 454 | 417 |
| Farm Bureau Mutual Ins. Co | 1,787 | 1,453 | 914 | 893 | 617 | 527 |
| Farmers Ins. Exchange | 590 | 573 | 582 | 502 | 347 | 336 |
| Farmers Mutual Ins. Co. of Nebr. | 1,859 | 1,307 | 1,213 | 914 | 494 | 457 |

*(Continued)*

**Exhibit 23.6** (continued)

**Wide Variation in Auto Insurance Premiums for Omaha, Nebraska (Six-Month Premiums: August 1, 2010 Rates)**

| | Premiums: Southwest Omaha | | | | | |
| | Example 1 | Example 2 | Example 3 | Example 4 | Example 5 | Example 6 |
| Company | 17-yr-old Single Male | 17-yr-old Single Female | 21-yr-old Single Male | 21-yr-old Single Female | 44-yr-old Married Female | 65-yr-old Married Male |
|---|---|---|---|---|---|---|
| GEICO General Insurance Co. | 1,457 | 1,083 | 693 | 667 | 347 | 314 |
| Motor Club Insurance Association | 3,401 | 2,434 | 2,072 | 1,503 | 718 | 649 |
| Nationwide Agribusiness Ins. Co. | 1,444 | 1,082 | 965 | 764 | 388 | 337 |
| Progressive Northern Ins. Co. | 3,140 | 2,627 | 1,052 | 812 | 486 | 470 |
| Progressive Universal Ins. Co. | 2,687 | 2,257 | 928 | 708 | 516 | 501 |
| Shelter Mutual Insurance Co. | 2,168 | 1,435 | 1,314 | 985 | 582 | 458 |
| State Farm Fire & Casualty Co. | 2,257 | 1,669 | 1,315 | 1,043 | 538 | 479 |
| State Farm Mutual Auto Ins. Co. | 1,969 | 1,459 | 1,147 | 909 | 470 | 418 |
| United Services Automobile Ass'n | 1,100 | 943 | 527 | 459 | 305 | 313 |

Source: Excerpted from Nebraska Department of Insurance, *Auto Insurance: A Rate Comparison Guide*, Revised October 2010.

## Take Advantage of Discounts

When shopping for auto insurance, you should determine whether you are eligible for one or more discounts. All insurers do not offer the same discounts, and certain discounts are not available in all states. Common discounts include the following:

- *Multicar discount*—10 to 15 percent
- *No accidents in three years*—5 to 10 percent
- *Drivers over age 50*—5 to 15 percent
- *Defensive driving course*—5 to 10 percent
- *Antitheft device*—5 to 50 percent discount for comprehensive (other-than-collision loss)
- *Antilock brakes*—5 to 10 percent
- *Good student discount*—5 to 25 percent
- *Auto and homeowners policy with same insurer*—5 to 15 percent
- *College student away from home without a car*—10 to 40 percent

## Improve Your Driving Record

If you are a high-risk driver and are paying exorbitant premiums, improving your driving record will substantially reduce your premiums. Obviously, a driving record cannot be improved overnight as it reflects experience over a period of time. In the meantime, you should consider other alternatives. Although physical damage insurance on a new or late-model car can easily double the premiums for a high-risk driver, an older car can be driven without collision insurance. You might also consider riding a motorcycle or bicycle or using mass transit. Nevertheless, there is no substitute for a good driving record.

To earn and maintain a good driving record, you should not drive after you have been drinking alcohol. Impaired drivers account for a relatively high proportion of auto accidents in which someone is seriously injured or killed. *A conviction for driving under the influence (DUI) can have a devastating effect on the premiums you are charged.* Premiums can easily double or triple after a DUI conviction.

## Maintain Good Credit

Another important suggestion is to maintain good credit. As noted earlier, many auto insurers use an applicant's credit record for purposes to underwriting or rating. Applicants with good or superior credit records may be able to purchase auto insurance at lower rates than applicants with poor credit records. A good credit record can also result in lower interest rates on credit cards and mortgage loans and higher credit limits. If your credit history is poor, clean it up if you wish to pay lower premiums.

---

### CASE APPLICATION

Paige, age 26, has purchased a new Ford sedan. She has a clean driving record. Collision coverage on the car in a small midwestern city where she lives would cost approximately $630 every six months with a $100 deductible, $566 with a $250 deductible, $492 with a $500 deductible, and $368 with a $1000 deductible. The state has a compulsory insurance law that requires minimum liability limits of $25,000/$50,000/$25,000. Paige would like to purchase collision insurance with a $100 deductible because the out-of-pocket cost to repair her car in an accident where she is at fault would be relatively small. She wants to purchase the minimum liability limits, because she has few financial assets to protect. Paige is also concerned that she might be seriously injured by a driver who has no insurance.

Assume that Paige asks your advice concerning her auto insurance coverages. Based on the above facts, answer the following questions.

a. Paige wants to know why auto insurance costs so much. Explain to her the factors that determine auto insurance rates.

b. Do you recommend that Paige purchase collision insurance with a $100 deductible? Explain your answer.

c. Do you agree with Paige that only minimum liability limits should be purchased because she has few financial assets to protect? Explain your answer.

d. Assume that Paige adds uninsured motorists coverage to her policy. Would she be completely protected against the financial consequences of a bodily injury caused by an uninsured driver? Explain your answer.

e. Paige would like to reduce her auto premiums because her monthly car payments are high. Explain to Paige the various methods for reducing or holding down auto insurance premiums.

---

## SUMMARY

- Financial responsibility laws require motorists to show proof of financial responsibility after an accident involving bodily injury or property damage over a certain amount, for conviction of certain offenses, and for failure to pay a final judgment resulting from an auto accident. Most motorists meet the financial responsibility law requirements by carrying auto liability insurance limits of a certain amount.

- Compulsory insurance laws require motorists to carry auto liability insurance at least equal to a certain amount before the vehicle can be licensed or registered.

- A few states have unsatisfied judgment funds to compensate accident victims who have exhausted all other means of recovery. The accident victim must obtain a judgment against the negligent driver who caused the accident and show that the judgment cannot be collected.

- Uninsured motorists coverage is another approach for compensating auto accident victims. Uninsured motorists coverage compensates the accident victim who has a bodily injury caused by an uninsured motorist, by a hit-and-run driver, or by a negligent driver whose company is insolvent.

- No-fault auto insurance means that after an auto accident involving a bodily injury, each party collects from his or her own insurer, regardless of fault. There are several types of no-fault plans and no-fault proposals: pure no-fault plan; modified no-fault plan; add-on plan; and choice no-fault plan.

■ The arguments for no-fault auto insurance laws are summarized as follows:

   Difficulty in determining fault

   Inequity in claim payments

   High transactions costs and attorney fees

   Fraudulent and excessive claims

   Delay in payments

■ The arguments against no-fault auto insurance laws are summarized as follows:

   Defects of the negligence system are exaggerated.

   Claims of efficiency and premium savings are exaggerated.

   Court delays are not universal.

   Safe drivers may be penalized.

   There is no payment for pain and suffering.

   The tort liability system needs to be reformed instead.

■ Several approaches are used to provide auto insurance to high-risk drivers:

   Automobile insurance plan

   Joint underwriting association (JUA)

   Reinsurance facility

   Maryland Automobile Insurance Fund

   Specialty insurers

■ The premium charged for auto insurance is a function of numerous variables, including:

   Territory

   Age, gender, and marital status

   Use of the auto

   Driver education

   Good student discount

   Number and types of cars

   Individual driving record

   Insurance score

■ Consumer experts suggest several rules to follow when shopping for auto insurance:

   Carry adequate liability insurance.

   Carry higher deductibles.

   Drop collision insurance on older vehicles.

   Shop around for auto insurance.

   Take advantage of discounts.

   Improve your driving record.

   Maintain good credit.

## KEY CONCEPTS AND TERMS

Add-on plan (513)

Automobile insurance plan (assigned risk plan) (516)

Choice no-fault plan (513)

Compulsory insurance law (509)

Data recorder (519)

Essential services expenses (514)

Financial responsibility law (506)

Good student discount (520)

Insurance score (521)

Joint underwriting association (JUA) (517)

Low-cost auto insurance (512)

Maryland Automobile Insurance Fund (517)

Modified no-fault plan (513)

Monetary threshold (513)

Multicar discount (521)

No-fault auto insurance (512)

"No pay, no play" laws (512)

Optional deductibles (514)

Optional no-fault benefits (514)

Pure no-fault plan (513)

Reinsurance facility (or pool) (517)

Safe driver plans (521)

Shared market (residual market) (516)

Specialty insurers (517)

Survivors' loss benefits (514)

Uninsured motorists coverage (509)

Unsatisfied judgment fund (509)

Verbal threshold (513)

## REVIEW QUESTIONS

1. a. What is a financial responsibility law?
   b. What is a compulsory insurance law?

2. a. Describe the characteristics of unsatisfied judgment funds.
   b. How are unsatisfied judgment funds financed?

3. a. Describe the characteristics of a low-cost auto insurance plan.
   b. What is a "no pay, no play" law?

4. a. What is no-fault auto insurance?
   b. What is the difference between a monetary threshold and a verbal threshold?
   c. Describe the major types of no-fault laws.
   d. List the arguments for and against no-fault auto insurance.

5. Describe the characteristics of automobile insurance plans.

6. What is a joint underwriting association (JUA)?

7. Describe the characteristics of a reinsurance facility.

8. Describe the characteristics of specialty insurers.

9. a. Identify the factors that determine the premiums charged for auto insurance.

   b. Explain the significance of an applicant's credit score in auto insurance underwriting and rating.

10. Explain the suggestions that consumers should follow when shopping for an auto insurance policy.

## APPLICATION QUESTIONS

1. All states have financial responsibility or compulsory insurance laws that require motorists to carry at least minimum amounts of auto liability insurance.

   a. Does a financial responsibility law or compulsory insurance law guarantee that injured auto accident victims will be adequately compensated for their injuries? Explain your answer.

   b. How effective are compulsory insurance laws in reducing the problem of uninsured drivers?

2. Uninsured motorists coverage is another approach to the problem of uninsured drivers.

   a. Explain the advantages of uninsured motorists coverage in meeting the problem of uninsured drivers.

   b. Explain the defects of uninsured motorists coverage as a technique for compensating people who are injured by uninsured drivers.

3. A number of states have passed some type of no-fault auto insurance laws to compensate injured auto accident victims.

   a. Describe the no-fault benefits that are typically paid in a state with a no-fault law.

   b. Why have no-fault auto insurance laws been enacted?

   c. Explain the arguments against no-fault auto insurance laws.

   d. How well have no-fault auto insurance laws worked? Explain your answer.

4. Compensating innocent victims of high-risk drivers is problematic for society. An automobile insurance plan (assigned risk plan) is one approach to the problem of providing auto insurance to high-risk drivers.

   a. What is an automobile insurance plan?

   b. Describe the eligibility requirements for obtaining insurance from an automobile insurance plan.

   c. Explain the process for assigning high-risk drivers to individual insurers.

   d. Explain the disadvantages of automobile insurance plans.

## INTERNET RESOURCES

- The **Insurance Research Council (IRC),** a division of The Institutes (The American Institute for CPCU), provides the insurance industry and the public with timely research studies that are relevant to public policy issues dealing with risk and insurance. Visit the site at

  www.insurance-research.org

- The **RAND Institute for Civil Justice, a RAND law, business, and regulation center,** is an organization within the RAND Corporation that conducts independent, objective research and analysis concerning the civil justice system. Many research studies deal with auto insurance and the insurance industry. Visit the site at

  rand.org/law-business-regulation/centers/civil-justice.html

- **GEICO** sells auto insurance directly over the phone (800-861-8380). The company claims that a 15-minute call can save you 15 percent or more on auto insurance rates. GEICO's Web site provides similar premium quotes online. Visit the site at

  geico.com

- The **Insurance Information Institute** provides timely information on auto insurance and other personal property and liability insurance coverages. Numerous consumer brochures and articles on auto insurance and other property and liability coverages can be accessed directly online. Visit the site at

  iii.org

- **Insure.com** provides premium quotes for auto insurance, homeowners insurance, and other insurance products. The site also provides timely information and news releases about auto insurance and events that affect the insurance industry. Visit the site at

  insure.com

- **InsWeb** provides premium quotes for auto, homeowners, and other insurance products. In addition, the site has a learning center and provides information and articles from consumer, industry, and regulatory groups. Visit the site at

  insweb.com

- The **International Risk Management Institute (IRMI)** is an online source that provides valuable information about personal lines and commercial lines. The site provides timely articles on a wide range of risk management and insurance topics and offers a number of free e-mail newsletters. Visit the site at

irmi.com

■ The **Progressive Casualty Insurance Company** has a user-friendly site that provides auto insurance quotes. Progressive claims its rates are highly competitive. Progressive also provides comparison rates from other insurers. Visit the site at

progressive.com

## SELECTED REFERENCES

"A Consumer's Guide to Auto Insurance—Choosing and Using your Auto Insurance Coverage," Washington State Office of the Insurance Commissioner.

"Compulsory Auto / Uninsured Motorists," *Issues Updates*, Insurance Information Institute, August 2012. This source is periodically updated.

Doerpinghaus, Helen I., Joan T. Schmit, and Jason Jis-Hsing Yeh, "Age and Gender Effects on Auto Liability Insurance Payouts," *Journal of Risk and Insurance*, Vol. 75, No. 3 (September 2008), pp. 527–550.

*Fire, Casualty & Surety Bulletins*, Personal Lines volume, Personal Auto section, Erlanger, KY: National Underwriter Company. The bulletins are updated monthly.

Hartwig, Robert P. *No Evidence of Disparate Impact in Texas Due to Use of Credit Information by Personal Lines Insurers*, Insurance Information Institute, January 2005.

Kinzler, Peter, "*Issue Analysis, Auto Insurance Reform Options: How to Change State Tort and No-Fault Laws to Reduce Premiums and Increase Consumer Choice*," National Association of Mutual Insurance Companies, August 2006.

National Association of Insurance Commissioners, *Uninsured Motorists: A Growing Problem for Consumers, An NAIC White Paper*, Prepared by the NAIC Property and Casualty Insurance Committee, Draft Date, December 6, 2005.

"No-Fault Auto Insurance," *Issues Updates,* New York: Insurance Information Institute, June 2012. This source is periodically updated.

Nyce, Charles, ed. *Personal Insurance,* 2nd ed. Malvern, PA.: American Institute for Chartered Property Casualty Underwriters/Insurance Institute of America, 2008.

"Residual Markets," *White Papers*, Insurance Information Institute, April 2012.

Wiening, Eric A. and David D. Thamann. *Personal Auto, Personal Lines Coverage Guide*, 2nd ed., second printing. Erlanger, KY: The National Underwriter Company, 2009.

## NOTES

1. A complete discussion of these laws can be found in *Fire, Casualty & Surety Bulletins*, Personal Lines volume, Personal Auto section (Erlanger, KY: National Underwriter Company). Discussion of financial responsibility laws is based on this source.

2. The first two figures refer to bodily injury liability limits, and the third figure refers to property damage liability. The liability limits apply to each accident.

3. A recent study by the Insurance Research Council (IRC) estimated 13.8 percent of drivers were uninsured in 2009, despite mandatory insurance statutes. The percentage uninsured varied from 4 percent in Maine and Massachusetts, to 28 percent in Mississippi. "Recession Marked by Bump in Uninsured Drivers," Insurance Research Council, April 21, 2011.

4. "Mandatory Auto Insurance Does Not Reduce Number of Uninsured Drivers, Says Insurer Trade Group," insurancejournal.com, national news, July 25, 2004.

5. See "Compulsory Auto/Uninsured Motorists," *Issues Update*, Insurance Information Institute, May 2012. The short-term duration of auto insurance contracts, typically six months, further compounds the problem.

6. Unsatisfied Judgment Funds are used in Michigan, New York, and North Dakota. Maryland's Automobile Insurance Fund was created to replace the Maryland Automobile Insurance Plan and the Unsatisfied Claim and Judgment Fund in 1973. See "Maryland Automobile Insurance Fund, Origins and Objectives," February 2001. In 2003, New Jersey began to phase-out the state's unsatisfied judgement fund. See "Residual Markets," The Insurance Information Institute, *White Papers*, April 2012.

7. Eric A. Wiening, et al., *Personal Insurance*, 1st ed. Malvern, PA: American Institute for Chartered Property Casualty Underwriters/Insurance Institute of America, 2002, pp. 2.8–2.10.

8. A description of these coverages is available at State of New Jersey Department of Banking & Insurance Web site. See state.nj.us/bodi.

9. "Compulsory Auto/Uninsured Motorists," *Issues Updates,* Insurance Information Institute, August 2012.

10. Ibid.

11. This section is based on "No-Fault Automobile Insurance," in *Fire, Casualty & Surety Bulletins*, Personal Lines volume, Personal Auto section (Erlanger, KY: National Underwriter Company) and "No-Fault Auto Insurance," *Issues Updates*, Insurance Information Institute, June 2012.

12. Insurance Research Council, *Auto Injury Victims Who Hire an Attorney Are Less Likely to Be Satisfied with Their Total Payment: Findings from a New IRC Study*, news release, August 19, 2004.

13. James M. Anderson, Paul Heaton, and Stephen H. Carroll, *The U.S. Experience with No-Fault Automobile Insurance: A Retrospective,* Santa Monica, CA: RAND, Institute for Civil Justice, 2010.

14. Ibid., pp. 131–132. The explanations provided were suggested by stakeholder interviews.

15. *The Insurance Fact Book 2012,* New York: Insurance Information Institute, p. 153.

16. The Consumer Federation of America (CFA) recently examined rates in 15 cities and compared quotes from different insurers for the same risk. In one city, the premiums quoted for a woman's auto coverage ranged from $762 to $3390. See "Rates for Good Drivers in Cities Too High, Too Variable, Says Consumer Group," *Insurance Journal*, June 19, 2012.

Students may take a self-administered test on this chapter at
**www.pearsonhighered.com/rejda**

# CHAPTER 24

# OTHER PROPERTY AND LIABILITY INSURANCE COVERAGES

*"Variety is the very spice of life."*

William Cowper,
Olney Hymns (1779)

*David is an avid stamp collector. Last Saturday, he visited a stamp dealer and spent $500 on a rare stamp. As he drove home from purchasing the stamp, he thought about his collection and how much it was worth. Then another thought crossed his mind—what if someone stole his collection or if there was a fire? He decided to stop by his insurance agent's office.*

*David's agent showed him the limited coverage that the homeowners policy provides for his stamp collection. David purchased a separate insurance policy to cover the stamps. The agent also told David that because he only has $100,000 in liability coverage through his homeowners policy and $100,000 per-person in bodily injury liability under his auto insurance, he should consider buying a personal umbrella policy. For just $190, David purchased an additional $1 million in liability insurance.*

*David had a specialized property insurance need. He also wanted protection against large liability claims. Fortunately, there are insurance coverages available to address these concerns.*

*In this chapter, we discuss several property and liability insurance coverages that meet specific needs of insureds. Topics discussed include the Insurance Services Office (ISO) dwelling program, mobile home insurance, inland marine floaters, insurance on boats, title insurance, and government property insurance programs, including flood insurance and FAIR plans. The chapter concludes with a discussion of the personal umbrella policy.*

## ISO DWELLING PROGRAM

Although the majority of homeowners are insured under a homeowners policy, certain dwellings are ineligible for coverage under a homeowners policy. For example, if the home is not occupied by the owner but is rented to a tenant, the property owner is ineligible for a homeowners policy. Also, some property owners do not need a homeowners policy, or they may want a less costly policy. Most of these homes can be insured under a dwelling policy drafted by the Insurance Services Office (ISO).

The ISO dwelling forms are narrower in coverage than the current homeowners forms. One major difference is that the dwelling forms do not include coverage for theft or for personal liability insurance without appropriate endorsements. In contrast, the homeowners forms automatically include theft coverage and personal liability insurance as part of a standard policy.

The current ISO dwelling program includes the following forms:[1]

- Dwelling Property 1—Basic Form
- Dwelling Property 2—Broad Form
- Dwelling Property 3—Special Form

### Dwelling Property 1 (Basic Form)

The basic form provides coverages similar to the homeowners policies discussed in Chapter 20.

- Coverage A insures the dwelling shown in the declarations; materials and supplies located on or next to the described location used to construct or repair the dwelling; and if not otherwise covered in the policy, building equipment and outdoor equipment used to service the described location.
- Coverage B covers other structures set apart from the dwelling by clear space, such as a detached garage or storage shed.
- Coverage C covers the personal property of the named insured and resident family members while the property is at the described location. Up to 10 percent of the Coverage C limit can be

applied to cover personal property anywhere else in the world.

- Coverage D covers the fair rental value if a loss makes part of the dwelling rented to others unfit for normal use. A maximum of 20 percent of the insurance on the dwelling can be applied to cover the loss of rents, subject to a maximum monthly limit of one-twelfth of that amount.
- Finally, Coverage E can be added as an endorsement to the basic form, which provides coverage for additional living expenses.

The basic form covers only a limited number of perils that apply to both the dwelling and personal property. Coverage for fire, lightning, and internal explosion can be purchased alone. An internal explosion is one that occurs in the dwelling or other covered structure. For an additional premium, extended coverage perils[2] and coverage for vandalism and malicious mischief can be added to the policy. Thus, the basic form can provide coverage for the following named perils:

- *Fire or lightning*
- *Windstorm or hail*
- *Explosion*
- *Riot or civil commotion*
- *Aircraft*
- *Vehicles*
- *Smoke*
- *Volcanic eruption*
- *Vandalism or malicious mischief*

All covered property losses are paid on an actual cash value basis. However, for losses to the dwelling and other structures, some states require that a modified loss settlement endorsement be attached to the policy. Under this endorsement, if the building is repaired or replaced at the same site within 180 days of the loss, the insurer pays the lesser of (1) the limit of insurance or (2) the amount actually spent to repair or replace using common construction materials and methods. If the insured elects not to repair or replace the building, the insurer pays the lowest of the limit of insurance, the market value, or the amount it would cost to repair or replace.

## Dwelling Property 2 (Broad Form)

The broad form provides broader coverage than the basic form. Covered losses to the dwelling and other structures are indemnified on the basis of *replacement cost* rather than actual cash value. The replacement cost provisions are similar to those found in the homeowner contracts. The broad form also includes coverage for additional living expense (Coverage E). If a covered loss makes the property unfit for normal use, the additional increase in living expenses is paid.

The broad form includes all of the perils listed in the basic form (fire, lightning, and internal explosion) plus the extended coverage perils (wind, hail, smoke, etc.) and the following additional perils:

- *Damage by burglars*
- *Falling objects*
- *Weight of ice, snow, or sleet*
- *Accidental discharge or overflow of water or steam*
- *Explosion of a steam or hot water heating system, an air conditioning or automatic fire protective sprinkler system, or an appliance for heating water*
- *Freezing of a plumbing, heating, air conditioning or automatic fire protective sprinkler system, or household appliance*
- *Sudden and accidental tearing apart, cracking, burning, or bulging of a steam or hot water heating system, air conditioning or sprinkler system, or an appliance for heating water*
- *Sudden and accidental damage from an artificially generated electrical current*
- *Volcanic eruption*

## Dwelling Property 3 (Special Form)

The special form provides the broadest coverage in the ISO dwelling program. The dwelling and other structures are insured against direct loss to covered property. This means that coverage is provided on an "open perils" basis. *Direct physical losses to the dwelling and other structures are covered except those losses specifically excluded.* However, personal property is covered for the same named perils found in the broad form discussed earlier.

## Endorsements to the Dwelling Program

Numerous endorsements are available that can be added to a dwelling form, depending on the needs and desires of the property owner. Two of the most commonly added coverages are theft and personal liability. *Theft coverage* can be written on a limited or broad basis under the endorsement. Personal liability insurance is available by adding a *personal liability supplement* to the policy, which provides personal liability insurance similar to the liability coverage found in the homeowners policy.

# MOBILE HOME INSURANCE

Mobile homes generally cost less than conventional housing. Because of cost, some families have purchased mobile homes as an alternative to conventional housing. Mobile homes are also purchased as a vacation home or second home.

Under the ISO program, **mobile home insurance** is written by adding an endorsement to either a Homeowners 2 or Homeowners 3 policy, which tailors the homeowners policy to meet the special characteristics of mobile homes. A number of specialty insurers also write mobile home insurance based on their own forms tailored to mobile home exposures. The following discussion of mobile home insurance is based on the ISO program.[3]

## Eligibility

An eligible mobile home typically must be at least 10 feet wide and 40 feet long, must be designed for portability, and must be designed for year-round living. These requirements are imposed to eliminate coverage for camper trailers pulled by autos and insured under auto insurance policies.

## Mobile Home Coverages

The coverages on a mobile home are similar to those found in a homeowners policy. The major coverages are summarized as follows:

- *Dwelling.* Coverage A insures the mobile home against physical damage losses on a replacement cost basis. Coverage also applies to permanently installed floor coverings, household appliances, cabinets, dressers, and other built-in furniture.

  Some mobile homes have depreciated to the point where replacement cost coverage is inappropriate. An optional actual cash value endorsement can be added.

- *Other structures.* Coverage B insures other structures and is 10 percent of Coverage A, with a minimum limit of $2000. For example, a shed damaged in a windstorm would be covered.
- *Unscheduled personal property.* Coverage C insures unscheduled personal property and is 40 percent of the Coverage A limit. Because some furniture is built in and is a permanent part of the mobile home, the Coverage C limit is only 40 percent of Coverage A rather than 50 percent or higher under a typical homeowners policy.
- *Loss-of-use.* Coverage D provides for loss-of-use coverage, which is 20 percent of the Coverage A limit. For example, additional living expenses are covered if the insured rents a furnished apartment after a covered loss to the mobile home occurs.
- *Additional coverages.* This provision pays up to $500 for the cost incurred in transporting the mobile home to a safe place to avoid damage when it is endangered by a covered peril, such as a forest fire or a hurricane. The limit can be increased by an endorsement and no deductible applies to the coverage.
- *Personal liability insurance.* Coverages E and F provide for comprehensive personal liability insurance and medical payments to others. This coverage is similar to the coverage provided in the homeowners policies.

# INLAND MARINE FLOATERS

Many people own certain types of valuable personal property—such as jewelry, furs, and cameras—that are frequently moved from one location to another. This property can be insured by an appropriate inland marine floater. *An* **inland marine floater** *provides broad coverage on property frequently moved from one location to another* and on property used in transportation and communications.

## Basic Characteristics of Inland Marine Floaters

Although inland marine floaters are not uniform, they have certain common characteristics:[4]

- *Coverages are tailored to the specific type of personal property to be insured.* For example, under a personal articles floater, several types of property can be insured, such as jewelry, coins, or stamps. The insured can select the appropriate coverages needed.

- *Desired amounts of insurance can be selected.* The homeowners policy has several sublimits on personal property. For example, there is a $200 limit on money and coins, a $1500 limit on stamp collections, and a $2500 limit for the theft of silverware or goldware. Higher limits are available through a floater policy.
- *Broader coverage can be obtained.* For example, a personal articles floater insures against direct physical loss to covered property. Consequently, direct physical losses are covered except those losses specifically excluded.
- *Most floaters cover insured property anywhere in the world.* This protection is especially valuable for international travelers.
- *Inland marine floaters are often written without a deductible.*

### Personal Articles Floater

The **personal articles floater (PAF)** is an inland marine floater that provides comprehensive protection on valuable personal property.[5] The coverage can be added as an endorsement to a homeowners policy, or it can be written separately as a stand-alone contract. When written as a separate contract, the PAF insures certain optional classes of personal property on a "direct physical loss" or an "open perils" basis. *Direct physical losses are covered except certain losses specifically excluded.*

The classes of personal property that can be covered include the following:

- *Jewelry.* Because of moral hazard, insurance on jewelry is underwritten carefully. Each item is described with a specific amount of insurance.
- *Furs.* Each item is listed separately with a specific amount of insurance.
- *Cameras.* Most photographic equipment can be covered under the PAF. Each item must be individually described and valued.
- *Musical instruments.* Musical instruments, cases, amplifying equipment, and similar articles can also be covered. Instruments played for pay are not covered unless a higher premium is paid.

- *Silverware.* The PAF can also be written to cover silverware and goldware.
- *Golfer's equipment.* Golf clubs and equipment are covered anywhere in the world. Golfer's clothes in a locker while the insured is playing golf are also covered.
- *Fine arts.* Fine arts include paintings, etchings, lithographs, antique furniture, rare books, rare glass, bric-a-brac, and manuscripts.
- *Stamp and coin collections.* Stamp and coin collections can be insured on a *blanket basis;* the stamps or coins are not described, and the insurance applies to the entire collection. The amount paid is the market value of the stamps and coins at the time of loss, with a $1000 maximum limit on any unscheduled coin collection and a $250 maximum limit on any single stamp or coin.

However, if the stamps or coins are valuable, they can be individually *scheduled.* The policyholder and insurer can agree on the value of the coins or stamps that are scheduled. The agreed value amount is the amount paid if a loss occurs.

### Scheduled Personal Property Endorsement

Coverage provided by a PAF can be added to a homeowners policy by use of a **scheduled personal property endorsement**. The endorsement provides essentially the same coverages provided by the freestanding personal articles floater.

## WATERCRAFT INSURANCE

Millions of Americans own or operate boats for pleasure and recreation. The homeowners policy, however, provides only limited coverage of boats. Coverage on a boat, its equipment, and boat trailer is limited to $1500. Direct loss from windstorm or hail is covered only if the boat is inside a fully enclosed building. Theft of the boat or its equipment away from the premises is excluded. Also, boats are covered for only a limited number of named (broad form) perils, and more comprehensive protection may be desired. Finally, legal liability arising out of the operation or ownership of larger boats is not covered under the homeowners policy. For these reasons, boat owners often purchase separate insurance contracts that provide broader protection.[6]

Insurance on recreational boats generally can be classified into two categories:

- Boatowners package policy
- Yacht insurance

## Boatowners Package Policy

Many insurers have designed a **boatowners package policy** that combines physical damage insurance on the boat, medical expense insurance, liability insurance, and other coverages into one policy. Although the package policies are not uniform, they have certain common characteristics.

**Physical Damage Coverage**  A boatowners policy provides physical damage insurance on the boat on a "direct physical loss" or an "open perils" basis. *Direct physical losses are covered except certain losses specifically excluded.* Thus, if the boat collides with another boat, is stranded on a reef, or is damaged by heavy winds, the loss is covered. Certain exclusions apply, including wear and tear, gradual deterioration, mechanical breakdown, use of the boat for commercial purposes, and use of the boat (except sailboats in some policies) in any race or speed contest.

**Liability Coverage**  The insured is covered for property damage and bodily injury liability arising out of the negligent ownership or operation of the boat. For example, if an operator carelessly damages another boat, swamps another boat, or accidentally injures some swimmers, the loss is covered. Certain exclusions apply, including intentional injury, use of the boat for commercial purposes, and use of the boat (sailboats sometimes excepted) in any race or speed test.

**Medical Expense Coverage**  This coverage is similar to that found in auto insurance contracts. The coverage pays the reasonable and necessary medical expenses of a covered person who is injured while in the boat or while boarding or leaving the boat. Most policies impose a limit of one to three years during which time the medical expenses must be incurred. In addition, many policies cover the medical expenses of waterskiers who are injured while being towed. If not covered, coverage can be obtained by an endorsement to the policy.

**Uninsured Boaters Coverage**  Some boatowners policies have an optional uninsured boaters coverage for bodily injury caused by an uninsured boater, which is similar to the uninsured motorists coverage in auto insurance.

## Yacht Insurance

**Yacht insurance** is designed for larger and more valuable boats, such as cabin cruisers, inboard motorboats, and sailboats over 26 feet in length. Yacht policies are not standard, but certain coverages typically appear in all policies. The following section summarizes the major provisions of a yacht policy of one insurer.

**Property Damage**  This coverage, often referred to as hull coverage, insures the yacht and its equipment for property damage on an "all-risks" or "open perils" basis. The policy covers direct physical loss or damage to the yacht except certain losses specifically excluded. Thus, if the yacht is damaged or sinks because of heavy seas, high winds, or collision with another vessel, the loss is covered. Exclusions include wear and tear; weathering; damage from insects, mold, animals, and marine life; marring, scratching, denting, and blistering; and freezing or extremes of temperature. A deductible applies to property damage losses.

**Liability Coverage**  Liability coverage insures the legal liability of an insured arising out of the ownership, operation, or maintenance of the yacht. For example, collision with another boat or damage to a dock or marina would be covered. The coverage also includes the cost of raising, removing, or destroying a sunken or wrecked yacht.

**Medical Payments Coverage**  This coverage pays for necessary and reasonable medical expenses because of accidental bodily injury. Covered expenses include medical, hospital, ambulance, professional nursing, and funeral costs.

**Uninsured Boaters Coverage**  This coverage pays the bodily injury damages up to the policy limit that the insured is legally entitled to recover from an uninsured owner or operator of another yacht.

**Other Coverages** The policy may include additional coverages. These coverages include coverage for legal liability incurred by the insured to maritime workers who are injured in the course of employment and who are covered under the U.S. Longshoremen's and Harbor Workers' Compensation Act; physical damage insurance on a vessel trailer listed in the declarations; and coverage for personal property while aboard the yacht. Personal property includes clothing, personal effects, fishing gear, and sports equipment, but not money, jewelry, traveler's checks, or other valuables.

## GOVERNMENT PROPERTY INSURANCE PROGRAMS

Government insurance programs are often necessary because certain perils are difficult to insure privately, and coverage may not be available at affordable premiums from private insurers. Two government property insurance programs merit discussion here:

- National Flood Insurance Program
- FAIR plans

### National Flood Insurance Program

Buildings in flood plains are difficult to insure by private insurers because the ideal requirements of an insurable risk discussed in Chapter 2 are not easily met. The exposure units in flood plains are not independent of each other, and the potential for a catastrophic loss is present. Also, adverse selection is a problem because owners of property who believe their property is susceptible to flooding are likely to seek protection.

Because of increasing flood losses and the escalating costs of disaster relief to the taxpayers, Congress created the **National Flood Insurance Program (NFIP)** in 1968.[7] The purposes of the legislation are to reduce flood damage in communities by floodplain management ordinances and to provide flood insurance to property owners.

Flood insurance can be purchased from agents or brokers who represent private insurers. Agents or brokers who are not affiliated with private insurers can also write federal flood insurance directly with the NFIP.

Most flood insurance policies are written with private insurers. Under the *write-your-own program* enacted in 1983, private insurers sell federal flood insurance under their own names, collect the premiums, and receive an expense allowance for policies written and claims paid. The federal government is responsible for all underwriting losses. The NFIP is self-supporting for the average historical loss year, which means that unless a widespread disaster occurs, claims and operating expenses are paid by flood insurance premiums, not by the taxpayers. Hurricane Katrina and other hurricanes in 2005 resulted in the payment of billions of dollars for flood damage losses. Problems with the program and an $18 billion deficit led to short-term extensions, uncertainty, and calls for reforming the program. Congress acted in the summer of 2012 to reform and extend the program for five years.

Federal law requires individuals to purchase flood insurance if they have federal guaranteed financing to build, buy, refinance, or repair structures located in special hazard flood areas in the participating community. This financing requirement includes federal FHA and VA loans as well as most conventional mortgage loans.

**Eligibility Requirements** Most buildings and their contents can be covered by flood insurance if the community agrees to adopt and enforce sound flood control and land use measures.

Communities that meet the eligibility requirements are initially covered under the *emergency program*. When a community joins the program, it is provided with a flood hazard boundary map that shows the general area of flood losses, and residents are allowed to purchase limited amounts of insurance at subsidized rates under the emergency portion of the program.

A flood insurance rate map is then prepared that divides the community into specific zones to determine the probability of flooding in each zone. When this map is prepared, and the community agrees to adopt more stringent flood control and land use measures, the community enters the *regular program*. Higher amounts of flood insurance can then be purchased.

**Definition of Flood** In the Standard Flood Insurance Policy, flood is defined, in part, as:

*A general and temporary condition of partial or complete inundation of two or more acres of normally*

**EXHIBIT 24.1**

**Amount of Federal Flood Insurance under the Emergency and Regular Programs**

| Building Coverage | Emergency Program | Regular Program |
|---|---|---|
| Single-family dwelling | $ 35,000* | $250,000 |
| Two- to four-family | 35,000* | 250,000 |
| Other residential | 100,000* | 250,000 |
| Non-residential | 100,000* | 500,000 |
| Contents Coverage | | |
| Residential | $ 10,000 | $100,000 |
| Nonresidential including Small Business | 100,000 | 500,000 |

*Under the Emergency Program, higher limits of building coverage are available in Alaska, Hawaii, the U.S. Virgin Islands, and Guam.

SOURCE: National Flood Insurance Program, Flood Insurance Manual, Federal Emergency Management Agency (FEMA), Revised May 2012.

*dry land area or of two or more properties (at least one of which is your property) from overflow of inland or tidal waters, from unusual and rapid accumulation or runoff of surface waters from any source, or from mudflow.*

For example, flood damage caused by an overflow of rivers, streams, or other bodies of water, by abnormally high waves, or by severe storms is covered. Note that the accumulation or runoff of surface water can come from any source, such as melting snow, ice, or heavy rain. If the flooding causes damage from mudflow, the loss is also covered.

**Amounts of Insurance**   Under the *emergency program,* maximum coverage on single-family and two- to four-family dwellings is limited to $35,000 on the building and $10,000 on the contents. For other residential and nonresidential buildings, maximum coverage is limited to $100,000 on the building and $10,000 on the contents for residential coverage and $100,000 on the contents for nonresidential coverage (see Exhibit 24.1).

Under the *regular program,* maximum coverage on single-family and two- to four-family dwellings is limited to $250,000 on the building and $100,000 on the contents. Commercial structures can be insured up to a limit of $500,000 on the building and $500,000 on the contents.

Losses to single family dwellings and residential condominium buildings can be indemnified on a *replacement cost* basis if certain conditions are met. The insured must carry insurance equal to 80 percent of the replacement cost of the dwelling at the time of loss, or the maximum amount of insurance available at the inception of the policy, whichever is less. If the amount of insurance carried is less than 80 percent of the full replacement cost at the time of the loss, the amount paid is subject to a coinsurance penalty. Losses to contents are always settled on an actual cash value basis (replacement cost less depreciation).

**Policy Forms**   There are three Standard Policy Forms that provide policyholders with a description of the coverage provided:

- The *Dwelling Form* is used to insure one- to four-family residential buildings and single-family dwelling units in a condominium building. Thus, homeowners can insure their dwelling and/or unscheduled personal property with this form; renters can also insure their unscheduled personal property with this form.
- The *General Property Policy Form* is used to insure five or more family residential buildings and non-residential buildings. Examples include hotels or motels; apartment buildings; shops, restaurants, or other businesses; schools; factories; churches; and non-residential condominiums.
- The *Residential Condominium Building Association Policy Form* is issued to residential condominium associations on behalf of association and unit owners.

A detailed analysis of the coverages in each form is beyond the scope of this text. However, Exhibit 24.2 provides general information on the property covered and not covered under the three forms.

**EXHIBIT 24.2**

**Summary of Property Covered under the National Flood Insurance Program (NFIP)**

**What Is Covered by Flood Insurance—and What's Not**

Generally, physical damage to your building or personal property "directly" caused by a flood is covered by your flood insurance policy. For example, damages caused by a sewer backup are covered if the backup is a direct result of flooding. However, if the backup is caused by some other problem, the damages are not covered.

The following chart provides general guidance on items covered and not covered by flood insurance.

### General Guidance on Flood Insurance Coverage

**What is insured under Building Property coverage?**

- The insured building and its foundation.
- The electrical and plumbing systems.
- Central air conditioning equipment, furnaces, and water heaters.
- Refrigerators, cooking stoves, and built-in appliances such as dishwashers.
- Permanently installed carpeting over an unfinished floor.
- Permanently installed paneling, wallboard, bookcases, and cabinets.
- Window blinds.
- Detached garages (up to 10 percent of Building Property coverage). Detached buildings (other than garages) require a separate Building Property policy.
- Debris removal.

**What is Insured under Personal Property coverage?**

- Personal belongings such as clothing, furniture, and electronic equipment.
- Curtains.
- Portable and window air conditioners.

- Portable microwave ovens and portable dishwashers.
- Carpets not included in building coverage (see above).
- Clothes washers and dryers.
- Food freezers and the food in them.
- Certain valuable items such as original artwork and furs (up to $2500).

**What is not insured by either Building Property or Personal Property coverage?**

- Damage caused by moisture, mildew, or mold that could have been avoided by the property owner.
- Currency, precious metals, and valuable papers such as stock certificates.
- Property and belongings outside of a building such as trees, plants, wells, septic systems, walks, decks, patios, fences, seawalls, hot tubs, and swimming pools.
- Living expenses such as temporary housing.
- Financial losses caused by business interruption or loss of use of insured property.
- Most self-propelled vehicles such as cars, including their parts.

SOURCE: FEMA. *National Flood Insurance Program, Summary of Coverage,* available at flloodsmart.gov

**Waiting Period** With certain exceptions, there is a 30-day waiting period for new applications and for endorsements to increase the amount of insurance on existing policies. Without a waiting period, property owners in flood zones could delay purchasing insurance until an imminent flood threatens their property.

**Deductible** A deductible applies separately to both the building and contents. For example, the purchaser might select a $2000 deductible on the structure and a $1000 deductible on the contents; or a $1000 deductible on the structure and a $1000 deductible on contents. Higher deductibles are available with a saving in premiums.

**Premiums** The cost of the protection is relatively low, given the risk. For example, a purchaser who lived in a low-risk area who qualified for a preferred risk policy would pay $247 annually for $100,000 in coverage on the home and $40,000 in coverage on the contents; both assuming a $1000 deductible on the home and contents. For an insured in a high-risk area, the cost for $100,000 in coverage on the home and $30,000 on the contents would be $1129; both assuming a $2000 deductible on the home and contents.[8]

There are numerous misconceptions and myths about the federal flood insurance program. Insight 24.1 discusses some common misunderstandings about the program.

## INSIGHT 24.1

# Dispelling Myths about Flood Insurance

Buying flood insurance can provide protection and peace of mind. Flooding is one of the most common natural hazards in the United States. Below are some common myths and misconceptions about flood insurance.

- **MYTH:** *Only homeowners can purchase flood insurance.*

  **FACT:** Most homeowners, condo unit owners, renters, and businesses in NFIP participating communities can purchase flood insurance. To find out if your community participates, go to www.floodsmart.gov or contact a community official or insurance agent. The maximum coverage amounts are:
  - Condominium unit owners: up to $250,000 in structural coverage and up to $100,000 in contents coverage
  - Renters: up to $100,000 in contents coverage
  - Businesses: up to $500,000 in commercial structural coverage and up to $500,000 in contents coverage

- **MYTH:** *You can't buy flood insurance if you are located in a high-flood-risk area.*

  **FACT:** You can buy National Flood Insurance no matter where you live, as long as your community participates in the NFIP. The NFIP was created in 1968 to make federally backed flood insurance available to property owners, renters, and businesses in participating communities.

- **MYTH:** *If you live in an unmapped area, you don't need flood insurance.*

  **FACT:** Even areas in unmapped flood zones are susceptible to flooding, although to varying degrees. If you live in a mapped flood zone, it is advisable to have flood insurance. However, between 20 and 25 percent of the NFIP's claims come from outside mapped flood zones. Residential and commercial property owners located in unmapped zones should ask their insurance agents if they are eligible for the Preferred Risk Policy, which provides very inexpensive flood insurance.

- **MYTH:** *You can't buy flood insurance if your property has been flooded before.*

  **FACT:** You are still eligible to purchase a flood insurance policy after your home, condo, apartment, or business has been flooded, provided that your community is participating in the NFIP.

- **MYTH:** *Homeowners insurance policies cover flooding.*

  **FACT:** Unfortunately, many home and business owners do not find out until it is too late that their homeowners and business insurance policies do not cover flooding. The NFIP offers a separate policy that protects the single most important financial asset, which for most people is their home or business. Homeowners can include contents coverage in their NFIP policy. Residential and commercial renters can purchase flood insurance coverage for their buildings and contents/inventory and, by doing so, protect their livelihood.

- **MYTH:** *Federal disaster assistance will pay for flood damage.*

  **FACT:** Before a community is eligible for disaster assistance, it must be declared a federal disaster area. Federal disaster assistance declarations are issued in fewer than 50 percent of flooding events. Furthermore, if you are uninsured and receive federal disaster assistance after a flood, you must purchase flood insurance to remain eligible for future disaster relief. Disaster assistance does not cover as much as flood insurance, and flood insurance claims can be paid very rapidly after the event.

- **MYTH:** *You can't buy flood insurance immediately before or during a flood.*

  **FACT:** You can purchase National Flood Insurance at any time. There is usually a 30-day waiting period after you buy flood insurance before the policy is effective. In most cases, the policy does not cover a "loss in progress," which is defined as a loss occurring as of midnight on the first day your policy goes into effect. Basically, if you buy flood insurance after a flood, it will not cover your past losses, only losses after the policy goes into effect.

- **MYTH:** *The NFIP does not offer basement coverage.*

  **FACT:** While basement improvements such as finished walls and floors, and personal belongings in a basement are not covered by flood insurance, structural elements and essential equipment within a basement are. The following items are covered under building coverage, as long as they are connected to a power source, if required, and installed in their functioning location:

  - Sump pumps
  - Well water tanks and pumps, cisterns, and the water in them
  - Oil tanks and the oil in them, natural gas tanks and the gas in them
  - Pumps and/or tanks used in conjunction with solar energy
  - Furnaces, water heaters, air conditioners, and heat pumps
  - Electrical junction and circuit breaker boxes and required utility connections
  - Foundation elements
  - Stairways, staircases, elevators, and dumbwaiters
  - Unpainted drywall walls and ceilings, including fiberglass insulation
  - Cleanup

SOURCE: Adapted from FEMA B-690, Catalog No. 09094-3, *Myths and Facts About the National Flood Insurance Program*, February 2010.

**Critical Problems and Issues** The federal flood insurance program faces several critical problems and issues at this time. The Government Accountability Office (GAO) has performed several studies of the National Flood Insurance Program,[9] and GAO officials have testified before Congress several times on the program. Results of the most recent study were presented to the U.S. Senate Committee on Banking, Housing, and Urban Affairs in September of 2010. Among the key findings of the study were the following problems:[10]

- *Substantial financial deficit.* As of August, 2010, the NFIP owed $18.8 billion to the U.S. Department of Treasury. The deficit is due largely to catastrophic losses from Hurricane Katrina in 2005 and other hurricanes.
- *Inadequate rates.* Many property owners do not pay premiums that adequately reflect the risk of flooding. Almost 25 percent of policyholders pay subsidized rates, and "full-risk" premiums do not reflect the actual flood risk. Also, the NFIP allows some policyholders to continue to pay "old rates" ("grandfathered rates") after their properties were reassessed as being higher risk. Furthermore, annual rate increases are capped.
- *NFIP is required to insure multiple loss properties.* The GAO report noted that "repetitive loss properties" account for one percent of the flood insurance policies in force, but generate 25-30 percent of the claims.
- *Operational and management issues plague the program.* FEMA does not systematically consider flood insurance expense data when calculating payments to write-your-own (WYO) insurers or implement controls in the WYO program. FEMA does not monitor non-WYO contractors or efficiently coordinate monitoring responsibilities among contractors.

**Extension of the National Flood Insurance Program** After 2008, there were several short-term extensions of the NFIP program, and the program expired several times in 2010. During the summer of 2012, Congress passed and the president signed the "Biggert-Waters Flood Insurance Reform and Modernization Act of 2012." The Biggert-Waters Act extends the NFIP program through September of 2017. In drafting the legislation, Congress addressed several key points raised by the GAO studies and other deficiencies. Some key provisions of the Biggert-Waters Act include:[11]

- Rate subsidies on certain properties are phased-out over four years.
- Rate subsidies on newly-insured NFIP properties and on properties where NFIP coverage has lapsed previously are prohibited.
- Annual premium rate increases of up to 20 percent are allowed (vs. 10 percent previously).
- Flood insurance premiums can be paid through installments.
- A reserve fund is created to help fund claims in years when catastrophic losses occur.
- Minimum deductibles of $1000 to $2000 are required depending on the amount of coverage and age of the property.
- The NFIP is required to create a repayment schedule for money owed to the U.S. Treasury.
- The National Flood Mapping Program is created and federal agencies are required to cooperate in improving flood mapping.
- Oversight reimbursement regulations are created for insurers under the Write-Your-Own program.

**FAIR Plans** During the 1960s, major riots occurred in many cities in the United States, resulting in millions of dollars in property damage. Subsequently, many property owners in riot-prone areas were unable to obtain property insurance at affordable premiums. This problem resulted in the creation of **FAIR plans** (Fair Access to Insurance Requirements), which were enacted into law as a result of the Urban Property and Reinsurance Act of 1968. *The basic purpose of a FAIR plan is to make property insurance available to urban property owners who are unable to obtain coverage in the standard markets.* FAIR plans typically provide coverage for fire and extended-coverage perils, vandalism, and malicious mischief. FAIR plans have been established in 32 states and the District of Columbia.[12]

Each state with a FAIR plan has a pool or syndicate that provides basic property insurance to persons who cannot obtain insurance in the standard markets. The pools or syndicates are operated by private insurers. Each insurer in the pool or syndicate is assessed its proportionate share of losses and expenses based on the proportion of property insurance premiums written in the state.

FAIR plan premiums are higher than premiums paid in the standard market. However, basic insurance is made available where coverage otherwise would not exist. All FAIR plans cover fire, vandalism, riot, and windstorm. About a dozen states provide some type of homeowners policy, which includes personal liability coverage.

Before a building is insured under a FAIR plan, it must meet certain underwriting standards. If these standards are met, a policy is issued. If the building is substandard, the property owner must make certain improvements that reduce the risk of fire, theft, or water damage, such as upgrading the electrical wiring, heating, or plumbing systems, repairing the roof, or improving security. If the property owner does not correct the conditions that make the home prone to losses, the FAIR plan administrator may deny coverage.

The original intent of FAIR plans was to make coverage available in high-crime areas. Several states along the Atlantic and Gulf Coasts have expanded their residual property insurance programs. These states offer beach and windstorm plans to property susceptible to damage from windstorms and hurricanes. Two states established insurance companies to write coverage: the Florida Citizens Property Insurance Company and the Louisiana Citizens Property Insurance Company. In 2011, 3.31 million residential and commercial policies were written by state-run property insurance programs.[13] Since Florida Citizens was established in 2002, it has grown to be the largest property insurer in the state. In 2012, Florida Citizens insured 1.4 million policyholders and property valued at $499 billion.[14]

## TITLE INSURANCE

Our discussion of property insurance coverages would not be complete without a brief description of title insurance. **Title insurance** *protects the owner of property or the lender of money for the purchase of property against any unknown defects in the title to the property under consideration.* Defects to a clear title can result from an invalid will, incorrect description of the property, defective probate of a will, undisclosed liens, easements, and numerous other legal defects that occurred sometime in the past. Without a clear title, the owner could lose the property to someone with a superior claim or incur other losses because of an unknown lien, unmarketability of the title, and attorney expenses. Title insurance is designed to provide protection against these losses.

Any liens, encumbrances, or easements against real estate are normally recorded in a courthouse in the area where the property is located. This information is recorded in a legal document known as an *abstract,* which is a history of ownership and title to the property. When real estate is purchased, the purchaser may hire an attorney to search the abstract to determine whether there are any defects to a clear title to the property. However, the purchaser is not fully protected by this method, because there may be an unknown lien, encumbrance, or other title defect not recorded in the abstract. The owner could still incur a loss despite a diligent and careful title search. Thus, the owner needs a stronger guarantee that he or she will be indemnified if a loss occurs. Title insurance can provide that guarantee.

Title insurance policies have certain characteristics that distinguish them from other contracts:

- *The policy provides protection against title defects that have occurred in the past, prior to the effective date of the policy.*
- *The policy is written by the insurer based on the assumption that no losses will occur.* Any known title defects or facts that have a bearing on the title are listed in the policy and excluded from coverage.
- *The premium is paid only once when the policy is issued.* No additional premiums are required.
- *The policy term runs indefinitely into the future.* As long as the title defect occurred before the issue date of the policy, any insured loss is covered, no matter when it is discovered in the future.
- *If a loss occurs, the insured is indemnified in dollar amounts up to the policy limits.* The policy does not guarantee possession by the owner, removal of any title defects, or a legal remedy against known defects.

The policy limit is usually the purchase price of the property. If the property appreciates in value over the years, the homeowner could be underinsured at the time of loss. This consideration is important in those areas where inflation in housing prices occurs. The cost of title insurance is typically included in the closing costs when you purchase a home.

Although title insurance is often viewed as a necessity, the coverage is poorly understood by consumers. The market for title insurance is highly concentrated, and consumer advocates argue that the market has several major defects. Among the defects are:[15]

- Homeowners do not shop around for title insurance; it's often selected by a real estate agent or lending institution and included in the closing costs.
- Home buyers are over-charged for title insurance– several studies allege consumers pay more for the coverage than loss ratios indicate is a fair price.

- The title insurance market is flawed by reverse competition–title insurers spend money to induce real estate agents, mortgage lenders and brokers, and homebuilders to steer home purchasers to specific title agents and companies, driving the cost of coverage up.
- Although illegal, kickbacks to real estate agents, lenders, and builders are widespread.

Given the lack of consumer knowledge about title insurance and some of the problems in the title insurance marketplace, the National Association of Insurance Commissioners (NAIC) issued a "Consumer Alert" about title insurance (see Insight 24.2).

---

## INSIGHT 24.2

### Title Insurance:
### Protecting Your Home Investment Against Unknown Title Defects

*Most first-time home buyers are familiar with various types of insurance (e.g., auto, life), but are unaware of what title insurance is, and the role it plays in real estate transactions. In the rush to close such transactions as quickly as possible, title insurance is typically an area that consumers commonly overlook in the home buying process.*

*If you borrow money to finance the purchase of a home or property, a lending institution will likely require you to buy a title insurance policy to protect its interest. As a consumer, it is in your best interest to be well-informed about title insurance, how title insurance works and key areas to be addressed when purchasing title insurance.*

**What is Title Insurance?**
Title insurance can help provide the home buyer and/or the mortgage lender necessary protection against losses resulting from unknown defects in the title to your property that occur prior to the closing of a real estate transaction.

Unknown defects in a title, such as any outstanding liens on the property (e.g., unpaid real estate taxes by a prior owner) or encumbrances (anything that might hinder the owner's right of ownership; e.g., errors or omissions in deeds, undisclosed errors, fraud, forgery, mistakes in examining records), can result in additional costs in the future or even invalidate a home buyer's right of ownership in the property, and might also invalidate the lender's security interest in the policy. Title insurance policies will cover the insured party for any covered losses and legal fees that might arise out of such problems.

**What Do Title Insurance Agents/Companies Do?**
Title insurance agents/companies search public records to develop and document the chain of ownership of a property. If any liens or encumbrances are found, the title company might require that the home buyer take steps to eliminate them before issuing a title policy. Title insurance agents might also hold money in escrow and perform closing services for an additional fee.

**How Does Title Insurance Work?**
Title insurance policies are indemnity policies — typically, they protect against losses arising from events that occur prior to the date of the policy, which is the date of closing. This is unlike other types of insurance policies, such as auto or life insurance, which protect against losses resulting from accidents or events that occur after the policy is issued. A title policy is usually paid for with a one-time premium that is handled at the closing of the real estate transaction.

**Who Needs Title Insurance?**
**Lenders**—If a mortgage is obtained in order to purchase property, nearly all lenders require that the home buyer purchase the lender's title insurance policy for an amount equal to the loan. A lender's policy is issued to a mortgage lender. The policy provides the lender protection from covered losses arising from any previously unknown defects in the title that have become known only after the insured property has been financed. The lender's insurance policy will remain in effect until the amount financed has been repaid, the property is resold or until refinancing has occurred.

## INSIGHT 24.2

**Owners**—Either the home seller or the home buyer may buy an owner's policy. In many areas, sellers pay for owner title policies as part of their obligation in the transfer of title to the home buyer. The party paying for the owner's policy can be negotiated during the purchasing process. An owner's policy is issued to a home buyer, and provides the home buyer protection from covered losses arising from any previously unknown defects in the title that existed at the time of purchase, and became known only after ownership of the property was acquired. An owner's policy remains in effect as long as you own or maintain an ownership interest in the insured property.

### Marketing and Sales Practices

Although home buyers are free to shop around for a title agent or a title insurer, many home buyers do not do so. Because of unfamiliarity with title insurance, home buyers tend to defer such decisions to lenders and/or real estate professionals who are parties to the home buying transaction. As a result, conflicts of interest can occur if the entities making such decisions have a financial interest in a title agency/title company.

Section 8 of the federal Real Estate Settlement Procedures Act (RESPA) prohibits the giving or accepting of kickbacks and referral fees among persons involved in the real estate settlement process.

### Key Points to Remember

- Although a title insurance company will most likely be provided for you during the mortgage transaction process, be aware that you are not obligated to use the suggested title company.
- Be sure to inquire about the services and fees included in the title insurance premium and any fees (e.g., cost of search and examination, closing services, etc.) that may be charged to you separately.
- A lender policy only covers a lender's loss; that is, it does not protect the home buyer from losses arising from defects in title. Consult with a local, reputable real estate attorney not involved in the real estate transaction to find out if it is in your best interest to purchase an owner's title insurance policy.
- Make sure to inquire about any discounts available on title insurance policies. Premium discounts might be available if both owner's and lender's policies are purchased from the same title insurance company or if you are refinancing your loan.
- Read all title insurance documents provided at closing, including the fine print. Ask questions if any items are unclear; or if any terms, conditions or amounts are not in line with those provided in previous discussions.
- If you believe that the title agent or title company in a real estate transaction is not following standard business practices (e.g., unexpected or undocumented fees), you can report the activity to your state's insurance department. A map linking to state insurance department Web sites is provided at www.naic.org. Contact information regarding the reporting of consumer complaints is provided on these Web sites.

For more information about title insurance in your state, please contact your state's insurance department. Access the U.S. Government Accountability Office's April 2007 report on title insurance at http://www.gao.gov/new.items/d07401.pdf. The U.S. Department of Housing and Urban Development Web page http://www.hud.gov/ is also a good source of information about title insurance.

## PERSONAL UMBRELLA POLICY

Personal liability claims occasionally reach catastrophic levels and can exceed the liability limits of a homeowners or auto insurance policy. For example, catastrophic losses can result from a chain-reaction accident on an icy highway where cars collide and several people are killed or injured; a boating accident in which a boat is swamped by another boat and several people are injured or drown; or a defamation-of-character lawsuit by someone who claims that his or her reputation is ruined.

The **personal umbrella policy** *provides protection against a catastrophic lawsuit or judgment.* Most insurers write this coverage in amounts ranging from $1 million to $10 million. Coverage is broad and covers catastrophic liability loss exposures arising out of the home, cars, boats, recreational vehicles, sports, and other personal activities.

### Basic Characteristics

Although personal umbrella policies differ among insurers, they share several common characteristics, including the following:[16]

- Excess liability insurance
- Broad coverage
- Self-insured retention or deductible
- Reasonable cost

**Typical Underlying Coverage Amounts Required to Qualify for a Personal Umbrella Policy**

| | |
|---|---|
| Auto liability insurance | $250,000 / $500,000 / $50,000 or $500,000 single limit |
| Personal liability insurance (separate contract or homeowners policy) | $100,000 or $300,000 |
| Large watercraft | $500,000 |

**Excess Liability Insurance**    *The personal umbrella policy provides excess liability insurance over underlying insurance contracts that apply.* The umbrella policy pays after the underlying insurance limits are exhausted. The insured is required to carry certain minimum amounts of liability insurance on the underlying contracts. Although the required amounts vary among insurers, the amounts shown in Exhibit 24.3 are typical.

If the required amounts of underlying insurance are not maintained, the umbrella insurer pays only the amount that it would have paid had the underlying insurance been kept in force.

**Broad Coverage**    *The umbrella policy provides broad coverage of personal liability loss exposures.* The policy covers bodily injury and property damage liability, as well as personal injury. **Personal injury** typically includes false arrest, wrongful detention or imprisonment; malicious prosecution; wrongful eviction or wrongful entry; libel, slander, and defamation of character; and oral or written publication of material that violates a person's right to privacy.

The umbrella policy also covers certain losses not covered by any underlying contract after a self-insured retention or deductible is met. In addition to the policy limits, most umbrella policies pay legal defense costs as well.

**Self-Insured Retention**    The umbrella policy typically contains a self-insured retention or deductible. *The* **self-insured retention,** *or deductible, applies only to losses covered by the umbrella policy but not by any underlying contract.* The self-insured retention is typically $250 but can be higher. Examples of claims not covered by the underlying contracts but insured under an umbrella policy include libel, slander, defamation of character, and a variety of additional claims.

To illustrate, assume that Andrea has a $1 million personal umbrella policy and an auto insurance policy with limits of $250,000 per person and $500,000 per accident for bodily injury liability. If she negligently injures another motorist and must pay damages of $650,000, the auto policy pays the first $250,000, its per-person liability limit. The umbrella policy pays the remaining $400,000, because the underlying limit of $250,000 per person under the auto policy has been exhausted. The self-insured retention does not apply here as the umbrella is excess coverage.

Now assume that Andrea is sued by her ex-husband for defamation of character and must pay damages of $50,000. If there is no underlying coverage and the self-insured retention is $250, her umbrella policy would pay $49,750. The self-insured retention must be paid by Andrea in this case.

**Reasonable Cost**    An umbrella policy is reasonable in cost. The policy costs less than you might think, given the high limit. Recall, however, that most claims will be covered by the underlying policies. The actual cost depends on several variables, including the number of cars, boats, and motorcycles to be covered. For most families, the annual premium for a $1 million umbrella policy is less than $350.

## ISO Personal Umbrella Policy

In 1998, the Insurance Services Office (ISO) introduced a personal umbrella policy. ISO revised the policy in 2006. Some insurers use the ISO policy, but other insurers have designed their own policies. The basic characteristics, however, are similar.

The following discussion summarizes the basic characteristics of the ISO policy.

**Persons Insured**    The ISO umbrella policy covers the following people:

■ *Named insured and spouse if a resident of the same household*

- *Resident relatives, including a ward of the court or foster child*
- *Household residents younger than age 21 in the care of the named insured or an insured age 21 or older*
- *Any person using an auto, recreational motor vehicle, or watercraft that is owned by the named insured and covered under the umbrella policy*
- *Any other person or organization legally responsible for the named insured or family member while using an auto or recreational motor vehicle covered under the policy.* For example, if James does volunteer work and negligently injures another motorist while delivering food baskets for a local church, the church is also covered.

**Coverages**  The umbrella policy pays for damages in excess of the retained limit for bodily injury, property damage, or personal injury for which the insured is legally liable because of a covered loss. *The* **retained limit** *is (1) the total limits of the underlying insurance or any other insurance available to an insured, or (2) the deductible stated in the declarations if the loss is covered by the umbrella policy but not by any underlying insurance or other insurance.*

In addition to the liability limit, the policy pays legal defense costs; expenses incurred by the insurer while defending the suit; premiums on any required bonds; reasonable expenses incurred by an insured at the insurer's request, including the loss of earnings up to $250 daily; and interest on any unpaid judgment.

**Exclusions**  The ISO policy contains numerous exclusions. Major exclusions include the following:

- *Expected or intentional injury.* Expected or intentional injury is excluded. However, the exclusion does not apply to intentional bodily injury resulting from reasonable force to protect people or property, such as acting in self-defense against an intruder who is breaking into your home.
- *Certain personal injury losses.* The policy excludes coverage for certain personal injury losses. Examples include loss arising out of material published before the beginning of the policy, or criminal acts committed by or at the direction of an insured.
- *Rental of the premises.* With certain exceptions, the ISO policy excludes liability arising out of

rental of the residence premises to someone else. This exclusion does not apply to the occasional rental of the residence premises, such as a professor who goes on a sabbatical leave and rents out his or her home for six months. The exclusion also does not apply if part of the residence premises is rented as an office, school, studio, or private garage.

- *Business liability.* The policy excludes liability arising out of business activities by the insured. This exclusion does not apply to an insured who performs civic or public activities without compensation other than reimbursement for expenses, such as a Girl or Boy Scout leader. Likewise, it does not apply to minors younger than age 18 (21 if a full-time student) who are self-employed, such as delivering newspapers, mowing lawns, baby-sitting, or removing snow.
- *Professional services.* The policy excludes liability arising out of the rendering of or failure to render professional services.
- *Aircraft, watercraft, and recreational vehicles.* The policy excludes liability arising out of the ownership or use of aircraft, except model or hobby aircraft. Also excluded are activities involving watercraft or recreational motor vehicles unless coverage is provided by underlying insurance.
- *No reasonable belief.* The ISO personal umbrella policy excludes coverage for a person using an auto, recreational motor vehicle, or watercraft without a reasonable belief that he or she is entitled to do so. This exclusion does not apply to a family member who uses a vehicle owned by the named insured, such as a teenager who drives a family car without first getting permission.
- *Vehicles used in racing.* The policy excludes the use of autos, recreational motor vehicles, or watercraft in a prearranged race or speed contest. The exclusion does not apply to sailboats or to watercraft involved in predicted log cruises.
- *Communicable disease, sexual molestation, or use of a controlled substance.* The policy excludes liability arising out of the transmission of a communicable disease; sexual molestation; corporal punishment; physical or mental abuse; or the use or sale of a controlled substance, such as methamphetamine, cocaine, marijuana, and narcotic drugs (except prescription drugs).

■ *Directors and officers.* The ISO policy excludes acts or omissions of an insured as an officer or member of a board of directors. This exclusion does not apply to nonprofit organizations in which the insured receives no compensation other than reimbursement for expenses.

■ *Care, custody, and control.* The policy excludes coverage for damage to property rented to, used by, or in the care, custody, and control of the insured to the extent that the insured is required by contract to provide insurance for such property.

This exclusion does not apply to property damage caused by fire, smoke, or explosion.

In addition, the ISO personal umbrella policy excludes liability arising out of bodily injury to the named insured or any family member; damage to property owned by an insured; bodily injury to any person eligible to receive workers compensation benefits; and liability arising out of the escape of fuel from a fuel system, absorption or inhalation of lead, or lead contamination.

## CASE APPLICATION

Fred purchased an old house near a river. Although the house needs major repairs, it will be his main residence. The river overflows periodically, which has caused substantial damage to several homes in the area. Fred lives alone, but he keeps two German shepherd dogs on the premises as watchdogs. He also has a small 15-horsepower boat, which is used for fishing.

An insurance agent has informed Fred that the house cannot be insured under a Homeowners 3 (HO-3) policy because the house did not meet the underwriting requirements. The agent stated he would try to get the underwriter to approve a Dwelling Property 3 policy (DP-3) or a Dwelling Property 1 policy (DP-1). As a last resort, the agent stated that coverage might be available through the state's FAIR plan.

a. Assume you are a risk management consultant. Identify the major loss exposures that Fred faces.
b. Explain the major differences among the HO-3, DP-3, and DP-1 policies discussed by the agent.
c. To what extent will each of the coverage alternatives discussed by the agent cover the loss exposures identified in (a)?
d. Assume that Fred buys a DP-3 policy. Do you recommend that he also purchase the personal liability supplement? Explain.
e. Assume that Fred obtains a DP-1 policy. Do you recommend that he also purchase flood insurance through the National Flood Insurance Program? Explain.

## SUMMARY

■ The ISO dwelling program is designed for dwellings that are ineligible for coverage under a homeowners policy and for persons who do not want or need a homeowners policy.

■ The *Dwelling Property 1 policy* is a basic form that provides coverage for a limited number of named perils. The *Dwelling Property 2 policy* is a broad form that includes all perils covered under the basic form and some additional perils. The *Dwelling Property 3 policy* is a special form that covers the dwelling and other structures against direct loss to property. Direct physical losses are covered except for those losses specifically excluded; personal property is covered on a named-perils basis.

■ A mobile home can be insured through an endorsement to a Homeowners 2 or Homeowners 3 policy. Thus, the coverages on a mobile home are similar to those found in homeowner contracts.

■ An *inland marine floater* provides broad and comprehensive protection on personal property that is frequently moved from one location to another. Although inland marine floaters are not uniform, they share certain common characteristics. Insurance is tailored to the specific types of personal property to be insured; desired amounts of insurance and type of coverage can be selected; broader coverage can be obtained; most floaters cover insured property anywhere in the world; and floaters are often written without a deductible.

■ A *personal articles floater (PAF)* insures certain personal property on an "all-risks" or "open perils" basis. Direct physical losses are covered except losses that are specifically excluded. The classes are jewelry, furs, cameras, musical instruments, silverware, golfer's equipment, fine arts, postage stamps, and coin collections. Individual items are listed and insured for specific amounts.

- A *scheduled personal property endorsement* is an endorsement that can be added to the homeowners policy that provides essentially the same coverages provided by a personal articles floater.

- Insurance on recreational boats generally can be divided into two categories. A *boatowners package policy* combines physical damage insurance, medical expense insurance, liability insurance, and other coverages into one contract. *Yacht insurance* is designed for larger and more valuable boats such as cabin cruisers and inboard motorboats. Yacht insurance provides physical damage insurance on the boat and equipment, liability insurance, medical payments insurance, and other coverages.

- The flood peril is difficult to insure privately because of the problems of a catastrophic loss, prohibitively high premiums, and adverse selection. Federal flood insurance is available to cover buildings and personal property in flood zones.

- Under the *write-your-own program,* private insurers write flood insurance, collect premiums, and pay claims. They are reimbursed for any underwriting losses by the federal government.

- *FAIR plans* provide basic property insurance to individuals who are unable to obtain coverage in the normal markets. If the property meets certain underwriting standards, it can be insured at standard or surcharged rates. In some cases, the owner may be required to make certain improvements in the property before the policy is issued.

- *Title insurance* protects the owner of property or secured lender against any unknown defects in the title to the property.

- A *personal umbrella policy* is designed to provide protection against a catastrophic lawsuit or judgment. The major features of a personal umbrella policy are as follows:

  > The policy provides excess liability insurance over basic underlying insurance contracts.

  > Coverage is broad and includes protection against certain losses not covered by the underlying contracts.

  > A self-insured retention must be met for certain losses covered by the umbrella policy but not by any underlying contract.

  > The umbrella policy is reasonable in cost.

## KEY CONCEPTS AND TERMS

Boatowners package
  policy (537)
Dwelling Property 1
  (basic form) (533)
Dwelling Property 2
  (broad form) (533)
Dwelling Property 3
  (special form) (533)
FAIR plans (542)
Inland marine floater (535)
Mobile home insurance (535)
National Flood Insurance
  Program (NFIP) (538)

Personal articles floater
  (PAF) (536)
Personal injury (546)
Personal umbrella
  policy (545)
Retained limit (547)
Scheduled personal
  property
  endorsement (536)
Self-insured
  retention (546)
Title insurance (543)
Yacht insurance (537)

## REVIEW QUESTIONS

1. The ISO dwelling program has several forms. Describe the characteristics of each of the following:
   a. Dwelling Property 1 (basic form)
   b. Dwelling Property 2 (broad form)
   c. Dwelling Property 3 (special form)

2. Explain how personal liability insurance can be added to a dwelling policy.

3. Describe the basic characteristics of inland marine floaters.

4. A personal articles floater (PAF) provides broad protection for valuable personal property. Give three examples of property that might require coverage under a PAF instead of a standard homeowners policy.

5. Identify the coverages found in a typical boatowners package policy.

6. Why are buildings in flood plains difficult to insure by private insurers?

7. The National Flood Insurance Program (NFIP) has numerous provisions. Briefly explain each of the following:
   a. Write-your-own program
   b. Meaning of a flood
   c. Waiting period

8. What is the purpose of a FAIR plan?

9. Describe the basic characteristics of title insurance.

10. Briefly explain the basic characteristics of a personal umbrella policy.

## APPLICATION QUESTIONS

1. Pedro owns a sixplex apartment building and lives in one unit. The building is insured under the Dwelling Property 1 (basic form) policy for $320,000. The replacement cost of the building is $400,000. Explain to what extent, if any, Pedro will recover for the following losses:
   a. A fire occurs in one of the apartments because of defective wiring. The actual cash value of the damage is $20,000, and the replacement cost is $24,000.
   b. The tenants move out because the apartment is unfit for normal living. It will take three months to restore the apartment to its former condition. The apartment is normally rented for $900 monthly.
   c. A tenant's personal property is damaged in the fire. The actual cash value of the damaged property is $5000, and its replacement cost is $7000.

2. Matthew owns a mobile home that is insured by an endorsement to a Homeowners 3 policy. Explain to what extent, if at all, this policy would pay for each of the following losses:
   a. A severe windstorm damages the roof of the mobile home.
   b. A built-in range and oven are also damaged in the storm.
   c. A window air conditioner is badly damaged in the storm.
   d. Matthew must move to a furnished apartment for three months while the mobile home is being repaired.

3. Morgan has an outboard motorboat insured under a boatowners package policy. Indicate whether each of the following losses would be covered under Morgan's policy. If the loss is not covered, or not completely covered, explain why.
   a. Morgan's boat was badly damaged when it struck a log floating in the water.
   b. An occupant in Morgan's boat was injured and incurred medical expenses when the boat struck a concrete abutment.
   c. The motor was stolen when the boat was docked at a marina.

   d. A small child in Morgan's boat was not wearing a life jacket. The child fell overboard and drowned. The child's parents have sued Morgan.

4. Dan has a personal umbrella policy with a $1 million limit. The self-insured retention is $250. Dan has a homeowners policy with no special endorsements and an auto insurance policy. The policies have the following liability limits:

   Homeowners policy: $300,000
   Personal auto policy: $250,000/$500,000/$50,000

   The liability limits meet the umbrella insurer's requirements with respect to the minimum amounts of liability insurance on the underlying contracts. Indicate whether each of the following losses would be covered under Dan's personal umbrella policy. If the loss is not covered, or not covered fully, explain why.
   a. Dan coaches a Little League baseball team. A team member sitting behind third base was struck in the face by a line drive and lost the sight in one eye. Dan is sued by the parents, who allege that his coaching and supervision are inadequate. The team member is awarded damages of $1 million.
   b. Dan is a member of the board of directors for the local YMCA. The YMCA is a nonprofit organization. Dan is sued by a YMCA member who was seriously injured when a trampoline collapsed. The injured member is awarded damages of $500,000.
   c. Dan accuses a male teenager, age 14, of stealing his racing bike valued at $2000. The police arrest the youth and book him. The police later arrest the actual thief and recover the bicycle. Dan is sued by the youth's parents for false arrest. The teenager is awarded damages of $100,000.
   d. Dan is driving to his son's soccer game. He fails to stop at a red light, and his car strikes another motorist. The injured motorist is awarded damages of $200,000.

5. Lori has a personal umbrella policy with a $1 million limit. The self-insured retention is $250. Lori has a homeowners policy with no special endorsements and an auto insurance policy. The policies have the following liability limits:

   Homeowners policy: $300,000
   Personal auto policy: $250,000/$500,000/ $50,000

   The liability limits meet the umbrella insurer's requirements with respect to the minimum amounts of liability insurance on the underlying contracts.

Indicate the amount, if any, that would be paid by Lori's umbrella policy for each of the following losses.

a. Lori's dog bites a small child. The parents sue Lori and are awarded damages of $25,000.

b. Lori failed to stop at a red light, and her car hit a school bus. Two children are severely injured. A court awards each child damages in the amount of $350,000.

c. Lori is a volunteer for a local nonprofit charity. While being interviewed on television with other guests, Lori calls one of the guests a "bag lady." The guest sues Lori for defamation of character and is awarded damages of $25,000.

d. Lori is a member of the board of directors for a local bank. She receives an annual fee of $50,000 for her service as a board member. She is also a member of the board's audit committee. The shareholders sue Lori and other board members for not discovering several fraudulent accounting transactions that caused millions of dollars of losses to the shareholders. A court awards the shareholders damages of $5 million.

## INTERNET RESOURCES

- The **Federal Emergency Management Agency (FEMA)** provides valuable consumer information about the National Flood Insurance Program. Check out this site at

  fema.gov/national-flood-insurance-program

- **FloodSmart.gov** is the official site of the National Flood Insurance Program (NFIP). The site provides important information about NFIP, flooding and flooding risks, and choice of flood coverages. Visit the site at

  floodsmart.gov

- The **Insurance Information Institute (III)** provides valuable consumer information on a number of property and liability insurance contracts for individuals and families. A timely feature is "Issues Updates." The III sponsors a site at

  iii.org

- Another site with useful information about home, auto, and other property and liability insurance coverages is sponsored by the **Independent Insurance Agents & Brokers of America.** You can find this site at

  iiaba.net

- **Insure.com** provides consumers with information on a variety of insurance products, including homeowners and auto insurance. Check out this interesting site at

  insure.com

- **InsWeb** provides premium quotes for auto, homeowners, and other insurance products. The site also has an insurance learning center. Visit the site at

  insweb.com

- The **National Association of Insurance Commissioners (NAIC)** has a link to all state insurance departments. This site also provides a number of articles for consumers. Visit the site at

  naic.org

## SELECTED REFERENCES

*Fire, Casualty & Surety Bulletins.* Fire and Marine volume and Casualty and Surety volume. Erlanger, KY: National Underwriter Company. See also the Personal Lines volume and Guide to Policies I volume. The bulletins are published monthly.

*Flood Insurance Manual*, National Flood Insurance Program, FEMA, Revised May 2012.

Hartwig, Robert P. and Claire Wilkinson, "Residual Market Property Plans: From Markets of Last Resort to Markets of First Choice," Insurance Information Institute, July 2012.

Hunter, J. Robert. *Title Insurance Cost and Competition*, testimony before the House Committee on Financial Services Subcommittee on Housing and Community Opportunity, Consumer Federation of America, April 26, 2006.

Nyce, Charles, ed. *Personal Insurance,* 2nd ed. Malvern, PA.: American Institute for Chartered Property Casualty Underwriters/Insurance Institute of America, 2008.

"Personal Umbrella Liability Policy." *The Institutes' Handbook of Insurance Policies*, 10th ed. Malvern, PA: American Institute for CPCU, 2011, pp. 116-123.

"Study: Flood Program Premiums Do Not Adequately Reflect Flood Risk," *Insurance Journal*, National News, December 9, 2008.

United States Government Accountability Office, *Flood Insurance, FEMA's Rate Setting Process Warrants Attention*, GAO-09-12, Washington, DC, October 2008.

United States Government Accountability Office, National Flood Insurance Program: Continued Actions Needed to Address Financial and Operational Issues, Testimony before the Committee on Banking, Housing, and Urban Affairs, U.S. Senate, Statement of Orice Williams Brown, Director, Financial Markets and Community Investment, Sept. 22, 2010. GAO-10-1063T.

United States Government Accountability Office, *National Flood Insurance Program, FEMA's Management and Oversight of Payments for Insurance Company Services Should Be Improved*, GAO-07-1078, Washington DC, September 2007.

United States Government Accountability Office, *Natural Catastrophe Insurance Coverage Remains a Challenge for State Programs*, GAO-10-1568R, Washington DC, April 16, 2010.

## NOTES

1. The ISO dwelling program is described in detail in *Fire, Casualty & Surety Bulletins,* Personal Lines volume, Dwelling section. The Dwelling program is also discussed in IRMI.com, the International Risk Management Institute's on-line library. The Insurance Services Office (ISO) dwelling forms were also used in preparing this section.

2. These perils are called "extended coverage" perils as they are included in an endorsement that was popular when the standard fire policy was used. That policy covered fire, lightning, and removal only. An extended coverage endorsement was often added to provide coverage for wind, hail, explosion, riot, civil commotion, aircraft, vehicles, and smoke. Explosion coverage under the extended coverage perils replaces the "internal explosion" coverage in the basic form.

3. For a detailed explanation of insuring mobile homes, see "Mobile Home Insurance," *Fire, Casualty & Surety Bulletins,* Personal Lines volume, Dwelling section. IRMI.com's on-line discussion of mobile home insurance was also used in preparing this section.

4. Eric A. Wiening, George E. Rejda, Constance M. Luthardt, and Cheryl L. Ferguson, *Personal Insurance,* 1st ed. (Malvern, PA.: American Institute for Chartered Property Casualty Underwriters/Insurance Institute of America, 2002), p. 9.4.; and the discussion of inland marine floaters at IRMI.com were used in preparing this section.

5. Discussion of the personal articles floater is based on *Fire, Casualty & Surety Bulletins*, Personal Lines volume, Misc. Personal lines section, and discussion on IRMI.com.

6. Insurance on recreational boats is based on *Fire, Casualty & Surety Bulletins,* Companies and Coverages volume, Aircraft-Marine section and the coverage on IRMI.com.

7. Current details of the federal flood insurance program can be found in the *Fire, Casualty & Surety Bulletins,* Fire and Marine volume, Catastrophe section. See also, Federal Emergency Management Agency, *Flood Insurance* at fema.gov/national-flood-insurance-program.

8. These flood insurance premiums were taken from floodsmart.gov.

9. See, for example, *Federal Emergency Management Agency: Challenges Facing the National Flood Insurance Program,* Statement of William O. Jenkins Jr., Director, Homeland Security and Justice Issues, GAO-06-174T, Washington, DC, October 18, 2005; *FEMA's Rate-Setting Process Warrants Attention,* GAO-09-12, Washington, DC, October 2008; and *National Flood Insurance Program: Continued Actions Needed to Address Financial and Operational Issues* , Statement of Orice Williams Brown, Director, Financial Markets and Community Investment, GAO-10-1063T, Washington DC, September 22, 2010.

10. *National Flood Insurance Program: Continued Actions Needed to Address Financial and Operational Issues*, Statement of Orice Williams Brown, Director, Financial Markets and Community Investment, GAO-10-1063T, Washington DC, September 22, 2010.

11. Selected provisions of the Biggert-Waters Flood Insurance Reform and Modernization Act of 2012.

12. FAIR plans exist in Arkansas (rural), California, Connecticut, Delaware, District of Columbia, Florida (Citizens Property Insurance Corporation), Georgia, Hawaii, Illinois, Indiana, Iowa, Kansas, Kentucky, Louisiana (Citizens), Maryland, Massachusetts, Michigan, Minnesota, Mississippi, Missouri, New Jersey, New Mexico, New York, North Carolina, Ohio, Oregon, Pennsylvania, Rhode Island, Virginia, Washington, West Virginia, and Wisconsin. Beach and windstorm plans exist in Alabama, Mississippi, North Carolina, South Carolina, and Texas. Florida and Louisiana Beach Plans merged their FAIR plans. This information was provided by the Insurance Information Institute's *2012 Insurance Fact Book*, pp. 92-94.

13. Robert P. Hartwig and Claire Wilkerson, "Residual Market Property Plans: From Markets of Last Resort to Markets of First Choice," Insurance Information Institute, July 2012, Figure 1, page 4.

14. Ibid., page 26.

15. These defects were enumerated by J. Robert Hunter, Director of Insurance, Consumer Federation of America. *Title Insurance Cost and Competition*, testimony before the House Committee on Financial Services Subcommittee on Housing and Community Opportunity, April 26, 2006.

16. Discussion of the personal umbrella policy is based on John R. Chesebrough and George E. Rejda, "Personal Umbrella Liability Insurance—A Critical Analysis," *CPCU Journal*, vol. 48, no. 2 (June 1995), pp. 98–104; "Personal Umbrella Liability Insurance," in *Fire, Casualty & Surety Bulletins*, Companies and Coverage volume, Personal Packages section (Erlanger, KY: National Underwriter Company); "Personal Umbrella Liability Policy," *The Institutes' Handbook of Insurance Policies*, 10th ed. (Malvern, PA: American Institute for Chartered Property Casualty Underwriters, 2011), pp. 116–123, and discussion on the IRMI.com Web site.

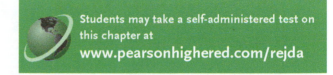

# CHAPTER 25

# COMMERCIAL PROPERTY INSURANCE

*"Protecting the company assets and the impact on earnings from a loss is a key function of the risk manager's job. Commercial property insurance is one of the most important techniques for financing the risks associated with damage to these assets."*

Rebecca A. McQuade
Director of Risk Management, PACCAR Inc

## LEARNING OBJECTIVES

**After studying this chapter, you should be able to**

◆ Explain the basic provisions in the building and personal property coverage form, including

| | |
|---|---|
| Covered property | Optional coverages |
| Additional coverages | Extensions of coverage |

◆ Identify the causes of loss that are covered under the following forms:

| | |
|---|---|
| Causes-of-loss basic form | Causes-of-loss special form |
| Causes-of-loss broad form | |

◆ Explain how a business income loss is determined under the business income (and extra expense) coverage form.

◆ Explain what is covered by each of the following ocean marine policies:

| | |
|---|---|
| Hull insurance | Protection and indemnity (P&I) insurance |
| Cargo insurance | Freight insurance |

◆ Identify the types of property that can be covered by an inland marine insurance policy.

◆ Describe the major provisions of the property insurance in a businessowners policy (BOP), including

| | |
|---|---|
| Coverages provided | Optional coverages |
| Additional coverages | |

*"This can't be good news,"* Devin Mitchell said to himself as he answered the phone. The call roused him from a deep sleep. It was 2 a.m. and the caller was Sheila Gordon, risk manager of Diversified Chemical Company. She was calling to inform Mitchell, president of the company, that there had been an explosion and fire at Diversified Chemical's largest production facility.

*The explosion and fire destroyed three buildings, damaged valuable production equipment, and destroyed finished goods and goods in process. Diversified Chemical Company lost profits that it could have earned and incurred continuing expenses while the plant was closed. Fortunately, Diversified Chemical Company was protected by several property insurance coverages that responded to most of the direct and indirect losses caused by the fire and explosion.*

*In this chapter, we discuss commercial property insurance, with emphasis on the commercial property insurance program developed by the Insurance Services Office (ISO). More specifically, the chapter discusses the commercial package policy, the building and personal property coverage form, business income insurance, and other property coverages. The chapter also discusses ocean marine insurance and inland marine insurance, which cover transportation and other commercial risks. The chapter concludes with an analysis of the property coverage of the ISO businessowners policy, which is designed for small- to medium-sized business firms.*[1]

## COMMERCIAL PACKAGE POLICY

The Insurance Services Office (ISO) makes available package policies tailored to meet the specific needs of business firms. *A package policy is one that combines two or more coverages into a single policy.* If property and liability insurance coverages are combined into a single policy, it is also known as a *multiple-line policy.* In contrast, a policy that provides only one type of coverage is known as a *monoline policy.*

When compared with individual policies, a package policy has several advantages. There are fewer gaps in coverage; insureds pay relatively lower premiums because individual policies are not purchased; savings in insurer expenses can be passed on to the policyholder; and the insured has the convenience of a single policy.

This section discusses the format of a **commercial package policy** (CPP), which is widely used by business firms. A CPP can be used to insure motels, hotels, apartment houses, office buildings, retail stores, churches and schools, processing firms such as dry cleaners, manufacturing firms, and a wide variety of other commercial firms. The various coverages can be specifically tailored to cover most property and liability loss exposures in a single policy, with the major exceptions of professional liability, workers compensation, and surety bonds.

Under the ISO program, each commercial package policy contains (1) a common policy declarations page, (2) a common policy conditions page, and (3) one or more coverage forms.[2] Exhibit 25.1 shows in greater detail the various parts of a commercial package policy.

### Common Policy Declarations

Each commercial package policy contains a *common policy declarations page* that shows the name and address of the insured, policy period, description of the insured property, a list of coverage parts that apply, and the premium amount.

EXHIBIT 25.1
**Components of a Sample Commercial Package Policy (CPP) (Endorsements omitted)**

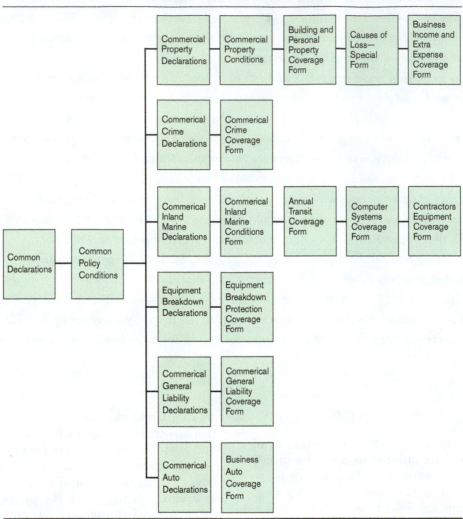

SOURCE: *Commercial Property Risk Management and Insurance*, Edited by Mary Ann Cook, 1st ed., p. 1.14, 2.5, © 2010 American Institute for Chartered Property Casualty Underwriters. Reprinted with permission.

## Common Policy Conditions

Each commercial package policy also contains a *common policy conditions page* that applies to all commercial lines of insurance. The common conditions are summarized as follows:

- *Cancellation.* Either party can cancel by giving the other party advance notice. The insurer can cancel by giving notice of cancellation for non-payment of premiums at least 10 days in advance and 30 days in advance for any other reason. If the insurer cancels, a pro rata refund of the premium is made. If the insured cancels, the refund may be less than pro rata.
- *Changes.* Any changes in the policy can be made only by an endorsement issued by the insurer.
- *Examination of books and records.* The insurer has the right to audit the insured's books and records anytime during the policy period and up to three years after the policy period ends.
- *Inspections and surveys.* The insurer has the right to make inspections and surveys that relate to insurability of the property and premiums to be charged.

- *Premiums.* More than one party may be named as an insured on the declarations page. The *first named insured* in the declarations is the party responsible for the payment of premiums.
- *Transfer of rights and duties.* The insured's rights and duties under the policy cannot be transferred without the insurer's written consent. One exception is that the rights and duties can be transferred to a legal representative if an individual named insured should die.

### Coverage Forms

Each commercial package policy includes one or more coverage forms. Depending on need, business firms can select among several coverages. Coverage forms include the following:

- Building and personal property coverage form
- Business income and extra expense coverage form
- Commercial crime coverage form
- Inland marine coverage form(s)
- Equipment breakdown protection coverage form
- Commercial general liability coverage form
- Business auto coverage form

Each coverage part, in turn, contains (1) its own declarations page that applies to that coverage, (2) the specific conditions that apply to that coverage part, (3) coverage forms that describe the various coverages provided, and (4) where applicable, a causes-of-loss form that describes the various perils that are covered.

## BUILDING AND PERSONAL PROPERTY COVERAGE FORM

The **building and personal property (BPP) coverage form** is a commercial property coverage form that is widely used to cover a direct physical damage loss to commercial buildings and business personal property.

### Covered Property

The insured selects the property to be covered. Covered property can include the following:

- Buildings
- Named insured's business personal property
- Personal property of others in the care, custody, or control of the named insured

For any of these coverages to apply, the declarations page must show a limit of insurance for that category. Depending on its needs, a business firm can elect one or all three coverages.

**Building** The form covers the building described in the declarations and includes any completed additions and fixtures and permanently installed machinery and equipment. Equipment used to maintain or service the building (such as fire-extinguishing equipment, appliances for cooking and dishwashing, floor buffers, and vacuum cleaners) is also covered.

Finally, if not covered by other insurance, the form also covers additions, alterations, or repairs to the building, which includes materials and supplies on or within 100 feet of the premises.

**Business Personal Property** Business personal property of the named insured inside or on the building or within 100 feet of the premises is also covered.[3] It includes furniture and fixtures; computer systems, machinery and equipment; stock[4] or inventory; and all other personal property owned by the insured and used in the insured's business.

In addition, the insured's interest in the personal property of others is covered to the extent of labor, materials, and other charges. For example, a machine shop may repair a piece of machinery owned by a customer. If parts and labor are $1000 and the machinery is damaged from an insured peril before it is delivered to the customer, the insured's interest of $1000 is covered.

The insured's use interest in improvements and betterments as a tenant is also covered as business personal property. Improvements and betterments include fixtures, alterations, installations, or additions that are made part of the building at the insured's expense. An example of an improvement is the installation of a new air conditioning unit by an insured who leases a building to open a new bar and restaurant.

The improvements belong to the landlord and cannot be removed legally without the landlord's consent. The tenant, however, has an insurable interest in use of the improvements during the lease or rental period.

Finally, business personal property includes leased personal property that the insured has a contractual obligation to insure. An example would be leased computer equipment for which the insured is required to provide insurance.

**Personal Property of Others** Personal property of others in the care, custody, or control of the named insured also can be covered. For example, if a tornado destroys a machinery repair shop, and equipment that belongs to customers is damaged, the loss would be covered.

**Additional Coverages** Several additional coverages are provided, summarized as follows:

- *Debris removal.* The cost of debris removal is paid up to certain limits specified in the policy. Debris removal coverage does not apply to the cost of extracting pollutants from land or water.
- *Preservation of property.* If property is moved to another location for safekeeping because of a covered loss, any direct physical loss or damage to the property while being moved or while stored at the other location is covered. Coverage applies only if the loss or damage occurs within 30 days after the property is first moved.
- *Fire department service charge.* A maximum of $1000 can be paid for a fire department service charge. No deductible applies to this coverage.
- *Pollutant cleanup and removal.* The insurer also pays the cost to clean up and remove pollutants from land or water at the described premises if the release or discharge of the pollutants results from a covered cause of loss. The maximum paid is limited to $10,000 during each separate 12-month policy period.
- *Increased cost of construction.* An additional coverage is the increased cost of construction because of an ordinance or law. A building code may increase the cost of restoring a building if a loss occurs. The additional coverage applies only to buildings insured on a replacement cost basis. The maximum amount of additional insurance that applies to each described building insured under this form is $10,000, or 5 percent of the limit of insurance that applies to that building, whichever is less.
- *Electronic data.* The policy pays the cost to replace or restore electronic data destroyed or corrupted by a covered cause of loss, including CDs, hard drives, and similar equipment. Covered causes of loss include damage caused by

a computer virus except if caused by an employee or leased employee. The maximum paid is $2500 during any policy year, regardless of the number of occurrences.

**Extensions of Coverage** If a coinsurance requirement of 80 percent or higher is shown in the declarations, or a value-reporting period symbol is shown on the declarations page, the insurance can be extended to cover other property. The extensions of coverage are summarized as follows:

- *Newly acquired or constructed property.* Insurance on the building is extended to cover new buildings while being built on the described premises and to newly acquired buildings at other locations. The insurance applies for a maximum period of 30 days and is limited to a maximum of $250,000 for each building. In addition, the insurance on business personal property ($100,000 maximum) can be applied to business personal property at newly acquired locations. This insurance also applies for a maximum period of 30 days.
- *Personal effects and property of others.* Insurance on business personal property can be extended to cover the personal effects of the named insured, officers, partners, or employees. However, the extension does not apply to theft. The extension also applies to personal property of others in the named insured's care, custody, or control. The maximum paid is limited to $2500.
- *Valuable papers and records (other than electronic data).* Insurance on business personal property can also be extended to cover the costs of researching, replacing, or restoring lost information on lost or damaged valuable papers and records. The maximum paid is limited to $2500 at each described premises.
- *Property off the premises.* Covered property that is temporarily at a location not owned, leased, or operated by the insured is covered up to $10,000. The extension of coverage does not apply to property in or on a vehicle or to property in the care, custody, or control of salespersons. However, if the property is in the care, custody, or control of salespersons at a trade show, fair, or exhibition, the extension of coverage will apply.
- *Outdoor property.* Outdoor fences, radio and television antennas, detached signs, and trees,

plants, and shrubs are covered up to a maximum of $1000, but not more than $250 for any single tree, shrub, or plant. The insurance applies only to losses caused by fire, lightning, explosion, riot or civil commotion, or aircraft.

- *Nonowned detached trailers.* Coverage can also be extended to nonowned detached trailers under certain circumstances. The trailer must be used in the business and in the insured's care, custody, and control; the insured must also have a contractual obligation to pay for any loss or damage to the trailer. However, coverage ceases if the trailer is attached to any motor vehicle whether in motion or not. For example, a construction company may rent a trailer that is used as a temporary office while at a worksite; coverage applies as long as the trailer is not attached to any motorized vehicle. The maximum paid under this extension is $5000.

## Other Provisions

Numerous additional provisions are included in the building and personal property coverage form, but it is beyond the scope of this text to discuss each of them. Several important provisions, however, are summarized here.

**Deductible**   A standard deductible of $500 applies to each occurrence. Higher deductible amounts are available. Only one deductible must be satisfied if different types of covered property are damaged in the same occurrence.

**Coinsurance**   If a coinsurance percentage is stated in the declarations, the coinsurance requirement must be met to avoid a coinsurance penalty. To reduce misunderstanding and confusion, the form contains several examples of how coinsurance works.

**Optional Coverages**   Several optional coverages are preprinted in the form, which eliminates the need for separate endorsements. If these optional coverages are selected, it is noted on the declarations page.

- *Agreed value.* The agreed value option suspends the coinsurance clause while the option is in force. For losses to be paid in full, the amount of insurance carried must equal the agreed value. For example, if the agreed value is $100,000, and the limit of insurance is $100,000, all covered losses will be paid in full (minus the deductible) up to the limit of insurance. However, if the amount of insurance carried is $75,000, only three-fourths of a covered loss will be paid. The purpose of this option is to avoid a penalty if the coinsurance requirement is not met.
- *Inflation guard.* This option automatically increases the amount of insurance by an annual percentage shown in the declarations. The increase is prorated throughout the year on a daily basis.
- *Replacement cost.* Under the replacement cost option, there is no deduction for depreciation if a loss occurs. However, this option does not apply to the property of others; contents of a residence; manuscripts; works of art, antiques, and similar property; and stock (unless designated in the declarations). Replacement cost insurance generally is recommended when the insured's buildings and their contents are insured. If this option is not selected, losses are paid on an actual cash-value basis.
- *Extension of replacement cost to personal property of others.* Another optional coverage is the extension of replacement cost to personal property of others in the named insured's care, custody, or control.

## CAUSES-OF-LOSS FORMS

A *causes-of-loss form* is part of the complete contract. Insureds can select one of the following forms:

- Causes-of-loss basic form
- Causes-of-loss broad form
- Causes-of-loss special form

The difference among these forms is the perils covered. The basic and broad forms provide named-perils coverage. The special form provides open perils coverage and insures against direct physical loss to covered property.[5]

### Causes-of-Loss Basic Form

The **causes-of-loss basic form** provides coverage for 11 basic causes of loss (perils) to covered property:

- Fire
- Lightning

- Explosion
- Windstorm or hail
- Smoke
- Aircraft or vehicles
- Riot or civil commotion
- Vandalism
- Sprinkler leakage
- Sinkhole collapse
- Volcanic action

### Causes-of-Loss Broad Form

The **causes-of-loss broad form** includes causes of loss covered by the basic form plus several additional causes:

- Falling objects
- Weight of snow, ice, or sleet
- Water damage

The broad form also covers collapse of a building as an additional coverage. Collapse is covered only if caused by the following:

- Certain specified causes of loss (the broad form perils)
- Hidden decay
- Hidden insect or vermin damage
- Weight of people or personal property
- Weight of rain that collects on a roof
- Use of defective materials or methods in construction or remodeling if collapse occurs during the course of construction or remodeling

### Causes-of-Loss Special Form

The **causes-of-loss special form** provides open perils coverage and insures against direct physical loss to covered property. *That is, direct physical damage losses to insured property are covered unless specifically excluded or limited in the form itself.* Important exclusions include loss due to the enforcement of an ordinance or law, flood, earth movement, and mold. The burden of proof falls on the insurer to show that the loss is not covered because of a specific exclusion or limitation that applies. In addition, collapse is included as an additional coverage.

The special form provides for three additional extensions of coverage. First, personal property in transit is covered for certain causes of loss while the property is in or on a motor vehicle owned, leased, or operated by the insured. The maximum paid is $5000.

Second, if the damage results from a covered water damage loss or from other liquids, powder, or molten material; the cost of tearing out and replacing part of the building or structure to repair the leaking water system or appliance is covered.

Finally, the special form covers glass damage as an additional extension of coverage. The insurer will pay for the cost of boarding up openings and repair or replacement of the damaged glass. The insurer will also pay the expense of removing or replacing obstructions when glass that is part of the building is being repaired or replaced. The cost of removing or replacing window displays, however, is not covered.

Because of its advantages, most risk managers prefer the special form.

## REPORTING FORMS

Some business firms have wide fluctuations in the value of business personal property during the policy period, especially in the value of inventories held for sale. A **reporting form** requires the insured to report periodically the value of insured business personal property.[6] The major advantage of the reporting form is that premiums are based on the actual value of the covered property if the insured reports accurately and on time rather than on the limit of insurance, which may be greater than the value of the covered property on hand. However, coverage is subject to the policy limits even if values in excess of those limits are reported.

Under the ISO commercial property program, the *value reporting form* is used to insure fluctuations in business personal property. An advance premium is paid at the inception of the policy based on the limit of insurance. The final premium is determined at the end of the policy period based on the values reported. The insured has the option of reporting daily, weekly, monthly, quarterly, or at the end of the policy year. As long as the insured reports the correct values, the full amount of the loss is covered (subject to the policy limit and deductible) even if the value of the property on hand exceeds the value reported at the last reporting date. For example, assume that the insured correctly reports business personal property of $1 million at the last reporting date. Before the next reporting date, the value of covered property increases to $5 million.

If a total loss occurs, the loss is covered in full up to the policy limit (less a deductible).

If the insured is dishonest or careless and under-reports, the insured will be penalized if a loss occurs. *If the insured underreports the insured property value and a loss occurs, recovery is limited to the proportion that the last value reported bears to the correct value that should have been reported.* For example, if the actual value of business personal property on hand, including inventory, is $500,000, and the insured reports only $400,000, only four-fifths of any loss will be paid (less the deductible).

Some businesses are seasonal. For example, a winter apparel company or a snow shovel manufacturer may have higher inventory during the fall months. Such a business will be under-insured during high inventory months if the amount of insurance purchased is based on average inventory. Conversely, the business will be over-insured in most months if the amount of insurance purchased is based on the seasonal higher inventory value. One solution to this problem is a peak season endorsement. A **peak season endorsement** *increases the amount of insurance in force during a specified period to reflect higher inventory values.*

## BUSINESS INCOME INSURANCE

Business firms often experience an indirect loss as a result of a direct physical damage loss to covered property, such as the loss of profits, rents, or extra expenses during the period of restoration. **Business income insurance** (formerly called *business interruption insurance*) is designed to cover the loss of business income, expenses that continue during the shutdown period, and extra expenses because of loss from a covered peril.

Two basic ISO forms may be used to insure business income losses:[7]

- Business income (and extra expense) coverage form
- Extra expense coverage form

### Business Income (and Extra Expense) Coverage Form

The **business income (and extra expense) coverage form** is used to cover the loss of business income whether the income is derived from retail or service operations, manufacturing, or rents. When a firm has a business income loss, profits are lost, and certain expenses may still continue, such as rent, interest, insurance premiums, and some salaries. The form covers both the loss of business income and extra expenses that result from a physical damage loss to covered property.

The **business income (without extra expense) coverage form** is also available. This form covers business income and continuing expenses. Extra expenses are covered only to the extent that such expenses reduce the loss.

**Loss of Business Income** The business income and extra expense coverage form covers the loss of business income due to the suspension of operations during the period of restoration. The suspension of operations must result from the direct physical loss or damage to property caused by an insured peril at the described premises. The insured perils are listed in the causes-of-loss form attached to the policy. *Business income is defined as the net profit or loss before income taxes that would have been earned, and continuing normal operating expenses, including payroll.* The business income loss is the difference between expected net income if the loss did not occur and actual net income after the loss. For example, assume that a retail shoe store has a fire and experiences a reduction in its net income during a three-month rebuilding period. Based on past and projected future earnings, the firm expected to earn net income of $75,000 during the three-month period if the loss did not occur. However, because of limited operations following the loss, actual net income was only $25,000. The business income loss is $50,000 ($75,000 − $25,000).

Consider a second example. In this case, the firm has no earnings during the shutdown period but has continuing expenses. Assume that Sal's Pizza is totally destroyed by a tornado, and it will take six months to rebuild. Based on past earnings and projected future income, Sal expected to earn a net income of $100,000 during the six-month period if the loss did not occur. During the shutdown period, however, there were no revenues, and Sal had continuing expenses of $10,000. As a result, the firm experienced a net loss of $10,000. As in the previous example, actual net income is subtracted from expected net income to determine the business income loss. In this case, the business income loss is

$110,000, calculated as $100,000 − (−$10,000). The loss payment covers the net income that would have been earned if the loss had not occurred and continuing expenses during the shutdown period.

**Extra Expenses** The business income (and extra expense) coverage form also covers extra expenses. Extra expenses *are the necessary expenses incurred by the firm during the period of restoration that would not have been incurred if the loss had not taken place.* Examples of covered expenses are the cost of relocating temporarily to another location, increased rent at another location, and the rental of substitute equipment.

**Additional Coverages** The business income form provides several additional coverages, summarized as follows:

- *Action of civil authority.* Loss of business income and extra expenses caused by action of a civil authority that prohibits access to the described premises are also paid. In this case, a covered cause of loss is responsible for a loss to property not owned by the insured. The coverage for business income begins 72 hours after the time of that action and continues for up to four consecutive weeks after the coverage begins.
- *Alterations and new buildings.* The loss of business income as a result of a direct physical damage loss to a new building on the premises (whether completed or under construction) is covered. The loss of business income because of alterations or additions to existing buildings is covered as well.
- *Extended business income.* A business that reopens may experience reduced earnings after the repairs are completed, and additional time may be needed to rebuild a customer base. For example, a restaurant that reopens after a fire may need time to attract former customers back. The extended business income provision covers the reduction in earnings for a limited period after the business reopens. The extended period begins on the date the property is repaired and operations are resumed and ends after 30 consecutive days or when business income returns to normal, whichever occurs first.[8]
- *Interruption of computer operations.* Coverage also applies to the suspension of operations caused by an interruption of computer operations from a covered cause of loss. For example, business operations may be temporarily suspended because a computer "hacker" breaks into the company's computer system, causing it to crash. The maximum paid is $2500 during any policy year.

**Coinsurance** The business income coverage form can be purchased with coinsurance of 50, 60, 70, 80, 90, 100, or 125 percent. *The basis for coinsurance is the sum of net income that would have been earned and continuing normal operating expenses, including payroll, for the 12 months following the inception of the policy or the last anniversary date, whichever is later.* This sum is then multiplied by the coinsurance percentage to determine the amount of insurance needed to avoid a coinsurance penalty. For example, assume that net income and operating expenses for the 12 months of the current policy term are $400,000, and that the coinsurance percentage is 50 percent; the required amount of insurance would be $200,000.

The actual coinsurance percentage selected depends on the expected length of time it will take to resume operations, and on the period of time during which most of the business is done. If the firm expects to be shut down for more than one year, the 125 percent option should be selected. If the firm expects to be shut down for no more than six months and business is uniform throughout the year, a coinsurance percentage of 50 percent should be selected. However, when seasonal peak periods are considered, this percentage may be inadequate, because 50 percent of the firm's business may not occur within a consecutive six-month period. Thus, when business income is seasonal or has peak periods, a coinsurance percentage higher than 50 percent is advisable to provide greater protection during a prolonged shutdown period that continues during the peak period.

Ordinary payroll is covered under the business income coverage form unless it is excluded by an endorsement to the policy. The endorsement can exclude ordinary payroll, or it can be covered for a limited period, such as 90 days. Limiting or excluding ordinary payroll reduces the premium.

**Optional Coverages** The business income form also has coverages that can be activated by an appropriate entry on the declarations page. The optional coverages are summarized as follows:

- *Maximum period of indemnity.* This optional coverage eliminates coinsurance and pays for the loss of business income for a maximum period of 120 days. The amount paid cannot exceed the policy limit. This option can be used by smaller firms that will not be shut down for more than 120 days if a loss occurs.
- *Monthly limit of indemnity.* This optional coverage eliminates coinsurance and limits the maximum monthly amount that will be paid for each consecutive 30-day period to a fraction of the policy limit. The fractions are one-third, one-fourth, and one-sixth. For example, if the fraction selected is one-third, and the policy limit is $120,000, the maximum paid for each consecutive 30-day period is $40,000.
- *Business income agreed value.* This option suspends the coinsurance clause and places no limit on the monthly amount paid, provided that the agreed amount of business income insurance is carried. The agreed amount is the coinsurance percentage (50 percent or higher) multiplied by an estimate of net income and operating expenses for the 12 months of the policy period.
- *Extended period of indemnity.* This option extends the recovery period following completion of repairs from 30 days to a longer period stated in the declarations.[9] The extended period of indemnity can be up to two years. This option is advantageous for those firms that need a longer recovery period to recapture old business and resume normal operations.

### Extra Expense Coverage Form

Certain firms such as banks, newspapers, and dairies must continue to operate after a loss occurs; otherwise, customers will be lost to competitors. The **extra expense coverage form** is a separate form that can be used to cover the extra expenses incurred by the firm in continuing operations during a period of restoration. The extra expense form does not cover the loss of business income because of the interruption of operations. However, the additional expenses to continue operating are covered, subject to certain limits stated in the declarations on the amount of insurance that can be used. A common limitation is

40 percent, 80 percent, and 100 percent. A maximum of 40 percent can be paid when the recovery period is 30 days or less, 80 percent when the recovery period is longer than 30 days but does not exceed 60 days, and 100 percent when the recovery period is longer than 60 days.

### Business Income from Dependent Properties

In some cases, a loss to someone else's property might cause a loss of income for the insured. For example, some firms depend on a single supplier for raw materials and supplies or on a single customer to purchase most or all of the firm's products. The insured's business may incur a loss because of property damage incurred by the sole supplier or customer. An appropriate endorsement can be added to a business income policy that covers loss of income to the insured resulting from direct damage to property at other locations.

There are four types of dependent properties situations for which this coverage may be needed.[10]

- *Contributing location.* A contributing location is a location that furnishes materials or services to the insured. For example, the insured may depend on one supplier for raw materials. If the supplier's factory is damaged, the insured's business may be forced to close.
- *Recipient location.* A recipient location is a location that purchases the insured's products or services. For example, a specialized cheese manufacturer may sell most of the cheese it produces to a resort hotel. If the hotel is closed because of fire, the cheese factory may have to shut down.
- *Manufacturing location.* A manufacturing location is a location that manufactures products for delivery to the insured's customers. If the manufacturer's plant is damaged, the products cannot be delivered, and the insured would incur a loss.
- *Leader location.* A leader location is a location that attracts customers to the insured's place of business. For example, a major department store in a shopping center may have a fire. As a result, a small specialty store in the shopping center may experience a decline in sales as it relied on the department store to generate customers.

# OTHER COMMERCIAL PROPERTY COVERAGES

The building and personal property coverage form discussed earlier is designed to meet the commercial property insurance needs of most business firms. However, many firms have certain needs that require the use of specialized coverages, which include the following:

- Builders risk insurance
- Condominium insurance
- Equipment breakdown insurance
- Difference in conditions (DIC) insurance

## Builders Risk Insurance

A building under construction is exposed to numerous perils, especially the peril of fire. The value of the building under construction changes as various stages of construction are completed. Under the simplified commercial property program by ISO, the **builders risk coverage form** can be used to insure buildings under construction. This form can be used to cover the insurable interest of a general contractor, subcontractor, or building owner.

Under the builders risk coverage form, insurance is purchased equal to the *full value* of the completed building. Because the building is substantially overinsured during the initial stages of construction, the rate charged is adjusted to reflect the average value exposed.

If desired, a *builders risk reporting form* can be attached as an endorsement, which requires the builder to report monthly the value of the building under construction. The initial premium reflects the value of the building at the inception of the policy period and not the completed value of the building. As construction progresses, the amount of insurance on the building is increased based on the reported values. The premiums are adjusted during the policy period based on the values reported by the builder.

## Condominium Association Coverage Form

Condominiums can be either commercial or residential. Owners of individual condominium units have a common interest in the building, which includes the exterior walls, the roof, and the plumbing, heating, and air conditioning systems. However, property insurance on the building and common elements of other condominium property is purchased in the name of the condominium owners association (named insured).

The **condominium association coverage form** covers both commercial and residential condominiums. The form covers the following types of property:

- Building(s)
- Named insured's business personal property
- Personal property of others

The form covers the condominium building and equipment used to maintain or service the building, such as fire extinguishing equipment and outdoor furniture. If required by the condominium association agreement, the form also covers fixtures, improvements and alterations that are part of the building, and appliances within individual units (such as a dishwasher or stove).

The form also covers the named insured's business personal property. The named insured is the condominium owners association. One example of business personal property is equipment in a condominium health club, such as treadmills, weights, stationary bikes, and similar equipment. Another example is furniture in a community clubhouse or around a community pool.

Finally, the condominium association form covers personal property of others in the named insured's care, custody, and control.

## Condominium Commercial Unit-Owners Coverage Form

Business or professional firms may own individual units in a commercial condominium. For example, a physician, dentist, or business firm may own individual office space in a commercial office building that is legally organized as a condominium.

The condominium commercial unit-owners coverage form is used to insure only the owners of commercial condominium units. Owners of residential condominium units normally insure their personal property under the Homeowners 6 policy (unit-owner form).

The **condominium commercial unit-owners coverage form** covers the following categories of property:

- Business personal property of the unit owner
- Personal property of others in the named insured's care, custody, or control

Business personal property includes the following:

- Furniture
- Fixtures and improvements that are part of the building and owned by the unit owner
- Machinery and equipment
- Stock (goods for sale)
- All other personal property owned by the unit owner and used in the business
- Labor, materials, or services furnished by the unit owner on personal property of others
- Leased personal property that the unit owner has a contractual obligation to insure

The condominium form also covers the personal property of others in the care, custody, or control of the unit owner. The personal property must be in or on the building described in the declarations or within 100 feet of the described premises if in the open or in a vehicle.

### Equipment Breakdown Insurance

**Equipment breakdown insurance** (formerly known as *boiler and machinery insurance*) covers losses due to the accidental breakdown of covered equipment. Such equipment includes steam boilers; air conditioning and refrigeration equipment; electrical generating equipment; pumps, compressors, turbines, and engines; machinery used in manufacturing; and computer equipment.

The causes-of-loss forms discussed earlier exclude steam boiler explosions, electrical breakdown, and mechanical breakdown. The **equipment breakdown protection coverage form** can be used to provide such coverage. Coverage can be written separately as a monoline policy, or it can be part of a commercial package policy.

**Covered Cause of Loss** The covered cause of loss is a breakdown to covered equipment. A *breakdown* is a direct physical loss that causes damage to covered equipment. *Covered equipment* refers to the boiler, machinery, or electrical or mechanical equipment insured under the policy, including communication equipment and computer equipment. Covered equipment also includes equipment owned by a public or private utility used solely to support utility services to the premises. Insight 25.1 gives examples of covered equipment breakdown claims.

**Coverages Provided** The current ISO form contains numerous coverages that can be included or omitted depending on the needs of the business firm. A specific coverage is in force if the declarations page indicates either a limit of insurance, or if the word "INCLUDED" is shown for the coverage. If neither is indicated, there is no coverage for that benefit.

- *Property damage.* The form pays for direct damage to covered property located at the premises described in the declarations. Covered property is property owned by the insured or property in the insured's care, custody, or control for which the insured is legally liable.
- *Expediting expenses.* Expediting expenses are the reasonable extra costs the insured must pay to make temporary repairs or to expedite the permanent repair or replacement of the damaged property. For example, the extra transportation charges to speed up delivery of a replacement part would be covered.
- *Business income and extra expense–extra expense only.* This coverage pays for the loss of business income and extra expenses. Business income refers to the loss of business income and extra expenses incurred during the period of restoration. However, if shown in the declarations, only extra expenses can be covered. For example, a firm may have its own power plant and an emergency standby connection with an outside public utility firm in case power is interrupted because of a covered loss. The extra costs of the outside power would be covered.
- *Spoilage damage.* This coverage pays for spoilage damage to raw materials, property in process, or finished products. For example, the loss of refrigeration in a meatpacking plant that results in the spoilage of meat would be covered.
- *Utility interruption.* This coverage extends the protection provided by the business income and extra expense coverages. For example, if a power generator owned by a local public utility has a mechanical failure, and the insured firm loses power and must shut down its business operations, the resulting loss of business income would be covered. However, the insured must select a waiting period—such as 12 hours—before coverage applies.
- *Newly acquired premises.* Coverage automatically applies to newly acquired premises leased

## INSIGHT 25.1

### Examples of Equipment Breakdown Claims

#### Recent Paid Claims

**Spoiled Squid**

Approximately 100,000 pounds of frozen packaged squid thawed out and had to be discarded after a compressor broke down. It cost less than $4,000 to replace the freezer compressor—spoilage accounted for the rest of the loss.

| | |
|---|---|
| Repair Cost | $3,384 |
| Spoilage | $102,527 |
| Total Paid Loss | $105,911 |

**Can't Take Your Order**

A chain restaurant was closed for 10 days after loose connections and severe arcing damaged the main electrical panel. The operators could not recall doing any electrical maintenance that might have prevented the accident.

| | |
|---|---|
| Repair Cost | $37,746 |
| Business Interruption | $14,264 |
| Total Paid Loss | $52,010 |

**Shocked the Robot**

A power surge in a medical laboratory shorted out equipment throughout the facility. The loss included a "bio-robot," computers, a centrifuge, timers, and DNA workstations.

| | |
|---|---|
| Total Paid Loss | $103,070 |

**Tainted Juice**

A capping machine in a beverage bottling plant failed to properly seal containers of fruit juice when drive clutches that controlled torque broke and cracked. In addition to the damage, some of the juice was contaminated and had to be destroyed.

| | |
|---|---|
| Repair Cost | $4,187 |
| Business Interruption | $43,279 |
| Perishable Goods | $103,760 |
| Total Paid Loss | $151,226 |

**Snake Shuts Down City**

A snake squeezed into a breaker box in a municipal utility substation, knocking out power to a city in a $342,707 equipment breakdown loss. Damage from electric arcing was so severe that temporary rental equipment was brought in to restore service.

| | |
|---|---|
| Repair Cost | $260,954 |
| Extra Expense | $81,754 |
| Total Paid Loss | $342,708 |

**Cool college classes**

Air conditioning, electrical and lighting equipment were damaged in two buildings on a community college campus when an underground feeder cable arced and burned out. A chiller unit was rented so classes could start for the fall semester.

| | |
|---|---|
| Repair Cost | $44,163 |
| Extra Expense | $12,103 |
| Total Paid Loss | $56,266 |

SOURCE: "Recent Paid Claims," *Whistle Stop*, © The Hartford Steam Boiler Inspection and Insurance Co. (accessed on hsbwhistlestop.com). Reprinted by permission of the Hartford Steam Boiler Inspection and Insurance Company.

or purchased. The insured is required to notify the insurer of the newly acquired premises as soon as practical.

- *Ordinance or law coverage.* This coverage pays for the increase in loss that results from an ordinance or law regulating the demolition, construction, repair, or use of the building. The form describes in detail what losses will be paid or not paid because of some ordinance or law.

- *Errors and omissions.* If the insured has made an unintentional error or mistake in describing the property or premises to be insured, the loss or damage will still be covered.
- *Brands and labels.* If there is a loss to covered property, the insurer may take any part of the property at an agreed or appraised value. This coverage allows the insured to stamp the word *salvage* on the merchandise or to remove the brand or label

from the damaged merchandise at the insurer's expense. The insurer pays the reasonable cost provided the total cost of the activity and the value of the damaged property do not exceed the limit of insurance for such coverage.

■ *Contingent business income and extra expense—extra expense only coverage.* This coverage extends the firm's business income coverage to insure the loss of income that results from a breakdown at a nonowned premises critical to the firm's operation. For example, assume that the insured does business in a shopping mall and that the entire mall is blacked out because of a short circuit in an electrical generator in another store. As a result, the firm must shut down and loses sales. The loss of income would be covered.

Insurers that write equipment breakdown coverage often provide loss-control services to their insureds. Covered equipment (boilers, refrigeration units, etc.) may be periodically inspected by the insurer's loss-control engineers. This line of insurance is characterized by higher expenses and lower losses per dollar of premium paid.

### Difference in Conditions Insurance

**Difference in conditions (DIC) insurance** is an "all-risks" (direct physical loss not excluded) policy that covers other perils not insured by basic property insurance contracts.[11] DIC insurance is written as a separate contract to supplement the coverage provided by the underlying contracts. As such, it excludes perils covered by the underlying contracts (such as fire and extended coverage perils,[12] vandalism and malicious mischief, and sprinkler leakage). This coverage is often purchased to obtain coverage for some perils that are usually excluded by other property forms, notably flood and earthquake, although additional perils are covered. A substantial deductible must be satisfied for losses not covered by the underlying contracts.

DIC insurance has two major advantages. First, it can be used to fill gaps in coverage. Many large multinational corporations use a DIC policy to insure their overseas property. Many foreign countries require property insurance to be purchased locally; if the local coverage is inadequate, a DIC policy can fill the gap in coverage.

Second, DIC insurance can be used to insure unusual and catastrophic exposures that are not covered by the underlying contracts. Some unusual losses that have been paid include the following:[13]

■ An accident caused molasses to spill into a machine. The cost to clean the machine was $38,000.
■ Dust collected on a roof and solidified, and the weight caused the roof to collapse.
■ A city water main broke, which flooded the basement of an industrial plant, causing hundreds of thousands of dollars of damage.

## TRANSPORTATION INSURANCE

Billions of dollars of goods are shipped by business firms each year. These goods are exposed to damage or loss from numerous transportation perils. The goods can be protected by ocean marine and inland marine contracts. **Ocean marine insurance** *provides protection for goods transported over water.* All types of oceangoing vessels and their cargo can be insured by ocean marine contracts; the legal liability of ship owners and cargo owners can also be insured.

**Inland marine insurance** *provides protection for goods shipped on land.* It includes insurance on imports and exports, domestic shipments, and means of transportation such as bridges and tunnels. In addition, inland marine insurance can be used to insure fine arts, jewelry, furs, and other property.[14]

### Ocean Marine Insurance

Ocean marine insurance is one of the oldest forms of transportation insurance. Ocean marine contracts are complex, reflecting maritime law, trade customs, and court interpretations of the various policy provisions.

There are several types of ocean marine contracts. Some basic coverages include the following:

■ **Hull insurance** *covers physical damage to the ship or vessel.* It is similar to collision insurance that covers physical damage to an automobile caused by a collision. Hull insurance is always written with a deductible. In addition, it contains a **collision liability clause** (also called a **running down clause**) that covers the owner's legal liability if the ship collides with another vessel or damages its cargo. However, the running down clause does not cover legal liability arising out of injury or death to other persons, damage to piers and docks, and personal injury and death of crew members.

- **Cargo insurance** *covers the shipper of the goods if the goods are damaged or lost.* The policy can be written to cover a single shipment. If regular shipments are made, an open-cargo policy can be used that insures the goods automatically when a shipment is made. The shipper is required to periodically report the shipments that are made. The open-cargo policy has no expiration date and remains in force until it is canceled.

- **Protection and indemnity (P&I) insurance** *is usually written as a separate contract that provides comprehensive liability insurance for property damage or bodily injury to third parties.* P&I insurance protects the ship owner for damage caused by the ship to piers, docks, and harbor installations, damage to the ship's cargo, illness or injury to the passengers or crew, and fines and penalties.

- **Freight insurance** *indemnifies the ship owner for the loss of earnings if the goods are damaged or lost and are not delivered.*

## Basic Concepts in Ocean Marine Insurance

Ocean marine insurance is based on certain fundamental concepts. The following section discusses these concepts and related contractual provisions.

**Implied Warranties** Ocean marine contracts contain three **implied warranties:**

- Seaworthy vessel
- No deviation from planned course
- Legal purpose

The ship owner implicitly warrants that the vessel is seaworthy, which means that the ship is properly constructed, maintained, and equipped for the voyage to be undertaken.

The warranty of no deviation means that the ship cannot deviate from its original course. However, an intentional deviation is permitted in the event of an unavoidable accident, to avoid bad weather, to save the life of an individual on board, or to rescue persons from some other vessel.

The warranty of legal purpose means that the voyage should not be for some illegal venture, such as smuggling drugs into a country.

The implied warranties described above are subject to numerous exceptions and qualifications. Discussion of the various exceptions, however, is beyond the scope of this text.

**Covered Perils** An ocean marine policy provides broad coverage for certain specified perils, including **perils of the sea,** such as damage or loss from bad weather, high waves, collision, sinking, and stranding. Other covered perils include loss from fire, enemies, pirates, thieves, jettison (throwing goods overboard to save the ship), barratry (fraud by the master or crew at the expense of the ship or cargo owners), and similar perils.

Ocean marine insurance can also be written on an open-perils ("all-risks") basis. All unexpected and fortuitous losses are covered except those losses specifically excluded. Common exclusions are losses due to delay, war, inherent vice (tendency of certain types of property to decompose), and strikes, riots, or civil commotion.

**Particular Average** In marine insurance, the word *average* refers to a partial loss. *A particular average is a loss that falls entirely on a particular interest,* as contrasted with a general average loss that falls on all parties to the voyage. Under the *free-of-particular-average clause* (FPA), partial losses are not covered unless the loss is caused by certain perils, such as stranding, sinking, burning, or collision of the vessel.

The FPA clause can be written with a percentage, such as 3 percent. If the loss exceeds the stated percentage, the entire loss is payable. For example, if cargo is insured for $100,000, a partial loss under $3000 falls entirely on the insured; if the loss is $3000 or more, the insurer pays the loss in full.

**General Average** *A general average is a loss incurred for the common good and consequently is shared by all parties to the venture.* For example, if a ship damaged by heavy waves is in danger of sinking, part of the cargo may be jettisoned to save the ship. The loss falls on all parties to the voyage: the ship owner, cargo owners, and freight interests. In this context, *freight* refers to the revenue that a cargo ship earns. Each party must pay its share of the loss based on the proportion that its interest bears to the total value in the venture. For example, assume that the captain must jettison $1 million of steel to save the ship. Also assume that the various interests are as follows:

| Value of steel | $2 million |
| Value of other cargo | + 3 million |
| Value of ship and freight | + 15 million |
| Total | $20 million |

The owner of the steel would absorb 2/20 of the $1 million loss, or $100,000. The owners of the other cargo would pay 3/20 of the loss, or $150,000. Finally, the ship and freight interests would pay 15/20 of the loss, or $750,000.

Certain conditions must be satisfied to have a general average loss:[15]

- *Imminent peril.* There must be an imminent peril to all interests in the venture—ship, cargo, and freight.
- *Voluntary.* The sacrifice must be voluntary, and the special expense incurred must be reasonable.
- *Preservation of at least part of the value.* The effort must be successful. At least part of the value must be saved.
- *Free from fault.* Any party that claims a general average contribution from other interests in the voyage must be free from fault with respect to the risk that threatens the venture.

### Inland Marine Insurance

Inland marine insurance grew out of ocean marine insurance. Ocean marine insurance first covered property from the point of embarkation to the place where the goods landed. As commerce and trade developed, goods had to be shipped over land as well. Inland marine insurance developed in the 1920s to cover property being transported over land, means of transportation such as bridges and tunnels, and property of a mobile nature.

### Nationwide Marine Definition

As inland marine insurance developed, conflicts arose between fire insurers and marine insurers. To resolve the confusion and conflict, the companies drafted a **nationwide marine definition** in 1933 to define the property that marine insurers could write. The definition was approved by the National Association of Insurance Commissioners (NAIC) and was later revised and broadened in 1953. In 1976, the NAIC drafted a new definition of marine insurance that has been adopted by most states. At present, marine insurance can be written on the following types of property:

- Imports
- Exports
- Domestic shipments
- Instrumentalities of transportation and communication
- Personal property floater risks
- Commercial property floater risks

### Major Classes of Inland Marine Insurance

Commercial property that can be insured by inland marine contracts can be classified into the following categories:

- Domestic goods in transit
- Property held by bailees
- Mobile equipment and property
- Property of certain dealers
- Instrumentalities of transportation and communication

**Domestic Goods in Transit** Domestic goods may be shipped by a common carrier, such as a trucking company, railroad, or airline, or by the company's own trucks. The goods can be damaged because of fire, lightning, flood, earthquake, or other perils. They can also be damaged from the collision, derailment, or overturn of the transportation vehicle. These losses can be insured by one of the various inland marine policies.

Although a common carrier is legally liable for safe delivery of the goods, liability does not extend to all losses. For example, a common carrier is not responsible for losses due to acts of God (such as a tornado), acts of public authority, acts of public enemies (war), improper packaging by the shipper, and inherent vice.

In addition, shipping charges are reduced if the shipper agrees to limit the carrier's liability for the goods at less than their full value (called a *released bill of lading*). Consequently, the shipper can save money by agreeing to a released bill of lading and then purchase insurance to cover the shipment.

**Property Held by Bailees** Inland marine insurance can be used to insure property held by a bailee. A **bailee** *is someone who has temporary possession of property that belongs to another.* Examples of bailees are dry cleaners, laundries, and television repair shops. Under common law, bailees are legally liable for damage to customers' property only if they or their employees are negligent. However, to ensure customer goodwill, many bailees purchase bailees customers insurance that covers the damage or loss to customers' property while in the bailee's possession regardless of fault, normally from certain named perils.

**Mobile Equipment and Property** Inland marine property floaters can be used to cover property that is frequently moved from one location to another, such as a tractor, crane, or bulldozer. Also, plumbing, heating, or air conditioning equipment can be covered while being transported to a job site or while being installed.

In addition, a property floater policy can be used to insure certain other types of property, such as fine arts, livestock, theatrical property, computers, and signs.

**Property of Certain Dealers** Inland marine insurance is also used to insure the property of certain dealers. Specialized inland marine policies or inland marine "block" policies are used to insure the property of jewelers, furriers, and dealers in diamonds, fine art, cameras, and musical instruments, and other dealers. Most of these policies provide coverage on an open-perils ("all-risks") basis.

**Instrumentalities of Transportation and Communication** Instrumentalities of transportation and communication *refers to property at a fixed location that is used in transportation or communication.* Inland marine insurance can be used to cover bridges, tunnels, piers, docks, wharves, pipelines, power transmission lines, radio and television towers, cranes, and similar equipment for loading, unloading, or transporting. For example, a bridge may be damaged by a flood, an ice jam, or a ship that collides with the bridge; a television tower or a power line may be damaged in a windstorm; or a fire may start in a tunnel when a gasoline truck overturns and explodes. These losses can be insured under inland marine contracts.

## ISO Inland Marine Forms

A variety of ISO forms are used to insure commercial inland marine loss exposures. The major forms are summarized here:

- The **accounts receivable coverage form** indemnifies the firm if it is unable to collect outstanding customer balances because of damage or destruction of the records. A firm may incur a sizable loss if its accounts receivable records are lost because of a fire, theft, or other peril, and the amount owed by customers cannot be collected.
- The **camera and musical instrument dealers coverage form** is used to cover stock in trade consisting principally of cameras or musical instruments and related equipment and accessories. The property of others in the insured's care, custody, or control is also covered.
- The **commercial articles coverage form** covers photographic equipment and musical instruments that are used commercially by photographers, professional musicians, motion picture producers, production companies, and other persons.
- The **equipment dealers form** covers the stock in trade of dealers in agricultural implements and construction equipment. The form can also be extended to cover furniture, fixtures, office supplies, and machinery used in the business.
- The **film coverage form** covers exposed motion picture film as well as magnetic or video tapes.
- The **floor plan coverage form** refers to a financing plan in which the dealer borrows money to buy merchandise to display and sell, but the title is held by the lending institution or manufacturer. The form can be used to cover the interest of the dealer, the lending institution, or both. The property covered is the merchandise that is financed.
- The **jewelers block coverage form** covers jewelry, watches, and precious stones of retail and wholesale jewelers, jewelry manufacturers, and diamond wholesalers.
- The **mail coverage form** covers securities in transit by first-class mail, registered or certified mail, or express mail. It is designed for stock brokerage firms, banks, and other financial institutions that ship securities by mail.
- The **physicians and surgeons equipment coverage form** covers the medical, surgical, or dental

equipment of physicians and dentists, including furniture, fixtures, and improvements.

- The **signs coverage form** covers neon, mechanical, and electrical signs. Each covered sign must be scheduled.
- The **theatrical property coverage form** covers costumes, stage scenery, and similar property used in theatrical productions. For example, a Broadway show may be presented in another city, which requires the shipment of stage props and scenery to that city. The theatrical property can be covered under this form.
- The **valuable papers and records coverage form** covers loss to valuable papers and records, such as student transcripts at a university, plans and blueprints of an architectural firm, and prescription records in a drugstore. The form covers the cost of reconstructing the damaged or destroyed records. It can also be used to insure the loss of irreplaceable records, such as a rare manuscript.

### Other Inland Marine Forms

Other inland marine forms are also available to meet the specialized or unique needs of commercial firms. Only a few of them are discussed here.

**Shipment of Goods**    As noted earlier, inland marine insurance can be used to cover the domestic shipment of goods. An **annual transit policy** can be used by manufacturers, wholesalers, and retailers to cover the shipment of goods on public trucks, railroads, and coastal vessels. Both outgoing and incoming shipments can be insured. Although these forms are not standardized, they have similar characteristics. They can be written either on an open perils ("all risks") or named-perils basis.

Although a transit policy provides broad coverage, it contains certain exclusions. The policy can be written to cover the theft of an entire shipment, but pilferage of the goods generally is not covered. Other common exclusions are losses from strikes, riots or civil commotion, leakage and breakage (unless caused by an insured peril), marring, scratching, dampness, molding, and rotting.

A **trip transit policy** is used by firms and individuals to cover a single shipment. For example, an electrical transformer worth thousands of dollars that is shipped from an Eastern factory to the West Coast or the household goods of executives who are transferred can be insured under a variation of the trip transit policy.

**Bailee Forms**    As stated earlier, a bailee is someone who has temporary possession of property that belongs to others. A *bailees liability policy* can be used to cover the firm's liability for the property of customers, such as clothes at a laundry. A bailees liability policy, however, covers the loss only if the firm is legally liable. In contrast, a *bailees customers policy* can be used to cover the loss or damage to the property of others regardless of legal liability. A bailees customers policy generally is designed for firms that hold the property of others that have high value, such as fur coats. A covered loss is paid regardless of legal liability, and the goodwill of customers is maintained.

**Business Floaters**    A **business floater** is an inland marine policy that covers property that frequently moves (floats) from one location to another. Numerous business floaters are available. For example, a *contractors equipment floater* can be used to insure the property of contractors, such as bulldozers, tractors, cranes, earthmovers, and scaffolding equipment. A *garment contractors floater* covers garments and parts of garments that are sent by a garment manufacturer for processing to outside firms, such as buttonhole makers, pleaters, or embroiderers.

**Instrumentalities of Transportation and Communication**    Inland marine contracts can be used to cover bridges, tunnels, towers, pipelines, power lines, and similar property. For example, a toll bridge lost revenues because a ship ran into a bridge pylon, forcing the bridge to close. A business income policy can be written to cover this exposure.

This type of property can be insured either on an open perils ("all risks)" basis or on a named-perils basis, depending on the specific needs of the insured.

## BUSINESSOWNERS POLICY (BOP)

A **businessowners policy (BOP)** is a package policy specifically designed for small- to medium-sized retail stores, office buildings, apartment buildings, and similar firms. There are different BOP policies on the market today. In this section, we discuss the BOP designed by the Insurance Services Office (ISO). The ISO form provides both property and liability insurance in one policy. The following section discusses only the property insurance coverages; the liability insurance coverages are discussed in the following chapter.[16]

## Eligible Business Firms

A BOP can be written to cover buildings and/or business personal property of the owners of apartments and residential condominium associations; office and office condominium associations; retail establishments; and eligible mercantile, service, or processing firms such as appliance firms, beauty parlors, and photocopy services. BOP coverage is also available for certain contractors, "limited-cooking" restaurants, and convenience stores.[17]

Some business firms are ineligible for a BOP because the loss exposures are outside those contemplated for the average small- to medium-sized firm. They include auto repair or service stations; automobile dealers, motorcycles, or mobile homes; parking lots; certain bars; places of amusement such as a bowling alley; and banks and financial institutions.

## BOP Coverages

The current ISO version of the BOP is a *special form,* which insures property on an open-perils basis. The policy pays for direct physical loss or damage to covered property; losses are covered except those losses specifically excluded. However, if desired, named-perils coverage is available by an endorsement to the policy; only those perils named in the policy are covered.

The present BOP form is a self-contained policy that incorporates the property coverages, liability coverages, and policy conditions into one contract. The following discussion summarizes the basic characteristics of the property coverages in the ISO form.

1. *Buildings.* The BOP covers the buildings that are described in the declarations, including completed additions, fixtures and outdoor fixtures, and permanently installed machinery and equipment. The building coverage also includes personal property in apartments or rooms furnished by the named insured as a landlord, and personal property owned by the named insured to maintain or service the premises, such as fire-extinguishing equipment and refrigerating and dishwashing appliances. The limit of insurance on the building is automatically increased each year by a stated percentage shown in the declarations to keep pace with inflation.

2. *Business personal property.* Business personal property is also covered. It includes property owned by the named insured used in the business; property of others in the insured's care, custody, and control; tenant's improvements and betterments; and leased personal property for which the named insured has a contractual responsibility to insure. Business personal property also includes exterior building glass if the named insured is a tenant, and no limit of insurance is shown in the declarations. The glass must be owned by the named insured or in the insured's care, custody, and control. A peak season provision provides for a temporary increase of 25 percent of the amount of insurance when inventory values are at their peak.

In addition, business personal property at newly acquired locations is covered for a maximum of $100,000 for 30 days at each premises. This provision provides automatic protection until the BOP can be endorsed to cover the new location. Business personal property in transit or temporarily away from the insured location is covered up to a maximum of $10,000.

3. *Covered causes of loss.* The latest edition of the BOP insures property against direct physical loss, which means that direct physical losses are covered unless specifically excluded or limited in the form itself.

The BOP can also be issued on a named-perils basis by an endorsement. Covered causes of loss include fire, lightning, explosion, windstorm or hail, smoke, aircraft or vehicles, riot or civil commotion, vandalism, sprinkler leakage, sinkhole collapse, volcanic action, and certain transportation perils. The named-perils endorsement also includes an optional coverage for burglary and robbery.

4. *Additional coverages.* The BOP includes several additional coverages that might be needed by the typical businessowner:
   - Debris removal
   - Preservation of covered property after a loss occurs

- Fire department service charge
- Collapse
- Water damage, other liquids, powder, or molten material damage
- Business income, extended business income, and extra expense
- Pollutant clean-up and removal
- Loss of business income and extra expense because of action by a civil authority
- Money orders and counterfeit money ($1000 maximum)
- Forgery and alteration losses ($2500 maximum)
- Increased cost of construction because of an ordinance or law ($10,000 maximum for each described building insured on a replacement cost basis)
- Business income from dependent properties ($5000 maximum)
- Glass expenses incurred to put up temporary plates or board up openings if repair or replacement of damaged glass is delayed
- Fire extinguisher systems recharge expense ($5000 maximum for any one occurrence)
- Replacing or restoring electronic data destroyed or corrupted by a covered cause of loss ($10,000 maximum)
- Interruption of computer operations ($10,000 maximum)

- Limited coverage for "fungi," and wet or dry rot ($15,000 maximum)

5. *Optional coverages.* The BOP provides several optional coverages to meet the specialized needs of businessowners by payment of an additional premium:

- Outdoor signs
- Money and securities
- Employee dishonesty
- Equipment breakdown

6. *Deductible.* A standard deductible of $500 per occurrence applies to all property coverages. Optional deductibles of $250, $1000, and $2500 are also available. The deductible does not apply, however, to the fire department service charge, business income losses, extra expenses, action by a civil authority, and the recharge expense for a fire extinguisher system.

7. *Business liability insurance.* The businessowners policy also has business liability coverage similar to the commercial general liability policy (CGL). The businessowner is insured for bodily injury and property damage liability, and advertising and personal injury liability. Medical expense insurance is also provided. Commercial general liability insurance is discussed in Chapter 26.

## CASE APPLICATION

Kimberly owns and operates a tennis shop in a resort area. The business is seasonal. A large part of the annual revenues are due to sales in June, July, and August. Kimberly keeps the shop open during the remaining months of the year, but the inventory carried during those months is reduced. During the summer months, the amount of inventory on hand is substantially increased. Kimberly has the business insured under the special form businessowners policy (BOP) with no endorsements attached.

a. Assume you are a risk management consultant. Identify the major loss exposures that Kimberly faces.

b. Assume that a covered loss occurs in July, which damages part of the inventory. Does the BOP provide any protection for the increase in inventory during the summer months? Explain your answer.

c. Kimberly plans to hire an additional employee during the summer months when sales are increasing. She is concerned about possible employee theft and dishonesty. Explain to Kimberly how this loss exposure can be handled under the BOP.

d. A fire damaged the building. As a result, Kimberly incurred a business income loss because the business was closed for three months. Is this loss covered by the BOP? Explain your answer.

e. Vandals broke an exterior glass window of the business, which caused substantial damage to the building. Is this loss covered by the BOP? Explain your answer.

## SUMMARY

- A commercial package policy (CPP) contains a common declarations page, a common policy conditions page, and one or more coverage forms.

- When compared with individual policies, a package policy has fewer gaps in coverage; premiums are relatively lower because individual policies are not purchased; savings in insurer expenses can be passed on to the policyholder; and the insured has the convenience of a single policy.

- Each commercial package policy includes one or more coverage forms. They include the following:

  Building and personal property (BPP) coverage form

  Business income and extra expense coverage form

  Commercial crime coverage form

  Inland marine coverage form(s)

  Equipment breakdown protection coverage form

  Commercial general liability coverage form

  Business auto coverage form

- The *building and personal property coverage form* can be used to insure the commercial building, business personal property, and personal property of others in the care and custody of the insured.

- Under the ISO commercial property insurance program, a causes-of-loss form is part of the complete contract. Insureds can select one of the following forms:

  Causes-of-loss basic form

  Causes-of-loss broad form

  Causes-of-loss special form

- The *business income (and extra expense) coverage form* covers the loss of business income due to the suspension of business operations because of a covered loss. Business income is the net profit or loss before income taxes that would have been earned if the loss had not occurred, and continuing normal operating expenses, including payroll. Extra expenses incurred as a result of a loss are also covered.

- The *extra expense coverage form* covers only the extra expenses incurred by the firm in continuing operations during the period of restoration. Loss of profits is not covered.

- Certain miscellaneous commercial coverages are important to business firms that have unique or specialized needs, including builders risk insurance, condominium insurance, equipment breakdown protection insurance, and difference in conditions insurance.

- Ocean marine insurance can be classified into four categories that reflect the various insurable interests:

  Hull insurance

  Cargo insurance

  Protection and indemnity (P&I) insurance

  Freight insurance

- A particular average in ocean marine insurance is a loss that falls entirely on a particular interest, as contrasted with a general average loss that falls on all parties to the voyage.

- Inland marine contracts are used to insure the following classes of commercial property:

  Domestic goods in transit

  Property held by bailees

  Mobile equipment and property

  Property of certain dealers

  Instrumentalities of transportation and communication

- For purposes of regulation, inland marine contracts are classified into filed forms and nonfiled forms. Filed forms are policy forms and rates that are filed with the state insurance department. Nonfiled forms are not filed with the state insurance department.

- Inland marine coverage forms include the following:

  Accounts receivable coverage form

  Camera and musical instrument dealers coverage form

  Commercial articles coverage form

  Equipment dealers form

  Film coverage form

  Floor plan coverage form

  Jewelers block coverage form

  Mail coverage form

  Physicians and surgeons equipment coverage form

  Signs coverage form

  Theatrical property coverage form

  Valuable papers and records coverage form

- Inland marine forms also include the following:

  Annual transit policy

  Trip transit policy

Bailee forms

Business floaters

Instrumentalities of transportation and communication

- A *businessowners policy* is a package policy for small-to medium-sized business firms. It covers the building, business personal property, loss of business income, extra expenses, and business liability exposures. Optional coverages are available for outdoor signs, money and securities, employee dishonesty, and mechanical breakdown.

## KEY CONCEPTS AND TERMS

Accounts receivable coverage form (570)

Annual transit policy (571)

Bailee (570)

Builders risk coverage form (564)

Building and personal property (BPP) coverage form (557)

Business floater (571)

Business income (and extra expense) coverage form (561)

Business income (without extra expense) coverage form (561)

Business income insurance (561)

Businessowners policy (BOP) (571)

Camera and musical instrument dealers coverage form (570)

Cargo insurance (568)

Causes-of-loss forms (basic, broad, special) (559–560)

Collision liability clause (running down clause) (567)

Commercial articles coverage form (570)

Commercial package policy (CPP) (555)

Condominium association coverage form (564)

Condominium commercial unit-owners coverage form (564)

Difference in conditions (DIC) insurance (567)

Equipment breakdown insurance (565)

Equipment breakdown protection coverage form (565)

Equipment dealers form (570)

Extra expense coverage form (563)

Extra expenses (562)

Film coverage form (570)

Floor plan coverage form (570)

Freight insurance (568)

General average (568)

Hull insurance (567)

Implied warranties (568)

Inland marine insurance (567)

Instrumentalities of transportation and communication (570)

Jewelers block coverage form (570)

Mail coverage form (570)

Nationwide marine definition (569)

Ocean marine insurance (567)

Package policy (555)

Particular average (568)

Peak season endorsement (561)

Perils of the sea (568)

Physicians and surgeons equipment coverage form (570)

Protection and indemnity (P&I) insurance (568)

Reporting form (560)

Signs coverage form (571)

Theatrical property coverage form (571)

Trip transit policy (571)

Valuable papers and records coverage form (571)

## REVIEW QUESTIONS

1. a. What is a package policy?
   b. Explain the advantages of a commercial package policy to a business firm as compared to the purchase of separate policies.

2. Identify the causes of loss that are covered under the following forms:
   a. Causes-of-loss basic form
   b. Causes-of-loss broad form
   c. Causes-of-loss special form

3. Explain the following provisions in the *building and personal property coverage form*:
   a. Covered property
   b. Additional coverages
   c. Optional coverages

4. The *business income (and extra expense) coverage form* has a number of policy provisions. Explain the following provisions:
   a. Business income loss
   b. Coverage of extra expenses

5. Briefly describe the following commercial property insurance coverages:
   a. Builders risk insurance
   b. Condominium insurance
   c. Equipment breakdown insurance
   d. Difference in conditions (DIC) insurance

6. Explain the following ocean marine insurance coverages:
   a. Hull insurance
   b. Cargo insurance
   c. Protection and indemnity (P&I) insurance
   d. Freight insurance

7. a. What is the difference between a particular average loss and a general average loss in ocean marine insurance?
   b. What conditions must be fulfilled to have a general average loss?

8. Identify the major types of commercial property that can be insured under an inland marine insurance policy.

9. Briefly describe the following inland marine coverages:
   a. Accounts receivable coverage form
   b. Valuable papers and records coverage form
   c. Bailees customer policy

10. A *businessowners policy* (BOP) contains a number of coverages. Explain the following:
    a. Coverage of buildings
    b. Coverage of business personal property
    c. Covered causes of loss
    d. Additional coverages provided by the BOP

## APPLICATION QUESTIONS

1. Michael owns a television repair shop that is insured under a commercial package policy. The policy includes the *building and personal property coverage form* and the *causes-of-loss broad form*. The declarations page indicates that coverage applies to both the building and the named insured's business property. Explain whether or not the following losses would be covered under his policy.
   a. A fire occurs on the premises, and the building is badly damaged.
   b. A burglar steals some money and securities from an unlocked safe.
   c. A business computer is damaged by vandals who break into the shop after business hours.
   d. A tornado touches down near the store. Several television sets of customers in the shop for repair are damaged in the storm.

2. Never-Die Battery manufactures batteries for industrial and consumer use. The company purchased a commercial package policy (CPP) to cover its property exposures. In addition to common policy conditions and declarations, the policy contains a *building and personal property coverage form and an equipment breakdown protection coverage form*. The policy also contains the *causes-of-loss broad form*. With respect to each of the following losses, indicate whether or not the loss is covered.
   a. An explosion occurred that damaged the building where finished batteries are stored.
   b. Because of the explosion, the company incurred expenses for expedited shipping of replacement parts for machines used to manufacture the batteries.

   c. The explosion injured several employees who received emergency treatment at a local hospital.
   d. An automatic sprinkler system accidentally discharged in the finished goods building. Some recently manufactured batteries were ruined because of water damage and corrosion.

3. Ashley owns a retail shoe store that is insured for $120,000 under the *business income (and extra expense) coverage form*. Because of a fire, Ashley was forced to close the store for three months. Based on past and projected future earnings, Ashley expected the store to earn a net income of $30,000 during the three-month shutdown period if the loss had not occurred. During the shutdown period, there were no revenues, and Ashley had continuing expenses of $10,000. How much will Ashley recover for the business income loss? Explain your answer.

4. a. Janet is the risk manager of *Daily News*, a daily publication in a highly competitive market. She wants to be certain that the newspaper will continue to be published if the company's printing facilities are damaged or destroyed by a covered cause of loss. What type of insurance can Janet purchase to cover the added cost of continuing to print the paper after a physical damage loss has occurred?
   b. James opened a bookstore in a mall. His store was located between a theater and a department store. James counts on the theater and department store to generate walk-in business for his store. James knows that if either of the other businesses closes, his store would incur a substantial financial loss. What type of insurance can James purchase to cover this type of loss exposure?

5. The *Mary Queen,* an ocean-going oil tanker, negligently collided with a large freighter. The *Mary Queen* is insured by an ocean marine hull insurance policy with a running down clause. For each of the following losses, explain whether the ocean marine coverage would apply to the loss.
   a. Damage to the *Mary Queen*
   b. Damage to the freighter
   c. Death or injury to the crew members on the freighter

6. An Ocean Transfer cargo ship was forced to jettison some cargo during a severe storm. The various interests in the voyage at the time the property was jettisoned are the following:

| | |
|---|---|
| Value of the ship | $4.0 million |
| Value of iron ore | $2.0 million |
| Value of lumber and wood chips | $2.0 million |

The captain jettisoned iron ore valued at $800,000. What is the amount that Ocean Transfer must pay under a general average loss? Explain your answer.

7. The value of business personal property at Kim's business fluctuates periodically, which is due largely to fluctuations in the value of inventory on hand. Kim's property insurance policy requires the periodic reporting of business personal property. The limit of insurance is $500,000. Kim believes she can save money by underreporting the value of inventory. Last period, she reported only $200,000 when the actual value was $400,000. Shortly after filing the last report, the value of the inventory increased to $500,000. The inventory was totally destroyed when a fire occurred. Ignoring any deductible, what is the amount that Kim's insurer will pay? Explain your answer.

8. Richard owns and operates a small furniture store. In addition to Richard, the firm employs two sales representatives. Richard's insurance agent advises him that the store can be insured under a *businessowners policy* (BOP). Identify the various property loss exposures to Richard's furniture store that can be covered by a businessowners policy.

## INTERNET RESOURCES

- **A. M. Best Company** is an organization that rates insurers and publishes books and periodicals relating to the insurance industry, including property and liability insurance. Visit the site at

  aibest.com

- The **American Association of Insurance Services** is an insurance organization that develops policy forms, manual rates, and rating information used by more than 700 property and casualty insurers in the United States. Visit the site at

  aaisonline.com

- The **American Insurance Association** is a trade and service organization representing 300 property and casualty insurers that provides a forum for discussing problems as well as safety, promotional, and legislative issues. Visit the site at

  aiadc.org

- The **Independent Insurance Agents & Brokers of America** sponsors a site that provides a considerable amount of information on commercial property and liability insurance. The site is designed for agents, brokers, risk managers, and consumers. Visit the site at

  iiaba.net

- The **Insurance Information Institute** is a primary source of information, analysis, and referral on subjects dealing with property and liability insurance. Visit the site at

  iii.org

- The **Inland Marine Underwriters Association** provides a forum for discussing common problems encountered by inland marine insurers. Visit the site at

  http://www.imua.org/

- The **Insurance Services Office (ISO)** provides statistical information, actuarial analysis, policy language, and technical information to participants in property and liability insurance markets. ISO has drafted a considerable number of commercial property forms, as discussed in this chapter. Visit the site at

  iso.com

- The **Insurance Research Council** is a division of the American Institute for CPCU. It provides the public and the insurance industry with timely research information relating to property and liability insurance. Visit the site at

  http://www.insurance-research.org/

- The **Mutual Service Office (MSO)** is a rating bureau that assists small and mid-size insurers. MSO offers customized rating and statistical services, and develops policy forms. Visit their site at

  msonet.com/

- The **Property Casualty Insurers Association of America—PCI** is the nation's premier trade association of property and casualty insurers. PCI advocates the public policy position of its members on important issues and provides members with targeted industry information. Visit the site at

  pciaa.net

- The **Risk Management Society (RIMS)** is the premier organization of corporate risk managers that makes known to insurers the insurance needs of business and industry, supports loss prevention, and provides a forum for discussing common objectives and problems. RIMS also publishes *Risk Management* magazine. Visit the site at

  rims.org

## SELECTED REFERENCES

Cook, Mary Ann (editor), *Commercial Property Risk Management and Insurance,* 1st ed., Malvern, PA: American Institute for Chartered Property Casualty Underwriters, 2010.

*Fire, Casualty & Surety Bulletins,* Fire and Marine volume, Erlanger, KY: National Underwriter Company. The various commercial coverages are discussed in the Commercial Property section, Business Income section, Inland Marine section, and Boiler & Machinery section.

Flitner, Arthur L. and Arthur E. Brunck, *Ocean Marine Insurance,* 2nd ed., vols. 1 and 2. Malvern, PA: Insurance Institute of America, 1992.

Flitner, Arthur L. and Jerome Trupin, *Commercial Insurance,* 2nd ed., Third printing. Malvern, PA: American Institute for Chartered Property Casualty Underwriters/Insurance Institute of America, November 2008.

*The Institutes' Handbook of Insurance Policies,* 10th ed., Malvern, PA: American Institute for CPCU, 2011.

Trupin, Jerome, and Arthur L. Flitner, *Commercial Property Risk Management and Insurance,* 8th ed. Malvern, PA: American Institute for CPCU/Insurance Institute of America, 2008.

## NOTES

1. This chapter is based on *Fire, Casualty & Surety Bulletins,* Fire and Marine volume, Commercial Property section (Erlanger, KY: National Underwriter Company); Arthur L. Flitner and Jerome Trupin, *Commercial Insurance,* 2nd ed., Third printing (Malvern, PA: American Institute for Chartered Property Casualty Underwriters/Insurance Institute of America, November 2008); Jerome Trupin and Arthur L. Flitner, *Commercial Property Risk Management and Insurance,* 8th ed. (Malvern, PA: American Institute for Chartered Property Casualty Underwriters/ Insurance Institute of America, 2008); *Commercial Property Risk Management and Insurance,* 1st ed., edited by Mary Ann Cook (Malvern, PA: American Institute for Chartered Property Casualty Underwriters, 2010), *The Institute's Handbook of Insurance Policies,* 10th ed. (Malvern, PA: American Institute for Chartered Property Casualty Underwriters 2011), and The International Risk Management Institute's on-line library, IRMI.com. The authors also drew on the various copyrighted commercial property and liability forms of the Insurance Services Office (ISO).

2. At the time of this writing, ISO had filed some revisions to its commercial property forms, with a proposed effective date in 2013. Some of the proposed changes will be noted.

3. The proposed revisions for business personal property and personal property of others state that the coverage applies to such property located in or on a structure described in the declarations.

4. Stock is defined in the policy as raw materials, goods in process, finished goods, merchandise in storage or for sale, and packing/shipping supplies.

5. In the proposed revision, the special form will eliminate the words "risk of" and cover "direct physical loss unless it is excluded or limited."

6. Some other lines of insurance are also subject to a reporting form.

7. This section is based on *Fire, Casualty & Surety Bulletins,* Fire and Marine volume, Business Income section (Erlanger: KY: National Underwriter Company); Flitner and Trupin, *Commercial Insurance,* ch. 4, and Cook, *Commercial Property Risk Management and Insurance,* ch. 7.

8. Under the proposed revision, the period is changed from 30 to 60 days.

9. Under the proposed revision, the period following completion of repairs will be changed from 30 days or longer to 60 days or longer (up to two years).

10. Flitner and Trupin, *Commercial Insurance,* ch. 4, and Cook, *Commercial Property Risk Management and Insurance,* ch. 7.

11. DIC insurance is discussed in detail in Trupin and Flitner, *Commercial Property Risk Management and Insurance,* 8th ed., pp. 7.13–7.14 and in Cook, *Commercial Property Risk Management and Insurance,* ch. 6, pp. 6.21–6.26.

12. The extended coverage endorsement was popular when the fire insurance policy provided narrow coverage. The extended coverage perils are: wind, hail, explosion, riot, civil commotion, aircraft, vehicles, and smoke.

13. William H. Rodda et al., *Commercial Property Risk Management and Insurance,* 2nd ed., vol. 1, (Malvern: PA: American Institute for Property and Liability Underwriters, 1983), pp. 221–222.

14. Transportation insurance is discussed in detail in *Fire, Casualty & Surety Bulletins,* Fire and Marine volume, Inland Marine section; Trupin and Flitner, *Commercial Property Risk Management and Insurance,* ch. 10;

Philip Gordis, *Property and Casualty Insurance,* 33rd ed. (Indianapolis, IN: Rough Notes Co., 1995), chs. 16 and 20; Cook, *Commercial Property Risk Management and Insurance,* ch. 8, pp. 8.1-8.40; and the International Risk Management Institute's Web site, IRMI.com. The authors drew on these sources in preparing this section.

15. Gordis, pp. 336–337.

16. The businessowners policy is discussed in *Fire, Casualty & Surety Bulletins,* Fire and Marine volume, Commercial Property section; Flitner and Trupin, *Commercial Insurance,* ch. 11; and Cook, *Commercial Property Risk Management and Insurance,* ch. 11.

17. Changes in the BOP in 2010 extended eligibility to casual and upscale restaurants, convenience stores, and supermarkets with gasoline sales provided certain conditions are met. The square footage and annual gross sales limits were increased to 35,000 and $6 million, respectively.

# CHAPTER 26

# COMMERCIAL LIABILITY INSURANCE

*"The litigious nature of American society is a risk that can impact a company's bottom line. Liability insurance is a key tool for managing this risk."*

William B. Hedrick,
Managing Director, Marsh USA, Inc.

**After studying this chapter, you should be able to**

◆ Identify the major liability loss exposures of business firms.

◆ Describe the basic coverages provided by the commercial general liability (CGL) policy.

◆ Explain the coverage provided by a workers compensation and employers liability policy.

◆ Describe the important provisions of a commercial umbrella policy.

◆ Identify the liability coverages provided by a businessowners policy (BOP).

◆ Describe the basic characteristics of a professional liability policy for physicians.

◆ Explain the coverage provided by directors and officers (D&O) liability insurance.

*State health department officials shut down Harris Produce Company's processing plant after several cases of E. coli infection were traced to the facility. Robert Harris started the business 10 years ago as a seasonal produce stand. The business grew, and soon he was selling bags of processed lettuce to four area supermarkets, local franchises of two national fast-food chains, and two local restaurants. So far, there have been 15 confirmed cases and 10 suspected cases of E. coli infection traced to Harris Produce lettuce. An elderly woman died, an elderly man suffered permanent kidney damage, and six others remain hospitalized with E. coli infection symptoms. All of these people consumed lettuce processed by the company.*

*Harris Produce contacted the fast-food franchises and restaurants and told them to stop using the lettuce. Harris went to the supermarkets and helped remove the lettuce from the shelves. When asked to comment on the situation, he said, "We're looking to find the cause of the contamination and bracing ourselves for lawsuits."*

*In the above case, the produce company faced possible lawsuits because of the sale of contaminated lettuce. Like the produce company, many business firms today operate in competitive markets where lawsuits for bodily injury and property damage are routine. The lawsuits range from small nuisance claims to multimillion-dollar demands. Firms are sued for defective products, injuries and death to customers, damage to the property of others, pollution of the environment, sexual harassment, illegal discrimination against employees, financial loss by investors, and numerous other reasons. Commercial liability insurance can provide firms with the protection needed to deal with these loss exposures.*

*In this chapter, we discuss the major liability loss exposures of business firms and the commercial liability coverages available for insuring these exposures. Topics discussed include the commercial general liability (CGL) policy, employment practices liability insurance, workers compensation and employers liability, directors and officers liability insurance, and other commercial liability coverages.*

## GENERAL LIABILITY LOSS EXPOSURES

General liability refers to legal liability arising out of business operations other than auto or aviation accidents and employee injuries. A business firm typically purchases a commercial general liability (CGL) policy or a businessowners policy (BOP) to cover its general liability loss exposures. As noted in the previous chapter, general liability insurance is often purchased as part of a commercial package policy. Important general liability loss exposures include the following:

- Premises and operations liability
- Products liability
- Completed operations liability
- Contractual liability
- Contingent liability

### Premises and Operations Liability

Legal liability can arise out of the *ownership and maintenance of the premises* where the firm does business. Firms are legally required to maintain the premises in a safe condition and are responsible for the actions of their employees. Customers in a store legally may be considered to be *invitees,* and the highest degree of care is owed to them. The customers must be warned and protected against any dangerous condition on the premises. For example, a firm may be held liable if a customer slips on a wet floor and breaks a leg.

Legal liability can also arise out of the firm's operations, either on or off the premises. For example, employees unloading lumber in a lumberyard may accidentally damage a customer's truck, or a construction worker on a high-rise building may carelessly drop a tool that injures a pedestrian.

### Products Liability

**Products liability** *refers to the legal liability of manufacturers, wholesalers, and retailers to persons who are injured or incur property damage from defective products.* Firms can be successfully sued on the basis of negligence, breach of warranty, and strict liability. These topics were discussed earlier in Chapter 19, and additional treatment is not needed here.

### Completed Operations Liability

**Completed operations liability** *refers to liability arising out of faulty work performed away from the premises after the work or operation is completed.* Contractors, plumbers, electricians, repair shops, and similar firms can be held liable for bodily injuries and property damage to others after their work is completed. When the work is in progress, it is part of the operations exposure. However, after the work is completed, it is a completed operations exposure. For example, a new boiler may explode if it is improperly installed, or ductwork in a supermarket may collapse and injure a customer because of improper installation.

A general liability policy provides coverage for both products liability and completed operations. Both products liability and completed operations loss exposures are now included in a definition called **products-completed operations hazard.** *The policy covers liability losses that occur away from the premises and arise out of the insured's product or work after the insured has relinquished possession of the product or the work has been completed.* For example, assume that a gas furnace is improperly installed, and an explosion occurs one month later. The installer's liability is insured under the products-completed operations coverage.

### Contractual Liability

**Contractual liability** *means that the business firm agrees by a written or oral contract to assume the legal liability of another party.* For example, a manufacturing firm rents a building, and the lease specifies that the building

owner is to be held harmless for any liability arising out of use of the building. Thus, by a written lease, the manufacturing firm assumes some potential legal liability that ordinarily would be the owner's responsibility.

### Contingent Liability

**Contingent liability** *refers to liability arising out of work done by independent contractors.* As a general rule, business firms are not legally liable for work done by independent contractors. However, a firm can be held liable if (1) the activity is illegal, (2) the situation or type of work does not permit delegation of authority, or (3) the work done by the independent contractor is inherently dangerous.[1] For example, a general contractor may hire a subcontractor to perform a blasting operation. If someone is injured by the blast, the general contractor can be held liable even though the subcontractor is primarily responsible.

### Other Liability Loss Exposures

Because of various exclusions, CGL policies do not cover all liability loss exposures of business firms. Other important liability loss exposures include the following:

- Liability arising out of the ownership or use of autos, aircraft, or watercraft
- Occupational injury or disease of employees
- Suits by employees alleging sexual harassment, discrimination, failure to hire or promote, wrongful dismissal, and other employment-related practices
- Professional liability
- Directors and officers liability

Specialized coverages are avilable for insuring the above exposures. We discuss these coverages later in the chapter.

## COMMERCIAL GENERAL LIABILITY POLICY

The **commercial general liability (CGL) policy** is widely used by business firms to cover their general liability loss exposures. Two alternate coverage forms are available: an occurrence form and a claims-made form. The following section discusses both forms of the CGL policy drafted by the Insurance Services Office (ISO).[2]

## Overview of the CGL Occurrence Policy

The CGL occurrence policy can be written alone or as part of a commercial package policy (CPP) discussed in the previous chapter. The occurrence form has five major sections:

- Section I—Coverages
  Coverage A: Bodily injury and property damage liability
  Coverage B: Personal and advertising injury liability
  Coverage C: Medical payments
  Supplementary payments: Coverages A and B
- Section II—Who Is an Insured?
- Section III—Limits of Insurance
- Section IV—Commercial General Liability Conditions
- Section V—Definitions

## Section I—Coverages

Section I provides coverage for bodily injury and property damage liability, personal and advertising injury liability, medical payments, and certain supplementary payments.

**Coverage A: Bodily Injury and Property Damage Liability**   The insurer agrees to pay on behalf of the insured all sums up to the policy limits that the insured is legally obligated to pay as damages because of **bodily injury or property damage** to which the insurance applies. The bodily injury or property damage must be caused by an occurrence. *An occurrence is defined as an accident, including continuous or repeated exposure to substantially the same general harmful conditions.* For example, an explosion occurs in a store, and several customers are injured, or a meat company processes a batch of contaminated hamburger, and over a period of time several persons become ill. These incidents would be considered occurrences and would be covered by the CGL.

In addition, the current CGL policy contains a provision for a known loss. Under this provision, coverage does not apply when a loss is known or is apparent before the policy's inception date, such as a loss in progress. Bodily injury or property damage is covered only if (1) it is caused by an occurrence during the policy period, and (2) no insured or employee authorized to receive notice of an occurrence or claim knew prior to the policy inception date that the bodily injury or property damage had occurred in whole or in part. For example, if an insured knew that prior to the policy period, actions by the firm had caused bodily injury or property damage, any bodily injury or property damage claims arising out of this known occurrence would not be covered.

**Defense Costs**   The insurer also pays legal defense costs. The insurer has the right to investigate a claim or suit and settle it at its discretion. The insurer's duty to defend the insured ends when the applicable limits of insurance are paid out in a judgment or settlement. Legal defense costs are generally paid in addition to the policy limits. The insurer has a vested interest in making certain that the suit is defended properly, as it will pay damages if the insured is determined to be legally responsible.

**Exclusions**   A lengthy list of exclusions applies to both bodily injury and property damage liability. Major exclusions include the following:

- *Expected or intended injury.* Bodily injury or property damage that is expected or intended by the insured is not covered. For example, a suit arising out of an assault on an umpire with a softball bat by an employee on the company's softball team would not be covered. The intention is to injure the umpire. The exclusion does not apply to bodily injury that results from the use of reasonable force to protect persons or property.
- *Contractual liability.* The policy excludes liability assumed by a contract or agreement. However, the exclusion does not apply to liability that the insured would have in the absence of the contract or agreement. The exclusion also does not apply to liability assumed under an *insured contract.* An insured contract refers to a lease of the premises, a railroad sidetrack agreement, an easement or license agreement, an obligation to indemnify a municipality, an elevator maintenance agreement, or a tort liability assumption (liability imposed by law in the absence of any contract or agreement) for bodily injury and property damage.
- *Liquor liability.* The exclusion applies only to firms in the business of manufacturing, distributing, selling, serving, or furnishing alcohol. For example, if a bartender continues to serve a drunken customer who injures another person,

the bar owner is not covered for any claim or suit. However, the liquor exclusion does not apply to firms that are not in the liquor business. For example, an insured that serves alcohol at a company-sponsored party would be covered. Coverage can be obtained by firms in the liquor manufacturing and distribution business by adding the liquor liability coverage form to the policy or by purchasing a separate policy.

- *Workers compensation.* Any legal obligation of the insured to pay benefits under a workers compensation law or similar law is excluded.
- *Employers liability.* The policy excludes liability for bodily injury to an employee arising out of and in the course of employment. It also excludes a claim by a spouse or close relative who is seeking damages as a result of a job-related injury to an employee of the insured. For example, a suit by a spouse who seeks damages for the loss of consortium (loss of companionship, affection, and comfort) following a work-related injury is not covered.
- *Pollution exclusion.* Chemical, manufacturing, and other firms may pollute the environment with smoke, fumes, acids, toxic chemicals, waste materials, and other pollutants. Leaking underground storage tanks can also damage the environment. The CGL policy excludes bodily injury or property damage arising out of the discharge or seepage of pollutants. The exclusion also applies to cleanup costs incurred because of a government order. There are several exceptions to the pollution exclusion, which go beyond the scope of the text to discuss. Pollution coverage can be obtained by a pollution endorsement or by adding a separate pollution liability coverage form to the policy.
- *Aircraft, auto, and watercraft exclusion.* Liability arising out of the ownership or operation of aircraft, autos, and watercraft is specifically excluded. The intent here is to exclude legal liability that should be covered by other policies. The exclusion does not apply to watercraft while ashore on premises owned or rented by the insured and to nonowned watercraft less than 26 feet in length and not used to carry people or property for a fee. In addition, the exclusion does not apply to bodily injury to customers resulting from parking autos on the premises or next to the premises, which is important for firms that park the cars of customers. However, physical damage to the car

being parked is not covered because of the care, custody, or control exclusion (discussed later).

- *Mobile equipment.* Mobile equipment is not covered when the equipment is (a) being transported by an auto owned by the insured or (b) used in or in preparation for any racing, speed, or demolition contest. For example, a bulldozer is excluded while being transported to a job site on a trailer.
- *War.* Bodily injury or property damage due to war is specifically excluded. War is defined to include civil war, insurrection, rebellion, or revolution.
- *Damage to property.* The CGL policy excludes property owned, rented, or occupied by the insured, premises that the insured sells or abandons, property loaned to the named insured, and personal property in the insured's care, custody, or control. Other excluded losses are property damage to that particular part of real property on which the insured, contractors, or subcontractors are working, and part of any property that must be restored, repaired, or replaced because the insured's work is performed incorrectly.
- *Damage to the insured's product.* The policy excludes **damage to the insured's product** if the damage results from a defect in the product. For example, a defective hot water heater may explode. The damage to the tank itself is not covered. However, the insured's liability for the explosion damage to other property would be covered under the manufacturer's liability policy.
- *Damage to the insured's work.* The policy also excludes **damage to the insured's work** that is included in the "products-completed operations hazard." The insured's work refers to the work or operations of the insured as well as material, parts, and equipment used in the work. For example, an employee of a heating contractor may improperly install a gas furnace that explodes after it is installed. Although the property damage to the customer's building is covered, the value of the employee's work is specifically excluded. The exclusion does not apply if the work is performed by a subcontractor on behalf of the insured.
- *Damage to impaired property.* The policy also excludes **damage to impaired property.** If property is impaired because of a defect in the insured's product or work, or failure to perform, the loss is not covered. Impaired property is tangible property that cannot be used or is less useful

because (1) it incorporates the insured's product or work, or (2) the insured fails to perform the terms of a contract or agreement, and (3) the property can be restored to use by correction of the insured's product or work or fulfillment of the contract. For example, assume that the insured manufactures airplane parts, and a faulty part causes several jets to be grounded. The planes are considered impaired property. The loss of use of the jets is not covered by the insured's CGL policy.

- *Recall of products.* Expenses arising out of the recall of defective products are also excluded. In recent years, firms have incurred substantial expenses in recalling defective products such as autos, drugs, or food products. The CGL specifically excludes such expenses. Product recall expenses can be covered through an endorsement.
- *Personal and advertising injury.* Coverage A does not apply to bodily injury arising out of personal and advertising injury. For example, Coverage A would not apply to a customer who is falsely arrested for shoplifting and later submits a claim that he or she was physically injured in the same incident. (However, there would be coverage for the incident under Coverage B—Personal and Advertising Injury Liability.)
- *Electronic data.* The CGL excludes damages arising out of the loss, loss of use, damage, corruption, inability to access, or inability to manipulate electronic data. The CGL excludes liability for electronic data, which is not considered tangible property for purposes of property damage liability insurance.
- *Distribution of material in violation of statutes.* Federal and state laws have been enacted to reduce unwanted telephone calls and e-mail messages. This exclusion excludes bodily injury or property damage suits arising out of violation of the Telephone Consumer Protection Act, the CAN-SPAM Act of 2003, or any other statute or regulation that prohibits or limits the sending, transmitting, communicating, or distribution of material or information. For example, a company that violates federal law by calling customers on a do-not-call list would not be covered under its CGL policy for any suits arising out of such calls.

**Fire Legal Liability Coverage** The final provision under Coverage A is a statement that certain exclusions in the preceding list (technically exclusions c. through n.) do not apply to fire damage to premises rented to the named insured or temporarily occupied by the named insured with the permission of the owner. This exception to certain exclusions is also known as **fire legal liability coverage**. A separate limit of insurance applies to this coverage. For example, assume that the named insured rents a building, and an employee negligently starts a fire. We noted earlier that legal liability arising out of property rented to or occupied by the named insured would not be covered. However, the exclusion does not apply to the fire damage. Thus, if the named insured is sued by the landlord for the fire damage, he or she has coverage under the CGL policy.

**Coverage B: Personal and Advertising Injury Liability** Under this coverage, the insurer agrees to pay those sums that the insured is legally obligated to pay as damages because of **personal injury** and **advertising injury**. This term is defined in the policy and includes the following:

- False arrest, detention, or imprisonment
- Malicious prosecution
- Wrongful eviction or entry
- Oral or written publication that slanders or libels
- Oral or written publication that violates a person's right to privacy
- Use of another's advertising idea in your advertisement
- Infringing upon another's copyright, slogan, or trade dress (total image and appearance of a product, including graphics, size, and shape)

For example, if a customer is falsely arrested for stealing, coverage applies if the firm is sued. Likewise, if a marketing manager uses an ad based on advertising ideas owned by an outside ad agency, coverage applies if the firm is sued.

**Coverage C: Medical Payments** Medical payments cover the medical expenses of persons who are injured in an accident on the premises or on ways next to the premises, or as a result of the insured's operations. The medical expenses must be incurred within one year of the accident and are paid without regard to legal liability. For example, if a customer falls on a slippery floor in a supermarket, the medical expenses are covered up to the policy limits.

The insured does not have to be legally liable for medical payments coverage to apply. The insurance limit for this coverage is relatively low in comparison to the limits for Coverage A and Coverage B.

### Supplementary Payments: Coverages A and B

Certain supplementary payments are included under Coverages A and B in addition to the policy limits:

- All expenses incurred by the insurer (e.g., outside legal counsel)
- Up to $250 for the cost of a bail bond because of an accident or traffic violation arising out of the use of a vehicle to which the insurance applies
- Cost of bonds to release attachments
- Actual loss of earnings by the insured up to $250 a day because of time off from work and other reasonable expenses incurred to assist the insurer
- All costs levied against the insured in the suit such as court costs
- Prejudgment interest
- All interest that accrues after entry of the judgment (postjudgment interest)

### Section II—Who Is an Insured?

The CGL policy can be used to insure a variety of individuals and organizations. If designated in the declarations, insureds include the following:

- Owner and spouse if a sole proprietorship
- Partners, members, and their spouses if a partnership or joint venture
- Members and managers if a limited liability company

- Officers, directors, and stockholders if a corporation
- A trust and trustees, but only with respect to their duties as trustees

The following are also insured under the policy:

- Volunteer workers, but only while performing duties related to the named insured's business
- Employees acting within the scope of their employment
- Any person or organization acting as a real estate manager
- A legal representative if the named insured should die
- Any newly acquired or formed organization, other than a partnership, joint venture, or limited liability company

### Section III—Limits of Insurance

The limits of insurance state the maximum amount that the insurer will pay regardless of the number of insureds, claims made or suits brought, or persons or organization making such claims or bringing suits. Several limits apply (see Exhibit 26.1).

1. *General aggregate limit*. The **general aggregate limit** is the maximum amount that the insurer will pay during the policy term for the sum of the following: damages under Coverage A (except bodily injury and property damage included

**EXHIBIT 26.1**
**Illustration of the CGL Limits of Insurance**

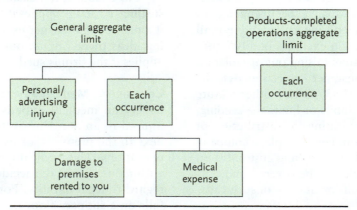

SOURCE: Adapted with permission from International Risk Management Institute, Inc. *Commercial Liability Insurance*, vol. 1, p. IV.E 14. Copyright 1994.

in the "products-completed operations hazard"), damages under Coverage B, and medical expenses under Coverage C.

2. *Products-completed operations aggregate limit.* The **product-completed operations aggregate limit** is the maximum amount that the insurer will pay during the policy term under Coverage A because of bodily injury and property damage included in the "products-completed operations hazard." There is no separate insuring agreement for products-completed operations. These claims are covered because they are not excluded. There is a separate limit of insurance that applies to products-completed operations claims.

3. *Personal and advertising injury limit.* This limit is the maximum amount that the insurer will pay under Coverage B to any one person or organization for personal injury and advertising injury.

4. *Each-occurrence limit.* This limit is the maximum amount that the insurer will pay for the sum of all damages under Coverage A and the medical expenses under Coverage C arising out of any one occurrence.

5. *Damage to rented premises.* This limit is the maximum amount that the insurer will pay for damages under Coverage A for property damage to rented premises from a single fire.

6. *Medical expense limit.* This limit is the maximum amount that the insurer will pay under medical expenses because of a bodily injury sustained by any one person.

## Section IV—Commercial General Liability Conditions

This section states the various conditions that apply to the commercial general liability coverage form. The conditions include provisions dealing with bankruptcy; duties in the event of an occurrence, claim, or suit; legal action against the insurer; other insurance; premium audit; and numerous additional conditions. However, space limitations preclude a discussion of these conditions here.

## Section V—Definitions

This section in the CGL policy defines more precisely the various terms used in the policy. Numerous definitions are stated in some detail. However, space limitations preclude a discussion of these definitions here.

## Overview of the CGL Claims-Made Policy

The Insurance Services Office (ISO) also offers a claims-made CGL policy, which is similar to the occurrence policy with the major exceptions of payment of claims on a claims-made basis, inclusion of an extended reporting period (Section V), and moving the definitions to Section VI.

**Meaning of "Claims-Made"** An **occurrence policy** is one that covers claims arising out of occurrences that take place during the policy period, regardless of when the claim is made. In contrast, *the* **claims-made** **policy** *covers only claims that are first reported during the policy period, provided the event occurred after the retroactive date (if any) stated in the policy.* The retroactive date is an extremely important concept that is discussed later.

To illustrate the difference between the two concepts, assume a building contractor purchased an occurrence policy three years ago, and the policy has been kept in force up to the present time. The contractor replaces the occurrence policy with a claims-made policy. If the contractor is sued because of a defect in a building constructed three years earlier, the occurrence policy would cover the claim. However, assuming no retroactive coverage, the claims-made policy would not cover the loss because it occurred prior to the inception date of the policy.

**Rationale for Claims-Made Policies** Insurers have developed claims-made policies as an alternative to occurrence policies because of the problem of **long-tail claims**. The long-tail refers to a relatively small number of claims that are reported years after the policy was first written. Under an occurrence policy, the insurer that provided coverage when the incident occurred was responsible for the claim. As a result, insurers had to pay claims on policies that expired years earlier. This problem made it difficult for actuaries to estimate accurately the correct premiums to charge and the correct loss reserve to establish for incurred but not yet reported (IBNR) claims. Under a claims-made policy, premiums, losses, and loss reserves can be estimated with greater accuracy.

**Retroactive Date** A claims-made policy can be written to cover events that occur prior to the inception date of the policy. Coverage will depend on the retroactive date, if any, inserted in the policy. To be covered, the occurrence must take place after the retroactive date, and the claim must be reported during the current policy term. If the occurrence takes place before the retroactive date, the claims-made policy will not respond.

For example, assume that the retroactive date is the issue date of the original claims-made policy. The issue date of the original claims-made policy is January 1, 2010. The most recent claims-made policy is issued on January 1, 2012. The insured would be covered under the current policy for all occurrences that take place after January 1, 2010 and are reported during the current policy period.

**Extended Reporting Periods** The claims-made policy also contains a provision that extends the period for reporting claims. *The purpose is to provide coverage under an expired claims-made policy for claims first reported after the policy expires.* The extended reporting period does not extend the period of protection. To be covered, the injury must occur after the retroactive date but before the end of the policy period. Injuries that occur before the retroactive date or after the policy expires are not covered.

The **basic extended reporting period** is automatically provided without an extra charge whenever one of the following occurs:

- The policy is canceled or not renewed.
- The insurer renews or replaces the policy with a retroactive date that is later than the retroactive date in the original policy.
- The claims-made policy is replaced with an occurrence policy.

The basic extended reporting period provides for two separate reporting periods or "tails." The first tail is a five-year period after the policy expires; the second tail is a 60-day period after the expiration date.

The five-year tail applies to claims arising out of an occurrence reported to the company during the policy period or no later than 60 days after the end of the policy period. (However, the occurrence must take place during the policy period or after the retroactive date.) For example, assume that a customer in a supermarket slips and falls on a wet floor during the policy period. The insured reports the occurrence promptly to the company, but no actual claim is made against the insured during the policy period. Any resulting claim arising out of that reported occurrence is covered by the expired policy if the claim is made before the end of the five-year period.

The second tail of 60 days applies to all other claims; these claims result from occurrences that take place during the policy period (or after the retroactive date), but are not reported to the insurer during the policy period. Coverage applies if the occurrence is reported to the insurer within 60 days after the policy expires. For example, referring back to our earlier example, the insured may have been unaware that the customer fell, so the incident was not reported to the company. However, if a claim is made against the insured after the policy expires, coverage applies if the occurrence is reported to the insurer within 60 days after the expiration date.

If the insured wants a longer reporting period after the policy expires, the supplemental extended reporting period can be added by an endorsement and payment of an additional premium. The insured must request the endorsement in writing within 60 days after the policy expires.

## EMPLOYMENT-RELATED PRACTICES LIABILITY INSURANCE

Employers may be sued by employees, former employees, and job applicants because of wrongful termination, discrimination, sexual harassment, failure to promote, failure to hire, and other employment-related practices. In recent years, the number of such suits has increased, but the median awards for damages have declined. The median award reached a high of $266,024 in 2008 but declined to $182,500 in 2010.[3] General liability insurance policies typically exclude or offer limited protection against liability arising out of the employment practices of employers. Many insurers now offer a separate policy or have specific endorsements to deal with these exposures.

ISO makes available an **employment-related practices liability coverage form**, which addresses employment practices loss exposures. The following discussion is based on the ISO form.

## Insuring Agreement

Under the ISO form, the insurer agrees to pay damages resulting from a "wrongful act" to which the insurance applies. A "wrongful act," as defined in the policy, is an offense to an employee arising out of one or more of the following:

- Wrongful demotion or failure to promote, negative evaluation, reassignment or discipline of an employee, or wrongful refusal to employ
- Wrongful termination of employment, wrongful denial of training or deprivation of career opportunity, breach of employment contract
- Negligent hiring or supervision
- Retaliatory action against employees
- Coercing an employee to commit an unlawful act or omission
- Work-related harassment
- Employment-related libel, slander, invasion of privacy, defamation, or humiliation
- Other work-related verbal, physical, mental, or emotional abuse, such as discrimination based on race, age, gender, or sexual orientation

## Legal Defense

The ISO form also provides for a legal defense; however, legal defense costs are included as part of the policy limit. Payment of legal defense costs reduces the amount of insurance available to pay damages.

Note that a claim cannot be settled without the insured's consent. This provision is designed to protect the employer's image and reputation. However, if the insurer works out a settlement with a claimant but the employer refuses to settle, any final settlement above the initial settlement is the employer's responsibility.

## Exclusions

The ISO form contains a number of exclusions. Some of these exclusions are as follows:

- Criminal, fraudulent, or malicious acts
- Contractual liability
- Workers compensation and similar laws
- Violation of laws applicable to employers, such as the Age Discrimination in Employment Act and the Family and Medical Leave Act of 1993
- Strikes and lockouts of employees

- Prior or pending litigation
- Prior notice

Because of the growing number of sexual harassment suits filed in recent years, interest in employment-related practices liability insurance is increasing. Most insurers will check an employer's policies on sexual harassment very carefully as part of the underwriting process.

## WORKERS COMPENSATION INSURANCE

Millions of workers are injured or become sick each year because of job-related accidents and diseases. All states have workers compensation laws that provide benefits to workers who have a job-related injury or occupational disease. Employers can meet their legal obligations to injured workers by purchasing a workers compensation insurance policy, through self-insurance, or by purchasing the coverage from a competitive or monopolistic state fund in some states.

As stated in Chapter 18, workers compensation insurance provides medical care, cash benefits, survivor benefits, and rehabilitation services to workers who are injured or die from job-related accidents or diseases. The benefits paid are based on the principle of **liability without fault**. *The employer is held absolutely liable for job-related accidents and diseases regardless of fault.* Workers receive benefits according to state law and are not required to sue their employers to receive benefits. The benefits are extremely important to workers who are injured or die as a result of job-related accidents or diseases. Insight 26.1 provides some basic facts about workers compensation laws.

This section discusses the current version of the **workers compensation and employers liability insurance policy** drafted by the National Council on Compensation Insurance.[4] The historical development of workers compensation as a form of social insurance was treated earlier in Chapter 18.

The workers compensation and employers liability policy provides the following coverages:

- Part One: Workers Compensation Insurance
- Part Two: Employers Liability Insurance
- Part Three: Other-States Insurance

## INSIGHT 26.1

### Basic Facts about Workers Compensation

Workers compensation benefits are payable to workers injured on the job and survivors of workers injured on the job. Workers compensation is the "exclusive remedy" for providing compensation for such injuries or fatalities. To qualify for workers compensation benefits, the injury or fatality must arise out of and in the course of employment. Background and facts about workers compensation:

- It is the nation's oldest social insurance program.
- It is a state-based program that protects injured workers and their survivors against the financial consequences of work-related accidents, disease, and deaths.
- The percentage of the workforce eligible to receive workers compensation benefits is estimated at 97 percent.
- Workers compensation does not exclude any type of treatment or service. The only coverage criteria are that the injury, illness, or death is work-related, and that the treatment or service provided is reasonable and necessary.
- Generally, employers are mandated by law to provide workers compensation coverage for their employees.
- Workers compensation is financed by employers, either through self-insurance or, more commonly, by securing insurance with an insurer licensed to write workers compensation insurance.

Although state workers compensation programs and laws differ, common features include:

- All state workers compensation laws require payment of all reasonable and necessary medical treatment, at no cost to the worker, with no co-payments or deductibles for as long as necessary to rehabilitate the injured worker, even for life.
- All workers compensation laws also provide tax-free benefits for lost wages, typically at two-thirds of a worker's wage.
- The duration, and sometimes the level, of wage loss benefits depends on whether there is any permanent injury and, if so, the extent of permanency.
- All workers compensation laws also provide benefits for the survivors and dependents of workers whose deaths were work-related; these benefits continue for the life of the surviving spouse or until remarriage.
- Dependency benefits are usually provided until at least age 18 but sometimes longer, as in the case of a dependent who's attending college or another educational institution.

Source: Excerpted with permission from American Insurance Association, "Protecting Workers Compensation from Terrorism," *AIA Advocate*, February 10, 2003.

---

The other three parts of the policy are: Duties if an Injury Occurs, Premiums, and Conditions.

### Part One: Workers Compensation Insurance

Part One is **workers compensation insurance**. Under this section, the insurer agrees to pay all workers compensation benefits and other benefits that the employer must legally provide to covered employees who have a job-related injury or an occupational disease. There are no policy limits for Part One. The insurer instead pays all benefits required by the workers compensation law of any state listed in the declarations.

Under certain conditions, the employer is responsible for payments made by the insurer that exceed regular workers compensation benefits. These situations generally involve fines or penalties associated with intentional misconduct by the employer. The employer must reimburse the insurer for any

payments that exceed regular workers compensation benefits because of the following:

- Serious and willful misconduct by the employer
- Knowingly employing workers in violation of law
- Failure to comply with a health or safety regulation
- Discharge, coercion, or discrimination against any employee in violation of the workers compensation law

### Part Two: Employers Liability Insurance

Part Two provides **employers liability insurance**, which covers employers against lawsuits by employees who are injured in the course of employment, but whose injuries (or diseases) are not compensable under the state's workers compensation law. This part is similar to other liability insurance policies where negligence must be established before the insurer is legally obligated to pay.

Employers liability insurance is needed for several reasons. First, a few states do not require workers compensation insurance for smaller employers with fewer than a certain number of employees, such as three or fewer. In such cases, an employer can be covered under the employers liability section if an employee with a work-related injury or disease sues for damages.

Second, an injury or disease that occurs on the job or at the workplace may not be considered work-related, and, therefore, would not be covered under the state's workers compensation law. However, the injured employee may still believe that the employer should be held accountable, and the employer would be covered if sued.

Third, some state workers compensation laws permit lawsuits by spouses and dependents for the *loss of consortium*. The employer would be covered under Part Two in such a case.

Finally, some employers are confronted with lawsuits because of *third-party-over cases*. An injured employee may sue a negligent third party, and the third party, in turn, sues the employer for contributory negligence. The lawsuit would be covered under Part Two (unless the employer assumed the liability of the third party, in which case it may be covered by the employer's CGL policy). For example, assume that a machine is defective, and its operator is injured. In addition to the payment of workers compensation benefits, the state may allow the injured employee to sue the negligent third party. If the injured employee sues the manufacturer of the defective machine, the manufacturer, in turn, could sue the employer for failure to provide proper operating instructions or failure to enforce safety rules. The employer would be covered in such cases.

The employers liability section of the ISO policy also contains several exclusions. Major exclusions include the following:

- Liability assumed under contract
- Punitive damages because of a bodily injury to an employee who is hired in violation of the law
- Bodily injury to an employee employed in violation of the law with the knowledge of the insured or executive officers of the insured

- Obligations imposed on the employer because of a workers compensation, occupational disease, unemployment compensation, or disability benefits law
- Intentional bodily injury caused by the employer
- Bodily injury outside the United States and its territories or Canada
- Damages resulting from coercion, demotion, evaluation, reassignment, harassment, discrimination, or termination of any employee
- Bodily injury to any person subject to the Longshore and Harbor Workers Compensation Act and similar federal workers compensation laws
- Bodily injury to any person subject to the Federal Employers Liability Act
- Bodily injury to a master or crew member of any vessel
- Fines or penalties because of violation of federal or state law
- Damages payable under the Migrant and Seasonal Agricultural Worker Protection Act

### Part Three: Other-States Insurance

Part Three of the workers compensation and employers liability policy provides **other-states insurance**. Workers compensation coverage (Part One) applies only to those states listed on the information page (declarations page) of the policy. However, the employer may face a workers compensation claim under the law of another state. This possibility could arise if an employee is injured while on a business trip in a state that was not considered when the workers compensation policy was first written, or if the law of a particular state is broadened so that employees are now covered under that state's workers compensation law.

Other-states insurance applies only if one or more states are shown on the information page of the policy. The information page is the equivalent of a declarations page. *In such cases, if the employer begins work in any of the states listed, the policy applies as if that state were listed in the policy for workers compensation purposes.* Thus, the employer has coverage for any workers compensation benefits that it may have to make under that state's workers compensation law. As workers compensation is a state-based program, benefits vary from state to state.

# COMMERCIAL AUTO INSURANCE

Legal liability arising out of the ownership and use of cars, trucks, and trailers is another important loss exposure for many businesses. This section examines several commercial auto coverages that can be used to meet this exposure.[5]

## Business Auto Coverage Form

The ISO **business auto coverage form** is widely used by business firms to insure their commercial auto exposures. Firms have considerable flexibility with respect to the autos that can be covered. There are 10 numerical classifications, each of which is referred to by a symbol:

1. Any auto
2. Owned autos only
3. Owned private passenger autos only
4. Owned autos other than private passenger autos only
5. Owned autos subject to no-fault plans
6. Owned autos subject to a compulsory uninsured motorists law
7. Specifically described autos
8. Hired autos only
9. Nonowned autos only
10. (This tenth classification is referred to as "Symbol 19".) Mobile equipment subject to compulsory or financial responsibility or other motor vehicle insurance law only

If one or more of the symbols 1 through 6 or 19 are selected, there is automatic coverage on newly acquired autos of the same type that the named insured acquires during the policy period. If symbol 7 is used, newly-acquired autos are covered only if two conditions are met: (1) the insurer must already cover all autos that the named insured owns for the coverage provided, or the new auto must replace an auto that the named insured previously owned that had such coverage, and (2) the named insured informs the insurer within 30 days after acquisition that he or she wants the auto insured for that coverage.

**Liability Insurance Coverage**   An insured is covered for a bodily injury or property damage claim to which the insurance applies, which is caused by an accident that results from the ownership, maintenance, or use of a covered auto. For example, if an employee drives a company car during the course of employment and injures another motorist, the employer has coverage for any resulting lawsuit. The employee has coverage as well.

The insuring agreement also provides limited coverage for pollution losses. The business auto coverage form has a broad pollution exclusion that excludes liability coverage for almost all pollution losses. However, there are limited exceptions. The insurer will pay all "covered pollution cost or expense" to which the insurance applies. To be covered, the pollution cost or expense must be caused by an accident that results from the ownership, maintenance, or use of a covered auto. However, the pollution cost or expense is covered only if there is either bodily injury or property damage to which the insurance applies, which is caused by the same accident. For example, a company employee driving a company car may negligently smash into an oil truck on a crowded expressway, which causes the truck to overturn, and the oil to spill. The cleanup cost that the insured might have to pay is covered. Covered pollution cost or expense is counted against the limit of liability.

Finally, the insurer agrees to defend any insured and pay all legal defense costs. Defense costs are in addition to the policy limit. The duty to defend or settle ends when the limit of insurance is exhausted by the payment of judgments or settlements.

**Physical Damage Coverage**   Three physical damage coverages are available to insure covered autos against damage or loss, summarized as follows:

- *Comprehensive coverage.* The insurer will pay for loss to a covered auto or its equipment from any cause except the covered auto's collision with another object or its overturn.
- *Specified causes-of-loss coverage.* As an alternative to comprehensive coverage, only losses from certain specified perils are covered: fire, lightning, or explosion; theft; windstorm, hail, or earthquake; flood; mischief or vandalism; or the sinking, burning, collision, or derailment of any conveyance transporting the covered auto.
- *Collision coverage.* Loss caused by the covered auto's collision with another object or its overturn is covered under this provision.

Coverage for towing and labor costs can be added if desired. The insurer will pay towing and labor costs up to the limit shown in the declarations each time a covered auto of the private passenger type is disabled. However, the labor must be performed at the place of disablement.

In addition, if a damaged covered auto has comprehensive coverage, the coverage applies to glass breakage, to loss caused by hitting a bird or animal, and to loss caused by falling objects or missiles. If glass breakage results from a collision, the insured can elect to have it covered as a collision loss. Without this option, the insured would have to meet two deductibles if both glass breakage and body damage result from the same collision. By treating glass breakage as part of the collision loss, only the collision deductible must be satisfied.

The insurer will also pay up to $20 per day (after 48 hours) up to a maximum of $600 for transportation expenses incurred by the insured because of the theft of a covered private passenger auto. The coverage applies only to covered autos that are insured for either comprehensive or specified causes-of-loss coverage.

## Garage Coverage Form

The **garage coverage form** is a specialized form for auto dealers. Auto dealers include both franchised auto dealers (such as a new car dealer) and nonfranchised dealers (such as a used car dealer). The major coverages include liability coverage, garagekeepers coverage, and physical damage coverage.

**Liability Coverage**   The insurer agrees to pay all sums that an insured must legally pay as damages because of bodily injury or property damage to which the insurance applies caused by an accident in the course of garage operations. *Garage operations* are defined to include garage business locations, autos covered under the form, and all operations necessary or incidental to a garage business. As such, the liability section includes coverage for premises and operations liability, auto liability, incidental contractual liability, and products and completed operations.

The insured has a choice of autos that can be covered, and numerical symbols are used to denote the covered autos, an approach similar to the business auto policy.

The liability section of the garage policy contains numerous exclusions. Because of space constraints, only two of them are discussed here. *First, damage to the property of others in the insured's care, custody, or control is excluded.* Thus, damage to a customer's car on an automobile servicing hoist, or damage to a customer's car while it is being road tested by a mechanic, would not be covered. These common exposures can be covered by adding garagekeepers coverage to the policy.

*Second, there is no coverage for property damage to any of the insured's products if the product is defective at the time it is sold.* For example, assume that a dealer sells a tire that has a hidden defect. The defective tire later blows out, and the car is damaged in a collision. This exclusion eliminates coverage for the defective tire, but the property damage caused by the defective tire would be covered. The intent of this exclusion is to cover property damage or bodily injury caused by a defective product but not any damage to the product itself.

**Garagekeepers Coverage**   As noted earlier, the garage coverage form excludes coverage for property of others in the care, custody, or control of the insured. Adding garagekeepers coverage to the policy provides this coverage. The insurer agrees to pay all sums the insured must legally pay as damages for loss to a customer's car left in the insured's care while the insured is attending, servicing, repairing, parking, or storing the vehicle in its garage operations.

Three coverages are available: (1) comprehensive coverage, (2) specified causes of loss coverage, and (3) collision coverage. These coverages apply only if the insured is legally liable for the loss. For example, if a customer's car were stolen because the dealer carelessly left the garage door unlocked, the loss would be covered. In contrast, if a customer's car were damaged by a tornado, the loss would not be covered because the insured could not be held liable for a tornado. It is possible, however, to broaden the coverage by adding direct physical damage coverage on customers' cars by payment of an additional premium. This approach is called direct coverage, which indemnifies customers for their losses even though the garage has no legal liability to do so. The insured checks a box on the declarations page to activate the option.

**Physical Damage Coverage**  Physical damage insurance on covered autos can also be included in the garage policy. The following three coverages are available to cover the autos the dealer owns:

- *Comprehensive coverage.* The insurer will pay for a loss from any cause except for the covered auto's collision with another object or its overturn.
- *Specified causes of loss coverage.* Covered perils are fire, lightning or explosion, theft, windstorm, hail, earthquake, flood, mischief or vandalism, and the sinking, burning, collision, or derailment of any conveyance transporting the covered auto.
- *Collision coverage.* Loss caused by the covered auto's collision with another object or its overturn is covered under this provision.

## AIRCRAFT INSURANCE

Major commercial airlines own fleets of expensive jets, and the liability exposure is enormous. Occasionally, a commercial jet will crash accidentally because of mechanical or human error, killing hundreds of passengers and causing extensive property damage to surrounding buildings. Legal liability losses arising out of the crash of a fully loaded jet airliner can be catastrophic. In addition, many firms own aircraft used for company business. Company planes sometimes crash, resulting in death or bodily injury to the passengers, as well as death or injury to people on the ground and substantial property damage to surrounding buildings where the crash occurs. Finally, thousands of Americans own or operate small planes, which may crash because of mechanical problems, adverse weather conditions, pilot error, or inexperience of the pilot.

Most states apply the common-law rules of negligence to aviation accidents. However, some states have absolute or strict liability laws that hold the owners or operators of aircraft absolutely liable for aviation accidents. As a result of international treaties and agreements among countries, absolute liability is also imposed on commercial airlines for aviation accidents that occur during international flights.

### Aircraft Insurers

**Aircraft insurance** is a package policy that can provide property, liability, and medical payments coverage. It is highly specialized line that is underwritten by a relatively small number of insurer organizations.[6] Most of the aviation insurance in the United States on commercial planes, aircraft manufacturers, and large domestic airports is underwritten by two multicompany aviation pools—United States Aircraft Insurance Group (USAIG) and Global Aerospace (formerly Associated Aviation Underwriters). Chartis (AIG), XL, and C.V. Starr are other underwriters in this market. Outside of the United States, another pool—La Reunion Aerienne based in Paris—provides aviation insurance to its members. There is also a national market pool in Japan that basically operates as a reinsurance facility for its members. The pools underwrite and manage aviation insurance loss exposures on behalf of individual insurers that belong to the pools. However, some large insurers or groups with sufficient capacity and underwriting experience underwrite aviation insurance coverages individually rather than through a pool.

The liability coverages on commercial jets are substantial. Major airlines that operate wide-bodied aircraft, such as a Boeing 747 or Boeing 777, generally buy a minimum of $2 billion of liability coverage on their jets. Narrow bodied carriers (e.g., "low-cost" carriers) typically purchase between $750 million and $1 billion of liability insurance on their aircraft.[7]

Major airlines also carry substantial amounts of hull insurance on their planes. **Hull insurance** is similar to collision insurance on cars; the insurance covers physical damage losses to covered aircraft. The amount of hull insurance varies depending on the type and age of the aircraft, but the highest insurance amounts currently carried on a commercial jet generally are around $275 million, with a high of $300 million. An operator of narrow-bodied aircraft, such as a Boeing 737, may carry a maximum insurance amount of $75 million on the jet.[8]

### Aircraft Insurance for Private Business and Pleasure Aircraft

Aircraft insurers offer policies designed for the owners and operators of private business and pleasure aircraft. These policies provide liability coverage for property damage and bodily injury arising out of the ownership or use of insured aircraft, medical expense coverage, and physical damage coverage for damage to the aircraft.[9]

**Physical Damage Coverages** A plane on the ground can be damaged by wind, fire, collapse, theft, vandalism, or other perils. While taxiing, the plane can collide with vehicles, buildings, or other aircraft. The most severe exposure is present when the plane is in flight. A plane can collide with another plane, it can be struck by lightning or damaged by turbulent winds, or it can experience mechanical difficulties from a fire or explosion. Planes can also be damaged or destroyed by acts of terrorism.

Physical damage insurance provides coverage for direct damage to the aircraft. The insured has a choice of physical damage coverages. There are three insuring agreements for physical damage to the aircraft:

- *"All-risks" basis, ground and flight.* All physical damage losses to the aircraft, including disappearance, are covered except those losses excluded.
- *"All-risks" basis, not in flight.* The aircraft is covered on an "all-risks" basis only when it is on the ground and not in flight. Fire or explosion following a crash is not covered.
- *"All-risks" basis, not in motion.* The aircraft is covered on an "all-risks" basis only when it is standing still. Fire or explosion after a crash is not covered.

Although aircraft can be covered on an "all-risks" basis, certain exclusions apply. Excluded losses include damage to tires (unless caused by fire, theft, or vandalism), wear and tear, deterioration, mechanical or electrical breakdown, and failure of installed equipment. However, these exclusions do not apply if such physical damage is coincident with and results from the same cause as other loss covered by the policy.

**Liability Coverages** Several liability coverages are available: (1) bodily injury liability excluding passengers, (2) passenger bodily injury liability, and (3) property damage liability. Separate limits of insurance typically apply to each coverage. However, liability insurance for all three coverages can be written as a single limit if desired.

Liability coverages have several important exclusions. The policy does not apply to bodily injury or property damage arising out of the following:

- Liability assumed in a contract

- Workers compensation, unemployment compensation, disability benefits, or similar law
- Bodily injury to any employee arising out of and in the course of employment by the insured
- Damage to property in the insured's care, custody, and control (except personal effects of passengers up to a stated limit)
- War, hijacking, and other perils
- Noise, such as a sonic boom or interference with the quiet enjoyment of property caused by an aircraft or any of its parts
- Discharge, seepage, or escape of pollutants, except from a crash, fire, or in-flight emergency
- Intentional injury, except to prevent a hijacking or other interference with the operation of the plane

**Medical Expense Coverage** This coverage pays all reasonable medical expenses incurred within one year from the date of injury for each passenger while the aircraft is being used by or with the permission of the named insured. Crew members are excluded unless listed in the declarations. The exclusion also applies to claims under a workers compensation or similar law.

## COMMERCIAL UMBRELLA POLICY

Because firms can be sued for large amounts, they may seek protection against catastrophic loss exposures not adequately insured under general liability policies. A **commercial umbrella policy** can provide protection against catastrophic liability judgments that might otherwise bankrupt a firm.

Most insurers that write commercial umbrella policies use their own forms. However, the Insurance Services Office (ISO) has designed a standard umbrella policy for commercial firms. The following discussion summarizes the major provisions in the ISO **commercial liability umbrella coverage form.**[10]

### Coverages

The ISO commercial umbrella policy pays the ultimate net loss in excess of the retained limit for bodily injury, property damage, and personal and advertising injury to which the insurance applies. *The* **ultimate net loss** *is the total sum the insured is legally obligated to pay as damages. The* **retained limit** *refers* to (1) the available limits of underlying insurance listed in the declarations, or (2) the self-insured retention, whichever applies.

If the loss is covered by both an underlying insurance contract and the umbrella policy, the umbrella policy pays only after the underlying limits are exhausted. For example, assume that an umbrella policy has a limit of $5 million. Assume also that the underlying limit under a commercial general liability (CGL) policy is $1 million for each occurrence, and a judgment against the insured amounts to $3 million. The underlying insurance (CGL policy) would pay $1 million, and the umbrella policy would pay the remaining $2 million.

If the loss is not covered by any underlying insurance but is covered by the umbrella policy, the insured must satisfy a **self-insured retention (SIR)**. The SIR can range from $500 for small firms to $1 million or more for large corporations. For example, assume that a firm's SIR amount is $25,000. A customer in the firm's store who is falsely accused and arrested for shoplifting wins a judgment against the insured in the amount of $100,000. If the loss is not covered by an underlying policy, the insured would pay $25,000. The umbrella policy would pay the remaining $75,000.

Legal defense costs are also paid when the underlying insurance does not provide coverage or the underlying limits are exhausted.

## Required Underlying Coverages

Insureds are required to carry certain minimum amounts of liability insurance before the umbrella insurer will pay any claims. The following underlying coverages and limits are typically required:

*Commercial general liability insurance*

$1,000,000 (each occurrence)
$2,000,000 (general aggregate)
$2,000,000 (products and completed-
             operations aggregate)

*Business auto liability insurance*

$1,000,000 (combined single limit)

*Employers liability insurance*

$500,000 (bodily injury per accident)
$500,000 (bodily injury by disease per employee)
$500,000 (disease aggregate)

## Exclusions

The ISO commercial umbrella form contains a lengthy list of exclusions. Under bodily injury and property damage liability, losses arising out of the following are excluded:

- Expected or intended injury
- Contractual liability (with certain exceptions)
- Liquor liability
- Any obligation of the insured under a workers compensation or similar law
- Any obligation of the insured under the Employees Retirement Income Security Act (ERISA)
- Any auto that is not a covered auto
- Bodily injury to an employee in the course of employment
- Liability arising out of employment-related practices
- Pollution
- Liability arising out of aircraft or watercraft unless provided by underlying insurance
- Racing activities
- War
- Property in the insured's care, custody, or control
- Damage to your product or work
- Damage to impaired property or property not physically impaired
- Recall of products, work, or impaired property
- Bodily injury arising out of personal and advertising injury
- Liability arising out of professional services
- Electronic data
- Distribution of material in violation of statutes

A lengthy set of exclusions also applies to personal and advertising injury liability. Under personal and advertising injury, claims arising out of the following are not covered:

- Knowingly violating the rights of another
- Oral or written publication of material that the insured knows to be false
- Oral or written publication of material prior to the policy period
- Criminal acts of the insured
- Contractual liability
- Breach of contract except an implied contract to use someone else's idea in your ad
- Failure of the product to perform as stated in the ad

- Wrong description of the price of products
- Infringement of copyright or patent
- An insured whose business is advertising, broadcasting, publishing, or telecasting; Web site design; and internet search, content, or provider service
- Electronic chatrooms or bulletin boards
- Unauthorized use of another's name or product
- Pollution
- Employment-related practices, such as failure to hire, harassment, and humiliation
- Professional services
- War
- Distribution of material in violation of statutes

## BUSINESSOWNERS POLICY

The **businessowners policy (BOP)** provides property and liability insurance for small businesses. The property coverages of the ISO businessowners policy were discussed in Chapter 25. The liability coverage is written on an occurrence basis, and, with certain exceptions, it is similar to the commercial general liability coverage (CGL) form discussed earlier.[11] The following discussion is based on the ISO form.

### Business Liability

Business liability coverage pays those sums the insured becomes legally obligated to pay as damages because of bodily injury, property damage (including fire damage to rented premises), or personal and advertising injury. For example, if an escalator in a clothing store is defective and a customer is injured, the loss would be covered. Likewise, if a customer in the clothing store is erroneously arrested for shoplifting, any suit for false arrest would be covered.

### Medical Expenses

Coverage for medical expenses is also provided. The insured does not have to be legally liable, and medical expenses are paid up to the policy limit regardless of fault. The medical expenses must result from a bodily injury caused by an accident on the premises owned or occupied by the named insured, or on ways next to the premises, or from business operations. Medical bills must be incurred and reported to the insurer within one year from the date of the accident. For example, if a customer slips on a wet floor in a supermarket and is injured, the medical expenses are paid without regard to legal liability up to the medical expense limit.

### Legal Defense

The insurer pays the legal costs of defending the insured. The legal costs are paid in addition to the amount that the insurer is legally obligated to pay as damages on the insured's behalf. The duty to defend applies only to claims covered under the policy and ends when the applicable limit of insurance is paid out as judgments, settlements, or medical expenses.

The definition of an insured also includes employees while they are acting in the scope of their employment. This provision protects a negligent employee who might be named in the lawsuit along with the employer.

### Exclusions

In general, the BOP business liability coverage exclusions are similar to those in the CGL policy. One important difference, however, deals with professional liability. Although the BOP excludes liability arising from professional services, a pharmacist's professional liability endorsement is available to a retail druggist or drugstore. In addition, professional liability endorsements are available for barbers, beauticians, funeral directors, optical and hearing aid establishments, printers, and veterinarians.

## PROFESSIONAL LIABILITY INSURANCE

Lawsuits against physicians, attorneys, engineers, and other professionals are common. This section briefly discusses professional liability insurance that provides protection against lawsuits alleging a substantial error or omission.

### Physicians Professional Liability Insurance

Professional liability insurance forms are not uniform, and insurers typically use their own forms. For medical professionals, the coverage is typically called **physicians, surgeons, and dentists professional**

**liability insurance.** The following section discusses some typical provisions of this coverage.[12]

- *Two insuring agreements.* The first insuring agreement covers the individual liability of each person named as an insured on the declarations page. The insurer agrees to pay all sums that the insured is legally obligated to pay as damages because of injury to which the insurance applies. The injury must result from a medical incident. A *medical incident* is any act or omission that arises out of the rendering or failing to render medical or dental services by the insured, or by any person acting under the direction and supervision of the insured. For example, if Dr. Smith operates on a patient and the patient is paralyzed after the operation, any resulting malpractice lawsuit would be covered. Likewise, if the office nurse gives a wrong shot to a patient, and the patient is harmed, Dr. Smith has liability coverage for the incident. However, the nurse is typically not included as an insured under the physician's policy but must secure his or her own professional liability policy. Thus, the nurse is not covered under Dr. Smith's policy for the medical incident unless an endorsement is added to the policy.

    The second insuring agreement applies to group liability, which refers to liability arising out of a partnership, limited liability company, association, or professional corporation. For example, if a physician insured under the first insuring agreement is a partner in a medical group, the physician is not insured under the first insuring agreement for any acts of malpractice committed by other partners. The second insuring agreement is needed to cover this exposure.

- *Liability is not restricted to accidental acts of the physician or surgeon.* In many cases the physician or surgeon deliberately intends to do a certain act; however, the professional diagnosis or the performance of the act may be faulty, and the patient is injured. For example, Dr. Smith may intend to operate on a patient by using a certain surgical procedure. If the patient is harmed or injured by the operation, Dr. Smith would still be covered for his intentional act to operate in a certain way.

- *There is a maximum limit per medical incident and an aggregate limit for each coverage.* For example, a patient and the patient's family may file separate claims against a physician for damages arising out of the same medical incident. Under current forms, the per-medical-incident limit is the maximum that would be paid for both claims. The aggregate limit is the maximum amount that would be paid as damages during any policy year.

- *Current forms permit the insurer to settle the claim without the physician's or surgeon's consent.* Payment of a claim could be viewed as an admission of guilt. Older forms required the insurer to obtain the physician's consent before a claim could be settled. However, current forms permit the insurer to settle without the physician's consent because an occasional claim against a physician in certain high-risk categories is not viewed as being overly detrimental to his or her character.

- *An extended reporting period endorsement can be added.* A physician with a claims-made policy may retire, change insurers, or drop the malpractice insurance. To protect the physician, an extended reporting period endorsement can be added, which covers future claims arising out of incidents that occurred during the period in which the claims-made policy was in force.

- *Professional liability insurance is not a substitute for other necessary forms of liability insurance.* General liability insurance is also needed to cover liability arising out of a hazardous condition on the premises or acts of the insured that are not professional in nature. For example, a patient may trip on a torn carpet in the doctor's office and break an arm. The professional liability policy would not cover this event.

In summary, a professional liability policy for physicians and surgeons provides considerable protection. The insurance is expensive, however. Malpractice insurance covering certain high-risk specialties can cost $100,000 or more each year in certain parts of the country. Physicians have responded to the medical malpractice problem by practicing defensive medicine, by abandoning high-risk specialties such as obstetrics and neurosurgery, and by pushing for legislation to limit malpractice awards. As a practical matter, however, a relatively large percentage of medical malpractice claims are groundless. Nevertheless, insurers must still defend the claims, which is expensive and increases the cost of malpractice insurance.

### Errors and Omissions Insurance

Some types of professional liability policies are referred to as "errors and omissions" policies. **Errors and omissions (E&O) insurance** provides protection against loss incurred by a client because of negligent acts, errors, or omissions by the insured. Professionals who need errors and omissions insurance include insurance agents and brokers, travel agents, real estate agents, stockbrokers, attorneys, consultants, engineers, architects, and other individuals who give advice to clients. The errors and omissions coverage is designed to meet the needs of each profession, including the growing number of self-employed professionals.

For example, in one policy for insurance agents, the insurer agrees to pay all sums that the insured is legally obligated to pay because of any negligent act, error, or omission by the insured (or by any other person for whose acts the insured is legally liable) in the conduct of business as general agents, insurance agents, or insurance brokers. For example, assume that Mark is an independent agent who fails to renew a property insurance policy for a client. The policy lapses, and a subsequent loss is not covered. If the client sues for damages, Mark would be covered for the omission. The policy is normally sold with a sizable deductible so that the agent has an incentive to minimize mistakes and errors.

Errors and omissions policies are generally issued on a claims-made basis covering claims made against the agent or broker only because of errors during the current policy period (and after the retroactive date).

Finally, the policy contains relatively few exclusions. However, claims that result from dishonest, fraudulent, criminal, or malicious acts by the insured, libel and slander, bodily injury, and destruction of tangible property are specifically excluded.

## DIRECTORS AND OFFICERS LIABILITY INSURANCE

Officers and directors of corporations are increasingly being sued by shareholders, employees, retirees, competing firms, government agencies, and other parties because of alleged mismanagement. **Directors and officers (D&O) liability insurance** provides financial protection for the directors and officers and the corporation if the directors and officers are sued for mismanagement of the company's affairs. Most corporations have bylaws that require the company to bear the financial responsibility of indemnifying directors and officers for claims alleging mismanagement. In addition to covering lawsuits against a company's directors and officers, a D&O policy reimburses the company for its costs of indemnifying directors and officers for such suits.

D&O policies are not uniform, but they have certain common features. The following discussion summarizes the major characteristics of D&O policies.

**Insuring Agreements** Most policies contain the following insuring agreements:

- *Personal liability of directors and officers.* The first agreement covers the personal liability of directors and officers. The insurer agrees to pay damages on behalf of insured persons because of a wrongful act. Insured persons include directors and officers and employees.

    The definition of a wrongful act varies among insurers. One policy defines a wrongful act broadly as any employment practices wrongful act, errors and omissions by a director or officer, any matter against an insured person solely because the person is a director or officer, errors and omissions by insured persons in their capacity as a director or officer of an outside entity, and any other errors and omissions by the corporation.

- *Corporate reimbursement coverage.* The second insuring agreement pays on behalf of the corporation. This coverage reimburses the corporation for loss resulting from the company's obligation to reimburse directors and officers to the extent required or permitted by law for suits alleging wrongful acts by such directors and officers.

- *Entity coverage.* Some D&O policies offer a third insuring agreement that covers the legal liability of a corporation arising out of the wrongful acts of directors and officers. *Entity coverage* covers the corporation if it is named as a defendant in a covered suit alleging wrongful acts by directors and officers. The insurer will defend the corporation and settle claims made directly against the corporation.

Typically, D&O policies are written on a claims-made basis. The policies usually have a discovery or extended reporting period in the event the insurer cancels the policy or refuses to renew. The reporting period varies by insurers—such as 90 days to 12 months—and applies only to claims for wrongful acts committed prior to termination of the policy but reported during the reporting period.

**Exclusions**    D&O policies contain numerous exclusions. Common exclusions are as follows:

- Bodily injury and property damage (covered under the CGL policy)
- Libel and slander (covered under the CGL policy)
- Personal profit, such as profit from insider trading
- Certain violations of the Securities Exchange Act of 1934 or similar provisions of state law
- Return of salaries or bonuses illegally received without stockholder approval
- Deliberate dishonesty by an insured
- Failure to procure or maintain insurance
- Violation of ERISA law
- Illegal discrimination
- Insured vs. insured claims (e.g., one director suing another director)

---

## CASE APPLICATION

1. Lastovica Construction is insured under a commercial general liability (CGL) policy. The firm agreed to build a new manufacturing facility for the Smith Corporation. A heavy machine used by Lastovica Construction accidentally fell from the roof of a partially completed building. Bill, an employee of the construction firm, was severely injured when the falling machine crushed his foot. Heather, a pedestrian, was also injured by the machine while walking on a public sidewalk in front of the building.

   a. Heather sued both Lastovica Construction and the Smith Corporation for her injury. Indicate the extent, if any, of the CGL insurer's obligation to provide a legal defense for Lastovica Construction.

   b. What legal defense could the Smith Corporation use to counter Heather's claim based on the nature of its relationship with Lastovica Construction? Explain your answer.

   c. Does Lastovica Construction have any responsibility for Bill's medical expenses and lost wages? Explain.

2. James is director of research for a pharmaceutical company. The company recently introduced a new drug to reduce the symptoms of arthritis. The company is insured under a claims-made CGL policy. The policy term is January 1, 2012 through December 31, 2012. On December 15, 2012, a patient of a physician that prescribed the drug became seriously ill after taking the prescribed dosage. On February 1, 2013, the patient filed a claim against the company for the illness. James had no prior notice that the patient had become ill. Explain whether the company's claims-made policy will cover the loss.

# SUMMARY

- General liability refers to the legal liability of business firms arising out of business operations other than liability for auto or aviation accidents or employee injuries. Important general liability loss exposures are as follows:

  Premises and operations

  Products liability

  Completed operations liability

  Contractual liability

  Contingent liability

- Legal liability can arise out of the *ownership and maintenance of the premises* where the firm does business. *Products liability* means that the firm can be held liable for property damage or bodily injury arising out of a defective product. *Completed operations liability* refers to liability arising out of faulty work performed away from the premises after the work is completed. *Contractual liability* means that the business firm agrees to assume the legal liability of another party by a written or oral contract. *Contingent liability* means that the firm can be held liable for work by independent contractors.

- Other important general liability loss exposures include environmental pollution; property in the insured's care, custody, or control; fire legal liability; liability arising out of the selling or serving of alcoholic beverages; directors and officers liability; personal and advertising injury; and liability arising out of wrongful termination, sexual harassment, and other employment-related practices.

- The *commercial general liability (CGL) policy* can be used to cover most general liability loss exposures of business firms. The CGL provides coverage for the following:

  Bodily injury and property damage liability

  Personal and advertising injury liability

  Medical payments

  Supplementary payments

- An *occurrence policy* covers liability claims arising out of occurrences that take place during the policy period, regardless of when the claim is made.

- A *claims-made policy* covers only claims that are first reported during the policy period or extended reporting period, provided that the event occurred after the retroactive date, if any, stated in the policy.

- Insurers use claims-made policies in some cases because of the problem of the *long tail*. The long tail refers to the relatively small number of claims that are reported years after the policy is first written. As a result of these claims, it is difficult to estimate premiums, losses, and loss reserves accurately. A claims-made policy enables an insurer to estimate premiums and losses more accurately.

- *Employment-related practices liability insurance* covers employers against suits arising out of wrongful termination, discrimination against employees, sexual harassment, and other employment-related practices.

- All states have workers compensation laws that require covered employers to provide workers compensation benefits to employees who become disabled because of work-related accidents or occupational disease. The workers compensation insurer pays all benefits that the employer must legally provide to employees who are occupationally disabled.

- The *business auto coverage form* can be used by business firms to insure their liability exposures from automobiles. The employer can select those autos to be covered under the policy.

- The *garage coverage form* is designed to meet the insurance needs of auto dealers. The major coverages include liability insurance, garagekeepers insurance, and physical damage insurance. *Garagekeepers insurance* covers the garage owner's liability for damage to customers' autos while the autos are in the dealer's care for service, repairs, or storage.

- Aircraft insurance covering private business and pleasure aircraft provides physical damage coverage on the aircraft and liability coverage for injury to passengers and to people on the ground.

- A *commercial umbrella policy* provides protection to firms against a catastrophic liability judgment. An umbrella policy is excess insurance over the underlying coverages.

- A *businessowners policy* (BOP) provides business liability coverage and medical expense coverage to small- to medium-sized business firms. The insured's employees are also covered for their negligent acts while acting within the scope of their employment.

- The *physicians, surgeons, and dentists professional liability coverage form* covers acts of malpractice by physicians, surgeons, and dentists. The policy has several important features:

  There are two insuring agreements.

  Liability is not restricted to accidental acts.

  There is a maximum limit for each medical incident and an aggregate limit for each coverage.

Current forms permit the company to settle a claim without the physician's or surgeon's consent.

An extended reporting period endorsement can be added.

Professional liability insurance is not a substitute for other necessary forms of liability insurance.

- *Errors and omissions insurance* provides protection against loss incurred by a client because of negligent acts, errors, or omissions by the insured.

- *Directors and officers (D&O) liability insurance* provides financial protection for the directors and officers and the corporation if the directors and officers are sued for mismanagement of the company's affairs.

## KEY CONCEPTS AND TERMS

Advertising injury (585)
Aircraft insurance (594)
Basic extended reporting period (588)
Bodily injury or property damage (583)
Business auto coverage form (592)
Businessowners policy (BOP) (597)
Claims-made policy (587)
Commercial general liability (CGL) policy (582)
Commercial liability umbrella coverage form (595)
Commercial umbrella policy (595)
Completed operations liability (582)
Contingent liability (582)
Contractual liability (582)
Damage to impaired property (584)
Damage to the insured's product (584)
Damage to the insured's work (584)
Directors and officers (D&O) liability insurance (599)

Employers liability insurance (590)
Employment-related practices liability coverage form (588)
Errors and omissions (E&O) insurance (599)
Fire legal liability coverage (585)
Garage coverage form (593)
General aggregate limit (586)
Hull insurance (594)
Liability without fault (589)
Long-tail claims (587)
Medical payments (584)
Occurrence (583)
Occurrence policy (587)
Other-states insurance (591)
Personal injury (584)
Physicians, surgeons, and dentists professional liability insurance (597)
Products-completed operations aggregate limit (587)

Products-completed operations hazard (581)
Products liability (582)
Retained limit (595)
Self-insured retention (SIR) (596)
Ultimate net loss (595)
Workers compensation and employers liability insurance policy (589)
Workers compensation insurance (590)

## REVIEW QUESTIONS

1. Identify the major general liability loss exposures of business firms.

2. Define each of the following:
   a. Products liability
   b. Completed operations liability
   c. Contractual liability
   d. Contingent liability

3. Briefly describe the meaning of "products and completed operations hazard."

4. The commercial general liability policy (CGL) contains several coverages. Briefly explain each of the following coverages:
   a. Bodily injury and property damage liability
   b. Personal and advertising injury liability
   c. Medical payments

5. Explain the difference between an occurrence policy and a claims-made policy.

6. A workers compensation policy contains several coverages. Briefly explain each of the following coverages:
   a. Part One: Workers Compensation Insurance
   b. Part Two: Employers Liability Insurance
   c. Part Three: Other States Insurance

7. a. Identify the major coverages in the business auto coverage form.
   b. Describe the major characteristics of the garage coverage form.

8. Briefly describe the following coverages that appear in an aircraft policy:
   a. Physical damage coverage
   b. Liability coverage

9. Explain the following characteristics in a commercial umbrella policy:
   a. Coverages provided
   b. Required underlying coverages
   c. Self-insured retention (SIR)

10. Briefly describe the major characteristics of a physicians, surgeons, and dentists professional liability insurance policy.

11. Explain the insuring agreements that typically appear in a directors & officers (D&O) liability policy.

## APPLICATION QUESTIONS

1. Ben owns an appliance and furniture store and is insured under a commercial general liability (CGL) policy written on an occurrence basis. Explain whether Ben's CGL policy would provide coverage for each of the following situations:
   a. Ben forcibly detained a customer whom he erroneously accused of shoplifting. One month later, after the policy had expired, the customer sued Ben for defamation of character.
   b. Ben's employees were delivering a large desk to a customer's house. The customer's front door was scratched and damaged when the desk hit the door. The customer immediately filed a claim for the damage to the door.
   c. An advertising firm sues Ben for using copyrighted material without permission when the material first appeared in a special holiday ad. Ben maintains that the ad material is original and belongs to him.
   d. Unknown to Ben, an automatic dishwasher had a defective part. One week after the dishwasher was installed in a customer's house, it malfunctioned and caused considerable water damage to the kitchen carpet. The homeowner sues Ben for the damage.
   e. An employee accidentally knocked over a heavy lamp that injured a customer's foot. The customer later presents a bill for medical expenses to Ben for payment.

2. Jill operates a sporting goods store in a rented location at a shopping mall. She is insured under a CGL policy with the following limits:

| | |
|---|---|
| General aggregate limit | $1,000,000 |
| Products-completed operations aggregate limit | 1,000,000 |
| Personal and advertising injury limit | 250,000 |
| Each-occurrence limit | 300,000 |
| Damage to rented premises | 100,000 |
| Medical expense limit (any one person) | 5,000 |

A propane tank in the store exploded. Indicate the dollar amount, if any, that Jill's insurer will pay for each of the following losses:
   a. Three customers were injured by flying debris from the explosion and had medical expenses of $6000, $7500, and $5000, respectively.
   b. A fire resulted from the explosion. Damages to the rented building are $50,000.
   c. A customer injured by the explosion sues Jill for $200,000 for the bodily injury.

3. Allison owns and operates a small retail food store in a suburban shopping center. The store is insured for liability coverage under a businessowners policy. Explain whether the following situations are covered under Allison's businessowners policy. Treat each situation separately.
   a. A clerk accidentally injures a customer with a shopping cart. Both Allison and the clerk are sued.
   b. A customer slips on a wet floor and breaks her leg.
   c. Allison has a customer arrested for shoplifting. The customer is innocent and sues for damages.
   d. A woman returns a spoiled package of gourmet cheese and demands her money back.

4. A surgeon is insured under a physicians, surgeons, and dentists professional liability policy. Explain whether the following situations are covered by the professional liability policy. Treat each situation separately.
   a. An office nurse gives a patient a wrong drug. Both the physician and the nurse are sued.
   b. The surgeon sets the broken arm of a patient. The patient sues because the arm becomes deformed and crooked.
   c. A patient waiting to see the doctor is injured when the legs of an office chair collapse.

5. Delivery Service purchased a commercial umbrella policy with a $10 million liability limit and a $100,000 self-insured retention. The umbrella insurer required Delivery Service to carry a $1 million per-occurrence limit on its general liability policy and a $1 million per-occurrence limit on its business auto policy. A Delivery Service driver was intoxicated while driving a company van and killed another motorist. The court ruled that Delivery Service must pay damages in the amount of $5 million. How much, if any, of this amount will the umbrella insurer pay? Explain your answer.

6. Electrical Services is an electrical contractor that employs 10 electricians. Electrical Services faces numerous loss exposures. One general liability loss

exposure arises out of faulty work that an electrician performs in a customer's home, which can cause property damage to the home. Identify the general liability loss exposure to which this example refers.

7. Fast Pizza hires college students who drive their own cars to deliver pizzas to customers. Fast Pizza is concerned that the company may be liable for damages caused by company employees while they are driving their cars on company business. Identify a liability coverage form that Fast Pizza could purchase to deal with this exposure.

## INTERNET RESOURCES

■ The **Defense Research Institute (DRI)** is a service organization created to improve the administration of justice and the skills of defense attorneys and in-house counsel. Visit the site at

dri.org

■ The **RAND Institute for Civil Justice** is a research unit within the RAND Organization that conducts independent, objective research on the civil justice system. Visit the site at

rand.org/law-business-regulation/centers/civil-justice.html

■ The **Insurance Information Institute** is a primary source of information, analysis, and referral on subjects dealing with property and liability insurance. Visit the site at

iii.org

■ The **Insurance Services Office (ISO)** provides statistical information, actuarial analyses, policy language, and technical information to participants in property and liability insurance markets. Visit the site at

iso.com

■ The **National Council on Compensation Insurance** is the most comprehensive source of workers compensation insurance information. The NCCI develops and administers rating plans and systems. Visit the site at

ncci.com

■ The **National Safety Council** provides national support and leadership in the field of safety, publishes safety materials of all kinds, and conducts a public information and publicity program to support safety. Visit the site at

nsc.org

■ The **Risk Management Society (RIMS)** is the premier professional organization for corporate risk managers and buyers of insurance. RIMS makes known to insurers the insurance needs of business and industry, supports loss prevention programs, and provides a forum for discussing common risk management objectives and problems. RIMS also publishes *Risk Management* magazine. Visit the site at

rims.org

## SELECTED REFERENCES

*Commercial Liability Risk Management and Insurance,* edited by Mary Ann Cook, First ed., second printing. Malvern, PA: American Institute for Chartered Property Casualty Underwriters, June 2012.

*Fire, Casualty & Surety Bulletins*, Erlanger, KY: National Underwriter Company, Casualty & Surety volume. The bulletins are published monthly. Detailed information on all forms of commercial liability insurance can be found in this volume.

Flitner, Arthur L. and Jerome Trupin, *Commercial Insurance,* 2nd ed., Third printing. Malvern, PA: American Institute for Property Casualty Underwriters/Insurance of America, November 2008.

*The Institutes' Handbook of Insurance Policies*, 10th ed., Malvern PA: American Institute of Chartered Property Casualty Underwriters, 2011.

Malecki, Donald S., *Commercial Liability Risk Management and Insurance*, 7th ed. Malvern, PA: American Institute for Chartered Property Casualty Underwriters/Insurance Institute of America, 2008.

Malecki, Donald S. and Arthur L. Flitner, *CGL Commercial General Liability,* 8th ed. Cincinnati, OH: The National Underwriter Company, 2005.

Rejda, George E., *Social Insurance and Economic Security*, 7th ed., Armonk, NY: M.E. Sharpe Inc., 2012.

Wells, Alexander T. and Bruce D., Chadbourne. *Introduction to Aviation Insurance and Risk Management,* 2nd ed. Malabar, FL: Krieger Publishing Company, 2000.

## NOTES

1. Emmett J. Vaughan and Therese M. Vaughan, *Fundamentals of Risk and Insurance,* 10th ed. (New York: Wiley, 2008), p. 610.

2. This section is based on *Fire, Casualty & Surety Bulletins,* Casualty and Surety volume, Public Liability section (Erlanger, KY: National Underwriter Company); Donald S. Malecki, et al, *Commercial Liability Risk Management and Insurance*, 7th ed. (Malvern, PA: American Institute for Chartered Property Casualty Underwriters/Insurance Institute of America, 2008); *Commercial Liability Risk Management and Insurance*, edited by Mary Ann Cook, American Institute for Chartered Property Casualty Underwriters (2011); and the International Risk Management Institute's Web site, IRMI.com. The authors also used various commercial liability forms prepared by the Insurance Services Office. The authors drew heavily on these sources in the preparation of this chapter.

3. *The Insurance Fact Book 2012,* New York: Insurance Information Institute, p. 185.

4. The workers compensation and employers liability policy is discussed in detail in *Fire, Casualty & Surety Bulletins,* Casualty and Surety volume, Workers Compensation section (Erlanger, KY: National Underwriter Company); *Commercial Liability Risk Management and Insurance*, Edited by Mary Ann Cook (Malvern, PA: American Institute for Chartered Property and Casualty Underwriters, 2011); and on the International Risk Management Institute's Web site, IRMI.com. The National Council on Compensation Insurance (NCCI) released an updated version of their workers compensation and employers liability policy effective July 1, 2011.

5. This section is based on the *Fire, Casualty & Surety Bulletins,* Casualty and Surety volume, Auto section (Erlanger, KY: National Underwriter Company); *Commercial Liability Risk Management and Insurance*, edited by Mary Ann Cook (2011); the International Risk Management Institute's Web site, IRMI.com; and the ISO business auto coverage form and garage coverage form.

6. Aircraft insurance is discussed in *Fire, Casualty & Surety Bulletins,* Companies & Coverages volume, Aircraft-Marine section (Erlanger, KY: National Underwriter). See also Alexander T. Wells and Bruce D. Chadbourne, *Introduction to Aviation Insurance and Risk Management,* 2nd ed. (Malabar, FL: Krieger Publishing Company, 2000), *Commercial Liability Risk Management and Insurance*, edited by Mary Ann Cook (2011), and the International Risk Management Institute's Web site, IRMI.com.

7. This information was provided by Nick Brown, Chief Underwriting Officer, Global Aerospace, United Kingdom in July, 2012.

8. Ibid.

9. This section is based on "Marine and Aviation Loss Exposures and Insurance," in *Commercial Liability Risk Management and Insurance*, edited by Mary Ann Cook (2011) and "Aircraft," Liability Risks and Insurance, Topic G-11, *Practical Risk Management*, June 2009.

10. A detailed discussion of the commercial umbrella policy can be found in *Fire, Casualty & Surety Bulletins,* Casualty and Surety volume, Public Liability section (Erlanger, KY: National Underwriter). See also Flitner and Trupin, *Commercial Insurance*, pp. 13.3–13.11; Cook, *Commercial Liability Risk Management and Insurance*, p. 3.17 and 11.6; and IRMI.com.

11. A detailed discussion of the businessowners policy can be found in *Fire, Casualty & Surety Bulletins,* Fire and Marine volume, Commercial Property section (Erlanger, KY: National Underwriter Company). The property and liability sections of the businessowners policy are discussed in *Commercial Property Risk Management and Insurance*, edited by Mary Ann Cook, first edition (Malvern, PA: American Institute for Chartered Property Casualty Underwriters, 2010). The ISO Businessowners Coverage Form is included in *The Institutes' Handbook of Insurance Policies*, 10th edition (Malvern, PA: American Institute for Chartered Property Casualty Underwriters, 2011).

12. Professional liability insurance for physicians is discussed in *Fire, Casualty & Surety Bulletins,* Casualty and Surety volume, Public Liability section (Erlanger, KY: National Underwriter Company). The subject is also discussed on the International Risk Management Institute's Web site, IRMI.com. A specimen policy is included in *The Institute's Handbook of Insurance Policies*, 10th edition (Malvern PA: American Institute for Chartered Property Casualty Underwriters, 2011).

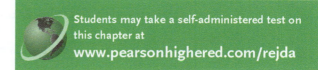

# CHAPTER 27

# CRIME INSURANCE AND SURETY BONDS

*"Thieves respect property. They merely wish the property to become their property that they may more perfectly respect it."*

G. K. Chesterton

## LEARNING OBJECTIVES

**After studying this chapter, you should be able to**

◆ Define theft, robbery, burglary, and safe burglary.

◆ Identify the insuring agreements in the commercial crime coverage form (loss-sustained form).

◆ Explain the difference between the discovery form and the loss-sustained form.

◆ Identify the basic insuring agreements in a financial institution bond for a commercial bank.

◆ Show how surety bonds differ from insurance.

◆ Identify the major types of surety bonds and give an example of where each can be used.

*Syd Davis owns Syd's Discount Drugs, a neighborhood pharmacy. The store closes at 9 pm on weeknights. Last Friday evening, just before closing, two men armed with handguns entered the store. They demanded money from the cash register and threatened to kill the cashier if she did not cooperate. The cashier gave the robbers over $400 in cash. One of the robbers smashed a display case beside the cash register and took some watches and cameras that were in the case. The robbers fled from the store with the cash and merchandise, and they have not been apprehended.*

*When Syd heard about the robbery, his first concern was the welfare of the cashier. She was not injured, but she was badly shaken by the event. Next, Syd thought about the broken display case, the stolen money, and the stolen merchandise. He remembers his insurance agent asking whether he wanted to add crime coverage to the insurance covering the business. Syd agreed to add the crime coverage. He's not really sure what the insurance covers, but he plans to call his agent to see how much of his loss he can recover.*

*Most firms need protection against crime loss exposures. Business firms lose billions of dollars annually because of robbery, burglary, larceny, and employee theft. Other crimes are widespread, including fraud, embezzlement, and other illegal activities. Computer crimes are also increasing.*

*In this chapter, we discuss the Insurance Services Office (ISO) commercial crime insurance program that protects business firms against robbery, burglary, employee theft, and other crime losses. The chapter also discusses financial institution bonds that cover the crime exposures of commercial banks and other financial institutions. This chapter concludes with a discussion of surety bonds that provide indemnification to one party if another bonded party fails to perform an agreed upon act.*

## ISO COMMERCIAL CRIME INSURANCE PROGRAM

Crime insurance coverage can either be added to a commercial package policy or purchased separately as a stand-alone (monoline) policy. There are five basic crime coverage forms and policies: (1) commercial crime coverage form, (2) commercial crime policy, (3) government crime coverage form, (4) government crime policy, and (5) employee theft and forgery policy. Each coverage form or policy is written in two versions—a discovery version and a loss-sustained version (see Exhibit 27.1). The *discovery version* covers a loss that is discovered during the policy period or within 60 days after the policy expires even

though the loss may have occurred before the policy's inception date. The *loss-sustained version* covers a loss that occurs during the policy period if the loss is discovered during the policy period or within one year after the policy expires. The loss-sustained version also covers a loss that would have been covered under a prior policy if the insurance had been kept in force.

The commercial crime coverage form and the commercial crime policy are designed for most private firms and nonprofit organizations other than financial institutions, such as banks and savings and loan institutions.

The government crime coverage form and government crime policy are designed for governmental

**EXHIBIT 27.1**
**ISO Commercial Crime Coverage Forms and Policies**

- Commercial Crime Coverage Form (discovery version and loss-sustained version).
- Commercial Crime Policy (discovery version and loss-sustained version).
- Government Crime Coverage Form (discovery version and loss-sustained version).
- Government Crime Policy (discovery version and loss-sustained version).
- Employee Theft and Forgery Policy (discovery version and loss-sustained version).

entities, such as states, cities, counties, state universities, and public utilities.

The employee theft and forgery policy is designed for business firms that need coverage only for employee theft and forgery losses. With certain exceptions, the crime coverage forms and policies follow a similar format with respect to insuring agreements, exclusions, and policy conditions.

As the five coverage forms and policies listed in Exhibit 27.1 can each be written on a loss sustained or discovery basis, a total of 10 coverage forms and policies are available. It is beyond the scope of the text to discuss each of these forms and policies in detail. Instead, the fundamentals of commercial crime insurance can be illustrated by a discussion of the ISO commercial crime coverage form (loss-sustained form).[1]

# COMMERCIAL CRIME COVERAGE FORM (LOSS-SUSTAINED FORM)

The **commercial crime coverage form** (**loss-sustained form**) can be added to a commercial package policy to cover the crime exposures of business firms or purchased as a separate policy.

## Basic Definitions

Most property crimes against business firms are due to robbery, burglary, or theft. The commercial crime coverage form has a lengthy definitions section that defines key terms. **Robbery** is the unlawful taking of property from the care and custody of a person by someone who (1) has caused or threatens to cause that person bodily harm, or (2) has committed an obviously unlawful act witnessed by that person.

Burglary is not defined in the ISO commercial crime policy (loss-sustained form). However, **burglary** typically is defined as the unlawful taking of property from inside the premises by a person who unlawfully enters or leaves the premises, as evidenced by marks of forcible entry or exit.

**Safe burglary** is the unlawful taking of property from within a locked safe or vault by someone who unlawfully enters the safe or vault as evidenced by marks of forcible entry upon the exterior. For coverage to apply, there must be marks of forcible entry upon the exterior of the safe. The definition of safe burglary also includes the unlawful taking of a safe or vault from the premises. Coverage applies if the entire safe is taken from inside the premises, which some burglars may do.

**Theft** is a broader term and is defined under the policy as the unlawful taking of property to the deprivation of the insured. It includes robbery and burglary as well as shoplifting, employee theft, and forgery.

## Insuring Agreements

The commercial crime coverage form contains several insuring agreements. Firms can select one or more of the following coverages:

- Employee Theft
- Forgery or Alteration
- Inside the Premises—Theft of Money and Securities
- Inside the Premises—Robbery or Safe Burglary of Other Property
- Outside the Premises
- Computer Fraud
- Funds Transfer Fraud
- Money Orders and Counterfeit Currency

**Employee Theft** This coverage pays for the loss of money, securities, and other property that results directly from theft committed by an employee. The theft is covered even if the employee cannot be identified, or the employee is acting alone or in collusion with other persons. For example, if an employee steals money from a cash register, the loss is covered.

Other types of employee theft are common, especially for small business firms.

Coverage of employee theft includes the theft of other property. **Other property** is any tangible property other than money or securities that has intrinsic value. However, other property does not include computer programs, electronic data, or any property excluded under the policy. For example, if an employee in an appliance store steals a television, the loss is covered.

The insuring agreement applies on a *blanket basis* to all persons who meet the definition of an employee—that is, covered employees are not specifically named in the policy. If desired, employers can instead use a *schedule approach,* which identifies covered employees in the policy by name or by position. Most employers prefer to cover employees on a blanket basis.

**Forgery or Alteration**    This coverage pays for a loss that results directly from forgery or from the alteration of checks, drafts, promissory notes, or similar instruments made or drawn by the insured or insured's agent. For example, if a thief steals some company checks and forges the insured's signature, the resulting loss is covered. Likewise, if a check signed by the insured is altered from $100 to $1000, that loss is covered. Note that this coverage applies only to forgery or alteration of the insured's checks or instruments and not to losses that result from the acceptance of forged checks or the instruments of others.[2]

**Inside the Premises—Theft of Money and Securities**
This coverage pays for the loss of money and securities inside the premises or banking premises that result directly from theft committed by a person present inside the premises, or from disappearance, or destruction. Coverage also applies to (1) damage to the premises or its exterior resulting from the actual or attempted theft of money or securities if the insured owns the premises or is liable for damage to it, and (2) damage to a locked safe, vault, cash register, or cash box inside the premises because of an actual or attempted theft or an unlawful entry into those containers.

Coverage is broad because of the words "theft, disappearance, or destruction." For example, covered losses include losses that occur when a cashier inside a liquor store is held up; money is destroyed in a fire or tornado; or a cash register or safe is damaged in a

burglary. In addition, damage to the premises or its exterior is covered if the insured owns the building or is liable for any damage to it.

**Inside the Premises—Robbery or Safe Burglary of Other Property**    This provision complements the previous insuring agreement of money and securities. This coverage pays for the loss or damage to *other property* inside the premises by the actual or attempted robbery of a custodian, or by safe burglary inside the premises. The term "custodian" is defined in the policy and includes the named insured, partners, and employees but not a janitor or watchperson. For example, if the owner of a pawn shop is robbed of several guns, the loss is covered. Likewise, if a cashier in a liquor store sees a customer take a bottle of liquor and then sprint out of the store without paying, that loss is covered.

Safe burglary of other property inside the premises is also covered. As stated earlier, safe burglary is (1) the unlawful taking of property from within a locked safe or vault by a person unlawfully entering the safe as evidenced by marks of forcible entry upon its exterior, or (2) the unlawful taking of a safe or vault from inside the premises. For example, if a burglar breaks into a locked safe and steals a watch and rings owned by the insured, the loss is covered.

Note that the burglary coverage in this insuring agreement applies only to safe burglary of other property inside the premises. For coverage to apply, property classified as other property must be in a locked safe or vault. Thus, if a burglar breaks into a clothing store and steals several suits and dresses off the rack, the burglary loss of other property would not be covered.

If broader coverage of burglary losses is desired, the policy can be endorsed with an optional insuring agreement to cover such losses. One optional agreement is **inside the premises—robbery or burglary of other property**. This insuring agreement covers actual or attempted burglary as well as robbery of a watchperson.

**Outside the Premises**    The **outside the premises** insuring agreement covers the theft, disappearance, or destruction of money and securities outside the premises while in the custody of a messenger or an armored-car company. A "messenger" is someone who has care and custody of the property outside the premises. For example, if an employee is robbed while taking the daily cash receipts to the bank, the loss is covered. Likewise, the loss of money or securities in the custody of an armored-car company is also covered.

In addition, actual or attempted robbery of other property outside the premises in the care of a messenger or armored-car company is covered. For example, if an employee is robbed while taking the insured's diamond ring and other jewelry to a jewelry store to be cleaned, the loss is covered. It is important to remember that it is not only large businesses that are subject to theft and burglary. Insight 27.1 discusses what small businesses can do to prevent crime.

**Computer Fraud**   This provision covers the loss of money, securities, and other property if a computer is used to transfer property fraudulently from inside

the premises or banking premises to a person or place outside the premises. For example, if a computer hacker breaks into a business computer and a check is issued to a fictitious person and cashed, the loss is covered.

**Funds Transfer Fraud**   The insuring agreement covers the loss of funds that results directly from fraudulent instructions that direct a financial institution to transfer or pay funds from the insured's account. For example, assume that a bank transfers funds from the insured's account to a bank in Switzerland. If the instruction to transfer the funds (such as electronic, cable, or telephone) is fraudulently made without the insured's knowledge or consent, the loss of money or securities is covered.

---

## INSIGHT 27.1

### Small Business Crime Prevention Guide

Crime—burglary, robbery, and vandalism—can be particularly devastating to small businesses in terms of money, customers, and employee safety. Through crime prevention, business owners can protect their assets as well as their employees.

**Laying a Foundation for Prevention**
Business owners should take a hard look at their businesses in areas such as physical layout, number of employees, hiring practices, and overall security to determine vulnerability to various kinds of crime, from burglary to embezzlement. Once this step has been taken, crime prevention measures can then be implemented.

- Establish and enforce clear policies about employee theft, employee substance abuse, crime reporting, opening and closing the business, and other security procedures.
- Provide training for all employees on security procedures.
- Use good locks, safes, and alarm systems. Refer questions about the best products available to local law enforcement officials.
- Keep detailed, up-to-date business records, such as inventories and banking records, and store back-up copies off premises. If a business is ever victimized, the owner can assess losses more easily and provide useful information for law enforcement investigations.
- Engrave all valuable office equipment and tools with an identification number such as a tax identification, license, or other unique number. Check with law enforcement officials for their recommendations.
- Mark equipment such as cash registers, printers, and computers, with an identification number (for example, tax identification or license number).

- Post the Operation Identification warning sticker in a storefront window to discourage burglary and theft. Operation Identification is the citizen's burglary prevention program for use in homes and business.
- Keep a record of all identification numbers off premises along with other important records.
- Consider the cost of each security improvement made against the potential savings through loss reduction. Remember to assess the impact on employees and customers. Since crimes against businesses are usually crimes of opportunity, failure to take good security precautions invites crime into a business.

**Burglary Prevention**

- Make sure all outside entrances and inside security doors have deadbolt locks. If padlocks are used, they should be made of steel and kept locked at all times. Remember to remove serial numbers from locks to prevent unauthorized keys from being made.
- All outside or security doors should be metal-lined and secured with metal security crossbars. Pin all exposed hinges to prevent removal, install security hinges or peen hinge pins.
- Windows should have secure locks and burglar-resistant glass. Consider installing metal grates on all windows except display windows.
- Remove all expensive items from window displays at night and make sure law enforcement officials can easily see into the business after closing.
- Light the inside and outside of the business, especially around doors, windows, skylights, or other entry points.

# INSIGHT 27.1

Consider installing covers over exterior lights and power sources to deter tampering.

- Check the parking lot for good lighting and unobstructed views.
- Keep the cash register in plain view from the outside of the business, so law enforcement can monitor it at all times. Leave it open and empty after closing.
- Be sure the safe is fireproof, securely anchored and kept in plain view. Leave it open when empty and use it to lock up valuables at close. Remember to change the combination when an employee who has had access to it leaves the business.
- Before investing in an alarm system, check with several companies and decide what level of security fits the needs of the business. Local law enforcement can recommend established companies. Learn how to use the system properly, check it daily, and run a test when closing.

## Robbery Prevention

Robbery doesn't occur as often as other crimes against businesses, but the potential for loss can be much greater from a single incident. Also, robbery involves force or threat of force and can result in serious injury or death.

- Most experts agree that, upon being confronted by a robber, you should cooperate with them. Merchandise and cash can always be replaced—people can't!
- Employees should greet every person who enters the business in a friendly manner. Personal contact can discourage a would-be criminal.
- Keep windows clear of displays or signs and make sure the business is well lighted. Check the layout of the store to eliminate any blind spots that may hide a robbery in progress.
- Provide information about the security systems to employees only on a "need-to-know" basis.
- Instruct employees to report any suspicious activity or person immediately and write down the information for future reference.
- Keep only small amounts of cash in the register to reduce possible losses. Use a drop safe into which large bills and excess cash are dropped by employees and cannot be retrieved by them. Post signs alerting would-be robbers of this procedure.
- Instruct employees to report any suspicious activity or person immediately and write down the information for future reference.
- Make bank deposits often and during business hours. Don't establish a pattern; take different routes at different times during the day. Ask local law enforcement to provide escort to the bank whenever possible.
- Ask local law enforcement what to do in the event of robbery.

- Ensure the address is visible so emergency vehicles can easily find the business.
- Secure the properly. Ask local law enforcement officials to conduct a security survey of the business. Ask for advice on lights, alarms, locks, and other security measures.

## Vandalism Prevention

Annual damage estimates due to vandalism are in the billions, and businesses pass the costs on to customers through higher prices. Most vandals are young people—from grade school children to teens to young adults.

- Clean up vandalism as soon as it happens—replace signs, repair equipment, paint over graffiti. Then, use landscape designs, building materials, lighting or fences to discourage vandals. Prickly shrubs, closely planted hedges and hard-to-mark surfaces can be effective in many circumstances.
- Work with law enforcement to set up a hotline to report vandalism. Remember, vandalism is a crime.
- Protect the business by installing and using good lighting and locking gates.
- Host a community meeting on vandalism to discuss its victims, costs, and solutions.
- Include young people in all vandalism prevention efforts.

## Organizing a Business Watch

Modeled after the Neighborhood Watch concept, Business Watch seeks to reduce commercial crime and the fear of crime from both the customer's and the business owner's point of view. There are important concepts behind Business Watch that business owners can use to prevent crime.

- Get to know the people who operate the neighboring residences and businesses—including schools, civic groups, libraries, and clubs. Making personal contact is the best way to get acquainted.
- Be alert and report suspicious behavior to law enforcement immediately, even if it means taking a chance on being wrong.
- Develop a telephone tree to share information with neighboring residents and businesses. Should a problem develop, each business is responsible for calling one or two others on the tree.
- Aggressively advertise the Business Watch group. Post signs and stickers saying that the neighboring block of businesses is organized to prevent crime by watching out for and reporting suspicious activities to law enforcement.

SOURCE: *Small Business Crime Prevention Guide*, Texas Department of Insurance, Oct. 2010.

**Money Orders and Counterfeit Paper Currency**   This coverage pays for losses resulting directly from the good-faith acceptance of money orders that are not paid upon presentation or from counterfeit currency acquired in the course of business. For example, if a sales clerk accepts a $50 counterfeit bill in exchange for merchandise, the loss is covered.

## Exclusions

The commercial crime coverage form contains numerous exclusions. It is beyond the scope of the text to discuss each exclusion. However, certain exclusions merit a brief discussion and are summarized here.

- *Dishonest acts or theft committed by the named insured, partners, or members.* Loss due to dishonest acts or theft by the insured or the insured's partners or members is specifically excluded.
- *Knowledge of dishonest acts of employees prior to policy period.* Loss caused by an employee is not covered if the employee committed theft or any other dishonest act prior to the effective date of the insurance, and the named insured or any partner, manager, officer, director, or trustee not in collusion with the employee learned of that theft or dishonest act prior to the policy period.
- *Dishonest acts or theft by employees, managers, directors, trustees, or representatives.* With the exception of the employee theft insuring agreement, dishonest acts or theft committed by employees, managers, directors, trustees, or representatives are excluded.
- *Confidential information.* Loss from the unauthorized disclosure of confidential information is excluded. Confidential information includes patents, trade secrets, processing methods, and customer lists. The exclusion also applies to the unauthorized disclosure of information of another person or party, including financial information, personal information, and credit card information.
- *Indirect loss.* An indirect loss that results from a covered loss is excluded. For example, if the business is temporarily closed because of a burglary, the loss of business income under this form is not covered.

- *Inventory shortages.* This exclusion applies to the employee theft insuring agreement. There is no coverage for any loss if proof of loss depends on an inventory computation or on a profit and loss computation. The intent here is to exclude inventory losses that may be due to errors in record keeping rather than employee dishonesty.
- *Trading losses.* This exclusion applies to the employee theft insuring agreement. Trading losses whether in the named insured's name or in a fictitious account are specifically excluded. Thus, unauthorized trading in stocks, bonds, futures, and derivatives is not covered. However, unauthorized trading losses can be catastrophic. An endorsement is available to cover trading losses that meet the criteria for employee theft.

## Policy Conditions

The policy conditions section in the commercial crime coverage form contains numerous conditions. Four important policy conditions are discussed here.

**Discovery Form**   As stated earlier, the crime coverage forms and policies are written in two versions—a discovery version and a loss-sustained version.

*The* **discovery form** *covers losses that are discovered during the policy period or within 60 days after the policy's expiration date, regardless of when the loss occurred.* Thus, losses that occur prior to a policy's inception date are covered if they are discovered within the policy period or within 60 days after termination or cancellation of the policy. In the case of employee benefit plans, the discovery period extends to one year after the policy's expiration date.

Employee theft can go undetected for years. The discovery form can be especially valuable for a business firm that has been in business for several years but is uninsured for employee theft losses. If the new insurance were written on a discovery basis, it would cover any losses that occurred years earlier but were only discovered during the current policy period (or within 60 days after expiration of the policy).

However, an underwriter may believe that large undiscovered losses might exist prior to the policy's inception date. To deal with adverse selection, a **retroactive date endorsement** could be added to the policy, which covers losses that occur only after the retroactive date and are discovered during the current policy period. If the retroactive date is the same as the policy's inception date, losses that occurred prior to the policy's inception date would not be covered.[3]

**Loss-Sustained Form**    *The* **loss-sustained form** *covers losses that occur during the policy period and are discovered during the policy period or within one year after the policy expires.* For example, if an employee steals $25,000 in cash during the policy period, the loss is covered if it is discovered during the current policy period or within one year after the policy's expiration date.

**Loss Sustained during Prior Insurance Not Issued by Us or Any Affiliate**    Under the **loss sustained during prior insurance not issued by us or any affiliate** provision, the current policy provides coverage for a loss that occurred during the term of the prior policy but was discovered only after the discovery period under the prior policy had expired. This provision enables the policyholder to change insurers without penalty. This provision applies only if there is no break in the continuity of coverage under both policies; that is, the present insurance became effective at the time of expiration of the prior insurance. Another requirement is that the loss is one that would have been covered by the current policy if it had been in force when the loss occurred.

The maximum amount paid is the policy limit under the previous policy, or the limit of insurance under the current policy, whichever is less. For example, assume that the policy limit under the previous policy is $10,000, and the policy limit under the current policy is $50,000. The current policy will pay only a maximum of $10,000 for any covered loss that occurred while the previous policy was in force.

**Termination as to Any Employee**    The **termination as to any employee** provision states that the employee theft insuring agreement terminates as to any employee once the insured has knowledge that the employee has committed a theft or dishonest act. Once the insured becomes aware of the theft or dishonest act committed by the employee either before or after the worker is employed, employee theft coverage on that worker is terminated.

# FINANCIAL INSTITUTION BONDS

Commercial banks, savings and loan institutions, credit unions, stock brokerage firms, and other financial institutions are faced with crime loss exposures that can result in enormous financial losses. These exposures include bank holdups, employee dishonesty, forgery and alteration of checks, acceptance of counterfeit money, theft of securities, armored-car exposures, and numerous additional crime exposures. Because of the size and complexity of their crime exposures, financial institutions use some type of financial institution bond to deal with these exposures. In its application to financial institutions, the word "bond" is synonymous with "insurance policy" and should not be confused with surety bonds discussed later in this chapter.

The Surety Association of America makes available a number of financial institution bonds that banks and other financial institutions can use. One widely used form is **Financial Institution Bond, Standard Form No. 24**, which is designed for commercial banks, savings banks, and savings and loan institutions. The following discussion is based on this form.

The financial institution bond contains a number of insuring agreements. Agreements A, B, C, and F are part of the basic bond coverage. Agreements D, E, and G are optional.[4]

- Insuring Agreement A—Fidelity
- Insuring Agreement B—On Premises
- Insuring Agreement C—In Transit
- Insuring Agreement D—Forgery or Alteration
- Insuring Agreement E—Securities
- Insuring Agreement F—Counterfeit Currency
- Insuring Agreement G—Fraudulent Mortgages

## Fidelity Coverage

Financial institutions frequently experience fidelity losses due to employee dishonesty. **Fidelity coverage** *covers losses that result directly from the dishonest or fraudulent acts of employees acting alone or in collusion with others, for the purpose of causing the insured to sustain such loss.* For example, if a bank teller steals cash from a cash register or vault, the loss is covered.

## On Premises Coverage

This provision covers the loss of property on the premises from robbery, burglary, misplacement, mysterious unexplainable disappearance, theft, and a number of additional perils. For example, if a bank robber threatens a bank teller with bodily harm and escapes with $25,000, the loss is covered.

## In-Transit Coverage

This provision covers in-transit losses, which include losses from robbery, larceny, theft, misplacement, mysterious unexplainable disappearance, and other specified perils. The property must be in the custody of a messenger or in the custody of a transportation company. For example, if a bank loses money in an armored car robbery, the loss is covered.

## Forgery or Alteration Coverage

This optional provision covers loss from forgery or alteration of most negotiable instruments and certain financial instruments specified in the bond. For example, if a bank officer's name is forged on a check payable to a fictitious person, the loss is covered.

## Securities Coverage

This optional provision covers losses to the insured because securities accepted in good faith have been forged, altered, lost, or stolen. For example, if a bank in good faith accepts some stolen stock certificates as collateral for a loan and the bank later tries to sell the certificates when the borrower defaults, any resulting loss is covered.

## Counterfeit Money

This provision is part of the basic bond coverage and covers loss to the insured from counterfeit money. For example, if a bank teller accepts a fake $100 bill, the loss to the bank is covered.

## Fraudulent Mortgages

This optional provision covers loss that results directly from having accepted or acted upon any mortgage on real property that proves defective because of a fraudulent signature. For example, if a bank accepts a mortgage on a building as collateral for a loan, and the mortgage is defective because the mortgagee's signature on the document is a forgery, any resulting loss would be covered.

# SURETY BONDS

A **surety bond** *is a contract in which the surety guarantees to a second party (the obligee) that a third party (the principal) will faithfully perform its obligations to the obligee.* For example, a contractor may be financially overextended and unable to complete a building project. A public official may embezzle public funds, or the executor of an estate may illegally convert part of the estate assets to his or her own use. Surety bonds can be used to meet these loss exposures.

## Parties to a Surety Bond

There are three parties to a surety bond:

- Principal
- Obligee
- Surety (obligor)

The **principal** *is the party that agrees to perform certain acts or fulfill certain obligations.* For example, a construction company may agree to build an office building for a commercial bank. The construction company may be required to obtain a performance bond before the contract is awarded. The construction company would be the principal.

The **obligee** *is the party that receives the proceeds of the bond if the principal fails to perform.* In the previous example, the bank would be reimbursed for any loss that resulted from failure of the construction company to complete the building on time or according to contract specifications.

The surety is the final party to the bond. *The* **surety (obligor)** *is the party that agrees to answer for the debt, default, or obligation of another.* For example, the construction company may have purchased a performance bond from a commercial insurer. If the construction company (principal) fails to perform, the bank (obligee) would be reimbursed for any loss by the commercial insurer (surety).

## Comparison of Surety Bonds and Insurance

Surety bonds are similar to insurance contracts in that both provide protection against specified losses. However, there are some important differences between them, as listed in Exhibit 27.2.

## Types of Surety Bonds

Different types of surety bonds can be used to meet specific needs and situations. Although surety bonds are not uniform and have different characteristics, they can generally be grouped into the following categories:[5]

- Contract bonds
    Bid bond
    Performance bond
    Payment bond
    Maintenance bond
    Completion bond
- License and permit bonds
- Public official bonds
- Judicial bonds
    Fiduciary bond
    Court bond
- Miscellaneous surety bonds

**Contract Bonds**   Contract bonds are used in connection with construction contracts. *A contract bond guarantees that the principal will fulfill all contractual obligations.* There are several types of contract bonds. Under a *bid bond,* the owner (obligee) is guaranteed that the party awarded a bid on a project will sign a contract and furnish a performance bond.

Under a **performance bond,** the owner is guaranteed that work will be completed according to the contract specifications. For example, if a building is not completed, the surety is responsible for completion of the project and the extra expense of hiring another contractor. Performance bonds are especially important in the construction industry where a large number of construction firms fail each year.

A *payment bond* guarantees that the bills for labor and materials used in a building project will be paid by the contractor when the bills are due.

A *maintenance bond* guarantees that poor workmanship by the principal will be corrected, or defective materials will be replaced. This maintenance guarantee is often included in a performance bond for one year.

A *completion bond* deals with contracts that involve the financing and design of projects. The completion bond guarantees the completion of a building or project. It is designed to protect lending institutions and lessors of property.

Exhibit 27.3 compares the various types of contract bonds.

**License and Permit Bonds**   These types of bonds are commonly required of parties that must obtain a license or permit from a city or town before they can engage in certain activities. *A license and permit bond guarantees that the party bonded will comply with all laws and regulations that govern the party's activities.* For example, a liquor store owner may post a bond guaranteeing that liquor will be sold according to the law. A plumber or electrician may post a bond guaranteeing that the work performed will comply with the local building code.

**EXHIBIT 27.2**
**Comparison of Insurance and Surety Bonds**

| *Insurance* | *Surety Bonds* |
|---|---|
| 1. There are two parties to an insurance contract. | 1. There are three parties to a surety bond. |
| 2. The insurer expects to pay losses. The premium reflects expected loss costs. | 2. The surety, theoretically, expects no losses to occur. The premium is viewed as a service fee, by which the surety's credit is substituted for that of the principal. |
| 3. The insurer normally does not have the right to recover a loss payment from the insured. | 3. The surety has the legal right to recover a loss payment from the defaulting principal. |
| 4. Insurance is designed to cover unintentional losses that ideally are outside of the insured's control. | 4. The surety guarantees the principal's character, honesty, integrity, and ability to perform. These qualities are within the principal's control. |

**EXHIBIT 27.3**
**Comparison of Five Contract Bonds**

| Type of Bond | Obligee | Principal | Guarantee |
|---|---|---|---|
| 1. Bid Bond | Property owner or party requesting bids | Firm or party submitting the bid | Party whose bid is accepted will sign a contract and furnish a performance bond |
| 2. Performance Bond | Property owner or party having work done | Contractor doing the work | Work will be completed according to contract specifications |
| 3. Payment Bond | Property owner or party having work done | Contractor doing the work | Bills for labor and materials will be paid when due |
| 4. Maintenance Bond | Party having work done | Contractor doing the work | Faulty work of principal will be corrected, or defective materials replaced |
| 5. Completion Bond | Lending institution or lessor | Contractor doing the work | Guarantees completion of the building or improvement |

**Public Official Bonds**   This type of bond is usually required by law for public officials who are elected or appointed to public office. A **public official bond** *guarantees that public officials will faithfully perform their duties for the protection of the public.* For example, a state treasurer must comply with state law governing the deposit of public funds.

**Judicial Bonds**   Judicial bonds *guarantee that the party bonded will fulfill certain obligations specified by law.* There are several types of judicial bonds. A **fiduciary bond** guarantees that the person who is responsible for the property of another will faithfully perform all required duties, give an accounting of all property, and make up any deficiency for which the courts hold the fiduciary liable. For example, administrators of estates, receivers or liquidators, or guardians of minor children may be required to post a bond guaranteeing their performance.

A **court bond** is designed to protect one person (obligee) against loss in the event that the person

bonded does not prove that he or she is legally entitled to the remedy sought against the obligee. For example, an **attachment bond** guarantees that if the court rules against the plaintiff who has attached the property of the defendant in a lawsuit, the defendant will be reimbursed for damages as a result of having the property attached.

Finally, a **bail bond** is another type of court bond. If the bonded person fails to appear in court at the appointed time, the entire bond is forfeited.

**Miscellaneous Surety Bonds**   This category consists of bonds that cannot be classified in any other group. For example, an *auctioneer's bond* guarantees the accounting of sales proceeds by an auctioneer; a *lost-instrument bond* guarantees the obligee against loss if the original instrument (such as a lost stock certificate) shows up later in the possession of another party; and an *insurance agent bond* indemnifies the insurer the agent represents for any penalties that result from the unlawful acts of agents.

## CASE APPLICATION

The ISO commercial crime coverage form can be used to insure specific crime exposures of most business firms. Assume that you are a risk management consultant. For each of the following losses, identify an appropriate insuring agreement that would have covered the loss.

a. Jennifer owns a restaurant and is taking the daily cash receipts to the bank. While walking to her car, she is confronted by a person with a gun and is told to hand over the cash. Fearing for her life, she surrenders the money.

b. Travis owns a large supermarket. After the store closed, a burglar broke into a locked safe and stole several thousand dollars.

c. Rebecca is a cashier at a 24-hour convenience store. In the early morning, a drug addict confronts her with a knife and threatens her with bodily harm if she does not give him all the cash in the cash drawer.

d. Kevin is the manager of a retail store that sells lamps and lighting accessories. A company audit reveals that a long-time accountant had embezzled several thousand dollars.

e. Josh sells merchandise over the Internet. A thief hacked into his business computer and transferred company funds to another party.

## SUMMARY

- *Theft* is the unlawful taking of money, securities, or other property to the deprivation of the insured. Robbery and burglary are forms of theft.

- *Robbery* is the unlawful taking of property from the care and custody of a person by someone who has (1) caused or threatened to cause that person bodily harm or (2) committed an obviously unlawful act witnessed by that person.

- *Burglary* is usually defined as the unlawful taking of property from inside the premises by a person who unlawfully enters or leaves the premises, as evidenced by marks of forcible entry or exit.

- *Safe burglary* is the unlawful taking of property from within a locked safe or vault by someone who unlawfully enters the safe or vault as evidenced by marks of forcible entry upon the exterior. The definition of safe burglary also includes the unlawful taking of a safe or vault from the premises.

- There are five basic ISO crime coverage forms and policies:

  Commercial Crime Coverage Form

  Commercial Crime Policy

  Government Crime Coverage Form

  Government Crime Policy

  Employee Theft and Forgery Policy

  Each crime coverage form or policy is written in two versions—a discovery version and a loss-sustained version.

- The *discovery form* covers losses that are discovered during the policy period or within 60 days after the policy's expiration date, regardless of when the loss occurred.

- The *loss-sustained form* covers losses that occur during the policy period and are discovered during the policy period or within one year after the policy expires.

- The commercial crime coverage form (loss-sustained form) contains several insuring agreements. Firms can select one or more of the following coverages:

  Employee Theft

  Forgery or Alteration

  Inside the Premises—Theft of Money and Securities

  Inside the Premises—Robbery or Safe Burglary of Other Property

  Outside the Premises

  Computer Fraud

  Funds Transfer Fraud

  Money Orders and Counterfeit Currency

- *Loss Sustained during Prior Insurance Not Issued by Us or Any Affiliate* is a provision by which the current policy provides coverage for a loss that occurred during the term of the prior policy but was not discovered until after the discovery period under the prior policy had expired. The purpose is to enable an insured to change insurers without penalty. The provision applies only if there is no break in the continuity of coverage under both policies, and the loss is one that would have been covered by the current policy if it had been in force when the loss occurred.

- A financial institution bond is designed for banks and similar institutions. The following coverages are available:

  Insuring Agreement A—Fidelity

  Insuring Agreement B—On Premises

  Insuring Agreement C—In Transit

  Insuring Agreement D—Forgery or Alteration

  Insuring Agreement E—Securities

Insuring Agreement F—Counterfeit Currency

Insuring Agreement G—Fraudulent Mortgages

- There are three parties to a surety bond. The *principal* is the party that agrees to perform certain obligations. The *obligee* is the party that receives the proceeds of the bond if the principal fails to perform. The *surety* (obligor) is the party that agrees to answer for the debt, default, or obligation of another.

- Surety bonds are similar to insurance contracts in that losses are paid if they occur. However, there are several major differences between surety bonds and insurance.

    There are two parties to an insurance contract; there are three parties to a surety bond.

    The insurer expects to pay losses; the surety theoretically expects no losses to occur.

    The insurer normally does not have the right to recover a loss payment from an insured; the surety has the right to recover from a defaulting principal.

    Insurance covers unintentional losses outside of the insured's control; the surety guarantees the principal's character and ability to perform, which are within the principal's control.

- Surety bonds guarantee the performance of the principal. They include various contract bonds, license and permit bonds, public official bonds, judicial bonds, federal surety bonds, and miscellaneous surety bonds.

## KEY CONCEPTS AND TERMS

Attachment bond (616)
Bail bond (616)
Burglary (608)
Commercial crime coverage form (loss-sustained form) (608)
Contract bond (615)
Court bond (616)
Discovery form (612)
Fidelity coverage (613)
Fiduciary bond (616)
Financial institution bond, Standard Form No. 24 (613)
Inside the premises—robbery or burglary of other property (609)
Inside the premises—theft of money and securities (609)
Judicial bonds (616)
License and permit bonds (615)
Loss sustained during prior insurance not issued by us or any affiliate (613)
Loss-sustained form (613)
Obligee (614)
Other property (609)
Outside the premises (609)
Performance bond (615)
Principal (614)
Public official bond (616)
Retroactive date endorsement (612)
Robbery (608)
Safe burglary (608)
Surety bonds (614)
Surety (obligor) (614)
Termination as to any employee (613)
Theft (608)

## REVIEW QUESTIONS

1. Define robbery, burglary, safe burglary, and theft.

2. Briefly describe the following insuring agreements in the commercial crime coverage form (loss-sustained form):
   a. Employee Theft
   b. Forgery or Alteration
   c. Inside the Premises—Theft of Money and Securities
   d. Inside the Premises—Robbery or Safe Burglary of Other Property
   e. Outside the Premises

3. a. Explain the difference between the discovery form and the loss-sustained form.
   b. What is the purpose of the retroactive date endorsement that may be attached to a policy written on a discovery basis?

4. Identify the major exclusions in the commercial crime coverage form (loss-sustained form).

5. An important policy provision is called *termination as to any employee*. Explain the meaning of this provision.

6. When commercial crime insurance is written on a loss-sustained basis, the policy contains a provision called *loss sustained during prior insurance not issued by us or any affiliate*. Explain the meaning of this provision.

7. Briefly describe the following insuring agreements that appear in a financial institutions bond.
   a. Fidelity coverage
   b. On premises coverage
   c. In transit coverage
   d. Forgery or alteration

8. Identify the three parties to a surety bond.

9. How do surety bonds differ from insurance contracts?

10. Identify three types of surety bonds and give an example where each can be used.

# APPLICATION QUESTIONS

1. Patrick is the owner of a liquor store that is insured under an ISO commercial crime coverage form (loss-sustained form) with the following insuring agreements:
   - Employee Theft
   - Inside the Premises—Theft of Money and Securities
   - Inside the Premises—Robbery or Safe Burglary of Other Property
   - Outside the Premises

   For each of the following losses, indicate whether any of the above insuring agreements would cover the loss. Explain your answer.
   a. Patrick withdrew money from a bank on a Friday afternoon to cash the payroll checks of customers over the weekend. He drove back to the liquor store and parked his car in the store's parking lot. As he was walking toward the liquor store, he was robbed of the cash at gunpoint.
   b. A video surveillance tape revealed that a newly-hired employee was stealing money from the cash register.
   c. Patrick suspected that one employee was taking liquor from the stock of inventory without paying. A physical inventory revealed a shortage of five cases of Canadian whiskey.
   d. A burglar forced open a locked safe and money inside the safe was taken. Also, the interior of the store was badly damaged in the burglary.
   e. Because of the burglary, the business was closed for two days. Patrick's sales receipts for the week were substantially reduced.
   f. A robber threatened a cashier with a knife and demanded the cash receipts. The cashier resisted giving the robber the money. The robber stabbed her and fled from the store with a substantial amount of cash.
   g. A customer paid for merchandise by giving the cashier a $50 money order drawn on a commercial bank. When the money order was presented to the bank for payment, the bank refused to pay because the money order had been stolen.

2. Kathy owns a large retail electrical store that sells light fixtures, lamps, and electrical equipment. The firm is not insured for employee theft. A risk management consultant recommended adding an ISO commercial crime coverage form to the firm's package policy, including coverage for employee theft. The crime form was issued on a *discovery basis* on July 1, 2011 without a retroactive date endorsement. The coverage amount for employee theft is $25,000. A routine audit in December 2011 by an accounting firm revealed that one of the bookkeepers had embezzled $20,000 over a three-month period in 2009.
   a. What dollar amount, if any, will the insurer pay for the loss?
   b. Would your answer to part (a) be the same or different if the crime coverage form were issued on a loss-sustained basis? Explain.

3. Richard owns several retail stores. The employees are insured for employee theft under a commercial crime coverage form (loss-sustained form) with an insurance limit of $10,000. Richard discovered that Vera, a long-time accountant, had embezzled $5000 during the current policy period to pay the gambling debts of her son, who had been threatened with bodily harm. What is the liability of the insurer, if any, for the preceding loss? Explain your answer.

4. Vasquez Construction has been awarded a contract by a local school board to build a new public school and must provide a performance bond.
   a. With respect to the performance bond, identify the principal, surety, and obligee.
   b. If Vasquez Construction fails to complete the building according to the terms of the contract, what would be the surety's obligation?
   c. Does the surety have any recourse against Vasquez Construction in this example? Explain your answer.

# INTERNET RESOURCES

- The **Coalition Against Insurance Fraud** is a nonprofit alliance of consumer, law enforcement, and insurance industry groups that attempts to reduce all types of insurance fraud by public advocacy and education. Visit the site at

  insurancefraud.org

- The **Insurance Committee for Arson Control** is an industry group that works to increase public awareness of arson and what can be done to reduce the arson problem. The organization also helps insurers recognize arson-prone risks and resist payment of fraudulent arson claims. Visit the site at

  arsoncontrol.org

- The **National Association of Surety Bond Producers** is a trade association serving the interests of over 5,000 surety bond producers. Visit the site at

  nasbp.org

- The **National Insurance Crime Bureau** is a nonprofit organization dedicated to combating insurance fraud and crime. Visit the site at

  nicb.org

- The **Surety & Fidelity Association of America** is a trade association that represents companies that write the majority of surety and fidelity bonds in the United States. Visit the site at

  surety.org

- The **Surety Information Office** is a source of information about contract surety bonds. Visit the site at

  sio.org

## SELECTED REFERENCES

Cook, Mary Ann (editor), *Commercial Property Risk Management and Insurance*, 1st ed. Malvern, PA: American Institute for Chartered Property and Casualty Underwriters, 2010.

*Fire, Casualty & Surety Bulletins*, Casualty and Surety volume, Crime section and Surety section. Erlanger, KY: National Underwriter Company. The bulletins are updated monthly. Detailed information on commercial crime insurance and surety bonds can be found in this volume.

Flinter, Arthur L. and Jerome Trupin, *Commercial Insurance*, 2nd ed., 3rd printing. Malvern, PA: American Institute for Chartered Property Casualty Underwriters/Insurance Institute of America, November 2008.

Trupin, Jerome, and Arthur L. Flitner, *Commercial Property Risk Management and Insurance*, 8th ed. Malvern, PA: American Institute for Chartered Property Casualty Underwriters/Insurance Institute of America, 2008.

## NOTES

1. The commercial crime coverages discussed in this chapter are based on Arthur L. Flitner and Jerome Trupin, *Commercial Insurance*, 2nd ed., 3rd printing (Malvern, PA: American Institute for Chartered Property Casualty Underwriters/Insurance Institute of America, November 2008), ch. 5; Jerome Trupin and Arthur L. Flitner, *Commercial Property Risk Management and Insurance*, 8th ed. (Malvern, PA: American Institute for Chartered Property Casualty Underwriters/Insurance Institute of America, 2008); Chapter 9 of *Commercial Property Risk Management and Insurance*, edited by Mary Ann Cook, 1st ed. (Malvern, PA: American Institute for Chartered Property and Casualty Underwriters, 2010); the International Risk Management Institute's Web site IRMI.com; and *Fire, Casualty & Surety Bulletins*, Casualty and Surety volume, Crime section and Surety section (Erlanger, KY: National Underwriter Company). The authors also drew on the copyrighted commercial crime coverage forms and contractual provisions of the Insurance Services Office (ISO).

2. Flitner and Trupin, *Commercial Insurance,* p. 5.10, and Cook, *Property Risk Management and Insurance*, p. 9.11.

3. Trupin and Flitner, *Commercial Property Risk Management and Insurance*, pp. 11.31, 11.32.

4. The discussion of financial institution bonds is based on *Fire, Casualty & Surety Bulletins*, Casualty and Surety volume, Financial Institutions section (Erlanger, KY: National Underwriter Company). The authors also drew on the Financial Institution Bond, Standard Form No. 24, the Surety Association of America, for purposes of discussing relevant contractual provisions.

5. Discussion of surety bonds is based on *Fire, Casualty & Surety Bulletins,* Casualty and Surety volume, Surety section (Erlanger, KY: National Underwriter Company).

Students may take a self-administered test on this chapter at **www.pearsonhighered.com/rejda**

## Homeowners Policy Declarations

**POLICYHOLDER:** Chris and Karen Swift
(Named Insured) 8110 Lake Street
Lincoln, Nebraska 68506

**POLICY NUMBER:** 296 H 578661

**POLICY PERIOD:** **Inception:** June 1, 2013
**Expiration:** June 1, 2014

Policy period begins 12:01 A.M. standard time
at the residence premises.

**FIRST MORTGAGEE AND MAILING ADDRESS:**

First National Bank of Lincoln
7000 Pioneer Blvd.
Lincoln, NE 68506

We will provide the insurance described in this policy in return for the premium and compliance with all
applicable policy provisions.

| SECTION I COVERAGES | LIMIT | |
|---|---|---|
| A—Dwelling | $ 250,000 | **SECTION I DEDUCTIBLE:** $ 1000 |
| B—Other Structures | $ 25,000 | (In case of loss under Section I, we cover |
| C—Personal Property | $ 125,000 | only that part of the loss over the |
| D—Loss of Use | $ 75,000 | deductible amount shown above.) |

| SECTION II COVERAGES | LIMIT | |
|---|---|---|
| E—Personal Liability | $ 300,000 | Each Occurrence |
| F—Medical Payments to Others | $ 1,000 | Each Person |

**CONSTRUCTION:** Masonry Veneer    **NO. FAMILIES:** One    **TYPE ROOF:** Approved

**YEAR BUILT:** 1985    **PROTECTION CLASS:** 7    **FIRE DISTRICT:** City of Lincoln

**NOT MORE THAN 1000 FEET FROM HYDRANT**

**NOT MORE THAN 5 MILES FROM FIRE DEPT.**

**FORMS AND ENDORSEMENTS IN POLICY:** HO 00 03 10 00

**POLICY PREMIUM:** $780.00    **COUNTERSIGNATURE DATE:** May 1, 2013    **AGENT:** Patrick Rejda

SAMPLE

# HOMEOWNERS 3 – SPECIAL FORM

## AGREEMENT

We will provide the insurance described in this policy in return for the premium and compliance with all applicable provisions of this policy.

## DEFINITIONS

**A.** In this policy, "you" and "your" refer to the "named insured" shown in the Declarations and the spouse if a resident of the same household. "We", "us" and "our" refer to the Company providing this insurance.

**B.** In addition, certain words and phrases are defined as follows:

**1.** "Aircraft Liability", "Hovercraft Liability", "Motor Vehicle Liability" and "Watercraft Liability", subject to the provisions in **b.** below, mean the following:

   **a.** Liability for "bodily injury" or "property damage" arising out of the:

   **(1)** Ownership of such vehicle or craft by an "insured";

   **(2)** Maintenance, occupancy, operation, use, loading or unloading of such vehicle or craft by any person;

   **(3)** Entrustment of such vehicle or craft by an "insured" to any person;

   **(4)** Failure to supervise or negligent supervision of any person involving such vehicle or craft by an "insured"; or

   **(5)** Vicarious liability, whether or not imposed by law, for the actions of a child or minor involving such vehicle or craft.

   **b.** For the purpose of this definition:

   **(1)** Aircraft means any contrivance used or designed for flight except model or hobby aircraft not used or designed to carry people or cargo;

   **(2)** Hovercraft means a self-propelled motorized ground effect vehicle and includes, but is not limited to, flarecraft and air cushion vehicles;

   **(3)** Watercraft means a craft principally designed to be propelled on or in water by wind, engine power or electric motor; and

   **(4)** Motor vehicle means a "motor vehicle" as defined in **7.** below.

**2.** "Bodily injury" means bodily harm, sickness or disease, including required care, loss of services and death that results.

**3.** "Business" means:

   **a.** A trade, profession or occupation engaged in on a full-time, part-time or occasional basis; or

   **b.** Any other activity engaged in for money or other compensation, except the following:

   **(1)** One or more activities, not described in **(2)** through **(4)** below, for which no "insured" receives more than $2,000 in total compensation for the 12 months before the beginning of the policy period;

   **(2)** Volunteer activities for which no money is received other than payment for expenses incurred to perform the activity;

   **(3)** Providing home day care services for which no compensation is received, other than the mutual exchange of such services; or

   **(4)** The rendering of home day care services to a relative of an "insured".

**4.** "Employee" means an employee of an "insured", or an employee leased to an "insured" by a labor leasing firm under an agreement between an "insured" and the labor leasing firm, whose duties are other than those performed by a "residence employee".

**5.** "Insured" means:

   **a.** You and residents of your household who are:

   **(1)** Your relatives; or

   **(2)** Other persons under the age of 21 and in your care or the care of a resident of your household who is your relative;

   **b.** A student enrolled in school full-time, as defined by the school, who was a resident of your household before moving out to attend school, provided the student is under the age of:

   **(1)** 24 and your relative; or

SAMPLE

**(2)** 21 and in your care or the care of a resident of your household who is your relative; or

**c.** Under Section **II**:

**(1)** With respect to animals or watercraft to which this policy applies, any person or organization legally responsible for these animals or watercraft which are owned by you or any person described in **5.a.** or **b.** "Insured" does not mean a person or organization using or having custody of these animals or watercraft in the course of any "business" or without consent of the owner; or

**(2)** With respect to a "motor vehicle" to which this policy applies:

**(a)** Persons while engaged in your employ or that of any person described in **5.a.** or **b.;** or

**(b)** Other persons using the vehicle on an "insured location" with your consent.

Under both Sections **I** and **II,** when the word an immediately precedes the word "insured", the words an "insured" together mean one or more "insureds".

**6.** "Insured location" means:

**a.** The "residence premises";

**b.** The part of other premises, other structures and grounds used by you as a residence; and

**(1)** Which is shown in the Declarations; or

**(2)** Which is acquired by you during the policy period for your use as a residence;

**c.** Any premises used by you in connection with a premises described in **a.** and **b.** above;

**d.** Any part of a premises:

**(1)** Not owned by an "insured"; and

**(2)** Where an "insured" is temporarily residing;

**e.** Vacant land, other than farm land, owned by or rented to an "insured";

**f.** Land owned by or rented to an "insured" on which a one-, two-, three- or four-family dwelling is being built as a residence for an "insured";

**g.** Individual or family cemetery plots or burial vaults of an "insured"; or

**h.** Any part of a premises occasionally rented to an "insured" for other than "business" use.

**7.** "Motor vehicle" means:

**a.** A self-propelled land or amphibious vehicle; or

**b.** Any trailer or semitrailer which is being carried on, towed by or hitched for towing by a vehicle described in **a.** above.

**8.** "Occurrence" means an accident, including continuous or repeated exposure to substantially the same general harmful conditions, which results, during the policy period, in:

**a.** "Bodily injury"; or

**b.** "Property damage".

**9.** "Property damage" means physical injury to, destruction of, or loss of use of tangible property.

**10.** "Residence employee" means:

**a.** An employee of an "insured", or an employee leased to an "insured" by a labor leasing firm, under an agreement between an "insured" and the labor leasing firm, whose duties are related to the maintenance or use of the "residence premises", including household or domestic services; or

**b.** One who performs similar duties elsewhere not related to the "business" of an "insured".

A "residence employee" does not include a temporary employee who is furnished to an "insured" to substitute for a permanent "residence employee" on leave or to meet seasonal or short-term workload conditions.

**11.** "Residence premises" means:

**a.** The one-family dwelling where you reside;

**b.** The two-, three- or four-family dwelling where you reside in at least one of the family units; or

**c.** That part of any other building where you reside;

and which is shown as the "residence premises" in the Declarations.

"Residence premises" also includes other structures and grounds at that location.

 PP 00 03 05 11

SAMPLE

**SECTION I – PROPERTY COVERAGES**

**A. Coverage A – Dwelling**

1. We cover:

   a. The dwelling on the "residence premises" shown in the Declarations, including structures attached to the dwelling; and

   b. Materials and supplies located on or next to the "residence premises" used to construct, alter or repair the dwelling or other structures on the "residence premises".

2. We do not cover land, including land on which the dwelling is located.

**B. Coverage B – Other Structures**

1. We cover other structures on the "residence premises" set apart from the dwelling by clear space. This includes structures connected to the dwelling by only a fence, utility line, or similar connection.

2. We do not cover:

   a. Land, including land on which the other structures are located;

   b. Other structures rented or held for rental to any person not a tenant of the dwelling, unless used solely as a private garage;

   c. Other structures from which any "business" is conducted; or

   d. Other structures used to store "business" property. However, we do cover a structure that contains "business" property solely owned by an "insured" or a tenant of the dwelling, provided that "business" property does not include gaseous or liquid fuel, other than fuel in a permanently installed fuel tank of a vehicle or craft parked or stored in the structure.

3. The limit of liability for this coverage will not be more than 10% of the limit of liability that applies to Coverage **A**. Use of this coverage does not reduce the Coverage **A** limit of liability.

**C. Coverage C – Personal Property**

1. **Covered Property**

   We cover personal property owned or used by an "insured" while it is anywhere in the world. After a loss and at your request, we will cover personal property owned by:

   a. Others while the property is on the part of the "residence premises" occupied by an "insured"; or

   b. A guest or a "residence employee", while the property is in any residence occupied by an "insured".

2. **Limit For Property At Other Locations**

   a. **Other Residences**

   Our limit of liability for personal property usually located at an "insured's" residence, other than the "residence premises", is 10% of the limit of liability for Coverage **C**, or $1,000, whichever is greater. However, this limitation does not apply to personal property:

   (1) Moved from the "residence premises" because it is:

      (a) Being repaired, renovated or rebuilt; and

      (b) Not fit to live in or store property in; or

   (2) In a newly acquired principal residence for 30 days from the time you begin to move the property there.

   b. **Self-storage Facilities**

   Our limit of liability for personal property owned or used by an "insured" and located in a self-storage facility is 10% of the limit of liability for Coverage **C**, or $1,000, whichever is greater. However, this limitation does not apply to personal property:

   (1) Moved from the "residence premises" because it is:

      (a) Being repaired, renovated or rebuilt; and

      (b) Not fit to live in or store property in; or

   (2) Usually located in an "insured's" residence, other than the "residence premises".

SAMPLE

**3. Special Limits Of Liability**

The special limit for each category shown below is the total limit for each loss for all property in that category. These special limits do not increase the Coverage **C** limit of liability.

**a.** $200 on money, bank notes, bullion, gold other than goldware, silver other than silverware, platinum other than platinumware, coins, medals, scrip, stored value cards and smart cards.

**b.** $1,500 on securities, accounts, deeds, evidences of debt, letters of credit, notes other than bank notes, manuscripts, personal records, passports, tickets and stamps. This dollar limit applies to these categories regardless of the medium (such as paper or computer software) on which the material exists.

This limit includes the cost to research, replace or restore the information from the lost or damaged material.

**c.** $1,500 on watercraft of all types, including their trailers, furnishings, equipment and outboard engines or motors.

**d.** $1,500 on trailers or semitrailers not used with watercraft of all types.

**e.** $1,500 for loss by theft of jewelry, watches, furs, precious and semiprecious stones.

**f.** $2,500 for loss by theft of firearms and related equipment.

**g.** $2,500 for loss by theft of silverware, silver-plated ware, goldware, gold-plated ware, platinumware, platinum-plated ware and pewterware. This includes flatware, hollowware, tea sets, trays and trophies made of or including silver, gold or pewter.

**h.** $2,500 on property, on the "residence premises", used primarily for "business" purposes.

**i.** $1,500 on property, away from the "residence premises", used primarily for "business" purposes. However, this limit does not apply to antennas, tapes, wires, records, disks or other media that are:

**(1)** Used with electronic equipment that reproduces, receives or transmits audio, visual or data signals; and

**(2)** In or upon a "motor vehicle".

**j.** $1,500 on portable electronic equipment that:

**(1)** Reproduces, receives or transmits audio, visual or data signals;

**(2)** Is designed to be operated by more than one power source, one of which is a "motor vehicle's" electrical system; and

**(3)** Is in or upon a "motor vehicle".

**k.** $250 for antennas, tapes, wires, records, disks or other media that are:

**(1)** Used with electronic equipment that reproduces, receives or transmits audio, visual or data signals; and

**(2)** In or upon a "motor vehicle".

**4. Property Not Covered**

We do not cover:

**a.** Articles separately described and specifically insured, regardless of the limit for which they are insured, in this or other insurance;

**b.** Animals, birds or fish;

**c.** "Motor vehicles".

This includes a "motor vehicle's" equipment and parts. However, this Paragraph **4.c.** does not apply to:

**(1)** Portable electronic equipment that:

**(a)** Reproduces, receives or transmits audio, visual or data signals; and

**(b)** Is designed so that it may be operated from a power source other than a "motor vehicle's" electrical system.

**(2)** "Motor vehicles" not required to be registered for use on public roads or property which are:

**(a)** Used solely to service a residence; or

**(b)** Designed to assist the handicapped;

**d.** Aircraft, meaning any contrivance used or designed for flight, including any parts whether or not attached to the aircraft.

We do cover model or hobby aircraft not used or designed to carry people or cargo;

**e.** Hovercraft and parts. Hovercraft means a self-propelled motorized ground effect vehicle and includes, but is not limited to, flarecraft and air cushion vehicles;

**f.** Property of roomers, boarders and other tenants, except property of roomers and boarders related to an "insured";

SAMPLE

g. Property in an apartment regularly rented or held for rental to others by an "insured", except as provided in **E.10.** Landlord's Furnishings under Section **I** – Property Coverages;

h. Property rented or held for rental to others off the "residence premises";

i. "Business" data, including such data stored in:

   **(1)** Books of account, drawings or other paper records; or

   **(2)** Computers and related equipment.

   We do cover the cost of blank recording or storage media and of prerecorded computer programs available on the retail market;

j. Credit cards, electronic fund transfer cards or access devices used solely for deposit, withdrawal or transfer of funds except as provided in **E.6.** Credit Card, Electronic Fund Transfer Card Or Access Device, Forgery And Counterfeit Money under Section **I** – Property Coverages; or

k. Water or steam.

**D. Coverage D – Loss Of Use**

The limit of liability for Coverage **D** is the total limit for the coverages in **1.** Additional Living Expense, **2.** Fair Rental Value and **3.** Civil Authority Prohibits Use below.

**1. Additional Living Expense**

If a loss covered under Section **I** makes that part of the "residence premises" where you reside not fit to live in, we cover any necessary increase in living expenses incurred by you so that your household can maintain its normal standard of living.

Payment will be for the shortest time required to repair or replace the damage or, if you permanently relocate, the shortest time required for your household to settle elsewhere.

**2. Fair Rental Value**

If a loss covered under Section **I** makes that part of the "residence premises" rented to others or held for rental by you not fit to live in, we cover the fair rental value of such premises less any expenses that do not continue while it is not fit to live in.

Payment will be for the shortest time required to repair or replace such premises.

**3. Civil Authority Prohibits Use**

If a civil authority prohibits you from use of the "residence premises" as a result of direct damage to neighboring premises by a Peril Insured Against, we cover the loss as provided in **1.** Additional Living Expense and **2.** Fair Rental Value above for no more than two weeks.

**4. Loss Or Expense Not Covered**

We do not cover loss or expense due to cancellation of a lease or agreement.

The periods of time under **1.** Additional Living Expense, **2.** Fair Rental Value and **3.** Civil Authority Prohibits Use above are not limited by expiration of this policy.

**E. Additional Coverages**

**1. Debris Removal**

a. We will pay your reasonable expense for the removal of:

   **(1)** Debris of covered property if a Peril Insured Against that applies to the damaged property causes the loss; or

   **(2)** Ash, dust or particles from a volcanic eruption that has caused direct loss to a building or property contained in a building.

   This expense is included in the limit of liability that applies to the damaged property. If the amount to be paid for the actual damage to the property plus the debris removal expense is more than the limit of liability for the damaged property, an additional 5% of that limit is available for such expense.

b. We will also pay your reasonable expense, up to $1,000, for the removal from the "residence premises" of:

   **(1)** Your trees felled by the peril of Windstorm or Hail or Weight of Ice, Snow or Sleet; or

   **(2)** A neighbor's trees felled by a Peril Insured Against under Coverage **C;**

   provided the trees:

   **(3)** Damage a covered structure; or

   **(4)** Do not damage a covered structure, but:

      **(a)** Block a driveway on the "residence premises" which prevents a "motor vehicle", that is registered for use on public roads or property, from entering or leaving the "residence premises"; or

SAMPLE

**(b)** Block a ramp or other fixture designed to assist a handicapped person to enter or leave the dwelling building.

The $1,000 limit is the most we will pay in any one loss, regardless of the number of fallen trees. No more than $500 of this limit will be paid for the removal of any one tree.

This coverage is additional insurance.

**2. Reasonable Repairs**

**a.** We will pay the reasonable cost incurred by you for the necessary measures taken solely to protect covered property that is damaged by a Peril Insured Against from further damage.

**b.** If the measures taken involve repair to other damaged property, we will only pay if that property is covered under this policy and the damage is caused by a Peril Insured Against. This coverage does not:

**(1)** Increase the limit of liability that applies to the covered property; or

**(2)** Relieve you of your duties, in case of a loss to covered property, described in **C.4.** under Section I – Conditions.

**3. Trees, Shrubs And Other Plants**

We cover trees, shrubs, plants or lawns, on the "residence premises", for loss caused by the following Perils Insured Against:

**a.** Fire or Lightning;

**b.** Explosion;

**c.** Riot or Civil Commotion;

**d.** Aircraft;

**e.** Vehicles not owned or operated by a resident of the "residence premises";

**f.** Vandalism or Malicious Mischief; or

**g.** Theft.

We will pay up to 5% of the limit of liability that applies to the dwelling for all trees, shrubs, plants or lawns. No more than $500 of this limit will be paid for any one tree, shrub or plant. We do not cover property grown for "business" purposes.

This coverage is additional insurance.

**4. Fire Department Service Charge**

We will pay up to $500 for your liability assumed by contract or agreement for fire department charges incurred when the fire department is called to save or protect covered property from a Peril Insured Against. We do not cover fire department service charges if the property is located within the limits of the city, municipality or protection district furnishing the fire department response.

This coverage is additional insurance. No deductible applies to this coverage.

**5. Property Removed**

We insure covered property against direct loss from any cause while being removed from a premises endangered by a Peril Insured Against and for no more than 30 days while removed.

This coverage does not change the limit of liability that applies to the property being removed.

**6. Credit Card, Electronic Fund Transfer Card Or Access Device, Forgery And Counterfeit Money**

**a.** We will pay up to $500 for:

**(1)** The legal obligation of an "insured" to pay because of the theft or unauthorized use of credit cards issued to or registered in an "insured's" name;

**(2)** Loss resulting from theft or unauthorized use of an electronic fund transfer card or access device used for deposit, withdrawal or transfer of funds, issued to or registered in an "insured's" name;

**(3)** Loss to an "insured" caused by forgery or alteration of any check or negotiable instrument; and

**(4)** Loss to an "insured" through acceptance in good faith of counterfeit United States or Canadian paper currency.

All loss resulting from a series of acts committed by any one person or in which any one person is concerned or implicated is considered to be one loss.

SAMPLE

This coverage is additional insurance. No deductible applies to this coverage.

**b.** We do not cover:

**(1)** Use of a credit card, electronic fund transfer card or access device:

**(a)** By a resident of your household;

**(b)** By a person who has been entrusted with either type of card or access device; or

**(c)** If an "insured" has not complied with all terms and conditions under which the cards are issued or the devices accessed; or

**(2)** Loss arising out of "business" use or dishonesty of an "insured".

**c.** If the coverage in **a.** above applies, the following defense provisions also apply:

**(1)** We may investigate and settle any claim or suit that we decide is appropriate. Our duty to defend a claim or suit ends when the amount we pay for the loss equals our limit of liability.

**(2)** If a suit is brought against an "insured" for liability under **a.(1)** or **(2)** above, we will provide a defense at our expense by counsel of our choice.

**(3)** We have the option to defend at our expense an "insured" or an "insured's" bank against any suit for the enforcement of payment under **a.(3)** above.

**7. Loss Assessment**

**a.** We will pay up to $1,000 for your share of loss assessment charged during the policy period against you, as owner or tenant of the "residence premises", by a corporation or association of property owners. The assessment must be made as a result of direct loss to property, owned by all members collectively, of the type that would be covered by this policy if owned by you, caused by a Peril Insured Against under Coverage **A**, other than:

**(1)** Earthquake; or

**(2)** Land shock waves or tremors before, during or after a volcanic eruption.

The limit of $1,000 is the most we will pay with respect to any one loss, regardless of the number of assessments. We will only apply one deductible, per unit, to the total amount of any one loss to the property described above, regardless of the number of assessments.

**b.** We do not cover assessments charged against you or a corporation or association of property owners by any governmental body.

**c.** Paragraph **Q.** Policy Period under Section **I** – Conditions does not apply to this coverage.

This coverage is additional insurance.

**8. Collapse**

**a.** The coverage provided under this Additional Coverage – Collapse applies only to an abrupt collapse.

**b.** For the purpose of this Additional Coverage – Collapse, abrupt collapse means an abrupt falling down or caving in of a building or any part of a building with the result that the building or part of the building cannot be occupied for its intended purpose.

**c.** This Additional Coverage – Collapse does not apply to:

**(1)** A building or any part of a building that is in danger of falling down or caving in;

**(2)** A part of a building that is standing, even if it has separated from another part of the building; or

**(3)** A building or any part of a building that is standing, even if it shows evidence of cracking, bulging, sagging, bending, leaning, settling, shrinkage or expansion.

**d.** We insure for direct physical loss to covered property involving abrupt collapse of a building or any part of a building if such collapse was caused by one or more of the following:

**(1)** The Perils Insured Against named under Coverage **C**;

**(2)** Decay, of a building or any part of a building, that is hidden from view, unless the presence of such decay is known to an "insured" prior to collapse;

**(3)** Insect or vermin damage, to a building or any part of a building, that is hidden from view, unless the presence of such damage is known to an "insured" prior to collapse;

**(4)** Weight of contents, equipment, animals or people;

**(5)** Weight of rain which collects on a roof; or

SAMPLE

**(6)** Use of defective material or methods in construction, remodeling or renovation if the collapse occurs during the course of the construction, remodeling or renovation.

**e.** Loss to an awning, fence, patio, deck, pavement, swimming pool, underground pipe, flue, drain, cesspool, septic tank, foundation, retaining wall, bulkhead, pier, wharf or dock is not included under **d.(2)** through **(6)** above, unless the loss is a direct result of the collapse of a building or any part of a building.

**f.** This coverage does not increase the limit of liability that applies to the damaged covered property.

**9. Glass Or Safety Glazing Material**

**a.** We cover:

**(1)** The breakage of glass or safety glazing material which is part of a covered building, storm door or storm window;

**(2)** The breakage of glass or safety glazing material which is part of a covered building, storm door or storm window when caused directly by earth movement; and

**(3)** The direct physical loss to covered property caused solely by the pieces, fragments or splinters of broken glass or safety glazing material which is part of a building, storm door or storm window.

**b.** This coverage does not include loss:

**(1)** To covered property which results because the glass or safety glazing material has been broken, except as provided in **a.(3)** above; or

**(2)** On the "residence premises" if the dwelling has been vacant for more than 60 consecutive days immediately before the loss, except when the breakage results directly from earth movement as provided in **a.(2)** above. A dwelling being constructed is not considered vacant.

**c.** This coverage does not increase the limit of liability that applies to the damaged property.

**10. Landlord's Furnishings**

We will pay up to $2,500 for your appliances, carpeting and other household furnishings, in each apartment on the "residence premises" regularly rented or held for rental to others by an "insured", for loss caused by a Peril Insured Against in Coverage **C**, other than Theft.

This limit is the most we will pay in any one loss regardless of the number of appliances, carpeting or other household furnishings involved in the loss.

This coverage does not increase the limit of liability applying to the damaged property.

**11. Ordinance Or Law**

**a.** You may use up to 10% of the limit of liability that applies to Coverage **A** for the increased costs you incur due to the enforcement of any ordinance or law which requires or regulates:

**(1)** The construction, demolition, remodeling, renovation or repair of that part of a covered building or other structure damaged by a Peril Insured Against;

**(2)** The demolition and reconstruction of the undamaged part of a covered building or other structure, when that building or other structure must be totally demolished because of damage by a Peril Insured Against to another part of that covered building or other structure; or

**(3)** The remodeling, removal or replacement of the portion of the undamaged part of a covered building or other structure necessary to complete the remodeling, repair or replacement of that part of the covered building or other structure damaged by a Peril Insured Against.

**b.** You may use all or part of this ordinance or law coverage to pay for the increased costs you incur to remove debris resulting from the construction, demolition, remodeling, renovation, repair or replacement of property as stated in **a.** above.

**c.** We do not cover:

**(1)** The loss in value to any covered building or other structure due to the requirements of any ordinance or law; or

**(2)** The costs to comply with any ordinance or law which requires any "insured" or others to test for, monitor, clean up, remove, contain, treat, detoxify or neutralize, or in any way respond to, or assess the effects of, pollutants in or on any covered building or other structure.

SAMPLE

Pollutants means any solid, liquid, gaseous or thermal irritant or contaminant, including smoke, vapor, soot, fumes, acids, alkalis, chemicals and waste. Waste includes materials to be recycled, reconditioned or reclaimed.

This coverage is additional insurance.

**12. Grave Markers**

We will pay up to $5,000 for grave markers, including mausoleums, on or away from the "residence premises" for loss caused by a Peril Insured Against under Coverage **C.**

This coverage does not increase the limits of liability that apply to the damaged covered property.

## SECTION I – PERILS INSURED AGAINST

### A. Coverage A – Dwelling And Coverage B – Other Structures

1. We insure against direct physical loss to property described in Coverages **A** and **B.**

2. We do not insure, however, for loss:

   **a.** Excluded under Section **I** – Exclusions;

   **b.** Involving collapse, including any of the following conditions of property or any part of the property:

      **(1)** An abrupt falling down or caving in;

      **(2)** Loss of structural integrity, including separation of parts of the property or property in danger of falling down or caving in; or

      **(3)** Any cracking, bulging, sagging, bending, leaning, settling, shrinkage or expansion as such condition relates to **(1)** or **(2)** above;

      except as provided in **E.8.** Collapse under Section **I** – Property Coverages; or

   **c.** Caused by:

      **(1)** Freezing of a plumbing, heating, air conditioning or automatic fire protective sprinkler system or of a household appliance, or by discharge, leakage or overflow from within the system or appliance caused by freezing. This provision does not apply if you have used reasonable care to:

         **(a)** Maintain heat in the building; or

         **(b)** Shut off the water supply and drain all systems and appliances of water.

However, if the building is protected by an automatic fire protective sprinkler system, you must use reasonable care to continue the water supply and maintain heat in the building for coverage to apply.

For purposes of this provision, a plumbing system or household appliance does not include a sump, sump pump or related equipment or a roof drain, gutter, downspout or similar fixtures or equipment;

**(2)** Freezing, thawing, pressure or weight of water or ice, whether driven by wind or not, to a:

   **(a)** Fence, pavement, patio or swimming pool;

   **(b)** Footing, foundation, bulkhead, wall, or any other structure or device that supports all or part of a building, or other structure;

   **(c)** Retaining wall or bulkhead that does not support all or part of a building or other structure; or

   **(d)** Pier, wharf or dock;

**(3)** Theft in or to a dwelling under construction, or of materials and supplies for use in the construction until the dwelling is finished and occupied;

**(4)** Vandalism and malicious mischief, and any ensuing loss caused by any intentional and wrongful act committed in the course of the vandalism or malicious mischief, if the dwelling has been vacant for more than 60 consecutive days immediately before the loss. A dwelling being constructed is not considered vacant;

**(5)** Mold, fungus or wet rot. However, we do insure for loss caused by mold, fungus or wet rot that is hidden within the walls or ceilings or beneath the floors or above the ceilings of a structure if such loss results from the accidental discharge or overflow of water or steam from within:

   **(a)** A plumbing, heating, air conditioning or automatic fire protective sprinkler system, or a household appliance, on the "residence premises"; or

   **(b)** A storm drain, or water, steam or sewer pipes, off the "residence premises".

SAMPLE

For purposes of this provision, a plumbing system or household appliance does not include a sump, sump pump or related equipment or a roof drain, gutter, downspout or similar fixtures or equipment; or

**(6)** Any of the following:

**(a)** Wear and tear, marring, deterioration;

**(b)** Mechanical breakdown, latent defect, inherent vice or any quality in property that causes it to damage or destroy itself;

**(c)** Smog, rust or other corrosion, or dry rot;

**(d)** Smoke from agricultural smudging or industrial operations;

**(e)** Discharge, dispersal, seepage, migration, release or escape of pollutants unless the discharge, dispersal, seepage, migration, release or escape is itself caused by a Peril Insured Against named under Coverage **C**.

Pollutants means any solid, liquid, gaseous or thermal irritant or contaminant, including smoke, vapor, soot, fumes, acids, alkalis, chemicals and waste. Waste includes materials to be recycled, reconditioned or reclaimed;

**(f)** Settling, shrinking, bulging or expansion, including resultant cracking, of bulkheads, pavements, patios, footings, foundations, walls, floors, roofs or ceilings;

**(g)** Birds, rodents or insects;

**(h)** Nesting or infestation, or discharge or release of waste products or secretions, by any animals; or

**(i)** Animals owned or kept by an "insured".

**Exception To c.(6)**

Unless the loss is otherwise excluded, we cover loss to property covered under Coverage **A** or **B** resulting from an accidental discharge or overflow of water or steam from within a:

**(i)** Storm drain, or water, steam or sewer pipe, off the "residence premises"; or

**(ii)** Plumbing, heating, air conditioning or automatic fire protective sprinkler system or household appliance on the "residence premises". This includes the cost to tear out and replace any part of a building, or other structure, on the "residence premises", but only when necessary to repair the system or appliance. However, such tear out and replacement coverage only applies to other structures if the water or steam causes actual damage to a building on the "residence premises".

We do not cover loss to the system or appliance from which this water or steam escaped.

For purposes of this provision, a plumbing system or household appliance does not include a sump, sump pump or related equipment or a roof drain, gutter, downspout or similar fixtures or equipment.

Section I – Exclusion **A.3.** Water, Paragraphs **a.** and **c.** that apply to surface water and water below the surface of the ground do not apply to loss by water covered under **c.(5)** and **(6)** above.

Under **2.b.** and **c.** above, any ensuing loss to property described in Coverages **A** and **B** not precluded by any other provision in this policy is covered.

**B. Coverage C – Personal Property**

We insure for direct physical loss to the property described in Coverage **C** caused by any of the following perils unless the loss is excluded in Section I – Exclusions.

**1. Fire Or Lightning**

**2. Windstorm Or Hail**

This peril includes loss to watercraft of all types and their trailers, furnishings, equipment, and outboard engines or motors, only while inside a fully enclosed building.

This peril does not include loss to the property contained in a building caused by rain, snow, sleet, sand or dust unless the direct force of wind or hail damages the building causing an opening in a roof or wall and the rain, snow, sleet, sand or dust enters through this opening.

 PP 00 03 05 11

3. **Explosion**

4. **Riot Or Civil Commotion**

5. **Aircraft**

   This peril includes self-propelled missiles and spacecraft.

6. **Vehicles**

7. **Smoke**

   This peril means sudden and accidental damage from smoke, including the emission or puffback of smoke, soot, fumes or vapors from a boiler, furnace or related equipment.

   This peril does not include loss caused by smoke from agricultural smudging or industrial operations.

8. **Vandalism Or Malicious Mischief**

9. **Theft**

   a. This peril includes attempted theft and loss of property from a known place when it is likely that the property has been stolen.

   b. This peril does not include loss caused by theft:

      (1) Committed by an "insured";

      (2) In or to a dwelling under construction, or of materials and supplies for use in the construction until the dwelling is finished and occupied;

      (3) From that part of a "residence premises" rented by an "insured" to someone other than another "insured"; or

      (4) That occurs off the "residence premises" of:

         (a) Trailers, semitrailers and campers;

         (b) Watercraft of all types, and their furnishings, equipment and outboard engines or motors; or

         (c) Property while at any other residence owned by, rented to, or occupied by an "insured", except while an "insured" is temporarily living there. Property of an "insured" who is a student is covered while at the residence the student occupies to attend school as long as the student has been there at any time during the 90 days immediately before the loss.

10. **Falling Objects**

    This peril does not include loss to property contained in a building unless the roof or an outside wall of the building is first damaged by a falling object. Damage to the falling object itself is not included.

11. **Weight Of Ice, Snow Or Sleet**

    This peril means weight of ice, snow or sleet which causes damage to property contained in a building.

12. **Accidental Discharge Or Overflow Of Water Or Steam**

    a. This peril means accidental discharge or overflow of water or steam from within a plumbing, heating, air conditioning or automatic fire protective sprinkler system or from within a household appliance.

    b. This peril does not include loss:

       (1) To the system or appliance from which the water or steam escaped;

       (2) Caused by or resulting from freezing except as provided in Peril Insured Against **14.** Freezing;

       (3) On the "residence premises" caused by accidental discharge or overflow which occurs off the "residence premises"; or

       (4) Caused by mold, fungus or wet rot unless hidden within the walls or ceilings or beneath the floors or above the ceilings of a structure.

    c. In this peril, a plumbing system or household appliance does not include a sump, sump pump or related equipment or a roof drain, gutter, downspout or similar fixtures or equipment.

    d. Section I – Exclusion **A.3.** Water, Paragraphs **a.** and **c.** that apply to surface water and water below the surface of the ground do not apply to loss by water covered under this peril.

13. **Sudden And Accidental Tearing Apart, Cracking, Burning Or Bulging**

    This peril means sudden and accidental tearing apart, cracking, burning or bulging of a steam or hot water heating system, an air conditioning or automatic fire protective sprinkler system, or an appliance for heating water.

    We do not cover loss caused by or resulting from freezing under this peril.

SAMPLE

**14. Freezing**

**a.** This peril means freezing of a plumbing, heating, air conditioning or automatic fire protective sprinkler system or of a household appliance, but only if you have used reasonable care to:

**(1)** Maintain heat in the building; or

**(2)** Shut off the water supply and drain all systems and appliances of water.

However, if the building is protected by an automatic fire protective sprinkler system, you must use reasonable care to continue the water supply and maintain heat in the building for coverage to apply.

**b.** In this peril, a plumbing system or household appliance does not include a sump, sump pump or related equipment or a roof drain, gutter, downspout or similar fixtures or equipment.

**15. Sudden And Accidental Damage From Artificially Generated Electrical Current**

This peril does not include loss to tubes, transistors, electronic components or circuitry that is a part of appliances, fixtures, computers, home entertainment units or other types of electronic apparatus.

**16. Volcanic Eruption**

This peril does not include loss caused by earthquake, land shock waves or tremors.

**SECTION I – EXCLUSIONS**

**A.** We do not insure for loss caused directly or indirectly by any of the following. Such loss is excluded regardless of any other cause or event contributing concurrently or in any sequence to the loss. These exclusions apply whether or not the loss event results in widespread damage or affects a substantial area.

**1. Ordinance Or Law**

Ordinance Or Law means any ordinance or law:

**a.** Requiring or regulating the construction, demolition, remodeling, renovation or repair of property, including removal of any resulting debris. This Exclusion **A.1.a.** does not apply to the amount of coverage that may be provided for in **E.11.** Ordinance Or Law under Section I – Property Coverages;

**b.** The requirements of which result in a loss in value to property; or

**c.** Requiring any "insured" or others to test for, monitor, clean up, remove, contain, treat, detoxify or neutralize, or in any way respond to, or assess the effects of, pollutants.

Pollutants means any solid, liquid, gaseous or thermal irritant or contaminant, including smoke, vapor, soot, fumes, acids, alkalis, chemicals and waste. Waste includes materials to be recycled, reconditioned or reclaimed.

This Exclusion **A.1.** applies whether or not the property has been physically damaged.

**2. Earth Movement**

Earth Movement means:

**a.** Earthquake, including land shock waves or tremors before, during or after a volcanic eruption;

**b.** Landslide, mudslide or mudflow;

**c.** Subsidence or sinkhole; or

**d.** Any other earth movement including earth sinking, rising or shifting.

This Exclusion **A.2.** applies regardless of whether any of the above, in **A.2.a.** through **A.2.d.**, is caused by an act of nature or is otherwise caused.

However, direct loss by fire, explosion or theft resulting from any of the above, in **A.2.a.** through **A.2.d.**, is covered.

**3. Water**

This means:

**a.** Flood, surface water, waves, including tidal wave and tsunami, tides, tidal water, overflow of any body of water, or spray from any of these, all whether or not driven by wind, including storm surge;

**b.** Water which:

**(1)** Backs up through sewers or drains; or

**(2)** Overflows or is otherwise discharged from a sump, sump pump or related equipment;

**c.** Water below the surface of the ground, including water which exerts pressure on, or seeps, leaks or flows through a building, sidewalk, driveway, patio, foundation, swimming pool or other structure; or

**d.** Waterborne material carried or otherwise moved by any of the water referred to in **A.3.a.** through **A.3.c.** of this exclusion.

SAMPLE

This Exclusion **A.3.** applies regardless of whether any of the above, in **A.3.a.** through **A.3.d.**, is caused by an act of nature or is otherwise caused.

This Exclusion **A.3.** applies to, but is not limited to, escape, overflow or discharge, for any reason, of water or waterborne material from a dam, levee, seawall or any other boundary or containment system.

However, direct loss by fire, explosion or theft resulting from any of the above, in **A.3.a.** through **A.3.d.**, is covered.

**4. Power Failure**

Power Failure means the failure of power or other utility service if the failure takes place off the "residence premises". But if the failure results in a loss, from a Peril Insured Against on the "residence premises", we will pay for the loss caused by that peril.

**5. Neglect**

Neglect means neglect of an "insured" to use all reasonable means to save and preserve property at and after the time of a loss.

**6. War**

War includes the following and any consequence of any of the following:

**a.** Undeclared war, civil war, insurrection, rebellion or revolution;

**b.** Warlike act by a military force or military personnel; or

**c.** Destruction, seizure or use for a military purpose.

Discharge of a nuclear weapon will be deemed a warlike act even if accidental.

**7. Nuclear Hazard**

This Exclusion **A.7.** pertains to Nuclear Hazard to the extent set forth in **N.** Nuclear Hazard Clause under Section I – Conditions.

**8. Intentional Loss**

Intentional Loss means any loss arising out of any act an "insured" commits or conspires to commit with the intent to cause a loss.

In the event of such loss, no "insured" is entitled to coverage, even "insureds" who did not commit or conspire to commit the act causing the loss.

**9. Governmental Action**

Governmental Action means the destruction, confiscation or seizure of property described in Coverage **A**, **B** or **C** by order of any governmental or public authority.

This exclusion does not apply to such acts ordered by any governmental or public authority that are taken at the time of a fire to prevent its spread, if the loss caused by fire would be covered under this policy.

**B.** We do not insure for loss to property described in Coverages **A** and **B** caused by any of the following. However, any ensuing loss to property described in Coverages **A** and **B** not precluded by any other provision in this policy is covered.

**1.** Weather conditions. However, this exclusion only applies if weather conditions contribute in any way with a cause or event excluded in **A.** above to produce the loss.

**2.** Acts or decisions, including the failure to act or decide, of any person, group, organization or governmental body.

**3.** Faulty, inadequate or defective:

**a.** Planning, zoning, development, surveying, siting;

**b.** Design, specifications, workmanship, repair, construction, renovation, remodeling, grading, compaction;

**c.** Materials used in repair, construction, renovation or remodeling; or

**d.** Maintenance;

of part or all of any property whether on or off the "residence premises".

**SECTION I – CONDITIONS**

**A. Insurable Interest And Limit Of Liability**

Even if more than one person has an insurable interest in the property covered, we will not be liable in any one loss:

**1.** To an "insured" for more than the amount of such "insured's" interest at the time of loss; or

**2.** For more than the applicable limit of liability.

**B. Deductible**

Unless otherwise noted in this policy, the following deductible provision applies:

With respect to any one loss:

**1.** Subject to the applicable limit of liability, we will pay only that part of the total of all loss payable that exceeds the deductible amount shown in the Declarations.

**2.** If two or more deductibles under this policy apply to the loss, only the highest deductible amount will apply.

SAMPLE

**C. Duties After Loss**

In case of a loss to covered property, we have no duty to provide coverage under this policy if the failure to comply with the following duties is prejudicial to us. These duties must be performed either by you, an "insured" seeking coverage, or a representative of either:

1. Give prompt notice to us or our agent;

2. Notify the police in case of loss by theft;

3. Notify the credit card or electronic fund transfer card or access device company in case of loss as provided for in **E.6.** Credit Card, Electronic Fund Transfer Card Or Access Device, Forgery And Counterfeit Money under Section I – Property Coverages;

4. Protect the property from further damage. If repairs to the property are required, you must:

   a. Make reasonable and necessary repairs to protect the property; and

   b. Keep an accurate record of repair expenses;

5. Cooperate with us in the investigation of a claim;

6. Prepare an inventory of damaged personal property showing the quantity, description, actual cash value and amount of loss. Attach all bills, receipts and related documents that justify the figures in the inventory;

7. As often as we reasonably require:

   a. Show the damaged property;

   b. Provide us with records and documents we request and permit us to make copies; and

   c. Submit to examination under oath, while not in the presence of another "insured", and sign the same;

8. Send to us, within 60 days after our request, your signed, sworn proof of loss which sets forth, to the best of your knowledge and belief:

   a. The time and cause of loss;

   b. The interests of all "insureds" and all others in the property involved and all liens on the property;

   c. Other insurance which may cover the loss;

   d. Changes in title or occupancy of the property during the term of the policy;

   e. Specifications of damaged buildings and detailed repair estimates;

   f. The inventory of damaged personal property described in **6.** above;

   g. Receipts for additional living expenses incurred and records that support the fair rental value loss; and

   h. Evidence or affidavit that supports a claim under **E.6.** Credit Card, Electronic Fund Transfer Card Or Access Device, Forgery And Counterfeit Money under Section I – Property Coverages, stating the amount and cause of loss.

**D. Loss Settlement**

In this Condition **D.**, the terms "cost to repair or replace" and "replacement cost" do not include the increased costs incurred to comply with the enforcement of any ordinance or law, except to the extent that coverage for these increased costs is provided in **E.11.** Ordinance Or Law under Section I – Property Coverages. Covered property losses are settled as follows:

1. Property of the following types:

   a. Personal property;

   b. Awnings, carpeting, household appliances, outdoor antennas and outdoor equipment, whether or not attached to buildings;

   c. Structures that are not buildings; and

   d. Grave markers, including mausoleums;

   at actual cash value at the time of loss but not more than the amount required to repair or replace.

2. Buildings covered under Coverage **A** or **B** at replacement cost without deduction for depreciation, subject to the following:

   a. If, at the time of loss, the amount of insurance in this policy on the damaged building is 80% or more of the full replacement cost of the building immediately before the loss, we will pay the cost to repair or replace, without deduction for depreciation, but not more than the least of the following amounts:

      (1) The limit of liability under this policy that applies to the building;

      (2) The replacement cost of that part of the building damaged with material of like kind and quality and for like use; or

      (3) The necessary amount actually spent to repair or replace the damaged building.

      If the building is rebuilt at a new premises, the cost described in **(2)** above is limited to the cost which would have been incurred if the building had been built at the original premises.

SAMPLE

**b.** If, at the time of loss, the amount of insurance in this policy on the damaged building is less than 80% of the full replacement cost of the building immediately before the loss, we will pay the greater of the following amounts, but not more than the limit of liability under this policy that applies to the building:

**(1)** The actual cash value of that part of the building damaged; or

**(2)** That proportion of the cost to repair or replace, without deduction for depreciation, that part of the building damaged, which the total amount of insurance in this policy on the damaged building bears to 80% of the replacement cost of the building.

**c.** To determine the amount of insurance required to equal 80% of the full replacement cost of the building immediately before the loss, do not include the value of:

**(1)** Excavations, footings, foundations, piers, or any other structures or devices that support all or part of the building, which are below the undersurface of the lowest basement floor;

**(2)** Those supports described in **(1)** above which are below the surface of the ground inside the foundation walls, if there is no basement; and

**(3)** Underground flues, pipes, wiring and drains.

**d.** We will pay no more than the actual cash value of the damage until actual repair or replacement is complete. Once actual repair or replacement is complete, we will settle the loss as noted in **2.a.** and **b.** above.

However, if the cost to repair or replace the damage is both:

**(1)** Less than 5% of the amount of insurance in this policy on the building; and

**(2)** Less than $2,500;

we will settle the loss as noted in **2.a.** and **b.** above whether or not actual repair or replacement is complete.

**e.** You may disregard the replacement cost loss settlement provisions and make claim under this policy for loss to buildings on an actual cash value basis. You may then make claim for any additional liability according to the provisions of this Condition **D.** Loss Settlement, provided you notify us, within 180 days after the date of loss, of your intent to repair or replace the damaged building.

**E. Loss To A Pair Or Set**

In case of loss to a pair or set we may elect to:

**1.** Repair or replace any part to restore the pair or set to its value before the loss; or

**2.** Pay the difference between actual cash value of the property before and after the loss.

**F. Appraisal**

If you and we fail to agree on the amount of loss, either may demand an appraisal of the loss. In this event, each party will choose a competent and impartial appraiser within 20 days after receiving a written request from the other. The two appraisers will choose an umpire. If they cannot agree upon an umpire within 15 days, you or we may request that the choice be made by a judge of a court of record in the state where the "residence premises" is located. The appraisers will separately set the amount of loss. If the appraisers submit a written report of an agreement to us, the amount agreed upon will be the amount of loss. If they fail to agree, they will submit their differences to the umpire. A decision agreed to by any two will set the amount of loss.

Each party will:

**1.** Pay its own appraiser; and

**2.** Bear the other expenses of the appraisal and umpire equally.

**G. Other Insurance And Service Agreement**

If a loss covered by this policy is also covered by:

**1.** Other insurance, we will pay only the proportion of the loss that the limit of liability that applies under this policy bears to the total amount of insurance covering the loss; or

**2.** A service agreement, this insurance is excess over any amounts payable under any such agreement. Service agreement means a service plan, property restoration plan, home warranty or other similar service warranty agreement, even if it is characterized as insurance.

SAMPLE

**H. Suit Against Us**

No action can be brought against us unless there has been full compliance with all of the terms under Section I of this policy and the action is started within two years after the date of loss.

**I. Our Option**

If we give you written notice within 30 days after we receive your signed, sworn proof of loss, we may repair or replace any part of the damaged property with material or property of like kind and quality.

**J. Loss Payment**

We will adjust all losses with you. We will pay you unless some other person is named in the policy or is legally entitled to receive payment. Loss will be payable 60 days after we receive your proof of loss and:

1. Reach an agreement with you;
2. There is an entry of a final judgment; or
3. There is a filing of an appraisal award with us.

**K. Abandonment Of Property**

We need not accept any property abandoned by an "insured".

**L. Mortgage Clause**

1. If a mortgagee is named in this policy, any loss payable under Coverage **A** or **B** will be paid to the mortgagee and you, as interests appear. If more than one mortgagee is named, the order of payment will be the same as the order of precedence of the mortgages.

2. If we deny your claim, that denial will not apply to a valid claim of the mortgagee, if the mortgagee:

   a. Notifies us of any change in ownership, occupancy or substantial change in risk of which the mortgagee is aware;

   b. Pays any premium due under this policy on demand if you have neglected to pay the premium; and

   c. Submits a signed, sworn statement of loss within 60 days after receiving notice from us of your failure to do so. Paragraphs **F.** Appraisal, **H.** Suit Against Us and **J.** Loss Payment under Section I – Conditions also apply to the mortgagee.

3. If we decide to cancel or not to renew this policy, the mortgagee will be notified at least 10 days before the date cancellation or nonrenewal takes effect.

4. If we pay the mortgagee for any loss and deny payment to you:

   a. We are subrogated to all the rights of the mortgagee granted under the mortgage on the property; or

   b. At our option, we may pay to the mortgagee the whole principal on the mortgage plus any accrued interest. In this event, we will receive a full assignment and transfer of the mortgage and all securities held as collateral to the mortgage debt.

5. Subrogation will not impair the right of the mortgagee to recover the full amount of the mortgagee's claim.

**M. No Benefit To Bailee**

We will not recognize any assignment or grant any coverage that benefits a person or organization holding, storing or moving property for a fee regardless of any other provision of this policy.

**N. Nuclear Hazard Clause**

1. "Nuclear Hazard" means any nuclear reaction, radiation, or radioactive contamination, all whether controlled or uncontrolled or however caused, or any consequence of any of these.

2. Loss caused by the nuclear hazard will not be considered loss caused by fire, explosion, or smoke, whether these perils are specifically named in or otherwise included within the Perils Insured Against.

3. This policy does not apply under Section I to loss caused directly or indirectly by nuclear hazard, except that direct loss by fire resulting from the nuclear hazard is covered.

**O. Recovered Property**

If you or we recover any property for which we have made payment under this policy, you or we will notify the other of the recovery. At your option, the property will be returned to or retained by you or it will become our property. If the recovered property is returned to or retained by you, the loss payment will be adjusted based on the amount you received for the recovered property.

**P. Volcanic Eruption Period**

One or more volcanic eruptions that occur within a 72-hour period will be considered as one volcanic eruption.

**Q. Policy Period**

This policy applies only to loss which occurs during the policy period.

 PP 00 03 05 11

SAMPLE

**R. Concealment Or Fraud**

We provide coverage to no "insureds" under this policy if, whether before or after a loss, an "insured" has:

1. Intentionally concealed or misrepresented any material fact or circumstance;

2. Engaged in fraudulent conduct; or

3. Made false statements;

relating to this insurance.

**S. Loss Payable Clause**

If the Declarations shows a loss payee for certain listed insured personal property, the definition of "insured" is changed to include that loss payee with respect to that property.

If we decide to cancel or not renew this policy, that loss payee will be notified in writing.

**SECTION II – LIABILITY COVERAGES**

**A. Coverage E – Personal Liability**

If a claim is made or a suit is brought against an "insured" for damages because of "bodily injury" or "property damage" caused by an "occurrence" to which this coverage applies, we will:

1. Pay up to our limit of liability for the damages for which an "insured" is legally liable. Damages include prejudgment interest awarded against an "insured"; and

2. Provide a defense at our expense by counsel of our choice, even if the suit is groundless, false or fraudulent. We may investigate and settle any claim or suit that we decide is appropriate. Our duty to settle or defend ends when our limit of liability for the "occurrence" has been exhausted by payment of a judgment or settlement.

**B. Coverage F – Medical Payments To Others**

We will pay the necessary medical expenses that are incurred or medically ascertained within three years from the date of an accident causing "bodily injury". Medical expenses means reasonable charges for medical, surgical, x-ray, dental, ambulance, hospital, professional nursing, prosthetic devices and funeral services. This coverage does not apply to you or regular residents of your household except "residence employees". As to others, this coverage applies only:

1. To a person on the "insured location" with the permission of an "insured"; or

2. To a person off the "insured location", if the "bodily injury":

a. Arises out of a condition on the "insured location" or the ways immediately adjoining;

b. Is caused by the activities of an "insured";

c. Is caused by a "residence employee" in the course of the "residence employee's" employment by an "insured"; or

d. Is caused by an animal owned by or in the care of an "insured".

**SECTION II – EXCLUSIONS**

**A. "Motor Vehicle Liability"**

1. Coverages **E** and **F** do not apply to any "motor vehicle liability" if, at the time and place of an "occurrence", the involved "motor vehicle":

a. Is registered for use on public roads or property;

b. Is not registered for use on public roads or property, but such registration is required by a law, or regulation issued by a government agency, for it to be used at the place of the "occurrence"; or

c. Is being:

(1) Operated in, or practicing for, any prearranged or organized race, speed contest or other competition;

(2) Rented to others;

(3) Used to carry persons or cargo for a charge; or

(4) Used for any "business" purpose except for a motorized golf cart while on a golfing facility.

2. If Exclusion **A.1.** does not apply, there is still no coverage for "motor vehicle liability", unless the "motor vehicle" is:

a. In dead storage on an "insured location";

b. Used solely to service a residence;

c. Designed to assist the handicapped and, at the time of an "occurrence", it is:

(1) Being used to assist a handicapped person; or

(2) Parked on an "insured location";

d. Designed for recreational use off public roads and:

(1) Not owned by an "insured"; or

SAMPLE

**(2)** Owned by an "insured" provided the "occurrence" takes place:

**(a)** On an "insured location" as defined in Definition **B.6.a., b., d., e.** or **h.;** or

**(b)** Off an "insured location" and the "motor vehicle" is:

**(i)** Designed as a toy vehicle for use by children under seven years of age;

**(ii)** Powered by one or more batteries; and

**(iii)** Not built or modified after manufacture to exceed a speed of five miles per hour on level ground;

**e.** A motorized golf cart that is owned by an "insured", designed to carry up to four persons, not built or modified after manufacture to exceed a speed of 25 miles per hour on level ground and, at the time of an "occurrence", is within the legal boundaries of:

**(1)** A golfing facility and is parked or stored there, or being used by an "insured" to:

**(a)** Play the game of golf or for other recreational or leisure activity allowed by the facility;

**(b)** Travel to or from an area where "motor vehicles" or golf carts are parked or stored; or

**(c)** Cross public roads at designated points to access other parts of the golfing facility; or

**(2)** A private residential community, including its public roads upon which a motorized golf cart can legally travel, which is subject to the authority of a property owners association and contains an "insured's" residence.

**B. "Watercraft Liability"**

**1.** Coverages **E** and **F** do not apply to any "watercraft liability" if, at the time of an "occurrence", the involved watercraft is being:

**a.** Operated in, or practicing for, any prearranged or organized race, speed contest or other competition. This exclusion does not apply to a sailing vessel or a predicted log cruise;

**b.** Rented to others;

**c.** Used to carry persons or cargo for a charge; or

**d.** Used for any "business" purpose.

**2.** If Exclusion **B.1.** does not apply, there is still no coverage for "watercraft liability" unless, at the time of the "occurrence", the watercraft:

**a.** Is stored;

**b.** Is a sailing vessel, with or without auxiliary power, that is:

**(1)** Less than 26 feet in overall length; or

**(2)** 26 feet or more in overall length and not owned by or rented to an "insured"; or

**c.** Is not a sailing vessel and is powered by:

**(1)** An inboard or inboard-outdrive engine or motor, including those that power a water jet pump, of:

**(a)** 50 horsepower or less and not owned by an "insured"; or

**(b)** More than 50 horsepower and not owned by or rented to an "insured"; or

**(2)** One or more outboard engines or motors with:

**(a)** 25 total horsepower or less;

**(b)** More than 25 horsepower if the outboard engine or motor is not owned by an "insured";

**(c)** More than 25 horsepower if the outboard engine or motor is owned by an "insured" who acquired it during the policy period; or

**(d)** More than 25 horsepower if the outboard engine or motor is owned by an "insured" who acquired it before the policy period, but only if:

**(i)** You declare them at policy inception; or

**(ii)** Your intent to insure them is reported to us in writing within 45 days after you acquire them.

The coverages in **(c)** and **(d)** above apply for the policy period.

Horsepower means the maximum power rating assigned to the engine or motor by the manufacturer.

**C. "Aircraft Liability"**

This policy does not cover "aircraft liability".

**D. "Hovercraft Liability"**

This policy does not cover "hovercraft liability".

     PP 00 03 05 11

SAMPLE

E. Coverage E – Personal Liability And Coverage F – Medical Payments To Others

Coverages **E** and **F** do not apply to the following:

1. **Expected Or Intended Injury**

   "Bodily injury" or "property damage" which is expected or intended by an "insured", even if the resulting "bodily injury" or "property damage":

   a. Is of a different kind, quality or degree than initially expected or intended; or

   b. Is sustained by a different person, entity or property than initially expected or intended.

   However, this Exclusion **E.1.** does not apply to "bodily injury" or "property damage" resulting from the use of reasonable force by an "insured" to protect persons or property;

2. **"Business"**

   a. "Bodily injury" or "property damage" arising out of or in connection with a "business" conducted from an "insured location" or engaged in by an "insured", whether or not the "business" is owned or operated by an "insured" or employs an "insured".

   This Exclusion **E.2.** applies but is not limited to an act or omission, regardless of its nature or circumstance, involving a service or duty rendered, promised, owed, or implied to be provided because of the nature of the "business".

   b. This Exclusion **E.2.** does not apply to:

   (1) The rental or holding for rental of an "insured location";

      (a) On an occasional basis if used only as a residence;

      (b) In part for use only as a residence, unless a single-family unit is intended for use by the occupying family to lodge more than two roomers or boarders; or

      (c) In part, as an office, school, studio or private garage; and

   (2) An "insured" under the age of 21 years involved in a part-time or occasional, self-employed "business" with no employees;

3. **Professional Services**

   "Bodily injury" or "property damage" arising out of the rendering of or failure to render professional services;

4. **"Insured's" Premises Not An "Insured Location"**

   "Bodily injury" or "property damage" arising out of a premises:

   a. Owned by an "insured";

   b. Rented to an "insured"; or

   c. Rented to others by an "insured";

   that is not an "insured location";

5. **War**

   "Bodily injury" or "property damage" caused directly or indirectly by war, including the following and any consequence of any of the following:

   a. Undeclared war, civil war, insurrection, rebellion or revolution;

   b. Warlike act by a military force or military personnel; or

   c. Destruction, seizure or use for a military purpose.

   Discharge of a nuclear weapon will be deemed a warlike act even if accidental;

6. **Communicable Disease**

   "Bodily injury" or "property damage" which arises out of the transmission of a communicable disease by an "insured";

7. **Sexual Molestation, Corporal Punishment Or Physical Or Mental Abuse**

   "Bodily injury" or "property damage" arising out of sexual molestation, corporal punishment or physical or mental abuse; or

8. **Controlled Substance**

   "Bodily injury" or "property damage" arising out of the use, sale, manufacture, delivery, transfer or possession by any person of a Controlled Substance as defined by the Federal Food and Drug Law at 21 U.S.C.A. Sections 811 and 812. Controlled Substances include but are not limited to cocaine, LSD, marijuana and all narcotic drugs. However, this exclusion does not apply to the legitimate use of prescription drugs by a person following the lawful orders of a licensed health care professional.

Exclusions **A.** "Motor Vehicle Liability", **B.** "Watercraft Liability", **C.** "Aircraft Liability", **D.** "Hovercraft Liability" and **E.4.** "Insured's" Premises Not An "Insured Location" do not apply to "bodily injury" to a "residence employee" arising out of and in the course of the "residence employee's" employment by an "insured".

SAMPLE

**F. Coverage E – Personal Liability**

Coverage **E** does not apply to:

1. Liability:

   a. For any loss assessment charged against you as a member of an association, corporation or community of property owners, except as provided in **D. Loss Assessment** under **Section II – Additional Coverages;**

   b. Under any contract or agreement entered into by an "insured". However, this exclusion does not apply to written contracts:

      (1) That directly relate to the ownership, maintenance or use of an "insured location"; or

      (2) Where the liability of others is assumed by you prior to an "occurrence";

      unless excluded in **a.** above or elsewhere in this policy;

2. "Property damage" to property owned by an "insured". This includes costs or expenses incurred by an "insured" or others to repair, replace, enhance, restore or maintain such property to prevent injury to a person or damage to property of others, whether on or away from an "insured location";

3. "Property damage" to property rented to, occupied or used by or in the care of an "insured". This exclusion does not apply to "property damage" caused by fire, smoke or explosion;

4. "Bodily injury" to any person eligible to receive any benefits voluntarily provided or required to be provided by an "insured" under any:

   a. Workers' compensation law;

   b. Non-occupational disability law; or

   c. Occupational disease law;

5. "Bodily injury" or "property damage" for which an "insured" under this policy:

   a. Is also an insured under a nuclear energy liability policy issued by the:

      (1) Nuclear Energy Liability Insurance Association;

      (2) Mutual Atomic Energy Liability Underwriters;

      (3) Nuclear Insurance Association of Canada;

      or any of their successors; or

   b. Would be an insured under such a policy but for the exhaustion of its limit of liability; or

6. "Bodily injury" to you or an "insured" as defined under Definition **5.a.** or **b.**

   This exclusion also applies to any claim made or suit brought against you or an "insured" to:

   a. Repay; or

   b. Share damages with;

   another person who may be obligated to pay damages because of "bodily injury" to an "insured".

**G. Coverage F – Medical Payments To Others**

Coverage **F** does not apply to "bodily injury":

1. To a "residence employee" if the "bodily injury":

   a. Occurs off the "insured location"; and

   b. Does not arise out of or in the course of the "residence employee's" employment by an "insured";

2. To any person eligible to receive benefits voluntarily provided or required to be provided under any:

   a. Workers' compensation law;

   b. Non-occupational disability law; or

   c. Occupational disease law;

3. From any:

   a. Nuclear reaction;

   b. Nuclear radiation; or

   c. Radioactive contamination;

   all whether controlled or uncontrolled or however caused; or

   d. Any consequence of any of these; or

4. To any person, other than a "residence employee" of an "insured", regularly residing on any part of the "insured location".

**SECTION II – ADDITIONAL COVERAGES**

We cover the following in addition to the limits of liability:

**A. Claim Expenses**

We pay:

1. Expenses we incur and costs taxed against an "insured" in any suit we defend;

2. Premiums on bonds required in a suit we defend, but not for bond amounts more than the Coverage **E** limit of liability. We need not apply for or furnish any bond;

SAMPLE

3. Reasonable expenses incurred by an "insured" at our request, including actual loss of earnings (but not loss of other income) up to $250 per day, for assisting us in the investigation or defense of a claim or suit; and

4. Interest on the entire judgment which accrues after entry of the judgment and before we pay or tender, or deposit in court that part of the judgment which does not exceed the limit of liability that applies.

## B. First Aid Expenses

We will pay expenses for first aid to others incurred by an "insured" for "bodily injury" covered under this policy. We will not pay for first aid to an "insured".

## C. Damage To Property Of Others

1. We will pay, at replacement cost, up to $1,000 per "occurrence" for "property damage" to property of others caused by an "insured".

2. We will not pay for "property damage":

   a. To the extent of any amount recoverable under Section I;

   b. Caused intentionally by an "insured" who is 13 years of age or older;

   c. To property owned by an "insured";

   d. To property owned by or rented to a tenant of an "insured" or a resident in your household; or

   e. Arising out of:

      (1) A "business" engaged in by an "insured";

      (2) Any act or omission in connection with a premises owned, rented or controlled by an "insured", other than the "insured location"; or

      (3) The ownership, maintenance, occupancy, operation, use, loading or unloading of aircraft, hovercraft, watercraft or "motor vehicles".

      This Exclusion e.(3) does not apply to a "motor vehicle" that:

      (a) Is designed for recreational use off public roads;

      (b) Is not owned by an "insured"; and

      (c) At the time of the "occurrence", is not required by law, or regulation issued by a government agency, to have been registered for it to be used on public roads or property.

## D. Loss Assessment

1. We will pay up to $1,000 for your share of loss assessment charged against you, as owner or tenant of the "residence premises", during the policy period by a corporation or association of property owners, when the assessment is made as a result of:

   a. "Bodily injury" or "property damage" not excluded from coverage under Section II – Exclusions; or

   b. Liability for an act of a director, officer or trustee in the capacity as a director, officer or trustee, provided such person:

      (1) Is elected by the members of a corporation or association of property owners; and

      (2) Serves without deriving any income from the exercise of duties which are solely on behalf of a corporation or association of property owners.

2. Paragraph I. Policy Period under Section II – Conditions does not apply to this Loss Assessment Coverage.

3. Regardless of the number of assessments, the limit of $1,000 is the most we will pay for loss arising out of:

   a. One accident, including continuous or repeated exposure to substantially the same general harmful condition; or

   b. A covered act of a director, officer or trustee. An act involving more than one director, officer or trustee is considered to be a single act.

4. We do not cover assessments charged against you or a corporation or association of property owners by any governmental body.

## SECTION II – CONDITIONS

## A. Limit Of Liability

Our total liability under Coverage E for all damages resulting from any one "occurrence" will not be more than the Coverage E Limit Of Liability shown in the Declarations. This limit is the same regardless of the number of "insureds", claims made or persons injured. All "bodily injury" and "property damage" resulting from any one accident or from continuous or repeated exposure to substantially the same general harmful conditions shall be considered to be the result of one "occurrence".

SAMPLE

Our total liability under Coverage **F** for all medical expense payable for "bodily injury" to one person as the result of one accident will not be more than the Coverage **F** Limit Of Liability shown in the Declarations.

**B. Severability Of Insurance**

This insurance applies separately to each "insured". This condition will not increase our limit of liability for any one "occurrence".

**C. Duties After "Occurrence"**

In case of an "occurrence", you or another "insured" will perform the following duties that apply. We have no duty to provide coverage under this policy if your failure to comply with the following duties is prejudicial to us. You will help us by seeing that these duties are performed:

1. Give written notice to us or our agent as soon as is practical, which sets forth:

   a. The identity of the policy and the "named insured" shown in the Declarations;

   b. Reasonably available information on the time, place and circumstances of the "occurrence"; and

   c. Names and addresses of any claimants and witnesses;

2. Cooperate with us in the investigation, settlement or defense of any claim or suit;

3. Promptly forward to us every notice, demand, summons or other process relating to the "occurrence";

4. At our request, help us:

   a. To make settlement;

   b. To enforce any right of contribution or indemnity against any person or organization who may be liable to an "insured";

   c. With the conduct of suits and attend hearings and trials; and

   d. To secure and give evidence and obtain the attendance of witnesses;

5. With respect to **C.** Damage To Property Of Others under Section **II** – Additional Coverages, submit to us within 60 days after the loss a sworn statement of loss and show the damaged property, if in an "insured's" control;

6. No "insured" shall, except at such "insured's" own cost, voluntarily make payment, assume obligation or incur expense other than for first aid to others at the time of the "bodily injury".

**D. Duties Of An Injured Person – Coverage F – Medical Payments To Others**

1. The injured person or someone acting for the injured person will:

   a. Give us written proof of claim, under oath if required, as soon as is practical; and

   b. Authorize us to obtain copies of medical reports and records.

2. The injured person will submit to a physical exam by a doctor of our choice when and as often as we reasonably require.

**E. Payment Of Claim – Coverage F – Medical Payments To Others**

Payment under this coverage is not an admission of liability by an "insured" or us.

**F. Suit Against Us**

1. No action can be brought against us unless there has been full compliance with all of the terms under this Section **II**.

2. No one will have the right to join us as a party to any action against an "insured".

3. Also, no action with respect to Coverage **E** can be brought against us until the obligation of such "insured" has been determined by final judgment or agreement signed by us.

**G. Bankruptcy Of An "Insured"**

Bankruptcy or insolvency of an "insured" will not relieve us of our obligations under this policy.

**H. Other Insurance**

This insurance is excess over other valid and collectible insurance except insurance written specifically to cover as excess over the limits of liability that apply in this policy.

**I. Policy Period**

This policy applies only to "bodily injury" or "property damage" which occurs during the policy period.

**J. Concealment Or Fraud**

We do not provide coverage to an "insured" who, whether before or after a loss, has:

1. Intentionally concealed or misrepresented any material fact or circumstance;

2. Engaged in fraudulent conduct; or

3. Made false statements;

relating to this insurance.

PP 00 03 05 11

SAMPLE

## SECTIONS I AND II – CONDITIONS

### A. Liberalization Clause

If we make a change which broadens coverage under this edition of our policy without additional premium charge, that change will automatically apply to your insurance as of the date we implement the change in your state, provided that this implementation date falls within 60 days prior to or during the policy period stated in the Declarations.

This Liberalization Clause does not apply to changes implemented with a general program revision that includes both broadenings and restrictions in coverage, whether that general program revision is implemented through introduction of:

1. A subsequent edition of this policy; or
2. An amendatory endorsement.

### B. Waiver Or Change Of Policy Provisions

A waiver or change of a provision of this policy must be in writing by us to be valid. Our request for an appraisal or examination will not waive any of our rights.

### C. Cancellation

1. You may cancel this policy at any time by returning it to us or by letting us know in writing of the date cancellation is to take effect.

2. We may cancel this policy only for the reasons stated below by letting you know in writing of the date cancellation takes effect. This cancellation notice may be delivered to you, or mailed to you at your mailing address shown in the Declarations. Proof of mailing will be sufficient proof of notice.

   a. When you have not paid the premium, we may cancel at any time by letting you know at least 10 days before the date cancellation takes effect.

   b. When this policy has been in effect for less than 60 days and is not a renewal with us, we may cancel for any reason by letting you know at least 10 days before the date cancellation takes effect.

   c. When this policy has been in effect for 60 days or more, or at any time if it is a renewal with us, we may cancel:

      (1) If there has been a material misrepresentation of fact which if known to us would have caused us not to issue the policy; or

      (2) If the risk has changed substantially since the policy was issued.

      This can be done by letting you know at least 30 days before the date cancellation takes effect.

   d. When this policy is written for a period of more than one year, we may cancel for any reason at anniversary by letting you know at least 30 days before the date cancellation takes effect.

3. When this policy is canceled, the premium for the period from the date of cancellation to the expiration date will be refunded pro rata.

4. If the return premium is not refunded with the notice of cancellation or when this policy is returned to us, we will refund it within a reasonable time after the date cancellation takes effect.

### D. Nonrenewal

We may elect not to renew this policy. We may do so by delivering to you, or mailing to you at your mailing address shown in the Declarations, written notice at least 30 days before the expiration date of this policy. Proof of mailing will be sufficient proof of notice.

### E. Assignment

Assignment of this policy will not be valid unless we give our written consent.

### F. Subrogation

An "insured" may waive in writing before a loss all rights of recovery against any person. If not waived, we may require an assignment of rights of recovery for a loss to the extent that payment is made by us.

If an assignment is sought, an "insured" must sign and deliver all related papers and cooperate with us.

Subrogation does not apply to Coverage **F** or Paragraph **C.** Damage To Property Of Others under Section **II** – Additional Coverages.

### G. Death

If any person named in the Declarations or the spouse, if a resident of the same household, dies, the following apply:

1. We insure the legal representative of the deceased but only with respect to the premises and property of the deceased covered under the policy at the time of death; and

SAMPLE

2. "Insured" includes:

    **a.** An "insured" who is a member of your household at the time of your death, but only while a resident of the "residence premises"; and

    **b.** With respect to your property, the person having proper temporary custody of the property until appointment and qualification of a legal representative.

## Personal Auto Policy Declarations

**POLICYHOLDER:**
**(Named Insured)**
Chris and Karen Swift
8110 Lake Street
Lincoln, Nebraska 68506

**POLICY NUMBER:** 296 S 468211

**POLICY PERIOD:**
**FROM:** August 1, 2013
**TO:** February 1, 2014

But only if the required premium for this period has been paid, and for six-month renewal periods if renewal premiums are paid as required. Each period begins and ends at 12:01 A.M. standard time at the address of the policyholder.

**INSURED VEHICLES AND
SCHEDULE OF COVERAGES**

| VEHICLE | COVERAGES | LIMITS OF INSURANCE | PREMIUM |
|---|---|---|---|
| 1 | 2004 Toyota Corolla | ID #JT2AL21E8B3306553 | |
| | Coverage A—Liability: | | |
| | Bodily Injury Liability | $100,000 **Each Person** | $130.00 |
| | | $300,000 **Each Accident** | |
| | Property Damage Liability | $ 50,000 **Each Accident** | $ 62.00 |
| | Coverage B—Medical Payments | $ 5,000 **Each Person** | $ 46.00 |
| | Coverage C—Uninsured Motorists: | | |
| | Bodily Injury | $100,000 **Each Person** | $ 42.00 |
| | | $300,000 **Each Accident** | |
| | | **TOTAL** | $280.00 |
| 2 | 2011 Ford Taurus | ID #1FABP3OU7GG212619 | |
| | Coverage A—Liability: | | |
| | Bodily Injury Liability | $100,000 **Each Person** | $170.00 |
| | | $300,000 **Each Accident** | |
| | Property Damage Liability | $ 50,000 **Each Accident** | $ 90.00 |
| | Coverage B—Medical Payments | $ 5,000 **Each Person** | $ 46.00 |
| | Coverage C—Uninsured Motorists: | | |
| | Bodily Injury | $100,000 **Each Person** | $ 42.00 |
| | | $300,000 **Each Accident** | |
| | Coverage D—Other Than Collision | **Actual Cash Value Less** $250 | $ 80.00 |
| | —Collision | **Actual Cash Value Less** $500 | $160.00 |
| | | **TOTAL** | $588.00 |

**POLICY FORM AND ENDORSEMENTS:** PP 00 01 01 05
**COUNTERSIGNATURE DATE:** July 1, 2013
**AGENT:** Patrick Rejda

SAMPLE

PERSONAL AUTO
PP 00 01 01 05

## PERSONAL AUTO POLICY

### AGREEMENT

In return for payment of the premium and subject to all the terms of this policy, we agree with you as follows:

### DEFINITIONS

**A.** Throughout this policy, "you" and "your" refer to:

1. The "named insured" shown in the Declarations; and

2. The spouse if a resident of the same household.

If the spouse ceases to be a resident of the same household during the policy period or prior to the inception of this policy, the spouse will be considered "you" and "your" under this policy but only until the earlier of:

1. The end of 90 days following the spouse's change of residency;

2. The effective date of another policy listing the spouse as a named insured; or

3. The end of the policy period.

**B.** "We", "us" and "our" refer to the Company providing this insurance.

**C.** For purposes of this policy, a private passenger type auto, pickup or van shall be deemed to be owned by a person if leased:

1. Under a written agreement to that person; and

2. For a continuous period of at least 6 months.

Other words and phrases are defined. They are in quotation marks when used.

**D.** "Bodily injury" means bodily harm, sickness or disease, including death that results.

**E.** "Business" includes trade, profession or occupation.

**F.** "Family member" means a person related to you by blood, marriage or adoption who is a resident of your household. This includes a ward or foster child.

**G.** "Occupying" means:

1. In;

2. Upon; or

3. Getting in, on, out or off.

**H.** "Property damage" means physical injury to, destruction of or loss of use of tangible property.

**I.** "Trailer" means a vehicle designed to be pulled by a:

1. Private passenger auto; or

2. Pickup or van.

It also means a farm wagon or farm implement while towed by a vehicle listed in **1.** or **2.** above.

**J.** "Your covered auto" means:

1. Any vehicle shown in the Declarations.

2. A "newly acquired auto".

3. Any "trailer" you own.

4. Any auto or "trailer" you do not own while used as a temporary substitute for any other vehicle described in this definition which is out of normal use because of its:

   **a.** Breakdown;

   **b.** Repair;

   **c.** Servicing;

   **d.** Loss; or

   **e.** Destruction.

   This Provision (**J.4.**) does not apply to Coverage For Damage To Your Auto.

**K.** "Newly acquired auto":

1. "Newly acquired auto" means any of the following types of vehicles you become the owner of during the policy period:

   **a.** A private passenger auto; or

   **b.** A pickup or van, for which no other insurance policy provides coverage, that:

      **(1)** Has a Gross Vehicle Weight Rating of 10,000 lbs. or less; and

      **(2)** Is not used for the delivery or transportation of goods and materials unless such use is:

         **(a)** Incidental to your "business" of installing, maintaining or repairing furnishings or equipment; or

         **(b)** For farming or ranching.

2. Coverage for a "newly acquired auto" is provided as described below. If you ask us to insure a "newly acquired auto" after a specified time period described below has elapsed, any coverage we provide for a "newly acquired auto" will begin at the time you request the coverage.

SAMPLE

a. For any coverage provided in this policy except Coverage For Damage To Your Auto, a "newly acquired auto" will have the broadest coverage we now provide for any vehicle shown in the Declarations. Coverage begins on the date you become the owner. However, for this coverage to apply to a "newly acquired auto" which is in addition to any vehicle shown in the Declarations, you must ask us to insure it within 14 days after you become the owner.

If a "newly acquired auto" replaces a vehicle shown in the Declarations, coverage is provided for this vehicle without your having to ask us to insure it.

b. Collision Coverage for a "newly acquired auto" begins on the date you become the owner. However, for this coverage to apply, you must ask us to insure it within:

(1) 14 days after you become the owner if the Declarations indicate that Collision Coverage applies to at least one auto. In this case, the "newly acquired auto" will have the broadest coverage we now provide for any auto shown in the Declarations.

(2) Four days after you become the owner if the Declarations do not indicate that Collision Coverage applies to at least one auto. If you comply with the 4 day requirement and a loss occurred before you asked us to insure the "newly acquired", a Collision deductible of $500 will apply.

c. Other Than Collision Coverage for a "newly acquired auto" begins on the date you become the owner. However, for this coverage to apply, you must ask us to insure it within:

(1) 14 days after you become the owner if the Declarations indicate that Other Than Collision Coverage applies to at least one auto. In this case, the "newly acquired auto" will have the broadest coverage we now provide for any auto shown in the Declarations.

(2) Four days after you become the owner if the Declarations do not indicate that Other Than Collision Coverage applies to at least one auto. If you comply with the 4 day requirement and a loss occurred before you asked us to insure the "newly acquired auto", an Other Than Collision deductible of $500 will apply.

---

## PART A – LIABILITY COVERAGE

### INSURING AGREEMENT

**A.** We will pay damages for "bodily injury" or "property damage" for which any "insured" becomes legally responsible because of an auto accident. Damages include prejudgment interest awarded against the "insured". We will settle or defend, as we consider appropriate, any claim or suit asking for these damages. In addition to our limit of liability, we will pay all defense costs we incur. Our duty to settle or defend ends when our limit of liability for this coverage has been exhausted by payment of judgments or settlements. We have no duty to defend any suit or settle any claim for "bodily injury" or "property damage" not covered under this policy.

**B.** "Insured" as used in this Part means:

1. You or any "family member" for the ownership, maintenance or use of any auto or "trailer".

2. Any person using "your covered auto".

3. For "your covered auto", any person or organization but only with respect to legal responsibility for acts or omissions of a person for whom coverage is afforded under this Part.

4. For any auto or "trailer", other than "your covered auto", any other person or organization but only with respect to legal responsibility for acts or omissions of you or any "family member" for whom coverage is afforded under this Part. This Provision (**B.4.**) applies only if the person or organization does not own or hire the auto or "trailer".

### SUPPLEMENTARY PAYMENTS

We will pay on behalf of an "insured":

1. Up to $250 for the cost of bail bonds required because of an accident, including related traffic law violations. The accident must result in "bodily injury" or "property damage" covered under this policy.

2. Premiums on appeal bonds and bonds to release attachments in any suit we defend.

3. Interest accruing after a judgment is entered in any suit we defend. Our duty to pay interest ends when we offer to pay that part of the judgment which does not exceed our limit of liability for this coverage.

SAMPLE

4. Up to $200 a day for loss of earnings, but not other income, because of attendance at hearings or trials at our request.

5. Other reasonable expenses incurred at our request.

These payments will not reduce the limit of liability.

**EXCLUSIONS**

A. We do not provide Liability Coverage for any "insured":

1. Who intentionally causes "bodily injury" or "property damage".

2. For "property damage" to property owned or being transported by that "insured".

3. For "property damage" to property:

   a. Rented to;

   b. Used by; or

   c. In the care of;

   that "insured".

   This Exclusion (**A.3.**) does not apply to "property damage" to a residence or private garage.

4. For "bodily injury" to an employee of that "insured" during the course of employment. This Exclusion (**A.4.**) does not apply to "bodily injury" to a domestic employee unless workers' compensation benefits are required or available for that domestic employee.

5. For that "insured's" liability arising out of the ownership or operation of a vehicle while it is being used as a public or livery conveyance. This Exclusion (**A.5.**) does not apply to a share-the-expense car pool.

6. While employed or otherwise engaged in the "business" of:

   a. Selling;

   b. Repairing;

   c. Servicing;

   d. Storing; or

   e. Parking;

   vehicles designed for use mainly on public highways. This includes road testing and delivery. This Exclusion (**A.6.**) does not apply to the ownership, maintenance or use of "your covered auto" by:

   a. You;

   b. Any "family member"; or

   c. Any partner, agent or employee of you or any "family member".

7. Maintaining or using any vehicle while that "insured" is employed or otherwise engaged in any "business" (other than farming or ranching) not described in Exclusion **A.6.**

   This Exclusion (**A.7.**) does not apply to the maintenance or use of a:

   a. Private passenger auto;

   b. Pickup or van; or

   c. "Trailer" used with a vehicle described in **a.** or **b.** above.

8. Using a vehicle without a reasonable belief that that "insured" is entitled to do so. This Exclusion (**A.8.**) does not apply to a "family member" using "your covered auto" which is owned by you.

9. For "bodily injury" or "property damage" for which that "insured":

   a. Is an insured under a nuclear energy liability policy; or

   b. Would be an insured under a nuclear energy liability policy but for its termination upon exhaustion of its limit of liability.

   A nuclear energy liability policy is a policy issued by any of the following or their successors:

   a. Nuclear Energy Liability Insurance Association;

   b. Mutual Atomic Energy Liability Underwriters; or

   c. Nuclear Insurance Association of Canada.

B. We do not provide Liability Coverage for the ownership, maintenance or use of:

1. Any vehicle which:

   a. Has fewer than four wheels; or

   b. Is designed mainly for use off public roads.

   This Exclusion (**B.1.**) does not apply:

   a. While such vehicle is being used by an "insured" in a medical emergency;

   b. To any "trailer"; or

   c. To any non-owned golf cart.

2. Any vehicle, other than "your covered auto", which is:

   a. Owned by you; or

   b. Furnished or available for your regular use.

3. Any vehicle, other than "your covered auto", which is:

   a. Owned by any "family member"; or

   b. Furnished or available for the regular use of any "family member".

SAMPLE

However, this Exclusion (**B.3.**) does not apply to you while you are maintaining or "occupying" any vehicle which is:

**a.** Owned by a "family member"; or

**b.** Furnished or available for the regular use of a "family member".

**4.** Any vehicle, located inside a facility designed for racing, for the purpose of:

**a.** Competing in; or

**b.** Practicing or preparing for;

any prearranged or organized racing or speed contest.

### LIMIT OF LIABILITY

**A.** The limit of liability shown in the Declarations for each person for Bodily Injury Liability is our maximum limit of liability for all damages, including damages for care, loss of services or death, arising out of "bodily injury" sustained by any one person in any one auto accident. Subject to this limit for each person, the limit of liability shown in the Declarations for each accident for Bodily Injury Liability is our maximum limit of liability for all damages for "bodily injury" resulting from any one auto accident.

The limit of liability shown in the Declarations for each accident for Property Damage Liability is our maximum limit of liability for all "property damage" resulting from any one auto accident.

This is the most we will pay regardless of the number of:

**1.** "Insureds";

**2.** Claims made;

**3.** Vehicles or premiums shown in the Declarations; or

**4.** Vehicles involved in the auto accident.

**B.** No one will be entitled to receive duplicate payments for the same elements of loss under this coverage and:

**1.** Part **B** or Part **C** of this policy; or

**2.** Any Underinsured Motorists Coverage provided by this policy.

### OUT OF STATE COVERAGE

If an auto accident to which this policy applies occurs in any state or province other than the one in which "your covered auto" is principally garaged, we will interpret your policy for that accident as follows:

**A.** If the state or province has:

**1.** A financial responsibility or similar law specifying limits of liability for "bodily injury" or "property damage" higher than the limit shown in the Declarations, your policy will provide the higher specified limit.

**2.** A compulsory insurance or similar law requiring a nonresident to maintain insurance whenever the nonresident uses a vehicle in that state or province, your policy will provide at least the required minimum amounts and types of coverage.

**B.** No one will be entitled to duplicate payments for the same elements of loss.

### FINANCIAL RESPONSIBILITY

When this policy is certified as future proof of financial responsibility, this policy shall comply with the law to the extent required.

### OTHER INSURANCE

If there is other applicable liability insurance we will pay only our share of the loss. Our share is the proportion that our limit of liability bears to the total of all applicable limits. However, any insurance we provide for a vehicle you do not own, including any vehicle while used as a temporary substitute for "your covered auto", shall be excess over any other collectible insurance.

---

## PART B – MEDICAL PAYMENTS COVERAGE

### INSURING AGREEMENT

**A.** We will pay reasonable expenses incurred for necessary medical and funeral services because of "bodily injury":

**1.** Caused by accident; and

**2.** Sustained by an "insured".

We will pay only those expenses incurred for services rendered within 3 years from the date of the accident.

**B.** "Insured" as used in this Part means:

**1.** You or any "family member":

**a.** While "occupying"; or

**b.** As a pedestrian when struck by;

a motor vehicle designed for use mainly on public roads or a trailer of any type.

**2.** Any other person while "occupying" "your covered auto".

SAMPLE

## EXCLUSIONS

We do not provide Medical Payments Coverage for any "insured" for "bodily injury":

1. Sustained while "occupying" any motorized vehicle having fewer than four wheels.

2. Sustained while "occupying" "your covered auto" when it is being used as a public or livery conveyance. This Exclusion (2.) does not apply to a share-the-expense car pool.

3. Sustained while "occupying" any vehicle located for use as a residence or premises.

4. Occurring during the course of employment if workers' compensation benefits are required or available for the "bodily injury".

5. Sustained while "occupying", or when struck by, any vehicle (other than "your covered auto") which is:

    a. Owned by you; or

    b. Furnished or available for your regular use.

6. Sustained while "occupying", or when struck by, any vehicle (other than "your covered auto") which is:

    a. Owned by any "family member"; or

    b. Furnished or available for the regular use of any "family member".

    However, this Exclusion (6.) does not apply to you.

7. Sustained while "occupying" a vehicle without a reasonable belief that that "insured" is entitled to do so. This Exclusion (7.) does not apply to a "family member" using "your covered auto" which is owned by you.

8. Sustained while "occupying" a vehicle when it is being used in the "business" of an "insured". This Exclusion (8.) does not apply to "bodily injury" sustained while "occupying" a:

    a. Private passenger auto;

    b. Pickup or van; or

    c. "Trailer" used with a vehicle described in a. or b. above.

9. Caused by or as a consequence of:

    a. Discharge of a nuclear weapon (even if accidental);

    b. War (declared or undeclared);

    c. Civil war;

    d. Insurrection; or

    e. Rebellion or revolution.

10. From or as a consequence of the following, whether controlled or uncontrolled or however caused:

    a. Nuclear reaction;

    b. Radiation; or

    c. Radioactive contamination.

11. Sustained while "occupying" any vehicle located inside a facility designed for racing, for the purpose of:

    a. Competing in; or

    b. Practicing or preparing for;

    any prearranged or organized racing or speed contest.

## LIMIT OF LIABILITY

A. The limit of liability shown in the Declarations for this coverage is our maximum limit of liability for each person injured in any one accident. This is the most we will pay regardless of the number of:

1. "Insureds";

2. Claims made;

3. Vehicles or premiums shown in the Declarations; or

4. Vehicles involved in the accident.

B. No one will be entitled to receive duplicate payments for the same elements of loss under this coverage and:

1. Part A or Part C of this policy; or

2. Any Underinsured Motorists Coverage provided by this policy.

## OTHER INSURANCE

If there is other applicable auto medical payments insurance we will pay only our share of the loss. Our share is the proportion that our limit of liability bears to the total of all applicable limits. However, any insurance we provide with respect to a vehicle you do not own, including any vehicle while used as a temporary substitute for "your covered auto", shall be excess over any other collectible auto insurance providing payments for medical or funeral expenses.

SAMPLE

---

**PART C – UNINSURED MOTORISTS COVERAGE**

**INSURING AGREEMENT**

**A.** We will pay compensatory damages which an "insured" is legally entitled to recover from the owner or operator of an "uninsured motor vehicle" because of "bodily injury":

1. Sustained by an "insured"; and

2. Caused by an accident.

The owner's or operator's liability for these damages must arise out of the ownership, maintenance or use of the "uninsured motor vehicle".

Any judgment for damages arising out of a suit brought without our written consent is not binding on us.

**B.** "Insured" as used in this Part means:

1. You or any "family member".

2. Any other person "occupying" "your covered auto".

3. Any person for damages that person is entitled to recover because of "bodily injury" to which this coverage applies sustained by a person described in **1.** or **2.** above.

**C.** "Uninsured motor vehicle" means a land motor vehicle or trailer of any type:

1. To which no bodily injury liability bond or policy applies at the time of the accident.

2. To which a bodily injury liability bond or policy applies at the time of the accident. In this case its limit for bodily injury liability must be less than the minimum limit for bodily injury liability specified by the financial responsibility law of the state in which "your covered auto" is principally garaged.

3. Which is a hit-and-run vehicle whose operator or owner cannot be identified and which hits:

   **a.** You or any "family member";

   **b.** A vehicle which you or any "family member" are "occupying"; or

   **c.** "Your covered auto".

4. To which a bodily injury liability bond or policy applies at the time of the accident but the bonding or insuring company:

   **a.** Denies coverage; or

   **b.** Is or becomes insolvent.

However, "uninsured motor vehicle" does not include any vehicle or equipment:

1. Owned by or furnished or available for the regular use of you or any "family member".

2. Owned or operated by a self-insurer under any applicable motor vehicle law, except a self-insurer which is or becomes insolvent.

3. Owned by any governmental unit or agency.

4. Operated on rails or crawler treads.

5. Designed mainly for use off public roads while not on public roads.

6. While located for use as a residence or premises.

**EXCLUSIONS**

**A.** We do not provide Uninsured Motorists Coverage for "bodily injury" sustained:

1. By an "insured" while "occupying", or when struck by, any motor vehicle owned by that "insured" which is not insured for this coverage under this policy. This includes a trailer of any type used with that vehicle.

2. By any "family member" while "occupying", or when struck by, any motor vehicle you own which is insured for this coverage on a primary basis under any other policy.

**B.** We do not provide Uninsured Motorists Coverage for "bodily injury" sustained by any "insured":

1. If that "insured" or the legal representative settles the "bodily injury" claim and such settlement prejudices our right to recover payment.

2. While "occupying" "your covered auto" when it is being used as a public or livery conveyance. This Exclusion (**B.2.**) does not apply to a share-the-expense car pool.

3. Using a vehicle without a reasonable belief that that "insured" is entitled to do so. This Exclusion (**B.3.**) does not apply to a "family member" using "your covered auto" which is owned by you.

**C.** This coverage shall not apply directly or indirectly to benefit any insurer or self-insurer under any of the following or similar law:

1. Workers' compensation law; or

2. Disability benefits law.

**D.** We do not provide Uninsured Motorists Coverage for punitive or exemplary damages.

SAMPLE

## LIMIT OF LIABILITY

**A.** The limit of liability shown in the Declarations for each person for Uninsured Motorists Coverage is our maximum limit of liability for all damages, including damages for care, loss of services or death, arising out of "bodily injury" sustained by any one person in any one accident. Subject to this limit for each person, the limit of liability shown in the Declarations for each accident for Uninsured Motorists Coverage is our maximum limit of liability for all damages for "bodily injury" resulting from any one accident.

This is the most we will pay regardless of the number of:

1. "Insureds";

2. Claims made;

3. Vehicles or premiums shown in the Declarations; or

4. Vehicles involved in the accident.

**B.** No one will be entitled to receive duplicate payments for the same elements of loss under this coverage and:

1. Part **A** or Part **B** of this policy; or

2. Any Underinsured Motorists Coverage provided by this policy.

**C.** We will not make a duplicate payment under this coverage for any element of loss for which payment has been made by or on behalf of persons or organizations who may be legally responsible.

**D.** We will not pay for any element of loss if a person is entitled to receive payment for the same element of loss under any of the following or similar law:

1. Workers' compensation law; or

2. Disability benefits law.

## OTHER INSURANCE

If there is other applicable insurance available under one or more policies or provisions of coverage that is similar to the insurance provided under this Part of the policy:

1. Any recovery for damages under all such policies or provisions of coverage may equal but not exceed the highest applicable limit for any one vehicle under any insurance providing coverage on either a primary or excess basis.

2. Any insurance we provide with respect to a vehicle you do not own, including any vehicle while used as a temporary substitute for "your covered auto", shall be excess over any collectible insurance providing such coverage on a primary basis.

3. If the coverage under this policy is provided:

**a.** On a primary basis, we will pay only our share of the loss that must be paid under insurance providing coverage on a primary basis. Our share is the proportion that our limit of liability bears to the total of all applicable limits of liability for coverage provided on a primary basis.

**b.** On an excess basis, we will pay only our share of the loss that must be paid under insurance providing coverage on an excess basis. Our share is the proportion that our limit of liability bears to the total of all applicable limits of liability for coverage provided on an excess basis.

## ARBITRATION

**A.** If we and an "insured" do not agree:

1. Whether that "insured" is legally entitled to recover damages; or

2. As to the amount of damages which are recoverable by that "insured";

from the owner or operator of an "uninsured motor vehicle", then the matter may be arbitrated. However, disputes concerning coverage under this Part may not be arbitrated.

Both parties must agree to arbitration. If so agreed, each party will select an arbitrator. The two arbitrators will select a third. If they cannot agree within 30 days, either may request that selection be made by a judge of a court having jurisdiction.

**B.** Each party will:

1. Pay the expenses it incurs; and

2. Bear the expenses of the third arbitrator equally.

**C.** Unless both parties agree otherwise, arbitration will take place in the county in which the "insured" lives. Local rules of law as to procedure and evidence will apply. A decision agreed to by at least two of the arbitrators will be binding as to:

1. Whether the "insured" is legally entitled to recover damages; and

2. The amount of damages. This applies only if the amount does not exceed the minimum limit for bodily injury liability specified by the financial responsibility law of the state in which "your covered auto" is principally garaged. If the amount exceeds that limit, either party may demand the right to a trial. This demand must be made within 60 days of the arbitrators' decision. If this demand is not made, the amount of damages agreed to by the arbitrators will be binding.

SAMPLE

---

**PART D – COVERAGE FOR DAMAGE TO YOUR AUTO**

---

**INSURING AGREEMENT**

**A.** We will pay for direct and accidental loss to "your covered auto" or any "non-owned auto", including their equipment, minus any applicable deductible shown in the Declarations. If loss to more than one "your covered auto" or "non-owned auto" results from the same "collision", only the highest applicable deductible will apply. We will pay for loss to "your covered auto" caused by:

  **1.** Other than "collision" only if the Declarations indicate that Other Than Collision Coverage is provided for that auto.

  **2.** "Collision" only if the Declarations indicate that Collision Coverage is provided for that auto.

If there is a loss to a "non-owned auto", we will provide the broadest coverage applicable to any "your covered auto" shown in the Declarations.

**B.** "Collision" means the upset of "your covered auto" or a "non-owned auto" or their impact with another vehicle or object.

Loss caused by the following is considered other than "collision":

  **1.** Missiles or falling objects;

  **2.** Fire;

  **3.** Theft or larceny;

  **4.** Explosion or earthquake;

  **5.** Windstorm;

  **6.** Hail, water or flood;

  **7.** Malicious mischief or vandalism;

  **8.** Riot or civil commotion;

  **9.** Contact with bird or animal; or

  **10.** Breakage of glass.

If breakage of glass is caused by a "collision", you may elect to have it considered a loss caused by "collision".

**C.** "Non-owned auto" means:

  **1.** Any private passenger auto, pickup, van or "trailer" not owned by or furnished or available for the regular use of you or any "family member" while in the custody of or being operated by you or any "family member"; or

  **2.** Any auto or "trailer" you do not own while used as a temporary substitute for "your covered auto" which is out of normal use because of its:

    **a.** Breakdown;

    **b.** Repair;

    **c.** Servicing;

    **d.** Loss; or

    **e.** Destruction.

**TRANSPORTATION EXPENSES**

**A.** In addition, we will pay, without application of a deductible, up to a maximum of $600 for:

  **1.** Temporary transportation expenses not exceeding $20 per day incurred by you in the event of a loss to "your covered auto". We will pay for such expenses if the loss is caused by:

    **a.** Other than "collision" only if the Declarations indicate that Other Than Collision Coverage is provided for that auto.

    **b.** "Collision" only if the Declarations indicate that Collision Coverage is provided for that auto.

  **2.** Expenses for which you become legally responsible in the event of loss to a "non-owned auto". We will pay for such expenses if the loss is caused by:

    **a.** Other than "collision" only if the Declarations indicate that Other Than Collision Coverage is provided for any "your covered auto".

    **b.** "Collision" only if the Declarations indicate that Collision Coverage is provided for any "your covered auto".

However, the most we will pay for any expenses for loss of use is $20 per day.

**B.** Subject to the provisions of Paragraph **A.**, if the loss is caused by:

  **1.** A total theft of "your covered auto" or a "non-owned auto", we will pay only expenses incurred during the period:

    **a.** Beginning 48 hours after the theft; and

    **b.** Ending when "your covered auto" or the "non-owned auto" is returned to use or we pay for its loss.

  **2.** Other than theft of a "your covered auto" or a "non-owned auto", we will pay only expenses beginning when the auto is withdrawn from use for more than 24 hours.

Our payment will be limited to that period of time reasonably required to repair or replace the "your covered auto" or the "non-owned auto".

SAMPLE

## EXCLUSIONS

We will not pay for:

1. Loss to "your covered auto" or any "non-owned auto" which occurs while it is being used as a public or livery conveyance. This Exclusion (1.) does not apply to a share-the-expense car pool.

2. Damage due and confined to:

   a. Wear and tear;

   b. Freezing;

   c. Mechanical or electrical breakdown or failure; or

   d. Road damage to tires.

   This Exclusion (2.) does not apply if the damage results from the total theft of "your covered auto" or any "non-owned auto".

3. Loss due to or as a consequence of:

   a. Radioactive contamination;

   b. Discharge of any nuclear weapon (even if accidental);

   c. War (declared or undeclared);

   d. Civil war;

   e. Insurrection; or

   f. Rebellion or revolution.

4. Loss to any electronic equipment that reproduces, receives or transmits audio, visual or data signals. This includes but is not limited to:

   a. Radios and stereos;

   b. Tape decks;

   c. Compact disk systems;

   d. Navigation systems;

   e. Internet access systems;

   f. Personal computers;

   g. Video entertainment systems;

   h. Telephones;

   i. Televisions;

   j. Two-way mobile radios;

   k. Scanners; or

   l. Citizens band radios.

   This Exclusion (4.) does not apply to electronic equipment that is permanently installed in "your covered auto" or any "non-owned auto".

5. Loss to tapes, records, disks or other media used with equipment described in Exclusion 4.

6. A total loss to "your covered auto" or any "non-owned auto" due to destruction or confiscation by governmental or civil authorities.

   This Exclusion (6.) does not apply to the interests of Loss Payees in "your covered auto".

7. Loss to:

   a. A "trailer", camper body, or motor home, which is not shown in the Declarations; or

   b. Facilities or equipment used with such "trailer", camper body or motor home. Facilities or equipment include but are not limited to:

      (1) Cooking, dining, plumbing or refrigeration facilities;

      (2) Awnings or cabanas; or

      (3) Any other facilities or equipment used with a "trailer", camper body, or motor home.

   This Exclusion (7.) does not apply to a:

   a. "Trailer", and its facilities or equipment, which you do not own; or

   b. "Trailer", camper body, or the facilities or equipment in or attached to the "trailer" or camper body, which you:

      (1) Acquire during the policy period; and

      (2) Ask us to insure within 14 days after you become the owner.

8. Loss to any "non-owned auto" when used by you or any "family member" without a reasonable belief that you or that "family member" are entitled to do so.

9. Loss to equipment designed or used for the detection or location of radar or laser.

10. Loss to any custom furnishings or equipment in or upon any pickup or van. Custom furnishings or equipment include but are not limited to:

    a. Special carpeting or insulation;

    b. Furniture or bars;

    c. Height-extending roofs; or

    d. Custom murals, paintings or other decals or graphics.

    This Exclusion (10.) does not apply to a cap, cover or bedliner in or upon any "your covered auto" which is a pickup.

11. Loss to any "non-owned auto" being maintained or used by any person while employed or otherwise engaged in the "business" of:

    a. Selling;

    b. Repairing;

SAMPLE

c. Servicing;

d. Storing; or

e. Parking;

vehicles designed for use on public highways. This includes road testing and delivery.

12. Loss to "your covered auto" or any "non-owned auto", located inside a facility designed for racing, for the purpose of:

a. Competing in; or

b. Practicing or preparing for;

any prearranged or organized racing or speed contest.

13. Loss to, or loss of use of, a "non-owned auto" rented by:

a. You; or

b. Any "family member";

if a rental vehicle company is precluded from recovering such loss or loss of use, from you or that "family member", pursuant to the provisions of any applicable rental agreement or state law.

**LIMIT OF LIABILITY**

A. Our limit of liability for loss will be the lesser of the:

1. Actual cash value of the stolen or damaged property; or

2. Amount necessary to repair or replace the property with other property of like kind and quality.

However, the most we will pay for loss to:

1. Any "non-owned auto" which is a trailer is $1500.

2. Electronic equipment that reproduces, receives or transmits audio, visual or data signals, which is permanently installed in the auto in locations not used by the auto manufacturer for installation of such equipment, is $1,000.

B. An adjustment for depreciation and physical condition will be made in determining actual cash value in the event of a total loss.

C. If a repair or replacement results in better than like kind or quality, we will not pay for the amount of the betterment.

**PAYMENT OF LOSS**

We may pay for loss in money or repair or replace the damaged or stolen property. We may, at our expense, return any stolen property to:

1. You; or

2. The address shown in this policy.

If we return stolen property we will pay for any damage resulting from the theft. We may keep all or part of the property at an agreed or appraised value.

If we pay for loss in money, our payment will include the applicable sales tax for the damaged or stolen property.

**NO BENEFIT TO BAILEE**

This insurance shall not directly or indirectly benefit any carrier or other bailee for hire.

**OTHER SOURCES OF RECOVERY**

If other sources of recovery also cover the loss, we will pay only our share of the loss. Our share is the proportion that our limit of liability bears to the total of all applicable limits. However, any insurance we provide with respect to a "non-owned auto" shall be excess over any other collectible source of recovery including, but not limited to:

1. Any coverage provided by the owner of the "non-owned auto";

2. Any other applicable physical damage insurance;

3. Any other source of recovery applicable to the loss.

**APPRAISAL**

A. If we and you do not agree on the amount of loss, either may demand an appraisal of the loss. In this event, each party will select a competent and impartial appraiser. The two appraisers will select an umpire. The appraisers will state separately the actual cash value and the amount of loss. If they fail to agree, they will submit their differences to the umpire. A decision agreed to by any two will be binding. Each party will:

1. Pay its chosen appraiser; and

2. Bear the expenses of the appraisal and umpire equally.

B. We do not waive any of our rights under this policy by agreeing to an appraisal.

 PP 00 01 01 05

SAMPLE

## PART E – DUTIES AFTER AN ACCIDENT OR LOSS

We have no duty to provide coverage under this policy if the failure to comply with the following duties is prejudicial to us:

**A.** We must be notified promptly of how, when and where the accident or loss happened. Notice should also include the names and addresses of any injured persons and of any witnesses.

**B.** A person seeking any coverage must:

  **1.** Cooperate with us in the investigation, settlement or defense of any claim or suit.

  **2.** Promptly send us copies of any notices or legal papers received in connection with the accident or loss.

  **3.** Submit, as often as we reasonably require:

    **a.** To physical exams by physicians we select. We will pay for these exams.

    **b.** To examination under oath and subscribe the same.

  **4.** Authorize us to obtain:

    **a.** Medical reports; and

    **b.** Other pertinent records.

  **5.** Submit a proof of loss when required by us.

**C.** A person seeking Uninsured Motorists Coverage must also:

  **1.** Promptly notify the police if a hit-and-run driver is involved.

  **2.** Promptly send us copies of the legal papers if a suit is brought.

**D.** A person seeking Coverage For Damage To Your Auto must also:

  **1.** Take reasonable steps after loss to protect "your covered auto" or any "non-owned auto" and their equipment from further loss. We will pay reasonable expenses incurred to do this.

  **2.** Promptly notify the police if "your covered auto" or any "non-owned auto" is stolen.

  **3.** Permit us to inspect and appraise the damaged property before its repair or disposal.

## PART F – GENERAL PROVISIONS

### BANKRUPTCY

Bankruptcy or insolvency of the "insured" shall not relieve us of any obligations under this policy.

### CHANGES

**A.** This policy contains all the agreements between you and us. Its terms may not be changed or waived except by endorsement issued by us.

**B.** If there is a change to the information used to develop the policy premium, we may adjust your premium. Changes during the policy term that may result in a premium increase or decrease include, but are not limited to, changes in:

  **1.** The number, type or use classification of insured vehicles;

  **2.** Operators using insured vehicles;

  **3.** The place of principal garaging of insured vehicles;

  **4.** Coverage, deductible or limits.

If a change resulting from **A.** or **B.** requires a premium adjustment, we will make the premium adjustment in accordance with our manual rules.

**C.** If we make a change which broadens coverage under this edition of your policy without additional premium charge, that change will automatically apply to your policy as of the date we implement the change in your state. This Paragraph (**C.**) does not apply to changes implemented with a general program revision that includes both broadenings and restrictions in coverage, whether that general program revision is implemented through introduction of:

  **1.** A subsequent edition of your policy; or

  **2.** An Amendatory Endorsement.

### FRAUD

We do not provide coverage for any "insured" who has made fraudulent statements or engaged in fraudulent conduct in connection with any accident or loss for which coverage is sought under this policy.

### LEGAL ACTION AGAINST US

**A.** No legal action may be brought against us until there has been full compliance with all the terms of this policy. In addition, under Part **A,** no legal action may be brought against us until:

  **1.** We agree in writing that the "insured" has an obligation to pay; or

  **2.** The amount of that obligation has been finally determined by judgment after trial.

SAMPLE

**B.** No person or organization has any right under this policy to bring us into any action to determine the liability of an "insured".

**OUR RIGHT TO RECOVER PAYMENT**

**A.** If we make a payment under this policy and the person to or for whom payment was made has a right to recover damages from another we shall be subrogated to that right. That person shall do:

1. Whatever is necessary to enable us to exercise our rights; and

2. Nothing after loss to prejudice them.

However, our rights in this Paragraph **(A.)** do not apply under Part **D**, against any person using "your covered auto" with a reasonable belief that that person is entitled to do so.

**B.** If we make a payment under this policy and the person to or for whom payment is made recovers damages from another, that person shall:

1. Hold in trust for us the proceeds of the recovery; and

2. Reimburse us to the extent of our payment.

**POLICY PERIOD AND TERRITORY**

**A.** This policy applies only to accidents and losses which occur:

1. During the policy period as shown in the Declarations; and

2. Within the policy territory.

**B.** The policy territory is:

1. The United States of America, its territories or possessions;

2. Puerto Rico; or

3. Canada.

This policy also applies to loss to, or accidents involving, "your covered auto" while being transported between their ports.

**TERMINATION**

**A. Cancellation**

This policy may be cancelled during the policy period as follows:

1. The named insured shown in the Declarations may cancel by:

   **a.** Returning this policy to us; or

   **b.** Giving us advance written notice of the date cancellation is to take effect.

2. We may cancel by mailing to the named insured shown in the Declarations at the address shown in this policy:

   **a.** At least 10 days notice:

   **(1)** If cancellation is for nonpayment of premium; or

**(2)** If notice is mailed during the first 60 days this policy is in effect and this is not a renewal or continuation policy; or

**b.** At least 20 days notice in all other cases.

3. After this policy is in effect for 60 days, or if this is a renewal or continuation policy, we will cancel only:

   **a.** For nonpayment of premium; or

   **b.** If your driver's license or that of:

   **(1)** Any driver who lives with you; or

   **(2)** Any driver who customarily uses "your covered auto";

   has been suspended or revoked. This must have occurred:

   **(1)** During the policy period; or

   **(2)** Since the last anniversary of the original effective date if the policy period is other than 1 year; or

   **c.** If the policy was obtained through material misrepresentation.

**B. Nonrenewal**

If we decide not to renew or continue this policy, we will mail notice to the named insured shown in the Declarations at the address shown in this policy. Notice will be mailed at least 20 days before the end of the policy period. Subject to this notice requirement, if the policy period is:

1. Less than 6 months, we will have the right not to renew or continue this policy every 6 months, beginning 6 months after its original effective date.

2. 6 months or longer, but less than one year, we will have the right not to renew or continue this policy at the end of the policy period.

3. 1 year or longer, we will have the right not to renew or continue this policy at each anniversary of its original effective date.

**C. Automatic Termination**

If we offer to renew or continue and you or your representative do not accept, this policy will automatically terminate at the end of the current policy period. Failure to pay the required renewal or continuation premium when due shall mean that you have not accepted our offer.

If you obtain other insurance on "your covered auto", any similar insurance provided by this policy will terminate as to that auto on the effective date of the other insurance.

PP 00 01 01 05

SAMPLE

**D. Other Termination Provisions**

1. We may deliver any notice instead of mailing it. Proof of mailing of any notice shall be sufficient proof of notice.

2. If this policy is cancelled, you may be entitled to a premium refund. If so, we will send you the refund. The premium refund, if any, will be computed according to our manuals. However, making or offering to make the refund is not a condition of cancellation.

3. The effective date of cancellation stated in the notice shall become the end of the policy period.

**TRANSFER OF YOUR INTEREST IN THIS POLICY**

**A.** Your rights and duties under this policy may not be assigned without our written consent. However, if a named insured shown in the Declarations dies, coverage will be provided for:

1. The surviving spouse if resident in the same household at the time of death. Coverage applies to the spouse as if a named insured shown in the Declarations; and

2. The legal representative of the deceased person as if a named insured shown in the Declarations. This applies only with respect to the representative's legal responsibility to maintain or use "your covered auto".

**B.** Coverage will only be provided until the end of the policy period.

**TWO OR MORE AUTO POLICIES**

If this policy and any other auto insurance policy issued to you by us apply to the same accident, the maximum limit of our liability under all the policies shall not exceed the highest applicable limit of liability under any one policy.

# GLOSSARY

**Absolute liability**  *See* **Strict liability**.

**Accidental death and dismemberment (AD&D) benefits**  Additional benefits payable in life insurance if the insured dies in an accident or incurs certain types of bodily injury.

**Accelerated death benefits**  A rider or benefit in a life insurance policy that allows insureds who are terminally ill or who suffer from certain catastrophic diseases to receive part or all of their life insurance benefits before they die, primarily to pay for the care they require.

**Accident**  A loss-causing event that is sudden, unforeseen, and unintentional. *See also* **Occurrence**.

**Accidental bodily injury**  Bodily injury resulting from an act whose result was accidental or unexpected.

**Actual cash value**  Value of property at the time of its damage or loss, determined by subtracting depreciation of the item from its replacement cost.

**Additional insured**  Person or party who is added to the named insured's policy by an endorsement.

**Add-on plan**  Pays benefits to an automobile accident victim without regard to fault, but the injured person still has the right to sue the negligent driver who caused the accident.

**Adjustment bureau**  Organization for adjusting insurance claims that is supported by insurers using the bureau's services.

**Advance funding**  Pension-funding method in which the employer systematically and periodically sets aside funds prior to the employee's retirement.

**Advance premium mutual**  Mutual insurance company owned by the policyholders that does not issue assessable policies but charges premiums expected to be sufficient to pay all claims and expenses.

**Adverse selection**  Tendency of persons with a higher-than-average chance of loss to seek insurance at standard (average) rates, which, if not controlled by underwriting, results in higher-than-expected loss levels.

**Affordable Care Act**  Legislation enacted in 2010 that extends health-care coverage to millions of uninsured Americans, provides substantial subsidies to uninsured individuals and small business firms to purchase health insurance, contains provisions to lower health-care costs, and prohibits insurers from engaging in certain abusive practices. The full law becomes effective January 1, 2014.

**Affordable Insurance Exchange**  A provision under the Affordable Care Act that creates an Affordable Insurance Exchange in each state, which is a new transparent and competitive insurance marketplace in which individuals and small firms with fewer than 100 employees can purchase affordable and qualified health insurance plans.

**Agency agreement**  Contract between an insurance agent and insurance company that describes the powers, rights, and duties of the agent.

**Agent**  Someone who legally represents the insurer, has the authority to act on the insurer's behalf, and can bind the insurer (principal) by expressed authority, by implied authority, and by apparent authority.

**Aggregate deductible**  Deductible in some property and health insurance contracts in which all covered losses during a year are added together and the insurer pays only when the aggregate deductible amount is exceeded.

**Aleatory contract**  One in which the values exchanged may not be equal but depend on an uncertain event.

**Alien insurer**  Insurance company chartered by a foreign country and meeting certain licensing requirements.

**"All-risks" policy**  Coverage by an insurance contract that promises to cover all losses except those losses specifically excluded in the policy. Also called an **open perils policy** and a **special coverage policy**.

**Alternative dispute resolution (ADR) techniques**  Techniques to resolve a legal dispute without litigation.

**Annuitant**  Person who receives the periodic payment from an annuity.

**Annuity**  Periodic payment to an individual that continues for a fixed period or for the duration of a designated life or lives.

**Appraisal clause**  Used when the insured and insurer agree that the loss is covered, but the amount of the loss is in dispute.

**Assessment mutual**  Mutual insurance company that has the right to assess policyholders for losses and expenses.

**Assigned risk plan**  *See* **Automobile insurance plan**.

**Assumption-of-risk**  Defense against a negligence claim that bars recovery for damages if a person understands and recognizes the danger inherent in a particular activity or occupation.

**Attitudinal hazard**  Carelessness or indifference to a loss, which increases the frequency or severity of a loss. Also known as **morale hazard**.

**Attractive nuisance**  Condition that can attract and injure children. Occupants of land on which such a condition exists are liable for injuries to children.

**Automatic premium loan**   Cash borrowed from a life insurance policy's cash value to pay an overdue premium after the grace period for paying the premium has expired.

**Automobile insurance plan**   Formerly called **assigned risk plan**. Method for providing auto insurance to persons considered to be high-risk drivers who cannot obtain protection in the voluntary markets. All auto insurers in the state are assigned their share of such drivers based on the volume of auto insurance business written in the state.

**Average indexed monthly earnings (AIME)**   Under the OASDI program, the person's actual earnings are indexed to determine his or her primary insurance amount (PIA).

**Avoidance**   A risk control technique in which a certain loss exposure is never acquired, or an existing loss exposure is abandoned.

**Bailee's customer policy**   Policy that covers the loss or damage to property of customers regardless of a bailee's legal liability.

**Basic form**   *See* **Dwelling Property 1**.

**Benefit period**   Length of time benefits are paid in a disability income policy or long-term care policy after the elimination period is met.

**Binder**   Authorization of coverage by an agent given before the company has formally approved a policy. Provides evidence that the insurance is in force.

**Blackout period**   The period during which Social Security benefits are not paid to a surviving spouse—between the time the youngest child reaches age 16 and the surviving spouse's sixtieth birthday.

**Blue Cross plans**   Typically nonprofit, community-oriented prepayment plans that provide health insurance coverage primarily for hospital services.

**Blue Shield plans**   Typically nonprofit prepayment plans that provide health insurance coverage mainly for physicians' services.

**Boatowners package policy**   A special package policy for boat owners that combines physical damage insurance, medical expense insurance, liability insurance, and other coverages in one contract.

**Boiler and machinery insurance**   Commercial insurance that covers damage caused by the malfunction or breakdown of boilers, or other equipment, including air conditioners, heating, electrical, telephone, and computer systems. Also called **Equipment breakdown** or **Systems breakdown insurance**.

**Broad form**   *See* **Dwelling Property 2; Homeowners 2 policy**.

**Broker**   Someone who legally represents the insured, soliciting or accepting applications for insurance that are not in force until the company accepts the business.

**Burglary**   The unlawful taking of property from inside the premises by a person who unlawfully enters or leaves the premises, as evidenced by marks of forcible entry or exit.

**Business income (and extra expense) coverage form**   A form that can be added to a commercial package policy that covers both the loss of business income and extra expenses

that may still continue as a result of a physical damage loss to covered property.

**Business income (without extra expense) coverage form**   A form that covers the loss of business income from a covered loss. Extra expenses are covered only to the extent that such expenses reduce the loss, and coverage is limited to the amount of loss that is reduced.

**Businessowners policy**   Package policy specifically designed to meet the basic property and liability insurance needs of smaller business firms in one contract.

**Cafeteria plan**   Generic term for an employee benefit plan that allows employees to select among the various group life, medical expense, disability, dental, and other plans that best meet their specific needs.

**Calendar-year deductible**   Amount payable by an insured during a calendar year before a group or individual health insurance policy begins to pay for medical expenses.

**Capacity**   Term used in the property and casualty insurance industry that refers to the relative level of surplus; the greater the industry's surplus position, the more willing underwriters will be to write new business or reduce premiums.

**Capital budgeting**   Method of determining which capital investment projects a company should undertake based on the time value of money.

**Capital retention approach**   A method used to estimate the amount of life insurance to own. Under this method, the insurance proceeds are retained and are not liquidated.

**Capitation fee**   A method of payment in managed care plans by which a physician or hospital receives a fixed annual payment for each plan member regardless of the frequency or type of service provided.

**Captive agent**   A term to describe agents who represent only one insurer or a group of insurers that are financially interrelated or under common ownership.

**Captive insurer**   Insurance company established and owned by a parent firm in order to insure its loss exposures while reducing premium costs, providing easier access to a reinsurer, and perhaps easing tax burdens.

**Cargo insurance**   Type of ocean marine insurance that protects the shipper of the goods against financial loss if the goods are damaged or lost.

**Cash refund annuity**   The balance is paid in one lump sum to the beneficiary after the death of the annuitant, if total payments do not equal the annuity purchase price.

**Cash surrender value**   Amount payable to the owner of a cash-value life insurance policy if he or she decides the insurance is no longer wanted. Calculated separately from the legal reserve.

**Casualty insurance**   Field of insurance that covers whatever is not covered by fire, marine, and life insurance. Includes auto, liability, burglary and theft, workers compensation, glass, and health insurance.

**Catastrophe bonds**   Corporate bonds that permit the issuer of the bond to skip or defer scheduled payments of principal or interest if a catastrophic loss occurs.

**Causes-of-loss form** Form added to commercial property insurance policy that indicates the causes of loss that are covered. There are three causes-of-loss forms: basic, broad, and special.

**Ceding company** Insurer that writes the policy initially and later transfers part or all of the coverage to a reinsurer.

**Certified Financial Planner (CFP)** Professional who has attained a high degree of technical competency in financial planning and has passed a series of professional examinations.

**Certified Insurance Counselor (CIC)** Professional in property and casualty insurance who has passed a series of examinations sponsored by the Society of Certified Insurance Counselors.

**Chance of loss** The probability that an event will occur.

**Change-of-plan provision** Allows life insurance policyholders to exchange their present policies for different contracts; provides flexibility.

**Chartered Financial Consultant (ChFC)** An individual who has attained a high degree of technical competency in the fields of financial planning, investments, and life and health insurance and has passed professional examinations administered by The American College.

**Chartered Life Underwriter (CLU)** An individual who has attained a high degree of technical competency in the fields of life and health insurance and has passed professional examinations administered by The American College.

**Chartered Property Casualty Underwriter (CPCU)** Professional who has attained a high degree of technical competency in property and liability insurance and has passed professional examinations administered by the Institutes (formerly known as the American Institute for Chartered Property Casualty Underwriters).

**Chief risk officer (CRO)** Person responsible for the treatment of pure and speculative risks faced by an organization.

**Choice no-fault plans** Motorists can elect to be covered under a state's no-fault automobile insurance law with lower premiums or they can retain the right to sue under the tort liability system with higher premiums.

**Claims adjustor** Person who settles claims: an agent, company adjustor, independent adjustor, or public adjustor.

**Claims-made policy** A liability insurance policy that only covers claims that are first reported during the policy period, provided the event occurred after the retroactive date (if any) stated in the policy.

**Class rating** Rate-making method in which similar insureds are placed in the same underwriting class and each is charged the same rate. Also called manual rating.

**CLU** See **Chartered Life Underwriter**.

**Coinsurance provision** Common provision in property insurance contracts that requires the insured to maintain insurance on the property at a stated percentage of its actual cash value or its replacement cost. Payment for a loss is determined by multiplying the amount of the loss by the fraction derived from the amount of insurance required. If the coinsurance requirement is not met at the time of loss, the insured will be penalized. In health insurance, coinsurance is a provision that requires the insured to pay a specified percentage of covered medical expenses in excess of the deductible.

**Collateral source rule** Under this rule, the defendant cannot introduce any evidence that shows the injured party has received compensation from other collateral sources.

**Collision loss** Damages to an automobile caused by the upset of the automobile or its impact with another vehicle or object. Collision losses are paid by the insurer regardless of fault.

**Commercial crime coverage form** Insurance Services Office (ISO) form that can be added to a package policy to cover crime exposures of business firms.

**Commercial general liability policy (CGL)** Commercial liability policy drafted by the Insurance Services Office containing two coverage forms—an occurrence form and a claims-made form.

**Commercial lines** Property and casualty coverages for business firms, nonprofit organizations, and government agencies.

**Commercial package policy (CPP)** A commercial policy that can be designed to meet the specific insurance needs of business firms. Property and liability coverage forms are combined to form a single policy.

**Commercial risks** Risks faced by business firms, including property risks, liability risks, loss of business income, and other risks.

**Commodity price risk** Risk of losing money if the price of a commodity changes.

**Commutative contract** One in which the values exchanged by both parties are theoretically even.

**Company adjustor** Claims adjustor who is a salaried employee representing only one company.

**Comparative negligence laws** Laws enacted by many jurisdictions permitting an injured person to recover damages even though he or she may have contributed to the accident. The financial burden is shared by both parties according to their respective degrees of fault.

**Compensatory damages** An award for damages that compensates an injured victim for losses actually incurred. Compensatory damages include both special damages and general damages.

**Completed operations** Liability arising out of faulty work performed away from the premises after the work or operations are completed; applicable to contractors, plumbers, electricians, repair shops, and similar firms.

**Compulsory insurance law** Law protecting accident victims against irresponsible motorists by requiring owners and operators of automobiles to carry certain amounts of liability insurance in order to license the vehicle and drive legally within the state.

**Concealment** Deliberate failure of an applicant for insurance to reveal a material fact to the insurer.

**Conditions**   Provisions inserted in an insurance contract that qualify or place limitations on the insurer's promise to perform.

**Consequential loss**   Financial loss occurring as the consequence of some other loss. Often called an indirect loss.

**Consolidation**   Combining of business organizations through mergers and acquisitions.

**Consumer-directed health plan (CDHP)**   A generic term for a plan that combines a high-deductible health insurance plan with a health savings account (HSA) or health reimbursement arrangement (HRA). The plans are designed to make employees more sensitive to health-care costs, to provide a financial incentive to avoid unnecessary care, and to seek out low-cost providers.

**Contingent beneficiary**   Beneficiary of a life insurance policy who is entitled to receive the policy proceeds on the insured's death if the primary beneficiary dies before the insured; or the beneficiary who receives the remaining payments if the primary beneficiary dies before receiving the guaranteed number of payments.

**Contingent liability**   Liability arising out of work done by independent contractors for a firm. A firm may be liable for the work done by an independent contractor if the activity is illegal, the situation does not permit delegation of authority, or the work is inherently dangerous.

**Contract bond**   Type of surety bond guaranteeing that the principal will fulfill all contractual obligations.

**Contract of adhesion**   The insured must accept the entire contract, with all of its terms and conditions; if there is ambiguity in the contract it is construed against the insurer.

**Contractual liability**   Legal liability of another party that the business firm agrees to assume by a written or oral contract.

**Contribution by equal shares**   Type of other-insurance provision often found in liability insurance contracts that requires each company to share equally in the loss until the share of each insurer equals the lowest limit of liability under any policy or until the full amount of loss is paid.

**Contributory negligence**   Common law defense blocking an injured person from recovering damages if he or she has contributed in any way to the accident.

**Contributory plan**   Group life or health insurance plan in which the employees pay part of the premiums.

**Coordination-of-benefits provision**   Provision in a group medical expense plan that prevents over-insurance and duplication of benefits when one person is covered under more than one group plan. The provision specifies the order of payment when more than one group medical expense plan covers the loss.

**Copayment**   Flat amount that the insured must pay for certain benefits, such as an office visit or prescription drug. Not to be confused with **coinsurance**.

**Cost-of-living rider**   Benefit that can be added to a life insurance policy under which the policyholder can purchase one-year term insurance equal to the cumulative percentage change in the consumer price index with no evidence of insurability.

**Cost of risk**   A risk management tool that measures certain costs in a risk management program, including insurance premiums paid, retained losses, outside risk management services, financial guarantees, internal administrative costs, taxes and fees, and certain other expenses.

**Coverage for damage to your auto**   That part of the personal auto policy that pays for damage or theft of the insured automobile. This optional coverage can be used to insure both collision and other-than-collision losses.

**CPCU**   *See* **Chartered Property Casualty Underwriter.**

**Credit default swap**   An agreement in which the risk of default of a financial instrument is transferred from the owner of the financial instrument to the issuer of the instrument.

**Currency exchange rate risk**   Risk of loss of value caused by changes in exchange rates between countries.

**Current assumption whole life insurance**   Nonparticipating whole life policy in which the cash values are based on the insurer's current mortality, investment, and expense experience. An accumulation account is credited with a current interest rate that changes over time. Also called interest-sensitive whole life insurance.

**Currently insured**   Status of a covered person under the Old-Age, Survivors, and Disability Insurance (OASDI) program who has at least six credits out of the last thirteen quarters, ending with the quarter of death, disability, or entitlement to retirement benefits.

**Damage to property of others**   Provision in Section II of a homeowners policy that pays up to $1000 per occurrence on behalf of an insured who damages someone's property. Payment is made without regard to legal liability.

**Declarations**   Statements in an insurance contract that provide information about the property to be insured and used for underwriting and rating purposes and identification of the property to be insured.

**Deductible**   A provision by which a specified amount is subtracted from the total loss payment that would otherwise be paid.

**Deferred annuity**   A retirement annuity that provides benefits at some future date.

**Defined-benefit plan**   Type of pension plan in which the retirement benefit is known in advance but the contributions vary depending on the amount necessary to fund the desired benefit.

**Defined-contribution plan**   Type of pension plan in which the contribution rate is fixed but the retirement benefit is variable. Most qualified retirement plans are defined-contribution plans.

**Demutualization**   A term to describe the conversion of a mutual insurer into a stock insurer.

**Dependency period**   Period of time following the readjustment period during which the surviving spouse's children are under eighteen and, therefore, dependent on the parent.

**Diagnosis-related groups (DRGs)** Method for reimbursing hospitals under the Medicare program. Under this system, a flat, uniform amount is paid to each hospital for the same type of medical care or treatment.

**Difference in conditions insurance (DIC)** An open perils ("all-risks") policy that covers other perils not insured by basic property insurance contracts, supplemental to and excluding the coverage provided by underlying contracts.

**Direct loss** Financial loss that results directly from an insured peril.

**Directors and officer liability (D&O) insurance** A commercial liability coverage that provides financial protection for the directors, officers, and the corporation if the directors and officers are sued for mismanagement of the company's affairs.

**Direct-response system** A marketing method where insurance is sold without the services of an agent. Potential customers are solicited by advertising in the mails, newspapers, magazines, television, radio, and other media.

**Direct writer** Insurance company in which the salesperson is an employee of the insurer, not an independent contractor, and which pays all selling expenses, including salary. In property and casualty insurance, the term "direct writer" is also used to describe insurers that use the exclusive agency system. *See also* **exclusive agency system.**

**Disability-insured** Status of an individual who is insured for disability benefits under the Old-Age, Survivors, and Disability Insurance (OASDI) program.

**Diversifiable risk** A risk that affects only individuals or small groups and not the entire economy, which can be reduced or eliminated by diversification. Also called **nonsystematic risk** or **particular risk.**

**Dividend accumulations** A dividend option in a participating life insurance policy in which the dividend is retained by the insurer and accumulated at interest.

**Domestic insurer** Insurance company domiciled and licensed in the state in which it does business.

**Double indemnity rider** Benefit that can be added to a life insurance policy doubling the face amount of life insurance if death occurs as the result of an accident.

**Dram shop law** Law that imputes negligence to the owner of a business that sells liquor in the event that an intoxicated customer causes injury or property damage to another person.

**Driver education credit** Student discount or reduction in premium amount for which young drivers become eligible on completion of a driver education course.

**Dwelling Property 1** Property insurance policy that insures the dwelling, other structures, personal property, fair rental value, and certain other coverages; covers a limited number of perils.

**Dwelling Property 2** Property insurance policy that insures the dwelling and other structures at replacement cost. It adds additional coverages and has a greater number of covered perils than the Dwelling Property 1 policy.

**Dwelling Property 3** Property insurance policy that covers the dwelling and other structures against direct physical loss from any peril except for those perils otherwise excluded. However, personal property is covered on a named-perils basis.

**Earned premiums** Premiums actually earned during the accounting period as contrasted with premiums written. Earned premiums represent the portion of written premiums that can be recognized as income for the portion of the policy period that has already elapsed.

**Earnings test (retirement test)** Test under the Old-Age, Survivors, and Disability Insurance (OASDI) program that reduces monthly cash benefits to those beneficiaries who have annual earned incomes in excess of the maximums allowed.

**Eligibility period** Brief period of time during which an employee can sign up for group insurance without furnishing evidence of insurability.

**Elimination period (waiting period)** Waiting period in health insurance during which benefits are not paid. Also a period of time that must be met before disability benefits are payable.

**Employee Retirement Income Security Act (ERISA)** Legislation passed in 1974 applying to most private pension and welfare plans that requires certain standards to protect participating employees.

**Employers liability insurance** Covers employers against lawsuits by employees who are injured in the course of employment, but whose injuries (or disease) are not compensable under the state's workers compensation law.

**Endorsement** Written provision that adds to, deletes, or modifies the provisions in the original contract. *See also* **Rider.**

**Endowment insurance** Type of life insurance that pays the face amount of insurance to the beneficiary if the insured dies within a specified period or to the policyholder if the insured survives to the end of the period.

**Enterprise risk** A term that encompasses all major risks faced by a business, including pure risk, speculative risk, strategic risk, operational risk, and financial risk.

**Enterprise risk management** Comprehensive risk management program that considers an organization's pure risks, speculative risks, strategic risks, and operational risks.

**Entire-contract clause** Provision in life insurance policies stating that the life insurance policy and attached application constitute the entire contract between the parties.

**Equipment breakdown insurance** Insurance that covers losses due to accidental breakdown of covered equipment. *See also* **boiler and machinery insurance.**

**Equity in the unearned premium reserve** Amount by which an unearned premium reserve is overstated because it is established on the basis of gross premiums rather than net premiums.

**Equity indexed annuity** A fixed, deferred annuity that allows limited participation in the stock market but guarantees the principal against loss if the contract is held to term.

**ERISA** *See* **Employee Retirement Income Security Act.**

**Errors and omissions insurance** Liability insurance policy that provides protection against loss incurred by a client because of some negligent act, error, or omission by the insured.

**Estate planning** Process designed to conserve estate assets before and after death, distribute property according to the individual's wishes, minimize federal estate and state inheritance taxes, provide estate liquidity to meet costs of estate settlement, and provide for the family's financial needs.

**Estoppel** Legal doctrine that prevents a person from denying the truth of a previous representation of fact, especially when such representation has been relied on by the one to whom the statement was made.

**Excess insurance** Under an excess insurance plan, the insurer does not participate in the loss until the actual loss exceeds a certain amount.

**Exclusion ratio** Calculation to determine the taxable and nontaxable portions of annuity payments, which is determined by dividing the investment in the contract by the expected return.

**Exclusions** Provisions in an insurance contract that list the perils, losses, and property excluded from coverage.

**Exclusive agency system** Type of insurance marketing system under which the agent represents only one company or group of companies under common ownership. In the property and casualty industry, insurers that use this marketing system are also called "direct writers."

**Exclusive provider organization (EPO)** A plan that does not cover medical care received outside of a network of preferred providers.

**Exclusive remedy doctrine** Doctrine in workers compensation insurance that states that workers compensation benefits should be the exclusive or sole source of recovery for workers who have a job-related accident or disease; doctrine has been eroded by legal decisions.

**Expense loading** *See* **Loading.**

**Expense ratio** That proportion of the gross rate available for expenses and profit. Ratio of expenses incurred to premiums written.

**Experience rating** (1) Method of rating group life and health insurance plans that uses the loss experience of the group to determine the premiums to be charged. (2) As applied to property and casualty insurance, the class or manual rate is adjusted upward or downward based on past loss experience. (3) As applied to state unemployment insurance programs, firms with favorable employment records pay lower unemployment compensation tax rates.

**Exposure unit** Unit of measurement used in insurance pricing.

**Extended nonowned coverage** Endorsement that can be added to an auto liability insurance policy that covers the insured while driving any nonowned automobile on a regular basis.

**Extra expense coverage form** A separate form that can be used to cover the extra expenses incurred by a firm to continue business operations during a period of restoration.

**Factory mutual** Mutual insurance company insuring only properties that meet high underwriting standards; emphasizes loss prevention.

**Facultative reinsurance** Optional, case-by-case method of reinsurance used when the ceding company receives an application for insurance that exceeds its retention limit.

**Fair Access to Insurance Requirements (FAIR plan)** Property insurance plan that provides basic property insurance to property owners in areas where they are unable to obtain insurance in the normal markets.

**Fair rental value** Amount payable to an insured homeowner for loss of rental income due to damage that makes the premises uninhabitable.

**Family purpose doctrine** Concept that imputes negligence committed by immediate family members while operating a family car to the owner of the car.

**File-and-use law** Law for regulating insurance rates under which companies are required only to file the rates with the state insurance department before putting them into effect.

**Financial institution bond** Bond that covers crime loss exposures of commercial banks, savings and loan institutions, and other financial institutions; used to cover bank holdups, employee dishonesty, forgery, alteration of checks, armored car exposures, and other crime exposures of financial institutions.

**Financial Modernization Act of 1999** A federal law that allows banks, insurers, investment firms, and other financial institutions to enter and compete in each other's financial markets.

**Financial responsibility law** Law that requires persons involved in automobile accidents to furnish proof of financial responsibility up to a minimum dollar limit or face having driving privileges revoked or suspended.

**Financial risk** A risk that business firms face because of adverse changes in commodity prices, interest rates, foreign exchange rates, and the value of money.

**Fire legal liability** Liability of a firm or person for fire damage caused by negligence and damage to property of others.

**First named insured** The first name that appears on the declarations page of the policy as an insured who has certain additional rights and responsibilities that do not apply to other named insureds.

**Fixed-amount option** Life insurance settlement option in which the policy proceeds are paid out in fixed amounts.

**Fixed annuity** Annuity whose periodic payment is a guaranteed fixed amount.

**Fixed-period option** Life insurance settlement option in which the policy proceeds are paid out over a fixed period of time.

**Flexible-premium annuity** An annuity contract that permits the owner to vary the size and frequency of premium payments. The amount of retirement income depends on the accumulated sum in the annuity at retirement.

**Flexible-spending account** An arrangement by which the employee agrees to a salary reduction, which can be used to pay for plan benefits, unreimbursed medical and dental expenses, and other expenses permitted by the Internal Revenue Code.

**Flex-rating law** Type of rating law in which prior approval of the rates is required only if the rates exceed a certain percentage above and below the rates previously filed.

**Foreign insurer** Insurance company chartered by one state but licensed to do business in another.

**Fortuitous loss** Unforeseen and unexpected loss that occurs as a result of chance.

**Fraternal insurer** Mutual insurance company that provides life and health insurance to members of a religious faith, ethnic group, or social organization.

**Full retirement age** Age at which full unreduced retirement benefits are payable to beneficiaries under the Social Security program.

**Fully insured** Insured status of a covered person under the Old-Age, Survivors, and Disability Insurance (OASDI) program. To be fully insured for retirement benefits, 40 credits are required.

**Fundamental risk** A risk that affects the entire economy or large numbers of persons or groups within the economy.

**Funding agency** A financial institution that provides for the accumulation or administration of the contributions that will be used to pay pension benefits.

**Funding instrument** An insurance contract or trust agreement that states the terms under which the funding agency will accumulate, administer, and disburse the pension funds.

**General aggregate limit** In the commercial general liability policy, it is the maximum amount the insurer will pay for the sum of the following—damages under Coverage A and B, and medical expenses under Coverage C.

**General average** In ocean marine insurance, a loss incurred for the common good that is shared by all parties to the venture.

**General damages** An award for damages that cannot be specifically measured or itemized, such as compensation for pain and suffering, disfigurement, or loss of companionship of a spouse.

**Good student discount** Reduction of automobile premium for a young driver at least sixteen who ranks in the upper 20 percent of his or her class, has a B or 3.0 average or better, or is on the Dean's list or honor roll. It is based on the premise that good students are better drivers.

**Grace period** Period of time during which a policyholder can pay an overdue life insurance or health insurance premium without causing the policy to lapse.

**Gross estate** The market value of the property that you own when you die. Also includes value of jointly owned property, life insurance, death proceeds, and certain other items.

**Gross premium** Amount paid by the insured, consisting of the gross rate multiplied by the number of exposure units.

**Gross rate** The sum of the pure premium and a loading element.

**Group life insurance** Life insurance provided on a number of persons in a single master contract. Physical examinations are not required, and certificates of insurance are issued to members of the group as evidence of insurance.

**Group term life insurance** Most common form of group life insurance. Yearly renewable term insurance on employees during their working careers.

**Group universal life products (GULP)** Universal life insurance plans sold to members of a group, such as individual employees of an employer. There are some differences between GULP plans and individual universal life plans; for instance, GULP expense charges are generally lower than those assessed against individual policies.

**Guaranteed issue** A term used to describe applicants for health insurance; coverage for medical expense insurance is guaranteed, and applicants cannot be turned down regardless of their medical condition.

**Guaranteed investment contract (GIC)** An arrangement in private pension plans in which the insurer guarantees the interest rate on a lump-sum pension deposit and also guarantees the principal against loss.

**Guaranteed purchase option** Benefit that can be added to a life insurance policy permitting the insured to purchase additional amounts of life insurance at specified times in the future without requiring evidence of insurability.

**Guaranteed renewable** Continuance provision of a health insurance policy under which the company guarantees to renew the policy to a stated age, and whose renewal is at the insured's option. Premiums can be increased for broad classes of insureds.

**Guaranteed replacement cost** In the event of a total loss, the insurer agrees to replace the home exactly as it was before the loss even though the replacement cost exceeds the amount of insurance stated in the policy.

**Hard insurance market** A period in the underwriting cycle during which underwriting standards are strict and premiums are high. *See also* **Soft insurance market** and **Underwriting cycle.**

**Hazard** Condition that creates or increases the chance of loss.

**Health maintenance organization (HMO)** A managed care plan that provides comprehensive health-care services to its members for a fixed prepaid fee. HMOs may also have cost-sharing provisions.

**Health savings account (HSA)** A tax-exempt or custodial account established exclusively for the purpose of paying qualified medical expenses of the account beneficiary who is covered under a high-deductible health insurance plan.

**Hedging**  Technique for transferring the risk of unfavorable price fluctuations to a speculator by purchasing and selling options and futures contracts on an organized exchange.

**High-deductible health plan (HDHP)**  A consumer-directed health plan that consists of major medical health insurance with a high deductible and a health savings account (HSA).

**HMO**  See **Health maintenance organization.**

**Hold-harmless clause**  Clause written into a contract by which one party agrees to release another party from all legal liability, such as a retailer who agrees to release the manufacturer from legal liability if the product injures someone.

**Home service life insurance**  Industrial life insurance and monthly debit ordinary life insurance contracts that are serviced by agents who earlier called on the policyholders at their homes to collect the premiums.

**Homeowners 2 policy (broad form)**  Homeowners insurance policy that provides coverage on a named-perils basis on the dwelling, other structures, and personal property. Personal liability insurance is also provided.

**Homeowners 3 policy (special form)**  Homeowners insurance policy that covers the dwelling and other structures on an open-perils basis and personal property on a named-perils basis. Personal liability insurance is also provided.

**Homeowners 4 policy (contents broad form)**  Homeowners insurance policy that applies to tenants renting a home or apartment. Covers the tenant's personal property and provides personal liability insurance.

**Homeowners 5 policy (comprehensive form)**  Homeowners insurance policy that provides open-perils coverage on both the building and personal property. The dwelling, other structures, and personal property are insured against direct physical loss to property; all losses are covered except those losses specifically excluded. Personal liability insurance is also provided.

**Homeowners 6 policy (unit-owners form)**  Homeowners insurance policy that covers personal property of insured owners of condominium units and cooperative apartments on a broad form, named-perils basis. Personal liability insurance is also provided.

**Homeowners 8 policy (modified coverage form)**  Homeowner policy that is designed for older homes. Dwelling and other structures are indemnified on the basis of repair cost using common construction materials and methods. Personal liability insurance is also provided.

**Hospital Insurance (Part A)**  Part A of Medicare that covers inpatient hospital care, skilled nursing facility care, home health-care services, and hospice care for Medicare beneficiaries.

**Hull insurance**  (1) Class of ocean marine insurance that covers physical damage to the ship or vessel insured. Typically written on an open perils ("all-risks") basis. (2) Physical damage insurance on aircraft—similar to collision insurance in an auto policy.

**Human life value**  For purposes of life insurance, the present value of the family's share of the deceased breadwinner's future earnings.

**Identity theft endorsement**  An endorsement to a homeowners policy that reimburses crime victims for the cost of restoring their identity and cleaning up their credit reports.

**Immediate annuity**  An annuity where the first payment is due one payment period from the date of purchase.

**Imputed negligence**  Case in which responsibility for damage can be transferred from the negligent party to another person, such as an employer.

**Incontestable clause**  Contractual provision in a life insurance policy stating that the insurer cannot contest the policy after it has been in force two years during the insured's lifetime.

**Indemnification**  Compensation to the victim of a loss, in whole or in part, by payment, repair, or replacement.

**Independent adjustor**  Claims adjustor who offers his or her services to insurance companies and is compensated by a fee.

**Independent agency system**  Type of property and casualty insurance marketing system, sometimes called the American agency system, in which the agent is an independent businessperson representing several insurers. The agency owns the expirations or renewal rights to the business, and the agent is compensated by commissions that vary by line of insurance.

**Indexed universal life insurance**  A variation of universal life insurance with certain key characteristics; there is a minimum interest rate guarantee; additional interest is credited to the policy based on the investment gains of a specific stock market index; and a formula determines the amount of enhanced (additional) interest credited to the policy.

**Indirect loss**  See **Consequential loss.**

**Individual 401(k) plan**  A qualified retirement plan with significant tax savings for self-employed individuals or businessowners with no employees other than a spouse, which combines a profit-sharing plan with an individual 401(k) plan.

**Individual Retirement Account (IRA)**  Individual retirement plan that can be established by a person with earned income. An IRA plan enjoys favorable income tax advantages.

**Industrial life insurance**  Type of life insurance in which policies are sold in small amounts and the premiums are collected weekly or monthly by a debit agent at the policyholder's home. See also **Home service life insurance.**

**Inflation-guard endorsement**  Endorsement added at the insured's request to a homeowners policy to increase periodically the face amount of insurance on the dwelling and other policy coverages by a specified percentage.

**Information systems**  Use of computer technology in the processing and storage of information and elimination of many routine tasks.

**Initial reserve** In life insurance, the reserve at the beginning of any policy year.

**Inland marine insurance** Transportation insurance that provides protection for goods shipped on land, including imports, exports, domestic shipments, instrumentalities of transportation, personal property floater risks, and commercial property floater risks.

**Installment refund annuity** Pays the annuitant a lifetime income, but if death occurs before receiving payments equal to the purchase price, the income payments continue to the beneficiary.

**Insurance** Pooling of fortuitous losses by transfer of risks to insurers who agree to indemnify insureds for such losses, to provide other pecuniary benefits on their occurrence, or to render services connected with the risk.

**Insurance guaranty funds** State funds that provide for the payment of unpaid claims of insolvent insurers.

**Insurance option** An option that derives value from specific insurable losses or from an index of values.

**Insurance score** A credit-based score based on an individual's credit record and other factors that is highly predictive of future claim costs; insureds with low insurance scores generally file more homeowners and auto insurance claims than insureds with good credit and higher insurance scores.

**Insurance Services Office (ISO)** Major rating organization in property and casualty insurance that drafts policy forms for personal and commercial lines of insurance and provides rate data on loss costs for property and liability insurance lines.

**Insuring agreement** That part of an insurance contract that states the promises of the insurer.

**Integrated risk management** A risk management technique that combines coverage for pure and speculative risks in the same insurance contract.

**Interest-adjusted method** Method of determining cost to an insured of a life insurance policy that considers the time value of money by applying an interest factor to each element of cost. *See also* **Net payment cost index; Surrender cost index.**

**Interest option** Life insurance settlement option in which the principal is retained by the insurer and interest is paid periodically.

**Interest rate risk** Risk of loss caused by adverse interest rate movements.

**Invitee** Someone who is invited onto the premises for the benefit of the occupant.

**IRA** *See* **Individual Retirement Account.**

**Irrevocable beneficiary** Beneficiary designation allowing no change to be made in the beneficiary of an insurance policy without the beneficiary's consent.

**ISO** *See* **Insurance Services Office.**

**Joint and several liability** Rule under which several parties may be responsible for the injury, but a defendant who is only slightly responsible may be required to pay the full amount of damages.

**Joint-and-survivor annuity** Annuity based on the lives of two or more annuitants. The annuity income (either the full amount of the original income or only two-thirds or one-half of the original income when the first annuitant dies) is paid until the death of the last annuitant.

**Joint underwriting association (JUA)** Organization of auto insurers operating in a state that makes auto insurance available to high-risk drivers. All underwriting losses are proportionately shared by insurers on the basis of premiums written in the state.

**Judgment rating** Rate-making method for which each exposure is individually evaluated and the rate is determined largely by the underwriter's judgment.

**Judicial bond** Type of surety bond used for court proceedings and guaranteeing that the party bonded will fulfill certain obligations specified by law, for example, fiduciary responsibilities.

**Juvenile insurance** Life insurance purchased by parents on children under a specified age.

**Keogh plan for the self-employed** Retirement plan individually adopted by self-employed persons that allows a tax deductible contribution to a defined-contribution or defined-benefit plan.

**Lapsed policy** One that is not in force because premiums have not been paid.

**Last clear chance rule** Statutory modification of the contributory negligence law allowing the claimant endangered by his or her own negligence to recover damages from a defendant if the defendant has a last clear chance to avoid the accident but fails to do so.

**Law of large numbers** Concept that the greater the number of exposures, the more closely will actual results approach the probable results expected from an infinite number of exposures.

**Legal hazard** Characteristics of the legal system or regulatory environment that increase the frequency or severity of losses.

**Legal reserve** Liability item on a life insurer's balance sheet representing the redundant or excessive premiums paid under the level-premium method during the early years. Assets must be accumulated to offset the legal reserve liability. Purpose of the legal reserve is to provide lifetime protection.

**Liability coverage** That part of the personal auto policy that protects a covered person against a suit or claim for bodily injury or property damage arising out of the negligent ownership or operation of an automobile. Liability coverage is also included in the homeowner's policy, which provides coverage for bodily injury and property damage liability.

**Liability without fault** Principle on which workers compensation is based, holding the employer absolutely liable for occupational injuries or disease suffered by workers, regardless of who is at fault.

**License and permit bond** Type of surety bond guaranteeing that the person bonded will comply with all laws and regulations that govern his or her activities.

**Licensee** Someone who enters or remains on the premises with the occupant's expressed or implied permission.

**Life annuity with guaranteed payments** Pays a life income to the annuitant with a certain number of guaranteed payments.

**Life income option** Life insurance settlement option in which the policy proceeds are paid during the lifetime of the beneficiary. A certain number of guaranteed payments may also be payable.

**Life insurance planning** Systematic method of determining the insured's financial goals, which are translated into specific amounts of life insurance, then periodically reviewed for possible changes.

**Limited-payment policy** Type of whole life insurance providing protection throughout the insured's lifetime and for which relatively high premiums are paid only for a limited period.

**Liquor liability law** See **Dram shop law**.

**Loading** The amount that must be added to the pure premium for expenses, profit, and a margin for contingencies.

**Longevity insurance** A generic name for a single-premium deferred annuity that begins paying benefits only at an advanced age, typically age 85.

**Long-term-care insurance** A form of health insurance that pays a daily benefit for medical or custodial care received in a nursing facility or hospital. Home health benefits may also be provided.

**Loss exposure** Any situation or circumstance in which a loss is possible, regardless of whether a loss occurs.

**Loss frequency** The probable number of losses that may occur during some given time period.

**Loss ratio** The ratio of incurred losses and loss adjustment expenses to earned premiums.

**Loss ratio method of rating** A rating system in property and casualty insurance by which the actual loss ratio is compared with the expected loss ratio, and the rate is adjusted accordingly.

**Loss reserve** Amount set aside by property and casualty insurers for claims reported and adjusted but not yet paid, claims reported and filed but not yet adjusted, and claims incurred but not yet reported to the insurer.

**Loss severity** The probable size of the losses that may occur.

**McCarran-Ferguson Act** Federal law passed in 1945 stating that continued regulation of the insurance industry by the states is in the public interest and that federal antitrust laws apply to insurance only to the extent that the industry is not regulated by state law.

**Major medical insurance** Health insurance designed to pay a large proportion of the covered expenses of a catastrophic illness or injury.

**Malpractice liability insurance** Covers acts of malpractice resulting in harm or injury to patients.

**Managed care** A generic name for medical expense plans that provide covered services to the members in a cost-effective manner, which includes HMOs, PPOs, and POS plans.

**Manual rating** See **Class rating**.

**Manuscript policy** Policy designed for a firm's specific needs and requirements.

**Mass merchandising** Plan for insuring individual members of a group, such as employees of firms or members of labor unions, under a single program of insurance at reduced premiums. Property and liability insurance is sold to individual members using group insurance marketing methods.

**Master contract** Contract between the insurer and group policyholder for the benefit of the individual members.

**Maximum possible loss** Worst loss that could happen to a firm during its lifetime.

**Mean reserve** In life insurance, the average of the terminal and initial reserves.

**Medical expense insurance** An individual or group plan that pays covered medical expenses as a result of disease or injury, including fees to physicians and surgeons, hospital costs, prescription drugs, outpatient tests, and a wide variety of ancillary benefits.

**Medical payments coverage** That part of the personal auto policy that pays all reasonable medical and funeral expenses incurred by a covered person within three years from the date of an accident.

**Medical payments to others** Pays for medical expenses of others under a homeowners policy in the event that a person (not an insured) is accidentally injured on the premises, or by the activities of an insured, resident employee, or animal owned by or in the care of an insured.

**Medicare** Part of the total Social Security program that covers the medical expenses of most people aged 65 and older and certain disabled people under age 65.

**Medicare Advantage plans** Private health plans that are part of Medicare that allow beneficiaries to choose alternates to the Original Medicare Plan, such as Medicare HMOs, Medicare PPOs, Medicare special needs plans, and Medicare private-fee-for-service plans.

**Medicare Part B** Part B of the Medicare program that covers physicians' fees and other related medical services. Most eligible Medicare recipients are automatically included unless they voluntarily refuse this coverage.

**Medicare prescription drug plans** Plans that provide coverage for prescription drugs under the Medicare program; beneficiaries have a choice of plans.

**Merit rating** Rate-making method in which class rates are adjusted upward or downward based on individual loss experience.

**MIB Group, Inc. (Medical Information Bureau)** Bureau whose purpose is to supply underwriting information in life insurance to member companies, which report any health impairments of an applicant for insurance.

**Minimum coverage requirement** A test that must be met to prevent employers from establishing a qualified pension plan that covers only the highly compensated. *See also* **Ratio percentage test.**

**Minimum distribution requirements** A provision in the income tax code that requires plan distributions from qualified retirement plans to start no later than April 1 of the calendar year following the year in which the individual attains age 70 1/2.

**Misstatement of age or sex clause** Contractual provision in a life insurance policy stating that if the insured's age or sex is misstated, the amount payable is the amount that the premium would have purchased at the correct age or gender.

**Mobilehome insurance** A package policy that provides property insurance and personal liability insurance to mobilehome owners.

**Modified life policy** Whole life policy for which premiums are reduced for the first three to five years and are higher thereafter.

**Modified no-fault plan** An injured person has the right to sue a negligent driver only if the bodily injury claim exceeds the dollar or verbal threshold.

**Modified prior-approval law** A state rating law where rate changes are based solely on loss experience; the rates must be filed with the state insurance department and can be used immediately. However, if the rate change is based on a change in rate classification or expense relationship, prior approval of the rates is necessary.

**Monetary threshold** Term used in states with no-fault auto insurance laws. An injured motorist is not permitted to sue a negligent driver but instead collects from his or her insurer, unless the claim exceeds the dollar threshold amount.

**Money purchase plan** A defined-contribution retirement plan in which each participant has an individual account, and the employer's contribution is a fixed percentage of the participant's compensation.

**Moral hazard** Dishonesty or character defects in an individual that increase the chance of loss.

**Morale hazard** Carelessness or indifference to a loss. *See also* **Attitudinal hazard.**

**Multicar discount** Reduction in auto insurance premiums for an insured who owns two or more automobiles, on the assumption that two such autos owned by the same person will not be driven as frequently as only one.

**Multiple distribution systems** Insurance marketing method that refers to the use of several distribution systems by an insurer; for example, a property and casualty insurer may use the independent agency method and direct response system to sell insurance.

**Multiple line exclusive agency system** Under this marketing system, agents who sell primarily property and casualty insurance also sell individual life and health insurance products. The agents represent only one insurer or

group of insurers that are financially interrelated or under common ownership. The agents are also called **captive agents.**

**Multiple-line insurance** Type of insurance that combines several lines of insurance into one contract, for example, property insurance and casualty insurance.

**Mutual insurer** Insurance corporation owned by the policyholders, who elect the board of directors. The board appoints managing executives, and the company may pay a dividend or give a rate reduction in advance to insureds.

**NAIC** *See* **National Association of Insurance Commissioners.**

**NALP** *See* **Net annual level premium.**

**Named insured** The person or persons named in the declarations section of the policy, as opposed to someone who may have an interest in the policy but is not named as an insured.

**Named-perils policy** Coverage by an insurance contract that promises to pay only for those losses caused by perils specifically listed in the policy.

**National Association of Insurance Commissioners (NAIC)** Group founded in 1871 that meets periodically to discuss industry problems and draft model laws in various areas and recommends adoption of these proposals by state legislatures. Members include the ranking insurance regulator from each state.

**Needs approach** Method for estimating amount of life insurance appropriate for a family by analyzing various family needs that must be met if the family head should die and converting them into specific amounts of life insurance. Financial assets are considered in determining the amount of life insurance needed.

**Negligence** Failure to exercise the standard of care required by law to protect others from harm.

**Net amount at risk** Concept associated with a level-premium life insurance policy. Calculated as the difference between the face amount of the policy and the legal reserve.

**Net annual level premium (NALP)** Annual level premium for a life insurance policy with no expense loading. Mathematically equivalent to the net single premium.

**Net payment cost index** Method of measuring the cost of an insurance policy to an insured if death occurs at the end of some specified time period. The time value of money is taken into consideration.

**Net present value** Used in capital budgeting and is the sum of the present values of the future cash flows minus the cost of the project. A positive net present value represents an increase in value for the firm.

**Net retention** *See* **Retention limit.**

**Net single premium (NSP)** Present value of the future death benefit of a life insurance policy.

**No-fault insurance** A tort reform proposal in which the injured person collects benefits from his or her insurer and does not have to sue a negligent third party who caused the accident and prove legal liability.

**No-filing law**    Rating law where insurers are not required to file their rates with the state insurance department but may be required to furnish rate schedules and supporting data to state officials. Also called an **open competition law.**

**Noncancellable**    Continuance provision in a health insurance policy stipulating that the policy cannot be canceled, that the renewal is guaranteed to a stated age, and that the premium rates cannot be increased.

**Noncontributory plan**    Employer pays the entire cost of a group insurance or private pension plan. All eligible employees are covered.

**Nondiversifiable risk**    A risk that affects the entire economy or large numbers of persons or groups within the economy, which cannot be reduced or eliminated by diversification. Also called **systematic risk** or **fundamental risk.**

**Nonforfeiture law**    State law requiring insurance companies to provide at least a minimum nonforfeiture value to policyholders who surrender their cash-value life insurance policies.

**Noninsurance transfers**    Various methods other than insurance by which a pure risk and its potential financial consequences can be transferred to another party, for example, contracts, leases, and hold-harmless agreements.

**Nonoccupational disability**    The accident or illness causing the disability must occur off the job.

**Nonparticipating policy**    Term used to describe a life insurance policy that does not pay dividends.

**Objective risk**    Relative variation of actual loss from expected loss, which varies inversely with the square root of the number of cases under observation.

**Obligee**    The party to a surety bond who is reimbursed for damages if the principal to the bond fails to perform.

**Occurrence**    An accident, including continuous or repeated exposure to substantially the same general, harmful conditions, which results in bodily injury or property damage during the policy period. *See also* **Accident.**

**Occurrence policy**    A liability insurance policy that covers claims arising out of occurrences that take place during the policy period, regardless of when the claim is made. *See also* **Claims-made policy.**

**Ocean marine insurance**    Type of insurance that provides protection for all types of oceangoing vessels and their cargoes as well as legal liability of owners and shippers.

**Open-competition law**    Law for regulating insurance rates under which insurers are not required to file rates with the state insurance department but may be required to furnish rate schedules and supporting data to state officials.

**Open perils policy**    Coverage by an insurance contract that promises to cover all losses except those losses specifically excluded in the policy. *See also* "**All-risks**" **policy.**

**Ordinary life insurance**    Type of whole life insurance providing protection throughout the insured's lifetime and for which premiums are paid throughout the insured's lifetime.

**Original Medicare Plan**    The traditional plan for beneficiaries run by the federal government that provides Hospital Insurance (Medicare Part A) benefits and Medical Insurance (Medicare Part B) benefits.

**Other insureds**    Persons or parties who are insured under the named insured's policy even though they are not specifically named in the policy.

**Other-insurance provisions**    Provisions whose purpose is to prevent profiting from insurance and violation of the principle of indemnity when more than one policy covers a loss.

**Other-than-collision loss**    Part of the coverage available under Part D: Coverage for Damage to Your Auto in the personal auto policy. All physical damage losses to an insured vehicle are covered except collision losses and those losses specifically excluded.

**Out-of-pocket limit**    Provision in medical expense policies by which 100 percent of covered medical expenses in excess of the deductible are paid after the insured incurs a certain annual amount of out-of-pocket expenses. Also called a **stop-loss limit.**

**Out-of-pocket maximum**    *See* **out-of-pocket limit.**

**Ownership clause**    Provision in life insurance policies under which the policyholder possesses all contractual rights in the policy while the insured is living. These rights can generally be exercised without the beneficiary's consent.

**P&I Insurance**    *See* **Protection and indemnity insurance.**

**Package policy**    Policy that combines two or more separate contracts of insurance in one policy, for example, homeowners insurance.

**Partial disability**    Inability of the insured to perform one or more important duties of his or her occupation.

**Participating policy**    Life insurance policy that pays dividends to the policyholders.

**Particular average**    An ocean marine loss that falls entirely on a particular interest as contrasted with a general average loss that falls on all parties to the voyage.

**Particular risk**    A risk that affects only individuals and not the entire community.

**Past-service credits**    Pension benefits awarded to employees based on service with the employer prior to the inception of the plan.

**Paul v. Virginia**    Landmark legal decision of 1869 establishing the right of the states, and not the federal government, to regulate insurance. Ruled that insurance was not interstate commerce.

**Peak season endorsement**    An endorsement to a business income policy for a business firm with seasonal fluctuations in inventory, which adjusts the amount of insurance in force for a specified period to reflect higher inventory values.

**Pension accrual benefit**    A disability income benefit that makes a pension contribution so that the disabled employee's pension benefit remains intact.

**Pension Benefit Guaranty Corporation (PBGC)** A federal corporation that guarantees the payment of vested or nonforfeitable benefits up to certain limits if a private defined benefit pension plan is terminated.

**Peril** Cause or source of loss.

**Personal injury** Injury for which legal liability arises (such as for false arrest, detention or imprisonment, malicious prosecution, libel, slander, defamation of character, violation of the right of privacy, and unlawful entry or eviction) and which may be covered by an endorsement to the homeowners policy. Also included in the coverage by a personal umbrella policy.

**Personal liability insurance** Liability insurance that protects the insured for an amount up to policy limits against a claim or suit for damages because of bodily injury or property damage caused by the insured's negligence. This coverage is provided by Section II of the homeowners policy.

**Personal lines** Property and liability insurance coverages that insure the home and personal property of individuals and families or provide protection against legal liability.

**Personal-producing general agent** Term used to describe an above-average salesperson with a proven sales record who is hired primarily to sell life insurance under a contract that provides both direct and overriding commissions.

**Preferred provider organization (PPO)** A managed care plan that contracts with health-care providers to provide certain medical services to the plan members at discounted fees. To encourage patients to use PPO providers, deductibles and coinsurance charges are reduced.

**Personal selling distribution system** A distribution system in which commissioned agents solicit and sell life insurance products to prospective insureds.

**Personal umbrella policy liability** Policy designed to provide protection against a catastrophic lawsuit or judgment, whose coverage ranges generally from $1 million to $10 million and extends to the entire family. Insurance is excess over underlying coverages.

**Physical hazard** Physical condition that increases the chance of loss.

**PIA** *See* **Primary insurance amount.**

**Point-of-service plan (POS)** A managed care plan that establishes a network of preferred providers. If patients see a preferred provider, they pay lower deductibles and coinsurance charges. If care is received outside the network, the care is covered, but the insured must pay substantially higher deductibles and coinsurance charges.

**Policy loan** Cash value of a life insurance policy that can be borrowed by the policyholder in lieu of surrendering the policy.

**Policyholders' surplus** Difference between an insurance company's assets and its liabilities.

**Pooling** Spreading of losses incurred by the few over the entire group, so that in the process, average loss is substituted for actual loss.

**Preexisting condition** A term to describe a physical or mental condition that existed during some specified time period prior to the effective date of the policy for which the insured received medical treatment.

**Preexisting-conditions clause** Contractual provision in a health insurance policy stating that preexisting conditions are not covered or are covered only after the policy has been in force for a specified period. Prohibited under the Affordable Care Act in individual and group medical expense insurance policies beginning January 1, 2014.

**Preferred risk** Individuals whose mortality experience is expected to be better than average.

**Primary and excess insurance** Type of other-insurance provision that requires the primary insurer to pay first in the case of a loss; when the policy limits under the primary policy are exhausted, the second insurer pays the excess.

**Primary beneficiary** Beneficiary of a life insurance policy who is first entitled to receive the policy proceeds on the insured's death.

**Primary insurance amount (PIA)** Monthly cash benefit paid to a retired worker at the full retirement age, or to a disabled worker eligible for benefits under the Old-Age, Survivors, and Disability Insurance (OASDI) program.

**Principal** The bonded party in the purchase of a surety bond who agrees to perform certain acts or fulfill certain obligations.

**Principle of indemnity** A principle that states the insurer agrees to pay no more than the actual amount of the loss. The insured should not profit from a covered loss but should be restored to approximately the same financial position that existed prior to the loss.

**Prior-approval law** Law for regulating insurance rates under which the rates must be filed and approved by the state insurance department before they can be used.

**Pro rata liability** A generic term for a provision that applies when two or more policies of the same type cover the same insurable interest in the property. Each insurer pays based on the proportion that its insurance bears to the total amount of insurance on the property.

**Probable maximum loss** Worst loss that is likely to happen to a firm during its lifetime.

**Probationary period** Waiting period of one to six months required of an employee before he or she is allowed to participate in a group insurance plan.

**Products-completed operations hazard** Liability losses that occur away from the premises and arise out of the insured's product or work after the insured has relinquished possession of the product, or the work has been completed.

**Products liability** The legal liability of manufacturers, wholesalers, and retailers to persons who are injured or who incur property damage from defective products.

**Prospective reserve** In life insurance, the difference between the present value of future benefits and the present value of future net premiums.

**Protection and indemnity insurance (P&I)** Coverage that can be added to an ocean marine insurance policy to provide liability insurance for property damage and bodily injury to third parties.

**Proximate cause** Factor causing damage to property for which there is an unbroken chain of events between the occurrence of an insured peril and damage or destruction of the property.

**Public adjustor** Claims adjustor who represents the insured rather than the insurance company and is paid a fee based on the amount of the claim settlement. A public adjustor may be employed in those cases where the insured and insurer cannot resolve a dispute over a claim, or if the insured needs technical assistance in a complex loss situation.

**Public official bond** Type of surety bond guaranteeing that public officials will faithfully perform their duties for the protection of the public.

**Punitive damages** An award for damages designed to punish people and organizations so that others are deterred from committing the same wrongful act. Awards for punitive damages are often several times the amount awarded for compensatory damages.

**Pure no-fault plan** The injured person cannot sue at all, regardless of the seriousness of the claim, and no payments are made for pain and suffering.

**Pure premium** That portion of the insurance rate needed to pay losses and loss-adjustment expenses.

**Pure premium method of rating** A rating system used in property and casualty insurance. The pure premium is determined by dividing the dollar amount of incurred losses and loss-adjustment expenses by the number of exposure units.

**Pure risk** Situation in which there are only the possibilities of loss or no loss.

**Rate** Price per unit of insurance.

**Rate making** Process by which insurance pricing or premium rates are determined for an insurance company.

**Ratio percentage test** A test that a qualified pension plan must meet to receive favorable income-tax treatment. Under this test, the percentage of non-highly compensated employees covered under the plan must be at least 70 percent of the percentage of highly compensated employees who are covered.

**Readjustment period** One- to two-year period immediately following the breadwinner's death during which time the family should receive approximately the same amount of income it received while the breadwinner was alive.

**Reasonable and customary charges** Payment of physicians' normal fees if they are reasonable and customary, such as a fee that does not exceed the 80th or 90th percentile for a similar procedure performed by physicians in the area.

**Rebating** A practice—illegal in virtually all states—of giving a premium reduction or some other financial advantage to an individual as an inducement to purchase the policy.

**Reciprocal exchange** Unincorporated mutual insuring organization in which insurance is exchanged among members and which is managed by an attorney-in-fact.

**Regression analysis** Method of characterizing the relationship between two or more variables, and then using this characterization as a predictor.

**Reinstatement clause** Contractual provision in a life insurance policy that permits the owner to reinstate a lapsed policy within three or five years if certain requirements are fulfilled; for example, evidence of insurability is required and overdue premiums plus interest must be paid.

**Reinstatement provision** Provision of a health insurance policy that allows the insured to reinstate a lapsed policy by payment of premium either with or without an application.

**Reinsurance** An arrangement by which the primary insurer that initially writes the insurance transfers to another insurer (called the reinsurer) part or all of the potential losses associated with such insurance.

**Reinsurance facility** Pool for placing high-risk automobile drivers that arranges for an insurer to accept all applicants for insurance. Underwriting losses are shared by all auto insurers in the state.

**Replacement cost insurance** Property insurance by which the insured is indemnified on the basis of replacement cost with no deduction for depreciation.

**Reporting form** Coverage for commercial property insurance that requires the insured to report monthly or quarterly the value of the insured inventory, with automatic adjustment of the insurance amount to cover the accurately reported inventory up to the policy limit.

**Representations** Statements made by an applicant for insurance (for example, in life insurance) such as the applicant's occupation, state of health, and family history.

**Residual disability** Residual disability means that a proportionate disability-income benefit is paid to an insured whose earned income is reduced because of an accident or illness.

**Residual market** The residual market refers to plans in which auto insurers participate to make insurance available to high-risk drivers who are unable to obtain coverage in the standard markets. Examples include an automobile insurance plan, joint underwriting association, and a reinsurance facility. Also called the **shared market**.

**Res ipsa loquitur** Literally, "the thing speaks for itself." Under this doctrine, the very fact that the event occurred establishes a presumption of negligence on behalf of the defendant.

**Retained limit** Term found in an umbrella liability policy that refers to (1) the total limits of the underlying insurance or any other insurance available to the insured, or (2) the deductible stated in the declarations if the loss is covered by the umbrella policy but not by any underlying insurance or other insurance, whichever is applicable.

**Retention**   Risk management technique in which an individual or a firm retains part or all of the losses resulting from a given loss exposure. Used when no other method is available, the worst possible loss is not serious, and losses are highly predictable.

**Retention limit**   Amount of insurance retained by a ceding company for its own account in a reinsurance operation.

**Retirement test**   *See* **Earnings test**.

**Retrocession**   Process by which a reinsurer obtains reinsurance from another company.

**Retrospective rating**   Type of merit-rating method in which the insured's loss experience during the current policy period determines the actual premium paid for that period.

**Retrospective reserve**   In life insurance, the net premiums collected by the insurer for a particular block of policies, plus interest earnings at an assumed rate, less the amounts paid out as death claims.

**Revocable beneficiary**   Beneficiary designation allowing the policyholder the right to change the beneficiary without consent of the beneficiary.

**Rider**   Term used in insurance contracts to describe a document that amends or changes the original policy. *See also* **Endorsement**.

**Risk**   Based on the historical definition, risk is defined as uncertainty concerning the occurrence of a loss. Numerous definitions of risk exist in the professional literature. Because of ambiguity, the term "loss exposure" is often used instead of "risk."

**Risk-based capital (RBC)**   Under NAIC standards, insurers are required to have a certain amount of capital that is based on the riskiness of their investments and operations.

**Risk control**   Risk management techniques that reduce the frequency or severity of losses, such as avoidance, loss prevention, and loss reduction.

**Risk financing**   Risk management techniques that provide for the funding of losses after they occur, such as retention, noninsurance transfers, and commercial insurance.

**Risk management**   Systematic process for the identification and evaluation of loss exposures faced by an organization or individual, and for the selection and implementation of the most appropriate techniques for treating such exposures.

**Risk management information system (RMIS)**   Computerized data base that permits the risk manager to store and analyze risk management data and to use such data to predict future loss levels.

**Risk map**   Map used in risk management that shows grids detailing the potential frequency and severity of risks faced by the organization.

**Robbery**   Taking of property from a person by someone who has (1) caused or threatens to cause bodily harm to that person, or (2) committed an obviously unlawful act witnessed by that person.

**Roth IRA**   An IRA in which the contributions are not income-tax deductible but distributions are received income-tax free if certain conditions are met.

**Roth 401(k) plan**   A qualified retirement plan in which contributions are made with after-tax dollars and qualified distributions at retirement are received income-tax free; investment earnings also accumulate on a tax-free basis.

**Safe driver plan**   Rating plan in which the premiums paid are based in large part on the individual driving record of the insured and vehicle operators who live with the insured.

**Savings bank life insurance**   Life insurance originally sold by mutual savings banks in Massachusetts, New York, and Connecticut. Now sold in other states as well.

**Scheduled personal property endorsement**   Special coverage added at the insured's request to a homeowners policy to insure items specifically listed. Used to insure valuable property such as jewelry, furs, and paintings.

**Schedule rating**   Type of merit-rating method in which each exposure is individually rated and given a basis rate that is then modified by debits or credits for undesirable or desirable physical features.

**Section 401(k) plan**   A qualified profit-sharing or thrift plan that allows participants the option of putting money into the plan or receiving the funds as cash. The employee can voluntarily elect to have his or her salary reduced up to some maximum annual limit, which is then invested in the employer's Section 401(k) plan.

**Section 403(B) plan**   A qualified retirement plan designed for employees of public educational systems and tax-exempt organization, such as hospitals, nonprofit groups, and churches. Also known as **tax-sheltered annuities**.

**Securitization of risk**   Term to describe the transfer of an insurable risk to the capital markets through the creation of a financial instrument, such as a catastrophe bond, futures contract, options contract, or other financial instrument.

**Self-insurance**   Retention program in which the employer self-funds or pays part or all of the losses.

**Self-insured retention**   *See* **Retained limit**.

**SEP**   *See* **Simplified Employee Pension**.

**Separate investment account**   Used in group pension plans in which the plan administrator has the option to invest in separate accounts offered by the insurer, such as stock funds, bond funds, and similar investments. Assets are segregated from the insurer's general investment account and are not subject to claims by the insurer's creditors.

**Service benefits**   Health insurance benefits that pay hospital charges or payment for care received by the insured directly to the hospital or providers of care. The plan provides service rather than cash benefits to the insured.

**Settlement options**   Ways in which life insurance policy proceeds can be paid other than in a lump sum, including interest, fixed period, fixed amount, and life income options.

**SEUA case**   *See* **South-Eastern Underwriters Association (SEUA) case**.

**Shared market**   *See* **Residual market**.

**SIMPLE retirement plan**  A qualified retirement plan for smaller employers who are exempt from most non-discrimination and administrative rules. Employees can elect to contribute up to certain annual limits.

**Simplified Employee Pension (SEP)**  An employer-sponsored individual retirement account that meets certain requirements. Paper work is reduced for employers who wish to cover employees in a retirement plan.

**Single limit**  The total amount of liability insurance that applies to the entire accident without a separate limit for each person. The total amount of insurance applies to both bodily injury liability and property damage liability.

**Single-premium deferred annuity**  A retirement annuity that is purchased with a single premium with benefits to start at some future date.

**Single-premium whole life insurance**  A whole life policy that provides lifetime protection with a single premium payment.

**Social insurance**  Government insurance programs with certain characteristics that distinguish them from other government insurance programs. Programs are generally compulsory; specific earmarked taxes fund the programs; benefits are heavily weighted in favor of low-income groups; and programs are designed to achieve certain social goals.

**Soft insurance market**  A period during which underwriting standards are more liberal and premiums are relatively low. *See also* **Hard insurance market** and **Underwriting cycle**.

**South-Eastern Underwriters Association (SEUA) case**  Legal landmark decision in 1944 overruling the *Paul v. Virginia* ruling and finding that insurance was interstate commerce when conducted across state lines and was subject to federal regulation.

**Special coverage policy**  *See* **Open perils policy**.

**Special damages**  An award for damages that can be determined and documented, such as medical expenses, lost earnings, or property damage.

**Specified (dread) disease policy**  A limited policy that covers only certain diseases listed in the policy, such as cancer, multiple sclerosis, or muscular dystrophy. Also called a **dread disease policy**.

**Speculative risk**  Situation in which either profit or loss are clear possibilities.

**Split limits**  The amounts of insurance for bodily injury liability and property damage liability are stated separately.

**Stop-loss limit**  Modification of the coinsurance provision in major medical plans that places a dollar limit on the maximum amount that an individual must pay out of pocket. *See also* **Out-of-pocket limit**.

**Straight deductible**  Deductible in an insurance contract by which the insured must pay a certain number of dollars of loss before the insurer is required to make a payment.

**Strict liability**  Liability for damages even though fault or negligence cannot be proven, for example, in such situations as occupational injury of employees under a workers compensation law. Also known as **absolute liability**.

**Subjective risk**  Uncertainty based on one's mental condition or state of mind.

**Subrogation**  Substitution of the insurer in place of the insured for the purpose of claiming indemnity from a negligent third party for a loss covered by insurance.

**Suicide clause**  Contractual provision in a life insurance policy stating that if the insured commits suicide within two years after the policy is issued, the face amount of insurance will not be paid; only premiums paid will be refunded.

**Surety**  Party who agrees to answer for the debt, default, or obligation of another in the purchase of a bond.

**Surety bond**  A contract in which the surety guarantees to a second party (the obligee) that a third party (the principal) will faithfully perform its obligations to the obligee.

**Surplus line broker**  Specialized insurance broker licensed to place business with a nonadmitted insurer (a company not licensed to do business in the state).

**Surrender-cost index**  Method of measuring the cost of an insurance policy to an insured if the policy is surrendered at the end of some specified time period. The time value of money is taken into consideration.

**Systemic risk**  Risk of collapse of an entire financial system or financial market in which the failure of a single entity or group of entities can result in the breakdown of the entire financial system.

**Term insurance**  Type of life insurance that provides temporary protection for a specified number of years with no savings element. It is usually renewable and convertible.

**Terminal reserve**  In life insurance, the reserve at the end of any given policy year.

**Theft**  Unlawful taking of money, securities, or other property to the deprivation of the insured; includes burglary and robbery. *See also* **Burglary** and **Robbery**.

**Time limit on certain defenses provision**  Provision in an individual health insurance policy that prohibits the company from canceling the policy or denying a claim on the basis of a preexisting condition or misstatement in the application after the policy has been in force for two or three years, except for fraudulent misstatements. Modified by the Affordable Care Act.

**Total disability**  A term that varies by insurers and type of policy. In individual disability income policies, total disability can be defined as (1) inability to perform the material and substantial duties of your regular occupation; or (2) inability to perform the duties of any occupation for which you are reasonably fitted by education, training, and experience; or (3) inability to perform the duties of any gainful occupation; or (4) loss-of-income test. In many waiver-of-premium provisions in life insurance, total disability means that, because of disease or bodily injury, the insured cannot do any of the essential duties of his or her job, or of any job for which he or she is suited based on schooling, training, or experience.

**Traditional IRA**  An IRA that allows workers to deduct part or all of their IRA contributions if taxable compensation is under a certain limit. Distributions are taxed as ordinary income.

**Traditional net cost method**  Method of determining cost to an insured of a life insurance policy, determined by subtracting the total dividends received and cash value at the end of a period from the total premiums paid during that period. Does not consider the time value of money.

**Treaty reinsurance**  Type of reinsurance in which the primary company must cede insurance to the reinsurer and the reinsurer must accept. The ceding company is automatically reinsured according to the terms of the reinsurance contract.

**Trespasser**  A person who enters or remains on the owner's property without the owner's consent.

**Trust**  Arrangement in which property is legally transferred to a trustee who manages it for the benefit of named beneficiaries for their security and to insure competent management of estate property.

**Trust-fund plan**  Type of pension plan in which all pension contributions are deposited with a trustee who invests the funds according to a trust agreement between employer and trustee. Benefits are paid directly out of the trust fund.

**Twisting**  Illegal practice of inducing a policyholder to drop an existing policy in one company and then replace it with a new policy in another company through misrepresentation or incomplete information.

**Ultimate net loss**  The total amount that the insurer is legally obligated to pay in a commercial umbrella policy.

**Underinsured motorists coverage**  Coverage that can be added to the personal auto policy. Coverage pays damages for a bodily injury to an insured caused by the ownership or operation of an underinsured vehicle by another driver. The negligent driver may have insurance that meets the state's financial responsibility or compulsory insurance law requirement, but the amount carried is insufficient to cover the loss sustained by the insured.

**Underwriting**  The selection and classification of applicants for insurance through a clearly stated company policy consistent with company objectives.

**Underwriting cycle**  A term to describe the cyclical pattern in underwriting standards, premium levels, and profitability. *See also* **Hard insurance market** and **Soft insurance market.**

**Unearned premium reserve**  Liability reserve of an insurance company that represents the unearned part of gross premiums on all outstanding policies at the time of valuation.

**Unified tax credit**  Tax credit that can be used to reduce the amount of the federal estate or gift tax.

**Unilateral contract**  Only one party makes a legally enforceable promise.

**Uninsured motorists coverage**  That part of the personal auto policy designed to insure against bodily injury caused by an uninsured motorist, a hit-and-run driver, or a driver whose company is insolvent.

**Unisex rating**  A rating system in which the pooled loss experience of both sexes is used to determine the rates charged.

**Unit-owners form**  *See* **Homeowners 6 policy.**

**Universal life insurance**  A flexible-premium whole life policy that provides lifetime protection under a contract that separates the protection and saving components. The contract is an interest-sensitive product that unbundles the protection, saving, and expense components.

**Unsatisfied judgment fund**  Fund established by a small number of states to compensate accident victims who have exhausted all other means of recovery.

**Use-and-file law**  A rating law that is a variation of a file-and-use; insurers can put into effect immediately any rate changes, but the rates must be filed with regulatory authorities within a certain period after first being used.

**Utmost good faith**  A higher degree of honesty is imposed on both parties to an insurance contract than is imposed on parties to other contracts.

**Value at risk (VAR)**  The value of the worst probable loss likely to occur in a given time period under regular market conditions at some level of confidence.

**Valued policy**  Policy that pays the face amount of insurance, regardless of actual cash value, if a total loss occurs.

**Valued policy laws**  Laws requiring payment to an insured of the face amount of insurance if a total loss to real property occurs from a peril specified in the law, even though the policy may state that only the actual cash value will be paid.

**Variable annuity**  Annuity whose periodic lifetime payments vary depending on the level of common stock prices (or other investments), based on the assumption that cost of living and common stock prices are correlated in the long run. Its purpose is to provide an inflation hedge.

**Variable life insurance**  Life insurance policy in which the death benefit and cash surrender values vary according to the investment experience of a separate account maintained by the insurer.

**Variable universal life insurance**  Similar to universal life insurance with certain exceptions. Cash values can be invested in a wide variety of investments; there is no minimum interest rate guarantee; and the investment risk falls entirely on the policyholder.

**Verbal threshold**  A suit for damages in some no-fault states that is allowed only in serious cases, such as those involving death or dismemberment.

**Vesting**  Characteristic of pension plans guaranteeing the employee's right to part or all of the employer's contributions if employment terminates prior to retirement.

**Vicarious liability** Responsibility for damage done by the driver of an automobile that is imputed to the vehicle's owner.

**Waiver** Voluntary relinquishment of a known legal right.

**Waiver-of-premium provision** Benefit that can be added to a life insurance policy providing for waiver of all premiums coming due during a period of total disability of the insured.

**War clause** Restriction in a life insurance policy that excludes payment if the insured dies as a direct result of war.

**Warranty** Statement of fact or a promise made by the insured, which is part of the insurance contract and which must be true if the insurer is to be liable under the contract.

**Weather option** Provides a payment if a specified weather contingency (e.g., temperatures higher or lower than normal) occurs.

**Workers compensation insurance** Insurance that covers payment of all workers compensation and other benefits that the employer must legally provide to covered employees who are occupationally disabled because of a job-related accident or disease.

# INDEX

## A

AAIS (American Association of Insurance Services), 427, 577
Abandonment of property, 446
Absolute assignment, 236, 262
Absolute liability, 407, 412
Abstract, 543
Abuse, liability arising out of, 459
Accelerated death benefits rider, 248–249
Acceptance, and offer, 174–175
Access devices, 435–436
Accidental death and dismemberment (AD&D) insurance, 222, 318, 332
Accidental death rider, 247–248
Accidental loss, 23
Accounting department, 54, 118
Accounts receivable coverage form, 570
Accumulation period, 277
Accumulation units, 279
ACLI. *See* American Council of Life Insurers
Acquisitions, 70
Active retention, 13–14
Activities of daily living (ADLs), 314
Actual cash value, 166–167, 443–444, 534
Actual deferral percentage (ADP) test, 362
Actuary, 104–105
AD&D (accidental death and dismemberment) insurance, 222, 332
Additional insured, 189
Additional living expense, 435
Additional vehicle, 479
Add-on plan, 513
Adhesion, contract of, 176–177
ADLs (activities of daily living), 314
Administrative charge, 280
Administrative services only (ASO) contract, 333
Admitted assets, 146
ADP (actual deferral percentage) test, 362
ADR (alternative dispute resolution), 417
Advance premium mutual, 90
Advance purchase privilege, 247
Advantage Plans, Medicare, 309, 386, 390
Adverse selection, 26, 106
Advertising injury, 585, 587, 596
Affiliated agents, 95

Affordable Care Act
  abusive insurer practices and, 302–303
  Affordable Insurance Exchange, 306, 338
  basic provisions of, 303–309
  cost and financing, 308–309
  cost-containment provisions, 392
  employer requirements, 306, 338
  essential health benefits, 305–306
  grandfathered plans, 304, 338
  group medical expense insurance and, 337–338
  guaranteed access, 304
  impact on Medicare, 389–390
  improving quality, 308
  individual mandate, 304, 338
  limited waiting periods, 305
  lowering costs, 308
  Medicaid expansion, 307
  NAIC implementation of, 155
  preexisting conditions and, 26, 102, 304, 307, 320, 338
  tax credits, 306–307
Affordable Insurance Exchange, 306, 338
After market parts, 496, 511
*Against the Gods* (Bernstein), 1, 43
Age and aging population
  auto insurance cost influenced by, 518–521
  health-care problem of, 299
  minimum requirement for, 355
  misstatement of, 234
  for retirement plans, 355–356, 376–380
  workers compensation and, 398–399
Age Discrimination in Employment Act, 355
Agency agreement, 177–178
Agents
  affiliated, 95
  basic concepts, 93–95
  career, 95
  as claims adjusters, 109
  competent, 265
  as first underwriters, 106
  Independent Insurance Agents & Brokers of America and, 491, 551, 577
  legal principles and, 177–178
  licensing of, 150

  life insurance, 93–94
  limitations on, 178
  principal responsible for acts of, 178
  property and casualty insurance, 93–94, 96
  special, 108
Agents report, 106
Aggregate deductible, 190
Agreed value coverage, 192, 559
AHIP (America's Health Insurance Plans), 323, 351
AIA. *See* American Insurance Association
AIG (American International Group), 65, 67, 156
AIME (average indexed monthly earnings), 377
Aircraft
  business, 594–595
  commercial insurance, 594–595
  damage to, 439, 461
  exclusion, 584
  homeowners insurance, 434
  liability exclusions for, 458, 547
  personal insurance, 29
  pleasure, 594–595
Aleatory contract, 175–176
Alien insurer, 146
Allen, Woody, 198
Allied lines, 28
"All-risks" basis
  aircraft insurance, 595
  described, 572
  DIC insurance, 567
  in insuring agreement, 186
  ocean marine insurance, 568
  yacht insurance and, 537
Alternative dispute resolution (ADR), 417
A.M. Best Company, 52, 81, 228–229, 577
Amendments, entire-contract clause and, 233
American Academy of Actuaries, 138, 391
American agency system, 97
American Association of Insurance Services (AAIS), 427, 577
American Benefits Council, 370
The American College, 100, 108, 121, 229
American Council of Life Insurers (ACLI), 100, 121, 138–139, 157, 229, 253

American Institute for CPCU, 83, 101, 108, 121

American Insurance Association (AIA), 37, 100, 121, 157, 577

American International Group (AIG), 65, 67, 156

American Medical Association (AMA), 332

American Risk and Insurance Association (ARIA), 18

American Society of Pension Professionals & Actuaries, 139

American Tort Reform Association (ATRA), 414, 423

America's Health Insurance Plans (AHIP), 323, 351

Ameriks, John, 381–382

Ameritas Advisors Services, 264, 268

Animals
    liability and, 412, 455
    as property not covered, 434

Annual pro rata method, 126

Annual reset method, 282

Annual transit policy, 571

Annuitant, 276

Annuities
    accumulation units, 279
    annuity units, 280
    bonus, 277
    deferred, 277
    definition of, 276
    due factor, 257
    equity-indexed, 281–282
    fixed, 277–279
    flexible-premium deferred, 277
    immediate, 277, 293
    individual, 276–277, 283–284
    life, 271, 278
    life insurance v., 276
    nonqualified, 283
    settlement options for, 278–279
    single-premium deferred, 277
    tax-sheltered, 363
    variable, 279–281, 284

Annuity.com site, 293

Annuityshopper.com site, 293

AnnuitySpecs.com site, 293

Annuity units, 280

Antirebating laws, 150–151

Antitrust exemption, 144–145, 154–155

Apparent authority, 93, 177

Appeal bond, 481

Application, underwriting, 106

Appraisal clause, 445, 497

A priori probabilities, 4

Arbitration, 417

ARIA (American Risk and Insurance Association), 18

Arizona, homeowners premium variations in, 467–470

ARM (Associate in Risk Management), 60, 83

Artificially generated electrical current, 440

ASO (administrative services only) contract, 333

Assessment method, 148

Assessment mutual, 90

Asset(s)
    admitted, 146
    on balance sheets, 124–125, 130, 206
    nonadmitted, 146
    risks for, 147

Asset valuation reserve (AVR), 130

Assigned risk plan, 516–517

Assignment clause, 236–237

Associate in Risk Management (ARM), 60, 83

Association captive, 49

Assumption of risk doctrine, 395, 409

ATRA (American Tort Reform Association), 414, 423

Attachment bonds, 616

Attained-age method, 208

Attending physician's report, 107

Attitudinal (morale) hazard, 5, 186–187

Attractive nuisance doctrine, 410–411

Auctioneer's bond, 616

Authority
    apparent, 93, 177
    civil, 562
    express, 93, 177
    implied, 93, 177–178

Auto accident victims, compensation of
    compulsory insurance laws and, 509
    financial responsibility laws and, 506–509
    indemnification and, 509
    from low-cost auto insurance, 512
    from no-fault auto insurance, 512–516
    from "no pay, no play" laws, 512
    property damage and, 514
    from uninsured motorists coverage, 509–512
    unsatisfied judgment funds and, 509

Auto insurance. *See also* Auto accident victims, compensation of; Motor vehicles; Personal Auto Policy
    adequate, 522
    collision, 523, 592, 594
    commercial, 28, 592–594
    complaints about, 151
    comprehensive, 592
    compulsory, 509

cost of, 512, 517–522, 523–527

deductible, 522–523

discounts, 526

disparity in rates, 153–154

financial responsibility laws and, 506–509

fraud, 32

fraudulent claims and, 514–515

for high-risk drivers, 516–517

information quality for, 143

JUA and, 517

liability, 472, 592–594

low-cost, 512

Maryland Automobile Insurance Fund for, 517

material misrepresentation and, 172

no-fault, 512–516

premium variations in, 523–526

as private insurance, 27, 143

reinsurance facility and, 517

shopping for, 522–527

society and, 506–527

state automobile insurance plan, 516–517

state funds for, 31

use of auto and, 519

for young drivers, 519–521

Automatic fire protective sprinkler system, 440

Automatic premium loan provision, 237–238

Automatic termination, 498

Automobile financial responsibility laws, 506–509

Automobile owners and operators, law of negligence and, 411

Average benefits test, 355

Average high-cost multiple, 395

Average indexed monthly earnings (AIME), 377

Average value method, 125–126

Aviation exclusions, 236

Avoidance, 12–13, 47, 56

AVR (asset valuation reserve), 130

**B**

Bail bonds, 481, 616

Bailees, 570, 571

Bailees customers policy, 571

Bailees liability policy, 571

Balance sheet
    assets on, 124–125, 130
    definition of, 124
    liabilities on, 125–126, 130–131
    life insurance, 130–131, 206
    policyholders' surplus on, 126–127, 131
    property and casualty insurance, 124–127

Barriere, Victor and Olga, 33
Basic extended reporting period, 588
Basic form (causes-of-loss), 559–560
Basic form (Dwelling Property 1), 533–534
Beach and Windstorm Plans, 31
Belth, Joseph M., 261–262
Benchmark prices, 261
Beneficiaries, 235, 244–245, 388
Benefit period, 315, 318, 384
Benefits. *See also* Defined-benefit plans
    abusive insurer practices, 302–303
    automatic determination of, 329
    average benefits test and, 355
    disability-income insurance, 318, 383
    earnings loosely related to, 374
    employee, 46, 327, 328
    extended, 394
    health insurance reforms, 304–306
    individual medical expense
        insurance, 310
    life insurance, 246–250
    long-term care insurance, 314
    lump-sum death, 383
    major medical insurance, 309–310
    maximum limits on, 345
    medical necessity trigger, 314
    nonforfeiture, 315
    optional no-fault, 514
    payment of, 277
    pension accrual, 346
    return of premium, 315
    service, 333
    social insurance, 376–384
    state-mandated, 297–299
    survivor, 346, 380–383, 514
    unemployment insurance, 393–394
    variable annuities, 280–281
    workers compensation, 397–398
Bernstein, Peter L., 1, 43
Betterment, 496
Bierce, Ambrose, 19
Biggert-Waters Flood Insurance Reform
        and Modernization Act of 2012, 542
Bilateral contract, 176
Binders, 93–94, 106, 174
Blackout period, 203
Blanket basis, 536, 609
Blue Cross and Blue Shield
    described, 351
        group insurance, 333
        health insurance, 92, 333
        HMOs, 92, 333
        PPOs, 92, 333
        as private insurers, 92
Boards of directors, 420
Boatowners package, 537
Bodily injury, 460, 482, 583
Boiler and machinery insurance, 28–29

Bonds
    appeal, 481
    attachment, 616
    auctioneer's, 616
    bail, 481, 616
    catastrophe, 71, 115
    completion, 615–616
    contract, 615
    court, 616
    fidelity, 29, 613
    fiduciary, 616
    financial institution, 613–614
    insurance agent, 616
    judicial, 616
    license and permit, 615–616
    maintenance, 615–616
    payment, 615–616
    performance, 615–616
    premiums on, 481
    public official, 616
    surety, 29, 614–616
    USAA, 71
Bonus annuity, 277
BOP. *See* Businessowners policy
Breakdown, equipment, 565–567
Broad evidence rule, 167
Broad form (causes-of-loss), 560
Broad form (Dwelling Property 2), 534
Broad form (HO-2), 427–429
Brochures, regulation of, 151
Brokers
    basic concepts, 94–95
    definition of, 70
    Independent Insurance Agents &
        Brokers of America, 491, 551, 577
    licensing of, 150
    marketing systems for, 96
    stock, 96
    surplus lines, 95
Builders risk coverage form, 564
Builders risk insurance, 564
Builders risk reporting form, 564
Building and personal property coverage
        form, 557–559
Burglary, 608, 609, 610–611
Burns, George, 353
Business aircraft, 594–595
Business auto coverage form, 592
Business floaters, 571
Business income insurance
    coverage for, 561–563, 572–573
    definition of, 561
    from dependent properties, 563
    equipment breakdown and, 565
    extra expense coverage form, 563
    without extra expense coverage form,
        561–563
Business income loss, 11, 46, 561–562

Business liability
    businessowners policy and, 597
    personal umbrella policy and, 547
    Section II coverage, 461
    Section II exclusions, 458
Business objectives, of rate making, 132
Businessowners policy (BOP)
    coverages for, 572–573
    deductible, 573
    definition of, 571–572
    eligible business firms, 572
    exclusions, 597
    general liability insurance from, 597
    medical expenses and, 597
Business personal property, 557–558,
        564, 572
Business records, 435
Business risk, 147
Business vehicles, 482, 484–485
Business Watch, 611

**C**

Cafeteria plans, 346–347
Calendar-year deductible
    definition of, 190
    in group plans, 337, 345
    individual medical expense insurance,
        310–311
California Earthquake Authority (CEA),
        31, 463
Camera and musical instrument dealers
        coverage form, 570
Campers, 440, 494
Cancellation
    of CPP, 556
    of homeowners insurance, 447
    noncancellable policies and, 319
    of PAP, 498
CAN-SPAM Act of 2003, 585
Capacity, 69
Capital budgeting, 78
Capital gains, 284
Capital market risk financing
        alternatives, 71
Capital retention approach, 206–207
Capitation fee, 335
Captive.com, 60
Captive insurers, 49–50, 93
Career agents, 95
Career-average earnings, 358
Cargo insurance, 568
Carinsurance.com site, 503
Case reserve, 125–126
Cash-balance plan, 359
Cash dividend, 238
Cash refund option, 279
Cash settlement option, 242, 278
Cash-surrender value, 210

Cash-value life insurance
  on children, 222
  as investment, 212
  nonforfeiture options, 239
  policy loan provision on, 237
  surrender charge, 264
  yearly rate-of-return method, 261
Casualty Actuarial Society, 83, 105, 139
Casualty insurance. *See also* Property and
  casualty insurance
  definition of, 27
  top groups by revenues, 89
Catastrophe bonds, 71, 115
Catastrophe modeling, 80–81
Catastrophic loss
  health insurance coverage, 248
  insurable risks and, 23–24
  modeling of, 80–81
  prediction of, 47
  prescription drugs and, 388
  reinsurance and, 111–112
Causes-of-loss coverage, 559–560, 592
CBO (Congressional Budget Office), 297,
  299, 308–309, 417–418
CDC (Centers for Disease Control and
  Prevention), 351
CDHP (consumer-directed health plan), 340
CDW (collision damage waiver), 490–492
CEA (California Earthquake Authority),
  31, 463
Ceding commission, 14
Ceding company, 110–111
Center for Retirement Research (Boston
  College), 402
Centers for Disease Control and
  Prevention (CDC), 351
Centers for Medicare & Medicaid Services
  (CMS), 34, 296, 390, 402
Central Limit Theorem, 41
Certified Financial Planner (CFP), 108, 265
Certified Insurance Counselor (CIC), 108
Certified Risk Manager (CRM), 83
Cession, 111
CFA (Consumer Federation of America),
  143, 220, 229, 253, 261
CFP (Certified Financial Planner), 108, 265
CGL (commercial general liability) policy,
  582–588
Chance of loss, 3–4, 24
Change-of-plan provision, 235–236
Charitable institutions, 411
Charles Schwab, 293, 370
Chartered Financial Consultant (ChFC),
  108, 265
Chartered Life Underwriter (CLU), 108, 265
Chartered Property Casualty Underwriter
  (CPCU), 60, 108
Chesterton, G. K., 606

ChFC (Chartered Financial Consultant),
  108, 265
Chief risk officer (CRO), 7, 65
Children
  attractive nuisance doctrine and,
    410–411
  CHIP for, 390
  minor, 175, 235
  parents' liability for, 412
  SCHIP for, 30
  Social Security benefits for, 377, 382
Children's Health Insurance Program
  (CHIP), 390
Choice no-fault plans, 513
ChoicePoint, 522
CIC (Certified Insurance Counselor), 108
Citizens Property Insurance Company
  (CPIC), 31
Civil authority, 562
Civil commotion, 439
Civil Service Retirement System, 30
Claimant, 406
Claim forms provision, 320
Claims
  adjusters for, 109
  contested, 233
  for dog bites, 455
  expenses with, 460
  fraudulent, 32–34, 109, 514–515
  IBNR, 597
  individual health insurance contractual
    provisions, 320
  inflated, 33–34, 514–515
  investigating, 110
  settling, 108–110
  third-party, 510–511
  unfair practices, 109
  workers compensation, 75–76
Claims-made policy, 587–588
Claims record, 111
Clash loss, 69
Class-action lawsuits, 413
Class beneficiary, 235
Classification, risk, 5–7
Class rating, 133–134
Clean risk, 517
Climate change risk, 67
CLU (Chartered Life Underwriter),
  108, 265
CLUE (Comprehensive Loss Underwriting
  Exchange) report, 466
CME Group, 73–74
CMS (Centers for Medicare & Medicaid
  Services), 34, 296, 390, 402
Coalition Against Insurance Fraud, 33,
  37, 619
COBRA (Consolidated Omnibus Budget
  Reconciliation Act of 1985), 344

Coinsurance
  CPP, 559, 562
  definition of, 190
  for dental insurance, 345
  health insurance reforms, 305
  HSAs and, 312
  individual medical expense insurance, 311
  in managed care plans, 335–336
  Medicare, 388
  nature of, 190–191
  problems with, 192
  purpose of, 191–192
Coinsurance clause, 190–192
Collapse, 437, 573
Collateral assignment, 236
Collateral source rule, 417
Collision
  in auto insurance, 489, 523, 592, 594
  in marine insurance, 568–569
Collision damage waiver (CDW), 490–492
Combined income, 383
Combined ratio, 68–69, 128–129
Commercial articles coverage form, 570
Commercial crime policy
  basic definitions, 608
  coverage form, 608–613
  exclusions, 612
  insuring agreements, 608–610
  overview, 607–608
  policy conditions, 612–613
Commercial general liability (CGL) policy,
  582–588
Commercial insurance. *See also*
  Commercial crime policy;
  Commercial liability insurance;
  Commercial property insurance
  advantages and disadvantages of, 53
  aircraft, 594–595
  auto, 28, 592–594
  multiple-peril, 28
  risk financing with, 51–53
  terrorism exclusion in, 67
Commercial insurers, 332–333
Commercial liability insurance
  auto, 592–594
  BOP, 597
  CGL policy, 582–588
  claims-made policy, 587–588
  conditions, 587
  coverages, 583–587
  definitions, 587
  D&O, 29, 582, 599–600
  employment-related practices, 588–589
  exclusions, 583–585, 589, 596–597, 600
  general liability loss exposures, 581–582
  insureds of, 586
  limits of, 586–587
  medical expense coverage, 595

medical payments coverage, 585–586
personal injury and, 585, 587, 596
professional liability insurance, 29, 597–599
required underlying coverages, 596
supplementary payments, 586
umbrella policy, 595–597
workers compensation and, 584
Commercial lines, 28–29, 149–150
Commercial package policy (CPP)
building and personal property coverage form, 557–559
business income (and extra expense) coverage form, 561–563
cancellation of, 556
causes-of-loss forms, 559–560
CGL in, 583
coinsurance, 559, 562
common policy conditions, 556–557
common policy declarations, 555
components of, 556
deductible, 559
definition of, 555
extra expense coverage form, 563
ISO, 555
optional coverages, 562–563
premiums, 557
replacement cost in, 559
reporting forms, 560–561, 564
Commercial property insurance. *See also* Commercial package policy
BOP, 571–573
builders risk insurance, 564
condominium association coverage form, 564
condominium commercial unit-owners coverage form, 564–565
DIC insurance, 567
equipment breakdown protection coverage form, 565
ISO simplified, 564
transportation, 567–571
Commercial risk management, 6
Commercial risks, 7, 11
Commercial umbrella policy, 595–597
Commissioners Standard Ordinary (CSO) Mortality Table, 269–270, 273
Commodity price risk, 63–64
Common policy conditions page, 556
Common policy declarations page, 555
Communicable disease exclusion, 459, 547
Community Care Transitions Program, 390
Commutative contract, 175–176
Company adjuster, 109
Company stock, 361, 366
Comparative negligence, 408–409
Compensation of auto accident victims. *See* Auto accident victims, compensation of

Compensatory damages, 408
Competent parties, 175
Competitive state fund, 396
Complaint division, 151
Completed operations liability, 582
Completion bonds, 615–616
Compounding, 77
Comprehensive auto insurance, 592
Comprehensive form (HO-5), 428, 430
Comprehensive Loss Underwriting Exchange (CLUE) report, 466
Compulsory insurance laws, 509
Compulsory programs, 374
Compulsory temporary disability insurance, 30
Computer fraud, 610
Computer operations, interruption of, 562, 573
Concealment, 173, 447
Concurrent causation losses, 440
Conditional contract, 176
Conditionally renewable policy, 319
Conditional premium receipt, 174–175
Conditions, 176, 187
Condominium association coverage form, 564
Condominium commercial unit-owners coverage form, 564–565
Conference of Consulting Actuaries, 139
Congressional Budget Office (CBO), 297, 299, 308–309, 417–418
Consequential loss, 10
Consideration, 175
Consolidated Omnibus Budget Reconciliation Act of 1985 (COBRA), 344
Consolidation, 70–71, 88
Consortium, loss of, 591
Construction, 134, 465–466, 558, 573
Consumer-directed health plan (CDHP), 340
Consumer Federation of America (CFA), 143, 220, 229, 253, 261
Consumer knowledge, 143
Consumer price index (CPI), 248, 315
Consumer protection, 153, 158–159
Consumers Union, 255
Contents broad form (HO-4), 428–429
Contingent beneficiary, 235
Contingent liability, 582
Contingent nonforfeiture benefits upon lapse, 315
Contract bonds, 615
Contract loans, 130
Contractors equipment floater, 571
Contracts. *See also* Insurance contracts
futures, 64
terms of, 52
Contractual liability, 459, 582
Contractual rights, 169

Contributing location, 563
Contribution by equal shares, 193
Contribution limits, HSA, 312
Contributory negligence, 395, 408
Contributory plan, 329
Controlled substance exclusion, 459, 547
Convergence, 88
Convertible, 208
Convertible policies, 208
Coordination-of-benefits provision, 194, 344
Copayments, 305, 311, 337
Corporal punishment, 459
Corporate governance, 419–420
Corporate reimbursement coverage, 599
Cost indexes, 257–260
Cost-of-living adjustment
for disability-income insurance, 318
for group disability-income insurance, 346
for life insurance, 248
for Social Security, 380
Cost of risk, 55
Cost Plans, Medicare, 387
Council for Disability Awareness, 324
Counterfeit money, 436, 573, 612, 614
Court bonds, 616
Courts, regulation by, 145
Coverage gap, 388, 390
Covered autos, 478
Cowper, William, 532
CPCU (Chartered Property Casualty Underwriter), 60, 108
CPI (consumer price index), 248, 315
CPP. *See* Commercial package policy
CRBN attack, 67
Credibility factor, 135
Credit, Social Security, 375–376
Credit-based insurance scores, 158–159, 521–522, 527
Credit cards, 435–436
Credit default swaps, 67, 156
Credit enhancement, 32
Credit insurance, 29
Credit life insurance, 222
Credit line, 49
Credit organizations, 466, 522
Creditors, secured, 169
Credit record, 466, 471
Crime exposures, 11, 46
Crime insurance, 29. *See also* Commercial crime policy
CRM (Certified Risk Manager), 83
Cross-industry consolidation, 70–71
CSO (Commissioners Standard Ordinary) Mortality Table, 269–270, 273
Currency exchange rate risk, 65
Current assumption whole life insurance, 220–221, 223

Currently insured status, 375
Current net income, 48
Custom furnishings and equipment, 495

**D**
Damage
    aircraft, 439, 461
    appraisal provision, 497
    CDW and, 490–492
    collision loss, 489
    compensatory, 408
    as element of negligence, 407–408
    exclusions for, 493–495
    general, 408
    to the insured's product or work, 584
    insuring agreement, 489–491
    limit of liability, 495–496
    noneconomic, 417, 513–515
    other recovery sources, 496–497
    other-than-collision loss, 489–490
    PAP covering, 489–497
    payment of loss, 496
    property, 438–440, 461, 514, 583–585
    punitive, 408, 417, 488
    rental cars, 490–492
    special, 408
    spoilage, 565
    steam, 435, 440
    transportation expenses and, 493
    water, 435, 440–441, 573
Dead storage, 457
Death
    accelerated death benefits rider and,
        248–249
    accidental, 247–248, 318, 332
    enhanced earning benefit, 280
    guaranteed benefit, 280
    lump-sum benefit, 383
    from motor vehicles, 22
    of named insured or spouse, 448
    premature, 7, 199–201
    rising-floor benefit, 280
    suicide and, 26, 233–234
    workers compensation benefits for, 397
Debris removal, 435–436, 558, 572
Decision making, risk
        management, 76–78
Declarations in insurance contracts, 185
Decreasing term insurance, 209–210
Deductibles
    aggregate, 190
    auto insurance, 522–523
    BOP, 573
    calendar-year, 190, 310–311, 337, 345
    collision coverage, 491
    CPP, 559
    definition of, 52, 189
    family deductible provision for, 337
    in health insurance, 190

health insurance reforms, 305
health savings accounts, 312
    in high-deductible health plan, 312,
        340–341
homeowners insurance, 466, 471
hurricane, 442
large-loss principle, 189
major medical policy, 310–311
Medicare prescription drug coverage, 388
NFIP, 540
optional, 514
in property insurance, 190
purposes of, 189–190
special form, 442
straight, 190
tax, 49–50
Deductive reasoning, 3
Defendant, 406
Defense costs, 583
Defense Research Institute, 604
Defensive medicine, 299
Deferred annuity, 277
Deferred retirement age, 356
Defined-benefit plans
    advantages of, 359
    cash-balance, 359
    definition of, 358
    disadvantages of, 359
    formulas for, 358
    Keogh, 364
    limits on, 358
    Pension Benefit Guaranty Corporation,
        358–359
    qualified, 358–359
    traditional, 358
    vesting and, 356
Defined-contribution plans
    definition of, 360
    health, 340
    Keogh plans, 364
    limits on, 360
    money purchase plans, 360
    profit-sharing, 363–364
    qualified, 360–365
    Section 401(k) plans, 360–363
    Section 403(b) plans, 363
    SEP, 365
    SIMPLE, 365
    vesting and, 356
Definitions in insurance contracts, 185
Degree of risk, 3, 4, 26–27
Delayed retirement credit, 377–380
Demutualization, 90
Dental insurance, group, 344–345
Dentists, 597–598
Dependency period, 203
Dependent events, 72
Dependent properties, 563
Depreciation, 167–168

Deregulation, commercial lines, 149–150
Determinable loss, 23
Diagnosis-related groups (DRGs), 385
DIC (difference in conditions)
        insurance, 567
Dickens, Charles, 275
Difference in conditions (DIC)
        insurance, 567
Diminution in value, 496
Direct (physical) loss
    causes-of-loss forms, 572
    definition of, 10
    DIC insurance, 567
    dwelling property, 534
    personal articles floater, 536
Directors and officers (D&O) liability
        insurance, 29, 582, 599–600
Direct response system, 96–98
Direct writer, 97
Disability
    blindness and, 318, 376
    definition of, 346, 383
    income, 397
    long-term, 8–9
    nonoccupational, 346
    partial, 317
    presumptive, 317
    residual, 317–318
    Social Security benefits for, 383
    total, 246, 316–317
Disability Income Forums, 323
Disability-income insurance
    for accidental death, dismemberment,
        and loss of sight, 318
    benefit period, 318
    benefits, 383
    compulsory temporary, 30
    definition of, 316
    as determinable and measurable loss, 23
    elimination period, 190, 318
    group, 345–346
    partial disability and, 317
    rehabilitation provision, 318
    residual disability and, 317–318
    Social Security and, 319, 383
    total disability and, 316–317
    waiver-of-premium provision, 246, 318
Disability insured status, 375–376
Discounting, 77
Discovery form, 607, 612–613
Discriminatory rates, 131
Disease management program, 343
Dismemberment, 318
Dispersion, measures of, 3, 21–22, 40
Distribution of material in violation of
        statutes, 585
Distribution systems
    direct response, 96–98
    financial institution, 96

financial planners, 96
personal selling, 95–96
stock brokers, 96
worksite marketing, 96
Diversifiable risk, 6
Dividend accumulations option, 240
Dividend options, life insurance, 238–239, 264
Dividend policy, 148
Dodd-Frank Wall Street Reform and Consumer Protection Act, 156, 420
Dog bites, 455–456
D&O (Directors and officers) liability insurance, 29, 582, 599–600
Domestic goods in transit, 569
Domestic insurer, 146
Do-not-call list, 585
Donut hole, 388, 390
Double-counting, 75
Double indemnity, 247–248
Double-trigger option, 65–66
Dram shop law, 409–410
DRGs (diagnosis-related groups), 385
Driver education, 520
Driving record, 521, 526–527
Driving under the influence (DUI), 526–527
Drug card program, 310
Drugs. *See* Prescription drug coverage
Dry rot, 438
DUI (driving under the influence), 526–527
Duration of work test, 375–376
Duties
  after loss, 442–443, 497–498
  legal, 407
Dwelling Form, NFIP, 539
Dwelling Property 1, 533–534
Dwelling Property 2, 534
Dwelling Property 3, 534

**E**

Each-occurrence limit, 587
Early distribution penalty, 356–357
Early retirement age, 355, 377
Earned income loss, 7
Earned premiums, 127–128
Earnings
  AIME, 377
  benefits loosely related to, 374
  career-average, 358
  enhanced earning benefit and, 280
  flat percentage of annual, 358
  stability of, 45
Earnings test, 380
Earth movement, 441–442
Earthquake endorsement, 28, 463, 467
EB (extended benefits) program, 394

EBRI (Employee Benefit Research Institute), 351, 370
EBSA (Employee Benefits Security Administration), 370
Economically feasible premiums, 24
Educational fund, 203
eHealthInsurance.com site, 324
Elective deferrals, 361–362
Electrical current damage, 440
Electronic data, 558, 573, 585
Electronic equipment, 493–494
Electronic fund transfer cards, 435–436
Elements of negligence, 407–408
Eligibility
  BOP, 572
  group insurance, 330
  homeowners insurance, 427
  HSA, 312
  IRA, 285
  long-term care insurance, 314
  Medicaid, 301
  mobile home insurance, 535
  NFIP, 538
  unemployment insurance, 393
  vehicle, 478
  workers compensation, 397
Eligibility period, 330
Elimination period
  for disability-income insurance, 190, 318
  health insurance reforms, 305
  for long-term care insurance, 314
  NFIP, 540
  for unemployment insurance, 393
Emergency fund, 12, 203
Emergency NFIP program, 538–539
Emergency Unemployment Compensation (EUC) program, 394
Employee Benefit Research Institute (EBRI), 351, 370
Employee benefits. *See also* Group insurance; Retirement plans
  definition of, 328
  handbook of, 327
  loss exposures, 46
Employee Benefits Security Administration (EBSA), 370
Employee Retirement Income Security Act of 1974 (ERISA)
  commercial umbrella policy and, 596
  described, 145, 354
  D&O insurance and, 600
  on self-insured plans, 333
Employee theft and forgery policy, 607–609
Employers liability
  employers liability insurance for, 588–589

enactment of laws, 395–396
exclusions for, 584
Federal Employers Liability Act and, 591
law of negligence on, 411–412
workers compensation insurance for, 395–396, 589–591
Employment and Training Administration (ETA), 402
Employment-based health insurance, 297
Employment-related practices liability insurance, 588–589
Endorsements
  earthquake, 28, 463, 467
  extended nonowned coverage, 483
  extended replacement cost, 445
  extended reporting period, 598
  home business insurance coverage, 464
  homeowners insurance, 462–465, 467
  identity theft, 464–465
  inflation guard, 462–463, 467, 559
  in insurance contracts, 189
  ISO dwelling program, 534–535
  miscellaneous-type vehicle, 499
  necessary, 467
  personal injury, 464
  PIP, 513
  replacement cost, 462–463, 467
  scheduled personal property, 464, 467, 536
  underinsured motorists, 488–489
  watercraft, 464
Endowment insurance, 213
Enhanced earning benefit, 280
Enterprise risk, 6–7
Enterprise risk management (ERM), 6, 66–67
Entire-contract clause, 232–233
Equal shares, contribution by, 193
Equipment breakdown insurance, 28–29
Equipment breakdown protection coverage form, 565
Equipment dealers form, 570
Equity-indexed annuity, 281–282
Equity in rating, 191–192
ERISA. *See* Employee Retirement Income Security Act of 1974
ERM (enterprise risk management), 6, 66–67
Errors and omissions, 566, 599
Essential health benefits, 305–306
Essential services expenses, 514
Estate clearance fund, 202
Estate tax, 262–263
Estoppel, 178
ETA (Employment and Training Administration), 402
EUC (Emergency Unemployment Compensation) program, 394

Excess insurance, 52, 483, 488, 546
Excess-of-loss sharing methods, 113–115
Exchange-traded weather contracts, 73
Exclusion ratio, 283
Exclusions
 aircraft, 584
 aviation, 236
 BOP, 597
 commercial crime coverage, 612
 commercial liability insurance, 583–585,
  589, 596–597, 600
 communicable disease, 459, 547
 controlled substance, 459, 547
 damage, 493–495
 D&O, 600
 employers liability, 584
 flood, 541
 individual health insurance contractual
  provisions, 320
 individual medical expense
  insurance, 311
 in insurance contracts, 186–187
 life insurance, 236
 long-term care insurance, 315
 major medical insurance, 311
 PAP, 481–483, 484–485, 487–488,
  493–495
 passenger hazard, 499
 personal injury, 547
 personal umbrella insurance, 547–548
 special form Section I, 437–438,
  439–442
 special form Section II, 457–460
 terrorism, 67
 uninsured motorists coverage, 487–488
 watercraft, 584
Exclusive agency system, 97
Exclusive remedy doctrine, 590
Expected or intended injury, 458, 481,
  547, 583
Expected return, 283
Expediting expenses, 565
Expense loading, 32
Expense ratio, 128
Expenses. See Income and expense statement
Experience rating, 135, 329, 394
Explosions, 439
Exposure of buildings, 134
Exposure units
 number of, 22–23
 in rate making, 104, 132
Express authority, 93, 177
Extended benefits (EB) program, 394
Extended nonowned coverage
  endorsement, 483
Extended replacement cost endorsement, 445
Extended reporting periods, 588, 598
Extended term insurance, 240–241

Extra expenses, 562
Extra expenses coverage form, 563

**F**

Facility-only policy, 314
Facultative reinsurance, 113
Fair Access to Insurance Requirements
  (FAIR) plans, 30–31, 542–543
Fair Isaac Corporation (FICO), 466, 522
Fair market value, 167
Fair payment, 109
Fair rental value, 435
Falling objects damage, 440
Families USA, 300, 324
Family deductible provision, 337
Family purpose doctrine, 409
FAST (Financial Analysis Solvency
  Tracking), 158
Faulty, inadequate, or defective planning
  and design, 442
FDIC (Federal Deposit Insurance
  Corporation), 30
Federal Bureau of Investigation (FBI), 34
Federal charters, 157
Federal Deposit Insurance Corporation
  (FDIC), 30
Federal Emergency Management Agency
  (FEMA), 542
Federal Employees Retirement System, 30
Federal Employers Liability Act, 591
Federal estate tax, 262–263
Federal flood insurance program. See
  National Flood Insurance Program
Federal income tax, 262
Federal Insurance Office (FIO), 156
Federal regulation, 151–155
Federal Reserve, 145
Federal Trade Commission (FTC), 145
Fee-for-service plans
 defects in, 302
 group, 333–334
 Medicare, 387
Fellow-servant doctrine, 395
FEMA (Federal Emergency Management
  Agency), 542
Fences, damage to, 438
FICO (Fair Isaac Corporation), 466, 522
Fidelity bonds, 29, 613
Fidelity Investments, 293, 370
Fiduciary bonds, 616
Field examinations, 158
Field underwriting, 106
Fifth dividend option, 239
50 percent rule, 409
51 percent rule, 409
File-and-use law, 149
Film coverage form, 570
Final average pay, 358

Finance department, 54
Financial analysis
 applications for, 77–78
 in risk management, 76–78
 time value of money in, 76–77
Financial Analysis Solvency Tracking
  (FAST), 158
Financial crisis
 AIG in, 65, 67, 156
 EUC program and, 394
 homeowners insurance during, 471
 of Medicare, 391–392
 regulation and, 156–157
 uninsured motorists and, 485
Financial guaranty insurance, 29
Financial Institution Bond, Standard Form
  No. 24, 613
Financial institution bonds, 613–614
Financial institution distribution systems, 96
Financial Modernization Act of 1999,
  88, 145
Financial operations of insurers
 life insurance, 130–131, 135
 property and casualty insurers,
  124–130, 131–135
Financial planners, 96
Financial responsibility laws, 506–509
Financial risk, 6, 24
Financial risk management
 basic concepts in, 65–66
 commodity price risk and, 63–64
 currency exchange rate risk and, 65
 interest rate risk and, 65
Financial services industry, 87–88
Financial Services Modernization Act of
  1999, 70–71
Financial Stability Oversight Council
  (FSOC), 156
Financial statements, 46, 158
FIO (Federal Insurance Office), 156
Fire
 apartment, 430–431
 automatic fire protective sprinkler
  system for, 440
 liability insurance, 585
 private insurance, 24–25, 28
 risk of, 24–25
 in special form, 438
Fire department service charge, 436,
  558, 573
Fire-protection class, 465
First-aid expenses, 460–461
First named insured, 188
Five-year cliff vesting, 356
Five-year term insurance, 270–271
Fixed-amount option, 242–243
Fixed annuity, 277–279
Fixed-period option, 242

Flat dollar amount for all employees, 358
Flat dollar amount for each year of
service, 358
Flat percentage of annual earnings, 358
Flexible-premium deferred annuity, 277
Flexible spending accounts, 338, 347
Flex-rating law, 149
Flight insurance at airports, 222
Flood exclusion, 541
Flooding, 442, 538–539
Flood insurance. *See also* National Flood
Insurance Program
dropping, 472
government programs for, 6, 28
tips on buying, 471
FloodSmart.gov, 541, 551
Floor of income, 374, 377
Floor plan coverage form, 570
Florida Hurricane Catastrophe Fund, 31
Flowcharts, 46
Foreign insurer, 146
Foreign loss exposures, 11, 46
Forgery
BOP coverage, 573
employee theft and forgery policy,
607–609
financial institution bonds, 613–614
homeowners insurance and, 436
Fortuitous loss, 22
401(k) plans. *See* Section 401(k) plans
403(b) plans, 363
FPA (free-of-particular-average) clause,
568
Fraternal insurer, 90
Fraud
auto insurance, 32
auto insurance and, 514–515
claims and, 32–34, 109, 233
Coalition Against Insurance Fraud and,
33, 37, 619
computer, 610
corporate governance and, 419–420
costs of, 33–34
funds transfer, 610
Hall of Shame, 33
health insurance reforms and, 308, 390
homeowners insurance and, 447
material misrepresentation and,
172–173
mortgage, 614
no-fault insurance and, 514–515
valued policy laws and, 168
workers compensation insurance, 398
FreeAdvice.com site, 182, 423
Free-of-particular-average (FPA)
clause, 568
Freezing, 437–438, 440
Freight insurance, 568

FSOC (Financial Stability Oversight
Council), 156
FTC (Federal Trade Commission), 145
Full choice cafeteria plans, 347
Full retirement age, 376–377, 380
Full-time student away from home, 431,
439, 526
Fully funded program, 374–375
Fully insured status, 375
Fundamental risk, 6
*Fundamentals of Insurance* (Mehr), 231
Funded reserve, 49
Funding agency and instruments, 365–366
Funds transfer fraud, 610
Fungus, 438, 573
Futures contracts, 64

**G**

GAAP (Generally Accepted Accounting
Principles), 118, 146
Gambling
contract regarding, 176
insurable interest and, 169
insurance *v.*, 26
slot machines, 4
speculative risk of, 5
GAO (Government Accountability Office),
141, 153, 542
Gap insurance, 496
Garage coverage form, 593–594
Garagekeepers coverage, 593
Garage operations, 593
Garment contractors floater, 571
Gatekeeper physician, 335
GEICO, 503, 529
Gender, auto insurance cost influenced by,
518–519
General aggregate limit, 586–587
General average, 568–569
General damages, 408
General investment account, 116–117
General liability insurance, 28,
581–582, 597
Generally Accepted Accounting Principles
(GAAP), 118, 146
General Property Policy Form, NFIP, 539
GIC (guaranteed investment contract), 366
Glass breakage, 437, 573
Global Aerospace, 594
GLWB (guaranteed lifetime withdrawal
benefits), 281
GMAB (guaranteed minimum
accumulation benefit), 281
GMIB (guaranteed minimum income
benefit), 281
GMWB (guaranteed minimum withdrawal
benefits), 281
Golay, Helen, 33

Golf carts, 457
Good student discount, 520–521, 526
Government Accountability Office (GAO),
141, 153, 542
Governmental action, loss due to, 442
Governmental functions, 411
Government crime coverage form,
607–608
Government crime policy, 607–608
Government destruction or confiscation, 494
Government entities, liability of, 411
Government exposures, 11
Government insurance. *See also* National
Flood Insurance Program; Social
insurance
FAIR plans, 542–543
nondiversifiable risks and, 6
nonsocial types of, 30
property, 538–543
social insurance programs, 29–30
at state level, 30–31
Grace period, 233, 320
Gramm-Leach-Bliley Act, 88, 145
Grandfathered plans, 304–305, 338
Grave markers, 437
Gross estate, 263–264
Gross premium, 132, 272
Gross rate, 132
Group captive, 49–50
Group insurance
AD&D, 332
Blue Cross and Blue Shield, 333
cafeteria plans, 346–347
CDHP, 340
dental, 344–345
disability-income, 345–346
eligibility requirements, 330
fee-for-service plans, 333–334
fundamentals of, 328–330
health, 332–344
individual insurance *v.*, 328–329
life, 224, 330–332
managed care and, 333, 334–336
marketing, 98
self-insurance and, 333
for small employers, 338
tax treatment of, 297
term life, 331
underwriting, 329–330
universal life, 332
Group medical expense contractual
provisions
COBRA law and, 344
coordination of benefits, 344
preexisting conditions, 343–344
Group medical expense insurance
Affordable Care Act requirements and,
337–338

coinsurance, 337
comprehensive, 336–337
contractual provisions, 343–344
copayments, 337
deductibles, 310–311, 337
definition of, 309–310
exclusions, 311
key features of, 336–337
out-of-pocket limit of, 311, 337
Group model HMO, 335
Guaranteed death benefit, 280
Guaranteed investment contract (GIC), 366
Guaranteed issue laws, 304, 320, 338
Guaranteed lifetime withdrawal benefits
    (GLWB), 281
Guaranteed minimum accumulation
    benefit (GMAB), 281
Guaranteed minimum income benefit
    (GMIB), 281
Guaranteed minimum interest rate, 214, 220
Guaranteed minimum value, 282
Guaranteed minimum withdrawal benefits
    (GMWB), 281
Guaranteed purchase option, 246–247
Guaranteed rate, 277
Guaranteed renewable policy, 317, 319
Guaranteed replacement cost policy, 445
Guaranteed values, 241
Guaranty funds, 148
Guardians, 235

**H**
Hail damage, 438–439
*The Handbook of Employee Benefits*
    (Rosenbloom), 327
Hard market conditions, 54, 68
Harvard School of Public Health, 301
Hazards. *See also* Moral hazard
    attitudinal, 5
    legal, 5
    nuclear, 441
    passenger, 499
    physical, 4
    products-completed operations, 582, 584
    risk *v.*, 4–5
HDHP (High-deductible health plan), 312,
    340–341
HealthCare.gov site, 324, 351
Health-care problems, in U.S.
    abusive insurer practices, 302–303
    aging population and, 299
    bankruptcies and, 303
    defects in financing health care, 302
    foreign nations compared with,
        296–298
    individual medical expense insurance
        and, 309–312
    reform of, 303–309

rising expenditures, 296–299
    uneven quality of medical care, 301
    uninsured population, 299–301, 339
    waste and inefficiency, 301–302
HealthGrades.com site, 324, 351
Health insurance. *See also* Medical expense
        insurance; specific plans
    accident and, 29
    catastrophic, 248
    coinsurance in, 192
    deductibles in, 190
    definition of, 27
    employment-based, 297
    essential health benefits, 305–306
    guaranteed issue laws for, 304, 320
    high-deductible, 312
    inadequate, 8–9
    medical payments coverage, 455–457,
        483–485, 585–586
    other-insurance provisions, 192
    preexisting conditions clause and,
        26, 320
    as private insurance, 27
    SCHIP, 30
    special high-risk pools, 30
    top groups by revenues, 89
Health Insurance Portability and
        Accountability Act (HIPAA),
        313–314, 343–344
Health insurance reforms. *See also*
        Affordable Care Act
    Affordable Insurance Exchange,
        306, 338
    basic provisions of, 303–309
    cost and financing, 308–309
    cost-containment provisions, 392
    employer requirements, 306, 338
    essential health benefits, 305–306
    grandfathered plans, 304, 338
    guaranteed access, 304
    important provisions, 304–305
    improving quality, 308
    individual mandate, 304, 338
    limited waiting periods, 305
    lowering costs, 308
    Medicaid expansion, 307
    preexisting conditions, 26, 102, 304,
        307, 320, 338
    tax credits, 306–307, 338
Health maintenance organizations
        (HMOs)
    Blue Cross and Blue Shield, 92, 333
    characteristics of, 334–335
    cost of, 341
    definition of, 334
    dental, 345
    market control for, 332
    Medicare, 384

PPOs *v.*, 336
    as private insurers, 93
    types of, 335–336
Health reimbursement account (HRA), 340
Health risk assessment, 343
Health savings account (HSA)
    coinsurance and, 312
    contribution limits, 312
    deductibles, 312
    definition of, 312
    eligibility requirements of, 312
    out-of-pocket limits, 305–306
    rationale for, 313
    tax treatment of, 312–313
Hedging
    of commodity price risk, 64
    definition of, 14–15
    insurance *v.*, 26–27
Hedrick, William B., 580
Hersman, Deborah A.P., 494
High-deductible health plan (HDHP), 312,
    340–341
Highly compensated employees, 355, 362
High-risk drivers, auto insurance for,
    516–517
HIPAA (Health Insurance Portability
        and Accountability Act), 313–314,
        343–344
Historical loss data, 46
Hit-and-run vehicle, 486–487
HMOs. *See* Health maintenance
        organizations
HO-2 (broad form), 427–429
HO-3. *See* Special form
HO-4 (contents broad form), 428–429
HO-5 (comprehensive form), 428, 430
HO-6 (unit-owners form), 428, 430
HO-8 (modified coverage form), 428, 430
Hold-harmless clause, 14
Holding company, 91
Home business insurance coverage
        endorsement, 464
Home health care, 314, 385
Home inventory, 443
Homeland Security Act of 2002, 12
Homeowners insurance. *See also*
        Special form
    adequate, 467
    apartment fire and, 430–431
    broad form, 427–429
    cancellation of, 447
    comparison of coverages, 429–430
    comprehensive form, 428, 430
    contents broad form, 428–429
    cost of, 465–471
    deductible, 466, 471
    definition of, 27–28
    discounts on, 471

eligible dwellings, 427
endorsements to, 462–465, 467
during financial crisis, 471
fraud and, 447
information quality for, 143
modified coverage form, 428, 430
motor vehicles and, 431–432, 434, 457–458
as multiple-line policy, 28
overview of policies, 427–430
premium variations of, 467–470
schedule for, 433
subrogation and, 447–448
tips for buying, 466–471
unit-owners form, 428, 430
workers compensation and, 460
Home service (industrial) life insurance, 224
Hospice care, 385
Hospital Insurance, in Original Medicare Plan, 384–385, 391
Household appliances, 440
Hovercraft, 434, 458, 461
HRA (health reimbursement account), 340
HSA. See Health savings account
Hubbard, Kin, 353
Huebner Foundation and Geneva Association, 18
Hull insurance, 567–568, 594
Human life value, 7, 201–202
Human resources department, 11, 46, 54
Hunter, J. Robert, 153
Hurricane(s)
    deductibles, 442
    Florida Hurricane Catastrophe Fund for, 31
    Katrina, 69, 80, 112, 440, 471, 542

I
IBNR (incurred-but-not-reported), 126, 587
Ice damage, 440
Identity theft endorsement, 464–465
IFRI (International Financial Risk Institute), 60
III. See Insurance Information Institute
ImmediateAnnuities.com site, 293
Immediate annuity, 277, 293
Implied authority, 93, 177
Implied warranties, 568
Imputed negligence, 409–410
"I'm sorry laws," 419
Income. See also Business income; Disability-income insurance; Retirement income
    combined, 383
    floor of, 374, 377
    in investment income ratio, 129
    IRA limits, 287

joint-and-survivor, 243, 245
in life income settlement option, 243
loss of, 7, 11, 46, 561–562
net, 48
taxes on, 262
Income and expense statement
    expenses on, 128
    life insurance, 131
    property and casualty insurance, 127–128
    revenues on, 127–128
Incontestable clause, 233
Incorporation, 15
Incurred-but-not-reported (IBNR) reserve, claims, 126, 587
Indemnity
    actual cash value and, 166–167
    auto accidents and, 509
    definition of, 22, 166
    double, 247–248
    exceptions to, 167–169
    legal principle of, 166–169
    life insurance and, 168–169
    for loss, 31
    maximum period of, 563
    monthly limit of, 563
    purposes of, 166
    traditional indemnity plans and, 333–334
Independent adjuster, 109
Independent agency system, 97
Independent events, 71–75
Independent Insurance Agents & Brokers of America, 491, 551, 577
Independent Payment Advisory Board, 390
Independent property and casualty agents, 96
Indexed universal life insurance, 219
Indexing method, 282
Indirect loss, 10
Individual 401(k) plans, 362–363
Individual annuities, 276–277, 283–284
Individual driving record, 521
Individual equity, 374
Individual health insurance
    contractual provisions and, 319–321
    disability-income insurance, 316–318
    guaranteed issue laws for, 304, 320
    health-care problems and, 296–309
    HSAs and, 305–306, 312–313
    long-term care insurance, 313–316
Individual health insurance contractual provisions
    on claims, 320
    grace period, 320
    notice of 10-day right to examine policy, 320
    preexisting-conditions exclusions, 320

reinstatement, 320
renewal provisions, 319
time limit on certain defenses, 320–321
Individual medical expense insurance
    broad range of benefits, 310
    calendar-year deductible, 310–311
    coinsurance in, 311
    contractual provisions and, 319–321
    copayments, 311
    definition of, 309
    exclusions, 311
    guaranteed issue laws for, 304, 320
    health-care problems and, 296–303
    major medical benefits, 309–310
    managed care plans and, 311–312
    mandate for, 304
    out-of-pocket limits, 311
Individual practice association plan (IPA), 336
Individual retirement accounts (IRAs)
    adequacy of, 288
    contribution limits, 285
    definition of, 284
    eligibility requirements, 285
    establishing, 286–287
    income limits on, 287
    investments, 287
    minimum distribution requirements and, 357
    nondeductible, 285
    retirement needs and, 203
    rollover, 287
    Roth, 287–288, 293, 357
    SEP-IRA and, 365
    SIMPLE-IRA and, 365
    spousal, 285
    taxes and, 285–286
    traditional, 285–288
Inductive reasoning, 4
Industrial (home service) life insurance, 224
Inefficiency, in health care, 301–302
Inflated claims, 33–34, 514–515
Inflation guard endorsement, 462–463, 467, 559
Inflation-indexed annuity option, 279
Inflation protection, 314–315
Information systems, 117–118
Inherent vice, 186
Initial reserve, 274
Injury
    advertising, 585, 587, 596
    bodily, 460, 482, 583
    as element of negligence, 407–408
    expected or intended, 458, 481, 547, 583
    personal, 464, 514, 546, 585, 587, 596
    PIP for, 513
Inland marine floaters, 535–536

Inland marine insurance
   definition of, 29, 567, 569
   inland marine floaters insurance,
      535–536
   ISO forms, 570–571
   major classes of, 569–570
   Nationwide Marine Definition for, 569
   other forms, 571
Inland Marine Underwriters
      Association, 577
Innocent misrepresentation, 173
Inpatient hospital care, 310, 384
Inside the premises-robbery or burglary of
      other property, 609
Insolvency of insurers, 142, 157–158
Inspection report, 106–107
Installment refund option, 279
The Institutes, 60, 101, 121
Instrumentalities of transportation and
      communication, 570–571
Insufficient retirement income risk, 7–8
Insurability premium receipt, 174–175
Insurable interest, 169–170, 442
Insurable risk
   applications of, 24–25
   catastrophic loss and, 23–24
   characteristics of, 22–24
Insurance. *See also specific types of insurance*
   adverse selection and, 26, 106
   applications for, 106
   availability of, 144, 154
   basic characteristics of, 20–22
   contracts, 52, 174–177
   definition of, 20
   excess, 52, 483, 488, 546
   gambling *v.*, 26
   gap, 496
   government regulation of, 141–159
   hedging *v.*, 26–27
   industry capacity, 69
   as investment fund source, 31
   in personal risk management, 57
   pooling in, 15, 20–22, 115, 517
   risk and, 20–34, 147
   self-, 14, 50, 333
   social costs and benefits of, 31–34
   statistics and, 39–40
   surety bonds *v.*, 615
   terrorism risk and, 67
   types of, 27–31
   weak competition in, 153–154
Insurance agent bonds, 616
Insurance agents. *See* Agents
Insurance brokers
   basic concepts, 94–95
   definition of, 70
   Independent Insurance Agents &
      Brokers of America, 491, 551, 577

licensing of, 150
   marketing systems for, 96
   surplus lines, 95
Insurance commissioner, 145–146
Insurance Committee for Arson Control, 619
Insurance.com site, 268, 451
Insurance contracts
   abusive insurer practices, 302–303
   analysis of, 184–194
   basic parts of, 185–187
   coinsurance in, 190–192
   deductibles in, 189–190
   definition of "insured" in, 187–189
   endorsements and riders in, 189
   health insurance reforms, 304
   insurance agents and, 177–178
   legal characteristics of, 175–177
   other-insurance provisions, 192–194
   requirements of, 174–175
Insurance Information Institute (III)
   described, 18, 37, 83, 100–101, 121,
      139, 197, 451, 475, 503, 529, 551,
      577, 604
   on fraud, 398
   quote attributed to, 86, 103
   on underinsurance, 471
*Insurance Journal*, 37, 101, 139
Insurance Law Communities site, 182
Insurance options, 71
Insurance Regulatory Examiners
      Society, 162
Insurance Regulatory Information System
      (IRIS), 158
Insurance Research Council (IRC)
   on claim payments, 515
   described, 37, 503, 529, 577
   on uninsured motorists, 485
Insurancesavenow.com site, 475
Insurance scores
   credit-based, 158–159, 521–522, 527
   definition of, 466, 521
Insurance Services Office (ISO)
   A-PLUS, 466
   on BOP, 572
   business auto coverage form, 592
   CGL policy, 582
   claims-made policy, 587–588
   commercial crime insurance program,
      607–608
   commercial liability umbrella coverage
      form, 595–597
   CPP, 555
   described, 105, 139, 604
   dwelling program, 533–535
   employment-related practices liability
      coverage form, 588–589
   on gap insurance, 496
   homeowners forms, 427

inland marine insurance forms,
      570–571
   mobile home insurance, 535
   personal umbrella policy, 546–548
   physicians, surgeons, and dentists
      professional liability insurance form,
      597–598
   rating fire department quality, 465
   simplified commercial property
      program, 564
Insure.com site, 101, 229, 253, 268, 293,
      451, 475, 529, 551
Insured contract, 583
Insured locations, 456–457, 460
Insured plan, 365
Insurers
   abusive practices, 302–303
   accounting department of, 118
   agents and brokers of, 70, 93–95
   alien, 146
   captive, 49–50, 93
   claims record of, 111
   claims settlement by, 108–110
   commercial, 332–333
   competence of, 175
   cost variation among, 258–259
   domestic, 146
   financial operations of, 124–135
   financial strength of, 265
   foreign, 146
   formation and licensing regulation, 146
   fraternal, 90
   information systems of, 117–118
   investments by, 116–117
   lawsuits against, 446
   legal function of, 118
   life insurance, 100, 121, 130–131, 139,
      157, 253
   liquidation of, 148–149
   loss-control services of, 118
   marketing systems of, 95–98
   moral hazard controlled by, 5
   mutual, 88–91
   nonadmitted, 95
   operations of, 104–118
   private, 5, 88–93
   production by, 108
   property and casualty, 124–130,
      131–135
   reinsurance and, 110–115
   selection of, 52
   small, 155
   solvency of, 142–143, 146–149,
      157–158, 272
   specialty, 517
   stock, 88, 90–91
   taxation of, 49–50, 151
   underwriting by, 105–108

Insurers Supervision, Rehabilitation, and Liquidation Model Act, 148
Insuring agreement, 186
InsWeb site, 101, 229, 253, 268, 451, 475, 503, 529, 551
Intangible property exposures, 11, 46
Integrated risk program, 65
Intended injury, 458, 481, 547, 583
Intentional loss, 441
Intentional torts, 406
Interest
    on cash-value life insurance, 237
    insurable, 169–170, 442
    settlement option, 242
Interest-adjusted cost method, 257
Interest credit, 359
Interest rate
    current, 277
    guaranteed, 277
    risk, 65, 147
    for universal life insurance, 214, 218–219
Interest-sensitive whole life insurance, 220–221
Interinsurance exchange, 92
Internal rate of return (IRR), 78
Internal Revenue Service (IRS), 49–50, 283, 354
International Financial Risk Institute (IFRI), 60
International Foundation of Employee Benefit Plans, 351
International Risk Management Institute (IRMI), 37, 60, 82–83, 451, 475, 503, 529–530
Intranets, risk management, 79
In-transit coverage, 614
Investment income ratio, 129
Investment management charge, 280
Investments
    in general investment account, 116–117
    GIC and, 366
    by insurers, 116–117
    IRA, 287
    life insurance, 116–117, 148, 212, 220
    in mortgages, 116
    property and casualty insurance, 117, 148
    regulation of, 148
    returns on, 69–70
    revenues from, 127
    risk-control, 78
    separate investment account and, 116–117, 366
Invitees, 410, 581
Involuntary market plans, 30
Ionesco, Eugene, 198
IPA (individual practice association plan), 336

IRAs. *See* Individual retirement accounts
IRC. *See* Insurance Research Council
IRIS (Insurance Regulatory Information System), 158
IRMI. *See* International Risk Management Institute
IRR (internal rate of return), 78
Irrevocable beneficiary, 235
IRS (Internal Revenue Service), 49–50, 283, 354
ISO. *See* Insurance Services Office

**J**
James, Richard, 33
Jewelers block coverage form, 570
Joint and several liability rule, 417
Joint-and-survivor annuity option, 279
Joint-and-survivor income, 243, 245
Joint business venture, 409
Joint Economic Committee, 505
Joint underwriting association (JUA), 517
JUA (joint underwriting association), 517
Judgment method, 125
Judgment rating, 133
Judicial bonds, 616
Judicial hellholes, 415–416
Jury awards, 414

**K**
Kaiser Family Foundation, 299–300, 301
Keogh plans, 364
Keyes, Mike, 123
Kickbacks, 544–545
Known loss, 583

**L**
Landlord's furnishings, 437
Large-loss principle, 189
Last clear chance rule, 409
Law of agency, 177–178
Law of large numbers
    definition of, 3, 15, 21–22
    objective risk reduced by, 26–27
    pooling and, 21–22
    probability and, 21
    pure risk and, 5
    random occurrences in, 22–23
    sampling distribution and, 40–42
Law of negligence, 410–411
Lawsuits. *See also* Tort liability system
    class-action, 413
    against insurers, 446
    liability and, 10–11
    against physicians, 418–419
    sovereign immunity from, 411
    stockholder, 414
    uninsured motorists coverage and, 512

Voltaire quote, 405
    workers compensation and, 395–396
Lawyers.com, 182
LDW (loss damage waiver), 490–492
Leader location, 563
Legal defense, 589, 592, 595, 596
Legal duty, 407
Legal hazard, 5
Legal Information Institute, 423
Legal liability. *See* Liability
Legally competent, 175
Legal obligations, as pre-loss objective, 45
Legal principles, fundamental
    agents and, 177–178
    contract characteristics and, 175–177
    contract requirements and, 174–175
    indemnity, 166–169
    insurable interest, 169–170
    of reasonable expectations, 177
    subrogation, 170–172
    of utmost good faith, 172–174
Legal purpose, 175
Legal reserves, 210–211
Legal wrong, 406
Legislation, regulation by, 145
Liability. *See also* Tort liability system
    absolute, 407, 412
    aircraft, 458, 547
    animals and, 412, 455
    on balance sheets, 125–126, 130–131
    basis of, 406–407
    bodily injury, 583
    business, 458, 461, 547, 597
    children, parents and, 412
    completed operations, 582
    contingent, 582
    contractual, 459, 582
    employer, 395–396, 584, 588–589
    of government entities, 411
    hovercraft, 458
    insurable interest and, 169
    joint and several liability rule and, 417
    lawsuits and, 10–11
    limit of, 433, 442, 483, 486, 495–496
    liquor, 583–584
    loss exposures, 46, 56, 581–582
    motor vehicle, 457–458, 472
    premises and operations liability, 581–582
    products, 28, 582
    professional services, 459, 547, 582
    property damage, 583
    pro rata, 192–193, 446
    recreational vehicles, 547
    strict, 407
    watercraft, 458, 537, 547
    without fault, 396, 589

Liability insurance. *See also* Commercial
    liability insurance
  adequate, 522
  auto, 472, 479–483, 486, 495–496,
    592–594
  combined ratio exhibit, 68
  commercial lines, 28–29
  contribution by equal shares
    provision, 193
  definition of, 27
  excess, 546
  fire, 585
  general, 28, 581–588, 597
  in PAP, 479–483, 486, 495–496
  personal lines, 27–28, 454–455, 471,
    535–536
  private, 27–29
  products, 28
  professional, 29, 597–599
Liability risk
  basis of, 406–407
  commercial, 11
  current tort liability problems, 412–420
  negligence and, 407–412
  personal, 10–11
Liability without fault principle, 396, 589
Liberalization clause, 447
License and permit bonds, 615–616
Licensees, 410
Lieberman, Gerald F., 165
Liens, 10
Life and Health Insurance Foundation for
    Education (LIFE), 229
Life annuity (no refund), 278
Life annuity with guaranteed payments,
    278–279
Life expectancy, 200, 283
Life income settlement option, 243–244
Life insurance
  actuaries for, 105
  additional benefits of, 246–250
  agents of, 93–94, 106
  amount to own, 201–208, 264
  annuities *v.*, 276
  balance sheet, 130–131
  best type of, 264
  buying, 255–265
  capital retention approach, 206–207
  cash-value, 212, 237, 239, 261–262, 264
  contractual provisions, 231–238
  cost of, 256–260
  definition of, 27
  dependency period, 203
  as determinable loss, 23
  dividend options, 238–239, 264
  endowment, 213
  exclusions and restrictions of, 236
  financial performance of, 131

  government programs for, 30
  group, 224, 330–332
  human life value approach to, 201–202
  income and expense statements, 131
  indemnity and, 168–169
  industrial, 224
  insurable interest and, 169–170
  insurers, 100, 121, 130–131, 139,
    157, 253
  investments of, 116–117, 148, 212, 220
  Loan provision, 237
  low-load, 264
  marketing systems for, 95–96
  need for, 263–264
  needs approach to, 202–206
  nonforfeiture options, 239–241
  offer and acceptance in, 174–175
  opportunity costs of buying, 207–208
  optional federal charter for, 157
  ordinary, 210–211, 223, 271–272
  permanent, 130
  policyowners' surplus in, 147
  premature death, 199–201
  premiums for, 116, 269–274
  private, 27
  rate making in, 135
  rate of return on saving component,
    260–262
  rate regulation of, 150
  reduced paid-up, 240
  replacing policies, 259
  SBLI, 93, 222–224
  second-to-die, 222
  settlement options, 241–246
  shopping for, 263–265
  subrogation and, 172
  suicide clause in, 26, 233–234
  taxation of, 262–263
  term, 208–210, 223, 239–241,
    269–271, 331
  top groups by revenues, 89
  types of, 208–213, 221–224
  underwriting information sources for,
    106–107
  unfair trade practices in, 109
  universal, 214–220, 223
  variable, 213–214, 223
  variations of whole life insurance,
    213–221
  whole, 210–221, 223, 240
Life Insurance Policy Illustration Model
    Regulation, 260
Life Office Management Association
    (LOMA), 121, 229
Life settlement, 249–250
Lifetime reserve days, 384
Lightening damage, 438, 441
Limited-payment policy, 213

LIMRA International, Inc., 101, 121,
    207, 229
Line underwriters, 107
Linton, M. Albert, 260
Linton yield, 260–261
Liquidation period, 277
Liquor liability, 583–584
Livery conveyance, 482, 484, 488, 493
Lloyd's of London, 91–92, 101
Loading, 132
Location in homeowners insurance, 465
LOMA (Life Office Management
    Association), 121, 229
Longevity insurance, 282–283
Long-range actuarial deficit, of Social
    Security, 390–391
Longshore and Harbor Workers
    Compensation Act, 538, 591
Long tail claims, 587
Long-term care insurance
  chances of needing, 313
  characteristics of, 313–315
  choice of benefits, 314
  definition of, 313
  eligibility, 314
  elimination period, 314
  exclusions, 315
  expensive coverage, 315
  guaranteed renewable policies, 315
  inflation protection, 314–315
  partnership programs, 315–316
  taxation of, 315
  variations in policies, 314
Long-term-care rider, 248
Long-term disability, financial impact of,
    8–9
Long-term group disability-income
    insurance, 346
Loss. *See also* Catastrophic loss; Loss
    exposures
  accidental, 23
  of business income, 11, 46, 561–562
  chance of, 3–4, 24
  clash, 69
  collision, 489
  concurrent causation, 440
  of consortium, 591
  determinable, 23
  direct, 10, 534, 536, 537, 567
  due to governmental action, 442
  due to ordinance or law, 440–441
  duties after, 442–443, 497–498
  excluded in insurance contracts, 186
  expected, 21
  forecasting, 71–75
  fortuitous, 22
  frequency of, 47
  of goods and services, 12

hazards and, 4–5
income, 7, 11, 46
indemnification for, 31
indirect, 10
intentional, 441
known, 583
large-loss principle, 189
maximum possible, 47
measuring of, 23, 128–129
other-than-collision, 489–490
paying, 48–49, 496
peril and, 4
pooling of, 15, 20–22, 115, 517
prevention of, 13, 31–32, 47–48, 51
probable maximum, 47
proof of, 110, 173, 320, 443
reduction of, 13, 48
severity of, 47
sharing methods, 113–115
sustained during prior insurance, 613
ultimate net, 595
underwriting, 117
unintentional, 23
of use, 435, 535
verification of, 109
Loss-adjustment expenses, 126
Loss assessment, 436–437, 461
Loss control
    rate making objectives, 132
    risk control and, 12–13, 47–48
    in risk management, 118
Loss damage waiver (LDW), 490–492
Loss distributions, 75–76
Loss exposures
    analysis of, 46–47, 56
    business income, 46
    crime, 11, 46
    definition of, 2, 44
    employee benefit, 46
    foreign, 11, 46
    government, 11
    human resources, 11, 46
    identification of, 46, 55–56
    liability, 46, 56, 581–582
    measurement of, 46–47
    personal, 55–56
    property, 11, 46, 56
    in risk management matrix, 53–54
    techniques for treating, 47–54, 56–57
    units of, 22–23, 104
Loss forecasting
    based on loss distributions, 75–76
    probability analysis in, 71–75
    regression analysis in, 75
    in risk management, 71–75
Loss history reports, 466
Loss ratio, 126, 128, 133–134
Loss reserves, 125

Loss settlement, 443–445, 491
Loss-sustained form, 607, 613
Loss to pair or set, 445
Lost-instrument bond, 616
Low-cost auto insurance, 512
Low-load life insurance, 264
Lump-sum death benefit, 383

**M**
Madoff, Bernard, 420
Mail coverage form, 570
Maintenance, of buildings, 134
Maintenance bonds, 615–616
Major medical insurance
    benefits, 309–310
    coinsurance in, 311
Malicious mischief, 438, 439
Malingering, 346
Malpractice insurance, 29, 418–419,
        597–598
Managed care. See also Health
        maintenance organizations; Preferred
        provider organizations
    coinsurance in, 335–336
    definition of, 334
    dental plans in, 345
    group insurance and, 333, 334–336
    individual medical expense insurance
        and, 311–312
    POS plans, 336
Manual, risk management, 54
Manual rating, 133
Manufacturing location, 563
Manuscript policy, 52
Maps, risk, 79
Marine insurance, 29. See also Inland marine
        insurance; Ocean marine insurance
Marital deduction, 263
Marital status, auto insurance cost
        influenced by, 518–519
Market conditions, risk management and,
        54, 68
Market conduct examinations, 154
Market dynamics
    capital market risk financing alternatives
        and, 71
    consolidation in, 70–71
    risk management and, 68–71
    underwriting cycle in, 68–70
Marketing department, 54
Marketing systems
    life insurance, 95–96
    property and casualty, 96–98
Market risks, 24
Maryland Automobile Insurance Fund,
        31, 517
Mass merchandising, 98
Master contract, 328

Material fact, 172
Material misrepresentation, 172–173
Maximum cap rate, 282
Maximum possible loss, 47
McCarran-Ferguson Act
    passage of, 144–145
    repeal of, 145, 155
McQuade, Rebecca A., 554
M&E (mortality and expense risk charge),
        220, 280
Mean reserve, 274
Means test, 374
Measurable loss, 23
Mediation, 417
Medicaid
    cost shifting by, 299
    eligibility, 301
    expansion of, 307
    health insurance reforms, 307–309
    long-term care partnership program,
        315–316
Medical care
    consumer demand for, 297
    uneven quality of, 301
    as workers compensation benefit, 397
Medical errors, 418
Medical expense insurance. See also
        Group medical expense insurance;
        Individual medical expense insurance
    in boatowners package, 537
    BOP and, 597
    commercial liability insurance and, 595
Medical Information Bureau, 107
Medical loss ratio, 305
Medical malpractice, 29, 418–419,
        597–598
Medical necessity trigger, 314
Medical payments coverage
    commercial liability insurance, 585–586
    PAP, 483–485
    payments to others and, 455–457
Medical savings accounts (MSA) plans, 387
Medicare
    Advantage Plans, 309, 386–387, 390
    coinsurance, 388
    Cost Plans, 387
    cost shifting by, 299
    definition of, 30, 384
    demonstration and pilot programs, 387
    fee-for-service plans, 387
    financial crisis of, 391–392
    financing of, 396
    health insurance reforms, 308–309
    HMO, 386
    Independent Payment Advisory
        Board, 390
    low-income beneficiaries of, 388
    medical savings accounts plans, 387

Medigap policy for, 389
monthly premiums, 386
Original Plan, 384–386, 390, 391
PACE, 387
Part A, 384–385, 386, 391
Part B, 385–386
Part C, 386
Part D, 388–389, 390
PPO, 387
prescription drug coverage, 388–389
Special Needs Plans, 387
web site for, 402
Medigap policy, 389
Mehr, Robert I., 231
Mental abuse, 459
Mergers, 70, 90
Merit rating, 134–135
MIB Group, Inc., 107
Middle Class Tax Relief and Job Creation
 Act of 2012, 394
Migrant and Seasonal Agricultural Worker
 Protection Act, 591
Minimum age and service requirement,
 355–356
Minimum coverage requirements, 355
Minimum distribution requirements, 357
Minimum participation requirements, 329
Minimum vesting standards, 356
Minor children, 175, 235
Minorities, credit-based insurance scores
 and, 158–159
Miscellaneous surety bonds, 616
Miscellaneous-type vehicle endorsement, 499
Misstatement of age or sex clause, 234
Mobile equipment, 584
Mobile home insurance, 535
Modified coverage form (HO-8), 428, 430
Modified life policy, 221
Modified no-fault plan, 513
Modified prior-approval law, 149
Mold, 438
Monetary threshold, 513
Money
 counterfeit, 436, 573, 612, 614
 theft of, 609
 time value of, 76–77
Money orders, 573, 612
Money purchase plans, 360
Monoline policy, 555
Monopoly state fund, 396
Monte Carlo simulation, 288–289
Monthly retirement benefits, 377
Mopeds, 499
Morale (attitudinal) hazard, 5, 186–187
Moral hazard
 definition of, 4–5
 disability-income insurance and, 346
 indemnity principle and, 166, 168

insurable interest principle and, 169
 insurance contracts on, 187
Morgan, Henry, 477
Mortality and expense risk charge (M&E),
 220, 280
Mortality charge, 214, 219
Mortgage clause, 446–447
Mortgage redemption fund, 203
Mortgages
 fraudulent, 614
 investment in, 116
Motorcycles, 499
Motor homes, 494
Motor vehicles. *See also* Auto insurance
 additional, 479
 business, 482, 484–485
 death from, 22
 hit-and-run, 486–487
 homeowners insurance and, 431–432,
  434, 457–458
 liability from, 457–458, 472
 newly acquired, 479
 nonowned, 483, 485, 490, 495
 owned, 483, 485
 property damage from, 439, 461
 racing, 483, 495, 547
 rental cars, 490–492, 495
 replacement, 479
 temporary substitute, 479
 uninsured, 487
MSA (medical savings accounts) plans, 387
MSO (Mutual Service Office), 577
Multicar discount, 521
Multiple distribution systems, 98
Multiple line exclusive agency system,
 95–96
Multiple-line policy, 28, 555
Multiple-peril insurance, 28
Mutual holding company, 91
Mutual insurers, 88–91
Mutually exclusive events, 75
Mutual Service Office (MSO), 577
Myers, Robert J., 372

**N**

NAIC. *See* National Association of
 Insurance Commissioners
NALP (net annual level premium),
 271–272
Named insured, 188
Named-perils policy, 186
Narrative summary, 260
National Academy of Social Insurance,
 402
National Alliance for Insurance Education
 and Research, 83
National Association of Health
 Underwriters, 324

National Association of Insurance and
 Financial Advisors, 229
National Association of Insurance
 Commissioners (NAIC)
 Consumer Information Source, 111
 on coordination of benefits, 344
 described, 110, 121, 146, 162, 229, 254,
  324, 451, 503, 551
 interest-adjusted cost method, 257
 Life Insurance Policy Illustration
  Model, 260
 on liquidation of insurers, 148
 model laws of, 109, 146, 158
 on nationwide marine definition, 569
 promotion of uniform laws by, 153
 on total adjusted capital, 147
National Association of Mutual Insurance
 Companies, 37, 101, 121
National Association of Surety Bond
 Producers, 620
National Commission to Preserve Social
 Security, 402
National Committee for Quality Assurance
 (NCQA), 301, 351–352
National Conference of Insurance
 Guaranty Funds, 157, 162
National Conference of Insurance
 Legislators, 162
National Council on Compensation
 Insurance (NCCI), 398–399, 402,
  589, 604
National Flood Insurance Program (NFIP)
 basic concepts in, 30
 deductible, 540
 definition of, 538
 eligibility, 538
 emergency program, 538–539
 policy forms, 539–540
 premiums, 540
 problems and issues with, 542
 Standard Policy Forms, 539
 waiting period, 540
National Insurance Crime Bureau, 398, 620
National Organization of Life & Health
 Insurance Guaranty Associations
 (NOLHGA), 162
National Public Radio, 301
National Safety Council, 21–22, 604
National Transportation Safety Board
 (NTSB), 494–495
National Underwriter Company, 229, 254
Nationwide marine definition, 569
NCCI (National Council on Compensation
 Insurance), 398–399, 402, 589, 604
NCQA (National Committee for Quality
 Assurance), 301, 351–352
Needs approach to life insurance, 202–206
Neglect, loss due to, 441

Negligence
   comparative, 408–409
   contributory, 395, 408
   defenses against, 408–409
   definition of, 407
   dog bites and, 456
   elements of, 407–408
   imputed, 409–410
   law regarding, 407–409
   liability risk and, 407–412
   *res ipsa loquitur* and, 410
   specific applications of law of, 410–412
Net amount at risk, 210–211
Net annual level premium (NALP),
      271–272
Net gain from operations, 131
Net income, 48
Net payment cost index, 257–258
Net present value (NPV), 78
Net retention, 111
Net single premium (NSP), 135, 269–271
Network model HMO, 336
Network providers, in POS plans, 336
Never events, 419
Newly acquired auto, 479
New York State Insurance Department, 197
NFIP. *See* National Flood Insurance
      Program
Nicholls, Timothy, 33
No-fault auto insurance
   arguments for and against, 514–515
   characteristics of, 513–514
   compensation from, 512–516
   definition of, 512–513
   evaluation of, 515–516
   inflated claims, fraud and, 514–515
No filing required, 149
No-lapse guarantees, 214
Nolo.com site, 423
Nonadmitted assets, 146
Nonadmitted insurer, 95
Noncancellable policy, 319
Noncontributory plan, 329
Nondeductible IRA, 285
Nondiversifiable risk, 6
Noneconomic damages, 417, 513–515
Nonelective contribution option, 365
Nonforfeiture provision, 239–241, 315, 363
Noninsurance transfers, 14–15, 51, 57
Nonoccupational disability, 346
Nonowned detached trailers, 559
Nonowned vehicles, 483, 485, 490, 495
Nonparticipating policy, 238
Nonprofit organizations, 393
Nonprofit Risk Management Center, 60, 83
Nonqualified annuity, 283
Nonrenewable policy, 319–320
Nonsystematic risk, 6

Nontransferable provision, 363
Nonwaiver clause, 178
"No pay, no play" laws, 512
Normal retirement age, 355
Notice of claim provision, 320
NPV (net present value), 78
NSP (net single premium), 135, 269–271
NTSB (National Transportation Safety
      Board), 494–495
Nuclear energy, 460, 482
Nuclear hazard, 441
Nuclear weapon, 485
Numeric summary, 260
Nursing homes, 313, 384–385

**O**

OASDI. *See* Social Security
Obama Administration, 155, 303
Objective probability, 3–4
Objective risk, 3, 4, 26–27
Obligee, 614
Obligor, 614
Occupancy, 134
Occurrence, 454, 583
Ocean marine insurance
   basic concepts in, 568–569
   definition of, 29, 567
   utmost good faith principle and, 172
OECD (Organisation for Economic
      Co-operation and Development), 298
OEM (original equipment manufacturer),
      496, 511
Offer and acceptance, 174–175
Office of the Chief Actuary, 402
Office of Thrift Supervision (OTS), 88
Oklahoma City attack (1995), 67
Old-Age, Survivors, and Disability Insurance
      (OASDI). *See* Social Security
On premises coverage, 614
"Open-perils" basis
   dwelling property and, 534
   insuring agreement, 186
   personal articles floater and, 536
   yacht insurance and, 537
Operational risk, 6
Operations liability, 581–582
Operation Watch, 610
Opportunity costs of buying life insurance,
      207–208
Optional deductibles, 514
Optional federal charter, 157
Optional no-fault benefits, 514
Ordinance or law
   commercial property coverages, 566
   increased costs from, 437
   loss due to, 440–441
Ordinary life insurance
   calculating premiums, 271–272

comparison of, 223
   definition of, 210
   limitations of, 211
   uses of, 211
Organisation for Economic Co-operation
      and Development (OECD), 298
Original-age method, 208
Original equipment manufacturer (OEM),
      496, 511
Other-insurance provisions
   contribution by equal shares, 193
   definition of, 192
   primary and excess insurance, 194
   pro rata liability, 192–193, 446
Other insureds provision, 188
Other property provision, 609
Other-states insurance, 591
Other-than-collision loss, 489–490
OTS (Office of Thrift Supervision), 88
Out-of-pocket limits, 305–306, 311, 337
Out-of-state coverage, 483
Outpatient hospital services, 310,
      385–386
Outpatient prescription drugs, 310
Outside the premises, 609–610
Overall operating ratio, 129
Overdue premiums, 233, 237–238
Owned vehicles, 483, 485
Ownership clause, 232

**P**

PACE, 387
Package policy, 555
PAF (personal articles floater), 536
Paid-up additions option, 238
Paid-up contract, 238
Pair, loss to set or, 445
PAP. *See* Personal Auto Policy
Part A, Medicare, 384–385, 386, 391
Part B, Medicare, 385–386
Part C, Medicare, 386
Part D, Medicare, 388–389, 390
Partial disability, 317
Participating policy, 238
Participation rate, 282
Particular average, 568
Particular risk, 6
Passenger hazard exclusion, 499
Passive retention, 14
Past-service credits, 358
Patio, damage to, 438
*Paul v. Virginia*, 144
Pavement, damage to, 438
Pay credit, 359
Payment bonds, 615–616
Payout period, 277
PBGC (Pension Benefit Guaranty
      Corporation), 30, 358–359, 371

PCI (Property Casualty Insurers Association of America), 509, 577
Peak season endorsement, 561
Pecuniary interest, 170
PEDs (portable electronic devices), 494–495
Pension accrual benefit, 346
Pension Benefit Guaranty Corporation (PBGC), 30, 358–359, 371
Pension Protection Act of 2006, 354
Per diem policies, 314
Performance bonds, 615–616
Perils
    excluded in insurance contracts, 186
    in multiple-peril insurance, 28
    named-perils policy, 186
    open-perils basis, 186, 534, 536, 537
    risks *v.*, 4
    of the sea, 568
    Section I, 437–440
Permitted disparity rules, 357
Personal articles floater (PAF), 536
Personal Auto Policy (PAP)
    cancellation of, 498
    damage to your auto, 489–497
    duties after accident or loss, 497–498
    eligible vehicles, 478
    exclusions in, 481–483, 484–485, 487–488, 493–495
    general provisions of, 498–499
    insured persons in, 480–481, 484, 487
    insuring agreement in, 480, 483–484, 486–487, 489–491
    liability coverage, 479–483, 486, 495–496
    medical payments coverage in, 483–485
    miscellaneous-type vehicle endorsement for, 499
    termination of, 498–499
    underinsured motorists coverage, 488–489
    uninsured motorists coverage, 485–489, 497
    uninsured vehicles in, 487
    your covered auto, 478–479
Personal contract, 176
Personal injury
    commercial liability insurance and, 585, 587, 596
    definition of, 464, 546
    endorsements for, 464
    exclusions for, 547
    PIP for, 513
Personal injury protection (PIP), 513
Personal liability insurance
    dwelling program endorsement, 535
    in homeowners insurance, 27
    inland marine floaters, 535–536

purchasing, 471
Section II coverage, 454–455
Personal lines, 27–28
Personal loss exposures, 55–56
Personal-producing general agent (PPGA), 96
Personal property
    building and personal property coverage form, 557–559
    business, 557–558, 564, 572
    loss settlement, 443
    replacement cost endorsement, 463, 467
    scheduled, 464, 467, 536
    special form and, 432–435, 438–440
Personal risk
    definition of, 7
    insufficient retirement income, 7–8
    liability, 10–11
    managing, 55–57
    poor health, 8
    premature death, 7
    property, 10
    unemployment, 7, 10, 24–25
Personal selling distribution systems, 95–96
Personal umbrella liability insurance
    definition of, 471, 545
    exclusions, 547–548
    ISO, 546–548
PFFS (private fee-for-services) plans, 387
Physical abuse, 459
Physical hazard, 4
Physical inspection, 46, 107
Physicians, surgeons, and dentists professional liability insurance, 597–598
Physicians and surgeons equipment coverage form, 570–571
Physician services, 310, 385–386
PIA (primary insurance amount), 377
P&I (protection and indemnity) insurance, 568
PIP (personal injury protection), 513
Plaintiff, 406
Point-of-service (POS) plan, 336
Policies. *See also specific types of policies*
    additional insured in, 189
    assignment of, 447
    convertible, 208
    first named insured in, 188
    mature as an endowment, 239
    named insured in, 188
    no-lapse guarantees, 214
    nonparticipating, 238
    nonrenewal of, 447, 498
    other insureds in, 188
    participating, 238
    reinstating, 233–234

renewable, 208
    10-day right to examine, 320
    valued, 167–168
Policy forms, regulation of, 150
Policy loan provision, 237
Policyowners' surplus, 126–127, 131, 146–147
Policy reserves, 130, 272–274
Political risk, 24
Pollutant cleanup and removal, 558, 573
Pooling of losses
    definition of, 15, 20–21
    law of large numbers and, 21–22
    reinsurance pool, 115, 517
Poor health risk, 8–9
Portable electronic devices (PEDs), 494–495
Portable term insurance, 331
POS (point-of-service) plan, 336
Post-loss risk management objectives, 45
Power failure, 441
PPOs. *See* Preferred provider organizations
Predetermination-of-benefits provision, 345
Preexisting Condition Insurance Plan (PCIP), 307
Preexisting conditions
    abusive insurer practices and, 302–303
    definition of, 102, 343
    group medical expense contractual provisions, 343–344
    health insurance reforms, 26, 102, 304, 307, 320, 338
    individual health insurance contractual provisions, 320
Preferred provider organizations (PPOs)
    Blue Cross and Blue Shield, 92, 333
    cost of, 341
    definition of, 312, 336
    dental, 345
    HMOs *v.*, 336
    market control for, 332
    Medicare, 387
Preferred risks, 221–222
Pre-loss risk management objectives, 45
Premature death
    costs of, 199
    declining problem of, 199
    definition of, 7, 199
    economic justification for life insurance, 200
    financial impact of, 200–201
Premises and operations liability, 581–582
Premium conversion plans, 347
Premiums
    auto insurance, variations in, 523–526
    automatic premium loan provision and, 237–238
    bond, 481
    calculation of, 269–274

conditional premium receipt and, 174–175
CPP, 557
dividends reducing, 238
earned, 127–128
economically feasible, 24
FAIR plan, 542–543
flexible, 277
gross, 132, 272
health insurance reforms, 306–307
homeowners insurance, variations in, 467–470
insurability premium receipt and, 174–175
life insurance, 116, 269–274
Medicare, 386
NALP, 271–272
NFIP, 540
NSP, 269–271
overdue, 233, 237–238
payment of, 236
pure, 132–134
return of, 315
revenues from, 127
single, 277
subsidies, 303
tax on, 151
unearned reserve and, 112, 126
for universal life insurance, 214, 219
waived, 246, 318
Prescription drug coverage
catastrophic, 388
drug card program and, 310
increased spending and, 299
Medicare, 388–389, 390
of outpatient prescription drugs, 310
tiered pricing for, 342–343
Presumptive disability, 317
Prevention and Public Health Fund, 308
Primary and excess insurance, 194
Primary beneficiary, 235
Primary insurance amount (PIA), 377
Principal, 614
Principal sum, 332
Principles. See Legal principles, fundamental
Prior-approval law, 149
Private fee-for-services (PFFS) plans, 387
Private firm, 393
Private insurance
aircraft, 29
auto, 27, 143
basic characteristics of, 20–22
casualty, 27–29
commercial multiple-peril, 28
credit, 29
crime, 29
equipment breakdown, 28–29

financial guaranty, 29
in financial services industry, 87–88
fire, 24–25, 28
health, 27
homeowners, 27–28, 143
liability, 27–29
life, 27
marine, 29
medical malpractice, 29, 418–419, 597–598
personal umbrella liability, 28, 471, 545–548
PMI, 29
property, 27–29
pure risk and, 5
unemployment and, 24–25
workers compensation, 28
Private insurers
Blue Cross and Blue Shield, 92
HMOs, 93
Lloyd's of London, 91–92, 101
mutual, 88–91
pure risk and, 5
reciprocal exchange, 92
stock, 88, 90–91
types of, 88–93
Private mortgage insurance (PMI), 29
Probability
insurance and, 39–42
law of large numbers and, 21
in loss forecasting, 71–75
objective, 3–4
a priori, 4
subjective, 4
Probable maximum loss, 47
Probationary period, 330
Problem physicians, 419
Production, definition of, 108
Production department, 54
Production risk, 24
Product recalls, 585
Products-completed operations aggregate limit, 587
Products-completed operations hazard, 582, 584
Products liability, 28, 582
Professionalism, in selling, 108
Professional liability insurance
commercial, 29
errors and omissions, 599
physicians, surgeons, and dentists, 597–598
Professional services liability, 459, 547, 582
Profits
measuring, 128–129
stabilized, 111–112
Profit-sharing plans, 363–364

Progressive Casualty Insurance Company, 503, 530
Progressive indexing, 391
Prohibited use, 435
Proof of loss, 110, 173, 320, 443
Property
abandonment of, 446
commercial risks, 11
excluded in insurance contracts, 186–187
inherent vice and, 187
loss exposures, 11, 46, 56
removal of, 436
Property and casualty insurance
actuaries for, 105
agents of, 93–94, 96, 106
balance sheet of, 124–127
commercial lines of, 28–29
contract characteristics of, 176
definition of, 27
income and expense statement, 127–128
insurable interest and, 169
insurers, 124–130, 131–135
investments of, 117, 148
marketing systems, 96–98
offer and acceptance in, 174
other-insurance provisions, 192
personal lines of, 27–28
policyowners' surplus in, 147
profitability of, 129
rate making in, 131–135
title insurance, 543–545
top groups by revenues, 89
underwriting cycle in, 54
underwriting information sources for, 107
Property Casualty Insurers Association of America (PCI), 509, 577
Property damage
auto insurance and, 514
commercial liability insurance, 583–585
Section I coverage, 438–440
Section II coverage, 461
Property insurance. See also Commercial property insurance; Property and casualty insurance
combined ratio exhibit, 68
deductibles in, 190
definition of, 27
government, 538–543
inland marine floaters, 535–536
inland marine insurance, 29
ISO dwelling program, 533–535
lines of coverage for, 27–29
mobile home insurance, 535
private, 27–29
pro rata liability, 192–193, 446

top groups by revenues, 89
watercraft insurance, 536–538
Property owners, law of negligence and, 410
Proprietary function, 411
Pro rata liability, 192–193, 446
Pro rata loss sharing methods, 113
Prospective reserve, 273
Protection, 134
Protection and indemnity (P&I)
 insurance, 568
Proximate cause, 408, 438
Public adjuster, 109
Publications, regulation of, 151
Public conveyance, 482, 484, 488, 493
Public official bonds, 616
Public Risk Management Association,
 60, 83
Punitive damages, 408, 417, 488
Pure captive, 49
Pure no-fault plan, 513
Pure premium, 132–134
Pure risk
 definition of, 5
 managing, 65
 noninsurance transfers and, 57
 types of, 10–11
Pure (comparative negligence) rule, 409

**Q**

Qualified plans
 defined-benefits, 358–359
 defined-contribution, 360–365
 definition of, 354–355, 357
 Keogh plans, 364
 profit-sharing plans, 363–364
 SIMPLE plans, 365
 simplified employee pension plans, 365
Quarter of coverage, 375
QuickQuote site, 268
Quota-share treaty, 113–114

**R**

Racing vehicle, 485, 495, 547
Radar detection equipment, 495
Radiation, 485
Radioactive contamination, 493
Railroad Retirement Act, 30
Railroad Unemployment Insurance
 Act, 30
RAND Institute for Civil Justice, 423, 503,
 529, 604
Ratchet method, 282
Rate making
 definition of, 104–105
 definitions for, 132–133
 exposure units in, 104, 132
 in life insurance, 135
 methods, 133–135

objectives of, 131–135
 in property and casualty insurance,
  131–135
Rate of return
 internal, 78
 on saving component, 260–262
 universal life insurance and, 218
Rates
 adequacy of, 107, 131–132, 150
 definition of, 104–105, 132
 discriminatory, 131–132
 disparity in, 153–154
 excessive, 131–132
 gross, 132
 guaranteed, 277
 reasonable, 143–144
 regulation of, 149–150
 state-made, 149
 subrogation and, 171
Rating, equity in, 191–192
Rating agencies, 265
Ratio percentage test, 355
RBC (risk-based capital), 147–148, 157
Readjustment period, 202
Real Estate Settlement Procedures Act, 545
Real estate value, 472
Reasonable and customary charges,
 333, 345
Reasonable belief of permission, 481–482,
 484, 488, 547
Reasonable expectations, principle of, 177
Reasonable repairs, 436
Rebating, 150–151, 305
Rebuilding, cost of, 472
Recall of products, 585
Recent work test, 375
Recipient location, 563
Reciprocal exchange, 92
Recreational vehicles liability, 547
Redetermination provision, 221
Reduced paid-up insurance, 240
Reentry term, 209
Reform. *See also* Health insurance reforms
 Social Security, 391
 of tort liability system, 417–418, 515
Regression analysis, 75
Regular NFIP program, 539
Regulation
 consumer protection and, 158–159
 by courts, 145
 federal, 151–155
 financial crisis and, 156–157
 historical development of, 144–145
 insolvency and, 157–158
 of insurer formation and licensing, 146
 of insurer taxation, 151
 of investments, 148
 by legislation, 145

methods, 145–146
 modernizing, 156–157
 of policy forms, 150
 of rates, 149–150
 RBC, 147–148
 reasons for, 142–144
 of reserves, 146
 of sales practices, 158–159
 solvency, 146–149
 state, 145–146, 149, 151–155
 surplus, 146–147
 of taxes, 151
Regulatory objectives, of rate making,
 131–132
Rehabilitation provision, 318
Rehabilitation services, 397
Reimbursement policies, 314
Reinstatement provision, 233–234, 320
Reinsurance
 alternatives to, 115
 catastrophic loss and, 111–112
 definition of, 23–24, 110
 early retirement program, 307
 facultative, 113
 insurers and, 110–115
 loss sharing methods and, 113–115
 pool, 115
 reasons for, 111–113
 SPRV and, 115
 treaty, 113
 underwriting and, 108
 unearned premium and, 126
Reinsurance facility, 517
Released bill of lading, 569
Renewable policies, 208
Renewal provisions, 319–320
Renewal underwriting, 108
Rental cars, 490–492, 495, 511
Renters insurance, 430–431, 472
Replacement cost
 CPP and, 559
 definition of, 444
 dwelling property, 534
 endorsements for, 445, 462–463, 467
 guaranteed, 445
 indemnity principle on, 167
Replacement cost insurance, 168
Replacement vehicle, 479
Reporting forms, 192, 560–561, 564
Reports and examinations, 148, 154, 158
Representations, 172–173
Reserves
 for amounts held on deposit, 130
 AVR, 130–131
 case, 125–126
 definition of, 272–273
 funded and unfunded, 48–49
 IBNR, 126

initial, 274
legal, 210–211
loss, 125
mean, 274
policy, 130, 272–274
prospective, 273
regulation of, 146
retrospective, 273
terminal, 274
unearned premium, 112, 126
Residential Condominium Building
    Association Form, NFIP, 539
Resident relatives, 431
Residual disability, 317–318
Residual market, 30, 516
*Res ipsa loquitur*, 410
*Respondeat superior* doctrine, 411–412
Restricted application, 382
Retained limit, 595–596
Retaliatory tax laws, 151
Retention. *See* Risk retention
Retention limit, 111
Retirement income. *See also* Social Security;
    Individual retirement accounts
  calculator for, 289
  Civil Service Retirement System for, 30
  delayed, 377–380
  ERISA and, 145, 333, 354, 596, 600
  Federal Employees Retirement System
    for, 30
  insufficient, 7–8
  monthly, 377
  PBGC and, 30
Retirement plans
  ages for, 355–356, 376–380
  defined-benefit plans, 358–359
  defined-contribution plans, 360–363
  fundamentals of, 354–357
  funding agency and instruments for,
    365–366
  matching contributions to, 284, 361, 365
  problems and issues in, 366–367
  profit-sharing plans, 363–364
  qualified, 354, 358–365
  for self-employed, 364
  SIMPLE, 365
  simplified employee pension, 365
  Social Security integrated with, 357
  tax treatment of, 354–356, 362, 364,
    366–367
  top-heavy, 357
  types of, 357
Retirement test, 380
Retroactive date, 588, 612–613
Retrocession, 111
Retrocessionaire, 111
Retrospective rating, 135
Retrospective reserve, 273

Return of premium benefits, 315
Return of premium term insurance, 209
Return on equity (ROE), 131
Revenues, 127–128
Reverse competition, 544
Revocable beneficiary, 235
Riders in insurance contracts. *See*
    Endorsements
RIMS (Risk and Insurance Management
    Society), 61, 66, 83, 577, 604
Riots, 439
Rising-floor death benefit, 280
Risk. *See also* Liability risk
  asset, 147
  assigned risk plan for, 516–517
  burdens of, 12
  business, 147
  classification of, 5–7
  clean, 517
  commercial, 7, 11
  commodity price, 63–64
  cost of, 55
  currency exchange rate, 65
  definition of, 2–3, 15–16
  diversifiable, 6
  emerging, 67
  enterprise, 6–7
  financial, 6, 24
  fire, 24–25
  fundamental, 6
  hazard $v.$, 4–5
  insurable, 22–25
  insurance and, 20–34, 147
  interest rate, 65, 147
  and its treatment, 2–18
  market, 24
  net amount at, 210–211
  nondiversifiable, 6
  objective, 3–4, 26–27
  operational, 7
  peril $v.$, 4
  personal, 7–10, 24–25, 55–57
  political, 24
  preferred, 221–222
  production, 24
  property, 11
  pure, 5, 10–11, 57, 65
  securitization of, 71, 115
  in society, 2–18
  speculative, 5–6, 65
  strategic, 6
  subjective, 3
  systematic, 6
  systemic, 152
  tolerance for, 284
  underwriting, 42, 67
Risk analysis questionnaires and
    checklists, 46

Risk and Insurance Management Society
    (RIMS), 61, 66, 83, 577, 604
Risk-based capital (RBC), 147–148, 157
Risk control
  avoidance and, 12–13, 47, 56
  definition of, 12, 47
  investment decisions based on, 78
  loss prevention and, 13, 47–48
  loss reduction and, 13, 48
  in personal risk management, 56
  techniques for, 12–13
  terrorism and, 67
Risk financing
  capital market alternatives, 71
  with commercial insurance, 51–53
  definition of, 12, 48
  with noninsurance transfers, 14–15, 51
  with retention, 13–14, 48–51
  techniques for, 13–15, 48–51
Risk management
  advanced topics in, 63–81
  benefits of, 55
  catastrophe modeling for, 80–81
  changing scope of, 63–67
  commercial, 6
  decision making, 76–78
  definition of, 44
  enterprise, 6, 66–67
  financial, 63–66
  financial analysis in, 76–78
  implementation of, 54–55, 57
  insurance market dynamics and, 68–71
  intranets, 79
  IRMI and, 37
  loss forecasting in, 71–75
  manual for, 54
  maps for, 79
  matrix, 53–54
  medical malpractice and, 419
  monitoring of, 54–55, 57
  objectives, 44–45
  personal, 55–57
  policy statement for, 54
  RMIS for, 79
  steps of, 45–57
  techniques for, 12–15, 53–54
  VAR analysis for, 79–80
Risk management information system
    (RMIS), 79
Risk managers, 46, 54–55
Risk maps, 79
Risk retention
  advantages of, 51
  captive insurers and, 49
  definition of, 13–14, 48
  determining levels, 48
  disadvantages of, 51
  insurance market dynamics and, 68

paying losses and, 48–49
in personal risk management, 56–57
retention limit, 111
risk financing and, 13–14
RRGs, 50–51
self-insurance and, 50, 596
tax treatment of captives, 49–50
Risk retention groups (RRGs), 50–51
Risk Theory Society, 18
Risk transfer
by contracts, 14
definition of, 22
insurance market dynamics and, 68
noninsurance, 14–15, 51, 57
purpose of, 15
RMIS (risk management information system), 79
Robbery, 608, 609, 611
ROE (return on equity), 131
Roomers, property of, 435
Rosenbloom, Jerry S., 327
Roth 401(k) plans, 362, 371
Roth 403(b) plans, 363
Roth IRAs, 287–288, 293, 357
Running down clause, 568–569
Rutterschmidt, Olga, 33

**S**

Safe burglary, 608, 609
Safe driver plans, 521
Safety glazing material, 437
SAIP (Special Auto Insurance Policy), 512
Sales practices, regulation of, 158–159
Sampling distribution, 40–42
SAP (statutory accounting principles), 146
Sarbanes-Oxley Act, 420
Saving component, rate of return on, 260–262
Savings Bank Life Insurance (SBLI), 93, 222–224
Savings Incentive Match Plan for Employees (SIMPLE), 365
SBLI (Savings Bank Life Insurance), 93, 222–224
Schedule, for homeowners insurance, 433
Schedule approach, to employee theft, 609
Scheduled personal property endorsement, 464, 467, 536
Schedule rating, 134
SCHIP (state children's health insurance programs), 30
SD (standard deviation), 21
Second-to-die life insurance, 222
Section 401(k) plans
ADP test and, 362
common mistakes with, 361
as defined-contribution plans, 360–363
definition of, 360

distribution limits for, 362
elective deferrals and, 361–362
individual, 362–363
Pension Protection Act of 2006 and, 354
Roth, 362, 371
Section 403(b) plans, 363
Section I, special form
conditions, 442–448
coverages, 432–437
exclusions, 437–438, 439–442
perils insured against, 437–440
Section II, special form
conditions, 447–448, 462
coverages, 429, 454–457, 460–461
exclusions, 457–460
Secured creditors, 169
Securities and Exchange Commission, 145, 419
Securities coverage, 614
Securities Exchange Act of 1934, 600
Securities theft, 609
Securitization of risk, 71, 115
Select Quote site, 268
Self-employed plans, 364
Self-funding, 333
Self-insurance, 14, 50, 333
Self-Insurance Institute of America, 61, 83
Self-insured retention (SIR), 546, 596
Selling, professionalism in, 108
SEP (simplified employee pension), 365
Separate investment account, 116–117, 366
SEP-IRA, 365
September 11, 2001 attacks
clash loss and, 69
loss of goods and services, 12
reinsurance and, 112
terrorism risk and, 67
Service benefits, 333
Set, loss to pair or, 445
Settlement options
advantages of, 243–244
for annuities, 278–279
cash, 242, 278
definition of, 241
disadvantages of, 244–245
fixed-amount, 242–243
fixed-period, 242
interest, 242
life income, 243
life insurance, 241–246
trusts, 245–246
SEUA (South-Eastern Underwriters Association), 144
Seven-year graded vesting, 356
Severe cognitive impairment, 314
Sex, misstatement of, 235
Sexual molestation, 459, 547
Shakespeare, William, 184

Shared market, 30, 516
Shortened benefit period, 315
Short-term group disability-income insurance, 346
Short-term involuntary unemployment, 392
Sight, loss of, 318, 376
Signs coverage form, 571
SIMPLE (Savings Incentive Match Plan for Employees), 365
SIMPLE-IRA, 365
Simplified commercial property program, 564
Simplified employee pension (SEP), 365
Single limit, 480
Single parent captive, 49
Single-parent families, 200
Single-premium deferred annuity, 277
Single premium immediate annuities (SPIAs), 278
Single-premium whole life insurance, 213
SIR (self-insured retention), 546, 596
Skilled nursing facility care, 384–385
Sleet, weight of, 440
Small business owners, 609–610
Smoke damage, 439
Snow, weight of, 440
Social adequacy, 374, 377
Social insurance. *See also* Medicare; Social Security
basic characteristics of, 373–375
benefit types of, 376–384
compulsory temporary disability, 30
financially self-supporting, 375
as government insurance, 29–30
impact of Affordable Care Act on Medicare, 389–390
nondiversifiable risks and, 6
Railroad Retirement Act and, 30
reasons for, 373
unemployment, 6, 29–30, 392–395
workers compensation, 30, 395–399
Social responsibility, 45
Social Security. *See also* Medicare
Advisory Board, 402
children receiving, 377, 382
cost-of-living adjustment to, 380
credits, 375–376
definition of, 30, 375
disability benefits, 319, 383
financing, 384
financing of, 391
full funding unnecessary for, 374–375
insured status determined for, 375–376
long-range actuarial deficit of, 390–391
occupations covered by, 375
reducing long-range deficit, 391
retirement benefits of, 376–380
retirement plans integrated with, 357

right time to draw, 381–382
survivor benefits, 380–383
taxation of, 383–384
website for, 402
Social Security Act of 1935, 375, 392
Society
auto insurance and, 506–527
burdens on, 12
costs and benefits of insurance to, 31–34
risk in, 2–18
Society for Risk Analysis (SRA), 18
Society of Actuaries, 105, 139
Society of Financial Service
Professionals, 229
Soft market conditions, 54, 68
Solvency, 142–143, 146–149, 157–158, 272
South-Eastern Underwriters Association
(SEUA), 144
Sovereign immunity, 411
Special agents, 108
Special Auto Insurance Policy (SAIP), 512
Special coverage policy, 186
Special damages, 408
Special form (causes-of-loss), 560
Special form (Dwelling Property 3), 534
Special form (HO-3)
deductible, 442
described, 428–429
dwelling covered by, 432, 437–438
fire coverage, 438
loss of use covered by, 435
other structures covered by, 432
personal property and, 432–435,
438–440
persons insured, 431–432
property not covered by, 433–435
Section I conditions, 442–448
Section I coverages, 432–437
Section I exclusions, 437–438, 439–442
Section I perils insured against, 437–440
Section II conditions, 447–448, 462
Section II coverages, 429, 454–457,
460–461
Section II exclusions, 457–460
Special Needs Plans, Medicare, 387
Special purpose reinsurance vehicle
(SPRV), 115
Specialty insurers, 517
Specific beneficiary, 235
Speculative risk, 5–6, 65
SPIAs (single premium immediate
annuities), 278
Split-funded combination plan, 365
Split limit, 480
Spoilage damage, 565
Spousal IRA, 285
Sprinkel, Elizabeth, 485
SPRV (special purpose reinsurance
vehicle), 115

SRA (Society for Risk Analysis), 18
Staff model HMO, 335
Standard coverage, of prescription
drugs, 388
Standard deviation (SD), 21, 40
Standard error of sampling distribution, 41
Standard Policy Forms, NFIP, 539
Stanford, Allen, 420
State automobile insurance plan, 516–517
State children's health insurance programs
(SCHIP), 30
State insurance programs, 30–31
State-of-the-art defense, 417
State regulations
federal v., 151–155
state insurance departments and,
145–146
state-made rates and, 149
state-mandated benefits, 297–299
for unemployment insurance, 393–394
Statistics, insurance and, 39–40
Statutory accounting principles (SAP), 146
Steam damage, 435, 440
Stenroos, Jeff, 33
Stepped-up benefit, 280
Stock brokers, 96
Stockholder lawsuits, 414
Stock insurers, 88, 90–91
Stop-loss limit, 50, 311
Straight deductible, 190
Strategic risk, 6
Strict liability, 407
Students
full-time, away from home, 431,
439, 526
good student discount for, 520–521, 526
Subjective probability, 4
Subjective risk, 3
Subrogation
definition of, 170
homeowners insurance and, 447–448
importance of, 171–172
life insurance and, 172
principle of, 170–172
purposes of, 171
Suicide clause, 26, 233–234
Supplemental term insurance, 331
Supplementary payments, 481
Surety bonds
definition of, 29, 614
insurance contracts v., 615
miscellaneous, 616
types of, 615
Surety & Fidelity Association of
America, 620
Surety Information Office, 620
Surgeons
equipment coverage form, 570–571
professional liability insurance, 597–598

Surgery, wrong-site, 418
Surplus, 69
Surplus lines broker, 95
Surplus-share treaty, 114
Surrender charge, 264, 280
Surrender cost index, 257
Survivor benefits, 346, 380–383, 514
Swimming pools, damage to, 438
Systematic risk, 6
Systemic risk, 152

**T**
T. Rowe Price, 289
Tabular value method, 126
Target premium, 214
Taxable estate, 263
Taxes
on capital gains, 284
deductibles for, 49–50
deferring, 276–277, 355
on distributions, 286
dividend accumulations and, 238
estate, 262–263
flexible spending accounts and, 347
on group insurance, 297
health insurance reforms, 306–307, 338
on HSAs, 312–313
immediate annuity and, 278
income, 262
individual annuities and, 283–284
of insurers, 49–50, 151
IRAs and, 285–286
life insurance and, 262–263
on long-term care insurance, 315
as penalties, 356, 362, 364
premium, 151
premium tax credits, 306
regulation of, 151
retaliatory laws influencing, 151
retention and, 49–50
on retirement plans, 354–356, 362, 364
on Social Security, 383–384
unemployment, 394
universal life insurance and, 216
Tax-sheltered annuities (TSAs), 363
TDI (Texas Department of Insurance), 197
Technological advances, 297
Telemarketing, 96
Telephone Consumer Protection Act, 585
Temporary life annuity due, 271
Temporary residence, 439
Temporary substitute vehicle, 479
10-day right to examine policy, 320
Term4Sale site, 268
Terminal reserve, 274
Terminated illness rider, 248
Termination
as to any employee, 613
PAP, 498–499

Term insurance
  calculating premiums for, 269–272
  comparison of, 223
  definition of, 208
  extended, 240–241
  group, 331
  limitations of, 210
  types of, 208–209
  uses of, 209
Territory, auto insurance cost influenced
    by, 518
Terrorism
  catastrophic loss and, 81, 112
  as emerging risk, 67
  loss of goods and services and, 12
Terrorism Risk Insurance Act (TRIA),
    67, 112
Terrorism Risk Insurance Program
    Reauthorization Act (TRIPRA),
    67, 112
Texas Department of Insurance (TDI), 197
Theatrical property coverage form, 571
Theft
  burglary, 608, 609, 610–611
  definition of, 608
  dwelling program endorsements,
    534–535
  employee, 607–609
  homeowners insurance coverage,
    439–440
  identity, 464–465
  of money and securities, 609
  robbery, 608, 609, 611
Third-party administrator (TPA), 79
Third-party claims, 510–511
Third-party cost sharing, 329–330
Third-party-over cases, 591
TIAA-CREF site, 293, 371
Time limit on certain defenses provision, 320
Time value of money, 76–77
Title insurance, 543–545
Top-heavy plans, 357
Tortfeasor, 406
Tort liability system
  corporate governance and, 419–420
  defective, 412–418
  delays in settling and, 414
  high jury awards in, 414
  inefficient compensation from, 414
  medical malpractice and, 418–419
  reform of, 417–418, 515
  rising costs of, 412–414
  uncertain legal outcomes of, 414
  uninsured motorists coverage and, 512
Torts, intentional, 406
Total adjusted capital, 147
Total disability, 246, 316–317
Towers Watson, 101, 121, 139
Towing costs, 493, 593

TPA (third-party administrator), 79
Traditional defined-benefit plans, 358
Traditional indemnity plans, 333–334
Traditional IRAs, 285–288
Traditional net cost method, 256–257
Trailers, 440, 479, 494, 559
Transportation expenses, 491–493
Transportation insurance, 567–571
Treaty reinsurance, 113
Trees, shrubs, and other plants, 436
Trespassers, 410
TRIA (Terrorism Risk Insurance Act),
    67, 112
Trucious, Thomas, 33
Trustees, 235, 245–246
Trust-fund plan, 366
Trusts, 245–246
TSAs (tax-sheltered annuities), 363
Twisting, 150

U
Ultimate net loss, 595
Umbrella policies
  commercial liability insurance, 595–597
  personal liability insurance, 28, 471,
    545–548
Underinsurance, 207, 471
Underinsured motorists coverage, 488–489
Underwriting
  by agents, 106
  capacity, increased, 111
  credit-based insurance scores in,
    158–159
  cycle in, 54, 68–70
  decision making in, 107
  definition of, 26, 105
  field, 106
  of group insurance, 329–330
  guide for, 105
  information sources for, 106–107
  by insurance companies, 105–108
  insurance industry capacity and, 69
  line, 107
  losses, 117
  policy statement for, 105
  principles, 105–106
  rate adequacy and, 107
  recent results of, 129–130
  reinsurance and, 108
  renewal, 108
  risks in, 42, 67
  steps in, 106
Unearned premium reserve, 112, 126
Unemployment
  categories of benefits, 393–394
  compensation, 6
  eligibility requirements and, 393
  EUC program for, 394
  financing for, 394

  personal risk of, 7, 10, 24–25
  private insurance and, 24–25
  Railroad Unemployment Insurance Act
    for, 30
  short-term involuntary, 392
  social insurance for, 6, 29–30, 392–395
  tax, 394
Unfair claims practices, 109
Unfair trade practices, 150
Unfunded reserve, 48
Unified credit, 262
Unilateral contract, 176
Uninsured boaters coverage, 537
Uninsured locations, 459
Uninsured motorists coverage
  auto accident victims compensation
    from, 509–512
  duties and, 497
  exclusions, 487–488
  financial crisis and, 485
  insured persons in, 487
  PAP, 485–489, 497
  tort liability lawsuits and, 512
  uninsured vehicles, 487
  workers compensation and, 488
Uninsured persons, 299–301, 339
Unintentional loss, 23
Unit-benefit formula, 358
United States. See Health-care problems,
    in U.S.
United States Aircraft Insurance Group
    (USAIG), 594
Unit-owners form (HO-6), 428, 430
Universal life insurance
  cash withdrawals from, 216
  comparison of, 223
  definition of, 214
  flexibility in, 216
  forms of, 215–216
  group, 332
  illustration of, 216–218
  indexed, 219
  limitations of, 218–219
  tax treatment of, 216
  unbundling component parts,
    214–215
  variable, 219–220
Unsatisfied judgment funds, 509
Urban Property and Reinsurance Act of
    1968, 542
U.S. See Health-care problems, in U.S.
U.S. v. South-Eastern Underwriters
    Association, 144
USAA bonds, 71
USAA Life Insurance, 264
USAIG (United States Aircraft Insurance
    Group), 594
Use-and-file law, 149
Utility interruption, 565

Utmost good faith
    concealment and, 173
    principle of, 172–174
    representations and, 172–173
    warranty and, 173–174

**V**

Valuable papers and records coverage,
    558, 571
Value at risk (VAR) analysis, 79–80
Value-Based Purchasing (VBP)
    program, 390
Valued policy, 167–168
Valued policy law, 168
Value reporting form, 560–561
Vandalism, 438, 611
Vanguard Group, 293, 371
VAR (value at risk) analysis, 79–80
Variable annuity
    buying, 284
    characteristics of, 279–280
    fees and expenses, 280–281
    guaranteed death benefit of, 280
Variable life insurance
    comparison of, 223
    described, 213–214
    universal, 219–220
Variance, 40
VBP (Value-Based Purchasing) program,
    390
Verbal threshold, 513
Vesting provisions, 356
Viatical and Life Settlement Association of
    America, 254
Viatical settlement, 249
Vicarious liability law, 409
Volcanic eruption, 440
Voltaire, 405

**W**

Wachter, Robert, 33
Waiting periods
    for disability-income insurance, 190, 318
    health insurance reforms, 305

    for long-term care insurance, 314
    NFIP, 540
    for unemployment insurance, 393
Waiver
    collision damage, 490–492
    doctrine of, 178
    nonwaiver clause and, 178
    written approval of, 447
Waiver-of-premium provision, 246, 318
War
    auto insurance exclusions, 493
    commercial liability insurance
        exclusions, 584
    life insurance provisions and, 236
    PAP exclusion for, 485
    property damage from, 441
    Section II special form, 459
Warranty, 173–174, 568
Waste, health care, 301–302
Watercraft endorsements, 464
Watercraft provisions
    in commercial liability insurance, 584
    in insurance policies, 536–538
    involving property damage, 461
    in personal umbrella policies, 547
    Section II exclusion, 458
    in special form, 440
Water damage, 435, 440–441, 573
Weather conditions, 442
Weather options, 71
Whitehouse.gov site, 295
Whole life annuity due, 271
Whole life insurance
    current assumption, 220–221, 223
    definition of, 210
    dividend options, 240
    indexed universal life insurance, 219
    interest-sensitive, 220–221
    limited-payment policy, 213
    ordinary life insurance, 210–211
    single-premium, 213
    universal life insurance, 214–219, 223
    variable universal life insurance, 219–220
Windstorm damage, 438–439, 440–441

Wisconsin State Life Insurance Fund, 31
Wisconsin Office of the Commissioner of
    Insurance, 197
Workers compensation insurance
    aging workforce and, 398–399
    basic facts about, 30, 589
    benefits, 397–398
    claims, 75–76
    commercial liability insurance and, 584
    cost considerations, 398–399
    covered occupations, 396–397
    death and, 397
    development of, 395–396
    eligibility requirements for, 397
    and employers liability insurance policy,
        589–591
    fraud and abuse, 398
    homeowners insurance and, 460
    laws for, 395–396
    litigation and, 395–396
    Longshore and Harbor Workers
        Compensation Act for, 538, 591
    objectives of, 396
    private insurance for, 28
    social insurance for, 30, 395–399
    state, 30
    uninsured motorists coverage and, 488
Workers Compensation Research Institute,
    402–403
Workman, Millicent, 62
Worksite marketing programs, 96, 332
Work tests, 375–376
Wrongful act, 589
Wrong-site surgery, 418

**Y**

Yacht insurance, 537
Yearly rate-of-return method, 261–262
Yearly renewable term insurance, 208,
    270, 331